11:00-11:50 MWF

fifth edition

Biopsychology

John P. J. Pinel

University of British Columbia

Boston ■ New York ■ San Francisco
Mexico City ■ Montreal ■ Toronto ■ London ■ Madrid ■ Munich ■ Paris
Hong Kong ■ Singapore ■ Tokyo ■ Cape Town ■ Sydney

■ To Maggie and Greg
for your love, care, and support

Executive Editor: Carolyn Merrill

Series Editorial Assistant: Jonathan Bender

Developmental Editor: Kelly Perkins

Marketing Managers: Brad Parkins and Wendy Gordon

Production Editor: Michael Granger

Editorial Production Service: Lifland et al., Bookmakers

Composition Buyer: Linda Cox

Manufacturing Buyer: Megan Cochran

Cover Administrator: Linda Knowles

Electronic Composition: Omegatype Typography, Inc.

Photo Researcher: Sarah Evertson, ImageQuest

Text Design: Carol Somberg

For related titles and support materials, visit our online catalog at www.ablongman.com.

Between the time Website information is gathered and then published, it is not
unusual for some sites to have closed. Also, the transcription of URLs can result
in unintended typographical erros. The publisher would appreciate notification
where these errors occur so that they may be corrected in subsequent editions.

Library of Congress Cataloging-in-Publication Data

Pinel, John P. J.
    Biopsychology / John P. J. Pinel. — 5th ed.
        p.   cm.
    Include bibliographical references and index.
    ISBN 0-205-34984-6 (hardcover)
    1. Psychobiology.   I. Title.
QP360.P463   2002
612.8–dc21   2002020660

Printed in the United States of America

10 9 8 7 6 5 4 3 2 1   VHP   08 07 06 04 03 02

Illustration and photo credits appear on pages 549 and 550, which constitute a continuation of the
copyright page.

Brief Contents

Contents

PART 1   WHAT IS BIOPSYCHOLOGY?

chapter 1

Biopsychology as a Neuroscience   1

What Is Biopsychology, Anyway?

PART 2   FOUNDATIONS OF BIOPSYCHOLOGY

chapter 2

Evolution, Genetics, and Experience   19

Thinking about the Biology of Behavior

chapter 3

The Anatomy of the Nervous System

51

The Systems, Structures, and Cells That Make Up Your Nervous System

chapter 4

Neural Conduction and Synaptic Transmission

79

How Neurons Send and Receive Signals

chapter **5**

The Research Methods of Biopsychology

Understanding What Biopsychologists Do — **104**

The Ironic Case of Professor P. — *105*

PART 3   SENSORY AND MOTOR SYSTEMS

chapter **6**

The Visual System

From Your Eyes to Your Cortex — **132**

*The Case of Mrs. Richards: Fortification
   Illusions and the Astronomer* — *133*

chapter 7

Mechanisms of Perception, Conscious Awareness, and Attention

161

How You Know the World

chapter **8**

The Sensorimotor System

How You Do What You Do   194

PART 4 BRAIN PLASTICITY

chapter **9**

Development of the Nervous System

From Fertilized Egg to You   221

chapter 10
Brain Damage and Neuroplasticity
240
Can the Brain Recover from Damage?

chapter 11
Learning, Memory, and Amnesia
268
How Your Brain Stores Information

PART 5 BIOPSYCHOLOGY OF MOTIVATION

chapter 12
Hunger, Eating, and Health
297
Why Do Many People Eat Too Much?

chapter 13

Hormones and Sex
324

What's Wrong with the Mamawawa?

chapter 17
Biopsychology of Emotion, Stress, and Health
437
Fear, the Dark Side of Emotion

chapter 18
Biopsychology of Psychiatric Disorders
461
The Brain Unhinged

Preface

Welcome to the fifth and newest edition of *Biopsychology*. I have been through four editions of this text—all successful—but never have I been as excited as I am about this one. This edition builds on the strengths of the previous ones, but it also takes important new steps: In addition to introducing cutting-edge research topics, it sharpens the focus on the human element of biopsychology and promotes interactive learning.

I originally wrote *Biopsychology* as a clear, engaging introduction to current biopsychological theory and research—and five editions later, it continues to fill this role. It is intended for use as a primary text in one- or two-semester courses in biopsychology—variously titled Biopsychology, Physiological Psychology, Brain and Behavior, Psychobiology, Behavioral Neuroscience, or Behavioral Neurobiology.

The defining feature of *Biopsychology* is its unique combination of biopsychological science and personal, reader-oriented discourse. It is a textbook that is "untextbooklike." Rather than introducing biopsychology in the usual textbook fashion, it interweaves the fundamentals of the field with clinical case studies, social issues, personal implications, and humorous anecdotes. It tries to be a friendly mentor that speaks directly to the reader, enthusiastically relating recent advances in biopsychological science.

My intention was that the friendly persona of *Biopsychology* would be more than just window dressing. I hope that *Biopsychology*'s engaging pedagogical approach facilitates the acquisition and retention of information so that the text delivers more biopsychology and more enjoyment for less effort.

Writing this preface is my final task for preparation of this edition. It marks the end of a year in which I have dedicated myself to further strengthening *Biopsychology*. Following are the major new features of this edition.

New Features for the Fifth Edition

A NEW FOCUS ON FOUR BIOPSYCHOLOGICAL THEMES ■ Throughout the text, the following four themes are highlighted with distinctive icons:

- Thinking about Biopsychology

- Clinical Implications

- The Evolutionary Perspective

- Cognitive Neuroscience

In order to emphasize "the big picture," I have selected these four themes for special prominence. I have expanded their coverage in every chapter, and a *Themes Revisited* section at the end of each chapter briefly summarizes how they were developed therein. The four themes provide excellent topics for essay assignments and exam questions.

AN INCREASED EMPHASIS ON THE HUMAN AND CLINICAL ELEMENTS OF BIOPSYCHOLOGY ■

Many new case studies have been added to this edition, and all case studies are now highlighted in the text. These provocative true stories stimulate interest and allow students to learn how biopsychological principles apply to the real world. Also, new chapter-opening photos emphasize the personal and social relevance of biopsychological principles. In addition, several additional psychiatric and neuropsychological disorders are covered.

A SIGNIFICANT INCREASE IN STUDENT ACCESSIBILITY ■

This edition of *Biopsychology* is the most student-friendly version to date. For example, provocative chapter subtitles and case study titles have been added to pique students' interest. Moreover, the difficulty of the text has been reduced somewhat (10–15%) by eliminating some difficult passages, clarifying others, and adding human illustrations and applications.

■ Features Carried Over from Previous Editions

The following are features of the first four editions of *Biopsychology* that have been maintained and strengthened in this edition.

AN EMPHASIS ON BEHAVIOR ■

In some biopsychological textbooks, the coverage of neurophysiology, neuro-chemistry, and neuroanatomy subverts the coverage of behavioral research. *Biopsychology* gives top billing to behavior: It stresses that neuroscience is a team effort and that the unique contribution made by biopsychologists to this effort is their behavioral expertise.

A BROAD DEFINITION OF BIOPSYCHOLOGY ■

Biopsychology is the study of the biology of behavior. *Biopsychology* focuses on the neural mechanisms of behavior but also emphasizes the evolution, genetics, and adaptiveness of behavioral processes.

A FOCUS ON THE SCIENTIFIC METHOD ■

Biopsychology emphasizes important—but frequently misunderstood—points about the scientific method, including these three: (1) The scientific method is a means of answering questions that is as applicable to daily life as it is to the laboratory. (2) The scientific method is fun—it is basically the same as the method used by detectives to solve crimes. (3) Widely accepted scientific theories are current best estimates—not statements of absolute fact.

AN INTEGRATIVE APPROACH ■

Biopsychology has not taken the modular approach, dispensing biopsychological information as a series of brief, independent subject modules. *Biopsychology*'s approach is integrative. It creates a strong fabric of research and ideas by weaving together related subject areas and research findings into chapters of intermediate length.

**AN EMPHASIS ON PERSONAL AND SOCIAL RELE-
VANCE** ■ Several chapters of *Biopsychology*—particularly
those on eating, sleeping, sex, and drug addiction—carry
strong personal and social messages. In these chapters, students are encouraged to consider the relevance of biopsychological research to their lives outside the classroom.

WIT AND ENTHUSIASM ■ Most biopsychology laboratories are places of enthusiasm, dedication, and good
humor. *Biopsychology* communicates these important
aspects of the "biopsychological life."

REMARKABLE ILLUSTRATIONS ■ The illustrations
in *Biopsychology* are special. This is because each one was
conceptualized and meticulously designed by a scientist–
artist team uniquely qualified to clarify and reinforce the
text: Pinel and his artist wife, Maggie Edwards.

■ | New Coverage in the Fifth Edition

Biopsychology remains one of the most rapidly
progressing scientific fields. Like previous editions, this
edition of *Biopsychology* has kept abreast of recent developments; it contains approximately 500 references to
articles that were not cited in the last edition. Indeed,
these additions have dictated changes to many parts of
this text. The following is a list of major content changes
to this edition, organized by chapter:

**IMPROVEMENTS AND REORGANIZATION OF
CHAPTERS** ■

- A new chapter has been added on the biopsychology
  of psychiatric disorders, and several chapters have
  received extensive reorganization.

- The chapters of the text are now organized into six
  parts:

  1. What Is Biopsychology?
  2. Foundations of Biopsychology
  3. Sensory and Motor Systems
  4. Brain Plasticity
  5. Biopsychology of Motivation
  6. Disorders of Cognition and Emotion

CHAPTER 1
Biopsychology as a Neuroscience:
What Is Biopsychology, Anyway?

- Introduction of the four major themes of the book
  and their related icons

CHAPTER 2
Evolution, Genetics, and Experience:
Thinking about the Biology of Behavior

- Introduction of two important evolutionary concepts: spandrels and exaptations

- Clearer discussion of the evolutionary concepts of
  homologous and analogous structures and convergent evolution

- New coverage of the field of evolutionary psychology

- Discussion of evolutionary theories of mate bonding

- Update on the human genome project

- Discussion of the relevance of the human genome
  project to the study of behavior

CHAPTER 3
The Anatomy of the Nervous System:
The Systems, Structures, and Cells
That Make Up Your Nervous System

- Introduction of the recent finding that glial cells
  play more than supporting roles in the nervous
  system

- Introduction of the concepts of proximal and distal

CHAPTER 4
Neural Conduction and Synaptic Transmission:
How Neurons Send and Receive Signals

- Introduction of the changing view of dendritic
  function

- Discussion of the role of glial cells in nervous system
  function

CHAPTER 5
The Research Methods of Biopsychology:
Understanding What Biopsychologists Do

- A new chapter-opening case study illustrating clinical applications of biopsychology research methods

- Introduction of magnetoencephalography (MEG)

- Simplified description of gene knockout techniques

- Introduction of the elevated plus maze

CHAPTER 6
The Visual System: From Your Eyes to Your Cortex

- Formerly Chapter 7

- A new chapter-opening case study: migraines and
  fortification illusions

CHAPTER 7
Mechanisms of Perception, Conscious Awareness,
and Attention: How You Know the World

- Formerly Chapter 8

- A new chapter-opening case study: simultagnosia

- Updated coverage of olfaction and gustation, with
  the suggestion of a fifth primary taste

- More systematic treatment of attention

CHAPTER 8
The Sensorimotor System: How You Do What You Do
- Formerly Chapter 9
- Discussion of the interesting finding that contralateral neglect is often not defined in terms of gravitational coordinates
- Description of the shifting visual receptive fields of bimodal neurons in premotor cortex
- Coverage of the concept of motor equivalence
- Demonstration of the independence of conscious experience and the sensory control of movement in normal subjects

CHAPTER 9
Development of the Nervous System: From Fertilized Egg to You
- Begins a new three-chapter sequence on neuroplasticity
- Focuses on development and developmental disorders
- A new chapter-opening case study: Genie
- Integrates material from former Chapter 15 with new material that provides a more human orientation
- A new section on postnatal brain development in human infants
- A new focus on disorders of neurodevelopment: autism, savantism, and Williams syndrome
- Expanded coverage of the effects of experience on brain development
- Extensive coverage of stem cell research

CHAPTER 10
Brain Damage and Neuroplasticity: Can the Brain Recover from Damage?
- Second in the new three-chapter sequence on neuroplasticity
- Focuses on brain damage and recovery
- Integrates former Chapter 6 with parts of former Chapter 15
- Updated coverage of the genetics of neuropsychological diseases
- Introduction of the role of cognitive reserve in recovery of cognitive function after brain damage
- New section on the applications of neuroplasticity (e.g., use of stem cells) to the treatment of nervous system damage
- New section on rehabilitative training, focusing on phantom limbs
- A new case study on phantom limbs

CHAPTER 11
Learning, Memory, and Amnesia: How Your Brain Stores Information
- Last of the three-chapter sequence on neuroplasticity
- Focuses on learning, memory, and amnesia
- Integrates material from former Chapters 14 and 15
- More systematic discussion of the mechanisms of memory consolidation
- Intensive coverage of theories of hippocampal function
- New section on memory and the prefrontal cortex
- Revised treatment of LTP
- Discussion of infantile amnesia

CHAPTER 12
Hunger, Eating, and Health: Why Do Many People Eat Too Much?
- Formerly Chapter 10
- Focuses on eating-related health problems
- A new chapter-opening case study: amnesia and eating
- Discussion of serotonin and satiety
- Introduction of nonexercise activity thermogenesis (NEAT)
- Update on leptin research
- Expanded coverage of anorexia

CHAPTER 13
Hormones and Sex: What's Wrong with the Mamawawa?
- Formerly Chapter 11
- New section on the regulation of hormone release
- New case study on androgenital syndrome
- Updated case study: the twin with ablatio penis (John/Joan)
- Update on the effects of anabolic steroids
- Recent evidence that anabolic steroids influence aggression
- Update on the role of the hypothalamus in sexual behavior

CHAPTER 14
Sleep, Dreaming, and Circadian Rhythms: How Much Do You Need to Sleep?
- Formerly Chapter 12
- New section on the comparative analysis of sleep
- A new section introducing the fundamental questions about sleep
- A clear concluding statement about what circadian research has taught us about sleep
- A discussion of the difficulties in interpreting the personal experiences of sleep loss
- A new section on the effects of sleep reduction on sleep efficiency
- New section on the basal forebrain and sleep

- New section on the genetics of circadian rhythms
- Introduction of sleep restriction therapy
- New section on sleep disorders that emphasizes recent advances in narcolepsy research

CHAPTER 15
Drug Addiction and the Brain's Reward Circuits: Chemicals That Harm with Pleasure

- Formerly Chapter 13
- Discussion of false claims that nicotine reduces tension
- Report on the heritability of nicotine and alcohol addiction
- Discussion of "crack baby syndrome"
- Discussion of the Swiss experiment
- Improved description of the mesocorticolimbic pathway and its role in addiction
- Clearer explanation of the involvement of dopamine in drug addiction
- More detailed description of the role of the nucleus accumbens in addiction

CHAPTER 16
Lateralization, Language, and the Split Brain: The Left Brain and the Right Brain of Language

- New coverage of gender differences in lateralization
- New discussion of split-brain patients tormented by conflict
- Improved explanation of misconceptions about lateralization
- Clarification of the fact that broad clusters of cognitive abilities (e.g., spatial abilities, musical abilities) are not the units of lateralization
- Description of new research on the lateralization of elements of cortical microcircuitry
- A new case study on aphasia for sign language
- Discussion of the evolution of cerebral laterality
- Update on the current status of the Wernicke-Geschwind model
- Systematic discussion of the cognitive neuroscience approach to language and language disorders
- New section on brain imaging and language
- Introduction of the provocative finding that different areas of the temporal lobe mediate the naming of different classes of objects (e.g., animals vs. tools)
- New section on the cognitive neuroscience of dyslexia
- Discussion of the remarkable finding that dyslexia is less common among Italian-speaking than English-speaking people

- New chapter-ending case study: a woman who experienced a total left hemispherectomy

CHAPTER 17
Biopsychology of Emotion, Stress, and Health: Fear, the Dark Side of Emotion

- New chapter-opening case study on Phineas Gage, featuring computerized reconstruction of his brain damage
- New table listing the major early milestones in the study of emotion
- Recent evidence that people tend to mimic facial expressions subliminally
- Introduction of the concept of subordination stress
- Improved section on stress and increased susceptibility to infection
- Improved section on factors that influence the reactivity to stress in adulthood
- Improved section on the effects of stress on the hippocampus
- Improved section on fear conditioning
- Explication of the complexity of amygdalar anatomy
- Discussion of contextual fear conditioning
- Systematic discussion of the human brain mechanisms of emotion
- New case study: a woman who could not recognize facial expressions of fear
- Introduction of Urbach-Wiethe disease (calcification of the amygdala)
- New discussion of the lateralization of emotion
- New discussion of individual differences in the cerebral organization of human emotion
- New chapter-ending case study about a man with an amygdalar tumor: the Texas tower sniper

CHAPTER 18
Biopsychology of Psychiatric Disorders: The Brain Unhinged

- New chapter created in part from sections of former Chapter 17
- Discussion of the arbitrariness of distinctions between psychiatric and neurological disorders
- New case study of schizophrenia
- New systematic discussion of atypical neuroleptics
- Update on the current status of the dopamine theory of schizophrenia
- New case study of depression
- Updated description of the diathesis-stress model of depression
- Update on the monoamine theory of depression
- New case study of anxiety

- New discussion of the etiology of anxiety disorders
- New section on Tourette's syndrome
- New case study: a neuroscientist with Tourette's syndrome
- New section on clinical trials, the development and testing of new psychiatric drugs
- Chapter-ending case study: a biopsychology student who used his critical thinking skills to direct his own treatment

■ Learning Aids

Biopsychology has several features that are expressly designed to help students learn and remember the material:

- Boldfaced **key terms**—additional terms of less importance appear in italics
- **Brain Scans,** study exercises that occur in the chapters at key transition points, where students can benefit most from pausing to consolidate preceding material before continuing
- **Themes Revisited,** sections that act as the conclusion to each chapter, summarizing the ways the book's four major themes have impacted that particular topic
- **Think about It,** discussion questions that challenge students to think critically about chapter information
- **Log On,** a list of weblinks that direct students to interesting, relevant websites at the conclusion of each chapter
- **Appendices,** which serve as convenient sources of important information that is too detailed for some students of biopsychology

■ Ancillary Materials Available with *Biopsychology*

THE NEW *BEYOND THE BRAIN & BEHAVIOR* CD-ROM ■ Packaged free with every new textbook, the CD-ROM titled *Beyond the Brain & Behavior* contains many activities and demonstrations designed to increase students' interest and encourage them to relate to biopsychology in an active way. Marginal annotations in *Biopsychology* direct students to CD components at the appropriate points in each chapter. Here some of the key elements featured on *Beyond the Brain & Behavior*:

ON THE CD

Visit the *Change Blindness* module. Change blindness needs to be experienced to be appreciated. This is one you'll want to share with your friends.

- **Animations and other demonstrations.** Media demonstrations specially designed for this CD allow students to experience important textual concepts for themselves. This CD includes demonstrations of the perception of motion and eye movement, synaptic transmission, Mach bands, change blindness, surface interpolation, and the leaky-barrel model of settling-point regulation.

- **Neural modules.** Ten animated neural modules from the acclaimed A.D.A.M. Interactive Physiology CD-ROM (Benjamin/Cummings) help students understand fundamental physiological principles. Through audio explanations and visual demonstrations, each module brings a complex aspect of biopsychology to life on students' own computer monitors.

- **Video clips.** Pinel speaks personally to students and communicates his enthusiasm for biopsychology in seven video clips, most filmed in his own home. These video clips focus on the following topics: (1) introduction to biopsychology, (2) four themes of the book, (3) hunger and eating, (4) drug addiction, (5) Pinel's personal experience with a brain tumor, (6) sleep, and (7) sensorimotor learning, illustrated by a demonstration of African drumming.

- **Practice Tests.** Here, students will find 15 multiple-choice questions per chapter, written by Pinel himself. These self-scoring tests will help students prepare for exams.

- **Electronic flash cards.** Students can review key terms and their definitions for each chapter using these convenient electronic flash cards.

TEST BANK ■ The test bank for this edition of *Biopsychology* comprises more than 2,000 multiple-choice questions. The difficulty of each item is rated—easy (1), moderate (2), or difficult (3)—to assist instructors with their test construction. Textbook authors rarely prepare their own test banks; the fact that Pinel insisted on preparing his own attests to its quality—and his commitment to helping students learn.

COMPUTERIZED TEST BANK ■ This computerized version of the test bank is available with Tamarack's easy-to-use TestGen software, which lets instructors prepare tests for printing as well for network and online testing. Full editing capability for Windows and Macintosh.

INSTRUCTOR'S MANUAL ■ The instructor's manual, skillfully prepared by Michael Mana of Western Washington University, includes a set of lectures. Each lecture is divided into an outline, lecture notes, and suggested Web resources.

STUDY GUIDE ■ Each chapter of the study guide, prepared by Michael Mana of Western Washington University, includes three sections. Section I is composed of *Jeopardy*-style study items—similar to the popular television quiz show, these uncharacteristically require the students to respond to the answers with the correct questions. The study items in Section I are arranged in two columns: questions on the left and answers on the right. Sometimes there is nothing in the space to the right of the question, and the student's task is to write in the correct question. Once these *Jeopardy*-style study items are completed, the student has a bidirectional list of questions and answers that summarize the main points of the chapter, conveniently arranged for studying.

Section II of each chapter of the study guide is composed of essay study questions. Spaces are provided for the student to write outlines of the correct answers to each question. The essay study questions encourage students to consider broad issues and themes.

Section III of each chapter of the study guide is a practice examination. Students are advised to use their results on the practice examination to guide the final stages of their preparation for in-class examinations.

DIGITAL IMAGE ARCHIVE ■ Allyn & Bacon's Digital Image Archive for Physiological Psychology, Version 2.0, is available to adopters of the book. This instructor's resource, available on CD-ROM from your Allyn & Bacon sales representative, provides more than 400 full-color images—including PowerPoint presentations and figures—from the text and from other sources. A booklet listing the images by chapter accompanies the CD-ROM, for easy reference.

BIOPSYCHOLOGY VIDEO ■ Instructors who adopt *Biopsychology* can obtain a 60-minute biopsychology videotape. Based on the *Films for the Humanities* series, this video provides students with glimpses of important biopsychological phenomena such as sleep recording, axon growth, memory testing in monkeys, the formation of synapses, gender differences in brain structure, human amnesic patients, rewarding brain stimulation, and brain scans.

Additional ancillary materials are also available to instructors. Please consult your Allyn & Bacon sales representative for details.

■ Acknowledgments

I wrote *Biopsychology*, but Maggie Edwards took the responsibility for all other aspects of the manuscript and CD preparation—Maggie is my partner in life. I am grateful for her encouragement and support and for her many contributions to this book. I also thank her on behalf of the many students who will benefit from her efforts.

Allyn and Bacon did a remarkable job of producing this book. They shared my dream of a textbook that meets the highest standards of pedagogy but is also personal, attractive, and enjoyable. Thank you to Bill Barke, Carolyn Merrill, and the other executives at Allyn and Bacon for having faith in *Biopsychology* and providing the financial and personal support necessary for it to stay at the forefront of its field. A special thank you goes to Kelly Perkins for development assistance and to Michael Granger and Jane Hoover for coordinating the production—an excruciatingly difficult and often thankless job. Copyeditor Denise Throckmorton spotted several errors in the text and art, which was greatly appreciated.

I thank the following biopsychology instructors for providing me or Allyn and Bacon with reviews of various editions of *Biopsychology*. Their comments have contributed substantially to the evolution of this edition.

L. Joseph Acher, Baylor University
Michael Babcock, Montana State University–Bozeman
Carol Batt, Sacred Heart University
Thomas Bennett, Colorado State University
Linda Brannon, McNeese State University
Peter Brunjes, University of Virginia
Michelle Butler, Colorado State University
Donald Peter Cain, University of Western Ontario
Deborah A. Carroll, Southern Connecticut State University
John Conklin, Camosun College
Gregory Ervin, Brigham Young University
Robert B. Fischer, Ball State University
Allison Fox, University of Wollongong
Thomas Goettsche, SAS Institute, Inc.
Arnold M. Golub, California State University–Sacramento
Mary Gotch, Solano College
Kenneth Guttman, Citrus College
Melody Smith Harrington, St. Gregory's University
Theresa D. Hernandez, University of Colorado
Cindy Ellen Herzog, Frostburg State University
Peter Hickmott, University of California–Riverside
Tony Jelsma, Atlantic Baptist University
Roger Johnson, Ramapo College
John Jonides, University of Michigan
Jon Kahane, Springfield College
Craig Kinsley, University of Richmond
Ora Kofman, Ben Gurion University of the Niger
Louis Koppel, Utah State University
Victoria Littlefield, Augsburg College
Linda Lockwood, Metropolitan State College of Denver
Charles Malsbury, Memorial University
Michael R. Markham, Florida International University
Michael P. Matthews, Drury College
Lin Meyers, California State University–Stanislaus
Russ Morgan, Western Illinois University
Henry Morlock, SUNY–Plattsburg
Lauretta Park, Clemson University
Ted Parsons, University of Wisconsin–Platteville

Jim H. Patton, Baylor University
Michael Peters, University of Guelph
David Robbins, Ohio Wesleyan University
Jeanne P. Ryan, SUNY–Plattsburgh
David Soderquist, University of North Carolina
    at Greensboro
Michael Stoloff, James Madison University

Dallas Treit, University of Alberta
Stuart Tousman, Rockford College
Dennis Vincenzi, University of Central Florida
Linda Walsh, University of Northern Iowa
Jon Williams, Kenyon College
David Yager, University of Maryland

To The Student

In the 1960s, I was, in the parlance of the times, "turned on" by an undergraduate course in biopsychology. I could not imagine anything more interesting than a field of science dedicated to studying the relation between psychological processes and the brain. My initial fascination led to a long career as a student, researcher, and teacher of biopsychological science. *Biopsychology* is my attempt to share this fascination with you.

I have tried to make *Biopsychology* a different kind of textbook, a textbook that includes clear, concise, and well-organized explanations of the key points but is still interesting to read—a book from which you might suggest a suitable chapter to an interested friend or relative. To accomplish this goal, I thought about what kind of textbook I would have liked when I was a student, and I decided immediately to avoid the stern formality and ponderous style of conventional textbook writing.

I wanted *Biopsychology* to have a relaxed and personal style. In order to accomplish this, I imagined that you and I were chatting as I wrote, and that I was telling you—usually over a glass of something—about the interesting things that go on in the field of biopsychology.

Imagining these chats kept my writing from drifting back into conventional "textbookese," and it never let me forget that I was writing this book for you, the student.

I am particularly excited, and a bit nervous, about this edition of *Biopsychology* because it's the first one to come with a CD. I believe you'll find a lot on the CD that will prove interesting and useful, but your reaction to the video clips concerns me the most. These clips allow me to communicate with you more naturally—most of them were shot in my home. I hope you like them because it is going to take me quite a while to fully recover from the shock of seeing and hearing myself on my own computer monitor.

I hope that *Biopsychology* teaches you much, and that reading it generates in you the same personal feeling that writing it did in me. If you are so inclined, I welcome your comments and suggestions. You can contact me at the Department of Psychology, University of British Columbia, Vancouver, B. C., Canada, V6T 1Z4 or at the following e-mail address:

jpinel@cortex.psych.ubc.ca

About the Author

John Pinel, the author of *Biopsychology*, obtained his PhD from McGill University in Montreal. He worked briefly at the Massachusetts Institute of Technology before taking up his current position at the University of British Columbia in Vancouver. Professor Pinel is an award-winning teacher and the author of over 200 scientific papers; however, he feels that *Biopsychology* is his major career-related accomplishment. "It ties together everything that I love about my job: students, teaching, writing, and research."

When we asked him about his personal interests, Professor Pinel spoke glowingly of his partner, Maggie, and son, Greg. The high quality of the illustrations in *Biopsychology* is largely attributable to the effort and talent of Maggie, who is an artist and professional designer. Greg is currently completing his PhD at the London School of Economics, specializing in social and educational programs for indigenous peoples.

"I get my exercise by working out regularly and by drumming," Pinel says. "I am an enthusiastic African hand drummer, and for a peak mental and physical experience a bit of Kpanlogo with my friends Kwasi and Dido is hard to beat." (Be sure to view *The Beat Goes On* video clip on the *Beyond the Brain & Behavior* CD-ROM—free with the purchase of a new text—for a hand-drumming demonstration by Pinel!) "In contrast, my rest and relaxation comes largely from one activity: cuddling our cats, Sambala and Rastaman."

Biopsychology as a Neuroscience
What Is Biopsychology, Anyway?

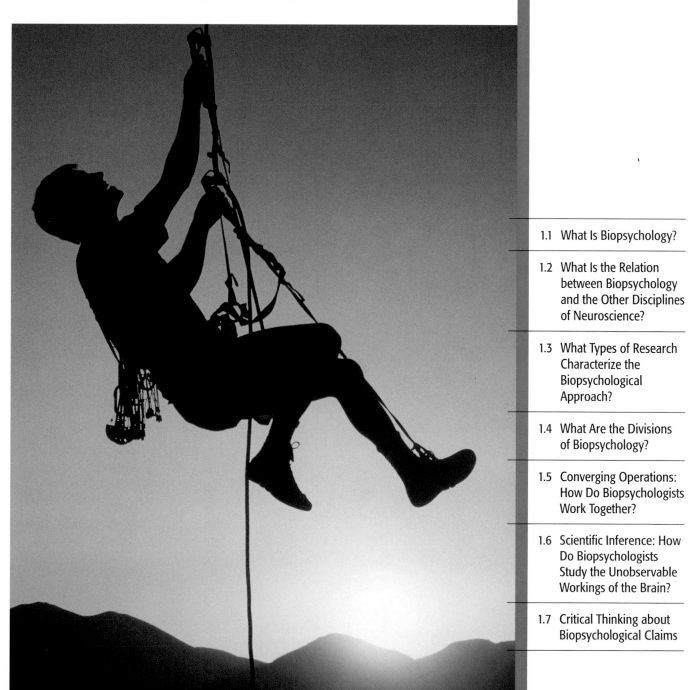

The appearance of the human brain is far from impressive (see Figure 1.1). The human brain is a squishy, wrinkled, walnut-shaped hunk of tissue weighing about 1.3 kilograms. It looks more like something that you might find washed up on a beach than like one of the wonders of the world—which it surely is. Despite its disagreeable external appearance, the human brain is an amazingly intricate network of **neurons** (cells that receive and transmit electrochemical signals). Contemplate for a moment the complexity of your own brain's neural circuits. Consider the 100 billion neurons in complex array, the estimated 100 trillion connections among them, and the almost infinite number of paths that neural signals can follow through this morass.

The complexity of the human brain is hardly surprising, considering what it can do. An organ capable of creating a *Mona Lisa,* an artificial limb, and a supersonic aircraft; of traveling to the moon and to the depths of the sea; and of experiencing the wonders of an alpine sunset, a newborn infant, and a reverse slam dunk must itself be complex. Paradoxically, **neuroscience** (the scientific study of the nervous system) may prove to be the brain's ultimate challenge: Does the brain have the capacity to understand something as complex as itself?

ON THE CD Visit the *Greetings from the Author* module. Pinel welcomes you personally and explains an often overlooked aspect of biopsychology he has included in this text.

Neuroscience comprises several related disciplines. The primary purpose of this chapter is to introduce you to one of them: biopsychology. Each of this chapter's seven sections characterizes biopsychology from a different perspective.

Before you proceed to the body of this chapter, I would like to tell you about two things: the case of Jimmie G., which will give you a taste of the interesting things that lie ahead, and the major themes of this book.

The Case of Jimmie G., the Man Frozen in Time

[In 1975] Jimmie was a fine-looking man, with a curly bush of grey hair, a healthy and handsome forty-nine-year-old. He was cheerful, friendly, and warm.

"Hiya, Doc!" he said. "Nice morning! Do I take this chair here?" . . . He spoke of the houses where his family had lived. . . . He spoke of school and school days, the friends he'd had, and his special fondness for mathematics and science . . . he was seventeen, had just graduated from high school when he was drafted in 1943. . . . He remembered the names of the various submarines on which he had served, their missions, where they were stationed, the names of his shipmates. . . . But there for some reason his reminiscences stopped. . . .

. . . I was very struck by the change of tense in his recollections as he passed from his school days to his days in the navy. He had been using the past tense, but now used the present. . . .

A sudden, improbable suspicion seized me.

"What year is this, Mr. G.?" I asked, concealing my perplexity under a casual manner.

"Forty-five, man. What do you mean?" He went on, "We've won the war, FDR's dead, Truman's at the helm. There are great times ahead."

"And you, Jimmie, how old would you be?" . . .

"Why, I guess I'm nineteen, Doc. I'll be twenty next birthday."

Looking at the grey-haired man before me, I had an impulse for which I have never forgiven myself. . . .

"Here," I said, and thrust a mirror toward him. "Look in the mirror and tell me what you see. . . ."

He suddenly turned ashen and gripped the sides of the chair. "Jesus Christ," he whispered. "Christ, what's going on? What's happened to me? Is this a nightmare? Am I crazy? Is this a joke?"—and he became frantic, panicked.

. . . I stole away, taking the hateful mirror with me.

Two minutes later I re-entered the room. . . . "Hiya, Doc!" he said. "Nice morning! You want to talk to me—do I take this chair here?" There was no sign of recognition on his frank, open face.

"Haven't we met before, Mr. G.?" I asked casually.

"No, I can't say we have. Quite a beard you got there. I wouldn't forget you, Doc!"

. . . "Where do you think you are?"

FIGURE 1.1 The human brain.

"I see these beds, and these patients everywhere. Looks like a sort of hospital to me. But hell, what would I be doing in a hospital—and with all these old people, years older than me. . . . Maybe I *work* here. . . . If I don't work here, I've been *put* here. Am I a patient, am I sick and don't know it, Doc? It's crazy, it's scary. . . ."

On intelligence testing he showed excellent ability. He was quick-witted, observant, and logical, and had no difficulty solving complex problems and puzzles—no difficulty, that is, if they could be done quickly. If much time was required, he forgot what he was doing. . . .

Homing in on his memory, I found an extreme and extraordinary loss of recent memory—so that whatever was said or shown to him was apt to be forgotten in a few seconds' time. Thus I laid out my watch, my tie, and my glasses on the desk, covered them, and asked him to remember these. Then, after a minute's chat, I asked him what I had put under the cover. He remembered none of them—or indeed that I had even asked him to remember. I repeated the test, this time getting him to write down the names of the three objects; again he forgot, and when I showed him the paper with his writing on it he was astounded. . . .

"What is this?" I asked, showing him a photo in the magazine I was holding.

"It's the moon," he replied.

"No, it's not," I answered. "It's a picture of the earth taken from the moon."

"Doc, you're kidding! Someone would've had to get a camera up there! . . . how the hell would you do that?" . . .

He was becoming fatigued, and somewhat irritable and anxious, under the continuing pressure of anomaly and contradiction, and their fearful implications. . . . And I myself was wrung with emotion—it was heartbreaking . . . to think of his life lost in limbo, dissolving.

He is, as it were . . . isolated in a single moment of being, with a moat . . . of forgetting all round him. . . . He is a man without a past (or future), stuck in a constantly changing, meaningless moment. (pp. 22–28)[1]

Remember Jimmie G.; you will encounter him again, later in this chapter.

■ Four Major Themes of This Book

You will learn many new facts in this book—new findings, concepts, brain structures, and the like—but what is more important is that, many years from now, long after you have forgotten most of these facts, you will still be carrying with you from this book productive ways of thinking. I have selected four of these for special emphasis: They are the major themes of this book.

To help you give these themes the special attention they deserve and to help you follow their development as you progress though the book, I have marked relevant

passages with icons. The following are the four major themes and their related icons.

THINKING ABOUT BIOPSYCHOLOGY ■ Because many biopsychological topics are so interesting (as you have already seen in the case of Jimmie G.) and often relevant to everyday life, we are fed a steady diet of biopsychological information and opinion—by television, newspapers, the Internet, friends, relatives, books, teachers, etc. One major purpose of this book is to help you make the transition from being a passive consumer of biopsychological claims to being an effective thinker, a person who takes nothing at face value, judges the reasonableness of various claims, and assesses their relevance to her or his own social views and lifestyle. To help you achieve this goal, I have marked each directly relevant passage in this book with a thinking-about-biopsychology icon.

CLINICAL IMPLICATIONS ■ **Clinical** (pertaining to illness or treatment) considerations are woven through the fabric of biopsychology. Much of what biopsychologists learn about the functioning of the normal brain comes from studying the diseased or damaged brain; and, conversely, much of what biopsychologists discover has relevance for the treatment of brain disorders. This book focuses on the interplay between brain dysfunction and biopsychology, and each major example of that interplay is highlighted by a clinical implications icon.

THE EVOLUTIONARY PERSPECTIVE ■ Although the events that led to the evolution of the human species can never be determined with certainty, thinking of the environmental pressures that likely led to the evolution of our brains and behavior often leads to important biopsychological insights. This approach is called the **evolutionary perspective.** An important aspect of the evolutionary perspective is the *comparative approach* (trying to understand biological phenomena by comparing them in different species). You will learn throughout the text that we humans have learned much about ourselves by studying species that are related to us through evolution. The evolutionary approach has proven to be one of the cornerstones of modern biopsychological inquiry; discussions that relate to its contributions are marked by evolutionary perspective icons.

COGNITIVE NEUROSCIENCE ■ The advances in any field of science are driven to a large degree by technological innovation: The development of an effective new research instrument is often followed by a series of discoveries. There is no better example of this than *cognitive neuroscience,* a relatively new field of

---

biopsychology that has been fueled by the development of methods for creating images of the activity of the living human brain. Using these functional brain-imaging methods, cognitive neuroscientists study the areas of the human brain that become active while subjects engage in particular *cognitive* (pertaining to thinking) processes, such as memory, attention, and perception. Discussions involving this area of inquiry are highlighted by cognitive neuroscience icons.

1.1 What Is Biopsychology?

Biopsychology is the scientific study of the biology of behavior—see Dewsbury (1991). Some refer to this field as *psychobiology, behavioral biology,* or *behavioral neuroscience;* but I prefer the term *biopsychology* because it denotes a biological approach to the study of psychology rather than a psychological approach to the study of biology: Psychology commands center stage in this text. *Psychology* is the scientific study of behavior—the scientific study of all overt activities of the organism as well as all the internal processes that are presumed to underlie them (e.g., learning, memory, motivation, perception, and emotion).

The study of the biology of behavior has a long history, but biopsychology did not develop into a major neuroscientific discipline until the 20th century. Although it is not possible to specify the exact date of biopsychology's birth, the publication of *The Organization of Behavior* in 1949 by D. O. Hebb played a key role in its emergence (see Milner, 1993; Milner & White, 1987). In his book, Hebb developed the first comprehensive theory of how complex psychological phenomena, such as perceptions, emotions, thoughts, and memories, might be produced by brain activity. Hebb's theory did much to discredit the view that psychological functioning is too complex to have its roots in the physiology and chemistry of the brain. Hebb based his theory on experiments involving both humans and laboratory animals, on clinical case studies, and on logical arguments developed from his own insightful observations of daily life. This eclectic approach has become a hallmark of biopsychological inquiry.

In comparison to physics, chemistry, and biology, biopsychology is an infant—a healthy, rapidly growing infant, but an infant nonetheless. In this book, you will reap the benefits of biopsychology's youth. Because biopsychology does not have a long and complex history, you will be able to move directly to the excitement of current research.

1.2 What Is the Relation between Biopsychology and the Other Disciplines of Neuroscience?

Neuroscience is a team effort, and biopsychologists are important members of the team (Kandel & Squire, 2000). This section of the chapter further defines biopsychology by discussing its relation to other neuroscientific disciplines.

Biopsychologists are neuroscientists who bring to their research a knowledge of behavior and of the methods of behavioral research. It is their behavioral orientation and expertise that make their contribution to neuroscience unique. You will be able to better appreciate the importance of this contribution if you consider that the ultimate purpose of the nervous system is to produce and control behavior.

Biopsychology is an integrative discipline. Biopsychologists draw together knowledge from the other neuroscientific disciplines and apply it to the study of behavior. The following are a few of the disciplines of neuroscience that are particularly relevant to biopsychology:

Neuroanatomy. The study of the structure of the nervous system (see Chapter 3).

Neurochemistry. The study of the chemical bases of neural activity (see Chapter 4).

Neuroendocrinology. The study of interactions between the nervous system and the endocrine system (see Chapters 13 and 17).

Neuropathology. The study of nervous system disorders (see Chapter 10).

Neuropharmacology. The study of the effects of drugs on neural activity (see Chapters 4, 15, and 18).

Neurophysiology. The study of the functions and activities of the nervous system (see Chapter 4).

1.3 What Types of Research Characterize the Biopsychological Approach?

Although biopsychology is only one of many disciplines that contribute to neuroscience, it is itself broad and diverse. Biopsychologists study many different phenomena, and they approach their research in many different ways. In order to characterize biopsychological research, this section discusses three major dimensions along which approaches to biopsychological research vary. Biopsychological research can involve either human or nonhuman subjects; it can take the form of either formal experiments or nonexperimental studies; and it can be either pure or applied.

Human and Nonhuman Subjects

Both human and nonhuman animals are the subject of biopsychological research. Of the nonhumans, rats are the most common subjects; however, mice, cats, dogs, and nonhuman primates are also widely studied.

Humans have several advantages over other animals as experimental subjects of biopsychological research: They can follow instructions, they can report their subjective experiences, and their cages are easier to clean. Of course, I am joking about the cages, but the joke does serve to draw attention to one advantage that humans have over other species of experimental subjects: Humans are often cheaper. Because only the highest standards of animal care are acceptable, the cost of maintaining an animal laboratory can be prohibitive for all but the most well-funded researchers.

Of course, the greatest advantage that humans have as subjects in a field aimed at understanding the intricacies of human brain function is that they have human brains. In fact, you might wonder why biopsychologists would bother studying nonhuman subjects at all. The answer lies in the evolutionary continuity of the brain. The brains of humans differ from the brains of other mammals primarily in their overall size and the extent of their cortical development. In other words, the differences between the brains of humans and those of related species are more quantitative than qualitative, and thus many of the principles of human brain function can be derived from the study of nonhumans.

Conversely, nonhuman animals have three advantages over humans as subjects in biopsychological research. The first is that the brains and behavior of nonhuman subjects are simpler than those of human subjects. Hence, the study of nonhuman species is more likely to reveal fundamental brain–behavior interactions.

The second is that insights frequently arise from the **comparative approach,** the study of biological processes by comparing different species. For example, comparing the behavior of species that do not have a cerebral cortex with the behavior of species that do can provide valuable clues about cortical function. The third is that it is possible to conduct research on laboratory animals that, for ethical reasons, is not possible with human subjects. This is not to say that the study of nonhuman animals is not governed by a strict code of ethics (see Institute of Laboratory Animal Resources, 1996)—it is. However, there are fewer ethical constraints on the study of laboratory species than on the study of humans.

In my experience, most biopsychologists display considerable concern for their subjects, whether they are of their own species or not; however, ethical issues are not left to the discretion of the individual researcher. All biopsychological research, whether it involves human or nonhuman subjects, is regulated by independent committees according to strict ethical guidelines: "Researchers cannot escape the logic that if the animals we observe are reasonable models of our own most intricate actions, then they must be respected as we would respect our own sensibilities" (Ulrich, 1991, p. 197).

Experiments and Nonexperiments

Biopsychological research involves both experiments and nonexperimental studies. Two common types of nonexperimental studies are quasiexperimental studies and case studies.

EXPERIMENTS ■ The experiment is the method used by scientists to find out what causes what, and, as such, it is almost single-handedly responsible for our modern way of life. It is paradoxical that a method capable of such complex feats is itself so simple. To conduct an experiment involving living subjects, the experimenter first designs two or more conditions under which the subjects will be tested. Usually, a different group of subjects is tested under each condition (**between-subjects design**), but sometimes it is possible to test the same group of subjects under each condition (**within-subjects design**). The experimenter assigns the subjects to conditions, administers the treatments, and measures the outcome in such a way that there is only one relevant difference between the conditions that are being compared.

This difference between the conditions is called the **independent variable.** The variable that is measured by the experimenter to assess the effect of the independent variable is called the **dependent variable.**

Why is it critical that there be no differences between conditions other than the independent variable? The reason is that when there is more than one difference that could affect the dependent variable, it is difficult to determine whether it was the independent variable or the unintended difference—called a **confounded variable**—that led to the observed effects on the dependent variable. Although the experimental method is conceptually simple, eliminating all confounded variables can be quite difficult. Readers of research papers must be constantly on the alert for confounded variables that have gone unnoticed by the experimenters themselves.

An experiment by Lester and Gorzalka (1988) illustrates the experimental method in action. The experiment was a demonstration of the Coolidge effect. The **Coolidge effect** is the fact that a copulating male who becomes incapable of continuing to copulate with one sex partner can often recommence copulating with a new sex partner (see Figure 1.2). Before your imagination starts running wild, I should mention that the subjects in Lester and Gorzalka's experiment were hamsters, not students from the undergraduate subject pool.

Lester and Gorzalka argued that the Coolidge effect had not been demonstrated in females because it is more difficult to conduct well-controlled Coolidge-effect experiments with females—not because females do not display a Coolidge effect. The confusion, according to Lester and Gorzalka, stemmed from the fact that the males of most mammalian species become sexually fatigued more readily than do the females. As a result, attempts to demonstrate the Coolidge effect in females are often confounded by the fatigue of the males. When, in the midst of copulation, a female is provided with a new sex partner, the increase in her sexual receptivity could be either a legitimate Coolidge effect or a reaction to the greater vigor of the new male. Because female mammals usually display little sexual fatigue, this confounded variable is not a serious problem in demonstrations of the Coolidge effect in males.

Lester and Gorzalka devised a clever procedure to control for this confounded variable. At the same time that a female subject was copulating with one male (the familiar male), the other male to be used in the test (the unfamiliar male) was copulating with another female. Then, both males were given a rest while the female was copulating with a third male. Finally, the female subject was tested with either the familiar male or the unfamiliar male. The dependent variable was the amount of time that the female displayed **lordosis** (the arched-back, rump-up, tail-diverted posture of female rodent sexual receptivity) during each sex test. As Figure 1.3 illustrates,

FIGURE 1.2 President Calvin Coolidge and Mrs. Grace Coolidge. Many students think that the Coolidge effect is named after a biopsychologist named Coolidge. In fact, it is named after President Calvin Coolidge, of whom the following story is told. (If the story isn't true, it should be.) During a tour of a poultry farm, Mrs. Coolidge inquired of the farmer how his farm managed to produce so many eggs with such a small number of roosters. The farmer proudly explained that his roosters performed their duty dozens of times each day.

"Perhaps you could point that out to Mr. Coolidge," replied the First Lady in a pointedly loud voice.

The President, overhearing the remark, asked the farmer, "Does each rooster service the same hen each time?"

"No," replied the farmer, "there are many hens for each rooster."

"Perhaps you could point that out to Mrs. Coolidge," replied the President.

the females responded more vigorously to the unfamiliar males than they did to the familiar males during the third test, despite the fact that both the unfamiliar and familiar males were equally fatigued and both mounted the females with equal vigor. This experiment illustrates the importance of good experimental design as well as a

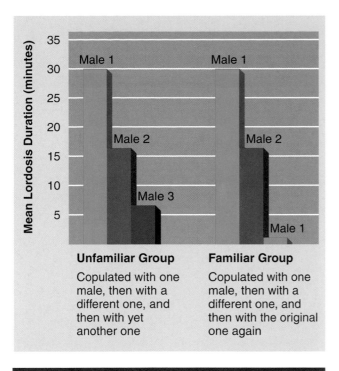

FIGURE 1.3   The experimental design and results of Lester and Gorzalka (1988). On the third test, the female hamsters were more sexually receptive to unfamiliar males than they were to the males with which they had copulated on the first test.

point made in Chapter 13: that males and females are more similar than most people appreciate.

QUASIEXPERIMENTAL STUDIES   ■   It is not possible for biopsychologists to bring the experimental method to bear on all problems of interest to them. There are frequently physical or ethical impediments that make it impossible to assign subjects to particular conditions or to administer the conditions once the subjects have been assigned to them. For example, experiments on the causes of brain damage in human alcoholics are not feasible because it would not be ethical to assign a subject to a condition that involves years of alcohol consumption. (Some of you may be more concerned about the ethics of assigning subjects to a control condition that involves years of sobriety.) In such prohibitive situations, biopsychologists sometimes conduct **quasi-experimental studies**—studies of groups of subjects who have been exposed to the conditions of interest in the real world. These studies have the appearance of experiments, but they are not true experiments because potential confounded variables have not been controlled—for example, by the random assignment of subjects to conditions.

In one quasiexperimental study, a team of researchers compared 100 detoxified male alcoholics from an alcoholism treatment unit with 50 male nondrinkers obtained from various sources (Acker et al., 1984). The alcoholics as a group performed more poorly on various tests of perceptual, motor, and cognitive ability, and their brain scans revealed extensive brain damage. Although this quasiexperimental study seems like an experiment, it is not. Because the subjects themselves decided which group they would be in—by drinking alcohol or not—the researchers had no means of ensuring that exposure to alcohol was the only variable that distinguished the two groups. Can you think of differences other than exposure to alcohol that could reasonably be expected to exist between a group of alcoholics and a group of abstainers—differences that could have contributed to the neuroanatomical or intellectual differences that were observed between them? There are several. For example, alcoholics as a group tend to be more poorly educated, more prone to accidental head injury, more likely to use other drugs, and more likely to have poor diets. Accordingly, quasiexperimental studies have revealed that alcoholics tend to have more brain damage than nonalcoholics, but they have not proved why.

Have you forgotten Jimmie G.? He was a product of long-term alcohol consumption.

CASE STUDIES   ■   Studies that focus on a single case or subject are called **case studies.** Because they focus on a single case, they often provide a more in-depth picture than that provided by an experiment or a quasi-experimental study, and they are an excellent source of testable hypotheses. On the other hand, a major problem with case studies is their **generalizability**—the degree to which their results can be applied to other cases. Because humans differ from one another in both brain function and behavior, it is important to be skeptical of any biopsychological theory based entirely on a few case studies.

■ Pure and Applied Research

Biopsychological research can be either pure or applied. Pure research and applied research differ in a number of respects, but they are distinguished less by their own attributes than by the motives of the individuals involved in their pursuit. **Pure research** is research motivated primarily by the curiosity of the researcher—it is done solely for the purpose of acquiring knowledge. In contrast, **applied research** is research intended to bring about some direct benefit to humankind.

Many scientists believe that pure research will ultimately prove to be of more practical benefit than applied research. Their view is that applications flow readily from an understanding of basic principles and that attempts to move directly to application without first gaining a basic understanding are shortsighted. Of course, it is not

Table 1.1   Some of the Nobel Prizes Awarded for Studies Related to the Nervous System or Behavior

NOBEL WINNER	DATE	ACCOMPLISHMENT
Ivan Pavlov	1904	Research on the physiology of digestion
Camillo Golgi and Santiago Ramón y Cajal	1906	Research on the structure of the nervous system
Charles Sherrington and Edgar Adrian	1932	Discoveries about the functions of neurons
Henry Dale and Otto Loewi	1936	Discoveries about the transmissions of nerve impulses
Joseph Erlanger and Herbert Gasser	1944	Research on the functions of single nerve fibers
Walter Hess	1949	Research on the role of the brain in controlling behavior
Egas Moniz	1949	Development of prefrontal lobotomy
Georg von Békésy	1961	Research on the auditory system
John Eccles, Alan Hodgkin, and Andrew Huxley	1963	Research on the ionic basis of neural transmission
Ragnor Granit, Haldan Hartline, and George Wald	1967	Research on the chemistry and physiology of vision
Bernard Katz, Ulf von Euler, and Julius Axelrod	1970	Discoveries related to synaptic transmission
Karl Von Frisch, Konrad Lorenz, and Nikolass Tinbergen	1973	Studies of animal behavior
Roger Guillemin and Andrew Schally	1977	Discoveries related to hormone production by the brain
Herbert Simon	1979	Research on human cognition
Roger Sperry	1981	Research on differences between the cerebral hemispheres
David Hubel and Torsten Wiesel	1981	Research on information processing in the visual system
Rita Levi-Montalcini and Stanley Cohen	1986	Discovery and study of nerve and epidermal growth factors
Erwin Neher and Bert Sakmann	1991	Research on ion channels
Alfred Gilman and Martin Rodbell	1994	Discovery of G protein–coupled receptors
Arvid Carlsson, Paul Greengard, and Eric Kandel	2000	Discoveries related to synaptic transmission

necessary for a research project to be completely pure or completely applied; many research programs have elements of both approaches.

One important difference between pure and applied research is that pure research is more vulnerable to the vagaries of political regulation because politicians and the voting public have difficulty understanding why research of no immediate practical benefit should be supported. If the decision were yours, would you be willing to grant hundreds of thousands of dollars to support the study of squid *motor neurons* (neurons that control muscles), learning in recently hatched geese, the activity of single nerve cells in the visual systems of monkeys, the hormones released by the *hypothalamus* (a small neural structure at the base of

the brain) of pigs and sheep, or the function of the *corpus callosum* (the large neural pathway that connects the left and right halves of the brain)? Which, if any, of these projects would you consider worthy of support? Each of these seemingly esoteric projects was supported, and each earned a Nobel Prize for its author.

Table 1.1 lists some of the Nobel Prizes awarded for research related to the brain and behavior. The purpose of this list is to give you a general sense of the official recognition that behavioral and brain research has received, not to have you memorize the list. You will learn later in the chapter that, when it comes to evaluating science, the Nobel committee has not been infallible.

1.4   What Are the Divisions of Biopsychology?

As you have just learned, biopsychologists conduct their research in a variety of fundamentally different ways. Biopsychologists who take the same approaches to their research tend to publish their research in the same journals, attend the same scientific meetings, and belong to the same professional societies. The particular ap-

proaches to biopsychology that have flourished and grown have gained wide recognition as separate divisions of biopsychological research. The purpose of this section of the chapter is to give you a clearer sense of biopsychology and its diversity by describing six of its major divisions: (1) physiological psychology, (2) psychopharmacology,

(3) neuropsychology, (4) psychophysiology, (5) cognitive neuroscience, and (6) comparative psychology. For simplicity, they are presented as distinct approaches; but there is much overlap among them, and many biopsychologists regularly follow more than one approach.

Physiological Psychology

Physiological psychology is the division of biopsychology that studies the neural mechanisms of behavior through the direct manipulation of the brain in controlled experiments—surgical and electrical methods of brain manipulation are most common. The subjects of physiological psychology research are almost always laboratory animals, because the focus on direct brain manipulation and controlled experiments precludes the use of human subjects in most instances. There is also a tradition of pure research in physiological psychology; the emphasis is usually on research that contributes to the development of theories of the neural control of behavior rather than on research that is of immediate practical benefit.

Psychopharmacology

Psychopharmacology is similar to physiological psychology, except that it focuses on the manipulation of neural activity and behavior with drugs. In fact, many of the early psychopharmacologists were simply physiological psychologists who moved into drug research, and many of today's biopsychologists identify closely with both approaches. However, the study of the effects of drugs on the brain and behavior has become so specialized that psychopharmacology is widely regarded as a separate discipline.

A substantial portion of psychopharmacological research is applied (see Brady, 1993). Although drugs are sometimes used by psychopharmacologists to study the basic principles of brain–behavior interaction, the purpose of many psychopharmacological experiments is to develop therapeutic drugs (see Chapter 18) or to reduce drug abuse (see Chapter 15). Psychopharmacologists study the effects of drugs on laboratory species—and on humans, if the ethics of the situation permits it.

Neuropsychology

Neuropsychology is the study of the psychological effects of brain damage in human patients. Obviously, human subjects cannot ethically be exposed to experimental treatments that endanger normal brain function. Consequently, neuropsychology deals almost exclusively with case studies and quasiexperimental studies of patients with brain damage resulting from disease, accident, or neurosurgery. The outer layer of the cerebral hemispheres—the **cerebral cortex**—is most likely to be damaged by accident or surgery; this is one reason why neuropsychology has focused on this important part of the human brain.

Neuropsychology is the most applied of the biopsychological subdisciplines; the neuropsychological assessment of human patients, even when part of a program of pure research, is always done with an eye toward benefiting them in some way. Neuropsychological tests facilitate diagnosis and thus help the attending physician prescribe effective treatment (see Benton, 1994). They can also be an important basis for patient care and counseling; Kolb and Whishaw (1990) described such an application.

The Case of Mr. R., the Brain-Damaged Student Who Switched to Architecture

Mr. R., a 21-year-old left-handed man, struck his head on the dashboard in a car accident. . . . Prior to his accident Mr. R. was an honor student at a university. . . . However, a year after the accident he had become a mediocre student who had particular trouble completing his term papers. . . . He was referred to us for neuropsychological assessment, which revealed several interesting facts.

First, Mr. R. was one of about one-third of left-handers whose language functions are represented in the right rather than left hemisphere. . . . In addition, although Mr. R. had a superior IQ, his verbal memory and reading speed were only low-average, which is highly unusual for a person of his intelligence and education. These deficits indicated that his right temporal lobe may have been slightly damaged in the car accident, resulting in an impairment of his language skills. On the basis of our neuropsychological investigation we were able to recommend vocations to Mr. R. that did not require superior verbal memory skills, and he is currently studying architecture. (p. 128)[2]

Psychophysiology

Psychophysiology is the division of biopsychology that studies the relation between physiological activity and psychological processes in human subjects (see Andreassi, 1989). Because the subjects of psychophysiological research are human, psychophysiological recording

---

[2]From *Fundamentals of Human Neuropsychology*, 3rd Edition, by Bryan Kolb and Ian Q. Whishaw. Copyright © 1980, 1985, 1990 W. H. Freeman and Company. Reprinted with permission.

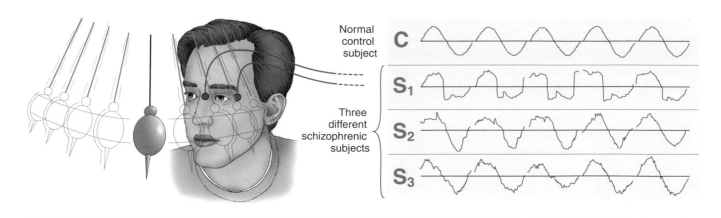

FIGURE 1.4 Visual tracking of a pendulum by a normal control subject (top) and three schizophrenics. (Adapted from Iacono & Koenig, 1983.)

procedures are typically noninvasive; that is, the physiological activity is recorded from the surface of the body. The usual measure of brain activity is the scalp **electroencephalogram (EEG).** Other common psychophysiological measures are muscle tension, eye movement, and several indicators of autonomic nervous system activity (e.g., heart rate, blood pressure, pupil dilation, and electrical conductance of the skin). The **autonomic nervous system** is the division of the nervous system that regulates the body's inner environment.

Most psychophysiological research focuses on understanding the physiology of psychological processes, such as attention, emotion, and information processing, but there have also been a number of interesting clinical applications of the psychophysiological method (see Iacono, 1985). For example, psychopsychological experiments have indicated that schizophrenics have difficulty smoothly tracking a moving object such as a pendulum (Iacono & Koenig, 1983)—see Figure 1.4.

Cognitive Neuroscience

Cognitive neuroscience is the youngest division of biopsychology, but it is currently among the most active and exciting. Cognitive neuroscientists study the neural bases of **cognition,** a term that generally refers to higher intellectual processes such as thought, memory, attention, and complex perceptual processes (see Sperry, 1993). Because of its focus on cognition, most cognitive neuroscience research involves human subjects; and because of its focus on human subjects, its major method is noninvasive recording rather than the direct manipulation of the brain.

The major method of cognitive neuroscience is functional brain imaging (recording images of the activ-

ity of the living human brain; see Chapter 5) while the subjects are engaged in particular cognitive activities. For example, in Figure 1.5, you will notice how an area of the left cerebral cortex became active when the subject tapped a finger of her right hand.

Because the theory and methods of cognitive neuroscience are so complex and interesting to people in so many fields, most cognitive neuroscientific research is an interdisciplinary collaboration among individuals with different types of training. For example, in addition to conventionally trained biopsychologists, cognitive psy-

FIGURE 1.5 Functional brain imaging is the major method of cognitive neuroscience. This functional brain image shows the top of the brain, with the front on your left. It illustrates the area of the left hemisphere that became active when the subject repeatedly tapped her right index finger. (Courtesy of Peter Liddle, Department of Psychiatry, University of British Columbia.)

chologists, computing and mathematics experts, and various types of neuroscientists commonly contribute to the field. Cognitive neuroscience research sometimes involves noninvasive electrophysiological recording, and it sometimes focuses on subjects with brain pathology; in these cases, the boundaries between cognitive neuroscience and psychophysiology and neuropsychology, respectively, are blurry.

Comparative Psychology

Although most biopsychologists study the neural mechanisms of behavior, there is more to biopsychology than this. As Dewsbury (1991) asserted:

> The "biology" in "psychobiology" should include the whole-animal approaches of ethology, ecology, evolution . . . as well as the latest in physiological methods and thought. . . . The "compleat psychobiologist" should use whatever explanatory power can be found with modern physiological techniques, but never lose sight of the problems that got us going in the first place: the integrated behavior of whole, functioning, adapted organisms. (p. 198)

The division of biopsychology that deals generally with the biology of behavior, rather than specifically with the neural mechanisms of behavior, is **comparative psychology.** Comparative psychologists compare the behavior of different species in order to understand the evolution, genetics, and adaptiveness of behavior (see Timberlake, 1993). Comparative research is the main method of those biopsychologists who study behavior from an evolutionary perspective.

Historically, comparative psychologists have focused on the experimental investigation of animal behavior in controlled laboratory environments. However, today, comparative psychology also encompasses **ethological research**—the study of animal behavior in its natural environment. Also, in the last few decades, as major advances have been made in the field of genetics, advances in *behavior genetics* (study of the genetics of behavior and other psychological processes) have kept apace.

In case you have forgotten, the purpose of this section has been to characterize biopsychology and its diversity by describing its divisions. You will learn much more about the exciting progress being made by the various divisions of biopsychology in subsequent chapters.

BrainScan

To see if you are ready to proceed to the next section of the chapter, scan your brain by filling in each of the following blanks with one of the six biopsychology divisions. The correct answers are provided at the bottom of the page. Before proceeding, review material related to your errors and omissions.

1. A biopsychologist who studies the memory deficits of human patients with brain damage would likely identify with the division of biopsychology termed _____ .

2. Psychologists who study the physiological correlates of psychological processes by recording physiological signals from the surface of the human body are often referred to as _____ .

3. The biopsychological research of _____ _____ frequently involves the direct manipulation or recording of the neural activity of laboratory animals by various invasive surgical, electrical, and chemical means.

4. The division of biopsychology that focuses on the study of the effects of drugs on behavior is often referred to as _____ .

5. Although _____ can be considered to be a division of biopsychology because it focuses on the neural bases of cognition, it is a collaborative interdisciplinary field.

6. _____ are biopsychologists who study the genetics, evolution, and adaptiveness of behavior, often by using the comparative approach.

1.5 Converging Operations: How Do Biopsychologists Work Together?

Because none of the six biopsychological approaches to research is without its shortcomings and because of the complexity of the brain and its role in psychological processes, major biopsychological issues are rarely resolved by a single experiment or even by a single series of experiments taking the same general approach. Progress is most likely when different approaches are focused on a single problem in such a way that the strengths of one approach compensate for the weaknesses of the others; this is called **converging operations.**

Consider, for example, the relative strengths and weaknesses of neuropsychology and physiological psychology in the study of the psychological effects of damage to the human cerebral cortex. In this instance, the strength of the neuropsychological approach is that it deals directly with human patients; its weakness is that its focus on human patients precludes experiments. In contrast, the strength of the physiological psychology approach is that it can bring the power of the experimental method and neuroscientific technology to bear through research on nonhuman animals; its weakness is that the relevance of research on laboratory animals to human neuropsychological deficits is always open to question. Clearly these two approaches complement each other well; together they can answer questions that neither can answer individually.

To examine converging operations in action, let's return to the case of Jimmie G. The neuropsychological disorder from which Jimmie G. suffered was first described in the late 19th century by S. S. Korsakoff, a Russian physician, and subsequently became known as **Korsakoff's syndrome.** The primary symptom of Korsakoff's syndrome is severe memory loss, which is made all the more heartbreaking—as you have seen in Jimmie G.'s case—by the fact that its sufferers are often otherwise quite capable. Because Korsakoff's syndrome commonly occurs in alcoholics, it was initially believed to be a direct consequence of the toxic effects of alcohol on the brain. This conclusion proved to be a good illustration of the inadvisability of basing causal conclusions on quasiexperimental research. Subsequent research showed that Korsakoff's syndrome is largely caused by the brain damage associated with *thiamine* (vitamin B_1) deficiency—see Butterworth, Kril, and Harper (1993) and Lishman (1990).

The first support for the thiamine-deficiency interpretation of Korsakoff's syndrome came from the discovery of the syndrome in malnourished persons who consumed little or no alcohol. Additional support came from experiments in which thiamine-deficient rats were compared with otherwise identical groups of control rats. The thiamine-deficient rats displayed memory deficits and patterns of brain damage similar to those observed in human alcoholics (Knoth & Mair, 1991; Mair, Knoth, et al., 1991; Mair, Otto, et al., 1991). Alcoholics often develop Korsakoff's syndrome because most of their caloric intake comes in the form of alcohol, which lacks vitamins, and because alcohol interferes with the metabolism of what little thiamine they do consume (Rindi, 1989). However, alcohol has been shown to accelerate the development of brain damage in thiamine-deficient rats, so it may have a direct toxic effect on the brain as well (Zimitat et al., 1990).

The point of all this (in case you have forgotten) is that progress in biopsychology typically comes from converging operations—in this case, from the convergence of neuropsychological case studies, quasiexperiments on human subjects, and controlled experiments on laboratory animals. The strength of biopsychology lies in the diversity of its methods and approaches. This means that, in evaluating biopsychological claims, it is rarely sufficient to consider the results of one study or even of one line of experiments using the same method or approach.

So what has all the research on Korsakoff's syndrome done for Jimmie G. and others like him? Today, alcoholics are often counseled to stop drinking and are treated with massive doses of thiamine. The thiamine limits the development of further brain damage and often leads to a slight improvement in the patient's condition; but, unfortunately, brain damage, once produced, is largely permanent. In some parts of the world, the fortification of alcoholic beverages with thiamine has been considered (Wodak, Richmond, & Wilson, 1990). What do you think of this plan?

1.6 Scientific Inference: How Do Biopsychologists Study the Unobservable Workings of the Brain?

Scientific inference is the fundamental method of biopsychology and of most other sciences—it is what makes being a scientist fun. This section provides further insight into the nature of biopsychology by defining, illustrating, and discussing scientific inference.

The scientific method is a system for finding things out by careful observation, but many of the processes studied by scientists cannot be observed. For example, scientists use empirical (observational) methods to study ice ages, gravity, evaporation, electricity, and nuclear fission—none of which can be directly observed; their effects can be observed, but the processes themselves cannot. Biopsychology is no different from other sciences in this respect. One of its main goals is to characterize, through empirical methods, the unobservable processes by which the nervous system controls behavior.

The empirical method that biopsychologists and other scientists use to study the unobservable is called **scientific inference.** The scientists carefully measure key events that they can observe and then use these measures as a basis for logically inferring the nature of events that they cannot observe. Like a detective carefully gathering clues from which to recreate an unwitnessed crime, a biopsychologist carefully gathers relevant measures of behavior and neural activity from which to infer the nature of the neural processes that regulate behavior. The fact that the neural mechanisms of behavior cannot be directly observed and must be studied through scientific inference is what makes biopsychological research such a challenge—and, as I said before, so much fun.

To illustrate scientific inference, I have selected a research project in which you can participate. By making a few simple observations about your own visual abilities under different conditions, you will be able to discover the principle by which your brain translates the movement of images on your retinas into perceptions of movement (see Figure 1.6). One feature of the mechanism is immediately obvious. Hold your hand in front of your face, and then move its image across your retinas by

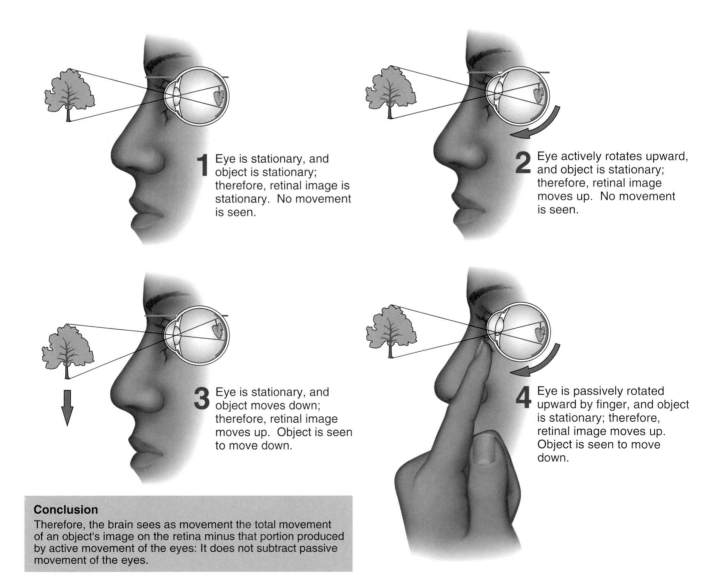

1 Eye is stationary, and object is stationary; therefore, retinal image is stationary. No movement is seen.

2 Eye actively rotates upward, and object is stationary; therefore, retinal image moves up. No movement is seen.

3 Eye is stationary, and object moves down; therefore, retinal image moves up. Object is seen to move down.

4 Eye is passively rotated upward by finger, and object is stationary; therefore, retinal image moves up. Object is seen to move down.

Conclusion
Therefore, the brain sees as movement the total movement of an object's image on the retina minus that portion produced by active movement of the eyes: It does not subtract passive movement of the eyes.

FIGURE 1.6 The perception of motion under four different conditions.

moving your eyes, by moving your hand, or by moving both at once. You will notice that only those movements of the retinal image that are produced by the movement of your hand are translated into the sight of motion; movements of the retinal image that are produced by your own eye movements are not. Obviously, there must be a part of your brain that monitors the movements of your retinal image and subtracts from the total those image movements that are produced by your own eye movements, leaving the remainder to be perceived as motion.

ON THE CD
Visit the *Perception of Motion* module. As you protect the earth from interstellar invasion, you demonstrate to yourself how your brain perceives motion.

Now, let's try to characterize the nature of the information about your eye movements that is used by your brain in its perception of motion (see Bridgeman, Van der Heijden, & Velichkovsky, 1994). Try the following. Shut one eye, then rotate your other eye slightly upward by gently pressing on your lower eyelid with your fingertip. What do you see? You see all of the objects in your visual field moving downward. Why? It seems that the brain mechanism that is responsible for the perception of motion does not consider eye movement per se. It considers only those eye movements that are actively produced by neural signals from the brain to the eye muscles, not those that are passively produced by external means (e.g., by your finger). Thus when your eye was moved passively, your brain assumed that it had remained still and attributed the movement of your retinal image to the movement of objects in your visual field.

It is possible to trick the visual system in the opposite way; instead of the eyes being moved when no active signals have been sent to the eye muscles, the eyes can be held stationary despite the brain's attempts to move them. Because this experiment involves paralyzing the eye muscles, you cannot participate. Hammond, Merton, and Sutton (1956) injected the active ingredient of *curare,* the paralytic substance with which some South American natives coat their blow darts, into the eye muscles of their subject—who was Merton himself. What do you think Merton saw when he tried to move his eyes? He saw the stationary visual world moving in the same direction as his attempted eye movements. If a visual object is focused on part of your retina, and it stays focused there despite the fact that you have moved your eyes to the right, it too must have moved to the right. Consequently, when Merton sent signals to his eye muscles to move his eyes to the right, his brain assumed that the movement had been carried out, and it perceived stationary objects as moving to the right.

The point of the eye-movement example is that biopsychologists can learn much about the activities of the brain without directly observing them—and so can you. Understanding that biopsychology, like most sciences, is based on scientific inference is a critical early step in developing your ability to think about it.

1.7 Critical Thinking about Biopsychological Claims

We have all heard or read that we use only a small portion of our brains, that it is important to eat three meals a day, that intelligence is inherited, that everybody needs at least 8 hours of sleep per night, that there is a gene for schizophrenia, that morphine is a particularly dangerous (hard) drug, that neurological diseases can now be cured by genetic engineering, and that homosexuality is caused by inappropriate upbringing—to name just a few claims about biopsychological phenomena that have been widely disseminated. You may believe some of these claims. But are they true? How does one find out? And if they are not true, why do so many people believe them?

As you have already learned, one of the major goals of this book is to teach you how to think effectively about biopsychological information. The purpose of this final section of the chapter is to begin the development of your *critical thinking ability,* the ability to evaluate scientific claims by identifying potential omissions or weaknesses in the evidence. Accordingly, the chapter concludes with two cases that were the bases for claims once widely accepted by many but subsequently shown to be unfounded. Notice that if you keep your wits about you, you do not have to be an expert to spot the weaknesses.

The first step in judging the validity of any scientific claim is to determine whether or not the claim and the research on which it is based were published in a scientific journal (Rensberger, 2000). The reason is that, in order to be published in a scientific journal, an article must first be reviewed by experts in the field—usually three or four of them—and judged to be of good quality. Indeed, many scientific journals publish only a small proportion of the manuscripts submitted to them. You should be particularly skeptical of scientific claims that have not gone through this rigorous review process, but, as you are about to learn, even articles judged to be important by other scientists are not necessarily free of unrecognized flaws.

The first of the two cases deals with an unpublished claim that was largely dispensed through the news media. The second deals with a claim that was initially supported by numerous scientific publications.

Case 1: José and the Bull

José Delgado demonstrated to a group of newspaper reporters a remarkable new procedure for controlling aggression. Delgado strode into a Spanish bull ring carrying only a red cape and a small radio transmitter. With the transmitter, he could activate a battery-powered stimulator that had previously been mounted on the horns of the other inhabitant of the ring. As the raging bull charged, Delgado calmly activated the stimulator and sent a weak train of electrical current from the stimulator through an electrode that had been implanted in the caudate nucleus, a structure deep in the bull's brain. The bull immediately veered from its charge. After a few such interrupted charges, the bull stood tamely as Delgado swaggered about the ring. According to Delgado, this demonstration marked a significant scientific breakthrough—the discovery of a caudate taming center and the fact that stimulation of this structure could eliminate aggressive behavior, even in bulls specially bred for their ferocity.

To those present at this carefully orchestrated event and to most of the millions who subsequently read about it, Delgado's conclusion was compelling. Surely, if caudate stimulation could stop the charge of a raging bull, the caudate must be a taming center. It was even suggested that caudate stimulation through implanted electrodes might be an effective treatment for human psychopaths. What do you think?

■ **ANALYSIS OF CASE 1** The fact of the matter is that Delgado's demonstration provided little or no support for his conclusion. It should have been obvious to anyone who did not get caught up in the provocative nature of Delgado's media event that there are numerous ways in which brain stimulation can abort a bull's charge, most of which are simpler or more direct, and thus more probable, than the one suggested by Delgado. For example, the stimulation may have simply rendered the bull confused, dizzy, nauseous, sleepy, or temporarily blind rather than nonaggressive; or the stimulation could have been painful. Clearly, any observation that can be interpreted in so many different ways provides little support for any one interpretation. When there are several possible interpretations for a behavioral observation, the rule is to give precedence to the simplest one; this rule is called **Morgan's Canon.** The following comments of Valenstein (1973) provide a reasoned view of Delgado's demonstration:

Actually there is no good reason for believing that the stimulation had any direct effect on the bull's aggressive tendencies. An examination of the film record makes it apparent that the charging bull was stopped because as long as the stimulation was on it was forced to turn around in the same direction continuously. After examining the film, any scientist with knowledge in this field could conclude only that the stimulation had been activating a neural pathway controlling movement. (p. 98)

. . . he [Delgado] seems to capitalize on every individual effect his electrodes happen to produce and presents little, if any, experimental evidence that his impression of the underlying cause is correct. (p. 103)

. . . his propensity for dramatic, albeit ambiguous, demonstrations has been a constant source of material for those whose purposes are served by exaggerating the omnipotence of brain stimulation. (p. 99)

Case 2: Becky, Moniz, and Prefrontal Lobotomy

In 1949, Dr. Egas Moniz was awarded the Nobel Prize in Physiology and Medicine for the development of **prefrontal lobotomy**—a surgical procedure in which the connections between the prefrontal lobes and the rest of the brain are cut—as a treatment for mental illness. The **prefrontal lobes** are the large areas, left and right, at the very front of the brain (see Figure 1.7).

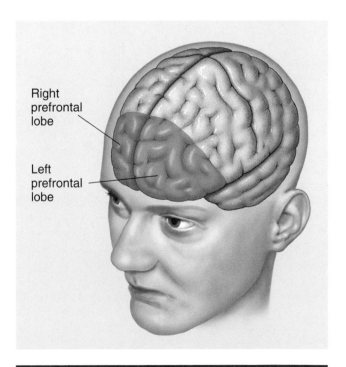

Right prefrontal lobe

Left prefrontal lobe

FIGURE 1.7 The right and left prefrontal lobes, whose connections to the rest of the brain are disrupted by prefrontal lobotomy.

Moniz's discovery was based on the report that Becky, a chimpanzee that frequently became upset when she made errors during the performance of a food-rewarded task, did not do so following the creation of a large *bilateral lesion* (an area of damage to both sides of the brain) of her prefrontal lobes. After hearing about this isolated observation at a scientific meeting in 1935, Moniz persuaded neurosurgeon Almeida Lima to operate on a series of psychiatric patients; Lima cut out six large cores of prefrontal tissue with a surgical device called a **leucotome** (see Figure 1.8).

Following Moniz's claims that prefrontal surgery was therapeutically successful and had no significant side effects, there was a rapid proliferation of various forms of prefrontal psychosurgery (see O'Callaghan & Carroll, 1982; Valenstein, 1980, 1986). One such variation was **transorbital lobotomy,** which was developed in Italy and then popularized in the United States by Walter Freeman in the late 1940s. It involved inserting an ice-pick–like device under the eyelid, driving it through the orbit (the eye socket) with a few taps of a mallet, and pushing it into the frontal lobes, where it was waved back and forth to sever the connections between the prefrontal lobes and the rest of the brain (see Figure 1.9). This operation was frequently performed in the surgeon's office.

■ **ANALYSIS OF CASE 2** Incredible as it may seem, Moniz's program of psychosurgery was largely based

The leucotome was inserted six times into the patient's brain with the cutting wire retracted.

After each insertion, the cutting wire was extruded and the leucotome rotated to cut out a core of tissue.

FIGURE 1.8 The prefrontal lobotomy procedure developed by Moniz and Lima.

FIGURE 1.9 The transorbital procedure for performing prefrontal lobotomy.

on the observation of a single chimpanzee in a single situation, thus displaying a complete lack of appreciation for the diversity of brain and behavior, both within and between species. No program of psychosurgery should ever be initiated without a thorough assessment of the effects of the surgery on a large sample of subjects from various nonhuman mammalian species.

A second major weakness in the scientific case for prefrontal psychosurgery was the failure of Moniz and others to carefully evaluate the consequences of the surgery in the first patients to undergo the operation. The early reports that the operation was therapeutically successful were based on the impressions of the individuals who were the least objective—the physicians who had prescribed the surgery and their colleagues. Patients were frequently judged as improved if they were more manageable, and little effort was made to evaluate more important aspects of their psychological adjustment or to document the existence of adverse side effects.

Eventually, it became clear that prefrontal lobotomies are of little therapeutic benefit and that they produce a wide range of undesirable side effects, such as amorality, lack of foresight, emotional unresponsiveness, epilepsy, and urinary incontinence. This led to the abandonment of prefrontal lobotomy in many parts of the world—but not before over 40,000 patients had been lobotomized in the United States alone. Still, prefrontal lobotomies continue to be performed in some countries.

Some regard sound scientific methods as unnecessary obstacles in the paths of patients seeking treatment and therapists striving to provide it. However, the unforeseen consequences of prefrontal lobotomy should caution us against abandoning science for expediency. Only by observing the rules of science can scientists protect the public from bogus scientific claims (Carroll, 1984).

There is a somber postscript to this story. Moniz was shot by one of his patients. The bullet became lodged in his spine, rendering him *paraplegic* (paralyzed below the waist).

Themes — Revisited

The seeds for all four major themes of this book were planted in this chapter, but the thinking-about-biopsychology theme predominated. You learned three important ideas that will help you think about many scientific claims: (1) the experimental method, (2) converging operations, and (3) scientific inference. You were then introduced to two biopsychological claims that were widely believed, even though the evidence for them was weak, and you saw critical thinking in action as the weaknesses were identified and the claims dismissed.

You also learned that the three other major themes of the book—clinical implications, the evolutionary perspective, and cognitive neuroscience—tend to be associated with particular divisions of biopsychology. Clinical implications most commonly emerge from neuropsychological and psychopharmacological research; the evolutionary perspective is a defining feature of comparative psychology; and, of course, modern cognitive neuroscientific research is a product of the burgeoning field of cognitive neuroscience.

You are about to enter a world of amazing discovery and intriguing ideas: the world of biopsychology. I hope that your brain enjoys learning about itself.

ON THE CD

Looking for more information about the topics in this chapter? For recommended additional readings, see Hard Copy for Chapter 1.

Log On

- **http://faculty.washington.edu/chudler/hist.html** Milestones in Neuroscience Research is a timeline of key historical events in the neurosciences and biopsychology.

- **http://www.epub.org.br/cm/n02/historia.psicocirg_i.html** This site offers an easy-to-read, comprehensive history of psychosurgical procedures.

- **http://www.brainconnection.com/** Featured here is a great collection of articles and links focusing on brain–behavior issues, illusions, and neuroanatomical illustrations.

Think about It

1. This chapter tells you in general conceptual terms what biopsychology is. Another, and perhaps better, way of defining biopsychology is to describe what biopsychologists do. Ask your instructor what she or he did to become a biopsychologist and what she or he does each workday. I think that you will be surprised. Is your instructor predominantly a physiological psychologist, a psychopharmacologist, a neuropsychologist, a psychophysiologist, a cognitive neuroscientist, or a comparative psychologist?

2. What ethical considerations should guide biopsychological research on nonhuman animals? How should these ethical considerations differ from those that should guide biopsychological research on humans?

ON THE CD
Studying for an exam? Try the Practice Tests for Chapter 1.

3. In retrospect, the entire story of prefrontal lobotomies is shocking. How could physicians, who are generally intelligent, highly educated, and dedicated to helping their patients, participate in such a travesty? How could somebody win a Nobel Prize for developing a form of surgery that left over 40,000 mental cripples in the United States alone? Why did this happen? Could it happen today?

Key Terms

Applied research *(p. 7)*
Autonomic nervous system *(p. 10)*
Between-subjects design *(p. 5)*
Biopsychology *(p. 4)*
Case studies *(p. 7)*
Cerebral cortex *(p. 9)*
Clinical *(p. 3)*
Cognition *(p. 10)*
Cognitive neuroscience *(p. 10)*
Comparative approach *(p. 5)*
Comparative psychology *(p. 11)*
Confounded variable *(p. 6)*
Converging operations *(p. 12)*

Coolidge effect *(p. 6)*
Dependent variable *(p. 6)*
Electroencephalogram (EEG) *(p. 10)*
Ethological research *(p. 11)*
Evolutionary perspective *(p. 3)*
Generalizability *(p. 7)*
Independent variable *(p. 6)*
Korsakoff's syndrome *(p. 12)*
Leucotome *(p. 16)*
Lordosis *(p. 6)*
Morgan's Canon *(p. 15)*
Neuroanatomy *(p. 4)*
Neurochemistry *(p. 4)*

Neuroendocrinology *(p. 4)*
Neurons *(p. 2)*
Neuropathology *(p. 4)*
Neuropharmacology *(p. 4)*
Neurophysiology *(p. 4)*
Neuropsychology *(p. 9)*
Neuroscience *(p. 2)*
Physiological psychology *(p. 9)*
Prefrontal lobes *(p. 15)*
Prefrontal lobotomy *(p. 15)*
Psychopharmacology *(p. 9)*
Psychophysiology *(p. 9)*
Pure research *(p. 7)*
Quasiexperimental studies *(p. 7)*

Scientific inference *(p. 13)*
Transorbital lobotomy *(p. 16)*
Within-subjects design *(p. 5)*

ON THE CD
Need some help studying the key terms for this chapter? Check out the electronic flash cards for Chapter 1.

chapter 2

Evolution, Genetics, and Experience

Thinking about the Biology of Behavior

We all tend to think about things in ways that have been ingrained in us by our **Zeitgeist** (pronounced "ZYTE-gyste"), the general intellectual climate of our culture. That is why this is a particularly important chapter for you. You see, you are the intellec-tual product of a Zeitgeist that promotes ways of thinking about the biological bases of behavior that are inconsistent with the facts. The primary purpose of this chapter is to help you bring your thinking about the biology of behavior in line with modern biopsychological science.

2.1 Thinking about the Biology of Behavior: From Dichotomies to Relations and Interactions

We tend to ignore the subtleties, inconsistencies, and complexities of our existence and to think in terms of simple, mutually exclusive dichotomies: right–wrong, good–bad, attractive–unattractive, and so on. The allure of this way of thinking is its simplicity.

The tendency to think about behavior in terms of dichotomies is illustrated by two kinds of questions that people commonly ask about behavior: (1) Is it physiological, or is it psychological? (2) Is it inherited, or is it learned? Both questions have proved to be misguided; yet they are among the most common kinds of questions asked in biopsychology classrooms. That is why I am dwelling on them here.

Is It Physiological, or Is It Psychological?

The idea that human processes fall into one of two categories, physiological or psychological, grew out of a 17th-century conflict between science and the Roman Church. For much of the history of Western civiliza-tion, truth was whatever was decreed to be true by the Church. Then, in about 1400, things started to change. The famines, plagues, and marauding armies that had repeatedly swept Europe during the Middle Ages sub-sided, and interest turned to art, commerce, and scholar-ship—this was the period of the *Renaissance*, or rebirth (1400 to 1700). Some Renaissance scholars were not con-tent to follow the dictates of the Church; instead, they started to study things directly by observing them—and so it was that modern science was born.

Much of the scientific knowledge that accumulated during the Renaissance was at odds with Church dictates. However, the conflict was resolved by the prominent French philosopher René Descartes (pronounced "day-CART"). Descartes (1596–1650) proposed a philosophy that, in a sense, gave one part of the universe to science and the other part to the Church. He argued that the universe is composed of two elements: (1) physical matter, which behaves according to the laws of nature and is thus a suitable object of scientific investigation; and (2) the human mind (soul or spirit), which lacks physical sub-stance, controls human behavior, obeys no natural laws, and is thus the appropriate purview of the Church. The human body, including the brain, was assumed to be en-tirely physical, and so were nonhuman animals.

Cartesian dualism, as Descartes's philosophy be-came known, was sanctioned by the Roman Church, and so the idea that the human brain and the mind are sepa-rate entities became widely accepted. It has survived to this day, despite the intervening centuries of scientific progress. Most people now understand that human be-havior has a physiological basis, but many still cling to the dualistic assumption that there is a category of hu-man activity that somehow transcends the human brain (Searle, 2000).

Is It Inherited, or Is It Learned?

The tendency to think in terms of dichotomies extends to the way people think about the development of behavioral capacities. For centuries, scholars have de-bated whether humans and other animals inherit their behavioral capacities or whether they acquire them through learning. This debate is commonly referred to as the **nature–nurture issue.**

Most of the early North American experimental psychologists were totally committed to the nurture (learning) side of the nature–nurture issue (de Waal, 1999). The degree of this commitment is illustrated by the oft-cited words of John B. Watson, the father of *behaviorism:*

> We have no real evidence of the inheritance of [behavioral] traits. I would feel perfectly confident in the ultimately favor-able outcome of careful upbringing of a healthy, well-formed baby born of a long line of crooks, murderers and thieves, and prostitutes. Who has any evidence to the contrary?
>
> . . . Give me a dozen healthy infants, well-formed, and my own specified world to bring them up in and I'll guarantee to take any one at random and train him to become any type of specialist I might select—doctor, lawyer, artist, merchant-chief and, yes even beggar-man and thief. (Watson, 1930, pp. 103–104)

At the same time that experimental psychology was taking root in North America, **ethology** (the study of animal behavior in the wild) was becoming the dominant approach to the study of behavior in Europe. European ethology, in contrast to North American experimental psychology, focused on the study of **instinctive behaviors** (behaviors that occur in all like members of a species, even when there seems to have been no opportunity for them to have been learned), and it emphasized the role of nature, or inherited factors, in behavioral development. Because instinctive behaviors do not seem to be learned, the early ethologists assumed that they are entirely inherited. They were wrong, but then so were the early experimental psychologists.

Problems with Thinking about the Biology of Behavior in Terms of Traditional Dichotomies

The physiological-or-psychological and nature-or-nurture debates are based on incorrect ways of thinking about the biology of behavior, and a new generation of questions is directing the current boom in biopsychological research. What is wrong with these old ways of thinking about the biology of behavior, and what are the new ways?

PHYSIOLOGICAL-OR-PSYCHOLOGICAL THINKING RUNS INTO DIFFICULTY ■ Not long after Descartes's mind–brain dualism was officially sanctioned by the Roman Church, it started to come under public attack.

> In 1747, Julien Offroy de la Mettrie anonymously published a pamphlet that scandalized Europe. . . . La Mettrie fled to Berlin, where he was forced to live in exile for the rest of his life. His crime? He had argued that thought was produced by the brain—a dangerous assault, in the eyes of his contemporaries. (Corsi, 1991, cover)

There are two lines of evidence against *physiological-or-psychological thinking* (the assumption that some aspects of human psychological functioning are so complex that they could not possibly be the product of a physical brain). The first line is composed of the many demonstrations that even the most complex psychological changes (e.g., changes in self-awareness, memory, or emotion) can be effected by damage to, or stimulation of, parts of the brain (see Kosslyn & Andersen, 1992). The second line of evidence is composed of the many demonstrations that some non-human species possess abilities that were once assumed to be purely psychological and thus purely human (see Cheney & Seyfarth, 1992; Hauser, 2000). The following two cases illustrate these two kinds of evidence. Both cases deal with self-awareness, which is

Right parietal lobe

FIGURE 2.1 Asomatognosia typically involves damage to the right parietal lobe.

widely regarded as the hallmark of the human mind (see Damasio, 1999).

The first case is Oliver Sacks's (1985) account of "the man who fell out of bed."[1] He—the patient, not Sacks—was suffering from **asomatognosia,** a deficiency in the awareness of parts of one's own body. Asomatognosia typically involves the left side of the body and usually results from damage to the *right parietal lobe* (see Figure 2.1). The second case describes G. G. Gallup's (1983) research on self-awareness in chimpanzees (see Parker, Mitchell, & Boccia, 1994; and Figure 2.2 on page 22).[2]

---

[1]Reprinted with the permission of Simon & Schuster from *The Man Who Mistook His Wife for a Hat and Other Clinical Tales* by Oliver Sacks. Copyright © 1970, 1981, 1983, 1984, 1985 by Oliver Sacks.

[2]From *Toward a Comparative Psychology of Mind* (pp. 474–477) by G. G. Gallup, Jr. In R. L. Mellgren, ed., *Animal Cognition and Behavior.* Amsterdam: North-Holland Publishing Co. Copyright © 1983. Reprinted by permission of North-Holland Publishing Co. and G. G. Gallup, Jr.

FIGURE 2.2 The reactions of chimpanzees to their own images indicate that they are self-aware. In this photo, the chimpanzee is reacting to the bright red, odorless dye that was painted on its eyebrow ridge while it was anesthetized. (Photograph by Donna Bierschwale, courtesy of the New Iberia Research Center.)

The Case of the Man Who Fell Out of Bed

He had felt fine all day, and fallen asleep towards evening. When he woke up he felt fine too, until he moved in the bed. Then he found, as he put it, "someone's leg" in the bed—*a severed human leg,* a horrible thing! He was stunned, at first, with amazement and disgust.... [Then] he had a brainwave.... Obviously one of the nurses ... had stolen into the Dissecting Room and nabbed a leg, and then slipped it under his bedclothes as a joke.... *When he threw it out of bed, he somehow came after it—and now it was attached to him.*

"Look at it!" he cried.... "Have you ever seen such a creepy, horrible thing?" ...

"Easy!" I said. "Be calm! Take it easy!" ...

"... why ... " he asked irritably, belligerently.

"Because it's *your* leg," I answered. "Don't you know your own leg?" ...

... "Ah Doc!" he said. "You're fooling me! You're in cahoots with that nurse." ...

"Listen," I said. "I don't think you're well. Please allow us to return you to bed. But I want to ask you one final question. If this—this thing—is *not* your left leg ... then where is your own left leg?"

Once more he became pale—so pale that I thought he was going to faint. "I don't know," he said. "I have no idea. It's disappeared. It's gone. It's nowhere to be found." (Sacks, 1985, pp. 53–55)

The Case of the Chimps and the Mirrors

An organism is self-aware to the extent that it can be shown capable of becoming the object of its own attention.... One way to assess an organism's capacity to become the object of its own attention is to confront it with a mirror.

... I gave a number of group-reared, preadolescent chimpanzees individual exposure to themselves in mirrors.... Invariably, their first reaction to the mirror was to respond as if they were seeing another chimpanzee.... After about two days, however, ... they ... started to use the mirror to groom and inspect parts of their bodies they had not seen before, and progressively began to experiment with the reflection by making faces, looking at themselves upside down, and assuming unusual postures while monitoring the results in the mirror....

So in an attempt to provide a more convincing demonstration of self-recognition, I devised an unobtrusive and more rigorous test.... [E]ach chimpanzee was anesthetized.... I carefully painted the uppermost portion of an eyebrow ridge and the top half of the opposite ear with a bright red, odorless, alcohol soluble dye....

Following recovery from anesthesia ... the mirror was then reintroduced as an explicit test of self-recognition. Upon seeing their painted faces in the mirror, all the chimpanzees showed repeated mark-directed responses, consisting of attempts to touch and inspect marked areas on their eyebrow and ear while watching the image. In addition, there was over a three-fold increase in viewing time.... Several chimpanzees also showed noteworthy attempts to visually examine and smell the fingers which had been used to touch these facial marks. I suspect that you would respond pretty much the same way, if upon awakening one morning you saw yourself in the mirror with red spots on your face. (Gallup, 1983, pp. 474–477)

NATURE-OR-NURTURE THINKING RUNS INTO DIFFICULTY ■ The history of nature-or-nurture thinking can be summed up by paraphrasing Mark Twain: "Reports of its death have been greatly exaggerated." Each time it has been discredited, it has resurfaced in a slightly modified form. First, factors other than genetics and learning were shown to influence behavioral development; factors such as the fetal environment, nutrition, stress, and sensory stimulation also proved to be influential. This led to a broadening of the concept of nurture to include a variety of experiential factors in addition to learning. In effect, it changed the nature-or-nurture dichotomy from "genetic factors or learning" to "genetic factors or experience."

Next, it was argued convincingly that behavior always develops under the combined control of both nature and nurture (see Johnston, 1987; Rutter, 1997), not under the control of one or the other. Faced with this discovery, many people merely substituted one kind of nature-or-nurture thinking for another. They stopped asking, "Is it genetic, or is it the result of experience?" and started asking, "How much of it is genetic, and how much of it is the result of experience?"

Like earlier versions of the nature-or-nurture question, the how-much-of-it-is-genetic-and-how-much-of-it-is-the-result-of-experience version is fundamentally flawed. The problem is that it is based on the premise that genetic factors and experiential factors combine in an additive fashion—that a behavioral capacity, such as intelligence, is created through the combination or mixture of so many parts of genetics and so many parts of experience, rather than through the interaction of genetics and experience. Once you learn more about how genetic factors and experience interact, you will better appreciate the folly of this assumption. For the time being, however, let me illustrate its weakness with a metaphor embedded in an anecdote.

The Case of the Thinking Student

One of my students told me that she had read that intelligence was one-third genetic and two-thirds experience, and she wondered whether this was true. She must have been puzzled when I began my response by describing an alpine experience. "I was lazily wandering up a summit ridge when I heard an unexpected sound. Ahead, with his back to me, was a young man sitting on the edge of a precipice, blowing into a peculiar musical instrument. I sat down behind him on a large sun-soaked rock, ate my lunch, and shared his experience with him. Then, I got up and wandered back down the ridge, leaving him undisturbed."

I put the following question to my student: "If I wanted to get a better understanding of this music, would it be reasonable for me to begin by asking how much of it came from the musician and how much of it came from the instrument?"

"That would be dumb," she said. "The music comes from both; it makes no sense to ask how much comes from the musician and how much comes from the instrument. Somehow the music results from the interaction of the two together. You would have to ask about the interaction."

"That's exactly right," I said. "Now, do you see why . . ."

"Don't say any more," she interrupted. "I see what you're getting at. Intelligence is the product of the interaction of genes and experience, and it is dumb to try to find how much comes from genes and how much comes from experience."

"And the same is true of any other behavioral trait," I added.

Several days later, the student strode into my office, reached into her pack, and pulled out a familiar object. "I believe that this is your mystery musical instrument," she said. "It's a Peruvian panpipe." She was right . . . again.

The point of this metaphor, in case you have forgotten, is to illustrate why it is nonsensical to try to understand interactions between two factors by asking how much each factor contributes. We would not ask how much the musician and how much the panpipe contributes to panpipe music; we would not ask how much the water and how much the temperature contributes to evaporation; and we would not ask how much the male and how much the female contributes to copulation. Similarly, we shouldn't ask how much genetic and experiential factors contribute to behavioral development. In each case, the answers lie in understanding the nature of the interactions (Lederhendler & Schulkin, 2000). The importance of thinking in this interactive way about development will become obvious to you in Chapter 9, which focuses on the mechanisms of neural development. At this point, however, it is sufficient for you to realize that neurons become active long before they are fully developed and that the subsequent course of their development (e.g., the number of connections they form or whether or not they survive) depends greatly on their activity, much of which is triggered by external experience.

A MODEL OF THE BIOLOGY OF BEHAVIOR ■ So far in this section, you have learned why people tend to think about the biology of behavior in terms of dichotomies, and you have learned some of the reasons why this way of thinking is inappropriate. Now, let's look at the way of thinking about the biology of behavior that has been adopted by many biopsychologists (see Kimble, 1989). It is illustrated in Figure 2.3 on page 24. Like other powerful ideas, it is simple and logical. This model boils down to the single premise that all behavior is the product of interactions among three factors: (1) the organism's genetic endowment, which is a product of its evolution; (2) its experience; and (3) its perception of the current situation. Please examine the model carefully, and consider its implications.

The next three sections of this chapter deal with three elements of this model of behavior: evolution, genetics, and the interaction of genetics and experience in behavioral development. The final section deals with the genetics of human psychological differences.

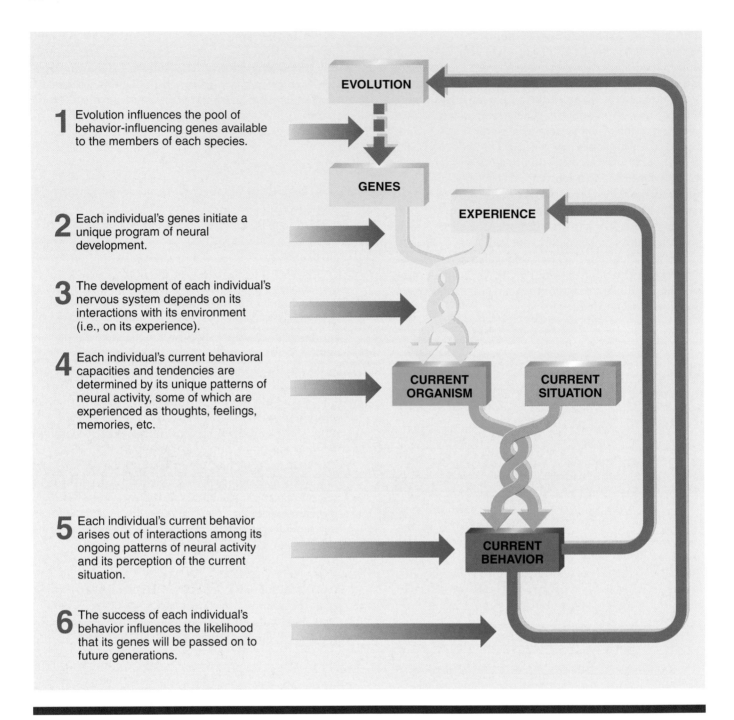

1 Evolution influences the pool of behavior-influencing genes available to the members of each species.

2 Each individual's genes initiate a unique program of neural development.

3 The development of each individual's nervous system depends on its interactions with its environment (i.e., on its experience).

4 Each individual's current behavioral capacities and tendencies are determined by its unique patterns of neural activity, some of which are experienced as thoughts, feelings, memories, etc.

5 Each individual's current behavior arises out of interactions among its ongoing patterns of neural activity and its perception of the current situation.

6 The success of each individual's behavior influences the likelihood that its genes will be passed on to future generations.

EVOLUTION

GENES

EXPERIENCE

CURRENT ORGANISM

CURRENT SITUATION

CURRENT BEHAVIOR

FIGURE 2.3   A schematic illustration of the way in which many biopsychologists think about the biology of behavior.

2.2   Human Evolution

Modern biology began in 1859 with the publication of Charles Darwin's *On the Origin of Species*. In this monumental work, Darwin described his theory of evolution—the single most influential theory in the biological sciences.

Darwin was not the first to suggest that species **evolve** (undergo gradual orderly change) from preexisting species, but he was the first to amass a large body of supporting evidence and the first to suggest how evolution occurs.

Darwin presented three kinds of evidence to support his assertion that species evolve: (1) He documented the evolution of fossil records through progressively more recent geological layers. (2) He described striking structural similarities among living species (e.g., a human's hand, a bird's wing, and a cat's paw), which suggested that they had evolved from common ancestors. (3) He pointed to the major changes that had been brought about in domestic plants and animals by programs of selective breeding. However, the most convincing evidence of evolution comes from direct observations of evolution in progress. For example, Grant (1991) observed evolution of the finches of the Galápagos Islands—a population studied by Darwin himself—after only a single season of drought. Figure 2.4 illustrates these four kinds of evidence.

Darwin argued that evolution occurs through **natural selection.** He pointed out that the members of each species vary greatly in their structure, physiology, and be-

havior, and that the heritable traits that are associated with high rates of survival and reproduction are the most likely ones to be passed on to future generations. He argued that natural selection, when repeated generation after generation, leads to the evolution of species that are better adapted to surviving and reproducing in their particular environmental niche. Darwin called this process *natural selection* to emphasize its similarity to the artificial selective breeding practices employed by breeders of domestic animals. Just as horse breeders create faster horses by selectively breeding the fastest of their existing stock, nature creates fitter animals by selectively breeding the fittest. **Fitness,** in the Darwinian sense, is the ability of an organism to survive and contribute its genes to the next generation.

The theory of evolution was at odds with the various dogmatic views that were embedded in the 19th-century Zeitgeist, so it met with initial resistance. Although traces

Fossil records change systematically through geological layers. Illustrated here is the evolution of the hominid skull.

Major changes have been created in domestic plants and animals by programs of selective breeding.

Evolution has been observed in progress. For example, an 18-month drought on one of the Galápagos Islands left only large, difficult-to-eat seeds and increased the beak size in one species of finch.

There are striking structural similarities among diverse living species (e.g., between a human arm and a bat's wing).

FIGURE 2.4   Four kinds of evidence supporting the theory that species evolve.

of this resistance still exist, virtually none comes from people who understand the evidence:

> Evolution by natural selection meets no significant opposition within biological science. The principle of natural selection has a logical necessity to it; indeed, some have argued that it is a tautology rather than an empirical law . . . [S]ubsequent development of biology in major new areas like genetics and biochemistry has only reinforced Darwin's conclusion that the facts make a belief in the theory of evolution by natural selection "inescapable." (Daly & Wilson, 1983, p. 7)

■ Evolution and Behavior

Some behaviors play an obvious role in evolution. For example, the ability to find food, avoid predation, and defend one's young obviously increases an animal's ability to pass on its genes to future generations. Other behaviors play a role that is less obvious but no less important; two examples are social dominance and courtship display.

SOCIAL DOMINANCE ■ The males of many species establish a stable *hierarchy of social dominance* through combative encounters with other males. In some species, these encounters often involve physical damage; in others, they involve mainly posturing and threatening until one of the two combatants backs down. The dominant male usually wins encounters with all other males of the group; the number 2 male usually wins encounters with all males except the dominant male; and so on down the line. Once a hierarchy is established, hostilities diminish because the low-ranking males learn to avoid or quickly submit to the dominant males. Because most of the fighting goes on between males competing for positions high in the social hierarchy, low-ranking males fight little; thus, the lower levels of the hierarchy tend to be only vaguely recognizable.

Why is social dominance an important factor in evolution? One reason is that in some species dominant males copulate more than nondominant males and thus are more effective in passing on their characteristics to future generations. McCann (1981) studied the effect of social dominance on the rate of copulation in 10 bull elephant seals that cohabited the same breeding beach. Figure 2.5 illustrates how these massive animals challenge each other by raising themselves to full height and pushing chest to chest. Usually, the smaller of the two backs down; if it does not, a vicious neck-biting battle ensues. McCann found that the dominant male accounted for about 37% of the copulations during the study, whereas poor number 10 accounted for only about 1% (see Figure 2.5).

Another reason why social dominance is an important factor in evolution is that in some species dominant females are more likely to produce more, and more healthy, offspring. For example, Pusey, Williams, and Goodall (1997) found that high-ranking female chimpanzees produced more offspring and that these offspring were more likely to survive to sexual maturity. They attributed these advantages to the fact that higher-ranking female chimpanzees are more likely to maintain access to productive food foraging areas.

COURTSHIP DISPLAY ■ An intricate series of courtship displays precedes copulation in many species. The male approaches the female and signals his interest. His signal (which may be olfactory, visual, auditory, or tactual) may elicit a signal in the female, which may elicit another response in the male, and so on until copulation ensues. But copulation is unlikely to occur if one of the pair fails to react appropriately to the signals of the other.

FIGURE 2.5 Two massive bull elephant seals challenge one another. Dominant bull elephant seals copulate more frequently than those that are lower in the dominance hierarchy. (Adapted from McCann, 1981.)

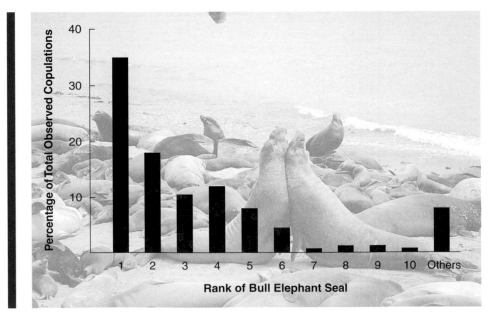

Courtship displays are thought to promote the evolution of new species. Let me explain. A **species** is a group of organisms that is reproductively isolated from other organisms; that is, the members of one species can produce fertile offspring only by mating with members of the same species. A new species begins to branch off from an existing species when some barrier discourages breeding between a subpopulation of the existing species and the remainder of the species (Peterson, Soberón, & Sánchez-Cordero, 1999). Once such a reproductive barrier forms, the subpopulation evolves independently of the remainder of the species until cross-fertilization becomes impossible.

The reproductive barrier may be geographic; for example, a few birds may fly together to an isolated island, where many generations of their offspring breed among themselves and evolve into a separate species. Alternatively—to get back to the main point—the reproductive barrier may be behavioral. A few members of a species may develop different courtship displays, and these may form a reproductive barrier between themselves and the rest of their **conspecifics** (members of the same species).

◼ Course of Human Evolution

By studying fossil records and comparing current species, we humans have looked back in time and pieced together the evolutionary history of our species—although some of the details are still controversial. Human evolution, as it is currently understood, is summarized in this section.

EVOLUTION OF VERTEBRATES ◼ Complex multicellular water-dwelling organisms first appeared on earth about 600 million years ago (Vermeij, 1996). About 150 million years later, the first chordates evolved. **Chordates** (pronounced "KOR-dates") are animals with dorsal nerve cords (large nerves that run along the center of the back, or *dorsum*); they are 1 of the 20 or so large categories, or *phyla* (pronounced "FY-la"), into which zoologists group animal species. The first chordates with spinal bones to protect their dorsal nerve cords evolved about 25 million years later. The spinal bones are called *vertebrae* (pronounced "VERT-eh-bray"), and the chordates that possess them are called **vertebrates**. The first vertebrates were primitive bony fishes. Today, there are seven classes of vertebrates: three classes of fishes, plus amphibians, reptiles, birds, and mammals.

EVOLUTION OF AMPHIBIANS ◼ About 410 million years ago, the first bony fishes ventured out of the water. Fishes that could survive on land for brief periods of time had two great advantages: They could escape from stagnant pools to nearby fresh water, and they could take advantage of terrestrial food sources. The advantages of life on land were so great that natural selection transformed the fins and gills of bony fishes to legs and lungs,

respectively—and so it was that the first **amphibians** evolved about 400 million years ago. Amphibians (e.g., frogs, toads, and salamanders) in their larval form must live in the water; only adult amphibians can survive on land.

EVOLUTION OF REPTILES ◼ About 300 million years ago, reptiles (e.g., lizards, snakes, and turtles) evolved from amphibians. Reptiles were the first vertebrates to lay shell-covered eggs and to be covered by dry scales. Both of these adaptations reduced the reliance of reptiles on watery habitats. A reptile does not have to spend the first stage of its life in the watery environment of a pond or lake; instead it spends the first stage of its life in the watery environment of a shell-covered egg. And once hatched, a reptile can live far from water, because its dry scales greatly reduce water loss through its water-permeable skin.

EVOLUTION OF MAMMALS ◼ About 180 million years ago, during the height of the age of dinosaurs, a new class of vertebrates evolved from one line of small reptiles. The females of this new class fed their young with secretions from special glands called *mammary glands,* and the members of this line are called **mammals** after these glands. Eventually, mammals stopped laying eggs; instead, the females nurtured their young in the watery environment of their bodies until the young were mature enough to be born. The duck-billed platypus is one surviving mammalian species that lays eggs.

Spending the first stage of life inside one's mother proved to have considerable survival value; it provided the long-term security and environmental stability necessary for complex programs of development to unfold. Today, there are 14 different orders of mammals. The one to which we belong is the order **primates**. We humans—in our usual humble way—named our order after the Latin *primus,* which means "first" or "foremost." There are five families of primates: prosimians, New-World monkeys, Old-World monkeys, apes, and hominids. Examples of the five primate families appear in Figure 2.6 on page 28.

Apes (gibbons, orangutans, gorillas, and chimpanzees) are thought to have evolved from a line of Old-World monkeys. Like Old-World monkeys, apes have long arms and grasping hind feet that are specialized for arboreal travel, and they have opposable thumbs that are not long enough to be of much use for precise manipulation (see Figure 2.7 on page 29). Unlike Old-World monkeys, though, apes have no tails and can walk upright for short distances. Chimpanzees are the closest living relatives of humans; approximately 99% of the genetic material is identical in the two species (see O'Neill, Murphy, & Gallagher, 1994).

EMERGENCE OF HUMANKIND ◼ The family of primates that includes humans is the **hominids;** it is composed of two genera (the plural of genus): *Australopithecus* and *Homo (Homo erectus* and *Homo sapiens).*

OLD-WORLD MONKEY
Hussar Monkey

APE
Silver-Backed Lowland Gorilla

PROSIMIAN
Tarsus Monkey

NEW-WORLD MONKEY
Squirrel Monkey

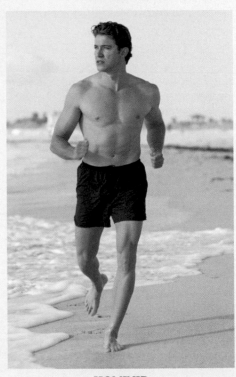

HOMINID
Human

FIGURE 2.6 Examples of the five different families of primates.

However, humans (*Homo sapiens*) are the only surviving hominid species. The *taxonomy* (classification) of the human species is illustrated in Figure 2.8.

The fossil and genetic evidence suggests that the Australopithecines evolved about 6 million years ago in Africa from a line of apes (*australo* means "southern,"

FIGURE 2.7 A comparison of the feet and hands of a human and a chimpanzee.

FIGURE 2.8 The taxonomy of the human species.

and *pithecus* means "ape")—the same line of apes that evolved into chimpanzees in West Africa (see Leakey & Walker, 1997). Several species of *Australopithecus* are thought to have roamed the plains of Africa in small groups for about 5 million years before becoming extinct. Australopithecines were only about 1.3 meters (4 feet) tall, and they had small brains; but analysis of their pelvis and leg bones indicates that their posture was as upright as yours or mine. Any doubts about their upright posture were erased by the discovery of the fossilized footprints pictured in Figure 2.9 (Agnew & Demas, 1998).

The first *Homo* species are thought to have evolved from a species of *Australopithecus* about 2 million years ago (Wood & Collard, 1999). The most distinctive

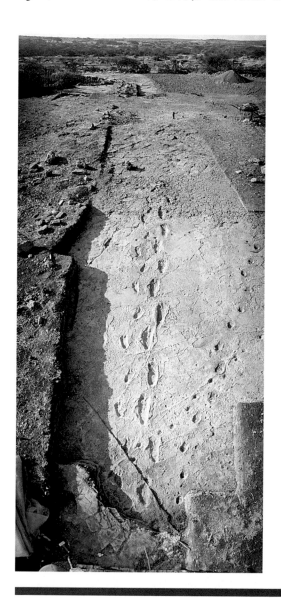

FIGURE 2.9 Fossilized footprints of Australopithecine hominids who strode across African volcanic ash about 3.6 million years ago. They left a 70-meter trail. There were two adults and a child; the child often walked in the footsteps of the adults.

feature of the early *Homo* species was their large brain cavity (about 850 cubic centimeters), larger than that of *Australopithecus* (about 500 cubic centimeters), but smaller than that of modern humans (about 1,330 cubic centimeters). The early *Homo* species used fire and tools (see Susman, 1994), coexisted in Africa with *Australopithecus* for about a half-million years until *Australopithecus* died out, and began to move out of Africa into Europe and Asia about 1.7 million years ago (Tattersall, 1997).

About 200,000 years ago (Pääbo, 1995), early *Homo* species were gradually replaced in the fossil record by modern humans (*Homo sapiens*). Paradoxically, although the big three human attributes—large brain, upright posture, and free hands with an opposable thumb—have been evident for hundreds of thousands of years, most human accomplishments are of recent origin. Artistic products (e.g., wall paintings and carvings) did not appear until about 40,000 years ago, ranching and farming

were not established until about 10,000 years ago, and writing was not invented until about 3,500 years ago.

■ Thinking about Human Evolution

Figure 2.10 illustrates the main branches of vertebrate evolution. As you examine it, put human evolution into perspective by considering the following eight often-misunderstood points about evolution:

1. Evolution does not proceed in a single line. Although it is common to think of an evolutionary ladder or scale, a far better metaphor for evolution is a dense bush.
2. We humans have little reason to claim evolutionary supremacy. We are the last surviving species of a

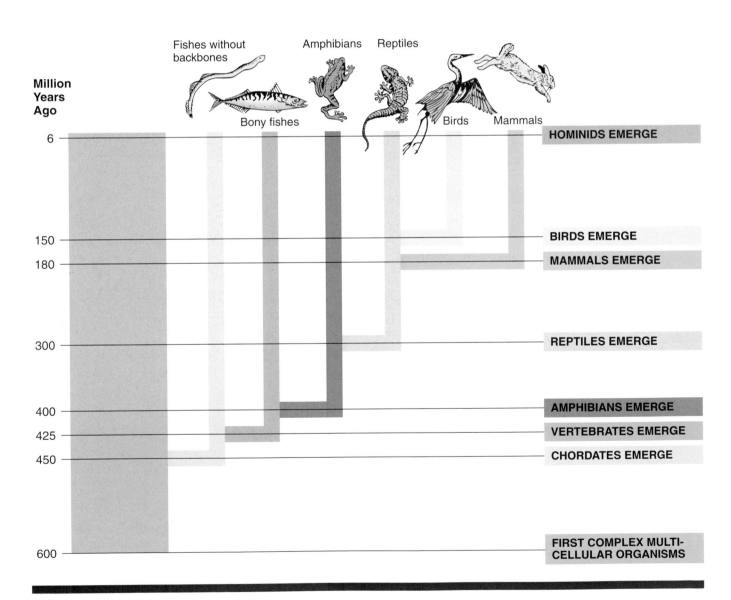

FIGURE 2.10 Vertebrate evolution.

family (i.e., hominids) that has existed for only a blip of evolutionary time.

3. Evolution does not always proceed slowly and gradually. Rapid evolutionary changes (i.e., in a few generations) can be triggered by sudden changes in the environment (see Potts, 1996) or by adaptive genetic mutations (see Elena, Cooper, & Lenski, 1996). Whether human evolution occurred gradually or suddenly is still a matter of intense debate among *paleontologists* (those who scientifically study fossils)—see Kerr (1996). About the time that hominids evolved, there was a sudden cooling of the earth leading to a decrease in African forests and an increase in African grasslands. This may have accelerated human evolution.

4. Few products of evolution have survived to the present day—only the tips of the evolutionary bush have survived. Fewer than 1% of all known species are still in existence.

5. Evolution does not progress to preordained perfection—evolution is a tinkerer, not an architect. Increases in adaptation occur through changes to existing programs of development; and the results, although improvements in their particular environmental context, are never perfect designs (see Nesse & Williams, 1998). For example, the fact that mammalian sperm do not develop effectively at body temperature led to the evolution of the scrotum— hardly a perfect solution to any design problem.

6. Not all existing behaviors or structures are adaptive. Evolution often occurs through changes in developmental programs that lead to several related characteristics, only one of which might be adaptive—the incidental nonadaptive evolutionary by-products are called **spandrels.** Also, behaviors or structures that were once adaptive might become nonadaptive, or even maladaptive, if the environment changes. The human belly button is a spandrel; it serves no adaptive function and is merely the by-product of the umbilical cord.

7. Not all existing adaptive characteristics evolved to perform their current function. Some characteristics, called **exaptations,** evolved to perform one function and were later co-opted to perform another (Buss et al., 1998). For example, bird wings are exaptations—they are limbs that first evolved for the purpose of walking.

8. Similarities among species do not necessarily mean that the species have common evolutionary origins. Structures that are similar because they have a common evolutionary origin are termed **homologous;** structures that are similar but do not have a common evolutionary origin are termed **analogous.** The similarities between analogous structures result from **convergent evolution,** the evolution of similar solutions to the same environmental demands by unrelated species. Deciding whether a structural similarity is analogous or homologous depends on a careful analysis of the similarity. For example, a bird's wing and a human's arm have a basic underlying commonality of skeletal structure that suggests a common ancestor (see Burke & Feduccia, 1997); in contrast, a bird's wing and a bee's wing have few structural similarities, although they do serve the same function.

■ Evolution of the Human Brain

Early research on the evolution of the human brain focused on size. This research was stimulated by the assumption that brain size and intellectual capacity are closely related—an assumption that quickly ran into two problems. First, it was shown that modern humans, whom modern humans believe to be the most intelligent of all creatures, do not have the biggest brains. With brains weighing about 1,350 grams, humans rank far behind whales and elephants, whose brains weigh between 5,000 and 8,000 grams (Harvey & Krebs, 1990). Second, the sizes of the brains of acclaimed intellectuals (e.g., Einstein) were found to be unremarkable, certainly no match for their gigantic intellects. It is now clear that, although healthy adult human brains vary greatly in size—between about 1,000 and 2,000 grams—there is no clear relationship between brain size and intelligence.

One obvious problem in relating brain size to intelligence is the fact that larger animals tend to have larger brains, presumably because larger bodies require more brain tissue to control and regulate them. Thus, the facts that large men tend to have larger brains than small men, that men tend to have larger brains than women, and that elephants have larger brains than humans do not suggest anything about the relative intelligence of these populations. This problem led to the proposal that brain weight expressed as a percentage of total body weight might be a better measure of intellectual capacity. This measure allows humans (2.33%) to take their rightful place ahead of elephants (0.20%), but it also allows both humans and elephants to be surpassed by that intellectual giant of the animal kingdom, the shrew (3.33%).

A more reasonable approach to the study of brain evolution has been to compare the evolution of different brain regions (Finlay & Darlington, 1995; Killacky, 1995). For example, it has been informative to consider the evolution of the **brain stem** separately from the evolution of the **cerebrum** (cerebral hemispheres). In general, the brain stem regulates reflex activities that are critical for survival (e.g., heart rate, respiration, and blood glucose level), whereas the cerebrum is involved in more complex adaptive processes such as learning, perception, and motivation.

Figure 2.11 on page 32 is a schematic representation of the relative size of the brain stems and cerebrums of

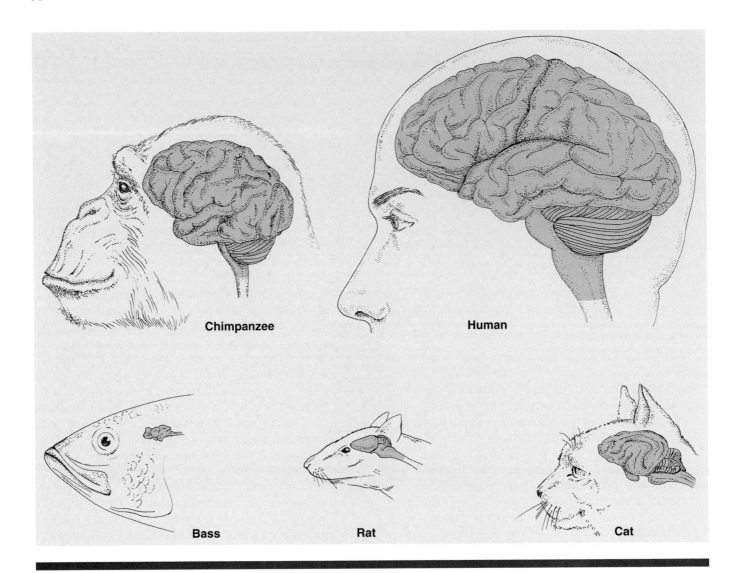

FIGURE 2.11 The brains of animals of different evolutionary age. Cerebrums are shown in beige; brain stems are shown in blue.

several species that are living descendants of species from which humans evolved. This figure makes three important points about the evolution of the human brain. The first is that it has increased in size during evolution; the second is that most of the increase in size has occurred in the cerebrum; and the third is that there has been an increase in the number of **convolutions**—folds on the cerebral surface—that has greatly increased the volume of the cerebral cortex (the outermost layer of cerebral tissue).

More significant than the differences among the brains of various related species are the similarities. All brains are constructed of neurons, and the neural structures that compose the brains of one species can almost always be found in the brains of related species. For example, the brains of humans, monkeys, rats, and mice contain the same gross structures connected in the same way.

Evolutionary Psychology: Understanding Mate Bonding

The evolutionary approach has been embraced by many psychologists. Indeed, a new field of psychology, termed *evolutionary psychology*, has coalesced around it. Evolutionary psychologists try to understand human behaviors through a consideration of the pressures that led to their evolution. Some of the most interesting and controversial work in this field has focused on questions of mate bonding, questions you may be dealing with in your own life.

In most species, mating is totally promiscuous. *Promiscuity* is a mating arrangement in which the members of both sexes indiscriminately copulate with many different partners during each mating period. Although such indiscriminate copulation is the predominant mode of reproduction (see Small, 1992), the males and females of some species form *mating bonds* (enduring mating relationships) with members of the other sex.

Most mammals tend to form mating bonds. Why? An influential theory, originally proposed by Trivers (1972), attributes the evolution of mating-bond formation in mammals to the fact that female mammals give birth to relatively small numbers of helpless, slow-developing young. As a result, it is adaptive for mammalian males to stay with the females who are carrying their offspring and to promote the successful development of those offspring. A male mammal that behaves in this way is more likely to pass his heritable characteristics on to future generations. Thus, natural selection has promoted the evolution in mammalian males of the tendency to bond with the females with which they have copulated. Similarly, there is selection pressure on female mammals to behave in ways that will induce males to bond to them because this improves their ability to pass on their own heritable characteristics to future generations. In many species, mating bonds last a lifetime.

The pattern of mate bonding that is most prevalent in mammals is **polygyny** (pronounced "pol-IG-in-ee"), an arrangement in which one male forms mating bonds with more than one female. Why did polygyny evolve in so many mammalian species? The evidence suggests that polygyny evolved as the predominant mating system in mammals because female mammals make a far greater contribution to the rearing of their young than do males (Trivers, 1972). Mammalian mothers carry their developing young in their bodies, sometimes for many months, and then suckle and care for them after they are born. In contrast, mammalian fathers often do not contribute much more to reproduction than sperm. One major consequence of this one-sided mammalian parenting arrangement is that female mammals can produce only a few offspring during their lifetimes, whereas males have the capacity to sire many offspring.

Because each female mammal can produce only a few offspring, she must make the best of her chances if her heritable characteristics are going to be passed on to future generations in significant numbers. In particular, it is important that she mate with particularly fit males. Mating with fit males increases the likelihood that her offspring will be fit and will pass on her genes, along with those of her mate, to the next generation; it also increases the likelihood that what little parental support her offspring will receive from their father will be effective. Thus, according to current theory, the tendency to establish mating bonds with only the fittest males evolved in females of many mammalian species. In contrast, because male mammals can sire so many offspring, there has been little evolutionary pressure on them to become selective in their bonding—the males of most mammalian species will form mating bonds with as many

females as possible. The inevitable consequence of the selective bonding of female mammals and the nonselective bonding of male mammals is polygyny—see Figure 2.12.

The strongest evidence in support of the theory that polygyny evolves when females make a far greater contribution to reproduction and parenting than males do comes from the studies of **polyandry** (pronounced "pol-ee-AN-dree"). Polyandry is a mating arrangement in which one female forms mating bonds with more than one male. Polyandry does not occur in mammals; it occurs only in species in which the contributions of the males to reproduction are greater than those of the females. For example, in one polyandrous species, the seahorse, the female deposits her eggs in the male's pouch, and he fertilizes them and carries them until they are mature enough to venture out on their own (see Daly & Wilson, 1983).

The current thinking is that both large body size and the tendency to engage in aggression evolved in male mammals because female mammals tend to be more selective in their reproductive bonding. Because of the selectivity of the females, the competition among the males for reproductive partners becomes fierce, with only the successful competitors passing on their genes. In contrast, the females of most species have little difficulty finding reproductive partners.

Although most mammals are polygynous, 3% of mammalian species, including humans, are primarily monogamous. **Monogamy** is a mate-bonding pattern in which enduring bonds are formed between one male and one female. Although monogamy is the most common human mate-bonding system, it is important to remember that it is not the predominant mammalian system.

FIGURE 2.12 Horses, like most mammals, are polygynous. The stallion breeds with all the mares in the herd by virtue of his victories over other males.

Monogamy is thought to have evolved in those mammalian species in which each female could raise more young, or more fit young, if she had undivided help (see Dewsbury, 1988). In such species, any change in the behavior of a female that would encourage a male to bond exclusively with her would increase the likelihood that her heritable characteristics would be passed on to future generations. One such behavioral change is for each female to drive other females of reproductive age away from her mate. This strategy is particularly effective if a female will not copulate with a male until he has stayed with her for a period of time. Once this pattern of behavior evolved in the females of a particular species, the optimal mating strategy for males would change. It would become difficult for each male to bond with many females, and a male's best chance of producing many fit offspring would be for him to bond with a fit female and to put most of his reproductive effort into her and their offspring. Of course, in a monogamous relationship, it is important that males select fertile females and that females select males that can effectively protect them and their offspring.

It is important not to lose sight of the fact that the significance of evolutionary psychology does not lie in the many theories it has generated. It is easy to speculate about how particular human behaviors evolved without ever having one's theories disproved, because it is not possible to know for sure how an existing behavior evolved. Good theories of behavioral evolution have predictions about current behaviors built into them so that the predictions—and thus the theory—can be tested. Theories that cannot be tested have little use.

The foregoing evolutionary theory of mate selection is one that has led to many predictions about current aspects of human mate selection. Buss (1992) has confirmed several of them: (1) Men in most cultures value youth and attractiveness (both indicators of fertility) in their mates more than women do; in contrast, women value power and earning capacity more than men do. (2) Physical attractiveness best predicts which women will bond with men of high occupational status. (3) The major mate-attraction strategy of women is increasing their physical attractiveness; in men, it is displaying their power and resources. (4) Men are more likely than women to commit adultery.

The forgoing evolutionary psychological analysis— and others like it—drives home three key points. First, it illustrates the ability of evolutionary analysis to generate insights into even the most complex psychological processes. Second, it emphasizes that we humans are products of over 600 million years of adaptation. And third, it stresses the fact that we humans are related to all other animal species— in some cases, more closely than we like to admit (see Dess & Chapman, 1998). Even our most personal hopes and desires are products of evolution. It is extremely important, however, to appreciate that the behavioral tendencies stamped in by evolution exist in humans without any need for their understanding or even awareness. Think about it.

2.3 Fundamental Genetics

Darwin did not understand two of the key facts on which his theory of evolution was based. He did not understand why conspecifics differ from one another, and he did not understand how anatomical, physiological, and behavioral characteristics are passed from parent to offspring. While Darwin puzzled over these questions, there was an unread manuscript in his files that contained the answers. It had been sent to him by an unknown Augustinian monk, Gregor Mendel. Unfortunately for Darwin (1809–1882) and for Mendel (1822–1884), the significance of Mendel's research was not recognized until the early part of the 20th century, well after both of their deaths.

Mendelian Genetics

Mendel studied inheritance in pea plants. In designing his experiments, he made two wise decisions. He decided to study dichotomous traits, and he decided to begin his experiments by crossing the offspring of true-breeding lines. **Dichotomous traits** are traits that occur in one form or the other, never in combination. For example, seed color is a dichotomous pea plant trait: Every pea plant has either brown seeds or white seeds. **True-breeding lines** are breeding lines in which interbred members always produce offspring with the same trait (e.g., brown seeds), generation after generation.

In one of his early experiments, Mendel studied the inheritance of seed color: brown or white. He began by cross breeding the offspring of a line of pea plants that had bred true for brown seeds with the offspring of a line of pea plants that had bred true for white seeds. The offspring of this cross all had brown seeds. Then, Mendel bred these first-generation offspring with one another, and he found that about three-quarters of the resulting second-generation offspring had brown seeds and about one-quarter had white seeds. Mendel repeated this experiment many times with various pairs of dichotomous pea plant traits, and each time the result was the same. One trait, which Mendel called the **dominant trait,** appeared in all of the first-generation offspring; the other trait, which he called the **recessive trait,** appeared in about one-quarter of the second-generation offspring. Mendel would have obtained a similar result if he had conducted an experiment with true-breeding lines of brown-eyed (dominant) and blue-eyed (recessive) humans.

The results of Mendel's experiment challenged the central premise upon which all previous ideas about inheritance had rested: that offspring inherit the traits of their parents. Somehow, the recessive trait (white seeds) was passed on to one-quarter of the second-generation pea plants by first-generation pea plants that did not themselves possess it. An organism's observable traits are referred to as its **phenotype;** the traits that it can pass on to its offspring through its genetic material are referred to as its **genotype.**

Mendel devised a theory to explain his results. It comprised four ideas. First, Mendel proposed that there are two kinds of inherited factors for each dichotomous

trait—for example, that a brown-seed factor and a white-seed factor control seed color. Today, we call each inherited factor a **gene.** Second, Mendel proposed that each organism possesses two genes for each of its dichotomous traits; for example, each pea plant possesses either two brown-seed genes, two white-seed genes, or one of each. The two genes that control the same trait are called **alleles** (pronounced "a-LEELZ"). Organisms that possess two identical genes for a trait are said to be **homozygous** for that trait; those that possess two different genes for a trait are said to be **heterozygous** for that trait. Third, Mendel proposed that one of the two kinds of genes for each dichotomous trait dominates the other in heterozygous organisms. For example, pea plants with a brown-seed gene and a white-seed gene always have brown seeds because the brown-seed gene always dominates the white-seed gene. And fourth, Mendel proposed that for each trait each organism randomly inherits one of its "father's" two factors and one of its "mother's" two factors. Figure 2.13 illustrates how Mendel's theory accounts for the result of his experiment on the inheritance of seed color in pea plants.

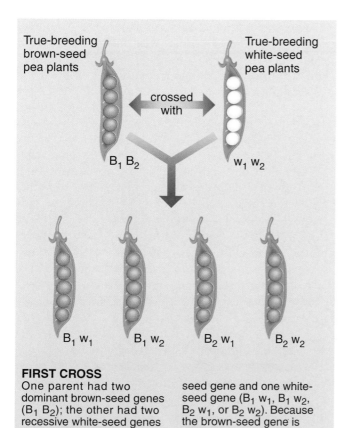

FIRST CROSS
One parent had two dominant brown-seed genes ($B_1 B_2$); the other had two recessive white-seed genes ($w_1 w_2$). Therefore, all offspring had one brown-seed gene and one white-seed gene ($B_1 w_1$, $B_1 w_2$, $B_2 w_1$, or $B_2 w_2$). Because the brown-seed gene is dominant, all had brown seeds.

SECOND CROSS
Each parent had one brown-seed gene and one white-seed gene. Therefore, 25% of the offspring had two brown-seed genes ($B_1 B_2$), 50% had a brown-seed gene and a white-seed gene ($B_1 w_2$ or $B_2 w_1$), and 25% had two white-seed genes ($w_1 w_2$). Because the brown-seed gene is dominant, 75% had brown seeds.

FIGURE 2.13 How Mendel's theory accounts for the results of his experiment on the inheritance of seed color in pea plants.

Chromosomes, Reproduction, and Linkage

It was not until the early 20th century that genes were found to be located on **chromosomes**—the thread-like structures in the *nucleus* of each cell. Chromosomes occur in matched pairs, and each species has a characteristic number of pairs in each of its body cells; humans have 23 pairs. The two genes (alleles) that control each trait are situated at the same locus, one on each chromosome of a particular pair.

The process of cell division that produces **gametes** (egg cells and sperm cells) is called **meiosis** (pronounced "my-OH-sis")—see Slunder and McCollum (2000). In meiosis, the chromosomes divide, and one chromosome of each pair goes to each of the two gametes that results from the division. As a result, each gamete has only half the usual number of chromosomes (23 in humans); and when a sperm cell and an egg cell combine during fertilization (see Figure 2.14), a **zygote** (a fertilized egg cell) with the full complement of chromosomes is produced. All other cell division in the body occurs by **mitosis** (pronounced "my-TOE-sis"). Just prior to mitotic division, the number of chromosomes doubles so that, when the division occurs, both daughter cells end up with the full complement of chromosomes. Figure 2.15 illustrates meiosis, fertilization, and mitosis.

Meiosis accounts for much of the genetic diversity within each species. In humans, for example, each meiotic division produces two gametes; each gamete contains one chromosome from each of the 23 pairs contained in each body cell. Because each of the 23 pairs is randomly sorted into the two gametes, each human can produce gametes with 2^{23} (8,388,608) different combinations of chromosomes.

The first comprehensive study of **linkage** was conducted in the early 20th century by Morgan and his col-

leagues. They found that there are four different clusters of fruit fly genes. If the gene for one trait in a cluster was inherited from one parent, that fruit fly had a higher probability (greater than 0.5) of inheriting genes for other traits in the cluster from the same parent. Because fruit flies have four pairs of chromosomes, Morgan and his colleagues concluded that linkage occurs between traits that are encoded on the same chromosome. They were correct; in every species in which linkage has been assessed, the number of clusters of linked traits has been found to equal the number of pairs of chromosomes.

If genes are passed from generation to generation on chromosomes, why are the genes on the same chromosome not always inherited together? The linkage between pairs of genes on a single chromosome varies from almost complete (close to 1.0) to just above chance (just over 0.5).

Morgan and his colleagues proposed that **crossing over** provided the solution to the puzzle of partial linkage. Figure 2.16 on page 38 illustrates how crossing over works. During the first stage of meiosis, after the chromosomes have replicated, they line up in their pairs. Then they usually cross over one another at random points, break apart at the points of contact, and exchange sections of themselves. As a result, parents rarely pass on intact chromosomal clusters of genes to their children. Each of your gametes contains chromosomes that are unique spliced-together combinations of chromosomes inherited from your mother and father.

The phenomenon of crossing over is important for two reasons. First, by ensuring that chromosomes are not passed intact from generation to generation, crossovers increase the diversity of the species; in a sense, crossing over shuffles the genetic deck before the chromosomes are randomly dealt out to the next generation. Second, the study of crossovers was the first means by which geneticists could construct **gene maps.** Because each crossover occurs at a random point along the length of a chromosome, the degree of linkage between two genes indicates how close they are together on the chromosome. Crossovers rarely occur between adjacent genes, and they frequently occur between genes at opposite ends of a chromosome.

Sex Chromosomes and Sex-Linked Traits

There is one exception to the rule that chromosomes always come in matched pairs. That exception is the **sex chromosomes**—the pair of chromosomes that determines an individual's sex. There are two types of sex chromosomes, X and Y, and the two look different and carry different genes. Female mammals have two X chromosomes, and male mammals have an X and a Y. Traits that are influenced by genes on the sex chromosomes are referred to as **sex-linked traits.** Virtually all sex-linked traits are controlled by genes on the X chro-

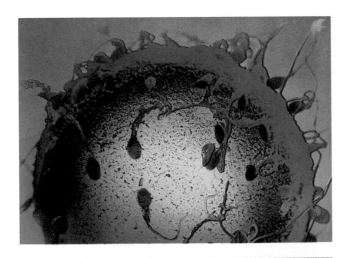

FIGURE 2.14 During fertilization, sperm cells attach themselves to the surface of an egg cell; only one will enter the egg cell and fertilize it.

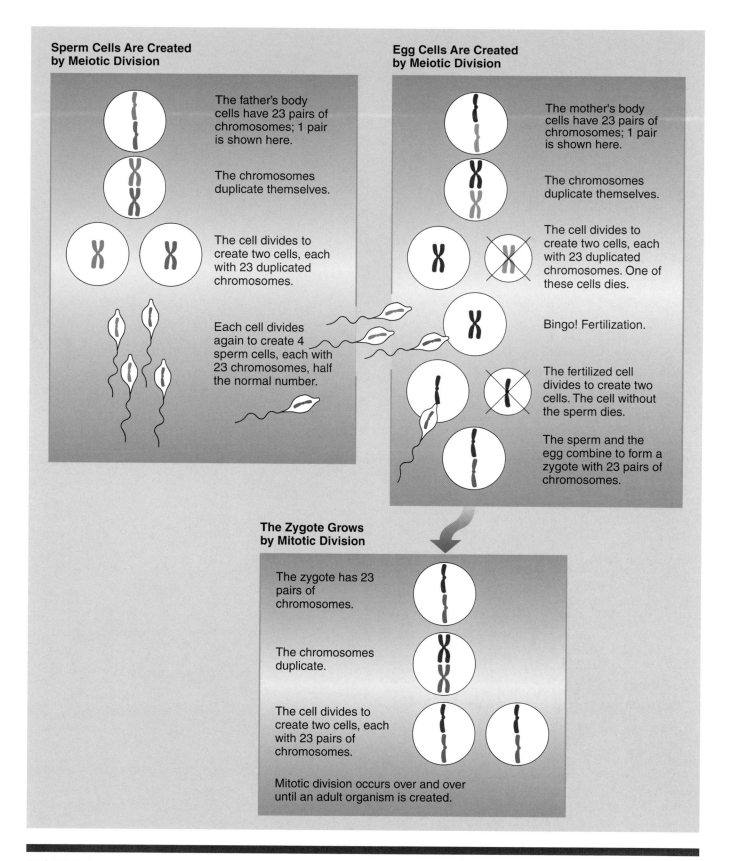

FIGURE 2.15 Meiotic cell division, fertilization, and mitotic cell division.

mosome because the Y chromosome is small and carries few genes other than those that cause an individual to develop into a male (see Rice, 1994).

Traits that are controlled by genes on the X chromosome occur more frequently in one sex than the other. If the trait is dominant, it occurs more frequently in females.

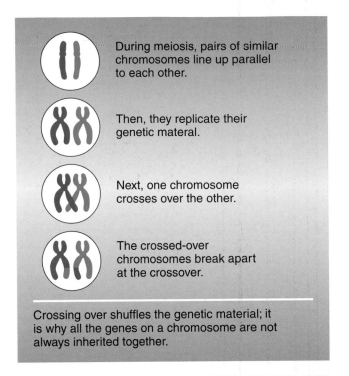

During meiosis, pairs of similar chromosomes line up parallel to each other.

Then, they replicate their genetic materal.

Next, one chromosome crosses over the other.

The crossed-over chromosomes break apart at the crossover.

Crossing over shuffles the genetic material; it is why all the genes on a chromosome are not always inherited together.

FIGURE 2.16   Crossing over.

Females have twice the chance of inheriting the dominant gene because they have twice the number of X chromosomes. In contrast, recessive sex-linked traits occur more frequently in males. The reason is that recessive sex-linked traits are manifested only in females who possess two of the recessive genes—one on each of their X chromosomes—whereas the traits are manifested in all males who possess the gene because they have only one X chromosome. The classic example of a recessive sex-linked trait is color blindness. Because the color blindness gene is quite rare, females almost never inherit two of them and thus almost never possess the disorder; in contrast, every male who possesses one color blindness gene is color blind.

■ | Chromosome Structure and Replication

Each chromosome is a double-stranded molecule of **deoxyribonucleic acid (DNA).** Each strand is a sequence of **nucleotide bases** attached to a chain of *phosphate* and *deoxyribose*; there are four nucleotide bases: *adenine, thymine, guanine,* and *cytosine.* It is the sequence of these bases on each chromosome that constitutes the genetic code—just as the sequence of letters constitutes the code of our language.

The two strands that compose each chromosome are coiled around each other and bonded together by the attraction of adenine for thymine and guanine for cytosine. This specific bonding pattern has an important consequence: The two strands that compose each chromosome are exact complements of each other. For

Adenine and thymine bind

Guanine and cytosine bind

FIGURE 2.17   A schematic illustration of the structure of a DNA molecule. Notice the complementary binding of nucleotide bases: thymine to adenine, and guanine to cytosine.

example, the sequence of adenine, guanine, thymine, cytosine, and guanine on one strand is always attached to the complementary sequence of thymine, cytosine, adenine, guanine, and cytosine on the other. Figure 2.17 illustrates the structure of DNA.

Replication is a critical process of the DNA molecule. Without it, mitotic cell division would not be possible. Figure 2.18 illustrates how DNA replication is thought to work (see Losick & Shapiro, 1998). The two strands of DNA start to unwind. Then the exposed nucleotide bases on each of the two strands attract loose complementary bases from the fluid of the nucleus. Thus, when the unwinding is complete, two double-stranded DNA molecules, both of which are identical to the original, have been created.

Chromosome replication does not always go according to plan; there may be errors. Sometimes, these errors are gross errors. For example, in *Down syndrome,* which you will learn about in Chapter 10, there is an extra chromosome in each cell. But more commonly, errors in duplication take the form of **mutations**—accidental alterations in individual genes. In most cases, mutations disappear from the genetic pool within a few generations because the organisms that inherit them are less fit. However, in rare instances, mutations increase fitness and in so doing contribute to rapid evolution.

■ | The Genetic Code and Gene Expression

There are several different kinds of genes. The most well understood are the **structural genes**—genes that contain the information necessary for the synthesis of a single protein. **Proteins** are long chains of **amino acids;** they control the physiological activities of cells and are important components of their structure. All the cells in the body (e.g., brain cells, hair cells, and bone cells) contain exactly the same structural genes. How then do different kinds of cells develop? The answer lies in a complex category of genes, the **operator genes.**

Each operator gene controls a structural gene or a group of related structural genes. The function of an operator gene is to determine whether or not each of its structural genes initiates the synthesis of a protein (i.e., whether or not the structural gene will be *expressed*) and at what rate.

The control of **gene expression** by operator genes is an important process because it determines how a cell

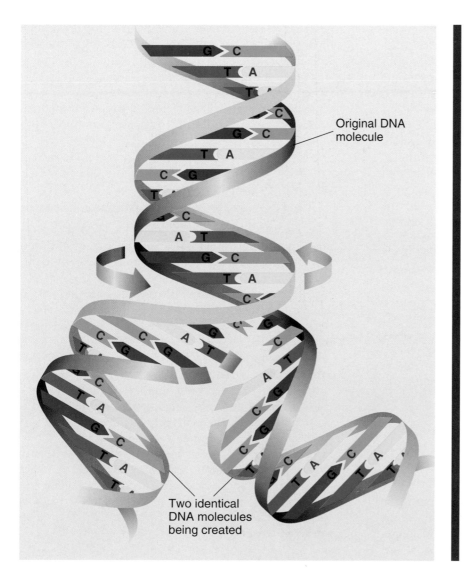

Original DNA molecule

Two identical DNA molecules being created

FIGURE 2.18 DNA replication. As the two strands of the original DNA molecule unwind, the nucleotide bases on each strand attract loose complementary bases. Once the unwinding is complete, two DNA molecules, each identical to the first, have been created.

will develop and how it will function once it reaches maturity. Operator genes are like switches; and, like switches, they can be regulated in two ways. Some operator genes are normally off, and they are regulated by **DNA-binding proteins** that turn them on; others are normally on, and they are regulated by DNA-binding proteins that turn them up, down, or off. Many of the DNA-binding proteins that control operator genes are influenced by signals received by the cell from its environment (see Darnell, 1997). This, then—if it has not already occurred to you—is the major mechanism by which experience interacts with genes to influence development.

The expression of a structural gene is illustrated in Figure 2.19. First, the small section of the chromosome that contains the structural gene unravels, and the unraveled section of one of the DNA strands serves as a template for the transcription of a short strand of **ribonucleic acid (RNA)**. RNA is like DNA except that it contains the nucleotide base uracil instead of thymine and has a phosphate and ribose backbone instead of a phosphate and deoxyribose backbone. The strand of transcribed RNA is called **messenger RNA** because it carries the genetic code from the nucleus of the cell. Once it has left the nucleus, the messenger RNA attaches itself to one of the many **ribosomes** in the cell's *cytoplasm* (the clear inner fluid of the cell). The ribosome then moves along the strand of messenger RNA, translating the genetic code as it proceeds.

Each group of three consecutive nucleotide bases along the messenger RNA strand is called a **codon.** Each codon instructs the ribosome to add 1 of the 20 different kinds of amino acids to the protein that it is constructing; for example, the sequence guanine-guanine-adenine instructs the ribosome to add the amino acid glycine. Each kind of amino acid is carried to the ribosome by molecules of **transfer RNA;** as the ribosome reads a codon, it attracts a transfer RNA molecule that is attached to the appropriate amino acid. The ribosome reads codon after codon and adds amino acid after amino acid until it reaches a codon that tells it the protein is complete, whereupon the completed protein is released into the cytoplasm. Thus, the process of gene expression involves two phases: the *transcription* of the DNA base-sequence code to an RNA base-sequence code and the *translation* of the RNA base-sequence code into a sequence of amino acids.

Human Genome Project

Arguably the most ambitious scientific project of all time began in 1990. Known as the **human genome project,** it is a loosely knit collaboration of major research institutions and individual research teams in several countries. The initial purpose of this collaboration was to determine the base sequence of each human gene. As I write these words, this task has just been accomplished.

Many people overestimate the degree to which deciphering the human genome will contribute to the understanding of human development: It is a major step, but it still leaves us a great distance from total understanding (see Collins et al., 1997, 1998). Still to come are the daunting tasks of identifying the millions of variations that occur among human genes and figuring out how each of these variations interacts with other genes and the environment to influence the development of human structures and functions (Plomin, 2000).

Although biopsychologists are most interested in what knowledge of the human genome can ultimately teach them about development of the human brain and its psychological processes, that knowledge will inevitably lead to other contributions. For example, identifying those genes involved in disease will greatly accelerate the development of preventive and therapeutic drugs (Hazeltine, 1997), and determining the genetic differences among various human populations will provide an alternative to paleontological analysis for inferring the evolution and migration patterns of our species (Bertranpetit, 2000).

Much progress will be realized during your lifetime. What once seemed the stuff of science fiction is within our grasp.

Mitochondrial DNA

So far, we have discussed only the DNA that composes the chromosomes in the cell nucleus. Indeed, you may have the impression that all the DNA is in the nucleus: It isn't. The cells' mitochondria also contain DNA (i.e., *mitochondrial DNA*). **Mitochondria** are the energy-generating structures located in the cytoplasm of every cell. All mitochondrial genes are inherited from one's mother.

Mitochondrial DNA is of great interest to scientists for two reasons. The first is that mutations in mitochondrial DNA have been implicated in the cause of several disorders. The second is that because mutations seem to develop in mitochondrial DNA at a reasonably consistent rate, mitochondrial DNA can be used as an evolutionary clock. Analysis of mutations of mitochondrial DNA have confirmed the theory, based on paleontological evidence, that hominids evolved in Africa and spread over the earth in a series of migrations (Wallace, 1997)—see Figure 2.20 on page 42.

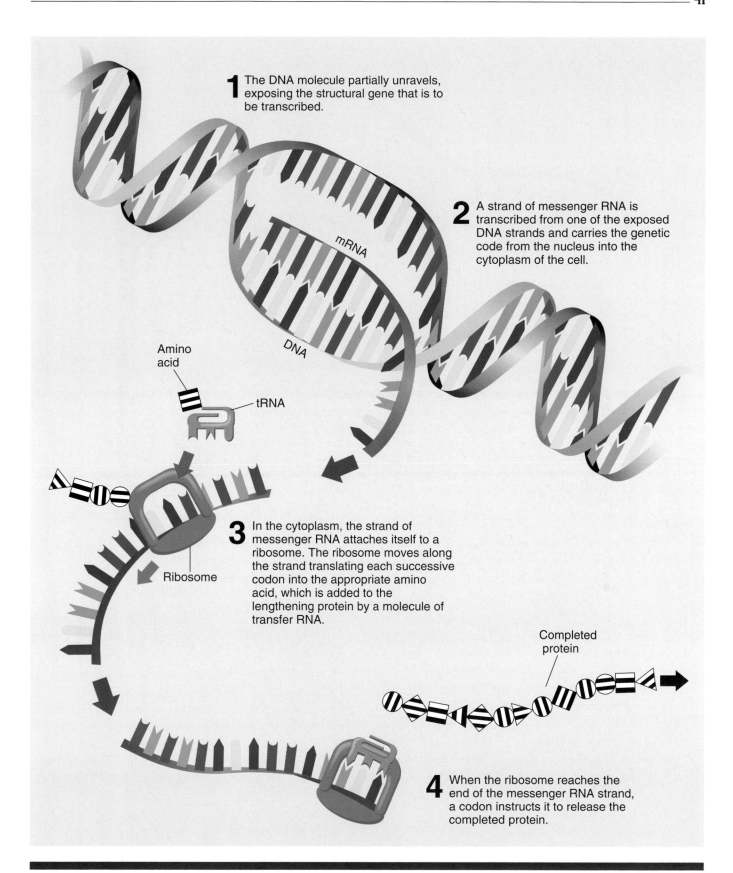

1 The DNA molecule partially unravels, exposing the structural gene that is to be transcribed.

2 A strand of messenger RNA is transcribed from one of the exposed DNA strands and carries the genetic code from the nucleus into the cytoplasm of the cell.

mRNA

DNA

Amino acid

tRNA

Ribosome

3 In the cytoplasm, the strand of messenger RNA attaches itself to a ribosome. The ribosome moves along the strand translating each successive codon into the appropriate amino acid, which is added to the lengthening protein by a molecule of transfer RNA.

Completed protein

4 When the ribosome reaches the end of the messenger RNA strand, a codon instructs it to release the completed protein.

FIGURE 2.19   Gene expression. Transcription of a section of DNA into a complementary strand of messenger RNA is followed by the translation of the messenger RNA strand into a protein.

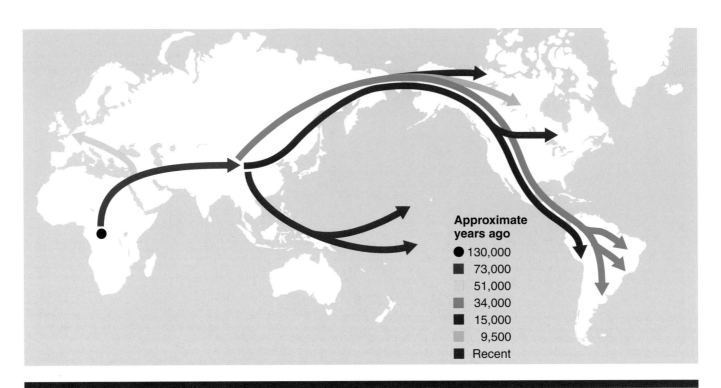

FIGURE 2.20 The analysis of mitochondrial DNA indicates that hominids evolved in Africa and spread over the earth in a series of migrations. (Adapted from Wallace, 1997.)

 BrainScan

This is a good place for you to pause to scan your brain to see if you are ready to proceed. Fill in the following blanks with the most appropriate terms from the first three sections of the chapter. The correct answers are provided at the bottom of the next page. Before proceeding, review material related to your errors and omissions.

1. The _____ side of the nature–nurture controversy is that all behavior is learned.

2. Physiological-or-psychological thinking was given official recognition in the 17th century when the Roman Church sanctioned _____ .

3. In the Darwinian sense, _____ refers to the ability of an organism to survive and produce large numbers of fertile offspring.

4. A _____ is a group of reproductively isolated organisms.

5. Mammals are thought to have evolved from _____ about 180 million years ago.

6. There are five different families of primates: prosimians, New-World monkeys, Old-World monkeys, _____ , and _____ .

7. _____ are the closest living relatives of humans; they have about 99% of the same genetic material.

8. The first hominids were _____ .

9. An organism's observable traits are its _____ ; the traits that it can pass to its offspring through its genetic material are its _____ .

10. The degree of _____ between two genes is a measure of how close they are together on a chromosome.

11. Each structural gene contains the information for the production of a single _____ .

12. Structural genes can be turned off or on by _____ genes.

13. The massive international effort to physically map human chromosomes is known as the _____ project.

2.4 Behavioral Development: The Interaction of Genetic Factors and Experience

This section of the chapter provides three classic examples of how genetic factors and experience interact to direct behavioral ontogeny. **Ontogeny** is the development of individuals through their life span. **Phylogeny,** in contrast, is the evolutionary development of species through the ages.

Selective Breeding of "Maze-Bright" and "Maze-Dull" Rats

You have already learned in this chapter that nature-or-nurture thinking dominated the study of behavior during the first half of the 20th century and that most psychologists of that era assumed that behavior develops largely through learning. Tryon (1934) undermined this assumption by showing that behavioral traits can be selectively bred.

Tryon focused his selective-breeding experiments on the very behavior that had been the focus of early psychologists in their investigations of learning: the maze running of laboratory rats. Tryon began by training a large heterogeneous group of laboratory rats to run a complex maze; the rats received a food reward when they reached the goal box. Tryon then mated the females and males that least frequently entered incorrect alleys during training—he referred to these rats as *maze-bright*. And he bred the females and males that most frequently entered incorrect alleys during training—he referred to these rats as *maze-dull.*

When the offspring of the maze-bright and of the maze-dull rats matured, their maze-learning performance was assessed. Then, the brightest of the maze-bright offspring were mated with one another and so were the dullest of the maze-dull offspring. This selective breeding procedure was continued for 21 generations, and the descendants of Tryon's original strains are available today to those interested in studying them. By the eighth generation, there was almost no overlap in the maze-learning performance of the two strains. With a few exceptions, the worst of the maze-bright strain made fewer errors than the best of the maze-dull strain (see Figure 2.21 on page 44).

To control for the possibility that good maze-running performance was somehow being passed from parent to offspring through learning, Tryon used a *cross-fostering control procedure:* He tested maze-bright offspring that had been reared by maze-dull parents and maze-dull offspring that had been reared by maze-bright parents. However, the offspring of maze-bright rats made few errors even when they were reared by maze-dull rats, and the offspring of maze-dull rats made many errors even when they were reared by maze-bright rats.

Since Tryon's seminal selective-breeding experiments, many behavioral traits have been selectively bred. Among them are open-field activity in mice, susceptibility to alcohol-induced sleep in mice, susceptibility to alcohol-withdrawal seizures in mice, nest building in mice, avoidance learning in rats, and mating in fruit flies. Indeed, it appears that any measurable behavioral trait that varies among members of a species can be selectively bred.

An important general point made by studies of selective breeding is that selective breeding based on one behavioral trait usually brings a host of other behavioral traits along with it. This indicates that the behavioral trait used as the criterion for selective breeding is not the only behavioral trait that is influenced by the genes segregated by the breeding. Thus, in order to characterize the behavioral function of the segregated genes, it is necessary to compare the performance of the selectively bred strains on a variety of tests. For example, Searle (1949) compared maze-dull and maze-bright rats on 30 different behavioral tests and found that they differed on many of them; the pattern of differences suggested that the maze-bright rats were superior maze learners not because they were more intelligent but because they were less emotional.

Selective-breeding studies have proved that genes influence the development of behavior. This conclusion in no way implies that experience does not. This point was clearly illustrated by Cooper and Zubek (1958) in a classic study of maze-bright and maze-dull rats. The researchers reared maze-bright and maze-dull rats in one of two environments: (1) an impoverished environment (a barren wire-mesh group cage) or (2) an enriched environment (a wire-mesh group cage that contained tunnels, ramps, visual displays, and other objects designed to stimulate interest). When the maze-dull rats reached maturity, they made significantly more errors than the maze-bright rats only if they had been reared in the impoverished environment (see Figure 2.22 on page 44). Apparently, enriched early environments can overcome the negative effects of disadvantaged genes. Indeed, rats reared in enriched environments develop thicker cerebral cortexes than those reared in impoverished environments (Bennett et al., 1964).

Brain Scan answers: (1) nurture, (2) Cartesian dualism, (3) fitness, (4) species, (5) reptiles, (6) apes, (7) hominids, (8) Australopithecines, (9) phenotype, genotype, (10) linkage, (11) protein, (12) operator, (13) human genome.

FIGURE 2.21 Selective breeding of maze-bright and maze-dull strains of rats by Tryon (1934).

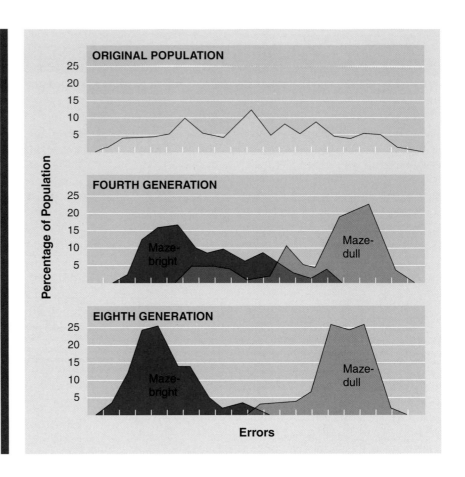

FIGURE 2.22 Maze-dull rats did not make significantly more errors than maze-bright rats when both groups were reared in an enriched environment. (Adapted from Cooper & Zubek, 1958.)

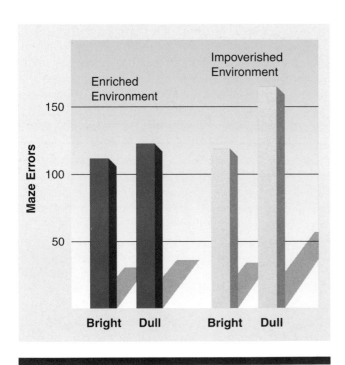

Phenylketonuria: A Single-Gene Metabolic Disorder

In contrast to what you might expect, it is often easier to understand the genetics of a behavioral disorder than it is to understand the genetics of normal behavior. The reason is that many genes influence the development of a normal behavioral trait, but it often takes only one abnormal gene to screw it up (see Plomin, 1995). A good example of this point is the neurological disorder **phenylketonuria (PKU).**

PKU was discovered in 1934 when a Norwegian dentist, Asbjörn Fölling, noticed a peculiar odor in the urine of his two mentally retarded children. He correctly assumed that the odor was related to their disorder, and he had their urine analyzed. High levels of **phenylpyruvic acid** were found in both samples. Spurred on by his discovery, Fölling identified other retarded children who had abnormally high levels of urinary phenylpyruvic acid, and he concluded that this subpopulation of retarded children was suffering from the same disorder. In addition to mental retardation, the symptoms of PKU include vomiting, seizures, hyperactivity, and hyperirritability.

The pattern of transmission of PKU through the family trees of afflicted individuals indicates that it is transmitted by a single gene mutation. About 1 in 100 people of European descent carry the PKU gene; but because the gene is recessive, PKU develops only in homozygous individuals (those who inherit a PKU gene from both their mother and their father). In the United States, about 1 in 10,000 white infants is born with PKU; the incidence is much lower among infants of African heritage.

The biochemistry of PKU turned out to be reasonably straightforward. PKU homozygotes lack *phenylalanine hydroxylase,* an enzyme that is required for the conversion of the amino acid *phenylalanine* to *tyrosine.* As a result, phenylalanine accumulates in the body; and levels of *dopamine,* a neurotransmitter normally synthesized from tyrosine, are low. The consequence is abnormal brain development.

Like other behavioral traits, the behavioral symptoms of PKU result from an interaction between genetic and environmental factors: between the PKU gene and diet. Accordingly, in most modern hospitals, the blood of each newborn infant is routinely screened for a high phenylalanine level. If the level is high, the infant is immediately placed on a special phenylalanine-reduced diet; this diet reduces both the amount of phenylalanine in the blood and the development of mental retardation. The timing of the treatment is extremely important. The phenylalanine-reduced diet does not significantly reduce the development of mental retardation in PKU homozygotes unless it is initiated within the first few weeks of life; conversely, the restriction of phenylalanine in the diet is usually relaxed in late childhood, with few obvious adverse consequences. The period of development, usually early in life, during which a particular experience must occur to have a major effect on development is its **sensitive period.**

Diamond and her colleagues (e.g., Diamond et al., 1997) showed that early application of the standard phenylalanine-reduced diet reduces, but does not prevent, the development of cognitive deficits. PKU children on the special diet performed more poorly than healthy children on several tests of cognitive ability. This finding is consistent with the fact that the blood levels of phenylalanine in PKU children on the standard phenylalanine-reduced diets tend to remain above normal. The cognitive deficits observed by Diamond and her colleagues (e.g., deficits in the ability to inhibit inappropriate responses) suggest prefrontal lobe damage. Diamond recommends putting all PKU children with elevated phenylalanine levels on stricter phenylalanine-reduced diets.

■ Development of Birdsong

In the spring, the songs of male songbirds threaten conspecific male trespassers and attract potential mates. The males of each species sing similar songs that are readily distinguishable from the songs of other species, and there are recognizable local dialects within each species, (see Ball & Hulse, 1998).

Studies of the ontogenetic development of birdsong suggest that birdsong develops in two phases (see Mooney, 1999). The first phase, called the **sensory phase,** begins several days after hatching. Although the young birds do not sing during this phase, they form memories of the adult songs they hear—usually sung by their own male relatives—that later guide the development of their own singing. The young males of many songbird species are genetically prepared to acquire the songs of their own species during the sensory phase. They cannot readily acquire the songs of other species; nor can they acquire the songs of their own species if they do not hear them during the sensory phase. Males who do not hear the songs of their own species early in their lives may later develop a song, but it is likely to be highly abnormal with only a few recognizable features of their species' mature songs.

The second phase of birdsong development, the **sensorimotor phase,** begins when the juvenile males begin to twitter subsongs (the immature songs of young birds), usually when they are several months old. During this phase, the rambling vocalizations of subsongs are gradually refined until they resemble the songs of the birds' earlier adult tutors. Auditory feedback is necessary for the development of singing during the sensorimotor phase; unless the young birds are able to hear themselves sing, their subsongs do not develop into adult songs. However, once stable adult song has crystallized, songbirds are much less dependent on hearing for normal song production; the disruptive effects of deafening on adult song are usually less severe, and they require several months to be fully realized (Lombardino & Nottebohm, 2000).

When it comes to the retention of their initial crystallized adult songs, there are two common patterns among songbird species. Most songbird species, such as the widely studied zebra finches and white-crowned sparrows, are *age-limited learners;* in these species, adult songs, once crystallized, remain unchanged for the rest of the birds' lives. In contrast, some species are *open-ended learners;* they are able to add new songs to their repertoire throughout their lives. For example, at the end of each mating season, male canaries return from a period of stable song to a period of plastic song—a period during which they can add new songs for the next mating season. Male zebra finches (age-limited learners) and male canaries (open-ended learners) are shown in Figure 2.23 on page 46.

Figure 2.24 on page 46 is a simplified version of the neural circuit that controls birdsong in the canary. It has two major components: the descending motor pathway and the anterior forebrain pathway. The *descending motor pathway* descends from the high vocal center on each side of the brain to the syrinx (voice box) on the same side; it mediates song production. The *anterior forebrain pathway* mediates song learning (Doupe, 1993; Vicario, 1991).

The canary song circuit is remarkable in four respects (see Mooney, 1999). First, the left descending motor

FIGURE 2.23 Male zebra finches (age-limited song learners) and male canaries (open-ended song learners) are common subjects of research on birdsong development. (Illustration kindly provided by *Trends in Neuroscience;* original photograph by Arturo Alvarez-Buylla.)

pathway plays a more important role in singing than the right descending motor pathway (which duplicates the left-hemisphere dominance for language in humans). Second, the high vocal center is four times larger in male canaries than in females (see MacDougall-Shackleton & Ball, 1999). Third, each spring, as the male canary prepares its new repertoire of songs for the summer seduction, the song-control structures of its brain double in size, only to shrink back in the fall; this springtime burst of brain growth and singing is triggered by elevated levels of the hormone testosterone that result from the increasing daylight (Tramontin & Brenowitz, 2000). Fourth, the seasonal increase in size of the song-control brain structures results from the growth of new neurons, not from an increase in the size of existing ones (Tramontin, Hartman, & Brenowitz, 2000)—a result that is remarkable because the growth of new neurons in adult vertebrate brains was until recently assumed to be impossible.

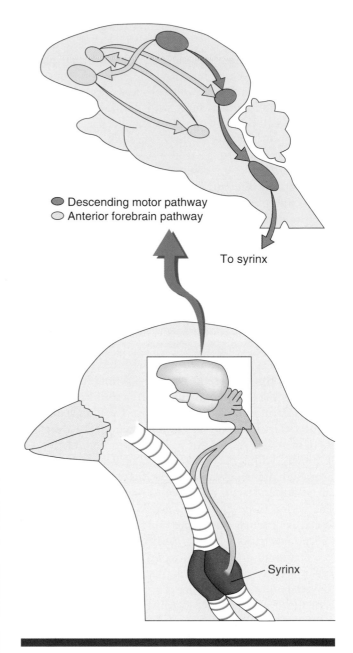

FIGURE 2.24 The neural pathway responsible for the production and learning of song in the male canary.

2.5 The Genetics of Human Psychological Differences

So far, this chapter has focused on three topics—human evolution, genetics, and the interaction of genetics and experience in the ontological development of psychological traits. All three topics converge on one fundamental question: Why are we the way we are? You have learned that each of us is a product of gene–experience interac-

tions and that the effects of genes and experience on individual development are inseparable—remember the metaphor of the musical mountaineer and the panpipe. In view of the fact that I have emphasized these points at every opportunity throughout the chapter, I am certain that you appreciate them by now. However, I am raising them again one last time because this final section of the chapter focuses on a developmental issue that is fundamentally different from the ones that we have been discussing.

Development of Individuals versus Development of Differences among Individuals

So far, this chapter has dealt with the development of individuals. The remainder of the chapter deals with the development of differences among individuals. In the development of the individual, the effects of genes and experience are inseparable. In the development of differences among individuals, they are separable. This distinction is extremely important, but it confuses many people. Let me return to the mountaineer-and-panpipe metaphor to explain it.

The music of an individual panpipe player is the product of the interaction of the musician and the panpipe, and it is nonsensical to ask what proportion of the music is produced by the musician and what proportion by the panpipe. However, if we measured the panpipe playing of a large sample of subjects, we could statistically estimate the degree to which the differences among them in the quality of their music resulted from differences in the subjects themselves as opposed to differences in their instruments. For example, if we selected 100 Peruvians at random and gave each a test on a professional-quality panpipe, we would likely find that most of the variation in the quality of the music resulted from differences in the subjects, some being experienced players and some never having played before. In the same way, behavioral geneticists measure a behavioral attribute of a group of subjects (e.g., the IQ of human subjects) and ask what proportion of the variation among the subjects resulted from genetic differences as opposed to experiential differences.

To assess the relative contributions of genes and experience to the development of differences in psychological attributes, behavioral geneticists study individuals of varying genetic similarity. For example, they often compare **identical twins** (monozygotic twins), who developed from the same zygote and thus are genetically identical, with **fraternal twins** (dizygotic twins), who developed from two zygotes and thus are no more similar than any pair of siblings. Studies of identical and fraternal twins who have been separated at infancy by adoption are particularly informative about the relative contributions of genetics and experience to differences in human psychological development. The most extensive of such studies is the Minnesota Study of Twins Reared Apart (see Bouchard & Pedersen, 1998).

Minnesota Study of Twins Reared Apart

The Minnesota Study of Twins Reared Apart involved 59 pairs of identical twins and 47 pairs of fraternal twins who had been reared apart, as well as many pairs of identical and fraternal twins who had been reared together. Their ages ranged from 19 to 68 years. Each twin was brought to the University of Minnesota for approximately 50 hours of testing, which focused on the assessment of intelligence and personality. Would the adult identical twins reared apart prove to be similar because they were genetically identical, or would they prove to be different because they had been brought up in different family environments?

The results of the Minnesota Study of Twins Reared Apart proved to be remarkably consistent—both internally, between the various cognitive and personality dimensions that were studied, and externally, with the findings of other, similar studies. In general, adult identical twins were substantially more similar to one another on all psychological dimensions than were adult fraternal twins, whether or not both twins of a pair were raised in the same family environment (see Turkheimer, 2000). The effect on general intelligence (as measured by the Wechsler Adult Intelligence Scale) has been the most widely studied of the twinship and adoption effects; Figure 2.25 illustrates the general pattern of findings (see Bouchard, 1998).

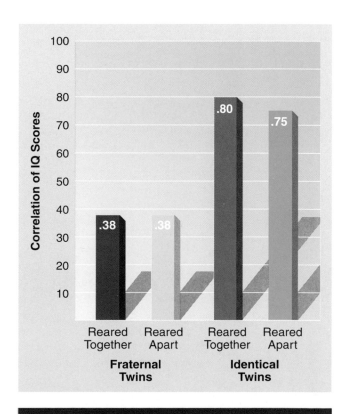

FIGURE 2.25 The correlation of the intelligence quotients (IQs) of identical and fraternal twins, reared together or apart.

The results of the Minnesota study have been widely disseminated by the popular press. Unfortunately, the meaning of the results has often been distorted. Sometimes, the misrepresentation of science by the popular press does not matter—at least not much. This is not one of those times. People's misbeliefs about the origins of human intelligence and personality are often translated into inappropriate and discriminatory social attitudes and practices. The following newspaper story illustrates

how the results of the Minnesota study have been misrepresented to the public.

This story is misleading in four ways. You should have no difficulty spotting the first: it oozes nature-or-nurture thinking and all of the misconceptions associated with it. Second, by focusing on the similarities of Bob and Bob, the story creates the impression that Bob and Bob (and the other monozygotic pairs of twins reared apart) are cognitively identical. They are not. It is easy to come up with a long list of similarities between any two people if one asks them enough questions and ignores the dissimilarities. Third, the story creates the impression that the results of the Minnesota study are revolutionary. On the contrary, the importance of the Minnesota study lies mainly in the fact that it constitutes a particularly thorough confirmation of the results of previous adoption studies. Fourth, and most important, the story creates the false impression that the results of the Minnesota study make some general point about the relative contributions of genes and experience to the development of intelligence and personality in individuals. They do not, and neither do the results of any other adoption study. True, Bouchard and his colleagues estimated the heritability of IQ to be 0.70, but they did not conclude that IQ is 70% genetic. A **heritability estimate** is not about individual development; it is a numerical estimate of the proportion of variability occurring in a particular trait in a particular study that resulted from the genetic variation in that study (see Plomin & DeFries, 1998). Thus, heritability estimates tell us about the contribution of genetic differences to phenotypic differences among subjects; they have nothing to say about the relative contributions of genes and experience to the development of individuals.

The concept of heritability estimates can be quite confusing. I suggest that you pause here and carefully think through the definition. The panpipe metaphor will help.

The magnitude of a study's heritability estimate depends on the amount of genetic and environmental variation from which it was calculated, and it cannot be applied to other kinds of situations. For example, in the Minnesota study, there was relatively little environmental variation. All subjects were raised in industrialized countries (e.g., Great Britain, Canada, and the United States) by parents who could meet the strict standards required for adoption. Accordingly, most of the variation in the subjects' intelligence and personality resulted from genetic variation. If the twins had been separately adopted by European royalty, African Bushmen, Hungarian Gypsies, Los Angeles rap stars, London advertising executives, and Argentinian army officers, the resulting heritability estimates for IQ and personality would likely have been lower. Bouchard and his colleagues emphasize this point in their papers. Still, selective-breeding studies

---

The Minnesota Signal,
Tuesday, November 19

Twins prove intelligence and personality inherited

Bob and Bob don't know each other. But they were born on the same day, graduated with engineering degrees in the same year, and both married teachers named Brenda. They both wear glasses, have mustaches, and smoke a pipe.

Bob and Bob are 38-year-old identical twins who were separated by adoption shortly after birth.

Dr. Thomas Bouchard and his colleagues recently brought Bob and Bob and 55 other pairs of genetically identical twins reared apart to the University of Minnesota.

Each twin underwent 50 hours of intensive psychological testing.

Dr. Bouchard found that the pairs of twins were almost identical in their intelligence and personality, despite having been reared by different families.

These findings are spearheading a psychological revolution.

They show that intelligence and personality are mostly genetic rather than being the result of experience, as thought by most psychologists.

The heritability estimates for IQ were found to be 70.

Nancy Baynes, chairperson of the school board, when contacted said, "We will certainly be discussing the implications of these important findings at our next meeting."

in laboratory animals and twin studies in humans have revealed no psychological differences that do not have a significant genetic component—even in twins over 80 years old (McClearn et al., 1997). Indeed, between childhood and adolescence, adopted children grow more and more similar to their biological parents in cognitive ability (Plomin et al., 1997).

A commonly overlooked point about the role of genetic factors in the development of human psychological differences is that genetic differences promote psychological differences by influencing experience (see Plomin & Neiderhiser, 1992). At first, this statement seems paradoxical because we have been conditioned to think of genes and experience as separate developmental influences. However, there is now ample evidence that individuals of similar genetic endowment tend to seek out similar environments and experiences. For example, individuals whose genetic endowments promote aggression are likely to become involved in aggressive activities (e.g., football or competitive fighting), and these experiences are likely to further contribute to the development of aggressive tendencies.

Themes Revisited

This chapter introduced the topics of evolution, genetics, and development, but its unifying focus was thinking clearly about the biology of behavior. Not surprisingly, then, of this book's four major themes, the thinking-about-biopsychology theme received the most attention. This chapter singled out several biopsychological issues about which there tends to be a lot of fuzzy thinking and tried to convince you that there are better ways to think about them. Thinking-about-biopsychology icons marked points in the chapter where you were encouraged to sharpen up your thinking about the physiological-or-psychological dichotomy, the nature–nurture issue, human evolution, the biopsychological implications of the human genome project, and the genetics of human psychological differences.

Two of this book's other themes also received coverage in this chapter and were marked by the appropriate icons. The evolutionary perspective was illustrated by comparative research on self-awareness in chimps, by efforts to understand human mate bonding, and by the use of mitochondrial DNA to study human evolution. The clinical implications theme was illustrated by the case of the man who fell out of bed and the discussion of phenylketonuria (PKU).

> **ON THE CD**
> Looking for more information about the topics in this chapter? For recommended additional readings, see Hard Copy for Chapter 2.

Log On

- **http://serendip.brynmawr.edu/Mind/Table.html** This site focuses on the history of the mind–brain problem from the time of Descartes.

- **http://home.att.net/~xchar/tna/ledoux.htm** Nature or nurture, genetics or experience? Dr. Joseph E. LeDoux describes the problems of the nature–nurture dichotomy.

- **http://www.anth.ucsb.edu/projects/human/evpsychfaq.html** This site is devoted to frequently asked questions about evolutionary psychology.

Think about It

1. Nature-or-nurture thinking about intelligence is sometimes used as an excuse for racial discrimination. How can the interactionist approach, which is championed in this chapter, be used as a basis for arguing against discriminatory practices?

2. Imagine that you are a biopsychology instructor. One of your students asks you whether depression is physiological or psychological. What would you say?

3. Modern genetics can prevent the tragedy of a life doomed by heredity; embryos can now be screened for some genetic diseases. But what constitutes a disease? Should

> **ON THE CD**
> Studying for an exam? Try the Practice Tests for Chapter 2.

genetic testing be used to select a child's characteristics? If so, what characteristics?

4. In the year 2030, a major company demands that all prospective executives take a gene test. As a result, some lose their jobs, and others fail to qualify for health insurance. Discuss.

5. "All men are created equal." Discuss.

Key Terms

Alleles *(p. 35)*
Amino acids *(p. 39)*
Amphibians *(p. 27)*
Analogous *(p. 31)*
Asomatognosia *(p. 21)*
Brain stem *(p. 31)*
Cartesian dualism *(p. 20)*
Cerebrum *(p. 31)*
Chordates *(p. 27)*
Chromosomes *(p. 36)*
Codon *(p. 40)*
Conspecifics *(p. 27)*
Convergent evolution *(p. 31)*
Convolutions *(p. 32)*
Crossing over *(p. 36)*
Deoxyribonucleic acid (DNA) *(p. 38)*
Dichotomous traits *(p. 34)*
DNA-binding proteins *(p. 40)*
Dominant trait *(p. 35)*
Ethology *(p. 21)*

Evolve *(p. 24)*
Exaptation *(p. 31)*
Fitness *(p. 25)*
Fraternal twins *(p. 47)*
Gametes *(p. 36)*
Gene *(p. 35)*
Gene expression *(p. 39)*
Gene maps *(p. 36)*
Genotype *(p. 35)*
Heritability estimate *(p. 48)*
Heterozygous *(p. 35)*
Hominids *(p. 27)*
Homologous *(p. 31)*
Homozygous *(p. 35)*
Human genome project *(p. 40)*
Identical twins *(p. 47)*
Instinctive behaviors *(p. 21)*
Linkage *(p. 36)*
Mammals *(p. 27)*
Meiosis *(p. 36)*
Messenger RNA *(p. 40)*

Mitochondria *(p. 40)*
Mitosis *(p. 36)*
Monogamy *(p. 33)*
Mutations *(p. 39)*
Natural selection *(p. 25)*
Nature–nurture issue *(p. 20)*
Nucleotide bases *(p. 38)*
Ontogeny *(p. 43)*
Operator genes *(p. 39)*
Phenotype *(p. 35)*
Phenylketonuria (PKU) *(p. 44)*
Phenylpyruvic acid *(p. 44)*
Phylogeny *(p. 43)*
Polyandry *(p. 33)*
Polygyny *(p. 33)*
Primates *(p. 27)*
Proteins *(p. 39)*
Recessive trait *(p. 35)*
Replication *(p. 39)*
Ribonucleic acid (RNA) *(p. 40)*
Ribosomes *(p. 40)*

Sensitive period *(p. 45)*
Sensorimotor phase *(p. 45)*
Sensory phase *(p. 45)*
Sex chromosomes *(p. 36)*
Sex-linked traits *(p. 36)*
Spandrels *(p. 31)*
Species *(p. 27)*
Structural genes *(p. 39)*
Transfer RNA *(p. 40)*
True-breeding lines *(p. 34)*
Vertebrates *(p. 27)*
Zeitgeist *(p. 20)*
Zygote *(p. 36)*

ON THE CD

Need some help studying the key terms for this chapter? Check out the electronic flash cards for Chapter 2.

The Anatomy of the Nervous System

The Systems, Structures, and Cells That Make Up Your Nervous System

chapter 3

I n order to understand what the brain does, it is essential to understand what it is—to know the names and locations of its major parts and how they are connected to one another. This chapter introduces you to these fundamentals of brain anatomy.

Before you begin this chapter, I want to apologize for the lack of foresight displayed by early neuroanatomists in their choice of names for neuroanatomical structures—but, then, how could they have anticipated that Latin and Greek, universal languages of the educated in their day, would not be compulsory university fare in our time? To help you, I have provided the literal English meanings of many of the neuroanatomical terms, and I have kept this chapter as brief and to the point as possible by covering only the most important structures. Still, there is no denying that this chapter will require extra effort. I can assure you, however, that it is effort well expended. Knowledge of your brain's basic structure is the necessary first step in understanding its psychological functions.

3.1   General Layout of the Nervous System

Divisions of the Nervous System

The vertebrate nervous system is composed of two divisions: the central nervous system and the peripheral nervous system (see Figure 3.1). The **central nervous system (CNS)** is the division of the nervous system that is located within the skull and spine. The **peripheral nervous system (PNS)** is the division that is located outside the skull and spine.

The central nervous system is composed of two divisions: the brain and the spinal cord. The *brain* is the part of the CNS that is located in the skull; the *spinal cord* is the part that is located in the spine.

The peripheral nervous system is also composed of two divisions: the somatic nervous system and the autonomic nervous system. The **somatic nervous system (SNS)** is the part of the PNS that interacts with the external environment. It is composed of **afferent nerves** that carry sensory signals from the skin, skeletal muscles, joints, eyes, ears, and so on, to the central nervous system, and **efferent nerves** that carry motor signals from the central nervous system to the skeletal muscles. The **autonomic nervous system (ANS)** is the part of the peripheral nervous system that participates in the regulation of the internal environment. It is composed of afferent nerves that carry sensory signals from internal organs to the CNS and efferent nerves that carry motor signals from the CNS to internal organs. You will not confuse the terms *afferent* and *efferent* if you remember that many words that involve the idea of going toward something—in this case, going toward the CNS—begin with an *a* (e.g., advance, approach, arrive) and that many words that involve the idea of going away from something begin with an *e* (e.g., exit, embark, escape).

The autonomic nervous system has two kinds of efferent nerves: sympathetic nerves and parasympathetic nerves. The **sympathetic nerves** are those autonomic motor nerves that project from the CNS in the *lumbar* (small of the back) and *thoracic* (chest area) regions of the spine. The **parasympathetic nerves** are those auto-

ON THE CD

You can review the differences between the efferent branches of the somatic and autonomic divisions of the PNS in the module titled *The Nervous System*. In particular, note the different transmitters used by the two divisions.

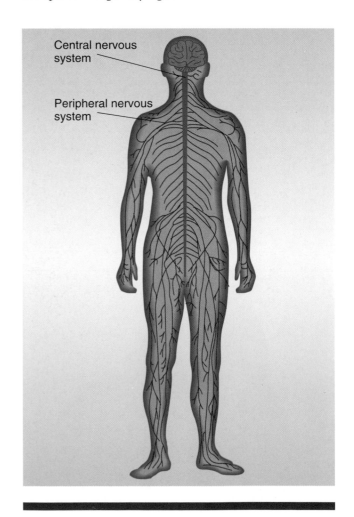

Central nervous system

Peripheral nervous system

FIGURE 3.1   The human central nervous system (CNS) and peripheral nervous system (PNS). The CNS is represented in red; the PNS in blue.

nomic motor nerves that project from the brain and *sacral* (lower back) region of the spine. See Appendix I. (Ask your instructor to specify the degree to which you are responsible for material in the appendices.) All sympathetic and parasympathetic nerves are two-stage neural paths: The sympathetic and parasympathetic neurons project from the CNS and go only part of the way to the target organs before they *synapse* on other neurons (second-stage neurons) that carry the signals the rest of the way. However, the sympathetic and parasympathetic systems differ in that the sympathetic neurons that project from the CNS synapse on second-stage neurons at a substantial distance from their target organs, whereas the parasympathetic neurons that project from the CNS synapse near their target organs on very short second-stage neurons (see Appendix I).

The conventional view of the respective functions of the sympathetic and parasympathetic systems stresses three important principles: (1) that sympathetic nerves stimulate, organize, and mobilize energy resources in threatening situations, whereas parasympathetic nerves act to conserve energy; (2) that each autonomic target organ receives opposing sympathetic and parasympathetic input, and its activity is thus controlled by relative levels of sympathetic and parasympathetic activity; and (3) that sympathetic changes are indicative of psychological arousal, whereas parasympathetic changes are indicative of psychological relaxation. Although these principles are generally correct, there are significant exceptions to each of them (see Blessing, 1997; Hugdahl, 1996)—see Appendix II.

Most of the nerves of the peripheral nervous system project from the spinal cord, but there are 12 pairs of exceptions: the 12 pairs of **cranial nerves,** which project from the brain. They are numbered in sequence from front to back. The cranial nerves include purely sensory nerves such as the olfactory nerves (I) and the optic nerves (II), but most contain both sensory and motor fibers. The longest cranial nerves are the vagus nerves (X), which contain motor and sensory fibers traveling to and from the gut. The 12 pairs of cranial nerves and their targets are illustrated in Appendix III; their functions are listed in Appendix IV. The autonomic motor fibers of the cranial nerves are parasympathetic.

The functions of the various cranial nerves are commonly assessed by neurologists as a basis for diagnosis. Because the functions and locations of the cranial nerves are specific, disruptions of particular cranial nerve functions provide excellent clues about the location and extent of tumors and other kinds of brain pathology.

Figure 3.2 summarizes the major divisions of the nervous system. Notice that the nervous system is a "system of twos."

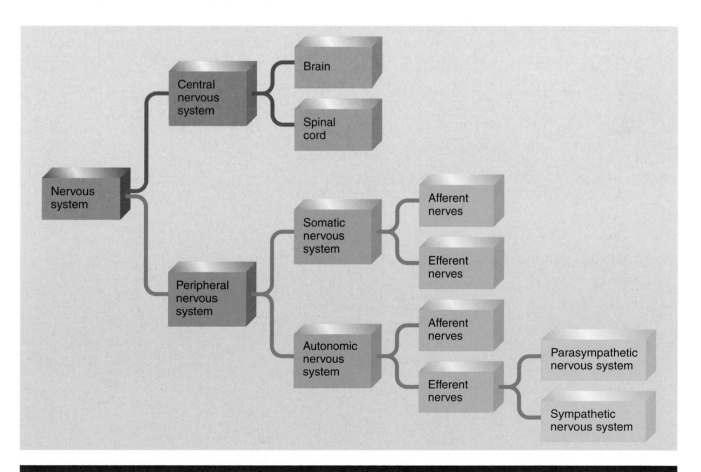

FIGURE 3.2   The major divisions of the nervous system.

Meninges, Ventricles, and Cerebrospinal Fluid

The brain and spinal cord (the CNS) are the most protected organs in the body. They are encased in bone and covered by three protective membranes, the three **meninges** (pronounced "men-IN-gees"). The outer *meninx* (which, believe it or not, is the singular of *meninges*) is a tough membrane called the **dura mater** (tough mother). Immediately inside the dura mater is the fine **arachnoid membrane** (spiderweblike membrane). Beneath the arachnoid membrane is a space called the **subarachnoid space,** which contains many large blood vessels and cerebrospinal fluid; then comes the innermost meninx, the delicate **pia mater** (pious mother), which adheres to the surface of the CNS.

Also protecting the CNS is the **cerebrospinal fluid (CSF),** which fills the subarachnoid space, the central canal of the spinal cord, and the cerebral ventricles of the brain. The **central canal** is a small central channel that runs the length of the spinal cord; the **cerebral ventricles** are the four large internal chambers of the brain: the two lateral ventricles, the third ventricle, and the fourth ventricles (see Figure 3.3). The subarachnoid space, central canal, and cerebral ventricles are interconnected by a series of openings and thus form a single reservoir.

The cerebrospinal fluid supports and cushions the brain. These functions are all too apparent to patients who have had some of their cerebrospinal fluid drained away; they suffer raging headaches and experience stabbing pain each time they jerk their heads.

Cerebrospinal fluid is continuously produced by the **choroid plexuses**—networks of capillaries (small blood vessels) that protrude into the ventricles from the pia mater lining. The excess cerebrospinal fluid is continuously absorbed from the subarachnoid space into large blood-filled spaces, or *dural sinuses,* which run through the dura mater and drain into the large jugular veins of the neck. Figure 3.4 illustrates the absorption of cerebrospinal fluid from the subarachnoid space into the large sinus that runs along the top of the brain between the two cerebral hemispheres.

Occasionally, the flow of cerebrospinal fluid is blocked by a tumor near one of the narrow channels that link the ventricles—for example, near the **cerebral aqueduct,** which connects the third and fourth ventricles. The resulting buildup of fluid in the ventricles causes the walls of the ventricles, and thus the entire brain, to expand, producing a condition called *hydrocephalus* (water head). Hydrocephalus is treated by draining the excess fluid from the ventricles and trying to remove the obstruction.

Blood–Brain Barrier

The brain is a finely tuned electrochemical organ whose function can be severely disturbed by the introduction of certain kinds of chemicals. Fortunately, there

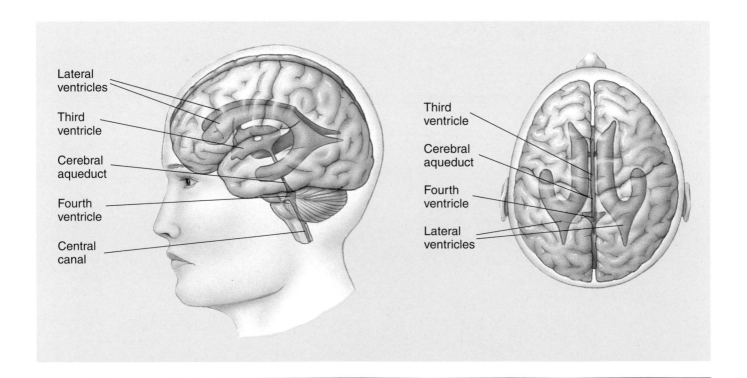

Lateral ventricles

Third ventricle

Cerebral aqueduct

Fourth ventricle

Central canal

Third ventricle

Cerebral aqueduct

Fourth ventricle

Lateral ventricles

FIGURE 3.3 The cerebral ventricles.

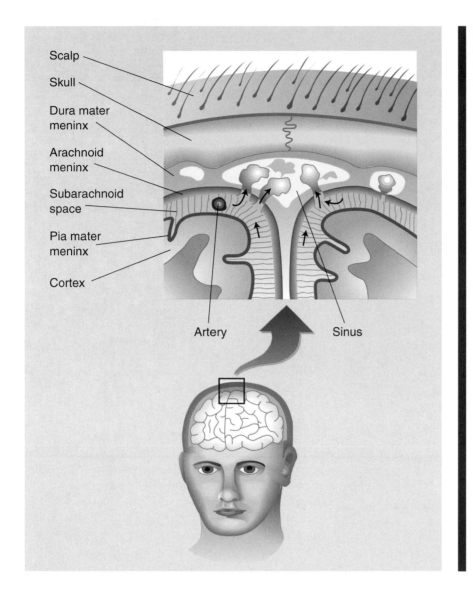

Scalp
Skull
Dura mater meninx
Arachnoid meninx
Subarachnoid space
Pia mater meninx
Cortex

Artery   Sinus

FIGURE 3.4 The absorption of cerebrospinal fluid from the subarachnoid space (blue) into a major sinus. Note the three meninges.

is a mechanism that impedes the passage of many toxic substances from the blood into the brain: the **blood–brain barrier.** This barrier is a consequence of the special structure of cerebral blood vessels. In the rest of the body, the cells that compose the walls of blood vessels are loosely packed; as a result, most molecules pass readily through them into surrounding tissue. In the brain, however, the cells of the blood vessel walls are tightly packed, thus forming a barrier to the passage of many molecules—particularly proteins and other large molecules. The degree to which psychoactive drugs in-fluence psychological processes depends on the ease with which they penetrate the blood–brain barrier.

The blood–brain barrier does not impede the passage of all large molecules. Some large molecules that are critical for normal brain function (e.g., glucose) are actively transported through cerebral blood vessel walls. Also, the blood vessel walls in some areas of the brain allow certain large molecules to pass through them unimpeded; for example, sex hormones, which have difficulty permeating some parts of the brain, readily enter those parts involved in sexual behavior.

3.2 Cells of the Nervous System

The cells of the nervous system are of two fundamentally different types: neurons and supportive cells. Their anatomy is discussed in the following two subsections.

Anatomy of Neurons

Neurons are cells that are specialized for the reception, conduction, and transmission of electrochemical signals. They come in an incredible variety of shapes and sizes; however, many are similar to the one illustrated in Figures 3.5 and 3.6.

EXTERNAL ANATOMY OF NEURONS ■ Figure 3.5 is an illustration of the major external features of a typical neuron. For your convenience, the definition of each feature is included in the illustration.

INTERNAL ANATOMY OF NEURONS ■ Figure 3.6 on page 58 is an illustration of the major internal features of a typical neuron. Again, the definition of each feature is included in the illustration.

NEURON CELL MEMBRANE ■ The neuron cell membrane is composed of a *lipid bilayer*—two layers of fat molecules (see Figure 3.7 on page 59). Embedded in the lipid bilayer are numerous protein molecules that are the basis of many of the cell membrane's functional properties. Some membrane proteins are *channel proteins*, through which certain molecules can pass; others are *signal proteins*, which transfer a signal to the inside of the neuron when particular molecules bind to them on the outside of the membrane.

CLASSES OF NEURONS ■ Figure 3.8 on page 59 illustrates a way of classifying neurons that is based on the number of processes emanating from their cell bodies. A neuron with more than two processes extending from its cell body is classified as a **multipolar neuron;** most neurons are multipolar. A neuron with one process extending from its cell body is classified as a **unipolar neuron,** and a neuron with two processes extending from its cell body is classified as a **bipolar neuron.** Neurons with short axons or no axon at all are called **interneurons;** their function is to integrate the neural activity within a single brain structure, not to conduct signals from one structure to another.

In general, there are two kinds of gross neural structures in the nervous system: those composed primarily of cell bodies and those composed primarily of axons. In the central nervous system, clusters of cell bodies are called **nuclei** (singular *nucleus*); in the peripheral nervous system, they are called **ganglia** (singular *ganglion*). (Note that the word *nucleus* has two different neuroanatomical meanings; it is a structure in the neuron cell body and a cluster of cell bodies in the CNS.) In the central nervous system, bundles of axons are called **tracts;** in the peripheral nervous system, they are called **nerves.**

Supportive Cells of the Nervous System: Glial Cells and Satellite Cells

Neurons are not the only cells in the nervous system. In the central nervous system, they are provided with physical and functional support by **glial cells;** in the peripheral nervous system, they are provided with physical and functional support by **satellite cells.** Among their many supportive functions, glial cells and satellite cells form a physical matrix that holds neural circuits together (*glia* means "glue"), and they absorb dead cells and other debris.

The largest glial cells are called **astrocytes,** or *astroglia* (see Chan-Ling & Stone, 1991), because they are star-shaped (*astron* means "star"). The armlike extensions of astrocytes cover the outer surface of blood vessels that course through the brain; they also make contact with neuron cell bodies (see Figure 3.9 on page 60). Accordingly, astrocytes are thought to play a role in the passage of chemicals from the blood into neurons.

Oligodendrocytes are another class of glial cells; they send out extensions that wrap around the axons of some neurons of the central nervous system. These extensions are rich in *myelin,* a fatty insulating substance, and the myelin sheaths that they form increase the speed and efficiency of axonal conduction. A similar function is performed by **Schwann cells** (a class of satellite cells) in the peripheral nervous system. Oligodendrocytes and Schwann cells are illustrated in Figure 3.10 on page 60. Notice that each Schwann cell constitutes one myelin segment, whereas each oligodendrocyte constitutes several segments, often on more than one axon. Another important difference between Schwann cells and oligodendrocytes is that only Schwann cells can guide axonal *regeneration* (regrowth) after damage. That is why there is normally little axonal regeneration in the mammalian CNS.

Although glial cells do play an important supportive role in the brain, the view that their role is restricted to the support of neural function is rapidly disappearing (LoTurco, 2000). In the last few years, the glial cells have been shown to participate in the transmission of chemical signals through the brain by sending signals to neurons and receiving signals from them (e.g., Yuan & Ganetsky, 1999). They have also been shown to control the establishment and maintenance of synapses between neurons (Ullian et al., 2001). Glial cells have been the forgotten majority—some estimates suggest that they outnumber neurons in the brain by almost 10 to 1. Now that the attention of neuroscientists has been focused on glial cells by the first wave of discoveries, our understanding of their function should improve quickly and markedly.

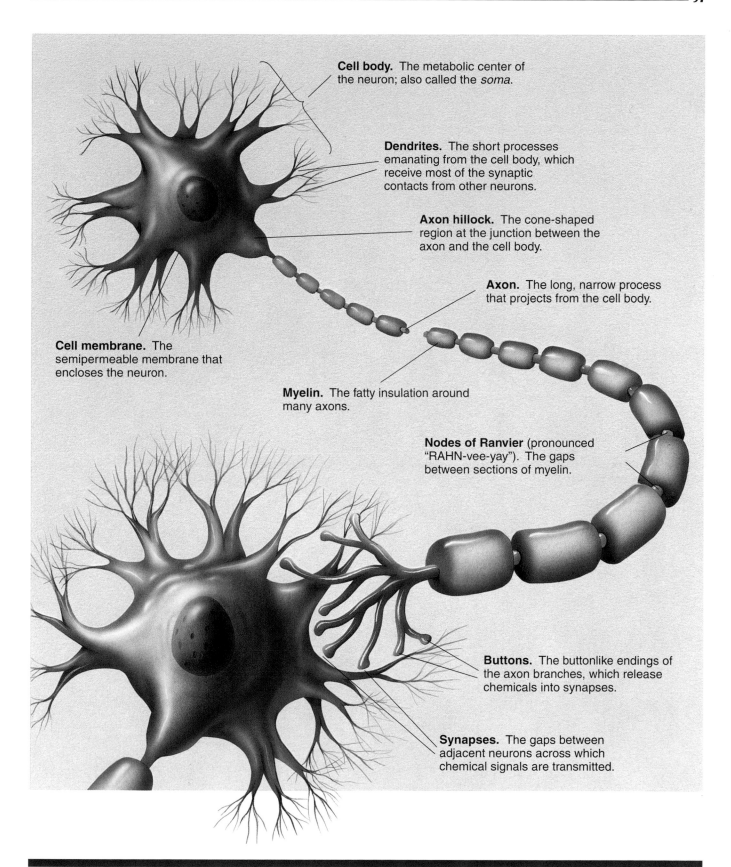

Cell body. The metabolic center of the neuron; also called the *soma*.

Dendrites. The short processes emanating from the cell body, which receive most of the synaptic contacts from other neurons.

Axon hillock. The cone-shaped region at the junction between the axon and the cell body.

Axon. The long, narrow process that projects from the cell body.

Cell membrane. The semipermeable membrane that encloses the neuron.

Myelin. The fatty insulation around many axons.

Nodes of Ranvier (pronounced "RAHN-vee-yay"). The gaps between sections of myelin.

Buttons. The buttonlike endings of the axon branches, which release chemicals into synapses.

Synapses. The gaps between adjacent neurons across which chemical signals are transmitted.

FIGURE 3.5   The major external features of a typical neuron.

Endoplasmic reticulum. A system of folded membranes in the cell body; rough portions (those with ribosomes) play a role in the synthesis of proteins; smooth portions (those without ribosomes) play a role in the synthesis of fats.

Cytoplasm. The clear internal fluid of the cell.

Ribosomes. Internal cellular structures on which proteins are synthesized; they are located on the endoplasmic reticulum.

Golgi complex. A system of membranes that packages molecules in vesicles.

Nucleus. The spherical DNA-containing structure of the cell body.

Mitochondria. Sites of aerobic (oxygen-consuming) energy release.

Microtubules. Tubules responsible for the rapid transport of material throughout neurons.

Synaptic vesicles. Spherical membrane packages that store neurotransmitter molecules ready for release near synapses.

Neurotransmitters. Molecules that are released from active neurons and influence the activity of other cells.

FIGURE 3.6   The major internal features of a typical neuron.

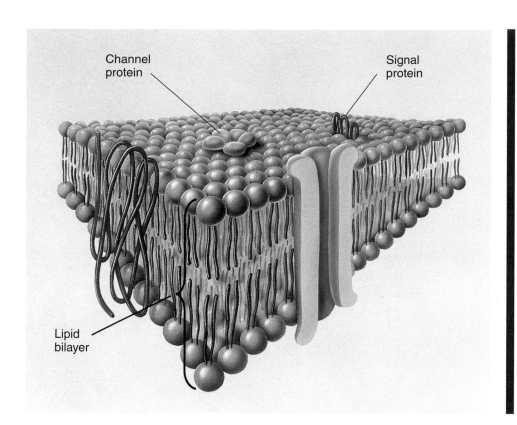

Channel protein

Signal protein

Lipid bilayer

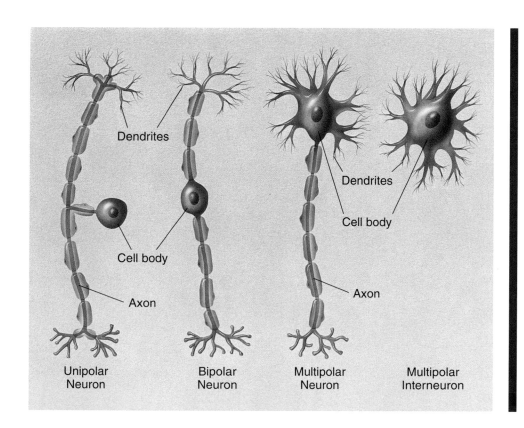

Dendrites

Cell body

Dendrites

Cell body

Axon

Axon

Unipolar Neuron

Bipolar Neuron

Multipolar Neuron

Multipolar Interneuron

FIGURE 3.9 Astrocytes have an affinity for blood vessels, and they form a supportive matrix for neurons. The photograph on the left is of a slice of brain tissue stained with a glial stain; the unstained channels are blood vessels. The illustration on the right is a three-dimensional representation of the image on the left showing how the feet of astrocytes cover blood vessels and contact neurons. **Compare the two panels.** (Photograph courtesy of T. Chan-Ling.)

Myelination in the Central Nervous System

Myelination in the Peripheral Nervous System

Nucleus

Axon

Oligodendrocyte

Axon

Nucleus

Schwann cell

FIGURE 3.10 The myelination of CNS axons by an oligodendrocyte and the myelination of PNS axons by Schwann cells.

3.3 Neuroanatomical Techniques and Directions

This section of the chapter first describes a few of the most common neuroanatomical techniques. Then, it explains the system of directions that neuroanatomists use to describe the location of structures in vertebrate nervous systems.

■ Neuroanatomical Techniques

The major problem in visualizing neurons is not their minuteness. The major problem is that neurons are so tightly packed and their axons and dendrites so intricately intertwined that looking through a microscope at unprepared neural tissue reveals almost nothing about them. The key to the study of neuroanatomy lies in preparing neural tissue in a variety of ways, each of which permits a clear view of a different aspect of neuronal structure, and then combining the knowledge obtained from each of the preparations. This point is illustrated by the following neuroanatomical techniques.

GOLGI STAIN ■ The greatest blessing to befall neuroscience in its early years was the accidental discovery of the **Golgi stain** by Camillo Golgi (pronounced "GOLE-jee"), an Italian physician, in the early 1870s. Golgi was trying to stain the meninges, by exposing a block of neural tissue to potassium dichromate and silver nitrate, when he noticed an amazing thing. For some unknown reason, the silver chromate created by the chemical reaction of the two substances Golgi was using invaded a few neurons in each slice of tissue and stained each invaded neuron entirely black. This discovery made it possible to see individual neurons for the first time, although only in silhouette (see Figure 3.11). Stains that totally dye all neurons on a slide reveal nothing of their structure because the neurons are so tightly packed.

NISSL STAIN ■ Although the Golgi stain permits an excellent view of the silhouettes of the few neurons that take up the stain, it provides no indication of the number of neurons in an area or the nature of their inner structure. The first neural staining procedure to overcome these shortcomings was the **Nissl stain,** which was developed by Franz Nissl, a German psychiatrist, in the 1880s. The most common dye used in the Nissl method is cresyl violet. Cresyl violet and other Nissl dyes penetrate all cells on a slide, but they bind effectively only to structures in neuron cell bodies. Thus, one can estimate the number of cell bodies in an area by counting the number of Nissl-stained dots. Figure 3.12 on page 62 is a

FIGURE 3.11 Neural tissue that has been stained by the Golgi method. Because only a few neurons take up the stain, their silhouettes are revealed in great detail, but their internal details are invisible. Usually, only part of a neuron is captured in a single slice. (Ed Reschke © Peter Arnold, Inc.)

photograph of a slice of brain tissue stained with cresyl violet. Notice that only the layers composed mainly of neuron cell bodies are densely stained.

ELECTRON MICROSCOPY ■ A neuroanatomical technique that provides information about the details of neuronal structure is **electron microscopy** (pronounced "my-CROSS-cuh-pee"). Because of the nature of light, the limit of magnification in light microscopy is about 1,500 times, a level of magnification that is insufficient to reveal the fine anatomical details of neurons. Greater detail can be obtained by first coating thin slices of neural tissue with an electron-absorbing substance that is taken

FIGURE 3.12   Neural tissue that has been stained by the Nissl method. Notice the densely stained cell body layers in this Nissl-stained section (slice) of the mouse hippocampus, a structure that plays an important role in learning and memory. (Courtesy of Jerold J. M. Chun, M.D., Ph.D.)

up by different parts of neurons to different degrees, then passing a beam of electrons through the tissue onto a photographic film. The result is an *electron micrograph,* which captures neuronal structure in exquisite detail (see Figure 4.10). A *scanning electron microscope* provides spectacular electron micrographs in three dimensions (see Figure 3.13), but is not capable of as much magnification as a conventional electron microscope.

FIGURE 3.13   A color-enhanced scanning electron micrograph of a neuron cell body (green) studded with terminal buttons (orange). Each neuron receives numerous synaptic contacts. (Courtesy of Jerold J. M. Chun, M.D., Ph.D.)

MYELIN STAINS ■ The first stains specifically developed for studying axons were **myelin stains**—stains that selectively dye the sheaths of myelinated axons. Figure 3.14 is a myelin-stained coronal section of the human brain. Notice that the subcortical white matter, which is composed largely of myelinated axons, is stained, while the cerebral cortex and various subcortical nuclear groups are not. Although myelin stains are useful for visualizing myelinated areas of the CNS, they are not very useful for tracking the pathways of individual axons—for three reasons. First, the stains are of no use in tracking unmyelinated axons. Second, because the initial segment and terminal branches of myelinated axons are not myelinated, the stains cannot reveal exactly where a myelinated axon originates or where it terminates. Third, because all myelinated axons are stained indiscriminately, once a myelinated axon becomes intermingled with others, it is impossible to trace it through a series of slices. Neuroanatomical tracing techniques circumvent these problems.

NEUROANATOMICAL TRACING TECHNIQUES ■ Neuroanatomical tracing techniques are of two types: anterograde (forward) tracing methods and retrograde (backward) tracing methods. *Anterograde tracing methods* are used when an investigator wants to trace the paths of axons projecting away from cell bodies located in a particular area. The investigator injects into the area one of several chemicals commonly used for anterograde

FIGURE 3.14   A myelin-stained section of the human brain. Notice that the white matter is stained black but the cortex and other nuclear groups are relatively unstained. (From *Fundamental Neuroanatomy* by Walle J. H. Nauta and Michael Feirtag. Copyright © 1986 W. H. Freeman and Company. Reprinted with permission.)

FIGURE 3.15 Retrograde tracing. Injection of a red fluorescent dye (rhodamine dextrans) into one visual cortex of a cat was taken up by neural buttons in the area and transported back to their cell bodies. Stained red in this section are the neural cell bodies in the contralateral visual cortex whose axons projected via the corpus callosum to the site of the injection. (Courtesy of Joanne Matsubara, Department of Ophthalmology, University of British Columbia.)

tracing—chemicals that are taken up by cell bodies and then transported forward along their axons to their terminal buttons. After a few days, the brain is removed and sliced; the slices are then treated to reveal the locations of the injected chemical. *Retrograde tracing methods* work in reverse; they are used when an investigator wants to trace the paths of axons projecting into a particular area. The investigator injects into the area one of several chemicals commonly used for retrograde tracing—chemicals that are taken up by terminal buttons and then transported backward along their axons to their cell bodies. After a few days, the brain is removed and sliced; the slices are then treated to reveal the locations of the injected chemical (see Figure 3.15).

Directions in the Vertebrate Nervous System

It would be difficult for you to develop an understanding of the layout of an unfamiliar city without a system of directional coordinates: north–south, east–west. The same goes for the nervous system. Thus, before introducing you to the locations of major nervous system structures, I will describe the three-dimensional system of directional coordinates used by neuroanatomists.

Directions in the vertebrate nervous system are described in relation to the orientation of the spinal cord. This system is straightforward for most vertebrates, as Figure 3.16 indicates. The vertebrate nervous system has three axes: anterior–posterior, dorsal–ventral, and medial–lateral. First, **anterior** means toward the nose end (the anterior end), and **posterior** means toward the tail end (the posterior end); these same directions are sometimes referred to as *rostral* and *caudal,* respectively. Second, **dorsal** means toward the surface of the back or the top of the head (the dorsal surface), and **ventral** means toward the surface of the chest or the bottom of the head (the ventral surface). Third, **medial** means toward the midline of the body, and **lateral** means away from the midline toward the body's lateral surfaces.

We humans complicate this simple three-axis (anterior–posterior, ventral–dorsal, medial–lateral) system of neuroanatomical directions by insisting on walking around on our hind legs. This changes the orientation of our cerebral hemispheres in relation to our spines and brain stems.

You can save yourself a lot of confusion if you remember that the system of vertebrate neuroanatomical directions was adapted for use in humans in such a way that the terms used to describe the positions of various

FIGURE 3.16 Anatomical directions in a representative vertebrate.

FIGURE 3.17 Anatomical directions in a human. Notice that the directions in the cerebral hemispheres are rotated by 90° in comparison to those in the spinal cord and brain stem because of the unusual upright posture of humans.

body surfaces are the same in humans as they are in more typical, non-upright vertebrates. Specifically, notice that the top of the human head and the back of the human body are both referred to as *dorsal* even though they are in different directions, and the bottom of the human head and the front of the human body are both referred to as *ventral* even though they are in different directions (see Figure 3.17). To circumvent this complication, the terms **superior** and **inferior** are often used to refer to the top and bottom of the primate head, respectively.

Proximal and distal are two other common directional terms. In general, *proximal* means "close," and *distal* means "far." Specifically, with regard to the peripheral nervous system, *proximal* means closer to the CNS, and *distal* means farther from the CNS—for example, the nerve terminals of the shoulders are proximal to those of the fingers.

In the next few pages, you will be seeing drawings of sections (slices) of the brain cut in one of three different planes: **horizontal sections, frontal** (also termed *coronal*) **sections,** and **sagittal sections.** These three planes are illustrated in Figure 3.18. A section cut down the center of the brain, between the two hemispheres, is called a

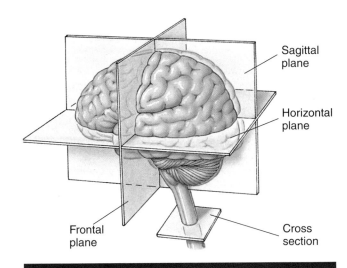

FIGURE 3.18 Horizontal, frontal (coronal), and sagittal planes in the human brain and a cross section of the human spinal cord.

midsagittal section. A section cut at a right angle to any long, narrow structure, such as the spinal cord or a nerve, is called a **cross section.**

3.4 The Spinal Cord

In the first three sections of this chapter, you learned about the divisions of the nervous system, the cells that compose it, and some of the neuroanatomical techniques that are used to study it. This section begins your ascent of the human CNS by focusing on the spinal cord. The final two sections of the chapter focus on the brain.

In cross section, it is apparent that the spinal cord comprises two different areas (see Figure 3.19): an inner H-shaped core of gray matter and a surrounding area of white matter. *Gray matter* is composed largely of cell bodies and unmyelinated interneurons, whereas *white matter* is composed largely of myelinated axons. (It is the myelin that gives the white matter its glossy white sheen.)

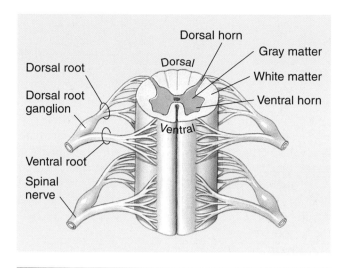

FIGURE 3.19 The dorsal and ventral roots of the spinal cord.

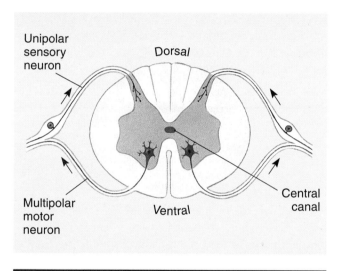

FIGURE 3.20 A schematic cross section of the spinal cord.

BrainScan

This is a good place for you to pause to scan your brain. Are you ready to proceed to the structures of the brain and spinal cord? Test your grasp of the preceding sections of this chapter by drawing a line between each term in the left column and the appropriate phrase in the right column. The correct answers are provided at the bottom of this page. Before proceeding, review material related to your incorrect answers.

1. Autonomic nervous system
2. Cerebral aqueduct
3. Axon hillock
4. Dorsal
5. Cell membrane
6. Cranial nerves
7. Superior or dorsal
8. Cell body
9. Synaptic vesicles
10. Oligodendrocytes
11. Nissl
12. Dura mater
13. Midsagittal section
14. Golgi

a. Packets of neurotransmitter molecules
b. PNS minus the somatic nervous system
c. Connects the third and fourth ventricles
d. Stains cell bodies
e. Top of a vertebrate's head
f. Outer meninx
g. Between the cell body and axon
h. Contains the nucleus of a neuron
i. Olfactory, visual, and vagus
j. Myelinate CNS axons
k. A slice down the center of the brain
l. Top of the primate head
m. Silhouette
n. Lipid bilayer

The two dorsal arms of the spinal gray matter are called the **dorsal horns,** and the two ventral arms are called the **ventral horns.**

Pairs of *spinal nerves* are attached to the spinal cord—one on the left and one on the right—at 31 different levels of the spine. Each of these 62 spinal nerves divides as it nears the cord (see Figure 3.19), and its axons are joined to the cord via one of two roots: the *dorsal root* or the *ventral root.*

All dorsal root axons, whether somatic or autonomic, are sensory (afferent) unipolar neurons with their cell bodies grouped together just outside the cord to form the *dorsal root ganglia.* Many of their synaptic terminals are in the dorsal horns of the spinal gray matter

(see Figure 3.20). In contrast, the neurons of the ventral root are motor (efferent) multipolar neurons with their cell bodies in the ventral horns. Those that are part of the somatic nervous system project to skeletal muscles; those that are part of the autonomic nervous system project to ganglia, where they synapse on neurons that in turn project to internal organs (heart, stomach, liver, etc.). See Appendix I.

Brain Scan answers: (1) b, (2) c, (3) g, (4) e, (5) n, (6) i, (7) l, (8) h, (9) a, (10) j, (11) d, (12) f, (13) k, (14) m.

3.5 The Five Major Divisions of the Brain

A necessary step in learning to live in an unfamiliar city is learning the names and locations of its major neighborhoods or districts. Those who possess this information can easily communicate the general location of any destination in the city. This section of the chapter introduces you to the five "neighborhoods," or divisions, of the brain—for much the same reason.

To understand why the brain is considered to be composed of five divisions, it is necessary to understand its early development (see Swanson, 2000). In the vertebrate embryo, the tissue that eventually develops into the CNS is recognizable as a fluid-filled tube (see Figure 3.21). The first indications of the developing brain are three swellings that occur at the anterior end of this tube. These three swellings eventually develop into the adult *forebrain, midbrain,* and *hindbrain.*

Before birth, the initial three swellings in the neural tube become five (see Figure 3.21). This occurs because the forebrain swelling grows into two different swellings,

and so does the hindbrain swelling. From anterior to posterior, the five swellings that compose the developing brain at birth are the *telencephalon,* the *diencephalon,* the *mesencephalon* (or midbrain), the *metencephalon,* and the *myelencephalon* (*encephalon* means "within the head"). These swellings ultimately develop into the five divisions of the adult brain. As a student, I memorized their order by remembering that the *te*lencephalon is on the *top* and the other four divisions are arrayed below it in alphabetical order.

Figure 3.22 illustrates the locations of the telencephalon, diencephalon, mesencephalon, metencephalon, and myelencephalon in the adult human brain. Notice that in humans, as in other higher vertebrates, the telencephalon (the left and right *cerebral hemispheres*) undergoes the greatest growth during development. The other four divisions of the brain are often referred to collectively as the **brain stem**—the stem on which the cerebral hemispheres sit. The myelencephalon is often referred to as the *medulla.*

3.6 Major Structures of the Brain

Now that you have learned the five major divisions of the brain, it is time to introduce you to their major structures. This section of the chapter begins its survey of

brain structures in the myelencephalon, then ascends through the other divisions to the telencephalon. The boldfaced brain structures introduced and defined in this

FIGURE 3.21 The early development of the mammalian brain illustrated in schematic horizontal sections. Compare with the adult human brain in Figure 3.22.

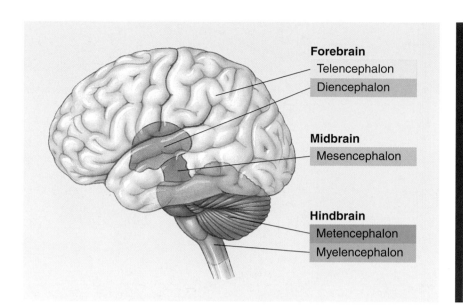

FIGURE 3.22 The divisions of the adult human brain.

section are not included in the Key Terms list at the end of the chapter. Rather, they are diagrammed according to their locations in Figure 3.32 on page 76.

Here is a reminder before you delve into the anatomy of the brain: The directional coordinates are the same for the brain stem as for the spinal cord, but they are rotated by 90° for the forebrain.

■ Myelencephalon

Not surprisingly, the **myelencephalon** (or **medulla**), the most posterior division of the brain, is composed largely of tracts carrying signals between the rest of the brain and the body. An interesting part of the myelencephalon from a psychological perspective is the **reticular formation** (see Figure 3.23 on page 68). It is a complex network of about 100 tiny nuclei that occupies the central core of the brain stem from the posterior boundary of the myelencephalon to the anterior boundary of the midbrain. It is so named because of its netlike appearance (*reticulum* means "little net"). Sometimes, the reticular formation is referred to as the *reticular activating system* because parts of it seem to play a role in arousal. The various nuclei of the reticular formation are involved in a variety of functions, however—including sleep, attention, movement, the maintenance of muscle tone, and various cardiac, circulatory, and respiratory reflexes. Accordingly, referring to this collection of nuclei as a system can be misleading.

■ Metencephalon

The **metencephalon,** like the myelencephalon, houses many ascending and descending tracts and part

of the reticular formation. These structures create a bulge, called the **pons,** on the brain stem's ventral surface. The pons is one major division of the metencephalon; the other is the cerebellum (little brain)—see Figure 3.23 on page 68. The **cerebellum** is the large, convoluted structure on the brain stem's dorsal surface. It is an important sensorimotor structure; cerebellar damage eliminates the ability to precisely control one's movements and to adapt them to changing conditions. However, the fact that cerebellar damage also produces a variety of cognitive deficits suggest that the function of the cerebellum is not restricted to sensorimotor control.

■ Mesencephalon

The **mesencephalon,** like the metencephalon, has two divisions. The two divisions of the mesencephalon are the tectum and the tegmentum (see Figure 3.24 on page 69). The **tectum** (roof) is the dorsal surface of the midbrain. In mammals, the tectum is composed of two pairs of bumps, the *colliculi* (little hills). The posterior pair, called the **inferior colliculi,** have an auditory function; the anterior pair, called the **superior colliculi,** have a visual function. In lower vertebrates, the function of the tectum is entirely visual; thus, the tectum is referred to as the *optic tectum.*

The **tegmentum** is the division of the mesencephalon ventral to the tectum. In addition to the reticular formation and tracts of passage, the tegmentum contains three colorful structures that are of particular interest to biopsychologists: the periaqueductal gray, the substantia nigra, and the red nucleus (see Figure 3.24 on page 69). The **periaqueductal gray** is the gray matter situated around the *cerebral aqueduct,* the duct connecting the

FIGURE 3.23 Structures of the human myelencephalon (medulla) and metencephalon.

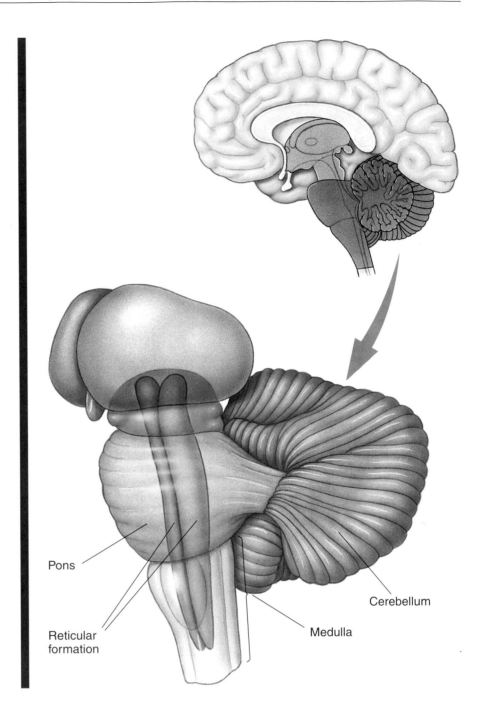

Pons

Reticular formation

Cerebellum

Medulla

third and fourth ventricles; it is of special interest because of its role in mediating the analgesic (pain-reducing) effects of opiate drugs. The **substantia nigra** (black substance) and the **red nucleus** are both important components of the sensorimotor system.

■ Diencephalon

The **diencephalon** is composed of two structures: the thalamus and the hypothalamus (see Figure 3.25 on page 70). The **thalamus** is the large, two-lobed structure that constitutes the top of the brain stem. One lobe sits

on each side of the third ventricle, and the two lobes are joined by the **massa intermedia,** which runs through the ventricle. Visible on the surface of the thalamus are white *lamina* (layers) that are composed of myelinated axons.

The thalamus comprises many different pairs of nuclei, most of which project to the cortex. Some are *sensory relay nuclei*—nuclei that receive signals from sensory receptors, process them, and then transmit them to the appropriate areas of sensory cortex. For example, the **lateral geniculate nuclei,** the **medial geniculate nuclei,** and the **ventral posterior nuclei** are important relay stations in the visual, auditory, and somatosensory systems, re-

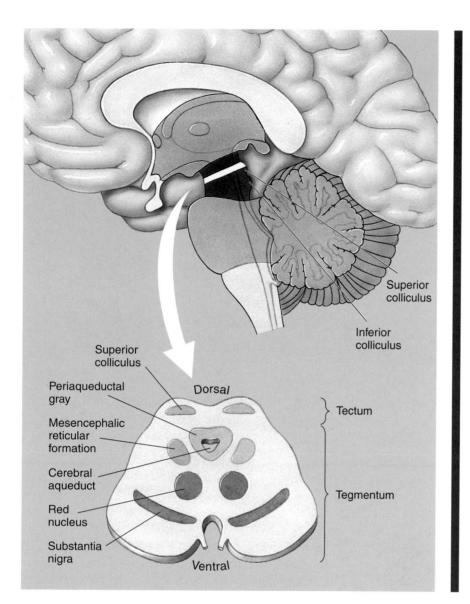

FIGURE 3.24 The human mesencephalon (midbrain).

spectively. The organization of the thalamus is illustrated in Appendix V.

The **hypothalamus** is located just below the anterior thalamus (*hypo* means "below")—see Figure 3.26 on page 71. It plays an important role in the regulation of several motivated behaviors. It exerts its effects in part by regulating the release of hormones from the **pituitary gland,** which dangles from it on the ventral surface of the brain. The literal meaning of *pituitary gland* is "snot gland"; it was discovered in a gelatinous state behind the nose of an unembalmed cadaver and was incorrectly assumed to be the main source of nasal mucus.

In addition to the pituitary gland, two other structures appear on the inferior surface of the hypothalamus: the optic chiasm and the mammillary bodies (see Figure 3.26). The **optic chiasm** is the point at which the *optic nerves* from each eye come together. The X shape is created because some of the axons of the optic nerve **de-**

cussate (cross over to the other side of the brain) via the optic chiasm. The decussating fibers are said to be **contralateral** (projecting from one side of the body to the other), and the nondecussating fibers are said to be **ipsilateral** (staying on the same side of the body). The **mammillary bodies** are a pair of spherical hypothalamic nuclei located on the inferior surface of the hypothalamus, just behind the pituitary. The mammillary bodies and the other nuclei of the hypothalamus are illustrated in Appendix VI.

■ Telencephalon

The **telencephalon** is the largest division of the human brain, and it mediates its most complex functions. It initiates voluntary movement, interprets sensory input, and mediates complex cognitive processes such as learning, speaking, and problem solving.

FIGURE 3.25 The human diencephalon.

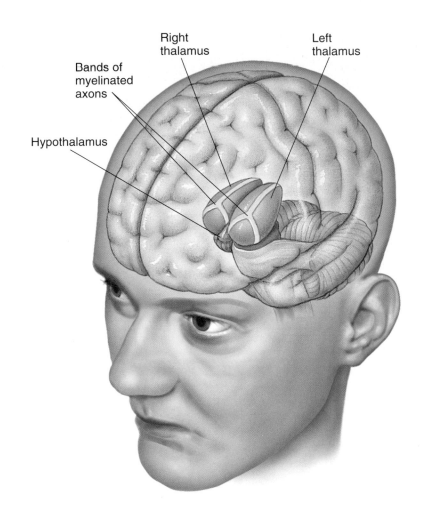

CEREBRAL CORTEX ■ The cerebral hemispheres are covered by a layer of tissue called the **cerebral cortex** (cerebral bark). In humans, the cerebral cortex is deeply convoluted (furrowed)—see Figure 3.27 on page 72. The *convolutions* have the effect of increasing the amount of cerebral cortex without increasing the overall volume of the brain. Not all mammals have convoluted cortexes; most mammals are *lissencephalic* (smooth-brained). It was once believed that the number and size of cortical convolutions determined a species' intellectual capacities; however, the number and size of cortical convolutions appear to be related more to body size. Every large mammal has an extremely convoluted cortex.

The large furrows in a convoluted cortex are called **fissures,** and the small ones are called *sulci* (singular *sulcus*). The ridges between fissures and sulci are called **gyri** (singular *gyrus*). It is apparent in Figure 3.27 that the cerebral hemispheres are almost completely separated by the largest of the fissures: the **longitudinal fissure.** The cerebral hemispheres are directly connected by only a few tracts spanning the longitudinal fissure; these hemisphere-connecting tracts are called **cerebral commissures.** The largest cerebral commissure, the **corpus callosum,** is clearly visible in Figure 3.27.

As Figure 3.28 on page 72 indicates, the two major landmarks on the lateral surface of each hemisphere are the **central fissure** and the **lateral fissure.** These fissures partially divide each hemisphere into four lobes: the **frontal lobe,** the **parietal lobe** (pronounced "pa-RYE-e-tal"), the **temporal lobe,** and the **occipital lobe** (pronounced "ok-SIP-i-tal"). Among the largest gyri are the **precentral gyri,** which contain motor cortex; the **postcentral gyri,** which contain somatosensory (body-sensation) cortex; and the **superior temporal gyri,** which contain auditory cortex. The function of occipital cortex is entirely visual.

About 90% of human cerebral cortex is **neocortex** (new cortex); that is, it is six-layered cortex of relatively recent evolution (Northcutt & Kaas, 1995). By convention, the layers of neocortex are numbered I through VI, starting at the surface. Figure 3.29 on page 73 illustrates two adjacent sections of neocortex. One has been stained with a Nissl stain to reveal the number and shape of its cell bodies; the other has been stained with a Golgi stain to reveal the silhouettes of a small proportion of its neurons.

Three important characteristics of neocortex anatomy are apparent from the sections in Figure 3.29. First, it is apparent that there are two fundamentally dif-

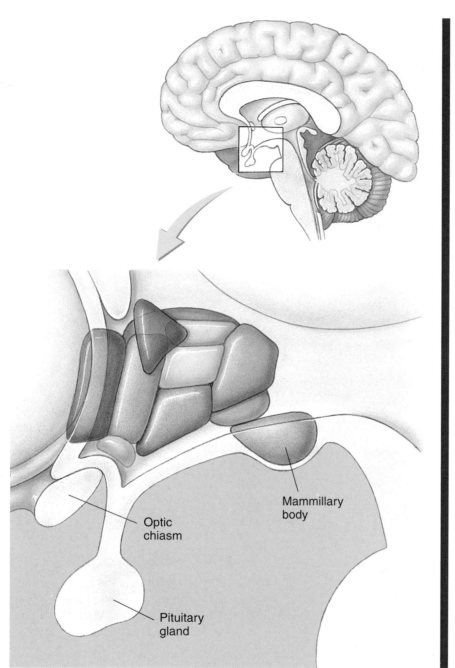

FIGURE 3.26 The human hypothalamus (in color) in relation to the optic chiasm and the pituitary gland.

Mammillary body

Optic chiasm

Pituitary gland

ferent kinds of cortical neurons: pyramidal (pyramid-shaped) cells and stellate (star-shaped) cells. **Pyramidal cells** are large multipolar neurons with pyramid-shaped cell bodies, a large dendrite called an *apical dendrite* that extends from the apex of the pyramid straight toward the cortex surface, and a very long axon. In contrast, **stellate cells** are small star-shaped interneurons (neurons with short axons or no axon). Second, it is apparent that the six layers of neocortex differ from one another in terms of the size and density of their cell bodies and the relative proportion of pyramidal and stellate cell bodies that they contain. Third, it is apparent that many long axons and dendrites course vertically (i.e., at right angles to the cortical layers) through the neocortex. This vertical

flow of information is the basis of the neocortex's **columnar organization;** neurons in a given vertical column of neocortex often form a mini-circuit that performs a single function.

A fourth important characteristic of neocortex anatomy is not apparent in Figure 3.29: Although all neocortex is six-layered, there are variations in the layers from area to area. For example, because the stellate cells of layer IV are specialized for receiving sensory signals from the thalamus, layer IV is extremely thick in areas of sensory cortex. Conversely, because the pyramidal cells of layer V conduct signals from the neocortex to the brain stem and spinal cord, layer V is extremely thick in areas of motor cortex.

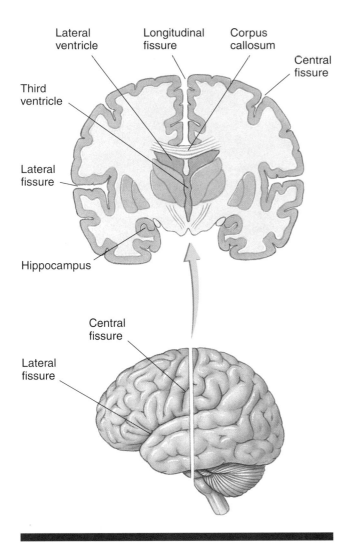

FIGURE 3.27   The major fissures of the human cerebral hemispheres.

The **hippocampus** is one important area of cortex that is not neocortex—it has only three layers. The hippocampus is located at the medial edge of the cerebral cortex as it folds back on itself in the medial temporal lobe (see Figure 3.27). This folding produces a shape that is, in cross section, somewhat reminiscent of a sea horse (*hippocampus* means "sea horse").

THE LIMBIC SYSTEM AND THE BASAL GANGLIA ■
Although much of the subcortical portion of the telencephalon is taken up by axons projecting to and from the neocortex, there are several large subcortical nuclear groups. Some of them are considered to be part of either the *limbic system* or the *basal ganglia motor system*. Don't be misled by the word *system* in these contexts; it implies a level of certainty that is unwarranted. It is not entirely clear exactly what these hypothetical systems do, exactly which structures should be included in them, or even whether it is appropriate to view them as unitary sys-

FIGURE 3.28   The lobes of the cerebral hemispheres.

tems. Nevertheless, if not taken too literally, the concepts of *limbic system* and *basal ganglia motor system* provide a useful means of conceptualizing the organization of the subcortex.

The **limbic system** is a circuit of midline structures that circle the thalamus (*limbic* means "ring"). The limbic system is involved in the regulation of motivated behaviors—including the four *F*s of motivation: fleeing, feeding, fighting, and sexual behavior. (This joke is as old

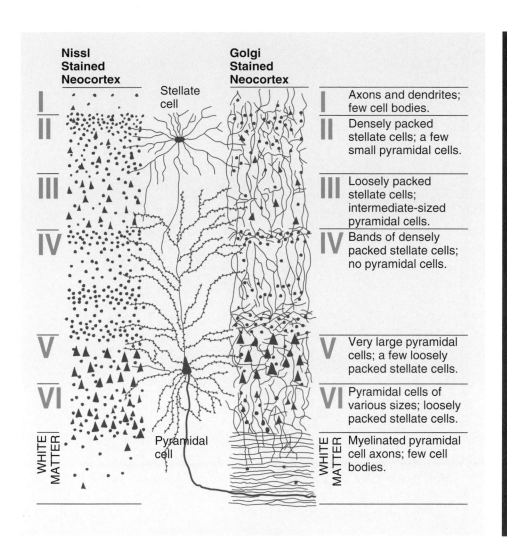

Nissl Stained Neocortex

Golgi Stained Neocortex

Stellate cell

Pyramidal cell

WHITE MATTER

I Axons and dendrites; few cell bodies.

II Densely packed stellate cells; a few small pyramidal cells.

III Loosely packed stellate cells; intermediate-sized pyramidal cells.

IV Bands of densely packed stellate cells; no pyramidal cells.

V Very large pyramidal cells; a few loosely packed stellate cells.

VI Pyramidal cells of various sizes; loosely packed stellate cells.

WHITE MATTER Myelinated pyramidal cell axons; few cell bodies.

FIGURE 3.29 The six layers of neocortex. (Adapted from Rakic, 1979.)

as biopsychology itself, but it is a good one.) In addition to several structures about which you have already read (e.g., the mammillary bodies and the hippocampus), major structures of the limbic system include the amygdala, the fornix, the cingulate cortex, and the septum.

Let's begin tracing the limbic circuit (see Figure 3.30 on page 74) at the **amygdala**—the almond-shaped nucleus in the anterior temporal lobe (*amygdala* means "almond")—see Swanson & Petrovich (1998). Posterior to the amygdala is the hippocampus, which runs beneath the thalamus in the medial temporal lobe. Next in the ring are the cingulate cortex and the fornix. The **cingulate cortex** is the large area of neocortex in the **cingulate gyrus** on the medial surface of the cerebral hemispheres, just superior to the corpus callosum; it encircles the dorsal thalamus (*cingulate* means "encircling"). The **fornix**, the major tract of the limbic system, also encircles the dorsal thalamus; it leaves the dorsal end of the hippocampus and sweeps forward in an arc coursing along the superior surface of the third ventricle and terminating in the septum and mammillary bodies (*fornix* means "arc"). The **septum** is a midline nucleus that is located at

the anterior tip of the cingulate cortex. Several tracts connect the septum and mammillary bodies with the amygdala and hippocampus, thereby completing the limbic ring.

The **basal ganglia** are illustrated in Figure 3.31 on page 74. As we did with the limbic system, let's begin our examination of the basal ganglia with the amygdala (pronounced "a-MIG-dah-lah"), which is considered to be part of both systems. Sweeping out of each amygdala, first in a posterior direction and then in an anterior direction, is the long tail-like **caudate** nucleus (*caudate* means "tail-like"). Each caudate nucleus forms an almost complete circle; in its center, connected to it by a series of fiber bridges, is the **putamen** (pronounced "pew-TAY-men"). Together, the caudate nucleus and putamen, which both have a striped appearance, are known as the **striatum** (striped structure). The remaining structure of the basal ganglia is the pale circular structure known as the globus pallidus (pale globe). The **globus pallidus** is located medial to the putamen, between the putamen and the thalamus.

FIGURE 3.30 The major structures of the limbic system: amygdala, hippocampus, cingulate cortex, fornix, septum, and mammillary body.

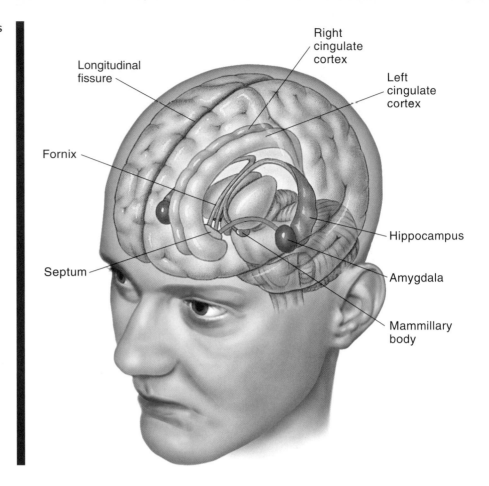

Longitudinal fissure

Fornix

Septum

Right cingulate cortex

Left cingulate cortex

Hippocampus

Amygdala

Mammillary body

FIGURE 3.31 The basal ganglia: amygdala, striatum (caudate plus putamen), and globus pallidus. Notice that, in this view, the right globus pallidus is largely hidden behind the right thalamus, and the left globus pallidus is totally hidden behind the left putamen.

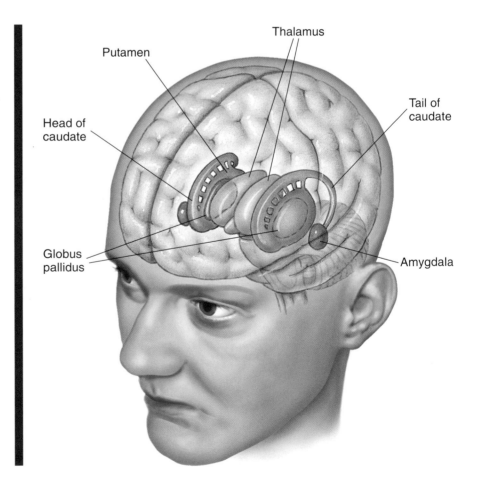

Putamen

Thalamus

Head of caudate

Tail of caudate

Globus pallidus

Amygdala

The basal ganglia play a major role in the performance of voluntary motor responses. Of particular interest is a pathway that projects to the striatum from the substantia nigra of the midbrain. *Parkinson's disease,* a disorder that is characterized by rigidity, tremors, and poverty of voluntary movement, is associated with the deterioration of this pathway.

Figure 3.32 on page 76 summarizes the major brain divisions and structures—those key terms that have appeared in boldface in this section.

Figure 3.33 on page 77 concludes this chapter for reasons that too often get lost in the shuffle of neuro-anatomical terms and technology. I have included it here to illustrate the beauty of the brain and the art of those who study its structure. I hope you are inspired by it. I wonder what thoughts its neural circuits once contained.

 BrainScan

If you have not previously studied the gross anatomy of the brain, your own brain is probably straining under the burden of new terms. To determine whether or not you are ready to proceed, scan your brain by labeling the following midsagittal view of a real human brain. (It will be challenging to switch from color-coded diagrams to a photograph.)

The correct answers are provided at the bottom of the page. Before proceeding, review material related to your errors and omissions. Notice that Figure 3.32 includes all the brain anatomy terms that have appeared in this chapter in bold type and thus is an excellent review tool.

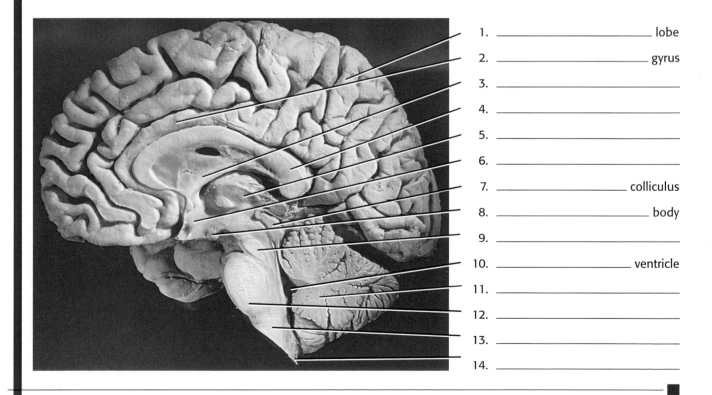

1. _____ lobe
2. _____ gyrus
3. _____
4. _____
5. _____
6. _____
7. _____ colliculus
8. _____ body
9. _____
10. _____ ventricle
11. _____
12. _____
13. _____
14. _____

Brain Scan answers: (1) parietal, (2) cingulate, (3) fornix, (4) corpus callosum, (5) thalamus, (6) hypothalamus, (7) superior, (8) mammillary, (9) tegmentum, (10) fourth, (11) cerebellum, (12) pons, (13) medulla, or myelencephalon, (14) spinal cord.

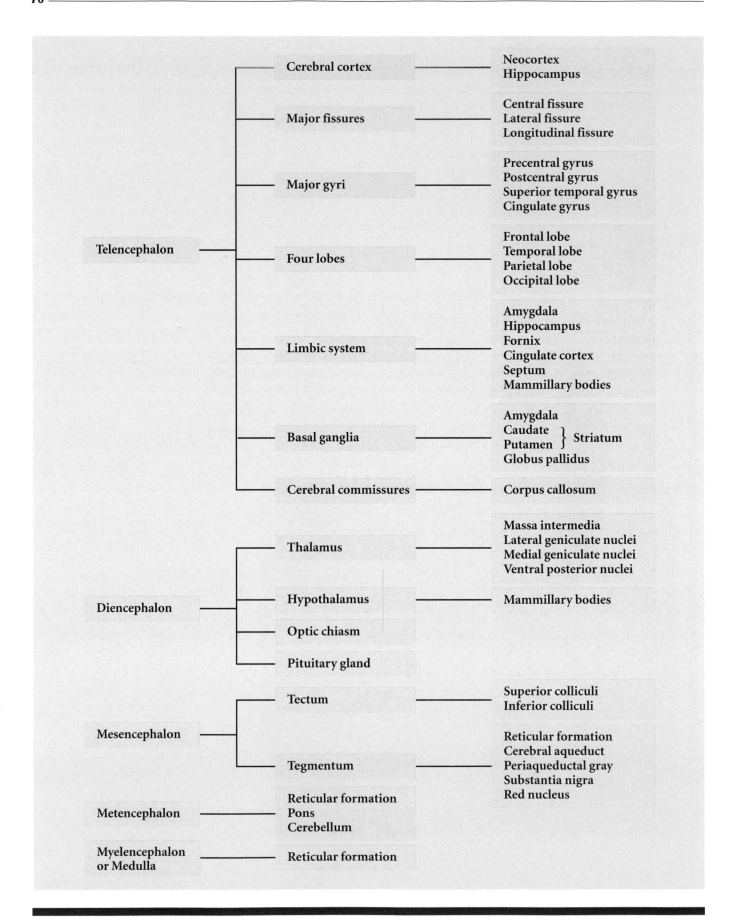

FIGURE 3.32 Summary of major brain structures. This hierarchy contains all the brain anatomy key terms that appear in boldface in this chapter.

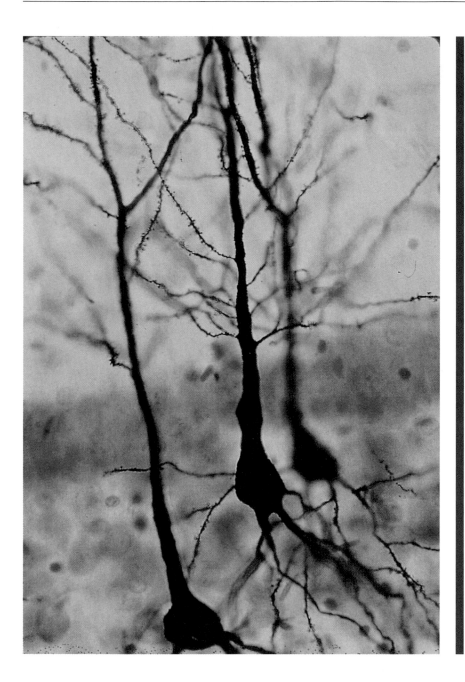

FIGURE 3.33 The art of neuro-anatomical staining. These pyramidal cells were stained with a Golgi stain and then with a Nissl stain. Clearly visible are the pyramid-shaped cell bodies and apical dendrites of the pyramidal cells. Each pyramidal cell has a long, narrow axon, which projects off the bottom of the slide. (Courtesy of Miles Herkenham, Unit of Functional Neuroanatomy, National Institute of Mental Health, Bethesda, MD.)

Themes 🩺💀💡🧬 Revisited

This chapter contributed relatively little to the development of the book's themes; that development was temporarily slowed while you were being introduced to the key areas and structures of the human brain. A knowledge of fundamental neuroanatomy will serve as the foundation of discussions of brain function in subsequent chapters. The clinical implications theme did arise three times: the importance of the cranial nerves in neurological diagnosis, the role of blockage of cerebral aqueducts in hydrocephalus, and the involvement of damage to the pathway from the substantia nigra to the striatum in Parkinson's disease.

ON THE CD 💿

Looking for more information about the topics in this chapter? For recommended additional readings, see Hard Copy for Chapter 3.

Log On

■ **http://www9.biostr.washington.edu/da.html** The Digital Anatomist Project presents the Interactive Brain Atlas, a fabulous collection of computer-generated brain images.

■ **http://faculty.washington.edu/chudler/gall1.html** If you would rather look at cells than brains, this site features beautiful photographs of various kinds of neurons.

■ **http://www.med.harvard.edu/AANLIB/** This site focuses on images of the living human brain, both normal and pathological. It also features good descriptions of the neuroimaging techniques that produce CT and MRI scans.

Think about It

1. Which of the following extreme positions do you think is closer to the truth? (a) The primary goal of all psychological research should be to relate psychological phenomena to the anatomy of neural circuits. (b) Psychologists should leave the study of neuroanatomy to neuroanatomists.

2. Perhaps the most famous mistake in the history of biopsychology was made by Olds and Milner (see Chapter 15). They botched an electrode implantation in the brain of a rat, and the tip of the stimulation electrode ended up in an unknown structure. When they subsequently tested the effects of electrical stimulation of this unknown structure, they made a fantastic discovery: The rat seemed to find the brain stimulation extremely pleasurable. In fact, the rat would press a lever for hours at an extremely high rate if every press produced a brief stimulation to its brain through the electrode. If you had accidentally stumbled on this intracranial self-stimulation phenomenon, what neuroanatomical procedures would you have used to identify the stimulation site and the neural circuits involved in the pleasurable effects of the stimulation?

ON THE CD
Studying for an exam? Try the Practice Tests for Chapter 3.

Key Terms

Afferent nerves *(p. 52)*
Anterior *(p. 63)*
Arachnoid membrane *(p. 54)*
Astrocytes *(p. 56)*
Autonomic nervous system (ANS) *(p. 52)*
Bipolar neuron *(p. 56)*
Blood-brain barrier *(p. 55)*
Brain stem *(p. 66)*
Central canal *(p. 54)*
Central nervous system (CNS) *(p. 52)*
Cerebral aqueduct *(p. 54)*
Cerebral ventricles *(p. 54)*
Cerebrospinal fluid (CSF) *(p. 54)*
Choroid plexuses *(p. 54)*
Columnar organization *(p. 71)*
Contralateral *(p. 69)*

Cranial nerves *(p. 53)*
Cross sections *(p. 64)*
Decussate *(p. 69)*
Dorsal *(p. 63)*
Dorsal horns *(p. 65)*
Dura mater *(p. 54)*
Efferent nerves *(p. 52)*
Electron microscopy *(p. 61)*
Frontal sections *(p. 64)*
Ganglia *(p. 56)*
Glial cells *(p. 56)*
Golgi stain *(p. 61)*
Horizontal sections *(p. 64)*
Inferior *(p. 64)*
Interneurons *(p. 56)*
Ipsilateral *(p. 69)*
Lateral *(p. 63)*
Medial *(p. 63)*
Meninges *(p. 54)*

Multipolar neuron *(p. 56)*
Myelin stains *(p. 62)*
Nerves *(p. 56)*
Nissl stain *(p. 61)*
Nuclei *(p. 56)*
Oligodendrocytes *(p. 56)*
Parasympathetic nerves *(p. 52)*
Peripheral nervous system (PNS) *(p. 52)*
Pia mater *(p. 54)*
Posterior *(p. 63)*
Pyramidal cells *(p. 71)*
Sagittal sections *(p. 64)*
Satellite cells *(p. 56)*
Schwann cells *(p. 56)*
Somatic nervous system (SNS) *(p. 52)*
Stellate cells *(p. 71)*
Subarachnoid space *(p. 54)*

Superior *(p. 64)*
Sympathetic nerves *(p. 52)*
Tracts *(p. 56)*
Unipolar neuron *(p. 56)*
Ventral *(p. 63)*
Ventral horns *(p. 65)*

ON THE CD
Need some help studying the key terms for this chapter? Check out the electronic flash cards for Chapter 3.

chapter 4

Neural Conduction and Synaptic Transmission

How Neurons Send and Receive Signals

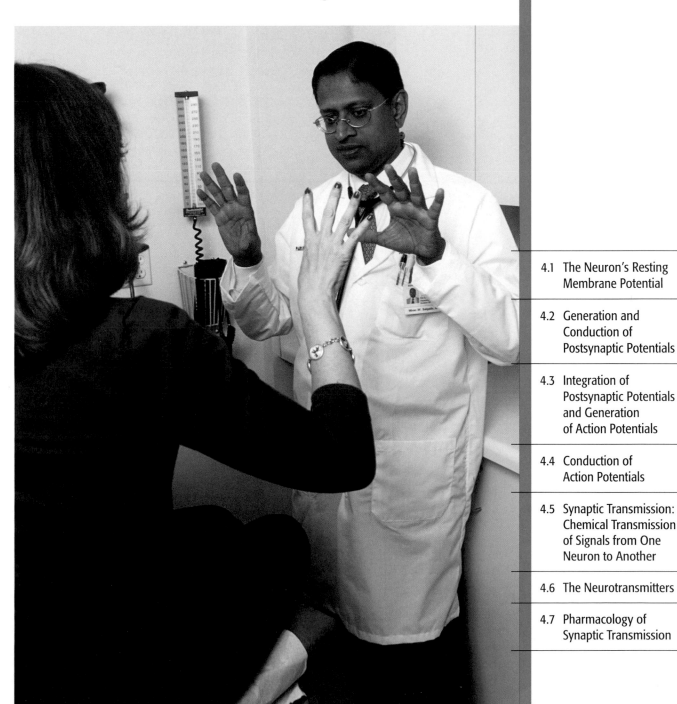

Chapter 3 introduced you to the anatomy of neurons. This chapter introduces you to their function—it is about how neurons conduct and transmit electrochemical signals. It begins with a description of how signals are generated in resting neurons; then, it follows the signals as they are conducted through neurons and transmitted across synapses to other neurons.

The Lizard, a case study of a patient with Parkinson's disease, Roberto Garcia d'Orta, will help you appreciate why a knowledge of neural conduction and synaptic transmission is an integral part of biopsychology.

The Lizard, a Case of Parkinson's Disease

"I have become a lizard," he began. "A great lizard frozen in a dark, cold, strange world."

His name was Roberto Garcia d'Orta. He was a tall thin man in his sixties, but like most patients with Parkinson's disease, he appeared to be much older than his actual age. Not many years before, he had been an active, vigorous business man. Then it happened—not all at once, not suddenly, but slowly, subtly, insidiously. Now he turned like a piece of granite, walked in slow shuffling steps, and spoke in a monotonous whisper.

What had been his first symptom?

A tremor.

Had his tremor been disabling?

"No," he said. "My hands shake worse when they are doing nothing at all"—a symptom called *tremor-at-rest.*

The other symptoms of Parkinson's disease are not quite so benign. They can change a vigorous man into a lizard. These include rigid muscles, a marked poverty of spontaneous movements, difficulty in starting to move, and slowness in executing voluntary movements once they have been initiated.

The term "reptilian stare" is often used to describe the characteristic lack of blinking and the widely opened eyes gazing out of a motionless face, a set of features that seems more reptilian than human. Truly a lizard in the eyes of the world.

What was happening in Mr. d'Orta's brain? A small group of nerve cells called the *substantia nigra* (black substance) were unaccountably dying. These neurons make a particular chemical neurotransmitter called dopamine, which they deliver to another part of the brain, known as the striatum. As the cells of the substantia nigra die, the amount of dopamine they can deliver goes down. The striatum helps control movement, and to do that normally, it needs dopamine. (Paraphrased from Klawans, 1990, pp. 53–57)[1]

Dopamine is not an effective treatment for Parkinson's disease because it does not readily penetrate the blood–brain barrier. However, knowledge of dopaminergic transmission has led to the development of an effective treatment: L-dopa, the chemical precursor of dopamine, which readily penetrates the blood–brain barrier and is converted to dopamine once inside the brain.

Mr. d'Orta's neurologist prescribed L-dopa, and it worked. He still had a bit of tremor; but his voice became stronger, his feet no longer shuffled, his reptilian stare faded away, and he was once again able to perform with ease many of the activities of daily life (e.g., eating, bathing, writing, speaking, and even making love with his wife). Mr. d'Orta had been destined to spend the rest of his life trapped inside a body that was becoming increasingly difficult to control, but his life sentence was repealed.

Mr. d'Orta's story does not end here. You will encounter him in a later chapter and should keep him in mind as you read this one. His situation will remind you that normal neural activity is necessary for normal psychological function. A knowledge of neural conduction and synaptic transmission is a major asset for any psychologist; it is a must for any biopsychologist.

---

[1]Paraphrased from *Newton's Madness: Further Tales of Clinical Neurology* by Harold L. Klawans. New York: Harper & Row, © Harold Klawans, 1990.

4.1 The Neuron's Resting Membrane Potential

One key to understanding neural function is the **membrane potential,** the difference in electrical charge between the inside and the outside of a cell.

Recording the Membrane Potential

To record a neuron's membrane potential, it is necessary to position the tip of one electrode inside the neuron and the tip of another electrode outside the neuron in the extracellular fluid. Although the size of the extracellular electrode is not critical, it is paramount that the tip of the intracellular electrode be fine enough to pierce the neural membrane without severely damaging it. The intracellular electrodes are called **microelectrodes;** their tips are less than one-thousandth of a millimeter in diameter—much too small to be seen by the naked eye.

The Resting Membrane Potential

When both electrode tips are in the extracellular fluid, the voltage difference between them is zero. However, when the tip of the intracellular electrode is inserted into a neuron, a steady potential of about −70 millivolts (mV) is recorded. This indicates that the potential inside the resting neuron is about 70 mV less than that outside the neuron. This steady membrane potential of about −70 mV is called the neuron's **resting potential.** In its resting state, with the −70 mV charge built up across its membrane, a neuron is said to be *polarized.*

The Ionic Basis of the Resting Potential

Why are resting neurons polarized? Like all salts in solution, the salts in neural tissue separate into positively and negatively charged particles called **ions.** The resting potential results from the fact that the ratio of negative to positive charges is greater inside the neuron than outside. Why this unequal distribution of charges occurs can be understood in terms of the interaction of four factors: two forces that act to distribute ions equally throughout the intracellular and extracellular fluids of the nervous system and two features of the neural membrane that counteract these homogenizing forces.

The first of the two homogenizing forces is *random motion.* The ions in neural tissue are in constant random motion, and particles in random motion tend to become evenly distributed because they are more likely to move down their *concentration gradients* than up them; that is, they are more likely to move from areas of high concentration to areas of low concentration than vice versa. The second force that promotes the even distribution of ions is *electrostatic pressure.* Any accumulation of charges, positive or negative, in one area tends to be dispersed by the repulsion among the like charges in the vicinity and the attraction of opposite charges concentrated elsewhere.

Despite the continuous homogenizing effects of random movement and electrostatic pressure, no single class of ions is distributed equally on the two sides of the neural membrane. Four kinds of ions contribute significantly to the resting potential: sodium ions (Na⁺), potassium ions (K⁺), chloride ions (Cl⁻), and various negatively charged protein ions. The concentration of both Na⁺ and Cl⁻ ions is greater outside a resting neuron than inside, whereas K⁺ ions are more concentrated on the inside. The negatively charged protein ions are synthesized inside the neuron and, for the most part, stay there. See Figure 4.1. By the way, the symbols for sodium and potassium were derived from their Latin names: *natrium* (Na⁺) and *kalium* (K⁺), respectively.

Two properties of the neural membrane are responsible for the unequal distribution of Na⁺, K⁺, Cl⁻, and protein ions in resting neurons. One of these properties

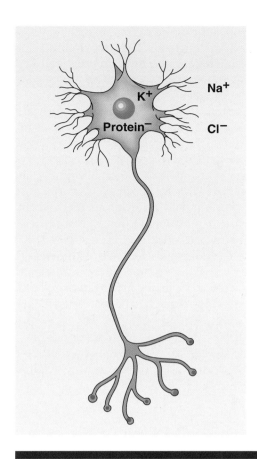

FIGURE 4.1 In its resting state, more Na⁺ and Cl⁻ ions are outside the neuron than inside, and more K⁺ ions and negatively charged protein ions are inside the neuron than outside.

is passive; that is, it does not involve the consumption of energy. The other is active and does involve the consumption of energy. The passive property of the neural membrane that contributes to the unequal disposition of ions is its differential permeability to Na⁺, K⁺, Cl⁻, and protein ions. In resting neurons, K⁺ and Cl⁻ ions pass readily through the neural membrane, Na⁺ ions pass through it with difficulty, and the negatively charged protein ions do not pass through it at all. Ions pass through the neural membrane at specialized pores called **ion channels,** each type of which is specialized for the passage of particular ions.

In the 1950s, the classic experiments of neurophysiologists Alan Hodgkin and Andrew Huxley provided the first evidence that an energy-consuming process is involved in the maintenance of the resting potential. Hodgkin and Huxley began by wondering why the high extracellular concentrations of Na⁺ and Cl⁻ ions and the high intracellular concentration of K⁺ ions were not eliminated by pressure for them to move down their concentration gradients to the side of lesser concentration. Could the electrostatic pressure of −70 mV across the membrane be the counteracting

ON THE CD

The *Ion Channels* module illustrates the regional specificity of the different types of ion channels and describes how each type is involved in a particular aspect of the membrane potential.

force that maintained the unequal distribution of ions? To answer this question, Hodgkin and Huxley calculated for each of the three ions the electrostatic charge that would be required to offset the pressure for them to move down their concentration gradients.

For Cl⁻ ions, this calculated electrostatic charge was −70 mV, the same as the actual resting potential. Hodgkin and Huxley thus concluded that when neurons are at rest, the unequal distribution of Cl⁻ ions across the neural membrane is maintained in equilibrium by the balance between the 70 mV force driving Cl⁻ ions down their concentration gradient into the neuron and the 70 mV of electrostatic pressure driving them out.

The situation turned out to be different for the K⁺ ions. Hodgkin and Huxley calculated that 90 mV of electrostatic pressure would be required to keep intracellular K⁺ ions from moving down their concentration gradient and leaving the neuron—some 20 mV more than the actual resting potential.

In the case of Na⁺ ions, the situation was much more extreme because the forces of both the concentration gradient and the electrostatic gradient act in the same direction. In the resting neuron, the concentration of Na⁺ ions outside the neuron creates 50 mV of pressure for Na⁺ ions to move down their concentration gradient into the neuron, which is added to the 70 mV of electrostatic pressure for them to move in the same direction. Thus, a whopping total of 120 mV of pressure is trying to force Na⁺ ions into resting neurons.

Subsequent experiments confirmed Hodgkin and Huxley's calculations. They showed that K⁺ ions are continuously being driven out of resting neurons by the 20 mV of pressure and that, despite the high resistance of the cell membrane to the passage of Na⁺ ions, the Na⁺ ions are continuously being driven in by the 120 mV of pressure. Why, then, do the intracellular and extracellular concentrations of Na⁺ and K⁺ remain constant in resting neurons? Hodgkin and Huxley discovered that there are active mechanisms in the cell membrane to counteract the *influx* (inflow) of Na⁺ ions by pumping Na⁺ ions out as rapidly as they leak in and to counteract the *efflux* (outflow) of K⁺ ions by pumping K⁺ ions in as rapidly as they leak out. Figure 4.2 summarizes Hodgkin and Huxley's findings and conclusions.

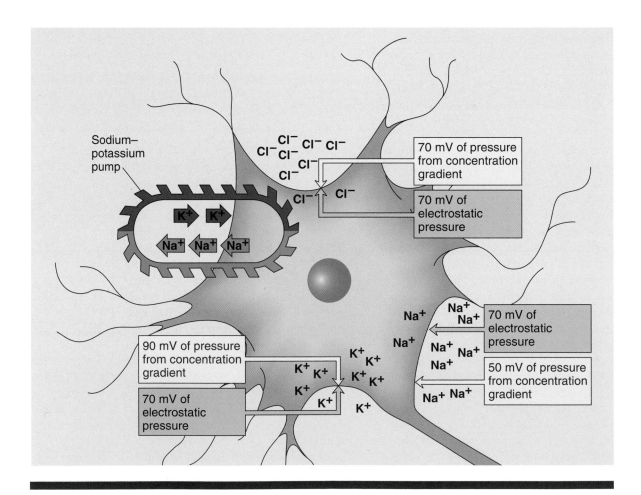

FIGURE 4.2   The passive and active forces that influence the distribution of Na⁺, K⁺, and Cl⁻ ions across the neural membrane. Passive forces continuously drive K⁺ ions out of the resting neuron and Na⁺ ions in; therefore, K⁺ ions must be actively pumped in and Na⁺ ions must be actively pumped out to maintain the resting equilibrium.

Table 4.1 The Factors Responsible for Maintaining the Differences in the Intracellular and Extracellular Concentrations of Na$^+$, K$^+$, and Cl$^-$ Ions in Resting Neurons

Na$^+$	Na$^+$ ions are driven into the neurons by both the high concentration of Na$^+$ ions outside the neuron and the negative internal resting potential of −70 mV. However, the membrane is resistant to the passive diffusion of Na$^+$, and the sodium–potassium pump is thus able to maintain the high external concentration of Na$^+$ ions by pumping them out at the same slow rate as they leak in.
K$^+$	K$^+$ ions are driven out of the neuron by their high internal concentration, although this pressure is partially offset by the internal negative potential. Despite the minimum pressure for the K$^+$ ions to leave the neuron, they do so at a substantial rate because the membrane offers little resistance to their passage. To maintain the high internal concentration of K$^+$ ions, mechanisms in the cell membrane pump K$^+$ ions into neurons at the same rate as they diffuse out.
Cl$^-$	There is little resistance in the neural membrane to the passage of Cl$^-$ ions. Thus, Cl$^-$ ions are readily forced out of the neuron by the negative internal potential. As chloride ions begin to accumulate on the outside, there is increased pressure for them to move down their concentration gradient back into the neuron. When the point is reached where the electrostatic pressure for Cl$^-$ ions to move out of the neuron is equal to the pressure for them to move back in, the distribution of Cl$^-$ ions is held in equilibrium. This point of equilibrium occurs at −70 mV.

ON THE CD

View the *Ionic Basis of the Resting Membrane Potential* module to review the role that K$^+$ ions and Na$^+$ ions play in determining the resting membrane potential.

It was subsequently discovered that the transport of Na$^+$ ions out of neurons and the transport of K$^+$ ions into them are not independent processes. Such ion transport is performed by energy-consuming mechanisms in the cell membrane that continually exchange three Na$^+$ ions inside the neuron for two K$^+$ ions outside. These transport mechanisms are commonly referred to as **sodium–potassium pumps.**

Table 4.1 summarizes the major factors that are responsible for maintaining the differences between the intracellular and extracellular concentrations of Na$^+$, K$^+$, and Cl$^-$ ions in resting neurons. These differences plus the negatively charged protein ions, which are trapped inside the neuron, are largely responsible for the resting membrane potential.

Now that you understand these basic properties of the resting neuron, you are prepared to consider how neurons respond to input.

4.2 Generation and Conduction of Postsynaptic Potentials

When neurons fire, they release from their terminal buttons chemicals called *neurotransmitters,* which diffuse across the synaptic clefts and interact with specialized receptor molecules on the receptive membranes of the next neurons in the circuit. When neurotransmitter molecules bind to postsynaptic receptors, they typically have one of two effects, depending on the structure of both the neurotransmitter and the receptor in question. They may **depolarize** the receptive membrane (decrease the resting membrane potential, from −70 to −67 mV, for example) or they may **hyperpolarize** it (increase the resting membrane potential, from −70 to −72 mV, for example).

Postsynaptic depolarizations are called **excitatory postsynaptic potentials (EPSPs)** because, as you will soon learn, they increase the likelihood that the neuron will fire. Postsynaptic hyperpolarizations are called **inhibitory postsynaptic potentials (IPSPs)** because they decrease the likelihood that the neuron will fire. Both EPSPs and IPSPs are **graded responses.** This means that the amplitudes of EPSPs and IPSPs are proportional to the intensity of the signals that elicit them: weak signals elicit small postsynaptic potentials, and strong signals elicit large ones.

EPSPs and IPSPs travel passively from their sites of generation at synapses, usually on the dendrites or cell body, in much the same way that electrical signals travel through a cable. Accordingly, the transmission of postsynaptic potentials has two important characteristics. First, it is rapid—so rapid that it can be assumed to be instantaneous for most purposes. It is important not to confuse the duration of EPSPs and IPSPs with their rate of transmission; although the duration of EPSPs and IPSPs varies considerably, all postsynaptic potentials, whether brief or enduring, are transmitted at great speed. Second, the transmission of EPSPs and IPSPs is *decremental:* EPSPs and IPSPs decrease in amplitude as they travel through the neuron, just as a sound wave grows fainter as it travels through air.

ON THE CD

To visualize the interactions between inputs from inhibitory neurons (which elicit IPSPs) and those from excitatory neurons (which elicit EPSPs), visit the *Interactions between EPSPs and IPSPs* module.

4.3 Integration of Postsynaptic Potentials and Generation of Action Potentials

The postsynaptic potentials created at a single synapse typically have little effect on the firing of the postsynaptic neuron. The receptive areas of most neurons are covered with thousands of synapses, and whether or not a neuron fires is determined by the net effect of their activity. More specifically, whether or not a neuron fires depends on the balance between the excitatory and inhibitory signals reaching its **axon hillock**—the conical structure at the junction between the cell body and the axon.

The graded EPSPs and IPSPs created by the action of neurotransmitters at particular receptive sites on the neural membrane are conducted instantly and decrementally to the axon hillock. If the sum of the depolarizations and hyperpolarizations reaching the axon hillock at any time is sufficient to depolarize the membrane to a level referred to as its **threshold of excitation**—usually about –65 mV—an action potential is generated at the axon hillock. The **action potential (AP)** is a massive momentary—about 1 millisecond—reversal of the membrane potential from about –70 to about +50 mV. Unlike postsynaptic potentials, action potentials are not graded responses; their magnitude is not related in any way to the intensity of the stimuli that elicit them. To the contrary, they are **all-or-none responses;** that is, they either occur full-blown or do not occur at all. See Figure 4.3 for an illustration of an EPSP, an IPSP, and an AP.

In effect, each multipolar neuron adds together all the graded excitatory and inhibitory postsynaptic potentials reaching its axon hillock and decides to fire or not to fire on the basis of their sum. Adding or combining a number of individual signals into one overall signal is called **integration.** Neurons integrate incoming signals in two ways: over space and over time.

Figure 4.4 illustrates the three possible combinations of **spatial summation.** It shows how local EPSPs that are produced simultaneously on different parts of the receptive membrane sum to form a greater EPSP, how simultaneous IPSPs sum to form a greater IPSP, and how simultaneous EPSPs and IPSPs sum to cancel each other out.

Figure 4.5 on page 86 illustrates **temporal summation.** It shows how postsynaptic potentials produced in rapid succession at the same synapse sum to form a greater signal. The reason that stimulations of a neuron can add together over time is that the postsynaptic potentials they produce often outlast them. Thus, if a particular sy-

ON THE CD 🖸

Visit the *Summation of EPSPs* module for an illustration of how temporal summation or spatial summation of EPSPs elicits an action potential if the threshold of activation at the axon hillock is exceeded.

An EPSP

An IPSP

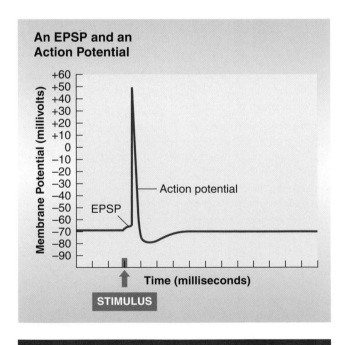

An EPSP and an Action Potential

FIGURE 4.3 An EPSP, an IPSP, and an EPSP followed by an AP.

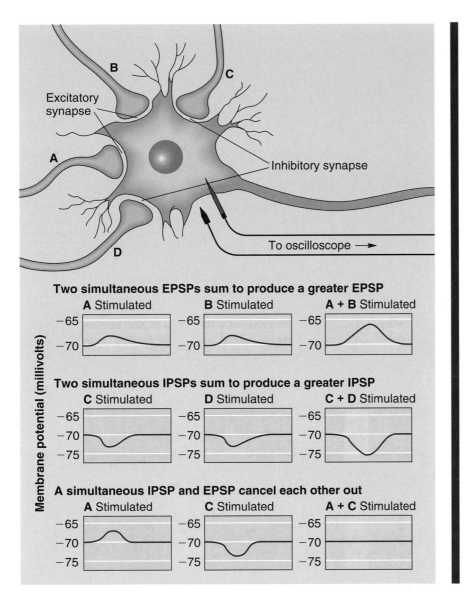

FIGURE 4.4   The three possible combinations of spatial summation.

napse is activated and then activated again before the original postsynaptic potential has completely dissipated, the effect of the second stimulus will be superimposed on the lingering postsynaptic potential produced by the first. Accordingly, it is possible for a brief subthreshold excitatory stimulus to fire a neuron if it is administered twice in rapid succession. In the same way, an inhibitory synapse activated twice in rapid succession can produce a greater IPSP than that produced by a single stimulation.

Each neuron continuously integrates signals over both time and space as it is continually bombarded with stimuli through the thousands of synapses covering its dendrites and cell body. Remember that, although schematic diagrams of neural circuitry rarely show neurons with more than a few representative synaptic contacts,

ON THE CD

For more about how the interactions between EPSPs and IPSPs determine whether or not a particular neuron will generate an action potential, take a look at the *Integration of Postsynaptic Potentials* module.

most neurons receive thousands of synaptic contacts. The location of a synapse on a receptive membrane is an important factor in determining its potential to influence neural firing. Because EPSPs and IPSPs are transmitted decrementally, synapses near the axon hillock trigger zone usually have the most influence on the firing of the neuron.

In some ways, the firing of a neuron is like the firing of a gun. Both are all-or-none reactions triggered by graded responses. As a trigger is squeezed, it gradually moves back until it causes the gun to fire; as a neuron is stimulated, it becomes less polarized until the threshold of excitation is reached and firing occurs. Furthermore, the firing of a gun and neural firing are both all-or-none events. Just as squeezing a trigger harder does not make the bullet travel faster or farther, stimulating a neuron more intensely does not increase the speed or amplitude of the resulting action potential.

FIGURE 4.5 The two possible combinations of temporal summation.

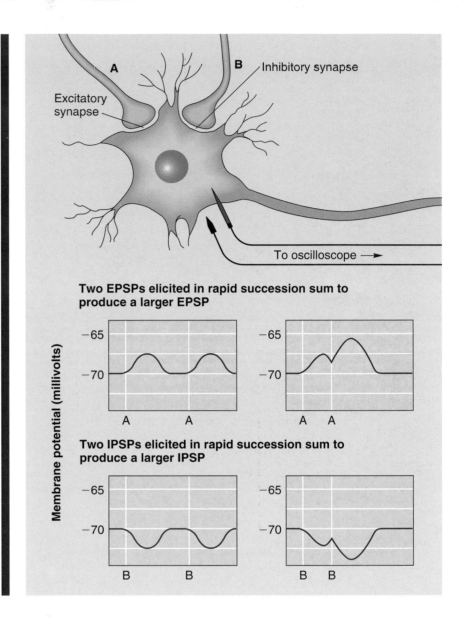

4.4 Conduction of Action Potentials

The Ionic Basis of Action Potentials

How are action potentials produced, and how are they conducted along the axon? The answer to both questions is basically the same: through the action of **voltage-activated ion channels**—ion channels that open or close in response to changes in the voltage of the membrane potential (see McCormick, 1999).

Recall that the membrane potential of a neuron at rest is relatively constant despite the great pressure for Na⁺ ions to flow into the cell. This is because the resting membrane is relatively impermeable to Na⁺ ions and because those few that leak in are pumped out. But things suddenly change when the membrane potential at the axon hillock is reduced to the threshold of excitation. The voltage-activated sodium channels in the hillock membrane open wide, and Na⁺ ions rush in, suddenly driving the membrane potential from about −70 to about +50 mV. The rapid change in the membrane potential that is associated with the *influx* of Na⁺ ions then triggers the opening of voltage-activated potassium channels. At this point, K⁺ ions near the membrane are driven out of the cell through these channels—first by their relatively high

ON THE CD

The *Generation of the Action Potential* module explains the threshold of activation for voltage-activated ion channels at the axon hillock of a neuron.

+60
+50
+30
+10
−10
−30
−50
−70

Membrane Potential (millivolts)

Sodium channels close

Potassium channels open

Sodium channels open

Potassium channels start to close

RISING PHASE
REPOLARIZATION
HYPERPOLARIZATION

1 2 3 4 5
Time (milliseconds)

FIGURE 4.6 The opening and closing of voltage-activated sodium and potassium channels during the three phases of the action potential: rising phase, repolarization, and hyperpolarization.

internal concentration and then, when the action potential is near its peak, by the positive internal charge. After about 1 millisecond, the sodium channels close. This marks the end of the *rising phase* of the action potential and the beginning of *repolarization* by the continued efflux of K$^+$ ions. Once repolarization has been achieved, the potassium channels gradually close. Because they close gradually, too many K$^+$ ions flow out of the neuron, and it is left hyperpolarized for a brief period of time. Figure 4.6 illustrates the timing of the opening and closing of the sodium and potassium channels during an action potential.

The number of ions that flow through the membrane during an action potential is extremely small in relation to the total number inside and around the neuron. The action potential involves only those ions right next to the membrane. Therefore, a single action potential has little effect on the relative concentrations of various ions inside and outside the neuron, and the resting ion concentrations next to the membrane are rapidly reestablished by the random movement of ions. The sodium–potassium pump plays only a minor role in the reestablishment of the resting potential.

ON THE CD
For a detailed review of the ionic basis of action potentials, see the aptly titled module *Ionic Basis of the Action Potential.*

Refractory Periods

There is a brief period of about 1 to 2 milliseconds after the initiation of an action potential during which it is impossible to elicit a second one. This period is called the **absolute refractory period.** The absolute refractory period is followed by the **relative refractory period**—the period during which it is possible to fire the neuron again, but only by applying higher-than-normal levels of stimulation. The end of the relative refractory period is

the point at which the amount of stimulation necessary to fire a neuron returns to baseline.

The refractory period is responsible for two important characteristics of neural activity. First, it is responsible for the fact that action potentials normally travel along axons in only one direction. Because the portions of an axon over which an action potential has just traveled are left momentarily refractory, an action potential cannot reverse direction. Second, the refractory period is responsible for the fact that the rate of neural firing is related to the intensity of the stimulation. If a neuron is subjected to a high level of continual stimulation, it fires and then fires again as soon as its absolute refractory period is over—a maximum of about 1,000 times per second. However, if the level of stimulation is of an intensity just sufficient to fire the neuron when it is at rest, the neuron does not fire again until both the absolute and the relative refractory periods have run their course. Intermediate levels of stimulation produce intermediate rates of neural firing.

Conduction of Action Potentials

The conduction of action potentials along an axon differs from the conduction of EPSPs and IPSPs in two important ways. First, the conduction of action potentials along an axon is *nondecremental*; action potentials do not grow weaker as they travel along the axonal membrane. Second, action potentials are conducted more slowly than postsynaptic potentials.

The reason for these two differences is that the conduction of EPSPs and IPSPs is passive, whereas the axonal conduction of action potentials is largely active. Once an action potential has been generated at the axon hillock, it travels passively along the axonal membrane to the adjacent voltage-activated sodium channels, which have yet to open. The arrival of the electrical signal opens these channels, thereby allowing Na$^+$ ions to rush into the neuron and generate a full-blown action potential on this portion of the membrane. This signal is then conducted passively to the next sodium channels, where another action potential is actively triggered. These events are repeated again and again until a full-blown action potential is triggered in the terminal buttons. However, because there are so many ion channels on the axonal membrane and they are so close together, it is usual to think of axonal conduction as a single wave of excitation spreading actively at a constant speed along the axon, rather than as a series of discrete events.

The wave of excitation triggered by the generation of an action potential on the hillock membrane also spreads back through the cell body and dendrites of the neuron. However, because the ion channels of cell bodies and dendrites are not usually voltage-activated, the conduction of action potentials back through the cell body and dendrites is usually passive (see Segev & Rall, 1998). Although little is yet known about the functions of these backward action potentials, they are the subject of much conjecture (e.g., Eilers & Konnerth, 1997; Sejnowski, 1997).

The following analogy may help you appreciate the major characteristics of axonal conduction. Consider a row of mousetraps on a wobbly shelf, all of them set and ready to be triggered. Each trap stores energy by holding back its striker against the pressure of the spring, in the same way that each sodium channel stores energy by holding back Na$^+$ ions, which are under pressure to move down their concentration and electrostatic gradients into the neuron. When the first trap in the row is triggered, the vibration is transmitted passively through the shelf, and the next trap is sprung—and so on down the line.

The nondecremental nature of action potential conduction is readily apparent from this analogy; the last trap on the shelf strikes with no less intensity than did the first. This analogy also illustrates the refractory period: A trap cannot respond again until it has been reset, just as a section of axon cannot fire again until it has been repolarized. Furthermore, the row of traps can transmit in either direction, just like an axon. If electrical stimulation of sufficient intensity is applied to the terminal end of an axon, an action potential will be generated and will travel along the axon back to the cell body; this is called **antidromic conduction.** Axonal conduction in the natural direction—from cell body to terminal buttons—is called **orthodromic conduction.**

Conduction in Myelinated Axons

In Chapter 3, you learned that the axons of many neurons are insulated from the extracellular fluid by segments of fatty tissue called *myelin.* In myelinated axons, ions can pass through the axonal membrane only at the **nodes of Ranvier**—the gaps between adjacent myelin

segments. How, then, are action potentials transmitted in myelinated axons?

When an action potential is generated at the axon hillock of a myelinated axon, the signal is conducted passively—that is, instantly and decrementally—along the first segment of myelin to the first node of Ranvier. Although the signal is somewhat diminished by the time it reaches the first node, it is still strong enough to open the voltage-activated sodium channels at the node and to generate another full-blown action potential. This action potential is conducted passively to the next node, where another full-blown action potential is elicited, and so on.

Myelination increases the speed of axonal conduction. Because conduction along the myelinated segments of the axon is passive, it occurs instantly, and the signal thus "jumps" down the axon from node to node. There is, of course, a slight delay at each node of Ranvier while the action potential is actively generated, but conduction is still much faster in myelinated axons than in unmyelinated axons, in which passive conduction plays a less prominent role. The transmission of action potentials in myelinated axons is called **saltatory conduction** (*saltare* means "to skip or jump").

The Velocity of Axonal Conduction

At what speed are action potentials conducted along an axon? The answer to this question depends on two properties of the axon. Conduction is faster in large-diameter axons, and—as you have just learned—it is faster in those that are myelinated. Mammalian *motor neurons* (neurons that synapse on skeletal muscles) are large and myelinated; thus, some can conduct at speeds of 100 meters per second (about 224 miles per hour). In contrast, small, unmyelinated axons conduct action potentials at about 1 meter per second.

There is a misconception about the velocity of motor neuron action potentials in humans. The maximum velocity of motor neuron action potentials was found to be about 100 meters per second in cats, and since then it has been assumed to be the same in humans: It is not. The maximum velocity of conduction in human motor neurons is about 60 meters per second (Peters & Brooke, 1998).

Conduction in Neurons without Axons

Action potentials are the means by which axons conduct all-or-none signals nondecrementally over relatively long distances. Thus, to keep what you have just learned about action potentials in perspective, it is important for you to remember that many neurons in the mammalian brain do not have axons and thus do not display action potentials. Neural conduction in these *interneurons* is typically by graded, decrementally conducted potentials (Juusola et al., 1996).

Changing View of Dendritic Function

Dendritic function is difficult to study, and dendrites have long been assumed to be merely passive conductors of postsynaptic potentials. Although this assumption may be true for some dendrites, it is now clear—thanks to recent technological advances—that the dendrites of some neurons function actively in diverse and complex ways (see Häuser, Spruston, & Stuart, 2000).

Two recent findings about dendrites have started to change theories of neural conduction. First, it has been shown that some dendrites are capable of generating action potentials, which can be actively conducted away from the site of generation in either direction (e.g., Chen, Midtgaard, & Shepherd, 1997). Second, some dendritic signals appear to be *compartmentalized*, that is, restricted to particular portions of the dendrite (Segev & London, 2000).

Such recent discoveries have increased awareness of the complexity and diversity of dendritic function, but it is not yet well understood how these newly recognized dendritic capabilities affect neural conduction. Still, a critical step has been taken: The first wave of important discoveries has focused the attention of neurophysiologists on dendrites, and more far-reaching discoveries and improved understanding are certain to follow.

4.5 Synaptic Transmission: Chemical Transmission of Signals from One Neuron to Another

You have learned in this chapter how postsynaptic potentials are generated on the receptive membrane of a resting neuron, how these graded potentials are conducted passively to the axon hillock, how the sum of these graded potentials can trigger action potentials, and how these all-or-none potentials are actively conducted down the axon to the terminal buttons. In the remaining sections of this chapter, you will learn how action potentials arriving at terminal buttons trigger the release of neurotransmitters into synapses and how neurotransmitters carry signals to other cells. This section provides an overview of five aspects of synaptic transmission: (1) the structure of synapses; (2) the synthesis, packaging, and transport of neurotransmitter molecules; (3) the release of neurotransmitter molecules; (4) the activation of receptors by neurotransmitter molecules; and (5) the reuptake, enzymatic degradation, and recycling of neurotransmitter molecules.

ON THE CD
Visit the *Synaptic Transmission* animation. See synaptic transmission in action before beginning to study its mechanisms.

Structure of Synapses

Most communication among neurons occurs across synapses such as the one illustrated in Figure 4.7 on page 90. Neurotransmitter molecules are released from buttons into synaptic clefts, where they induce EPSPs or IPSPs in other neurons by binding to receptors on their postsynaptic membranes. The synapses featured in Figure 4.7 are *axodendritic synapses*—synapses of axon terminal buttons on dendrites. Many axodendritic synapses terminate on **dendritic spines** (see Figure 3.33)—small synaptic buds that cover the surfaces of many dendrites (see Yuste, Majewska, & Holthoff, 2000). Also common are *axosomatic synapses*—synapses of axon terminal buttons on *somas* (cell bodies).

Although axodendritic and axosomatic synapses are the most common synaptic arrangements, there are several others (Shepherd & Erulkar, 1997). For example, there are *dendrodendritic synapses*, which are interesting because they are often capable of transmission in either direction; and there are *axoaxonal synapses*, which are interesting because some of them mediate presynaptic inhibition (see Wu & Saggau, 1997). **Presynaptic inhibition** is compared with **postsynaptic inhibition** in Figure 4.8 on page 91.

The synapses depicted in Figure 4.7 are **directed synapses**—synapses at which the site of neurotransmitter release and the site of neurotransmitter reception are in close proximity. This is a common arrangement, but there are also many nondirected synapses in the nervous system. **Nondirected synapses** are synapses at which the site of release is at some distance from the site of reception. One type of nondirected synapse is depicted in Figure 4.9 on page 92. In this type of arrangement, neurotransmitter molecules are released from a series of varicosities along the axon and its branches and thus are widely dispersed to surrounding targets. Because of their appearance, these synapses are often referred to as *string-of-beads synapses*.

ON THE CD
The *Action at the Synapse* module presents a variety of diagrams, explanations, and exercises that will help you understand and remember the principles and mechanisms of synaptic function.

FIGURE 4.7 The anatomy of a typical synapse.

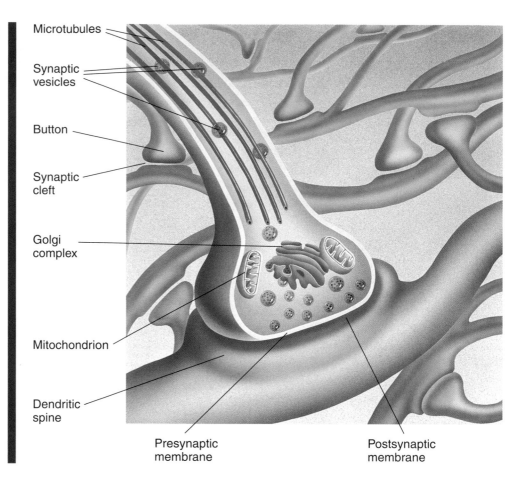

Microtubules

Synaptic vesicles

Button

Synaptic cleft

Golgi complex

Mitochondrion

Dendritic spine

Presynaptic membrane

Postsynaptic membrane

Synthesis, Packaging, and Transport of Neurotransmitter Molecules

Neurotransmitter molecules are of two basic types: small and large. The small neurotransmitters are of several types; large neurotransmitters are all peptides. **Peptides** are amino acid chains that are composed of 10 or fewer amino acids; in effect, they are short proteins. They may be small for proteins, but they are large for neurotransmitters.

Small-molecule neurotransmitters are typically synthesized in the cytoplasm of the button and packaged in **synaptic vesicles** by the button's **Golgi complex** (see Brittle & Waters, 2000; Rothman & Orci, 1996). Once filled with neurotransmitter, the vesicles are stored in clusters right next to the presynaptic membrane. In contrast, peptide neurotransmitters, like other proteins, are assembled in the cytoplasm of the cell body on *ribosomes;* they are then packaged in vesicles by the cell body's Golgi complex and transported by *microtubules* to the terminal buttons at a rate of about 40 centimeters per day (see Vallee & Bloom, 1991). The vesicles that contain large-molecule neurotransmitters are larger than those that contain small-molecule neurotransmitters, and they do not congregate as closely as the other vesicles

to the presynaptic membrane (see Thureson-Klein & Klein, 1990).

It may have escaped your notice that the button illustrated in Figure 4.7 contains synaptic vesicles of two sizes. This means that it contains two neurotransmitters: a peptide neurotransmitter in the larger vesicles and a small-molecule neurotransmitter in the smaller vesicles. It was once believed that each neuron synthesizes and releases only one neurotransmitter, but it is now clear that many neurons contain two neurotransmitters—a situation that is referred to as **coexistence.** So far, almost all documented cases of coexistence have involved one small-molecule neurotransmitter and one peptide neurotransmitter (see Nicoll & Malenka, 1998).

Release of Neurotransmitter Molecules

Exocytosis—the process of neurotransmitter release—is illustrated in Figure 4.10 on page 93 (see Zucker, Kullman, & Bennett, 1999). When a neuron is at rest, synaptic vesicles that contain small-molecule neurotransmitters congregate next to sections of the presynaptic membrane that are particularly rich in *voltage-*

Postsynaptic Inhibition

In postsynaptic inhibition, **B** inhibits the excitatory effects of **A** or any other excitatory neuron synapsing on **C** by hyperpolarizing **C**.

Presynaptic Inhibition

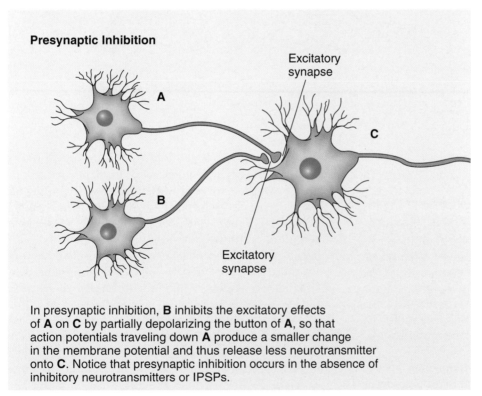

In presynaptic inhibition, **B** inhibits the excitatory effects of **A** on **C** by partially depolarizing the button of **A**, so that action potentials traveling down **A** produce a smaller change in the membrane potential and thus release less neurotransmitter onto **C**. Notice that presynaptic inhibition occurs in the absence of inhibitory neurotransmitters or IPSPs.

FIGURE 4.8 Postsynaptic and presynaptic inhibition.

activated calcium channels. When stimulated by action potentials, these channels open, and Ca^{2+} ions enter the button. The entry of the Ca^{2+} ions causes the synaptic vesicles to fuse with the presynaptic membrane and empty their contents into the synaptic cleft (see Kasai, 1999; Stanley, 1997).

The exocytosis of small-molecule neurotransmitters differs from the exocytosis of peptide neurotransmitters in one important respect. Small-molecule neurotransmitters are typically released in a pulse each time an action potential triggers a momentary influx of Ca^{2+} ions through the presynaptic membrane; in contrast, peptide neurotransmitters are typically released gradually in response to general increases in the level of intracellular Ca^{2+} ions, such as might occur during a general increase in the rate of neuron firing.

FIGURE 4.9 Nondirected neurotransmitter release. Some neurons release neurotransmitter molecules diffusely from varicosities along the axon and its branches.

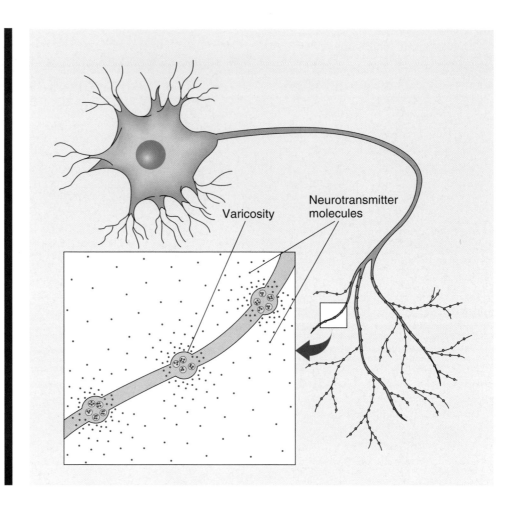

Varicosity

Neurotransmitter molecules

Activation of Receptors by Neurotransmitter Molecules

Once released, neurotransmitter molecules produce signals in postsynaptic neurons by binding to **receptors** in the postsynaptic membrane (see Changeux, 1993). Each receptor is a protein that contains binding sites for only particular neurotransmitters; thus, a neurotransmitter can influence only those cells that have receptors for it. Any molecule that binds to another is referred to as its **ligand,** and a neurotransmitter is thus said to be a ligand of its receptor.

It was initially assumed that there is only one type of receptor for each neurotransmitter, but this has not proved to be the case. As more receptors have been identified, it has become clear that most neurotransmitters bind to several different types of receptors. The different types of receptors to which a particular neurotransmitter can bind are called the **receptor subtypes** for that neurotransmitter. The various receptor subtypes for a neurotransmitter are typically located in different brain areas, and they typically respond to the neurotransmitter in different ways (see Darlison & Richter, 1999). Thus, one advantage of receptor subtypes is that they enable a neurotransmitter to transmit different kinds of messages to different parts of the brain.

The binding of a neurotransmitter to one of its receptor subtypes can influence a postsynaptic neuron in one of two fundamentally different ways, depending on whether the receptor is ionotropic or metabotropic (Heuss & Gerber, 2000; Waxham, 1999). **Ionotropic receptors** are those receptors that are associated with ligand-activated ion channels; **metabotropic receptors** are those receptors that are associated with signal proteins and *G proteins (guanosine-triphosphate–sensitive proteins)*—see Figure 4.11 on page 94.

When a neurotransmitter molecule binds to an ionotropic receptor, the associated ion channel usually opens or closes immediately, thereby inducing an immediate postsynaptic potential. For example, in some neurons, EPSPs (depolarizations) occur because the neurotransmitter opens sodium channels, thereby increasing the flow of Na^+ ions into the neuron. In contrast, IPSPs (hyperpolarizations) often occur because the neurotransmitter opens potassium channels or chloride channels, thereby increasing the flow of K^+ ions out of the neuron or the flow of Cl^- ions into it, respectively.

Metabotropic receptors are more prevalent than ionotropic receptors, and their effects are slower to develop, longer-lasting, more diffuse, and more varied (see Linder & Gilman, 1992). There are many different kinds

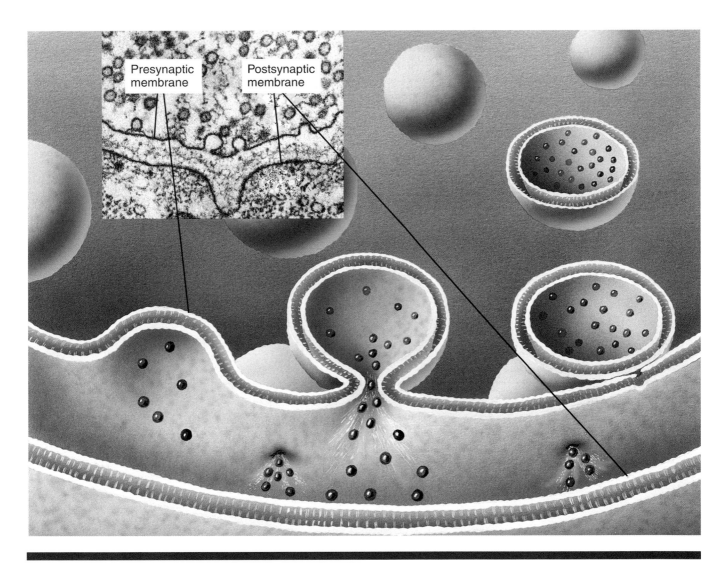

FIGURE 4.10   Schematic and photographic illustrations of exocytosis. (The photomicrograph was reproduced from J. E. Heuser et al., *Journal of Cell Biology*, 1979, *81*, 275–300, by copyright permission of The Rockefeller University Press.)

of metabotropic receptors, but each is attached to a signal protein that winds its way back and forth through the cell membrane seven times. The metabotropic receptor is attached to a portion of the signal protein outside the neuron; the G protein is attached to a portion of the signal protein inside the neuron.

When a neurotransmitter binds to a metabotropic receptor, a subunit of the associated G protein breaks away. Then, one of two things happens, depending on the particular G protein: The subunit may move along the inside surface of the membrane and bind to a nearby ion channel, thereby inducing an EPSP or IPSP (see Clapham, 1994); or it may trigger the synthesis of a chemical called a **second messenger** (neurotransmitters are considered to be the *first messengers*). Once created, a second messenger diffuses through the cytoplasm and may influence the activities of the neuron in a variety of ways (Schulman & Hyman, 1999)—for example, it may enter

the nucleus and bind to the DNA, thereby influencing genetic expression (see Gustafsson, 1999; Noselli & Perrimon, 2000). Thus, although a common consequence of a neurotransmitter's binding to a receptor is a brief postsynaptic potential, neurotransmitters can also have radical, long-lasting effects.

One type of metabotropic receptors—autoreceptors—warrants special mention (see Parnas et al., 2000). **Autoreceptors** are metabotropic receptors that have two unconventional characteristics: They bind to their neuron's own neurotransmitter molecules; and they are located on the presynaptic, rather than the postsynaptic, membrane. Their usual function is to monitor the number of neurotransmitter molecules in the synapse, to reduce subsequent release when the levels are high, and to increase subsequent release when they are low.

ON THE CD

The *Review of Synaptic Transmission* module takes an in-depth look at the different stages of synaptic transmission.

FIGURE 4.11   Ionotropic and metabotropic receptors.

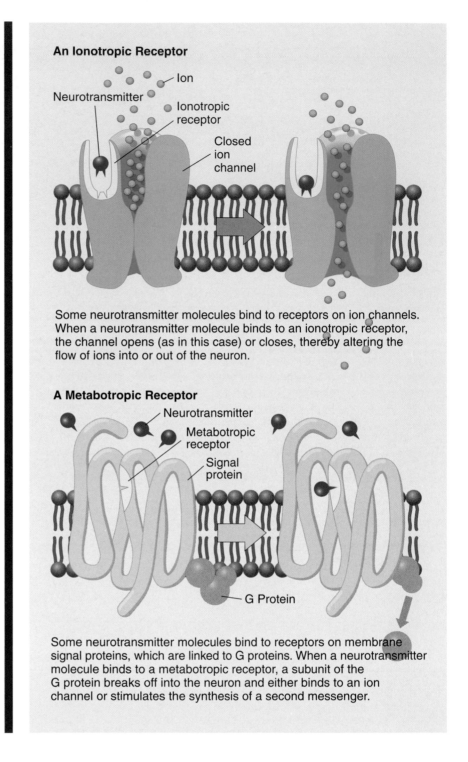

An Ionotropic Receptor

Some neurotransmitter molecules bind to receptors on ion channels. When a neurotransmitter molecule binds to an ionotropic receptor, the channel opens (as in this case) or closes, thereby altering the flow of ions into or out of the neuron.

A Metabotropic Receptor

Some neurotransmitter molecules bind to receptors on membrane signal proteins, which are linked to G proteins. When a neurotransmitter molecule binds to a metabotropic receptor, a subunit of the G protein breaks off into the neuron and either binds to an ion channel or stimulates the synthesis of a second messenger.

Differences between small-molecule and peptide neurotransmitters in patterns of release and receptor binding suggest that they serve different functions. Small-molecule neurotransmitters tend to be released into directed synapses and to activate either ionotropic receptors or metabotropic receptors that act directly on ion channels. In contrast, peptide neurotransmitters tend to be released diffusely and bind to metabotropic receptors that act through second messengers. Consequently, the function of small-molecule neurotransmitters appears to be the transmission of rapid, brief excitatory or

inhibitory signals to adjacent cells; and the function of peptide neurotransmitters appears to be the transmission of slow, diffuse, long-lasting signals.

Reuptake, Enzymatic Degradation, and Recycling

If nothing intervened, a neurotransmitter molecule would remain active in the synapse, in effect clogging

Two Mechanisms of Neurotransmitter Deactivation

Reuptake

Enzymatic Degradation

FIGURE 4.12   The two mechanisms for terminating neurotransmitter action in the synapse: reuptake and enzymatic degradation.

that channel of communication. However, two mechanisms terminate synaptic messages and keep that from happening. These two message-terminating mechanisms are **reuptake** and **enzymatic degradation** (see Figure 4.12).

Reuptake is the more common of the two deactivating mechanisms. The majority of neurotransmitters, once released, are almost immediately drawn back into the presynaptic buttons (see Clements et al., 1992), and their components are recycled.

In contrast, other neurotransmitters are degraded (broken apart) in the synapse by **enzymes**—chemicals that stimulate or inhibit chemical reactions without directly participating in them. For example, *acetylcholine,* one of the few neurotransmitters for which enzymatic degradation is the main mechanism of synaptic deactivation, is broken down by the enzyme **acetylcholinesterase.** Many of the breakdown products of enzymatic degradation are reabsorbed by the presynaptic button and used in the synthesis of more neurotransmitter molecules.

Changing View of Glial Function

Once overlooked as playing merely supportive roles in the nervous system, glial cells have recently been thrust to center stage by a wave of remarkable findings (Haydon, 2001; LoTurco, 2000; Ullian et al., 2001). Glial cells—particularly astrocytes—have been shown to release chemical transmitters, to contain receptors for neurotransmitters, to conduct signals, to influence the development of synapses, and to participate in neurotransmitter reuptake. Indeed, it is becoming inappropriate to think of brain function solely in terms of neuron–neuron connections. Although it is clear that neurons are essential for nervous system function, it is becoming increasingly apparent that they are only part of the story.

The importance of glial cells in brain function may be reflected in the greater prevalence of these cells in intelligent organisms. Many simple organisms have more neurons than glial cells, but glial cells outnumber neurons in the human brain by about 10 to 1. Will *neuroscience* prove to be a misnomer? Anybody for "gliascience"?

4.6   The Neurotransmitters

Now that you understand the basics of neurotransmitter function, let's take a closer look at some of the neurotransmitter substances (see Deutch & Roth, 1999). There are four classes of small-molecule neurotransmitters: the *amino acids,* the *monoamines,* the recently discovered soluble gases,* and *acetylcholine.* In addition, there is the one class of large-molecule neurotransmitters: the *neuropeptides.* Most neurotransmitters produce either excitation or inhibition, not both; but a few produce excitation when they bind to some of their receptor subtypes and inhibition when they bind to others. All of the neurotransmitter classes and individual neurotransmitters that appear in this section in boldface type are outlined in Figure 4.15 later in this section.

Amino Acid Neurotransmitters

The neurotransmitters in the vast majority of fast-acting, directed synapses in the central nervous system are **amino acids**—the molecular building blocks of proteins. The four most widely acknowledged amino acid neurotransmitters are **glutamate, aspartate, glycine,** and **gamma-aminobutyric acid (GABA).** The first three are common in the proteins we consume, whereas GABA is synthesized by a simple modification of the structure of glutamate. Glutamate is the most prevalent excitatory neurotransmitter in the mammalian central nervous system; GABA is the most prevalent inhibitory neurotransmitter.

ON THE CD

The *Amino Acid Synapses* module summarizes the effects of three amino acid neurotransmitters—glutamate, GABA, and glycine—on post-synaptic neurons.

Monoamine Neurotransmitters

Monoamines are another class of small-molecule neurotransmitters. Each is synthesized from a single amino acid—hence the name *monoamine* (one amine). Monoamine neurotransmitters are slightly larger than amino acid neurotransmitters, and their effects tend to be more diffuse (see Bunin & Wightman, 1999). The monoamines are present in small groups of neurons whose cell bodies are, for the most part, located in the brain stem. These neurons often have highly branched axons with many varicosities (string-of-beads axons), from which monoamine neurotransmitters are diffusely released into the extracellular fluid (see Figures 4.9 and 4.13).

There are four monoamine neurotransmitters: **dopamine, norepinephrine, epinephrine,** and **serotonin.** They are subdivided into two groups, **catecholamines** and **indolamines,** on the basis of their structure. Dopamine, norepinephrine, and epinephrine are catecholamines. Each is synthesized from the amino acid *tyrosine.* Tyrosine is converted to *L-dopa,* which in turn is converted to dopamine. Neurons that release norepinephrine have an extra enzyme (one that is not present in dopaminergic neurons), which converts the dopamine in them to norepinephrine. Similarly, neurons that release epinephrine have all the enzymes present in neurons that release norepinephrine, along with an extra enzyme that converts norepinephrine to epinephrine (see Figure 4.14). In contrast to the other monoamines, *serotonin* (also called *5-hydroxytryptamine,* or *5-HT*) is synthesized from the amino acid *tryptophan* and is classified as an indolamine.

FIGURE 4.13 String-of-beads noradrenergic nerve fibers in rat cerebellar cortex. The bright beaded structures represent sites in these multiply branched axons where the monoamine neurotransmitter norepinephrine is stored in high concentration and released into the surrounding extracellular fluid. (Courtesy of Floyd E. Bloom, M.D., The Scripps Research Institute, La Jolla, California.)

Neurons that release norepinephrine are called *noradrenergic;* those that release epinephrine are called *adrenergic.* There are two reasons for this naming. One is that epinephrine and norepinephrine used to be called *adrenaline* and *noradrenaline,* respectively, by many scientists, until a drug company registered *Adrenalin* as a brand name. The other reason will become apparent to you if you try to say *norepinephrinergic.*

Soluble-Gas Neurotransmitters

Another class of small-molecule neurotransmitters, the **soluble gases,** was discovered fairly recently; so far, the class includes **nitric oxide** and **carbon monoxide.** The soluble gases do not act like the other neurotransmitters (Brenman & Bredt, 1997; Hölscher, 1997). They are produced in the neural cytoplasm; and once produced, they immediately diffuse through the cell mem-

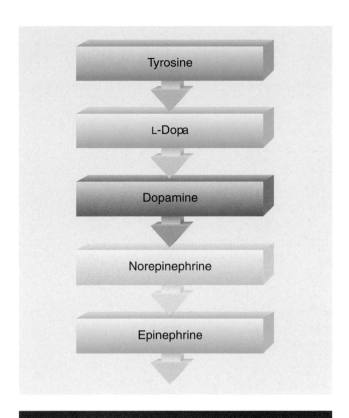

FIGURE 4.14 The steps in the synthesis of catecholamines from tyrosine.

brane into the extracellular fluid and then into nearby cells. They easily pass through cell membranes because they are soluble in lipids. Once in other cells, they stimulate the production of a second messenger and are im-

mediately broken down. They are difficult to study because they exist for only a few seconds.

At some synapses, nitric oxide has been shown to mediate *retrograde transmission*. That is, at some synapses, nitric oxide transmits feedback signals from the postsynaptic neuron back to the presynaptic neuron.

■ Acetylcholine

Acetylcholine (abbreviated Ach) is a small-molecule neurotransmitter that is in one major respect like a professor who is late for a lecture: It is in a class by itself. It is created by adding an *acetyl group* to a *choline molecule*. Acetylcholine is the neurotransmitter at neuromuscular junctions, at many of the synapses in the autonomic nervous system, and at synapses in several parts of the central nervous system. As you learned in the last section, acetylcholine is broken down in the synapse by the enzyme *acetylcholinesterase*. Neurons that release acetylcholine are said to be *cholinergic*.

■ Neuropeptides

Over 50 peptides currently qualify as neurotransmitters or putative neurotransmitters (see some of them in Appendix VII). A *putative neurotransmitter* is a suspected neurotransmitter—one for which the evidence is strong but not yet unequivocal.

Peptides that play a role in neurotransmission are referred to as **neuropeptides.** Among the most interesting

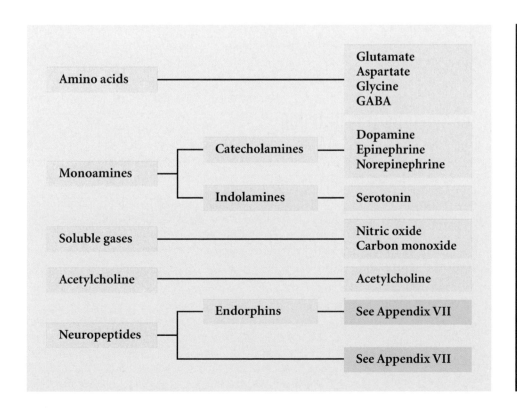

FIGURE 4.15 Classes of neurotransmitters and the particular neurotransmitters that have been introduced, and appear in boldface, in this chapter.

BrainScan

This is a good place for you to pause to scan your brain to see if you are ready to proceed. Are you familiar with the neurotransmitters to which you have just been introduced? Find out by filling in the blanks. The correct answers are provided at the bottom of this page. Before proceeding, review material related to your errors and omissions.

Amino acids are the neurotransmitters in the vast majority of (1) _____-acting, directed synapses. Four amino acids are widely recognized neurotransmitters: (2) _____ , (3) _____ , (4) _____ , and (5) _____. In contrast to the amino acid neurotransmitters, the (6) _____ are small-molecule neurotransmitters with slower, more diffuse effects; they belong to one of two categories: (7) _____ or indolamines. Belonging to the former category are epinephrine, (8) _____ , and (9) _____ ; (10) _____ is the only neurotransmitter belonging to the latter category. The neuropeptides, which are short chains of (11) _____ , are the only class of large-molecule neurotransmitters. (12) _____ , the neurotransmitter at neuromuscular junctions, is a neurotransmitter in a class by itself. Finally, there are the recently discovered (13) _____ neurotransmitters, nitric oxide and carbon monoxide.

neuropeptides are the **endorphins** (see Stefano et al., 2000); endorphins are endogenous opiates (opiumlike chemicals that are produced within the body). The existence of endorphins was first suggested by the discovery that opiate drugs (e.g., opium, morphine, and heroin) bind to receptors in the brain (Pert, Snowman, & Snyder, 1974); presumably, there would not be receptors in the brain for substances that are not themselves produced by the body. This suggestion was subsequently confirmed by the discovery of several different endorphins and several

subtypes of the endorphin receptor. Endorphins activate neural systems that produce *analgesia* (pain supression) and neural systems that mediate (underlie) the experience of pleasure. These effects are presumably why opiate drugs are so addictive.

Figure 4.15 (on page 97) summarizes the neurotransmitters that were introduced in this section. Consequently, they do not appear in the list of key terms at the end of the chapter.

4.7   Pharmacology of Synaptic Transmission

The more neuroscientists have discovered about synaptic transmission, the greater has been their ability to develop drugs to modify it in specific ways. The effects of synaptic-transmission–altering drugs on psychological processes is currently one of the most productive topics of biopsychological research. This research has taught us a great deal about the neural bases of psychological processes. Also, it has led to the development of effective pharmacological treatments for psychological disorders—recall the improvement of Roberto Garcia d'Orta. This section completes the chapter by explaining some of the ways drugs influence psychological processes through their effects on synaptic transmission.

Drugs have two fundamentally different kinds of effects on synaptic transmission: They facilitate it or they inhibit it. Drugs that facilitate the effects of a particular neurotransmitter are said to be **agonists** of that neuro-

Brain Scan answers: (1) fast; (2, 3, 4, 5) glutamate, aspartate, glycine, and GABA, in any order; (6) monoamines; (7) catecholamines; (8, 9) norepinephrine and dopamine, in either order; (10) serotonin; (11) amino acids; (12) Acetyl-choline; (13) soluble-gas.

transmitter. Drugs that inhibit the effects of a particular neurotransmitter are said to be its **antagonists.**

How Drugs Influence Synaptic Transmission

Although the synthesis, release, and action of neurotransmitters vary somewhat from neurotransmitter to neurotransmitter (see Walmsley, Alvarez, & Fyffe, 1998), the following seven general steps are common to most: (1) synthesis of the neurotransmitter, (2) storage in vesicles, (3) breakdown in the cytoplasm of any neurotransmitter that leaks from the vesicles, (4) exocytosis, (5) inhibitory feedback via autoreceptors, (6) activation of postsynaptic receptors, and (7) deactivation. Figure 4.16 illustrates these seven steps, and Figure 4.17 on page 100 illustrates some ways that agonistic and antagonistic drugs influence them. For example, some agonists

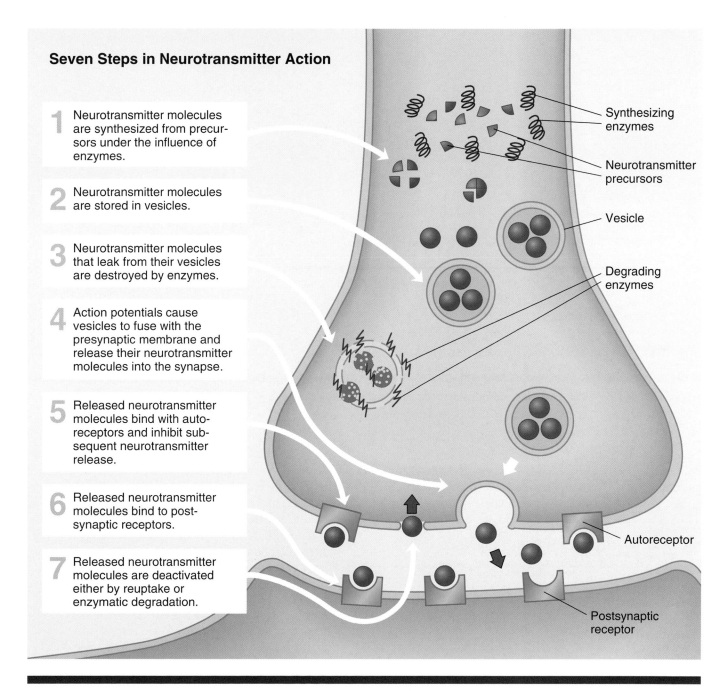

Seven Steps in Neurotransmitter Action

1 Neurotransmitter molecules are synthesized from precursors under the influence of enzymes.

2 Neurotransmitter molecules are stored in vesicles.

3 Neurotransmitter molecules that leak from their vesicles are destroyed by enzymes.

4 Action potentials cause vesicles to fuse with the presynaptic membrane and release their neurotransmitter molecules into the synapse.

5 Released neurotransmitter molecules bind with autoreceptors and inhibit subsequent neurotransmitter release.

6 Released neurotransmitter molecules bind to postsynaptic receptors.

7 Released neurotransmitter molecules are deactivated either by reuptake or enzymatic degradation.

Synthesizing enzymes
Neurotransmitter precursors
Vesicle
Degrading enzymes
Autoreceptor
Postsynaptic receptor

FIGURE 4.16 Seven steps in neurotransmitter action: (1) synthesis, (2) storage in vesicles, (3) breakdown of any neurotransmitter leaking from the vesicles, (4) exocytosis, (5) inhibitory feedback via autoreceptors, (6) activation of postsynaptic receptors, and (7) deactivation.

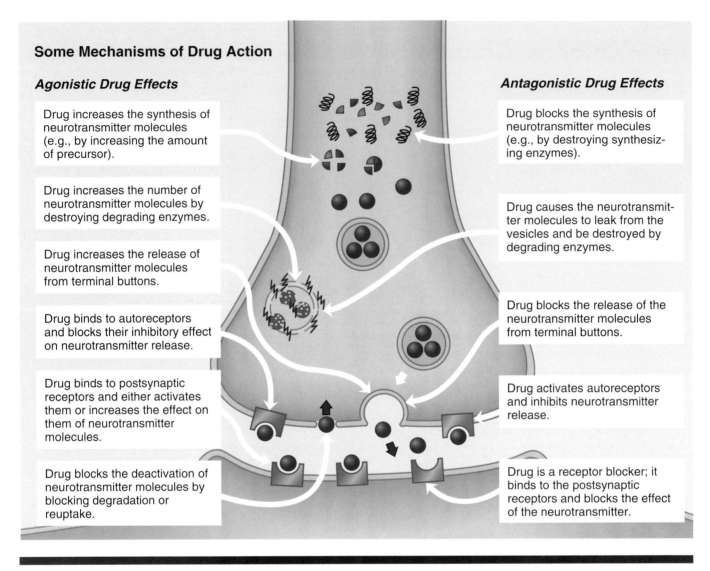

FIGURE 4.17 Some mechanisms of agonistic and antagonistic drug effects.

bind to postsynaptic receptors and activate them, whereas some antagonistic drugs, called **receptor blockers,** bind to postsynaptic receptors without activating them and, in so doing, block the access of the usual neurotransmitter.

Psychoactive Drugs: Four Examples

You will encounter many psychoactive drugs, their psychological effects, and their mechanisms of action in future chapters. Here are four examples: two agonists, cocaine and the benzodiazepines; and two antagonists, atropine and curare.

COCAINE ■ **Cocaine** is a potent catecholamine agonist that is highly addictive. It increases the activity of both dopamine and norepinephrine by blocking their reuptake from the synapse into the presynaptic button.

Accordingly, when there are high levels of cocaine in the brain, molecules of dopamine and norepinephrine, once released into the synapse, continue to activate postsynaptic receptors because their primary method of deactivation has been blocked. This produces a variety of psychological effects, including euphoria, loss of appetite, and insomnia. It is also responsible for the addictive potential of cocaine (see Chapter 15).

BENZODIAZEPINES ■ *Chlordiazepoxide* (marketed under the name *Librium*) and *diazepam* (marketed under the name *Valium*) belong to a class of drugs called *benzodiazepines*. **Benzodiazepines** have *anxiolytic* (anxiety-reducing), *sedative* (sleep-inducing), and *anticonvulsant* effects. They appear to exert their anxiolytic effects by serving as GABA agonists. Benzodiazepines bind to one subtype of the GABA receptor, the ionotropic GABA$_A$ receptor (see

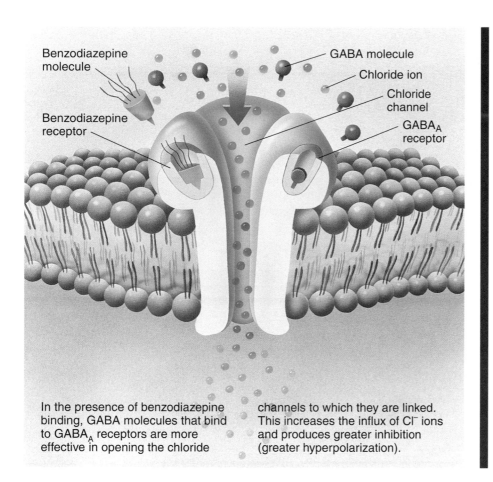

Benzodiazepine molecule

Benzodiazepine receptor

GABA molecule

Chloride ion

Chloride channel

GABA$_A$ receptor

In the presence of benzodiazepine binding, GABA molecules that bind to GABA$_A$ receptors are more effective in opening the chloride channels to which they are linked. This increases the influx of Cl⁻ ions and produces greater inhibition (greater hyperpolarization).

FIGURE 4.18 The GABA$_A$–benzodiazepine receptor complex.

Macdonald & Olsen, 1994), but they do not exert their agonistic effect by mimicking GABA's actions. Benzodiazepine molecules do not bind to the GABA$_A$ receptor at the same site at which GABA molecules bind. Instead they bind to another part of the molecule; by so doing, they increase the binding of GABA molecules to the receptor and thus increase GABA's inhibitory effects by increasing the influx of Cl⁻ ions and hyperpolarizing the neuron (see Figure 4.18).

ATROPINE ■ Many of the drugs that are used in research and in medicine are extracts of plants that have long been used for medicinal and recreational purposes. For example, in the time of Hippocrates, the Greeks consumed extracts of the belladonna plant to treat stomach ailments and to make themselves more attractive. Greek women believed that its pupil-dilating effects enhanced their beauty (*belladonna* means "beautiful lady"). **Atropine** is the active ingredient of belladonna. It is a receptor blocker that exerts its antagonist effect by binding to a metabotropic subtype of acetylcholine receptors called *muscarinic receptors,* thereby blocking the effects of acetylcholine on them. Many muscarinic receptors are located in the brain; the disruptive effect of high doses of atropine on memory was one of the earliest clues that

cholinergic mechanisms play a role in memory (see Chapter 11).

CURARE ■ South American Indians have long used **curare**—an extract of a certain class of woody vines—to kill their game and occasionally their enemies. Like atropine, curare is a receptor blocker at cholinergic synapses, but it acts at a different subtype of acetylcholine receptors: an ionotropic subtype called *nicotinic receptors.* By binding to nicotinic receptors, curare blocks transmission at **neuromuscular junctions,** thus paralyzing its recipients and killing them by blocking their respiration.

You may be surprised, then, to learn that the active ingredient of curare is sometimes administered to human patients during surgery to ensure that their muscles do not contract during an incision. When curare is used for this purpose, the patient's breathing must be artificially maintained by a respirator.

You may be wondering about the differences between muscarinic and nicotinic receptors and about the significance of their names. The existence of these cholinergic receptor subtypes was inferred from the discovery that some of the receptors to which acetylcholine binds also bind to *muscarine,* whereas others bind to *nicotine.*

Themes Revisited

The function of the nervous system, like the function of any circuit, depends on how signals travel through it. The primary purpose of this chapter was to introduce you to neural conduction and transmission. This introduction touched on three of the book's four themes.

The clinical implications theme was illustrated by the opening case of the Lizard, Roberto Garcia d'Orta, whose symptoms resulted from a disruption of dopaminergic transmission. Also, there were discussions of the therapeutic use of anxiolytic drugs and curare.

The evolutionary perspective theme was implicit throughout the entire chapter because almost all neurophysiological research is conducted on the neurons and synapses of nonhuman subjects. However, the evolutionary perspective received explicit emphasis from the particularly high glial-cell-to-neuron ratio (10:1) of human brains.

The thinking-about-biopsychology theme arose in two metaphors: the firing-gun metaphor of action potentials and the mouse-traps-on-a-wobbly-shelf metaphor of axonal conduction. Metaphors are useful in teaching, and scientists find them useful for thinking about the phenomena they study and for generating hypotheses about them.

ON THE CD
Looking for more information about the topics in this chapter? For recommended additional readings, see Hard Copy for Chapter 4.

Log On

- **http://psych.hanover.edu/Krantz/neural/actionpotential. html** This site features a series of simple animations illustrating the ionic basis of neural membrane potentials and the chemical and electrical forces that underlie postsynaptic and action potentials.

- **http://www.epub.org.br/cm/n06/historia/bioelectr_i.htm** This is a fascinating page on the history of electrophysiology and its role in neural signaling.

- **http://www.pbs.org/wnet/closetohome/science/html/ animations.html** Learn about how psychoactive drugs influence neural activity; this site includes simple animations illustrating synaptic transmission and how drugs such as cocaine, ethanol, and heroin produce their psychoactive effects.

- **http://vv.carleton.ca/~neil/neural/index.html** Once you've mastered neural conduction and synaptic transmission, you might try to construct your own simple neural network; the site includes downloadable software for doing so.

Think about It

1. Just as computers operate on binary (yes–no) signals, the all-or-none action potential is the basis of neural communication. The human brain is thus nothing more than a particularly complex computer. Discuss.

2. How have the findings described in this chapter changed your understanding of brain function?

3. Why is it important for biopsychologists to understand neural conduction and synaptic transmission? Is it important for all psychologists to have such knowledge? Discuss.

4. The discovery that neurotransmitters can act directly on DNA via G proteins uncovered a mechanism through which experience and genes can interact (see Chapter 2). Discuss.

5. Dendrites and glial cells are currently "hot" subjects of neuroscientific research. Discuss.

ON THE CD
Studying for an exam? Try the Practice Tests for Chapter 4.

Key Terms

Absolute refractory period *(p. 87)*
Acetylcholinesterase *(p. 95)*
Action potential (AP) *(p. 84)*
Agonists *(p. 98)*
All-or-none responses *(p. 84)*
Antagonists *(p. 99)*
Antidromic conduction *(p. 88)*
Atropine *(p. 101)*
Autoreceptors *(p. 93)*
Axon hillock *(p. 84)*
Benzodiazepines *(p. 100)*
Cocaine *(p. 100)*
Coexistence *(p. 90)*
Curare *(p. 101)*
Dendritic spines *(p. 89)*
Depolarize *(p. 83)*
Directed synapses *(p. 89)*

Enzymatic degradation *(p. 95)*
Enzymes *(p. 95)*
Excitatory postsynaptic potentials (EPSPs) *(p. 83)*
Exocytosis *(p. 90)*
Golgi complex *(p. 90)*
Graded responses *(p. 83)*
Hyperpolarize *(p. 83)*
Inhibitory postsynaptic potentials (IPSPs) *(p. 83)*
Integration *(p. 84)*
Ion channels *(p. 81)*
Ionotropic receptors *(p. 92)*
Ions *(p. 81)*
Ligand *(p. 92)*
Membrane potential *(p. 80)*
Metabotropic receptors *(p. 92)*
Microelectrodes *(p. 80)*

Neuromuscular junctions *(p. 101)*
Nodes of Ranvier *(p. 88)*
Nondirected synapses *(p. 89)*
Orthodromic conduction *(p. 88)*
Peptides *(p. 90)*
Postsynaptic inhibition *(p. 89)*
Presynaptic inhibition *(p. 89)*
Receptor blockers *(p. 100)*
Receptors *(p. 92)*
Receptor subtypes *(p. 92)*
Relative refractory period *(p. 87)*
Resting potential *(p. 81)*
Reuptake *(p. 95)*
Saltatory conduction *(p. 88)*
Second messenger *(p. 93)*

Sodium–potassium pumps *(p. 83)*
Spatial summation *(p. 84)*
Synaptic vesicles *(p. 90)*
Temporal summation *(p. 84)*
Threshold of excitation *(p. 84)*
Voltage-activated ion channels *(p. 86)*

ON THE CD
Need some help studying the key terms for this chapter? Check out the electronic flash cards for Chapter 4.

chapter 5

The Research Methods of Biopsychology

Understanding What Biopsychologists Do

Chapters 1 and 2 introduced you to the general interests, ideas, and approaches that characterize biopsychology. In Chapters 3 and 4, your introduction to biopsychology was temporarily curtailed while background material in neuroanatomy, neurophysiology, and neurochemistry was presented. This chapter gets down to the nitty-gritty of biopsychology; it describes the specific day-to-day activities of the biopsychology laboratory. It is intended to prepare you for later chapters and to sharpen your understanding of biopsychology by describing how biopsychologists do their research.

The organization of this chapter reflects biopsychology's intrinsic duality. The chapter has two major parts: one dealing with methods of studying the nervous system and the other dealing with methods of studying behavior.

As you read through this chapter, you should keep in mind that most of the methods that are used to study the human brain are also used for clinical purposes, for either diagnosis or treatment. The case of Professor P. makes this point.

The Ironic Case of Professor P.

Two weeks before his brain surgery, Professor P. reported to the hospital for a series of tests. What amazed Professor P. most about these tests was how familiar they seemed. No, Professor P. was not a psychic; he was a behavioral neuroscientist, and he was struck by how similar the tests performed on him were to the tests he had seen in his department.

Professor P. had a brain tumor on his right auditory-vestibular cranial nerve (cranial nerve VIII; see Appendices III and IV), and he had to have it *excised* (cut out). First, Professor P.'s auditory abilities were assessed by measuring his ability to detect sounds of various volumes and pitches and then by measuring the magnitude of the EEG signals evoked in his auditory cortex by clicks in his right ear.

Next, Professor P.'s vestibular function (balance) was tested by injecting cold water into his ear.

"Do you feel anything, Professor P.?"

"Well, a cold ear."

"Nothing else?"

"No."

So colder and colder water was tried with no effect until the final, coldest test was conducted. "Ah, that feels weird," said Professor P. "It's kind of like the bed is tipping."

The results of the tests were bad, or good, depending on your perspective. Professor P.'s hearing in his right ear was poor, and his right vestibular nerve was barely functioning. "At the temperatures we flushed down there, most people would have been on their hands and knees puking their guts out." Professor P. smiled at the technical terminology.

Of course, he was upset that his brain had deteriorated so badly, but he sensed that his neurosurgeon was secretly pleased: "We won't have to try to save the nerve; we'll just cut it."

There was one last test. The skin of his right cheek was lightly pricked while the EEG responses of his somatosensory cortex were recorded from his scalp. "This is just to establish a baseline for the surgery," it was explained. "One main risk of removing tumors on the auditory-vestibular cranial nerve (VIII), is damaging the facial cranial nerve (VII), and that would make the right side of your face sag. So during the surgery, electrodes will be inserted in your cheek, and your cheek will be repeatedly stimulated with tiny electrical pulses. The cortical responses will be recorded and fed into a loudspeaker so that the surgeon can immediately hear changes in the activity if his scalpel starts to stray into the area."

As Professor P. was driving home, his mind wandered from his own plight to his day at the hospital. "Quite interesting," he thought to himself. There were biopsychologists everywhere, doing biopsychological things. In all three labs he had visited, there were people who began their training as biopsychologists.

Two weeks later, Professor P. was rolled into the preparation room. "Sorry to do this, Professor P., you were one of my favorite instructors," the nurse said, as she inserted a large needle into Professor P.'s face and left it there.

Professor P. didn't mind; he was barely conscious. He did not know that he wouldn't regain consciousness for several days—at which point he would be incapable of talking, eating, or even breathing.

Don't forget Professor P.; you will learn more about his case in Chapter 10. But now that the case has demonstrated to you that many of the research methods of biopsychology are also used in clinical settings, let's move on to the methods themselves.

PART ONE METHODS OF STUDYING THE NERVOUS SYSTEM

5.1   Methods of Visualizing the Living Human Brain

Prior to the early 1970s, biopsychological research was impeded by the inability to obtain images of the organ of primary interest: the living human brain. Conventional X-ray photography is next to useless for this purpose. For an X-ray photograph to be taken, an X-ray beam is passed through an object and then onto a photographic plate. Each of the molecules through which the beam passes absorbs some of the radiation; thus, only the unabsorbed portions of the beam reach the photographic plate. X-ray photography is therefore effective in characterizing internal structures that differ substantially from their surroundings in the degree to which they absorb X-rays—for example, a revolver in a suitcase full of clothes or a bone in flesh. However, by the time an X-ray beam has passed through the numerous overlapping structures of the brain, which differ only slightly from one another in their ability to absorb X-rays, it carries little information about the shape of the individual structures through which it has passed.

Contrast X-Rays

Although conventional X-ray photography is not useful for visualizing the brain, contrast X-ray techniques are. **Contrast X-ray techniques** involve injecting into one compartment of the body a substance that absorbs X-rays either less then or more than the surrounding tissue. The injected substance then heightens the contrast between the compartment and the surrounding tissue during X-ray photography.

One contrast X-ray technique, **cerebral angiography,** uses the infusion of a radio-translucent dye into a cerebral artery to visualize the cerebral circulatory system during X-ray photography (see Figure 5.1). Cerebral angiograms are most useful for localizing vascular damage, but the displacement of blood vessels from their normal position also can indicate the location of a tumor.

X-Ray Computed Tomography

In the early 1970s, the study of the living human brain was revolutionized by the introduction of computed tomography. **Computed tomography (CT)** is a computer-assisted X-ray procedure that can be used to visualize the brain and other internal structures of the living body. During cerebral computed tomography, the neurological patient lies with his or her head positioned in the center of a large cylinder, as depicted in Figure 5.2. On one side of the cylinder is an X-ray tube that projects an X-ray beam through the head to an X-ray detector mounted on the other side. The X-ray tube and detector automatically rotate around the head of the patient at one level of the brain, taking many individual X-ray photographs as they rotate. The meager information in each X-ray photograph is combined by a computer to generate a CT scan of one horizontal section of the brain. Then, the X-ray tube and detector are moved along the axis of the patient's body to another level of the brain, and the process is repeated. Scans of eight or nine horizontal brain sections are typically obtained from a patient; combined, they provide a three-dimensional representation of the brain.

Magnetic Resonance Imaging

The success of computed tomography stimulated the development of other techniques for obtaining images of the inside of the living body. Among these techniques

FIGURE 5.1   A cerebral angiogram of a healthy subject.

X-ray source

X-ray detector

is **magnetic resonance imaging (MRI)**—a procedure in which high-resolution images are constructed from the measurement of waves that hydrogen atoms emit when they are activated by radio-frequency waves in a magnetic field. MRI provides clearer images of the brain than does CT. A color-coded two-dimensional MRI scan of the midsagittal brain is presented in Figure 5.3.

In addition to providing relatively high **spatial resolution** (the ability to detect differences in spatial location), MRI can produce images in three dimensions. Figure 5.4 on page 108 is a three-dimensional MRI scan. Figure 5.5 on page 108 shows two-dimensional MRI scans of a slice of a brain.

Positron Emission Tomography

Positron emission tomography (PET) is a brain-imaging technique that has been widely used in biopsychological research because it provides images of brain activity rather than brain structure. In one common version of PET, radioactive **2-deoxyglucose (2-DG)** is injected into the patient's *carotid artery* (an artery of the neck that feeds the ipsilateral cerebral hemisphere). Because of its similarity to glucose, the primary metabolic fuel of the brain, 2-deoxyglucose is rapidly taken up by active (energy-consuming) neurons. However, unlike glucose, 2-deoxyglucose cannot be metabolized; it therefore accumulates in active neurons until it is gradually broken down. Each PET scan is an image of the levels of radioactivity (indi-

cated by color coding) in various parts of one horizontal level of the brain. Thus, if a PET scan is taken of a patient who engages in an activity such as reading for about 30 seconds after the 2-DG injection, the resulting scan

FIGURE 5.3 A color-enhanced midsagittal MRI scan.

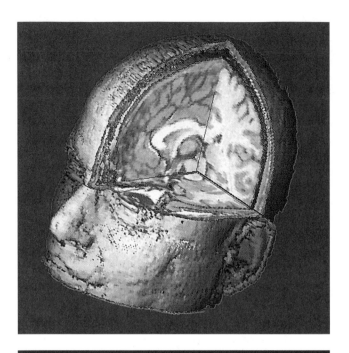

FIGURE 5.4 Structural (MRI) can be used to provide three-dimensional images of the entire brain. (Courtesy of Bruce Foster and Robert Hare, University of British Columbia.)

FIGURE 5.6 A series of PET scans. Each scan is a horizontal section recorded during a different psychological activity. Areas of high activity are indicated by reds and yellows. For example, notice the high level of activity in the visual cortex of the occipital lobe when the subject scanned a visual display. (From "Positron Tomography: Human Brain Function and Biochemistry" by Michael E. Phelps and John C. Mazziotta, *Science,* 228 [9701], May 17, 1985, p. 804. Copyright 1985 by the AAAS. Reprinted by permission. Courtesy of Drs. Michael E. Phelps and John Mazziotta, UCLA School of Medicine.)

FIGURE 5.5 Structural MRI can also be used to provide two-dimensional images of brain slices. The upper MRI scan shows a tumor shortly after radiotherapy, and the lower MRI scan shows the same tumor several weeks later. Ventricles are outlined in yellow; the tumor is outlined in red. (Adapted from Calmon et al., 1998; courtesy of Neil Roberts, University of Liverpool.)

will indicate the areas at that brain level that were most active during the 30 seconds of activity (see Figure 5.6). Usually, several different levels of the brain are scanned so that the extent of brain activity can be better assessed.

Another PET procedure (see Turner, 1995) takes advantage of the fact that there is an increase in blood flow to active areas of the brain because active neurons often release *nitric oxide,* a vasodilator (Iadecola, 1993). Accordingly, if radioactive water is injected into the brain's circulatory system as the subject engages in some activity, the PET scan will indicate the areas in which blood flow is increased during the activity (see Raichle, 1994).

Notice from Figure 5.6 that PET scans are not images of the brain. Each PET scan is merely a colored map of the amount of radioactivity in each of the tiny square voxels that compose the scan. One can only estimate exactly how each voxel maps onto a particular brain structure.

Functional MRI

MRI technology has been applied with great success to the measurement of brain activity (see Cabeza & Nyberg, 2000). **Functional MRI (fMRI)** produces images of the increase in oxygen flow in the blood to active areas of the brain.

Functional MRI has four advantages over PET: (1) Nothing has to be injected into the subject; (2) it provides both structural and functional information in the same image; (3) its spatial resolution is better; and (4) it can be used to produce three-dimensional images of activity over the entire brain. Like PET, fMRI offers poor **temporal resolution** (the ability to detect differences in time); it takes several seconds to collect enough information to form a single image, whereas neural events occur in milliseconds. Functional MRIs are shown in Figure 5.7.

Magnetoencephalography

Another technique that is used to monitor the brain activity of human subjects is **magnetoencephalography (MEG).** MEG measures changes in magnetic fields on the surface of the scalp that are produced by changes in underlying patterns of neural activity.

FIGURE 5.7 Functional magnetic resonance images (fMRIs). These images illustrate the areas of cortex that became more active when the subjects observed strings of letters and were asked to specify which strings were words; in the control condition, subjects viewed strings of asterisks (Liddle et al., in press). These fMRIs illustrate surface activity; but images of sections through the brain can also be displayed. (Courtesy of Kent Kiehl and Peter Liddle, Department of Psychiatry, University of British Columbia.)

5.2 ▶ Recording Human Psychophysiological Activity

The preceding section introduced you to functional brain imaging, the cornerstone of cognitive neuroscience research. This section deals with *psychophysiological recording methods* (methods of recording physiological activity from the surface of the human body). Five of the most widely studied psychophysiological measures are described: one measure of brain activity (the scalp EEG), two measures of somatic nervous system activity (muscle tension and eye movement), and two measures of autonomic nervous system activity (skin conductance and cardiovascular activity).

■ Scalp Electroencephalography

The *electroencephalogram (EEG)* is a gross measure of the electrical activity of the brain. It is recorded through large electrodes by a device called an *electroencephalograph (EEG machine),* and the technique is called **electroencephalography.** In EEG studies of human subjects, each channel of EEG activity is usually recorded from disk-shaped electrodes, about half the size of a dime, which are taped to the scalp.

The scalp EEG signal reflects the sum of electrical events throughout the head. These events include action potentials and postsynaptic potentials, as well as electrical signals from the skin, muscles, blood, and eyes. Thus the utility of the scalp EEG does not lie in its ability to provide an unclouded view of neural activity. Its value as a research and diagnostic tool rests on the fact that some EEG wave forms are associated with particular states of consciousness or particular types of cerebral pathology (e.g., epilepsy). For example, **alpha waves** are regular, 8- to 12-per-second, high-amplitude waves that are associated with relaxed wakefulness. A few examples of EEG wave forms and their psychological correlates are presented in Figure 5.8.

Because EEG signals decrease in amplitude as they spread from their source, a comparison of signals recorded from various sites on the scalp can sometimes indicate the origin of particular waves. This is why it is usual to record EEG activity from many sites simultaneously.

Psychophysiologists are often more interested in the EEG waves that accompany certain psychological events than they are in the background EEG signal. These accompanying EEG waves are generally referred to as

FIGURE 5.8 Some typical electroencephalograms and their psychological correlates.

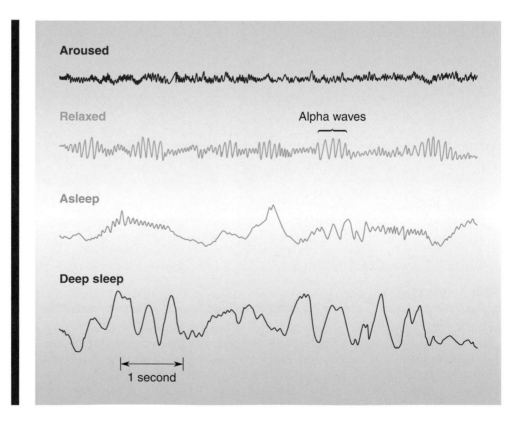

event-related potentials (ERPs). One commonly studied type of event-related potential is the **sensory evoked potential**—the change in the cortical EEG signal that is elicited by the momentary presentation of a sensory stimulus. As Figure 5.9 illustrates, the cortical EEG that follows a sensory stimulus has two components: the response to the stimulus (the signal) and the ongoing background EEG activity (the noise). The *signal* is the part of any recording that is of interest; the *noise* is the part that isn't. The problem in recording sensory evoked potentials is that the noise of the background EEG is often so great that the sensory evoked potential is masked. Measuring a sensory evoked potential can be like measuring a whisper at a rock concert.

A method used to reduce the noise of the background EEG is **signal averaging.** First, a subject's response to a stimulus, such as a click, is recorded many—let's say 1,000—times. Then, a computer identifies the millivolt value of each of the 1,000 traces at their starting points (i.e., at the click) and calculates the mean of these 1,000 scores. Next, it considers the value of each of the 1,000 traces 1 millisecond (msec) from their start, for example, and calculates the mean of these values. It repeats this process at the 2-msec mark, the 3-msec mark, and so on. When these averages are plotted, the average response evoked by the click

is more apparent because the random background EEG is canceled out by the averaging. See Figure 5.9, which illustrates the averaging of an auditory evoked potential.

The analysis of *average evoked potentials (AEPs)* focuses on the various waves in the averaged signal. Each wave is characterized by its direction, positive or negative, and by its latency. For example, the **P300 wave** illustrated in Figure 5.10 on page 112 is the positive wave that occurs about 300 msec after a momentary stimulus that has considerable meaning for the subject. In contrast, the small waves recorded in the first few milliseconds after a stimulus are not influenced by the meaning of the stimulus. These small waves are called **far-field potentials** because, although they are recorded from the scalp, they originate far away in the sensory nuclei of the brain stem.

Although electroencephalography scores high points when it comes to temporal resolution, it initially failed miserably on spatial resolution. With conventional electroencephalographic procedures, one can only roughly estimate the source of a particular signal. However, newer techniques employing sophisticated computer software and many electrodes can accurately locate the source of signals. The spatial resolution of these techniques is sufficient to enable the amplitude of evoked EEG signals recorded on the cortex to be color-coded

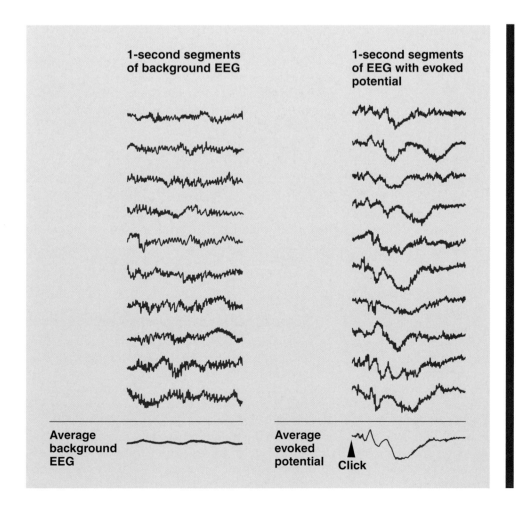

FIGURE 5.9 The averaging of an auditory evoked potential. Averaging increases the signal-to-noise ratio.

FIGURE 5.10   An average auditory evoked potential. Notice the P300 wave. This wave occurs only if the stimulus has meaning for the subject; in this case, the click signals the imminent delivery of a reward. By convention, positive EEG waves are always shown as downward deflections.

and plotted on the surface of a three-dimensional MRI scan (Gevins et al., 1995). This useful marriage of techniques is illustrated in Figure 5.11.

Muscle Tension

Each skeletal muscle is composed of millions of threadlike muscle fibers. Each muscle fiber contracts in an all-or-none fashion when activated by the motor neuron that innervates it. At any given time, a few fibers in each resting muscle are likely to be contracting, thus maintaining the overall tone (tension) of the muscle. Movement results when a large number of fibers contract at the same time.

In everyday language, anxious people are commonly referred to as "tense." This usage acknowledges the fact that anxious, or otherwise aroused, individuals typically display high resting levels of tension in their muscles. This is why psychophysiologists are interested in this measure; they use it as an indicator of psychological arousal.

Electromyography is the usual procedure for measuring muscle tension. The resulting record is called an *electromyogram (EMG)*. EMG activity is usually recorded between two electrodes taped to the surface of the skin over the muscle of interest. An EMG record is presented in Figure 5.12. You will notice from this figure that the main correlate of an increase in muscle contraction is an increase in the amplitude of the raw EMG signal, which reflects the number of muscle fibers contracting at any one time.

Most psychophysiologists do not work with raw EMG signals; they convert them to a more workable form. The raw signal is fed into a computer that calculates the total amount of EMG spiking per unit of time—

FIGURE 5.11   The marriage of electroencephalography and magnetic resonance imaging: The distribution of EEG signals can be represented on a structural cerebral MRI. Plotted in this illustration is the distribution of theta waves recorded while the subjects worked on a memory task. The highest incidence of theta waves (indicated by red in the three-dimensional MRI of the dorsal brain surface and by blue on the midsagittal section) occurred in the anterior cingulate cortex. (Alan Gevins, EEG Systems Laboratory & SAM Technology, San Francisco.)

in consecutive 0.1-second intervals, for example. The integrated signal (i.e., the total EMG activity per unit of time) is then plotted. The result is a smooth curve, the amplitude of which is a simple, continuous measure of the level of muscle tension (see Figure 5.12).

Eye Movement

The electrophysiological technique for recording eye movements is called **electrooculography,** and the resulting record is called an *electrooculogram (EOG)*. Electrooculography is based on the fact that there is a steady potential difference between the front (positive) and back (negative) of the eyeball. Because of this steady potential, when the eye moves, a change in the electrical potential between electrodes placed around the eye can be recorded. It is usual to record EOG activity between two electrodes placed on each side of the eye to measure its

Raw EMG signal

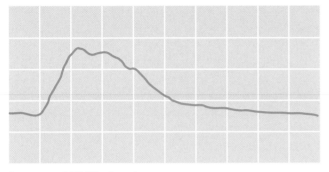

Integrated EMG signal

FIGURE 5.12 The relation between a raw EMG signal and its integrated version. The subject tensed the muscle beneath the electrodes and then gradually relaxed it.

horizontal movements and between two electrodes placed above and below the eye to measure its vertical movements (see Figure 5.13).

Electrooculograms of the subject as she scanned a circle

FIGURE 5.13 The typical placement of electrodes around the eye for electrooculography. The two electrooculogram traces were recorded as the subject scanned a circle.

■ Skin Conductance

Emotional thoughts and experiences are associated with increases in the ability of the skin to conduct electricity. The two most commonly employed indexes of *electrodermal activity* are the **skin conductance level (SCL)** and the **skin conductance response (SCR).** The SCL is a measure of the background level of skin conductance that is associated with a particular situation, whereas the SCR is a measure of the transient changes in skin conductance that are associated with discrete experiences.

The physiological bases of skin conductance changes are not fully understood, but there is considerable evidence implicating the sweat glands (see Boucsein, 1992). Although the main function of sweat glands is to cool the body, these glands tend to become active in emotional situations. Sweat glands are distributed over most of the body surface; but, as you are almost certainly aware, those of the hands, feet, armpits, and forehead are particularly responsive to emotional stimuli.

■ Cardiovascular Activity

The presence in our language of phrases such as *chicken-hearted, white with fear,* and *blushing bride* indicates that modern psychophysiologists were not the first to recognize the relationship between *cardiovascular activity* and emotion. The cardiovascular system has two parts: the blood vessels and the heart. It is a system for distributing oxygen and nutrients to the tissues of the body, removing metabolic wastes, and transmitting chemical messages. Three different measures of cardiovascular activity are frequently employed in psychophysiological research: heart rate, arterial blood pressure, and local blood volume.

HEART RATE ■ The electrical signal that is associated with each heartbeat can be recorded through electrodes placed on the chest. The recording is called an **electrocardiogram** (abbreviated either ECG, for obvious reasons, or **EKG,** from the original German). The average resting heart rate of a healthy adult is about 70 beats per minute, but it increases abruptly at the sound, or thought, of a dental drill.

BLOOD PRESSURE ■ Measuring arterial blood pressure involves two independent measurements: a measurement of the peak pressure during the periods of heart contraction, the *systoles,* and a measurement of the minimum pressure during the periods of relaxation, the *diastoles.* Blood pressure is usually expressed as a ratio of systolic over diastolic blood pressure in millimeters of mercury (mmHg). The normal resting blood pressure for an adult is about 130/70 mmHg. A chronic blood pressure of more than 140/90 mmHg is viewed as a serious health hazard and is called **hypertension.**

You have likely had your blood pressure measured with a *sphygmomanometer*—a crude device composed of a hollow cuff, a rubber bulb for inflating it, and a pressure gauge for measuring the pressure in the cuff (*sphygmos* means "pulse"). More reliable, fully automated methods are used in research.

BLOOD VOLUME ▪ Changes in the volume of blood in particular parts of the body are associated with psychological events. The best-known example of such a change is the engorgement of the genitals that is associ-

ated with sexual arousal in both males and females. **Plethysmography** refers to the various techniques for measuring changes in the volume of blood in a particular part of the body (*plethysmos* means "an enlargement").

One method of measuring these changes is to record the volume of the target tissue by wrapping a strain gauge around it. Although this method has utility in measuring blood flow in fingers or similarly shaped organs, the possibilities for employing it are somewhat limited. Another plethysmographic method is to shine a light through the tissue under investigation and to measure the amount of the light that is absorbed by it. The more blood there is in a structure, the more light it will absorb.

5.3 Invasive Physiological Research Methods

Efforts to study brain–behavior relations in human subjects are impeded by the necessity of adhering to lines of research that involve no direct interaction with the organ of interest: the brain. We turn now from a consideration of the noninvasive techniques employed in research on living human brains to a consideration of more direct techniques. This section introduces some of the physiological methods commonly employed in biopsychological studies of laboratory animals.

Most physiological techniques used in biopsychological research on laboratory animals fall into one of three categories: lesion methods, electrical stimulation methods, and invasive recording methods. Each of these three methods is discussed in this section of the chapter, but it begins with a description of *stereotaxic surgery.*

Stereotaxic Surgery

Stereotaxic surgery is the first step in many biopsychological experiments. *Stereotaxic surgery* is the means by which experimental devices are precisely positioned in the depths of the brain. Two things are required in stereotaxic surgery: an atlas to provide directions to the target site and an instrument for getting there.

The **stereotaxic atlas** is used to locate brain structures in much the same way that a geographic atlas is used to locate geographic landmarks. There is, however, one important difference. In contrast to the surface of the earth, which has only two dimensions, the brain has three. Accordingly, the brain is represented in a stereotaxic atlas by a series of individual maps, one per page, each representing the structure of a single, two-dimensional frontal brain slice. In stereotaxic atlases, all distances are given in

millimeters from a designated reference point. In some rat atlases, the reference point is **bregma**—the point on the top of the skull where two of the major *sutures* (seams in the skull) intersect.

The **stereotaxic instrument** has two parts: a *head holder,* which firmly holds each subject's brain in the prescribed position and orientation; and an *electrode holder,* which holds the device to be inserted. A system of precision gears allows the electrode holder to be moved in three dimensions: anterior–posterior, dorsal–ventral, and lateral–medial. The implantation by stereotaxic surgery of an electrode in the amygdala of a rat is illustrated in Figure 5.14.

Lesion Methods

Those of you with an unrelenting drive to dismantle objects to see how they work will appreciate the lesion methods. In those methods, a part of the brain is removed, damaged, or destroyed; then, the behavior of the subject is carefully assessed in an effort to determine the functions of the lesioned structure. Four types of lesions are discussed here: aspiration lesions, radio-frequency lesions, knife cuts, and cryogenic blockade.

ASPIRATION LESIONS ▪ When a lesion is to be made in an area of cortical tissue that is accessible to the eyes and instruments of the surgeon, **aspiration** is frequently the method of choice. The cortical tissue is drawn off by suction through a fine-tipped handheld glass pipette. Because the underlying white matter is slightly more resistant to suction than the cortical tissue itself, a skilled

1 The atlas indicates that the amygdala target site is 2.8 mm posterior to bregma, 4.5 mm lateral, and 8.5 mm ventral.

Amygdala

Bregma

2 A hole is drilled 2.8 mm posterior to bregma and 4.5 lateral to it. Then, the electrode holder is positioned over the hole, and the electrode is lowered 8.5 mm through the hole.

Electrode connector
Electrode

3 The electrode is anchored to the skull by letting dental acrylic harden around the electrode connector and several stainless steel skull screws.

FIGURE 5.14 Stereotaxic surgery: Implanting an electrode in the rat amygdala.

surgeon can delicately peel off the layers of cortical tissue from the surface of the brain, leaving the underlying white matter and major blood vessels undamaged.

RADIO-FREQUENCY LESIONS ■ Small subcortical lesions are commonly made by passing *radio-frequency current* (high-frequency current) through the target tissue from the tip of a stereotaxically positioned electrode. The heat from the current destroys the tissue. The size and shape of the lesion are determined by the duration and intensity of the current and the configuration of the electrode tip.

KNIFE CUTS ■ *Sectioning* (cutting) is used to eliminate conduction in a nerve or tract. A tiny, well-placed cut can unambiguously accomplish this task without producing extensive damage to surrounding tissue. How does one insert a knife into the brain to make a cut with-

out severely damaging the overlying tissue? One method is depicted in Figure 5.15 on page 116.

CRYOGENIC BLOCKADE ■ An alternative to destructive lesions is **cryogenic blockade.** When coolant is pumped through an implanted *cryoprobe,* such as the one depicted in Figure 5.16 on page 116, neurons near the tip are cooled until they stop firing. The temperature is maintained above the freezing level, so there is no structural damage. Then, when the tissue is allowed to warm up, normal neural activity returns. A cryogenic blockade is functionally similar to a lesion in that it eliminates the contribution of a particular area of the brain to the ongoing behavior of the subject. This is why cryogenic blockades are sometimes referred to as *reversible lesions.* Reversible lesions can also be produced with microinjections into the brain of local anesthetics such as lidocaine (see Floresco, Seamans, & Phillips, 1997).

FIGURE 5.15 A device for performing subcortical knife cuts. The device is stereotaxically positioned in the brain; then, the blade swings out to make the cut. Here, the anterior commissure is being sectioned.

FIGURE 5.16 A cryoprobe. The cryoprobe is implanted in the brain; then, the brain area at the uninsulated tip of the cryoprobe is cooled while the effects on behavior are assessed. Cryoprobes are slender so that they can be implanted in the brain without causing substantial damage; they are typically constructed of two gauges of hypodermic tubing.

INTERPRETING LESION EFFECTS ■ Before you leave this section on lesions, a word of caution is in order. Lesion effects are deceptively difficult to interpret. Because the structures of the brain are small, convoluted, and tightly packed together, even a highly skilled surgeon cannot completely destroy a structure without producing significant damage to adjacent structures. There is, however, an unfortunate tendency to lose sight of this fact. For example, a lesion that leaves major portions of the amygdala intact

and damages an assortment of neighboring structures comes to be thought of simplistically as an *amygdala lesion*. Such an apparently harmless abstraction can be misleading in two ways. If you believe that all lesions referred to as "amygdala lesions" include damage to no other brain structure, you may incorrectly attribute all of their behavioral effects to amygdala damage; conversely, if you believe that all lesions referred to as "amygdala lesions" include the entire amygdala, you may incorrectly conclude that the amygdala does not participate in behaviors uninfluenced by the lesion.

BILATERAL AND UNILATERAL LESIONS ■ As a general principle—but one with several notable exceptions—the behavioral effects of *unilateral lesions* (lesions restricted to one half of the brain) are much milder than those of symmetrical *bilateral lesions* (lesions involving both sides of the brain), particularly in nonhuman species. Indeed, behavioral effects of unilateral lesions to some brain structures can be difficult to detect. As a result, most experimental studies of lesion effects are studies of bilateral, rather than unilateral, lesions.

■ | Electrical Stimulation

Clues about the function of a neural structure can be obtained by stimulating it electrically. Electrical brain stimulation is usually delivered across the two tips of a *bipolar electrode*—two insulated wires wound tightly together and cut at the end. Weak pulses of current produce an immediate increase in the firing of neurons near the tip of the electrode.

Electrical stimulation of the brain is an important biopsychological research tool because it often has behavioral effects, usually opposite to those produced by a lesion to the same site. It can elicit a number of behavioral sequences, including eating, drinking, attacking,

copulating, and sleeping. The particular behavioral response that is elicited depends on the location of the electrode tip, the parameters of the current, and the test environment in which the stimulation is administered.

■ | Invasive Electrophysiological Recording Methods

This section describes four invasive electrophysiological recording methods: intracellular unit recording, extracellular unit recording, multiple-unit recording, and invasive EEG recording. See Figure 5.17 for an example of each method.

INTRACELLULAR UNIT RECORDING ■ A method whose findings were discussed at length in Chapter 4, *intracellular unit recording*, provides a moment-by-moment record of the graded fluctuations in one neuron's membrane potential. Most experiments using this

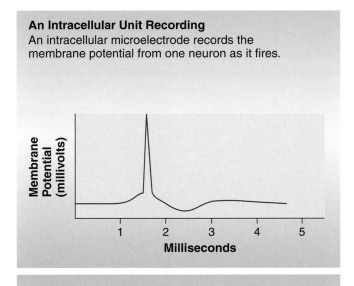

An Intracellular Unit Recording
An intracellular microelectrode records the membrane potential from one neuron as it fires.

A Multiple-Unit Recording
A small electrode records the action potentials of many nearby neurons. These are added up and plotted. In this example, firing in the area of the electrode tip gradually declined and then suddenly increased.

An Extracellular Unit Recording
An extracellular microelectrode records the electrical disturbance that is created each time an adjacent neuron fires.

An Invasive EEG Recording
A large implanted electrode picks up general changes in electrical brain activity. The EEG signal is not related to neural firing in any obvious way.

FIGURE 5.17 Four methods of recording electrical activity of the nervous system.

recording procedure are performed on chemically immobilized animals because it is next to impossible to keep the tip of a microelectrode positioned inside a neuron of a freely moving animal.

EXTRACELLULAR UNIT RECORDING ■ It is possible to record the action potentials of a neuron through a microelectrode whose tip is positioned in the extracellular fluid next to it. Each time the neuron fires, a blip is recorded on the oscilloscope. Accordingly, *extracellular unit recording* provides a record of the firing of a neuron but no information about the neuron's membrane potential. It is difficult to record extracellularly from a single neuron in a freely moving animal without the electrode tip shifting away from the neuron, but it can be accomplished with special flexible microelectrodes that can shift slightly with the brain. Initially, extracellular unit recording involved recording from one neuron at a time, each at the tip of a separately implanted electrode. However, it is now possible to simultaneously record extracellular signals from up to 100 or so neurons by analyzing the correlations among the signals picked up through several different electrodes implanted in the same general area. Most theories of the neural mediation of complex behavioral processes assume that they are encoded by relations among the firing of many functionally related neurons—together referred to as *ensembles* (see Deadwyler & Hampson, 1995). Accordingly, studying psychological processes by recording from single neurons can be like studying an animated computer image one pixel at a time.

MULTIPLE-UNIT RECORDING ■ In *multiple-unit recording,* the electrode tip is larger than that of a microelectrode; thus, it picks up signals from many neurons. (The larger the electrode, the more neurons contribute to the signal.) The action potentials picked up by the electrode are fed into an integrating circuit, which adds them together. A multiple-unit recording is a graph of the total number of recorded action potentials per unit of time (e.g., per 0.1 second).

INVASIVE EEG RECORDING ■ In laboratory animals, EEG signals are recorded through large implanted electrodes rather than through scalp electrodes. Cortical EEG signals are frequently recorded through stainless steel skull screws, whereas subcortical EEG signals are typically recorded through stereotaxically implanted wire electrodes.

5.4 Pharmacological Research Methods

In the preceding section, you learned how physiological psychologists study the brain by manipulating it and recording from it using surgical and electrical methods. In this section, you will learn how psychopharmacologists manipulate and record from the brain using chemical methods.

The major research strategy of psychopharmacology is to administer drugs that either increase or decrease the effects of particular neurotransmitters and to observe the behavioral consequences. You learned in Chapter 4 how *agonists* and *antagonists* affect neurotransmitter systems. Described here are routes of drug administration, methods of using chemicals to make selective brain lesions, methods of measuring the chemical activity of the brain that are particularly useful in biopsychological research, and methods for locating neurotransmitter systems.

Routes of Drug Administration

In most psychopharmacological experiments, drugs are administered in one of the following ways: (1) They are fed to the subject; (2) they are injected through a tube into the stomach (*intragastrically*); or (3) they are injected hypodermically into the peritoneal cavity of the abdomen (*intraperitonally, IP*), into a large muscle (*intramuscularly, IM*), into the fatty tissue beneath the skin (*subcutaneously, SC*), or into a large surface vein (*intravenously, IV*). A problem with these peripheral routes of administration is that many drugs do not readily pass through the blood–brain barrier. To overcome this problem, drugs can be administered in small amounts through a fine, hollow needle, called a **cannula,** that has been stereotaxically implanted in the brain.

Selective Chemical Lesions

The effects of surgical, electrolytic, and cryogenic lesions are frequently difficult to interpret because they affect all neurons in the target area. In some cases, it is possible to make more selective lesions by injecting **neurotoxins** (neural poisons) that have an affinity for certain components of the nervous system. There are many selective neurotoxins. For example, when either *kainic acid* or *ibotenic acid* is administered by microinjection, it is preferentially taken up by cell bodies at the tip of the cannula and destroys those neurons, while leaving neurons with axons passing through the area largely unscathed.

Another widely used selective neurotoxin is *6-hydroxydopamine (6-OHDA)*. It is taken up by only those neurons that release the neurotransmitters *norepinephrine* or *dopamine,* and it leaves other neurons at the injection site undamaged.

Measuring Chemical Activity of the Brain

There are many procedures for measuring the chemical activity of the brains of laboratory animals. Two techniques that have proved particularly useful in biopsychological research are the 2-deoxyglucose technique and cerebral dialysis.

2-DEOXYGLUCOSE TECHNIQUE ■ The *2-deoxyglucose (2-DG)* technique entails placing an animal that has been injected with radioactive 2-DG in a test situation in which it engages in the behavior of interest. Because 2-DG is similar in structure to glucose—the brain's main source of energy—neurons active during the test absorb it at a high rate but do not metabolize it. After the subject engages in the behavior, it is killed, and its brain is removed and sliced. The slices are then subjected to **autoradiography;** they are coated with a photographic emulsion, stored in the dark for a few days, and then developed much like film. Areas of the brain that absorbed

high levels of the radioactive 2-DG during the test appear as black spots on the slides. The density of the spots in various regions of the brain can then be color-coded (see Figure 5.18).

CEREBRAL DIALYSIS ■ The **cerebral dialysis** procedure is a method of measuring the extracellular concentration of specific neurochemicals in behaving animals (see Robinson & Justice, 1991)—most other techniques for measuring neurochemicals require that the animals be killed so that tissue can be extracted. Cerebral dialysis involves the implantation in the brain of a fine tube with a short semipermeable section. The semipermeable section is positioned in the brain structure of interest so that extracellular chemicals from the structure will diffuse into the tube. Once in the tube, they can be collected for freezing, storage, and later analysis; or they can be carried in solution directly to a *chromatograph* (a device for measuring the chemical constituents of liquids and gases).

Locating Neurotransmitters and Receptors in the Brain

A key step in trying to understand the psychological function of a particular neurotransmitter or receptor is finding out where it is located in the brain. Two of the techniques available for this purpose are immunocytochemistry and in situ hybridization. Each involves exposing brain slices to a labeled *ligand* of the molecule under investigation (the ligand of a molecule is another molecule that binds to it).

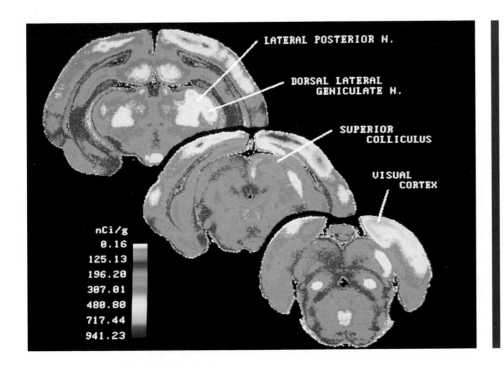

LATERAL POSTERIOR N.

DORSAL LATERAL GENICULATE N.

SUPERIOR COLLICULUS

VISUAL CORTEX

nCi/g
0.16
125.13
196.20
307.01
480.80
717.44
941.23

FIGURE 5.18 The 2-deoxyglucose technique. The accumulation of radioactivity is shown in three frontal sections taken from the brain of a Richardson's ground squirrel. The subject was injected with radioactive 2-deoxyglucose; then, for 45 minutes, it viewed brightly illuminated black and white stripes through its left eye while its right eye was covered. Because the ground squirrel visual system is largely crossed, most of the radioactivity accumulated in the visual structures of the right hemisphere (the hemisphere on your right). (Courtesy of Rod Cooper, Department of Psychology, University of Calgary.)

IMMUNOCYTOCHEMISTRY ■ When a foreign protein (an *antigen*) is injected into an animal, the animal creates *antibodies* that bind to it and then help the body remove or destroy it; this is known as the body's *immune reaction*. Neurochemists have created stocks of antibodies to most of the brain's peptide neurotransmitters and receptors. **Immunocytochemistry** is a procedure for locating particular neuroproteins in the brain by labeling their antibodies with a dye or radioactive element and then exposing slices of brain tissue to the labeled antibodies (see Figure 5.19). Regions of dye or radioactivity accumulation in the brain slices mark the locations of the target neuroprotein.

Because all enzymes are proteins and because only those neurons that release a particular neurotransmitter are likely to contain all the enzymes required for its synthesis, immunocytochemistry can be used to locate neurotransmitters by binding to their enzymes. This is done by exposing brain slices to labeled antibodies that bind to enzymes located in only those neurons that contain the neurotransmitter of interest (see Figure 5.20).

IN SITU HYBRIDIZATION ■ Another technique for locating peptides and other proteins in the brain is **in situ hybridization.** This technique takes advantage of the fact that all peptides and proteins are transcribed from sequences of nucleotide bases on strands of messenger RNA (see Chapter 2). The nucleotide base sequences that direct the synthesis of many neuroproteins have been identified, and hybrid strands of mRNA with the complementary base sequences have been artificially

FIGURE 5.20 Immunocytochemistry. This section through a rat's substantia nigra reveals dopaminergic neurons that have taken up the antibody for tyrosine hydroxylase, the enzyme that converts tyrosine to L-dopa. (Courtesy of Mark Klitenick and Chris Fibiger, Department of Psychiatry, University of British Columbia.)

created. In situ hybridization (see Figure 5.21) involves the following steps. First, hybrid RNA strands with the base sequence complementary to that of the mRNA that directs the synthesis of the target neuroprotein are obtained. Next, the hybrid RNA strands are labeled with a dye or radioactive element. Finally, the brain slices are exposed to the labeled hybrid RNA strands; they bind to the complementary mRNA strands, marking the location of neurons that release the target neuroprotein.

FIGURE 5.19 Immunocytochemistry. This section through a cat's visual cortex reveals GABAergic inhibitory interneurons that have taken up the antibody for GABA. (Courtesy of Joanne Matsubara, Department of Ophthalmology, University of British Columbia.)

FIGURE 5.21 In situ hybridization. This color-coded frontal section through a rat brain reveals high concentrations of mRNA expression for an endorphin in the striatum (in red and yellow). (Courtesy of Ningning Guo and Chris Fibiger, Department of Psychiatry, University of British Columbia.)

5.5 Genetic Engineering

Genetics is a science that has made amazing progress in the last decade, and biopsychologists are reaping the benefits. Modern genetic methods are now widely used in biopsychological research. Gene knockout and gene replacement techniques are two of them.

Gene Knockout Techniques

Gene knockout techniques are procedures for creating organisms that lack a particular gene under investigation. Once these subjects have been created, efforts are made to identify and then investigate any observable neural or behavioral anomalies they might possess. Mice (the favored mammalian subjects of genetic research), that are the products of gene knockout techniques are referred to as *knockout mice*. This term often makes me smile, as images of little mice with boxing gloves flit through my mind.

There has been much enthusiasm for gene knockout technology, and many gene knockout studies are in progress. However, behavioral studies of knockout mice may be more difficult to interpret than first anticipated (e.g., Crusio, 1996; Gerlai, 1996; Lathe, 1996). At least three warnings have been issued. First, most behavioral traits are influenced by the activities of many interacting genes; consequently, the elimination of a behavioral trait by knockout of a gene can at best identify only one small genetic contribution to the behavior. Second, elimination of a gene often influences the expression of other genes; as a result, any observed change in the behavior of knockout mice may be only indirectly related to the knocked-out gene (Mogil, Yu, & Basbaum, 2000). And, third, the expression of genes can be influenced by experience; thus, the effects of some gene knockouts may depend on the mouse's experience (Crabbe, Wahlsten, & Dudek, 1999).

Gene Replacement Techniques

It is now possible to replace one gene with another in mice (Tsien, 2000). **Gene replacement techniques** are creating some interesting possibilities for developmental research and therapy. For example, scientists have removed pathological genes from human cells and inserted them in mice (mice that contain the genetic material of another species are called **transgenic mice**). It is also possible to replace a gene with one that is identical except for the addition of

BrainScan

The research methods of biopsychology illustrate a psychological disorder suffered by many scientists. I call it "unabbreviaphobia"—the fear of leaving any term unabbreviated. To determine whether you have mastered Part One of this chapter and are ready for Part Two, supply the full term for each of the following abbreviations. The correct answers are provided on the next page. Before proceeding, review material related to your incorrect answers and omissions.

1. CT: _____
2. MRI: _____
3. PET: _____
4. 2-DG: _____
5. fMRI: _____
6. MEG: _____
7. EEG: _____

8. ERP: _____
9. AEP: _____
10. EMG: _____
11. EOG: _____
12. SCL: _____
13. SCR: _____
14. ECG: _____

15. EKG: _____
16. IP: _____
17. IM: _____
18. IV: _____
19. SC: _____
20. 6-OHDA: _____

a few bases that can act as a switch, turning the gene off or on in response to particular chemicals. These chemicals can be used to activate or suppress a gene at a particular point in development or in a particular brain structure (see Gingrich & Roder, 1998).

Gene knockout and gene replacement technologies are certainly amazing. How much they will teach us about psychological development and how useful they will be in the treatment of brain disorders remain to be determined.

Brain Scan answers: (1) computed tomography, (2) magnetic resonance imaging, (3) positron emission tomography, (4) 2-deoxyglucose, (5) functional MRI, (6) magnetoencephalography, (7) electroencephalogram, (8) event-related potential, (9) average evoked potential, (10) electromyogram, (11) electro-oculogram, (12) skin conductance level, (13) skin conductance response, (14) electrocardiogram, (15) electrocardiogram, (16) intraperitoneal, (17) intramuscular, (18) intravenous, (19) subcutaneous, (20) 6-hydroxydopamine.

PART TWO BEHAVIORAL RESEARCH METHODS OF BIOPSYCHOLOGY

We turn now from methods used by biopsychologists to study the nervous system to those that deal with the behavioral side of biopsychology. Because of the inherent invisibility of neural activity, the primary objective of the methods used in its investigation is to render the unobservable observable. In contrast, the major objectives of behavioral research methods are to control, to simplify, and to objectify.

A single set of procedures developed for the investigation of a particular behavioral phenomenon is commonly referred to as a **behavioral paradigm.** Each behavioral paradigm normally comprises a method for producing the behavioral phenomenon under investigation and a method for objectively measuring it.

There is an unfortunate tendency to underestimate both the critical role that effective behavioral paradigms play in the progress of neuroscience and the ingenuity and effort required to develop them (see Lederhendler & Schulkin, 2000). Perhaps this is a consequence of behavior's visibility—we all seem to undervalue the familiar. Do not make this mistake! Remember that behavior is the ultimate manifestation of nervous system activity. In the final analysis, the purpose of all neural activity is the production of behavior. Studying it is no simple matter.

5.6 | Neuropsychological Testing

A patient suspected of suffering from some sort of nervous system dysfunction is usually referred to a *neurologist*, who assesses simple sensory and motor functions. More subtle changes in perceptual, emotional, motivational, or cognitive functions are the domain of the *neuropsychologist.*

Because neuropsychological testing is so time consuming, it is typically prescribed for only a small portion of brain-damaged patients. This is unfortunate; the results of neuropsychological testing can help brain-damaged patients in three important ways: (1) by assisting in the diagnosis of neural disorders, particularly in cases in which brain imaging, EEG, and neurological testing have proved equivocal; (2) by serving as a basis for counseling and caring for the patients; or (3) by providing a basis for objectively evaluating the effectiveness of the treatment and the seriousness of its side effects.

Modern Approach to Neuropsychological Testing

The nature of neuropsychological testing has changed radically since the 1950s. Indeed, the dominant approach to psychological testing has evolved through three distinct phases: the *single-test approach,* the *standardized-test-battery approach,* and the modern *customized-test-battery approach.*

SINGLE-TEST APPROACH ■ Before the 1950s, the few existing neuropsychological tests were designed to detect the presence of brain damage; in particular, the goal of these early tests was to discriminate between patients with psychological problems resulting from structural brain damage and those with psychological problems resulting from functional, rather than structural, changes to the brain. This approach proved unsuccessful, in large part because no single test could be developed that would be sensitive to all the varied and complex psychological symptoms that could potentially occur in a brain-damaged patient.

STANDARDIZED-TEST-BATTERY APPROACH ■ The standardized-test-battery approach to neuropsychological testing grew out of the failures of the single-test approach, and by the 1960s, it was predominant. The objective stayed the same—to identify brain-damaged patients—but the testing involved standardized batteries of tests rather than a single test. The most widely used standardized test battery has been the *Halstead-Reitan Neuropsychological Test Battery.* The Halstead-Reitan is a collection of tests that tend to be performed poorly by brain-damaged patients in relation to other patients or healthy control subjects; the scores on each test are added together to form a single aggregate score. An aggregate score below the designated cutoff leads to a diagnosis of brain damage. The standardized-test-battery approach has proved only marginally successful; standardized test batteries discriminate effectively between neurological patients and healthy patients, but they are not so good at discriminating between neurological patients and psychiatric patients.

THE CUSTOMIZED-TEST-BATTERY APPROACH ■ The customized-test-battery approach began to be used routinely in a few elite neuropsychological research institutions in the 1960s. This approach proved highly successful in research, and it soon spread to clinical practice. It predominates today in both the research laboratory and the neurological ward (see Lezak, 1997; Strub & Black, 1997).

The objective of current neuropsychological testing is not merely to identify patients with brain damage; the objective is to characterize the nature of the psychological deficits of each brain-damaged patient. So how does the customized-test-battery approach to neuropsychological testing work? It usually begins in the same way for all patients: with a common battery of tests selected by the neuropsychologist to provide an indication of the general nature of the neuropsychological symptoms. Then, depending on the results of the common test battery, the neuropsychologist selects a series of tests customized to each patient in an effort to characterize in more detail the general symptoms revealed by the common battery. For example, if a patient were found to have a memory problem by the test battery, subsequent tests would include those designed to reveal the specific nature of the memory problem.

The tests used in the customized-test-battery approach differ in three respects from earlier tests. First, the newer tests are specifically designed to measure aspects of psychological function that have been spotlighted by modern theories and data. For example, modern theories, and the evidence on which they are based, suggest that the mechanisms of short-term and long-term memory are totally different; thus, the testing of patients with memory problems virtually always involves specific tests of both short-term and long-term memory. Second, the interpretation of the tests often does not rest entirely on how well the patient does; unlike early neuropsychological tests, currently used tests often require the neuropsychologist to assess the cognitive strategy that the patient employs in performing the test. Brain damage often changes the strategy that a neuropsychological patient uses to perform a test without lowering the overall score. Third, the customized-test-battery approach requires more skillful examination. Skill and knowledge are often required to select just the right battery of tests to expose a patient's deficits and to identify qualitative differences in cognitive strategy.

■ Tests of the Common Neuropsychological Test Battery

Because the customized-test-battery approach to neuropsychological testing typically involves two phases—a battery of general tests given to all patients followed by a series of specific tests customized to each patient—the following examples of neurological tests are presented in two subsections. First are some tests that are often administered as part of the initial common test battery, and second are some tests that might be used by a neuropsychologist to investigate in more depth particular problems revealed by the common battery.

INTELLIGENCE ■ Although the overall *intelligence quotient* (IQ) is a notoriously poor measure of brain damage, a test of general intelligence is nearly always included in the battery of neuropsychological tests routinely given to all patients. Many neuropsychological assessments begin with the **Wechsler Adult Intelligence Scale (WAIS).** This is because knowing a patient's IQ can help the neuropsychologist interpret the results of other tests. Also, a skilled neuropsychologist can sometimes draw inferences about a patient's neuropsychological dysfunction from the pattern of deficits on the various subtests of the WAIS. For example, low scores on subtests of verbal ability tend to be associated with left hemisphere damage, whereas right hemisphere damage tends to reduce scores on performance subtests. The 11 subtests of the WAIS are illustrated in Table 5.1 on page 124.

MEMORY ■ One weakness of the WAIS is that it often fails to detect memory deficits, despite including two subtests specifically designed to test memory function.

Table 5.1 The 11 Subtests of the Wechsler Adult Intelligence Scale (WAIS)

VERBAL SUBTESTS

Information Read to the subject are 29 questions of general information—for example "Who is the president of the United States?"

Digit-span Three digits are read to the subject at 1-second intervals, and the subject is asked to repeat them in the same order. Two trials are given at three digits, four digits, five digits, and so on until the subject fails both trials at one level.

Vocabulary The subject is asked to define a list of 35 words that range in difficulty.

Arithmetic The subject is presented with 14 arithmetic questions and must answer them without the benefit of pencil and paper.

Comprehension The subject is asked 16 questions that test the ability to understand general principles—for example, "Why should people vote?"

Similarities The subject is presented with pairs of items and is asked to explain how the items in each pair are similar.

PERFORMANCE SUBTESTS

Picture-completion The subject must identify the important part missing from 20 drawings—for example, a drawing of a squirrel with no tail.

Picture-arrangement The subject is presented with 10 sets of cartoon drawings and is asked to arrange each set so it will tell a sensible story.

Block-design The subject is presented with blocks that are red on two sides, white on two sides, and half red and half white on the other two. The subject is shown pictures of nine patterns and is asked to duplicate them by arranging the blocks appropriately.

Object-assembly The subject is asked to put together the pieces of four simple jigsaw puzzles to form familiar objects.

Digit-symbol The subject is presented with a key that matches each of a series of symbols with a different digit. On the same page is a series of digits, and the subject is given 90 seconds to write the correct symbol, according to the key, next to as many digits as possible.

The information subtest of the WAIS assesses memory for general knowledge (e.g., "Who is Queen Elizabeth?"), and the subtest focusing on **digit span** identifies the longest sequence of random digits that can be correctly repeated 50% of the time by the patient—most people have a digit span of 7. However, these two forms of memory are among the least likely to be disrupted by brain damage—patients with seriously disturbed memories often show no deficits on either the information or digit-span subtests of the WAIS. Be that as it may, memory problems rarely escape unnoticed. If present, they may be detected by other tests that are included in the common test battery; they may be noticed by the neuropsychologist during discussions with the patient; or they may be reported by the patient or the family of the patient.

LANGUAGE ■ If a neuropsychological patient has taken the WAIS, deficits in the use of language can be inferred from a low aggregate score on the six verbal subtests. If the WAIS has not been taken, patients can be quickly screened for language-related deficits with the **token test.** Twenty tokens of two different shapes (squares and circles), two different sizes (large and small), and five different colors (white, black, yellow, green, and red) are placed on a table in front of the subject. The test begins with the examiner reading simple instructions—for example, "Touch a red square"—and the subject trying to follow them. Then, the test progresses to more difficult instructions, such as "Touch the small, red circle and then the large, green square." Finally, the subject is asked to read the instructions aloud and follow them.

LANGUAGE LATERALIZATION ■ It is usual for one hemisphere to participate more than the other in language-related activities. In most people, the left hemisphere is dominant for language, but in some, the right hemisphere is dominant. A test of language lateralization is often included in the common test because knowing which hemisphere is dominant for language is often useful in interpreting the results of other tests. Furthermore, a test of language lateralization is virtually always given to patients before any surgery that might encroach on the cortical language areas. The results are used to plan the surgery, trying to avoid the language areas if possible.

There are two widely used tests of language lateralization. The sodium amytal test (Wada, 1949) is one, and the dichotic listening test (Kimura, 1973) is the other.

The **sodium amytal test** involves injecting the anesthetic sodium amytal into either the left or right carotid artery in the neck. This temporarily anesthetizes the *ipsilateral* (same-side) hemisphere while leaving the *contralateral* (opposite-side) hemisphere largely unaffected. Several tests of language function are quickly administered while the ipsilateral hemisphere is anesthetized. Later, the process is repeated for the other side of the brain. When the injection is on the side dominant for language, the patient is completely mute for about 2 minutes. When the injection is on the nondominant side, there are only a few minor speech problems. Because the sodium amytal test is invasive, it can be administered only for medical reasons—usually to determine the dominant language hemisphere prior to brain surgery.

In the standard version of the **dichotic listening test,** sequences of spoken digits are presented to subjects through stereo headphones. Three digits are presented to one ear at the same time that three different digits are presented to the other ear. Then the subjects are asked to report as many of the six digits as they can. Kimura found that subjects correctly report more of the digits heard by the ear contralateral to their dominant hemisphere for language, as determined by the sodium amytal test.

Tests of Specific Neuropsychological Function

Following analysis of the results of a neuropsychological patient's performance on the common test battery, the neuropsychologist selects a series of specific tests to clarify the nature of the general problems exposed by the common battery. There are thousands of tests that might be selected. This section describes a few of them and mentions some of the considerations that might influence their selection.

MEMORY ■ Following the discovery of a memory impairment by the common test battery, at least four fundamental questions about the memory impairment must be answered: (1) Does the memory impairment involve *short-term memory, long-term memory,* or both? (2) Are any deficits in long-term memory *anterograde* (affecting the retention of things learned after the damage), *retrograde* (affecting the retention of things learned before the damage), or both? (3) Do any deficits in long-term memory involve *semantic memory* (memory for knowledge of the world) or *episodic memory* (memory for personal experiences)? (4) Are any deficits in long-term memory deficits of *explicit memory* (memories of which the patient is aware and can thus express verbally), *implicit memory* (memories that are demonstrated by the improved performance of the patient without the patient being conscious of them), or both?

Many amnesic patients display severe deficits in explicit memory with no deficits at all in implicit memory (Curran & Schacter, 1997). **Repetition priming tests** have proven instrumental in the assessment and study of this pattern. Patients are first shown a list of words and asked to study them; they are not asked to remember them. Then, at a later time, they are asked to complete a list of word fragments, many of which are fragments of words from the initial list. For example, if "purple" had been in the initial test, "pu __ p __ __" could be one of the test word fragments. Amnesic patients often complete the fragments as well as healthy control subjects. But—and this is the really important part—they often have no conscious memory of any of the words in the initial list or even of ever having seen the list. In other words, they display good implicit memory of experiences without explicit memories of them.

LANGUAGE ■ If a neuropsychological patient turns out to have language-related deficits on the common test battery, a complex series of tests is administered to clarify the nature of the problem. For example, if there is a speech problem, there may be one of three fundamentally different problems: problems of *phonology* (the rules governing the sounds of the language), problems of *syntax* (the grammar of the language), or problems of *se-* *mantics* (the meanings of the language). Because brain-damaged patients may have one of these problems but not the others, it is imperative that the testing of all neuropsychological patients with speech problems include tests of each of these three capacities (Saffran, 1997).

Reading aloud can be disrupted in different ways by brain damage, and follow-up tests must be employed that can differentiate between the different patterns of disruption (Coslett, 1997). Some *dyslexic* patients (those with reading problems) remember the rules of pronunciation but have difficulties pronouncing words that do not follow rules but must be pronounced from memory of the specific words (e.g., *come* and *tongue*). Other dyslexic patients pronounce simple familiar words based on memory but have lost the ability to apply the rules of pronunciation—they cannot pronounce nonwords such as *trapple* or *fleeming*.

FRONTAL-LOBE FUNCTION ■ Injuries to the frontal lobes are common, and the **Wisconsin Card Sorting Test** (see Figure 5.22) is a component of many customized

FIGURE 5.22 The Wisconsin Card Sorting Test. This woman is just starting the test. In front of which of the four stimulus cards should she place her first card? She must guess until she can learn which principle—color, shape, or number—should guide her sorting. After she has placed a card, she is told whether or not her placement is correct.

test batteries because it is sensitive to frontal-lobe damage (Kimberg, D'Esposito, & Farah, 1997). On each Wisconsin card is either one symbol or two, three, or four identical symbols. The symbols are all either triangles, stars, circles, or crosses; and they are all either red, green, yellow, or blue. At the beginning of the test, the patient is confronted with four stimulus cards that differ from one another in form, color, and number. The task is to correctly sort cards from a deck into piles in front of the stimulus cards. However, the patient does not know whether to sort by form, by color, or by number. The patient begins by guessing and is told after each card has been sorted whether it was sorted correctly or incorrectly. At first, the task is to learn to sort by color. But as

soon as the patient makes several consecutive correct responses, the sorting principle is changed to shape or number without any indication other than the fact that responses based on color become incorrect. Thereafter, each time a new sorting principle is learned, the principle is changed.

Patients with damage to their frontal lobes often continue to sort on the basis of one sorting principle for 100 or more trials after it has become incorrect. They seem to have great difficulty learning and remembering that previously appropriate guidelines for effective behavior are no longer appropriate, a problem called *perseveration.*

5.7 Behavioral Methods of Cognitive Neuroscience

Cognitive neuroscience is predicated on two related assumptions (see Sarter, Berntson, & Cacioppo, 1996). The first premise is that each complex cognitive process results from the combined activity of simple cognitive processes called **constituent cognitive processes.** The second premise is that each constituent cognitive process is mediated by neural activity in a particular area of the brain. One of the main goals of cognitive neuroscience is to identify the parts of the brain that mediate various constituent cognitive processes.

With the central role played by PET and fMRI in cutting-edge cognitive neuroscience research, the **paired-image subtraction technique** has become one of the key behavioral research methods in cognitive neuroscience research (see Posner & Raichle, 1994). Let me illustrate this technique with an example from a PET study of single-word processing by Petersen and colleagues (1988). Petersen and his colleagues were interested in locating the parts of the brain that enable a subject to make a word association (to respond to a printed word by saying a related word). You might think this would be an easy task to accomplish by having a subject perform a word-association task while a PET image of the subject's brain is recorded. The problem with this approach is that many parts of the brain that would be active during the test period would have nothing to do with the constituent cognitive process of forming a word association; much of the activity recorded would be associated with other processes such as seeing the words, reading the words, and speaking. The paired-image subtraction technique was developed to deal with this problem.

The paired-image subtraction technique involves obtaining PET or fMRI images during several different

cognitive tasks. Ideally, the tasks are designed so that pairs of them differ from each other in terms of only a single constituent cognitive process. Then, the brain activity associated with that process can be estimated by subtracting the activity in the image associated with one of the two tasks from the activity in the image associated with the other. For example, in one of the tasks in the study by Petersen and colleagues, subjects spent a minute reading aloud printed nouns as they appeared on a screen; in another, they observed the same nouns on the screen but responded to each of them by saying aloud an associated verb (e.g., *truck—drive*). Then, Petersen and his colleagues subtracted the activity in the images that they recorded during the two tasks to obtain a *difference image.* The difference image illustrated the areas of the brain that were specifically involved in the constituent cognitive process of forming the word association; the activity associated with fixating on the screen, seeing the nouns, saying the words, and so on was eliminated by the subtraction (see Figure 5.23).

Another problem involved in using PET and fMRI to locate constituent cognitive processes is the *noise* associated with random cerebral events that occur during the test—for example, thinking about a sudden pang of hunger, noticing a fly on the screen, or wondering whether the test will last much longer. The noise created by such events can be significantly reduced with a technique discussed earlier in this chapter: *signal averaging.* By averaging the difference images obtained from repetitions of the same tests, the researchers can greatly increase the *signal-to-noise ratio.* It is standard practice to average the images obtained from several subjects; the resulting mean (averaged) difference image emphasizes areas of activity that are com-

FIGURE 5.23 The paired-image subtraction technique, which is commonly employed in cognitive neuroscience. Here we see that the brain of a subject is generally active when the subject looks at a flickering checkerboard pattern (visual stimulation condition). However, if the activity that occurred when the subject stared at a blank screen (control situation) is subtracted, it becomes apparent that the perception of the flashing checkerboard pattern was associated with an increase in activity that was largely restricted to the occipital lobe. The individual difference images of five subjects were averaged to produce the mean difference image. (PET scans courtesy of Marcus Raichle, Mallinckrodt Institute of Radiology, Washington University Medical Center.)

mon to most of the subjects and deemphasizes areas of activity that are peculiar to a few of them (see Figure 5.23). However, this averaging procedure can lead to a serious problem: If two subjects had specific but different patterns of cortical activity, the averaged image would reveal little about either.

5.8 Biopsychological Paradigms of Animal Behavior

Noteworthy examples of the behavioral paradigms used to study the biopsychology of laboratory species are provided here under three headings: (1) paradigms for the assessment of species-common behaviors, (2) traditional conditioning paradigms, and (3) seminatural animal learning paradigms. In each case, the focus is on methods used to study the behavior of the laboratory rat, the most common subject of biopsychological research.

Paradigms for Assessment of Species-Common Behaviors

Many of the behavioral paradigms that are used in biopsychological research are used to study species-common behaviors. **Species-common behaviors** are those that are displayed by virtually all members of a species, or at least by all those of the same age and sex. Commonly studied species-common behaviors include grooming, swimming, eating, drinking, copulating, fighting, and nest building. Described here are the open-field test, tests of aggressive and defensive behavior, and tests of sexual behavior.

OPEN-FIELD TEST ■ In the **open-field test,** the subject is placed in a large, barren chamber, and its activity is recorded. It is usual to measure general activity either with an automated activity recorder or by drawing lines on the floor of the chamber and counting the number of line-crossings during the test. It is also common in the open-field test to count the number of *boluses* (pieces of excrement) that were dropped by an animal during the test. Low activity scores and high bolus counts are frequently used as indicators of fearfulness. Fearful rats are highly **thigmotaxic;** that is, they rarely venture away from the walls of the test chamber and rarely engage in such activities as rearing and grooming. Rats are often fearful when they are first placed in a strange open field, but this fearfulness usually declines with repeated exposure to the same open field.

TESTS OF AGGRESSIVE AND DEFENSIVE BEHAV-IOR ■ Typical patterns of aggressive and defensive behavior can be observed and measured during combative encounters between the dominant male rat of an established colony and a smaller male intruder (see Blanchard & Blanchard, 1988). This is called the **colony–intruder paradigm.** The behaviors of the dominant male are considered to be aggressive and those of the hapless intruder defensive. The dominant male of the colony (the *alpha male*) moves sideways toward the intruder, with its hair erect. When it nears the intruder, it tries to push the intruder off balance and to deliver bites to its back and flanks. The defender tries to protect its back and flanks by rearing up on its hind legs and pushing the attacker away with its forepaws or by rolling onto its back. Thus, piloerection, lateral approach, and flank- and back-biting indicate conspecific aggression in the rat; freezing, boxing (rearing and pushing away), and rolling over indicate defensiveness.

Some tests of rat defensive behavior assess reactivity to the experimenter rather than to another rat. For example, it is common to rate the resistance of a rat to being picked up—no resistance being the lowest category and biting the highest—and to use the score as one measure of defensiveness (Kalynchuk et al., 1997).

The **elevated plus maze,** a four-armed, plus-sign-shaped maze that is typically mounted 50 centimeters above the floor, is a test of defensiveness that is commonly used to study in rats the *anxiolytic* (anxiety-reducing) effects of drugs. Two of the arms of the maze have sides, and two do not. The measure of defensiveness, or anxiety, is the proportion of time the rats spend in the protected closed arms rather than on the exposed arms. Many established anxiolytic drugs significantly increase the proportion of time that rats spend on the open arms (see Pellow et al., 1985), and, conversely, many new drugs that prove to be effective in reducing rats' defensiveness on the maze often turn out to be effective in the treatment of human anxiety.

TESTS OF SEXUAL BEHAVIOR ■ Most attempts to study the physiological bases of rat sexual behavior have focused on the copulatory act itself. The male mounts the female from behind and clasps her hindquarters. If the female is receptive, she responds by assuming the **lordosis** posture; that is, she sticks her hindquarters in the air, she bends her back in a U, and she deflects her tail to the side. During some mounts, the male inserts his penis into the female's vagina; this act is called **intromission.** After intromission, the male dismounts by jumping backwards. He then returns a few seconds later to mount and intromit once again. Following about 10 such cycles of mounting, intromitting, and dismounting, the male mounts, intromits, and **ejaculates** (ejects his sperm).

Three common measures of male rat sexual behavior are the number of mounts required to achieve intromission, the number of intromissions required to achieve ejaculation, and the interval between ejaculation and the reinitiation of mounting. The most common measure of female rat sexual behavior is the **lordosis quotient** (the proportion of mounts that elicit lordosis).

■ Traditional Conditioning Paradigms

Learning paradigms play a major role in biopsychological research for three reasons. The first is that learning is a phenomenon of primary interest to psychologists. The second is that learning paradigms provide an effective technology for producing and controlling animal behavior. Because animals cannot follow instructions from the experimenter, it is often necessary to train them to behave in a fashion consistent with the goals of the experiment. The third reason is that it is possible to infer much about the sensory, motor, motivational, and cognitive state of an animal from its ability to learn and perform various responses.

If you have taken a previous course in psychology, you will likely be familiar with the Pavlovian and operant conditioning paradigms. In the **Pavlovian conditioning paradigm,** the experimenter pairs an initially neutral stimulus called a *conditional stimulus* (e.g., a tone or a light) with an *unconditional stimulus* (e.g., meat powder)—a stimulus that elicits an *unconditional* (reflexive) *response* (e.g., salivation). As a result of these pairings, the conditional stimulus eventually acquires the capacity, when administered alone, to elicit a *conditional response* (e.g., salivation)—a response that is often, but not always, similar to the unconditional response.

In the **operant conditioning paradigm,** the rate at which a particular voluntary response (such as a lever press) is emitted is increased by *reinforcement* or decreased by *punishment.* One of the most widely used operant conditioning paradigms in biopsychology is the self-stimulation paradigm. In the **self-stimulation paradigm,** animals press a lever to deliver electrical stimulation to particular sites in their own brains; those structures in the brain that support self-stimulation are often called *pleasure centers.*

■ Seminatural Animal Learning Paradigms

In addition to Pavlovian and operant conditioning paradigms, biopsychologists use animal learning paradigms that have been specifically designed to mimic situations that an animal might encounter in its natural environment (see Gerlai & Clayton, 1999). Development of these paradigms stemmed in part from the reasonable assumption that forms of learning tending to benefit an animal's survival in the wild are likely to be more highly developed and more directly related to innate neural mechanisms. The following are four common seminatural learning paradigms: the conditioned taste aversion, radial arm maze, Morris water maze, and conditioned defensive burying.

CONDITIONED TASTE AVERSION ■ A **conditioned taste aversion** is the aversion that develops to tastes of food whose consumption has been followed by illness (see Garcia & Koelling, 1966). In the standard conditioned taste aversion experiment, rats receive an *emetic* (a nausea-inducing drug) after they consume a food with an unfamiliar taste. On the basis of this single conditioning trial, the rats learn to avoid the taste.

The ability of rats to readily learn the relationship between a particular taste and subsequent illness unquestionably increases their chances of survival in their natural environment, where potentially edible substances are not routinely screened by government agencies. Rats and many other animals are *neophobic* (afraid of new things); thus, when they first encounter a new food, they consume it in only small quantities. If they subsequently become ill, they will not consume it again. Conditioned aversions also develop to familiar tastes, but these typically require more than a single trial to be learned.

Humans also develop conditioned taste aversions. Cancer patients have been reported to develop aversions to foods consumed before nausea-inducing chemotherapy (Bernstein & Webster, 1980). Many of you will be able to testify on the basis of personal experience about the effectiveness of conditioned taste aversions. I still have vivid memories of a long-ago batch of laboratory punch that I overzealously consumed after eating two pieces of blueberry pie. But that is another story—albeit a particularly colorful one.

The following words communicate just how much the study of conditioned taste aversion changed the thinking of psychologists about conditioning:

The 1950s was a time of sock hops, sodas at Al's, crewcuts, and drive-in movies. In the animal-behavior laboratory, it was a time of lever presses, key pecks, and shuttles made in response to flashing lights, tones, and geometric patterns. Then, along came rock 'n' roll and the discovery of conditioned taste aversion: Things have not been the same since.

The discovery of conditioned taste aversion challenged three widely accepted principles of learning (see Revusky & Garcia, 1970) that had grown out of research on traditional operant and Pavlovian conditioning paradigms. First, it challenged the view that animal conditioning is always a gradual step-by-step process; robust taste aversions can be established in only a single trial. Second, it showed that *temporal contiguity* is not essential for conditioning; rats acquire taste aversions even when they do not become ill until several hours after eating. Third, it challenged the *principle of equipotentiality*—the view that conditioning proceeds in basically the same manner regardless of the particular stimuli and responses under investigation. Rats appear to have evolved to read-

ily learn associations between tastes and illness; it is only with great difficulty that they learn relations between the color of food and nausea or between taste and footshock.

RADIAL ARM MAZE ■ The radial arm maze taps the well-developed spatial abilities of rodents. The survival of rats in the wild depends on their ability to navigate quickly and accurately through their environment and to learn which locations in it are likely to contain food and water. This task is much more complex for a rodent than it is for us. Most of us obtain food from locations where the supply is continually replenished; we go to the market confident that we will find enough food to satisfy our needs. In contrast, the foraging rat must learn, and retain, a complex pattern of spatially coded details. It must not only learn where morsels of food are likely to be found but must also remember which of these sites it has recently stripped of their booty so as not to revisit them too soon. Designed by Olton and Samuelson (1976) to study these spatial abilities, the **radial arm maze** (see Figure 5.24) is an array of arms—usually eight or more—radiating from a central starting area. At the end of each arm is a food cup, which may or may not be baited, depending on the purpose of the experiment.

In one version of the radial arm maze paradigm, rats are placed each day in a maze that has the same arms baited each day. After a few days of experience, rats rarely visit unbaited arms at all, and they rarely visit baited arms more than once in the same day—even when control procedures make it impossible for them to recognize odors left during previous visits to an arm or to make their visits in a systematic sequence. Because the arms are identical, rats must orient themselves in the maze with reference to external room cues; thus, their performance can be disrupted by rotation of the maze or by changes in the appearance of the room.

FIGURE 5.24   A radial arm maze.

FIGURE 5.25 A rat burying a test object from which it has just received a single mild shock. (Photograph by Jack Wong.)

MORRIS WATER MAZE ■ Another seminatural learning paradigm that has been designed to study the spatial abilities of rats is the **Morris water maze** (Morris, 1981). The rats are placed in a circular, featureless pool of cool milky water, in which they must swim until they discover the escape platform—which is invisible just beneath the surface of the water. The rats are allowed to rest on the platform before being returned to the water for another trial. Despite the fact that the starting point is varied from trial to trial, the rats learn after only a few trials to swim directly to the platform, presumably by using spatial cues from the room as a reference. The Morris water maze has proved extremely useful for assessing the navigational skills of lesioned or drugged animals (e.g., Kolb, 1989).

CONDITIONED DEFENSIVE BURYING ■ Yet another seminatural learning paradigm that is useful in biopsychological research is conditioned defensive burying (e.g., Pinel & Mana, 1989; Pinel & Treit, 1978). In studies of **conditioned defensive burying,** rats receive a single aversive stimulus (e.g., a shock, airblast, or noxious odor) from an object mounted on the wall of the chamber just above the floor, which is littered with bedding material. After a single trial, almost every rat learns that the test ob-

ject is a threat and responds by spraying bedding material at the test object with its head and forepaws (see Figure 5.25). Antianxiety drugs reduce the amount of conditioned defensive burying, and thus the paradigm is used to study the neurochemistry of anxiety (e.g., Treit, 1987).

Before moving on to the next chapter, you need to appreciate that to be effective these research methods must be used together. Seldom, if ever, is an important biopsychological issue resolved by a single set of methods. The reason for this is that neither the methods used to manipulate the brain nor the methods used to assess the behavioral consequences of these manipulations are totally selective; there are no methods of manipulating the brain that change only a single aspect of brain function, and there are no measures of behavior that reflect only a single psychological process. Accordingly, lines of research that use a single set of methods can often be interpreted in more than one way and thus cannot provide unequivocal evidence for any one interpretation. Typically, important research questions are resolved only when several methods are brought to bear on a single problem. This approach, as you learned in Chapter 1, is called *converging operations.*

Themes Revisited

This chapter introduced you to the two kinds of research methods used by biopsychologists: methods of studying the brain and methods of studying behavior. In the descriptions of these methods, all four of the main themes of the book were apparent.

The clinical implications theme was most evident in the chapter-opening case of Professor P. This case alerted you to the fact that many of the methods used by biopsychologists to study the human brain are also used clinically, in either diagnosis or treatment. In addition, the clinical implications theme was repeatedly emphasized during the discussion of neuropsychological methods; all neuropsychological methods have direct clinical implications because the subjects of neuropsychological research are patients with brain damage.

Predictably, the cognitive neuroscience theme emerged repeatedly in the two sections dealing with the methods of that field. In contrast, the evolutionary perspective theme was evident only in the subsection that discussed seminatural paradigms of animal learning.

The thinking-about-biopsychology theme came up frequently in the chapter. Because the subject matter of biopsychology is so complex, all biopsychological research methods require thoughtful application. It is very important for both scientists and consumers of science to understand the weaknesses, as well as the strengths, of the various methods.

ON THE CD
Looking for more information about the topics in this chapter? For recommended additional readings, see Hard Copy for Chapter 5.

Log On

- **http://www.pbs.org/wgbh/aso/tryit/brain/#** "Probe the Brain" gives you a chance to experience how electrical stimulation is used to map the human motor cortex.

- **http://www.med.harvard.edu/AANLIB/hms1.html** This site has one of the best introductions to brain-imaging techniques; the Neuroimaging Primer includes links to the Whole Brain Atlas.

- **http://coglab.psych.purdue.edu/** If you are interested in the cognitive side of biopsychology, this site allows you to assess your own memory, perception, language, and other cognitive skills.

Think about It

1. The current rate of progress in the development of new and better brain scanning devices will soon render behavioral tests of brain damage obsolete. Discuss.

2. You are taking a physiological psychology course, and your laboratory instructor gives you two rats: one rat with a lesion in an unknown structure and one normal rat. How would you test the rats to determine which one has the lesion? How would your approach differ from that you might use to test a human patient suspected of having brain damage?

3. The search for the neural mechanisms of learning should focus on forms of learning necessary for survival in the wild. Discuss.

4. All patients should complete a battery of neuropsychological tests both before and after neurosurgery. Discuss.

ON THE CD
Studying for an exam? Try the Practice Tests for Chapter 5.

Key Terms

Alpha waves (p. 110)
Aspiration (p. 114)
Autoradiography (p. 119)
Behavioral paradigm (p. 122)
Bregma (p. 114)
Cannula (p. 118)
Cerebral angiography (p. 106)
Cerebral dialysis (p. 119)
Cognitive neuroscience (p. 126)
Colony–intruder paradigm (p. 128)
Computed tomography (CT) (p. 106)
Conditioned defensive burying (p. 130)
Conditioned taste aversion (p. 129)
Constituent cognitive processes (p. 126)
Contrast X-ray techniques (p. 106)
Cryogenic blockade (p. 115)
2-deoxyglucose (2-DG) (p. 107)
Dichotic listening test (p. 124)
Digit span (p. 124)

Ejaculates (p. 128)
Electrocardiogram (ECG or EKG) (p. 113)
Electroencephalography (p. 110)
Electromyography (p. 112)
Electrooculography (p. 112)
Elevated plus maze (p. 128)
Event-related potentials (ERPs) (p. 111)
Far-field potentials (p. 111)
Functional MRI (fMRI) (p. 109)
Gene knockout techniques (p. 121)
Gene replacement techniques (p. 121)
Hypertension (p. 114)
Immunocytochemistry (p. 120)
In situ hybridization (p. 120)
Intromission (p. 128)
Lordosis (p. 128)
Lordosis quotient (p. 128)
Magnetic resonance imaging (MRI) (p. 107)

Magnetoencephalography (MEG) (p. 109)
Morris water maze (p. 130)
Neurotoxins (p. 118)
Open-field test (p. 127)
Operant conditioning paradigm (p. 128)
P300 wave (p. 111)
Paired-image subtraction technique (p. 126)
Pavlovian conditioning paradigm (p. 128)
Plethysmography (p. 114)
Positron emission tomography (PET) (p. 107)
Radial arm maze (p. 129)
Repetition priming tests (p. 125)
Self-stimulation paradigm (p. 128)
Sensory evoked potential (p. 111)
Signal averaging (p. 111)
Skin conductance level (SCL) (p. 113)

Skin conductance response (SCR) (p. 113)
Sodium amytal test (p. 124)
Spatial resolution (p. 107)
Species-common behaviors (p. 127)
Stereotaxic atlas (p. 114)
Stereotaxic instrument (p. 114)
Temporal resolution (p. 109)
Thigmotaxic (p. 127)
Token test (p. 124)
Transgenic mice (p. 121)
Wechsler Adult Intelligence Scale (WAIS) (p. 123)
Wisconsin Card Sorting Test (p. 125)

ON THE CD
Need some help studying the key terms for this chapter? Check out the electronic flash cards for Chapter 5.

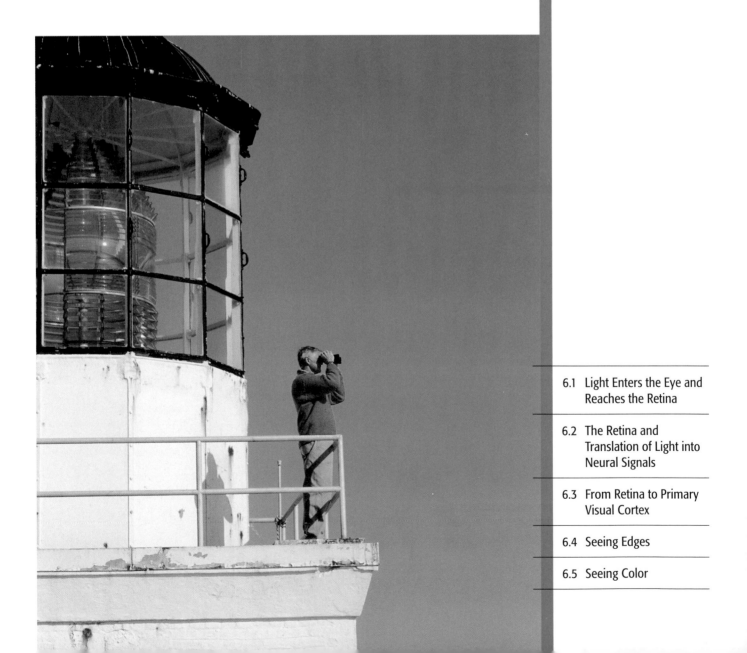

The Visual System

From Your Eyes to Your Cortex

This chapter is about the visual system. Most people think that their visual system has evolved to respond as accurately as possible to the patterns of light that enter their eyes. They recognize the obvious limitations in their visual system's accuracy, of course; and they appreciate those curious instances, termed *visual illusions,* in which it is "tricked" into seeing things the way they aren't. But such shortcomings are generally regarded as minor imperfections in a system that responds as faithfully as possible to the external world.

Despite its intuitive appeal, this way of thinking about the visual system is wrong. The visual system does not produce an accurate internal copy of the external world. It does much more. From the tiny, distorted, upside-down, two-dimensional retinal images projected upon the visual receptors lining the backs of the eyes, the visual system creates an accurate, richly detailed, three-dimensional perception that is—and this is the really important part—in some respects even better than the external reality from which it was created.

Regardless of what you may have heard to the contrary, "what you see is not necessarily what you get." One of my primary goals in this chapter is to help you recognize and appreciate the inherent creativity of your own visual system.

This chapter is composed of five sections. The first three sections take you on a journey from the external visual world to the visual receptors of the retina and from there over the major visual pathway to the primary visual cortex. The last two sections describe how the neurons of this pathway mediate the perception of two particularly important features of the visual world: edges and color.

You will learn in this chapter that understanding the visual system requires the integration of two types of research: (1) research that probes the visual system with sophisticated neuroanatomical, neurochemical, and neurophysiological techniques; and (2) research that focuses on the assessment of what we see. Both types of research receive substantial coverage in this chapter, but it is the second type that provides you with a unique educational opportunity: the opportunity to participate in the very research you are studying. Throughout this chapter, you will be encouraged to participate in demonstrations designed to give you a taste of the excitement of scientific discovery and to illustrate the relevance of what you are learning in this text to life outside its pages.

Before you begin the first section of the chapter, I'd like you to consider an interesting clinical case. Have you ever wondered whether one person's subjective experiences are like those of others? This case provides evidence that at least some of them are. It was reported by Whitman Richards (1971), and his subject was Mrs. Richards. Mrs. Richards suffered from migraine headaches, and like many migraine sufferers, she often experienced visual displays, called *fortification illusions,* prior to her attacks.

The Case of Mrs. Richards: Fortification Illusions and the Astronomer

Each fortification illusion began with a gray area of blindness near the center of her visual field—see Figure 6.1. During the next few minutes, the gray area would begin to expand into a horseshoe shape, with a zigzag pattern of flickering lines at its advancing edge. It normally took about 20

An attack began, often when reading, as a gray area of blindness near the center of the visual field.

Over the next 20 minutes, the gray area assumed a horseshoe shape and expanded into the periphery, at which point the headache began.

FIGURE 6.1   The fortification illusions associated with migraine headaches.

minutes for the lines and the trailing area of blindness to reach the periphery of her visual field. At this point, her headache would usually begin.

Because the illusion expanded so slowly, Mrs. Richards was able to stare at a point on the center of a blank sheet of paper and periodically trace on the sheet the details of her illusion. This method made it apparent that the lines became thicker and the expansion of the area of blindness occurred faster as the illusion spread into the periphery.

The features of fortification illusions are quite interesting, but they are not the most intriguing aspect of this case. Dr. Richards discovered that a similar set of drawings was published in 1870 by the famous British astronomer George Biddell Airy, and they were virtually identical to those done by Mrs. Richards. (By the way, the illusions got their name because their advancing edges reminded people of the plans for a fortification.)

We will return to fortification illusions after we have learned a bit about the visual system. At that point, you will be able to appreciate the significance of their features.

6.1 | Light Enters the Eye and Reaches the Retina

Everybody knows that cats, owls, and other nocturnal animals can see in the dark. Right? Wrong! Some animals have special adaptations that allow them to see under very dim illumination, but no animal can see in complete darkness. The light reflected into your eyes from the objects around you is the basis for your ability to see them; if there is no light, there is no vision.

You may recall from high-school physics that light can be thought of in two different ways: as discrete particles of energy, called *photons,* traveling through space at about 300,000 kilometers (186,000 miles) per second or as waves of energy. Both theories are useful; in some ways light behaves like a particle, and in others it behaves like a wave. Physicists have learned to live with this nagging inconsistency, and we must do the same.

Light is sometimes defined as waves of electromagnetic energy that are between 380 and 760 nanometers (billionths of a meter) in length (see Figure 6.2). There is nothing special about these wavelengths except that the human visual system responds to them. In fact, some animals can see wavelengths that we cannot. For example, rattlesnakes can see *infrared waves,* which are too long for humans to see; as a result, they can see warm-blooded prey in what for us would be complete darkness. Accordingly, if I were writing this book for rattlesnakes, I would be forced to provide another, equally arbitrary, definition of light.

Wavelength and intensity are two properties of light that are of particular interest—wavelength because it plays an important role in the perception of color, and

FIGURE 6.2 The electromagnetic spectrum and the colors associated with the wavelengths that are visible to humans.

intensity because it plays an important role in the perception of brightness. The concepts of *wavelength* and *color* are typically regarded as interchangeable, and so are *intensity* and *brightness*. For example, we commonly refer to an intense light with a wavelength of 700 nanometers as being a bright red light (see Figure 6.2), when in fact it is our perception of the light, not the light itself, that is bright and red. I know that these distinctions may seem trivial to you now, but by the end of the chapter you will appreciate their importance.

The amount of light reaching the retinas is regulated by the donut-shaped bands of contractile tissue, the *irises,* which give our eyes their characteristic color (see Figure 6.3). Light enters the eye through the *pupil,* the hole in the iris. The adjustment of pupil size in response to changes in illumination represents a compromise between **sensitivity** (the ability to detect the presence of dimly lit objects) and **acuity** (the ability to see the details of objects). When the level of illumination is high and sensitivity is thus not important, the visual system takes advantage of the situation by constricting the pupils. When the pupils are constricted, the image falling on each retina is sharper and there is a greater *depth of focus;* that is, a greater range of depths are simultaneously kept in focus on the retinas. However, when the level of illumination is too low to adequately activate the receptors,

FIGURE 6.3   The human eye. Light enters the eye through the pupil, whose size is regulated by the iris. The iris gives the eye its characteristic color—blue, brown, or other.

the pupils dilate to let in more light, thereby sacrificing acuity and depth of focus.

Behind each pupil is a *lens,* which focuses incoming light on the retina (see Figure 6.4). When we direct our gaze at something near, the tension on the ligaments

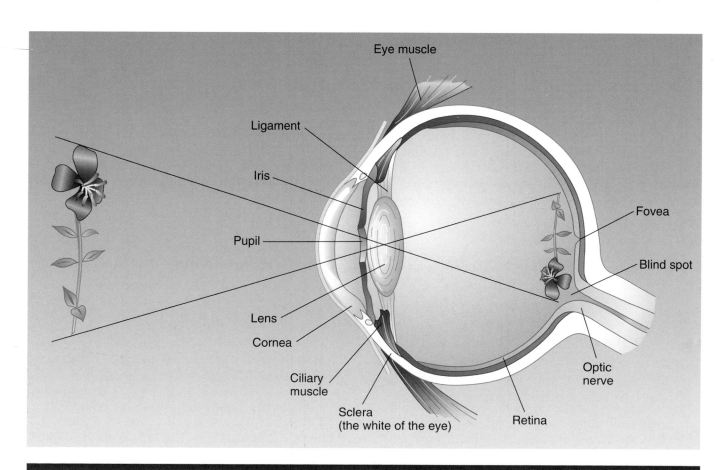

FIGURE 6.4   A diagram of the human eye.

holding each lens in place is reduced by the contraction of the **ciliary muscles,** and the lens assumes its natural cylindrical shape. (Be alert here: The fact that the tension on the lens is reduced by muscle contraction is counter-intuitive.) This increases the ability of the lens to *refract* (bend) light and thus brings close objects into sharp focus. When we focus on a distant object, the ciliary muscles relax, and the lens is flattened. The process of adjusting the configuration of the lenses to bring images into focus on the retina is called **accommodation.**

No description of the eyes of vertebrates would be complete without a discussion of their most obvious feature: the fact that they come in pairs. One reason vertebrates have two eyes is that vertebrates have two sides: left and right. By having one eye on each side, which is by far the most common arrangement, vertebrates can see in almost every direction without moving their heads. But then why do some mammals, including humans, have their eyes mounted side by side on the front of their heads? This arrangement sacrifices the ability to see behind so that what is in front can be viewed through both eyes simultaneously—an arrangement that is an important basis for our visual system's ability to create three-dimensional perceptions (to see depth) from two-dimensional retinal images. Why do you think the two-eyes-on-the-front arrangement has evolved in some species but not in others?

The movements of your eyes are coordinated so that each point in your visual world is projected to corresponding points on your two retinas. To accomplish this, your eyes must *converge* (turn slightly inward); convergence is greatest when you are inspecting things that are close. But the positions of the retinal images on your two eyes can never correspond exactly because your two eyes do not view the world from exactly the same position (see the accompanying demonstration). **Binocular disparity**—the difference in the position of the same image on the two retinas—is greater for close objects than for distant objects; therefore, your visual system can use the degree of binocular disparity to construct one three-dimensional perception from two two-dimensional retinal images.

Demonstration

The demonstration of binocular disparity and convergence is the first of the demonstrations that punctuate this chapter. If you compare the views from each eye (by quickly closing one eye and then the other) of objects at various distances in front of you—for example, your finger held at different distances—you will notice that the disparity between the two views is greater for closer objects. Now try the mysterious demonstration of the cocktail sausage. Face the farthest wall (or some other distant object) and bring the tips of your two pointing fingers together at arm's length in front of you—with the backs of your fingers away from you, unless you prefer sausages with fingernails. Now, with both eyes open, look through the notch between your touching fingertips, but focus on the wall. Do you see the cocktail sausage between your fingertips? Where did it come from? To prove to yourself that the sausage is a product of binocularity, make it disappear by shutting one eye. Warning: Do not eat this sausage.

6.2 The Retina and Translation of Light into Neural Signals

Figure 6.5 illustrates the cellular structure of the retina. Notice the five different layers of cells: **receptors, horizontal cells, bipolar cells, amacrine cells,** and **retinal ganglion cells** (see Hendry & Calkins, 1998; Sharpe & Stockman, 1999). Notice too that the amacrine cells and horizontal cells are specialized for *lateral communication* (communication across the major channels of sensory input).

Also notice in Figure 6.5 that the retina is in a sense inside-out: Light reaches the receptor layer only after passing through the other four layers. Then, once the receptors have been activated, the neural message is transmitted back out through the retinal layers to the retinal ganglion cells, whose axons project across the inside of the retina before gathering together in a bundle and exiting the eyeball. This inside-out arrangement creates two visual problems. One is that the incoming light is distorted by the retinal tissue through which it must pass before reaching the receptors. The other is that for the bundle of retinal

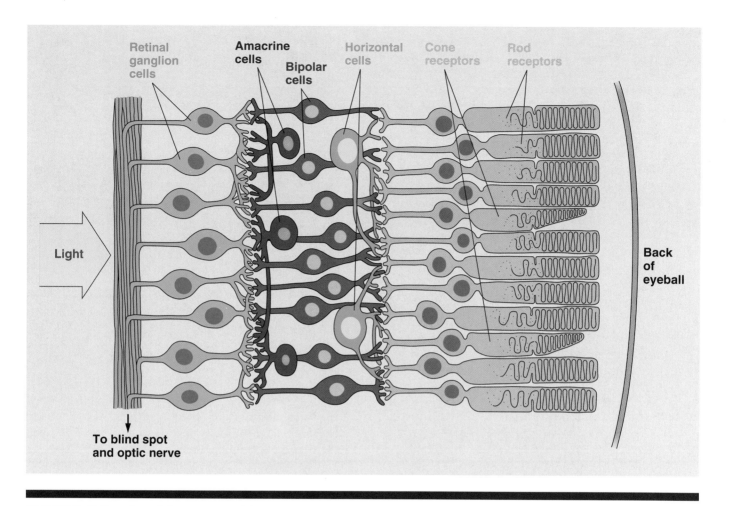

FIGURE 6.5 The cellular structure of the mammalian retina.

ganglion cell axons to leave the eye, there must be a gap in the receptor layer; this gap is called the **blind spot.**

The first of these two problems is minimized by the fovea (see Figure 6.6 on page 138). The **fovea** is an indentation, about 0.33 centimeter in diameter, at the center of the retina; it is the area of the retina that is specialized for high-acuity vision (for seeing fine details). The thinning of the retinal ganglion cell layer at the fovea reduces the distortion of incoming light. The blind spot, the second of the two visual problems created by the inside-out structure of the retina, requires a more creative solution—which is illustrated in the demonstration on page 139.

In this demonstration, you will experience **completion.** The visual system uses information provided by the receptors around the blind spot to fill in the gaps in your retinal images. When the visual system detects a straight bar going into one side of the blind spot and another straight bar leaving the other side, it fills in the missing bit for you; and what you see is a continuous straight bar, regardless of what is actually there. The completion phenomenon is one of the most compelling demonstrations that the visual system does much more than create a faithful copy of the external world.

It is a mistake to think that completion is merely a response to blind spots (see Ramachandran, 1992; Spillman & Werner, 1996). Indeed, completion is a fundamental visual system function. When you look at an object, your visual system does not conduct an image of that object from your retina to your cortex. Instead, it extracts key information about the object—primarily information about its edges and their location—and conducts that information to the cortex, where a perception of the entire object is created from that partial information. For example, the color and brightness of large unpatterned surfaces are not directly perceived but are filled in (completed) by a completion process, in this case called *surface interpolation.*

ON THE CD

Visit the *Surface Interpolation* module. The Cornsweet Illusion demonstrates that much of what you "see" is actually a creation of your visual system.

Cone and Rod Vision

You likely noticed in Figure 6.5 that there are two different types of receptors in the human retina: cone-

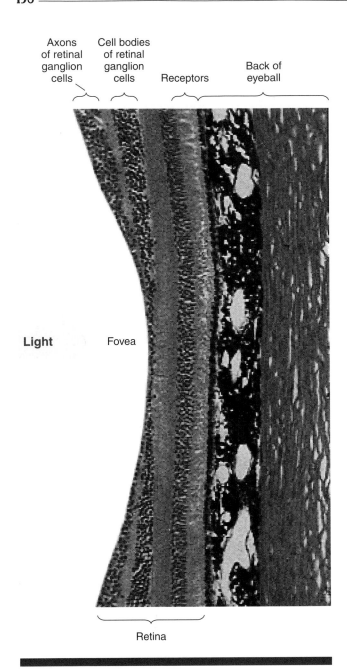

FIGURE 6.6 A section of the retina. The fovea is the indentation at the center of the retina; it is specialized for high-acuity vision.

FIGURE 6.7 Cones and rods. The smaller, conical cells are cones; the larger, cylindrical cells are rods.

shaped receptors called **cones,** and rod-shaped receptors called **rods** (see Figure 6.7). The existence of these two types of receptors puzzled researchers until 1866, when it was first noticed that species active only in the day tend to have cone-only retinas and that species active only at night tend to have rod-only retinas.

From this observation emerged the **duplexity theory** of vision—the theory that cones and rods mediate different kinds of vision. Cone-mediated vision (**photopic vision**) predominates in good lighting and provides high-acuity (finely detailed) colored perceptions of the world. In dim illumination, there is not enough light

to reliably excite the cones, and the more sensitive rod-mediated vision (**scotopic vision**) predominates. However, the sensitivity of scotopic vision is not achieved without cost: Scotopic vision lacks both the detail and the color of photopic vision.

The differences between photopic (cone) and scotopic (rod) vision result in part from a difference in the way the two systems are "wired." As Figure 6.8 illustrates, there is a large difference in *convergence* between the two systems. The output of several hundred rods may ultimately converge on a single retinal ganglion cell, whereas it is not uncommon for a retinal ganglion cell to receive input from only a few cones. As a result, the effects of dim light simultaneously stimulating many rods can summate to influence the firing of a retinal ganglion cell onto which the output of the stimulated rods converges, whereas the effects of the same dim light applied to a sheet of cones cannot summate to the same degree, and the retinal ganglion cells may not respond to the light.

The convergent scotopic system pays for its high degree of sensitivity with a low level of acuity. When a retinal ganglion cell that receives input from hundreds of rods changes its firing, the brain has no way of knowing which portion of the rods contributed to the change. Although a more intense light is required to change the firing of a retinal ganglion cell that receives signals from cones, when it does react, there is less ambiguity about the location of the stimulus that triggered the reaction.

Cones and rods differ in their distribution on the retina. As Figure 6.9 on page 140 illustrates, there are no rods at all in the fovea, only cones. At the boundaries of the foveal indentation, the proportion of cones declines markedly, and there is an increase in the number of rods. The density of rods reaches a maximum at 20° from the center of the fovea. Notice that there are many more rods

Demonstration

First, prove to yourself that you do have areas of blindness that correspond to your retinal blind spots. Close your left eye and stare directly at the A below, trying as hard as you can to not shift your gaze. While keeping the gaze of your right eye fixed on the A, hold the book at different distances from you until the black dot to the right of the A becomes focused on your blind spot and disappears (at about 20 centimeters, or 8 inches).

If each eye has a blind spot, why is there not a black hole in your perception of the world when you look at it with one eye? You will discover the answer by focusing on B with your right eye while holding the book at the same distance as before. Suddenly, the broken line to the right of B will become whole. Now focus on C at the same distance with your right eye. What do you see?

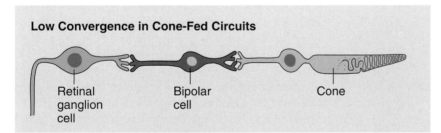

FIGURE 6.8 A schematic representation of the convergence of cones and rods on retinal ganglion cells. There is a low degree of convergence in cone-fed pathways and a high degree of convergence in rod-fed pathways.

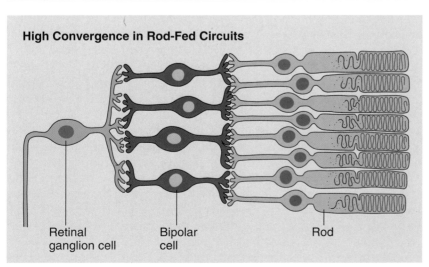

FIGURE 6.9 The distribution of cones and rods over the human retina. The figure illustrates the number of cones and rods per square millimeter as a function of distance from the center of the fovea. (Adapted from Lindsay & Norman, 1977.)

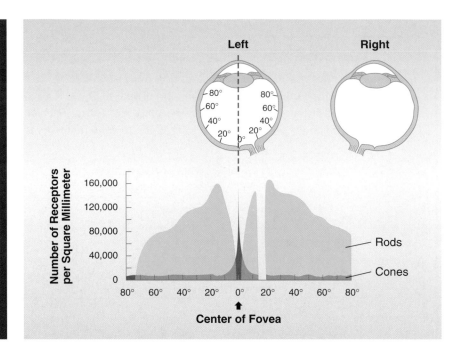

in the **nasal hemiretina** (the half of each retina next to the nose) than in the **temporal hemiretina** (the half next to the temples).

Generally speaking, more intense lights appear brighter. However, wavelength also has a substantial effect on the perception of brightness. Because our visual systems are not equally sensitive to all wavelengths in the visible spectrum, lights of the same intensity but of different wavelengths can differ markedly in brightness. A graph of the relative brightness of lights of the same intensity presented at different wavelengths is called a *spectral sensitivity curve.*

By far the most important thing to remember about spectral sensitivity curves is that humans and other animals with both cones and rods have two of them: a **photopic spectral sensitivity curve** and a **scotopic spectral sensitivity curve.** The photopic spectral sensitivity of humans can be determined by having subjects judge the relative brightness of different wavelengths of light shone on the fovea. Their scotopic spectral sensitivity can be determined by asking subjects to judge the relative brightness of different wavelengths of light shone on the periphery of the retina at an intensity too low to activate the few peripheral cones that are located there.

The photopic and scotopic spectral sensitivity curves of human subjects are plotted in Figure 6.10. Notice that under photopic conditions, the visual system is maximally sensitive to wavelengths of about 560 nanometers; thus, under photopic conditions, a light at 500 nanometers would have to be much more intense than one at 560 nanometers to be seen as equally bright. In contrast, under scotopic conditions, the visual system is maximally sensitive to wavelengths of about 500 nanometers; thus, under scotopic conditions, a light of 560 nanometers

would have to be much more intense than one at 500 nanometers to be seen as equally bright.

Because of the difference in photopic and scotopic spectral sensitivity, an interesting visual effect can be observed during the transition from photopic to scotopic vision. In 1825, Purkinje described the following occurrence, which has become known as the **Purkinje effect** (pronounced "pur-KIN-jee"). One evening, just before dusk, while Purkinje was walking in his garden, he noticed how bright most of his yellow and red flowers appeared in relation to his blue ones. What amazed him was that just a few minutes later the relative brightness of his flowers had somehow been reversed; the entire scene, when viewed at night, appeared completely in shades of gray, but most of the blue flowers appeared as brighter grays than did the yellow and red ones. Can you explain this shift in relative brightness by referring to the photopic and scotopic spectral sensitivity curves in Figure 6.10?

■ Eye Movement

If cones are in fact responsible for mediating high-acuity color vision under photopic conditions, how can they accomplish their task when most of them are crammed into the fovea? Look around you. What you see is not a few colored details at the center of a grayish scene. You seem to see an expansive, richly detailed, lavishly colored visual world. How can such a perception be the product of a photopic system that, for the most part, is restricted to a few degrees in the center of your visual field? The demonstration on the next page provides a clue.

What this demonstration shows is that what we see is determined not just by what is projected on the retina

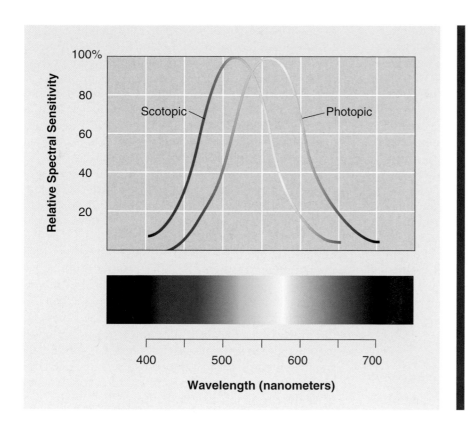

FIGURE 6.10 Human photopic (cone) and scotopic (rod) spectral sensitivity curves. The peak of each curve has been arbitrarily set at 100%.

at that instant. Although we are not aware of it, the eye continually scans the visual field by making a series of brief fixations. About three fixations occur every second, and they are connected by very quick eye movements called **saccades.** The visual system *integrates* (adds together) the foveal images from the preceding few fixations to produce a wide-angled, high-acuity, richly colored perception (see Irwin, 1996). It is because of this *temporal integration* that the world does not vanish momentarily each time we blink.

One way of demonstrating the critical role played by eye movement in vision is to study what happens to vision when all eye movement is stopped. However, be-

cause of the risks inherent in paralyzing the eye muscles, researchers have taken an alternative approach. Rather than stopping eye movement, they have stopped the primary consequence of eye movement—the movement of the retinal image across the retina. They have accomplished this by projecting test stimuli from a tiny projector mounted on a contact lens. Each time the eye moves, the lens and the projector move with it; this keeps the retinal image fixed on the same receptors, as if the eye had remained still.

The effect on vision of stabilizing the retinal image is dramatic (e.g., Pritchard, 1961). After a few seconds of viewing, a simple **stabilized retinal image** disappears,

Demonstration

Close your left eye, and with your right eye stare at the fixation point ✦ at a distance of about 12 centimeters (4.75 inches) from the page. Be very careful that your gaze does not shift. You will notice when your gaze is totally fixed that it is difficult to see detail and color at 20° or more from the fixation point because there are so few cones there. Now look at the page again with your right eye, but this time without fixing your gaze. Notice the difference that eye movement makes to your vision.

W		**F**	**D**	**M**	**E**	**A**	✦
50°		40°	30°	20°	10°	5°	0°

leaving a featureless gray field. The movements of the eyes then increase, presumably in an attempt to bring the image back. However, such movements are futile in this situation because the stabilized retinal image simply moves with the eyes. In a few seconds, the stimulus pattern, or part of it, spontaneously reappears, only to disappear once again.

Why do stabilized images disappear? The answer lies in the fact that the neurons of the visual system respond to change rather than to steady input. Most visual system neurons respond vigorously when a stimulus is presented, moved, or terminated; but they respond only weakly to a continuous, unchanging stimulus. Apparently, one function of eye movements is to keep the retinal image moving back and forth across the receptors, thus ensuring that the receptors and the neurons to which they are connected receive a continually changing pattern of stimulation. When a retinal image is stabilized, parts of the visual system stop responding to the image, and it disappears.

Visual Transduction: The Conversion of Light to Neural Signals

Transduction is the conversion of one form of energy to another. *Visual transduction* is the conversion of light to neural signals by the visual receptors. A break-

through in the study of visual transduction came in 1876, when a red *pigment* (a pigment is any substance that absorbs light) was extracted from the predominantly rod retina of the frog. This pigment had a curious property. When the pigment (which became known as **rhodopsin**), was exposed to continuous intense light, it was *bleached* (lost its color) and lost its ability to absorb light; but when it was returned to the dark, it regained both its redness and its light-absorbing capacity.

It is now clear that the absorption and bleaching of rhodopsin by light is the first step in rod-mediated vision. Evidence comes from demonstrations that the degree to which rhodopsin absorbs light in various situations predicts how humans see under the very same conditions. For example, it has been shown that the degree to which rhodopsin absorbs lights of different wavelengths is related to the ability of humans and other animals with rods to detect the presence of different wavelengths of light under scotopic conditions. Figure 6.11 illustrates the relationship between the **absorption spectrum** of rhodopsin and the human scotopic spectral sensitivity curve. The goodness of the fit leaves little doubt that, in dim light, our sensitivity to various wavelengths is a direct consequence of rhodopsin's ability to absorb them.

Rhodopsin is a G protein–linked receptor that responds to light rather than to neurotransmitter mole-

FIGURE 6.11 The absorption spectrum of rhodopsin compared with the human scotopic spectral sensitivity curve.

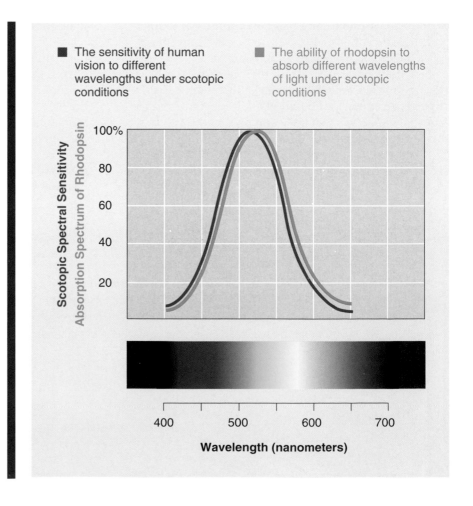

cules (see Koutalos & Yau, 1993; Molday & Hsu, 1995). Rhodopsin receptors, like other G protein–linked receptors, initiate a cascade of intracellular chemical events when they are activated (see Figure 6.12). When rods are in darkness, an intracellular chemical called *cyclic GMP* (guanosine monophosphate) keeps sodium channels partially open, thus keeping the rods slightly depolarized and a steady flow of excitatory glutamate neurotransmitter molecules emanating from them. However, when rhodopsin receptors are bleached by light, the resulting cascade of intracellular chemical events deactivates the cyclic GMP; and in so doing, it closes the sodium channels, hyperpolarizes the rods, and reduces the release of glutamate. The transduction of light by rods makes an important point: Signals are often transmitted through neural systems by inhibition.

Less is known about the cone photopigments than about rhodopsin. However, their structure and function appear to be similar to those of rhodopsin. For example, when stimulated, they become hyperpolarized, and the cones release glutamate (see Hendry & Calkins, 1998).

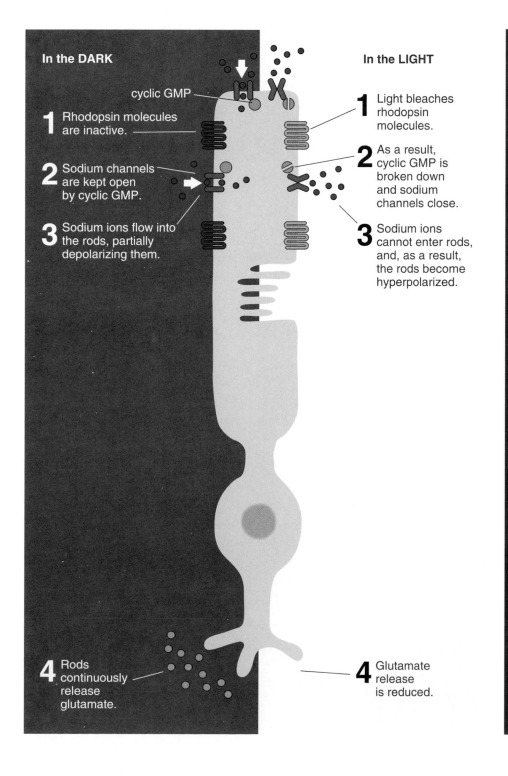

In the DARK

cyclic GMP

1 Rhodopsin molecules are inactive.

2 Sodium channels are kept open by cyclic GMP.

3 Sodium ions flow into the rods, partially depolarizing them.

In the LIGHT

1 Light bleaches rhodopsin molecules.

2 As a result, cyclic GMP is broken down and sodium channels close.

3 Sodium ions cannot enter rods, and, as a result, the rods become hyperpolarized.

4 Rods continuously release glutamate.

4 Glutamate release is reduced.

FIGURE 6.12   The inhibitory response of rods to light. When light bleaches rhodopsin molecules, the rods' sodium channels close; as a result, the rods become hyperpolarized and release less glutamate.

6.3 From Retina to Primary Visual Cortex

Many pathways in the brain carry visual information. By far the largest and most thoroughly studied visual pathway is the **retina-geniculate-striate pathway,** which conducts signals from the retina to the **primary visual cortex,** or *striate cortex,* via the **lateral geniculate nuclei** of the thalamus. The organization of this retina-geniculate-striate pathway is illustrated in Figure 6.13. Examine it carefully.

The main thing to notice from Figure 6.13 is that all signals from the left visual field reach the right primary visual cortex, either ipsilaterally via the *temporal hemiretina* of the right eye or contralaterally via the *nasal hemiretina* of the left eye—and that the opposite is true of all signals from the right visual field. Each lateral geniculate nucleus has six layers, and each layer receives input from all parts of the contralateral visual field of one eye. Most of the lateral geniculate neurons that project to the primary visual cortex terminate in the lower part of cortical layer IV (see Figure 3.29), producing a characteristic stripe, or striation, when viewed in cross section—hence the name *striate cortex.*

Retinotopic Organization

The retina-geniculate-striate system is **retinotopic;** each level of the system is organized like a map of the

FIGURE 6.13 The retina-geniculate-striate system: The neural projections from the retinas through the lateral geniculate nuclei to the left and right primary visual cortex (striate cortex). The colors indicate the flow of information from various parts of the receptive fields of each eye to various parts of the visual system. (Adapted from Netter, 1962.)

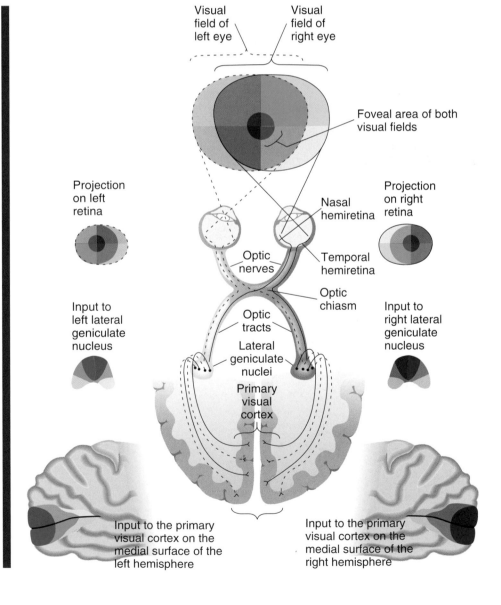

Visual field of left eye

Visual field of right eye

Foveal area of both visual fields

Projection on left retina

Projection on right retina

Nasal hemiretina

Temporal hemiretina

Optic nerves

Optic chiasm

Input to left lateral geniculate nucleus

Input to right lateral geniculate nucleus

Optic tracts

Lateral geniculate nuclei

Primary visual cortex

Input to the primary visual cortex on the medial surface of the left hemisphere

Input to the primary visual cortex on the medial surface of the right hemisphere retina. This means that two stimuli presented to adjacent areas of the retina excite adjacent neurons at all levels of the system. The retinotopic layout of the primary visual cortex has a disproportionate representation of the fovea; although the fovea is only a small part of the retina, a relatively large proportion of the primary visual cortex (about 25%) is dedicated to the analysis of its input.

A dramatic demonstration of the retinotopic organization of the primary visual cortex was provided by Dobelle, Mladejovsky, and Girvin (1974). They implanted an array of electrodes in the primary visual cortex of patients who were blind because of damage to their eyes. If electrical current was administered simultaneously through an array of electrodes forming a shape, such as a cross, on the surface of a patient's cortex, the patient reported "seeing" a glowing image of that shape.

■ | ## The M and P Layers

Not apparent in Figure 6.13 is the fact that at least two independent channels of communication flow through each lateral geniculate nucleus (see Hendry & Calkins, 1998). One channel runs through the top four layers. These layers are called the **parvocellular layers** (or *P layers*) because they are composed of neurons with small cell bodies (*parvo* means "small"). The other channel runs through the bottom two layers, which are called the **magnocellular layers** (or *M layers*) because they are composed of neurons with large cell bodies (*magno* means "large").

The parvocellular neurons are particularly responsive to color, to fine pattern details, and to stationary or slowly moving objects. In contrast, the magnocellular neurons are particularly responsive to movement. Cones provide the majority of the input to the P layers, whereas rods provide the majority of the input to the M layers.

The parvocellular and magnocellular neurons project to slightly different sites in the striate cortex. The magnocellular neurons terminate just above the parvocellular neurons, both in *lower layer IV* of the striate cortex (see Yabuta & Callaway, 1998). Lower layer IV is the major destination of the retina-geniculate-striate pathway.

BrainScan

This is a good place to pause to scan your brain. Are you ready to proceed to the last two sections of the chapter, which describe how the visual system mediates the perception of edges and color? Find out by filling in the following blanks. The correct answers are provided at the bottom of the page. Before proceeding, review material related to your errors and omissions.

1. Neural signals are carried from the retina to the lateral geniculate nuclei by the axons of _____ cells.

2. The axons of retinal ganglion cells leave the eyeball at the _____ .

3. The area of the retina that mediates high-acuity vision is the _____ .

4. Cones are the receptors of the _____ system, which functions only in good lighting.

5. The retinal ganglion cells from the nasal hemiretinas decussate (cross over to the other side of the brain) via the _____ .

6. The photopigment of rods is _____ .

7. The most important organizational principle of the retina-geniculate-striate system is that it is laid out _____ .

8. Evidence that rhodopsin is the scotopic photopigment is provided by the fit between the _____ spectrum of rhodopsin and the scotopic spectral sensitivity curve.

9. The high degree of _____ characteristic of the scotopic system increases its sensitivity but decreases its acuity.

Brain Scan answers: (1) retinal ganglion, (2) blind spot, (3) fovea, (4) photopic, (5) optic chiasm, (6) rhodopsin, (7) retinotopically, (8) absorption, (9) convergence.

6.4 Seeing Edges

Edge perception (seeing edges) does not sound like a particularly important topic, but it is. Edges are the most informative features of any visual display because they define the extent and position of the various objects in it. Given the importance of perceiving visual edges and the unrelenting pressure of natural selection, it is not surprising that the visual systems of many species are particularly good at edge perception.

Before considering the visual mechanisms underlying edge perception, it is important to appreciate exactly what a visual edge is. In a sense, a visual edge is nothing: It is merely the place where two different areas of a visual image meet. Accordingly, the perception of an edge is really the perception of a *contrast* between two adjacent areas of the visual field. This section of the chapter reviews the perception of edges (the perception of contrast) between areas that differ from one another in brightness. Color contrast is discussed in the following section.

■ Lateral Inhibition and Contrast Enhancement

Carefully examine the stripes in Figure 6.14. The intensity graph in the figure indicates what is there—a series of homogeneous stripes of different intensity. But this is not exactly what you see, is it? What you see is indicated in the brightness graph. Adjacent to each edge, the brighter stripe looks brighter than it really is and the darker stripe looks darker than it really is (see the demonstration). The nonexistent stripes of brightness and darkness running adjacent to the edges are sometimes called *Mach bands;* they enhance the contrast at each edge and make the edge easier to see.

── Demonstration ──

The Mach band demonstration is so compelling that you may be confused by it. You many think that the Mach bands in Figure 6.14 have been created by the printers of the book, rather than by your own visual system. To prove to yourself that the Mach bands are a creation of your own visual system, view each stripe individually by covering the adjacent ones with two pieces of paper, and you will see at once that each stripe is completely homogeneous. Then, take the paper away, and the Mach bands will suddenly reappear.

FIGURE 6.14 The illusory bands visible in this figure are often called Mach bands, but they were in fact discovered by French chemist M. Chevreul in the late 1800s while he was doing research on textile patterns. The Austrian physicist E. Mach discovered illusory bands in a different figure, but the term *Mach bands* is sometimes used in a general sense—as I have done here—to refer to both his and Chevreul's discoveries. (Thanks to David Burr of the Università Degli Studi di Roma for informing me, and now you, of Chevreul's contribution—see Ross, Morrone, & Burr, 1989.)

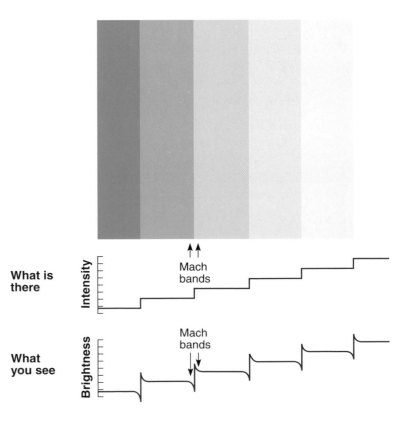

It is important to appreciate that **contrast enhancement** is not something that occurs just in books. Although we are normally unaware of it, every edge we look at is highlighted for us by the contrast-enhancing mechanisms of our nervous systems. In effect, our perception of edges is better than the real thing.

ON THE CD

Visit the *Contrast Enhancement* module. View the important Mach band demonstration in a particularly compelling way.

The classic studies of the physiological basis of contrast enhancement were conducted on the eyes of an unlikely subject: the *horseshoe crab* (e.g., Ratliff, 1972). The *lateral eyes* of the horseshoe crab are ideal for certain types of neurophysiological research. Unlike mammalian eyes, they are composed of very large receptors, called **ommatidia,** each with its own large axon. In each lateral eye, the axons of all the ommatidia are interconnected by a lateral neural network.

In order to understand the physiological basis of contrast enhancement in the horseshoe crab, you must know two things. The first is that if a single ommatidium is illuminated, it fires at a rate that is proportional to the intensity of the light striking it; more intense lights produce more firing. The second is that when a receptor fires, it inhibits its neighbors via the lateral neural network; this inhibition is called **lateral inhibition** because it spreads laterally across the array of receptors (or *mutual inhibition,* because neighboring receptors inhibit one another). The amount of lateral inhibition produced by a receptor is greatest when it is most intensely illuminated, and it has its greatest effect on its immediate neighbors.

The neural basis of contrast enhancement can be understood in terms of the firing rates of the receptors on each side of an edge, as indicated in Figure 6.15. Notice that the receptor adjacent to the edge on the more intense side (receptor D) fires more than the other intensely illuminated receptors (A, B, C), while the receptor adjacent to the edge on the less-well-illuminated side (receptor E) fires less than the other receptors on that side (F, G, H). Lateral inhibition accounts for these differences. Receptors A, B, and C all fire at the same rate, because they are all receiving the same high level of stimulation and the same high degree of lateral inhibition from all their highly stimulated neighbors. Receptor D fires more than A, B, and C, because it receives as much stimulation as they do but less inhibition from its neighbors, many of whom are on the dimmer side of the edge. Now consider the receptors on the dimmer side. Receptors F, G, and H fire at the same rate, because they are all being stimulated by the same low level of light and receiving the same low level of inhibition from their neighbors. However, receptor E fires even less, because it is receiving the same excitation but more inhibition from its neighbors, many of which are on the more intense side of the edge. Now that you understand the neural basis of contrast enhancement, take another look at Figure 6.14.

■ Receptive Fields of Visual Neurons

The Nobel Prize–winning research of Hubel and Wiesel is the fitting climax to this discussion of

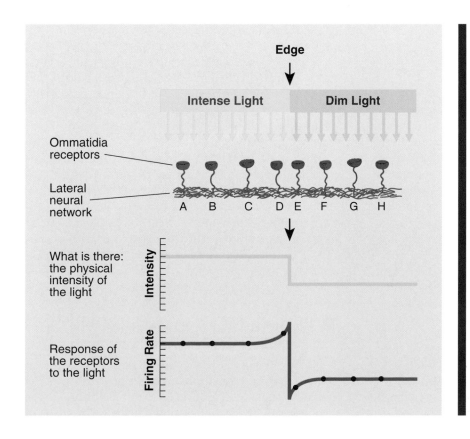

FIGURE 6.15 How lateral inhibition produces contrast enhancement. (Adapted from Ratliff, 1972.)

Edge

Intense Light   Dim Light

Ommatidia receptors

Lateral neural network

A   B   C   D   E   F   G   H

What is there: the physical intensity of the light

Intensity

Response of the receptors to the light

Firing Rate

brightness contrast. Their research has revealed much about the neural mechanisms of vision, and their methods have been adopted by a generation of sensory neurophysiologists. Hubel and Wiesel's subjects are single neurons in the visual systems of cats and monkeys; because it is invasive, their technique cannot be employed on human subjects.

First, the tip of a microelectrode is positioned near a single neuron in the visual area of interest. During testing, eye movements are blocked by *curare* (see Chapter 4), and the images on a screen in front of the subject are focused sharply on the retina by an experimenter using an adjustable lens. The next step in the procedure is to identify the receptive field of the neuron. The **receptive field** of a visual neuron is the area of the visual field within which it is possible for a visual stimulus to influence the firing of that neuron. Visual system neurons tend to be continually active; thus, effective stimuli are those that either increase or decrease the rate of firing. The final step in the method is to record the responses of the neuron to various stimuli within its receptive field in order to characterize the types of stimuli that most influence its activity. Then, the electrode is advanced slightly, and the entire process of identifying and characterizing the receptive field properties is repeated for another neuron, and then for another, and another, and so on. The general strategy is to begin by studying neurons near the receptors and gradually working up through "higher" and "higher" levels of the system in an effort to understand the increasing complexity of the neural responses at each level.

■ Receptive Fields: Neurons of the Retina-Geniculate-Striate Pathway

Hubel and Wiesel (e.g., 1979) began their studies of visual system neurons by recording from the three levels of the retina-geniculate-striate pathway: first from retinal ganglion cells, then from lateral geniculate neurons, and finally from the striate neurons of lower layer IV, the terminus of the pathway. They found little change in the receptive fields as they worked their way along the pathway.

When Hubel and Wiesel compared the receptive fields recorded from retinal ganglion cells, lateral geniculate nuclei, and lower layer IV neurons, four commonalties were readily apparent. First, at each level, the receptive fields in the foveal area of the retina were smaller than those at the periphery; this is consistent with the fact that the fovea mediates fine-grained (high-acuity) vision. Second, all the neurons (retinal ganglion cells, lateral geniculate neurons, *and* lower layer IV neurons) had receptive fields that were circular. Third, all the neurons were **monocular;** that is, each neuron had a receptive field in one eye but not the other. And fourth, many neurons at each of the three levels of the retina-geniculate-striate system had receptive fields that com-

prised an excitatory area and an inhibitory area separated by a circular boundary. It is this fourth point that is most important and most complex. Let me explain.

When Hubel and Wiesel shone a spot of white light onto the various parts of the receptive fields of neurons in the retina-geniculate-striate pathway, they discovered two different responses. The neuron responded with either "on" firing or "off" firing, depending on the location of the spot of light in the receptive field. That is, the neuron either displayed a burst of firing when the light was turned on (*"on" firing*), or it displayed an inhibition of firing when the light was turned on and a burst of firing when it was turned off (*"off" firing*).

For most neurons in the retina-geniculate-striate system, their reaction—"on" firing or "off" firing—to a light in a particular part of the receptive field was quite predictable. It depended on whether they were on-center cells or off-center cells, as illustrated in Figure 6.16. **On-center cells** respond to lights shone in the central region of their receptive fields with "on" firing and to lights shone in the periphery of their receptive fields with inhibition, followed by "off" firing when the light is turned off. **Off-center cells** display the opposite pattern: They respond with inhibition and "off" firing in response to lights in the center of their receptive fields and with "on" firing to lights in the periphery of their receptive fields.

In effect, on-center and off-center cells respond best to contrast. Figure 6.17 illustrates this point. The most effective way to influence the firing rate of an on-center or off-center cell is to maximize the contrast between the center and the periphery of its receptive field by illuminating either the entire center or the entire surround (periphery), while leaving the other region completely dark. Diffusely illuminating the entire receptive field has little effect on firing. Hubel and Wiesel thus concluded that one function of many neurons in the retina-geniculate-striate system is to respond to the degree of brightness contrast between the two areas of their receptive fields (see Livingstone & Hubel, 1988).

Before leaving Figures 6.16 and 6.17, notice one important thing about visual system neurons: They are continually active, even when there is no visual input (Tsodyks et al., 1999). Indeed, spontaneous activity is a characteristic of most cerebral neurons. Arieli and colleagues (1996) have shown that the level of activity of visual cortical neurons at the time that a visual stimulus is presented influences how the cells respond to the stimulus—this may be the means by which cognition influences perception.

■ Receptive Fields: Simple Cortical Cells

The striate cortex neurons that you just read about—that is, the neurons of lower layer IV—are exceptions. Their receptive fields are unlike those of the vast majority of striate neurons. The receptive fields of

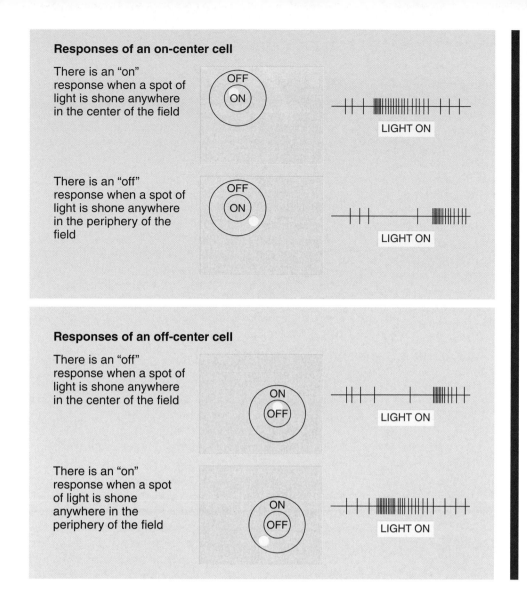

Responses of an on-center cell

There is an "on" response when a spot of light is shone anywhere in the center of the field

OFF
ON

LIGHT ON

There is an "off" response when a spot of light is shone anywhere in the periphery of the field

OFF
ON

LIGHT ON

Responses of an off-center cell

There is an "off" response when a spot of light is shone anywhere in the center of the field

ON
OFF

LIGHT ON

There is an "on" response when a spot of light is shone anywhere in the periphery of the field

ON
OFF

LIGHT ON

FIGURE 6.16 The receptive fields of an on-center cell and an off-center cell.

The most effective way of maximizing the firing of an on-center or off-center cell is to completely illuminate either the "on area" or the "off area" of its receptive field:

OFF
ON

LIGHT ON

OFF
ON

LIGHT ON

If both areas of a cell's receptive field are illuminated together, there is little reaction from the cell:

OFF
ON

LIGHT ON

FIGURE 6.17 The responses of an on-center cell to contrast.

most primary visual cortex neurons fall into one of two classes: simple or complex. Neither of these classes includes the neurons of lower layer IV.

Simple cells, like lower layer IV neurons, have receptive fields that can be divided into antagonistic "on" and "off" regions and are thus unresponsive to diffuse light. And like lower layer IV neurons, they are all monocular. The main difference is that the borders between the "on" and "off" regions of the cortical receptive fields of simple cells are straight lines rather than circles. Several examples of receptive fields of simple cortical cells are presented in Figure 6.18. Notice that simple cells respond best to bars of light in a dark field, dark bars in a light field, or single straight edges between dark and light areas; that each simple cell responds maximally only when its preferred straight-edge stimulus is in a particular position and in a particular orientation; and that the receptive fields of simple cortical cells are rectangular rather than circular.

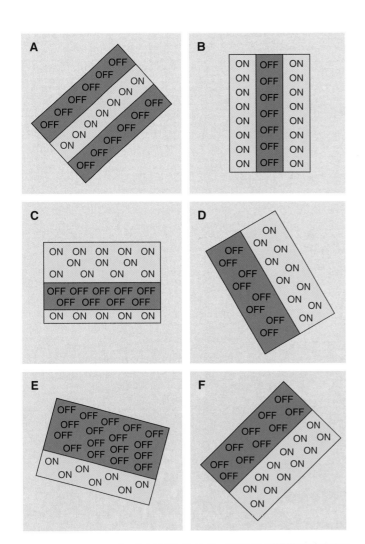

FIGURE 6.18 Examples of visual fields of simple cortical cells.

Receptive Fields: Complex Cortical Cells

Complex cells are more numerous than simple cells. Like simple cells, complex cells have rectangular receptive fields, respond best to straight-line stimuli in a specific orientation, and are unresponsive to diffuse light. However, complex cells differ from simple cells in three important ways. First, they have larger receptive fields. Second, it is not possible to divide the receptive fields of complex cells into static "on" and "off" regions: A complex cell responds to a particular straight-edge stimulus of a particular orientation regardless of its position within the receptive field of that cell. Thus, if a stimulus (e.g., a 45° bar of light) that produces "on" firing in a particular complex cell is swept across its receptive field, the cell will respond continuously to it as it moves across the field. Many complex cells respond more robustly to the movement of a straight line across their receptive fields in a particular direction. Third, unlike simple cortical cells, which are all monocular (respond to stimulation of only one of the eyes), many complex cells are **binocular** (respond to stimulation of either eye). Indeed, in monkeys, over half the complex cortical cells are binocular.

If the receptive field of a binocular complex cell is measured through one eye and then through the other, the receptive fields in each eye turn out to have almost exactly the same position in the visual field, as well as the same orientation preference. In other words, what you learn about the cell by stimulating one eye is confirmed by stimulating the other. What is more, if the appropriate stimulation is applied through both eyes simultaneously, a binocular cell usually fires more robustly than if only one eye is stimulated.

Most of the binocular cells in the primary visual cortex of monkeys display some degree of *ocular dominance;* that is, they respond more robustly to stimulation of one eye than they do to the same stimulation of the other. In addition, some binocular cells fire best when the preferred stimulus is presented to both eyes at the same time but in slightly different positions on the two retinas (e.g., Ohzawa, 1998). In other words, these cells respond best to *retinal disparity* and thus are likely to play a role in depth perception (e.g., Livingstone & Tsao, 1999).

Columnar Organization of Primary Visual Cortex

The study of the receptive fields of primary visual cortex neurons has led to two important conclusions. The first conclusion is that the characteristics of the receptive fields of visual cortex neurons are attributable to the flow of signals from neurons with simpler receptive fields to those with more complex fields (see Reid & Alonso, 1996). Specifically, it seems that signals flow from on-center and off-center cells in lower layer IV to simple cells and from simple cells to complex cells.

The second conclusion is that primary visual cortex neurons are grouped in functional vertical columns (in this context, *vertical* means at right angles to the cortical layers). Much of the evidence for this conclusion comes from studies of the receptive fields of neurons along various vertical and horizontal electrode tracks (see Figure 6.19). If one advances an electrode vertically through the layers of the visual cortex, stopping to plot the receptive fields of many neurons along the way, each cell in the column has a receptive field in the same area of the visual field. One would also find that all the cells in a column respond best to straight lines in the very same orienta-

tion, and those neurons in a column that are either monocular or binocular with ocular dominance are all most sensitive to light in the same eye, left or right.

In contrast, if an electrode is advanced horizontally through the tissue, each successive cell encountered is likely to have a receptive field in a slightly different location and to be maximally responsive to straight lines of a slightly different orientation. And during a horizontal electrode pass, the tip passes alternately through areas of left-eye dominance and right-eye dominance—commonly referred to as *ocular dominance columns.*

All of the functional columns in the primary visual cortex that analyze input from one area of the retina are clustered together. Half of a cluster receives input

FIGURE 6.19 The organization of the primary visual cortex: The receptive-field properties of cells encountered along typical vertical and horizontal electrode tracks in the primary visual cortex.

primarily from the left eye, and half receives input primarily from the right eye. Indeed, input from the eyes has been found to enter layer IV in alternating patches. The best kind of evidence of this alternating arrangement first came from a study (LeVay, Hubel, & Wiesel, 1975) in which a radioactive amino acid was injected into one eye in sufficient quantities to cross the synapses of the retina-geniculate-striate system and show up in lower layer IV of the primary visual cortex, and to a lesser degree in the layers just above and below it. The alternating patches of radioactivity and nonradioactivity in the autoradiograph in Figure 6.20 mark the alternating patches of input from the two eyes.

All of the clusters of functional columns that analyze input from one area of the retina are thought to include neurons with preferences for straight-line stimuli of various orientations. The columns of orientation specificity were visualized in a study (Hubel, Wiesel, & Stryker, 1977) in which radioactive 2-DG was injected into monkeys that then spent 45 minutes viewing a pattern of vertical stripes moving back and forth. As you know from previous chapters, radioactive 2-DG is taken up by active neurons and accumulates in them, thus identifying the location of neurons that are particularly active during the test period. The autoradiograph in Figure 6.21 reveals the columns of cells in the primary visual cortex that were activated by exposure to the moving vertical stripes. Notice that the neurons in lower layer IV show no orientation specificity—because they do not respond to straight-line stimuli. High-powered MRI techniques have recently been developed for visualizing columns of orientation specificity in human subjects (Kim, Duong, & Kim, 2000).

FIGURE 6.20 The alternation of input into lower layer IV of the primary visual cortex from the left and right eyes. Radioactive amino acids that were injected into one eye were subsequently revealed on autoradiographs of the visual cortex as patches of radioactivity alternating with patches of nonradioactivity. (From "Brain Mechanisms of Vision" by D. H. Hubel and T. N. Wiesel. Reprinted by permission of *Scientific American*, vol. 241, p. 151. Copyright © 1979 by Scientific American, Inc.)

FIGURE 6.21 The columns of orientation specificity in the primary visual cortex of a monkey as revealed by 2-DG autoradiography. (From "Orientation Columns in Macaque Monkey Visual Cortex Demonstrated by the 2-Deoxyglucose Autoradiographic Technique" by D. H. Hubel, T. N. Wiesel, and M. P. Stryker. Reprinted by permission from *Nature*, vol. 269, p. 329. Copyright © 1977 by Macmillan Magazines Ltd.)

Figure 6.22 summarizes Hubel and Wiesel's theory of how the vertical columns of the primary visual cortex are organized.

Spatial-Frequency Theory

Hubel and Wiesel barely had time to place their Nobel Prize medals on their mantels before an important qualification to their theory was proposed. DeValois, DeValois, and their colleagues (see DeValois & DeValois, 1988) proposed that the visual cortex operates on a code of spatial frequency, not on the code of straight lines and edges hypothesized by Hubel and Wiesel.

In support of the **spatial-frequency theory** is the observation that visual cortex neurons respond even more robustly to sine-wave gratings that are placed at specific angles in their receptive fields than they do to bars or edges. A **sine-wave grating** is a set of equally spaced, parallel, alternating light and dark stripes that is created by varying the light across the grating in a sine-wave pattern—see Figure 6.23. Sine-wave gratings differ from one another in frequency (the width of their stripes), amplitude (the magnitude of the difference in intensity between the dark and light stripes), and angle.

The spatial-frequency theory is based on two physical principles. The first is that any visual stimulus can be represented by a plotting of the intensity of light along lines running through it (see Figure 6.24). The second is that any curve, no matter how irregular, can be broken down into constituent sine waves by a mathematical procedure called **Fourier analysis** (see Figure 6.25 on page 154).

The spatial-frequency theory of visual cortex function (see DeValois & DeValois, 1988) is that each

A block of tissue such as this is assumed to analyze visual signals from one area of the visual field.

Half the block of tissue is presumed to be dominated by right-eye input and half by left-eye input.

Each slice of the block of tissue is presumed to specialize in the analysis of straight lines in a particular orientation.

FIGURE 6.22 Hubel and Wiesel's model of the organization of functional columns in the primary visual cortex.

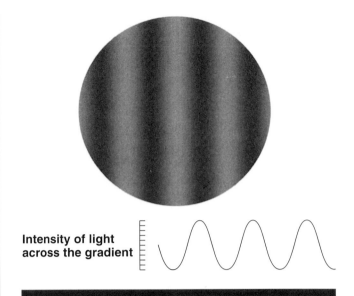

Intensity of light across the gradient

FIGURE 6.23 A sine-wave grating. (Adapted from DeValois & DeValois, 1988.)

functional module of the visual cortex performs a sort of Fourier analysis on the visual pattern in its receptive field; the neurons in each module are thought to respond selectively to various frequencies and orientations of sine-wave gratings. When all of the visual cortex neurons that are influenced by a particular scene respond together, a perception of the scene is created by the summation of its various constituent sine-wave gratings.

As I said before, the primary support for the spatial-frequency theory is that primary visual cortex neurons are more responsive to sine-wave gratings than they are to straight lines. Most neurons in the primary visual cortex respond best when a sine-wave grating of a particular frequency is presented at a particular angle in a particular location of the visual field. However, straight-edge stimuli, which have been used in most studies of

FIGURE 6.24 A visual stimulus represented by the plotting of changes in the intensity of light along slices running through it. For example, plotted here are the changes in intensity along one slice of a scene that would interest any hungry lion.

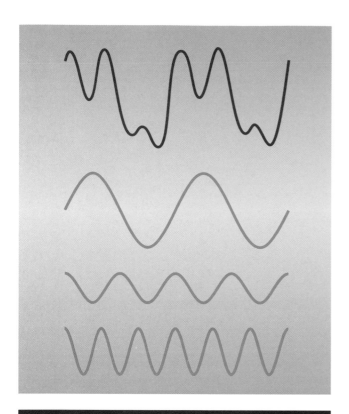

FIGURE 6.25   Any wave can be broken down into component sine waves by Fourier analysis. For example, the complex wave at the top is the sum of the sine waves shown beneath it. (Adapted from DeValois & DeValois, 1988.)

visual cortex neurons, can readily be translated into component sine-wave gratings of the same orientation. Thus, the research on spatial-frequency detection by visual neurons extends and complements previous research rather than refuting it.

This is a good point in the chapter to reconsider the case of Mrs. Richards, the woman who sketched her premigraine fortification illusions so that her husband could study them. Now that you have learned some of the fundamentals of visual system organization and function, you are in a better position to understand Mrs. Richards's symptoms.

The Case of Mrs. Richards, Revisited

There was obviously a disturbance in Mrs. Richards's visual system: But where? And what kind of disturbance? And why the straight lines? A simple test located the disturbance. Mrs. Richards was asked to shut one eye and then the other and to report what happened to her illusion. The answer was, "Nothing." This suggested that the disturbance was cortical, because the visual cortex is the first part of the retina-geniculate-striate pathway that contains neurons that receive input from both eyes.

This hypothesis was confirmed by a few simple calculations: The gradual acceleration of the illusion as it spread out to the periphery is consistent with a wave of disturbance expanding from the "foveal area" of the primary visual cortex to its boundaries at a constant rate of about 3 millimeters per minute—the illusion accelerated because proportionally less visual cortex is dedicated to receiving signals from the periphery of the visual field.

And why the lines? Would you expect anything else from an area of the cortex whose elements appear to be specialized for coding straight-line stimuli?

6.5 Seeing Color

Color is one of the most obvious qualities of human visual experience. So far in this chapter, we have largely limited our discussion of vision to the so-called **achromatic colors:** black, white, and gray. Black is experienced when there is an absence of light, the perception of white is produced by an intense mixture of a wide range of wavelengths in roughly equal proportion, and the perception of gray is produced by the same mixture at lower intensities. In this section, we deal with the perception of **chromatic colors**—colors such as blue, green, and yellow. The correct term for chromatic colors is *hues,* but in everyday language they are referred to as colors; and for the sake of simplicity, I will do the same.

What is there about a visual stimulus that determines the color we perceive? To a large degree, the perception of an object's color depends on the wavelengths of light that it reflects into the eye. Figure 6.2 (on page 134) is an illustration of the colors associated with individual wavelengths; however, outside the laboratory, one never encounters objects that reflect single wavelengths. Sunlight and most sources of artificial light contain complex mixtures of most visible wavelengths. Most objects absorb the different wavelengths of light that strike them to varying degrees and reflect the rest. The mixture of wavelengths that objects reflect influences our perception of their color.

With the development and refinement of methods for studying the responses of individual receptors and neurons in the visual system, an impressive amount has been learned in the last three decades about how the visual system responds to different wavelengths. However, in some ways, it is even more impressive that the basic mechanisms of color vision were derived in the 19th century by behaviorial scientists whose research technology was limited to their own ingenuity and observational skills. Through careful observation of the perceptual abilities of their subjects, these scientists were able to infer some of the major features of the physiological basis of color vision.

You have already encountered in this chapter many instances in which scientific gains have resulted from the convergence of behavioral, neurochemical, and neurophysiological research. However, the early advances in the study of the neural basis of color vision occurred long before it was possible to bring modern neurochemical and neurophysiological procedures to bear.

Component and Opponent Processing

The **component theory** (trichromatic theory) of color vision was proposed by Thomas Young in 1802 and refined by Hermann von Helmholtz in 1852. According to this theory, there are three different kinds of color receptors (cones), each with a different spectral sensitivity, and the color of a particular stimulus is presumed to be encoded by the ratio of activity in the three kinds of receptors. Young and Helmholtz derived their theory from the observation that any color of the visible spectrum can be matched by a mixing together of three different wavelengths of light in different proportions. This can be accomplished with any three wavelengths, provided that the color of any one of them cannot be matched by a mixing of the other two. The fact that three is normally the minimum number of different wavelengths necessary to match every color suggested that there were three types of receptors.

Another theory of color vision, the **opponent-process theory** of color vision, was proposed by Ewald Hering in 1878. He suggested that there are two different classes of cells in the visual system for encoding color and another class for encoding brightness. Hering hypothesized that each of the three classes of cells encoded two complementary color perceptions. One class of color-coding cells signaled red by changing its activity in one direction (e.g., hyperpolarization) and signaled red's complementary color, green, by changing its activity in the other direction (e.g., hypopolarization). Another class of color-coding cells was hypothesized to signal blue and its complement, yellow, in the same opponent fashion; and a class of brightness-coding cells was hypothesized to similarly signal both black and white. **Complementary colors** are pairs of colors that produce white or gray when combined in equal measure (e.g., green light and red light).

Hering based his opponent-process theory of color vision on several behavioral observations. One was that complementary colors cannot exist together: There is no such thing as bluish yellow or reddish green. Another was that the afterimage produced by staring at red is green and vice versa, and the afterimage produced by staring at yellow is blue and vice versa (see the demonstration below).

A somewhat misguided debate raged for many years between supporters of the component (trichromatic) and opponent theories of color vision. I say "misguided" because it was fueled more by the adversarial predisposition of scientists than by the incompatibility of the two theories. In fact, research subsequently proved that both color-coding mechanisms coexist in our visual systems (see Hurlbert, 1991).

It was the development in the early 1960s of **microspectrophotometry**—a technique for measuring the absorption spectrum of the photopigment contained in a single cone—that allowed researchers (e.g., Wald, 1964) to confirm the conclusion that had been reached by Young over a century and a half before. They found that there are indeed three different kinds of cones in the retinas of those vertebrates with good color vision, and they found that each of the three has a different photopigment with its own characteristic absorption spectrum. As Figure 6.26 on page 156 illustrates, some cones are most sensitive to short wavelengths, some are most sensitive to medium wavelengths, and some are most sensitive to long wavelengths.

Demonstration

Have you ever noticed complementary afterimages? To see them, stare at the fixation point in the left panel for 1 minute without moving your eyes; then quickly shift your gaze to the fixation point in the right panel. In the right panel, you will see four squares whose colors are complementary to those in the left panel.

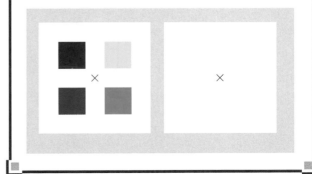

FIGURE 6.26 The absorption spectra of the three classes of cones.

Although the coding of color by cones operates on a purely component basis, there is evidence of opponent processing of color at all subsequent levels of the retina-geniculate-striate system. That is, at all subsequent levels, there are cells that respond in one direction (e.g., increased firing) to one color and in the opposite direction (e.g., decreased firing) to its complementary color. Figure 6.27 illustrates a circuit that can translate the component responses of the three types of cones into the red–green and blue–yellow opponent responses of bipolar cells.

■ Color Constancy and the Retinex Theory

Neither component nor opponent processing can account for the single most important characteristic of color vision: color constancy. **Color constancy** refers to the fact that the perceived color of an object is not a simple function of the wavelengths reflected by it.

As I write this at 7:15 on a December morning, it is dark outside, and I am working in my office by the light of a tiny incandescent desk lamp. Later in the morning, when students start to arrive, I turn on my nasty fluorescent office lights; and then, in the afternoon, when the sun has shifted to my side of the building, I turn off the lights and work by natural light. The point is that because these light sources differ markedly in the wavelengths they contain, the wavelengths reflected by various objects in my office—my blue shirt, for example—change substantially during the course of the day. However, although the wavelengths reflected by my shirt change markedly, its color does not. My shirt will be just as blue in midmorning and in late afternoon as it is now. Color constancy is the tendency for an object to stay the same color despite major changes in the wavelengths of light that it reflects.

Although the phenomenon of color constancy is counterintuitive, its advantage is obvious. Color constancy improves our ability to tell objects apart in a memorable way so that we can respond appropriately to them; our ability to recognize objects would be greatly lessened if their color changed every time there was a change in illumination. In essence, if it were not for color constancy, color vision would have little survival value.

Although color constancy is an important feature of our vision, we are normally unaware of it. Under everyday conditions, we have no way of appreciating just how much the wavelengths reflected by an object can change without the object changing its color. It is only in the controlled environment of the laboratory that one can fully appreciate that color constancy is more than an important factor in color vision: It is the essence of color vision.

Edwin Land (1977), the inventor of the Polaroid camera, developed several dramatic laboratory demonstrations of color constancy. The following is one of them. First, Land asked subjects to adjust the intensity of light coming from each of three different projectors until they judged the mixture to be a pure white when viewed in an otherwise dark room. Each projector emitted only one wavelength of light: one a short-wavelength

Short-Wavelength Cones respond best to blue.

Medium-Wavelength Cones respond best to green and yellow.

Long-Wavelength Cones respond best to red and yellow.

Excitatory   Inhibitory

A bipolar cell that is excited best by blue and inhibited best by yellow

It is inhibited best by yellow light because when medium- and long-wavelength cones are simultaneously stimulated by yellow light, their inhibitory effects summate.

A bipolar cell that is excited best by green and inhibited best by red

It does not respond when medium- and long-wavelength cones are simultaneously stimulated by yellow light because their excitatory and inhibitory effects cancel one another out.

FIGURE 6.27 A retinal circuit that can translate the component responses of the three types of cones into the red–green and blue–yellow opponent responses of bipolar cells.

light, one a medium-wavelength light, and one a long-wavelength light. Next, Land shone the three projectors on a test display like the one in Figure 6.28. (These dis-

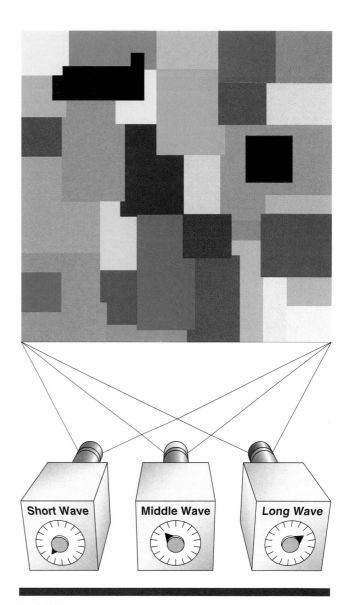

Short Wave   Middle Wave   Long Wave

FIGURE 6.28 Land's (1977) color-vision experiments. Subjects viewed Mondrians that were illuminated by various proportions of three different wavelengths: a short wavelength, a middle wavelength, and a long wavelength.

plays are called *Mondrians* because they resemble the paintings of the Dutch master painter Piet Mondrian.) Land himself adjusted the three projectors so that the mixture of the three that was being reflected from one particular area of the Mondrian—let's say the blue rectangular shape—was the exact mixture that had been judged as white by subjects in the first stage of the demonstration. To accomplish this, Land used a *photometer* to measure the amounts of the three wavelengths being reflected by the blue rectangle. Next, he repeated this process but this time for another area of the Mondrian—let's say the green rectangle—that is, he adjusted the three projectors until the mixture that had previously been judged as white was being reflected by the green rectangle.

What color was the blue rectangle when it was reflecting a pure white mixture of light, and what color was the green rectangle when it was reflecting the very same mixture of light? The answers to these questions astound many students: The blue rectangle appeared blue, and the green rectangle appeared green, even though they were reflecting the exact same mixture of white light. However, when the blue and green rectangles were viewed in isolation (not as part of a Mondrian) under the same illumination but in an otherwise dark room, they both appeared white.

The point of Land's demonstration is that blue objects stay blue, green objects stay green, and so forth, regardless of the wavelengths they reflect. This color constancy occurs as long as the object is illuminated with light that contains some short, medium, and long wavelengths (such as daylight, firelight, and virtually all manufactured lighting) and as long as the object is viewed as part of a scene, not in isolation.

According to Land's **retinex theory** of color vision, the color of an object is determined by its *reflectance*—the proportion of light of different wavelengths that a surface reflects. Although the wavelengths of light reflected by a surface change dramatically with changes in illumination, the efficiency with which a surface absorbs each wavelength and reflects the unabsorbed portion does not change. According to the retinex theory, the visual system calculates the reflectance of surfaces, and thus perceives their colors, by comparing the light reflected by adjacent surfaces in three different wavelength bands (short, medium, and long), which correspond to the three classes of cones.

Why is Land's research so critical for neuroscientists trying to discover the neural mechanisms of color vision? It is important because it indicates the type of cortical neurons that are likely to be involved in color vision. If the perception of color depends on the analysis of contrast between adjacent areas of the visual field, then the critical neurons should be responsive to color contrast. And they are. For example, **dual-opponent color cells** in the monkey visual cortex respond with vigorous "on" firing when the center of their circular receptive field is illuminated with one wavelength, such as green, and the surround (periphery) is simultaneously illuminated with another wavelength, such as red. And the same cells display vigorous "off" firing when the pattern of illumination is reversed—for example, red in the center and green in the surround. In essence, dual-opponent color cells respond to the contrast between wavelengths reflected by adjacent areas of their receptive field.

A major breakthrough in the understanding of the organization of the primary visual cortex came with the discovery that dual-opponent color cells are not distributed evenly throughout the primary visual cortex of monkeys (see Zeki, 1993a). Livingstone and Hubel (1984) found that these neurons are distributed in the primary visual cortex in peglike columns that penetrate the layers of the monkey primary visual cortex, with the exception of lower layer IV. The neurons in these peglike columns are particularly rich in the mitochondrial enzyme **cytochrome oxidase;** thus, their distribution in the primary visual cortex can be visualized if one stains slices of tissue with stains that have an affinity for this enzyme.

When a section of monkey striate tissue is cut parallel to the cortical layers and stained in this way, the pegs are seen as "blobs" of stain scattered over the cortex (unless the section is cut from lower layer IV). To the relief of instructors and students alike, the term **blobs** has become the accepted scientific label for peglike, cytochrome oxidase–rich, dual-opponent color columns. The blobs were found to be located in the middle of ocular dominance columns (see Figure 6.29, and compare it with Figure 6.22). Functional MRI studies have recently provided evidence of dual-opponent color cells in the human visual cortex (Engel, 1999).

A key goal of this chapter was to help you understand that vision is a creative process. The retina-geniculate-striate pathway does not conduct intact visual images to the cortex. It conducts information about a few critical features of the visual field—for example, information about location, movement, brightness contrast, and color contrast—and from these bits of information, it creates a perception that is better than the retinal image in all respects and better than the external reality in some. The study of the visual system is arguably the best example of the use of converging operations in biopsychology—significant insights into the neural bases of psychological processes have resulted from the con-

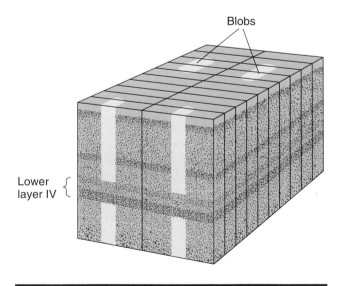

FIGURE 6.29 Hubel and Livingstone's model of primary visual cortex organization. The blobs are peglike columns that contain dual-opponent color cells.

vergence of neuroanatomical, neurochemical, neurophysiological, and behavioral research.

In this chapter, there were opportunities for you to experience firsthand the important principles of the visual process. I hope these demonstrations made you more aware of the amazing abilities of your own visual system and the relevance of what you have learned in this chapter to your everyday life.

Themes Revisited

All four major themes of this book were developed in this chapter, but two of them—the evolutionary perspective and thinking about biopsychology—predominated. The evolutionary perspective theme was emphasized for two reasons: because the vast majority of research on the neural mechanisms of human vision is comparative, and because evolutionary analyses have been important in developing an appreciation of the key roles played by edge perception and color constancy in human vision. The thinking-about-biopsychology theme was emphasized because many people think about their own visual systems in a way that is fundamentally incorrect: The visual system does not passively provide images of the external world; it actively extracts some features of the external visual world and from these it creates visual perceptions.

The cognitive neuroscience and clinical implications themes played lesser, but still significant, roles in this chapter. You learned that, although most of the research on the neural mechanisms of vision has been invasive and thus has involved nonhuman subjects, technological developments have made it possible for cognitive neuroscientists to study the neural mechanisms of vision in human subjects. Finally, you learned about two clinical implications that were based on the finding that the visual cortex is organized retinotopically: a better understanding of the fortification illusions associated with migraine headaches and the demonstration that brain stimulation can be used to produce images in patients who are blind but still have a functional visual cortex.

ON THE CD
Looking for more information about the topics in this chapter? For recommended additional readings, see Hard Copy for Chapter 6.

Log On

- **http://faculty.washington.edu/chudler/chvision.html** This site provides visual demonstrations of blind spots, color illusions, and illusions of depth.

- **http://www.brainconnection.com/library/?main=playhome/ illusions** The Brain Connection presents a page of visual illusions.

- **http://coglab.psych.purdue.edu/coglab/Labs/Receptive Field.html** If you want to try mapping the receptive field of a simulated visual system, this demonstration will give you an appreciation for the pioneering studies of Hubel and Weisel.

- **http://www.accessexcellence.org/AE/AEC/CC/vision_ background.html** For those interested in the process of visual transduction, this site also includes links to other pages on vision.

Think about It

1. In vision, as in photography, one frequently has to sacrifice sharpness (acuity) to increase sensitivity. Discuss.

2. Why is it important to distinguish between intensity and brightness and between wavelength and color?

3. If you mix equal proportions of red and green light, you get something close to white or gray light, depending on the exact wavelengths of red and green. However, if you mix equal portions of red and green paint, you get an approximation of black paint. Explain this paradox.

4. Is it appropriate to refer to the light being reflected by a red object as a red light? Why or why not?

5. The study of the neural mechanisms of human vision could not have progressed without research on other species. Discuss.

ON THE CD
Studying for an exam? Try the Practice Tests for Chapter 6.

Key Terms

Absorption spectrum (*p. 142*)
Accommodation (*p. 136*)
Achromatic colors (*p. 154*)
Acuity (*p. 135*)
Amacrine cells (*p. 136*)
Binocular (*p. 150*)
Binocular disparity (*p. 136*)
Bipolar cells (*p. 136*)
Blind spot (*p. 136*)
Blobs (*p. 158*)
Chromatic colors (*p. 154*)
Ciliary muscles (*p. 136*)
Color constancy (*p. 156*)
Complementary colors (*p. 155*)
Completion (*p. 137*)
Complex cells (*p. 150*)
Component theory (*p. 155*)
Cones (*p. 138*)
Contrast enhancement (*p. 147*)
Cytochrome oxidase (*p. 158*)

Dual-opponent color cells
    (*p. 158*)
Duplexity theory (*p. 138*)
Fourier analysis (*p. 152*)
Fovea (*p. 137*)
Horizontal cells (*p. 136*)
Lateral geniculate nucleus
    (*p. 144*)
Lateral inhibition (*p. 147*)
Magnocellular layers (*p. 145*)
Microspectrophotometry
    (*p. 155*)
Monocular (*p. 148*)
Nasal hemiretina (*p. 140*)
Off-center cells (*p. 148*)
Ommatidia (*p. 147*)
On-center cells (*p. 148*)
Opponent-process theory
    (*p. 155*)
Parvocellular layers (*p. 145*)

Photopic spectral sensitivity
    curve (*p. 140*)
Photopic vision (*p. 138*)
Primary visual cortex
    (*p. 144*)
Purkinje effect (*p. 140*)
Receptive field (*p. 148*)
Receptors (*p. 136*)
Retina-geniculate-striate
    pathway (*p. 144*)
Retinal ganglion cells (*p. 136*)
Retinex theory (*p. 158*)
Retinotopic (*p. 144*)
Rhodopsin (*p. 142*)
Rods (*p. 138*)
Saccades (*p. 141*)
Scotopic spectral sensitivity
    curve (*p. 140*)
Scotopic vision (*p. 138*)
Sensitivity (*p. 135*)

Simple cells (*p. 150*)
Sine-wave grating (*p. 152*)
Spatial-frequency theory
    (*p. 152*)
Stabilized retinal image
    (*p. 141*)
Temporal hemiretina (*p. 140*)
Transduction (*p. 142*)

ON THE CD

Need some
help studying the key
terms for this chapter?
Check out the elec-
tronic flash cards
for Chapter 6.

Mechanisms of Perception, Conscious Awareness, and Attention

How You Know the World

There are two chapters in this text whose primary focus is sensory: Chapter 6 was the first, and this is the second. Chapter 6 described how visual signals are translated into neural signals by cones and rods and how these neural signals are conducted by the retina-geniculate-striate system to the primary visual cortex.

This chapter differs from Chapter 6 in two major respects. First, rather than focusing on one sensory system, it discusses all five **exteroceptive sensory systems,** the five sensory systems that interpret stimuli from outside the body: vision, hearing, touch, smell, and taste. Second, rather than focusing on the conduction of sensory signals from receptors to cortex, this chapter focuses on cortical mechanisms and phenomena.

Before you begin the first section of this chapter, consider the following case from Williams (1970). By the time you have reached the final section, you will be prepared to diagnose the patient and interpret the case.

The Case of the Man Who Could See Only One Thing at a Time

A 68-year-old patient was referred because he had difficulty finding his way around—even around his own home. The patient attributed his problems to his "inability to see properly."

It was found that if two objects (e.g., two pencils) were held in front of him at the same time, he could see only one of them, whether they were held side by side, one above the other, or even one partially behind the other. Pictures of single objects or faces could be identified, even when quite complex; but if a picture included two objects, only one object could be identified at one time, though that one would sometimes fade, whereupon the other would enter the patient's perception. If a sentence were presented in a line, only the rightmost word could be read, but if one word were presented spread over the entire area covered by the previous sentence, the word could be read in its entirety. If the patient was shown overlapping drawings (i.e., one drawn on top of another), he would see one but deny the existence of the other.

As you read this chapter, think about this patient. Think about the nature of his deficit and the likely location of his brain damage.

7.1 Principles of Sensory System Organization

To understand the organization of the sensory areas of the cortex, it is important that you appreciate that they are of three fundamentally different types: primary, secondary, and association. The **primary sensory cortex** of a system is the area of sensory cortex that receives most of its input directly from the thalamic relay nuclei of that system. For example, as you learned in Chapter 6, the primary visual cortex is the area of the cerebral cortex that receives most of its input from the lateral geniculate nucleus of the thalamus. The **secondary sensory cortex** of a system comprises the areas of the sensory cortex that receive most of their input from the primary sensory cortex of that system or from other areas of the secondary sensory cortex of the same system. **Association cortex** is any area of cortex that receives input from more than one sensory system. Most input to areas of association cortex comes via areas of secondary sensory cortex.

The interactions among these three types of sensory cortex are characterized by three major principles: hierarchical organization, functional segregation, and parallel processing.

Hierarchical Organization

Sensory systems are characterized by **hierarchical organization.** A *hierarchy* is a system whose members can be assigned to specific levels or ranks in relation to one another. For example, the army is a hierarchical system because all soldiers are ranked with respect to their authority. In the same way, sensory structures are organized in a hierarchy on the basis of the specificity and complexity of their function (see Figure 7.1). As one moves through a sensory system from receptors, to thalamic nuclei, to primary sensory cortex, to secondary sensory cortex, to association cortex, one finds neurons that respond optimally to stimuli of greater and greater specificity and complexity. Each level of a sensory hierarchy receives its input from lower levels and adds another layer of analysis before passing it on up the hierarchy (see Hilgetag, O'Neill, & Young, 1996).

The hierarchical organization of sensory systems is apparent from a comparison of the effects of damage to various levels: The higher the level of damage, the more

FIGURE 7.1 The hierarchical organization of the sensory systems. The receptors perform the simplest and most general analyses, and the association cortex performs the most complex and specific analyses.

specific and complex the deficit. For example, destruction of a sensory system's receptors produces a complete loss of ability to perceive in that sensory modality (e.g., total blindness or deafness); in contrast, destruction of an area of association or secondary sensory cortex typically produces complex and specific sensory deficits, while leaving fundamental sensory abilities intact. Dr. P., the man who mistook his wife for a hat (Sacks, 1985), displayed such a pattern of deficits.

The Case of the Man Who Mistook His Wife for a Hat

Dr. P. was a musician of distinction, well-known for many years as a singer . . . and as a teacher. . . . It was obvious within a few seconds of meeting him that there was no trace of dementia [intellectual deterioration]. . . . He was a man of great cultivation and charm who talked well and fluently, with imagination and humour. . . .

"What seems to be the matter?" I asked him at length.

"Nothing that I know of," he replied with a smile, "but people seem to think that there's something wrong with my eyes."

"But *you* don't recognise any visual problems?"

"No, not directly, but I occasionally make mistakes." . . .

It was while examining his reflexes . . . that the first bizarre experience occurred. I had taken off his left shoe and scratched the sole of his foot with a key—a frivolous-seeming but essential test of a reflex—and then, excusing

myself to screw my ophthalmoscope together, left him to put on the shoe himself. To my surprise, a minute later, he had not done this.

"Can I help?" I asked.

"Help what? Help whom?" . . .

"Your shoe," I repeated. "Perhaps you'd put it on."

He continued to look downwards, though not at the shoe, with an intense but misplaced concentration. Finally his gaze settled on his foot.

"That is my shoe, yes?" Did I mis-hear? Did he mis-see?

"My eyes," he explained, and put his hand to his foot. "This is my shoe, no?"

"No, it is not. That is your foot. *There* is your shoe."

Was he joking? Was he mad? Was he blind? If this was one of his "strange mistakes," it was the strangest mistake I had ever come across.

I helped him on with his shoe (his foot), to avoid further complication. . . . I resumed my examination. His visual acuity was good; he had no difficulty seeing a pin on the floor. . . .

He saw all right, but what did he see? . . .

"What is this?" I asked, holding up a glove.

"May I examine it?" he asked, taking it from me.

"A continuous surface," he announced at last, "infolded on itself. It appears to have"—he hesitated—"five out-pouchings, if this is the word."

"Yes," I said cautiously. "You have given me a description. Now tell me what it is."

"A container of some sort?"

"Yes," I said, "and what would it contain?"

"It would contain its contents!" said Dr. P., with a laugh. "There are many possibilities. It could be a change purse, for example, for coins of five sizes. It could . . . "

"Does it not look familiar? Do you think it might contain, might fit, a part of the body?"

No light of recognition dawned on his face . . .

I must have looked aghast, but he seemed to think he had done rather well. There was a hint of a smile on his face. He also appeared to have decided the examination was over and started to look around for his hat. He reached out his hand and took hold of his wife's head, tried to lift it off, to put it on. He had apparently mistaken his wife for a hat! His wife looked as if she was used to such things.[1]

In recognition of the hierarchical organization of sensory systems, psychologists sometimes divide the general process of perceiving into two general phases: sensation and perception. **Sensation** is the process of detecting the presence of stimuli, and **perception** is the higher-order process of integrating, recognizing, and interpreting complete patterns of sensations. Dr. P.'s problem was clearly one of visual perception, not visual sensation.

---

[1]Reprinted with the permission of Simon & Schuster from *The Man Who Mistook His Wife for a Hat and Other Clinical Tales* by Oliver Sacks. Copyright © 1970, 1981, 1983, 1984, 1985 by Oliver Sacks.

Functional Segregation

It was once assumed that the primary, secondary, and association areas of a sensory system were each *functionally homogeneous.* That is, it was assumed that all areas of cortex at any given level of a sensory hierarchy acted together to perform the same function. However, research has shown that **functional segregation,** rather than functional homogeneity, characterizes the organization of sensory systems. It is now clear that each of the three levels of cerebral cortex—primary, secondary, and association—in each sensory system contains functionally distinct areas that specialize in different kinds of analysis.

Parallel Processing

It was once believed that the different levels of a sensory hierarchy were connected in a serial fashion. A *serial system* is a system in which information flows among the components over just one pathway, like a string through a strand of beads. However, there is now evidence that sensory systems are *parallel systems*—systems in which information flows through the components over multiple pathways. Parallel systems feature **parallel processing**—the simultaneous analysis of a signal in different ways by the multiple parallel pathways of a neural network.

An important type of parallel processing recurs throughout this chapter. There appear to be two kinds of parallel streams of analysis in our sensory systems: one that is capable of influencing our behavior without our conscious awareness and one that influences our behavior by engaging our conscious awareness (see Jeannerod et al., 1995). This finding is as counterintuitive as it is important. Pause for a moment to consider its implications. What do you think would happen if a lesion disrupted the conscious stream without disrupting its parallel unconscious stream? You will encounter patients in this chapter who have such damage: They can reach out and deftly pick up objects that they do not consciously see.

The Current Model of Sensory System Organization

Figure 7.2 summarizes the information in this section of the chapter by illustrating how thinking about the organization of sensory systems has changed. In the 1960s, sensory systems were believed to be hierarchical, functionally homogeneous, and serial. However, subsequent research has established that sensory systems are hierarchical, functionally segregated, and parallel (see Zeki, 1993a).

Sensory systems are characterized by a division of labor: multiple specialized areas, at multiple levels, inter-

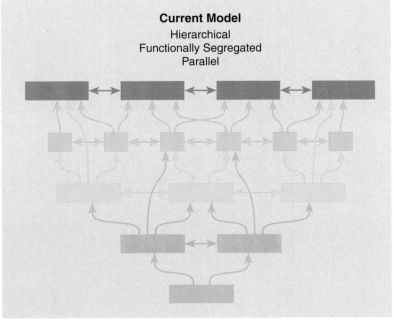

FIGURE 7.2 Two models of sensory system organization: The former model was hierarchical, functionally homogeneous, and serial; the current model, which is more consistent with the evidence, is hierarchical, functionally segregated, and parallel. Not shown in the current model are descending pathways that provide feedback from higher levels to lower levels.

connected by multiple parallel pathways. Yet, complex stimuli are normally perceived as integrated wholes, not as combinations of independent attributes. How does the brain combine individual sensory attributes to produce integrated perceptions? This is called the *binding problem* (see Bernstein & Robertson, 1998; de Gelder, 2000; Friedman-Hill, Robertson, & Treisman, 1995).

One possible solution to the binding problem is that there is a single area of the cortex at the top of the sensory hierarchy that receives signals from all other areas of the sensory system and puts them together to form perceptions; however, there are no areas of cortex to which all areas of a single sensory system report. It seems, then, that perceptions must be a product of the combined

activity of the many interconnected cortical areas (see Zeki, 1993a).

Not shown in Figure 7.2 are the many pathways that descend through the sensory hierarchies. Although most sensory pathways carry information from lower to higher levels of their respective sensory hierarchies, many less prominent pathways in these systems conduct in the opposite direction (from higher to lower levels). Those that conduct information from cortical sensory areas to subcortical areas are called **corticofugal pathways.** Corticofugal pathways are one of the means by which cognitive processes, such as attention, can influence perception (see Gao & Suga, 2000; Murphy, Duckett, & Sillito, 1999).

7.2 Cortical Mechanisms of Vision

We humans are visual animals. The entire occipital cortex as well as large areas of temporal cortex and parietal cortex are involved in vision (see Figure 7.3). The *primary visual cortex* is located in the posterior region of the occipital lobes, much of it hidden from view in the longitudinal fissure. The areas of *secondary visual cortex* are located in two general regions: in the prestriate cortex and in the inferotemporal cortex. The **prestriate cortex** is the band of tissue in the occipital lobe that surrounds the primary visual cortex. The **inferotemporal cortex** is the cortex of the inferior temporal lobe. Areas of association cortex that receive visual input are located in several parts of the cerebral cortex, but the largest single area is in the **posterior parietal cortex.**

In keeping with the general hierarchical organization of the sensory cortex, the major flow of visual information is from the primary visual cortex to the various areas of secondary visual cortex to the areas of association cortex. As one moves up this visual hierarchy, the neurons have larger receptive fields and the stimuli to which the neurons respond are more specific and more complex (see Zeki, 1993b).

Scotomas: Completion

Damage to an area of the primary visual cortex produces a **scotoma**—an area of blindness—in the

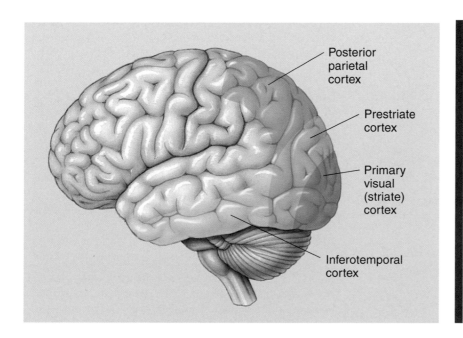

FIGURE 7.3 The visual areas of the human cerebral cortex.

Posterior parietal cortex

Prestriate cortex

Primary visual (striate) cortex

Inferotemporal cortex

corresponding area of the contralateral visual field of both eyes (see Figure 6.13). Neurological patients with suspected damage to the primary visual cortex are usually given a **perimetry test.** While the patient's head is held motionless on a chin rest, the patient stares with one eye at a fixation point on a screen. A small dot of light is then flashed on various parts of the screen, and the patient presses a button to record when the dot is seen. Then, the entire process is repeated for the other eye. The result is a map of the visual field of each eye, which indicates any areas of blindness. Figure 7.4 illustrates the perimetric maps of the visual fields of a man with a bullet wound in his left primary visual cortex. Notice the massive scotoma in the right visual field of each eye.

Many patients with extensive scotomas are unaware of their deficits. One of the factors that contributes to this lack of awareness is the phenomenon of **completion** (see Chapter 6). A patient with a scotoma who looks at a complex figure, part of which lies in the scotoma, often reports seeing a complete image. In some cases, this com-

pletion may depend on residual visual capacities in the scotoma; however, completion also occurs in cases in which this explanation can be ruled out. For example, patients who are **hemianopsic** (having a scotoma covering half of the visual field) may see an entire face when they focus on a person's nose, even when the side of the face in the scotoma has been covered by a blank card.

Consider the completion phenomenon experienced by the esteemed physiological psychologist Karl Lashley (1941). He often developed a large scotoma next to his fovea during a migraine attack (see Figure 7.5).

The Case of the Physiological Psychologist Who Made Faces Disappear

Talking with a friend I glanced just to the right of his face wherein his head disappeared. His shoulders and necktie were still visible but the vertical stripes on the wallpaper behind him seemed to extend down to the necktie. It was impossible to see this as a blank area when projected on the striped wallpaper of uniformly patterned surface although any intervening object failed to be seen. (p. 338)

Scotomas: Blindsight

Blindsight is another phenomenon displayed by patients with scotomas resulting from damage to primary visual cortex. Blindsight is the ability of such patients to respond to visual stimuli in their scotomas even though they have no conscious awareness of the stimuli (Weiskrantz, 1996). For example, a subject might reach out and grab an object in her scotoma, all the while claiming not to see it. If blindsight confuses you, imagine how it confuses people who experience it. Consider, for example, the reactions to blindsight of D.B., a patient who was blind in his left visual field following surgical removal of his right occipital lobe (Weiskrantz et al., 1974).

The Case of D.B., the Man Confused by His Own Blindsight

Even though the patient had no awareness of "seeing" in his blind [left] field, evidence was obtained that (a) he could reach for visual stimuli [in his left field] with considerable accuracy; (b) could differentiate the orientation of a vertical line from a horizontal or diagonal line; (c) could differentiate the letters "X" and "O." (p. 726)

Needless to say, he was questioned repeatedly about his vision in his left half-field, and his most common response was that he saw nothing at all. . . . When he was shown his results [through his good, right-half field] he expressed

FIGURE 7.4 The perimetric maps of a subject with a bullet wound in his left primary visual cortex. The scotomas (areas of blindness) are indicated in gray. (Adapted from Teuber, Battersby, & Bender, 1960b.)

FIGURE 7.5 The completion of a migraine-induced scotoma as described by Karl Lashley (1941).

surprise and insisted several times that he thought he was just "guessing." When he was shown a video film of his reaching and judging orientation of lines, he was openly astonished. (p. 721)

Two neurological interpretations of blindsight have been proposed. One is that the striate cortex is not completely destroyed and the remaining islands of functional cells are capable of mediating some visual abilities in the absence of conscious awareness (see Wessinger, Fendrich, & Gazzaniga, 1997). The other is that those visual pathways that ascend directly to the secondary visual cortex from subcortical visual structures without passing through the primary visual cortex are capable of maintaining some visual abilities in the absence of cognitive awareness (see Kentridge, Heywood, & Weiskrantz, 1997). There is some support for both theories, but the evidence is not conclusive for either (see Rosa, Tweedale, & Elston, 2000; Schärli, Harman, & Hogben, 1999a, 1999b). Indeed, it is possible that both mechanisms contribute to the phenomenon.

■ Visual Perception and Neural Activity

Do you recall the key point stressed in Chapter 6—that our visual perceptions are often different from the physical reality of visual input? This occurs because the activity of visual cortical neurons is often associated with the properties of the perception rather than the physical stimulus.

Figure 7.6 illustrates this point by showing that we often see visual contours where none exist (Albright, 1995); these are called **subjective contours.** Why do we see subjective contours? The reason is that prestriate neurons (Peterhans & von der Heydt, 1991), and even a

FIGURE 7.6 Subjective contours. You see the white bar in A and the white triangle in B even though they do not physically exist—they are subjective contours. Your ability to see subjective contours helps you see boundaries between objects of similar brightness, color, and pattern—for example, look at C.

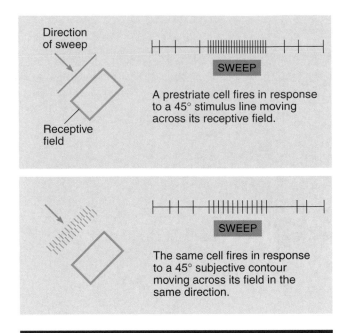

FIGURE 7.7   Neurons of the monkey prestriate cortex and primary visual cortex respond to subjective contours of a particular orientation. (Adapted from Peterhans & von der Heydt, 1991.)

few primary visual cortex neurons (Sheth et al., 1996), respond as if real contours are present when subjective contours of the appropriate orientation appear in their receptive fields (see Figure 7.7).

A similar point was made by a recent study using fMRI (functional magnetic resonance imaging) and subjects viewing a color illusion (Humphrey et al., 1999). Activity in areas of prestriate cortex was more closely related to the perceived colors than to the wavelengths of the actual stimuli.

Functional Areas of Secondary and Association Visual Cortex

Secondary visual cortex and the portions of association cortex that are involved in visual analysis are both composed of different areas, each specialized for a particular type of visual analysis. For example, in the macaque monkey, whose visual cortex has been thoroughly mapped, there are at least 30 different functional areas of visual cortex; in addition to primary visual cortex, 24 areas of secondary visual cortex and 7 areas of association visual cortex have been identified. The neurons in each functional area respond most vigorously to different aspects of visual stimuli (e.g., to their color, movement, or shape); selective lesions to the different areas produce different visual losses; and there are often subtle anatomical differences among the areas (see Tanaka, 1996).

The various functional areas of secondary and association visual cortex in the macaque are prodigiously interconnected. Anterograde and retrograde tracing studies have identified over 300 interconnecting pathways (Van Essen, Anderson, & Felleman, 1992). Although connections between areas are virtually always reciprocal, the major flow of information is up the hierarchy, from more simple to more complex areas.

PET (positron emission tomography) and fMRI have been used to identify various areas of visual cortex in humans. The activity of the subjects' brains has been monitored while they inspect various types of visual stimuli (e.g., Grossman et al., 2000; Kourtzi & Kanwisher, 2000). By identifying the areas of activation associated with various visual properties (e.g., movement or color), researchers have so far delineated about a dozen different functional areas of human visual cortex. A map of these areas is shown in Figure 7.8. Most are similar in terms of location, anatomical characteristics, and function to areas in the macaque (Courtney & Ungerleider, 1997), but each tends to be much larger than its macaque counterpart.

Dorsal and Ventral Streams

You learned in Chapter 6 that most visual information enters the primary visual cortex via the lateral geniculate nuclei. In the primary visual cortex, the information from the two lateral geniculate nuclei is received, combined, and then segregated into multiple pathways that project separately to the various functional areas of secondary, and then association, visual cortex (see Cabeza & Nyberg, 1997; Logothetis, 1998).

Many pathways that conduct information from the primary visual cortex through various specialized areas of secondary and association cortex are parts of two major streams: the dorsal stream and the ventral stream (Ungerleider & Mishkin, 1982; Courtney & Ungerleider, 1997). The **dorsal stream** flows from the primary visual cortex to the dorsal prestriate cortex to the posterior parietal cortex, and the **ventral stream** flows from the primary visual cortex to the ventral prestriate cortex to the inferotemporal cortex—see Figure 7.9.

Ungerleider and Mishkin (1982) proposed that the dorsal and ventral visual streams perform different visual functions. They suggested that the dorsal stream is involved in the perception of "where" objects are and the ventral stream is involved in the perception of "what" objects are.

The major implication of the **"where" versus "what" theory** and other parallel-processing theories of vision is that damage to some areas of cortex may abolish certain aspects of vision while leaving others unaffected. Indeed, the most convincing support for the influential "where" versus "what" theory has come from

Back and medial surface
of right hemisphere

Back and lateral surface
of right hemisphere

| ■ V1 | ■ V2 | ■ VP | ■ V3a | ■ V3 | □ V4v | ■ LO |

| □ MT/V5 | ■ VIP/SPO | ■ pMSTd/MSTd | □ LIP/LSPO |

FIGURE 7.8   Areas of visual cortex so far discovered in humans. Their names are based on similarities to areas of visual cortex in the more thoroughly studied macaque monkey.
(Based on Tootell et al., 1996.)

the comparison of the specific effects of damage to the dorsal and ventral streams (see Ungerleider & Haxby, 1994). Patients with damage to the posterior parietal cortex often have difficulty reaching accurately for objects that they have no difficulty describing; conversely, patients with damage to the inferotemporal cortex often have no difficulty reaching accurately for objects that they have difficulty describing.

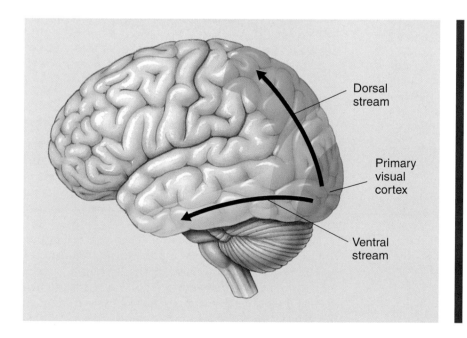

Dorsal
stream

Primary
visual
cortex

Ventral
stream

FIGURE 7.9   Information about particular aspects of a visual display flow out of the primary visual cortex over many pathways. The pathways can be grouped into two general streams: dorsal and ventral.

Although the "where" versus "what" theory has many advocates, there is an alternative interpretation for the same evidence (Goodale, 1993; Milner & Goodale, 1993). Goodale and Milner argued that the key difference between the dorsal and ventral streams is not the kinds of information they carry but the use to which that information is put. They suggested that the function of the dorsal stream is to direct behavioral interactions with objects, whereas the function of the ventral stream is to mediate the conscious perception of objects; this is the **"control of behavior" versus "conscious perception" theory** (see Logothetis & Sheinberg, 1996).

The "control of behavior" versus "conscious perception" theory can readily explain the two major neuropsychological findings that are the foundation of the "where" versus "what" theory. Namely, the "control of behavior" versus "conscious perception" theory suggests that patients with dorsal stream damage may do poorly on tests of location and movement because most tests of location and movement involve performance measures, and that patients with ventral stream damage may do poorly on tests of visual recognition because most tests of visual recognition involve verbal, and thus conscious, report.

The major strength of the "control of behavior" versus "conscious perception" theory is the confirmation of its two primary assertions: (1) that some patients with bilateral lesions to the ventral stream have no conscious experience of seeing and yet are able to interact with objects under visual guidance, and (2) that some patients with bilateral lesions to the dorsal stream can consciously see objects but cannot interact with them under visual guidance. Following are two such cases.

The Case of D.F., the Woman Who Could Grasp Objects She Did Not Consciously See

D.F. has bilateral damage to her ventral prestriate cortex, thus interrupting the flow of the ventral stream (Goodale et al., 1991). Amazingly, she can respond accurately to visual stimuli that she does not consciously see. Goodale and Milner (1992) describe her thusly:

> Despite her profound inability to recognize the size, shape and orientation of visual objects, D.F. showed strikingly accurate guidance of hand and finger movements directed at the very same objects. Thus, when she was presented with a pair of rectangular blocks of the same or different dimensions, she was unable to distinguish between them. When she was asked to indicate the width of a single block by means of her index finger and thumb, her matches bore no relationship to the dimensions of the object and showed considerable trial to trial variability. However, when she was asked simply to reach out and pick up the block, the aperture between her index finger and thumb changed systematically

> with the width of the object, just as in normal subjects. In other words, D.F. scaled her grip to the dimensions of the objects she was about to pick up, even though she appeared to be unable to [consciously] "perceive" those dimensions.
> A similar dissociation was seen in her responses to the orientation of stimuli. Thus, when presented with a large slot that could be placed in one of a number of different orientations, she showed great difficulty in indicating the orientation either verbally or manually (i.e., by rotating her hand or a hand-held card). Nevertheless, she was as good as normal subjects at reaching out and placing her hand or the card into the slot, turning her hand appropriately from the very onset of the movement. (p. 22)

The Case of A.T., the Woman Who Could Not Accurately Grasp Unfamiliar Objects That She Saw

The case of A.T. is in major respects complementary to that of D.F. The patient A.T. is a woman with a lesion of the occipitoparietal region, which likely interrupts her dorsal route.

> A.T. was able to recognize objects, and was also able to demonstrate their size with her fingers. By contrast, preshape of the hand during object-directed movements was incorrect. Correlation between object size and maximum grip size was lacking, with the consequence that objects could not be grasped between the fingertips; instead, the patient made awkward palmar grasps. The schema framework offers a compelling explanation for this deficit. Because the grasp schemas were destroyed by the lesion, or disconnected from visual input, the grip aperture did not stop at the required size, grip closure was delayed and the transport was prolonged in order to remain co-ordinated with the grasp.
> A.T. cannot preshape her hand for neutral objects like plastic cylinders, yet, when faced with a familiar object whose size is a semantic property, like a lipstick, she can grasp it with reasonable accuracy. This interaction reflects the role of the abundant anatomical interconnections between the two cortical systems. (Jeannerod et al., 1995, p. 320)

■ Prosopagnosia

A discussion of prosopagnosia completes this section of this chapter. It is an interesting, controversial, and important topic in its own right; but, as you will soon learn, its investigation has provided further support for the "control of behavior" versus "conscious perception" theory.

What is prosopagnosia? **Prosopagnosia,** briefly put, is visual agnosia for faces. Let me explain. **Agnosia** is a failure of recognition (*gnosis* means "to know") that is not attributable to a sensory deficit or to verbal or intellectual impairment; **visual agnosia** is a specific agnosia for visual stimuli. Visual agnosics can see visual stimuli, but they don't know what they are. (Recall the case of Dr. P., the man who mistook his wife for a hat.)

Visual agnosias themselves are often specific to a particular aspect of visual input and are named accordingly; for example, *movement agnosia, object agnosia,* and *color agnosia* are difficulties in recognizing movement, objects, and color, respectively. It is presumed that each specific visual agnosia results from damage to an area of secondary visual cortex that mediates the recognition of that particular attribute. Prosopagnosics are visual agnosics with a specific difficulty in recognizing faces.

Prosopagnosics can usually recognize a face as a face, but they have problems recognizing whose face it is. They often report seeing a jumble of individual facial parts (e.g., eyes, nose, chin, cheeks) that for some reason are never fused into an easy-to-recognize whole. In extreme cases, prosopagnosics cannot recognize themselves: Imagine what it would be like to stare in the mirror every morning and not recognize the face that is looking back.

Autopsy and structural MRI studies of prosopagnosics have linked prosopagnosia to the ventral stream: There is typically bilateral damage to the inferior prestriate area and to the adjacent portions of the inferotemporal cortex (see Gross & Sergent, 1992). Furthermore, a similar area has been shown by MRI studies to be activated in normal humans while they are viewing faces, as opposed to other pattern stimuli (see Courtney & Ungerleider, 1997; Gauthier et al., 2000).

Prosopagnosia was initially assumed to result from bilateral damage to a particular area of cortex dedicated to the recognition of faces. The faces of one's conspecifics (members of one's species) are among the most important visual stimuli for higher social primates, so it is conceivable that there is an area of the cortex specifically dedicated to face recognition. The main evidence for this interpretation is that patients who have difficulty recognizing faces have little difficulty recognizing other test objects (e.g., a chair, a pencil, or a door).

Stop reading for a moment and give this line of evidence some thought: It is seriously flawed. Because prosopagnosics have no difficulty recognizing faces as faces, the fact that they can recognize chairs as chairs, pencils as pencils, and doors as doors is not relevant. The critical question is whether they can recognize which chair, which pencil, and which door. Careful testing of some prosopagnosics has revealed that their recognition deficits are not restricted to faces: A farmer lost his ability to recognize particular cows when he became prosopagnosic, and a birdwatcher lost his ability to distinguish species of birds. These cases suggest that many prosopagnosics have a general problem recognizing specific objects that belong to complex classes of objects (e.g., particular automobiles or particular houses), not a specific problem recognizing faces (see Dixon, Bub, & Argin, 1998; Gauthier, Behrmann, & Tarr, 1999). However, there are some well-documented reports of neuropsychological patients who have difficulty recognizing particular faces but not other complex objects (DeRenzi, 1997; Farah, 1990).

Evidence that there is a specific region of visual cortex dedicated to the recognition of faces is provided by the case of C.K. (Moscovitch, Winocur, & Behrmann, 1997).

The Case of C.K., the Man Who Could Recognize a Face But Not Vegetables

C.K. did not have prosopagnosia; he had the opposite problem: He had severe visual object agnosia but no difficulty recognizing faces. For example, C.K. could recognize the inverted face in Figure 7.10 without being able to recognize the vegetables that compose it. C.K. had damage to his ventral stream.

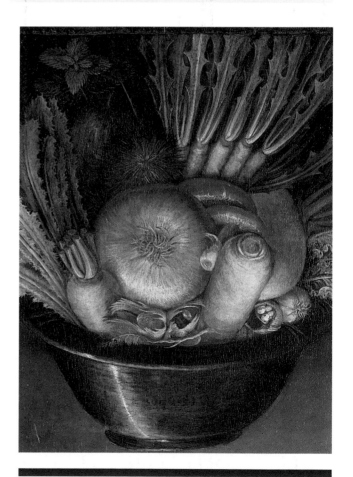

FIGURE 7.10 *The Vegetable Gardener* by Guiseppe Arcimbaldo, owned by Museo Civico Ala Ponzone, Cremona, Italy. Patient C.K. (Moscovitch, Winocur, & Behrmann, 1997) could see the face in this painting when he viewed it upside-down, as could all the control subjects. But C.K. could recognize none of the vegetables that compose the face. This is evidence that prosopagnosia and visual object agnosia can be independent.

FIGURE 7.11 The firing rate of a monkey inferotemporal cortex neuron before, during, and after the presentation of monkey faces at different angles. The profile view (100°) was most effective in increasing the firing rate of this cell. (Adapted from Gross et al., 1985.)

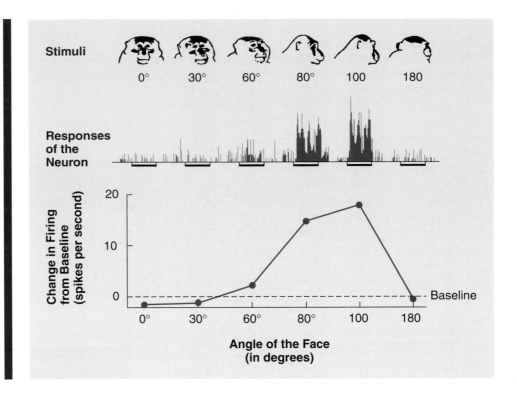

Consistent with the idea that bilateral lesions in the ventral stream might produce specific deficits in facial recognition is that neurons in the inferotemporal cortex of macaques seem to respond most robustly to macaque faces (see Logothetis & Sheinberg, 1996). They do not respond to other complex shapes, to mixed-up components of faces, or to upside-down faces. Some inferotemporal neurons, as illustrated in Figure 7.11, fire only when the face is in a specific orientation (Gross et al., 1985). Moreover, functional brain-imaging studies have identified an area of inferotemporal cortex—the same area implicated in prosopagnosia—that becomes active in both hemispheres when human subjects view human faces but not when they view equally complex control patterns (see Gauthier et al., 2000; Ishai et al., 2000).

An interesting hypothesis about prosopagnosia can be derived from the "control of behavior" versus "conscious perception" theory. The fact that prosopagnosia results from bilateral damage to the ventral stream suggests that dorsal-stream function may be intact. In other words, it suggests that prosopagnosics may be able to unconsciously recognize faces that they cannot recognize consciously. Remarkably, this is, indeed, the case.

Tranel and Damasio (1985) were the first to demonstrate unconscious facial recognition in prosopagnosics. They presented a series of photographs to each patient, some familiar to the patient, some not. The subjects claimed not to recognize any of the faces. However, when familiar, but not unfamiliar, faces were presented, the subjects displayed a large skin conductance response, thus indicating that the faces were being unconsciously recognized by undamaged portions of the brain.

■ Interim Conclusion

Before leaving this section on visual perception, review in your mind the topics that were discussed: completion, blindsight, subjective contours, functional cortical areas, dorsal and ventral streams, the cases of D.F., A.T., and C.K., and prosopagnosia. Advances in understanding of these topics have reinforced the three principles of perceptual processing that introduced the chapter: hierarchical organization, functional segregation, and parallel processing.

7.3 Audition

The function of the auditory system is the perception of sound—or, more accurately, the perception of objects and events through the sounds that they make (Masterton, 1992). Sounds are vibrations of air molecules that

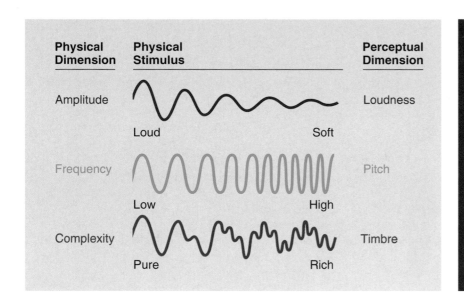

FIGURE 7.12   The relation between the physical and perceptual dimensions of sound.

stimulate the auditory system; humans hear only those molecular vibrations between about 20 and 20,000 hertz (cycles per second). Figure 7.12 illustrates how sounds are commonly recorded in the form of waves and the relation between the physical dimensions of sound vibrations and our perceptions of them. The *amplitude, frequency,* and *complexity* of the molecular vibrations are perceived as *loudness, pitch,* and *timbre,* respectively.

Pure tones (sine wave vibrations) exist only in laboratories and sound recording studios; in real life, sound is always associated with complex patterns of vibrations. For example, Figure 7.13 illustrates the complex sound wave associated with one note of a clarinet. The figure also illustrates that any complex sound wave can be broken down mathematically into a series of sine waves of various frequencies and amplitudes; these component sine waves produce the original sound when they are added together. As you learned in Chapter 6, *Fourier*

analysis is the mathematical procedure for breaking down complex waves into their component sine waves. One theory of audition is that the auditory system performs a Fourier-like analysis of complex sounds in terms of their component sine waves.

■ | The Ear

The ear is illustrated in Figure 7.14 on page 174. Sound waves travel down the *auditory canal* and cause the **tympanic membrane** (the eardrum) to vibrate. These vibrations are then transferred to the three **ossicles**—the small bones of the middle ear: the *malleus* (the hammer), the *incus* (the anvil), and the *stapes* (the stirrup). The vibrations of the stapes trigger vibrations of the membrane called the **oval window,** which in turn transfers the vibrations to the fluid of the snail-shaped **cochlea**

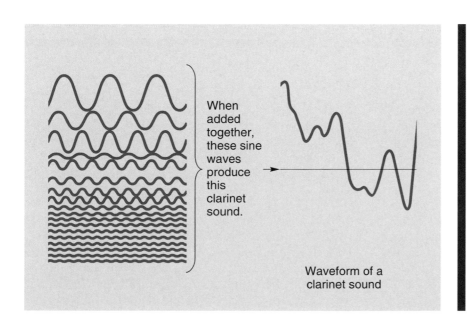

When added together, these sine waves produce this clarinet sound.

Waveform of a clarinet sound

FIGURE 7.13   The breaking down of a sound—in this case, the sound of a clarinet—into its component sine waves by Fourier analysis. When added together, the sine wave components produce the complex sound wave.

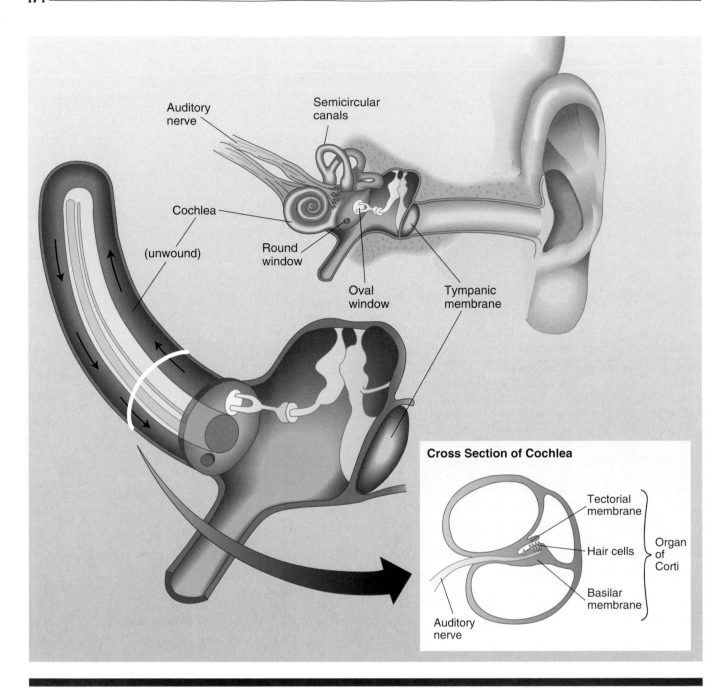

FIGURE 7.14 Anatomy of the ear.

(*kokhlos* means "land snail"). The cochlea is a long, coiled tube with an internal membrane running almost to its tip. This internal membrane is the auditory receptor organ, the **organ of Corti.**

Each pressure change at the oval window travels along the organ of Corti as a wave. The organ of Corti is composed of two membranes: the basilar membrane and the tectorial membrane. The auditory receptors, the **hair cells,** are mounted in the **basilar membrane,** and the **tectorial membrane** rests on the hair cells. Accordingly, a deflection of the organ of Corti at any point along its length produces a shearing force on the hair cells at the same point (Corwin & Warchol, 1991). This force stim-

ulates the hair cells and thereby triggers action potentials in axons of the **auditory nerve**—a branch of the eighth cranial nerve (the *auditory-vestibular nerve*). The vibrations of the cochlear fluid are ultimately dissipated by the *round window,* an elastic membrane in the cochlea wall.

The major principle of cochlear coding is that different frequencies produce maximal stimulation of hair cells at different points along the basilar membrane—with higher frequencies producing greater activation closer to the windows. Thus, the many component frequencies that compose each complex sound activate hair cells at many different points along the basilar membrane, and the many signals created by a single complex sound are carried out of the ear by many different auditory neurons. Like the cochlea, most other structures of the auditory system are arrayed according to frequency. Thus, in the same way that the organization of the visual system is primarily **retinotopic,** the organization of the auditory system is primarily **tonotopic.**

This brings us to the major unsolved mystery of auditory processing. Imagine yourself in a complex acoustic environment such as a party. The music is playing; people are dancing, eating, and drinking; and numerous conversations are going on around you. Because the component frequencies in each individual sound activate many sites along your basilar membrane, the number of sites simultaneously activated at any one time by the party noises is enormous. But somehow your auditory system manages to sort these individual frequency messages into separate categories and combine them so that you hear each source of complex sounds independently. For example, you hear the speech of the person

standing next to you as a separate sequence of sounds, despite the fact that it contains many of the same component frequencies coming from other sources.

Figure 7.14 also shows the **semicircular canals**—the receptive organs of the vestibular system. The **vestibular system** carries information about the direction and intensity of head movements, which helps us maintain our balance.

■ | From the Ear to the Primary Auditory Cortex

There is no major auditory pathway to the cortex comparable to the retina-geniculate-striate pathway of the visual system. Instead, there is a network of auditory pathways (see Masterton, 1992), some of which are illustrated in Figure 7.15. The axons of each *auditory nerve* synapse in the ipsilateral *cochlear nuclei,* from which many projections lead to the **superior olives** at the same level. The axons of the olivary neurons project via the

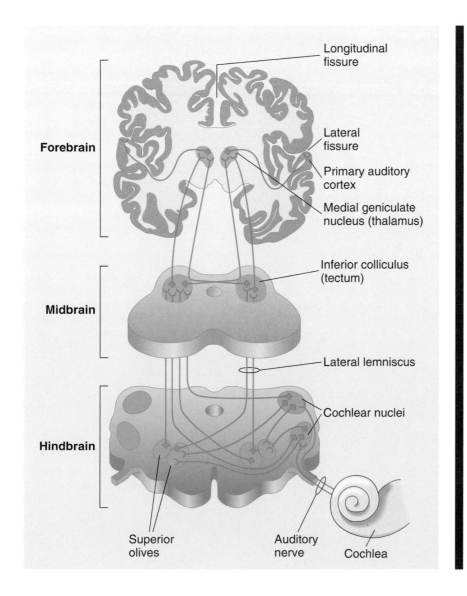

FIGURE 7.15 Some of the pathways of the auditory system that lead from one ear to the cortex.

lateral lemniscus to the **inferior colliculi,** where they synapse on neurons that project to the **medial geniculate nuclei** of the thalamus, which in turn project to the *primary auditory cortex.* Notice that signals from each ear are transmitted to both ipsilateral and contralateral auditory cortex.

Primary Auditory Cortex

In humans, the primary auditory cortex is located in the *lateral fissure* (see Figure 7.16). It is surrounded by secondary auditory cortex. There are thought to be three areas of primary auditory cortex and seven areas of secondary auditory cortex (see Kaas, Hackett, & Tramo, 1999).

Two important principles of organization of the primary auditory cortex have been identified. First, like other areas of the cerebral cortex, the primary auditory cortex is organized in functional columns (see Schreiner, 1992): All of the neurons encountered during a vertical microelectrode penetration of the primary auditory cortex (i.e., a penetration at right angles to the cortical layers) respond optimally to sounds in the same frequency range. Second, like the cochlea, each area of primary auditory cortex is organized tonotopically (see Schreiner, Read, & Sutter, 2000):

Little is known about the neurons in secondary auditory cortex because they respond weakly and inconsistently to the pure tones typically used by researchers. Rauschecker, Tian, and Hauser (1995) reasoned on the basis of what was known about the neurons of secondary visual cortex that they might have more success in studying secondary auditory cortex if they used more complex stimuli—secondary visual cortex neurons respond to complex visual stimuli but respond little to dots of light. These researchers found that monkey calls were more ef-

fective in activating secondary than primary auditory cortex neurons in monkeys. Hence, auditory cortical function, like visual cortical function, appears to be organized hierarchically.

Sound Localization

Localization of sounds in space is mediated by the lateral and medial superior olives, but in different ways. When a sound originates to a person's left, it reaches the left ear first, and it is louder at the left ear. Some neurons in the *medial superior olives* respond to slight differences in the time of arrival of signals from the two ears, whereas some neurons in the *lateral superior olives* respond to slight differences in the amplitude of sounds from the two ears (see Heffner & Masterton, 1990).

The medial and lateral superior olives project to the *superior colliculus* (not shown in Figure 7.15), as well as to the inferior colliculus. In contrast to the general tonotopic organization of the auditory system, the deep layers of the superior colliculi, which receive auditory input, are laid out according to a map of auditory space (King, Schnupp, & Thompson, 1998). The superficial layers of the superior colliculi, which receive visual input, are organized retinotopically. Thus, it appears that the general function of the superior colliculi is locating sources of sensory input in space.

Many researchers interested in sound localization have studied barn owls because these owls can locate sources of sounds better than any other animal whose hearing has been tested. They are nocturnal hunters and must be able to locate field mice solely by the rustling sounds the mice make in the dark. Not surprisingly, the auditory neurons of the barn owl's superior colliculus region are very finely

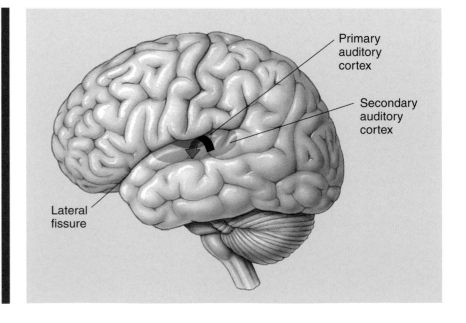

FIGURE 7.16 Location of the primary and secondary auditory cortex in the temporal cortex. Most of the auditory cortex is hidden in the lateral fissure.

Primary auditory cortex

Secondary auditory cortex

Lateral fissure

tuned; that is, each neuron responds only to those sounds from a particular small area around the subject (see Cohen & Knudsen, 1999).

Effects of Auditory Cortex Damage

Efforts to characterize the effects of damage to the auditory cortex have been complicated by the fact that most human auditory cortex is deep in the lateral fissure. Consequently, it is rarely destroyed in its entirety; and if it is, there is in-

evitably extensive damage to surrounding tissue. As a result of this problem, efforts to understand the effects of auditory cortex damage have relied largely on the study of nonhumans.

Surprisingly, complete bilateral lesions of the primary auditory cortex in laboratory mammals produce no permanent deficits in their ability to detect the presence of sounds (e.g., Kavanagh & Kelly, 1988), even when the lesions include substantial secondary auditory cortex. However, such lesions do disrupt the abilities to localize brief sounds and to recognize rapid complex sequences of sound.

7.4 Somatosensation: Touch and Pain

You have undoubtedly experienced a wide variety of sensations emanating from your body. These are generally referred to as *somatosensations*. The system that mediates these bodily sensations—the *somatosensory system*—is, in fact, three separate but interacting systems: (1) an *exteroceptive system*, which senses external stimuli that are applied to the skin; (2) a *proprioceptive system*, which monitors information about the position of the body that comes from receptors in the muscles, joints, and organs of balance; and (3) an *interoceptive system*, which provides general information about conditions within the body (e.g., temperature and blood pressure). This discussion deals almost exclusively with the exteroceptive system, which itself comprises three somewhat distinct divisions: a division for perceiving *mechanical stimuli* (touch), one for *thermal stimuli* (temperature), and one for *nociceptive stimuli* (pain).

Cutaneous Receptors

There are several different kinds of receptors in the skin. Figure 7.17 on page 178 illustrates four that are found in both hairy skin and hairless skin, such as that on the palms of your hands. The simplest cutaneous receptors are the **free nerve endings** (neuron endings with no specialized structures on them), which are particularly sensitive to temperature change and pain. The largest and deepest cutaneous receptors are the onionlike **Pacinian corpuscles;** because they adapt rapidly, they respond best to sudden displacements of the skin. In contrast, *Merkel's disks* and *Ruffini endings* both adapt slowly and respond best to gradual skin indentation and gradual skin stretch, respectively.

To appreciate the functional significance of fast and slow receptor adaptation, consider what happens when a constant pressure is applied to the skin. The pressure

evokes a burst of firing in all receptors, which corresponds to the sensation of being touched; however, after a few hundred milliseconds, only the slowly adapting receptors remain active, and the quality of the sensation changes. In fact, you are often totally unaware of constant skin pressure; for example, you are usually unaware of the feeling of your clothes against your body until you focus attention on it. As a consequence, when you try to identify objects by touch, you manipulate them in your hands so that the pattern of stimulation continually changes. The identification of objects by touch is called **stereognosis.**

Dermatomes

The neural fibers that carry information from cutaneous receptors and other somatosensory receptors gather together in nerves and enter the spinal cord via the *dorsal roots*. The area of the body that is innervated by the left and right dorsal roots of a given segment of the spinal cord is called a **dermatome.** Figure 7.18 on page 179 is a dermatomal map of the human body. Because there is considerable overlap between adjacent dermatomes, destruction of a single dorsal root typically produces little somatosensory loss.

The Two Major Ascending Somatosensory Pathways

Somatosensory information ascends to the human cortex over two major somatosensory system pathways: the dorsal-column medial-lemniscus system and the anterolateral system. The **dorsal-column medial-lemniscus system** carries information about touch and

FIGURE 7.17   Four cutaneous receptors that occur in both hairy and hairless skin.

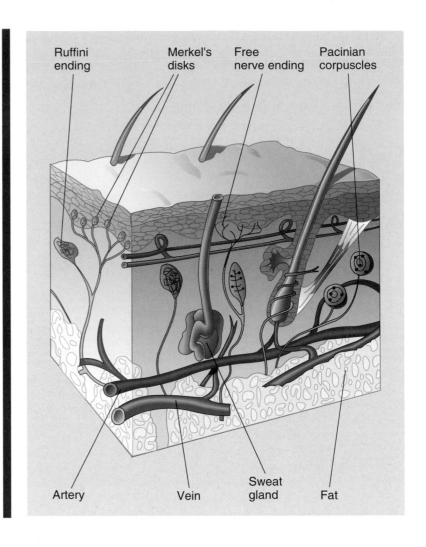

proprioception. The **anterolateral system** carries information about pain and temperature.

The dorsal-column medial-lemniscus system is illustrated in Figure 7.19 on page 180. The sensory neurons of this system enter the spinal cord via a dorsal root, ascend ipsilaterally in the **dorsal columns,** and synapse in the *dorsal column nuclei* of the medulla. The axons of dorsal column nuclei neurons *decussate* (cross over to the other side of the brain) and then ascend in the **medial lemniscus** to the contralateral **ventral posterior nucleus** of the thalamus. The ventral posterior nuclei also receive input via the three branches of the *trigeminal nerve,* which carry somatosensory information from the contralateral areas of the face. Most neurons of the ventral posterior nucleus project to the *primary somatosensory cortex (SI);* others project to the *secondary somatosensory cortex (SII)* or the posterior parietal cortex. Neuroscience trivia collectors will almost certainly want to add to their collection the fact that the dorsal column neurons that originate in the toes are the longest neurons in the human body.

The anterolateral system is illustrated in Figure 7.20 on page 181. Most dorsal root neurons of the anterolat-

eral system synapse as soon as they enter the spinal cord. The axons of most of the second-order neurons decussate but then ascend to the brain in the contralateral anterolateral portion of the spinal cord; however, some do not decussate but ascend ipsilaterally. The anterolateral system comprises three different tracts: the *spinothalamic tract,* which projects to the *ventral posterior nucleus* of the thalamus (as does the dorsal-column medial-lemniscus system); the *spinoreticular tract,* which projects to the *reticular formation* (and then to the *parafascicular nuclei* and *intralaminar nuclei* of the thalamus); and the *spinotectal tract,* which projects to the *tectum* (colliculi). The three branches of the trigeminal nerve carry pain and temperature information from the face to the same thalamic sites. The pain and temperature information that reaches the thalamus is then distributed to SI, SII, the posterior parietal cortex, and other parts of the brain.

Mark, Ervin, and Yakolev (1962) assessed the effects of lesions to the thalamus on the chronic pain of patients in the advanced stages of cancer. Lesions to the ventral posterior nuclei, which receive input from both the spinothalamic tract and the dorsal-column medial-lemniscus system, produced some

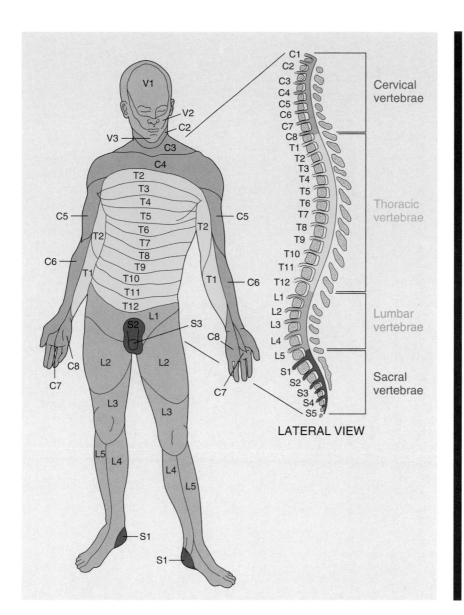

FIGURE 7.18 The dermatomes of the human body. S, L, T, and C refer respectively to the *sacral, lumbar, thoracic,* and *cervical* regions of the spinal cord. V1, V2, and V3 stand for the three branches of the trigeminal nerve.

loss of cutaneous sensitivity to touch, to temperature change, and to sharp pain; but the lesions had no effect on deep, chronic pain. In contrast, lesions of the parafascicular and intralaminar nuclei, both of which receive input from the spinoreticular tract, reduced deep chronic pain without disrupting cutaneous sensitivity.

■ Cortical Areas of Somatosensation

In 1937, Penfield and his colleagues mapped the primary somatosensory cortex of patients during neurosurgery (see Figure 7.21 on page 182). Penfield applied electrical stimulation to various sites on the cortical surface, and the patients, who were fully conscious under a local anesthetic, described what they felt. When stimulation was applied to the *postcentral gyrus,* the patients reported somatosensory sensations in various

parts of their bodies. When Penfield mapped the relation between each site of stimulation and the part of the body in which the sensation was felt, he discovered that the human primary somatosensory cortex (SI) is **somatotopic**—organized according to a map of the body surface. This somatotopic map is commonly referred to as the **somatosensory homunculus** (*homunculus* means "little man").

Evidence of a second somatotopically organized area (SII) was obtained in a similar manner. SII lies just ventral to SI in the postcentral gyrus, and much of it extends into the lateral fissure. SII receives much of its input from SI; but, in contrast to SI, whose input is largely contralateral, SII receives substantial input from both sides of the body.

Much of the output of SI and SII goes to the association cortex of the *posterior parietal lobe.* Notice in Figure 7.21 that the somatosensory homunculus is distorted;

FIGURE 7.19 The dorsal-column medial-lemniscus system.

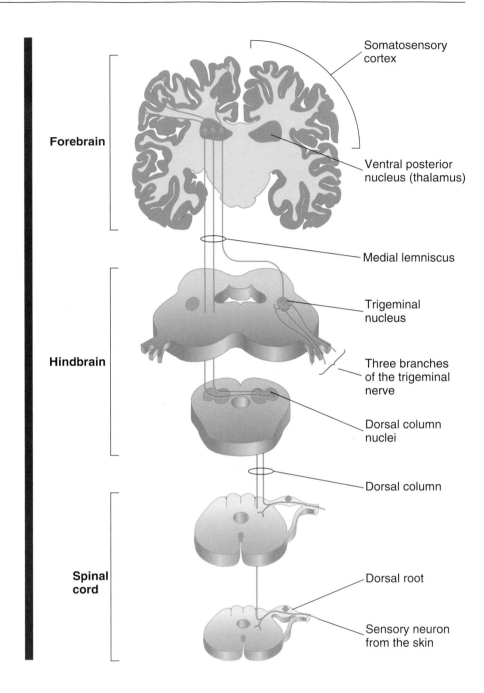

the greatest proportion of the primary somatosensory cortex is dedicated to receiving input from the parts of the body that are capable of the finest tactual discriminations (e.g., hands, lips, and tongue).

Kaas and others (1981) found that the primary somatosensory cortex is not a single area as described by Penfield. It is, in fact, four parallel strips, each with a similar, but separate, somatotopic organization. Each strip of primary somatosensory cortex is most sensitive to a different kind of somatosensory input (e.g., to light touch or temperature). Thus, if one were to record from neurons in a horizontal line across the four strips, one would find neurons that "preferred" four different kinds of tactile stimulation, all to the same part of the body. Also, one would find that as one moved from anterior to posterior, the preferences of the neurons would tend to become

more complex and specific (see Caselli, 1997), suggesting an anterior-to-posterior hierarchical scheme (Iwamura, 1998).

Like the primary visual and auditory cortexes, the primary somatosensory cortex is organized in columns; each neuron in a particular cortical column responds to the same kind of somatosensory stimuli and has a receptive field on the same part of the body. The receptive fields of many neurons in the primary somatosensory cortex, like those of visual system neurons, can be divided into antagonistic excitatory and inhibitory areas (DiCarlo & Johnson, 2000; DiCarlo, Johnson, & Hsaio, 1998). Figure 7.22 on page 182 illustrates the receptive field of a neuron of the primary somatosensory cortex that is responsive to light touch (Mountcastle & Powell, 1959).

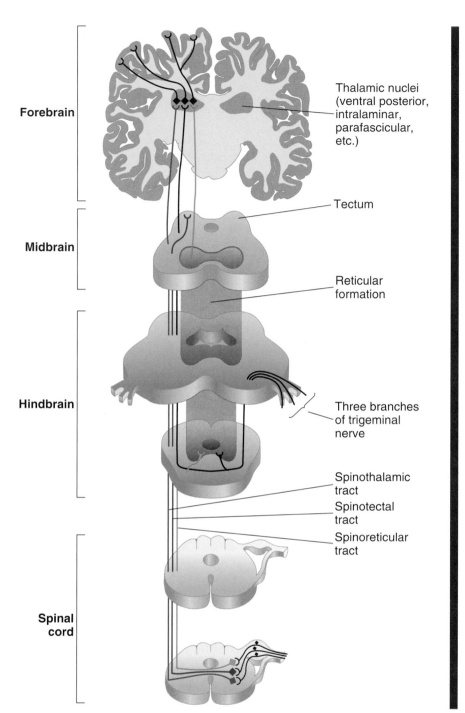

FIGURE 7.20 The anterolateral system.

Forebrain

Thalamic nuclei
(ventral posterior,
intralaminar,
parafascicular,
etc.)

Midbrain

Tectum

Reticular
formation

Hindbrain

Three branches
of trigeminal
nerve

Spinothalamic
tract

Spinotectal
tract

Spinoreticular
tract

Spinal
cord

Effects of Damage to the Primary Somatosensory Cortex

Like the effects of damage to the primary auditory cortex, the effects of damage to the primary somatosensory cortex are often remarkably mild. Corkin, Milner, and Rasmussen (1970) assessed the somatosensory abilities of patients both before and after unilateral excision of SI for the relief of epilepsy. Following surgery, the patients displayed two minor contralateral deficits: a reduced ability to detect light touch and a reduced ability to identify objects by touch (i.e., a deficit in stereognosis). These deficits were bilateral only in those cases in which the unilateral lesion encroached on SII.

Somatosensory Agnosias

There are two major types of somatosensory agnosia. One is **astereognosia**—the inability to recognize objects by touch. Cases of pure astereognosia— those that occur in the absence of simple sensory deficits—are rare (Corkin, Milner, & Rasmussen,

FIGURE 7.21 The location of human primary (SI) and secondary (SII) somatosensory cortex and an illustration of the primary somatosensory homunculus.

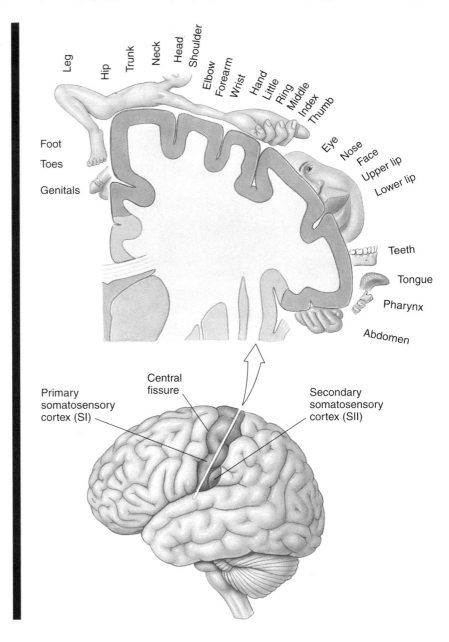

FIGURE 7.22 The receptive field of a neuron of the primary somatosensory cortex. Notice the antagonistic excitatory and inhibitory areas.

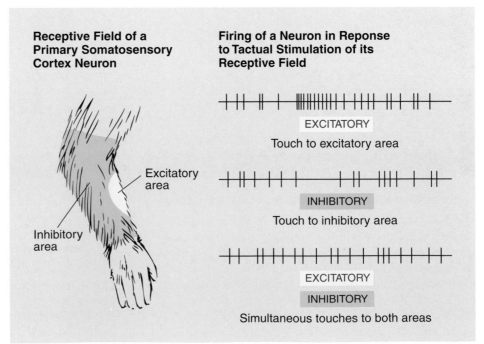

1970). The other type of somatosensory agnosia is **asomatognosia**—the failure to recognize parts of one's own body. Asomatognosia is usually unilateral, affecting only the left side of the body; and it is usually associated with extensive damage to the right posterior parietal lobe. You have already encountered one example of asomatognosia in this book, the case of the man who fell out of bed; the case of Aunt Betty is another (Klawans, 1990).

The Case of Aunt Betty, Who Lost Half of Her Body

It was time to see Aunt Betty—she wasn't really my aunt, but I grew up thinking that she was. She was my mother's best friend. She had had a stroke in her right hemisphere.

As we walked to her room, one of the medical students described the case. "Left hemiplegia [left-side paralysis]," I was told.

Aunt Betty was lying on her back with her head and eyes turned to the right. "Betty," I called out. Not Aunt Betty, but Betty. I was 37; I'd dropped the "Aunt" long ago—at least 2 years earlier.

I approached her bed from the left, but Aunt Betty did not turn her head or even her eyes to look towards me.

"Hal," she called out. "Where are you?"

I turned her head gently toward me. We talked. It was clear that she had no speech problems, no memory loss, and no confusion. She was as bright as ever. But her eyes still looked to the right as if the left side of her world did not exist.

I picked up her right hand and held it in front of her eyes. "What's this?" I asked.

"My hand, of course," she said with an intonation that suggested what she thought of my question.

"Well then, what's this?" I said, as I held up her limp left hand where she could see it.

"A hand."

"Whose hand?"

"Your hand, I guess," she replied. She seemed genuinely puzzled. I carefully placed her hand on the bed.

"Why have you come to this hospital?" I asked.

"To see you," she replied hesitantly. I could tell that she didn't really know the answer.

"Is there anything wrong with you?"

"No."

"How about your left hand and leg?"

"They're fine," she said. "How are yours?"

"They're fine too," I replied. There was nothing else to do. Aunt Betty was in trouble.[2]

As in the case of Aunt Betty, asomatognosia is often accompanied by **anosognosia**—the failure of neuropsychological patients to recognize their own symptoms. Asomatognosia may also be accompanied by **contralateral neglect**—the tendency not to respond to stimuli that are contralateral to a right-hemisphere injury. (You will learn more about contralateral neglect in Chapter 8).

◾ The Paradoxes of Pain

A paradox is a logical contradiction. The perception of pain is paradoxical in three important respects, which is why I have singled out pain for special discussion. The three paradoxes of pain are explained in the following three subsections.

ADAPTIVENESS OF PAIN ◾ One paradox of pain is that an experience that seems in every respect to be so bad is in fact extremely important for our survival. There is no special stimulus for pain; it is a response to excessive (potentially harmful) stimulation of any type (Cesare & McNaughton, 1997). The value of pain is best illustrated by the case of a person who does not experience it.

The Case of Miss C., the Woman Who Felt No Pain

The best documented of all cases of congenital insensitivity to pain is Miss C., a young Canadian girl who was a student at McGill University in Montreal. . . . The young lady was highly intelligent and seemed normal in every way except that she had never felt pain. As a child, she had bitten off the tip of her tongue while chewing food, and had suffered third-degree burns after kneeling on a radiator to look out of the window. . . . She felt no pain when parts of her body were subjected to strong electric shock, to hot water at temperatures that usually produce reports of burning pain, or to a prolonged ice-bath. Equally astonishing was the fact that she showed no changes in blood pressure, heart rate, or respiration when these stimuli were presented. Furthermore, she could not remember ever sneezing or coughing, the gag reflex could be elicited only with great difficulty, and corneal reflexes (to protect the eyes) were absent. A variety of other stimuli, such as inserting a stick up through the nostrils, pinching tendons, or injections of histamine under the skin—which are normally considered as forms of torture—also failed to produce pain.

Miss C. had severe medical problems. She exhibited pathological changes in her knees, hip, and spine, and underwent several orthopaedic operations. The surgeon attributed these changes to the lack of protection to joints usually given by pain sensation. She apparently failed to shift her weight when standing, to turn over in her sleep, or to avoid certain postures, which normally prevent inflammation of joints. . . .

Miss C. died at the age of twenty-nine of massive infections . . . and extensive skin and bone trauma.[3]

[2]Paraphrased from pp. 12–14 of *Newton's Madness: Further Tales of Clinical Neurology* by Harold L. Klawans (New York: Harper & Row, 1990).

[3]From *The Challenge of Pain* (pp. 16–17) by Ronald Melzack and Patrick D. Wall, 1982, London: Penguin Books Ltd. Copyright © Ronald Melzack and Patrick D. Wall, 1982.

LACK OF CORTICAL REPRESENTATION OF PAIN ■
The second paradox of pain is that it has no obvious cortical representation. Removal of SI and SII in humans is not associated with any change in the threshold for pain; indeed, *hemispherectomized* patients (patients with one cerebral hemisphere removed) can still perceive pain from both sides of their bodies.

There was initial optimism that functional brain-imaging would easily sort out the puzzle of the cortical representation of pain: Surely, PET or fMRI recordings from patients experiencing pain would reveal the particular area of cortex mediating the perception of pain. This optimism has largely dissipated.

It is now clear that the cortical representation of pain is much more complex than initially assumed. For example, the brief painful stimuli that are commonly used in pain experiments do not seem to activate the same cortical areas as chronic clinical pain, and many seemingly minor methodological variations seem to affect the areas of the cortex that are activated by painful stimuli (Apkarian, 1995). Apparently, pain is not mediated by cortical activity in the same way that sights, sounds, and touches are.

The one cortical area that has been most frequently linked to pain is the **anterior cingulate cortex** (see Figure 7.23). For example, Craig and colleagues (1996) used PET to demonstrate increases in anterior cingulate cortex activity when subjects placed a hand on painfully cold bars, painfully hot bars, or even on alternating cool and warm bars, which produce an illusion of painful stimulation (see Figure 7.23).

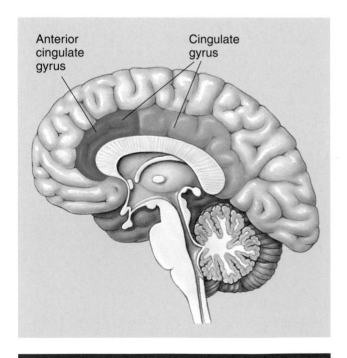

FIGURE 7.23 Location of anterior cingulate cortex in the cingulate gyrus.

Evidence suggests that the anterior cingulate cortex is involved in the emotional reaction to pain rather than to the perception of pain itself (Price, 2000). The following are two findings that support this view. First, conventional *prefrontal lobotomy,* which damages the anterior cingulate cortex and its connections, typically reduces the emotional reaction to pain without changing the threshold for pain. Second, increasing or decreasing the unpleasantness of painful stimulation by hypnosis produces corresponding changes in anterior cingulate PET activity.

DESCENDING PAIN CONTROL ■ The third paradox of pain is that this most compelling of all sensory experiences can be so effectively suppressed by cognitive and emotional factors. For example, men participating in a certain religious ceremony swing from ropes attached to giant meat hooks in their backs with little evidence of pain; severe wounds suffered by soldiers in battle are often associated with little pain; and people injured in life-threatening situations frequently feel no pain until the threat is over.

Melzack and Wall (1965) proposed the **gate-control theory** to account for the ability of cognitive and emotional factors to block pain. They theorized that signals descending in *centrifugal pathways* (pathways conducting from higher to lower levels of a sensory hierarchy; a more general term than *corticofugal* pathways) from the brain can activate neural gating circuits in the spinal cord to block incoming pain signals.

Three important discoveries led to the identification of the descending pain-control circuit. First was the discovery that electrical stimulation of the **periaqueductal gray (PAG)** has analgesic (pain-blocking) effects: Reynolds (1969) was able to perform abdominal surgery on rats with no analgesia other than that provided by PAG stimulation. Second was the discovery that the PAG and other areas of the brain contain specialized receptors for opiate analgesic drugs such as morphine, which suggested that such analgesic substances might occur naturally in the body: Why else would there be receptors for them? And third was the isolation of several endogenous (internally produced) opiate analgesics, the **endorphins,** which you learned about in Chapter 4 (e.g., Hughes et al., 1975). These three findings together suggested that analgesic drugs and psychological factors might block pain through an endorphin-sensitive circuit that descends from the PAG.

Figure 7.24 illustrates the descending analgesia circuit first hypothesized by Basbaum and Fields (1978). They proposed that the output of the PAG excites the serotonergic neurons of the *raphé nuclei* (a cluster of serotonergic nuclei in the core of the medulla), which in turn project down the dorsal columns of the spinal cord and excite interneurons that block incoming pain signals in the dorsal horn.

Descending analgesia pathways have been the subject of intensive investigation since the first model was

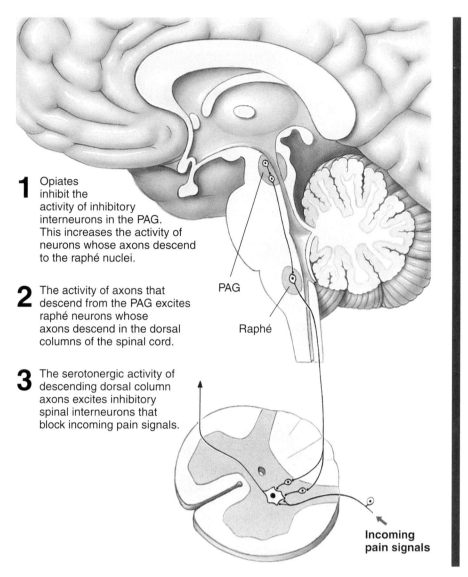

FIGURE 7.24 Basbaum and Fields's (1978) model of the descending analgesia circuit.

1 Opiates inhibit the activity of inhibitory interneurons in the PAG. This increases the activity of neurons whose axons descend to the raphé nuclei.

2 The activity of axons that descend from the PAG excites raphé neurons whose axons descend in the dorsal columns of the spinal cord.

3 The serotonergic activity of descending dorsal column axons excites inhibitory spinal interneurons that block incoming pain signals.

PAG

Raphé

**Incoming
pain signals**

proposed by Basbaum and Fields in 1978. In order to incorporate the mass of accumulated data, models of the descending analgesia circuits have grown much more complex (see Borszcz, 1999; McNally, 1999). Still, a descending component involving opiate activity in the PAG and serotonergic activity in the raphé nuclei remain key parts of most of these models.

7.5 The Chemical Senses: Smell and Taste

Olfaction (smell) and *gustation* (taste) are referred to as the chemical senses because their function is to monitor the chemical content of the environment (see Bartoshuk & Beauchamp, 1994). Smell is the response of the olfactory system to airborne chemicals that are drawn by inhalation over receptors in the nasal passages, and taste is the response of the gustatory system to chemicals in the solutions of the oral cavity.

When we are eating, smell and taste act in concert. Molecules of food excite both smell and taste receptors and produce an integrated sensory impression termed **flavor.** The contribution of olfaction to flavor is often underestimated, but you won't make this mistake if you remember that people with no sense of smell have difficulty distinguishing the flavors of apples and onions.

Smell and taste have the dubious distinction of being the least understood of the exteroceptive sensory systems (see Laurent, 1997). One reason is that chemical stimuli are inherently more difficult to control and administer than are lights, tones, and touches. Another is that loss of the ability to smell and taste does not pose many serious health problems for individuals living in societies, such as ours, in which potential foods are screened by government agencies. Be that as it may, the chemical senses continue to attract considerable interest.

Arguably, the single most interesting aspect of the chemical senses is their role in the social lives of many species (e.g., de Catanzaro et al., 2000). The members of many species release **pheromones**—chemicals that influence the behavior of *conspecifics* (members of the same species). For example, Murphy and Schneider (1970) showed that the sexual and aggressive behavior of hamsters is under pheromonal control. Normal male hamsters attack and kill unfamiliar males that are placed in their colonies, whereas they mount and impregnate unfamiliar sexually receptive females. However, male hamsters that are unable to smell the intruders engage in neither aggressive nor sexual behavior. Murphy and Schneider confirmed the olfactory basis of hamsters' aggressive and sexual behavior in a particularly devious fashion. They swabbed a male intruder with the vaginal secretions of a sexually receptive female before placing it in an unfamiliar colony; in so doing, they converted it from an object of hamster assassination to an object of hamster lust.

The possibility that humans may release sexual pheromones has received considerable attention because of its financial and recreational potential. There have been many suggestive findings. For example, (1) the olfactory sensitivity of women is greatest when they are ovulating; (2) the menstrual cycles of women living together tend to become synchronized; (3) humans—particularly women—can tell the sex of a person from the breath or the underarm odor; and (4) men can judge the stage of a woman's menstrual cycle on the basis of her vaginal odor. However, there is still no direct evidence that human odors can serve as sex attractants (Doty, 1986): To put it mildly, most subjects do not find the aforementioned body odors to be particularly attractive.

Another feature of the chemical senses that has attracted attention is that they are involved in some interesting forms of learning. As you discovered in Chapter 5, animals that suffer from gastrointestinal upset after consuming a particular food develop a *conditioned taste aversion.* Conversely, it has been shown that rats develop preferences for flavors they encounter in their mother's milk (Galef & Sherry, 1973) or on the breath of conspecifics (Galef, 1989). And adult male rats that were nursed as pups by lemon-scented mothers copulate more effectively with females that smell of lemons (Fillion &

Blass, 1986)—a phenomenon that has been aptly referred to as the *I-want-a-girl-just-like-the-girl-who-married-dear-old-dad phenomenon* (Diamond, 1986).

The Olfactory System

Because we can discriminate among thousands of different odors, it had long been assumed that olfaction, like color vision (see Chapter 6), is coded according to component principles—that is, that there are a few primary receptor types, and the perception of various odors is produced by different ratios of activity in them. This is not the case: About a thousand different kinds of olfactory receptor proteins have been identified, each maximally sensitive to a different odor (see Buck, 1996; Gibson & Garbers, 2000). In mammals, each olfactory receptor cell contains one type of receptor molecule (Duchamp-Viret, Chaput, & Duchamp, 1999; Yoshihara, Nagao, & Mori, 2001).

The olfactory system is illustrated in Figure 7.25. The olfactory receptors are located in the upper part of the nose, embedded in a layer of mucus-covered tissue called the **olfactory mucosa.** They have their own axons, which pass through a porous portion of the skull (the *cribriform plate*) and enter the **olfactory bulbs,** where they synapse on neurons that project via the *olfactory tracts* to the brain.

Taking the lead from research on other sensory systems, researchers have attempted to discover the functional principle by which the various receptors are distributed through the olfactory mucosa. If there is such a functional principle, it has not yet been discovered: Each type of receptor protein appears to be scattered throughout the mucosa, providing no clue about the organization of the system. However, all of the olfactory receptors with the same receptor protein seem to project to the same general location in the olfactory bulb (see Axel, 1995; Mombaerts, 1996; Mori, 1995).

Each olfactory tract projects to several structures of the medial temporal lobes, including the amygdala and the **piriform cortex**—an area of the medial temporal cortex adjacent to the amygdala. The olfactory system is the only sensory system whose major sensory pathway reaches the cerebral cortex without first passing through the thalamus.

Two major olfactory pathways leave the amygdala-piriform area. One projects diffusely to the limbic system, and the other projects via the **medial dorsal nuclei** of the thalamus to the **orbitofrontal cortex**—the area of cortex on the inferior surface of the frontal lobes, next to the *orbits* (eye sockets). The limbic projection is thought to mediate the emotional response to odors; the

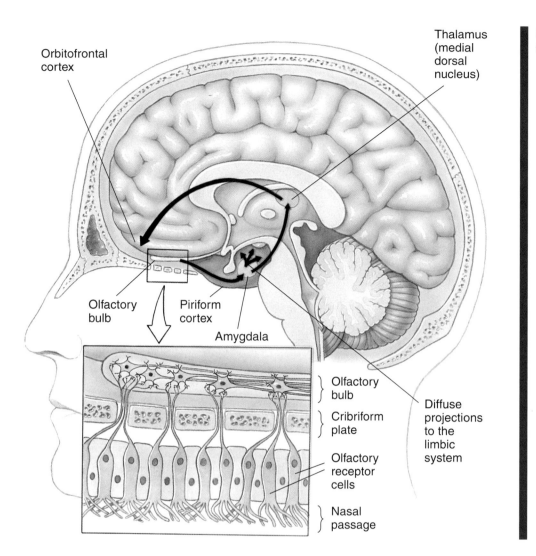

FIGURE 7.25 The olfactory system.

thalamic-orbitofrontal projection is thought to mediate the conscious perception of odors. Little is known about how neurons receptive to different odorants are organized in the cortex.

The Gustatory System

Taste receptors are found on the tongue and in parts of the oral cavity; they typically occur in clusters of about 50, called **taste buds.** On the tongue, taste buds are often located around small protuberances called *papillae* (singular *papilla*). The relation between taste receptors, taste buds, and papillae is illustrated in Figure 7.26 on page 188. Unlike olfactory receptors, taste receptors do not have their own axons; each neuron that carries impulses away from a taste bud receives input from many receptors.

Psychologically, there seem to be four primary tastes: sweet, sour, bitter, and salty. Consequently, it was once assumed that there are four kinds of taste receptors and that the perception of any taste stimulus is a consequence of the relative amounts of activity produced in these four receptors. Although this simple component-processing theory of taste is consistent with some of the data, it has several problems (see Smith & Margolskee, 2001). One is that there may be more than four primary tastes; for example, many believe *unami* (meaty or savory) is a fifth. Another problem is that many tastes cannot be created by combinations of the primaries (Schiffman & Erickson, 1980). Yet another is that some tastes (salty and sour) have been shown to influence receptor activity by acting directly through ion channels rather than on receptor molecules (see Kinnamon & Margolskee, 1996).

The major pathways over which gustatory signals are conducted to the cortex are illustrated in Figure 7.27 on page 189. Gustatory afferents leave the mouth as part of the *facial* (VII), *glossopharyngeal* (IX), and *vagus* (X) *cranial nerves,* which carry information from the front of the tongue, back of the tongue, and back of the oral cavity, respectively. These fibers all terminate in the **solitary nucleus** of the medulla, where they synapse on neurons that project to the *ventral posterior nucleus* of the thalamus. The gustatory axons of the ventral posterior nucleus

FIGURE 7.26 Taste receptors, taste buds, and papillae on the surface of the tongue. Two sizes of papillae are visible in the photograph; only the larger papillae contain taste buds and receptors.

Surface of Tongue

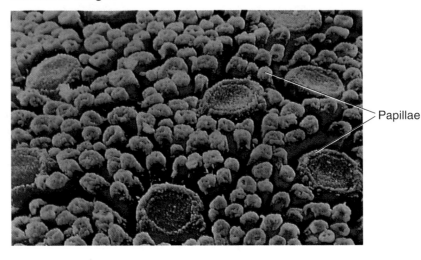

Papillae

Cross Section of a Papilla

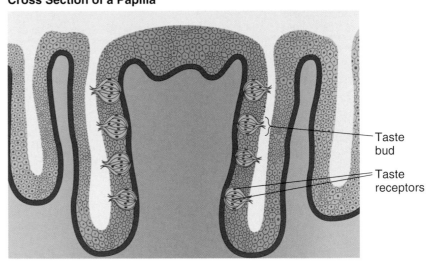

Taste bud

Taste receptors

project to the *primary gustatory cortex,* which is near the face area of the somatosensory homunculus, and to the *secondary gustatory cortex,* which is hidden from view in the lateral fissure (Pritchard, Macaluso, & Eslinger, 1999). Unlike the projections of other sensory systems, the projections of the gustatory system are primarily ipsilateral.

Although evidence for simple component processing of taste at the receptor level is still lacking, electrophysiological recordings of both peripheral and central neurons in the gustatory system suggest that some type of component processing is occurring (see Smith & Margolskee, 2001). Most gustatory neurons respond to a variety of dissimilar tastes, and particular tastes seem to be encoded in the brain by profiles of activity in groups of neurons (e.g., high in some and low in others).

■ | **Brain Damage and the Chemical Senses**

The inability to smell is called **anosmia;** the inability to taste is called **ageusia.** The most common neurological cause of anosmia is a blow to the head that causes a displacement of the brain within the skull and shears the olfactory nerves where they pass through the cribriform plate. Approximately 6% of patients hospitalized for traumatic head injuries are found to have olfactory deficits of some sort (e.g., Zusho, 1983).

In contrast to anosmia, ageusia is rare, presumably because sensory signals from the mouth are carried over three separate pathways. However, ageusia for the anterior two-thirds of the tongue on one side is sometimes observed after damage to the ear on the same side of the body. This is because the branch of the facial nerve (VII) that carries gustatory information from the anterior two-thirds of the tongue passes through the middle ear.

One noteworthy feature of ageusia and anosmia is that they sometimes occur together in neurological patients. This suggests that there is some as yet unidentified area in the brain where olfactory and gustatory information converges.

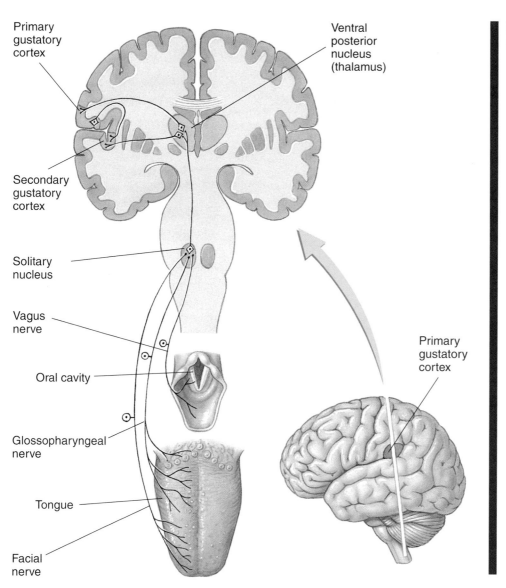

Primary gustatory cortex

Ventral posterior nucleus (thalamus)

Secondary gustatory cortex

Solitary nucleus

Vagus nerve

Oral cavity

Glossopharyngeal nerve

Tongue

Facial nerve

Primary gustatory cortex

FIGURE 7.27 The gustatory system.

7.6 Selective Attention

We consciously perceive only a small subset of the many stimuli that excite our sensory organs at any one time and largely ignore the rest. The process by which this occurs is **selective attention.**

There are two aspects to selective attention: It improves the perception of the stimuli that are its focus, and it interferes with the perception of the stimuli that are not its focus. For example, if you focus your attention on a potentially important announcement in a noisy airport, your chances of understanding it increase; but your chances of understanding a simultaneous comment from a traveling companion decrease.

Attention can be focused in two different ways: by internal cognitive processes (*endogenous attention*) or by

external events (*exogenous attention*)—see Rosen and others (1999). For example, your attention can be focued on a table top because you are searching for your keys (endogenous attention), or it can be drawn there because your cat tipped over a lamp (exogenous attention). Endogenous attention is thought to be mediated by *top-down* (from higher to lower levels) neural mechanisms, whereas exogenous attention is thought to be mediated by *bottom-up* (from lower to higher levels) neural mechanisms.

Attention is an extremely important aspect of perception. There is no better illustration of its importance than the phenomenon of **change blindness** (Henderson & Hollingworth, 1999; Rensink, O'Regan, & Clark, 1997). To

BrainScan

Now that you have reached this chapter's final section, on selective attention, you should scan your brain to test your knowledge of the sensory systems. Complete each sentence with the name of the appropriate system. The correct answers are provided at the bottom of this page. Before proceeding, review material related to your incorrect answers and omissions.

1. The inferotemporal cortex is an area of secondary _____ cortex.

2. The dorsal and ventral streams are part of the _____ system.

3. The primary _____ cortex is organized tonotopically.

4. The inferior colliculi and medial geniculate nuclei are components of the _____ system.

5. The dorsal-column medial-lemniscus system and the anterolateral system are pathways of the _____ system.

6. The ventral posterior nuclei, the intralaminar nuclei, and the parafascicular nuclei are all

thalamic nuclei of the _____ system.

7. The periaqueductal gray and the raphé nuclei are involved in blocking the perception of _____ .

8. One pathway of the _____ system projects from the amygdala and piriform cortex to the orbitofrontal cortex.

9. Parts of the ventral posterior nuclei are thalamic relay nuclei of both the somatosensory and _____ systems.

10. Unlike the projections of all other sensory systems, the projections of the _____ system are primarily ipsilateral.

study change blindness, a subject is shown a photographic image on a computer screen and is asked to report any change in the image as soon as it is noticed. In fact, the image is composed of two images that alternate with a delay of less than a tenth of a second between. The two photographic images are identical except for one gross feature. For example, the two images in Figure 7.28 are identical except that the picture in the center of the wall is missing from one. You might think that any subject would immediately notice the picture disappearing and reappearing. But this is not what happens—most subjects spend many seconds staring at the image—searching, as instructed, for some change—before they notice the disappearing and reappearing picture. When this finally happens, they wonder in amazement why it took them so long.

Why does change blindness occur? It occurs because, contrary to our impression, when we view a scene, we have absolutely no memory for parts of the scene that are not the focus of our attention (see Enns & DiLollo, 1997). When viewing the scene in Figure 7.28, most subjects attend to the two people and do not notice when the picture disappears from the wall between them. Because they have no memory of the parts of the image to which

they did not attend, they are not aware when those parts change.

The change blindness phenomenon does not occur without the brief (i.e., less than 0.1 second) intervals between images, although they barely produce a flicker. Without the intervals, no memory is required and the changes are immediately perceived.

ON THE CD

Visit the *Change Blindness* module. Change blindness needs to be experienced to be appreciated. This is one you'll want to share with your friends.

Moran and Desimone (1985) were the first to demonstrate the effects of attention on neural activity in the visual system (see also Spitzer, Desimone, & Moran, 1988). They trained monkeys to stare at a fixation point on the screen while they recorded the activity of neurons in a prestriate area that was part of the ventral stream and particularly sensitive to color. In one experiment, they recorded from individual neurons that responded to either red or green bars of light in their receptive fields. When the monkey was trained to perform a task that required attention to the red cue, the response to the red cue was increased, and the response to the green cue was reduced. The opposite happened when the monkey attended to green.

Experiments paralleling those in monkeys have been conducted in humans using functional brain imaging techniques (see Driver & Mattingley, 1995). For example, Corbetta and colleagues (1990) presented a collection of moving, colored stimuli of various shapes and asked their

Brain Scan answers: (1) visual, (2) visual, (3) auditory, (4) auditory, (5) somatosensory, (6) somatosensory, (7) pain, (8) olfactory, (9) gustatory, (10) gustatory.

0.1
second

FIGURE 7.28 The change blindness phenomenon. These two illustrations were continually alternated, with a brief (less than 0.1 second) interval between each presentation, and
the subjects were asked to report any changes that they noticed. Amazingly, it took them
many seconds to notice the disappearing and reappearing picture in the center of the wall.
(Photographs prepared by James Enns, Department of Psychology, University of British Columbia.)

subjects to discriminate among the stimuli based on their
movement, color, *or* shape. Attention to shape or color produced increased activity in areas of the ventral stream; attention to movement produced increased activity
in an area of the dorsal stream.

In another study of attention in human subjects, Ungerleider and Haxby (1994) showed
subjects a series of faces. The subjects were asked whether
the faces belonged to the same person or whether they
were located in the same position relative to the frame.
When the subjects were attending to identity, regions of
the ventral stream were more active; when the subjects
were attending to position, regions of the dorsal stream
were more active.

How do the mechanisms of selective attention work?
According to current theories (see Behrmann & Haimson, 1999; Kanwisher & Downing, 1998), neural representations of various aspects of a visual display compete
with one another. Selective attention is thought to work
by strengthening the representations of the attended-to
aspects and weakening the others.

A cognitive neuroscience experiment by Kastner and
colleagues (1998) illustrates the type of evidence on
which these theories are based. The researchers used
fMRI to measure activity in various areas of visual cortex during the visual presentation of one and then four
objects. First, they showed that the activity produced by
the presence of one single object declined markedly
when the other three objects were presented
along with it. Second, they showed that the magnitude of this decline was less if subjects were instructed to attend to the first object.

Eye movements often play an important role in visual
attention, but it is important to realize that visual attention can be shifted without shifting the direction of visual
focus. To prove this to yourself, see the Demonstration.

Demonstration

A
J   F
E   +   S
W   B
K

Fix your gaze on the +, concentrate on it. Next, shift
your attention to one of the letters without shifting
your gaze from +. Now, shift your attention to other
letters, again without shifting your gaze from the +.
You have experienced covert attention—a shift of
attention without corresponding eye movement.

Visual attention that involves a shift in gaze is called *overt attention;* visual attention that does not involve a shift in gaze is called *covert attention.*

One last important characteristic of selective attention is the cocktail-party phenomenon. The **cocktail-party phenomenon** is the fact that even when you are focusing so intently on one conversation that you are totally unaware of the content of other conversations going on around you, the mention of your name in one of the other conversations will immediately gain access to your consciousness. This phenomenon suggests that your brain can block from awareness all stimuli except those of a particular kind while still unconsciously monitoring the blocked-out stimuli just in case something comes up that requires attention.

No, I have not forgotten that I asked you to think about the patient whose case opened this chapter. He could identify objects in any part of his visual field if they were presented individually; thus, he was not suffering from blindness or other visual field defects. His was a disorder of visual attention. He suffered from visual **simultanagnosia,** a difficulty in attending to more than one visual object at a time. Because the dorsal stream is responsible for localizing objects in space, you may have hypothesized that the patient's problem was associated with damage to this area. If you did, you were correct. The damage associated with simultagnosia is typically bilateral.

Themes — Revisited

The clinical implications theme was the dominant one in this chapter, but you saw it in a different light. Previous chapters focused on how biopsychological research is leading to the development of new treatments; this chapter focused on what particular clinical cases reveal about the organization of healthy sensory systems. The following cases played a key role in this chapter: the patient with simultanagnosia; Dr. P., the visual agnosic who mistook his wife for a hat; D. B., the man with blindsight; Karl Lashley, the physiological psychologist who used his scotoma to turn a friend's head into a wallpaper pattern; D. F., who showed by her accurate reaching that she perceived the size, shape, and orientation of objects that she could not describe; A. T., who could describe the size and shape of objects that she could not accurately reach for; C. K., the visual agnosic who could still recognize faces; Aunt Betty, the asomatognosic who lost the left side of her body; and Miss C., the student who felt no pain and died as a result.

The other three major themes were also developed in this chapter. You learned how the study of the neural organization of the sensory systems has recently been extended to healthy human subjects by using the functional brain-imaging techniques of cognitive neuroscience. You learned that the comparative study of some species has been particularly informative because of their evolutionary specializations (e.g., the auditory localization abilities of the barn owl). And you learned how critical thinking has led to a re-evaluation of the concept of prosopagnosia.

ON THE CD
Looking for more information about the topics in this chapter? For recommended additional readings, see Hard Copy for Chapter 7.

Log On

- **http://www.monell.org/** If you are interested in olfaction and taste, check out this site of the Monell Chemical Senses Center.

- **http://kahuna.psych.uiuc.edu/ipl/aud/level_2_aud.html** This site provides a good overview of audition and an illustration of classic auditory illusions.

- **http://thalamus.wustl.edu/course/bassens.html** More interested in somatosensation? This site focuses on the somatosensory system and the consequences of lesions to its various parts.

- **http://coglab.psych.purdue.edu/coglab/Labs/Attentional Blink.html** Purdue University's Cognitive Psychology website demonstrates a phenomenon referred to as "attentional blink."

Think about It

1. How has this chapter changed your concept of perception?

2. Some sensory pathways control behavior directly without producing conscious perceptions, whereas others control behavior by mediating conscious perceptions. Discuss the evolutionary implications of this fact. Why did consciousness evolve?

3. Comparative biopsychological research often focuses on species that are similar to humans in key respects; however, such research sometimes focuses productively on species that differ from humans in key respects. Explain and discuss.

4. One purpose of biopsychological research is to help neuropsychological patients, but neuropsychological patients also help biopsychologists understand the neural mechanisms of psychological processes. Explain.

ON THE CD
Studying for an exam? Try the Practice Tests for Chapter 7.

Key Terms

Ageusia *(p. 188)*
Agnosia *(p. 170)*
Anosmia *(p. 188)*
Anosognosia *(p. 183)*
Anterior cingulate cortex *(p. 184)*
Anterolateral system *(p. 178)*
Asomatognosia *(p. 183)*
Association cortex *(p. 162)*
Astereognosia *(p. 181)*
Auditory nerve *(p. 174)*
Basilar membrane *(p. 174)*
Blindsight *(p. 166)*
Change blindness *(p. 189)*
Cochlea *(p. 173)*
Cocktail-party phenomenon *(p. 192)*
Completion *(p. 166)*
Contralateral neglect *(p. 183)*
"Control of behavior" versus "conscious perception" theory *(p. 170)*
Corticofugal pathways *(p. 165)*
Dermatome *(p. 177)*
Dorsal columns *(p. 178)*

Dorsal stream *(p. 168)*
Dorsal-column medial-lemniscus system *(p. 177)*
Endorphins *(p. 184)*
Exteroceptive sensory systems *(p. 162)*
Flavor *(p. 185)*
Free nerve endings *(p. 177)*
Functional segregation *(p. 164)*
Gate-control theory *(p. 184)*
Hair cells *(p. 174)*
Hemianopsic *(p. 166)*
Hierarchical organization *(p. 162)*
Inferior colliculi *(p. 176)*
Inferotemporal cortex *(p. 165)*
Medial dorsal nuclei *(p. 186)*
Medial geniculate nuclei *(p. 176)*
Medial lemniscus *(p. 178)*
Olfactory bulbs *(p. 186)*
Olfactory mucosa *(p. 186)*
Orbitofrontal cortex *(p. 186)*
Organ of Corti *(p. 174)*
Ossicles *(p. 173)*

Oval window *(p. 173)*
Pacinian corpuscles *(p. 177)*
Parallel processing *(p. 164)*
Perception *(p. 163)*
Periaqueductal gray (PAG) *(p. 184)*
Perimetry test *(p. 166)*
Pheromones *(p. 186)*
Piriform cortex *(p. 186)*
Posterior parietal cortex *(p. 165)*
Prestriate cortex *(p. 165)*
Primary sensory cortex *(p. 162)*
Prosopagnosia *(p. 170)*
Retinotopic *(p. 175)*
Scotoma *(p. 165)*
Secondary sensory cortex *(p. 162)*
Selective attention *(p. 189)*
Semicircular canals *(p. 175)*
Sensation *(p. 163)*
Simultanagnosia *(p. 192)*
Solitary nucleus *(p. 187)*
Somatosensory homunculus *(p. 179)*

Somatotopic *(p. 179)*
Stereognosis *(p. 177)*
Subjective contours *(p. 167)*
Superior olives *(p. 175)*
Taste buds *(p. 187)*
Tectorial membrane *(p. 174)*
Tonotopic *(p. 175)*
Tympanic membrane *(p. 173)*
Ventral posterior nucleus *(p. 178)*
Ventral stream *(p. 168)*
Vestibular system *(p. 175)*
Visual agnosia *(p. 170)*
"Where" versus "what" theory *(p. 168)*

ON THE CD
Need some help studying the key terms for this chapter? Check out the electronic flash cards for Chapter 7.

The Sensorimotor System

How You Do What You Do

Last evening, while standing in a checkout line at the local market, I furtively scanned the headlines on the prominently displayed magazines—WOMAN GIVES BIRTH TO CAT; FLYING SAUCER LANDS IN CLEVELAND SHOPPING MALL; HOW TO LOSE 20 POUNDS IN 2 DAYS. Then, my mind began to wander, and I started to think about beginning to write this chapter. That is when I began to watch Rhonda's movements and to wonder about the neural system that controlled them. Rhonda is the cashier—the best in the place.

The Case of Rhonda, the Dexterous Cashier

I was struck by the complexity of even Rhonda's simplest movements. As she deftly transferred a bag of tomatoes to the scale, there was a coordinated adjustment in almost every part of her body. In addition to her obvious finger, hand, arm, and shoulder movements, coordinated movements of her head and eyes tracked her hand to the tomatoes; and there were adjustments in the muscles of her feet, legs, trunk, and other arm, which kept her from lurching forward. The accuracy of these responses suggested that they were guided in part by the patterns of visual, somatosensory, and vestibular changes they produced. The term *sensorimotor* in the title of this chapter formally recognizes the critical contribution of sensory input to guiding motor output.

As my purchases flowed through her left hand, Rhonda registered the prices with her right hand and bantered with Rick, the bagger. I was intrigued by how little of what Rhonda was doing appeared to be under her conscious control. She made general decisions about which items to pick up and where to put them, but she seemed to give no thought to the exact means by which these decisions were carried out. Each of her responses could have been made with an infinite number of different combinations of finger, wrist, elbow, shoulder, and body adjustments; but somehow she unconsciously picked one. The higher parts of her sensorimotor system—perhaps her cortex—seemed to issue conscious general commands to other parts of the system, which unconsciously produced a specific pattern of muscular responses that carried them out.

The automaticity of Rhonda's performance was a far cry from the slow, effortful responses that had characterized her first days at the market. Somehow, experience had integrated her individual movements into smooth sequences, and it seemed to have transferred the movements' control from a mode that involved conscious effort to one that did not.

I was suddenly jarred from my contemplations by a voice. "Sir, excuse me, sir, that will be $18.65," Rhonda said, with just a hint of delight at catching me in mid-daydream. I hastily paid my bill, muttered "thank you," and scurried out of the market.

As I write this, I am smiling both at my own embarrassment and at the thought that Rhonda has unknowingly introduced you to three principles of sensorimotor control that are the foundations of this chapter: (1) The sensorimotor system is hierarchically organized. (2) Motor output is guided by sensory input. (3) Learning changes the nature and the locus of sensorimotor control.

8.1 Three Principles of Sensorimotor Function

Before getting into the details of the sensorimotor system, let's take a closer look at the three principles of sensorimotor function introduced by Rhonda. You will better appreciate these principles if you recognize that they are the very same principles that govern the operation of a large, efficient company—perhaps because both are systems of controlling output that have evolved in a competitive environment (Colarelli, 1998).

The Sensorimotor System Is Hierarchically Organized

The operation of both the sensorimotor system and a large, efficient company is directed by commands that cascade down through the levels of a hierarchy (see Sakata et al., 1997)— from the association cortex or the company president (the highest levels) to the muscles or the workers (the lowest levels). Like the orders that are issued from the office of a company president, the commands that emerge from the association cortex specify general goals rather than specific plans of action. Neither the association cortex nor the company president routinely gets involved in the details. The main advantage of this *hierarchical organization* is that the higher levels of the hierarchy are left free to perform more complex functions.

Both the sensorimotor system and large, efficient companies are parallel hierarchical systems; that is, they are hierarchical systems in which signals flow between levels over multiple paths (see Darian-Smith, Burman, & Darian-Smith, 1999). This parallel structure enables the association cortex or company president to exert control over the lower levels of the hierarchy in more than one way. For example, the association cortex may directly inhibit an eyeblink reflex to allow the insertion of a contact lens, and a company president may personally organize a delivery to an important customer.

The sensorimotor and company hierarchies are also characterized by *functional segregation.* That is, each level of the sensorimotor and company hierarchies tends to be composed of different units (neural structures or departments), each of which performs a different function.

In summary, the sensorimotor system—like the sensory systems you read about in Chapter 7—is a parallel, functionally segregated hierarchical system. The main difference between the sensory systems and the sensorimotor system is the primary direction of information flow. In sensory systems, information mainly flows up through the hierarchy; in the sensorimotor system, information mainly flows down.

Motor Output Is Guided by Sensory Input

Efficient companies continuously monitor the effects of their own activities, and they use this information to fine-tune those activities. The sensorimotor system does the same (Lemon, 1999; Weeks et al., 1999). The eyes, the organs of balance, and the receptors in skin, muscles, and joints all monitor the progress of our responses; and they feed their information back into sensorimotor circuits. In most instances, this **sensory feedback** plays an important role in directing the continuation of the responses that produced it. The only responses that are not normally influenced by sensory feedback are *ballistic movements*—brief, all-or-none, high-speed movements, such as swatting a fly.

Behavior in the absence of just one kind of sensory feedback—the feedback that is carried by the somatosensory nerves of the arms—was studied in G.O., a former darts champion (Rothwell et al., 1982).

The Case of G.O., the Man with Too Little Feedback

An infection had selectively destroyed the somatosensory nerves of G.O.'s arms. He had great difficulty performing intricate responses such as doing up his buttons or picking up coins, even under visual guidance. Other difficulties resulted from his inability to adjust his motor output in the light of unanticipated external disturbances; for example, he could not keep from spilling a cup of coffee if somebody brushed against him. However, G.O.'s greatest problem was his inability to maintain a constant level of muscle contraction:

The result of this deficit was that even in the simplest of tasks requiring a constant motor output to the hand, G.O. would have to keep a visual check on his progress. For example,

when carrying a suitcase, he would frequently glance at it to reassure himself that he had not dropped it some paces back. However, even visual feedback was of little use to him in many tasks. These tended to be those requiring a constant force output such as grasping a pen while writing or holding a cup. Here, visual information was insufficient for him to be able to correct any errors that were developing in the output since, after a period, he had no indication of the pressure that he was exerting on an object; all he saw was either the pen or cup slipping from his grasp. (Rothwell et al., 1982, p. 539)

Many adjustments in motor output that occur in response to sensory feedback are controlled unconsciously by the lower levels of the sensorimotor hierarchy without the involvement of the higher levels. In the same way, large companies run more efficiently if the clerks do not have to check with the company president each time they encounter a minor problem.

Learning Changes the Nature and Locus of Sensorimotor Control

When a company is just starting up, each individual decision is made by the company president after careful consideration. However, as the company develops, many individual actions are coordinated into sequences of prescribed procedures that are routinely carried out by personnel at lower levels of the hierarchy.

Similar changes occur during sensorimotor learning (see Willingham, 1999). During the initial stages of motor learning, each individual response is performed under conscious control; then, after much practice, individual responses become organized into continuous integrated sequences of action that flow smoothly and are adjusted by sensory feedback without conscious regulation. If you think for a moment about the sensorimotor skills you have acquired (e.g., typing, swimming, knitting, basketball playing, dancing, piano playing), you will appreciate that the organization of individual responses into continuous motor programs and the transfer of their control to lower levels of the nervous system characterizes most sensorimotor learning.

ON THE CD
Visit *The Beat Goes On.* In this module, Pinel demonstrates an important feature of the sensorimotor system.

A General Model of Sensorimotor System Function

Figure 8.1 is a model that illustrates several principles of sensorimotor system organization; it is the framework of this chapter. Notice its hierarchical structure, the functional segregation of the levels (e.g., of secondary motor cortex), the parallel connections between levels, and the numerous feedback pathways.

FIGURE 8.1 A general model of the sensorimotor system. Notice its hierarchical structure, its functional segregation, its parallel descending pathways, and its feedback circuits.

This chapter focuses on the neural structures that play important roles in the control of voluntary behavior (e.g., picking up an apple). It begins at the level of asso-

ciation cortex and traces major motor signals as they descend the sensorimotor hierarchy to the skeletal muscles that ultimately perform the movements.

8.2 | Sensorimotor Association Cortex

Association cortex is at the top of your sensorimotor hierarchy. There are two major areas of sensorimotor association cortex: the posterior parietal association cortex and the dorsolateral prefrontal association cortex (see Caminiti, Ferraina, & Mayer, 1998). Experts agree that the posterior parietal cortex and the dorsolateral prefrontal cortex are each composed of several different areas, each of which has a different function (see Fuster, 2000); however, the experts do not yet agree on how best to divide them up (see Rushworth, 2000).

■ Posterior Parietal Association Cortex

Before an effective movement can be initiated, certain information is required. The nervous system must know the original positions of the parts of the body that are to be moved, and it must know the positions of any external objects with which the body is going to interact. The **posterior**

parietal association cortex plays an important role in integrating these two kinds of information (see Andersen et al., 1997; Kalaska et al., 1997). You learned in Chapter 7 that the posterior parietal cortex is classified as *association cortex* because it receives input from more than one sensory system. It receives information from the three sensory systems that play roles in the localization of the body and external objects in space: the visual system, the auditory system, and the somatosensory system. In turn, much of the output of the posterior parietal cortex goes to areas of motor cortex, which are located in the frontal cortex (see Steinmetz, 1998): to the *dorsolateral prefrontal association cortex*, to the various areas of *secondary motor cortex*, and to the **frontal eye field**—a small area of prefrontal cortex that controls eye movements (see Figure 8.2 on page 198).

Damage to the posterior parietal cortex can produce a variety of sensorimotor deficits, including deficits in the perception and memory of spatial relationships, in accurate reaching and grasping, in the control of eye

FIGURE 8.2 The major cortical input and output pathways of the posterior parietal association cortex. Shown are the lateral surface of the left hemisphere and the medial surface of the right hemisphere.

movement, and in attention (Steinmetz, 1998). However, apraxia and contralateral neglect are the two most striking consequences of posterior parietal cortex damage.

Apraxia is a disorder of voluntary movement that is not attributable to a simple motor deficit (e.g., not to paralysis or weakness) or to any deficit in comprehension or motivation (see Heilman, Watson, & Rothi, 1997). Remarkably, apraxic patients have difficulty making specific movements when they are requested to do so, particularly when the movements are out of context; however, they can often readily perform the very same movements under natural conditions, when they are not thinking about doing so. For example, an apraxic carpenter who has no difficulty at all hammering a nail during the course of her work might not be able to demonstrate hammering movements when requested to make them, particularly in the absence of a hammer. Although its symptoms are bilateral, apraxia is often caused by unilateral damage to the left posterior parietal lobe or its connections.

Contralateral neglect is a disturbance of a patient's ability to respond to stimuli on the side of the body opposite (contralateral) to the side of a brain lesion, in the absence of simple sensory or motor deficits (see Heilman, Watson, & Valenstein, 1997). The disturbance is often associated with large lesions of the right posterior parietal lobe (see Weintraub & Mesulam, 1989). For example, Mrs. S. suffered

from contralateral neglect after a massive stroke to the posterior portions of her right hemisphere. Like many other neuropsychological patients, she developed ways of dealing with her deficiency.

The Case of Mrs. S., the Woman Who Turned in Circles

She has totally lost the idea of "left," with regard to both the world and her own body. Sometimes she complains that her portions are too small, but this is because she only eats from the right half of the plate—it does not occur to her that it has a left half as well. Sometimes, she will put on lipstick, and make up the right half of her face, leaving the left half completely neglected: it is almost impossible to treat these things, because her attention cannot be drawn to them. . . .

. . . She has worked out strategies for dealing with her [problem]. She cannot look left, directly, she cannot turn left, so what she does is turn right—and right through a circle. Thus she requested, and was given, a rotating wheelchair. And now if she cannot find something which she knows should be there, she swivels to the right, through a circle, until it comes into view. . . . If her portions seem too small, she will swivel to the right, keeping her eyes to the right, until the previously missed half now comes into view; she will eat this, or rather half of this, and feel less hungry than before. But if she is still hungry, or if she thinks on the

Contralateral neglect is sometimes manifested in terms of gravitational coordinates.

Contralateral neglect is sometimes manifested in terms of object-based coordinates.

FIGURE 8.3 Contralateral neglect is sometimes manifested in terms of gravitational coordinates, sometimes in terms of object-based coordinates.

matter, and realises that she may have perceived only half of the missing half, she will make a second rotation till the remaining quarter comes into view. (Sacks, 1985, pp. 73–74)[1]

---

[1]Reprinted with the permission of Simon & Schuster from *The Man Who Mistook His Wife for a Hat and Other Clinical Tales* by Oliver Sacks. Copyright © 1970, 1981, 1983, 1984, 1985 by Oliver Sacks.

What do you think happens when a patient with visual neglect tilts her or his head to the side? Remarkably, the field of neglect is not rotated with the patient's head; the patient still neglects visual stimuli to the left as defined by real-world (i.e., gravitational) vertical coordinates, not to the left of the rotated head (see Figure 8.3).

Although patients with contralateral neglect tend to neglect visual stimuli to the left as defined by gravitational coordinates, this is not always the case; their contralateral neglect can sometimes be manifested in terms of external object-based coordinates. Consider the following demonstration (see Figure 8.3). In one condition, the experimenter, strapped onto a vertically positioned wheel, was rotated counterclockwise. In this condition, the patient had more difficulty reacting to movements of the experimenter's right (lower) hand than to those of the left. In another condition, the experimenter was rotated clockwise. In this condition, the patient still had more difficulty responding to the right hand, even though it was now in the upper rather than lower position. In another interesting somatosensory study, patients suffering from contralateral neglect were found to be more responsive than usual to touches on their left hand if their arms were crossed (Aglioti, Smania, & Peru, 1999).

Dorsolateral Prefrontal Association Cortex

The other large area of association cortex that has important sensorimotor functions is the **dorsolateral prefrontal association cortex.** It receives projections from the posterior parietal cortex, and it sends projec-

tions to areas of *secondary motor cortex,* to *primary motor cortex,* and to the *frontal eye field* (see Figure 8.4).

The function of the dorsolateral prefrontal cortex seems to be the evaluation of external stimuli (Christoff & Gabrielli, 2000) and the initiation of reactions to them. This view is supported by the response characteristics of neurons in this area of association cortex.

Several studies have characterized the activity of individual neurons of monkeys' dorsolateral prefrontal association cortex as the monkeys identify and respond to objects (e.g., Di Pelligrino & Wise, 1991; Rao, Rainer, & Miller, 1997). The activity of some neurons depends on the characteristics of objects; the activity of others depends on the locations of objects; and the activity of still others depends on a combination of both. The activity of other dorsolateral prefrontal neurons is related to the response, rather than to the object. These neurons typically begin to fire before the response and continue to fire until the response is complete. There are neurons in all cortical motor areas that begin to fire in anticipation of a motor activity, but those in the dorsolateral prefrontal association cortex fire first. Thus, it seems that decisions to initiate voluntary actions may be made in this area (see Goldman-Rakic, Bates, & Chafee, 1992).

FIGURE 8.4 The major cortical input and output pathways of the dorsolateral prefrontal association cortex. Shown are the lateral surface of the left hemisphere and the medial surface of the right hemisphere.

Posterior parietal association cortex

Dorsolateral prefrontal association cortex

8.3 | Secondary Motor Cortex

Areas of **secondary motor cortex** are those that receive much of their input from association cortex and send much of their output to primary motor cortex (see Figure 8.5). For many years, only two areas of secondary motor cortex were known: the supplementary motor area and the premotor cortex. Both of these large areas are clearly visible on the lateral surface of the frontal lobe, just anterior to the *primary motor cortex*. The **supplementary motor area** wraps over the top of the frontal lobe and extends down its medial surface into the longitudinal fissure, and the **premotor cortex** runs in a strip from the supplementary motor area to the lateral fissure. However, two other areas of secondary motor cortex—the **cingulate motor areas**—were discovered, in the cortex of the cingulate gyrus of each hemisphere, just ventral to the supplementary motor area. Figure 8.5 shows the location of the supplementary motor area, the premotor cortex, and the two cingulate motor areas.

The areas of secondary motor cortex are anatomically similar to one another in the following four respects:

(1) Each sends many of its axons to primary motor cortex; (2) each receives axons back from primary motor cortex; (3) each is reciprocally connected to the other areas of secondary motor cortex; and (4) each sends axons directly into the motor circuits of the brain stem. They are functionally similar in the following three respects: (1) Electrical stimulation to particular sites within each area of secondary motor cortex results in complex movements of the body; (2) neurons in each area of secondary motor cortex fire prior to and during voluntary motor responses; and (3) movements of one side of the body are often associated with activation of each area of secondary motor cortex in both hemispheres.

In general, the areas of secondary motor cortex are thought to be involved in the programming of specific patterns of movements. Evidence of such a function comes from several brain-imaging studies in which the patterns of activity in the brain have been measured while the subject is either imagining his or her own performance of a particular

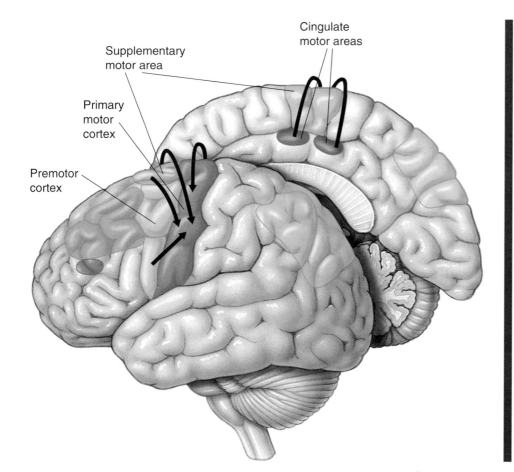

Supplementary motor area

Cingulate motor areas

Primary motor cortex

Premotor cortex

FIGURE 8.5 Four areas of secondary motor cortex—the supplementary motor area, the premotor cortex, and the two cingulate motor areas—and their output to the primary motor cortex. Shown are the lateral surface of the left hemisphere and the medial surface of the right hemisphere.

series of movements or planning the performance of the same movements. The specific results of these studies have varied widely, depending on the particular instructions and target movements they employed, but bilateral increases of activity in the various areas of secondary motor cortex are often observed (see Jeannerod & Decety, 1995; Roland & Zilles, 1996). For example, Parsons and colleagues (1995) found that there was increased PET activity in the supplementary motor area, premotor cortex, and cingulate motor areas while subjects imagined grasping and picking up an object.

Although the general function of secondary motor cortex is commonly held to be the programming of various movements into complex sequences of behavior, PET studies have found extensive activation in the various areas of secondary motor cortex even during the repetition of a simple response (e.g., finger tapping), which should entail little or no response sequencing (Roland & Zilles, 1996). Complex sequences of movements do not activate additional regions of secondary motor cortex, but they do produce more activity in the same areas.

Similarities among the areas of secondary motor cortex aside, the most effort has been put into discovering their differences. It is widely assumed that there are different areas of secondary motor cortex because the different areas play different roles in the planning, programming, and generation of movement. Although several theories have been proposed to explain the functional differences between various areas of secondary motor cortex, none has received consistent support (see Roland & Zilles, 1996; Tanji, 1996).

One interesting line of research on the premotor cortex has focused on how it encodes spatial relations (Graziano & Gross, 1998). Many premotor neurons respond to touch, and each of these has a somatosensory receptive field on a particular part of the body. Many of these neurons also respond to visual input and are thus referred to as *bimodal neurons* (neurons that can be affected by stimuli in two different stimulus modalities). The visual receptive field of a bimodal neuron is always adjacent to its somatosensory receptive field. For example, if a bimodal neuron has its somatosensory receptive field on the left hand, its visual receptive field is usually in the space adjacent to the left hand. Remarkably, the visual receptive field remains next to the left hand regardless of where the left hand is or where the eyes are focused. Clearly, such a neuron is dedicated to the programming of movements of the left hand.

8.4 Primary Motor Cortex

The **primary motor cortex** is located in the *precentral gyrus* of the frontal lobe (see Figures 8.5 and 8.6). It is the major point of convergence of cortical sensorimotor signals, and it is the major point of departure of sensorimotor signals from the cerebral cortex.

In 1937, Penfield and Boldrey mapped the primary motor cortex of conscious human patients during neurosurgery by applying electrical stimulation to various points on the cortical surface and noting which part of the body moved in response to each stimulation. They found that the primary motor cortex is somatotopically organized. The **somatotopic** (organized according to a map of the body) layout of the human primary motor cortex is commonly referred to as the **motor homunculus** (see Figure 8.6). Notice that most of the primary motor cortex is dedicated to controlling parts of the body that are capable of intricate movements, such as the hands and mouth.

More recent research has necessitated an important revision to the original motor homunculus proposed by Penfield and Boldrey, with respect to the hand areas. Recordings from individual primary motor cortex neurons in monkeys while they performed individual finger movements revealed that the control of any individual finger movement depended on the activity of a network of neurons that was widely distributed throughout the primary motor cortex hand area rather than being located in one somatotopically segregated finger area (Schieber & Hibbard, 1993). A similar pattern in the hand area of the human primary motor cortex has also been documented using fMRI (Sanes et al., 1995). Furthermore, small lesions in the hand area of the primary motor cortex of humans (Schieber, 1999) and monkeys (Schieber & Poliakov, 1998) never selectively disrupt the activity of a single finger. It is now clear that the area of primary motor cortex that controls any particular finger is large and overlaps areas controlling other fingers.

Each general area in the primary motor cortex controls the movements of particular groups of muscles, and each receives somatosensory feedback, via somatosensory cortex, from receptors in these muscles and in the joints that they influence. One interesting exception to this general pattern of feedback has been described in monkeys: Monkeys have two different hand areas in the primary motor cortex of each hemisphere, and one receives input from receptors in the skin rather than from receptors in the muscles and joints. Presumably, this adaptation facilitates **stereognosis**—the process of iden-

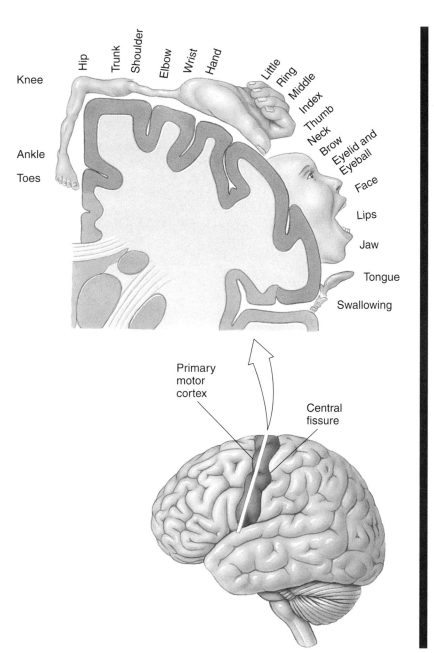

Knee

Hip
Trunk
Shoulder
Elbow
Wrist
Hand

Little
Ring
Middle
Index
Thumb
Neck
Brow
Eyelid and
Eyeball
Face

Lips

Jaw

Tongue

Swallowing

Ankle

Toes

Primary
motor
cortex

Central
fissure

FIGURE 8.6   The motor homunculus: the somatotopic map of the human primary motor cortex. Stimulation of sites in the primary motor cortex elicits simple movements in the indicated parts of the body. (Adapted from Penfield & Rasmussen, 1950.)

tifying objects by touch. Close your eyes and explore an object with your hands; notice how stereognosis depends on a complex interplay between motor responses and the somatosensory stimulation produced by them.

Neurons in the arm area of the primary motor cortex fire maximally when the arm reaches in a particular direction; each neuron has a different preferred direction. Georgopoulos (1995) dissociated the direction of force and the direction of movement by applying external forces to monkeys' arms while the arms reached in various directions. The firing of primary motor cortex neurons was correlated with the direction of the resulting movement rather than with the direction of the force that was generated to produce the movement. Each neuron fired most during and just before movements in a preferred

direction but also fired to movements in other directions; the closer to the preferred direction, the more it fired.

Extensive damage to the human primary motor cortex has less effect than you might expect, given that this cortex is the major point of departure of motor fibers from the cerebral cortex. Large lesions to the primary motor cortex may disrupt a patient's ability to move one body part (e.g., one finger) independently of others; may produce **astereognosia** (deficits in stereognosis), and may reduce the speed, accuracy, and force of a patient's movements. They do not, however, eliminate voluntary movement, presumably because there are pathways that descend directly from secondary motor areas to subcortical motor circuits without passing through primary motor cortex (see Schwartz, 1994).

8.5 | Cerebellum and Basal Ganglia

The cerebellum and the basal ganglia (see Figures 3.23 and 3.31) are both important sensorimotor structures, but neither is a major part of the pathway by which signals descend through the sensorimotor hierarchy. Instead, both the cerebellum and the basal ganglia interact with different levels of the sensorimotor hierarchy, and in so doing they coordinate and modulate its activities. The interconnections between sensory and motor areas via the cerebellum and basal ganglia are thought to be the reason why damage to cortical connections between visual cortex and frontal motor areas does not abolish visually guided responses (Glickstein, 2000).

Cerebellum

The complexity of the cerebellum is suggested by its structure. Although it constitutes only 10% of the mass of the brain, it contains more than half of its neurons (see Goldowitz & Hamre, 1998; Voogd & Glickstein, 1998). The cerebellum receives information from primary and secondary motor cortex, information about descending motor signals from brain stem motor nuclei, and feedback from motor responses via the somatosensory and vestibular systems. The cerebellum is thought to compare these three sources of input and correct ongoing movements that deviate from their intended course (see Ebner, 1998; Serrien & Weisendanger, 1999). By performing this function, it is believed to play a major role in motor learning (see Raymond, Lisberger, & Mauk, 1996; Thach, 1996).

The consequences of diffuse cerebellar damage for motor function are devastating. The patient loses the ability to control precisely the direction, force, velocity, and amplitude of movements and the ability to adapt patterns of motor output to changing conditions. It is difficult to maintain steady postures (e.g., standing), and attempts to do so frequently lead to tremor. There are also severe disturbances in balance, gait, speech, and the control of eye movement. Learning new motor patterns is virtually impossible.

Like theories of cerebellar function, theories of basal ganglia function are evolving. The traditional view that the function of the cerebellum is limited to the fine-tuning and learning of motor responses has been challenged. The basis for this challenge has come from the observation of activity in the cerebellum by functional brain imaging during the performance of a variety of nonmotor cognitive tasks by healthy human subjects (e.g., Allen et al., 1997; Lotz et al., 1999) and from the documenta-

tion of cognitive deficits in patients with cerebellar damage (e.g., Townsend et al., 1999; Tucker et al., 1996). Various alternative theories have been proposed, but the most parsimonious of them tend to argue that the cerebellum functions in the fine-tuning and learning of cognitive responses in the same way that it functions in the fine-tuning and learning of motor responses (e.g., Leiner, Leiner, & Dow, 1995).

Basal Ganglia

The basal ganglia do not contain as many neurons as the cerebellum, but in one sense they are more complex. Unlike the cerebellum, which is organized systematically in lobes, columns, and layers, the basal ganglia are a complex heterogeneous collection of interconnected nuclei (see Graybiel et al., 1994).

The anatomy of the basal ganglia suggests that, like the cerebellum, they perform a modulatory function. They contribute no fibers to descending motor pathways; instead, they are part of neural loops that receive cortical input from various cortical areas and transmit it back via the thalamus to the various areas of motor cortex (see Goldman-Rakic & Selemon, 1990; Middleton & Strick, 1994).

Theories of basal ganglia function have been modified—in much the same way that theories of cerebellar function have changed. The traditional view of the basal ganglia was that they, like the cerebellum, play a role in the modulation of motor output—for example, in the sequencing of movement (Aldridge & Berridge, 1998). This view has been greatly expanded. Now, the basal ganglia are thought to be involved in a variety of cognitive functions in addition to their role in the modulation of neural output (see Brown, Schneider, & Lidsky, 1997; Graybiel, 1995). This expanded view of the function of the basal ganglia is consistent with the fact that they project to cortical areas known to have cognitive functions (see Wichmann & DeLong, 1996).

In experiments on rats, the basal ganglia have been shown to participate in learning to respond correctly to learned associations, a type of response learning which characteristically progresses gradually, trial by trial (e.g., McDonald & White, 1993). However, the basal ganglia's cognitive functions do not appear to be limited to this form of response learning. For example, patients with basal ganglia damage often display difficulties in solving complex puzzles that require only a single key press to indicate the correct response (see Knowlton, Mangels, & Squire, 1996).

BrainScan

Are you ready to continue your descent into the sensorimotor circuits of the spinal cord? This is a good place for you to pause to scan your brain to evaluate your knowledge of the sensorimotor circuits of the cortex, cerebellum, and basal ganglia by completing the following statements. The correct answers are provided at the bottom of this page. Before proceeding, review material related to your incorrect answers and omissions.

1. Visual, auditory, and somatosensory input converges on the _____ association cortex.

2. A small area of frontal cortex called the frontal _____ plays a major role in the control of eye movement.

3. Contralateral neglect is often associated with large lesions of the right _____ lobe.

4. The _____ prefrontal cortex seems to play an important role in initiating complex voluntary responses.

5. The secondary motor area that is just dorsal to the premotor cortex and is largely hidden from view on the medial surface of each hemisphere is the _____ .

6. Most of the direct sensory input to the supplementary motor area comes from the _____ system.

7. Most of the direct sensory input to the premotor cortex comes from the _____ system.

8. The _____ cortex is the main point of departure of motor signals from the cerebral cortex to lower levels of the sensorimotor hierarchy.

9. The foot area of the motor homunculus is in the _____ fissure.

10. Although the _____ constitutes only 10% of the mass of the brain, it contains more than half of its neurons.

11. The _____ are part of neural loops that receive input from various cortical areas and transmit it back to various areas of motor cortex via the thalamus.

12. Although both are considered to be motor structures, damage to the _____ or the _____ produces cognitive deficits.

8.6 Descending Motor Pathways

Neural signals are conducted from the primary motor cortex to the motor neurons of the spinal cord over four different pathways. Two pathways descend in the *dorsolateral* region of the spinal cord, and two descend in the *ventromedial* region of the spinal cord. These pathways act together in the control of voluntary movement (see Iwaniuk & Whishaw, 2000).

■ Dorsolateral Corticospinal Tract and Dorsolateral Corticorubrospinal Tract

One group of axons that descends from the primary motor cortex descends through the *medullary pyramids*—two bulges on the ventral surface of the medulla—then decussates and continues to descend in the contralateral dorsolateral spinal white matter. This group of axons constitutes the **dorsolateral corticospinal tract.** Most notable among its neurons are the **Betz cells**—extremely large pyramidal neurons of the primary motor cortex. Their axons terminate in the lower regions of the spinal cord on motor neurons that project to the muscles of the legs. They are thought to be the means by which we exert rapid and powerful voluntary control over our legs.

Most axons of the dorsolateral corticospinal pathway synapse on small interneurons of the spinal gray matter, which synapse on the motor neurons of distal muscles of the wrist, hands, fingers, and toes. Primates and the few other mammals that are capable of moving their digits independently (e.g., hamsters and raccoons) have dorsolateral corticospinal tract neurons that synapse directly on digit motor neurons (see Porter & Lemon, 1993).

A second group of axons that descends from the primary motor cortex synapses in the *red nucleus* of the midbrain. The axons of neurons in the red nucleus then decussate and descend through the medulla, where some of them terminate in the nuclei of the cranial nerves that control the muscles of the face. The rest continue to descend in the dorsolateral portion of the spinal cord. This pathway is called the **dorsolateral corticorubrospinal tract** (*rubro* refers to the red nucleus). The axons of the dorsolateral corticorubrospinal tract synapse on interneurons that in turn synapse on motor neurons that project to the distal muscles of the arms and legs.

The two divisions of the dorsolateral motor pathway—the direct dorsolateral corticospinal tract and the indirect dorsolateral corticorubrospinal tract—are illustrated schematically in Figure 8.7.

Ventromedial Corticospinal Tract and Ventromedial Cortico-brainstem-spinal Tract

Just as there are two major divisions of the dorsolateral motor pathway, one direct (the corticospinal tract) and one indirect (the corticorubrospinal tract), there are two major divisions of the ventromedial motor pathway, one direct and one indirect. The direct ventromedial pathway is the **ventromedial corticospinal tract,** and the indirect one—as you might infer from its cumbersome but descriptive name—is the **ventromedial cortico-brainstem-spinal tract.**

The long axons of the ventromedial corticospinal tract descend ipsilaterally from the primary motor cortex directly into the ventromedial areas of the spinal white matter. As each axon of the ventromedial corticospinal tract descends, it branches diffusely and innervates the interneuron circuits in several different spinal segments on both sides of the spinal gray matter.

The ventromedial cortico-brainstem-spinal tract comprises motor cortex axons that feed into a complex network of brain stem structures. The axons of some of the neurons in this complex brain stem motor network then descend bilaterally in the ventromedial portion of the spinal cord. Each side carries signals from both hemispheres, and each neuron synapses on the interneurons of several different spinal cord segments that control the proximal muscles of the trunk and limbs.

Which brain stem structures interact with the ventromedial cortico-brainstem-spinal tract? There are four major ones: (1) the **tectum,** which receives auditory and visual information about spatial location; (2) the **vestibular nucleus,** which receives information about balance from receptors in the semicircular canals of the inner ear; (3) the **reticular formation,** which, among other things, contains motor programs for complex species-common movements such as walking, swimming, and jumping; and (4) the motor nuclei of the cranial nerves that control the muscles of the face.

The two divisions of the descending ventromedial pathway—the direct ventromedial corticospinal tract and the indirect ventromedial cortico-brainstem-spinal tract—are illustrated in Figure 8.8 on page 208.

Comparison of the Two Dorsolateral Motor Pathways and the Two Ventromedial Motor Pathways

The descending dorsolateral and ventromedial pathways are similar in that each is composed of two major tracts, one whose axons descend directly to the spinal cord and another whose axons synapse in the brain stem on neurons that in turn descend to the spinal cord. However, the two dorsolateral tracts differ from the two ventromedial tracts in two major respects:

1. The two ventromedial tracts are much more diffuse. Many of their axons innervate interneurons on both sides of the spinal gray matter and in several different segments, whereas the axons of the two dorsolateral tracts terminate in the contralateral half of one spinal cord segment, sometimes directly on a motor neuron.
2. The motor neurons that are activated by the two ventromedial tracts project to proximal muscles of the trunk and limbs (e.g., shoulder muscles), whereas the motor neurons that are activated by the two dorsolateral tracts project to distal muscles (e.g., finger muscles).

Because all four of the descending motor tracts originate in the cerebral cortex, all are presumed to mediate voluntary movement; however, major differences in their routes and destinations suggest that they have different functions. This difference was first demonstrated in two experiments that were reported by Lawrence and Kuypers in 1968.

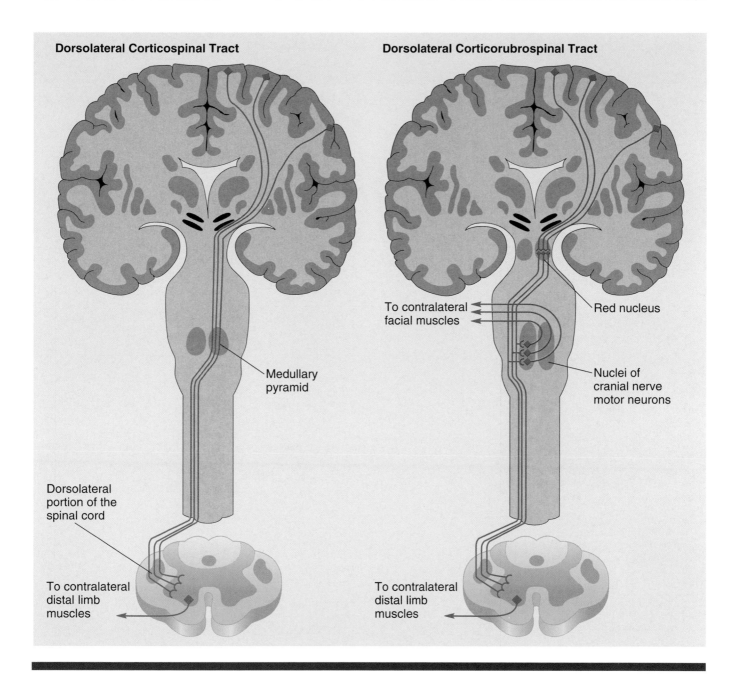

FIGURE 8.7   The two divisions of the dorsolateral motor pathway: the dorsolateral corticospinal tract and the dorsolateral corticorubrospinal motor tract. The projections from only one hemisphere are shown.

In their first experiment, Lawrence and Kuypers (1968a) transected (cut through) the left and right dorsolateral corticospinal tracts of their monkey subjects in the medullary pyramids, just above the decussation of the tracts. Following surgery, these monkeys could stand, walk, and climb quite normally; however, their ability to use their limbs for other activities was impaired. For example, their reaching movements were weak and poorly directed, particularly in the first few days following the surgery. Although there was substantial improvement in the monkeys' reaching ability over the ensuing weeks, two other

deficits remained unabated. First, the monkeys never regained the ability to move their fingers independently of one another; when they picked up pieces of food, they did so by using all of their fingers as a unit, as if they were glued together. And second, they never regained the ability to release objects from their grasp; as a result, once they picked up a piece of food, they often had to root for it in their hand like a pig rooting for truffles in the ground. In view of this latter problem, it is remarkable that they had no difficulty releasing their grasp on the bars of their cage when they were climbing. This point is important because it shows that the same response

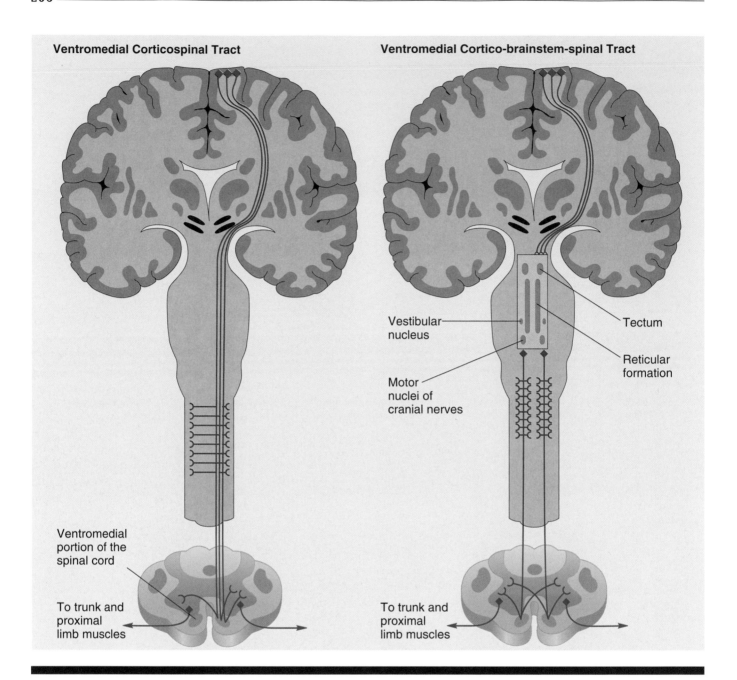

Ventromedial Corticospinal Tract

Ventromedial Cortico-brainstem-spinal Tract

Vestibular nucleus

Tectum

Reticular formation

Motor nuclei of cranial nerves

Ventromedial portion of the spinal cord

To trunk and proximal limb muscles

To trunk and proximal limb muscles

FIGURE 8.8 The two divisions of the ventromedial motor pathway: the ventromedial corticospinal tract and the ventromedial cortico-brainstem-spinal tract. The projections from only one hemisphere are shown.

performed in different contexts can be controlled by different parts of the central nervous system.

In their second experiment, Lawrence and Kuypers (1968b) made additional transections in the monkeys whose dorsolateral corticospinal tracts had already been transected in the first experiment. The dorsolateral corticorubrospinal tract was transected in one group of these monkeys. The monkeys could stand, walk, and climb after this second transection; but when they were sitting, their arms hung limply by their sides (remember that monkeys normally use their arms for standing and walking). In those few instances in which the monkeys

did use an arm for reaching, they used it like a rubber-handled rake—throwing it out from the shoulder and using it to draw small objects of interest back along the floor.

The other group of monkeys in the second experiment had both of their ventromedial tracts transected. In contrast to the first group, these subjects had severe postural abnormalities: They had great difficulty walking or sitting. If they did manage to sit or stand without clinging to the bars of their cages, the slightest disturbance, such as a loud noise, frequently made them fall. Although they had some use of their arms, the additional transection of the two ventromedial tracts eliminated their ability to control their shoulders. When they fed, they did so with elbow and whole-hand movements while their upper arms hung limply by their sides.

What do these experiments tell us about the roles of the various descending sensorimotor tracts in the control of movement? They suggest that the two ventromedial tracts are involved in the control of posture and whole-body movements (e.g., walking and climbing) and that

they can exert control over the limb movements involved in such activities. In contrast, both dorsolateral tracts—the corticospinal tract and the corticorubrospinal tract—control the reaching movements of the limbs. This redundancy was presumably the basis for the good recovery of limb movement after the initial lesions of the corticospinal dorsolateral tract. However, only the corticospinal division of the dorsolateral system is capable of mediating independent movements of the digits.

8.7 Sensorimotor Spinal Circuits

■ Muscles

Motor units are the smallest units of motor activity. Each motor unit comprises a single motor neuron and all of the individual skeletal muscle fibers that it innervates (see Figure 8.9). When the motor neuron fires, all the muscle fibers of its unit contract together. Motor units differ appreciably in the number of muscle fibers they contain; the units with the fewest fibers—those of the fingers and face—permit the highest degree of selective motor control.

A skeletal muscle comprises hundreds of thousands of threadlike muscle fibers bound together in a tough membrane and attached to a bone by a *tendon. Acetylcholine,* which is released by motor neurons at *neuromuscular junctions,* activates the **motor end-plate** on each muscle fiber and causes the fiber to contract. All of the motor neurons that innervate the fibers of a single muscle are called its **motor pool.**

Although it is an oversimplification (see Gollinick & Hodgson, 1986), skeletal muscle fibers are often considered to be of two basic types: fast and slow. *Fast muscle fibers,* as you might guess, are those that contract and relax quickly. Although they are capable of generating great force, they fatigue quickly because they are poorly vascularized (which gives them a pale color). In contrast, *slow muscle fibers,* although slower and weaker, are capable of more sustained contraction because they are more richly vascularized (and hence much redder). Depending on their function, muscles have different proportions of fast and slow fibers.

Many skeletal muscles belong unambiguously to one of two categories: flexors or extensors. **Flexors** act to bend or flex a joint, and **extensors** act to straighten or extend it. Figure 8.10 on page 210 illustrates the *biceps* and *triceps*—the flexor and extensor, respectively, of the elbow joint. Any two muscles whose contraction produces the same movement, be it flexion or extension, are said to be **synergistic muscles;** those that act in opposition, like the biceps and the triceps, are said to be **antagonistic muscles.**

To understand how muscles work, it is important to realize that muscles have elastic, rather than inflexible, cablelike, properties. If you think of an increase in muscle

FIGURE 8.9 An electron micrograph of a motor unit: a motor neuron (pink) and the muscle fibers that it innervates.

FIGURE 8.10 The biceps and triceps, which are the flexor and extensor, respectively, of the elbow joint.

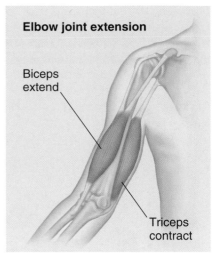

tension as being analogous to an increase in the tension of an elastic band joining two bones, you will appreciate that muscle contraction can be of two types. Activation of a muscle can increase the tension that it exerts on two bones without shortening and pulling them together; this is termed **isometric contraction.** Or it can shorten and pull them together; this is termed **dynamic contraction.** The tension in a muscle can be increased by increasing the number of neurons in its motor pool that are firing, by increasing the firing rates of those that are already firing, or more commonly by a combination of the two.

Receptor Organs of Tendons and Muscles

The activity of skeletal muscles is monitored by two kinds of receptors: Golgi tendon organs and muscle spindles. **Golgi tendon organs** are embedded in the *tendons,* which connect each skeletal muscle to bone; and **muscle spindles** are embedded in the muscle tissue itself. Because of their different locations, Golgi tendon organs and muscle spindles respond to different aspects of muscle contraction. Golgi tendon organs respond to increases in muscle tension (i.e., to the pull of the muscle on the tendon), but they are completely insensitive to changes in muscle length. In contrast, muscle spindles respond to changes in muscle length, but they do not respond to changes in muscle tension.

Under normal conditions, the function of Golgi tendon organs is to provide the central nervous system with information about muscle tension, but they also serve a protective function. When the contraction of a muscle is so extreme that there is a risk of damage, the Golgi tendon organs excite inhibitory interneurons in the spinal cord that cause the muscle to relax.

Figure 8.11 is a schematic diagram of the *muscle-spindle feedback circuit.* Examine it carefully. Notice that each muscle spindle has its own threadlike **intrafusal muscle,** which is innervated by its own **intrafusal motor neuron.** Why would a receptor have its own muscle and motor neuron? The reason becomes apparent when you consider what would happen to a muscle spindle without them. Without its intrafusal motor input, a muscle spindle would fall slack each time its **skeletal muscle (extrafusal muscle)** contracted. In this slack state, the muscle spindle could not do its job, which is to respond to slight changes in extrafusal muscle length. As Figure 8.12 illustrates, the intrafusal motor neuron solves this problem by shortening the intrafusal muscle each time the extrafusal muscle becomes shorter, thus keeping enough tension on the middle, stretch-sensitive portion of the muscle spindle to keep it responsive to slight changes in the length of the extrafusal muscle.

Stretch Reflex

When the word *reflex* is mentioned, many people think of themselves sitting on the edge of their doctor's examination table having their knees rapped with a little rubber-headed hammer. The resulting leg extension is called the **patellar tendon reflex** (*patella* means "knee"). This reflex is a **stretch reflex**—a reflex that is elicited by a sudden external stretching force on a muscle.

When your doctor strikes the tendon of your knee, the extensor muscle running along your thigh is stretched. This initiates the chain of events that is depicted in Figure 8.13 on page 212. The sudden stretch of the thigh muscle stretches its muscle-spindle stretch receptors, which in turn initiates a volley of action potentials that is carried from the stretch receptors into the spinal cord by **spindle afferent neurons** via the *dorsal root.* This volley of action potentials excites motor neurons in the *ventral horn* of the spinal cord, which respond by sending action potentials back to the muscle whose stretch originally excited them (see Illert & Kümmel, 1999). The arrival of these impulses back at the starting point results in a compensatory muscle contraction and a sudden leg extension.

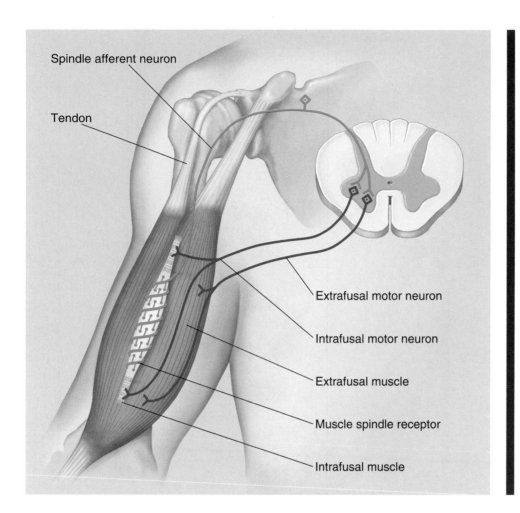

The method by which the patellar tendon reflex is typically elicited in a doctor's office—that is, by a sharp blow to the tendon of a completely relaxed muscle—is designed to make the reflex readily observable. However, it does little to communicate its functional significance. In real-life situations, the function of the stretch reflex is to keep external forces from altering the intended position of the body. When an external force, such as a push

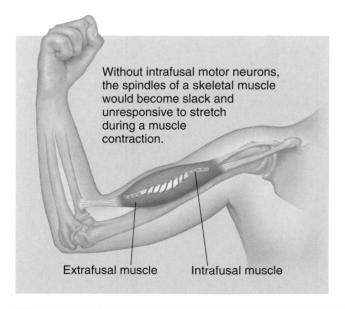

Without intrafusal motor neurons, the spindles of a skeletal muscle would become slack and unresponsive to stretch during a muscle contraction.

The function of intrafusal motor neurons is to adjust the length of intrafusal muscles, thus maintaining an appropriate degree of tension on muscle spindles, regardless of the length of the skeletal muscle.

FIGURE 8.12 The function of intrafusal motor neurons.

FIGURE 8.13   The elicitation of a stretch reflex. All of the muscle spindles in a muscle are activated during a stretch reflex, but only a single muscle spindle is depicted here.

Rap occurs here

The rap on the knee tendon stretches the spindles of the thigh muscle and elicits a burst of firing in their afferent neurons.

Rap occurs here

The burst of firing in the spindle afferent neurons triggers a burst of firing in the thigh muscle motor neurons, which causes the thigh muscle to contract.

on your arm while you are holding a cup of coffee, causes an unanticipated extrafusal muscle stretch, the muscle-spindle feedback circuit produces an immediate compensatory contraction of the muscle that counteracts the force and keeps you from spilling the coffee—unless, of course, you are wearing your best clothes.

The mechanism by which the stretch reflex maintains limb stability is illustrated in Figure 8.14. Examine it carefully because it illustrates two of the principles of sensorimotor system function that are the focus of this chapter: the important role played by sensory feedback in the regulation of motor output and the ability of lower circuits in the motor hierarchy to take care of "business details" without the involvement of higher levels.

■ | **Withdrawal Reflex**

I am sure that, at one time or another, you have touched something painful—a hot pot, for example—

and suddenly pulled back your hand. This is a **withdrawal reflex.** Unlike the stretch reflex, the withdrawal reflex is *not monosynaptic* (Eidelberg, 1987). When a painful stimulus is applied to the hand, the first responses are recorded in the motor neurons of the arm flexor muscles about 1.6 milliseconds later, about the time it takes a neural signal to cross two synapses. Thus, the shortest route in the withdrawal-reflex circuit involves one interneuron. Other responses are recorded in the motor neurons of the arm flexor muscles after the initial volley; these responses are triggered by signals that have traveled over multisynaptic pathways—some involving the cortex (see Matthews, 1991). See Figure 8.15 on page 214.

■ | **Reciprocal Innervation**

Reciprocal innervation is an important principle of spinal cord circuitry. It refers to the fact that antago-

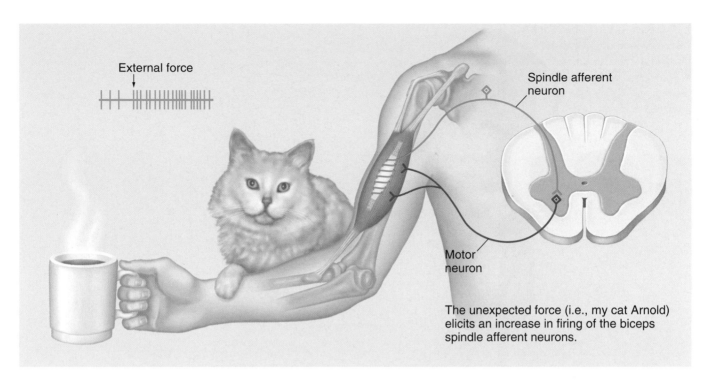

External force

Spindle afferent neuron

Motor neuron

The unexpected force (i.e., my cat Arnold) elicits an increase in firing of the biceps spindle afferent neurons.

External force

The increase in the firing of the biceps spindle afferent neurons increases firing in the biceps motor neurons, thus keeping the arm in its original position.

FIGURE 8.14   The automatic maintenance of limb position by the muscle-spindle feedback system.

nistic muscles are innervated in a way that permits a smooth, unimpeded motor response: When one is contracted, the other relaxes. Figure 8.15 illustrates the role of reciprocal innervation in the withdrawal reflex. "Bad news" of a sudden painful event in the hand arrives in the dorsal horn of the spinal cord and has two effects: The signals excite both excitatory and inhibitory interneu-

rons. The excitatory interneurons excite the motor neurons of the elbow flexor; the inhibitory interneurons inhibit the motor neurons of the elbow extensor. Thus a single sensory input produces a coordinated pattern of motor output; the activities of agonists and antagonists are automatically coordinated by the internal circuitry of the spinal cord.

FIGURE 8.15 The reciprocal innervation of antagonistic muscles in the arm. During a withdrawal reflex, elbow flexors are excited, and elbow extensors are inhibited.

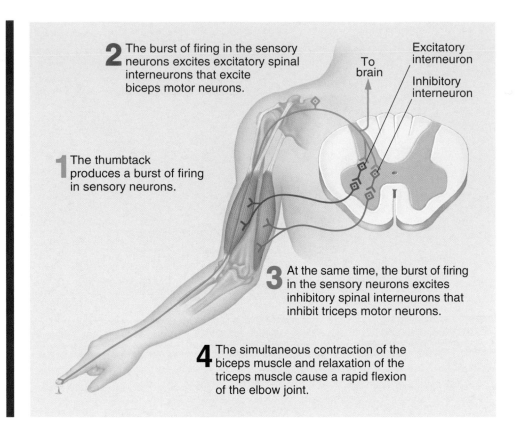

2 The burst of firing in the sensory neurons excites excitatory spinal interneurons that excite biceps motor neurons.

1 The thumbtack produces a burst of firing in sensory neurons.

To brain

Excitatory interneuron

Inhibitory interneuron

3 At the same time, the burst of firing in the sensory neurons excites inhibitory spinal interneurons that inhibit triceps motor neurons.

4 The simultaneous contraction of the biceps muscle and relaxation of the triceps muscle cause a rapid flexion of the elbow joint.

Movements are quickest when there is simultaneous excitation of all agonists and complete inhibition of all antagonists; however, this is not the way voluntary movement is normally produced. Most muscles are always contracted to some degree, and movements are produced by adjustment in the level of relative cocontraction between antagonists. Movements that are produced by **cocontraction** are smooth, and they can be stopped with precision by a slight increase in the contraction of the antagonistic muscles. Moreover, cocontraction insulates us from the effects of unexpected external forces.

Recurrent Collateral Inhibition

Like most workers, muscle fibers and the motor neurons that innervate them need an occasional break, and there are inhibitory neurons in the spinal cord that make sure they get it. Each motor neuron branches just before it leaves the spinal cord, and the branch synapses on a small inhibitory interneuron, which inhibits the very motor neuron from which it receives its input (see Illert & Kümmel, 1999). The inhibition produced by these local feedback circuits is called **recurrent collateral inhibition,** and the small inhibitory interneurons that mediate recurrent collateral inhibition are called *Renshaw cells.* As a consequence of recurrent collateral inhibition, each time a motor neuron fires, it momentarily inhibits itself and shifts the responsibility for the contraction of a particular muscle to other members of the muscle's motor pool.

Figure 8.16 provides a summary; it illustrates recurrent collateral inhibition and other factors that directly excite or inhibit motor neurons.

Walking: A Complex Sensorimotor Reflex

Most reflexes are much more complex than withdrawal and stretch reflexes. Think for a moment about the complexity of the program of reflexes that is needed to control an activity such as walking. Such a program must integrate visual information from the eyes; somatosensory information from the feet, knees, hips, arms, and so on; and information about balance from the semicircular canals of the inner ears. And it must produce, on the basis of this information, an integrated series of movements that involves the muscles of the trunk, legs, feet, and upper arms. This program of reflexes must also be incredibly flexible; it must be able to adjust its output immediately to changes in the slope of the terrain, to instructions from the brain, or to external forces such as a bag of groceries. Nobody has yet managed to build a robot that can come close to duplicating these feats.

Grillner (1985) showed that walking is controlled largely by circuits in the spinal cord. Grillner's subjects were cats whose spinal cords had been separated from their brains by transection. He suspended the cats in a sling over a treadmill; amazingly, when the treadmill was started so that the cats received sensory feedback of the sort that normally accompanies walking, they began to walk.

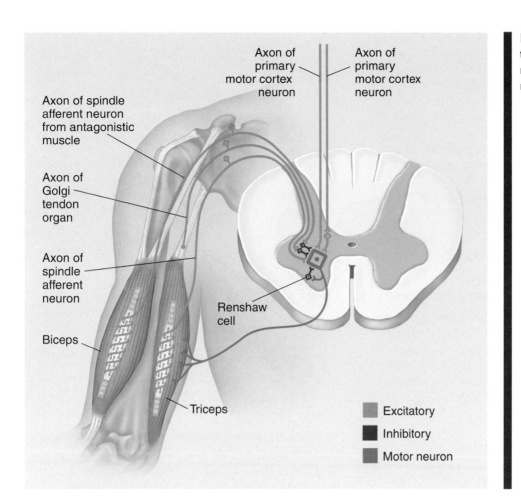

Axon of primary motor cortex neuron

Axon of primary motor cortex neuron

Axon of spindle afferent neuron from antagonistic muscle

Axon of Golgi tendon organ

Axon of spindle afferent neuron

Renshaw cell

Biceps

Triceps

Excitatory

Inhibitory

Motor neuron

FIGURE 8.16 The excitatory and inhibitory signals that directly influence the activity of a motor neuron.

8.8 Central Sensorimotor Programs

In this chapter, you have learned that the sensorimotor system is like the hierarchy of a large efficient company. You have learned how the executives—the dorsolateral prefrontal cortex, the supplementary motor area, and the premotor cortex—issue commands based on information supplied to them by the posterior parietal cortex. And you have learned how these commands are forwarded to the director of operations (the primary motor cortex) for distribution over four main channels of communication (the two dorsolateral and the two ventromedial spinal motor pathways) to the metaphoric office managers of the sensorimotor hierarchy (the spinal sensorimotor circuits). Finally, you have learned how spinal sensorimotor circuits direct the activities of the workers (the muscles).

One theory of sensorimotor function is that the sensorimotor system comprises a hierarchy of **central sensorimotor programs** (see Brooks, 1986; Georgopoulos, 1991). The central sensorimotor program theory suggests that all but the highest levels of the sensorimotor system have certain patterns of activity programmed into

them and that complex movements are produced by activating the appropriate combinations of these programs. Accordingly, if your association cortex decides that you might like to look at a magazine, it activates high-level cortical programs that in turn activate lower-level programs—perhaps in your brain stem—for walking, bending over, picking up, and thumbing through. These programs in turn activate specific spinal programs that control the various elements of the sequences and cause your muscles to complete the objective.

Once activated, each level of the sensorimotor system is capable of operating on the basis of current sensory feedback, without the direct control of higher levels. Thus, although the highest levels of your sensorimotor system retain the option of directly controlling your activities, most of the individual responses that you make are performed without direct cortical involvement, and you are barely aware of them.

In much the same way, a company president who wishes to open a new branch office simply issues the command to one of the executives, and the executive responds in the usual fashion by issuing a series of commands to the appropriate people lower in the hierarchy, who in turn do the same. Each of the executives and workers of the company knows how to complete many different tasks and executes them in the light of current conditions when instructed to do so. Good companies have mechanisms for ensuring that the programs of action at different levels of the hierarchy are well coordinated and effective. In the sensorimotor system, these mechanisms seem to be the responsibility of the cerebellum and basal ganglia.

Central Sensorimotor Programs Are Capable of Motor Equivalence

Like a large, efficient company, the sensorimotor system does not always accomplish a particular task in exactly the same way. The fact that the same basic movement can be carried out in different ways involving different muscles is called **motor equivalence.** For example, you have learned to sign your name with stereotypical finger and hand movements, yet if you signed your name with your toe on a sandy beach, your signature would still retain many of its typical characteristics. This example of motor equivalence suggests that the central sensorimotor programs for signing your name are not stored in the neural circuits that directly control your preferred hand, but higher in your sensorimotor hierarchy. Where?

In an fMRI study, Rijntjes and others (1999) showed that the central sensorimotor programs for signing one's name are stored in areas of secondary motor cortex that control the preferred hand. Remarkably, these same hand areas were also activated when the signature was made with a toe.

Sensory Information That Controls Central Sensorimotor Programs Is Not Necessarily Conscious

In Chapter 7, you learned that the neural mechanisms of conscious visual perception (ventral stream) are not necessarily the same as those that mediate the visual control of behavior (dorsal stream). Initial evidence for this theory came from neuropsychological patients who could respond to visual stimuli of which they had no conscious awareness and from patients who could not effectively interact with objects they consciously perceived.

Is there evidence for the separation of conscious perception and sensory control of behavior in intact subjects? Haffenden and Goodale (1998) supplied such evidence. They showed healthy subjects a three-dimensional version of the visual illusion in Figure 8.17—

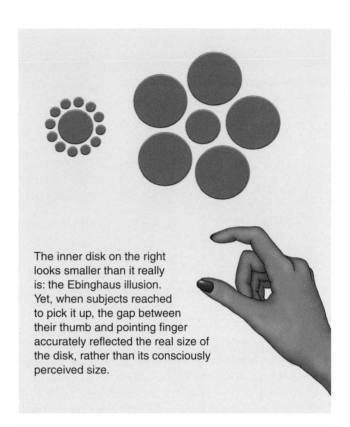

The inner disk on the right looks smaller than it really is: the Ebinghaus illusion. Yet, when subjects reached to pick it up, the gap between their thumb and pointing finger accurately reflected the real size of the disk, rather than its consciously perceived size.

FIGURE 8.17 The Ebinghaus illusion. Notice that the central disk on the left appears larger than the one on the right. Haffenden and Goodale (1998) found that when subjects reached out to pick up either of the central disks, the position of their fingers as they approached the disks indicated that their responses were being controlled by the actual sizes of the disks, not their consciously perceived sizes.

notice that the two central disks appear to be different sizes, even though they are identical. Remarkably, when subjects were asked to indicate the size of each central disk with their right thumb and pointing finger, they judged the disk on the left to be bigger than the one on the right; however, when they were asked to reach out and pick up the disks with the same two digits, the preparatory gap between the digits was a function of the actual size of each disk rather than its perceived size.

Central Sensorimotor Programs Can Develop without Practice

What type of experience is necessary for the normal development of central sensorimotor programs? In particular, is it necessary to practice a particular behavior for its central sensorimotor program to develop?

Although central sensorimotor programs for some behaviors can be established by practicing the behaviors, the central sensorimotor programs for many species-typical behaviors are established without explicit practice of the behaviors. This point was made clear by the classic study of Fentress (1973). Fentress showed that adult mice raised from birth without forelimbs still made the patterns of shoulder movements typical of grooming in their species—and that these movements were well coordinated with normal tongue, head, and eye movements. For example, the mice blinked each time they made the shoulder movements that would have swept their forepaws across their eyes. Fentress's study also demonstrated the importance of sensory feedback in the operation of central sensorimotor programs. The forelimbless mice, deprived of normal tongue–forepaw contact during face grooming, would often interrupt ostensible grooming sequences to lick a cage-mate or even the floor.

Practice Can Create Central Sensorimotor Programs

Although central sensorimotor programs for many species-typical behaviors develop without practice, practice is a certain way to generate or modify such programs. Theories of sensorimotor learning emphasize two kinds of processes that influence the learning of central sensorimotor programs: response chunking and shifting control to lower levels of the sensorimotor system.

RESPONSE CHUNKING ■ According to the **response-chunking hypothesis,** practice combines the central sensorimotor programs that control individual response into programs that control sequences (chunks) of behavior. In a novice typist, each response necessary to type a word is individually triggered and controlled; in a skilled typist, sequences of letters are activated as a unit, with a marked increase in speed and continuity.

An important principle of chunking is that chunks can themselves be combined into higher-order chunks. For example, the responses needed to type the individual letters and digits of one's address may be chunked into longer sequences necessary to produce the individual words and numbers, and these chunks may in turn be combined so that the entire address can be typed as a unit.

SHIFTING CONTROL TO LOWER LEVELS ■ During the development of a central sensorimotor program, control is shifted from higher levels of the sensorimotor hierarchy to lower levels. Shifting the level of control to lower levels of the sensorimotor system during training (see Seitz et al., 1990) has two advantages. One is that it frees up the higher levels of the system to deal with more esoteric aspects of performance. For example, skilled pianists can concentrate on interpreting a piece of music because they do not have to consciously focus on pressing the right keys. The other advantage of shifting the

level of control is that it permits great speed because different circuits at the lower levels of the hierarchy can act simultaneously, without interfering with one another. It is possible to type 120 words per minute only because the circuits responsible for activating each individual key press can become active before the preceding response has been completed.

Functional Brain Imaging of Sensorimotor Learning

Functional brain imaging techniques have provided new opportunities for studying the neural correlates of sensorimotor learning. By recording the brain activity of human subjects as they learn to perform new motor sequences, it is possible to develop hypotheses about the roles of various structures in sensorimotor learning. A good example of this approach is the PET study of Jenkins and colleagues (1994). These researchers recorded PET activity from human subjects who performed two different sequences of key presses. There were four different keys, and each sequence was four presses long. The presses were performed with the right hand, one every 3 seconds, and tones indicated when to press and whether or not a press was correct. There were three conditions: a rest control condition, a condition in which the subjects performed a newly learned sequence, and a condition in which the subjects performed a well-practiced sequence.

The following are six major findings of this study (see Figure 8.18 on page 218). They recapitulate important points that have already been made in this chapter.

Finding 1: Posterior parietal cortex was activated during the performance of both the newly learned sequence and the well-practiced sequence, but it was more active during the newly learned sequence. This finding is consistent with the hypothesis that the posterior parietal cortex integrates sensory stimuli (in this case, the tones) that are used to guide motor sequences, and it is consistent with the finding that the posterior parietal cortex is more active when subjects are attending more to the stimuli, as is often the case during the early stages of motor learning.

Finding 2: Dorsolateral prefrontal cortex was activated during the performance of the newly learned sequence but not during the well-practiced sequence (see Shadmehr & Holcomb, 1997). This suggests that the dorsolateral prefrontal cortex plays a particularly important role when motor sequences are being performed largely under conscious control, as is often the case during the early stages of motor learning.

Finding 3: The areas of secondary motor cortex responded differently. The contralateral premotor

FIGURE 8.18 The activity recorded by PET scans during the performance of newly learned and well-practiced sequences of finger movements. (Adapted from Jenkins et al., 1994.)

Sensorimotor areas activated by performing a well-practiced sequence of finger movements

Sensorimotor areas activated by performing a newly learned sequence of finger movements

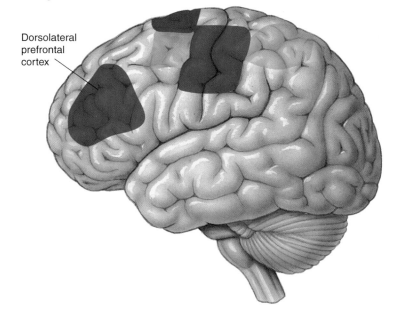

cortex was more active during the performance of the newly learned sequence, whereas the supplementary motor area was more active bilaterally during the well-practiced sequence. This finding is consistent with the hypothesis that the premotor cortex plays a more prominent role when performance is being guided largely by sensory stimuli, as is often the case in the early stages of motor learning, and that the supplementary motor area plays a more prominent role when performance is largely independent of sensory stimuli, as is often the case for well-practiced motor sequences, which can be run off automatically with little sensory feedback.

Finding 4: Contralateral primary motor and somatosensory cortexes were equally activated during the performance of both the newly learned and well-practiced motor sequences. This finding is consistent with the fact that the motor elements were the same during both sequences.

Finding 5: The contralateral basal ganglia were equally activated during the performance of the newly learned sequence and the well-practiced sequence. Jenkins and colleagues speculated that different subpopulations of basal ganglia neurons may have been active during the two conditions, but this could not be detected because of the poor spatial resolution of PET.

Finding 6: The cerebellum was activated bilaterally during the performance of both the newly learned and the well-practiced sequences, but it was more active during the newly learned sequence. This is consistent with the idea that the cerebellum plays a prominent role in motor learning (see Flament et al., 1996; Thach, 1996).

The Case of Rhonda, Revisited

Recently, I stopped off to pick up a few fresh vegetables and some fish for dinner, and I once again found myself waiting in Rhonda's line. It was the longest line, but I am a creature of habit. This time, I felt rather smug as I watched her. All of the reading and thinking that had gone into the preparation of this chapter had provided me with some new insights into what she was doing and how she was doing it. I wondered whether she appreciated her own finely tuned sensorimotor system as much as I did. Then I hatched my plot—a little test of Rhonda's muscle-spindle feedback system. How would Rhonda's finely tuned sensorimotor system react to a bag that looked heavy but was in fact extremely light? Next time, I would get one of those paper bags at the mushroom counter, blow it up, drop one mushroom in it, and then fold up the top so it looked completely full. I smiled at the thought. But I wasn't the only one smiling. My daydreaming ended abruptly, and the smile melted from my face, as I noticed Rhonda's extended hand and her amused grin. Will I never learn?

Themes Revisited

All four of this book's major themes were addressed in this chapter. Most prominent were the clinical implications and cognitive neuroscience themes: You learned how the convergence of research on neuropsychological patients with sensorimotor deficits and studies of functional brain images of human subjects engaging in sensorimotor activities has contributed to current theories of sensorimotor functioning.

The evolutionary perspective theme was evident in the discussion of several comparative experiments on the sensorimotor system, largely in nonhuman primates. An important point to keep in mind is that although the sensorimotor functions of nonhuman primates are similar to those of humans, they are not identical (e.g., monkeys walk on their hands).

Finally, you learned how metaphors can be used to think productively about science—in particular, how a large, efficient company can serve as a useful metaphor for the sensorimotor system.

ON THE CD Looking for more information about the topics in this chapter? For recommended additional readings, see Hard Copy for Chapter 8.

Log On

- **http://psychlab1.hanover.edu/Classes/Neuro/Internet/Stretch%20Reflex/index.html** Interested in learning more about muscle tone and the stretch reflex? Take a look at these animations.

- **http://www.ptd.neu.edu/neuroanatomy/cyberclass/spinalcontrol/** If you want more detail about spinal mechanisms of motor control in a readable form, go to this site for some simple animations and good explanations of sensorimotor phenomena.

- **http://thalamus.wustl.edu/course/cerebell.html** This site provides information about the role played by the cerebellum and the basal ganglia in movement.

Think about It

1. Both sensorimotor systems and large businesses are complex systems trying to survive in a competitive milieu. It is no accident that they function in similar ways. Discuss.

2. We humans tend to view cortical mechanisms as preeminent, presumably because we are the species with the largest cortexes. However, one might argue from several perspectives that the lower sensori-

motor functions are more important. Discuss.

3. This chapter has presented more evidence of parallel processing: Some neural circuits perform their function under conscious awareness, and other circuits perform the same function in the absence of consciousness. Discuss.

ON THE CD
Studying for an exam? Try the Practice Tests for Chapter 8.

Key Terms

Antagonistic muscles *(p. 209)*
Apraxia *(p. 198)*
Astereognosia *(p. 203)*
Betz cells *(p. 206)*
Central sensorimotor programs *(p. 215)*
Cingulate motor areas *(p. 201)*
Cocontraction *(p. 214)*
Contralateral neglect *(p. 198)*
Dorsolateral corticorubro-spinal tract *(p. 206)*
Dorsolateral corticospinal tract *(p. 206)*
Dorsolateral prefrontal association cortex *(p. 200)*
Dynamic contraction *(p. 210)*
Extensors *(p. 209)*
Flexors *(p. 209)*

Frontal eye field *(p. 197)*
Golgi tendon organs *(p. 210)*
Intrafusal motor neuron *(p. 210)*
Intrafusal muscle *(p. 210)*
Isometric contraction *(p. 210)*
Motor end-plate *(p. 209)*
Motor equivalence *(p. 216)*
Motor homunculus *(p. 202)*
Motor pool *(p. 209)*
Motor units *(p. 209)*
Muscle spindles *(p. 210)*
Patellar tendon reflex *(p. 210)*
Posterior parietal association cortex *(p. 197)*
Premotor cortex *(p. 201)*
Primary motor cortex *(p. 202)*

Reciprocal innervation *(p. 212)*
Recurrent collateral inhibition *(p. 214)*
Response-chunking hypothesis *(p. 217)*
Reticular formation *(p. 206)*
Secondary motor cortex *(p. 201)*
Sensory feedback *(p. 196)*
Skeletal muscle (extrafusal muscle) *(p. 210)*
Somatotopic *(p. 202)*
Spindle afferent neurons *(p. 210)*
Stereognosis *(p. 202)*
Stretch reflex *(p. 210)*
Supplementary motor area *(p. 201)*

Synergistic muscles *(p. 209)*
Tectum *(p. 206)*
Ventromedial cortico-brainstem-spinal tract *(p. 206)*
Ventromedial corticospinal tract *(p. 206)*
Vestibular nucleus *(p. 206)*
Withdrawal reflex *(p. 212)*

ON THE CD
Need some help studying the key terms for this chapter? Check out the electronic flash cards for Chapter 8.

chapter 9

Development of the Nervous System

From Fertilized Egg to You

Most of us tend to think of the nervous system as a three-dimensional array of neural elements "wired" together in a massive network of circuits. The sheer magnitude and complexity of such a wiring diagram would be staggering, but the analogy sells the nervous system short by failing to capture one of its most important features. The nervous system is not a static network of interconnected elements, as is implied by the wiring-diagram model; rather, it is a *plastic* (changeable), living organ that grows and changes continuously in response to its genetic programs and its interactions with its environment.

This chapter focuses on the amazing process of *neurodevelopment* (neural development), the neuroplastic process that begins with a single fertilized egg cell (see the chapter-opening photo) and ends with a functional adult brain. There are three key points: (1) the complexity and wonder of neurodevelopment, (2) the important role experience plays in neurodevelopment, and (3) the dire consequences when neurodevelopment goes wrong. The chapter is organized as a progression through these three points in the order given, culminating in a discussion of two devastating disorders of human neurodevelopment: *autism* and *Williams disorder*.

But first is the sad case of Genie. People tend to underestimate the role of experience in human neural and psychological development. One of the reasons is that most of us are reared in similar environments. Because there is so little variation in most people's early experience, the critical role of experience in human cerebral and psychological development is not obvious. This misconception can be corrected by considering cases in which children have been reared in grossly abnormal environments. Genie is such a case (Curtiss, 1977; Rymer, 1993).

The Case of Genie

When Genie was admitted to the hospital at the age of 13, she was only 1.35 meters (4 feet, 5 inches) tall and weighed only 28.1 kilograms (62 pounds). She could not stand erect, chew solid food, or control her bladder or bowels. Since the age of 20 months, Genie had spent most days tied to a potty in a small, dark, closed room. Her only clothing was a cloth harness, which kept her from moving anything other than her feet and hands. In the evening, Genie was transferred to a covered crib and a straitjacket. Her father was intolerant of noise, and he beat Genie if she made any sound whatsoever. According to her mother, who was almost totally blind, Genie's father and brother rarely spoke to Genie, although they sometimes barked at her like dogs. The mother was permitted only a few minutes with Genie each day, during which time she fed Genie cereal or baby food—Genie was allowed no solid food. Genie's severe childhood deprivation left her seriously scarred. When she was admitted to hospital, she made almost no sounds and was totally incapable of speech.

After Genie's discovery, a major effort was made to get her development back on track and to document her problems and improvements; however, after a few years, Genie "disappeared" in a series of legal proceedings, foster homes, and institutions (Rymer, 1993).

Although Genie did show some improvement in the years after her rescue, during which time she was receiving special care, it was readily apparent that she would never achieve anything approximating normal psychological development. The following were a few of her continuing problems: She did not react to extremes of warmth and cold; she tended to have silent tantrums during which she would flail, spit, scratch, urinate, and rub her own "snot" all over herself; she was easily terrified (e.g., of dogs and men wearing khaki); she could not chew; she could speak only short, poorly pronounced utterances. Genie is currently living in a home for retarded adults. Clearly, experience plays a major role in the processes of neurodevelopment, processes to which you are about to be introduced.

9.1 Phases of Neurodevelopment

In the beginning, there is a *zygote,* a single cell formed by the amalgamation of an *ovum* and a *sperm.* The zygote divides to form two daughter cells. These two divide to form four, the four divide to form eight, and so on, until a mature organism is produced. Of course, there must be more to development than this; if there were not, each of us would have ended up like a bowl of rice pudding: an amorphous mass of homogeneous cells.

To save us from this fate, three things other than cell multiplication must occur. First, cells must *differentiate;* some must become muscle cells, some must become multipolar neurons, some must become glial cells, and so on. Second, cells must make their way to appropriate sites and align themselves with the cells around them to form particular structures. And third, cells must establish appropriate functional relations with other cells. This section describes how developing neurons accomplish these things in five phases: (1) induction of the neural plate, (2) neural proliferation, (3) migration and aggregation, (4) axon growth and synapse formation, and (5) neuron death and synapse rearrangement.

■ | Induction of the Neural Plate

Three weeks after conception, the tissue that is destined to develop into the human nervous system becomes recognizable as the **neural plate**—a small patch of ectodermal tissue on the dorsal surface of the developing embryo. The ectoderm is the outermost of the three layers of embryonic cells: *ectoderm, mesoderm,* and *endoderm.* The development of the neural plate is the first major stage of neurodevelopment in all vertebrates.

As Figure 9.1 illustrates, the neural plate folds to form the *neural groove,* and then the lips of the neural groove fuse to form the **neural tube.** The inside of the neural tube eventually becomes the *cerebral ventricles* and *spinal canal.* By 40 days after conception, three swellings are visible at the anterior end of the human neural tube; these swellings ultimately develop into the *forebrain, midbrain,* and *hindbrain* (see Figure 3.21).

The first cells to develop in the embryo are **totipotent** (having the potential to develop into any type of mature body cell if transplanted into another part of the embryo). Developing cells that have this potential to become more than one type of cell are called **stem cells.**

With the development of the neural plate, the stem cells of the dorsal ectoderm lose some of their potential. Each cell of the neural plate still has the potential to develop into any type of mature nervous system cell, but it does not normally have the ability to develop into other kinds of cells, even if it were transplanted to a different part of the embryo. Stem cells whose destiny has been partially, but not totally, specified are called *pluripotent stem cells* (stem cells that have the potential to develop

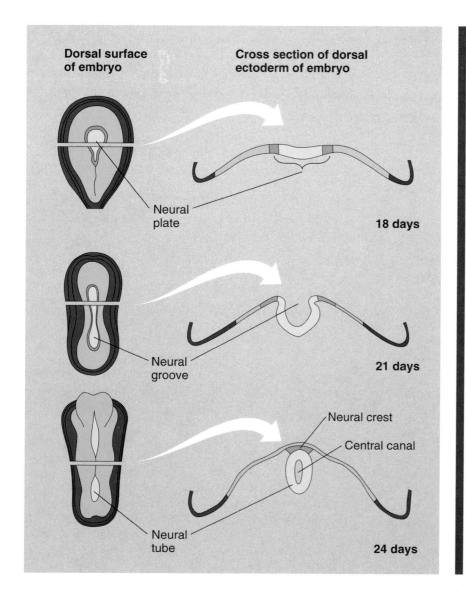

Dorsal surface of embryo

Cross section of dorsal ectoderm of embryo

Neural plate

18 days

Neural groove

21 days

Neural crest

Central canal

Neural tube

24 days

FIGURE 9.1 How the neural plate develops into the neural tube during the third and fourth weeks of human embryological development. (Adapted from Cowan, 1979.)

into more than one type of mature cell). The stem cells of the neural plate are called *neural stem cells.*

Because of the ability of stem cells to develop into different types of mature cells, their therapeutic potential is currently under intensive investigation (e.g., Temple & Alvarez-Buylla, 1999). Will stem cells injected into a damaged part of a mature brain develop into new brain structures and improve function? You will learn about the potential of stem-cell therapy in Chapter 10.

The development of the neural plate seems to be *induced* by chemical signals from the underlying **mesoderm layer** (see Dodd, Jessel, & Placzek, 1998; Kessler & Melton, 1994). Tissue taken from the dorsal mesoderm of one embryo (i.e., the *donor*) and implanted beneath the ventral ectoderm of another embryo (i.e., the *host*) induces the development of an extra neural plate on the ventral surface of the host.

One of the most fanciful demonstrations of **induction** is one that may require the abandonment of the expression "as scarce as hen's teeth." Kollar and Fisher (1980) induced teeth to grow from the ectodermal cells of chick embryos by implanting beneath them a tiny piece of mouse embryo mesoderm taken from beneath the portion of the ectoderm that would have normally developed into the mouse's mouth.

Neural Proliferation

Once the lips of the neural groove have fused to create the neural tube, the cells of the tube begin to *proliferate* (increase greatly in number). This **neural proliferation** does not occur simultaneously or equally in all parts of the tube. In each species, the cells in different parts of the neural tube proliferate in a characteristic sequence that is respon-

sible for the pattern of swelling and folding that gives each brain its species-characteristic shape. Most cell division in the neural tube occurs in the **ventricular zone**—the region adjacent to the *ventricle* (the fluid-filled center of the tube).

Migration and Aggregation

MIGRATION ■ Once cells have been created through cell division in the ventricular zone of the neural tube, they migrate to an appropriate location. During the period of **migration,** a temporary network of glial cells, called **radial glial cells** (see Figure 9.2), is present in the developing neural tube. Migrating neurons mainly move outward along these radial glial cells to their destinations (see Herrup & Silver, 1994), but there are also significant *tangential migrations,* migrations at right angles to the radial glial cells (Pearlman et al., 1998).

The first neurons to be created during the phase of proliferation migrate to the *intermediate zone* of the growing neural tube (see Figure 9.3). After the intermediate zone is well established, some of the migrating cells form a layer between the *ventricular zone* and the intermediate zone. The cells that migrate to this *subventricular zone* are destined to become either glial cells or interneurons. In the forebrain, new cells begin to migrate through these layers to establish a layer of cells called the *cortical plate,* which eventually develops into the cerebral cortex. Because the cells of the deepest of the six layers of neocortex arrive at their destination first, the cells of progressively higher layers must migrate through them (Parnavelas, 2000); this is referred to as the *inside-out pattern of cortical development.* When the migration of cells away from the ventricular zone is complete, the cells remain-

FIGURE 9.2 Newly created neurons migrate away from the ventricular zone along a network of radial glial cells.

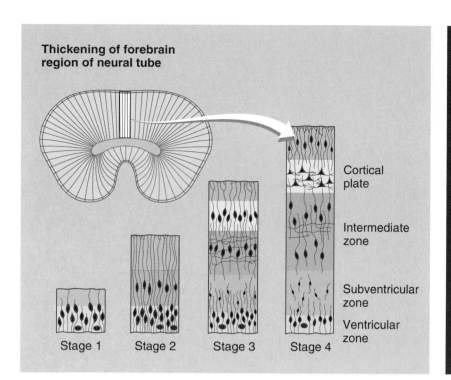

Thickening of forebrain region of neural tube

Stage 1 · Stage 2 · Stage 3 · Stage 4

Cortical plate

Intermediate zone

Subventricular zone

Ventricular zone

FIGURE 9.3 Neurons migrating out from the ventricular zone of the neural tube, creating new layers of cells. Illustrated here is the growth of the forebrain area of the neural tube.

ing there develop into *ependymal cells,* which form the lining of both the cerebral ventricles of the brain and the central canal of the spinal cord.

The **neural crest** is a structure that is situated just dorsal to the neural tube (see Figure 9.1). It is formed from cells that break off from the neural tube as it is being formed. Neural crest cells develop into the neurons and glial cells of the peripheral nervous system, and thus many of them must migrate over considerable distances. What directs them to their destinations? Their migration is directed by the media through which they travel, rather than information contained within the cells themselves. Consequently, cells transplanted from one part of the neural crest to another adopt the route characteristic of their new location. Numerous chemicals that guide migrating neurons by either attracting or repelling them have been discovered (see Gleeson & Walsh, 2000; Golman & Luskin, 1998).

AGGREGATION ■ Once developing neurons have migrated, they must align themselves with other developing neurons that have migrated to the same area to form the structures of the nervous system. This process is called **aggregation.** Both migration and aggregation are thought to be mediated by **cell-adhesion molecules (CAMs),** which are located on the surface of neurons and other cells. Cell-adhesion molecules have the ability to recognize molecules on other cells and adhere to them (see Fazeli & Walsh, 1996).

■ **Axon Growth and Synapse Formation**

Once neurons have migrated to their appropriate positions and aggregated into neural structures, axons

and dendrites begin to grow from them. For the nervous system to function, these neural projections must grow to appropriate targets. At each growing tip of an axon or dendrite is an amoebalike structure called a **growth cone** (see Stirling & Dunlop, 1995), which extends and retracts fingerlike cytoplasmic extensions called *filopodia* (see Figure 9.4), as if searching for the correct route. Three hypotheses have been proposed to explain how growth

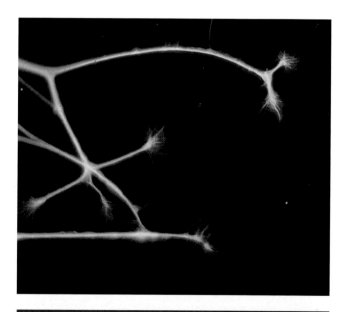

FIGURE 9.4 Growth cones. The cytoplasmic fingers (the filopodia) of growth cones seem to grope for the correct route. (Courtesy of Naweed I. Syed, Ph.D., Departments of Anatomy and Medical Physiology, the University of Calgary.)

cones find their way to their appropriate destinations: the chemoaffinity hypothesis, the blueprint hypothesis, and the topographic gradient hypothesis.

CHEMOAFFINITY HYPOTHESIS ■ In the early 1940s, Sperry conducted a classic series of experiments on the growth of axons in the frog visual system. In one of them, he cut the optic nerves of frogs, rotated their eyeballs 180°, and waited for the axons of the **retinal ganglion cells,** which compose the optic nerve, to *regenerate* (grow again). (Frogs, unlike mammals, have retinal ganglion cells that regenerate.) Once regeneration was complete, Sperry used a convenient behavioral test to assess the frogs' visual capacities (see Figure 9.5). When he dangled a lure behind the frogs, they struck forward, thus indicating that their visual world, like their eyes, had been rotated 180°. Frogs whose eyes had been rotated, but whose optic nerves had not been cut, responded in exactly the same way. This was strong behavioral evidence that each retinal ganglion cell had grown back to the same point of the **optic tectum** to which it had originally been connected. Neuroanatomical investigations have confirmed that this is exactly what happens (see Guo & Udin, 2000).

On the basis of his studies of regeneration, Sperry proposed the **chemoaffinity hypothesis** of axonal development (see Sperry, 1963). He hypothesized that each postsynaptic surface in the nervous system releases a specific chemical label and that each growing axon is attracted by the label to its postsynaptic target during both neural development and regeneration. Strong support for the chemoaffinity hypothesis has come from two important discoveries. First, it has been shown that in some cases developing neurons will grow to their normal targets *in vitro* (in tissue culture) (see Bolz, 1994); this supports the chemoaffinity hypothesis because none of the spatial cues that might guide axon growth *in vivo* (in living organisms) are present in a tissue culture. Second, numerous chemicals that either attract or repel growth cones have been isolated from extracellular neural tissue (see Cook, Tannahill, & Keynes, 1998; Stoekli & Landmesser, 1998).

Although the chemoaffinity hypothesis accounts for many aspects of axonal development (see Tessier-Lavigne & Placzek, 1991), it cannot explain three important facts. First, it cannot explain why targets transplanted to novel positions sometimes become incorrectly innervated. For example, when Whitelaw and Hollyday (1983) implanted an extra thigh segment in the legs of developing chick embryos so that the sequence was thigh, thigh, calf, foot—instead of the normal thigh, calf, foot—the second thigh segment became innervated by axons that normally would have innervated the calf. Second, the chemoaffinity hypothesis has difficulty explaining how some axons manage to follow exactly the same circuitous route to their target in every member of a species, rather than growing directly to the target (Bastiani et al., 1985;

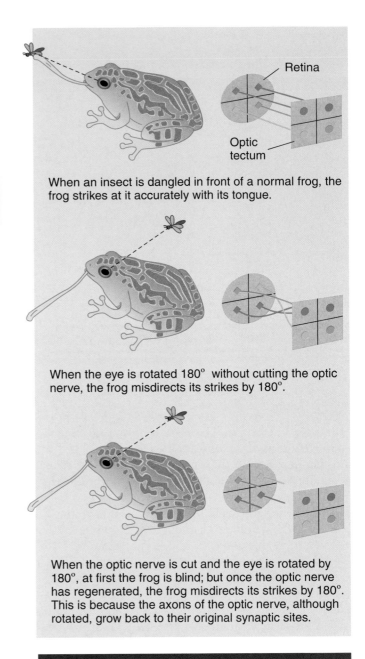

When an insect is dangled in front of a normal frog, the frog strikes at it accurately with its tongue.

When the eye is rotated 180° without cutting the optic nerve, the frog misdirects its strikes by 180°.

When the optic nerve is cut and the eye is rotated by 180°, at first the frog is blind; but once the optic nerve has regenerated, the frog misdirects its strikes by 180°. This is because the axons of the optic nerve, although rotated, grow back to their original synaptic sites.

FIGURE 9.5 Sperry's classic study of eye rotation and regeneration.

Kuwada, 1986). And third, there are not enough genes in each body cell for each neuron to produce and release its own distinctive chemical label.

BLUEPRINT HYPOTHESIS ■ The inability of the chemoaffinity hypothesis to account for certain aspects of axonal development led to the proposal of the blueprint hypothesis. According to the **blueprint hypothesis,** the undeveloped nervous system contains specific chemical or mechanical trails that growing axons follow to their destinations. **Pioneer growth cones**—the first growth cones to travel along a particular route in a developing nervous system—are presumed to follow the correct trail by interacting with the CAMs of cells along the route (see Tessier-Lavigne & Goodman, 1996; van Vactor, 1998). Then, subsequent growth cones embarking on the same journey follow the routes blazed by the pioneers. The tendency of developing axons to grow along the paths established by preceding axons is called **fasciculation.** When pioneer axons in the fish spinal cord were destroyed with a laser, subsequent axons of the same nerves did not reach their usual destinations.

Although the blueprint hypothesis can account for some aspects of axon growth, it cannot account for the ability of some developing axons to reach their correct destinations in vitro. Nor can it account for the ability of some developing axons to reach their correct destinations *in vivo* when their starting points have been surgically shifted. For example, when Lance-Jones and Landmesser (1980) cut a small portion of the spinal cord from a chick embryo, inverted it, and implanted it back into the same embryo, the axons grew out to their original target muscles despite the fact that they started from a new location (see Figure 9.6).

TOPOGRAPHIC GRADIENT HYPOTHESIS ■ Much of the axonal development in complex nervous systems involves growth from one topographic array of neurons to another. The neurons on one array project to another, maintaining the same topographic relation they had on the first; for example, the topographic map of the retina is maintained on the optic tectum (see Figure 9.7 on page 228).

It was initially assumed that the integrity of topographical relations in the developing nervous system was maintained by point-to-point chemoaffinity. Although this may be the primary mechanism of axonal development in invertebrate nervous systems, research on the development of vertebrate visual systems has led to the **topographic gradient hypothesis** (Easter et al., 1985). According to this hypothesis, axons that have grown out from one sheet of cell bodies (e.g., the retina) to another (e.g., the optic tectum) arrange their synaptic terminals according to the relative positions of their cell bodies on the original sheet, as defined by two intersecting right-angle gradients (e.g., an up-down gradient and a left-right gradient). Consistent with this hypothesis is the discovery of molecules whose concentration varies in a gradient across the tectum and retina (Holt & Harris, 1998).

Support for the topographic gradient hypothesis has come from both studies of development and studies of regeneration. For example, in studies of visual system development, it was found that the synaptic connections between eyes and optic tectums are established long before either reach their full size; then, as the eyes and the optic tectums grow at different rates, the initial synaptic connections shift to other tectal neurons so that the retina is always faithfully mapped onto the tectum, regardless of their relative sizes (Gaze et al., 1979; Reh & Constantine-Paton, 1984).

The pathways normally followed by the motor neuron axons growing out from the spinal cord of a chick embryo to two target muscles.

Before the motor neuron axons grew to their target muscles, Lance-Jones and Landmesser cut out a section from a developing chick spinal cord and reversed it.

Although the cell bodies of the motor neurons were then in an abnormal position, they grew out to their appropriate muscle.

FIGURE 9.6 Evidence against the blueprint hypothesis. When a section of spinal cord was cut from a chick embryo, inverted, and implanted back in the same location, the motor neuron axons grew out to their original target muscles. (Adapted from Lance-Jones & Landmesser, 1980.)

In studies of visual system regeneration (e.g., Gaze & Sharma, 1970; Yoon, 1971), the optic nerves of mature frogs or fish were cut and their pattern of regeneration was assessed after parts of either the retina or the optic tectum had been

FIGURE 9.7 The regeneration of the optic nerve of the frog after portions of either the retina or the optic tectum have been destroyed. These phenomena support the topographic gradient hypothesis.

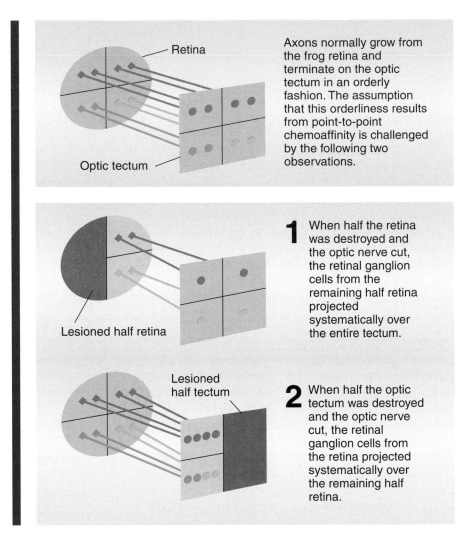

Retina

Optic tectum

Axons normally grow from the frog retina and terminate on the optic tectum in an orderly fashion. The assumption that this orderliness results from point-to-point chemoaffinity is challenged by the following two observations.

Lesioned half retina

1 When half the retina was destroyed and the optic nerve cut, the retinal ganglion cells from the remaining half retina projected systematically over the entire tectum.

Lesioned half tectum

2 When half the optic tectum was destroyed and the optic nerve cut, the retinal ganglion cells from the retina projected systematically over the remaining half retina.

destroyed. In both cases, the axons did not grow out to their original points of connection (as the chemoaffinity and blueprint hypotheses predicted they would); instead they grew out to fill the available space in an orderly fashion. Axons growing from the remaining portion of a lesioned retina "spread out" in an orderly fashion to fill all of the space on an intact tectum. Conversely, axons growing from an intact retina "squeeze in" in an orderly fashion to fill the remaining space on a lesioned tectum. These results are illustrated schematically in Figure 9.7.

AXON GROWTH AND SYNAPSE FORMATION: CONCLUSION ■ Over half a century of research on the miraculous ability of developing axons to grow to their correct targets has led to the conclusion that no single mechanism can account for all instances (see Holt & Harris, 1998). The main guiding force appears to be the growth cones' attraction to specific chemical signals that are released by their targets, but there are well-documented instances in which the growth cones follow specific circuitous routes through the cellular matrix,

presumably by following trails of CAMs in the substrate. Furthermore, the ability of growing axons to establish topographic gradients seems to require a spatially graded chemical signal from the target structure and a gradient-related mechanism of axon–axon interaction.

Neuron Death and Synapse Rearrangement

NEURON DEATH ■ Neuron death is a normal and important part of neurodevelopment. Such development seems to operate on the principle of survival of the fittest: Many more neurons—about 50% more—are produced than are required, and only the fittest survive. Large-scale death is not a time-limited stage of development; it occurs in waves in various parts of the brain throughout development.

Three findings suggest that developing neurons die because of their failure to compete successfully for **neurotrophins**—life-preserving chemicals that are supplied to neurons by their targets. First, the implantation of extra target sites decreases neuron death. For example, Hollyday and Hamburger (1976) grafted an extra limb on one side of a chick embryo and fewer motor neurons on that side died. Second, destroying some of the neurons growing into an area before the period of cell death increases the survival rate of the remaining neurons (e.g., Pilar, Landmesser, & Burstein, 1980). Third, increasing the number of axons that initially innervate a target decreases the proportion that survive.

Nerve growth factor (NGF) was the first neurotrophin to be isolated (see Levi-Montalcini, 1952, 1975). NGF is synthesized and released by the targets of *sympathetic neurons* during the period of cell death, and it is taken up by the sympathetic neurons, attracts them as they grow, and promotes their survival. Since the discovery of NGF, many other neurotrophins have been isolated. They may prove to have major therapeutic value in halting the course of neurodegenerative diseases (see Ibáñez, 1998).

Neuron death during development was initially assumed to be a passive process. It was assumed that the appropriate neurotrophins are needed for the survival of neurons and that without them neurons passively degenerate and die. However, it is now clear that cell death during development is usually an active process: The absence of the appropriate neurotrophins can trigger a genetic program inside neurons that causes them to actively commit suicide. Passive cell death is called

necrosis (ne-KROE-sis); active cell death is called **apoptosis** (a-poe-TOE-sis).

Apoptosis is safer than necrosis. Necrotic cells break apart and spill their contents into extracellular fluid, and the consequence is potentially harmful inflammation. In contrast, in apoptotic cell death, DNA and other internal structures are cleaved apart and packaged in membranes before the cell membrane disintegrates; consequently, no inflammation occurs (see Ashkenazi & Dixit, 1998; Green & Reed, 1998; Kuan et al., 2000).

During the phase of neuron death, apoptosis removes excess neurons in a safe, neat, and orderly way. But apoptosis has a dark side as well. If genetic programs for apoptotic cell death are inhibited, the consequence can be cancer; if the programs are inappropriately activated, the consequence can be neurodegenerative disease (Adams & Cory, 1998; Evan & Littlewood, 1998).

SYNAPSE REARRANGEMENT ■ During the period of cell death, neurons that have established incorrect connections are particularly likely to die. As they die, the space they vacate on postsynaptic membranes is filled by the sprouting axon terminals of surviving neurons. Thus cell death results in a massive rearrangement of synaptic connections. Synapse rearrangement focuses the output of each neuron on a smaller number of postsynaptic cells, thus increasing the selectivity of transmission (see Figure 9.8).

A diffuse pattern of synaptic contact is characteristic of early stages of development.

A more focused pattern of synaptic contact is present after synapse rearrangement.

FIGURE 9.8 The effect of neuron death and synapse rearrangement on the selectivity of synaptic transmission. The synaptic contacts of each axon become focused on a smaller number of cells.

BrainScan

Are you ready to focus on neurodevelopment in the human brain after birth? To find out, scan your brain by filling in the blanks in the following chronological list of stages of neuro-development. The correct answers are provided at the bottom of this page. Before proceeding, review material related to your errors and omissions.

1. Induction of the neural _____
2. Formation of the _____ tube
3. Neural _____
4. Neural _____
5. _____ aggregation
6. Growth of neural _____
7. Formation of _____
8. Neuron _____ and synapse _____

9.2   Postnatal Cerebral Development in Human Infants

Most of our knowledge of neurodevelopment comes from the study of nonhuman species. This fact emphasizes the value of the comparative approach and the evolutionary perspective. There is, however, one way in which the development of the human brain is unique and thus not amenable to comparative research: The human brain develops far more slowly than that of other species, not achieving full maturity until late adolescence (Spear, 2000).

This section deals with that part of the development of the human brain that occurs after birth. It focuses on the development of the prefrontal cortex (see Figure 1.8). The prefrontal cortex is the last part of the brain to reach maturity, and it is thought to mediate many higher cognitive abilities.

Postnatal Growth of the Human Brain

The human brain grows substantially after birth: Brain volume quadruples between birth and adulthood (see Johnson, 1997). This increase in size does not, however, result from the development of additional neurons. With the exception of a few structures (e.g., the olfactory bulb and the hippocampus) in which many new neurons continue to be created during the adult years, all of the neurons that will compose the adult human brain have developed and migrated to their appropriate location by

the seventh month of prenatal development. The postnatal growth of the human brain seems to result from three other kinds of growth: **synaptogenesis** (the formation of new synapses), myelination of many axons, and increased branching of dendrites.

There has been particular interest in the postnatal formation of synapses because the number of connections between neurons in a particular region of the brain is assumed to be an indicator of the analytic ability of that region. There seems to be an increase in the rate of formation of synapses throughout the human cortex shortly after birth, but there are differences among the cortical regions in the course of this development (Huttenlocher, 1994). For example, in the primary visual and auditory cortexes, there is a major burst of synaptogenesis in the fourth postnatal month, and maximum synapse density (150% of adult levels) is achieved in the seventh or eighth month; whereas synaptogenesis in the prefrontal cortex occurs at a relatively steady rate, reaching maximum synapse density in the second year.

Myelination increases the speed of axonal conduction, and the myelination of various areas of the human

Brain Scan answers: (1) plate, (2) neural, (3) proliferation, (4) migration, (5) Neural, (6) processes (axons and dendrites), (7) synapses, (8) death; rearrangement.

brain during development roughly parallels their functional development. Myelination of sensory areas occurs in the first few months after birth, and the myelination of the motor areas follows soon after that, whereas myelination of prefrontal cortex continues into adolescence.

In general, the pattern of dendritic branching duplicates the original pattern of neural migration. Just as the cells of the deeper layers are first to migrate into position, and the cells of progressively more superficial layers migrate through them to assume their positions, dendritic branching progresses from deeper to more superficial layers. For example, the growth of dendritic trees in layer V always seems to precede that in layers II and III, regardless of the cortical area.

Postnatal human brain development is not a one-way street; there are regressive changes as well as growth (Huttenlocher, 1994). For example, once maximum synaptic density has been achieved, there are periods of synaptic loss. Like periods of synaptogenesis, periods of synaptic loss occur at different times in different parts of the brain. For example, synaptic density in primary visual cortex declines to adult levels by about 3 years of age, whereas its decline to adult levels in prefrontal cortex is not achieved until adolescence. It has been suggested that the overproduction of synapses may underlie the greater plasticity of the young brain.

■ Development of the Prefrontal Cortex

As you have just learned, the prefrontal cortex displays the most prolonged period of development of any brain region. Its development is believed to be largely responsible for the course of human cognitive development, which occurs over the same period.

Given the size, complexity, and heterogeneity of the prefrontal cortex, it is hardly surprising that there is no single widely accepted theory explaining its function. Nevertheless, three types of cognitive functions have consistently been linked to this area in studies of adults with prefrontal damage. The prefrontal cortex seems to play a role in (1) *working memory,* that is, keeping relevant information accessible for short periods of time while a task is being completed; (2) planning and carry-

ing out sequences of actions; and (3) inhibiting responses that are inappropriate in the current context but not in others (see Hauser, 1999).

One interesting line of research on prefrontal cortex development is based on Piaget's classic studies of psychological development in human babies. In his studies of 7-month-old children, Piaget noticed an intriguing error. A small toy was shown to an infant; then it was placed, as the child watched, behind one of two screens, left or right. After a brief delay period, the infant was allowed to reach for the toy. Piaget found that almost all 7-month-old infants reached for the screen behind which they had seen the toy being placed. However, if, after being placed behind the same screen on several consecutive trials, the toy was placed behind the other screen (as the infant watched), most of the 7-month-old infants kept reaching for the previously correct screen, rather than the screen that currently hid the toy. Children tend to make this *perseverative error* between about 7 and 12 months, but not thereafter (Diamond, 1985). **Perseveration** is the tendency to continue making a formerly correct response when it is currently incorrect.

Diamond (1991) hypothesized that this perseverative error occurred in infants between 7 and 12 months because the neural circuitry of the prefrontal cortex is not yet fully developed during that period. Synaptogenesis in the prefrontal cortex is not maximal until early in the second year, and correct performance of the task involved two of the major functions of this brain area: holding information in working memory and suppressing previously correct, but currently incorrect, responses.

In support of her hypothesis, Diamond conducted a series of comparative experiments. First, she showed that infant monkeys, but not adult monkeys, make the same perseverative error as 7-to-12-month-old human infants on Piaget's test. Then, she tested adult monkeys with bilateral lesions to their dorsolateral prefrontal cortex (see Figure 8.2 for the location of this area of cortex), and she found that the lesioned adult monkeys made perseverative errors similar to those made by the infant monkeys. Control monkeys with lesions in the hippocampus or posterior parietal cortex did not make such errors.

9.3 ► Effects of Experience on Neurodevelopment

Genetic programs of neurodevelopment do not act in a vacuum. Neurodevelopment unfolds through interactions between neurons and their environment. You learned in the first section of this chapter how factors in a neuron's immediate environment (e.g., neurotrophins

and CAMs) can influence its migration, aggregation, and growth. This section focuses on how the experience of a developing organism and the activity of its newly formed neurons influence its subsequent development. The main principle that governs the effects of early experience on neurodevelopment is simple: Neurons and synapses that are not activated by experience do not usually survive (see Hockfield & Kalb, 1993; Kalil, 1989).

Early Studies of Experience and Neurodevelopment

Many of the first demonstrations of the impact of early experience on neurodevelopment came from two lines of research: the study of the effects of early visual deprivation and the study of early exposure to enriched environments. For example, animals reared in the dark were found to have fewer synapses and fewer dendritic spines in their primary visual cortexes, and they were found to have deficits in depth and pattern vision as adults. Conversely, rats that were raised in enriched (complex) group cages rather than by themselves in barren cages were found to have thicker cortexes with greater dendritic development and more synapses per neuron.

Competitive Nature of Experience and Neurodevelopment

Experience promotes the development of active neural circuits, but there seems to be a competitive aspect to this. This competitive aspect is clearly illustrated by the disruptive effects of early monocular deprivation.

Depriving one eye of input for a few days early in life blocks the development of vision in the deprived eye, but this does not happen if the other eye is also blindfolded. When only one eye is blindfolded during early development, the ability of that eye to activate the visual cortex is reduced or eliminated, whereas the ability of the other eye is increased. Both these effects occur because early monocular deprivation changes the pattern of synaptic input into layer IV of the primary visual cortex.

In newborn cats and monkeys, the input into layer IV from the left and right eyes is intermingled; then, during the course of normal development, it becomes segregated into equal-size alternating columns of ocular dominance (see Figure 6.20). Early monocular deprivation decreases the width of the columns of input from the deprived eye and increases the width of the columns of input from the nondeprived eye (Hata & Stryker, 1994; Hubel, Wiesel, & LeVay, 1977).

Because the adverse effects of early monocular deprivation manifest themselves so quickly (i.e., in a few days), it was believed that they could not be mediated by structural changes. This has proved not to be the case, however. For example, Antonini and Stryker (1993) found that a few days of monocular deprivation produces a massive decrease in the axonal branching of the lateral geniculate nucleus neurons that normally carry signals from the deprived eye to layer IV of the primary visual cortex (see Figure 9.9).

The competitive nature of the effects of neural activity on synapse rearrangement has also been demonstrated in experiments on motor neurons and muscle cells. In *neonates* (newborns), each muscle cell is normally innervated by several motor neurons, and then all but one are eliminated during the course of development. Lo and Poo (1991) developed an in vitro preparation in which one developing muscle cell was innervated by two developing motor neurons. Applying pulses of electrical stimulation to one of these neurons caused a rapid degradation in the synaptic contacts of the other. Apparently, motor neurons compete with one another for synaptic contacts on muscle cells, and active synapses take precedence.

Effects of Experience on the Development of Topographic Sensory Cortex Maps

Some of the most remarkable demonstrations of the effects of experience on neurodevelopment come

FIGURE 9.9 The effect of a few days of early monocular deprivation on the structure of axons projecting from the lateral geniculate nucleus into layer IV of the primary visual cortex. Axons carrying information from the deprived eye displayed substantially less branching. (Adapted from Antonini & Stryker, 1993.)

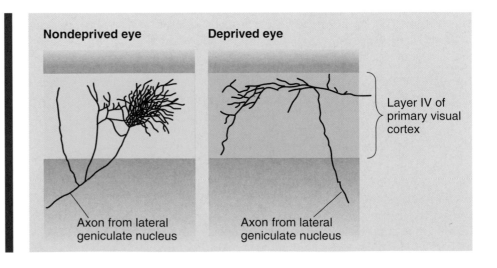

from lines of research on the development of cortical topographic maps of the sensory systems. The following are four key studies.

First, Roe and colleagues (1990) surgically altered the course of developing axons of ferrets' retinal ganglion cells so that the axons synapsed in the medial geniculate nucleus of the auditory system instead of in the lateral geniculate nucleus of the visual system. Remarkably, the experience of visual input caused the auditory cortex of the ferrets to become organized retinotopically (laid out like a map of the retina).

Second, Knudsen and Brainard (1991) raised barn owls with vision-displacing prisms over their eyes. This led to a corresponding change in the auditory spatial map in the tectum. For example, an owl that was raised wearing prisms that shifted its visual world 23° to the right had an auditory map that was also shifted 23° to the right, so that objects were heard to be where they were seen to be (see Knudsen, 1998; Miller & Knudsen, 1999).

Third, Weliky and Katz (1997) periodically disturbed the spontaneous optic nerve activity of neonatal ferrets that had yet to open their eyes. This disrupted the development of the orientation and direction selectivity of the ferrets' primary visual cortex neurons. Thus, it appears that patterns of spontaneous neural activity emanating from fetal eyes prior to the onset of vision play a role in the development of the visual cortex (see Katz & Shatz, 1996). Although visual cortex is largely developed in primates when they are born, subsequent lack of visual input leads to its deterioration (Crair, Gillespie, & Stryker, 1998).

Fourth, several studies have shown that early music training influences the organization of human auditory cortex (see Rauschecker, 1999). In particular, fMRI studies have shown

that early musical training tends to expand the area of auditory cortex that responds to complex musical tones, and behavioral studies have shown that early musical training leads to the development of absolute pitch (the ability to identify the pitch of any sound).

■ Mechanisms by Which Experience Might Influence Neurodevelopment

It is well established that experience has major effects on neurodevelopment, but the mechanisms through which this occurs are not well understood. However, recent experiments have revealed several possible mechanisms (see Gottlieb, 2000). The following are three of the possibilities.

First, neural activity has been shown to regulate the expression of genes that direct the synthesis of cell-adhesion molecules (CAMs). Thus, by influencing neural activity, experience could produce changes in cell adhesion (Fields & Itoh, 1996; Itoh et al., 1995).

Second, neural activity has been shown to influence the release of neurotrophins from neurons' dendrites (Thoenen, 1995). Thus, by influencing neural activity, experience could promote and direct the growth of presynaptic neurons and influence their survival (Schinder & Poo, 2000).

Third, some neural circuits are spontaneously active early in the course of brain development, and the activity of these circuits is necessary for the normal progression of some aspects of brain development (Crair, 1999). Thus, by influencing the activity of these spontaneously active neural circuits, experience could influence the course of brain development (see Levitt et al., 1997).

9.4 Neuroplasticity in Adults

The brain is clearly in its most plastic state during its developmental period. Indeed, until the last decade, neuroplastic phenomena were thought to be restricted to the developmental period. Mature brains were considered to be set in their ways, incapable of substantial reorganization. Now, it is generally acknowledged that adult brains, although not as plastic as developing brains, are still capable of major adaptation. Several different areas of research have contributed to this changed view; the following are two of these.

■ Neurogenesis in Adult Mammals

When I was a student, I learned two important principles of brain development. The first I learned through experience: The human brain starts to function in the womb and never stops working until one stands up to speak in public. The second I learned in a course on brain development: *Neurogenesis* (the growth of new neurons) does not occur in adults. While the first principle appears to be fundamentally correct, at least when applied to me, the second has been proved to be wrong (see Kempermann & Gage, 1999; Ormerod, Falconer, & Galea, 2001).

Prior to the early 1980s, all neurons were thought to be created during early stages of development. Accordingly, subsequent brain development was seen as a downhill slope: Neurons continually die throughout a person's life, and it was assumed that the lost cells are never replaced by new ones. Although researchers began to chip away at this misconception in the early 1980s, it persisted until recently as one of the central principles of neurodevelopment.

The first serious challenge to the assumption that neurogenesis is restricted to early stages of development came in the early 1980s, with the discovery of the growth of new neurons in the brains of adult birds. Nottebohm and colleagues (e.g., Goldman & Nottebohm, 1983) found that brain structures involved in singing begin to grow in songbirds just before each mating season and that this growth results from an increase in the number of neurons. This finding stimulated the re-examination of earlier unconfirmed claims that new neurons are created in the adult rat hippocampus. Armed with immunohistochemical markers that have a selective affinity for newly created neurons, researchers convincingly showed that adult neurogenesis does indeed occur in the rat hippocampus (Cameron et al., 1993). Also, new neurons are continually added to the olfactory bulbs of adult rats. Stem cells are created in the ventricular zone; these cells then migrate into the rats' olfactory bulbs and develop into neurons. Despite these findings, the belief that neurogenesis is almost totally restricted to the early stages of development persisted. The demonstrations of neurogenesis in adults were seen as rare exceptions to a valid general principle.

Today, adult neurogenesis is widely accepted as a reality. The following are three of the recent findings that have led to this change in thinking: (1) The number of new neurons created in the hippocampus of adult rats is substantial, an estimated 2,000 per hour (West, Slomianka, & Gunderson, 1991); (2) adult neurogenesis occurs in primates (e.g., Kornack & Rakic, 1999), including humans (Erikkson et al., 1998); and (3) adult neurogenesis has been reported in association cortex (Gould et al., 1999).

The discovery that new neurons are created in the brains of adult mammals has created quite a stir among neuroscientists, and many researchers are trying to understand the causes, mechanisms, and functions of the new cells, particularly those in the hippocampus, where adult neurogenesis is so robust (see Ormerod & Galea, 2001). One provocative finding has been that adult rats living in an enriched environment (a changing environment, with toys, running wheels, and other rats) produce 60% more new hippocampal neurons than do adult rats living in nonenriched environments (Kempermann & Gage, 1999). This increase appears to result largely, if not entirely, from the subjects' increased movement in an enriched environment (Van Praag et al., 1999).

■ Effects of Experience on the Reorganization of the Adult Cortex

A second influential area of research on adult neuroplasticity has focused on the degree to which experience in adulthood can lead to reorganization of sensory and motor cortical maps (e.g., Jones, 2000; Sanes & Donoghue, 2000). For example, Mühlnickel and colleagues (1998) found that *tinnitus* (ringing in the ears) produces a major reorganization of primary auditory cortex, and Elbert and colleagues (1995) showed that musicians who play stringed instruments that are fingered with the left hands (e.g., violin) have an enlarged hand area in their right somatosensory cortex.

In a more controlled demonstration of the ability of experience to reorganize the adult human brain, healthy human volunteers received 1 hour of tactual experience for 20 days (Braun et al., 2000). For the 20 hours, the subjects experienced patterns of touch simultaneously delivered to the tips of their left thumb and left little finger. There were two conditions: In one, the subjects sat passively while the stimuli were delivered; in the other, the subjects were required to identify the patterns. The areas of the right somatosensory cortex activated by stimulation of the tip of either the left thumb or the left little finger were measured by high-resolution EEG evoked potentials. The results differed with the experimental condition. In the passive condition, the areas of somatosensory cortex responding to touches of the thumb and little finger moved closer together as the experiment progressed. In the active identification condition, the areas of somatosensory cortex responding to touches of the thumb and little finger moved farther apart.

9.5 ▶ Disorders of Neurodevelopment: Autism and Williams Syndrome

I have tried to keep this chapter focused on fundamentals rather than on details. Still, I hope you have managed to

get a sense of the incredible complexity of neurodevelopment. Like all complex processes, neurodevelopment is easily thrown off track; and, unfortunately, one tiny screw-up can have far-reaching and tragic consequences because it can disrupt all subsequent stages. This fact will become apparent to you in this, the final, section of the chapter, which focuses on two disorders of neurodevelopment: autism and Williams syndrome.

■ Autism

Autism is a complex neurodevelopmental disorder that typically occurs in about 4 of every 10,000 individuals. It usually becomes apparent before the age of 3 and changes little thereafter (Happé & Frith, 1996). The diagnosis of autism is based on the presence of three core symptoms: (1) a reduced ability to interpret the emotions and intentions of others, (2) a reduced capacity for social interaction and communication; and (3) a preoccupation with a single subject or activity. Although this triad of symptoms defines the disorder, other signs are commonly, but not universally, associated with it. For example, about 75% of those with autism are male, about 75% suffer from mental retardation, and about 35% suffer from epilepsy.

Autism is a difficult disorder to treat. Intensive behavioral therapy can improve the lives of some individuals, but it is rarely possible for a person with autism to live independently, even if he or she represents one of those few cases in which intelligence is reasonably normal. How is a person who has no appreciation for the feelings and motivations of others, who has difficulty communicating, who compulsively bangs his head against the wall, and who is obsessed by bus schedules going to function in society?

AUTISM IS A HETEROGENEOUS DISORDER ■ Although many scientists who study autism do so in an effort to help those who have the disorder, many are attracted to study it because of one of its major features—its heterogeneity (Happé & Frith, 1996). In autism, some functions are severely impaired, whereas others are normal or even superior. It is these "spotty" patterns of neuropsychological deficits that have the most potential to teach us about the neural bases of psychological functions.

Unfortunately, not all autistic patients display the same pattern of deficits and spared abilities, which greatly complicates the study of this disorder. There are, however, some common patterns. For example, autistic individuals—even those who are severely retarded—commonly display the following preserved abilities: rote memory, the ability to complete jigsaw puzzles, musical ability, and artistic ability.

Even within the single category of speech disability, there is often a heterogeneous pattern of deficits. Many autistic individuals have sizable vocabularies, are good spellers, and can read aloud even those things they do not understand. However, the same individuals are often unable to use intonation to communicate emotion, to coordinate eye gaze and facial expression with speech, and to speak metaphorically. About one quarter of autistic individuals have little or no language ability.

AUTISTIC SAVANTS ■ Perhaps the single most remarkable aspect of autism is the tendency for autistic individuals to be savants. **Savants** are intellectually handicapped individuals who nevertheless display amazing and specific cognitive or artistic abilities. About 1 in 10 autistic individuals display savant abilities. Savant abilities can take many forms, but the following are common: feats of memory, naming the day of the week for any future or past date, identifying prime numbers (numbers that are divisible only by 1), drawing, and playing musical instruments.

Savant abilities may be the most puzzling phenomena in all of neuroscience. Consider the following cases (Ramachandran & Blakeslee, 1998; Sacks, 1985).

Some Cases of Amazing Savants

Nadia suffered from severe autism; her IQ was between 60 and 70. She could barely put two words together. Yet, by the time she reached the age of 6, she could draw gallery-quality pictures of people, animals, and other complex subjects.

One savant could tell the time of day to the exact second without ever referring to his watch. Even when he was asleep, he would mumble the correct time.

Another savant could specify the width of objects. For example, she was asked the width of a rock that lay on the ground about 20 feet away. "Exactly two feet, eleven and three-quarter inches," she replied. She was right; indeed, she was always right.

Tom was a blind, autistic 13-year-old who could not tie his own shoes. He had never had any musical training, but he could play the most difficult piano piece after hearing it just once, even if he was sitting with his back to the piano. Once, he played one song with one hand and a second with the other, while singing a third.

One pair of autistic twins had difficulty doing simple addition and subtraction and could not even comprehend multiplication and division. Yet, if given any date in the last or next 40,000 years, they could specify the day of week that it would fall on. Their short-term memory for digits was amazing: They were able to correctly repeat a list of 300 digits after hearing it only once. A box of matches fell on the floor: "One hundred and eleven," they immediately cried out together. There were 111.

These and many other well-documented savant cases remain a mystery. Savant abilities do not develop through rote learning or practice; they seem to emerge spontaneously. Even the savants with language abilities cannot explain their own feats. They seem naturally to recognize implicit patterns and relations that escape others. We can only regard these cases with wonder and speculate that somehow damage to certain parts of their brains has led to compensatory overdevelopment in other parts.

NEURAL BASIS OF AUTISM ■ Two lines of research show that genetic factors influence the development of autism (see Rodier, 2000). First, autism has been found to run in families; various studies have shown that siblings of people with autism have about a 5% chance of being diagnosed with the same disorder. This is well above the rate in the general population, but well below the 50% chance that would be expected if autism were caused solely by a single dominant gene or the 25% chance that would be expected if autism were caused solely by a single recessive gene. Second, several studies have shown that the development of autism is highly related in monozygotic twins; if one twin is diagnosed as autistic, the other has a 60% chance of receiving the same diagnosis. Although this high correlation shows that autism has a genetic basis, it also shows that it is not entirely genetic. If it were, the concordance rate would be 100% in individuals with identical genes. Together, these two lines of research suggest that autism is triggered by several genes interacting with the environment.

Although the etiology of autism is poorly understood, one line of research is particularly promising (see Rodier, 2000). First, Strömland and colleagues (1994) discovered that a pregnant woman's taking *thalidomide,* the morning-sickness pill that caused an epidemic of birth defects in the 1960s, greatly increased the probability that the child would be born with autism. Because a prescription for thalidomide was restricted to the early weeks of pregnancy, this relationship suggests that autism is created by a neurodevelopmental error occurring at this time.

Knowing when something happens provides *embryologists* (scientists who study embryos) with important clues. Knowing that thalidomide-induced autism develops in the first few weeks of embryological development has focused attention on the motor neurons of the cranial nerves that control the face, mouth, and eyes, because few neurons other than these are formed by the fourth week. Indeed, it was shown that both thalidomide-induced and typical autism are associated with various deficits in face, mouth, and eye control (e.g., Strömland et al., 1994).

Another clue came from analysis of the physical appearance of individuals with autism—whether or not the disorder was thalidomide-induced. Their appearance is typically good; however, there are a few minor anomalies of ear structure: square shape, positioned too low on the head, rotated slightly backward, tops flopped over (see Figure 9.10). This suggested that autism is triggered by an abnormal event occurring between 20 and 24 days after conception, when the ears are developing. Remarkably, most of the cases of thalidomide-induced autism did not display the stunted and misshapen limbs typical of most cases of thalidomide-induced birth defects; they did, however, display anomalies of external ear structure.

Rodier (2000) had the opportunity to conduct an autopsy examination of the brain of an autistic woman, and influenced by the research on thalidomide-induced autism, she focused her examination on the brain stem. She made a remarkable finding: The woman's brain stem was shortened, as if a slice had failed to develop. Nuclei in the slice were either underdeveloped (facial nucleus) or totally missing (superior olive) (see Figure 9.11).

As Rodier examined the shortened brain stem of the autistic woman, she experienced a "powerful shock of recognition." She had seen this pattern before. From the stacks of papers on her office floor, she retrieved an article about the brains of knockout mice, engineered to lack the expression of a gene known as *Hoxa 1.* These mice exhibited shortening of the brain stem, an underdeveloped facial nucleus, and no superior olive. Moreover, the mice had ear malformations and abnormal eye movements. Rodier (2000) subsequently discovered that some people have a variant form of *Hoxa 1,* which is located on chromosome 7, and that the form is prevalent in people with autism—it is found in 40% of autistic persons, compared with 20% of the general population.

Let's put this series of findings in perspective. First, it is unlikely that the developmental distortions in the midbrain are responsible for all of the symptoms of autism. These midbrain

FIGURE 9.10 A boy with autism shows the typical anomalies of ear structure.

FIGURE 9.11 The brain stem of a woman with autism was found to be shortened, missing a band of tissue at the junction of the pons and medulla. (Adapted from Rodier, 2000.)

distortions are only one manifestation of a more general developmental problem—for example, the adjacent cerebellum is abnormal in most individuals with autism (Bauman, Filipek, & Kemper, 1997). Second, the Hoxa 1 gene has been implicated in only some cases.

Williams Syndrome

Williams syndrome, like autism, is a neurodevelopmental disorder associated with mental retardation and a strikingly uneven pattern of abilities and disabilities. Williams syndrome occurs in approximately 1 of every 20,000 births.

In contrast to the withdrawn, emotionally insensitive, uncommunicative person with autism, people with Williams syndrome are sociable, empathetic, and talkative. It is their language abilities that have attracted the most attention. Although they display a delay in language development and language deficits in adulthood (Bishop, 1999; Paterson et al., 1999), their language skills are remarkable considering their characteristically poor IQs—which average around 60. For example, when asked about his infantile scribble on a piece of paper, one severely retarded Williams teenager, with an IQ of 49, identified it as an elephant and offered the following verbal commentary (Bellugi et al., 1999):

And what an elephant is it is one of the animals. And what the elephant does, it lives in the jungle. It can also live in the zoo. And what it has, it has long gray ears, fan ears, ears that can blow in the wind. It has a long trunk that can pick grass, or pick up hay . . . if they're in a bad mood it can be terrible. . . . If the elephant gets mad it could stomp; it could charge. Sometimes elephants can charge. They have long tusks. You don't want an elephant as a pet. You want a cat or a dog or a bird. . . . (p. 199)

The remarkable language skills of Williams children have also been demonstrated by objective tests (Bellugi et al., 1999). For example, in one test, Williams children were asked to name as many animals as they could in 60 seconds. Answers included koala, yak, ibex, condor, chihuahua, brontosaurus, and hippopotamus. When asked to look at a picture and tell a story about it, an animated narrative often ensued. As they told the story, Williams children altered the pitch, volume, rhythm, and vocabulary of their speech to engage the audience. Sadly, the verbal and social skills of these children often lead teachers to overestimate their cognitive abilities, and thus they do not always receive the extra academic support they need.

Williams people have other cognitive strengths, several of which involve music (Lenhoff et al., 1997). Although most cannot learn to read music, some have perfect or near-perfect pitch and an uncanny sense of rhythm. Many retain melodies for years, and some are professional musicians. As a group, Williams people show more interest in, and emotional reaction to, music than does the general population. One Williams child said, "Music is my favorite way of thinking." Yet another cognitive strength of Williams people is their remarkable ability to recognize faces.

Like any group of individuals with an average IQ of 60, Williams people display many severe cognitive deficits. Against this background, their strengths tend to stand out. However, there is one class of cognitive problems that is noteworthy because it is even more severe in them than it is in other people with similar IQs: They have a profound impairment in spatial cognition. For example, they have great difficulty remembering the location of a few blocks placed on a test board, their space-related speech is poor, and their ability to draw objects is almost nonexistent (Bellugi et al., 1999).

Williams syndrome is also associated with a variety of health problems, including several involving the heart. Ironically, the study of one of these disorders in people who did not have the syndrome led to the identification of a major genetic factor in the syndrome. This heart disorder was found to result from a mutation in a gene on chromosome 7 that controls the synthesis of *elastin*, a protein that imparts elasticity to many organs and tissues. Aware that the same cardiac problem is prevalent in Williams people, investigators assessed the status of this gene in that group. Remarkably, they found that the gene on one of the two copies of chromosome 7 was absent in 95% of Williams people. Other genes were missing as well; through an accident of reproduction, an entire region of chromosome 7 had been deleted. Once the other genes in this region have been identified and their functions determined, there will be a much fuller understanding of the etiology of Williams syndrome.

In general, Williams people display gross underdevelopment of occipital and parietal cortex, which could account for their poor spatial abilities; normal frontal and temporal cortex, which could account for their pre-

FIGURE 9.12   Williams people are characterized by their elfin appearance.

served speech; and changes in the limbic system, which could account for their heightened friendliness (see Bellugi et al., 1999).

You may have unknowingly encountered stories of Williams people. Many cultures feature tales involving magical little people: pixies, elves, leprechauns, etc. Remarkably, descriptions and drawings of these creatures portray them as virtually identical to Williams people, who are often described as elfin in appearance. Williams people tend to be short, and they have small upturned noses, oval ears, broad mouths with full lips, puffy eyes, and small chins (see Figure 9.12). Accordingly, many believe that folk tales about elves may have originally been based on Williams people. Even the typical behavioral characteristics of elves—engaging storytellers, talented musicians, loving, trusting, and sensitive to the feelings of others—match those of Williams people.

Themes Revisited

The clinical implications and evolutionary perspective themes were heavily emphasized in this chapter. One of the best ways to understand the principles of normal neurodevelopment is to consider what happens when it goes wrong: Accordingly, the chapter began with the tragic case of Genie and ended with a discussion of autism and Williams syndrome. The evolutionary perspective theme was emphasized because much of the information that we have about normal human neurodevelopment and human neurodevelopmental disorders has come from studying other species.

The thinking-about-biopsychology icon appeared infrequently in this chapter, but the theme was pervasive. Thinking-about-biopsychology icons highlighted discussions that made two general points. First, neurodevelopment always proceeds from gene–experience interactions rather than from either genetics or environment alone. Second, it is important not to overreact to the impressive recent advances in the study of neurodevelopment: Important

ON THE CD

Looking for more information about the topics in this chapter? For recommended additional readings, see Hard Copy for Chapter 9.

steps have been taken, but we are still a long way from a complete understanding.

The cognitive neuroscience theme came up infrequently in this chapter. Only recently has the power of brain-imaging techniques been brought to bear on the study of neurodevelopment and neurodevelopmental disorders.

Log On

■ **http://faculty.washington.edu/chudler/dev.html** This site provides a detailed summary of the development of the nervous system, including diagrams of the neural plate and neural tube, plus links to related sites.

■ **http://www.biorap.org/rg/rgagepd.html** Information on the aging brain, emphasizing changes in neural and behavioral function, is available here.

■ **http://www.autism-society.org/** The Autism Society of America presents an overview of the causes, symptoms, and treatment of autism.

Think about It

1. What does the case of Genie teach us about normal development?

2. Neuron death is a necessary stage in neurodevelopment. Discuss.

3. Even the adult brain displays plasticity. What do you think is the evolutionary significance of this ability?

4. Discuss the evolutionary significance of the slow development of the human brain.

5. Autism and Williams syndrome are opposites in several ways and could be fruitfully studied together. Discuss.

ON THE CD
Studying for an exam? Try the Practice Tests for Chapter 9.

Key Terms

Aggregation *(p. 225)*
Apoptosis *(p. 229)*
Autism *(p. 235)*
Blueprint hypothesis *(p. 226)*
Cell-adhesion molecules (CAMs) *(p. 225)*
Chemoaffinity hypothesis *(p. 226)*
Fasciculation *(p. 227)*
Growth cone *(p. 225)*
Induction *(p. 224)*

Mesoderm layer *(p. 224)*
Migration *(p. 224)*
Necrosis *(p. 229)*
Nerve growth factor (NGF) *(p. 229)*
Neural crest *(p. 225)*
Neural plate *(p. 223)*
Neural proliferation *(p. 224)*
Neural tube *(p. 223)*
Neurotrophins *(p. 228)*
Optic tectum *(p. 226)*

Perseveration *(p. 231)*
Pioneer growth cones *(p. 226)*
Radial glial cells *(p. 224)*
Retinal ganglion cells *(p. 226)*
Savants *(p. 235)*
Stem cells *(p. 223)*
Synaptogenesis *(p. 230)*
Topographic gradient hypothesis *(p. 227)*

Totipotent *(p. 223)*
Ventricular zone *(p. 224)*
Williams syndrome *(p. 237)*

ON THE CD
Need some help studying the key terms for this chapter? Check out the electronic flash cards for Chapter 9.

chapter 10

Brain Damage and Neuroplasticity

Can the Brain Recover from Damage?

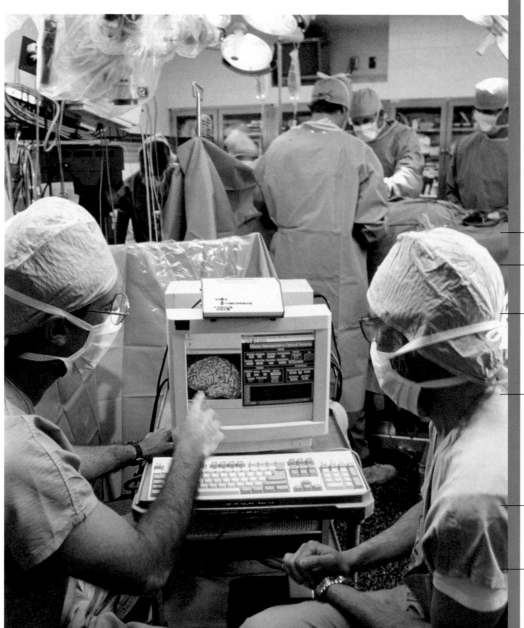

The study of human brain damage serves two purposes: It increases our understanding of the healthy human brain, and it serves as a basis for the development of new treatments. The first three sections of this chapter focus on human brain damage; the fourth section focuses on the recovery and reorganization of the brain after damage; and the fifth section describes current efforts to use recent discoveries to develop new treatments. But first, the ironic case of Professor P., to which you were introduced in Chapter 5, relates the personal tragedy of brain damage.

The Ironic Case of Professor P.

One night Professor P. sat at his desk staring at a drawing of the cranial nerves, much like the one in Appendix III of this book. As he mulled over the location and function of each cranial nerve (see Appendix IV), the painful truth became impossible for him to deny. The irony of the situation was that Professor P. was a neuroscientist, all too familiar with what he was experiencing.

His symptoms started subtly, with slight deficits in balance. He probably wouldn't have even noticed them except that his experience as a mountaineer had taught him to pay attention to such things. Professor P. chalked these occasional lurches up to aging—after all, he thought to himself, he was past his prime, and things like this happen. Similarly, his doctor didn't seem to think that it was a problem worth looking into, but Professor P. monitored his symptoms carefully nevertheless. Three years later, his balance problems still unabated, Professor P. really started to worry. He was trying to talk with a colleague on the phone but was not having much success because of what he thought was a bad connection. Then, he changed the phone to his other ear, and all of a sudden, the faint voice on the other end became louder. He tried this switch several times over the ensuing days, and the conclusion became inescapable: Professor P. was going deaf in his right ear.

Professor P. immediately made an appointment with his doctor, who referred him to a specialist. After a cursory and poorly controlled hearing test, the specialist gave him good news. "You're fine, Professor P.; lots of people experience hearing loss when they reach middle age, and your problems are not serious enough to worry about." To this day, Professor P. regrets that he did not insist on a second opinion; his problem would have been so much easier to deal with at that stage.

It was about a year later that Professor P. sat staring at the illustration of the cranial nerves. By then he had begun to experience numbness on the right side of his mouth; he was having minor problems swallowing; and his right tear ducts were not releasing enough tears. There he sat staring at the point where the auditory and vestibular nerves come together to form cranial nerve VIII (the auditory-vestibular nerve). He knew it was there, and he knew that it was large enough to be affecting cranial nerves V through X as well, but he didn't know what it was: a tumor, a stroke, an angioma, an infection? Was he going to die? Was his death going to be terrible and lingering as his brain and intellect gradually deteriorated?

He didn't make an appointment with his doctor right away. A friend of his was conducting a brain MRI study, and Professor P. volunteered to be a control subject, knowing that his problem would show up on the scan. It did: a large tumor sitting, as predicted, on the right cranial nerve VIII.

Then, MRI in hand, Professor P. went back to his doctor, who referred him to a neurologist, who in turn referred him to a neurosurgeon. Several stressful weeks later, Professor P. found himself on life support in the intensive care unit of his local hospital, hands tied to the bed and tubes emanating seemingly from every part of his body. You see, the tumor was so convoluted that it took 6 hours to remove; and during the 6 hours that Professor P.'s brain was exposed, air entered his circulatory system, and he developed pneumonia. Near death and hallucinating from the morphine, Professor P. thought he heard his wife, Maggie, calling for help and tried to go to her assistance: That is why he was tied down. One gentle morphine-steeped professor was no match for five burly nurses intent on saving his life.

Professor P.'s auditory-vestibular nerve was transected during his surgery, which has left him permanently deaf and without vestibular function on the right side. He was also left with partial hemifacial paralysis, including serious blinking and tearing problems, but these facial symptoms have largely cleared up.

Professor P. has now returned to his students, his research, and his writing, hoping that the tumor was completely removed and that he will not have to endure another surgery. Indeed, at the very moment that I am writing these words, Professor P. is working on the forthcoming edition of his textbook. . . . If it has not yet occurred to you, I am Professor P.

ON THE CD

Visit the module *My Tumor and Welcome To It.* Pinel, relaxing in his own garden, describes his struggle with a brain tumor.

10.1 Causes of Brain Damage

This section provides an introduction to six causes of brain damage: brain tumors, cerebrovascular disorders, closed-head injuries, infections of the brain, neurotoxins, and genetic factors. It concludes with a discussion of programmed cell death, which mediates many forms of brain damage.

Brain Tumors

A **tumor,** or **neoplasm** (literally, "new growth"), is a mass of cells that grows independently of the rest of the body. In other words, it is a cancer.

About 20% of tumors found in the human brain are **meningiomas** (see Figure 10.1)—tumors that grow between the *meninges,* the three membranes that cover the central nervous system. All meningiomas are **encapsulated tumors**—tumors that grow within their own membrane. As a result, they are particularly easy to identify on a CT scan, they can influence the function of the brain only by the pressure they exert on surrounding tissue, and they are almost always **benign tumors**—tumors that are surgically removable with little risk of further growth in the body (see Grimson et al., 1999).

Unfortunately, encapsulation is the exception rather than the rule when it comes to brain tumors. With the exception of meningiomas, most brain tumors are infiltrating. **Infiltrating tumors** are those that grow diffusely through surrounding tissue. As a result, they are usually **malignant tumors;** it is difficult to remove or destroy them completely, and any cancerous tissue that remains after surgery continues to grow.

FIGURE 10.1 **A meningioma.** (Courtesy of Kenneth Berry, Head of Neuropathology, Vancouver General Hospital.)

About 10% of brain tumors do not originate in the brain. They grow from infiltrating tumor fragments carried to the brain by the bloodstream from some other part of the body. (The brain is a particularly fertile ground for tumor growth.) These tumors are called **metastatic tumors;** *metastasis* refers to the transmission of disease from one organ to another. Most metastatic brain tumors originate as cancers of the lungs. Obviously, the chance of recovering from a cancer that has already attacked two or more separate sites is slim at best. Figure 10.2 illustrates the ravages of metastasis.

Fortunately, my tumor was encapsulated. Encapsulated tumors that grow on cranial nerve VIII are referred to as *acoustic neuromas* (neuromas are tumors that grow on nerves or tracts). Figure 10.3 is an MRI scan of my acoustic neuroma, the very same scan that I took to my doctor.

Cerebrovascular Disorders

Strokes are sudden-onset cerebrovascular disorders that cause brain damage. Two types of cerebrovascular disorders lead to strokes: cerebral hemorrhage and cerebral ischemia (pronounced "iss-KEEM-ee-a"). In the United States, stroke is the third leading cause of death and the most common cause of adult disability. Common consequences of stroke are amnesia, aphasia (language difficulties), paralysis, and coma (see Zivin & Choi, 1991). The area of dead or dying tissue produced by a stroke is called an *infarct.*

CEREBRAL HEMORRHAGE ■ Cerebral hemorrhage (bleeding in the brain) occurs when a cerebral blood vessel ruptures and blood seeps into the surrounding neural tissue and damages it. Bursting aneurysms are a common cause of intracerebral hemorrhage. An **aneurysm** is a pathological balloonlike dilation that forms in the wall of a blood vessel at a point where the elasticity of the vessel wall is defective. Aneurysms can be **congenital** (present at birth) or can result from exposure to vascular poisons or infection. Individuals who have aneurysms should make every effort to avoid high blood pressure.

CEREBRAL ISCHEMIA ■ Cerebral ischemia is a disruption of the blood supply to an area of the brain. The three main causes of cerebral ischemia are thrombosis, embolism, and arteriosclerosis. In **thrombosis,** a plug called a *thrombus* is formed and blocks blood flow at the site of its formation. A thrombus may be composed of a

FIGURE 10.2 Multiple metastatic brain tumors. The arrows indicate some of the more advanced areas of metastatic tumor development.

FIGURE 10.3 An MRI of Professor P.'s acoustic neuroma. The arrow indicates the tumor.

blood clot, fat, oil, an air bubble, tumor cells, or any combination thereof. **Embolism** is similar except that the plug, called an *embolus* in this case, is carried by the blood from a larger vessel, where it was formed, to a smaller one, where it becomes lodged; in essence, an embolus is just a thrombus that has taken a trip. In **arteriosclerosis,** the walls of blood vessels thicken and the channels narrow, usually as the result of fat deposits; this narrowing can eventually lead to complete blockage of the blood vessels. The *angiogram* in Figure 10.4 on page 244 illustrates partial blockage of one carotid artery.

Paradoxically, some of the brain's own neurotransmitters play a key role in the development of ischemia-produced brain damage. It was once assumed—quite reasonably—that disruption of the oxygen and glucose supply was the key causal factor in stroke-related brain damage; however, it now appears that much of the brain damage associated with stroke is a consequence of excessive release of excitatory amino acid neurotransmitters, in particular **glutamate,** the brain's most prevalent excitatory neurotransmitter.

Here is how this mechanism is thought to work (see Dirgnagl, Iadecola, & Moskowitz, 1999). After a blood vessel becomes blocked, many of the blood-deprived neurons become overactive and release excessive quantities of glutamate. The glutamate in turn overactivates glutamate receptors in the membranes of postsynaptic neurons; the glutamate receptors that are most involved in this reaction are the **NMDA (N-methyl-D-aspartate)**

FIGURE 10.4 An angiogram that illustrates narrowing of the carotid artery (see arrow), the main pathway of blood to the brain. Compare this angiogram with the normal angiogram in Figure 5.1.

receptors. As a result, large numbers of Na$^+$ and Ca^{2+} ions enter the postsynaptic neurons.

The excessive internal concentrations of Na$^+$ and Ca^{2+} ions affect the postsynaptic neurons in two ways: They trigger the release of excessive amounts of glutamate from them, thus spreading the toxic cascade to yet other neurons; and they trigger a sequence of internal reactions that ultimately kill the postsynaptic neurons. (See Figure 10.5.)

Ischemia-induced brain damage has three important properties (Krieglstein, 1997). First, it takes a while to develop. Soon after a temporary cerebral ischemic episode, say, one 10 minutes in duration, there usually is little or no evidence of brain damage; however, substantial neuron loss can often be detected several days later. Second, ischemia-induced brain damage does not occur equally in all parts of the brain; particularly susceptible are neurons in certain areas of the hippocampus. Third, the mechanisms of ischemia-induced brain damage vary somewhat from structure to structure.

An exciting implication of the discovery that excessive glutamate release causes much of the brain damage associated with stroke is the possibility of preventing stroke-related brain damage by blocking the glutaminergic cascade. The search is on for a glutamate antagonist that is effective and safe for use in human stroke victims (see De Keyser, Sulter, & Luiten, 1999; Emerich, 2000).

■ Closed-Head Injuries

It is not necessary for the skull to be penetrated for the brain to be seriously damaged. In fact, any blow to the head should be treated with extreme caution, particularly when confusion, sensorimotor disturbances, or loss of consciousness ensues. Brain injuries produced by blows that do not penetrate the skull are called *closed-head injuries.*

Contusions are closed-head injuries that involve damage to the cerebral circulatory system. Such damage produces internal hemorrhaging, which results in a hematoma. A **hematoma** is a localized collection of clotted blood in an organ or tissue—in other words, a bruise.

It is paradoxical that the very hardness of the skull, which protects the brain from penetrating injuries, is the major factor in the development of contusions. Contusions from closed-head injuries occur when the brain slams against the inside of the skull. As Figure 10.6 on page 246 illustrates, blood from such injuries can accumulate in the *subdural space*—the space between the dura mater and arachnoid membrane—and severely distort the surrounding neural tissue.

It may surprise you to learn that contusions frequently occur on the side of the brain opposite the side struck by a blow. The reason for such so-called **contrecoup injuries** is that the blow causes the brain to strike the inside of the skull on the other side of the head.

When there is a disturbance of consciousness following a blow to the head and there is no evidence of a contusion or other structural damage, the diagnosis is **concussion.** It is commonly assumed that concussions entail a temporary disruption of normal cerebral function with no long-term damage. However, the punch-drunk syndrome suggests otherwise. The **punch-drunk syndrome** is the **dementia** (general intellectual deterioration) and cerebral scarring that is observed in boxers and other individuals who experience repeated concussions. If there were no damage associated with a single concussion, the effects of many concussions could not summate to produce severe damage. One of the most dangerous aspects of concussion is the complacency with which it is regarded. Flippant references to it, such as "having one's bell rung," do little to communicate its hazards.

The Case of Jerry Quarry, Ex-Boxer

Jerry Quarry thumps his hard belly with both fists. Smiles at the sound. Like a stone against a tree.

"Feel it," he says proudly, punching himself again and again.

He pounds big, gnarled fists into meaty palms. Cocks his head. Stares. Vacant blue eyes. Punch-drunk at 50. Medical name: *Dementia pugilistic* [punch-drunk syndrome]. Cause: Thousands of punches to the head.

A top heavyweight contender in the 1960s and '70s, Quarry now needs help shaving, showering, putting on shoes and socks. Soon, probably, diapers. His older brother,

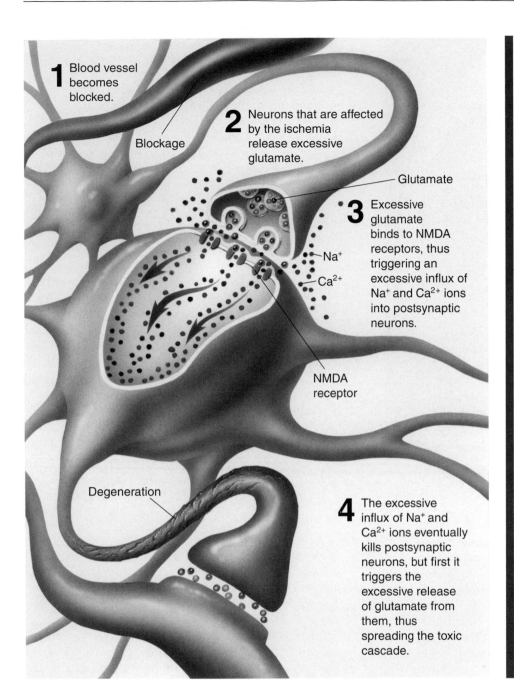

1 Blood vessel becomes blocked.

Blockage

2 Neurons that are affected by the ischemia release excessive glutamate.

Glutamate

3 Excessive glutamate binds to NMDA receptors, thus triggering an excessive influx of Na⁺ and Ca²⁺ ions into postsynaptic neurons.

Na⁺

Ca²⁺

NMDA receptor

Degeneration

4 The excessive influx of Na⁺ and Ca²⁺ ions eventually kills postsynaptic neurons, but first it triggers the excessive release of glutamate from them, thus spreading the toxic cascade.

FIGURE 10.5 The cascade of events by which the stroke-induced release of glutamate kills neurons.

James, cuts meat into little pieces so he won't choke. Jerry smiles like a kid. Shuffles like an old man.

Slow, slurred speech. Random thoughts snagged on branches in a dying brain. Memories twisted. Voices no one else hears. (Steve Wiltstein, Associated Press, 1995)

■ | Infections of the Brain

An invasion of the brain by microorganisms is a *brain infection,* and the resulting inflammation is **encephalitis.** There are two common types of brain infections: bacterial infections and viral infections.

BACTERIAL INFECTIONS ■ When bacteria infect the brain, they often lead to the formation of *cerebral abscesses*—pockets of pus in the brain. They also often attack and inflame the meninges, creating a disorder known as **meningitis.** Penicillin and other antibiotics can eliminate the infection, but they cannot reverse brain damage that has already been produced.

Syphilis is one bacterial brain infection you have likely heard about. Syphilis bacteria are passed from infected to noninfected individuals through contact with genital sores. The infecting bacteria then go into a dormant stage for several years before they become virulent and attack many parts of the body, including the brain.

FIGURE 10.6 A CT scan of a subdural hematoma. Notice that the subdural hematoma has displaced the left lateral ventricle.

The syndrome of insanity and dementia that results from a syphilitic infection is called **general paresis.**

Syphilis has a particularly interesting history (see Klawans, 1990). The first Europeans to visit America stripped the natives of their gold and left smallpox in return. But the deal was not totally one-sided; the booty carried back to Europe by Columbus's sailors and the adventurers that followed included a cargo of syphilis bacteria. Until then, syphilis had been restricted to the Americas, but it quickly spread to the rest of the world.

VIRAL INFECTIONS ■ There are two types of viral infections of the nervous system: those that have a particular affinity for neural tissue and those that attack neural tissue but have no greater affinity for it than for other tissues.

Rabies, which is usually transmitted through the bite of a rabid animal, is a well-known example of a viral infection that has a particular affinity for the nervous system. The fits of rage caused by the virus's effects on the brain increase the probability that rabid animals that normally attack by biting (e.g., dogs, cats, raccoons, bats, and mice) will spread the disorder. Although the effects of the rabies virus on the brain are ultimately lethal, the virus does have one redeeming feature: It does not usually attack the brain for at least a month after it has been contracted, thus allowing time for a preventive vaccination.

The *mumps* and *herpes* viruses are common examples of viruses that can attack the nervous system but have no special affinity for it. Although these viruses sometimes spread into the brain, they typically attack other tissues of the body.

Viruses may play a far greater role in neuropsychological disorders than is currently thought. Their involvement in the *etiology* (cause) of disorders is often difficult to recognize because they may lie dormant for many years before producing symptoms.

■ | **Neurotoxins**

The nervous system can be damaged by exposure to any one of a variety of toxic chemicals, which can enter general circulation from the gastrointestinal tract, from the lungs, or through the skin. For example, heavy metals such as mercury and lead can accumulate in the brain and permanently damage it, producing a **toxic psychosis** (chronic insanity produced by a neurotoxin). Have you ever wondered why Alice in Wonderland's Mad Hatter was a mad hatter and not a mad something else? In 18th- and 19th-century England, hatmakers were commonly driven mad by the mercury employed in the preparation of the felt used to make hats. In a similar vein, the word *crackpot* originally referred to the toxic psychosis observed in people—primarily the British poor—who steeped their tea in cracked ceramic pots with lead cores.

Sometimes, the very drugs used to treat neurological disorders prove to have toxic effects. For example, some of the antipsychotic drugs introduced in the early 1950s produced effects of distressing scope. By the late 1950s, millions of psychotic patients were being maintained on these new drugs. However, after several years of treatment, many of the patients developed a motor disorder termed **tardive dyskinesia (TD).** Its primary symptoms are involuntary smacking and sucking movements of the lips, thrusting and rolling of the tongue, lateral jaw movements, and puffing of the cheeks. Safer antipsychotic drugs have now been developed.

Brain damage from the effects of recreational drugs is also a serious problem. You learned in Chapter 1 that alcohol produces brain damage through a combination of its direct neurotoxic effects and its effects on thiamine metabolism. Do you remember the case of Jimmie G.?

Some neurotoxins are *endogenous* (produced by the patient's own body). For example, the body can produce antibodies that attack particular components of the nervous system (see Newsom-Davis & Vincent, 1991).

■ | **Genetic Factors**

Normal human cells have 23 pairs of chromosomes; however, sometimes accidents of cell division occur, and the fertilized egg ends up with an abnormal chromosome or with an abnormal number of normal chromosomes. Then, as the fertilized egg divides and redivides, these chromosomal anomalies are duplicated in every cell of the body.

Most neuropsychological diseases of genetic origin are caused by abnormal recessive genes that are passed from parent to offspring. (In Chapter 2, you learned about one such disorder, *phenylketonuria.*) Inherited neuropsychological disorders are rarely associated with dominant genes because dominant genes that disturb neuropsychological function tend to be eliminated from the gene pool—every individual who carries one is at a major survival and reproductive disadvantage. In contrast, individuals who inherit one abnormal recessive gene do not develop the disorder, and the gene is passed on to future generations.

There are, however, two situations in which neurological disorders are associated with dominant genes. One is the case in which an abnormal dominant gene manifests itself only in rare environmental circumstances. The other is the case in which an abnormal dominant gene is not expressed until the individual is well past puberty.

Down syndrome is a genetic disorder that is caused not by a faulty gene, but by a genetic accident, which occurs in 0.15% of births. During reproduction, an extra chromosome 21 is created: There are three rather than two. The consequences of the superfluous chromosome are unfortunate. In addition to characteristic disfigurement—flattened skull and nose, folds of skin over the inner corners of the eyes, and short fingers (see Figure 10.7)—intellectual development is retarded, and there are often serious medical complications. The probability of giving birth to a child with Down syndrome increases with advancing maternal age.

Rapid progress is being made in locating and characterizing the faulty genes that are associated with some neuropsychological disorders. Once this goal is achieved, it will open up a variety of new treatment and prevention strategies, such as splicing in healthy genes to replace faulty ones and developing specific DNA-binding proteins that can enter neurons and block the expression of faulty genes.

■ Programmed Cell Death

Neurons and other cells have genetic programs for suicide. The process by which cells destroy themselves is called **apoptosis** (pronounced "AP-oh-TOE-sis").

You learned in Chapter 9 that apoptosis plays a critical role in early development by eliminating the excessive numbers of neurons that are initially created. Here, we focus on the role of apoptosis in brain damage. Indeed, each of the six causes of brain damage that have already been discussed in this chapter (tumors, cerebrovascular disorders, closed-head injuries, infections, toxins, and genetic factors) appears to produce its effect, in part, by activating programs of cellular self-destruction (Allsop & Fazakerley, 2000; Nijhawan, Honarpour, & Wang, 2000).

Apoptosis is more adaptive than *necrosis* (passive cell death) because apoptosis does not involve inflammation. It seems that a damaged or dysfunctional neuron will commit suicide if it can (Roy & Sapolsky, 1999). However, if a neuron is severely damaged, it may not have the resources for self-destruction, and it may die by necrosis or by a combination of necrosis and apoptosis.

Apoptotic and necrotic cell death are readily distinguishable (see Kogure & Kogure, 1997). In apoptotic death, changes in the structure of the nucleus are among the first changes to be observed, whereas in necrotic death, they are among the last. Also, apoptosis is a slow death, often lasting several days, whereas necrosis is largely complete in a few hours.

FIGURE 10.7 A child with Down syndrome before and after plastic surgery. The purpose of these photographs is not to promote cosmetic surgery but to challenge our culture's reaction to patients with Down syndrome. The little girl on the left and the little girl on the right are the same girl; they deserve the same respect and consideration. (Courtesy of Kenneth E. Salyer, Director, International Craniofacial Institute.)

10.2 Neuropsychological Diseases

The preceding section focused on the causes of human brain damage. This section considers five diseases that are associated with brain damage: epilepsy, Parkinson's disease, Huntington's disease, multiple sclerosis, and Alzheimer's disease.

Epilepsy

The primary symptom of **epilepsy** is the epileptic seizure, but not all persons who suffer seizures are considered to have epilepsy. It is not uncommon for an otherwise healthy person to have a seizure during temporary illness or following exposure to a convulsive agent. The label *epilepsy* is applied to only those patients whose seizures appear to be generated by their own chronic brain dysfunction. About 1% of the population are diagnosed as epileptic at some point in their lives.

In view of the fact that epilepsy is characterized by epileptic seizures—or, more accurately, by spontaneously recurring epileptic seizures—you might think that the task of diagnosing this disorder would be an easy one. But you would be wrong. The task is made difficult by the diversity and complexity of epileptic seizures. You are probably familiar with seizures that take the form of **convulsions** (motor seizures); these often involve tremors (*clonus*), rigidity (*tonus*), and loss of both balance and consciousness. But many seizures do not take this form; instead, they involve subtle changes of thought, mood, or behavior that are not easily distinguishable from normal ongoing activity. In such cases, the diagnosis of epilepsy rests heavily on electroencephalographic (EEG) evidence.

The value of scalp electroencephalography in suspected cases of epilepsy stems from the fact that epileptic seizures are associated with bursts of high-amplitude EEG spikes, which are often apparent in the scalp EEG during an attack (see Figure 10.8), and from the fact that individual spikes often punctuate the scalp EEGs of epileptics between attacks. Although the observation of spontaneous epileptic discharges is incontrovertible evidence of epilepsy, the failure to observe them does not always mean that the patient is not epileptic. It could mean that the patient is epileptic but did not happen to experience epileptic discharges during the test or that epileptic discharges did occur during the test but were not recorded through the scalp electrodes.

Some epileptics experience peculiar psychological changes just before a convulsion. These changes, called **epileptic auras,** may take many different forms—for example, a bad smell, a specific thought, a vague feeling of familiarity, a hallucination, or a tightness of the chest.

Epileptic auras are important for two reasons. First, the nature of the auras provides clues concerning the location of the epileptic focus. Second, because the epileptic auras experienced by a particular patient are often similar from attack to attack, they warn the patient of an impending convulsion.

Once an individual has been diagnosed as epileptic, it is usual to assign the epilepsy to one of two general categories—*partial epilepsy* or *generalized epilepsy*—and then to one of their respective subcategories. The various seizure types are so different from one another that epilepsy is best viewed not as a single disease but as a number of different, but related, diseases. Supporting this view is the fact that epilepsy has no single cause; almost any kind of brain disturbance can cause seizures.

PARTIAL SEIZURES ■ A **partial seizure** is a seizure that does not involve the entire brain. For reasons unknown, the epileptic neurons at a focus begin to discharge together in bursts, and it is this synchronous bursting of neurons (see Figure 10.9) that produces epileptic spiking in the EEG. The synchronous activity may stay restricted to the focus until the seizure is over, or it may spread to other areas of the brain—but, in the case of partial seizures, not to the entire brain. The specific behavioral symptoms of a partial epileptic seizure depend on where the disruptive discharges begin

FIGURE 10.8 Cortical electroencephalogram (EEG) record from various locations on the scalp during the beginning of a complex partial seizure. The letters and numbers to the left of each trace indicate the conventional locations of the electrodes over the frontal (F), temporal (T), parietal (P), and occipital (O) lobes.

FIGURE 10.9 The bursting of an epileptic neuron, recorded by extracellular unit recording.

and into what structures they spread. Because partial seizures do not involve the entire brain, they are not usually accompanied by a total loss of consciousness or equilibrium.

There are two major categories of partial seizures: simple and complex. **Simple partial seizures** are partial seizures whose symptoms are primarily sensory or motor or both; they are sometimes called *Jacksonian seizures* after the famous 19th-century neurologist Hughlings Jackson. As the epileptic discharges spread through the sensory or motor areas of the brain, the symptoms spread systematically through the body.

In contrast, **complex partial seizures** are often restricted to the temporal lobes, and those who experience them are often said to have *temporal lobe epilepsy*. During a complex partial seizure, the patient engages in compulsive, repetitive, simple behaviors commonly referred to as *automatisms* (e.g., doing and undoing a button) and in more complex behaviors that appear almost normal. The diversity of complex partial seizures is illustrated by the following four cases reported by Lennox (1960).

The Subtlety of Complex Partial Seizures: Four Cases

A war veteran subject to many automatisms read in the newspaper about a man who had embraced a woman in a park, followed her into a women's toilet, and then boarded a bus. From the description given, he realized he was the man.

One morning a doctor left home to answer an emergency call from the hospital and returned several hours later, a trifle confused, feeling as though he had experienced a bad dream. At the hospital he had performed a difficult . . . [operation] with his usual competence, but later had done and said things deemed inappropriate.

A young man, a music teacher, when listening to a concert, walked down the aisle and onto the platform, circled the piano, jumped to the floor, did a hop, skip, and jump up the aisle, and regained his senses when part way home. He often found himself on a trolley [bus] far from his destination.

A man in an attack went to his employer and said, "I have to have more money or [I] quit." Later, to his surprise, he found that his salary had been raised. (pp. 237–238)

Although patients appear to be conscious throughout their complex partial seizures, they usually have little or no

subsequent recollection of them. About half of all cases of epilepsy are of the complex partial variety—the temporal lobes are particularly susceptible to epileptic discharges.

GENERALIZED SEIZURES ■ **Generalized seizures** involve the entire brain. Some begin as focal discharges that gradually spread through the entire brain. In other cases, the discharges seem to begin almost simultaneously in all parts of the brain. Such sudden-onset generalized seizures may result from diffuse pathology or may begin focally in a structure, such as the thalamus, that projects to many parts of the brain.

Like partial seizures, generalized seizures occur in many forms. One is the **grand mal** (literally, "big trouble") **seizure.** The primary symptoms of a grand mal seizure are loss of consciousness, loss of equilibrium, and a violent *tonic-clonic convulsion*—a convulsion involving both tonus and clonus. Tongue biting, urinary incontinence, and *cyanosis* (turning blue from excessive extraction of oxygen from the blood during the convulsion) are common manifestations of grand mal convulsions. The **hypoxia** (shortage of oxygen supply to tissue, for example, to the brain) that accompanies a grand mal seizure can itself cause brain damage, some of which develops slowly after the attack and is mediated by the excessive release of excitatory amino acid neurotransmitters.

A second major category of generalized seizure is the **petit mal** (literally, "small trouble") **seizure.** Petit mal seizures are not associated with convulsions; their primary behavioral symptom is the *petit mal absence*—a disruption of consciousness that is associated with a cessation of ongoing behavior, a vacant look, and sometimes fluttering eyelids. The EEG of a petit mal seizure is different from that of other seizures; it is a bilaterally symmetrical **3-per-second spike-and-wave discharge** (see Figure 10.10 on page 250). Petit mal seizures are most common in children, and they frequently cease at puberty. They often go undiagnosed; thus, children with petit mal epilepsy are sometimes considered to be "daydreamers" by their parents and teachers and "space cadets" by their playmates.

Although there is no cure for epilepsy, the frequency and severity of seizures can often be reduced by anticonvulsant medication. Brain surgery is sometimes prescribed in life-threatening situations.

■ Parkinson's Disease

Parkinson's disease is a movement disorder of middle and old age that affects about 0.5% of the population

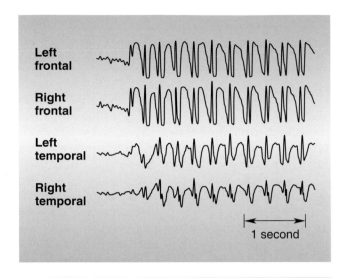

FIGURE 10.10 The bilaterally symmetrical, 3-per-second spike-and-wave EEG discharge that is associated with petit mal epileptic seizures.

(see Bodis-Wollner & Pfeiffer, 1998; Youdim & Riederer, 1997). It is about 2.5 times more prevalent in males (see Sawada & Shimohama, 2000).

The initial symptoms of Parkinson's disease are mild—perhaps no more than a slight stiffness or tremor of the fingers—but they inevitably increase in severity with advancing years. The most common symptoms of the full-blown disorder are a tremor that is pronounced during inactivity but not during voluntary movement or sleep, muscular rigidity, difficulty initiating movement, slowness of movement, and a masklike face.

Although Parkinson's patients often display some cognitive deficits, dementia is not associated with the disorder. In essence, Parkinson's disease victims are thinking people trapped inside bodies they cannot control. Do you remember from Chapter 4 the case of the "lizard"—Roberto Garcia d'Orta?

Like epilepsy, Parkinson's disease seems to have no single cause; faulty genes, brain infections, strokes, tumors, traumatic brain injury, and neurotoxins have all been implicated in specific cases. However, in the majority of cases, no cause is obvious, and there is no family history of the disorder (see Calne et al., 1987).

Parkinson's disease is associated with degeneration of the **substantia nigra**—the midbrain nucleus whose neurons project via the **nigrostriatal pathway** to the **striatum** of the basal ganglia. The neurotransmitter of substantia nigra neurons is *dopamine*, and there is almost a total lack of dopamine in the substantia nigra and striatum of long-term Parkinson's patients.

As you saw in the case of d'Orta, the symptoms of Parkinson's disease can be alleviated by injections of L-**dopa**—the chemical from which dopamine is synthesized. However, L-dopa is rarely a permanent solution; it typically becomes less and less effective with continued use, until its side effects outweigh its benefits. This is exactly what happened to d'Orta. L-Dopa therapy gave him a 3-year respite from his disease, but ultimately it became totally ineffective. His prescription was then changed to another dopamine agonist, and again his condition improved—but again the improvement was only temporary. You will return to d'Orta's roller-coaster case later in this chapter.

Several different gene mutations have been linked to Parkinson's disease (see Cowan, Harter, & Kandel, 2000; Lozano et al., 1998). This has led many people to believe that a cure is just around the corner. However, it is important to realize that each of these gene mutations has been discovered in a different family, each of which had members suffering from a rare form of early-onset Parkinson's disease that runs in families. Thus, these mutations are unlikely to be factors in typical forms of the disease. Still, the study of the effects of these gene mutations may eventually lead to a better understanding of the physiological changes that underlie the symptoms of the disorder.

■ | Huntington's Disease

Like Parkinson's disease, **Huntington's disease** is a progressive motor disorder of middle and old age; but, unlike Parkinson's disease, it is rare, it has a strong genetic basis, and it is associated with severe dementia.

The first motor signs of Huntington's disease are often increased fidgetiness; as the disorder develops, rapid, complex, jerky movements of entire limbs (rather than individual muscles) begin to predominate. Eventually the motor and intellectual deterioration become so severe that sufferers are incapable of feeding themselves, controlling their bowels, or recognizing their own children. There is no cure; death typically occurs about 15 years after the appearance of the first symptoms.

Huntington's disease is passed from generation to generation by a single dominant gene; thus, all of the individuals carrying the gene develop the disorder, as do about half their offspring. The Huntington's gene is readily passed from parent to child because the first symptoms of the disease do not appear until the parent is well past the peak reproductive years (at about age 40).

The abnormal dominant gene that causes Huntington's disease was identified and characterized in 1993. The abnormal protein produced by the Huntington's gene has also been isolated and characterized (see Albin & Tagle, 1995; MacDonald & Gusella, 1996; Paulson & Fischbeck, 1996). The precise effect of this protein, which has been named *huntingtin,* has not yet been determined (see Gusella & MacDonald, 1998; Reddy, Williams, & Tagle, 1999). Curiously, huntingtin is produced in all parts of the brains of Huntington's sufferers, yet brain damage is largely restricted to the striatum and cerebral cortex (see DiFiglia et al., 1997; Jakel & Maragos, 2000).

If one of your parents were to develop Huntington's disease, the chance would be 50/50 that you too would develop it. If you were in such a situation, would you want to know whether or not you would suffer the same fate? Medical geneticists have developed a test that can tell relatives of Huntington's patients whether they are carrying the gene (Gilliam, Gusella, & Lehrach, 1987; Martin, 1987). Some choose to take the test, and some do not. One advantage of the test is that it permits the relatives of Huntington's patients who have not inherited the gene to have children without the fear of passing on the disorder.

Shortly after the first edition of this textbook appeared in print, I received the letter reproduced on page 252. I have altered it slightly to protect the identity of its author and his family. It speaks for itself.

■ Multiple Sclerosis

Multiple sclerosis (MS), a progressive disease affecting CNS myelin, typically begins in early adult life. It occurs in about 0.15% of the population. First, there are microscopic areas of degeneration on myelin sheaths; but eventually there is a breakdown of both the myelin and the associated axons, along with the development of many areas of hard scar tissue (*sclerosis* means "hardening"). Figure 10.11 illustrates degeneration in the white matter of a patient with multiple sclerosis.

Diagnosing multiple sclerosis is difficult because the nature and severity of the disorder depend on the number, size, and position of the sclerotic lesions. Furthermore, in some cases, there are lengthy periods of remission (up to 2 years), during which the patient seems

FIGURE 10.11 Areas of sclerosis (see arrows) in the white matter of a patient with MS.

almost normal; however, these are usually just oases in the progression of the disorder. Common symptoms of advanced multiple sclerosis are urinary incontinence, visual disturbances, muscular weakness, numbness, tremor, and **ataxia** (loss of motor coordination).

Epidemiological studies of multiple sclerosis have provided evidence of the environmental and genetic factors that influence its development. **Epidemiology** is the study of the various factors, such as diet, geographic location, age, sex, and race, that influence the distribution of a disease in the general population.

Evidence that environmental factors influence the development of multiple sclerosis comes from the finding that the incidence of multiple sclerosis is far greater in people who spent their childhood in a cool climate, even if they subsequently moved to a warm climate. In contrast, evidence of genetic involvement comes from the finding that multiple sclerosis is rare among certain groups, such as gypsies and Asians, even when they live in environments in which the incidence of the disease is high in other groups. Further evidence of a genetic factor in multiple sclerosis comes from comparisons of the concordance of the disease in *monozygotic* (identical) twins (about 36%) and *dizygotic* (fraternal) twins (about 12%).

A model of multiple sclerosis can be induced in laboratory animals by injecting them with myelin and a preparation that stimulates the body's immune reaction (see Wekerle, 1993). Because the resulting disorder, which is termed **experimental autoimmune encephalomyelitis,** is similar in some respects to multiple sclerosis, it has led to the view that multiple sclerosis results from a faulty immune reaction that attacks the body's own myelin as if it were a foreign substance (see Allegretta et al., 1990). Many researchers believe that this faulty *autoimmune reaction* is the result of a slow-acting infection contracted early in life.

There are now a variety of drugs that combat the symptoms of multiple sclerosis. However, none of these totally blocks its progression (Hall, Compston, & Scolding, 1997; McFarland, 1996).

■ Alzheimer's Disease

Alzheimer's disease is the most common cause of *dementia*. It sometimes appears in individuals as young as 40, but the likelihood of its development becomes greater with advancing years. About 15% of the general population over the age of 65 suffer from the disease, and the proportion is about 35% in those over 85 (St. George-Hyslop, 2000).

Alzheimer's disease is progressive. Its early stages are characterized by depression and a general decline in cognitive ability; its intermediate stages are marked by irritability, anxiety, and deterioration of speech; and in its advanced stages, the patient deteriorates to the point that even simple responses such as swallowing and

Mr. Walter S. Miller
1500 N. Severn-Langdon Rd.
Manchester, Connecticut 22022
Z9/900-854
August 5, 1991

Dr. John P.J. Pinel
Department of Psychology
University of British Columbia
Vancouver, B.C. Canada V6T.,1Y7.

Dear Dr. Pinel:

I am worried about my children and their future. In fact, I am worried sick. After reading your book I feel that you are my friend and I have nowhere else to turn.

My wife came down with Huntington's disease 7 years ago, and today she can't walk or take care of herself. I have three young children. Where can I take them to see if they have inherited my wife's infected cells? I am presently incarcerated, which adds to my psychological pain. I look to be released soon, and could take my wife and kids just about any wheres to find help and get answers.

Any kind of advice that you could give us would be greatly appreciated by me and my family. I wish to thank you for any assistance that you can give.

God bless you and give you and yours His love and peace! I remain with warmest personal regards.

Very truly yours,

Walter S. Miller

Walter S. Miller

WSM:

THE UNIVERSITY OF BRITISH COLUMBIA

Department of Psychology
2136 West Mall
Vancouver, B. C. Canada V6T 1Z4
Tel: (604) 822-2755
Fax: (604) 822-6923

November 25, 1991

Mr. Walter S. Miller
1500 N. Severn-Langdon Road
Manchester, Connecticut 22022
U.S.A.

Dear Mr. Miller:

I was saddened to learn of your unhappy state of affairs. In requesting my advice, I hope that you understand that I am a scientist, not a physician. In any case, the following is my assessment.

If your wife does in fact have Huntington's disease and not some other neurological disorder, each of your children has a 50/50 chance of developing Huntington's disease in adulthood. I am sure that you are aware that there is currently no cure.

I advise you to seek the advice of a local neurologist, who can explain your options to you and provide you with the advice and support that you sorely need. You must decide whether or not to subject your children to the tests that are required to determine whether or not they are carrying the Huntington's gene. One option would be to wait for your children to reach legal age and then allow them to make the decision for themselves. Some people whose parents develop Huntington's disease decide to take the test; others decide not to. In either case, it is extremely important for them not to risk passing on the Huntington's gene to future generations.

I am sorry that I cannot provide you with a more optimistic assessment, but your children's situation is too serious for me to be less than totally frank. Again, please consult a neurologist as soon as possible.

Do not lose hope. There is a chance (1/8) that none of your children is carrying the Huntington's gene. I wish you, your wife, and your children good fortune.

Cordially,

John P. J. Pinel

John P. J. Pinel
Professor

controlling the bladder are difficult. Alzheimer's disease is terminal.

Because Alzheimer's disease is not the only cause of dementia, it cannot be diagnosed with certainty on the basis of its behavioral symptoms—definitive diagnosis of Alzheimer's disease must await autopsy. The two defining characteristics of the disease are neurofibrillary tangles and amyloid plaques. *Neurofibrillary tangles* are threadlike tangles of protein in the neural cytoplasm, and *amyloid plaques* are clumps of scar tissue composed of degenerating neurons and a protein called **amyloid,** which is present in normal brains in only very small amounts. In addition, there is substantial neuron loss. The presence of amyloid plaques in the brain of a patient who died of Alzheimer's disease is illustrated in Figure 10.12.

Although neurofibrillary tangles (see Goedert, 1993), amyloid plaques (see Fraser, Suh, & Djamgoz, 1997), and neuron loss (see O'Banion, Coleman, & Callahan, 1994)

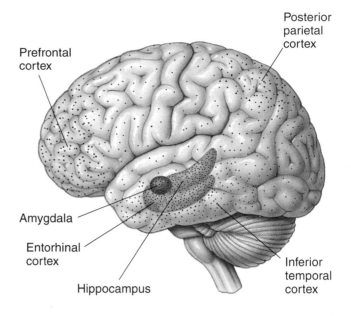

FIGURE 10.13 The typical distribution of neurofibrillary tangles and amyloid plaques in the brains of patients with advanced Alzheimer's disease. (Based on Goedert, 1993, and Selkoe, 1991.)

tend to occur throughout the brains of Alzheimer's patients, they are more prevalent in some areas than in others. For example, they are particularly prevalent in medial temporal lobe structures such as the *entorhinal cortex, amygdala,* and *hippocampus*—all structures that are involved in various aspects of memory. They are also prevalent in the inferior temporal cortex, posterior parietal cortex, and prefrontal cortex—all areas that mediate complex cognitive functions. (See Figure 10.13.)

There is a difficulty in studying the genetics of Alzheimer's disease: Its carriers often die of natural causes before their Alzheimer's symptoms can be manifested. Nevertheless, it is clear that Alzheimer's disease has a major genetic component. People with an Alzheimer's victim in their immediate family have a 50% chance of being stricken by the disease if they survive into their 80s (Breitner, 1990).

Because of the difficulties involved in studying the genetics of late-onset diseases, most of the research on the genetics of Alzheimer's disease has focused on rare early-onset *familial* forms of the disease. Several genes have been found to be associated with Alzheimer's disease, and mutations in all of them have been implicated in the synthesis of amyloid or *tau,* a protein found in neurofibrillary tangles (see Haass & De Strooper, 1999; St. George-Hyslop, 2000).

Because cholinergic neurons are particularly susceptible to Alzheimer's disease, cholinergic agonists are commonly used in its treatment. Although these substances sometimes have modest benefits in the early stages of the disorder, they are ineffective once cholinergic neurons have degenerated (see Shoulson, 1998).

FIGURE 10.12 Amyloid plaques (see arrows) in the brain of a patient with Alzheimer's disease.

BrainScan

This is a good place for you to pause to scan your brain. Are you ready to progress to the following section, which discusses animal models of some of the disorders that you have just learned about? Fill in the following blanks. The correct answers are provided at the bottom of this page. Before proceeding, review material related to your errors and omissions.

1. The two major categories of epileptic seizures are _____ and
   _____ .

2. _____ are simple repetitive responses that occur during complex partial seizures.

3. The disorder characterized by tremor at rest is _____ disease.

4. Parkinson's disease is associated with degeneration in the _____ dopamine pathway.

5. _____ disease is passed from generation to generation by a single dominant gene.

6. Genetic studies of Parkinson's disease and Alzheimer's disease have focused on early-onset _____ forms of the disorder.

7. Experimental autoimmune encephalomyelitis is an animal model _____ of _____ .

8. The most common cause of dementia is _____ disease.

9. Two major neuropathological symptoms of Alzheimer's disease are _____ tangles and _____ plaques.

10.3   Animal Models of Human Neuropsychological Diseases

The first two sections of this chapter focused on neuropsychological diseases and their causes, but they also provided some glimpses into the ways in which researchers have attempted to solve the many puzzles of neurological dysfunction. This section focuses on one of these ways: the experimental investigation of animal models. Because the experimentation necessary to identify the neuropathological basis of human neuropsychological diseases is seldom possible on the patients themselves, animal models of the diseases play an important role in such investigation.

It is important to appreciate that even the best animal models of neuropsychological diseases display only some of the features of the diseases they are modeling. Consequently, animal models must be employed with caution. Studying an animal model is like exploring a section of an unknown maze. One enters an unfamiliar section with little more than a hope that its exploration will prove fruitful, and it

is only after each of its arms has been carefully explored that it is possible to know whether the decision to enter the section was wise. In the same way, it is not possible to evaluate animal models of neuropsychological dysfunction that are currently under investigation until each has been thoroughly explored. Surely, only a few animal models will lead toward the goals of understanding and prevention, but only time and effort can tell which ones these are.

This section of the chapter discusses three animal models that are currently the focus of intensive investigation: the kindling model of epilepsy, the transgenic

---

Brain Scan answers: (1) partial and generalized in either order, (2) Automatisms, (3) Parkinson's, (4) nigrostriatal, (5) Huntington's, (6) familial, (7) multiple sclerosis, (8) Alzheimer's, (9) neurofibrillary and amyloid.

mouse model of Alzheimer's disease, and the MPTP model of Parkinson's disease.

Kindling Model of Epilepsy

In 1969, Goddard, McIntyre, and Leech delivered one mild electrical stimulation per day to rats through implanted amygdalar electrodes. There was no behavioral response to the first few stimulations, but soon each stimulation began to elicit a convulsive response. The first convulsions were mild, involving only a slight tremor of the face. However, with each subsequent stimulation, the elicited convulsions became more generalized, until each convulsion involved the entire body. The progressive development and intensification of convulsions elicited by a series of periodic brain stimulations became known as the **kindling phenomenon.**

Although kindling is most frequently studied in rats subjected to repeated amygdalar stimulation, it is a remarkably general phenomenon. For example, kindling has been reported in mice (Leech & McIntyre, 1976), rabbits (Tanaka, 1972), cats (Adamec, 1990), dogs (Wauquier, Ashton, & Melis, 1979), and various primates (Wada, 1990a). Moreover, kindling can be produced by the repeated stimulation of many brain sites other than the amygdala, and it can be produced by the repeated application of initially subconvulsive doses of convulsive chemicals (Cain, 1986; Mori & Wada, 1990; Post et al., 1990).

There are many interesting features of kindling (see Racine & Burnham, 1984; Wada, 1990b), but two warrant emphasis. The first is that the neural changes underlying kindling are permanent. A subject that has been kindled and then left unstimulated for several months still responds to each low-intensity stimulation with a generalized convulsion (Goddard, McIntyre, & Leech, 1969; Wada & Sato, 1974). The second is that kindling is produced by distributed, as opposed to massed, stimulations. If the intervals between successive stimulations are shorter than an hour or two, it usually requires many more stimulations to kindle a subject; and under normal circumstances, no kindling at all occurs at intervals of less than about 20 minutes (Racine et al., 1973).

Much of the interest in kindling stems from the fact that it models epilepsy in two ways. First, the convulsions elicited in kindled animals are similar in many respects to those observed in some types of human epilepsy. Second, the kindling phenomenon itself is comparable to the **epileptogenesis** (the development, or genesis, of epilepsy) that can follow a head injury: Some individuals who at first appear to have escaped serious injury after a blow to the head begin to experience convulsions a few weeks later, and these convulsions sometimes begin to recur more and more frequently and with greater and greater intensity.

It must be stressed that the kindling model as it is applied in most laboratories is different from epilepsy in one important respect. You will recall from earlier in this chapter that epilepsy is a disease in which epileptic attacks recur spontaneously; in contrast, kindled convulsions are elicited. However, a model that overcomes this shortcoming has been developed in several species. If subjects are kindled for a very long time—about 300 stimulations in rats—a syndrome can be induced that is truly epileptic, in the sense that the subjects begin to display spontaneous seizures and continue to display them even after the regimen of stimulation is curtailed (e.g., Pinel, 1981; Shouse et al., 1990; Wada, Sato, & Corcoran, 1974).

One interesting and potentially important development in the study of kindling is that some researchers have started to focus on *interictal behavior* (behavior that occurs in epileptics between their seizures). For some human epileptics, particularly those who suffer from complex partial epilepsy, pathological changes in their interictal behavior are more distressing and more difficult to treat than the seizures themselves (Leung, Ma, & McLachlin, 2000). Several studies of kindling have shown that kindled subjects display a variety of changes in interictal emotional behavior that are similar to those observed in human epileptics (Kalynchuk, 2000).

Transgenic Mouse Model of Alzheimer's Disease

Perhaps the most exciting development in the study of Alzheimer's disease has been the transgenic model of the disorder. **Transgenic** refers to animals into which the genes of another species have been introduced (see Carter et al., 1999).

One difficulty in studying Alzheimer's disease is that only humans and a few related primates develop amyloid plaques, considered by many to be the primary symptom of the disorder. As a result, experimental studies of Alzheimer's disease have been difficult to conduct, and fundamental questions of causation have been difficult to address. For example, the causal role of amyloid deposits in Alzheimer's disease has not yet been sorted out: Some investigators believe that amyloid deposition triggers neuron degeneration, thereby causing the behavioral symptoms; others believe that the amyloid plaques are the result, not the cause, of the neural degeneration (Neve & Robakis, 1998). This lack of progress in answering fundamental causal questions about Alzheimer's disease is why the development of the transgenic mouse model of the disorder is such an important contribution.

There are several forms of the transgenic mouse model. In one (Hsiao et al., 1996), genes that accelerate the synthesis of human amyloid are injected into newly fertilized mouse eggs, which are then injected into a foster mother to develop. When the transgenic mice mature, their brains contain many amyloid plaques like those of human Alzheimer's patients. Moreover, the distribution of the amyloid plaques is comparable to that observed in human Alzheimer's patients, with the highest concentrations occurring in the hippocampus and surrounding areas.

Although the transgenic mice of Hsiao and her colleagues arguably provide the best animal model of Alzheimer's disease, the model is not without its problems (Routtenberg, 1997). For example, the mice show no neurofibrillary tangles, and the degree of memory impairment changes little as the mice mature and develop more plaques. However, an animal model does not have to mimic the human disorder in every respect to be useful: Skovronsky and colleagues (2000) recently used the transgenic mouse model to develop a radioactive ligand for amyloid plaques, which may prove to be useful for visualizing amyloid plaques in human patients.

■ | MPTP Model of Parkinson's Disease

The preeminent animal model of Parkinson's disease grew out of an unfortunate accident, which resulted in the following anomalous cases of Parkinson's disease.

The Case of the Frozen Addicts

Parkinson's disease . . . rarely occurs before the age of 50. It was somewhat of a surprise then to see a group of young drug addicts at our hospital in 1982 who had developed symptoms of severe and what proved to be irreversible parkinsonism. The only link between these patients was the recent use of a new "synthetic heroin." They exhibited virtually all of the typical motor features of Parkinson's disease, including the classic triad of bradykinesia (slowness of movement), tremor and rigidity of their muscles. Even the subtle features, such as seborrhea (oiliness of the skin) and micrographia (small handwriting), that are typical of Parkinson's disease were present. After tracking down samples of this substance, the offending agent was tentatively identified as 1-methyl-4-phenyl-1,2,3,6-tetrahydropyridine or **MPTP**. . . . There has been no sign of remission, and most are becoming increasingly severe management problems. (Langston, 1985, p. 79)

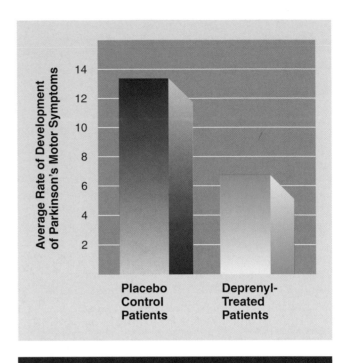

FIGURE 10.14 Average rate of motor symptom development in early Parkinson's patients treated with deprenyl (a monoamine oxidase inhibitor) or with a placebo. Deprenyl slowed the progression of the disease by 50%. (Based on Tetrud and Langston, 1989.)

Researchers immediately tried to turn the misfortune of these few to the advantage of many by developing a much-needed animal model of Parkinson's disease (Langston, 1986). It was quickly established that nonhuman primates respond like humans to MPTP (Burns et al., 1983; Langston et al., 1984).

The brains of primates exposed to MPTP have cell loss in the substantia nigra similar to that observed in the brains of Parkinson's patients. Considering that the substantia nigra is the major source of the brain's dopamine, it is not surprising that the level of dopamine is greatly reduced in both the MPTP model and in the naturally occurring disorder. However, it is curious that in a few monkeys MPTP produces a major depletion of dopamine without producing any gross motor symptoms (Taylor et al., 1990).

The development of the MPTP animal model has already benefitted patients with Parkinson's disease. For example, it was discovered that **deprenyl,** a monoamine agonist, blocks the effects of MPTP in an animal model, and it was subsequently shown that deprenyl administered to early Parkinson's patients retards the progression of the disease (Tetrud & Langston, 1989)—see Figure 10.14.

10.4 Neuroplastic Responses to Nervous System Damage: Degeneration, Regeneration, Reorganization, and Recovery

Damage to the nervous system may trigger four neuroplastic responses: degeneration, regeneration, reorganization, and recovery. Each of these four responses is discussed in this section.

Neural Degeneration

A widely used method for the controlled study of the responses of neurons to damage is to sever their axons. Two kinds of neural degeneration (deterioration) ensue: anterograde degeneration and retrograde degeneration. **Anterograde degeneration** is the degeneration of the **distal segment**—the segment of a cut axon between the cut and the synaptic terminals. **Retrograde degeneration** is the degeneration of the **proximal segment**—the segment of a cut axon between the cut and the cell body.

Anterograde degeneration occurs quickly following *axotomy,* because the cut separates the distal segment of the axon from the cell body, which is the metabolic center of the neuron. The entire distal segment becomes badly swollen within a few hours, and it breaks into fragments within a few days.

The course of retrograde degeneration is different; it progresses gradually back from the cut to the cell body. In about 2 or 3 days, major changes become apparent in the cell bodies of most axotomized neurons. These early cell body changes are either degenerative or regenerative in nature. Early degenerative changes to the cell body (e.g., a decrease in size) suggest that the neuron will ultimately die—usually by apoptosis but sometimes by necrosis (Goldberg & Barres, 2000). Early regenerative changes (e.g., an increase in size) indicate that the cell body is involved in a massive synthesis of the proteins that will be used to replace the degenerated axon. But early regenerative changes in the cell body do not guarantee the long-term survival of the neuron; if the regenerating axon does not manage to make synaptic contact with an appropriate target, the neuron eventually dies.

Sometimes, degeneration spreads from damaged neurons to neurons that are linked to them by synapses; this is called **transneuronal degeneration.** In some cases, transneuronal degeneration spreads from damaged neurons to the neurons on which they synapse; this is called *anterograde transneuronal degeneration.* And in some cases, it spreads from damaged neurons to the neurons that synapse on them; this is called *retrograde trans-*

neuronal degeneration. Neural and transneuronal degeneration are illustrated in Figure 10.15 on page 258.

Neural Regeneration

Neural regeneration—the regrowth of damaged neurons—does not proceed as successfully in mammals and other higher vertebrates as it does in most invertebrates and lower vertebrates. The capacity for accurate axon growth, which is possessed by higher vertebrates during their original development, is lost once they reach maturity. Regeneration is virtually nonexistent in the CNS of adult mammals, and regeneration in their PNS is at best a hit-or-miss affair.

In the mammalian PNS, regrowth from the proximal stump of a damaged nerve usually begins 2 or 3 days after axonal damage. What happens next depends on the nature of the injury (see Tonge & Golding, 1993); there are three possibilities. First, if the original Schwann cell myelin sheaths remain intact, the regenerating peripheral axons grow through them to their original targets at a rate of a few millimeters per day. Second, if the peripheral nerve is severed and the cut ends become separated by a few millimeters, regenerating axon tips often grow into incorrect sheaths and are guided by them to incorrect destinations; that is why it is often difficult to regain the coordinated use of a limb affected by nerve damage even if there has been substantial regeneration. And third, if the cut ends of a severed mammalian peripheral nerve become widely separated or if a lengthy section of the nerve is damaged, there may be no meaningful regeneration at all; regenerating axon tips grow in a tangled mass around the proximal stump, and the neurons ultimately die. These three patterns of mammalian peripheral nerve regeneration are illustrated in Figure 10.16 on page 259.

Why do mammalian PNS neurons regenerate, and mammalian CNS neurons do not? The obvious answer is that PNS neurons are inherently capable of regeneration while CNS neurons are not, but this answer has proved to be incorrect. CNS neurons are capable of regeneration if they are transplanted to the PNS, whereas PNS neurons are not capable of regeneration if they are transplanted to the CNS. Clearly, there is something about the environment of the PNS that promotes regeneration and something about the environment of the CNS that does not (Goldberg & Barres, 2000). Schwann cells are the key.

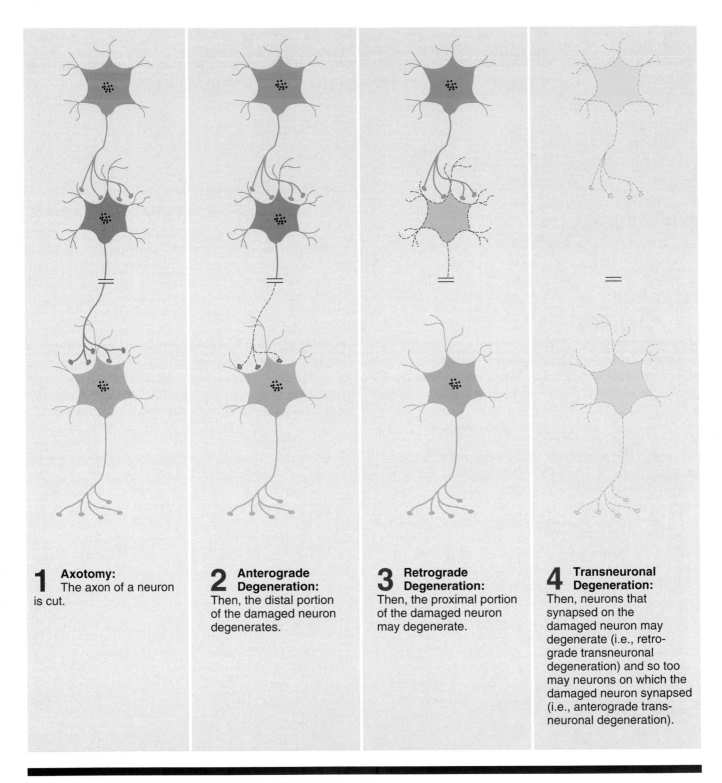

1 Axotomy:
The axon of a neuron is cut.

2 Anterograde Degeneration:
Then, the distal portion of the damaged neuron degenerates.

3 Retrograde Degeneration:
Then, the proximal portion of the damaged neuron may degenerate.

4 Transneuronal Degeneration:
Then, neurons that synapsed on the damaged neuron may degenerate (i.e., retrograde transneuronal degeneration) and so too may neurons on which the damaged neuron synapsed (i.e., anterograde transneuronal degeneration).

FIGURE 10.15   Neuronal and transneuronal degeneration following axotomy.

Schwann cells, which myelinate PNS axons, promote regeneration in the mammalian PNS by producing both neurotrophic factors and cell-adhesion molecules (CAMs). The neurotrophic factors released by Schwann cells stimulate the growth of new axons, and the cell-adhesion molecules on the cell membranes of Schwann cells provide the paths along which regenerating PNS axons grow. In contrast, **oligodendroglia,** which myelinate CNS axons, do not stimulate or guide regeneration; indeed, they release factors that actively block regeneration.

In contrast to neural regeneration in mammals, that in lower vertebrates is extremely accurate. It is accurate in both the CNS and the PNS, and it is accurate even when the regenerating

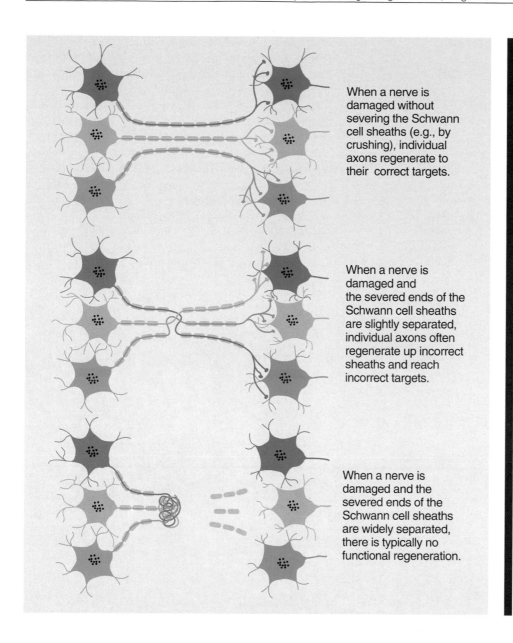

When a nerve is damaged without severing the Schwann cell sheaths (e.g., by crushing), individual axons regenerate to their correct targets.

When a nerve is damaged and the severed ends of the Schwann cell sheaths are slightly separated, individual axons often regenerate up incorrect sheaths and reach incorrect targets.

When a nerve is damaged and the severed ends of the Schwann cell sheaths are widely separated, there is typically no functional regeneration.

axons do not grow into remnant Schwann cell myelin sheaths. The accuracy of regeneration in lower vertebrates offers hope of a medical breakthrough: If the factors that promote accurate regeneration in lower vertebrates can be identified and applied to the human brain, it might be possible to cure currently untreatable brain injuries.

When an axon degenerates, axon branches grow out from adjacent healthy axons and synapse at the sites vacated by the degenerating axon; this is called **collateral sprouting.** Collateral sprouts may grow out from the axon terminal branches or the nodes of Ranvier on adjacent neurons. Collateral sprouting is illustrated in Figure 10.17 on page 260.

■ | Neural Reorganization

It has long been assumed that major changes in mammalian nervous systems were limited to the period of early development: Adult mammalian nervous systems were thought to be limited to the subtle functional changes that mediate learning and memory. However, as you learned in Chapter 9, it was recently discovered that adult mammalian brains retain the ability to reorganize themselves in response to experience. They also retain the ability to reorganize themselves in response to damage.

EXAMPLES OF CORTICAL REORGANIZATION FOLLOWING NERVOUS SYSTEM DAMAGE ■ Most studies of neural reorganization following damage have focused on adult sensory and motor systems (see Donoghue, 1995). Sensory and motor systems are ideally suited to the study of neural reorganization because of their topographic layout. The damage-induced reorganization of the primary sensory and motor systems has been studied in two fundamentally different conditions: following damage to peripheral nerves and following

Axotomy of neuron A

Degeneration of neuron A and collateral sprouting of neuron B.

FIGURE 10.17 Collateral sprouting after neural degeneration.

damage to the primary cortical areas (Buonomano & Merzenich, 1998). Let's consider some studies that illustrate these two approaches.

Kaas and colleagues (1990) assessed the effect of making a small lesion in one retina and removing the other. Several months after the retinal lesions were made, primary visual cortex neurons that originally had receptive fields in the lesioned area of the retina were found to have receptive fields in the area of the retina next to the lesion; remarkably, this change began within minutes of the lesion (Gilbert & Wiesel, 1992).

Pons and colleagues (1991) mapped the primary somatosensory cortex of monkeys whose contralateral arm sensory neurons had been cut 10 years before. They found that the cortical face representation had systematically expanded into the original arm area. This study created a stir because the scale of the reorganization was far greater than had been assumed to be possible: The primary somatosensory cortex face area had expanded its border by well over a centimeter, likely as a consequence of the particularly long (10-year) interval between surgery and testing.

Jenkins and Merzenich (1987) removed the area of monkey somatosensory cortex that responded to touches of the palm of the contralateral hand. Several weeks later, they found that neurons adjacent to the lesion now responded to touches of the palm.

Working with rats, Sanes, Suner, and Donoghue (1990) transected the motor neurons that controlled the muscles of the rats' *vibrissae* (whiskers). A few weeks later, stimulation of the area of motor cortex that had previously elicited vibrissae movement now activated other muscles of the face. This result is illustrated in Figure 10.18.

MECHANISMS OF NEURAL REORGANIZATION ■
Two kinds of mechanisms have been proposed to account for the reorganization of neural circuits: a strengthening of existing connections, possibly through release from inhibition, and the establishment of new connections by collateral sprouting (see O'Leary, Ruff, & Dyck, 1994). Support for the first mechanism comes from two observations: Reorganization often occurs too

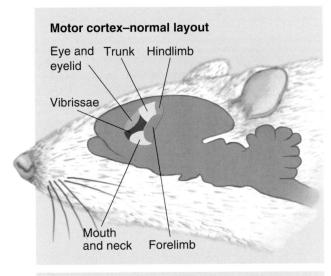

Motor cortex—normal layout

Eye and eyelid   Trunk   Hindlimb

Vibrissae

Mouth and neck   Forelimb

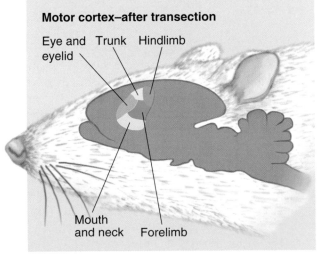

Motor cortex—after transection

Eye and eyelid   Trunk   Hindlimb

Mouth and neck   Forelimb

FIGURE 10.18 Reorganization of the rat motor cortex following transection of the motor neurons that control movements of the vibrissae. The motor cortex was mapped by brain stimulation before transection and then again a few weeks after. (Adapted from Sanes, Suner, & Donoghue, 1990.)

quickly to be explained by neural growth, and rapid reorganization never involves changes of more than 2 millimeters of cortical surface. Support for the second mechanism comes from the observation that the magnitude of long-term reorganization can be too great to be explained by changes in existing connections. Figure 10.19 illustrates how these two mechanisms might account for the reorganization that occurs after damage to a peripheral somatosensory nerve.

Recovery of Function after Brain Damage

Understanding the mechanisms that underlie the recovery of function after nervous system damage is a high priority for neuroscientists. If these mechanisms were understood, steps could be taken to promote recovery. However, recovery of function after nervous system damage is a poorly understood phenomenon.

Little is known about recovery of function after nervous system damage for two reasons. The first is that it is difficult to conduct controlled experiments on populations of brain-damaged patients. The second is that nervous system damage may result in a variety of compensatory changes that can easily be confused with true recovery of function. For example, any improvement in the week or two after damage could reflect a decline in *cerebral edema* (brain swelling) rather than a recovery from the neural damage itself, and any gradual improvement in the months after damage could reflect the learning of new cognitive and behavioral strategies (i.e., substitution of functions) rather than the return of lost functions (see Wilson, 1998). Consequently, true recovery of function is less

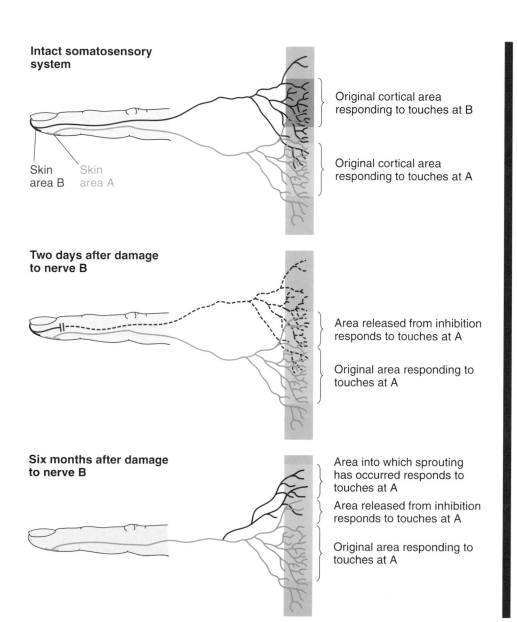

Intact somatosensory system

Skin area B   Skin area A

Original cortical area responding to touches at B

Original cortical area responding to touches at A

Two days after damage to nerve B

Area released from inhibition responds to touches at A

Original area responding to touches at A

Six months after damage to nerve B

Area into which sprouting has occurred responds to touches at A

Area released from inhibition responds to touches at A

Original area responding to touches at A

FIGURE 10.19 The two-stage model of neural reorganization: (1) strengthening of existing connections through release from inhibition and (2) establishment of new connections by collateral sprouting.

FIGURE 10.20 Percentage of patients showing improvement following brain injury. Teuber (1975) assessed the deficits of brain-damaged soldiers within a week of their injury and again 20 years later.

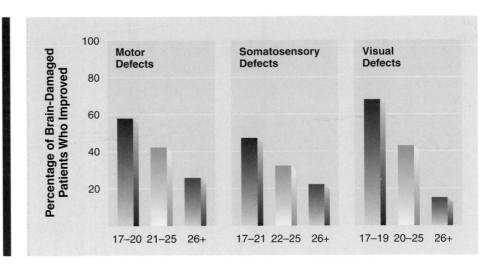

common and less complete than most people believe. Recovery of function is most likely when lesions are small and the patient is young (see Figure 10.20).

Cognitive reserve (roughly equivalent to education and intelligence) is thought to play an important role in the apparent recovery of cognitive function after brain damage. Kapur (1997) conducted a biographical study of doctors and neuroscientists with brain damage, and he observed a great deal of cognitive recovery. He concluded that the observed improvement did not occur because these patients had actually recovered lost cognitive function but because their cognitive reserve allowed them to accomplish cognitive tasks in alternative ways.

The role of neural reorganization in recovery of function after brain damage is controversial. It seems likely that neural reorganization contributes to such recovery, but so far most of the evidence for this hypothesis has been indirect. The strongest evidence comes from a recent study in which the degree of motor recovery in stroke patients was found to be correlated with the degree of motor cortex reorganization (Lipert et al., 2000).

10.5 | Neuroplasticity and the Treatment of Nervous System Damage

The study of neuroplasticity is currently one of the most active and exciting areas of research in neuroscience. This section reveals the reason for all the excitement: The dream that recent discoveries about neuroplasticity—with which you are now familiar—can be applied to the treatment of brain damage in human patients. This dream may be on the verge of being realized. Several recent studies have demonstrated effective new techniques for blocking neural degeneration or promoting regeneration in animal models. Trials in human patients are in progress, and more are sure to follow. The following are four particularly promising lines of research.

Blocking Neurodegeneration

Several studies have shown that it is possible to reduce the neurodegeneration caused by a cerebral accident. A study conducted by Xu and colleagues (1999) is particularly promising because these researchers showed that blocking neurodegeneration also blocked the development of behavioral deficits.

Xu and colleagues (1999) exposed rats to cerebral ischemia by limiting blood flow to the brain. This had two major effects in the control group of rats: It produced damage in the hippocampus, a structure that is particularly susceptible to ischemic damage, and it produced deficits in the rats' performance in the Morris water maze (see Chapter 5). The hippocampuses of rats in the experimental group were treated with viruses genetically engineered to release *apoptosis inhibitor protein*. Amazingly, the apoptosis inhibitor protein prevented both the loss of hippocampal neurons and the deficits in Morris water maze performance.

Promoting Recovery from CNS Damage by Promoting Regeneration

Although regeneration does not normally occur in the mammalian CNS, several studies have shown that it can be induced. The following two studies are particularly promising because they have shown that such regeneration can be associated with functional recovery.

Eitan and colleagues (1994) transected the left optic nerves of rats. In the control rats, the retinal ganglion cells, which compose the left optic nerve, permanently degenerated. The experimental rats received injections of an agent that is toxic to oligodendrocytes, thus eliminating these cells' ability to block regeneration. In these experimental subjects, the optic nerves regenerated, and 6 weeks after the injury, evoked potentials could be recorded from the optic nerve in response to light flashes presented to the left eye.

Cheng, Cao, and Olson (1996) transected the spinal cords of rats, thus rendering them *paraplegic* (paralyzed in the posterior portion of their bodies). The researchers then transplanted sections of myelinated peripheral nerve across the transection. As a result, spinal cord neurons regenerated through the implanted Schwann cell myelin sheaths, and the regeneration allowed the rats to regain use of their hindquarters. A similar finding was subsequently reported by Li, Field, and Raisman (1997).

■ Promoting Recovery from CNS Damage by Neurotransplantation

A few years ago, the idea of brain transplantation was little more than science fiction. Today, the treatment of brain damage by transplanting neural tissue is approaching reality. Efforts to treat CNS damage by neurotransplantation have taken two different approaches (see Björklund & Lindvall, 2000). The first is to transplant fetal tissue; the second is to transplant stem cells.

TRANSPLANTING FETAL TISSUE ■ The first approach to neurotransplantation was to replace a damaged structure with fetal tissue that would develop into the same structure. Could the *donor* tissue develop and become integrated into the *host* brain, and in so doing alleviate the symptoms? This approach focused on Parkinson's disease. Parkinson's patients lack the dopamine-releasing cells of the nigrostriatal pathway: Could they be cured by transplanting the appropriate fetal tissue into the site?

Early signs were very positive. Bilateral transplantation of fetal substantia nigra cells was successful in treating the MPTP monkey model of Parkinson's disease (Bankiewicz et al., 1990; Sladek et al., 1987). Fetal substantia nigra transplants survived in the MPTP-treated monkeys; they innervated adjacent striatal tissue, released dopamine, and, most importantly, alleviated the severe poverty of movement, tremor, and rigidity produced by the MPTP.

Soon after the favorable effects of neurotransplants in the MPTP monkey model were reported, neurotrans-

plantation was offered as a treatment for Parkinson's disease at major research hospitals. The results of the first case studies were promising. The fetal substantia nigra implants survived, and they released dopamine into the host striatum (see Sawle & Myers, 1993). More importantly, some of the patients improved.

The results of these case studies triggered a large-scale double-blind evaluation study on patients suffering from advanced Parkinson's disease. The study was extremely thorough; it even included placebo controls—patients who received surgery but no implants. The initial results were encouraging: Although control patients showed no improvement, the implants survived in the experimental patients, and some displayed a modest improvement. Unfortunately, however, about 15% of these patients started to display a variety of uncontrollable writhing and chewing movements about a year after the surgery (Greene et al., 1999).

In Chapter 4, you were introduced to Roberto Garcia d'Orta—the Lizard. D'Orta, who suffered from Parkinson's disease, initially responded to L-dopa therapy; but, after 3 years of therapy, his condition worsened. Then he responded to treatment with a dopamine agonist, but again the improvement was only temporary. D'Orta, was in a desperate state when he heard about *adrenal medulla autotransplantation* (transplanting a patient's own adrenal medulla cells into her or his striatum, usually for the treatment of Parkinson's disease). Adrenal medulla cells release small amounts of dopamine, and there were some early indications that adrenal medulla autotransplantation might alleviate the symptoms of Parkinson's disease.

D'Orta demanded adrenal medulla autotransplantation from his doctor. When his doctor refused, on the grounds that the effectiveness of the treatment was still in doubt, d'Orta found himself another doctor—a neurosurgeon who was not nearly so cautious.

The Case of Roberto Garcia d'Orta: The Lizard Gets an Autotransplant

Roberto flew to Juarez. The neurosurgeon there greeted him with open arms. As long as Roberto could afford the cost, he'd be happy to do an adrenal implant on him. . . .

Were there any dangers?

The neurosurgeon seemed insulted by the question. If Senor d'Orta didn't trust him, he could go elsewhere. . . .

Roberto underwent the procedure.

He flew back home two weeks later. He was no better. He was told that it took time for the cells to grow and make the needed chemicals. . . .

Then I received an unexpected call from Roberto's wife. Roberto was dead. . . .

He'd died of a stroke. . . . Had the stroke been a complication of his surgery? It was more than a mere possibility. (Klawans, 1990, pp. 63–64)

TRANSPLANTING STEM CELLS ■ In Chapter 9, you learned about *stem cells,* which are *pluripotent* (having the capacity to develop into many types of mature cells). Investigators are trying to develop procedures for correcting brain damage by injecting stem cells into the damaged site. Once injected, the stem cells could develop and replace the damaged cells, under guidance from surrounding tissue (see Svendsen & Smith, 1999). This line of research received a major boost from the development of renewable cultures of stems cells (see Gearhart, 1998; Wakayama et al., 2001), which can serve as a source for transplantation and research (Gage, 2000). The study by McDonald and colleagues (1999) illustrates the potential of this method.

McDonald and colleagues injected stem cells into an area of spinal damage. Their subjects were rats that had been rendered paraplegic by a blow. The stem cells migrated to different areas around the damaged area, where they developed into neurons and oligodendrocytes. Remarkably, the rats receiving the implants became capable of supporting their weight with their hindlimbs and walking, albeit awkwardly.

■ Promoting Recovery from CNS Damage by Rehabilitative Training

Recent demonstrations of the important role of experience in the organization of the developing and adult brain have kindled a renewed interest in the use of rehabilitative training to promote recovery from CNS damage. The following innovative rehabilitative training programs have been derived from recent findings.

STROKES ■ Small strokes produce a core of brain damage, which is often followed by a gradually expanding loss of neural function around this core. Nudo and colleagues (1996) produced small *ischemic lesions* (lesions produced by an interruption of blood supply) in the hand area of the motor cortex of monkeys. Then, 5 days later, a program of hand training and practice was initiated. During the ensuing 3 or 4 weeks, the monkeys plucked hundreds of tiny food pellets from food wells of different sizes. This practice substantially reduced the expansion of cortical damage. The monkeys that received the rehabilitative training also showed greater recovery in the use of their affected hand.

One of the principles that has emerged from the study of neurodevelopment is that neurons seem to be in a competitive situation: They compete with other neurons for synaptic sites and neurotrophins, and the losers die. Weiller and Rijntjes (1999) designed a rehabilitative program based on this principle, tested it on monkeys, and then tested it on unilateral stroke patients who had difficulty using one arm. Their procedure was to tie

down the functioning arm for 2 weeks while the affected arm received intensive training. Performance with the affected arm improved markedly over the 2 weeks, and there was an increase in the area of motor cortex controlling that arm.

SPINAL INJURY ■ In one approach to treating patients with spinal injuries (see Muir & Steeves, 1997), patients incapable of walking were supported by a harness over a moving treadmill. With most of their weight supported and the treadmill providing appropriate feedback, the patients gradually learned to make walking movements. Then, as they improved, the amount of support was gradually reduced. In one study using this technique, over 90% of the trained patients eventually became independent walkers, compared with only 50% of those receiving conventional physiotherapy.

PHANTOM LIMBS ■ Most amputees continue to experience limbs that have been amputated—a condition referred to as **phantom limb.** The most striking feature of phantom limbs is their reality. Their existence is so compelling that a patient may try to jump out of bed onto a nonexistent leg or to lift a cup with a nonexistent hand. In most cases, the amputated limb behaves like a normal limb; for example, as an amputee walks, a phantom arm seems to swing back and forth in perfect coordination with the intact arm. However, sometimes an amputee feels that the amputated limb is stuck in a peculiar position. For example, one amputee felt that his phantom arm extended straight out from the shoulder, and as a result, he turned sideways whenever he passed through doorways (Melzack, 1992).

About 50% of amputees experience chronic severe pain in their phantom limbs. A typical complaint is that an amputated hand is clenched so tightly that the fingernails are digging into the palm of the hand. Occasionally, phantom limb pain can be treated by having the amputee concentrate on opening the amputated hand. However, when this does not work, the pain can become so intense that desperate measures are attempted.

Based on the premise that phantom limb pain results from irritation at the stump, many efforts to control it involved cutting off the stump or surgical destruction of various parts of the neural pathway between the stump and the cortex. Unfortunately, none of these surgical interventions provided patients with relief from the pain or eliminated the phantom limb (see Melzack, 1992). Still, the idea that phantom limbs and phantom limb pain result from irritation of nerves in the stump persisted. There seemed to be no other possibility.

This chapter ends with the stories of two patients suffering from phantom limb pain and their exceptional doctor. The patients were Tom and Philip, and their physician was the neuropsychologist V. S. Ramachandran. In the process of treating Tom and Philip, Dr.

Ramachandran solved a long-standing neuropsychological puzzle and developed a new treatment to boot.

The Cases of Tom and Philip: Phantom Limbs and Ramachandran

Dr. Ramachandran read an article about a study you have already encountered in this chapter, the study by Pons and colleagues (1991). In this study, severing the sensory neurons in the arms of monkeys led to a reorganization of somatosensory cortex: The area of the somatosensory cortex that originally received input from the damaged arm now received input from areas of the body normally mapped onto adjacent areas of somatosensory cortex. Ramachandran was struck by a sudden insight: Perhaps phantom limbs were not in the stump at all, but in the brain; perhaps the perception of a phantom arm originated from parts of the body that now innervated the original arm area of the somatosensory cortex (see Ramachandran & Blakeslee, 1998).

Excited by his hypothesis, Dr. Ramachandran asked one of his patients, Tom, if he would participate in a simple test. He touched various parts of Tom's body and asked Tom what he felt. Remarkably, when he touched the side of Tom's face on the same side as his amputated arm, Tom felt sensations from various parts of his phantom hand as well as his face. Indeed, when some warm water was dropped on his face, he felt it running down his phantom hand. A second map of his hand was found on his shoulder (see Figure 10.21).

Philip, another patient of Dr. Ramachandran, suffered from severe chronic pain in his phantom arm. For a decade, Philip had been unable to move the joints of the phantom arm: It was frozen in an awkward position (Ramachandran & Rogers-Ramachandran, 2000), and Philip suffered great pain in all of its joints, particularly the elbow.

Dr. Ramachandran applied a bit of biopsychological ingenuity to the problem. Could he relieve Philip's pain by teaching him to move his phantom arm? Knowing how important feedback is in movement (see Chapter 8), Dr. Ramachandran constructed a special feedback apparatus for Philip. This was a box divided in two by a vertical mirror. Philip was instructed to put his good right hand into the box through a hole in the front and view it through a hole in the top. When he looked at his hand, he could see it and its mirror image. He was instructed to put his phantom limb in the box and try to position it, as best he could, so that it corresponded to the mirror image of his good hand. Then, he was instructed to make synchronous, bilaterally symmetrical movements of his

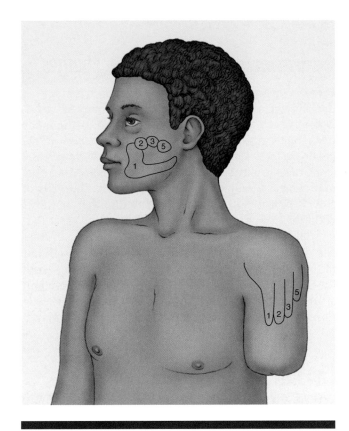

FIGURE 10.21 The places on Tom's body where touches elicited sensations in his phantom hand. (Adapted from Ramachandran & Blakeslee, 1998.)

arms—his actual right arm and his phantom left arm—while viewing his good arm and its mirror image.

> "Oh my God! Oh my God, doctor! This is unbelievable. It's mind-boggling." He was jumping up and down like a kid. "My left arm is plugged in again. It's as if I'm in the past. . . . I can move my arm again. I can feel my elbow moving, my wrist moving. It's all moving again. (pp. 47–48. Ramachandran & Blakeslee, 1998)

But when Philip shut his eyes or removed his arms from the apparatus, his phantom limb was frozen once again . . . and the pain was as bad as ever. So, Ramachandran sent Philip home with the box and instructions to use it. Three weeks later, Philip phoned.

> "Doctor," he exclaimed, "it's gone!"
> "What's gone?" (I thought maybe he had lost the mirror box.)
> "My phantom is gone."
> "What are you talking about?"
> "You know, my phantom arm, which I had for 10 years. It doesn't exist anymore. All I have is my phantom fingers and palm dangling from my shoulder."
> . . . "Philip—does this bother you?"
> "No, no, no. . . . On the contrary. You know the excruciating pain that I always had in my elbow? . . . Well, now I don't have an elbow and I don't have that pain anymore." (p. 49, Ramachandran & Blakeslee, 1998).

Themes Revisited

Because this entire chapter dealt with clinical issues, the clinical implications icon made numerous appearances. In particular, it drew attention to the many cases that appeared in the chapter: the ironic case of Professor P.; Jerry Quarry, the punch-drunk ex-boxer; the cases of complex partial epilepsy; Walter S. Miller, the man whose wife had Huntington's disease; the cases of MPTP poisoning; and Tom and Philip, the amputees with phantom limbs.

The chapter stressed clear thinking about biopsychology in several places. Attention was drawn to thinking about the cumulative effects of concussions, about the relation between genes and Parkinson's disease, about animal models of disease, and about recovery of function. Particularly interesting were the insightful approaches that Dr. Ramachandran took in treating Tom and Philip, who suffered from phantom limb pain.

The evolutionary perspective was also highlighted at several points. You were introduced to the concept of animal models, which is based on the comparative approach, and you learned that most of the research on neural regeneration and reorganization following brain damage has been done with animal models. Finally, you learned that research into the mechanisms of neural regeneration has been stimulated by the fact that this process occurs accurately in some species.

ON THE CD

Looking for more information about the topics in this chapter? For recommended additional readings, see Hard Copy for Chapter 10.

Log On

- **http://www.braincenter.org/help4new.htm** This easy-to-read site covers various aspects of brain injury.

- **http://www.hhmi.org/senses/e/e210.htm** This is a useful set of web pages describing the remapping of primary somatosensory cortex, from the Howard Hughes Medical Institute.

- **http://news.bbc.co.uk/hi/english/health/newsid_780000/780970.stm** This BBC News site features an article on control devices for neural prostheses, plus a set of related links.

Think about It

1. An epileptic is brought to trial for assault. The lawyer argues that her client is not a criminal and that the assaults in question were psychomotor attacks. She points out that her client takes her medication faithfully, but that it does not help. The prosecution lawyer argues that the defendant has a long history of violent assault and must be locked up. What do you think the judge should do?

2. Describe a bizarre incident you have observed that you think in retrospect might have been a complex partial or petit mal seizure.

3. The more that is known about a disease, the easier it is to diagnose; and the more accurately that it can be diagnosed, the easier it is to find things out about it. Explain and discuss.

4. Total dementia often creates less suffering than partial dementia. Discuss.

5. In order to be useful, animal models do not have to have all of the features of the disorder they are modeling. Discuss.

6. Major breakthroughs in the treatment of nervous system damage are on the horizon. Discuss.

7. The first evaluation of the effectiveness of neurotransplantation in the treatment of Parkinson's disease suggested that the treatment, as currently administered, is not effective. What do you think should be the next step?

ON THE CD

Studying for an exam? Try the Practice Tests for Chapter 10.

Key Terms

Alzheimer's disease *(p. 251)*
Amyloid *(p. 253)*
Aneurysm *(p. 242)*
Anterograde degeneration
  (p. 257)
Apoptosis *(p. 247)*
Arteriosclerosis *(p. 243)*
Ataxia *(p. 251)*
Benign tumors *(p. 242)*
Cerebral hemorrhage *(p. 242)*
Cerebral ischemia *(p. 242)*
Collateral sprouting *(p. 259)*
Complex partial seizures
  (p. 249)
Concussion *(p. 244)*
Congenital *(p. 242)*
Contrecoup injuries *(p. 244)*
Contusions *(p. 244)*
Convulsions *(p. 248)*
Dementia *(p. 244)*
Deprenyl *(p. 256)*
Distal segment *(p. 257)*

Down syndrome *(p. 247)*
Embolism *(p. 243)*
Encapsulated tumors *(p. 242)*
Encephalitis *(p. 245)*
Epidemiology *(p. 251)*
Epilepsy *(p. 248)*
Epileptic auras *(p. 248)*
Epileptogenesis *(p. 255)*
Experimental autoimmune
  encephalomyelitis *(p. 251)*
General paresis *(p. 246)*
Generalized seizures *(p. 249)*
Glutamate *(p. 243)*
Grand mal seizure *(p. 249)*
Hematoma *(p. 244)*
Huntington's disease *(p. 250)*
Hypoxia *(p. 249)*
Infiltrating tumors *(p. 242)*
Kindling phenomenon *(p. 255)*
L-Dopa *(p. 250)*
MPTP *(p. 256)*
Malignant tumors *(p. 242)*

Meningiomas *(p. 242)*
Meningitis *(p. 245)*
Metastatic tumors *(p. 242)*
Multiple sclerosis (MS) *(p. 251)*
NMDA (N-methyl-D-
  aspartate) receptors
  (p. 243)
Neural regeneration *(p. 257)*
Nigrostriatal pathway *(p. 250)*
Oligodendroglia *(p. 258)*
Parkinson's disease *(p. 249)*
Partial seizures *(p. 248)*
Petit mal seizure *(p. 249)*
Phantom limb *(p. 264)*
Proximal segment *(p. 257)*
Punch-drunk syndrome
  (p. 244)
Retrograde degeneration
  (p. 257)
Schwann cells *(p. 258)*
Simple partial seizures *(p. 249)*
Striatum *(p. 250)*

Strokes *(p. 242)*
Substantia nigra *(p. 250)*
Tardive dyskinesia (TD)
  (p. 246)
3-per-second spike-and-wave
  discharge *(p. 249)*
Thrombosis *(p. 242)*
Toxic psychosis *(p. 246)*
Transgenic *(p. 255)*
Transneuronal degeneration
  (p. 257)
Tumor (neoplasm) *(p. 242)*

ON THE CD

Need some
help studying the
key terms for this
chapter? Check out
the electronic flash
cards for Chapter 10.

chapter 11

Learning, Memory, and Amnesia

How Your Brain Stores Information

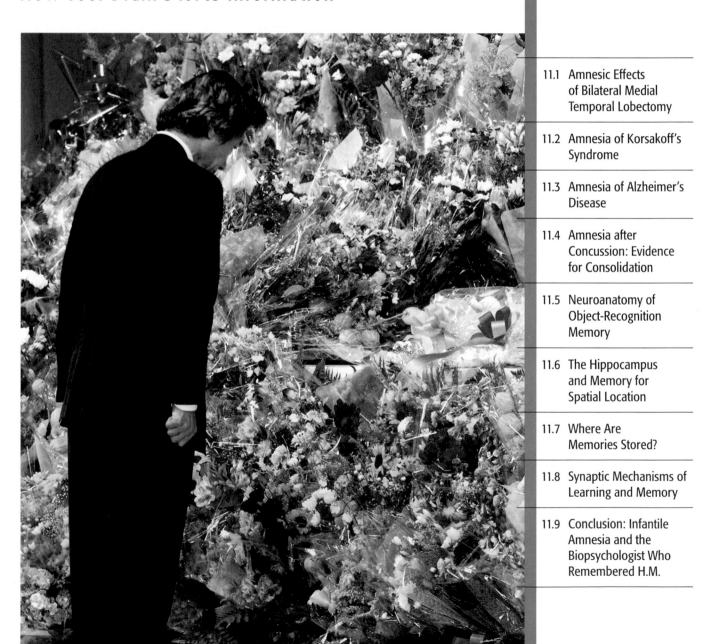

Learning and memory are two ways of thinking about the same thing: Both deal with the ability of the brain to change its functioning in response to experience. **Learning** deals with how experience changes the brain, and **memory** deals with how these changes are stored and subsequently reactivated. Without the ability to learn and remember, we would experience every moment as if waking from a lifelong sleep—each person would be a stranger, each act a new challenge, and each word incomprehensible.

The chapter focuses on the roles played by various brain structures in the processes of learning and memory. Knowledge of these roles is largely based on the study of amnesic patients with brain damage and on animal models of brain-damage–produced amnesia.

11.1 Amnesic Effects of Bilateral Medial Temporal Lobectomy

Ironically, the person who has contributed more than any other to our understanding of the neuropsychology of memory is not a neuropsychologist. In fact, although he has collaborated on dozens of studies of memory, he has no formal research training and not a single degree to his name. He is H.M., a man who in 1953, at the age of 27, had the medial portions of his temporal lobes removed for the treatment of a severe case of epilepsy. Just as the Rosetta Stone provided archaeologists with important clues to the meaning of Egyptian hieroglyphics, H.M.'s memory deficits have been instrumental in the achievement of our current understanding of the neural bases of memory.

The Case of H.M., the Man Who Changed the Study of Memory

During the 11 years preceding his surgery, H.M. suffered an average of one generalized convulsion each week and many partial convulsions each day, despite massive doses of anticonvulsant medication. Electroencephalography suggested that H.M.'s convulsions arose from foci in the medial portions of both his left and right temporal lobes. Because the removal of one medial temporal lobe had proved to be an effective treatment for patients with a unilateral temporal lobe focus, the decision was made to perform a **bilateral medial temporal lobectomy**—the removal of the medial portions of both temporal lobes, including most of the **hippocampus, amygdala,** and adjacent cortex (see Figure 11.1). (A **lobectomy** is an operation in which a lobe, or a major part of one, is removed from the brain; a **lobotomy** is an operation in which a lobe, or a major part of one, is separated from the rest of the brain by a large cut but is not removed.)

In several respects, H.M.'s bilateral medial temporal lobectomy was an unqualified success. His generalized convulsions were all but eliminated, and the incidence of his minor seizures was reduced to one or two per day, even though the level of his anticonvulsant medication was substantially reduced. Furthermore, H.M. entered surgery a reasonably well-adjusted individual with normal perceptual and motor abilities and superior intelligence, and he left it in the same condition. Indeed, H.M.'s IQ increased from 104 to 118 as a result of his surgery, presumably because of the decline in the incidence of his seizures. Be that as it may, H.M. was the last patient to receive a bilateral medial temporal lobectomy—because of its devastating amnesic effects.

In assessing the amnesic effects of brain surgery, it is usual to administer tests of the patient's ability to

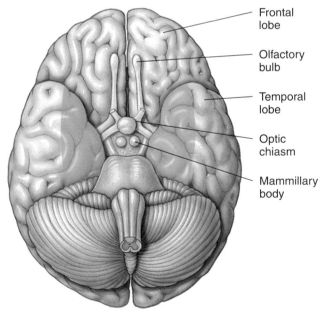

Frontal lobe

Olfactory bulb

Temporal lobe

Optic chiasm

Mammillary body

■ Tissue typically excised in medial-temporal lobectomy

FIGURE 11.1 Medial temporal lobectomy. The portions of the medial temporal lobes that were removed from H.M.'s brain are illustrated in a view of the inferior surface of the brain.

remember things learned before the surgery and tests of the patient's ability to remember things learned after the surgery. Deficits on the former tests lead to a diagnosis of **retrograde** (backward-acting) **amnesia;** those on the latter tests lead to a diagnosis of **antero-grade** (forward-acting) **amnesia.**

Like his intellectual abilities, H.M.'s memory for events predating his surgery remains largely intact. Although he has a mild retrograde amnesia for those events that occurred in the 2 years before his surgery, his memory for more remote events (e.g., for the events of his childhood) is reasonably normal.

In contrast, H.M. suffers from a severe antero-grade amnesia. His ability to hold information in short-term storage is well within the normal range—he has a **digit span** of six digits (Wickelgren, 1968); however, he has great difficulty forming new long-term memories. Once he stops thinking about a new experience, it is usually lost forever. In effect, H.M. became suspended in time on that day in 1953 when he regained his health but lost his future:

> As far as we can tell, this man has retained little if anything of events subsequent to the operation. . . . Ten months before I examined him, his family had moved from their old house to a new one a few blocks away on the same street. He still had not learned the new address (though remembering the old one perfectly), nor could he be trusted to find his way home alone. He did not know where objects in constant use were kept, and his mother stated that he would read the same magazines over and over again without finding their contents familiar. . . . [F]orgetting occurred the instant the patient's focus of attention shifted. (Milner, 1965, pp. 104–105)

> During three of the nights at the Clinical Research Center, the patient rang for the night nurse, asking her, with many apologies, if she would tell him where he was and how he came to be there. He clearly realized that he was in a hospital but seemed unable to reconstruct any of the events of the previous day. On another occasion he remarked "Every day is alone in itself, whatever enjoyment I've had, and whatever sorrow I've had." Our own impression is that . . . events fade for him long before the day is over. He often volunteers stereotyped descriptions of his own state, by saying that it is "like waking from a dream." His experience seems to be that of a person who is just becoming aware of his surroundings without fully comprehending the situation, because he does not remember what went before.

> He still fails to recognize people who are close neighbours or family friends but who got to know him only after the operation. When questioned, he tries to use accent as a clue to a person's place of origin and weather as a clue to the time of year. Although he gives his date of birth un-hesitatingly and accurately, he always underestimates his own age and can only make wild guesses as to the date. (Milner, Corkin, & Teuber, 1968, pp. 216–217)

H.M. has lived in a nursing home for many years. He spends much of each day doing crossword puzzles; his progress on a crossword puzzle is never lost because it is written down.

■ Formal Assessment of H.M.'s Anterograde Amnesia

This subsection describes H.M.'s performance on several objective tests of memory.

DIGIT SPAN + 1 TEST ■ H.M.'s inability to form long-term memories is illustrated by his performance on the *digit span + 1 test.* H.M. was asked to repeat 5 digits that were read to him at 1-second intervals. He repeated the sequence correctly. On the next trial, the same 5 digits were presented in the same sequence with 1 new digit added to the end. This same 6-digit sequence was presented a few times until he got it right, and then another digit was added to the end of it, and so on. After 25 trials, H.M. had not managed to repeat the 8-digit sequence. Normal subjects can repeat about 15 digits after 25 digit span + 1 trials (Drachman & Arbit, 1966).

BLOCK-TAPPING MEMORY-SPAN TEST ■ Milner (1971) demonstrated that H.M.'s amnesia was not restricted to verbal material by assessing his performance on the + 1 version of the *block-tapping memory span test.* An array of 9 blocks was spread out on a board in front of H.M., and he was asked to watch the neuropsychologist touch a sequence of them and then to repeat the same sequence of touches. H.M. had a *block-tapping span* of 5 blocks, which is in the normal range; but he could not learn to correctly touch a sequence of 6 blocks, even when the same sequence was repeated 12 times. H.M. has **global amnesia**—amnesia for information presented in all sensory modalities.

MIRROR-DRAWING TEST ■ The first indication that H.M.'s anterograde amnesia does not involve all long-term memories came from the results of a *mirror-drawing test* (Milner, 1965). H.M.'s task was to draw a line within the boundaries of a star-shaped target by watching his hand in a mirror. H.M. was asked to trace the star 10 times on each of 3 consecutive days, and the number of times he went outside the boundaries on each trial was recorded. As Figure 11.2 shows, H.M.'s performance improved over the 3 days, which indicates retention of the task. However, despite his improved performance, H.M. could not recall ever having seen the task before.

ROTARY-PURSUIT TEST ■ In the *rotary-pursuit test* (see Figure 11.3 on page 272), the subject tries to keep the tip of a stylus in contact with a target that rotates on a revolving turntable. Corkin (1968) found that H.M.'s performance on the rotary-pursuit test improved significantly over 9 daily practice sessions, despite the fact that H.M. claimed each day that he had never seen the pursuit rotor before. His improved performance was retained over a 7-day retention interval.

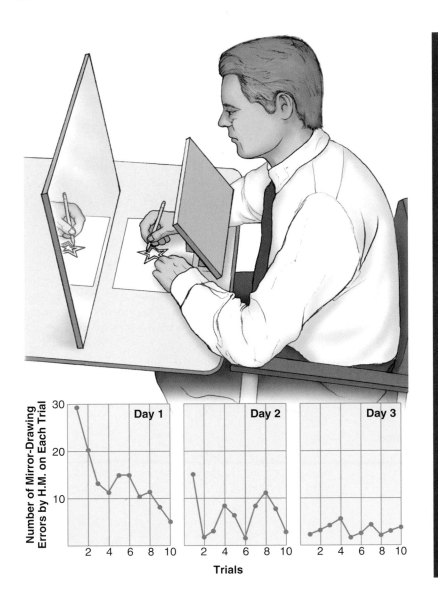

FIGURE 11.2 The learning and retention of the mirror-drawing task by H.M. Despite his good retention of the task, H.M. had no conscious recollection of having performed it before. (Adapted from Milner, 1965.)

INCOMPLETE-PICTURES TEST ■ The discovery that H.M. is capable of forming long-term memories for mirror drawing and rotary pursuit suggested that sensorimotor tasks were the one exception to his inability to form long-term memories. However, this view was challenged by the demonstration that H.M. could also form new long-term memories for the **incomplete-pictures test** (Gollin, 1960)—a nonsensorimotor test of memory that employs five sets of fragmented drawings. Each set contains drawings of the same 20 objects, but they differ in their degree of sketchiness: Set 1 contains the most fragmented drawings, and set 5 contains the complete drawings. The subject is asked to identify the 20 objects from the sketchiest set (set 1); then, those objects that go unrecognized are presented in their set 2 versions, and so on, until all 20 items have been identified. Figure 11.4 on page 273 illustrates the performance of H.M. on this test and his improved performance 1 hour later (Milner, Corkin, & Teuber, 1968). Despite his improved performance, H.M. could not recall previously performing the task.

PAVLOVIAN CONDITIONING ■ H.M. learned an eyeblink Pavlovian conditioning task, albeit at a retarded rate (Woodruff-Pak, 1993). A tone was sounded just before a puff of air was administered to his eye, until the tone alone elicited an eyeblink. Two years later, H.M. retained this conditioned response almost perfectly, although he had no conscious recollection of the training.

■ Scientific Contributions of H.M.'s Case

H.M.'s case is a story of personal tragedy, but his contributions to the study of the neural basis of memory have been immense. By showing that the medial temporal lobes play an especially important role in memory, H.M.'s case challenged the then prevalent view that memory functions are diffusely and equivalently distributed throughout the brain. In so doing, H.M.'s case renewed efforts to relate individual brain structures to specific mnemonic processes. Particularly, H.M.'s case spawned a massive research effort aimed at clarifying the

FIGURE 11.3   The rotary-pursuit task. The subject tries to keep the stylus in contact with the rotating target, and time-on-target is automatically recorded. H.M. learned and retained this task, although he had no conscious recollection of the learning trials.

mnemonic (memory-related) functions of the hippocampus and other medial temporal lobe structures.

The discovery that bilateral medial temporal lobectomy abolished H.M.'s ability to form certain kinds of long-term memories without disrupting his performance on tests of short-term memory supported the theory that there are different modes of storage for short-term and long-term memory. H.M.'s specific problem appears to be a difficulty in **memory consolidation** (the transfer of short-term memories to long-term storage).

Finally, H.M.'s case was the first to reveal that an amnesic patient might claim no recollection of a previous experience, while demonstrating memory for it by improved performance. Conscious memories are called **explicit memories,** whereas memories that are expressed by improved test performance without conscious awareness are called **implicit memories.**

Medial Temporal Lobe Amnesia

Neuropsychological patients with a profile of mnemonic deficits similar to those of H.M., with pre-

served intellectual functioning, and with evidence of medial temporal lobe damage are said to suffer from **medial temporal lobe amnesia.**

Research on medial temporal lobe amnesia has shown that H.M.'s difficulty in forming explicit long-term memories while retaining the ability to form implicit long-term memories of the same experiences is not unique to him (see Eichenbaum, 1999). This problem has proved to be a symptom of medial temporal lobe amnesia, as well as many other amnesic disorders. As a result, the assessment of implicit long-term memories has played an important role in the study of human amnesia.

Tests that have been developed to assess implicit memory are called **repetition priming tests.** The incomplete-pictures test is an example, but repetition priming tests that involve memory for words are more common. First, the subjects are asked to examine a list of words; they are not asked to learn or remember anything. Later, they are shown a series of word fragments (e.g., _ O B S _ _ E R) of words from the original list, and they are simply asked to complete them. Control subjects who have seen the original words perform well. Surprisingly, amnesic subjects often perform equally well, even though they have no explicit memory of seeing the original list.

Most medial temporal lobe amnesics have difficulty forming explicit long-term memories, but, unlike H.M., they do not completely lose this ability. Consequently, medial temporal lobe amnesics have been studied to determine whether particular kinds of explicit long-term memories are more susceptible to disruption by medial temporal lobe damage. Indeed, research on medial temporal lobe amnesics has shown that not all of their explicit long-term memories are equally effected. The semantic memories of medial temporal lobe amnesics are often quite normal, but their episodic memories are largely absent (see Eichenbaum, 1997). **Semantic memories** are explicit memories for general facts or information, whereas **episodic memories** are explicit memories for the particular events or experiences of one's life. For example, Vargha-Khadem and colleagues (1997) identified three individuals who had experienced bilateral medial temporal lobe damage early in life and then assessed the memory problems experienced by these amnesics as they developed. Remarkably, despite the fact that they remembered few of the experiences that they had during their daily lives (episodic memory), they progressed through mainstream schools and acquired reasonable levels of language ability and factual knowledge (semantic memory).

The symptoms of medial temporal lobe amnesia raise an important question: Why do we have two parallel memory systems, one conscious (explicit) and one unconscious (implicit)? Presumably, the implicit system was the first to

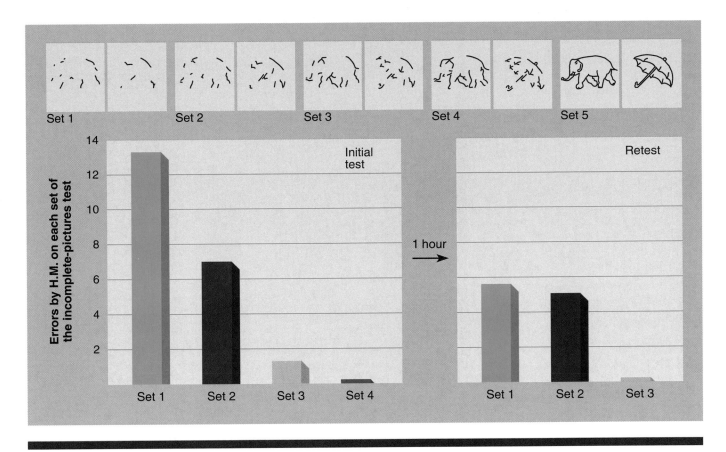

FIGURE 11.4 Two items from the incomplete-pictures test. H.M.'s memory for the 20 items on the test was indicated by his ability to recognize the more fragmented versions of them when he was retested. Nevertheless, he had no conscious awareness of having previously seen the items.

evolve, so the question is actually this: What advantage is there in having a second, conscious system?

Two experiments, one in amnesic patients (Reber, Knowlton, & Squire, 1996) and one in amnesic monkeys with medial temporal lobe lesions (Buckley & Gaffan, 1998), suggest that the answer is "flexibility." In both experiments, the amnesic subjects learned an implicit learning task as well as control subjects did; however, if they were asked to use their implicit knowledge in a different way or in a different context, they failed miserably. Presumably, the evolution of explicit memory systems provided for the flexible use of information.

◼ | Effects of Cerebral Ischemia on the Hippocampus and Memory

Patients who have experienced **cerebral ischemia**—that is, have experienced an interruption of blood supply to their brains—often suffer from medial temporal lobe amnesia. R.B. is one such individual (Zola-Morgan, Squire, & Amaral, 1986).

The Case of R.B., the Product of a Bungled Operation

At the age of 52, R.B. underwent cardiac bypass surgery. The surgery was bungled, and, as a consequence, R.B. suffered brain damage. The pump that was circulating R.B.'s blood to his body while his heart was disconnected broke down, and it was several minutes before a replacement arrived from another part of the hospital. R.B. lived, but the resulting ischemic brain damage left him amnesic.

Although R.B.'s amnesia was not as severe as H.M.'s, it was comparable in many aspects. R.B. died in 1983 of a heart attack, and a detailed postmortem examination of his brain was carried out with the permission of his family. Obvious brain damage was restricted largely to the **pyramidal cell layer** of just one part of the hippocampus—the **CA1 subfield** (see Figure 11.5 on page 274).

R.B.'s case suggested that hippocampal damage by itself can produce amnesia; however, this conclusion has been challenged—as you will learn later in this chapter.

FIGURE 11.5   The major components of the hippocampus: CA1, CA2, CA3, and CA4 subfields and the dentate gyrus. R.B.'s brain damage appeared to be restricted largely to the pyramidal cell layer of the CA1 subfield. (CA stands for *cornu ammonis,* another name for hippocampus.)

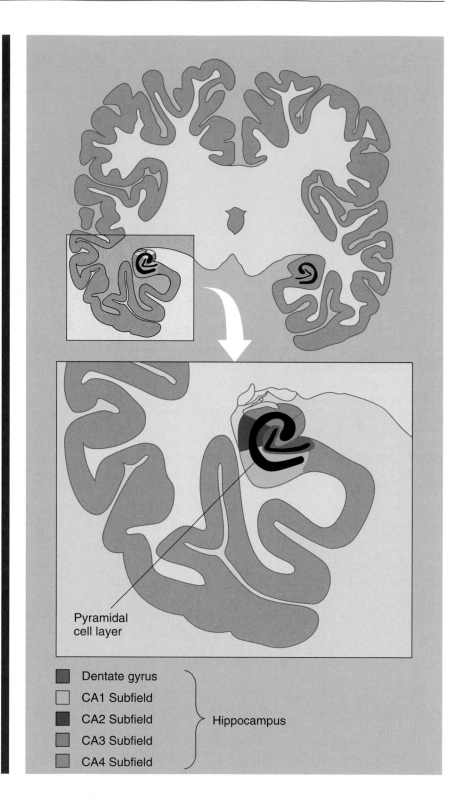

Pyramidal cell layer

⬛ Dentate gyrus	
⬜ CA1 Subfield	
⬛ CA2 Subfield	⎫
⬛ CA3 Subfield	⎬ Hippocampus
⬛ CA4 Subfield	⎭

11.2   Amnesia of Korsakoff's Syndrome

As you learned in Chapter 1, **Korsakoff's syndrome** is a disorder of memory that is common in people who have consumed large amounts of alcohol. In its advanced

stages, it is characterized by a variety of sensory and motor problems, extreme confusion, personality changes, and a risk of death from liver, gastrointestinal, or heart disorders. Postmortem examination typically reveals lesions to the *medial diencephalon* (the medial thalamus and the medial hypothalamus) and diffuse damage to several other brain structures, most notably the neocortex and cerebellum.

The amnesia of Korsakoff's syndrome is similar to medial temporal lobe amnesia in some respects. For example, during the early stages of the disorder, anterograde amnesia for explicit episodic memories is the most prominent symptom. However, as the disorder progresses, severe retrograde amnesia, which can extend back into childhood, also develops.

The gradual, insidious onset and progressive development of Korsakoff's syndrome complicate the study of the resulting retrograde amnesia. It is never entirely clear to what extent Korsakoff amnesia for recent events reflects the retrograde disruption of existing memories or the gradually increasing anterograde blockage of the formation of new ones.

Because the brain damage associated with Korsakoff's syndrome is diffuse, it has not been easy to identify the portion of it that is specifically responsible for the amnesia. The first hypothesis, which was based on several small postmortem studies, was that damage to the *mammillary bodies* of the hypothalamus was responsible for the memory deficits of Korsakoff patients; however, subsequent studies revealed cases of Korsakoff's amnesia with no mammillary body damage. But in all of these exceptional cases, there was damage to another pair of medial diencephalic nuclei: the **mediodorsal nuclei** of the thalamus. The occurrence of **medial diencephalic amnesia** (amnesia, such as Korsakoff's amnesia and similar memory disorders, associated with damage to the medial diencephalon) in stroke patients with small ischemic lesions to the mediodorsal nuclei provides additional evidence of the importance of these structures to mnemonic function (e.g., Graff-Radford et al., 1985; Winocur et al., 1984). However, it is unlikely that the memory deficits of Korsakoff's patients are attributable to the damage of any single diencephalic structure (see Paller et al., 1997).

The Up-Your-Nose Case of N.A.

After a year of junior college, N.A. joined the U.S. Air Force; he served as a radar technician until his accident in December of 1960. On that fateful day, N.A.

> was assembling a model airplane in his barracks room. His roommate had removed a miniature fencing foil from the wall and was making thrusts behind N.A.'s chair. N.A. turned suddenly and was stabbed through the right nostril. The foil penetrated the cribriform plate [the thin bone around the base of the frontal lobes], taking an upward course to the left into the forebrain. (Squire, 1987, p. 177)

> The examiners . . . noted that at first he seemed to be unable to recall any significant personal, national or international events for the two years preceding the accident, but this extensive retrograde amnesia appeared to shrink. . . . Two-and-a-half years after the accident, the retrograde amnesia was said to involve a span of perhaps two weeks immediately preceding the injury, but the exact extent of this retrograde loss was (and remains) impossible to determine. . . .

> During . . . convalescence (for the first six to eight months after the accident), the patient's recall of day-to-day events was described as extremely poor, but "occasionally some items sprang forth uncontrollably; he suddenly recalled something he seemed to have no business recalling." His physicians thus gained the impression that his memory was patchy; he appeared to have difficulty in calling up at will many things that at other times emerged spontaneously. . . .

> Since his injury, he has been unable to return to any gainful employment, although his memory has continued to improve, albeit slowly. (Teuber, Milner, & Vaughan, 1968, pp. 268–269)

An MRI of N.A.'s brain was taken in the late 1980s (Squire et al., 1989). It revealed extensive medial diencephalic damage, including damage to the mediodorsal nuclei and mammillary bodies.

11.3 Amnesia of Alzheimer's Disease

Alzheimer's disease is another major cause of amnesia. The first sign of Alzheimer's disease is often a mild deterioration of memory. However, the disorder is progressive: Eventually, *dementia* develops and becomes so severe that the patient is incapable of even simple activities (e.g., eating, speaking, recognizing a spouse, or bladder control). Alzheimer's disease is terminal.

Efforts to understand the neural basis of Alzheimer's amnesia have focused on *predementia Alzheimer's patients* (Alzheimer's patients who have yet to develop dementia). The memory deficits of these patients are more general than those associated with medial temporal lobe damage, medial diencephalic damage, or Korsakoff's syndrome (see Butters & Delis, 1995). In addition to major anterograde and retrograde deficits in tests of explicit memory, predementia Alzheimer's patients often display deficits in short-term memory and in some types of implicit memory: Implicit memory for verbal and perceptual material is often deficient, whereas implicit memory for sensorimotor learning is not (see Gabrieli et al., 1993; Postle, Corkin, & Growdon, 1996).

The level of acetylcholine is greatly reduced in the brains of Alzheimer's patients. This reduction results from the degeneration of the **basal forebrain** (a midline area located just above the hypothalamus; see Figure 11.16 on page 288), which is the brain's main source of acetylcholine. This finding, coupled with the finding that

strokes in the basal forebrain area can cause amnesia (Morris et al., 1992), led to the view that acetylcholine depletion is the cause of Alzheimer's amnesia. However, although acetylcholine depletion resulting from damage to the basal forebrain may contribute to Alzheimer's amnesia, it is unlikely to be the only factor. The brain damage associated with Alzheimer's disease is extremely diffuse (see Figure 10.13) and involves areas such as the medial temporal lobe and prefrontal cortex, which play major roles in memory. Furthermore, damage to some structures of the basal forebrain produces attentional deficits, which can easily be mistaken for memory problems (see Baxter & Chiba, 1999; Everitt & Robbins, 1997).

11.4 Amnesia after Concussion: Evidence for Consolidation

Blows to the head that do not penetrate the skull but are severe enough to produce *concussion* (a temporary disturbance of consciousness produced by a nonpenetrating head injury) are the most common causes of amnesia (see Levin, 1989). Amnesia following a nonpenetrating blow to the head is called **posttraumatic amnesia (PTA).**

Posttraumatic Amnesia

The *coma* (pathological state of unconsciousness) following a severe blow to the head usually lasts a few seconds or minutes, but in severe cases it can last weeks. Then, once the patient regains consciousness, there is a period of confusion. Victims of concussion are typically not tested by a neuropsychologist until after the period of confusion—if they are tested at all. Testing usually reveals that the patient has a permanent retrograde amnesia for the events that led up to the blow and a permanent anterograde amnesia for many of the events that occurred during the subsequent period of confusion.

The anterograde memory deficits that follow a nonpenetrating head injury are often quite puzzling to the friends and relatives who have talked to the patient during the period of confusion—for example, during a hospital visit. The patient may seem reasonably lucid at the time, because short-term memory is normal, but later may have no recollection whatsoever of the conversation.

Figure 11.6 summarizes the effects of a closed-head injury on memory. Note that the duration of the period of confusion and anterograde amnesia is typically longer than that of the coma, which is typically longer than the period of retrograde amnesia. More severe blows to the head tend to produce longer comas, longer periods of

confusion, and longer periods of amnesia (Levin, Papanicolaou, & Eisenberg, 1984). Not illustrated in Figure 11.6 are *islands of memory*—memories that sometimes survive for isolated events that occurred during periods that have otherwise been wiped out.

Gradients of Retrograde Amnesia and Memory Consolidation

Gradients of retrograde amnesia after concussion seem to provide evidence for memory consolidation. The fact that concussions preferentially disrupt recent memories suggests that the storage of older memories has been strengthened (i.e., consolidated).

The most prominent theory of memory consolidation is Hebb's theory. He argued that memories of experiences are stored in the short term by neural activity *reverberating* (circulating) in closed circuits. These reverberating patterns of neural activity are susceptible to disruption—for example, by a blow to the head—but eventually they induce structural changes in the involved synapses, which provide stable long-term storage.

Electroconvulsive shock seemed to provide a controlled method of studying memory consolidation. **Electroconvulsive shock (ECS)** is an intense, brief, diffuse, seizure-inducing current that is administered to the brain through large electrodes attached to the scalp. The rationale was that by disrupting neural activity, ECS would erase from storage only those memories that had not been converted to structural synaptic changes; the length of the period of retrograde amnesia produced by an ECS would thus provide an estimate of the amount of time needed for memory consolidation.

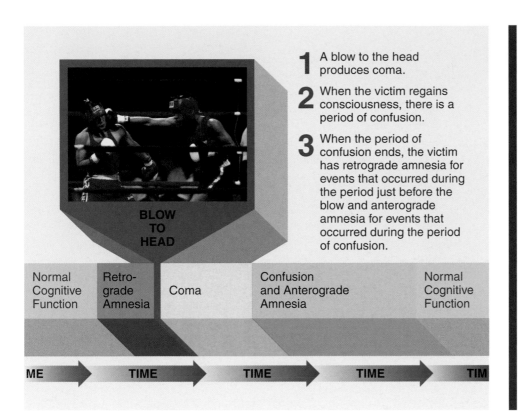

1 A blow to the head produces coma.

2 When the victim regains consciousness, there is a period of confusion.

3 When the period of confusion ends, the victim has retrograde amnesia for events that occurred during the period just before the blow and anterograde amnesia for events that occurred during the period of confusion.

BLOW TO HEAD

| Normal Cognitive Function | Retro-grade Amnesia | Coma | Confusion and Anterograde Amnesia | Normal Cognitive Function |

ME   TIME   TIME   TIME   TIM

FIGURE 11.6 The retrograde amnesia and anterograde amnesia that are associated with a concussion-producing blow to the head.

Many studies have employed ECS to study consolidation. Some studies have been conducted on human patients, who receive ECS for the treatment of depression. However, the most well-controlled studies have been conducted with laboratory animals.

In one such study, thirsty rats were placed for 10 minutes on each of 5 consecutive days in a test box that contained a small niche. By the 5th of these habituation sessions, most rats explored the niche only 1 or 2 times per session. On the 6th day, a water spout was placed in the niche, and each rat was allowed to drink for 15 seconds after it discovered the spout. This was the learning trial. Then, 10 seconds, 1 minute, 10 minutes, 1 hour, or 3 hours later, each experimental rat received a single ECS. The next day, the retention of all subjects was assessed on the basis of how many times each explored the niche when the water spout was not present. The control rats that experienced the learning trial but received no ECS explored the empty niche an average of 10 times during the 10-minute test session, thereby indicating that they remembered their discovery of water the previous day. The rats that had received ECS 1 hour or 3 hours after the learning trial also explored the niche about 10 times. In contrast, the rats that received the ECS 10 seconds, 1 minute, or 10 minutes after the learning trial explored the empty niche significantly less on the test day. This result suggested that the consolidation of the memory of the learning trial took between 10 minutes and 1 hour (see Figure 11.7 on page 278).

Numerous variations of this experiment were conducted in the 1950s and 1960s, with different learning tasks, different species, and different numbers and intensities of electroconvulsive shocks. Initially, there was some consistency in the findings: Most seemed to suggest a rather brief consolidation time of a few minutes or less (e.g., Chorover & Schiller, 1965). But some researchers observed very long gradients of ECS-produced retrograde amnesia. For example, Squire, Slater, and Chace (1975) measured the memory of a group of ECS-treated patients for television shows that had played for only one season in different years prior to their electroconvulsive therapy. They tested each subject twice on different forms of the test: once before they received a series of five electroconvulsive shocks and once after. The difference between the before-and-after scores served as an estimate of memory loss for the events of each year. Figure 11.8 on page 278 illustrates that five electroconvulsive shocks disrupted the retention of television shows that had played in the 3 years prior to treatment but not those that had played earlier.

Long gradients of retrograde amnesia are incompatible with Hebb's theory of consolidation. It is reasonable to think of the neural activity resulting from an experience reverberating through the brain for a few seconds or even a few minutes; but gradients of retrograde amnesia covering days, weeks, or years cannot be easily accounted for by the disruption of reverberatory neural activity (e.g., Squire & Spanis, 1984). Long gradients of retrograde amnesia indicate that memory consolidation can continue for a very long time after learning, perhaps indefinitely.

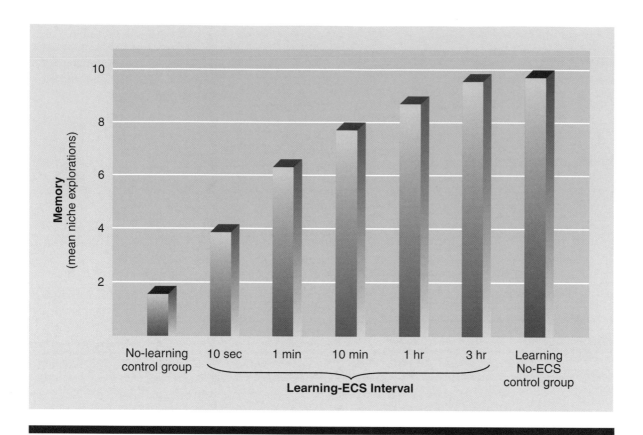

FIGURE 11.7   Retention of one-trial appetitive learning by a control group of rats and by groups of rats that received ECS at various intervals after the learning trial. Only the rats that received ECS within 10 minutes of the learning trial displayed significant retrograde amnesia for it. (Adapted from Pinel, 1969.)

FIGURE 11.8   A demonstration of ECS-produced amnesia. A series of five electroconvulsive shocks produced retrograde amnesia for television shows that played for only one season in the 3 years before the shocks; however, the shocks did not produce amnesia for one-season shows that had played prior to that. (Adapted from Squire, Slater & Chace, 1975.)

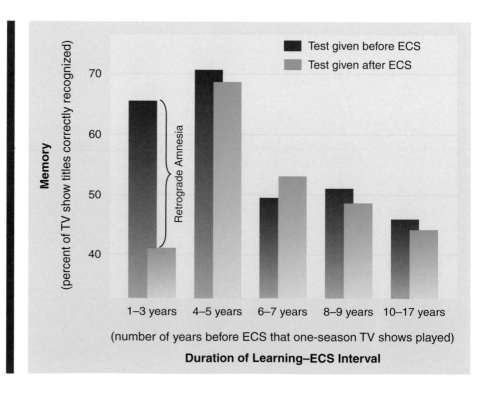

The Hippocampus and Consolidation

The discovery that H.M. was suffering from a temporally graded retrograde amnesia led Scoville and Milner (1957) to conclude that the hippocampus and related structures play a role in consolidation. To account for the fact that the bilateral medial temporal lobectomy disrupted only those retrograde memories acquired in the period just before H.M.'s surgery, they suggested that memories are temporarily stored in the hippocampus until they can be transferred to a more stable cortical storage system—a widely held theory that has changed little over the years (see Squire & Alvarez, 1995).

Nadel and Moscovitch (1997) have suggested an alternative theory of consolidation that is more consistent with the finding that gradients of retrograde amnesia are often very long. Nadel and Moscovitch proposed that the hippocampus and other structures involved in memory storage store memories for as long as they exist—not just during the period immediately after learning. When a conscious experience occurs, it is rapidly and sparsely encoded in a distributed fashion throughout the hippocampus and other involved structures (Moser & Moser, 1998). According to Nadel and Moscovitch, retained memories become progressively more resistant to disruption by hippocampal damage because each time a similar experience occurs or the original memory is recalled, a new **engram** (a change in the brain that stores a memory) is established and linked to the original engram, making the memory easier to recall and the original engram more difficult to disrupt.

 # BrainScan

This chapter is about to move from discussion of human memory disorders to consideration of animal models of human memory disorders. Are you ready? Scan your brain to assess your knowledge of human memory disorders by filling in the blanks in the following sentences. The correct answers are provided at the bottom of this page. Before proceeding, review the material related to your errors and omissions.

1. H.M. had his _____ temporal lobes removed.

2. The mirror-drawing test, the rotary pursuit test, the incomplete-pictures test, and the repetition priming test are all test of _____ memory.

3. H.M. appears incapable of forming new _____ long-term memories.

4. Support for the view that hippocampal damage can by itself cause amnesia comes from the study or R.B., who suffered _____ damage to the pyramidal cells of his CA1 hippocampal subfield.

5. The current view is that damage to the _____ diencephalon is responsible for most of the memory deficits of people with Korsakoff's disease.

6. The gradual onset of Korsakoff's syndrome complicates the study of the resulting _____ amnesia.

7. The _____ nuclei are the medial diencephalic nuclei that have been most frequently implicated in memory.

8. Alzheimer's disease is associated with degeneration of _____ neurons in the basal forebrain.

9. Posttraumatic amnesia can be induced with _____ shock, which is used in the treatment of depression.

10. The transfer of a memory from short-term storage to long-term storage is termed _____.

11. Because some gradients of retrograde amnesia are extremely long, it is unlikely that memory consolidation is mediated by _____ neural activity, as hypothesized by Hebb.

12. The changes in the brain that store memories are called _____.

Brain Scan answers: (1) medial, (2) implicit, (3) explicit, (4) ischemic, (5) medial, (6) retrograde, (7) mediodorsal, (8) cholinergic, (9) electroconvulsive, (10) consolidation, (11) reverberating, (12) engrams.

11.5 Neuroanatomy of Object-Recognition Memory

As interesting and informative as the study of amnesic patients can be, it has major limitations. Many important questions about the neural bases of amnesia can be answered only by controlled experiments. For example, in order to identify the particular structures of the brain that participate in various kinds of memory, it is necessary to make precise lesions in various structures and to control what and when the subjects learn, and how and when their retention is tested. Because such experiments are not feasible with human subjects, there has been a major effort to develop animal models of human brain-damage–produced amnesia.

The first reports of H.M.'s case in the 1950s triggered a massive effort to develop an animal model of his disorder so that it could be subjected to experimental analysis. In its early years, this effort was a dismal failure; lesions of medial temporal lobe structures did not produce severe anterograde amnesia in rats, monkeys, or other nonhuman species.

In retrospect, there were two reasons for the initial difficulty in developing an animal model of medial temporal lobe amnesia. First, it was not initially apparent that H.M.'s anterograde amnesia did not extend to all kinds of long-term memory—that is, that it was specific to explicit long-term memories; and most animal memory tests that were widely used in the 1950s and 1960s were tests of implicit memory (e.g., Pavlovian and operant conditioning). Second, it was incorrectly assumed that the amnesic effects of medial temporal lobe lesions were largely, if not entirely, attributable to hippocampal damage; and most efforts to develop animal models of medial temporal lobe amnesia thus focused on hippocampal lesions.

Monkey Model of Object-Recognition Amnesia: The Delayed Nonmatching-to-Sample Test

Finally, in the mid 1970s, over two decades after the first reports of H.M.'s remarkable case, an animal model of his disorder was developed. It was hailed as a major breakthrough because it opened up the neuroanatomy of medial temporal lobe amnesia to experimental investigation.

In separate laboratories, Gaffan (1974) and Mishkin and Delacour (1975) showed that monkeys with bilateral medial temporal lobec-

tomies have major problems forming long-term memories for objects encountered in the **delayed nonmatching-to-sample test.** In this test, a monkey is presented with a distinctive object (the *sample object*), under which it finds food (e.g., a banana pellet). Then, after a delay, the monkey is presented with two test objects: the sample object and an unfamiliar object. The monkey must remember the sample object so that it can select the unfamiliar object to obtain food concealed beneath it. The correct performance of a trial is illustrated in Figure 11.9.

Intact, well-trained monkeys performed correctly on about 90% of the delayed nonmatching-to-sample trials when the retention intervals were a few minutes or less. In contrast, monkeys with bilateral medial temporal lobe lesions had major object-recognition deficits (see Figure 11.10). These deficits modeled those of H.M. in key respects. For example, the monkeys' performance was normal at delays of a few seconds but fell off to near chance levels at delays of several minutes, and their performance was extremely susceptible to the disruptive effects of distraction (Squire & Zola-Morgan, 1985). In fact, human medial temporal lobe amnesics have been tested on the delayed nonmatching-to-sample test—their rewards were coins rather than banana pellets—and their performance mirrored the performance of monkeys with similar brain damage.

The development of the delayed nonmatching-to-sample test for monkeys provided a means of testing the assumption that the amnesia resulting from medial temporal lobe damage is entirely the consequence of hippocampal damage—Figure 11.11 on page 282 illustrates the locations in the monkey brain of the three major temporal lobe structures: hippocampus, amygdala, and adjacent **rhinal cortex.** But before we consider this important line of research, we need to look at a key methodological development—the rat version of the delayed nonmatching-to-sample test.

The Delayed Nonmatching-to-Sample Test for Rats

In order to understand why the development of the rat version of the delayed nonmatching-to-sample test played an important role in assessing the specific role of hippocampal damage in medial temporal lobe amnesia, examine Figure 11.12 on page 282, which illustrates the usual methods of making hippocampal lesions in monkeys and rats.

1 The monkey moves the sample object to obtain food from the well beneath it.

2 A screen is lowered in front of the monkey during the delay period.

3 The monkey is confronted with the sample object and an unfamiliar object.

4 The monkey must remember the sample object and then select the unfamiliar object to obtain the food beneath it.

FIGURE 11.9 The correct performance of a delayed nonmatching-to-sample trial. (Adapted from Mishkin & Appenzeller, 1987.)

FIGURE 11.10 The performance deficits of monkeys with large bilateral medial temporal lobe lesions on the delayed nonmatching-to-sample test. There were significant deficits at all but the shortest retention interval. These deficits parallel the memory deficits of human medial temporal lobe amnesics on the same task. (Adapted from Squire & Zola-Morgan, 1991.)

FIGURE 11.11 The three major structures of the medial temporal lobe, illustrated in the monkey brain: the hippocampus, the amygdala, and the rhinal cortex.

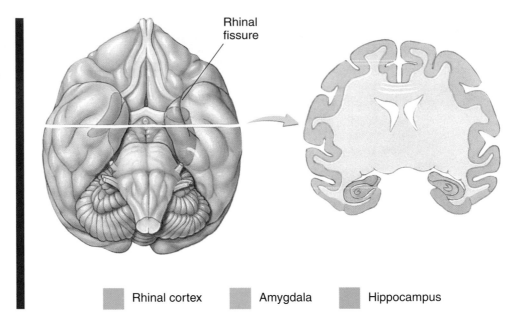

Rhinal fissure

Rhinal cortex   Amygdala   Hippocampus

FIGURE 11.12 Aspiration lesions of the hippocampus in monkeys and rats. Because of differences in the size and location of the hippocampus in monkeys and in rats, hippocampectomy typically involves the removal of large amounts of rhinal cortex in monkeys, but not in rats.

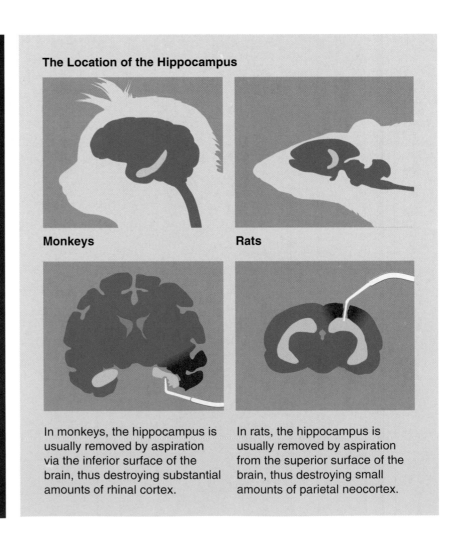

The Location of the Hippocampus

Monkeys   **Rats**

In monkeys, the hippocampus is usually removed by aspiration via the inferior surface of the brain, thus destroying substantial amounts of rhinal cortex.

In rats, the hippocampus is usually removed by aspiration from the superior surface of the brain, thus destroying small amounts of parietal neocortex.

Because of the size and location of the hippocampus, almost all studies of hippocampal lesions in monkeys have involved *aspiration* (suction) of large portions of the rhinal cortex in addition to the hippocampus. However, in rats the extraneous damage associated with aspiration lesions of the hippocampus is typically limited to a small area of parietal neocortex. Furthermore, the rat hippocampus is small enough that it can readily be lesioned electrolytically or with intracerebral neuro-toxin injections; in either case there is little extraneous damage.

The version of the delayed nonmatching-to-sample test for rats that most closely resembles that for monkeys was developed by David Mumby using an apparatus that has become known as the **Mumby box.** This rat version of the test is illustrated in Figure 11.13

It was once assumed that rats could not perform a task as complex as that required for the delayed

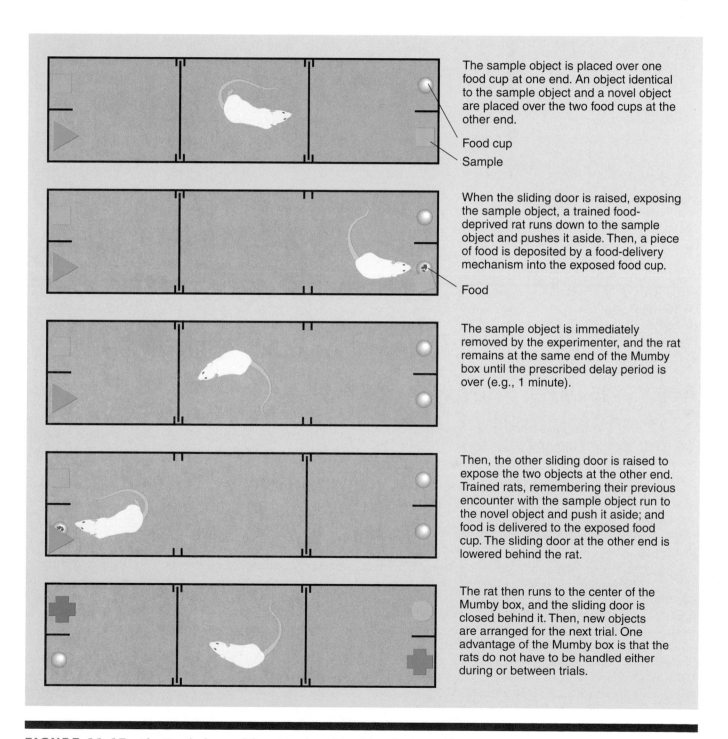

The sample object is placed over one food cup at one end. An object identical to the sample object and a novel object are placed over the two food cups at the other end.

Food cup
Sample

When the sliding door is raised, exposing the sample object, a trained food-deprived rat runs down to the sample object and pushes it aside. Then, a piece of food is deposited by a food-delivery mechanism into the exposed food cup.

Food

The sample object is immediately removed by the experimenter, and the rat remains at the same end of the Mumby box until the prescribed delay period is over (e.g., 1 minute).

Then, the other sliding door is raised to expose the two objects at the other end. Trained rats, remembering their previous encounter with the sample object run to the novel object and push it aside; and food is delivered to the exposed food cup. The sliding door at the other end is lowered behind the rat.

The rat then runs to the center of the Mumby box, and the sliding door is closed behind it. Then, new objects are arranged for the next trial. One advantage of the Mumby box is that the rats do not have to be handled either during or between trials.

FIGURE 11.13 The Mumby box and the rat version of the delayed nonmatching-to-sample test.

FIGURE 11.14 A comparison of the performance of intact monkeys (Zola-Morgan, Squire, & Mishkin, 1982) and intact rats (Mumby, Pinel, & Wood, 1989) on the delayed nonmatching-to-sample test.

nonmatching-to-sample test; Figure 11.14 indicates otherwise. Rats perform almost as well as monkeys at delays up to 1 minute (Mumby, Pinel, & Wood, 1989).

The validity of the rat version of the delayed nonmatching-to-sample test has been established by studies of the effects of medial temporal lobe lesions. Combined bilateral lesions of rats' hippocampus, amygdala, and rhinal cortex produce major retention deficits at all but the shortest retention intervals (Mumby, Wood, & Pinel, 1992).

Neuroanatomical Basis of the Object-Recognition Deficits Resulting from Medial Temporal Lobectomy

To what extent are the object-recognition deficits following bilateral medial temporal lobectomy a consequence of hippocampal damage? In the early 1990s, researchers began assessing the relative effects on performance in the delayed nonmatching-to-sample test of lesions to various medial temporal lobe structures in both monkeys and rats. Early challenges to the preeminence of the hippocampus (Meunier et al., 1990; Mumby, Wood, & Pinel, 1992; Zola-Morgan et al., 1989) attracted the interest of other researchers and yielded many relevant findings. Reviewers of this research (Brown & Aggleton, 2001; Duva, Kornecook, & Pinel, 2000; Murray, 1996) have reached similar conclusions. Bilateral surgical removal of the rhinal cortex has consistently produced severe and permanent deficits in performance on the delayed nonmatching-to-sample test and other tests of object recog-

nition. In contrast, bilateral surgical removal of the hippocampus has produced either moderate deficits or none at all, and bilateral destruction of the amygdala has had no effect. Figure 11.15 compares the effects of rhinal cortex lesions and hippocampus-plus-amygdala lesions in rats.

The recent reports that object-recognition memory is severely disrupted by rhinal cortex lesions but only moderately by hippocampal lesions have led to a resurgence of interest in the case of R.B. Earlier in this chapter, you learned that R.B. was left amnesic following an ischemic accident that occurred during heart surgery and that subsequent analysis of his brain revealed that obvious cell loss was restricted largely to the pyramidal cell layer of his CA1 hippocampal subfield (see Figure 11.5). This result has been replicated in both monkeys and rats. In both monkeys (Zola-Morgan et al., 1992) and rats (Wood et al., 1993), cerebral ischemia leads to a loss of CA1 hippocampal pyramidal cells and severe deficits in the delayed nonmatching-to-sample task.

The relation between ischemia-produced hippocampal damage and object-recognition deficits in humans, monkeys, and rats seems to provide strong support for the theory that the hippocampus plays a key role in object-recognition memory. But there is a gnawing problem with this line of evidence: How can ischemia-produced lesions to one small part of the hippocampus be associated with severe deficits in performance on the delayed nonmatching-to-sample test when the deficits associated with total removal of the hippocampus are only moderate?

Mumby and his colleagues (1996) conducted an experiment that appears to resolve this paradox. They

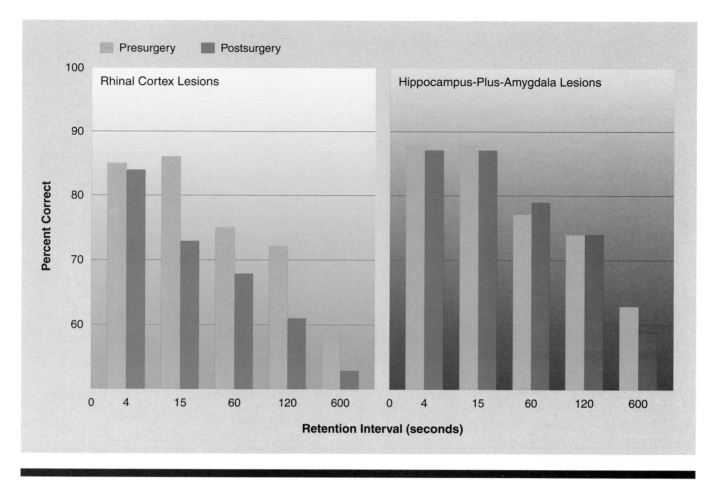

FIGURE 11.15 Effects of rhinal cortex lesions and hippocampus-plus-amygdala lesions in rats. Lesions of the rhinal cortex, but not of the hippocampus and amygdala combined, produced severe deficits in performance of the delayed nonmatching-to-sample test in rats. (Adapted from Mumby & Pinel, 1994; Mumby, Wood, & Pinel, 1992.)

hypothesized the following: (1) that the ischemia-produced hyperactivity of CA1 pyramidal cells damages neurons outside the hippocampus, possibly through the excessive release of excitatory amino acid neurotransmitters; (2) that this extrahippocampal damage is not readily detectable by conventional histological analysis (i.e., it does not involve concentrated cell loss); and (3) that this extrahippocampal damage is largely responsible for the object-recognition deficits that are produced by cerebral ischemia. Mumby and colleagues supported their hypothesis by showing that bilateral hippocampectomy actually blocks the development of ischemia-produced deficits in performance on the delayed nonmatching-to-sample test. First, they produced cerebral ischemia in rats by temporarily tying off their carotid arteries. Then, one group of the ischemic rats received a bilateral hippocampectomy 1 hour later, a second group received a bilateral hippocampectomy 1 week later, and a third group received no bilateral hippocampectomy. Following recovery, the latter two groups of is-

chemic rats displayed severe object-recognition deficits, whereas the rats whose hippocampus had been removed 1 hour after ischemia did not. Explaining how hippocampectomy can prevent the development of the object-recognition deficits normally produced by cerebral ischemia is a major problem for the theory that the hippocampus plays a critical role in object-recognition memory.

Support for the theory that the object-recognition deficits of ischemic patients result from extrahippocampal disturbances comes from functional brain-imaging studies. Widespread cerebral dysfunction is commonly observed in neuroanatomically intact areas distant from sites of ischemic cell loss (e.g., Baron, 1989; Fazio et al., 1992). Consequently, cases of ischemia-produced amnesia with hippocampal cell loss (cases such as that of R.B.) do provide only equivocal evidence that the hippocampus plays the major role in object recognition.

11.6 | The Hippocampus and Memory for Spatial Location

The discovery that the rhinal cortex plays a more important role than the hippocampus in object recognition does not mean that the hippocampus plays no significant role in memory. Indeed, the hippocampus plays a key role in memory for spatial location.

Hippocampal Lesions Disrupt Spatial Memory

Bilateral lesions of the hippocampus in laboratory animals often have little or no effect on the performance of memory tests. But there is one exception to this general result: Hippocampal lesions disrupt the performance of tasks that involve the memory for spatial location (e.g., McDonald & White, 1993; O'Keefe, 1993). For example, hippocampal lesions disrupt the performance of the *Morris water maze test* and the *radial arm maze test.*

In the **Morris water maze test,** intact rats placed at various locations in a circular pool of murky water rapidly learn to swim to a stationary platform hidden just below the surface. Rats with hippocampal lesions learn this simple task with great difficulty.

In the **radial arm maze test,** several arms (e.g., eight arms) radiate out from a central starting chamber, and the same few arms are baited with food each day. Intact rats readily learn to visit only those arms that contain food, without visiting the same arm more than once each day. The ability to visit only the baited arms of the radial arm maze is a measure of **reference memory** (memory for the general principles and skills that are required to perform a task), and the ability to refrain from visiting an arm more than once in a given day is a measure of **working memory** (temporary memory necessary for the successful performance of tasks on which one is currently working). Rats with hippocampal lesions display major deficits on both the reference memory and the working memory measures of radial arm maze performance.

Hippocampal Place Cells

Consistent with the observation that hippocampal lesions disrupt spatial memory is the fact that many hippocampal neurons are **place cells** (O'Keefe & Dostrovsky, 1971)—neurons that respond only when a subject is in specific locations (i.e., in the *place fields* of the neurons). For example, when a rat is first placed in an unfamiliar test environment, none of its hippocampal neurons have a place field in that environment; then, as the rat familiarizes itself with the environment, many hippocampal neurons acquire a place field in it—that is, each fires only when the rat is in a particular part of the test environment. Each place cell has a place field in a different part of the environment.

By placing a rat in an ambiguous situation in a familiar test environment, it is possible to determine where the rat thinks it is from the route that it takes to get to the location in the environment where it has previously been rewarded. Using this strategy, researchers (O'Keefe & Speakman, 1987; Wilson & McNaughton, 1993) have shown that the firing of a rat's place cells indicates where the rat "thinks" it is in the test environment, not necessarily where it actually is.

Comparative Studies of the Hippocampus and Spatial Memory

Although most of the evidence that the hippocampus plays a role in spatial memory comes from research on rats, the hippocampus seems to perform a similar function in many other species (see Colombo & Broadbent, 2000). Most noteworthy has been the research in food-caching birds. Food-caching birds must have remarkable spatial memories, because in order to survive, they must remember the locations of hundreds of food caches scattered around their territories. In one study, Sherry and colleagues (1989) found that food-caching species tended to have larger hippocampuses than related non–food-caching species.

Although research on a variety of species indicates that the hippocampus does play a role in spatial memory, the evidence from primate studies has been inconsistent. The hippocampal pyramidal cells of primates do have place fields (Rolls, Robertson, & Georges-François, 1995), but the effects of hippocampal damage on the performance of spatial memory tasks have been mixed (e.g., Henke et al., 1999; Maguire et al., 1998; Pigott & Milner, 1993). The problem may be that in humans and monkeys spatial memory is typically tested in stationary subjects making judgments of location on computer screens; whereas in rats, mice, and birds, spatial memory is typically studied in subjects navigating through controlled test environments. The results of two recent studies by Maguire and colleagues suggest that this is the case.

First, Maguire and colleagues (1998) used positron emission tomography (PET) to record the brain activity of subjects as they learned to find their way around a virtual-reality town. Activation of the right hippocampus was strongly associated with knowing where places were and navigating accurately to them. Second, Maguire and colleagues (2000) used structural magnetic resonance imaging (MRI) to estimate hippocampal volume in a group of humans who had intensive spatial training: London taxi drivers. They found that London taxi drivers with more than 20 years of experience had significantly more posterior hippocampal gray matter than usual.

Theories of Hippocampal Function

There are many theories of hippocampal function, all of which acknowledge the important role of the hippocampus in spatial memory. Let's take a look at three of these theories.

O'Keefe and Nadel (1978) proposed the **cognitive map theory** of hippocampal function. According to this theory, there are several systems in the brain that specialize in the memory for different kinds of information, and the specific function of the hippocampus is the storage of memories for spatial location. Specifically, Nadel and O'Keefe proposed that the hippocampus constructs and stores allocentric maps of the external world from the sensory input that it receives. *Allocentric* refers to representa-

tions of space based on relations among external objects and landmarks; in contrast, *egocentric* refers to representations of space based on relations to one's own position.

Another influential theory of hippocampal function is the *configural association theory* (Rudy & Sutherland, 1992). The configural association theory is based on the premise that spatial memory is one specific manifestation of the hippocampus's more general function. The configural association theory is that the hippocampus plays a role in the retention of the behavioral significance of combinations of stimuli but not of individual stimuli. For example, according to this theory, the hippocampus is involved in remembering that a flashing light in a particular context (i.e., at a particular location or time) signals food but not that a flashing light signals food irrespective of the context. There is substantial support for this theory; however, there have also been some failures to disrupt the performance of nonspatial configural tasks with hippocampal lesions (e.g., Bussey et al., 1998).

Finally, Brown and Aggleton (2001) have proposed a specific theory of the role of the hippocampus in object recognition and its relation to that of the rhinal cortex. They concur with recent evidence that the rhinal cortex, not the hippocampus, plays the major role in most object-recognition tasks. However, they suggest that the hippocampus plays the greater role in recognizing spatial arrangements of objects, as in a visual scene, for example (see Wan, Aggleton, & Brown, 1999).

11.7 Where Are Memories Stored?

Evidence suggests that each memory is stored diffusely throughout the structures of the brain that participated in its original experience (see Nyberg et al., 2000; Wheeler, Petersen, & Buckner, 2000). This chapter has focused on two structures of the medial temporal lobes—the hippocampus and the rhinal cortex—and their roles in spatial location and object recognition, respectively. Attention was also given to the mediodorsal nucleus and basal forebrain; the mnemonic functions of these structures is less well understood, but they have been implicated in memory by studies of Korsakoff's and Alzheimer's patients, respectively. In this section, we take a brief look at five other areas of the brain that have been implicated in memory storage: inferotemporal cortex, amygdala, prefrontal cortex, cerebellum, and striatum. See Figure 11.16 on page 288.

Inferotemporal Cortex

Areas of secondary sensory cortex are presumed to play an important role in storing sensory memories. For

example, because the **inferotemporal cortex** (the cortex of the inferior temporal lobe) is involved in the visual perception of objects, it is thought to participate in storing memories of visual patterns. In support of this view, Naya, Yoshida, and Miyashita (2001) recorded the responses of neurons in inferotemporal cortex and rhinal cortex while monkeys learned the relation between the two items in pairs of visual images. When a pair was presented, responses were first recorded in inferotemporal neurons and then in rhinal neurons; however, when the monkeys were required to recall the same pair, activity was recorded in rhinal neurons before inferotemporal neurons. Naya and colleagues concluded that this reversed pattern of activity reflected the retrieval of visual memories from inferotemporal cortex.

Amygdala

The amygdala seems to play a role in memory for the emotional significance of experiences. Rats with

FIGURE 11.16 The structures of the brain that have been shown to play a role in memory. Because it would have blocked the view of other structures, the striatum is not included. (See Figure 3.31.)

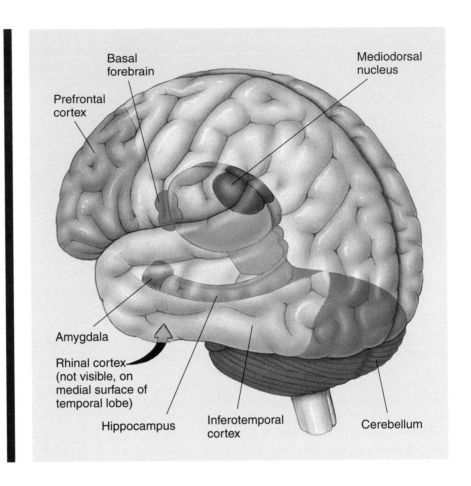

amygdalar lesions, unlike intact rats, do not respond with fear to a neutral stimulus that has been repeatedly followed by electric footshocks (see LeDoux, 1992). Also, Bechara and colleagues (1995) reported the case of a neuropsychological patient with bilateral damage to the amygdala who could not acquire conditioned autonomic startle responses to various visual or auditory stimuli but had good explicit memory for them.

Prefrontal Cortex

Patients with damage to the *prefrontal cortex* are not grossly amnesic; they often display no deficits at all on conventional tests of memory (see Petrides, 1996). They do, however, display deficits in memory for the temporal order of events, even when they can remember the events themselves as well as deficits in *working memory* (the ability to maintain relevant memories while a task is being completed)—see Kimberg, D'Esposito, & Farah, 1998; Smith, 2000). As a result of these two deficits, patients with prefrontal cortex damage have particular difficulty performing tasks that involve a series of responses.

The Case of the Cook Who Couldn't

The story of one patient with prefrontal cortex damage is very well known because she was the sister of Wilder Penfield, the famous Montreal neurosurgeon. Before her brain damage, she had been an excellent cook; and afterward, she retained all the prerequisite knowledge. She remembered her favorite recipes, and she remembered how to perform each individual cooking technique. However, she was incapable of preparing even simple meals because she could not carry out the various steps in proper sequence (Penfield & Evans, 1935).

The prefrontal cortex is a large heterogeneous structure; it is composed of numerous anatomically distinct areas that have different connections and, presumably, different functions. Do different areas of prefrontal cortex mediate different kinds of working memory—spatial, visual, verbal, and so forth? The answer seems to be, "yes and no." There appear to be regions of prefrontal cortex that perform fundamental cognitive processes (e.g., attention and task management) during all working memory tasks (Duncan & Owen, 2000; Smith & Jonidees, 1999). However, there are also regions of prefrontal cortex that seem to mediate specific kinds of working memory (Owen, Lee, & Williams, 2000; Petrides, 2000; Postle & D'Esposito, 2000).

Cerebellum and Striatum

Just as explicit memories of experiences are presumed to be stored in the circuits of the brain that mediated their original perception, implicit memories of sensorimotor learning are presumed to be stored in sensorimotor circuits (see Salmon & Butters, 1995). Most research on the neural mechanisms of memory for sensorimotor tasks have focused on two structures: the *cerebellum* and the *striatum*.

The **cerebellum** is thought to store memories of learned sensorimotor skills. Its role in the Pavlovian conditioning of the eyeblink response of rabbits has been most intensively investigated (see Daum & Schugens, 1996; Steinmetz, 1998). In this paradigm, a tone (conditional stimulus) is sounded just before a puff of air (unconditional stimulus) is delivered to the eye. After several trials, the tone comes to elicit an eyeblink. The convergence of evidence from stimulation, recording, and lesion studies suggests that the effects of this conditioning are stored in the form of changes in the way that cerebellar neurons respond to the tone (Kim & Thompson, 1997; Thompson & Krupa, 1994).

The **striatum** is thought to store memories for consistent relationships between stimuli and responses—the type of memories that develop incrementally over many trials (see White, 1997). Sometimes this striatum-based form of learning is referred to as *habit formation* (Jog et al., 1999).

One study of striatal function compared Parkinson's patients, who all have striatal damage, with patients suffering from medial temporal lobe damage. Knowlton, Mangels, and Squire (1996) found that the Parkinson's patients could not solve a probabilistic discrimination problem. The problem was a computer "weather forecasting" game, and the task of the subjects was to correctly predict the weather by pressing one of two keys, rain or shine. They based their predictions on stimulus cards presented on the screen—each card had a different probability of leading to sunshine. The Parkinson's patients did not improve over 50 trials, although they displayed normal explicit (conscious) memory for the training episode. In contrast, amnesic patients with medial temporal lobe or medial diencephalic damage displayed marked improvement in performance but had no explicit memory of their training.

11.8 Synaptic Mechanisms of Learning and Memory

So far, this chapter has focused on the particular structures of the human brain that are involved in learning and memory and what happens when these structures are damaged. In this section, the level of analysis changes: The focus shifts to the neuroplastic mechanisms within these structures that are thought to be the fundamental bases of learning and memory.

Most modern thinking about the neural mechanisms of memory began with Hebb (1949). Hebb argued so convincingly that enduring changes in the efficiency of synaptic transmission were the basis of long-term memory that the search for the neural bases of learning and memory has focused almost exclusively on the synapse.

Long-Term Potentiation

Because Hebb's hypothesis that enduring facilitations of synaptic transmission are the neural basis of learning and memory was so influential, there was great excitement when such an effect was discovered. In 1973, Bliss and Lømo showed that there is a facilitation of synaptic transmission following high-frequency electrical stimulation applied to presynaptic neurons. This phenomenon has been termed **long-term potentiation (LTP).**

LTP has been demonstrated in many species and in many parts of their brains, but it has been most frequently studied in the rat hippocampus. Figure 11.17 on page 290 illustrates the three hippocampal synapses at which LTP is commonly studied.

Figure 11.18 on page 291 is a demonstration of LTP in the granule cell layer of the rat hippocampal dentate gyrus. First, a single low-intensity pulse of current was delivered to the perforant path (the major input to the dentate gyrus), and the response was recorded through an extracellular multiple-unit electrode in the granule cell layer of the hippocampal dentate gyrus; the purpose of this initial stimulation was to determine the initial response baseline. Second, high-intensity, high-frequency stimulation lasting 10 seconds was delivered to the perforant path to induce the LTP. Third, the granule cells' responses to single pulses of low-intensity current were measured again after various delays. It is apparent in Figure 11.18 that

FIGURE 11.17 A slice of rat hippocampal tissue that illustrates the three synapses at which LTP is most commonly studied: (1) the dentate granule cell synapse, (2) the CA3 pyramidal cell synapse, and (3) the CA1 pyramidal cell synapse.

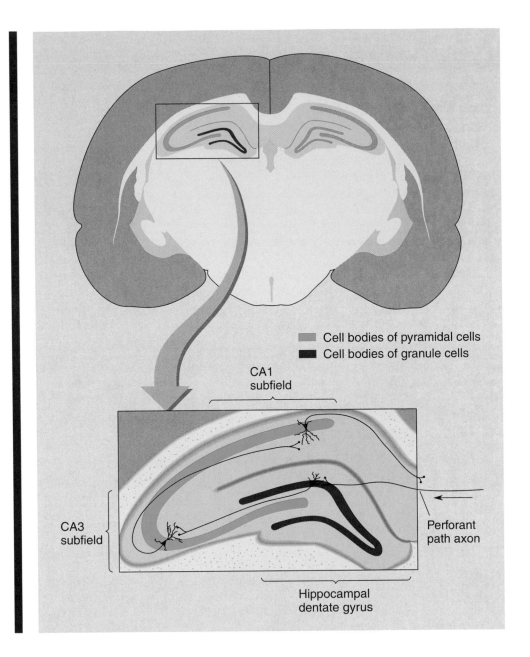

transmission at the granule cells' synapses was still potentiated 1 week after the high-frequency stimulation.

LTP is among the most widely studied neuroscientific phenomena. Why? The reason goes back to 1949 and Hebb's influential theory of memory. The synaptic changes that were hypothesized by Hebb to underlie long-term memory seemed to be the same kind of changes that underlie LTP.

LTP has two key properties that Hebb proposed as characteristics of the physiological mechanisms of learning and memory. First, LTP can last for a long time—for many weeks after multiple stimulations. Second, LTP develops only if the firing of the presynaptic neuron is followed by the firing of the postsynaptic neuron; it does not develop when the presynaptic neuron fires and the

postsynaptic neuron does not, and it does not develop when the presynaptic neuron does not fire and the postsynaptic neuron does (e.g., Kelso, Ganong, & Brown, 1986; Sastry, Goh, & Auyeung, 1986). The *co-occurrence* of firing in presynaptic and postsynaptic cells is now recognized as the critical factor in LTP, and the assumption that co-occurrence is a physiological necessity for learning and memory is often referred to as *Hebb's postulate for learning.*

Additional support for the idea that LTP is related to the neural mechanisms of learning and memory has come from several observations: (1) LTP can be elicited by low levels of stimulation that mimic normal neural activity; (2) LTP effects are most prominent in structures that have been implicated in learning and memory, such

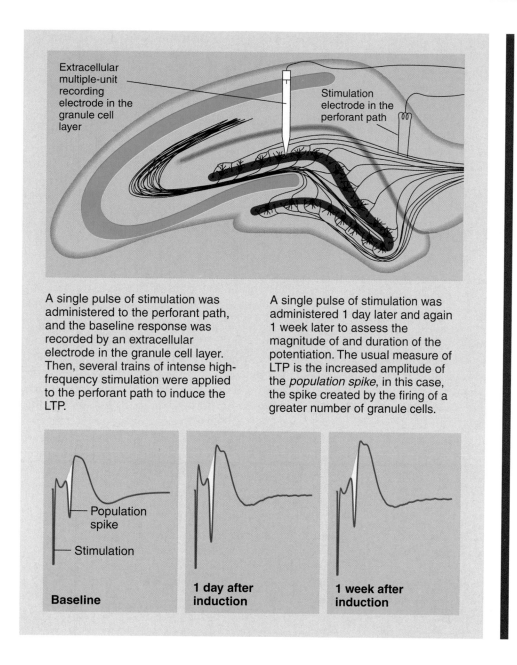

Extracellular
multiple-unit
recording
electrode in the
granule cell
layer

Stimulation
electrode in the
perforant path

A single pulse of stimulation was administered to the perforant path, and the baseline response was recorded by an extracellular electrode in the granule cell layer. Then, several trains of intense high-frequency stimulation were applied to the perforant path to induce the LTP.

A single pulse of stimulation was administered 1 day later and again 1 week later to assess the magnitude of and duration of the potentiation. The usual measure of LTP is the increased amplitude of the *population spike*, in this case, the spike created by the firing of a greater number of granule cells.

Population
spike

Stimulation

Baseline

1 day after induction

1 week after induction

FIGURE 11.18 Long-term potentiation in the granule cell layer of the rat hippocampal dentate gyrus. (Traces courtesy of Michael Corcoran, Department of Psychology, University of Saskatchewan.)

as the hippocampus; (3) behavioral conditioning can produce LTP-like changes in the hippocampus (e.g., Iriki et al., 1989); (4) many drugs that influence learning and memory have parallel effects on LTP (e.g., Brown et al., 1988; Skelton et al., 1987); (5) the induction of maximal LTP blocks the learning of a Morris water maze until the LTP has subsided (Castro et al., 1989); (6) mutant mice that display little hippocampal LTP have difficulty learning the Morris water maze (Silva et al., 1992); and (7) LTP occurs at specific synapses that have been shown to participate in learning and memory in simple invertebrate nervous systems (Johnston, 1997; Lin & Glanzman, 1994; Murphy & Glanzman, 1997). Still, it is important to keep in mind that all of this evidence is indirect and that LTP as induced in the laboratory by electrical stim-

ulation is at best a caricature of the subtle cellular events that underlie learning and memory (see Cain, 1997; Eichenbaum, 1996; Shors & Matzel, 1997).

■ | Induction of LTP: Learning

LTP has been studied most extensively at synapses at which the NMDA receptor is prominent. The **NMDA** (N-methyl-D-aspartate) **receptor** is a receptor for **glutamate**—the main excitatory neurotransmitter of the brain. The NMDA receptor has a special property. It does not respond maximally unless two events occur simultaneously: Glutamate must bind to it, and the postsynaptic neuron must already be partially depolarized. This dual requirement stems from the fact that the calcium channels that are linked to NMDA receptors allow only small numbers of calcium ions to enter the neuron unless the neuron is already depolarized when glutamate binds to the receptor; it is the influx of calcium ions that triggers action potentials and the cascade of events in the postsynaptic neuron that induces LTP. The study of calcium influx has been greatly facilitated by the development of *optical imaging techniques* for visualizing it (see Figure 11.19).

An important characteristic of the induction of LTP at glutaminergic synapses stems from the nature of the NMDA receptor and LTP's requirement for co-occurrence. This characteristic is not obvious under the usual, but unnatural, experimental condition in which LTP is induced by high-intensity, high-frequency stimulation, which always activates the postsynaptic neurons through massive temporal and spatial summation. However, when a more natural, low-intensity stimulation is applied, the postsynaptic neurons do not fire and thus LTP is not induced—unless the postsynaptic neurons are already partially depolarized so that their calcium channels open wide when glutamate binds to their NMDA receptors.

The requirement for the postsynaptic neurons to be partially depolarized when the glutamate binds to them is an extremely important characteristic of LTP because it permits neural networks to learn associations. Let me explain. If one glutaminergic neuron were to fire by itself and release its glutamate neurotransmitter across a synapse onto the NMDA receptors of a postsynaptic neuron, there would be no potentiation of transmission at that synapse because the postsynaptic cell would not fire. However, if the postsynaptic neuron were partially depolarized by input from other neurons when the presynaptic neuron fired, the binding of the glutamate to the NMDA receptors would open wide the calcium channels, calcium ions would flow into the postsynaptic neuron, and transmission across the synapses between the presynaptic and postsynaptic neuron would be potentiated. Accordingly, the requirement for co-occurrence and the dependence of NMDA receptors on simultaneous binding and partial depolarization mean that, under natural conditions, synaptic facilitation records the fact that there has been simultaneous activity in at least two converging inputs to the postsynaptic neuron—as would be produced by the "simultaneous" presentation of a conditional stimulus and an unconditional stimulus.

The exact mechanisms by which calcium influx induces LTP are unclear; however, there is substantial evidence that calcium exerts its effects by activating *protein kinases* (a class of enzymes that influence many chemical reactions of the cell) in the neural cytoplasm (see Grant & Silva, 1994; Linden & Routtenberg, 1989). A consistent finding has been that protein kinase inhibitors block the induction of LTP (see Bashir & Collingridge, 1992). Figure 11.20 summarizes the induction of NMDA-receptor–mediated LTP.

■ | Maintenance and Expression of LTP: Memory

Although there is a consensus that the chemical events that induce LTP occur in postsynaptic neurons, it is still not clear whether the mechanisms responsible for the maintenance and expression of LTP are presynaptic or postsynaptic (Edwards, 1995). Do the maintenance and expression of LTP depend on changes in presynaptic neurons that increase their release of the neurotransmitter or on changes in postsynaptic neurons that increase their responsiveness to the neurotransmitter? The difficulty in answering this question stems from the current difficulty in measuring neurotransmitter release at individual synapses (Malinow, 1994).

Although it is still not clear whether the maintenance and expression of LTP are presynaptic or postsynaptic, progress in understanding the mechanisms of maintenance and expression of NMDA-receptor–mediated LTP has recently been made on the following four fronts.

First, whether LTP is presynaptic or postsynaptic, there must be some mechanism to account for the fact that its maintenance and expression are restricted to specific synapses on the postsynaptic neuron (see Malgaroli et al., 1995). Some research has suggested that the specificity of LTP is attributable to **dendritic spines;** calcium that enters one dendritic spine does not diffuse

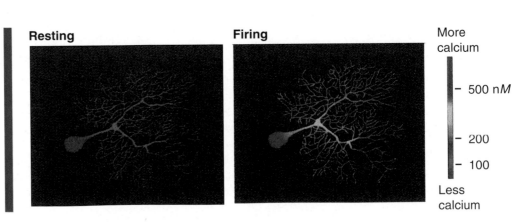

FIGURE 11.19   The influx of calcium ions into active neurons. This influx can be visualized with microfluorometric techniques. Notice that the greatest influx (measured in nanomolars) occurs in the axon terminal branches. (Courtesy of Tank et al., 1988.)

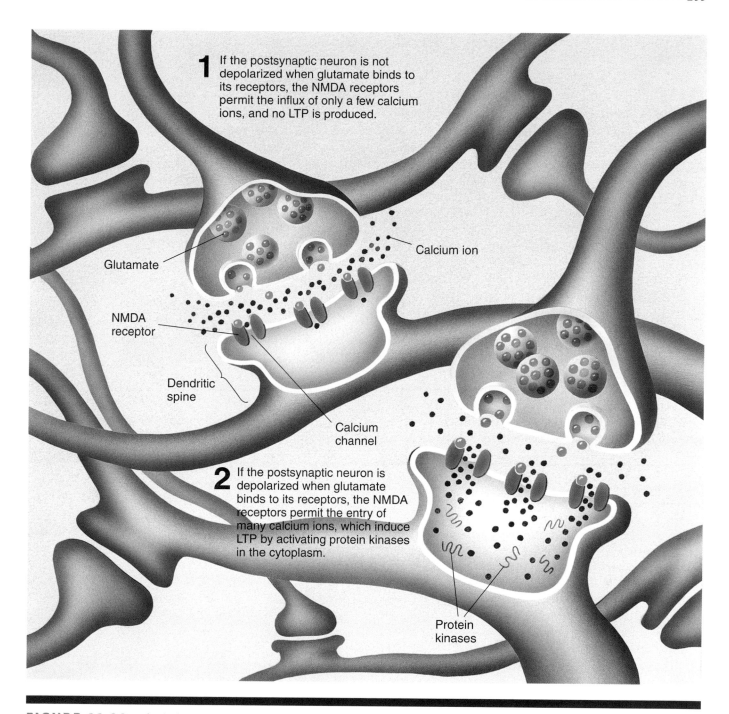

1 If the postsynaptic neuron is not depolarized when glutamate binds to its receptors, the NMDA receptors permit the influx of only a few calcium ions, and no LTP is produced.

Glutamate

Calcium ion

NMDA receptor

Dendritic spine

Calcium channel

2 If the postsynaptic neuron is depolarized when glutamate binds to its receptors, the NMDA receptors permit the entry of many calcium ions, which induce LTP by activating protein kinases in the cytoplasm.

Protein kinases

FIGURE 11.20   The induction of NMDA-receptor–mediated LTP.

out of it and thus exerts its effects locally (see Harris & Kater, 1994).

Second, whether LTP is presynaptic or postsynaptic, it seems likely that its maintenance over long intervals would require the synthesis of neural protein. Studies have shown that blocking of protein synthesis immediately after stimulation has no effect on the maintenance of LTP for 1 or 2 hours but prevents its maintenance for longer periods (e.g., Nguyen, Abel, & Kandel, 1994).

Third, if the maintenance and expression of LTP are presynaptic while its induction is postsynaptic, there

must be some signal that passes from the postsynaptic neuron back to the presynaptic neuron. Evidence suggests that the soluble-gas neurotransmitter **nitric oxide** serves this function; it appears to be synthesized in the postsynaptic neuron in response to calcium influx and then to diffuse back into the presynaptic button (see Harris, 1995; Larkman & Jack, 1995).

And fourth, studies have documented structural changes in synapses that are participating in the storage of LTP. For example, several studies have shown that the number of synapses between particular axons and dendrites increases following the induction of LTP (Stewart et al., 2000; Toni et al., 1999).

Variability of LTP

The neural mechanisms underlying the induction, maintenance, and expression of LTP are currently the focus of massive research efforts, and substantial progress is being made. However, it is important to keep this progress in perspective.

Almost all of the research on LTP has focused on NMDA-receptor–mediated LTP in the hippocampus, but more and more reports are emerging of LTP in non-

glutaminergic synapses in different parts of the brain (e.g., Buonomano, 1999; Teskey & Valentine, 1998). LTP at such synapses has properties different from those of the NMDA-receptor–mediated form. Accordingly, the discovery of the mechanisms of NMDA-receptor–mediated LTP will be only the first of many necessary steps toward complete understanding.

From the psychological perspective, it is not enough to understand LTP, even in its variable forms. The major psychological goal is to understand the properties of each type of LTP and how each type participates in learning and memory (see Martin, Grimwood, & Morris, 2000). This goal is not likely to be achieved in the near future.

11.9 Conclusion: Infantile Amnesia and the Biopsychologist Who Remembered H.M.

We tend to think of memory as a unitary ability. Nevertheless, brain-damaged individuals often display severe deficits in one memory process but not others. Because this chapter has so far focused on the amnesic affects of brain damage, you may have been left with the impression that the dissociations among various kinds of memory have little direct relevance to individuals with intact healthy brains. This, the final, section emphasizes that such is not the case. It makes the point with one interesting line of experiments and one provocative case study.

We all experience *infantile amnesia;* that is, we remember virtually nothing of the events of our infancy. Newcombe and her colleagues (2000) addressed the following question: Do normal children who fail explicitly to recall or recognize things from their early childhood display preserved implicit memory for these things? The results of two experiments indicate that the answer is "yes."

In one study of infantile amnesia (Newcombe & Fox, 1994), children were shown a series of photographs of preschool-aged children, some of whom had been their preschool classmates. The subjects recognized a few of their former preschool classmates. However, whether they explicitly remembered a former classmate or not, they consistently displayed a large skin conductance response to the photographs of those classmates.

In a second study of infantile amnesia, Drummey and Newcombe (1995) used a modern version of the incomplete-pictures test. They showed a series of drawings to 3-year-olds, 5-year-olds, and adults. Three months later, subjects' memory for these drawings was assessed by asking them to identify them and some control drawings as quickly as they could. The drawings were initially badly out of focus, but became progressively sharper.

Following this test of implicit memory, the subjects were asked which of the drawings they remembered seeing before. The 5-year-olds and adults showed better explicit memory than the 3-year-olds did; that is, they were more likely to recall seeing drawings from the original series. However, all three groups displayed substantial implicit memory: All subjects were able to identify more quickly the drawings they had seen before, even when they had no conscious recollection of having seen them before.

This chapter began with the case of H.M.; it ends with the case of R.M. The case of R.M. is one of the most ironic that I have encountered, which is why I have saved it for a chapter-ending treat. R.M. is a biopsychologist, and, as you will learn, his vocation played an important role in one of his symptoms.

The Case of R.M., the Biopsychologist Who Remembered H.M.

R.M. fell on his head while skiing; when he regained consciousness, he was suffering from both retrograde and anterograde amnesia. For several hours, he could recall few of the events of his previous life. He could not remember if he was married, where he lived, or where he worked. He had lost most of his episodic memory.

Also, many of the things that happened to him in the hours after his accident were forgotten as soon as his attention was diverted from them. For example, in the car on his way to the hospital, R.M. chatted with the person sitting next to him—a friend of a friend with whom he had skied all day. But each time his attention was drawn elsewhere—for example, by the mountain scenery—he completely forgot this person and their previous conversations, and subsequently reintroduced himself.

This was a classic case of posttraumatic amnesia. Like H.M., R.M. was trapped in the present, with only a cloudy past and seemingly no future. The irony of the situation was that during those few hours, when R.M. could recall few of the events of his own life, his thoughts repeatedly drifted to one semantic memory— his memory of a person he remembered learning

about somewhere in his muddled past. Through the haze, he remembered H.M., his fellow prisoner of the present and wondered if the same fate lay in store for him.

R.M. is now fully recovered and looks back on what he can recall of his experience with relief and with a feeling of empathy for H.M. Unlike H.M., R.M. received a reprieve, but his experience left him with a better appreciation for the situation of those amnesics, like H.M., who are serving life sentences.

Themes Revisited

Because this chapter was based almost entirely on the study of human memory disorders and animal models of them, the clinical implications and evolutionary perspective themes predominated. The clinical study of memory disorders has so far been a one-way street: We have learned much about memory and its neural mechanisms from studying amnesic patients, but we have not yet learned enough to treat their memory problems.

The cognitive neuroscience theme emerged infrequently in this chapter. However, modern functional brain-imaging methods are starting to play a major role in the study of brain-damage–produced memory disorders.

Finally, the thinking-about-biopsychology icon marked several points in the chapter where it was partic-

ularly important for you to think clearly and carefully. It warned you to (1) appreciate the limitations of case studies, (2) not think about memory as a unitary process, (3) appreciate the difficulty in distinguishing anterograde and retrograde effects when disorders have a gradual onset (e.g., Korsakoff's disease), (4) recognize that cases of cerebral ischemia (e.g., that of R.B.) do not provide conclusive evidence of the role of the hippocampus in memory, and (5) appreciate that, although LTP is a diverse phenomenon, most research has focused on NMDA-receptor–mediated LTP in the hippocampus.

ON THE CD
Looking for more information about the topics in this chapter? For recommended additional readings, see Hard Copy for Chapter 11.

Log On

- **http://www.exploratorium.edu/memory/** This is an interesting series of pages on memory, including a dissection of a sheep's brain and links to online lectures about various aspects of memory and amnesia.

- **http://www.alzheimers.org/mmedia.html** This site features a series of multimedia links to lectures and ani-

mations illustrating various aspects of early- and late-onset Alzheimer's disease.

- **http://www.sciam.com/askexpert/medicine/medicine40/medicine40.html** *Scientific American* presents an overview of what a concussion is and how it might affect the brain and behavior.

Think about It

1. The study of the anatomy of memory has come a long way since H.M.'s misfortune. What kind of advances do you think will be made in the next decade?

2. Using examples from your own experience, compare implicit and explicit memory.

3. What are the advantages and shortcomings of animal models of amnesia? Compare the usefulness of monkey and rat models.

ON THE CD
Studying for an exam? Try the Practice Tests for Chapter 11.

4. LTP is one of the most intensely studied of all neuroscientific phenomena. Why?

5. Case studies have played a particularly important role in the study of memory. Discuss.

Key Terms

Amygdala *(p. 269)*
Anterograde amnesia *(p. 270)*
Basal forebrain *(p. 276)*
Bilateral medial temporal lobectomy *(p. 269)*
CA1 subfield *(p. 273)*
Cerebellum *(p. 289)*
Cerebral ischemia *(p. 273)*
Cognitive map theory *(p. 287)*
Delayed nonmatching-to-sample test *(p. 280)*
Dendritic spines *(p. 292)*
Digit span *(p. 270)*
Electroconvulsive shock (ECS) *(p. 276)*
Engram *(p. 279)*
Episodic memories *(p. 272)*

Explicit memories *(p. 272)*
Global amnesia *(p. 270)*
Glutamate *(p. 291)*
Hippocampus *(p. 269)*
Implicit memories *(p. 272)*
Incomplete-pictures test *(p. 271)*
Inferotemporal cortex *(p. 287)*
Korsakoff's syndrome *(p. 274)*
Learning *(p. 269)*
Lobectomy *(p. 269)*
Lobotomy *(p. 269)*
Long-term potentiation (LTP) *(p. 289)*
Medial diencephalic amnesia *(p. 275)*

Medial temporal lobe amnesia *(p. 272)*
Mediodorsal nuclei *(p. 275)*
Memory *(p. 269)*
Memory consolidation *(p. 292)*
Morris water maze test *(p. 286)*
Mumby box *(p. 283)*
Nitric oxide *(p. 293)*
NMDA receptor *(p. 291)*
Place cells *(p. 286)*
Posttraumatic amnesia (PTA) *(p. 276)*
Pyramidal cell layer *(p. 273)*
Radial arm maze test *(p. 286)*
Reference memory *(p. 286)*

Repetition priming tests *(p. 272)*
Retrograde amnesia *(p. 270)*
Rhinal cortex *(p. 280)*
Semantic memories *(p. 272)*
Striatum *(p. 289)*
Working memory *(p. 286)*

ON THE CD

Need some help studying the key terms for this chapter? Check out the electronic flash cards for Chapter 11.

Hunger, Eating, and Health

Why Do Many People Eat Too Much?

ating is a behavior that is of interest to virtually everyone. We all do it, and most of us derive great pleasure from it. But for many of us, it becomes a source of serious personal and health problems.

Most eating-related health problems are associated with eating too much. For example, over half of the adult U.S. population meets the current criteria of clinical obesity, qualifying this problem for epidemic status. The resulting financial and personal costs are huge. Each year in the United States, $45 billion is spent treating obesity-related disorders; missed work costs another $23 billion; and $33 billion is spent on weight-loss products and services. Moreover, each year an estimated 300,000 U.S. citizens die from disorders caused by their excessive eating (e.g., diabetes, hypertension, cardiovascular diseases, and some cancers). Although the United States is the trend-setter when it comes to overeating and obesity, many other countries are not far behind.

Ironically, as overeating and obesity have reached epidemic proportions, there has been a related increase in disorders associated with eating too little. For example, about 3% of U.S. adolescents currently suffer from *anorexia nervosa,* which is life-threatening in extreme cases.

The message is clear: At some time in your life, you or somebody you care about will almost certainly suffer from an eating-related disorder.

The massive increases in obesity and other eating-related disorders that have occurred over the last few decades in many countries stand in stark contrast to most people's thinking about hunger and eating. Most people—and I assume that they include you—believe that hunger and eating are normally triggered when the body's energy resources fall below a prescribed optimal level, or **set point:** Most people appreciate that many factors influence hunger and eating, but they assume that the hunger and eating system has evolved to supply the body with just the right amount of energy.

The incompatibility of set-point thinking with the current epidemic of eating disorders is the focus of this chapter. If we all have hunger and eating systems whose primary function is to maintain energy resources at optimal levels, then eating disorders should be rare. The fact that they are so prevalent suggests that hunger and eating are regulated in some other way.

The first sections of this chapter examine some of the fundamental characteristics of hunger and eating; from this examination, a different way of thinking about hunger, eating, and health is derived. Armed with this new perspective, we will reexamine the clinical problems of obesity and anorexia nervosa in the final sections. This chapter will provide you with new insights of major personal relevance—I guarantee it.

Before you move on to the body of the chapter, I would like you to pause to consider a case study (Rozin et al., 1998). What would a severely amnesic patient do if offered a meal shortly after finishing one? If his hunger and eating were controlled by energy set points, he would refuse the second meal. Did he?

ON THE CD
In the module *Thinking about Hunger,* Pinel welcomes you to this chapter and talks about a common misconception about meal-time hunger.

The Case of the Man Who Forgot Not to Eat

R.H. was a 48-year-old male whose progress in graduate school was interrupted by the development of severe amnesia for long-term explicit memory. His amnesia was similar in pattern and severity to that of H.M., whom you met in Chapter 11, and an MRI examination revealed bilateral damage to the medial temporal lobes.

The meals offered to R.H. were selected on the basis of interviews with him about the foods he liked: veal parmigiana (about 750 calories) plus all the apple juice he wanted. On one occasion, he was offered a second meal about 15 minutes after he had eaten the first, and he ate it. When offered a third meal 15 minutes later, he ate that, too. When offered a fourth meal he rejected it, claiming that his "stomach was a little tight."

Then, a few minutes later, R.H. announced that he was going out for a good walk and a meal. When asked what he was going to eat, his answer was "veal parmigiana." Clearly, R.H.'s hunger (i.e., motivation to eat) did not result from an energy deficit.

12.1 Digestion and Energy Flow

The primary purpose of eating is to supply the body with the energy it needs to survive and function. This section provides a brief overview of the processes by which food is digested, stored, and converted to energy.

The *gastrointestinal tract* and the process of digestion are illustrated in Figure 12.1. **Digestion** is the gastrointestinal process of breaking down food and absorbing its constituents into the body. In order to appreciate the

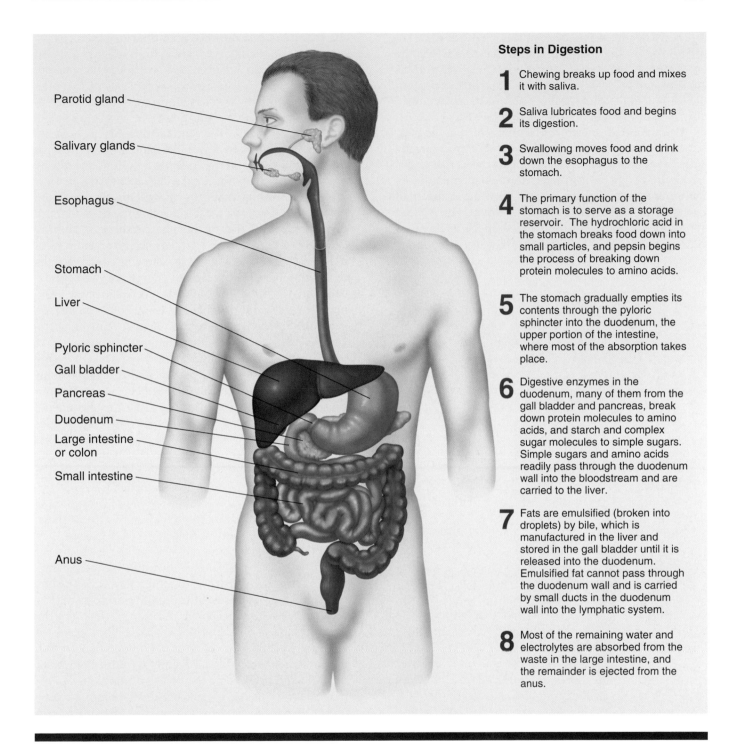

Steps in Digestion

1 Chewing breaks up food and mixes it with saliva.

2 Saliva lubricates food and begins its digestion.

3 Swallowing moves food and drink down the esophagus to the stomach.

4 The primary function of the stomach is to serve as a storage reservoir. The hydrochloric acid in the stomach breaks food down into small particles, and pepsin begins the process of breaking down protein molecules to amino acids.

5 The stomach gradually empties its contents through the pyloric sphincter into the duodenum, the upper portion of the intestine, where most of the absorption takes place.

6 Digestive enzymes in the duodenum, many of them from the gall bladder and pancreas, break down protein molecules to amino acids, and starch and complex sugar molecules to simple sugars. Simple sugars and amino acids readily pass through the duodenum wall into the bloodstream and are carried to the liver.

7 Fats are emulsified (broken into droplets) by bile, which is manufactured in the liver and stored in the gall bladder until it is released into the duodenum. Emulsified fat cannot pass through the duodenum wall and is carried by small ducts in the duodenum wall into the lymphatic system.

8 Most of the remaining water and electrolytes are absorbed from the waste in the large intestine, and the remainder is ejected from the anus.

Labels: Parotid gland, Salivary glands, Esophagus, Stomach, Liver, Pyloric sphincter, Gall bladder, Pancreas, Duodenum, Large intestine or colon, Small intestine, Anus

FIGURE 12.1   The gastrointestinal tract and the process of digestion.

basics of digestion, it is useful to consider the body without its protuberances, as a simple living tube with a hole at each end. To supply itself with energy and other nutrients, the tube puts food into one of its two holes—typically the one with teeth—and passes it along its internal canal so that it can be broken down and partially absorbed from the canal into the body. The leftovers are jettisoned from the other end. Although this is not a particularly appetizing description of eating, it does serve

to illustrate that, strictly speaking, food has not been consumed until it has been digested.

As a consequence of digestion, energy is delivered to the body in three forms: (1) **lipids** (fats), (2) **amino acids** (the breakdown products of proteins), and (3) **glucose** (a simple sugar that is the breakdown product of complex *carbohydrates,* that is, complex starches and sugars).

The body uses energy continuously, but its consumption is intermittent; therefore, it must store energy for use in the intervals between meals. Energy is stored in three forms: *fats, glycogen,* and *proteins.* Most of the body's energy reserves are stored as fats, relatively little as glycogen and proteins (see Figure 12.2). Thus, changes in the body weights of adult humans are largely a consequence of changes in the amount of body fat.

Because glycogen, which is largely stored in the liver, is readily converted to glucose—the body's main directly utilizable source of energy—one might expect that glycogen would be the body's preferred mode of energy storage. There are two main reasons why fat, rather than glycogen, is the primary mode of energy storage. One is that a gram of fat can store twice as much energy as a gram of glycogen; the other is that glycogen, unlike fat, at-

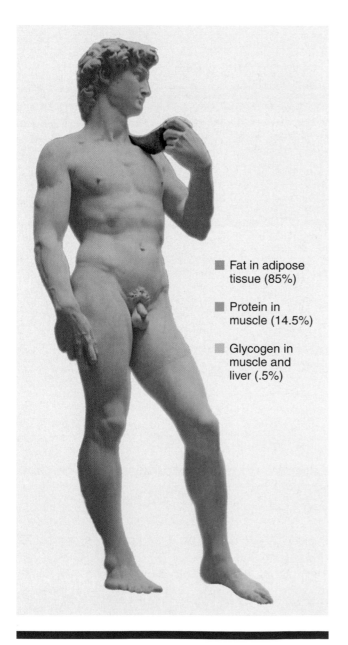

■ Fat in adipose tissue (85%)

■ Protein in muscle (14.5%)

■ Glycogen in muscle and liver (.5%)

FIGURE 12.2 Distribution of stored energy in an average person.

tracts and holds substantial quantities of water. Consequently, if your fat calories were all stored as glycogen, you would likely weigh well over 275 kilograms (600 pounds).

There are three phases of *energy metabolism* (the chemical changes by which energy is made available for an organism's use): the cephalic phase, the absorptive phase, and the fasting phase. The **cephalic phase** is the preparatory phase; it often begins with the sight, smell, or even just the thought of food, and it ends when the food starts to be absorbed into the bloodstream. The **absorptive phase** is the period during which the energy absorbed into the bloodstream from the meal is meeting the body's immediate energy needs. The **fasting phase** is the period during which all of the unstored energy from the previous meal has been used and the body is withdrawing energy from its reserves to meet its immediate energy requirements; it ends with the beginning of the next cephalic phase. During periods of rapid weight gain, people often go directly from one absorptive phase into the next cephalic phase, without experiencing an intervening fasting phase.

The flow of energy during the three phases of energy metabolism is controlled by two pancreatic hormones: insulin and glucagon. During the cephalic and absorptive phases, the pancreas releases a great deal of insulin into the bloodstream and very little glucagon. The **insulin** does three things: (1) It promotes the use of glucose as the primary source of energy by the body. (2) It promotes the conversion of bloodborne fuels to forms that can be stored: glucose to glycogen and fat, and amino acids to proteins. (3) It promotes the storage of glycogen in liver and muscle, fat in adipose tissue, and proteins in muscle. In short, the function of insulin during the cephalic phase is to lower the levels of bloodborne fuels, primarily glucose, in anticipation of the impending influx; and its function during the absorptive phase is to minimize the increasing levels of bloodborne fuels by utilizing and storing them.

In contrast to the cephalic and absorptive phases, the fasting phase is characterized by high blood levels of **glucagon** and low levels of insulin. Without high levels of insulin, glucose has difficulty entering most body cells; thus, glucose stops being the body's primary fuel. In effect, this saves the body's glucose for the brain, because insulin is not required for glucose to enter most brain cells. The low levels of insulin also promote the conversion of glycogen and protein to glucose. (The conversion of protein to glucose is called **gluconeogenesis.**)

On the other hand, the high levels of fasting-phase glucagon promote the release of **free fatty acids** from adipose tissue and their use as the body's primary fuel. The high glucagon levels also stimulate the conversion of free fatty acids to **ketones,** which are used by muscles as a source of energy during the fasting phase. After a prolonged period without food, however, the brain also starts to use ketones, thus further conserving the body's resources of glucose.

Figure 12.3 summarizes the major metabolic events associated with the three phases of energy metabolism.

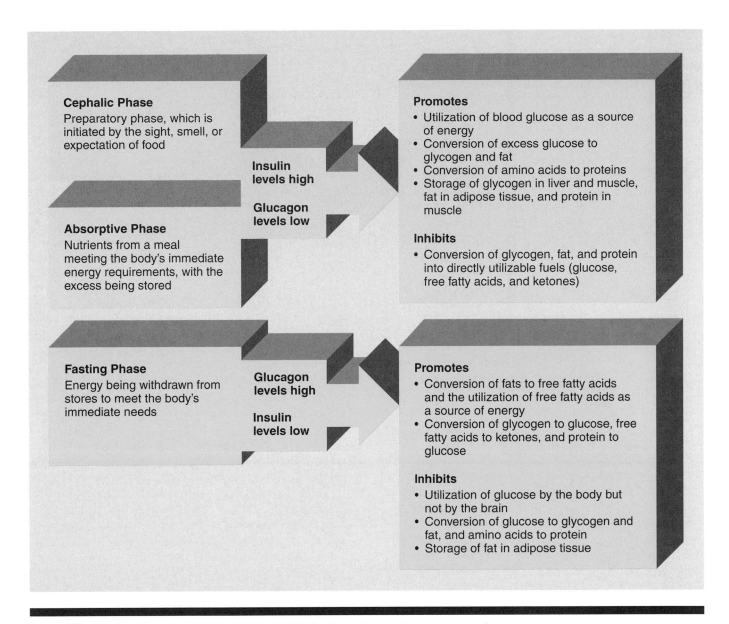

FIGURE 12.3 The major events associated with the three phases of energy metabolism: the cephalic, absorptive, and fasting phases.

12.2 Theories of Hunger and Eating: Set Points versus Positive Incentives

One of the main difficulties I have in teaching the fundamentals of hunger, eating, and body weight regulation is the **set-point assumption.** Although it dominates most people's thinking about hunger and eating (Assanand, Pinel, & Lehman, 1998a, 1998b), whether they realize it or not, it is inconsistent with the bulk of the evidence. What exactly is the set-point assumption?

Set-Point Assumption

Most people attribute *hunger* (the motivation to eat) to the presence of an energy deficit, and they view eating as the means by which the energy resources of the body are returned to their optimal level—that is, to the *energy set point*. Figure 12.4 on page 302 summarizes this

FIGURE 12.4 The energy set-point view that is the basis of many people's thinking about hunger and eating.

set-point assumption. After a *meal* (a bout of eating), a person's energy resources are thought to be near their set point and to decline thereafter as the body uses energy to fuel its physiological processes. When the level of the body's energy resources falls far enough below the set point, a person becomes motivated by hunger to initiate another meal. The meal continues, according to the set-point assumption, until the energy level returns to its set point and the person feels *satiated* (no longer hungry).

The set-point model of hunger and eating works in much the same way as a thermostat-regulated heating system in a cool climate. The heater increases the house temperature until it reaches its set point (the thermostat setting). This turns off the heat, and then the temperature of the house gradually declines until the decline is large enough to turn the heater back on. All set-point systems have three components: a set-point mechanism, a detector mechanism, and an effector mechanism. The *set-point mechanism* defines the set point, the *detector mechanism* detects deviations from the set point, and the *effector mechanism* acts to eliminate the deviations. For example, the set-point, detector, and effector mechanisms of a heating system are the thermostat, the thermometer, and the heater, respectively.

All set-point systems are **negative feedback systems**—systems in which feedback from changes in one direction elicit compensatory effects in the opposite direction. Negative feedback systems are common in mammals because they act to maintain **homeostasis**—a constant internal environment—which is critical for mammals' survival (see Wenning, 1999).

Glucostatic and Lipostatic Set-Point Theories of Hunger and Eating

In the 1940s and 1950s, researchers working under the assumption that eating is regulated by some type of

set-point system speculated about the nature of the regulation. Several researchers suggested that eating is regulated by a system that is designed to maintain a blood glucose set point—the idea being that we become hungry when our blood glucose levels drop significantly below their set point and that we become satiated when eating returns our blood glucose levels to their set point. Various versions of this theory are referred to as the **glucostatic theory.** It seemed to make good sense that the main purpose of eating is to defend a blood glucose set point because glucose is the brain's primary fuel.

The **lipostatic theory** is another set-point theory that was proposed in various forms in the 1940s and 1950s. According to this theory, every person has a set point for body fat, and deviations from this set point produce compensatory adjustments in the level of eating that return levels of body fat to their set point. The most frequently cited support for the theory is the fact that the body weights of adults stay relatively constant.

The glucostatic and lipostatic theories were viewed as complementary, not mutually exclusive. The glucostatic theory was thought to account for meal initiation and termination, whereas the lipostatic theory was thought to account for long-term regulation. Thus the dominant view in the 1950s was that eating is regulated by the interaction between two set-point systems: a short-term glucostatic system and a long-term lipostatic system. The simplicity of these 1950s theories is appealing. Remarkably, they are still being presented as the latest word in some textbooks; perhaps you have encountered them.

Problems with Set-Point Theories of Hunger and Eating

Set-point theories of hunger and eating have several serious weaknesses. You have already learned one fact that undermines these theories: the current epidemic of obesity and other eating disorders. Let's look at three more.

First, set-point theories of hunger and eating are inconsistent with basic eating-related evolutionary pressures as we understand them. The major eating-related problem faced by our ancestors was the inconsistency and unpredictability of the food supply. Thus, in order to survive, it was important for them to eat large quantities of good food when it was available so that calories could be banked in the form of body fat. Any ancestor—human or otherwise—that stopped feeling hungry as soon as immediate energy needs were met would not have survived the first hard winter or prolonged drought. For any warm-blooded species to survive under natural conditions, it needs a hunger and eating system that prevents energy deficits, rather than one that merely responds to them once they have developed. From this perspective, it is difficult to imagine how a set-point hunger and feeding system could have evolved in mammals (see Pinel, Assanand, & Lehman, 2000; Weingarten, 1985).

Second, major predictions of the set-point theories of hunger and eating have not been confirmed. Early studies seemed to support the set-point theories by showing that large reductions in body fat, produced by starvation, or large reductions in blood glucose, produced by insulin injections, induce increases in eating in laboratory animals. The problem is that reductions of the magnitude needed to reliably induce eating rarely occur naturally. Indeed, as you have already learned in this chapter, over 50% of the U.S. adult population have a significant excess of fat deposits when they begin a meal. Conversely, efforts to reduce meal size by having subjects consume a high-calorie drink before eating have been largely unsuccessful; indeed, beliefs about the caloric content of a premeal drink often influence the size of a subsequent meal more than does its actual caloric content (see Lowe, 1993).

Third, set-point theories of hunger and eating are deficient because they fail to recognize the major influences on hunger and eating of such important factors as taste, learning, and social factors. To convince yourself of the importance of these factors, pause for a minute and imagine the sight, smell, and taste of your favorite food. Perhaps it is a succulent morsel of lobster meat covered with melted garlic butter, a piece of chocolate cheesecake, or a plate of sizzling homemade french fries. Are you starting to feel a bit hungry? If the homemade french fries—my personal weakness—were sitting in front of you right now, wouldn't you reach out and have one, or maybe the whole plateful? Have you not on occasion felt discomfort after a large main course, only to polish off a substantial dessert? The usual positive answers to these questions lead unavoidably to the conclusion that hunger and eating are not rigidly controlled by deviations from energy set points. This same point can be easily demonstrated in laboratory rats by adding a small amount of saccharin to their laboratory chow; saccharin increases the sweetness of the chow without adding calories, and it produces a major increase in both eating and body weight.

■ Positive-Incentive Theory

The inability of set-point theories to account for the basic phenomena of eating and hunger has led to the development of an alternative theory. The central assertion of this new theoretical perspective, commonly referred to as the **positive-incentive theory,** is that humans and other animals are not driven to eat by internal energy deficits but are drawn to eat by the anticipated pleasure of eating—the anticipated pleasure of a behavior is called its **positive-incentive value** (see Bolles, 1980; Booth, 1981; Collier, 1980; Rolls, 1981; Toates, 1981).

The major tenet of the positive-incentive theory of eating is that eating is controlled in much the same way as sexual behavior: We engage in sexual behavior not because we have an internal deficit, but because we have evolved to crave it. The evolutionary pressures of unexpected food shortages have shaped us and all other warm-blooded animals, who need a continuous supply of energy to maintain their body temperatures, to take advantage of good food when it is present and eat it. According to the positive-incentive theory, it is the presence of good food, or the anticipation of it, that usually makes us hungry, not an energy deficit.

According to the positive-incentive theory, the degree of hunger you feel at any particular time depends on the interaction of all the factors that influence the positive-incentive value of eating. These include the following: the flavor of the food you are likely to consume, what you have learned about the effects of this food either from eating it previously or from other people, the amount of time since you last ate, the type and quantity of food in your gut, whether or not other people are present and eating, whether or not your blood glucose levels are within the normal range. This partial list illustrates one strength of the positive-incentive theory. Unlike the set-point theories, the positive-incentive theory does not single out one factor as the major determinant of hunger and ignore the others; it acknowledges that many factors interact to determine a person's hunger at any time, and it suggests that this interaction occurs through the influence of these various factors on the positive-incentive value of eating (see Cabanac, 1971).

In this section, you learned that most people think about hunger and eating in terms of energy set points, and you were introduced to an alternative: the positive-incentive theory. Which is correct? If you are like most people, you will have an attachment to familiar ways of thinking and a resistance to new ones. The principles of clear thinking, however, require that you put these tendencies aside and base your views about this important issue entirely on the evidence.

You have already learned about some of the major weaknesses of set-point theories. In the next section, you will learn some of the things that biopsychological research has taught us about eating. As you progress through the section, notice the superiority of positive-incentive theories over set-point theories in accounting for the basic facts of hunger and eating.

12.3 Factors That Determine What, When, and How Much We Eat

This section describes major factors that commonly determine what we eat, when we eat, and how much we eat. Notice that energy deficits are not included among these factors. Although major energy deficits clearly increase hunger and eating, they are not a common factor in the eating behavior of people like us, who live in food-replete societies. Although you may believe that your body is short of energy just before a meal, it is not. This misconception is one that is addressed in this section. Also, notice that research on nonhumans has played an important role in furthering understanding of eating by our species.

Factors That Determine What We Eat

Certain tastes have a high positive-incentive value for virtually all members of a species. For example, most humans have a special fondness for sweet, fatty, and salty tastes. This species-typical pattern of human taste preferences is adaptive because in nature sweet and fatty tastes are typically characteristic of high-energy foods that are rich in vitamins and minerals, and salty tastes are characteristic of sodium-rich foods. In contrast, bitter tastes, for which most humans have an aversion, are often associated with toxins. Superimposed on our species-typical taste preferences and aversions, each of us has the ability to learn specific taste preferences and aversions (see Rozin & Shulkin, 1990).

LEARNED TASTE PREFERENCES AND AVERSIONS
Animals learn to prefer tastes that are followed by an infusion of calories, and they learn to avoid tastes that are followed by illness (e.g., Baker & Booth, 1989; Lucas & Sclafani, 1989; Sclafani, 1990). In addition, humans and other animals learn what to eat from their conspecifics. For example, rats learn to prefer flavors that they experience in mother's milk and those that they smell on the breaths of other rats (see Galef, 1995, 1996; Galef, Whishkin, & Bielavska, 1997). Similarly, in humans, many food preferences are culturally specific—for example, in some cultures, various nontoxic insects are considered to be a delicacy. Galef and

Wright (1995) have shown that rats reared in groups, rather than in isolation, are more likely to learn to eat a healthy diet.

LEARNING TO EAT VITAMINS AND MINERALS
How do animals select a diet that provides all of the vitamins and minerals they need? To answer this question, researchers have studied how dietary deficiencies influence diet selection. Two patterns of results have emerged: one for sodium and one for the other essential vitamins and minerals. When an animal is deficient in sodium, it develops an immediate and compelling preference for the taste of sodium salt (see Rowland, 1990b). In contrast, an animal that is deficient in some vitamin or mineral other than sodium must learn to consume foods that are rich in the missing nutrient by experiencing their positive effects; this is because vitamins and minerals other than sodium normally have no detectable taste in food. For example, rats maintained on a diet deficient in *thiamine* (vitamin B_1) develop an aversion to the taste of that diet; and if they are offered two new diets, one deficient in thiamine and one rich in thiamine, they often develop a preference for the taste of the thiamine-rich diet over the ensuing days.

If we, like rats, are capable of learning to select diets that are rich in the vitamins and minerals we need, why are dietary deficiencies so prevalent in our society (see Willett, 1994)? One reason is that, in order to maximize profits, manufacturers produce foods with the tastes that we prefer but with most of the essential nutrients extracted from them. (Even rats prefer chocolate chip cookies to nutritionally complete rat chow.) The second reason is illustrated by the classic study of Harris and associates (1933). When thiamine-deficient rats were offered two new diets, one with thiamine and one without, almost all of them learned to eat the complete diet and avoid the deficient one. However, when they were offered ten new diets, only one of which contained the badly needed thiamine, few developed a preference for the complete diet. The number of different substances consumed each day by most people in industrialized societies is immense, and this makes it difficult, if not impossible, for their bodies to learn which foods are beneficial and which are not.

Factors That Influence When We Eat

Collier and his colleagues (see Collier, 1986) found that most mammals choose to eat many small meals (snacks) each day if they have ready access to a continuous supply of food. Only when there are physical costs involved in initiating meals— for example, having to travel a considerable distance— does an animal opt for a few large meals.

The number of times humans eat each day is influenced by cultural norms, work schedules, family routines, personal preferences, wealth, and a variety of other factors. However, in contrast to the usual mammalian preference, most people, particularly those living in family groups, tend to eat a few large meals each day at regular times. Interestingly, each person's regular mealtimes are the very same times at which that person is likely to feel most hungry; in fact, many people experience attacks of malaise (headache, nausea, and an inability to concentrate) when they miss a regularly scheduled meal.

PREMEAL HUNGER ■ I am sure that you have experienced attacks of premeal hunger. Subjectively, they seem to provide compelling support for set-point theories. Your body seems to be crying out: "I need more energy. I cannot function without it. Please feed me." But things are not always the way they seem. Woods has straightened out the confusion (see Woods, 1991; Woods & Ramsay, 2000; Woods & Strubbe, 1994).

According to Woods, the key to understanding hunger is to appreciate that eating meals stresses the body. Before a meal, the body's energy reserves are in reasonable homeostatic balance; then, as a meal is consumed, there is a homeostasis-disturbing influx of fuels into the bloodstream. The body does what it can to defend its homeostasis. At the first indication that a person will soon be eating—for example, when the usual mealtime approaches—the body enters the cephalic phase and takes steps to soften the impact of the impending homeostasis-disturbing influx by releasing insulin into the blood and thus reducing blood glucose. Woods's message is that the strong, unpleasant feelings of hunger that you may experience at mealtimes are not cries from your body for food; they are the sensations of your body's preparations for the expected homeostasis-disturbing meal. Mealtime hunger is caused by the expectation of food, not by an energy deficit.

As a high school student, I ate lunch at exactly 12:05 every day and was overwhelmed by hunger as the time approached. Now, my eating schedule is different, and I never experience noontime hunger pangs; I now get hungry just before the time at which I usually eat. Have you had a similar experience?

PAVLOVIAN CONDITIONING OF HUNGER ■ In a clever series of Pavlovian conditioning experiments on laboratory rats, Weingarten (1983, 1984, 1985) provided strong support for the view that hunger is often caused by the expectation of food, not by an energy deficit. During the conditioning phase of one of his experiments, Weingarten presented rats with six meals per day at irregular intervals, and he signaled the impending delivery of each meal with a buzzer-and-light conditional stimulus. This conditioning procedure was continued for 11 days. Throughout the ensuing test phase of the experiment, the food was continuously available. Despite the fact that the subjects were never deprived during the test phase, the rats started to eat each time the buzzer and light were presented—even if they had recently completed a meal.

Factors That Influence How Much We Eat

The motivational state that causes us to stop eating a meal when there is food remaining is **satiety**. Satiety mechanisms play a major role in determining how much we eat.

SATIETY SIGNALS ■ As you will learn in the next section of the chapter, food in the gut and glucose entering the blood can induce satiety signals, which inhibit subsequent consumption. These signals seem to depend on both the volume and **nutritive density** (calories per unit volume) of the food.

The effects of nutritive density have been demonstrated in studies in which laboratory rats have been maintained on a single diet. Once a stable baseline of consumption has been established, the nutritive density of the diet is changed. Many rats learn to adjust the volume of food they consume to keep their caloric intake and body weights relatively stable. However, there are limits to this adjustment: Rats often do not increase their intake sufficiently to maintain their body weights if the nutritive density of their conventional laboratory feed is reduced by more than 50%, and they do not maintain the constancy of their caloric intake if there are major changes in the diet's palatability.

SHAM EATING ■ The study of **sham eating** indicates that satiety signals from the gut or blood are not necessary to terminate a meal. In sham-eating experiments, food is chewed and swallowed by the subject; but rather than passing down the subject's esophagus into the stomach, it passes out of the body through an implanted tube (see Figure 12.5 on page 306).

Because sham eating adds no energy to the body, set-point theories predict that all sham-eaten meals should be huge. But this is not the case. Weingarten and Kulikovsky (1989) sham fed rats one of two differently flavored diets: one that the rats had naturally eaten many times before and one that they had never eaten before. The first sham meal of the rats that had previously eaten

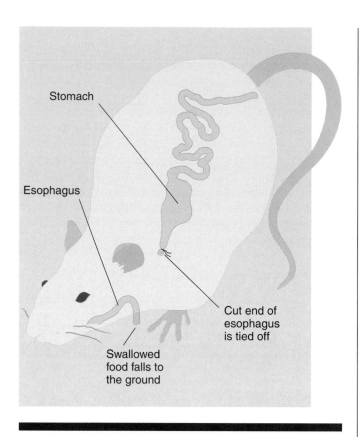

FIGURE 12.5 The sham-eating preparation.

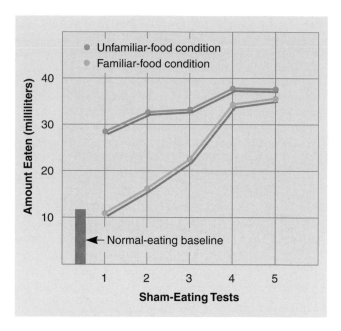

FIGURE 12.6 Change in the magnitude of sham eating over repeated sham-eating trials. The rats in one group sham ate the same diet they had eaten before the sham-eating phase; the rats in another group sham ate a diet different from the one they had previously eaten.
(Adapted from Weingarten, 1990.)

the diet was the same size as the previously eaten meals of that diet; then, on ensuing days they began to sham eat more and more (see Figure 12.6). In contrast, the rats that were presented with the unfamiliar diet sham ate large quantities right from the start. Weingarten and Kulikovsky concluded that the amount we eat is influenced largely by our previous experience with the particular food's postingestive effects, not by the immediate effect of the food on the body.

APPETIZER EFFECT AND SATIETY ■ The next time you attend a dinner party, you may experience a major weakness of the set-point theory of satiety. If appetizers are served, you will experience the fact that small amounts of food consumed before a meal actually increase hunger rather than reducing it. This is the **appetizer effect.** Presumably, it occurs because the consumption of a small amount of food is particularly effective in eliciting cephalic-phase responses.

SOCIAL INFLUENCES AND SATIETY ■ Feelings of satiety depend on whether we are eating alone or with others. Redd and de Castro (1992) found that their subjects consumed 60% more when eating with others. Laboratory rats also eat substantially more when fed in groups.

In humans, social factors have also been shown to reduce consumption. Many people eat less than they

would like in order to achieve their society's ideal of slenderness, and others refrain from eating large amounts in front of others so as not to appear gluttonous. Unfortunately, in our culture, females are greatly influenced by such pressures, and, as you will learn later in the chapter, some develop serious eating disorders as a result.

SENSORY-SPECIFIC SATIETY ■ The number of different tastes available at each meal has a major effect on meal size. For example, the effect of offering a laboratory rat a varied diet of highly palatable foods—a **cafeteria diet**—is dramatic. Adults rats that were offered bread and chocolate in addition to their usual laboratory diet increased their average intake of calories by 84%, and after 120 days they had increased their average body weights by 49% (Rogers & Blundell, 1980). The spectacular effects of cafeteria diets on consumption and body weight clearly run counter to the idea that satiety is rigidly controlled by internal energy set points.

The effect on meal size of cafeteria diets results from the fact that satiety is to a large degree taste-specific. As you eat one food, the positive-incentive value of all foods declines slightly, but the positive-incentive value of that particular food plummets. As a result, you soon become satiated on that food and stop eating it. However, if another food is offered to you, you will often begin eating again.

In one study of **sensory-specific satiety** (Rolls et al., 1981), human subjects were asked to rate the palatability of eight different foods, and then they ate a meal of one of them. After the meal, they were asked to rate the palatability of the eight foods once again, and it was found that their rating of the food they had just eaten had declined substantially more than had their ratings of the other seven foods. Moreover, when the subjects were offered an unexpected second meal, they consumed most of it unless it was the same as the first.

Booth (1981) asked subjects to rate the momentary pleasure produced by the flavor, the smell, the sight, or just the thought of various foods at different times after consuming a large, high-calorie, high-carbohydrate liquid meal. There was an immediate sensory-specific decrease in the palatability of foods of the same or similar flavor as soon as the liquid meal was consumed. This was followed by a general decrease in the palatability of all substances about 30 minutes later. Thus, it appears that signals from taste receptors produce an immediate decline in the positive-incentive value of similar tastes and that signals associated with the postingestive conse-quences of eating produce a general decrease in the positive-incentive value of all foods.

Rolls (1990) suggested that sensory-specific satiety has two kinds of effects: relatively brief effects that influence the selection of foods within a single meal and relatively enduring effects that influence the selection of foods from meal to meal. Some foods seem to be relatively immune to long-lasting sensory-specific satiety; foods such as rice, bread, potatoes, sweets, and green salads can be eaten almost every day with only a slight decline in their palatability (Rolls, 1986).

The phenomenon of sensory-specific satiety has two adaptive consequences. First, it encourages the consumption of a varied diet. If there were no sensory-specific satiety, a person would tend to eat her or his preferred food and nothing else, and the result would be malnutrition. Second, sensory-specific satiety encourages animals that have access to a variety of foods to eat a lot; an animal that has eaten its fill of one food will often begin eating again if it encounters a different one (Raynor & Epstein, 2001). This encourages animals to take full advantage of times of abundance, which are all too rare in nature.

12.4 Physiological Research on Hunger and Satiety

Now that you have been introduced to the set-point theory, the positive-incentive theory, and some basic eating-related facts, this section introduces you to five prominent lines of research on the physiology of hunger and satiety.

Role of Blood Glucose Levels in Hunger and Satiety

As I have already explained, efforts to link blood glucose levels to eating have been largely unsuccessful. However, there was a renewed interest in the role of glucose in the regulation of eating in the 1990s, following the development of methods of continually monitoring blood glucose levels. In the classic experiment of Campfield and Smith (1990), rats were housed individually, with free access to a mixed diet and water, and their blood glucose levels were continually monitored via a chronic intravenous catheter (i.e., a hypodermic needle located in a vein). In this situation, baseline blood glucose levels rarely fluctuated more than 2%. However, about 10 minutes before a meal was initiated, the levels suddenly dropped about 8% (see Figure 12.7 on page 308).

Myth of Hypothalamic Hunger and Satiety Centers

In the 1950s, experiments on rats seemed to suggest that eating behavior is controlled by two different regions of the hypothalamus: satiety by the **ventromedial hypothalamus (VMH)** and feeding by the **lateral hypothalamus (LH)**. Figure 12.8 on page 308 illustrates the locations of the VMH and the LH in the rat brain.

VMH SATIETY CENTER ■ In 1940, it was discovered that large bilateral electrolytic lesions to the ventromedial hypothalamus produce **hyperphagia** (excessive eating) and extreme obesity in rats (Hetherington & Ranson, 1940). This *VMH syndrome* has two different phases: dynamic and static. The **dynamic phase,** which begins as soon as the subject regains consciousness after the operation, is characterized by several weeks of grossly excessive eating and rapid weight gain. However, after that, consumption gradually declines to a level that is just sufficient to maintain a stable level of obesity; this marks the beginning of the **static phase.** Figure 12.9 on page 309 illustrates the weight gain and food intake of an adult rat with bilateral VMH lesions.

FIGURE 12.7 The meal-related changes in blood glucose levels observed by Campfield and Smith (1990).

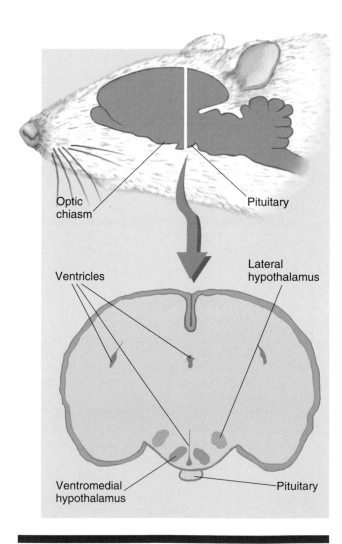

FIGURE 12.8 The locations in the rat brain of the ventromedial hypothalamus and the lateral hypothalamus.

The most important feature of the static phase of the VMH syndrome is that the animal maintains its new body weight. If a rat in the static phase is deprived of food until it has lost a substantial amount of weight, it will regain the lost weight once deprivation is curtailed; conversely, if it is made to gain weight by forced feeding, it will lose the excess once forced feeding is curtailed.

Paradoxically, despite their prodigious levels of consumption, VMH-lesioned rats in some ways seem less hungry than unlesioned controls. Although VMH-lesioned rats eat much more than normal rats when palatable food is readily available, they are less willing to work for it (Teitelbaum, 1957) or to consume it if it is slightly unpalatable (Miller, Bailey, & Stevenson, 1950). Weingarten, Chang, and Jarvie (1983) have shown that the finicky eating of VMH-lesioned rats is a consequence of their obesity, not a primary effect of their lesion; they are no less likely to consume unpalatable food than are unlesioned rats of equal obesity.

LH FEEDING CENTER ■ In 1951, Anand and Brobeck reported that bilateral electrolytic lesions to the *lateral hypothalamus* produce **aphagia**—a complete cessation of eating. Even rats that were first made hyperphagic by VMH lesions were rendered aphagic by the addition of LH lesions. Anand and Brobeck concluded that the lateral region of the hypothalamus is a feeding center. Teitelbaum and Epstein (1962) subsequently discovered two important features of the *LH syndrome*. First, they found that the aphagia was accompanied by **adipsia**—a complete cessation of drinking. Second, they found that LH-lesioned rats partially recover if they are kept alive by tube feeding. First, they begin to eat wet, palatable foods, such as chocolate chip cookies soaked in milk, and even-

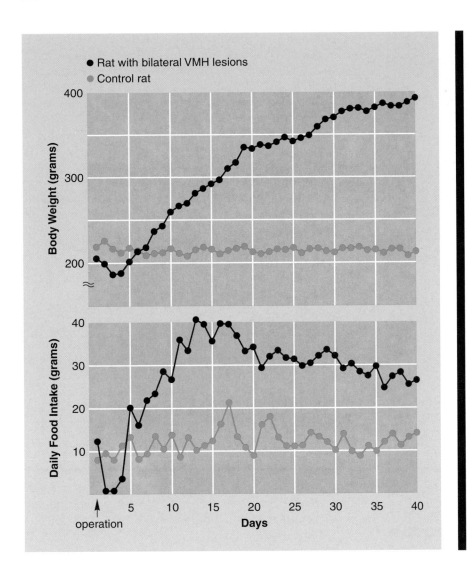

- ● Rat with bilateral VMH lesions
- ● Control rat

FIGURE 12.9 Postoperative hyperphagia and obesity in a rat with bilateral VMH lesions. (Adapted from Teitelbaum, 1961.)

tually they will eat dry food pellets if water is concurrently available.

REINTERPRETATION OF THE EFFECTS OF VMH AND LH LESIONS ■ The theory of VMH satiety and LH feeding centers became very popular, and it was served up to wave after wave of students as if the evidence for it were unassailable. However, little about it is true.

The theory that the VMH is a satiety center has crumbled in the face of two lines of evidence. One of these lines has shown that the primary role of the hypothalamus is the regulation of energy metabolism, not the regulation of eating. The initial interpretation was that VMH-lesioned animals become obese because they overeat; however, the evidence suggests the converse—that they overeat because they become obese. Bilateral VMH lesions increase blood insulin levels, which increases **lipogenesis** (the production of body fat) and decreases **lipolysis** (the breakdown of body fat to utilizable forms of energy)—see Powley et al. (1980). Both are likely to be the result of the increases in insulin levels that occur following the lesion. Because the calories of VMH-lesioned rats are converted to fat at a high rate, the rats must keep eating to ensure that they have enough calories in their blood to meet their immediate energy requirements (e.g., Hustvedt & Løvø, 1972); they are like misers who run to the bank each time they make a bit of money and deposit it in a savings account from which withdrawals cannot be made.

The second line of evidence that has undermined the theory of a VMH satiety center has shown that many of the effects of VMH lesions are not attributable to VMH damage. A large fiber bundle, the *ventral noradrenergic bundle,* courses past the VMH and is thus inevitably damaged by large electrolytic VMH lesions; in particular, fibers that project from the nearby **paraventricular nuclei** of the hypothalamus are damaged (see Figure 12.10 on page 310). Bilateral lesions of the noradrenergic bundle (e.g., Gold et al., 1977) or the paraventricular nuclei (Leibowitz, Hammer, & Chang, 1981) produce hyperphagia and obesity similar to those produced by VMH lesions.

Most of the evidence against the notion that the LH is a feeding center has come from a thorough analysis of the

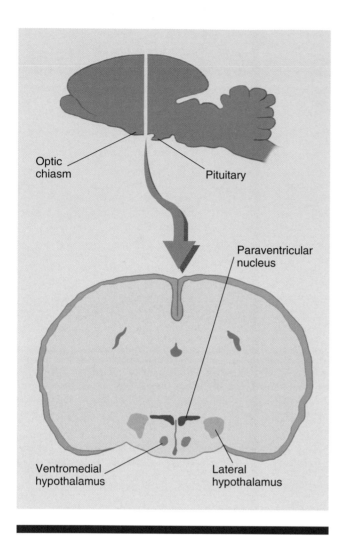

FIGURE 12.10 Location of the paraventricular nucleus in the rat hypothalamus. Note that the section through the hypothalamus is slightly different than the one in Figure 12.8.

effects of bilateral LH lesions. Early research focused exclusively on the aphagia and adipsia that are produced by LH lesions, but subsequent research has shown that LH lesions produce a wide range of severe motor disturbances and a general lack of responsiveness to sensory input (of which food and drink are but two examples). Consequently, the idea that the LH is a center specifically dedicated to feeding no longer warrants serious consideration.

Role of the Gastrointestinal Tract in Satiety

One of the most influential early studies of hunger was published by Cannon and Washburn in 1912. It was a perfect collaboration: Cannon had the ideas, and Washburn had the ability to swallow a balloon. First, Washburn swallowed an empty balloon tied to the end of a thin tube. Then, Cannon pumped some air into the balloon and connected the end of the tube to a water-filled glass U-tube so that Washburn's stomach contractions

produced a momentary increase in the level of the water at the other end of the U-tube. Washburn reported a "pang" of hunger each time that a large stomach contraction was recorded (see Figure 12.11).

Cannon and Washburn's finding led to the theory that hunger is the feeling of contractions caused by an empty stomach, whereas satiety is the feeling of stomach distention. However, support for this theory and interest in the role of the gastrointestinal tract in hunger and satiety quickly waned with the discovery that human patients whose stomachs had been surgically removed and whose esophaguses had been hooked up directly to their **duodenums** continued to report feelings of hunger and satiety and continued to maintain their normal body weights by eating more meals of smaller size.

In the 1980s, there was a resurgence of interest in the role of the gastrointestinal tract in eating. It was stimulated by a series of experiments that indicated that the gastrointestinal tract is the source of satiety signals. For example, Koopmans (1981) transplanted an extra stomach and length of intestine into rats and then joined the major arteries and veins of the implants to the recipients' circulatory systems (see Figure 12.12). Koopmans found that food injected into the transplanted stomach and kept there by a noose around the *pyloric sphincter* decreased eating in proportion to both its caloric content and volume. Because the transplanted stomach had no functional nerves, the gastrointestinal satiety signal had to be reaching the brain through the blood. And because nutrients are not absorbed from the stomach, the blood-borne satiety signal could not have been a nutrient. It had to be some chemical or chemicals that were released from the stomach in response to the caloric value and volume of the food.

Hunger and Satiety Peptides

Soon after the discovery that the stomach and other parts of the gastrointestinal tract release chemicals, evidence began to accumulate that these were *peptides* (see Seeley & Schwartz, 1997), short chains of amino acids that function as hormones and neurotransmitters. Ingested food interacts with receptors in the gastrointestinal tract and in so doing causes the tract to release peptides into the bloodstream. In 1973, Gibbs, Young, and Smith injected one of these gut peptides, **cholecystokinin (CCK),** into hungry rats and found that they ate smaller meals. This led to the hypothesis that circulating gut peptides provide the brain with information about the quantity and nature of food in the gastrointestinal tract and that this information plays a role in satiety.

There has been considerable support for the hypothesis that peptides can function as satiety signals (see Kuhar & Dall Vechia, 1999; Leibowitz, 1992). Several gut peptides have been shown to bind to receptors in the

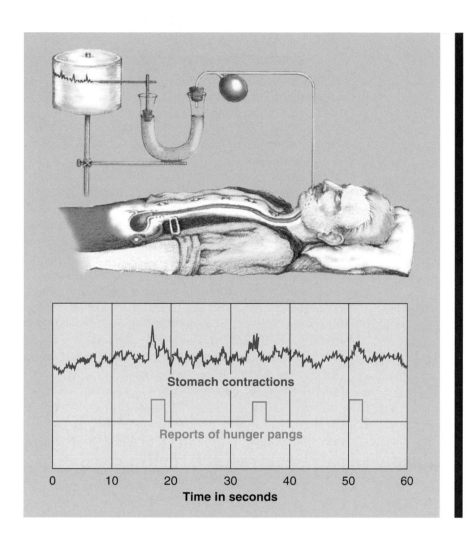

FIGURE 12.11 The system developed by Cannon and Washburn in 1912 for measuring stomach contractions. They found that large stomach contractions were related to pangs of hunger.

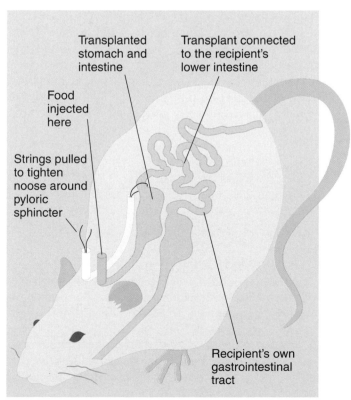

FIGURE 12.12 Transplantation of an extra stomach and length of intestine in a rat. Koopmans (1981) implanted an extra stomach and length of intestine in each of his experimental subjects. He then connected the major blood vessels of the implanted stomachs to the circulatory systems of the recipients. Food injected into the extra stomach and kept there by a noose around the pyloric sphincter decreased eating in proportion to its volume and caloric value.

brain, and a dozen or so (e.g., CCK, bombesin, glucagon, and somatostatin) have been reported to reduce food intake (see Halford & Blundell, 2000).

In studying the appetite-reducing effects of peptides, researchers had to rule out the possibility that these effects are not merely the consequence of illness. Indeed, there is evidence that CCK induces illness: CCK administered to rats after they have eaten an unfamiliar substance induces a *conditioned taste aversion* for that substance, and CCK induces nausea in human subjects. However, CCK reduces appetite and eating at doses substantially below those that are required to induce taste aversions in rats (Ervin et al., 1995; Mosher et al., 1998) or nausea in humans (Pi-Sunyer et al., 1982).

Although most peptides that affect eating have been shown to play an inhibitory role, there are a few exceptions: These are the hunger peptides (e.g., Sakurai et al., 1998). Most widely studied among the hunger peptides are *neuropeptide Y* (Billington & Levine, 1992) and *galanin* (Leibowitz, Akabayashi, & Wang, 1998). Both of these substances increase eating when injected into the *paraventricular nucleus* of the hypothalamus (Leibowitz, 1992).

■ Serotonin and Satiety

The monoaminergic neurotransmitter serotonin also plays a role in satiety. The initial evidence for this role came from a line of research on rats that was initiated in the 1970s. In these studies, *serotonin agonists* consistently reduced rats' food intake.

In rats, the satiety-inducing effects of serotonin have three major characteristics (see Blundell & Halford, 1998). First, they are powerful: They can even overcome the powerful attraction of highly palatable cafeteria diets. Second, they reduce the amount of food that is consumed during each meal rather than reducing the number of meals (see Clifton, 2000). And third, they are associated with a shift in food preferences away from fatty foods.

In humans, serotonin agonists (e.g., fenfluramine, dexfenfluramine, fluoxetine) have been shown to reduce hunger, eating, and body weight under a variety of conditions (see Blundell & Halford, 1998). Indeed, the potential of serotonin agonists as a partial solution to the problem of obesity is currently under intensive investigation. More will be said about this later in the chapter.

12.5 Body Weight Regulation: Set Points versus Settling Points

One strength of the set-point theory of eating is that it also explains body-weight regulation. You have already learned that the set-point theory is largely inconsistent with the facts of eating, but how well does it account for the regulation of body weight? Certainly, most people in our culture believe that body weight is regulated by a body-fat set point (Assanand, Pinel, & Lehman, 1998a, 1998b). They believe that when fat deposits are below a person's set point, a person becomes hungrier and eats more, which results in a return of body-fat levels to that person's set point; and, conversely, they believe that when fat deposits are above a person's set point, a person becomes less hungry and eats less, which results in a return of body fat levels to their set point.

■ Set-Point Assumptions about Body Weight and Eating

You have already learned that set-point theories do a poor job of predicting the major properties of hunger and eating. Do they do a better job of accounting for the facts of body-weight regulation? Let's begin by looking at three lines of evidence that challenge fundamental aspects of many set-point theories of body weight regulation.

VARIABILITY OF BODY WEIGHT ■ The set-point theory is expressly designed to explain why adult body weights remain constant. Indeed, a set-point mechanism should make it virtually impossible for an adult to gain or lose large amounts of weight. Yet, many adults experience large and lasting changes in body weight. Moreover, set-point thinking crumbles in the face of the epidemic of obesity that is currently sweeping fast-food societies.

Set-point theories of body weight regulation suggest that the best method of maintaining a constant body weight is to eat each time there is a motivation to eat—because the main function of these hunger motivations is to defend the set point. However, as I am sure many of you know from personal experience, many people avoid obesity only by resisting their strong drives to eat.

SET POINTS AND HEALTH ■ One implication of set-point theories of body weight regulation is that each person's set-point is optimal for that person's health—or at least not incompatible with good health. This is why media psychologists commonly advise people to "listen to the wisdom of their bodies" and eat as much as they need to satisfy their hunger. Experimental results indicate that this common prescription for good health could not be further from the truth.

Two kinds of evidence suggest that typical *ad libitum* (free-feeding) levels of consumption are unhealthy (see Brownell & Rodin, 1994). First are the results of studies of humans who consume fewer calories than others. For example, people living on the Japanese island of Okinawa seemed to eat so few calories that it was of concern to health officials. When they took a closer look, here is what they found (see Kagawa, 1978). Adult Okinawans were found to consume, on average, 20% fewer calories than other adult Japanese, and Okinawan schoolchildren were found to consume 38% fewer calories than recommended by public health officials. It was somewhat surprising then that rates of morbidity and mortality and of all aging-related diseases were found to be substantially lower in Okinawa than in other parts of Japan, a country in which overall levels of caloric intake and obesity are far below Western norms. For example, the death rates from stroke, cancer, and heart disease in Okinawa were only 59%, 69%, and 59%, respectively, of those in the rest of Japan. Indeed, the proportion of Okinawans living to be over 100 years of age was up to 40 times greater than that of inhabitants of various other regions of Japan.

The Okinawan study and the other studies that have reported major health benefits in humans who eat less (e.g., Manson et al., 1995; Walford & Walford, 1994) are not controlled experiments; therefore they must be interpreted with caution. For example, per- haps it is not the consumption of fewer calories per se that leads to the health and longevity; perhaps people who eat less tend to eat healthier diets. Fortunately, calorie-restriction experiments conducted in over a dozen different species, including monkeys, do not have these problems of interpretation.

The effects of calorie restriction are the second kind of evidence that *ad libitum* levels of consumption are unhealthy. In *calorie-restriction experiments,* one group of subjects is allowed to eat as much as they choose, while other groups of subjects have their caloric intake of the same diets substantially reduced (by between 25% and 65% in various studies). Results of such experiments have been remarkably consistent (see Bucci, 1992; Masoro, 1988; Weindruch, 1996; Weindruch & Walford, 1988): In experiment after experiment, substantial reductions in the caloric intake of balanced diets have improved numerous indices of health and increased longevity. For example, in one experiment (Weindruch et al., 1986), groups of mice had their caloric intake of a well-balanced commercial diet reduced by either 25%, 55%, or 65% after weaning. All levels of dietary restriction substantially improved health and increased longevity but the benefits were greatest in the mice whose intake was reduced the most. Those mice that consumed the least had the lowest incidence of cancer, the best immune responses, and the greatest maximum life span—they lived 67% longer than did mice that ate as much as they liked.

One surprising point about the results of the calorie-restriction experiments: They suggested that the health benefits of restricted diets are not entirely attributable to loss of body fat (see Weindruch, 1996). The subjects were not frankly obese when they commenced their calorie-reduced diets, and thus they did not lose a lot of weight; moreover, there was no correlation between the amount of weight loss and degree of improved health. The current thinking is that some by-product of energy consumption accumulates in cells and accelerates aging with all its attendant health problems (Sohal & Weindruch, 1996).

Please stop and think about the implications of these amazing calorie-restriction experiments. They are not well known in psychology because many were published in agriculture or nutrition journals.

REGULATION OF BODY WEIGHT BY CHANGES IN THE EFFICIENCY OF ENERGY UTILIZATION ■
Implicit in many set-point theories is the premise that body weight is largely a function of how much a person eats. Of course, how much someone eats plays a role in his or her body weight, but it is now clear that the body controls its fat levels, to a large degree, by changing the efficiency with which it uses energy. As a person's level of body fat declines, that person starts to use energy resources more efficiently, which limits further weight loss (see Martin, White, & Hulsey, 1991); conversely, weight gain is limited by a progressive decrease in the efficiency of energy utilization. Rothwell and Stock (1982) created a group of obese rats by maintaining them on a cafeteria diet, and they found that the resting level of energy expenditure in these obese rats was 45% greater than in control rats.

This point is illustrated by the progressively declining effectiveness of weight-loss programs. Initially, low-calorie diets produce substantial weight loss. But the rate of weight loss diminishes with each successive week on the diet, until an equilibrium is achieved and little or no further weight loss occurs. Most dieters are familiar with this disappointing trend. A similar effect occurs with weight-gain programs (see Figure 12.13 on page 314).

The mechanism by which the body adjusts the efficiency of its energy utilization in response to its levels of body fat has been termed **diet-induced thermogenesis.** Increases in the levels of body fat produce increases in body temperature, which require additional energy to maintain them—and decreases in the level of body fat have the opposite effects.

There are major differences among subjects both in their **basal metabolic rate** (the rate at which they utilize energy to maintain bodily processes when resting) and in their ability to adjust their metabolic rate in response to changes in the levels of body fat. We all know people who remain slim even though they eat gluttonously. However, the research on calorie-restricted diets suggests that these people may not eat with impunity: There may be a health cost to pay for overeating even in the absence of obesity.

FIGURE 12.13   The diminishing effects on body weight of a low-calorie diet and a high-calorie diet.

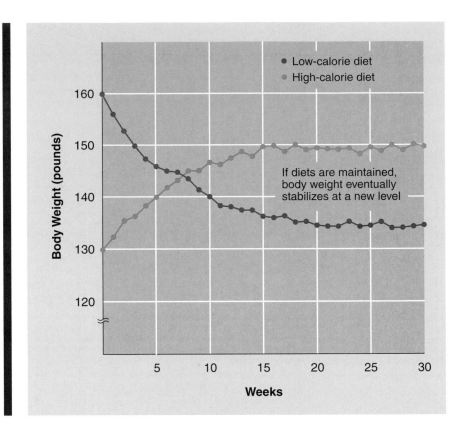

Set Points and Settling Points in Weight Control

Many investigators (see Booth, Fuller & Lewis, 1981; Wirtshafter & Davis, 1977) believe that eating is not part of a system that is designed to defend a body-fat set point. They argue that body weight tends to drift around a natural **settling point**—the level at which the various factors that influence body weight achieve an equilibrium. The idea is that as body-fat levels increase, changes occur that tend to limit further increases until a balance is achieved between all factors that encourage weight gain and all those that discourage it.

The settling-point model provides a loose kind of homeostatic regulation, without a set-point mechanism or mechanisms to return body weight to a set point. According to the settling-point model, body weight remains stable as long as there are no long-term changes in the factors that influence it; and if there are such changes, their impact is limited by negative feedback. In the settling-point model, the feedback merely limits further changes in the same direction, whereas in the set-point model, negative feedback triggers a return to the set point. A neuron's resting potential is a well-known biological settling point—see Chapter 4.

The seductiveness of the set-point theory is attributable in no small part to the existence of the thermostat model, which provides a vivid means of thinking about it. Figure 12.14 presents a model I like to use to think

about the settling-point theory. I call it the **leaky-barrel model.** It is an analogy: (1) The amount of water entering the hose is analogous to the amount of food available to the subject; (2) the water pressure at the nozzle is analogous to the positive-incentive value of the available food; (3) the amount of water entering the barrel is analogous to the amount of energy consumed; (4) the water level in the barrel is analogous to the level of body fat; (5) the amount of water leaking from the barrel is analogous to the amount of energy being expended; and (6) the weight of the barrel on the hose is analogous to the strength of the satiety signal.

The main advantage of the settling-point theory of body weight regulation over the body-fat set-point theory is that it is more consistent with the data. Another advantage is that in those cases in which both theories make the same prediction, the settling-point theory does so more parsimoniously—that is, with a simpler mechanism that requires fewer assumptions. Let's use the leaky-barrel model to see how the two theories account for four key facts of weight regulation.

ON THE CD
Visit the *Leaky Barrel* animation. See the leaky-barrel model of settling-point regulation in action.

Fact 1: Body weight remains relatively constant in many adult animals. On the basis of this fact, it has been argued that body fat must be regulated around a set point. However, constant body weight does not require, or even imply, a set

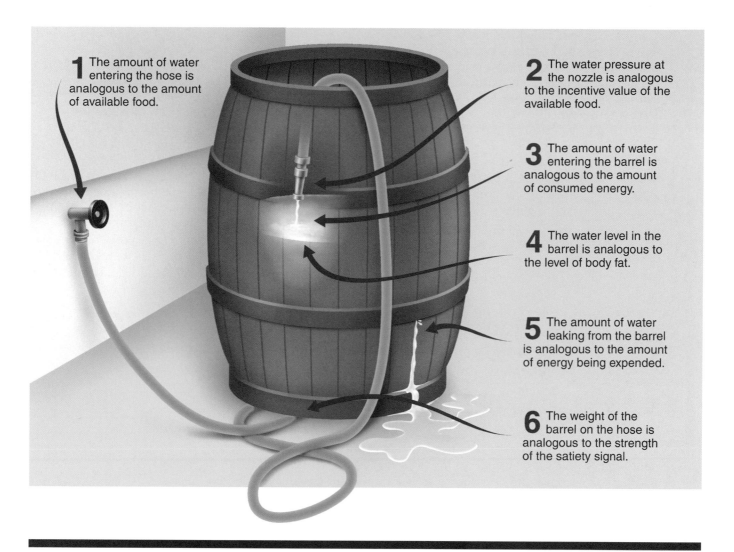

1 The amount of water entering the hose is analogous to the amount of available food.

2 The water pressure at the nozzle is analogous to the incentive value of the available food.

3 The amount of water entering the barrel is analogous to the amount of consumed energy.

4 The water level in the barrel is analogous to the level of body fat.

5 The amount of water leaking from the barrel is analogous to the amount of energy being expended.

6 The weight of the barrel on the hose is analogous to the strength of the satiety signal.

FIGURE 12.14 The leaky-barrel model: a settling-point model of eating and body weight homeostasis.

point. Consider the leaky-barrel model. As water from the tap begins to fill the barrel, the weight of the water in the barrel increases. This increases the amount of water leaking out of the barrel and decreases the amount of water entering the barrel by increasing the pressure of the barrel on the hose. Eventually, this system settles into an equilibrium where the water level stays constant; but because this level is neither predetermined nor actively defended, it is a settling point, not a set point.

Fact 2: Many adult animals experience enduring changes in body weight. Set-point systems are designed to maintain internal constancy in the face of fluctuations of the external environment. Thus, the fact that many adult animals experience long-term changes in body weight is a strong argument against the set-point theory. In contrast, the settling-point theory predicts that when there is an enduring change in one of the parameters that af-

fect body weight—for example, a major increase in the positive-incentive value of available food—body weight will drift to a new settling point.

Fact 3: If a subject's intake of food is reduced, metabolic changes that limit the loss of weight occur; the opposite happens when the subject overeats. This fact is often cited as evidence for set-point regulation of body weight; however, because the metabolic changes merely limit further weight changes rather than eliminating those that have occurred, they are more consistent with a settling-point model. For example, when water intake in the leaky-barrel model is reduced, the water level in the barrel begins to drop; but the drop is limited by a decrease in leakage and an increase in inflow attributable to the falling water pressure in the barrel. Eventually, a new settling point is achieved, but the reduction in water level is not as great as one might expect because of the loss-limiting changes.

Fact 4: After an individual has lost a substantial amount of weight (by dieting, exercise, or the surgical removal of fat), there is a tendency for the original weight to be regained once the subject returns to the previous eating- and energy-related lifestyle. Although this finding is often offered as irrefutable evidence of a body-weight set point, the settling-point theory readily accounts for it. When the water level in the leaky-barrel model is reduced—by temporarily decreasing input (dieting), by temporarily increasing output (exercising), or by scooping out some of the water (surgical removal of fat)—only a temporary drop in the settling point is produced. When the original conditions are reinstated, the water level inexorably drifts back to the original settling point.

Does it really matter whether we think about body weight regulation in terms of set points or settling points—or is it just splitting hairs? It certainly matters to biopsychologists: Understanding that body weight is regulated by a settling-point system helps them better understand and more accurately predict the changes in body weight that are likely to occur in various situations; it also indicates the kinds of physiological mechanisms that are likely to mediate these changes. And it should matter to you. If the set-point theory is correct, attempting to change your body weight would be a waste of time; you would inevitably be drawn back to your body-weight set point. On the other hand, the leaky-barrel model suggests that it is possible to permanently change your body weight by permanently changing any of the factors that influences energy intake and output.

BrainScan

Are you ready to move on to the final two sections of the chapter, which deal with eating disorders? This is a good place to pause and scan your brain to see if you understand the biopsychological principles of eating and weight regulation. Complete the following sentences by filling in the blanks. The correct answers are provided at the bottom of this page. Before proceeding, review material related to your incorrect answers and omissions.

1. The primary function of the _____ is to serve as a storage reservoir for undigested food.

2. Most of the absorption of nutrients into the body takes place through the wall of the _____, or upper intestine.

3. The phase of energy metabolism that is triggered by the expectation of food is the _____ phase.

4. During the absorptive phase, the pancreas releases a great deal of _____ into the bloodstream.

5. During the fasting phase, the primary fuels of the body are _____.

6. During the fasting phase, the primary fuel of the brain is _____.

7. The three components of a set-point system are a set-point mechanism, a detector, and an _____.

8. The theory that hunger and satiety are regulated by a blood glucose set point is the _____ theory.

9. Evidence suggests that hunger is a function of the current _____ value of food.

10. The _____ hypothalamus was once believed to be the satiety center.

11. Evidence suggests that the monoaminergic neurotransmitter _____ plays a role in satiety.

12. Research evidence supports a _____ model of body weight regulation rather than a set-point model.

12.6 Human Obesity

You have already learned that obesity is currently a major health problem in many parts of the world. What is more distressing is the rate at which the problem is growing; in the United States, for example, its incidence more than doubled during the 20th century (see Kuczmarski, 1992) and continues to rise. This rapid rate of increase indicates that environmental factors play a significant role in obesity.

Genetic factors also contribute to obesity. For example, it was estimated from a sample of U.S. twins that environmental and genetic factors contribute equally to individual differences in body fat in this population (see Price & Gottesman, 1991). However, the current surge in obesity is occurring too rapidly to be a product of genetic changes. Also, set-point theory is of no help in trying to understand the epidemic of obesity; according to that theory, permanent weight gain should not occur in healthy adults.

Why Is There an Epidemic of Obesity?

Let's begin our analysis of obesity by considering the pressures that are likely to have led to the evolution of our eating and weight-regulation systems (see Pinel et al., 2000). During the course of evolution, inconsistent food supplies were one of the main threats to survival. As a result, the fittest individuals were those who preferred high-calorie foods, ate to capacity when food was available, stored as many excess calories as possible in the form of body fat, and used their stores of calories as efficiently as possible. Individuals who did not have these characteristics were unlikely to survive a food shortage, and so these characteristics were passed on to future generations.

Augmenting the effects of evolution has been the development of numerous cultural practices and beliefs that promote consumption. For example, in my culture, it is commonly believed that one should eat three meals per day at regular times, whether one is hungry or not; that food should be the focus of most social gatherings; that meals should be served in courses of progressively increasing palatability; and that salt, sweets (e.g., sugar), and fats (e.g., butter) should be added to foods to improve their flavor and thus increase their consumption.

Each of us possesses an eating and weight-regulation system that evolved to deal effectively with periodic food shortages, and many of us live in cultures whose eating-related practices evolved for the same purpose. However, our current environment differs from our "natural" environment in critical food-related ways. We live in an environment in which an endless variety of foods of the highest positive-incentive value are readily and continuously available. The consequence is an appallingly high level of consumption.

Why Do Some People Become Obese While Others Do Not?

Why do some people become obese while others living under the same obesity-promoting conditions do not? At a superficial level, the answer is obvious: Those who are obese are those whose energy intake has grossly exceeded their energy output; those who are slim are those whose energy intake has not grossly exceeded their energy output. Although this answer provides little insight, it does serve to emphasize that two kinds of individual differences play a role in obesity: those that lead to differences in energy input and those that lead to differences in energy output. Let's consider examples of each kind.

There are many factors that lead some people to eat more than others who have comparable access to food. For example, some people consume more energy because they have strong preferences for the taste of high-calorie foods; some consume more because they were raised in families and/or cultures that promote excessive eating; and some consume more because they have particularly large cephalic-phase responses to the sight or smell of food (Rodin, 1985).

With respect to energy output, people differ markedly from one another in the degree to which they can dissipate excess consumed energy. The most obvious difference is that people differ substantially in the amount of exercise they get; however, there are others. You have already learned about two of them: differences in *basal metabolism rate* and in the ability to react to fat increases by *diet-induced thermogenesis*. The third factor is called **NEAT,** or *nonexercise activity thermogenesis,* which is generated by activities such as fidgeting and the maintenance of posture and muscle tone (Ravussin & Danforth, 1999). Although the effects of NEAT on body weight have not been investigated systematically, evidence suggests that it plays a significant role in dissipating excess energy (Levine, Eberhardt, & Jensen, 1999).

Why Are Weight-Loss Programs Typically Ineffective?

Figure 12.15 on page 318 describes the course of the typical dietary weight-loss program. Most weight-loss

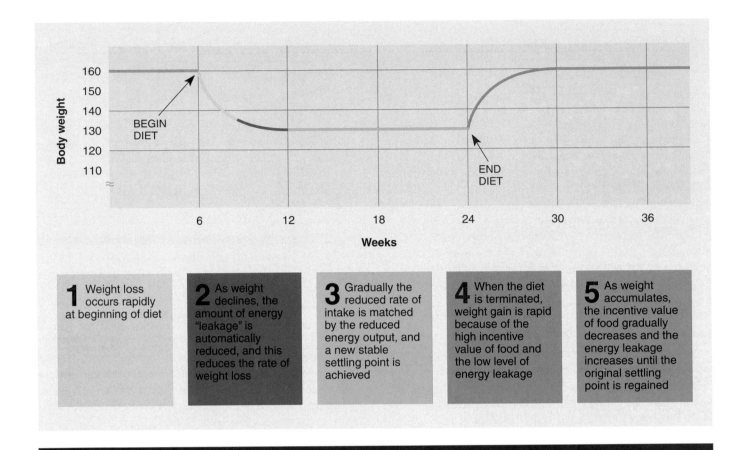

FIGURE 12.15   The five stages of a typical weight-loss program.

programs are unsuccessful in the sense that, as predicted by the settling-point model, most of the lost weight is regained once the program is terminated and the original conditions are reestablished. Clearly, the key to permanent weight loss is a permanent lifestyle change.

People who have difficulty controlling their weight may receive some solace by understanding that the tendency to eat large amounts of food, to accumulate body fat, and to use energy efficiently would all be highly adaptive tendencies in a natural environment. It is our current environment that is "pathological," not the people with weight problems.

Many people believe that exercise is the most effective method of losing weight; however, several studies have shown that exercise contributes little to weight loss (e.g., Sweeney et al., 1993). One reason is that physical activity normally accounts for only a small proportion of total energy expenditure: About 80% of your energy is used to maintain the resting physiological processes of your body and to digest your food (Calles-Escandon & Horton, 1992). Another reason is that after exercise, many people consume drinks and foods that contain more calories than the relatively small number that were expended during the exercise.

Severe cases of obesity are sometimes treated by wiring the jaw shut to limit consumption to liquid diets,

stapling part of the stomach together to reduce the size of meals, or cutting out a section of the duodenum to reduce the absorption of nutrients from the gastrointestinal tract. The main problems with jaw wiring are that some patients do not lose weight on a liquid diet and that those who do typically regain it once the wires are removed. Problems with the other two methods include diarrhea, flatulence, and vitamin and mineral deficiencies.

■ | Mutant Obese Mice and Leptin

In 1950, a genetic mutation occurred spontaneously in the mouse colony being maintained in the Jackson Laboratory at Bar Harbor, Maine. It was thought that this fortuitous development might prove to be the key to understanding and treating extreme forms of human obesity. You see, the mice that were *homozygous* for this mutant gene (ob) were grossly obese, weighing up to three times as much as typical mice (see Figure 12.16). These homozygous obese mice are commonly referred to as **ob/ob mice.**

Ob/ob mice eat more and convert calories to fat more efficiently than controls, and they use their fat calories more efficiently. Coleman

FIGURE 12.16   An ob/ob mouse and a control mouse.

(1979) hypothesized that ob/ob mice lack a critical hormone that normally inhibits fat production.

In 1994, Friedman and his colleagues characterized and cloned the gene that is mutated in ob/ob mice (Zhang et al., 1994). They found that this gene is *expressed* only in fat cells, and they characterized the protein hormone that it encodes. They named this protein **leptin.**

Research has shown that leptin satisfies three criteria for a negative feedback fat signal (Seeley & Schwartz, 1997): (1) levels of leptin in the blood have been found to be positively correlated with fat deposits in humans and other animals (Schwartz et al., 1996a); (2) injections of leptin at doses too low to be aversive have been shown to reduce eating and body fat in ob/ob mice (Campfield et al., 1995); and (3) receptors for leptin have been found in the brain (Schwartz et al., 1996b).

Do obese humans, like ob/ob mice, have a mutation to the ob gene, and do they have low levels of the satiety signal, leptin? The answer to both these questions is no. Genetic mutations are rare in obese humans, and most have high levels of circulating leptin. Moreover, injections of leptin have not reliably reduced the body fat of obese individuals (Heymsfield et al., 1999). Although few obese humans have a genetic mutation to the ob gene, leptin may prove to be a panacea for those few who do. Consider the following case (Farooqi et al., 1999).

The Case of the Child with No Leptin

The patient was of normal weight at birth, but soon it began to increase at an excessive rate. She demanded food continually and was disruptive when denied food. As a result of her extreme obesity, deformities of her legs developed, and surgery was required.

She was 9 when she was referred for treatment. At this point, she weighed 94.4 kilograms (about 210 pounds), and her weight was still increasing at an alarming rate. She was found to be homozygous for the ob gene and had no detectable leptin. Thus, leptin therapy was commenced.

The leptin therapy immediately curtailed the weight gain. She began to eat less, and she lost weight steadily over the 12-month period of the study, a total of 16.5 kilograms (about 36 pounds), almost all in the form of fat. There were no obvious side effects.

■ | Insulin: Another Negative Feedback Fat Signal

Although the discovery of leptin has received substantial publicity, leptin is not the only hormone to satisfy the three criteria for a negative feedback fat signal—it wasn't even the first (see Schwartz, 2000). The pancreatic peptide hormone insulin was identified as being such a signal more than 20 years ago by Woods and colleagues (1979).

At first, the suggestion that insulin serves as a negative feedback fat signal was viewed with a great deal of skepticism. After all, how could the level of insulin in the body, which goes up and then comes back down to normal following each meal, provide the brain with information about gradually changing levels of body fat? It turns out that insulin does not readily penetrate the blood–brain barrier, and the levels in the brain were found to stay relatively stable. More importantly, brain levels of insulin were found to be positively correlated with levels of body fat (Seeley et al., 1996); receptors for it were found in the brain (Baura et al., 1993); and infusions of insulin into the brains of laboratory animals, at doses too low to be aversive and too low to affect blood glucose levels, were found to reduce eating and body weight (Campfield et al., 1995; Chavez, Seeley, & Woods, 1995).

The role of insulin in the regulation of body fat was recently studied in *knockout mice.* Brüning and others (2000) studied the fat levels of mice that lacked the gene for the synthesis of the brain insulin receptor. If insulin inhibits fat accumulation by supplying the brain with information about high fat levels, then subjects without the brain insulin receptor should be fatter. Indeed, the knockout mice were substantially fatter than normal control mice.

■ | Serotonergic Drugs and the Treatment of Obesity

Because—as you have already learned—serotonin agonists have been shown to reduce food consumption in both human and nonhuman subjects, they have considerable potential in the treatment of obesity (Halford &

Blundell, 2000a). Serotonin agonists seem to act by a mechanism different from that for leptin and insulin, which produce long-term satiety signals based on fat stores. Serotonin agonists seem to increase short-term satiety signals associated with the consumption of a meal (Halford & Blundell, 2000b).

Serotonin agonists have been found in various studies of obese patients to reduce the following: the urge to eat high-calorie foods, the consumption of fat, the subjective intensity of hunger, the size of meals, the number of between-meal snacks, and bingeing. Because of this extremely positive profile of effects and the severity of

the obesity problem, serotonin agonists (fenfluramine and dexfenfluramine) were rushed into clinical use. However, they were subsequently withdrawn from the market because chronic use was found to be associated with heart disease in a small, but significant, number of users.

Currently, the search is on for serotonergic weight-loss medications that do not have dangerous side effects. There is reason for optimism. The variety of different serotonin receptor subtypes means that it may be possible to develop serotonin agonists that selectively promote weight loss.

12.7 Anorexia Nervosa

In contrast to obesity, **anorexia nervosa** is a disorder of underconsumption. Anorexics eat so little that they experience health-threatening weight loss; and despite their grotesquely emaciated appearance, they often perceive themselves as fat. About 50% of anorexics periodically engage in binges of eating, which are usually followed by purging with large doses of laxatives or by self-induced vomiting. Individuals who display the cycles of fasting, bingeing, and purging without the extreme weight loss are said to suffer from **bulimia nervosa.**

The incidence of anorexia nervosa among North American student populations is about 2.5%, with the vast majority of sufferers being female. Unfortunately, there are currently no proven effective treatments. In one study, only 29% of treated anorexics had shown significant recovery 20 years later. Approximately 15% of sufferers die from suicide or starvation (Ratnasuriya et al., 1991).

Anorexics are ambivalent about food. On the one hand, they display a higher than normal cephalic-phase insulin response (Broberg & Bernstein, 1989), and they are often preoccupied with the discussion, purchase, and preparation of food. However, eating food is a different matter; they are often disgusted by sweet and fatty tastes, and they often feel ill after a meal.

Anorexia and Dieting

Although some degree of dietary restraint appears to be essential for the maintenance of optimal health by most people in wealthy cultures, the practice of restrained eating is associated with risks. Virtually all patients with eating disorders have a history of strict dieting prior to the onset of the disorder. For example, in one study (Patton, 1988), 21% of teenage girls who were

dieting at the time of their initial interview had developed an eating disorder 1 year later, compared with only 3% of nondieters.

Evidence suggests that people—primarily adolescent females—under great pressure from a cultural emphasis on slenderness begin dieting, and those who are highly controlled, rigid, and obsessive overcome the attraction of food and develop the disorder (see Wilson, Heffernan, & Black, 1996). However, the new ideas about hunger and eating that you have encountered in this chapter point to another factor in the etiology of anorexia nervosa. Consider the following analysis.

Anorexia and Positive Incentives

The positive-incentive theory of hunger suggests that the decline in eating that defines anorexia nervosa is likely a consequence of a corresponding decline in the positive-incentive value of food. However, the positive-incentive value of food for anorexia patients has received little attention—in part, because anorexic patients often display substantial interest in food. The fact that many anorexic patients are obsessed with food—continually talking about it, thinking about it, and preparing it for others (Crisp, 1983)—seems to suggest that it still holds a high positive-incentive value for them. However, to avoid confusion, it is necessary to keep in mind the fact that the positive-incentive value of interacting with food is not necessarily the same as the positive-incentive value of eating food—and it is the positive-incentive value of eating food that is critical when considering anorexia nervosa.

A few studies have examined the positive-incentive value of various tastes in anorexic patients (see, e.g., Drewnowski et al., 1987; Sunday & Halmi, 1990). In general, these studies have found that the positive-incentive value of various tastes is lower in anorexic patients than in control participants. However, these studies grossly underestimate the importance of reductions in the positive-incentive value of food in the etiology of anorexia nervosa because the anorexic participants and the normal-weight control participants were not matched for weight.

People who have had starvation imposed on them—although difficult to find—are the suitable equal-weight comparison subjects for anorexic participants. Starvation normally triggers a radical increase in the positive-incentive value of food. This has been best documented by the descriptions and behavior of participants voluntarily undergoing experimental semistarvation. When asked how it felt to starve, one participant replied:

> I wait for mealtime. When it comes I eat slowly and make the food last as long as possible. The menu never gets monotonous even if it is the same each day or is of poor quality. It is food and all food tastes good. Even dirty crusts of bread in the street look appetizing. (Keys et al., 1950, p. 852)

■ The Puzzle of Anorexia

The domination of set-point theory over research into the regulation of hunger and eating has resulted in widespread inattention to one of the major puzzles of anorexia: Why does the adaptive massive increase in the positive-incentive value of eating that occurs in victims of starvation not occur in starving anorexics? The positive-incentive value of eating normally increases to such high levels under conditions of starvation that it is difficult to imagine how anybody who is starving—no matter how controlled, rigid, obsessive, and motivated—could refrain from eating in the presence of palatable food. Why this protective mechanism is not activated in severe anorexics is a pressing question about the etiology of anorexia nervosa. The answer will have to explain how anyone can overcome food's attraction enough to reach the level of starvation characteristic of extreme anorexia.

I believe that part of the answer lies in the research of Woods and his colleagues on the aversive physiological effects of meals. At the beginning of meals, people are normally in reasonably homeostatic balance, and this homeostasis is disrupted by the sudden infusion of calories. The other part of the answer lies in the finding that the aversive effects of meals are much greater in people who have been eating little (Brooks & Melnik, 1995). Meals, which produce adverse, but tolerable, effects in healthy individuals, may be extremely aversive for individuals who have undergone food deprivation. Evidence for the extremely noxious effects that eating meals has on starving humans is found in the reactions of World War II concentration camp victims to refeeding—many were rendered ill and some were even killed by the very food given to them by their liberators (Keys et al., 1950; see also Solomon & Kirby, 1990).

So why do severe anorexics not experience a massive increase in the positive-incentive value of eating, similar to the increase experienced by other starving individuals? In a word, the answer is *meals*—meals forced on these patients as a result of the misconception of our society that meals are the healthy way to eat. Each meal consumed by an anorexic may produce a variety of conditioned taste aversions that reduce the motivation to eat. This hypothesis needs to be addressed because of its implication for treatment: Anorexic patients—or anybody else who is severely undernourished—should not be encouraged, or even permitted, to eat meals. They should be fed—or infused with—small amounts of food intermittently throughout the day.

The Case of the Anorexic Student

In a society in which obesity is the main disorder of consumption, anorexics are out of step. People who are struggling to eat less have difficulty understanding those who have to struggle to eat. Still, when you stare anorexia in the face, it is difficult not to be touched by it.

She began by telling me how much she had been enjoying the course and how sorry she was to be dropping out of the university. She was articulate and personable, and her grades were high. Her problem was anorexia; she weighed only 82 pounds, and she was about to be hospitalized.

"But don't you want to eat?" I asked naively. "Don't you see that your plan to go to medical school will go up in smoke if you don't eat?"

"Of course I want to eat. I know I am terribly thin—my friends tell me I am. Believe me, I know this is wrecking my life. I try to eat, but I just can't force myself. In a strange way, I am pleased with my thinness."

She was upset, and I was embarrassed by my insensitivity. "It's too bad you're dropping out of the course before we cover the chapter on eating," I said, groping for safer ground.

"Oh, I've read it already," she responded. "It's the first chapter I looked at. It had quite an effect on me; a lot of things started to make more sense. The bit about positive incentives and learning was really good. I think my problem began when eating started to lose its positive-incentive value for me—in my mind, I kind of associated eating with being fat and all the boyfriend problems I was having. This made it easy to diet, but every once in a while I would get hungry and binge, or my parents would force me to eat a big meal. I would eat so much that I would feel ill. So I would put my finger down my throat and make myself throw up. This kept me from gaining weight, but I think it also taught my body to associate my favorite foods with illness—

kind of a conditioned taste aversion. What do you think of my theory?"

Her insightfulness impressed me; it made me feel all the more sorry that she was going to discontinue her studies. How could such a bright, personable young woman knowingly risk her health and everything that she had worked for?

After a lengthy chat, she got up to leave, and I walked her to the door of my office. I wished her luck and made her promise to come back for a visit. I never saw her again. The image of her emaciated body walking down the hallway from my office has stayed with me.

Themes — Revisited

Three of the book's four themes played prominent roles in this chapter. The thinking-about-biopsychology theme was common as you were challenged to critically evaluate your own beliefs and ambiguous research findings, to consider the scientific implications of your own experiences, and to think creatively about the personal and clinical implications of the new ideas you encountered. The chapter ended by using these new ideas to develop a potentially important hypothesis about the etiology of anorexia nervosa. Because of its emphasis on thinking, this chapter is my personal favorite.

Both aspects of the evolutionary theme were emphasized repeatedly. First, you saw how thinking about hunger and eating from an evolutionary perspective leads to important insights. Second, you saw how controlled research on nonhuman species has contributed to our current understanding of human hunger and eating.

Finally, the clinical implications theme was featured in the section on the eating disorders obesity and anorexia nervosa. Three clinical cases played important roles in this chapter: the man who forgot not to eat, the child with no leptin, and the anorexic student.

ON THE CD

Looking for more information about the topics in this chapter? For recommended additional readings, see Hard Copy for Chapter 12.

Log On

- **http://www.aabainc.org/home.html** The home page of the American Anorexia Bulimia Association gives descriptions of the symptoms, risk factors, and treatments for various eating disorders.

- **http://thalamus.wustl.edu/course/hypoANS.html** Washington University School of Medicine presents a review of the anatomy, physiology, and function of the hypothalamus.

- **http://www.findarticles.com/cf_0/m0961/2000_Annual/61855628/p1/article.jhtml?term=brain+eating** This excellent review article on food intake and body weight regulation by Dr. Stephen Woods is from the *Annual Review of Psychology*.

Think about It

1. Set-point theories suggest that attempts at permanent weight loss are a waste of time. On the basis of what you have learned in this chapter, design an effective weight-loss program.

2. Most of the dietary problems that people in our society face occur because the conditions in which we live are different from those in which our species evolved. Discuss.

3. On the basis of what you have learned in this chapter, develop a feeding program for laboratory rats that would lead to obesity. Compare this program with the eating habits prevalent in those cultures in which obesity is a serious problem.

ON THE CD

Studying for an exam? Try the Practice Tests for Chapter 12.

4. What causes anorexia nervosa? Summarize the evidence that supports your view.

Key Terms

Absorptive phase *(p. 300)*
Adipsia *(p. 308)*
Amino acids *(p. 299)*
Anorexia nervosa *(p. 320)*
Aphagia *(p. 308)*
Appetizer effect *(p. 313)*
Basal metabolic rate *(p. 320)*
Bulimia nervosa *(p. 306)*
Cafeteria diet *(p. 300)*
Cephalic phase *(p. 310)*
Cholecystokinin (CCK) *(p. 310)*
Diet-induced thermogenesis
 (p. 313)
Digestion *(p. 298)*
Duodenum *(p. 310)*
Dynamic phase *(p. 307)*

Fasting phase *(p. 300)*
Free fatty acid *(p. 300)*
Glucagon *(p. 300)*
Gluconeogenesis *(p. 300)*
Glucose *(p. 299)*
Glucostatic theory *(p. 302)*
Homeostasis *(p. 302)*
Hyperphagia *(p. 307)*
Insulin *(p. 300)*
Ketones *(p. 300)*
Lateral hypothalamus (LH)
 (p. 307)
Leaky-barrel model *(p. 314)*
Leptin *(p. 319)*
Lipids *(p. 299)*
Lipogenesis *(p. 309)*

Lipolysis *(p. 309)*
Lipostatic theory *(p. 309)*
NEAT *(p. 317)*
Negative feedback systems
 (p. 302)
Nutritive density *(p. 305)*
Ob/ob mice *(p. 318)*
Paraventricular nuclei *(p. 309)*
Positive-incentive theory
 (p. 303)
Positive-incentive value
 (p. 303)
Satiety *(p. 305)*
Sensory-specific satiety
 (p. 307)
Set point *(p. 298)*

Set-point assumption *(p. 301)*
Settling point *(p. 314)*
Sham eating *(p. 305)*
Static phase *(p. 307)*
Ventromedial hypothalamus
 (VMH) *(p. 307)*

ON THE CD

Need some
help studying the key
terms for this chapter?
Check out the elec-
tronic flash cards for
Chapter 12.

Hormones and Sex

What's Wrong with the Mamawawa?

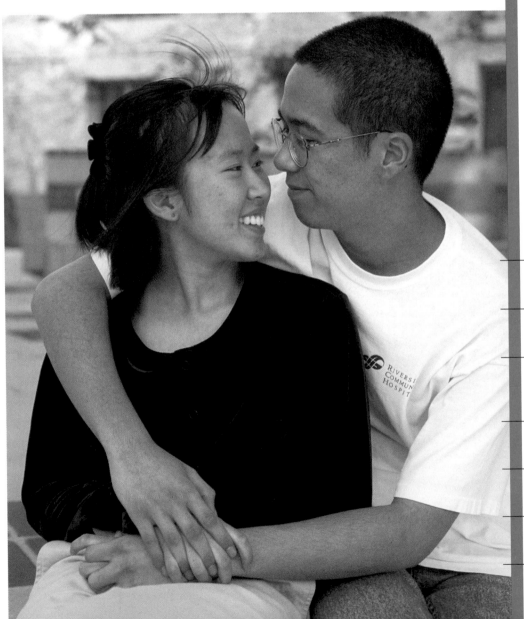

This chapter is about hormones and sex, a topic that fascinates most people. Perhaps it is because we hold our sexuality in such high esteem that we are intrigued by the fact that it is influenced by the secretions of a pair of glands that some regard as unfit topics of conversation. Perhaps it is because we each think of our gender as fundamental and immutable that we are fascinated by the fact that it can be altered with a snip or two and a few hormone injections. Perhaps what fascinates us is the idea that our sex lives might be enhanced by the application of a few hormones. For whatever reason, the topic of hormones and sex is always a hit. Some remarkable things await you in this chapter; let's go directly to them.

■ The Developmental and Activational Effects of Sex Hormones

Hormones influence sex in two ways: (1) by influencing the development from conception to sexual maturity of the anatomical, physiological, and behavioral characteristics that distinguish one as female or male; and (2) by activating the reproduction-related behavior of sexually mature

adults. Both the *developmental* and *activational* effects of sex hormones are discussed in this chapter.

■ The Men-Are-Men-and-Women-Are-Women Assumption

Almost everybody brings to the topic of hormones and sex a piece of excess baggage: the men-are-men-and-women-are-women assumption—or "mamawawa." This assumption is seductive; it seems so right that we are continually drawn to it without considering alternative views. Unfortunately, it is fundamentally flawed.

The men-are-men-and-women-are-women assumption is the tendency to think about femaleness and maleness as discrete, mutually exclusive, complementary categories. In thinking about hormones and sex, this general attitude leads one to assume that females have female sex hormones that give them female bodies and make them do female things, and that males have male sex hormones that give them male bodies and make them do opposite male things. Despite the fact that this approach to hormones and sex is totally wrong, its simplicity, symmetry, and comfortable social implications draw us to it. That's why this chapter grapples with it throughout.

13.1 ▶ The Neuroendocrine System

This section introduces the general principles of neuroendocrine function. It introduces these principles by focusing on the glands and hormones that are directly involved in sexual development and behavior.

The endocrine glands are illustrated in Figure 13.1 on page 326. By convention, only the organs whose primary function is the release of hormones are referred to as endocrine glands. However, other organs (e.g., the stomach, liver, and intestine) also release hormones into general circulation (see Chapter 12), and they are thus, strictly speaking, also part of the endocrine system.

■ Glands

There are two types of glands: exocrine glands and endocrine glands. **Exocrine glands** (e.g., sweat glands) release their chemicals into ducts, which carry them to their targets, mostly on the surface of the body. **Endocrine glands** (ductless glands) release their chemicals, which are called **hormones,** directly into the circulatory system. Once released by an endocrine gland, a hormone travels via the circulatory system until it reaches the tar-

gets on which it normally exerts its effect (e.g., other endocrine glands or sites in the nervous system).

■ Hormones

Most hormones fall into one of three categories: (1) amino acid derivatives, (2) peptides and proteins, and (3) steroids. **Amino acid derivative hormones** are hormones that are synthesized in a few simple steps from an amino acid molecule; an example is *epinephrine,* which is released from the *adrenal medulla* and synthesized from *tyrosine.* **Peptide hormones** and **protein hormones** are chains of amino acids—peptide hormones are short chains, and protein hormones are long chains. **Steroid hormones** are hormones that are synthesized from *cholesterol,* a type of fat molecule.

Steroid hormones play the major role in sexual development and behavior. Most other hormones produce their effects by binding to receptors in cell membranes. Steroid molecules can influence cells in this fashion; however, because they are small and fat-soluble, they can readily penetrate cell membranes and affect cells in a

FIGURE 13.1 The endocrine glands.

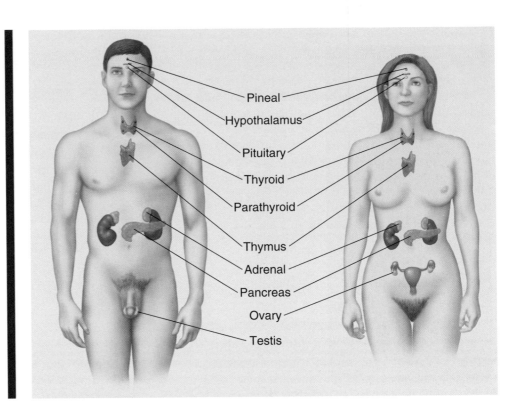

second way. Once inside a cell, the steroid molecules can bind to receptors in the cytoplasm or nucleus and, by so doing, can directly influence gene expression; amino acid derivative and peptide hormones affect gene expression by less direct mechanisms. Consequently, steroid hormones tend to have especially diverse and long-lasting effects on cellular function (Brown, 1994).

Gonads

Central to any discussion of hormones and sex are the **gonads**—the male **testes** (pronounced TEST-eez) and the female **ovaries** (see Figure 13.1). The primary function of the testes and ovaries is the production of *sperm cells* and *ova*, respectively. After **copulation** (sexual intercourse), a single sperm cell may combine with an *ovum* to form a cell called a **zygote,** which contains all of the information necessary for the normal growth of a complete adult organism in its natural environment.

With the exception of ova and sperm cells, each cell of the human body has 23 pairs of chromosomes. In contrast, the ova and sperm cells contain only half that number, one member of each of the 23 pairs. Thus, when a sperm cell fertilizes an ovum, the resulting zygote ends up with the full complement of 23 pairs of chromosomes, one of each pair from the father and one of each pair from the mother.

Of particular interest in the context of this chapter is the pair of chromosomes called the **sex chromosomes,** so named because they contain the genetic programs that direct sexual development. The cells of females have two large X-shaped sex chromosomes, called *X chromosomes.* In males, one sex chromosome is an X chromosome, and the other is a small X-shaped chromosome called a *Y chromosome.* (There must be a good reason for calling a small X-shaped chromosome a Y chromosome, but I don't know what it is.) Consequently, the sex chromosome of every ovum is an X chromosome, whereas half the sperm cells have X chromosomes and half have Y chromosomes. Your gender with all its social, economic, and personal ramifications was determined by which of your father's sperm cells won the dash to your mother's ovum. If a sperm cell with an X sex chromosome won, you are a female; if one with a Y sex chromosome won, you are a male.

Writing this section reminded me of my grade 7 basketball team, "The Nads." The name puzzled our teacher because it was not at all like the names usually favored by pubescent boys—names such as the "Avengers," the "Marauders," and the "Vikings." Her puzzlement ended abruptly at our first game as our fans began to chant their support. You guessed it; "Go Nads, Go! Go Nads, Go!" My 14-year-old spotted-faced teammates and I considered this to be humor of the most mature and sophisticated sort. The teacher didn't.

Sex Steroids

The gonads do more than create sperm and egg cells; they also produce and release hormones. Most people are surprised to learn that the testes and ovaries release the very same hormones. The two main classes of gonadal hormones are **androgens** and **estrogens; testosterone** is the most common androgen, and **estradiol** is the most common estrogen. The fact that adult ovaries tend to release more estrogens than they do androgens and that adult testes release more androgens than they do estrogens has led to the common, but misleading, practice of referring to androgens as "the *male* sex hormones" and to estrogens as "the *female* sex hormones." This practice should be avoided because of its men-are-men-and-women-are-women implication that androgens produce maleness and estrogens produce femaleness. They don't.

The ovaries and testes also release a third class of hormones called **progestins.** The most common progestin is **progesterone,** which in females prepares the uterus and the breasts for pregnancy. Its function in males is unclear.

Because the primary function of the **adrenal cortex**—the outer layer of the *adrenal gland* (see Figure 13.1)—is the regulation of glucose and salt levels in the blood, it is not generally thought of as a sex gland. However, in addition to its principal steroid hormones, it does release in small amounts all of the sex steroids that are released by the gonads.

◼ Hormones of the Pituitary

The pituitary gland is frequently referred to as the *master gland* because most of its hormones are tropic hormones. *Tropic hormones* are hormones whose primary function is to influence the release of hormones from other glands (*tropic* is an adjective that describes things that stimulate or change other things). For example, **gonadotropin** is a pituitary tropic hormone that travels through the circulatory system to the gonads, where it stimulates the release of gonadal hormones.

The pituitary gland is really two glands, the posterior pituitary and the anterior pituitary, which fuse during the course of embryological development. The **posterior pituitary** develops from a small outgrowth of hypothalamic tissue that eventually comes to dangle from the *hypothalamus* on the end of the **pituitary stalk** (see Figure 13.2). In contrast, the **anterior pituitary** begins as part of the same embryonic tissue that eventually develops into the roof of the mouth; during the course of development, it pinches off and migrates upward to assume its position next to the posterior pituitary. It is the anterior pituitary that releases tropic hormones; thus, it is the anterior pituitary in particular, rather than the pituitary in general, that qualifies as the master gland.

◼ Female Gonadal Hormone Levels Are Cyclic, Male Gonadal Hormone Levels Are Steady

The major difference between the endocrine function of women and men is that in women the levels of gonadal and gonadotropic hormones go through a cycle that repeats itself every 28 days or so (see Appendix VIII). It is these more-or-less regular hormone fluctuations that control the female **menstrual cycle.** In contrast, human males are, from a neuroendocrine perspective, rather dull creatures; the levels of their gonadal and gonadotropic hormones change little from day to day.

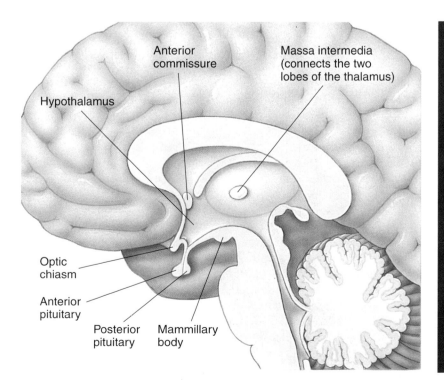

FIGURE 13.2 A midline view of the posterior and anterior pituitary and surrounding structures.

Anterior commissure

Massa intermedia (connects the two lobes of the thalamus)

Hypothalamus

Optic chiasm

Anterior pituitary

Posterior pituitary

Mammillary body

Because the anterior pituitary is the master gland, many early scientists assumed that an inherent difference between the male and female anterior pituitary was the basis for the difference in their patterns of gonadotropic and gonadal hormone release. However, this hypothesis was discounted by a series of clever transplant studies conducted by Geoffrey Harris in the 1950s (see Raisman, 1997). In these studies, a cycling pituitary removed from a mature female rat became a steady-state pituitary when transplanted at the appropriate site in a male, and a steady-state pituitary removed from a mature male rat began to cycle once transplanted in a female. What these studies established was that anterior pituitaries are not inherently female (cyclical) or male (steady-state); their patterns of hormone release are controlled by some other part of the body. The master gland seemed to have its own master. Where was it?

Neural Control of the Pituitary

The nervous system was implicated in the control of the anterior pituitary by behavioral research on birds and other animals that breed only during a specific time of the year. It was found that the seasonal variations in the light–dark cycle triggered many of the breeding-related changes in hormone release. If the lighting conditions under which the animals lived were reversed, for example, by having the animals transported across the equator, the breeding seasons were also reversed. Somehow, visual input to the nervous system was controlling the release of tropic hormones from the anterior pituitary.

The search for the particular neural structure that controlled the anterior pituitary turned, naturally enough, to the *hypothalamus,* the structure from which the pituitary is suspended. Hypothalamic stimulation and lesion experiments quickly established that the hypothalamus is the regulator of the anterior pituitary, but how the hypothalamus carries out this role remained a mystery. You see, the anterior pituitary, unlike the posterior pituitary, receives no neural input whatsoever from the hypothalamus, or from any other neural structure (see Figure 13.3).

Control of the Anterior and Posterior Pituitary by the Hypothalamus

There are two different mechanisms by which the hypothalamus controls the pituitary: one for the posterior pituitary and one for the anterior pituitary. The two major hormones of the posterior pituitary, **vasopressin** and **oxytocin,** are peptide hormones that are synthesized

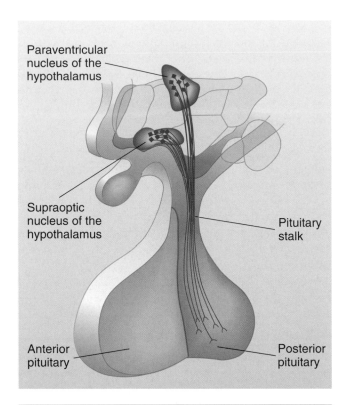

FIGURE 13.3   The neural connections between the hypothalamus and the pituitary. All neural input to the pituitary goes to the posterior pituitary; the anterior pituitary has no neural connections.

in the cell bodies of neurons in the **paraventricular nuclei** and **supraoptic nuclei** of the hypothalamus (see Figure 13.3). They are then transported along the axons of these neurons to their terminals in the posterior pituitary and are stored there until the arrival of action potentials causes them to be released into the bloodstream. (Neurons that release hormones into general circulation are called *neurosecretory cells.*) Oxytocin stimulates contractions of the uterus during labor and the ejection of milk during suckling. Vasopressin (also called *antidiuretic hormone*) facilitates the reabsorption of water by the kidneys.

The means by which the hypothalamus controls the release of hormones from the neuron-free anterior pituitary was more difficult to explain. Harris (1955) suggested that the release of hormones from the anterior pituitary was itself regulated by hormones released from the hypothalamus. Two findings provided early support for this hypothesis. The first was the discovery of a vascular network, the **hypothalamopituitary portal system,** that seemed well suited to the task of carrying hormones from the hypothalamus to the anterior pituitary. As Figure 13.4 illustrates, a network of hypothalamic capillaries feeds a bundle of portal veins that carries blood down the pituitary stalk into another network of

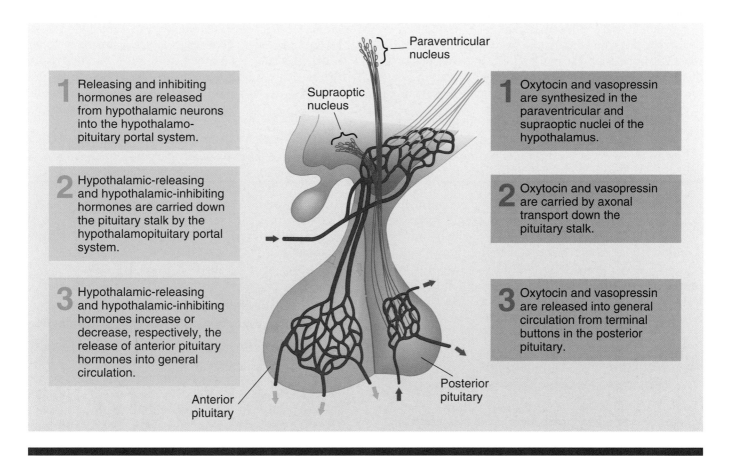

1 Releasing and inhibiting hormones are released from hypothalamic neurons into the hypothalamo-pituitary portal system.

2 Hypothalamic-releasing and hypothalamic-inhibiting hormones are carried down the pituitary stalk by the hypothalamopituitary portal system.

3 Hypothalamic-releasing and hypothalamic-inhibiting hormones increase or decrease, respectively, the release of anterior pituitary hormones into general circulation.

Paraventricular nucleus

Supraoptic nucleus

1 Oxytocin and vasopressin are synthesized in the paraventricular and supraoptic nuclei of the hypothalamus.

2 Oxytocin and vasopressin are carried by axonal transport down the pituitary stalk.

3 Oxytocin and vasopressin are released into general circulation from terminal buttons in the posterior pituitary.

Anterior pituitary

Posterior pituitary

FIGURE 13.4 Control of the anterior and posterior pituitary by the hypothalamus.

capillaries in the anterior pituitary. (A *portal vein* is a vein that connects one capillary network with another.) The second finding was the discovery that cutting the portal veins of the pituitary stalk disrupts the release of anterior pituitary hormones until the damaged veins regenerate (Harris, 1955).

■ Discovery of Hypothalamic Releasing Hormones

 It was hypothesized that the release of each anterior pituitary hormone is controlled by a different hypothalamic hormone. The hypothalamic hormones that were thought to stimulate the release of an anterior pituitary hormone were referred to as **releasing factors;** those thought to inhibit the release of an anterior pituitary hormone were referred to as **inhibitory factors.**

Efforts to isolate the putative (hypothesized) hypothalamic releasing and inhibitory factors led to a major breakthrough in the late 1960s. Guillemin and his colleagues isolated

thyrotropin-releasing hormone from the hypothalamus of sheep, and Schally and his colleagues isolated the same hormone from the hypothalamus of pigs. Thyrotropin-releasing hormone triggers the release of **thyrotropin** from the anterior pituitary, which in turn stimulates the release of hormones from the *thyroid gland.*

It is difficult to appreciate the effort that went into the initial isolation of thyrotropin-releasing hormone. Releasing and inhibiting factors exist in such small amounts that a mountain of hypothalamic tissue was required to extract even minute quantities. Schally reported that the work of his group required over 1 million pig hypothalami. And where did Schally get such a quantity of pig hypothalami? From Oscar Mayer & Company—where else?

Why would two research teams dedicate over a decade of their lives to accumulate a pitifully small quantity of thyrotropin-releasing hormone? The reason was that it enabled both Guillemin and Schally to determine the chemical composition of thyrotropin-releasing hormone and then to develop methods of synthesizing larger quantities of the hormone for research and clinical use. For their efforts, Guillemin and Schally were awarded Nobel Prizes in 1977.

You may have noticed a change in terminology during the preceding discussion: from *releasing factors* to **releasing hormones.** This shift reflects the usual practice of referring to a hormone as a "factor" or "substance" until it has been isolated and its chemical structure identified.

Schally's and Guillemin's isolation of thyrotropin-releasing hormone confirmed that hypothalamic-releasing hormones control the release of hormones from the anterior pituitary and thus provided the major impetus for the isolation and synthesis of several other releasing hormones. Of direct relevance to study of sex hormones was the subsequent isolation of **gonadotropin-releasing hormone** by Schally and his group (Schally, Kastin, & Arimura, 1971). This releasing hormone stimulates the release of both of the anterior pituitary's gonadotropins: **follicle-stimulating hormone (FSH)** and **luteinizing hormone (LH).** All releasing hormones, like all tropic hormones, have proven to be peptides.

Regulation of Hormone Levels

Hormone release is regulated by three different kinds of signals: signals from the nervous system, signals from other hormones, and signals from nonhormonal chemicals in the blood (Brown, 1994).

NEURAL REGULATION ■ All endocrine glands, with the exception of the anterior pituitary, are directly regulated by signals from the nervous system. Endocrine glands located in the brain (i.e., pituitary and pineal) are regulated by cerebral neurons; those located outside the CNS are innervated by the *autonomic nervous system*— usually by both the *sympathetic* and *parasympathetic* branches, which typically have opposite effects on hormone release.

The effects of experience on hormone release are usually mediated by signals from the nervous system. It is extremely important to remember that hormone release is regulated by experience. This means that hormonal explanations do not in any way rule out experiential explanations; they may be different parts of the same mechanism.

HORMONAL REGULATION ■ Signals from the hormones themselves also influence hormone release. You have already learned, for example, that the tropic hormones of the anterior pituitary influence the release of hormones from their respective target glands. However, the regulation of endocrine function by the anterior pituitary is not a one-way street. Circulating hormones often provide feedback to the very structures that influence their release: the pituitary gland, the hypothalamus, and other sites in the brain. The function of most hormonal feedback is the maintenance of stable blood levels of the hormones. Thus, high gonadal hormone levels usually have effects on the hypothalamus and pituitary that decrease subsequent gonadal hormone release, and low levels usually have effects that increase hormone release.

REGULATION BY NONHORMONAL CHEMICALS ■ Circulating chemicals other than hormones can play a role in regulating hormone levels. Glucose, calcium, and sodium levels in the blood all influence the release of particular hormones. For example, you learned in Chapter 12 that increases in blood glucose increase the release of *insulin* from the *pancreas,* and insulin, in turn, reduces blood glucose levels.

Pulsatile Hormone Release

Hormones tend to be released in pulses (Karsch, 1987); they are discharged several times per day in large surges, which typically last no more than a few minutes. Hormone levels in the blood are regulated by changes in the frequency and duration of the hormone pulses (Reame et al., 1984). One consequence of **pulsatile hormone release** is that there are often large minute-to-minute fluctuations in the levels of circulating hormones (e.g., Koolhaas, Schuurman, & Wierpkema, 1980). Accordingly, when the pattern of human male gonadal hormone release is referred to as "steady," it means that there are no major systematic changes in circulating gonadal hormone levels from day to day, not that the levels never vary.

A Summary Model of Gonadal Endocrine Regulation

Figure 13.5 is a summary model of the regulation of gonadal hormones. According to this model, the brain controls the release of gonadotropin-releasing hormone from the hypothalamus into the hypothalamopituitary portal system, which carries it to the anterior pituitary. In the anterior pituitary, the gonadotropin-releasing hormone stimulates the release of gonadotropin, which is carried by the circulatory system to the gonads. In response to the gonadotropin, the gonads release androgens, estrogens, and progestins, which feed back into the pituitary and hypothalamus to regulate subsequent gonadal hormone release.

Armed with this general perspective of neuroendocrine function, you are ready to consider how gonadal hormones direct sexual development and activate adult sexual behavior.

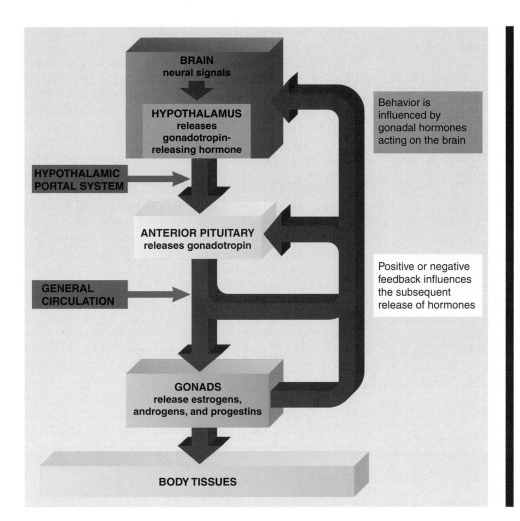

FIGURE 13.5 A summary model of the regulation of gonadal hormones.

13.2 Hormones and Sexual Development

You have undoubtedly noticed that humans are *dimorphic*—that is, they come in two standard models: female and male. This section describes how the development of female and male characteristics is directed by hormones.

The next section discusses three cases of exceptional sexual development. I am sure you will be intrigued by these three cases, but that is not the only reason why I have chosen to include them. My main reason is expressed by a proverb: The exception proves the rule. Most people think this proverb means that the exception "proves" the rule in the sense that it establishes its truth, but this is nonsense: The truth of a rule is challenged by, not confirmed by, exceptions to it. The word *proof* comes from the Latin *probare,* which means "to test"—as in *proving ground* or printer's *proof*—and this is the sense in which it is used in the pro-

verb. Hence, the proverb means that the explanation of exceptional cases is a major challenge for any theory. Accordingly, the primary purpose of discussing the three cases of exceptional sexual development is to test the theories presented in this section.

Sexual differentiation in mammals begins at fertilization with the production of one of two different kinds of zygotes: either one with an XX (female) pair of sex chromosomes or one with an XY (male) pair. (The opening photograph for Chapter 9 shows fertilization in progress.) It is the genetic information on the sex chromosomes that normally determines whether development will occur along female or male lines. But be cautious here: Do not fall into the seductive embrace of the men-are-men-and-women-are-women assumption. Do not begin by assuming that there are two parallel but opposite genetic programs for sexual development, one for female development and one for male development. As you are about to learn, sexual development unfolds according to an entirely different principle, one that many males—particularly those who still stubbornly adhere to notions of male preeminence—find unsettling. This principle is that we are all genetically programmed to develop female bodies; genetic males develop male bodies only because their fundamentally female program of development is overruled.

Fetal Hormones and the Development of Reproductive Organs

GONADS ■ Figure 13.6 illustrates the structure of the gonads as they appear 6 weeks after fertilization. Notice that at this stage of development, each fetus, regardless of its genetic sex, has the same pair of gonadal structures, called *primordial gonads* (*primordial* means "existing at the beginning"). Each primordial gonad has an outer covering, or *cortex,* which has the potential to develop

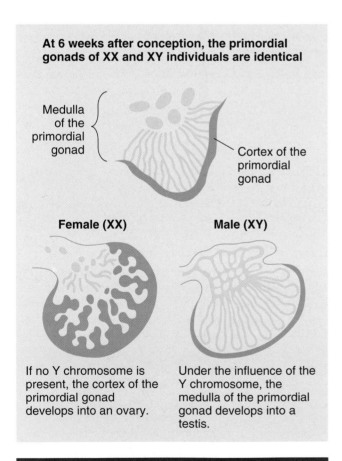

At 6 weeks after conception, the primordial gonads of XX and XY individuals are identical

Medulla of the primordial gonad

Cortex of the primordial gonad

Female (XX)

Male (XY)

If no Y chromosome is present, the cortex of the primordial gonad develops into an ovary.

Under the influence of the Y chromosome, the medulla of the primordial gonad develops into a testis.

FIGURE 13.6 The development of an ovary and a testis from the cortex and medulla, respectively, of the primordial gonadal structure that is present 6 weeks after conception.

into an ovary; and each has an internal core, or *medulla,* which has the potential to develop into a testis.

Six weeks after conception, the Y chromosome of the male triggers the synthesis of **H-Y antigen** (see Haqq et al., 1994; Wang et al., 1995), and this protein causes the medulla of each primordial gonad to grow and to develop into a testis. There is no female counterpart of H-Y antigen; in the absence of H-Y antigen, the cortical cells of the primordial gonads automatically develop into ovaries. Accordingly, if H-Y antigen is injected into a genetic female fetus 6 weeks after conception, the result is a genetic female with testes; or if drugs that block the effects of H-Y antigen are injected into a male fetus, the result is a genetic male with ovaries. Such "mixed-gender" individuals expose in a dramatic fashion the weakness of the "mamawawa" assumption.

INTERNAL REPRODUCTIVE DUCTS ■ Six weeks after fertilization, both males and females have two complete sets of reproductive ducts. They have a male **Wolffian system,** which has the capacity to develop into the male reproductive ducts (e.g., the *seminal vesicles,* which hold the fluid in which sperm cells are ejaculated; and the *vas deferens,* through which the sperm cells travel to the seminal vesicles). And they have a female **Müllerian system,** which has the capacity to develop into the female ducts (e.g., the *uterus;* the upper part of the *vagina;* and the *fallopian tubes,* through which ova travel from the ovaries to the uterus, where they can be fertilized).

In the third month of male fetal development, the testes secrete testosterone and **Müllerian-inhibiting substance.** As Figure 13.7 illustrates, the testosterone stimulates the development of the Wolffian system, and the Müllerian-inhibiting substance causes the Müllerian system to degenerate and the testes to descend into the **scrotum**—the sac that holds the testes outside the body cavity. Because it is testosterone—not the sex chromosomes—that triggers Wolffian development, genetic females who are injected with testosterone during the appropriate fetal period develop male reproductive ducts along with their female ones.

The differentiation of the internal ducts of the female reproductive system (see Figure 13.7) is not under the control of ovarian hormones; the ovaries are almost completely inactive during fetal development. The development of the Müllerian system occurs in any fetus that is not exposed to testicular hormones during the critical fetal period. Accordingly, normal female fetuses, ovariectomized female fetuses, and orchidectomized male fetuses all develop female reproductive ducts (Jost, 1972). **Ovariectomy** is the removal of the ovaries, and **orchidectomy** is the removal of the testes (*orchis* means "testicle"). **Gonadectomy,** or *castration,* is the surgical removal of gonads—either ovaries or testes.

EXTERNAL REPRODUCTIVE ORGANS ■ There is a basic difference between the differentiation of the exter-

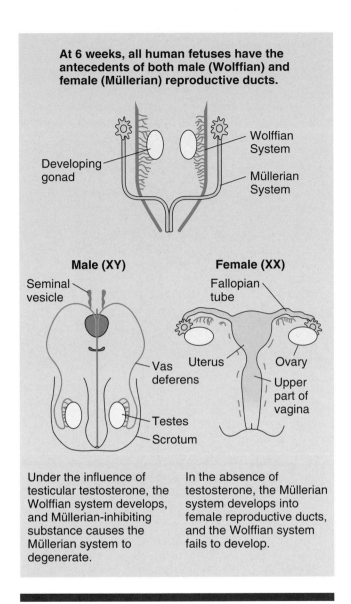

At 6 weeks, all human fetuses have the antecedents of both male (Wolffian) and female (Müllerian) reproductive ducts.

Developing gonad

Wolffian System

Müllerian System

Male (XY)

Seminal vesicle

Vas deferens

Testes

Scrotum

Female (XX)

Fallopian tube

Uterus

Ovary

Upper part of vagina

Under the influence of testicular testosterone, the Wolffian system develops, and Müllerian-inhibiting substance causes the Müllerian system to degenerate.

In the absence of testosterone, the Müllerian system develops into female reproductive ducts, and the Wolffian system fails to develop.

FIGURE 13.7 The development of the internal ducts of the male and female reproductive systems from the Wolffian and Müllerian systems, respectively.

nal reproductive organs and the differentiation of the internal reproductive organs (i.e., the gonads and reproductive ducts). As you have just read, every normal fetus develops separate precursors for the male (medulla) and female (cortex) gonads and for the male (Wolffian system) and female (Müllerian system) reproductive ducts; then, only one set, male or female, develops. In contrast, both male and female **genitals**—external reproductive organs—develop from the same precursor. This *bipotential precursor* and its subsequent differentiation are illustrated in Figure 13.8 on page 334.

In the second month of pregnancy, the bipotential precursor of the external reproductive organs consists of four parts: the glans, the urethral folds, the lateral bodies, and the labioscrotal swellings. Then it begins to differentiate. The *glans* grows into the head of the *penis* in the

male or the *clitoris* in the female, the *urethral folds* fuse in the male or enlarge to become the *labia minora* in the female, the *lateral bodies* form the shaft of the penis in the male or the hood of the clitoris in the female, and the *labioscrotal swellings* form the *scrotum* in the male or the *labia majora* in the female.

Like the development of the internal reproductive ducts, the development of the external genitals is controlled by the presence or absence of testosterone. If testosterone is present at the appropriate stage of fetal development, male external genitals develop from the bipotential precursor; if testosterone is not present, the development of the external genitals proceeds along female lines.

■ Development of Sex Differences in the Brain

The brains of men and women are alike, but they are not identical. The brains of men tend to be, on the average, about 15% larger. Also, a number of more subtle anatomical differences have been documented: slight differences in the anatomy of the hypothalamus, corpus callosum, anterior commissure, thalamus, and cortex (Frederikse et al., 1999; Gur et al., 1999). Positron emission tomography (PET) has revealed sex differences in brain function as well; for example, Gur et al. (1995) reported that men tend to have a higher level of baseline metabolic activity in several areas of the temporal lobe and limbic system, whereas women tend to have higher baseline activity in the cingulate gyrus. Presumably, some of these differences are related to differences in sexual behavior, whereas others are related to differences in cognitive and emotional function; but at the present time, the functional significance of cerebral sex differences remains a matter of conjecture.

How do sex differences in the brain develop? Most of our current understanding of the sexual differentiation of the human brain has come from experiments on rats. Rats are useful subjects for the study of brain development because they are born just 22 days after conception. At 22 days after conception, the period during which hormones can influence their genital development is largely over, but the period during which hormones can influence their brain development is just beginning. Accordingly, it is easy to study the effects of hormones on brain development, unconfounded by their effects on genital development.

PERINATAL ANDROGENS AND BRAIN DIFFERENTIATION ■ Most of the early experiments on the development of sex differences in the brain focused on the factors that control the development of the steady and cyclic patterns of gonadotropin release in males and females, respectively. The seminal experiments were conducted by Pfeiffer in 1936. In his experiments, some neonatal rats (males and females) were gonadectomized

FIGURE 13.8   The development of male and female external reproductive organs from the same bipotential precursor.

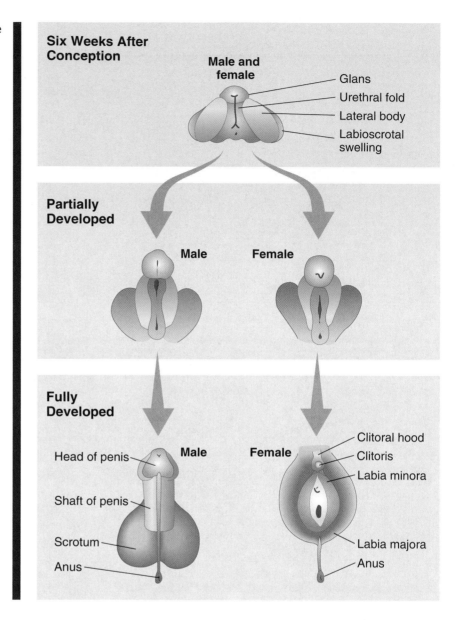

and some were not, and some received gonad transplants (ovaries or testes) and some did not.

Remarkably, Pfeiffer found that gonadectomizing neonatal rats of either genetic sex caused them to develop into adults with the female cyclic pattern of gonadotropin release. In contrast, transplantation of testes into gonadectomized or intact female neonatal rats caused them to develop into adults with the steady male pattern of gonadotropin release. Transplantation of ovaries had no effect on the pattern of hormone release. Pfeiffer concluded that the female cyclic pattern of gonadotropin release develops unless the preprogrammed female cyclicity is overridden by testosterone during perinatal development (see Harris & Levine, 1965).

Pfeiffer incorrectly concluded that the presence or absence of testicular hormones in neonatal rats influenced the development of the pituitary because he was not aware of what we know today: that the release of go-nadotropins from the anterior pituitary is controlled by the hypothalamus. Once this was discovered, it became apparent that Pfeiffer's experiments had provided the first evidence of the role of *perinatal* (around the time of birth) androgens in the sexual differentiation of the hypothalamus. Several other differences between male and female brains have been shown to be under similar hormonal control: The presence of perinatal testosterone leads to the development of male brain characteristics; its absence leads to the development of female brain characteristics, regardless of genetic sex.

AROMATIZATION AND BRAIN DIFFERENTIATION

■ All gonadal and adrenal sex hormones are steroid hormones, which are all derived from *cholesterol*. Because all steroid hormones have similar structures, they are readily converted from one to the other. For example, a slight change to one ring of the testosterone molecule changes that ring to a benzene ring and in so doing, converts testosterone to estradiol; this process is called **aromatization** (see Balthazart & Ball, 1998).

There is good evidence that aromatization is a critical step in the masculinization of the brain by testosterone in some species. According to this theory, perinatal testosterone does not directly masculinize the brain; the brain is masculinized by estradiol that has been aromatized from perinatal testosterone. Although the idea that estradiol—the alleged female hormone—masculinizes the brain is counterintuitive, there is strong evidence for it in several species. In the rat, for example, (1) the enzyme that is necessary for aromatization of testosterone is present in neonates; (2) neonatal injections of estradiol masculinize the brain; (3) **dihydrotestosterone**—an androgen that cannot be converted to estrogen—has no masculinizing effect on the brain; and (4) agents that block the aromatization of testosterone or block estrogen receptors interfere with the masculinizing effects of testosterone on the brain.

How do genetic females of species whose brains are masculinized by estradiol keep from being masculinized by their mothers' estradiol, which circulates through the fetal blood supply? In the rat, alpha fetoprotein is the answer. **Alpha fetoprotein** is present in the blood of rats during the perinatal period, and it deactivates circulating estradiol by binding to it. How, then, does estradiol masculinize the brain of the male fetus in the presence of the deactivating effects of alpha fetoprotein? Because testosterone is immune to alpha fetoprotein, it can travel unaffected from the testes to the brain, where it enters cells and is converted there to estradiol. The estradiol is not broken down in the brain because alpha fetoprotein does not readily penetrate the blood–brain barrier.

In humans, female fetuses are protected from the masculinizing effects of the mother's estrogens by a *placental barrier*. Unfortunately, this barrier is not as effective against some synthetic estrogens (e.g., *diethylstilbestrol*). As a result, the female offspring of mothers who have been exposed to synthetic estrogens while pregnant may display a variety of male characteristics (see McEwen, 1983).

▪ Perinatal Hormones and Behavioral Development

In view of the fact that perinatal hormones influence the development of the brain, it should come as no surprise that they also influence the development of behavior. Much of the research on hormones and behavioral development has focused on the role of perinatal hormones in the development of sexually dimorphic copulatory behaviors in laboratory animals.

Phoenix and colleagues (1959) were among the first to demonstrate that the perinatal injection of testosterone **masculinizes** and **defeminizes** a genetic female's adult copulatory behavior. First, they injected pregnant guinea pigs with testosterone. Then, when the litters were born, they ovariectomized the female offspring. Finally, when these ovariectomized female guinea pigs reached maturity, they injected them with testosterone and assessed their copulatory behavior. Phoenix and his colleagues found that the females that had been exposed to perinatal testosterone displayed more malelike mounting behavior in response to testosterone injections in adulthood than did adult females that had not been exposed to perinatal testosterone. And when as adults they were injected with progesterone and estradiol and mounted by males, they displayed less **lordosis**—the intromission-facilitating arched-back posture of female rodent receptivity.

In a study complementary to that of Phoenix and colleagues, Grady, Phoenix, and Young (1965) found that the lack of early exposure of male rats to testosterone both **feminizes** and **demasculinizes** their copulatory behavior as adults. Male rats castrated shortly after birth failed to display the normal male copulatory pattern of mounting, **intromission** (penis insertion), and **ejaculation** (ejection of sperm) when they were treated with testosterone and given access to a sexually receptive female; and when they were injected with estrogen and progesterone as adults, they exhibited more lordosis than did uncastrated controls. The aromatization of perinatal testosterone to estradiol seems to be important for both the defeminization and the masculinization of rodent copulatory behavior (Goy & McEwen, 1980; Shapiro, Levine, & Adler, 1980).

Because much of the research on hormones and behavioral development has focused on the copulatory act itself, we know less about the role of hormones in the development of **proceptive behaviors** (solicitation behaviors) and in the development of gender-related behaviors that are not directly related to reproduction. However, perinatal testosterone has been reported to disrupt the proceptive hopping, darting, and ear wiggling of receptive female rats; to increase the aggressiveness of female mice; to disrupt the maternal behavior of female rats; and to increase rough social play in female monkeys and rats.

In thinking about hormones and behavioral development, it is important to remember two things. First, feminizing and demasculinizing effects do not always go together; nor do defeminizing and masculinizing effects. Hormone treatments can enhance or disrupt female behavior without affecting male behavior, and vice versa (Bloch, Mills, & Gale, 1995). Second, timing is important. The ability of single injections of testosterone to masculinize and defeminize the rat brain seems to be restricted to the first 11 days after birth. However, large multiple doses of testosterone can have masculinizing effects outside this *sensitive period* (Bloch & Mills, 1995).

Puberty: Hormones and the Development of Secondary Sex Characteristics

During childhood, levels of circulating gonadal hormones are low, reproductive organs are immature, and males and females differ little in general appearance. This period of developmental quiescence ends abruptly with the onset of *puberty*—the transitional period between childhood and adulthood during which fertility is achieved, the adolescent growth spurt occurs, and the secondary sex characteristics develop. **Secondary sex characteristics** are those features other than the reproductive organs that distinguish sexually mature men and women. The body changes that occur during puberty are illustrated in Figure 13.9; you are undoubtedly familiar with at least half of them.

Puberty is associated with an increase in the release of hormones by the anterior pituitary. The increase in the release of **growth hormone**—the only anterior pituitary hormone that does not have an endocrine gland as its primary target—acts directly on bone and muscle tissue to produce the pubertal growth spurt. Increases in gonad-

otropic hormone and **adrenocorticotropic hormone** release cause the gonads and adrenal cortex to increase their release of gonadal and adrenal hormones, which in turn initiate the maturation of the genitals and the development of secondary sex characteristics.

The general principle guiding normal pubertal sexual maturation is a simple one: In pubertal males, androgen levels are higher than estrogen levels, and masculinization is the result; in pubertal females, estrogen predominates, and the result is feminization. Individuals castrated prior to puberty do not become sexually mature unless they receive replacement injections of androgen or estrogen.

But even during puberty, its only major time of relevance, the men-are-men-and-women-are-women assumption stumbles badly. You see, **androstenedione,** an androgen that is released primarily by the adrenal cortex, is normally responsible for the growth of pubic hair and *axillary hair* (underarm hair) in females. It is hard to take seriously the practice of referring to androgens as "male hormones" when one of them is responsible for the development of the female pattern of pubic hair growth. The male pattern is a pyramid, and the female pattern is an inverted pyramid (see Figure 13.9).

Do you remember how old you were when you started to go through puberty? In most North American

FIGURE 13.9 The changes that normally occur in males and females during puberty.

BrainScan

Before you proceed to a consideration of three cases of exceptional human sexual development, scan your brain to see whether you understand the basics of normal sexual development by completing the following exercise. The correct answers are provided at the bottom of this page. Review material related to your errors and omissions before proceeding.

1. Six weeks after conception, the Y chromosome of the human male triggers the production of _____ .

2. In the absence of H-Y antigen, the cortical cells of the primordial gonads develop into _____ .

3. In the third month of male fetal development, the testes secrete testosterone and _____ substance.

4. The hormonal factor that triggers the development of the human Müllerian system is the lack of _____ around the third month of fetal development.

5. The scrotum and the _____ develop from the same bipotential precursor.

6. The female pattern of cyclic _____ release from the anterior pituitary develops in adulthood unless androgens are present in the body during the perinatal period.

7. It has been hypothesized that perinatal testosterone must first be changed to estrogen before it can masculinize the male rat brain. This is called the _____ hypothesis.

8. _____ is normally responsible for pubic and axillary hair growth in human females during puberty.

9. Girls usually begin puberty _____ boys do.

and European countries, puberty begins at about 11 years of age for girls and 12 for boys. I am sure that you would have been unhappy if you had not started puberty until you were 15 or 16, but this was the norm in North America and Europe just a century and a half ago. Presumably, this 4-year acceleration of puberty has resulted from an improvement in dietary, medical, and socio-economic conditions.

13.3 Three Cases of Exceptional Human Sexual Development

So far in this chapter, you have learned the "rules" according to which hormones seem to influence normal sexual development. Now, three exceptional cases are offered to prove (to test) these rules.

The Case of Anne S., the Woman Who Wasn't

Anne S., an attractive 26-year-old female, sought treatment for two sex-related disorders: lack of menstruation and pain during sexual intercourse (Jones & Park, 1971). She sought help because she and her husband of 4 years had

been trying without success to have children, and she correctly surmised that her lack of a menstrual cycle was part of the problem. A physical examination revealed that Anne was a healthy young woman. Her only readily apparent peculiarity was the sparseness and fineness of her pubic and axillary hair. Examination of her external genitals revealed no abnormalities;

Brain Scan answers: (1) H-Y antigen, (2) ovaries, (3) Müllerian-inhibiting, (4) androgens (or testosterone), (5) labia majora, (6) gonadotropin, (7) aromatization, (8) androstenedione, (9) before.

however, there were some problems with her internal genitals. Her vagina was only 4 centimeters long, and her uterus was underdeveloped.

At the start of this chapter, I said that you would encounter some remarkable things, and the diagnosis of Anne's case certainly qualifies as one of them. Anne's doctors concluded that she was a man. No, this is not a misprint; they concluded that Anne, the attractive young housewife, was in fact Anne, the happily married man. Three lines of evidence supported this diagnosis. First, analysis of cells scraped from the inside of Anne's mouth revealed that they were of the male XY type. Second, a tiny incision in Anne's abdomen, which enabled Anne's physicians to look inside, revealed a pair of internalized testes but no ovaries. Finally, hormone tests revealed that Anne's hormone levels were those of a male.

Anne suffers from **androgenic insensitivity syndrome;** all her symptoms stem from a mutation to the androgen receptor gene that rendered her androgen receptors defective (see Fink et al., 1999; Goldstein, 2000). During development, Anne's testes released normal amounts of androgens for a male, but her body could not respond to them, and her development thus proceeded as if no androgens had been released. Her external genitals, her brain, and her behavior developed along preprogrammed female lines, without the effects of androgens to override the female program, and her testes could not descend from her body cavity with no scrotum for them to descend into. Furthermore, Anne did not develop normal internal female reproductive ducts because, like other genetic males, her testes released Müllerian-inhibiting substance; that is why her vagina was short and her uterus undeveloped. At puberty, Anne's testes released enough estrogens to feminize her body in the absence of the counteracting effects of androgens; however, adrenal androstenedione was not able to stimulate the growth of pubic and axillary hair.

Money and Ehrhardt (1972) studied the psychosexual development of 10 androgen-insensitive patients and concluded that the placidity of their childhood play, their goals, their fantasies, their sexual behavior, and their maternal tendencies—several had adopted children—all conformed to the idealized stereotype of what constitutes femininity in our culture. Apparently, without the masculinizing effects of androgens, infants who look like females and are raised as females come to think and act like females—even when they are genetic males.

An interesting issue of medical ethics is raised by the androgenic insensitivity syndrome. Many people believe that physicians should always disclose all relevant findings to their patients. If you were Anne's physician, would you tell her that she is a man? Would you tell her husband? Anne's vagina was surgically enlarged, she was

counseled to consider adoption, and, as far as I know, she is still happily married and unaware of her genetic sex.

The Case of the Little Girl Who Grew into a Boy

The patient—let's call her Elaine—sought treatment in 1972. Elaine was born with somewhat ambiguous external genitals, but she was raised by her parents as a girl without incident, until the onset of puberty, when she suddenly began to develop male secondary sex characteristics. This was extremely distressing. Her treatment had two aspects: surgical and hormonal. Surgical treatment was used to increase the size of her vagina and decrease the size of her clitoris; hormonal treatment was used to suppress androgen release so that her own estrogen could feminize her body. Following treatment, Elaine developed into an attractive young woman—narrow hips and a husky voice being the only signs of her brush with masculinity. Fifteen years later, she was married and enjoying a normal sex life (Money & Ehrhardt, 1972).

Elaine suffered from adrenogenital syndrome. **Adrogenital syndrome** is a disorder of sexual development caused by **congenital adrenal hyperplasia**—a congenital deficiency in the release of the hormone *cortisol* from the adrenal cortex, which results in compensatory adrenal hyperactivity and the excessive release of adrenal androgens. This has little effect on the development of males, other than accelerating the onset of puberty, but it has major effects on the development of genetic females. Females who suffer from the adrenogenital syndrome are usually born with an enlarged clitoris and partially fused labia. Their gonads and internal ducts are usually normal because the adrenal androgens are released too late to stimulate the development of the Wolffian system.

Most female cases of adrenogenital syndrome are diagnosed at birth. In such cases, the abnormalities of the external genitals are immediately corrected, and cortisol is administered to reduce the levels of circulating adrenal androgens. Following early treatment, adrenogenital females grow up to be physically normal except that the onset of menstruation is likely to be later than normal. This makes them good subjects for studies of the effects of fetal androgen exposure on psychosexual development.

Adrenogenital teenage girls who have received early treatment typically display a high degree of tomboyishness and little interest in maternity (e.g., Ehrhardt, Epstein, & Money, 1968). They prefer boys' clothes and toys, play mainly with boys, show little interest in handling babies, and tend to daydream about future careers rather than motherhood. It is important not to lose sight of the fact that many teenage girls display similar characteristics—and why not? Accordingly, the behavior of treated adrenogenital females, although perhaps tending toward the masculine, is well within the range considered normal by the current standards of our culture.

The most interesting questions about the development of females with adrenogenital syndrome concern their romantic and sexual preferences as adults. They seem to lag behind normal females in dating and marriage—perhaps because of the delayed onset of their menstrual cycle—but in other respects their sexual interests appear normal. Most are heterosexual, although it has been suggested that they have a slight tendency toward bisexuality. However, Zucker and others (1996) found that although females with adrenogenital syndrome had fewer heterosexual experiences and fantasies, they had no more homosexual experiences or fantasies.

Prior to the development of cortisol therapy in 1950, genetic females with adrenogenital syndrome were left untreated. Some were raised as boys and some as girls, but the direction of their pubertal development was unpredictable. In some cases, adrenal androgens predominated and masculinized their bodies; in others, ovarian estrogens predominated and feminized their bodies. Thus, some who were raised as boys were transformed at puberty into women, and some who were raised as girls were transformed into men, with devastating emotional consequences. Elaine was such a case.

The Case of the Twin Who Lost His Penis

One of the most famous cases in the literature on sexual development is that of a male identical twin whose penis was accidentally destroyed during circumcision at the age of 7 months. Because there was no satisfactory way of surgically replacing the lost penis, a respected expert in such matters, John Money, recommended that the boy be castrated, that an artificial vagina be created, that the boy be raised as a girl, and that estrogen be administered at puberty to feminize the body. After a great deal of consideration and anguish, the parents followed Money's advice.

Money's (1975) report of this case of **ablatio penis** has been influential. It has been seen by some as the ultimate test of the *nature–nurture controversy* (see Chapter 2) with respect to the development of sexual identity and behavior. It seemed to pit the masculinizing effects of male genes and male prenatal hormones against the effects of being reared as a female. And the availability of a genetically identical control subject, the twin brother, made the case all the more interesting.

According to Money, the outcome of this case strongly supports the *social-learning theory* of sexual identity. Money reported in 1975, when the patient was 12, that "she" had developed as a normal female, thus confirming his prediction that being gonadectomized, having the genitals surgically altered, and being raised as a girl would override the masculinizing effects of male genes and early androgens. Because it is such an interesting case, Money's description of it continues to be featured in some textbooks, each time carrying with it the message that the sexual identity and sexual behavior of men and women are largely a matter of upbringing.

However, a long-term follow-up study published by experts independent of the ones who initially prescribed the treatment tells an entirely different story (Diamond & Sigmundson, 1997). Despite having female genitalia and being treated as a female, John/Joan developed along male lines. Apparently, the organ that determines the course of psychosocial development is the brain, not the genitals (Reiner, 1997). The following paraphrases from Diamond and Sigmundson's report give you a glimpse of John/Joan's life:

From a very early age, Joan tended to act in a masculine way. She preferred boys' activities and games and displayed little interest in dolls, sewing, or other conventional female activities. When she was four, she was watching her father shave and her mother put on lipstick, and she began to put shaving cream on her face. When she was told to put makeup on like her mother, she said, "No, I don't want no makeup, I want to shave."

"Things happened very early. As a child, I began to see that I felt different about a lot of things than I was supposed to. I suspected I was a boy from the second grade on."

Despite the absence of a penis, Joan often tried to urinate while standing, and she would sometimes go to the boys' lavatory.

Joan was attractive as a girl, but as soon as she moved or talked her masculinity became apparent. She was teased incessantly by the other girls, and she often retaliated violently, which resulted in her expulsion from school.

Joan was put on an estrogen regimen at the age of 12 but rebelled against it. She did not want to feminize; she hated her developing breasts and refused to wear a bra.

At 14, Joan decided to live as a male and switched to John. At that time, John's father tearfully revealed John's entire early history to him. "All of a sudden everything clicked. For the first time I understood who and what I was."

John requested androgen treatment, a *mastectomy* (surgical removal of breasts), and *phaloplasty* (surgical creation of a penis). He became a handsome and popular young man. He married at the age of 25 and adopted his wife's children. He is strictly heterosexual.

John's ability to ejaculate and experience orgasm returned following his androgen treatments. However, his early castration permanently eliminated his reproductive capacity.

John is living a happy and productive life, but he remains bitter about his early treatment and his inability to produce offspring. He wants his story to be told to save others from his experience (Colapinto, 2000).

John's case suggests that the clinical practice of surgically modifying a person's sex at birth should be curtailed. Any such irrevocable treatments should await early puberty and the emergence of the patient's sexual identity and sexual attraction. Then, a compatible course of treatment can be selected.

■ Do the Exceptional Cases Prove the Rule?

Do current theories of hormones and sexual development pass the test imposed by the three preceding cases of exceptional sexual development? In my view, the answer is an em- phatic *yes*. Although current theories do not supply all of the answers, they have contributed greatly to the understanding of exceptional sexual development.

For centuries, cases of abnormal sexual development have befuddled scholars, but now, armed with a basic understanding of the role of hormones in sexual development, they have been able to make sense of even the most puzzling of such cases. Moreover, the modern science of sexual development has pointed the way to effective treatments. Judge these contributions for yourself by comparing your current understanding of these three cases with the understanding that you would have had if you had encountered them before beginning this chapter.

Notice one more thing about the three cases: Each of the three subjects was male in some respects and female in others. Accordingly, each case is a serious challenge to the men-are-men-and-women-are-women assumption.

13.4 Effects of Gonadal Hormones on Adults

Once an individual reaches sexual maturity, gonadal hormones begin to play a role in activating reproductive behavior. These activational effects are the focus of this section, which has three parts. The first deals with the role of hormones in activating the reproduction-related behavior of men. The second deals with the role of hormones in activating the reproduction-related behavior of women. And the third deals with the epidemic of anabolic steroid use.

■ Male Reproduction–Related Behavior and Testosterone

The important role played by gonadal hormones in the activation of male sexual behavior is clearly demonstrated by the asexualizing effects of orchidectomy. Bremer (1959) reviewed the cases of 157 orchidectomized Norwegians. Many had committed sex-related offenses and had agreed to castration to reduce the length of their prison terms.

Two important generalizations can be drawn from Bremer's study. The first is that orchidectomy leads to a reduction in sexual interest and behavior; the second is that the rate and degree of the loss is variable. About half the men became completely asexual within a few weeks of the operation; others quickly lost their ability to achieve an erection but continued to experience some sexual interest and pleasure; and a few continued to copulate successfully, although somewhat less enthusiastically, for the duration of the study. There were also body changes: a reduction of hair on the trunk, extremities, and face; the deposition of fat on the hips and chest; a softening of the skin; and a reduction in strength.

Of the 102 sex offenders in Bremer's study, only 3 were reconvicted of sex offenses. Accordingly, he recommended castration as an effective treatment of last resort for male sex offenders.

Why do some men remain sexually active for months after orchidectomy, despite the fact that testicular hormones are cleared from their bodies within days? It has been suggested that adrenal androgens may play some role in the maintenance of sexual activity in some castrated men, but there is no direct evidence for this hypothesis.

Orchidectomy, in one fell swoop—or, to put it more precisely, in two fell swoops—removes a pair of glands that release many hormones. Because testosterone is the major testicular hormone, the major symptoms of orchidectomy have been generally attributed to the loss of testosterone, rather than to the loss of some other testicular hormone or to some nonhormonal consequence of the surgery. The therapeutic effects of **replacement injections** of testosterone have confirmed this assumption.

The Case of the Man Who Lost and Regained His Manhood

The very first case report of the effects of testosterone replacement therapy concerned an unfortunate 38-year-old World War I veteran, who was castrated in 1918 at the age of 19 by a shell fragment that removed his testes but left his penis undamaged.

> His body was soft; it was as if he had almost no muscles at all; his hips had grown wider and his shoulders seemed narrower than when he was a soldier. He had very little drive. . . .
>
> Just the same this veteran had married, in 1924, and you'd wonder why, because the doctors had told him he would surely be **impotent** [unable to achieve an erection]. . . . he made some attempts at sexual intercourse "for his wife's satisfaction" but he confessed that he had been unable to satisfy her at all. . . .
>
> Dr. Foss began injecting it [testosterone] into the feeble muscles of the castrated man. . . .
>
> After the fifth injection, erections were rapid and prolonged. . . . But that wasn't all. During twelve weeks of treatment he had gained eighteen pounds, and all his clothes had become too small. Originally, he wore fourteen-and-a-half inch collars. Now fifteen-and-a-half were too tight. . . . testosterone had resurrected a broken man to a manhood he had lost forever. (de Kruif, 1945, pp. 97–100)

Since this first clinical trial, testosterone has breathed sexuality into the lives of many men. Testosterone does not, however, eliminate the *sterility* (inability to reproduce) of males who lack functional testes.

The fact that testosterone is necessary for male sexual behavior has led to two widespread assumptions: (1) that the level of a man's sexuality is a function of the amount of testosterone he has in his blood, and (2) that a man's sex drive can be increased by increasing his testosterone levels. Both assumptions are incorrect. Sex drive and testosterone levels are uncorrelated in healthy men, and testosterone injections do not increase their sex drive.

It seems that each healthy male has far more testosterone than is required to activate the neural circuits that produce his sexual behavior and that having more than the minimum is of no advantage in this respect (Sherwin, 1988). A classic experiment by Grunt and Young (1952) clearly illustrates this point.

First, Grunt and Young rated the sexual behavior of each of the male guinea pigs in their experiment. Then, on the basis of the ratings, the researchers divided the male guinea pigs into three experimental groups: low, medium, and high sex drive. Following castration, the sexual behavior of all of the guinea pigs fell to negligible levels within a few weeks (see Figure 13.10), but it recovered after the initiation of a series of testosterone replacement injections. The important point is that although each subject received the same, very large replacement injections of testosterone, the injections simply returned each to its previous level of copulatory activity. The conclusion is clear: With respect to the effects of testosterone on sexual behavior, more is not necessarily better.

Dihydrotestosterone, a nonaromatizable androgen, has failed to reactivate the copulatory behavior of castrated male rats in several studies (see MacLusky & Naftolin, 1981). This suggests that in male rats the activational effects of testosterone on sexual behavior may be produced by estradiol that has been aromatized from the testosterone. However, dihydrotestosterone has proved effective in activating sexual behavior in orchidectomized primates (e.g., Davidson, Kwan, & Greenleaf, 1982).

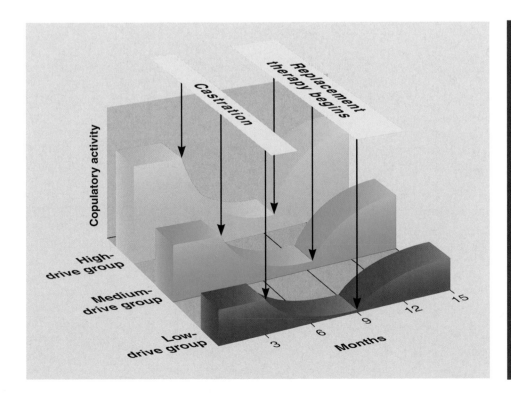

FIGURE 13.10 The sexual behavior of male guinea pigs with low, medium, and high sex drive. Sexual behavior was disrupted by castration and returned to its original level by very large replacement injections of testosterone. (Adapted from Grunt & Young, 1952.)

Female Reproduction–Related Behavior and Gonadal Hormones

Sexually mature female rats and guinea pigs display 4-day cycles of gonadal hormone release. There is a gradual increase in the secretion of estrogen by the developing follicle in the 2 days prior to ovulation, followed by a sudden surge in progesterone as the egg is released. These surges of estrogen and progesterone initiate **estrus**—a period of 12 to 18 hours during which the female is *fertile, receptive* (likely to assume the lordosis posture when mounted), *proceptive* (likely to engage in behaviors that serve to attract the male), and *sexually attractive* (smelling of chemicals that attract males).

The close relation between the cycle of hormone release and the **estrous cycle**—the cycle of sexual receptivity—in female rats and guinea pigs and in many other mammalian species suggests that female sexual behavior in these species is under hormonal control. The effects of ovariectomy confirm this conclusion; ovariectomy of female rats and guinea pigs produces a rapid decline of both proceptive and receptive behaviors. Furthermore, estrus can be induced in ovariectomized rats and guinea pigs by an injection of estradiol followed a day and a half later by an injection of progesterone.

Women are different from female rats and guinea pigs when it comes to the hormonal control of their sexual behavior. Neither the sexual motivation nor the sexual behavior of women is inextricably linked with their menstrual cycles (see Sanders & Bancroft, 1982). Moreover, ovariectomy has surprisingly little direct effect on either their sexual motivation or sexual behavior (e.g., Martin, Roberts, & Clayton, 1980). Other than sterility, the major consequences of ovariectomy in women is a decrease in vaginal lubrication.

Paradoxically, there is evidence that the sex drive of women is under the control of androgens, not estrogens (see Sherwin, 1988). Apparently, enough androgen is released from the human adrenal glands to maintain the sexual motivation of women even after their ovaries have been removed. Support for the theory that androgens control human female sexuality has come from three sources:

1. Experiments in nonhuman female primates: Replacement injections of testosterone, but not estradiol, increase the proceptivity of ovariectomized and adrenalectomized rhesus monkeys (see Everitt & Herbert, 1972; Everitt, Herbert, & Hamer, 1971).
2. Correlational studies in healthy women: Various measures of sexual motivation are correlated with testosterone levels but not with estradiol levels (see Bancroft et al., 1983; Morris et al., 1987).
3. Clinical studies of women following ovariectomy and adrenalectomy: Replacement injections of testosterone, but not of estradiol, rekindle their sexual moti-

vation (see Sherwin, 1985; Sherwin, Gelfand, & Brender, 1985).

Anabolic Steroid Abuse

Anabolic steroids are steroids, such as testosterone, that have *anabolic* (growth-promoting) effects. Testosterone itself is not very useful as an anabolic drug because it is broken down soon after injection and because it has undesirable side effects. Chemists have managed to synthesize a number of potent anabolic steroids that are long-acting, but they have not managed to synthesize one that does not have side effects.

We are currently in the midst of an epidemic of anabolic steroid abuse. Many competitive athletes and bodybuilders are self-administering appallingly large doses to increase their muscularity and strength, but the problem is even more extensive than this. In recent years, the cosmetic use of steroids has reached troubling proportions. For example, recent studies indicate that over a million young American males have used steroids (see Pope, Kouri, & Hudson, 2000).

Because steroids are illegal in most parts of the United States, it has been difficult to document their effects. Research is tightly regulated, and users are not forthcoming.

EFFECTS OF ANABOLIC STEROIDS ON ATHLETIC PERFORMANCE ■ Do anabolic steroids really increase the muscularity and strength of the athletes who use them? Surprisingly, the scientific evidence is inconsistent (see Yesalis & Bahrke, 1995), even though many athletes and coaches believe that it is impossible to compete successfully at the highest levels of their sports without an anabolic steroid boost. The failure of science to confirm the benefits that have been experienced by many athletes likely results from two shortcomings of the scientific research. First, the experimental studies have tended to use doses of steroids smaller than those used by athletes and for shorter periods of time. Second, the experimental studies have often been conducted on subjects who are not involved in intense anabolic training. However, despite the lack of firm scientific evidence, it is difficult to ignore the successes of steroid users such as the man pictured in Figure 13.11.

PHYSIOLOGICAL EFFECTS OF ANABOLIC STEROIDS ■ There is general agreement (see Yesalis & Bahrke, 1995) that people who take high doses of anabolic steroids risk several sex-related physiological side effects. In men, the negative feedback from high levels of anabolic steroids reduces gonadotropin release; this leads to a reduction in testicular activity, which can result in *testicular atrophy* (wasting away of the testes) and sterility. *Gynecomastia* (breast growth in men) can also occur, presumably as the result of the aromatization of anabolic steroids to estrogens. In women, anabolic steroids can

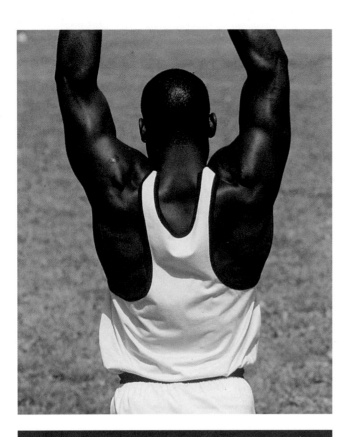

FIGURE 13.11 An athlete who used anabolic steroids to augment his training program.

produce *amenorrhea* (cessation of menstruation), sterility, *hirsutism* (excessive growth of body hair), growth of the clitoris, development of a masculine body shape, baldness, shrinking of the breasts, and deepening and coarsening of the voice. Unfortunately, many of the sex-related effects on women appear to be irreversible.

Both men and women who use anabolic steroids can suffer muscle spasms, muscle pains, blood in the urine, acne, general swelling from the retention of water, bleeding of the tongue, nausea, vomiting, and a variety of psychotic behaviors, including fits of depression and anger (Pope & Katz, 1987). Oral anabolic steroids produce cancerous liver tumors.

A controlled evaluation of the effects of exposure to anabolic steroids was conducted in adult male mice.

Mice were exposed for 6 months to a cocktail of four anabolic steroids at relative levels comparable to those used by human athletes (Bronson & Matherne, 1997). None of the mice died during the period of steroid exposure; however, by 20 months of age, 52% of the steroid-exposed mice had died, whereas only 12% of the controls had died.

BEHAVIORAL EFFECTS OF ANABOLIC STEROIDS ▪ There is no indication that the chronic use of high doses of steroids increases, improves, or redirects sexual motivation or behavior. Accordingly, most of the research on anabolic steroids and nonathletic behavior has focused on aggression.

There have been numerous anecdotal reports that steroid use increases aggression. However, these reports must be treated with caution for at least three reasons. First, because many people believe that testosterone is linked to aggression, reports of aggressive behavior in steroid users might be a consequence of expectation. Second, individuals (e.g., professional fighters or football players) who use steroids are likely to have been aggressive before they started treatment. And third, aggressive behavior might be an indirect consequence of increased size and muscularity.

Despite the need for experimental assessment of the effects of anabolic steroids on aggression, few such experiments have been conducted. The best is a recent experiment by Pope and colleagues (2000). They administered either testosterone or placebo injections in a double-blind study of 53 men. The subjects completed tests of aggression, as well as keeping daily aggression-related diaries—a similar diary was also kept by a "significant other" of each subject. Pope and colleagues found large increases in aggression in some of the subjects, but most experienced little or no change in aggression.

To put the findings of Pope and colleagues in perspective, it is important to realize that testosterone is less potent than other anabolic steroids in common use, that the doses were not large, and that they were administered for a relatively brief period of time. Thus, the fact that Pope and colleagues observed substantial increases in aggression in a few subjects may be only the tip of the iceberg. Clearly, much more research is required.

13.5 The Hypothalamus and Sexual Behavior

Many parts of the brain are involved in mammalian sexual behavior. In fact, the brain is often referred to as "the largest human sex organ." However, the discovery that gonado-tropin release is controlled by the hypothalamus focused the study of the neural bases of sexual behavior on this structure. Accordingly, this section also focuses on it.

Structural Differences between the Male Hypothalamus and the Female Hypothalamus

You have already learned that the male hypothalamus and the female hypothalamus are functionally different in their control of anterior pituitary hormones (steady versus cyclic release, respectively). In the 1970s, structural differences between the male and female hypothalamus were discovered in rats (Raisman & Field, 1971). Most notably, Gorski and his colleagues (1978) discovered a nucleus in the **medial preoptic area** of the rat hypothalamus that was several times larger in males (see Figure 13.12). They called this nucleus the **sexually dimorphic nucleus.**

At birth, the sexually dimorphic nuclei of male and female rats are the same size. In the first few days after birth, the male sexually dimorphic nuclei grow at a high rate and the female sexually dimorphic nuclei do not. The growth of the male sexually dimorphic nuclei is triggered by estradiol, which has been aromatized from testosterone (see McEwen, 1987). Accordingly, castrating day-old (but not 4-day-old) male rats significantly reduces the size of their sexually dimorphic nuclei as adults, whereas injecting neonatal (newborn) female rats with testosterone significantly increases the size of theirs (Gorski, 1980)—see Figure 13.13. Although the overall size of the sexually dimorphic nucleus diminishes only slightly in male rats that are castrated in adulthood, specific areas of the nucleus do display significant degeneration (Bloch & Gorski, 1988).

The size of a male rat's sexually dimorphic nucleus is correlated with the rat's testosterone levels and aspects of its sexual activity (Anderson et al., 1986). However, bilateral lesions of the sexually dimorphic nucleus have only slight disruptive effects on male rat sexual behavior (e.g., DeJonge et al., 1989; Turkenburg et al., 1988), and the specific function of this nucleus is unclear.

FIGURE 13.12 Nissl-stained coronal sections through the preoptic area of male and female rats. The sexually dimorphic nuclei are larger in male rats than in female rats. (Adapted from Gorski et al., 1978.)

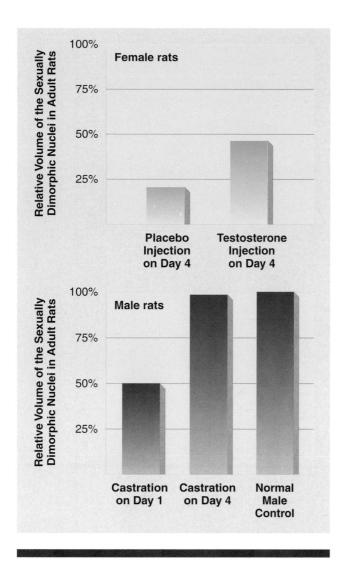

FIGURE 13.13 The effects of neonatal testosterone exposure on the size of the sexually dimorphic nuclei in male and female adult rats. (Adapted from Gorski, 1980.)

Since the discovery of the sexually dimorphic nuclei in rats, other sex differences in hypothalamic anatomy have been identified in rats and in other species (see Swaab & Hofman, 1995; Witelson, 1991). In humans, for example, there are nuclei in the preoptic (Swaab & Fliers, 1985), suprachiasmatic (Swaab et al., 1994), and anterior (Allen et al., 1989) regions of the hypothalamus that are substantially larger in men than in women.

The Hypothalamus and Male Sexual Behavior

The medial preoptic area of the hypothalamus (which includes the sexually dimorphic nucleus) plays a key role in male sexual behavior. Destruction of the entire area abolishes sexual behavior in the males of all mammalian species that have been studied (see Hull et

al., 1999). In contrast, medial preoptic area lesions do not eliminate the female sexual behaviors of females, but they do eliminate the male sexual behaviors (e.g., mount) that are often observed in females (Singer, 1968). Thus, bilateral medial preoptic lesions appear to abolish male copulatory behavior in both sexes. On the other side of the coin, electrical stimulation of the medial preoptic area elicits copulatory behavior in male rats (Malsbury, 1971; Rodriguez-Monzo et al., 2000), and copulatory behavior can be reinstated in castrated male rats by medial preoptic implants of testosterone (Davidson, 1980).

It is not clear why males with medial preoptic lesions stop copulating. These males vigorously approach and investigate receptive females, and they make clumsy attempts to mount them (e.g., Malsbury & Pfaff, 1974; Powers, Newman, & Bergondy, 1987). They seem to want to copulate, but for some unknown reason they can't. Everitt and Stacey (1987) confirmed this notion by assessing the effects of medial preoptic lesions on male rats that had been trained to press a lever for access to receptive females, which dropped into the test chamber through a trap door in the ceiling. Following medial-preoptic-area lesions, the male rats continued to press the lever at a high rate to receive the females, but they never managed to copulate with them. In contrast, orchidectomized males stopped pressing the lever.

The medial preoptic area appears to control male sexual behavior via a tract that projects to an area of the midbrain called the *lateral tegmental field*. Destruction of this tract disrupts the sexual behavior of male rats (Brackett & Edwards, 1984). Moreover, the activity of individual neurons in the lateral tegmental field of male rats is often correlated with aspects of the copulatory act (Shimura & Shimokochi, 1990); for example, some neurons in the lateral tegmental field fire at a high rate only during intromission.

The medial preoptic area seems to serve a somewhat different sexual function in female mammals. Although medial preoptic lesions do not abolish female copulatory behavior, they do reduce the amount of time that females choose to spend with sexually active males (e.g., Yang & Clemens, 2000).

The Hypothalamus and Female Sexual Behavior

The **ventromedial nucleus** (VMN) of the hypothalamus contains circuits that are critical for female sexual behavior. Electrical stimulation of the VMN facilitates the sexual behavior of female rats, and VMN lesions substantially reduce it (see Pfaff & Modianos, 1985). Indeed, female rats with bilateral lesions of the VMN do not display lordosis, and they are likely to attack suitors who become too ardent.

FIGURE 13.14 The hypothalamus-tegmentum circuits that play a role in female and male sexual behavior.

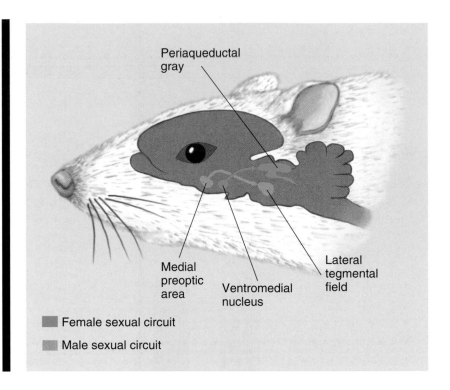

You have already learned that an injection of progesterone brings into estrus an ovariectomized female rat that received an injection of estradiol 48 hours before. Because the progesterone by itself does not induce estrus, the estradiol must in some way prime the nervous system so that the progesterone can exert its effect. This priming effect appears to be mediated by the large increase in the number of *progesterone receptors* that occurs in the VMN and surrounding area following an estradiol injection (Blaustein et al., 1988); the estradiol exerts this effect by entering VMN cells and influencing gene expression. Confirming the role of the VMN in estrus is the fact that microinjections of estradiol and progesterone directly into the VMN induce estrus in ovariectomized female rats (Pleim & Barfield, 1988).

The influence of the VMN on the sexual behavior of female rats appears to be mediated by a tract that descends to the *periaqueductal gray (PAG)* of the tegmentum. Destruction of this tract eliminates female sexual behavior (Hennessey et al., 1990), as do lesions of the PAG itself (Sakuma & Pfaff, 1979).

In summary, research on rodents suggests that tracts that run from the hypothalamus to the mesencephalon play important roles in sexual behavior. Male sexual behavior is influenced by a tract that runs from the medial preoptic area to the lateral tegmental field, and female sexual behavior is influenced by a tract that runs from the ventromedial nucleus to the periaqueductal gray (see Figure 13.14).

13.6 Sexual Orientation, Hormones, and the Brain

So far, this chapter has avoided the issue of sexual orientation. As you know, some people are **heterosexual** (sexually attracted to members of the other sex), some are **homosexual** (sexually attracted to members of the same sex), and some are **bisexual** (sexually attracted to members of both sexes). A discussion of recent research on sexual orientation is a fitting conclusion to this chapter because it brings together the information on sex hormones and the hypothalamus and the exception-proves-the-rule and anti-"mamawawa" messages.

Sexual Orientation and Genes

Research has shown that differences in sexual orientation have a genetic basis. For example, Bailey and Pillard (1991) studied a group of male homosexuals who had twin brothers, and they found that 52% of the monozygotic twin brothers and 22% of the dizygotic twin brothers were homosexual. In a comparable study of female twins by the same group of researchers (Bailey et al., 1993), the concordance rates for homosexuality were 48% for monozygotic twins and 16% for dizygotic twins.

Considerable excitement was created by the claim that a gene for male homosexuality had been localized on one end of the X chromosome (Hamer et al., 1993). However, subsequent research has not confirmed this claim (Rice et al., 1999). The search for specific genes involved in sexual orientation continues.

Sexual Orientation and Early Hormones

Many people mistakenly assume that homosexuals have lower levels of sex hormones. They don't: Heterosexuals and homosexuals do not differ in their levels of circulating hormones. Moreover, orchidectomy reduces the sexual behavior of both heterosexual and homosexual males, but it does not redirect it; and replacement injections simply reactivate the preferences that existed prior to surgery.

Efforts to determine whether perinatal hormone levels influence the development of sexual orientation have focused on nonhuman species. A consistent pattern of findings has emerged from this research (see Ellis & Ames, 1987). In rats, hamsters, ferrets, pigs, zebra finches, and dogs, perinatal castration of males and testosterone treatment of females have been shown to induce same-sex preferences (see Adkins-Regan, 1988; Baum et al., 1990).

On the one hand, prudence should be exercised in applying the results of experiments on laboratory species to the development of sexual preferences in humans; it would be a mistake to ignore the profound cognitive and emotional components of human sexuality, which have no counterpart in laboratory animals. On the other hand, it would also be a mistake to think that a pattern of results that runs so consistently through so many mammalian species has no relevance to humans.

Do perinatal hormone levels influence the sexual orientation of adult humans? Although directly relevant evidence is sparse, there are some indications that the answer is yes. The strongest support for this view comes from the quasiexperimental study of Ehrhardt and her colleagues (1985). They interviewed adult women whose mothers had been exposed to *diethylstilbestrol* (a synthetic estrogen) during pregnancy. The subjects' responses indicated that they were significantly more sexually attracted to women than was a group of matched control subjects. Ehrhardt and her colleagues concluded that perinatal estrogen exposure does encourage homosexuality and bisexuality in women but that its effect is relatively weak: The sexual behavior of all but 1 of the 30 subjects was still primarily heterosexual.

What Triggers the Development of Sexual Attraction?

The evidence indicates that most girls and boys living in Western countries experience their first feelings of sexual attraction at about 10 years of age. This finding is at odds with the usual assumption that sexual interest is triggered by puberty, which, as you have learned, currently tends to occur at 11 years of age in girls and at 12 years in boys.

McClintock and Herdt (1996) have suggested that the emergence of sexual attraction may be stimulated by adrenal cortex steroids. Unlike gonadal maturation, adrenal maturation occurs during childhood, at about the age of 10.

Is There a Difference in the Brains of Homosexuals and Heterosexuals?

There have been several reports of neuroanatomical, neuropsychological, and hormonal response differences between homosexuals and heterosexuals (see Gladue, 1994). Most studies have compared male heterosexuals and homosexuals; studies of lesbians are scarce. In some studies, but not all, male homosexuals have been found to be intermediate between female and male heterosexuals in their brain structure. The study of LeVay (1991) has received the most publicity.

LeVay compared the postmortem neuroanatomy of three groups of subjects: heterosexual men, homosexual men, and women (who were assumed to be heterosexual). Reports of gender differences in the anterior and preoptic areas of the hypothalamus of various species, including humans, focused LeVay's research on these areas. LeVay confirmed a previous report (Allen et al., 1989) that the *third interstitial nucleus of the anterior hypothalamus (INAH 3)* is more than twice as large in heterosexual men as it is in women. In addition, he found that it is more than twice as large in heterosexual men as it is in homosexual men (see Figure 13.15 on page 348). LeVay's report created a kerfuffle (fuss) in both the popular and the scientific media (Byne, 1994; LeVay & Hamer, 1994).

What does LeVay's finding mean? This finding does not prove, as implied in many newspaper articles, that homosexuality results from having a small INAH 3. Like all correlations, LeVay's observation is subject to a variety of causal interpretations. Being a homosexual may cause a small INAH 3, rather than vice versa, or some unrecognized third factor may affect both and be responsible for the correlation.

LeVay considered a third factor that might have led to the correlation, but he ruled it out: the possibility that AIDS was responsible for the correlation. Many of the homosexual brains in LeVay's study came from men who had died of AIDS, which is why LeVay was able to obtain such

FIGURE 13.15 The size of the third interstitial nucleus of the anterior hypothalamus (INAH 3) in heterosexual males and females and in homosexual males. (LeVay, 1991.)

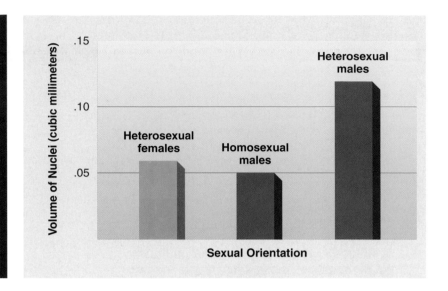

a large sample of male homosexual brains and why he did not include female homosexuals in his study. However, even when LeVay considered only those subjects who had died of other causes, there was still a weak correlation between sexual orientation and the size of the INAH 3.

LeVay's study is controversial; others have failed to replicate it. Still, it has been widely publicized and has stimulated a major effort to identify neural correlates of sexual orientation.

Themes Revisited

Three of the book's four major themes were repeatedly emphasized in this chapter: the evolutionary perspective, clinical implications, and thinking-about-biopsychology themes.

The evolutionary perspective was pervasive. It received frequent attention because most of the experimental studies of hormones and sex have been conducted in nonhuman species. The other major source of information about hormones and sex has been the study of human clinical cases, which is why the clinical implications theme was prominent in the cases of the woman who wasn't, the little girl who grew into a boy, the twin who lost his penis, and the man who lost and regained his manhood.

The thinking-about-biopsychology theme was emphasized throughout the chapter because conventional ways of thinking about hormones and sex have often been at odds with the results of biopsychological research. If you are now better able to resist the seductive appeal of the men-are-men-and-women-are-women assumption, you are leaving this chapter a more broadminded and understanding person than when you began it. I hope you have gained an abiding appreciation of the fact that maleness and femaleness are slight, multidimensional, and at times ambiguous variations of each other.

ON THE CD

Looking for more information about the topics in this chapter? For recommended additional readings, see Hard Copy for Chapter 13.

Log On

■ **http://www.epub.org.br/cm/n03/mente/sexo_i.htm** Dr. Silvia Helena Cardoso authored this review of the physiology of coitus and the influence the brain has on sexual preference and its control of sexual behavior.

■ **http://www.medhelp.org/www/ais/** This page was developed by the Androgen Insensitivity Syndrome Sup-

port Group; it includes complete descriptions of AIS and related conditions.

■ **http://www.apa.org/pubinfo/orient.html** The American Psychological Association provides this informative page on sexual orientation and homosexuality.

Think about It

1. Over the last century and a half, the onset of puberty has changed from age 15 or 16 to age 11 or 12, but there has been no corresponding acceleration in psychological and intellectual development. Precocious puberty is like a loaded gun in the hand of a child. Discuss.

2. Do you think adult sex-change operations should be permitted? Explain.

3. What should be done about the current epidemic of anabolic steroid abuse? Would you make the same recommendation if a safe anabolic steroid were developed? If a safe drug that would dramatically improve your memory were developed, would you take it?

4. Discuss LeVay's report of a difference in the brains of heterosexual and homosexual men with respect to the physiological-or-psychological and the learned-or-innate dichotomies.

5. Heterosexuality cannot be understood without studying homosexuality. Discuss.

6. What treatment should be received by infants born with ambiguous external genitals? Why?

ON THE CD
Studying for an exam? Try the Practice Tests for Chapter 13.

Key Terms

Ablatio penis *(p. 339)*
Adrenal cortex *(p. 327)*
Adrenocorticotropic hormone *(p. 336)*
Adrenogenital syndrome *(p. 338)*
Alpha fetoprotein *(p. 335)*
Amino acid derivative hormones *(p. 325)*
Anabolic steroids *(p. 342)*
Androgenic insensitivity syndrome *(p. 338)*
Androgens *(p. 327)*
Androstenedione *(p. 336)*
Anterior pituitary *(p. 327)*
Aromatization *(p. 335)*
Bisexual *(p. 346)*
Congenital adrenal hyperplasia *(p. 338)*
Copulation *(p. 326)*
Defeminizes *(p. 326)*
Demasculinizes *(p. 335)*
Dihydrotestosterone *(p. 335)*
Ejaculation *(p. 325)*
Endocrine glands *(p. 325)*
Estradiol *(p. 327)*

Estrogens *(p. 327)*
Estrous cycle *(p. 342)*
Estrus *(p. 342)*
Exocrine glands *(p. 325)*
Feminizes *(p. 335)*
Follicle-stimulating hormone (FSH) *(p. 330)*
Genitals *(p. 333)*
Gonadectomy *(p. 332)*
Gonadotropin-releasing hormone *(p. 330)*
Gonadotropins *(p. 327)*
Gonads *(p. 326)*
Growth hormone *(p. 336)*
H-Y antigen *(p. 332)*
Heterosexual *(p. 346)*
Homosexual *(p. 346)*
Hormones *(p. 325)*
Hypothalamopituitary portal system *(p. 328)*
Impotent *(p. 341)*
Inhibitory factors *(p. 329)*
Intromission *(p. 335)*
Lordosis *(p. 335)*
Luteinizing hormone (LH) *(p. 330)*

Masculinizes *(p. 335)*
Medial preoptic area *(p. 344)*
Menstrual cycle *(p. 327)*
Müllerian-inhibiting substance *(p. 332)*
Müllerian system *(p. 332)*
Orchidectomy *(p. 332)*
Ovariectomy *(p. 332)*
Ovaries *(p. 326)*
Oxytocin *(p. 328)*
Paraventricular nuclei *(p. 328)*
Peptide hormones *(p. 325)*
Pituitary stalk *(p. 327)*
Posterior pituitary *(p. 327)*
Proceptive behaviors *(p. 335)*
Progesterone *(p. 327)*
Progestins *(p. 327)*
Protein hormones *(p. 325)*
Pulsatile hormone release *(p. 330)*
Releasing factors *(p. 329)*
Releasing hormones *(p. 330)*
Replacement injections *(p. 340)*
Scrotum *(p. 332)*
Secondary sex characteristics *(p. 336)*

Sex chromosomes *(p. 326)*
Sexually dimorphic nucleus *(p. 344)*
Steroid hormones *(p. 325)*
Supraoptic nuclei *(p. 328)*
Testes *(p. 326)*
Testosterone *(p. 327)*
Thyrotropin *(p. 329)*
Thyrotropin-releasing hormone *(p. 329)*
Vasopressin *(p. 328)*
Ventromedial nucleus *(p. 345)*
Wolffian system *(p. 332)*
Zygote *(p. 326)*

ON THE CD
Need some help studying the key terms for this chapter? Check out the electronic flash cards for Chapter 13.

chapter 14

Sleep, Dreaming, and Circadian Rhythms

How Much Do You Need to Sleep?

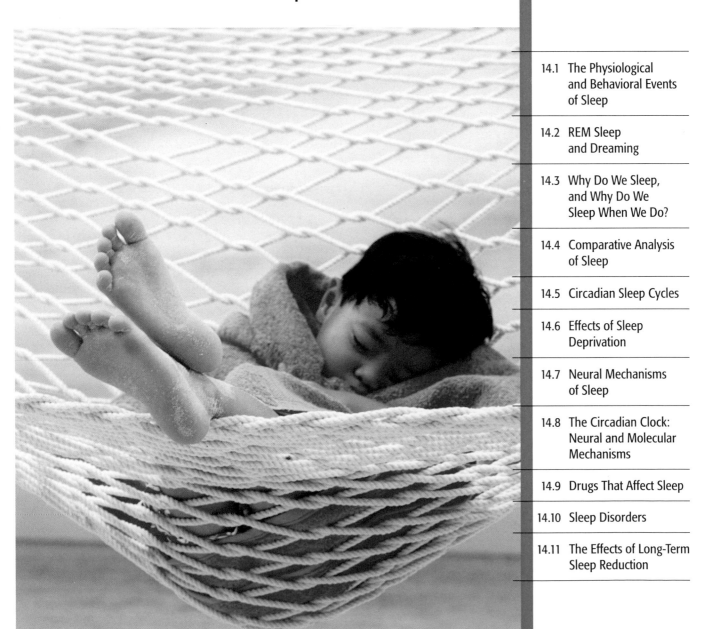

Most of us have a fondness for eating and sex—the two highly esteemed motivated behaviors discussed in Chapters 12 and 13. But the amount of time devoted to these behaviors by even the most amorous gourmands pales in comparison to the amount of time spent sleeping: Most of us will sleep for well over 175,000 hours in our lifetimes.

This extraordinary commitment of time implies that sleep fulfills a critical biological function. But what is it? And what about dreaming: Why do we spend so much time dreaming? And why do we tend to get sleepy at about the same time every day? Answers to these questions await you in this chapter.

Almost every time I give a lecture about sleep, somebody asks "How much sleep do we need?" and each time, I provide the same unsatisfying answer. I explain that there are two fundamentally different answers to this question, but that neither has emerged a clear winner. One answer stresses the presumed health-promoting and recuperative powers of sleep and suggests that people need as much sleep as they can comfortably get. The other answer is that many of us sleep more than we need to and are consequently sleeping part of our lives away. Just think how your life could change if you slept 5 hours per night instead of 8. You would have an extra 21 waking hours each week, a mind-boggling 10,952 hours each decade.

As I prepared to write this chapter, I began to think of some of the personal implications of the idea that we get more sleep than we need. That is when I decided to do something a bit unconventional. While I write this chapter, I am going to be your subject in a sleep-reduction experiment. I am going to try to get no more than 5 hours of sleep per night—11:00 P.M. to 4:00 A.M.—until this chapter is written. As I begin, I am excited by the prospect of having more time to write but a little worried that this extra time might be obtained at a personal cost that is too dear.

It is now the next day—4:50 Saturday morning to be exact—and I am just beginning to write. There was a party last night, and I didn't make it to bed by 11:00; but considering that I slept for only 3 hours and 35 minutes, I feel quite good. I wonder what I will feel like later in the day. In any case, I will report my experiences to you at the end of the chapter.

The following case study challenges several common beliefs about sleep. Ponder its implications before proceeding with the chapter

The Case of the Woman Who Wouldn't Sleep

Miss M . . . is a busy lady who finds her ration of twenty-three hours of wakefulness still insufficient for her needs. Even though she is now retired she is still busy in the community, helping sick friends whenever requested. She is an active painter and . . . writer. Although she becomes tired physically, when she needs to sit down to rest her legs, she does not ever report feeling sleepy. During the night she sits on her bed . . . reading, writing, crocheting or painting. At about 2:00 A.M. she falls asleep without any preceding drowsiness often while still holding a book in her hands. When she wakes about an hour later, she feels as wide awake as ever. It would be wrong to say that she woke refreshed because she did not complain of tiredness in the first place.

To test her claim we invited her along to the laboratory. She came willingly but on the first evening we hit our first snag. She announced that she did not sleep at all if she had interesting things to do, and by her reckoning a visit to a university sleep laboratory counted as very interesting. Moreover, for the first time in years, she had someone to talk to for the whole of the night. So we talked.

In the morning we broke into shifts so that some could sleep while at least one person stayed with her and entertained her during the next day. The second night was a repeat performance of the first night. . . . Things had not gone according to plan. So far we were very impressed by her cheerful response to two nights of sleep deprivation, but we had very little by way of hard data to show others.

In the end we prevailed upon her to allow us to apply EEG electrodes and to leave her sitting comfortably on the bed in the bedroom. She had promised that she would cooperate by not resisting sleep although she claimed not to be especially tired. . . . At approximately 1:30 A.M., the EEG record showed the first signs of sleep even though . . . she was still sitting with the book in her hands. . . .

The only substantial difference between her sleep and what we might have expected from any other . . . lady was that it was of short duration. . . . [After 99 minutes], she had no further interest in sleep and asked to . . . join our company again. (Meddis, 1977, pp. 42–44)[1]

14.1 The Physiological and Behavioral Events of Sleep

Many changes occur in the body during sleep. This section introduces you to the major ones.

[1]From *The Sleep Instinct* (pp. 42–44) by R. Meddis. Copyright © 1977, Routledge & Kegan Paul, London. Reprinted by permission.

The Three Standard Psychophysiological Measures of Sleep

There are major changes in the human EEG during the course of a night's sleep (Loomis, Harvey, & Hobart, 1936). Although the EEG waves that accompany sleep are generally high-voltage and slow, there are periods throughout the night that are dominated by low-voltage, fast waves similar to those in nonsleeping subjects. In 1953, Aserinsky and Kleitman discovered that *rapid eye movements (REMs)* occur under the closed eyelids of sleeping subjects during these periods of low-voltage, fast EEG activity. And in 1962, Berger and Oswald discovered that there is also a loss of electromyographic activity in the neck muscles during these same sleep periods. Subsequently, the **electroencephalogram (EEG),** the **electrooculogram (EOG),** and the neck **electromyogram (EMG)** became the three standard psychophysiological bases for defining stages of sleep (Rechtschaffen & Kales, 1968).

Figure 14.1 depicts a subject participating in a sleep experiment. A subject's first night's sleep in a sleep laboratory is often fitful. That's why it is the usual practice to have each subject sleep several nights in the laboratory before commencing a study. The disturbance of sleep observed during the first night in a sleep laboratory is called the *first-night phenomenon.* It is well known to markers of introductory psychology examinations because of the creative definitions of it that are offered by students who forget that it is a sleep-related, rather than a sex-related, phenomenon.

Four Stages of Sleep EEG

There are four stages of sleep EEG: stage 1, stage 2, stage 3, and stage 4. Examples of each are presented in Figure 14.2.

After the eyes are shut and a person prepares to go to sleep, **alpha waves**—waxing and waning bursts of 8- to 12-Hz EEG waves—begin to punctuate the low-voltage, high-frequency waves of active wakefulness. Then, as the person falls asleep, there is a sudden transition to a period of stage 1 sleep EEG. The stage 1 sleep EEG is a low-voltage, high-frequency signal that is similar to, but slower than, that of active wakefulness.

There is a gradual increase in EEG voltage and a decrease in EEG frequency as the person progresses from stage 1 sleep through stages 2, 3, and 4. Accordingly, the stage 2 sleep EEG has a slightly higher amplitude and a lower frequency than the stage 1 EEG; in addition, it is punctuated by two characteristic wave forms: K complexes and sleep spindles. Each *K complex* is a single large negative wave (upward deflection) followed immediately by a single large positive wave (downward deflection). Each *sleep spindle* is a 1- to 2-second waxing and waning burst of 12- to 14-Hz waves. The stage 3 sleep EEG is defined by the occasional presence of **delta waves**—the largest and slowest EEG waves, with a frequency of 1 to 2 Hz—whereas the stage 4 sleep EEG is defined by a predominance of delta waves.

Once subjects reach stage 4 EEG sleep, they stay there for a time, and then they retreat back through the stages of sleep to stage 1. However, when they return to stage 1, things are not at all the same as they were the first time through. The first period of stage 1 EEG during a night's sleep (**initial stage 1 EEG**) is not marked by any striking electromyographic or electrooculographic changes, whereas subsequent periods of stage 1 sleep EEG (**emergent stage 1 EEG**) are accompanied by REMs and by a loss of tone in the muscles of the body core.

After the first cycle of sleep EEG—from initial stage 1 to stage 4 and back to emergent stage 1—the rest of the night is spent going back and forth through the stages. Figure 14.3 illustrates the EEG cycles of a typical night's sleep and the close relation between emergent stage 1

FIGURE 14.1 A subject participating in a sleep experiment.

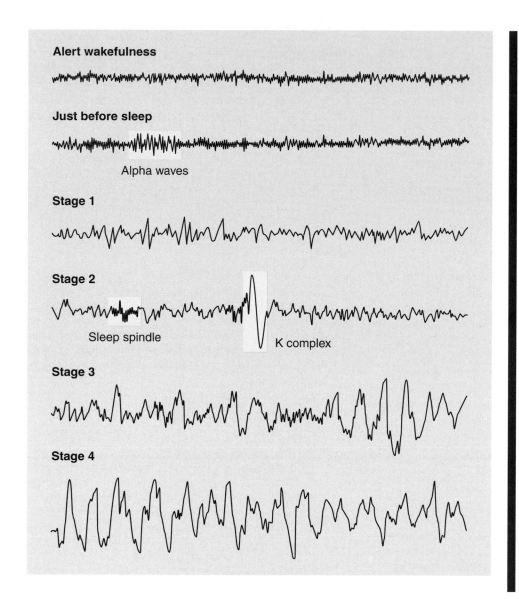

Alert wakefulness

Just before sleep

Alpha waves

Stage 1

Stage 2

Sleep spindle   K complex

Stage 3

Stage 4

FIGURE 14.2 The EEG of alert wakefulness, the EEG that precedes sleep onset, and the four stages of sleep EEG. Each trace is about 10 seconds long.

sleep, REMs, and the loss of tone in core muscles. Notice that each cycle tends to be about 90 minutes long and that, as the night progresses, more and more time is spent in emergent stage 1 sleep and less and less time is spent in the other stages, particularly stage 4. Notice also that there are brief periods during the night when the subject is awake; these periods of wakefulness are usually not remembered in the morning.

Let's pause here to get some sleep-stage terms straight. The sleep associated with emergent stage 1 EEG

Awake
Stage 1
Stage 2
Stage 3
Stage 4

Sleep EEG

Periods of REM   Lack of core-muscle tone

1 2 3 4 5 6 7 8 9

Hours

FIGURE 14.3 The course of EEG stages during a typical night's sleep and the relation of emergent stage 1 EEG to REMs and lack of tone in core muscles.

is usually called **REM sleep,** after the associated rapid eye movements; whereas all other stages of sleep together are called *NREM sleep* (non-REM sleep). Stages 3 and 4 together are referred to as **slow-wave sleep (SWS),** after the delta waves that characterize them.

REMs, loss of core muscle tone, and a low-amplitude, high-frequency EEG are not the only physiological correlates of REM sleep. Cerebral activity (e.g., oxygen consumption, blood flow, and neural firing) increases to waking levels in many brain structures, and there is a general increase in autonomic nervous system activity (e.g., in blood pressure, pulse, and respiration). Also, the muscles of the extremities occasionally twitch, and there is always some degree of clitoral or penile erection.

14.2 ▶ REM Sleep and Dreaming

Nathaniel Kleitman's laboratory was an exciting place in 1953. Kleitman's students had just discovered REM sleep, and they were driven by the fascinating implication of their discovery. With the exception of the loss of tone in the core muscles, all of the other measures suggested that REM sleep episodes were emotion-charged. Could REM sleep be the physiological correlate of dreaming? Could it provide researchers with a window into the subjective inner world of dreams? The researchers began by waking a few subjects in the middle of REM episodes and asking them if they had been dreaming. The results were remarkable:

> The vivid recall that could be elicited in the middle of the night when a subject was awakened while his eyes were moving rapidly was nothing short of miraculous. It [seemed to open] . . . an exciting new world to the subjects whose only previous dream memories had been the vague morning-after recall. Now, instead of perhaps some fleeting glimpse into the dream world each night, the subjects could be tuned into the middle of as many as ten or twelve dreams every night. (Dement, 1978, p. 37)[2]

Strong support for the theory that REM sleep is the physiological correlate of dreaming came from the observation that 80% of awakenings from REM sleep but only 7% of awakenings from NREM (non-REM) sleep led to dream recall. The dreams recalled from NREM sleep tended to be individual experiences (e.g., "I was falling"), unlike the stories associated with REM sleep. The phenomenon of dreaming, which for centuries had been the subject of wild speculation, was finally rendered accessible to scientific investigation. The following anecdote related by Dement (1978) communicates some of the excitement felt by those involved in the discovery:

> I decided to be a subject primarily out of envy; having listened with amazement and awe as many subjects recounted their dreams, I wished to enjoy the experience myself. . . .

> A hastily trained medical student . . . was monitoring the EEG and supervising my arousals. I went to sleep prepared for an exciting night and woke up with a certain urgency. . . . I searched my mind . . . I could remember nothing. . . . So I went back to sleep and was suddenly aware of being wrenched from the void once again. This time I could remember nothing except a very, very vague feeling of a name or a person. . . .

> The next time I was jolted awake—still unable to recall anything—I began to worry. Why didn't I remember a dream? I had expected to dazzle the medical student with my brilliant recall! After a fourth and fifth awakening with exactly the same results, I was really upset. . . .

> The experience had left me exhausted and extremely puzzled, and I was anxious to look at the polygraphic record of my miserable night. Upon examining the record I discovered, to my utter delight and relief, that the medical student had been mistakenly arousing me in NREM. Not once had I awakened during a REM period. . . .

> The next night, with additional instruction . . . the medical student hit the REM periods right on the button, and vivid recall flooded my mind with each awakening. (pp. 38–39)[3]

■ Testing Common Beliefs about Dreaming

The high correlation between REM sleep and dream recall provided an opportunity to test some common beliefs about dreaming. The following are five such beliefs that have been subjected to empirical tests.

1. Many people believe that external stimuli can become incorporated into their dreams. Dement and Wolpert (1958) sprayed water on sleeping subjects after they had been in REM sleep for a few minutes, and a few seconds after the spray, each subject was awakened. In 14 of 33 cases, the water was incor-

---

[2]From *Some Must Watch while Some Must Sleep* by William E. Dement, published by Portable Stanford Books, Stanford Alumni Association, Stanford University. Reprinted by permission.

[3]From *Some Must Watch while Some Must Sleep* by William E. Dement, published by Portable Stanford Books, Stanford Alumni Association, Stanford University. Reprinted by permission.

porated into the dream report. The following narrative was reported by a subject who had been dreaming that he was acting in a play:

> I was walking behind the leading lady when she suddenly collapsed and water was dripping on her. I ran over to her and water was dripping on my back and head. The roof was leaking. . . . I looked up and there was a hole in the roof. I dragged her over to the side of the stage and began pulling the curtains. Then I woke up. (p. 550)

2. Some people believe that dreams last only an instant, but research suggests that dreams run on "real time." In one study (Dement & Kleitman, 1957), subjects were awakened 5 or 15 minutes after the beginning of a REM episode and asked to decide on the basis of the duration of the events in their dreams whether they had been dreaming for 5 or 15 minutes. They were correct in 92 of 111 cases.

3. Some people claim that they do not dream. However, these people have just as much REM sleep as normal dreamers. Moreover, they report dreams if they are awakened during REM episodes (Goodenough et al., 1959), although they do so less frequently than do normal dreamers.

4. Penile erections are commonly assumed to be indicative of dreams with sexual content. However, erections are no more complete during dreams with frank sexual content than during those without it (Karacan et al., 1966). Even babies have REM-related penile erections.

5. Most people believe that sleeptalking and **somnambulism** (sleepwalking) occur during dreams. This is not so; sleeptalking and somnambulism occur least frequently during dreaming, when core muscles tend to be totally relaxed. They occur most frequently during stage 4 sleep.

■ | The Interpretation of Dreams

The idea that dreams are disguised messages has a long history. For example, the Bible describes how a dream of seven lean cattle following and devouring seven fat cattle warned that seven years of famine would follow seven years of plenty. It was Freud's theory of dreams that refined this view of dreams and gave it legitimacy.

Freud believed that dreams are triggered by unacceptable repressed wishes, often of a sexual nature. He argued that because dreams represent unacceptable wishes, the dreams we experience (our *manifest dreams*) are merely disguised versions of our real dreams (our *latent dreams*): An unconscious censor disguises and subtracts information from our real dreams so that we can endure them. Freud thus concluded that one of the keys to understanding people and dealing with their psychological problems is to expose the meaning of their latent dreams through the interpretation of their manifest dreams.

There is no convincing evidence for the Freudian theory of dreams; indeed, the brain science of the 1890s, which served as its foundation, is now obsolete. Nevertheless, the Freudian theory of dreams has been the basis for many interesting stories; as a result, it continues to be widely disseminated to the general public through the entertainment and communication media as if it were fact. Consequently, even today, the Freudian theory of dreams is deeply ingrained in many people's thinking. Many accept the notion that dreams bubble up from a troubled subconscious and that they represent repressed thoughts and wishes.

The modern alternative to the Freudian theory of dreams is Hobson's (1989) activation-synthesis theory. It is based on the observation that, during REM sleep, many brainstem circuits become active and bombard the cerebral cortex with neural signals. The essence of the **activation-synthesis theory** is that the information supplied to the cortex during REM sleep is largely random and that the resulting dream is the cortex's effort to make sense of these random signals.

Activation-synthesis theory does not deny that dreams have meaning, but it differs from Freudian theory in terms of where that meaning lies. Hobson's dreamers reveal themselves by what they add to the random jumble of brainstem signals in order to create a coherent story, not by the painful hidden message of their dreams.

■ | Lucid Dreams

The reality of dreams is usually quite distinct from the reality of consciousness (see Williams et al., 1992). However, there are dreams, called **lucid dreams,** in which this distinction becomes blurred. These are dreams in which the dreamer is aware at the time that she or he is dreaming and can influence the course of the dream. The experience of a lucid dream is something like being awake in a dream (see Blackmore, 1991).

Support for the existence of lucid dreams has come from demonstrations in which sleeping subjects signaled to the experimenter from their dreams (by a prearranged signal). For example, in one study, the subject was instructed to draw large triangles with his right arm as soon as he got into a dream and to signal to the experimenter with eye movements just before he drew each triangle. EMG activity that was consistent with triangle drawing was recorded from the right forearm each time the eye-movement signal was received (Schatzman, Worsley, & Fenwick, 1988). In another study, a woman who could create various positive sexual encounters in her lucid dreams was found to experience real physiological orgasms during some dream encounters (LaBerge, Greenleaf, & Kedzierski, 1983).

In various surveys, about 50% of respondents report having had at least one lucid dream (e.g., Gackenbach & LaBerge, 1988). However, because the concept of lucid dreaming is a difficult one to grasp, this figure is likely to be a gross overestimate.

14.3 Why Do We Sleep, and Why Do We Sleep When We Do?

Now that you have been introduced to the properties of sleep and its various stages, the focus of this chapter shifts to a consideration of two fundamental questions about sleep: Why do we sleep? And why do we sleep when we do? The first question deals with the functions of sleep; the second deals with its timing and duration.

Two kinds of theories for sleep have been proposed: *recuperation theories* and *circadian theories.* The differences between these two theoretical approaches are revealed by the answers they offer to the two fundamental questions about sleep.

The essence of **recuperation theories of sleep** is that being awake disrupts the *homeostasis* (internal physiological stability) of the body in some way and sleep is required to restore it. Various recuperation theories differ in terms of the particular physiological disruption they propose as the trigger for sleep—for example, it is commonly believed that the function of sleep is to restore energy levels. However, regardless of the particular function postulated by restoration theories of sleep, they all imply that sleepiness is triggered by a deviation from homeostasis caused by wakefulness and that sleep is terminated by a return to homeostasis.

The essence of **circadian theories of sleep** is that sleep is not a reaction to the disruptive effects of being awake but the result of an internal timing mechanism— that is, we humans are all programmed to sleep at night regardless of what happens to us during the day. According to these theories, we have evolved to sleep at night because sleep protects us from accident and predation during the night. (Remember that humans evolved long before the advent of artificial lighting.)

Circadian theories of sleep focus more on when we sleep than on the function of sleep. However, one extreme version of a circadian theory proposes that sleep plays no role in the efficient physiological functioning of the body. According to this theory, early humans had enough time to get their eating, drinking, and reproducing out of the way during the daytime, and their strong motivation to sleep at night evolved to conserve their energy resources and to make them less susceptible to mishap (e.g., predation) in the dark. This theory suggests that sleep is like reproductive behavior in the sense that we are highly motivated to engage in it, but we don't need it to stay healthy.

Some metaphors may help you think about the difference between the recuperation and circadian approaches to sleep. In essence, recuperation theories view sleep as a nightly repairman who fixes damage produced by wakefulness, while circadian theories regard sleep as a strict parent who demands inactivity because it keeps us out of trouble.

Choosing between the recuperation and circadian theories is the logical first step in the search for the physiological basis of sleep. Is the sleep system run by a biological clock that produces compelling urges to sleep at certain times of the day, perhaps to conserve energy and protect us from mishap; or is it a homeostatic system whose function is to correct some adverse consequence of staying awake? Several lines of research that have a bearing on the answer to this question will be discussed in the sections that follow.

14.4 Comparative Analysis of Sleep

All mammals and birds sleep, and their sleep is much like ours—characterized by high-amplitude, low-frequency EEG waves punctuated by periods of low-amplitude, high-frequency waves (see Winson, 1993). Even fish, reptiles, amphibians, and insects go through periods of inactivity and unresponsiveness that are similar to mammalian sleep (e.g., Shaw et al., 2000). Table 14.1 illustrates the average number of hours per day that various mammalian species spend sleeping.

The comparative investigation of sleep has led to several important conclusions. Let's consider four of these.

First, the fact that all mammals and birds sleep suggests that sleep serves some important physiological function, rather than merely protecting animals from mishap and conserving energy. The evidence is strongest in species that are at increased risk of predation when they sleep (e.g., antelopes) and in species that have evolved complex mechanisms that enable them to sleep

Table 14.1	The Average Number of Hours Slept per Day by Various Mammalian Species	
MAMMALIAN SPECIES		**HOURS OF SLEEP PER DAY**
Giant sloth		20
Opossum, brown bat		19
Giant armadillo		18
Owl monkey, nine-banded armadillo		17
Arctic ground squirrel		16
Tree shrew		15
Cat, golden hamster		14
Mouse, rat, gray wolf, ground squirrel		13
Arctic fox, chinchilla, gorilla, raccoon		12
Mountain beaver		11
Jaguar, vervet monkey, hedgehog		10
Rhesus monkey, chimpanzee, baboon, red fox		9
Human, rabbit, guinea pig, pig		8
Gray seal, gray hyrax, Brazilian tapir		6
Tree hyrax, rock hyrax		5
Cow, goat, elephant, donkey, sheep		3
Roe deer, horse		2

FIGURE 14.4 After gorging themselves on a kill, African lions sleep almost continuously for 2 or 3 days. And where do they sleep? Anywhere they want!

(e.g., some marine mammals sleep with only half of their brain at a time so that the other half can control resurfacing for air). It is against the logic of natural selection for some animals to risk predation while sleeping and for others to have evolved complex mechanisms to permit them to sleep unless sleep itself serves some critical function (Rechtschaffen, 1998).

Second, the fact that all mammals and birds sleep suggests that the function of sleep is not some special, higher-order human function. For example, suggestions that sleep helps humans reprogram our complex brains or that it permits some kind of emotional release to maintain our mental health seem to be ruled out by the comparative evidence.

Third, the large between-species differences in sleep time suggest that although sleep may be essential for survival, it is not necessarily needed in large quantities (see Table 14.1). Horses and many other animals get by quite nicely on 2 or 3 hours of sleep per day.

Fourth, many studies have tried to identify some characteristic that identifies various species as long sleepers or short sleepers. Why do cats tend to sleep about 14 hours a day and horses only about 2? Under the influence of recuperation theories, researchers have focused on energy-related factors in their efforts. However, there is no clear relationship between a species' sleep time and its level of activity, its body size, or its body temperature. The fact that giant sloths sleep 20 hours per day is a strong argument against the theory that sleep is a compensatory reaction to energy expenditure. In contrast, circadian theories correctly predict that the daily sleep time of each species is related to how vulnerable it is while it is asleep and how much time it must spend each day to feed itself and to take care of its other survival requirements. For example, zebras must graze almost continuously to get enough to eat and are extremely vulnerable to predatory attack when they are asleep—and they sleep only about 2 hours per day. In contrast, African lions often sleep more or less continuously for 2 or 3 days after they have gorged themselves on a kill. Figure 14.4 says it all.

14.5 Circadian Sleep Cycles

The world in which we live cycles from light to dark and back again once every 24 hours, and most surface-dwelling species have adapted to this regular change in their environment by developing a variety of so-called **circadian rhythms** (see Hastings, 1997). (*Circadian* means "lasting about 1 day.") For example, most species display a regular

circadian sleep–wake cycle. Humans take advantage of the light of day to take care of their biological needs, and then they sleep for much of the night; *nocturnal animals*, such as rats, sleep for much of the day and stay awake at night.

Although the sleep–wake cycle is the most obvious circadian rhythm, "it is virtually impossible to find a physiological, biochemical, or behavioral process in animals which does not display some measure of circadian rhythmicity" (Groos, 1983, p. 19). Each day, our bodies adjust themselves in a variety of ways to meet the demands of the two environments in which we live: light and dark.

Our circadian cycles are kept on their once-every-24-hours schedule by temporal cues in the environment. The most important of these cues for the regulation of mammalian circadian rhythms is the daily cycle of light and dark. Environmental cues, such as the light–dark cycle, that can *entrain* (control the timing of) circadian rhythms are called **zeitgebers** (pronounced "ZITE-gay-bers"), a German word that means "time givers." In controlled laboratory environments, it is possible to lengthen or shorten circadian cycles by adjusting the duration of the light–dark cycle; for example, when exposed to alternating 10-hour periods of light and 10-hour periods of dark, subjects' circadian cycles begin to conform to a 20-hour day. In a world without 24-hour cycles of light and dark, other *zeitgebers* can entrain circadian cycles. For example, the circadian sleep–wake cycles of hamsters living in continuous darkness or in continuous light can be entrained by regular daily bouts of social interaction, hoarding, eating, or exercise (see Mistlberger, 1994; Mistlberger et al., 1996; Sinclair & Mistlberger, 1997). Hamsters display particularly clear circadian cycles and thus are frequent subjects of research on circadian rhythms.

■ | Free-Running Circadian Sleep–Wake Cycles

The study of sleep in the absence of *zeitgebers* provides a powerful method for studying regulation of the temporal pattern of sleep. What happens to sleep–wake cycles and other circadian rhythms in an environment that is devoid of *zeitgebers?* Remarkably, under conditions in which there are absolutely no temporal cues, humans and other animals maintain all of their circadian rhythms. Circadian rhythms in constant environments are said to be **free-running rhythms,** and their duration is called the **free-running period.** Free-running periods vary in length from subject to subject, are of relatively constant duration within a given subject, and are usually longer than 24 hours—about 25 hours in most humans (Czeisler et al., 1999; Moore, 1999). It seems that we all have an internal *biological clock* that habitually runs a little slow unless it is entrained by time-related cues in the environment. A typical free-running circadian sleep–wake cycle is illustrated in Figure 14.5. Notice its regularity. Without any external cues, this man fell asleep approximately every 25.3 hours for an entire month.

Perhaps the most remarkable characteristic of free-running circadian cycles is that they do not have to be learned. Even rats that are born and raised in an unchanging laboratory environment (in continuous light

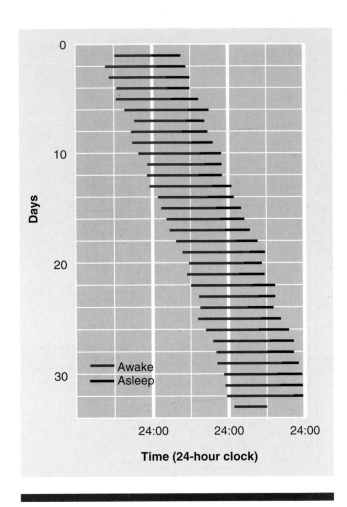

FIGURE 14.5 A typical free-running circadian sleep–wake cycle 25.3 hours in duration. Each day, the subject went to sleep approximately 1.3 hours later than he had the day before. (Adapted from Wever, 1979, p. 30.)

or in continuous darkness) display regular free-running sleep–wake cycles of about 25 hours (Richter, 1971).

Many animals display a circadian cycle of body temperature that is related to their circadian sleep–wake cycle: They tend to sleep during the falling phase of their circadian body temperature cycle and awaken during its rising phase. However, when subjects are housed in constant laboratory environments, their sleep–wake and body temperature cycles sometimes break away from one another. This phenomenon is called **internal desynchronization.** For example, in one case, the free-running periods of *both* the sleep–wake and body temperature cycles of a human subject were initially 25.7 hours; then, for some unknown reason, there was an increase in the free-running period of the sleep–wake cycle to 33.4 hours and a decrease in the free-running period of the body temperature cycle to 25.1 hours. The potential for the simultaneous existence of two different free-running periods suggests that there is more than one circadian timing mechanism, and that sleep is not causally related to the decreases in body temperature that are normally associated with it (see Harrington, Rusak, & Mistlberger, 1994).

So, what has research on circadian sleep–wake cycles taught us about the function of sleep? The fact that the regularity of the free-running period of such cycles is maintained despite day-to-day variations in physical and mental activity provides strong support for the dominance of circadian factors over recuperative factors in the regulation of sleep. Indeed, there have been several attempts to change the timing of sleep in both human and nonhuman subjects by having them engage in intensive physical or mental activity or by exposing them to infectious agents, but these attempts have had little, if any, effect on the subjects' subsequent sleep (see Rechtschaffen, 1998).

There is another point about free-running circadian sleep–wake cycles that is incompatible with recuperative theories of sleep. On occasions when subjects stay awake longer than usual, the following sleep time is shorter rather than longer (Wever, 1979). Humans and other animals are programmed to have sleep–wake cycles of approximately 24 hours; hence, the more wakefulness there is during a cycle, the less time there is for sleep.

Jet Lag and Shift Work

Modern industrialized societies are faced with two different disruptions of circadian rhythmicity: jet lag and shift work. **Jet lag** occurs when the *zeitgebers* that control the phases of various circadian rhythms are accelerated during eastern flights (*phase advances*) or decelerated during western flights (*phase delays*). In *shift work,* the *zeitgebers* stay the same but workers are forced to adjust their natural sleep–wake cycles in order to meet the demands of changing work schedules. Both of these disruptions produce sleep disturbances, fatigue, general malaise, and deficits on tests of physical and cognitive function. The disturbances can last for many days; for example, it typically takes about 10 days to completely adjust to a Tokyo-to-Boston flight—a phase advance of 10.5 hours.

What can be done to reduce the disruptive effects of jet lag and shift work? Two behavioral approaches have been proposed for the reduction of jet lag. One is gradually shifting one's sleep–wake cycle in the days prior to the flight (see Hobson, 1989). The other is administering treatments after the flight that promote the required shift in the circadian rhythm. For example, exposure to intense light early in the morning following an eastern flight accelerates adaptation to the phase advance. Similarly, the results of a study of hamsters (Mrosovsky & Salmon, 1987) suggest that a good workout early in the morning of the first day after an eastern flight might accelerate adaptation to the phase advance; hamsters that engaged in one 3-hour bout of wheel running 7 hours before their usual period of activity adapted quickly to an 8-hour advance in their light-dark cycle (see Figure 14.6 on page 360).

Companies that employ shift workers have had great success in improving the productivity and job satisfaction of those workers by scheduling phase delays rather than phase advances; whenever possible, shift workers are transferred from their current schedule to one that begins later in the day. It is much more difficult to go to sleep 4 hours earlier and get up 4 hours earlier (a phase advance) than it is to go to sleep 4 hours later and get up 4 hours later (a phase delay).

14.6   Effects of Sleep Deprivation

Recuperation theories of sleep make specific predictions about the effects of sleep deprivation. Because recuperation theories are based on the premise that sleep is a response to the accumulation of some debilitating effect of wakefulness, they predict (1) that long periods of wakefulness will produce physiological and behavioral disturbances, (2) that these disturbances will grow steadily worse as the sleep deprivation continues, and (3) that after a period of deprivation has ended, much of the missed sleep will be regained. Have these predictions been confirmed?

This section begins with a cautionary note about the personal experience of sleep deprivation. It next presents two classic sleep-deprivation case studies. Then, the major findings of sleep-deprivation studies in humans and laboratory animals are summarized. Finally, the evidence that sleep can become more efficient as a result of sleep deprivation is reviewed.

Personal Experience of Sleep Deprivation: A Cautionary Note

I am sure that you have experienced the negative effects of sleep deprivation. When you sleep substantially less than you are used to, the next day you feel crabby and unable to function as well as you usually do. Although such experiences of sleep deprivation are compelling, you need to be cautious in interpreting your own

FIGURE 14.6 A period of forced exercise accelerates adaptation to an 8-hour phase advance in the circadian light-dark cycle. Daily activity is shown in red; periods of darkness are shown in black; and the period of forced exercise is shown in green.
(Adapted from Mrosovsky & Salmon, 1987.)

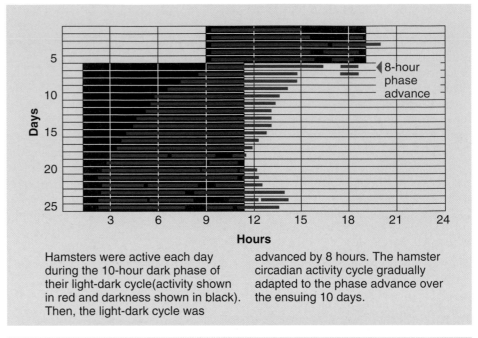

Hamsters were active each day during the 10-hour dark phase of their light-dark cycle (activity shown in red and darkness shown in black). Then, the light-dark cycle was advanced by 8 hours. The hamster circadian activity cycle gradually adapted to the phase advance over the ensuing 10 days.

Hamsters that were forced to run in a running wheel on the day of the phase advance, 7 hours prior to their normal activity time (forced running shown in green), adapted to the phase advance in 1 day.

experiences and the similar experiences of others. Let me illustrate this point by referring to a recurring news story.

Every few months, I see on the television news or read in the newspaper that most people need more sleep. To support this contention, an "expert" explains that many people in modern society work such long, irregular hours that they do not sleep enough and suffer all kinds of adverse effects as a result. To make this point, there are typically a few interviews with people such as long-distance truck drivers and shift workers who describe their sleep-related experiences. Two things never seem to occur to the news reporters or to the "expert." First, it never occurs to them that most people who sleep little

or irregularly do so because they are under stress. Second, it never occurs to them that people who are forced to change their schedule of sleep also experience a major disruption of their circadian rhythms. Accordingly, stress and circadian disruptions might be responsible for, or at least contribute to, some of the adverse effects commonly attributed to loss of sleep (see Taub & Berger, 1973).

Compounding these two possible causes is the fact that people have proven to be poor judges of the impact of sleep deprivation on their performance. Both types of errors have been reported: In some cases, people claim that they cannot function after sleep loss but perform without decrement; in other cases, people claim that sleep loss has not adversely affected their performance when the data tell a different story.

Consequently, your own experiences of sleep loss and the testimonials of others who have experienced sleep loss need to be interpreted cautiously. Documenting the effects of sleep loss requires systematic research.

■ Two Classic Sleep-Deprivation Case Studies

Let's begin our consideration of the research on sleep deprivation by looking at two classic case studies. First is the case study of a group of sleep-deprived students, described by Kleitman (1963); second is the case of Randy Gardner, described by Dement (1978).

The Case of the Sleep-Deprived Students

While there were differences in the many subjective experiences of the sleep-evading persons, there were several features common to most.... [D]uring the first night the subject did not feel very tired or sleepy. He could read or study or do laboratory work, without much attention from the watcher, but usually felt an attack of drowsiness between 3 A.M. and 6 A.M. . . . Next morning the subject felt well, except for a slight malaise which always appeared on sitting down and resting for any length of time. However, if he occupied himself with his ordinary daily tasks, he was likely to forget having spent a sleepless night. During the second night . . . reading or study was next to impossible because sitting quietly was conducive to even greater sleepiness. As during the first night, there came a 2–3 hour period in the early hours of the morning when the desire for sleep was almost overpowering. . . . Later in the morning the sleepiness diminished once more, and the subject could perform routine laboratory work, as usual. It was not safe for him to sit down, however, without danger of falling asleep, particularly if he attended lectures. . . .

The third night resembled the second, and the fourth day was like the third. . . . At the end of that time the individual was as sleepy as he was likely to be. Those who continued to stay awake experienced the wavelike increase and decrease in sleepiness with the greatest drowsiness at about the same time every night. (Kleitman, 1963, pp. 220–221)

The Case of Randy Gardner

As part of a 1965 science fair project, Randy Gardner and two classmates, who were entrusted with keeping him awake, planned to break the then world record of 260 hours of consecutive wakefulness. Dement read about the project in the newspaper and, seeing an opportunity to collect some important data, joined the team, much to the

comfort of Randy's worried parents. Randy proved to be a friendly and cooperative subject, although he did complain vigorously when his team would not permit him to close his eyes for more than a few seconds at a time. However, in no sense could Randy's behavior be considered abnormal or disturbed. Near the end of his vigil, Randy held a press conference attended by reporters and television crews from all over the United States, and he conducted himself impeccably. When asked how he had managed to stay awake for 11 days, he replied politely, "It's just mind over matter." Randy went to sleep exactly 264 hours and 12 minutes after his alarm clock had awakened him 11 days before. And how long did he sleep? Only 14 hours the first night, and thereafter he returned to his usual 8-hour schedule. Although it may seem amazing that Randy did not have to sleep longer to "catch up" on his lost sleep, the lack of substantial recovery sleep is typical of such cases.

Mrs. Maureen Weston later supplanted Randy Gardner in the *Guinness Book of World Records*. During a rocking-chair marathon in 1977, Mrs. Weston kept rocking for 449 hours (18 days, 17 hours)—an impressive bit of "rocking around the clock." By the way, my own modest program of sleep reduction is now in its 10th day.

■ Experimental Studies of Sleep Deprivation in Humans

Investigations have assessed the effects on human subjects of sleep-deprivation schedules ranging from a slightly reduced amount of sleep during one night to total sleep deprivation for several nights, and they have assessed the effects of these schedules on dozens of different objective measures: measures of sleepiness, mood, cognition, motor performance, and physiological function.

Even moderate amounts of sleep deprivation—for example, 3 or 4 hours in one night—have been found to have three consistent effects. First, sleep-deprived subjects display an increase in sleepiness: They report being more sleepy, and they fall asleep more quickly if given the opportunity. Second, sleep-deprived subjects display disturbances on various written tests of mood. And third, they perform poorly on tests of vigilance, such as listening to a series of tones and responding when one differs slightly from the rest.

After 2 or 3 days of continuous sleep deprivation, subjects experience microsleeps. **Microsleeps** are brief periods of sleep, typically about 2 or 3 seconds long, during which the eyelids droop and the subjects become less responsive to external stimuli, even though they remain sitting or standing. Microsleeps disrupt performance on passive tests, such as tests of vigilance, but they are not necessary for such performance deficits to occur (Dinges et al., 1997; Ferrara, De Gennaro, & Bertini, 1999).

Remarkably, the effects of sleep deprivation on complex cognitive function, motor performance, and physiological function have been much less consistent. Deficits have been observed in some studies but not in others, even after lengthy periods of deprivation (e.g., Bonnet & Arand, 1996; Dinges et al., 1997; Gillberg et al., 1996; Harrison & Horne, 1997). For example, Martin (1986) concluded that adverse physiological changes following sleep deprivation have yet to be convincingly documented; VanHelder and Radomski (1989) found that periods of sleep deprivation lasting up to 72 hours had no effect on strength or motor performance, except for reducing time to exhaustion; and active tests of complex cognitive ability (such as IQ tests) have proven to be largely immune to disruption by sleep deprivation (Binks, Waters, & Hurry, 1999; Percival, Horne, & Tilley, 1983). It should be pointed out, however, that although performance on intelligence tests is influenced little by sleep deprivation, Horne (1983) found that 32 hours of sleep deprivation greatly disrupted subjects' performance on several tests expressly designed to measure creativity.

To put the experimental and case-study research on human sleep deprivation in context, I like to compare sleep deprivation to deprivation of the motivated behaviors discussed in Chapters 12 and 13. If subjects were deprived of the opportunity to eat or engage in sexual activity, the effects would be devastating and unavoidable: In the first case, starvation and death would ensue; in the second, there would be a total loss of reproductive capacity. There have been no such dramatic effects reported in sleep-deprivation studies. Indeed, none of the three major predictions of the recuperation theories of sleep has been unambiguously confirmed. I suspect that the confusion stems from the fact that we do not understand the basic function of sleep: Without this knowledge, it is difficult to know what measures are likely to be most sensitive to sleep loss.

■ Sleep-Deprivation Studies with Laboratory Animals

Studies using a **carousel apparatus** (see Figure 14.7) to deprive rats of sleep suggest that sleep deprivation may not be as inconsequential as the research on human subjects suggests. Two rats, an experimental rat and its *yoked control,* are placed in separate chambers of the apparatus. Each time the EEG activity of the experimental rat indicates that it is sleeping, the disk, which serves as the floor of half of both chambers, starts to slowly rotate. As a result, if the sleeping experimental rat does not awaken immediately, it gets shoved off the disk into a shallow pool of water. The yoked control is exposed to exactly the same

FIGURE 14.7 The carousel apparatus used to deprive an experimental rat of sleep while a yoked control rat is exposed to the same number and pattern of disk rotations. The disk on which both rats rest rotates every time the experimental rat has a sleep EEG. If the sleeping rat does not awaken immediately, it is deposited in the water. (Adapted from Rechtschaffen et al., 1983.)

pattern of disk rotations; but if it is not sleeping, it can easily avoid getting dunked by walking in the direction opposite to the direction of disk rotation. The experimental rats typically died after several days, while the yoked controls stayed reasonably healthy (see Rechtschaffen & Bergmann, 1995).

The fact that human subjects have been sleep-deprived for similar periods of time without dire consequences argues for caution in interpreting the results of the carousel sleep-deprivation experiments. It may be that repeatedly being awakened by the moving platform or, worse yet, being plunged into water while sleeping kills the experimental rats not because it keeps them from sleeping but because it is stressful and physically damaging. This interpretation is consistent with the pathological symptoms that were revealed in the experimental rats by postmortem examination: for example, swollen adrenal glands, gastric ulcers, and internal bleeding. Indeed, it may not be possible to study the effects of sleep deprivation in nonhumans adequately because of the unavoidable confounding effects of stress (see Benington & Heller, 1999; D'Almeida et al., 1997).

■ REM-Sleep Deprivation

Because of its association with dreaming, REM sleep has been the subject of intensive investigation. In an effort to reveal the particular functions of REM sleep,

sleep researchers have specifically deprived sleeping subjects of REM sleep by waking them up each time a bout of REM sleep begins.

REM-sleep deprivation has been shown to have two consistent effects (see Figure 14.8). First, with each successive night of deprivation, there is a greater tendency for subjects to initiate REM sequences. Thus, as REM-sleep deprivation proceeds, subjects have to be awakened more and more frequently to keep them from accumulating significant amounts of REM sleep. For example, during the first night of REM-sleep deprivation in one experiment (Webb & Agnew, 1967), the subjects had to be awakened 17 times to keep them from having extended periods of REM sleep; but during the seventh night of deprivation, they had to be awakened 67 times. Second, following REM-sleep deprivation, subjects have more than their usual amount of REM sleep for the first two or three nights (Brunner et al., 1990).

The compensatory increase in REM sleep following a period of REM-sleep deprivation suggests that the amount of REM sleep is regulated separately from the amount of slow-wave sleep and that REM sleep serves a special function. Numerous theories of the functions of REM sleep have been proposed (see Webb, 1973; Winson, 1993). Most of them fall into one of three categories: (1) those that hypothesize that REM sleep is necessary for the maintenance of an individual's mental health, (2) those that hypothesize that REM sleep is necessary for the maintenance of normal levels of motivation, and (3) those that hypothesize that REM sleep is necessary for the processing of memories. None of these theories has emerged a clear winner. Reports that REM-sleep deprivation produces a variety of personality and motivational problems (e.g., Dement, 1960) have not proved replicable, and more recent reports that REM-sleep deprivation produces memory deficits for certain kinds of material learned the preceding day (e.g., Karni et al., 1994), while promising, are still controversial.

The main challenge faced by any theory of the function of REM sleep is to explain why **tricyclic antidepressant drugs** are not severely debilitating. Because tricyclic antidepressants selectively block REM sleep, patients who

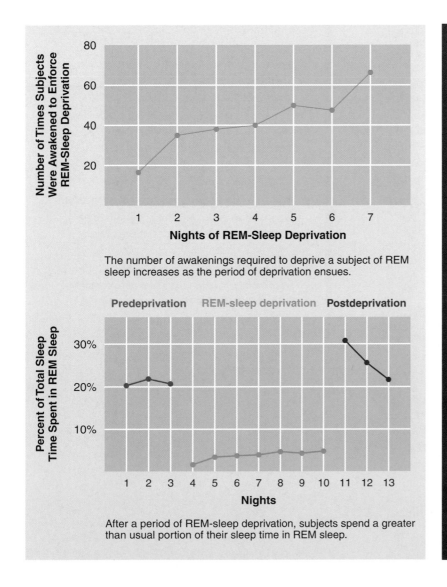

FIGURE 14.8 The two effects of REM-sleep deprivation.

The number of awakenings required to deprive a subject of REM sleep increases as the period of deprivation ensues.

After a period of REM-sleep deprivation, subjects spend a greater than usual portion of their sleep time in REM sleep.

regularly take large doses (e.g., for depression) get little REM sleep for months at a time—and yet they experience no serious side effects of this REM-sleep loss.

Sleep Deprivation Increases the Efficiency of Sleep

One of the most important findings of human sleep-deprivation research is that individuals who are deprived of sleep become more efficient sleepers. In particular, their sleep has a higher proportion of slow-wave sleep (stages 3 and 4), which seems to serve the main restorative function. Because this is such an important finding, let's take a look at six major pieces of evidence that support it.

First, although subjects regain only a small proportion of their total lost sleep after a period of sleep deprivation, they regain most of their lost stage 4 sleep (e.g., Borbély et al., 1981; De Gennaro et al., 2000; Lucidi et al., 1997). Second, after sleep deprivation, the slow-wave sleep EEG of humans is characterized by an even higher proportion than usual of slow waves (Borbély, 1981; Borbély et al., 1981). Third, short sleepers normally get as much slow-wave sleep as long sleepers do (e.g., Jones & Oswald, 1966; Webb & Agnew, 1970). Fourth, if subjects take an extra nap in the morning after a full night's sleep, their naptime EEG shows few slow waves, and the nap does not reduce the duration of the following night's sleep (e.g., Åkerstedt & Gillberg, 1981; Hume & Mills, 1977; Karacan et al., 1970). Fifth, subjects who gradually reduce their usual sleep time get less stage 1 and stage 2 sleep, but the duration of their slow-wave sleep remains about the same as before (Mullaney et al., 1977; Webb & Agnew, 1975). And sixth, repeatedly waking subjects up during REM sleep produces little, if any, increase in the sleepiness they experience the next day, whereas repeatedly waking subjects up during slow-wave sleep has major effects (Nykamp et al., 1998).

The fact that sleep becomes more efficient in people who sleep less means that conventional sleep-deprivation studies are virtually useless for discovering how much humans really need to sleep. The negative consequences of sleep loss in inefficient sleepers do not indicate whether the lost sleep was really needed; the true need for sleep can be assessed only by experiments in which sleep is regularly reduced for many weeks, to give the subjects an opportunity to adapt to less sleep by increasing their sleep to its maximum efficiency. Only when people are sleeping at their maximal efficiency is it possible to determine how much sleep they really need. Such sleep-reduction studies are discussed later in the chapter, but please pause here to think about this point—it is extremely important.

It is an appropriate time, here at the end of the section on sleep deprivation, for me to file a brief progress

ON THE CD

In the *Good Morning* module, the camera catches Pinel arriving at his office at 6:00 A.M. He discusses a common misconception about sleep.

BrainScan

Before continuing with this chapter, scan your brain by completing the following exercise to make sure you understand the fundamentals of sleep. The correct answers are provided at the bottom of this page. Before proceeding, review material related to your errors and omissions.

1. The three most commonly studied psychophysiological correlates of sleep are the EEG, EMG, and _____ .

2. Stage 4 sleep EEG is characterized by a predominance of _____ waves.

3. _____ stage 1 EEG is accompanied by neither REM nor loss of core muscle tone.

4. Dreaming occurs during _____ sleep.

5. The modern alternative to Freud's theory of dreaming is Hobson's _____ theory.

6. Environmental cues that can entrain circadian rhythms are called _____ , or time givers.

7. In contrast to the prediction of the recuperation theories of sleep, when a subject stays awake longer than usual under free-running conditions, the following period of sleep tends to be _____ .

8. The most convincing evidence that REM-sleep deprivation is not seriously debilitating comes from the study of patients taking _____ .

9. After a lengthy period of sleep deprivation (e.g., several days), a subject's first night of sleep is only slightly longer than usual, but it contains a much higher proportion of _____ waves.

10. _____ sleep in particular, rather than sleep in general, appears to play the major recuperative role.

report. It has now been 2 weeks since I began my 5-hours-per-night sleep schedule. Generally, things are going well. My progress on this chapter has been faster than usual. I am not having any difficulty getting up on time or getting my work done, but I am finding that it takes a major effort to stay awake in the evening. If I try to read or watch a bit of television after 10:30, I experience microsleeps. Luckily for me, my so-called friends delight in making sure that my transgressions last no more than a few seconds.

14.7 Neural Mechanisms of Sleep

The first influential theory of the physiology of sleep was proposed by Bremer in 1936. He hypothesized that sleep is caused by a reduction of sensory input to the forebrain. To test his hypothesis, he severed the brain stems of cats between their *inferior colliculi* and *superior colliculi* in order to disconnect their forebrains from ascending sensory input (see Figure 14.9 on page 366) This surgical preparation is called a **cerveau isolé preparation** (pronounced "ser-VOE ees-o-LAY"—literally, "isolated forebrain").

In support of his hypothesis, Bremer found that the cortical EEG of the isolated cat forebrains was indicative of almost continuous slow-wave sleep. Only when strong visual or olfactory stimuli were presented (the cerveau isolé has intact visual and olfactory input) could the continuous high-amplitude, slow-wave activity be changed to a **desynchronized EEG**—a low-amplitude, high-frequency EEG. However, this arousing effect barely outlasted the stimuli. Bremer's theory is classified as a *passive theory of sleep* because it postulated no mechanism of active sleep regulation; it viewed sleep as a passive consequence of a decline in sensory input to the forebrain.

■ Reticular Activating System Theory of Sleep

Bremer's passive sensory theory of sleep regulation was gradually replaced by the theory that sleep is actively regulated by an arousal mechanism in the *reticular formation*. This hypothetical arousal mechanism was the **reticular activating system.** Three findings contributed to wide acceptance of the reticular activating system theory of sleep (see Figure 14.9). The first finding came from a study of the **encéphale isolé preparation** (pronounced "on-say-FELL ees-o-LAY")—an experimental preparation in which the brain is disconnected from the rest of the nervous system by a transection of the caudal brain stem. Although it cut most of the same sensory fibers as the cerveau isolé transection, the encéphale isolé transection did not disrupt the normal cycle of sleep EEG and wakefulness EEG (Bremer, 1937). This suggested that a mechanism for maintaining wakefulness was located somewhere in the brain stem between the two transections. The second finding was that partial transections at the cerveau isolé level disrupted normal sleep–wake cycles of cortical EEG

only when they severed the reticular activating system core of the brain stem; when the partial transections were restricted to more lateral areas, which contain the ascending sensory tracts, they had little effect on the cortical EEG (Lindsey, Bowden, & Magoun, 1949). The third finding was that electrical stimulation of the reticular formation of sleeping cats awakened them and produced a lengthy period of EEG desynchronization (Moruzzi & Magoun, 1949). On the basis of these three early findings, Moruzzi and Magoun (1949) proposed that low levels of activity in the reticular formation produce sleep and that high levels produce wakefulness.

■ Three Important Discoveries about the Neural Basis of Sleep

The wave of research on the physiology of sleep that was stimulated by the reticular activating system theory led to several discoveries. The following three are particularly important (see Steriade & Hobson, 1976).

SLEEP IS NOT A STATE OF NEURAL QUIESCENCE
■ Because the body is inactive during sleep, it had long been assumed that sleep is a state of general neural quiescence. Neural recording and functional brain imaging (see Hobson et al., 1998) have revealed that this is not the case. Many areas of the brain are less active during slow-wave sleep than they are during relaxed wakefulness, but the reduction in average firing rates rarely exceeds 10%—a far cry from the total inactivity that was initially assumed. Moreover, during REM sleep, the neurons in some areas become even more active than they are during relaxed wakefulness.

THERE ARE SLEEP-PROMOTING CIRCUITS IN THE BRAIN ■ The reticular activating system theory suggested that sleep is a consequence of low levels of activity in circuits whose primary role is the maintenance of wakefulness. This view was altered by the discovery that brain stimulation can induce sleep and that brain lesions can disrupt it. Both of these findings suggest that there are structures in the brain whose function is the promotion of sleep.

THE VARIOUS CORRELATES OF SLEEP ARE DISSOCIABLE ■ Most neurophysiological theories of sleep

FIGURE 14.9 Evidence for the sensory theory of sleep (a passive theory) and the reticular activating system theory (an active theory).

Evidence for Bremer's 1937 Passive Sensory Theory of Sleep

Cats with a midcollicular transection (i.e., a cerveau isolé preparation) displayed a continuous cortical slow-wave sleep EEG.

Superior colliculus

Inferior colliculus

Thus Bremer concluded that sleep occurs when there is little sensory input to the forebrain.

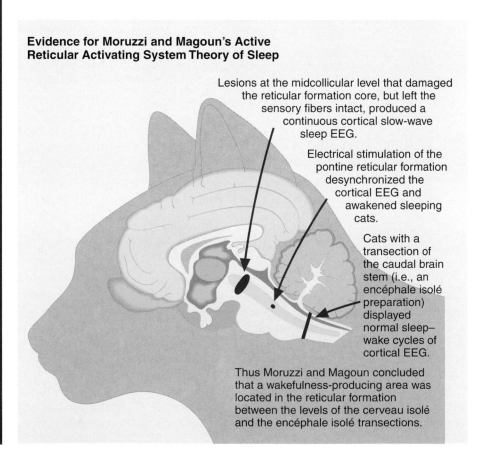

Evidence for Moruzzi and Magoun's Active Reticular Activating System Theory of Sleep

Lesions at the midcollicular level that damaged the reticular formation core, but left the sensory fibers intact, produced a continuous cortical slow-wave sleep EEG.

Electrical stimulation of the pontine reticular formation desynchronized the cortical EEG and awakened sleeping cats.

Cats with a transection of the caudal brain stem (i.e., an encéphale isolé preparation) displayed normal sleep–wake cycles of cortical EEG.

Thus Moruzzi and Magoun concluded that a wakefulness-producing area was located in the reticular formation between the levels of the cerveau isolé and the encéphale isolé transections.

have treated REM sleep and slow-wave sleep as if each were a unitary entity—and, for simplicity, I have followed this convention in this chapter. However, evidence has accumulated that the physiological changes that go together to define REM sleep sometimes break apart and go their separate ways—and the same is true of the changes that define slow-wave sleep. For example, during REM-sleep deprivation, penile erections, which normally occur during REM sleep, begin to occur during slow-wave sleep. And during total sleep deprivation, slow waves, which normally occur only during slow-wave sleep, begin to occur during wakefulness. This suggests that REM sleep, slow-wave sleep, and wakefulness are not each controlled by a single mechanism; each state seems to result from the interaction of a variety of mechanisms that are capable under certain conditions of operating independently of one another.

■ Three Brain Areas That Have Been Implicated in Sleep Regulation

Several areas of the brain have been implicated in sleep regulation by research on laboratory animals. The following are three of them: the raphé nuclei, the basal forebrain region, and the REM-sleep circuits in the caudal reticular formation.

RAPHÉ NUCLEI ■ The **raphé** (pronounced "ra-FAY") **nuclei** are a cluster of serotonin-producing nuclei running in a thin strip down the midline of the caudal retic-

ular formation (see Figure 14.10). Lesions that destroyed 80–90% of the raphé nuclei in cats produced complete insomnia for 3 or 4 days, and then there was a partial recovery that never exceeded more than 2.5 hours of sleep per day, all slow-wave sleep (Jouvet & Renault, 1966). Cats normally sleep about 14 hours per day.

The theory that the raphé nuclei promote sleep received initial support from the observation that an injection of **parachlorophenylalanine (PCPA)**—a chemical that temporarily blocks the synthesis of serotonin—produced temporary insomnia in cats (Mouret, Bobillier, & Jouvet, 1968). However, when PCPA was injected every day, both REM sleep and slow-wave sleep eventually recovered to 80% of their normal levels despite the fact that serotonin levels remained low (Dement, Mitler, & Henriksen, 1972). Further challenges to the raphé nuclei–serotonin theory of sleep came from the discovery that serotonin injections do not induce sleep and the discovery that PCPA injections do not disrupt sleep in species other than cats (see Vanderwolf, 1988).

BASAL FOREBRAIN REGION ■ Substantial evidence has implicated the **basal forebrain region** and the adjacent *anterior hypothalamus* in sleep. The location of this area is shown in Figure 14.11 on page 368. Attention was focused on the role of the basal forebrain region in sleep about a century ago, when it was observed that patients with small basal forebrain tumors had difficulty sleeping. Subsequently, it has been shown that basal forebrain lesions disrupt sleep in experimental animals (Lu et al., 2000). For example, bilateral lesions of the basal forebrain in cats produce a

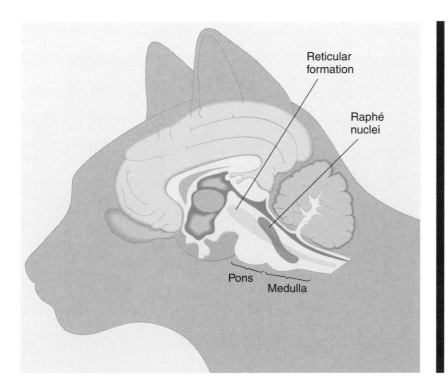

FIGURE 14.10 The location of the raphé nuclei in the caudal reticular formation.

substantial reduction of daily sleep time that is maximal 2 weeks after the lesion but recedes somewhat thereafter (McGinty & Sterman, 1968)—see Figure 14.11.

Further evidence of the involvement of the basal forebrain region has come from recording studies. Single-cell recording has revealed neurons in the area that increase their activity only during sleep (Sherin et al., 1996). Also, levels of the peptide neurotransmitter *adenosine* in the basal forebrain region increase with pro-longed wakefulness and decline with sleep—adenosine inhibits the cholinergic neurons of the basal forebrain.

CAUDAL RETICULAR FORMATION REM-SLEEP CIR-CUITS ■ REM sleep appears to be controlled from a variety of sites scattered throughout the caudal reticular formation. Each site is responsible for controlling one of the major indexes of REM sleep (Siegel, 1983; Vertes, 1983)—a site for the reduction of core muscle tone, a site for EEG desynchronization, a site for rapid eye movements, and so on. The approximate location in the caudal brain stem of each of these putative REM-sleep centers is illustrated in Figure 14.12. The coor-dinated activation of the REM-sleep centers is thought to be controlled by interplay between cholinergic and monoaminergic (nonadrenergic and serotonergic) neu-rons in the caudal reticular formation (see Hobson, 1989).

FIGURE 14.11 The effects of basal forebrain lesions on the sleep of cats. (Adapted from McGinty & Sterman, 1968.)

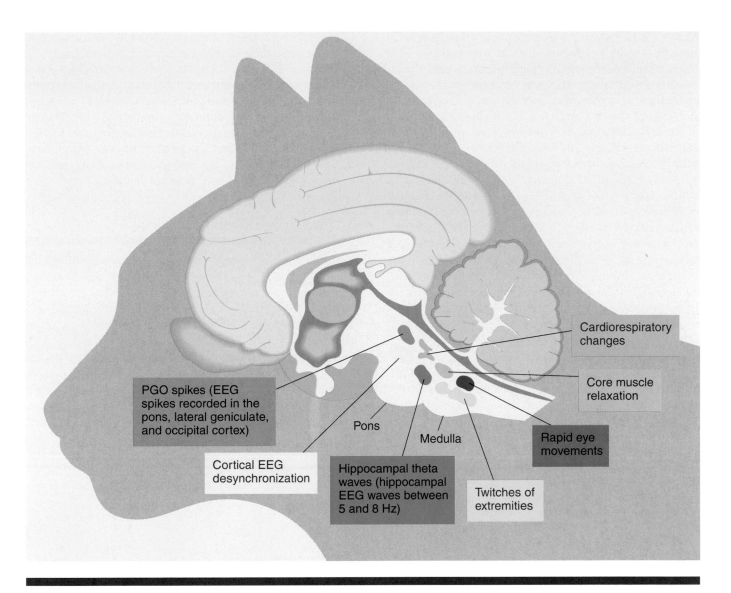

FIGURE 14.12 A sagittal section of the brain stem of the cat illustrating the areas that control the various physiological indexes of REM sleep. (Adapted from Vertes, 1983.)

14.8 The Circadian Clock: Neural and Molecular Mechanisms

The fact that circadian sleep–wake cycles persist in the absence of temporal cues from the environment indicates that the physiological systems that regulate sleep are controlled by an internal timing mechanism—the **circadian clock.** Where is this timing mechanism?

Location of the Circadian Clock in the Suprachiasmatic Nuclei

The first breakthrough in the search for the circadian clock was Richter's 1967 discovery that large medial hypothalamic lesions disrupt circadian cycles of eating, drinking, and activity in rats. Next, specific lesions of the **suprachiasmatic nuclei (SCN)** of the medial hypothalamus were shown to disrupt various circadian cycles, including sleep–wake cycles. Although SCN lesions do not reduce the amount of time mammals spend sleeping, they do abolish its circadian periodicity.

Further support for the conclusion that the suprachiasmatic nuclei contain a circadian timing mechanism comes from the observation that the nuclei display circadian cycles of electrical, metabolic, and biochemical activity (e.g.,

Moore, 1982)—even when they have been surgically isolated from the rest of the brain by circular knife cuts (Groos & Hendricks, 1982; Inouye & Kawamura, 1982). Also, electrical stimulation of the SCN has been shown to produce phase shifts in free-running cycles (Rusak & Groos, 1982).

If there was any lingering doubt about the location of the circadian clock, it was eliminated by the brilliant experiment of Ralph and his colleagues (1990). They removed the SCN from the fetuses of a strain of mutant hamsters that had an abnormally short (20-hour) free-running sleep–wake cycle. Then, they transplanted these SCN into normal adult hamsters whose free-running sleep–wake cycles of 25 hours had been abolished by SCN lesions. These transplants restored free-running sleep–wake cycles in the recipients; but, remarkably, the cycles were about 20 hours long rather than the original 25 hours. Transplants in the other direction—that is, from normal hamster fetuses to SCN-lesioned adult mutants—had the complementary effect: They restored free-running sleep–wake cycles that were about 25 hours long rather than the original 20 hours.

Although the suprachiasmatic nuclei are unquestionably the major circadian clocks in mammals, they are not the only ones. Three lines of evidence support this view. First, under certain conditions, bilateral SCN lesions have been shown to leave some circadian rhythms unaffected while abolishing others (e.g., Boulos & Terman, 1980). Second, bilateral SCN lesions do not eliminate the ability of all environmental stimuli to entrain circadian rhythms; for example, in hamsters, SCN lesions block entrainment by light but not by food or water availability (Mistlberger, 1993). Third, just as suprachiasmatic neurons do (Earnest et al., 1999), cells from other parts of the body display free-running circadian cycles of activity when maintained in tissue culture (e.g., Tosini & Menacker, 1996).

■ Mechanisms of Entrainment

How does the 24-hour light–dark cycle entrain the sleep–wake cycle and other circadian rhythms? To answer this question, researchers began at the obvious starting point: the eyes. They tried to identify and track the specific neurons that left the eyes and carried the information about light and dark that entrained the biological clock. Cutting the *optic nerves* before they reached the *optic chiasm* eliminated the ability of the light–dark cycle to entrain circadian rhythms; however, when the *optic tracts* were cut at the point where they left the optic chiasm, the ability of the light–dark cycle to entrain circadian

FIGURE 14.13 The discovery of the retinohypothalamic tracts. Neurons from each retina project to both suprachiasmatic nuclei.

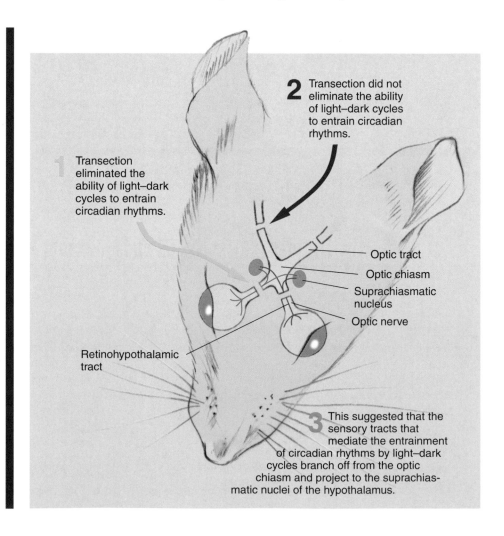

1 Transection eliminated the ability of light–dark cycles to entrain circadian rhythms.

2 Transection did not eliminate the ability of light–dark cycles to entrain circadian rhythms.

Optic tract

Optic chiasm

Suprachiasmatic nucleus

Optic nerve

Retinohypothalamic tract

3 This suggested that the sensory tracts that mediate the entrainment of circadian rhythms by light–dark cycles branch off from the optic chiasm and project to the suprachiasmatic nuclei of the hypothalamus.

rhythms was unaffected. As Figure 14.13 illustrates, these two findings indicated that visual axons critical for the entrainment of circadian rhythms branch off from the optic nerve in the vicinity of the optic chiasm. This finding led to the discovery of the *retinohypothalamic tracts,* which leave the optic chiasm and project to the adjacent suprachiasmatic nuclei.

Surprisingly, although the retinohypothalamic tracts mediate the ability of light to entrain photoreceptors, neither rods or cones are necessary for the entrainment. *Transgenic mice* lacking both rods and cones still show light-entrained circadian cycles of activity (Freedman et al., 1999) and melatonin release (Lucas et al., 1999).

■ | Genetics of Circadian Rhythms

An important breakthrough in the study of the genetic basis of circadian rhythms came in 1988 when routine screening of a shipment of hamsters revealed that some of them had abnormally short 20-hour free-running circadian rhythms. Subsequent breeding experiments showed that the abnormality was the result of a genetic mutation, and the gene that was found was named *tau* (Ralph & Menaker, 1988).

Although tau was the first mammalian circadian gene to be identified, it was not the first to have its molecular structure characterized. This honor went to *clock,* a mammalian circadian gene discovered in mice. The structure of the clock gene was characterized in 1997, and that of the tau gene was characterized in 2000 (Lowrey et al., 2000). The molecular structures of eight mammalian circadian genes have now been specified (see King & Takahashi, 2000).

Work on the circadian genes is progressing at a rapid rate. The proteins encoded by the genes have been identified, and investigators are trying to determine how these proteins interact with one another and with experience to regulate circadian timing (see King & Takahashi, 2000).

Although complete understanding of the genetic basis of circadian rhythms is not likely to be achieved in the near future, two important discoveries have already been made. First, it has been found that many tissues, not just the SCN, express the circadian genes—accounting for the fact that many tissues display free-running circadian rhythms in culture. Second, the same or similar circadian genes have been found in many species of different evolutionary ages (e.g., bacteria, flies, fish, frogs, mice, and humans). It seems that circadian rhythms evolved early in evolutionary history, and the same genes have been conserved in various descendant species (see Young, 2000a, 2000b).

14.9 ▶ Drugs That Affect Sleep

Most drugs that influence sleep fall into two different classes: hypnotic and antihypnotic. **Hypnotic drugs** are drugs that increase sleep; **antihypnotic drugs** are drugs that reduce sleep. A third class of sleep-influencing drugs comprises those that influence its circadian rhythmicity; the main drug of this class is **melatonin.**

■ | Hypnotic Drugs

The **benzodiazepines** (e.g., Valium and Librium) were developed and tested for the treatment of anxiety, yet they are the most commonly prescribed hypnotic medications. In the short term, they increase drowsiness, decrease the time it takes to fall asleep, reduce the number of awakenings during a night's sleep, and increase total sleep time. Thus, they can be effective in the treatment of occasional difficulties in sleeping.

Although benzodiazepines can be effective therapeutic hypnotic agents in the short term, their prescription for the treatment of chronic sleep difficulties is ill-advised. Still, they are commonly prescribed for this purpose—primarily by general practitioners. Following are four complications associated with the chronic use of benzodiazepines as hypnotic agents: First, tolerance develops to the hypnotic effects of benzodiazepines; thus, patients must take larger and larger doses to maintain their efficacy. Second, cessation of benzodiazepine therapy after chronic use causes *insomnia* (sleeplessness), which can exacerbate the very problem that the benzodiazepines were intended to correct. Third, chronic benzodiazepine use is addictive. Fourth, benzodiazepines distort the normal pattern of sleep; they increase the duration of sleep by increasing the duration of stage 2 sleep, while actually decreasing the duration of stage 4 and REM sleep.

Evidence that the raphé nuclei play a role in sleep suggested that serotonergic drugs might be effective hypnotics. Efforts to demonstrate the hypnotic effects of such drugs have focused on **5-hydroxytryptophan (5-HTP)**—the precursor of serotonin—because 5-HTP, but not serotonin, readily passes through the blood–brain barrier. Injections of 5-HTP do reverse the insomnia produced in both cats and rats by the serotonin antagonist PCPA; however, they are of no therapeutic benefit in the treatment of human insomnia (see Borbély, 1983).

Antihypnotic Drugs

There are two main classes of antihypnotic drugs: *stimulants* (e.g., cocaine and amphetamine) and *tricyclic antidepressants*. Both stimulants and antidepressants increase the activity of catecholamines (norepinephrine, epinephrine, and dopamine) by either increasing their release or blocking their reuptake from the synapse, or both.

From the perspective of the treatment of sleep disorders, the most important property of antihypnotic drugs is that they act preferentially on REM sleep. They can totally suppress REM sleep even at doses that have little effect on total sleep time.

Using stimulant drugs to treat chronic excessive sleepiness is a risky proposition. Most stimulants are highly addictive, and they produce a variety of adverse side effects, such as loss of appetite. Moreover, unless these drugs are taken at just the right doses and at just the right times, there is a danger that they will interfere with normal sleep.

Melatonin

Melatonin is a hormone that is synthesized from the neurotransmitter serotonin in the **pineal gland** (see Moore, 1996). The pineal gland is an inconspicuous gland that Descartes once believed to be the seat of the soul; it is located on the midline of the brain just ventral to the rear portion of the corpus callosum (see Figure 14.14).

The pineal gland has important functions in birds, reptiles, amphibians, and fish (see Cassone, 1990). The pineal gland of these species has inherent timing properties and regulates circadian rhythms and seasonal changes in reproductive behavior through its release of melatonin. In humans and other mammals, however, the functions of the pineal gland and melatonin are not as apparent.

In humans and other mammals, circulating levels of melatonin display circadian rhythms under control of the suprachiasmatic nuclei (see Gillette & McArthur, 1996), with the highest levels being associated with darkness and sleep (see Foulkes et al., 1997). On the basis of this correlation, it has long been assumed that melatonin plays a role in promoting sleep or in regulating its timing in mammals.

In order to put the facts about melatonin in perspective, it is important to keep one significant point firmly in mind. In adult mammals, pinealectomy and the consequent elimination of melatonin have little effect.

Pineal gland

FIGURE 14.14 The location of the pineal gland, the source of melatonin.

The pineal plays a role in the development of mammalian sexual maturity, but its functions after puberty are not at all obvious.

Does *exogenous* (externally produced) melatonin improve sleep, as widely believed? The evidence is mixed. Several studies have shown that large doses of melatonin during the day, when levels of *endogenous* (internally produced) melatonin are low, produce quicker and better sleep during subsequent nap tests (e.g., Haimov & Lavie, 1996). However, the effects of melatonin taken at bedtime have not been so consistent: A few studies have found subsequent sleep to be longer and more efficient (e.g., Attenburrow, Cowen, & Sharpley, 1996), but others have not (Dawson & Encel, 1993).

In contrast to the controversy over the soporific (sleep-promoting) effects of exogenous melatonin in mammals, there is good evidence that it can influence mammalian circadian cycles (see Lewy, Ahmed, & Sack, 1996). Exposure to exogenous melatonin acts much like exposure to a period of darkness, which makes sense because high levels of endogenous melatonin are associated with darkness. Thus, a dose of melatonin before dusk can help jet-lagged travelers adapt to eastern flights, whereas a dose after dawn can help with adaptation to western flights. The shift in circadian rhythms is, however, typically slight—less than an hour.

Exogenous melatonin has been shown to have a therapeutic potential in the treatment of two types of sleep problems. Melatonin before bedtime has been shown to improve the sleep of insomniacs who are melatonin-deficient (e.g., Haimov et al., 1995) and of blind patients who have sleep problems attributable to the lack of the synchronizing effects of the light–dark cycle (e.g., Lapierre & Dumont, 1995).

14.10 Sleep Disorders

Many sleep disorders fall into one of two complementary categories: insomnia and hypersomnia. **Insomnia** includes all disorders of initiating and maintaining sleep, whereas **hypersomnia** includes disorders of excessive sleep or sleepiness. A third major class of sleep disorders includes all those disorders that are specifically related to REM-sleep dysfunction.

In various surveys, approximately 30% of the respondents report significant sleep-related problems. However, it is important to recognize that complaints of sleep problems often come from people whose sleep appears normal in laboratory sleep tests. For example, many people who complain of insomnia actually sleep a reasonable amount (e.g., 6 hours a night), but they believe that they should sleep more (e.g., 8 hours a night). As a result, they spend more time in bed than they should and have difficulty getting to sleep. Often, the anxiety associated with their inability to sleep makes it even more difficult for them to sleep. Such patients can often be helped by counseling that convinces them to go to bed only when they are very sleepy (see Anch et al., 1988). Others with disturbed sleep have more serious problems.

Insomnia

Many cases of insomnia are **iatrogenic** (physician-created). Paradoxically, sleeping pills (e.g., benzodiazepines) prescribed by well-intentioned physicians are a major cause of insomnia. At first, hypnotic drugs are effective in increasing sleep, but soon the patient is trapped in a rising spiral of drug use, as *tolerance* to the drug develops and progressively more of it is required to produce its original hypnotic effect. Soon, the patient cannot stop taking the drug without running the risk of experiencing *withdrawal symptoms*, which include insomnia. The case of Mr. B. illustrates this problem.

Mr. B., the Case of Iatrogenic Insomnia

Mr. B. was studying for a civil service exam, the outcome of which would affect his entire future. He was terribly worried about the test and found it difficult to get to sleep at night. Feeling that the sleep loss was affecting his ability to study, he consulted his physician for the express purpose of getting "something to make me sleep." His doctor prescribed a moderate dose of barbiturate at bedtime, and Mr. B. found that this medication was very effective . . . for the first several nights. After about a week, he began having trouble sleeping again and decided to take two sleeping pills each night. Twice more the cycle was repeated, until on the night before the exam he was taking four times as many pills as his doctor had prescribed. The next night, with the pressure off, Mr. B. took no medication. He had tremendous difficulty falling asleep, and when he did, his sleep was terribly disrupted. . . . Mr. B. now decided that he had a serious case of insomnia, and returned to his sleeping pill habit. By the time he consulted our clinic several years later, he was taking approximately 1,000 mg sodium amytal every night, and his sleep was more disturbed than ever. . . . Patients may go on for years and years—from one sleeping pill to another—never realizing that their troubles are caused by the pills. (Dement, 1978, p. 80)[4]

Sleep apnea is another common cause of insomnia. In sleep apnea, the patient stops breathing many times each night. Each time, the patient awakens, begins to breathe again, and drifts back to sleep. Sleep apnea usually leads to a sense of having slept poorly and is thus often diagnosed as insomnia. However, some patients are totally unaware of their multiple awakenings and instead complain of excessive sleepiness during the day, which leads to a diagnosis of *hypersomnia* (Stepanski et al., 1984).

Sleep apnea disorders are thought to be of two types: (1) those resulting from obstruction of the respiratory passages by muscle spasms or *atonia* (lack of muscle tone) and (2) those resulting from the failure of the central nervous system to stimulate respiration. Sleep apnea is more common in males, in the overweight, and in the elderly.

Two other causes of insomnia—nocturnal myoclonus and restless legs—both involve the legs. **Nocturnal myoclonus** is a periodic twitching of the body, usually the legs, during sleep. Most patients suffering from this disorder complain of poor sleep and daytime sleepiness but are unaware of the nature of their problem. In contrast, people with **restless legs** are all too aware of their problem. They complain of a hard-to-describe tension or uneasiness in their legs that keeps them from falling asleep. Benzodiazepines are often prescribed in cases of nocturnal myoclonus and restless legs because of their hypnotic, *anxiolytic* (antianxiety), muscle-relaxant, and anticonvulsant properties; however, they are rarely effective.

In one study, insomniacs claimed to take an average of 1 hour to fall asleep and to sleep an average of only 4.5 hours per night; but when they were tested in a sleep laboratory, they were found to have an average *sleep latency* (time to fall asleep) of only 15 minutes and an average nightly sleep duration of 6.5 hours. It used to be common medical practice to assume that people who claimed to suffer from insomnia but slept more than 6.5 hours per night were neurotic. However, this practice stopped when some of those diagnosed as *neurotic pseudoinsomniacs* were subsequently found to be suffering from sleep apnea, nocturnal myoclonus, or other sleep-disturbing problems. Insomnia is not necessarily a problem of too little sleep; it is often a problem of too little undisturbed sleep (Stepanski et al., 1987).

Remarkably, one of the most effective treatments for insomnia is *sleep restriction therapy*. First, the amount of time that an insomniac is allowed to spend in bed is sub-

stantially reduced. Then, after a period of sleep restriction, the amount of time spent in bed is gradually increased in small increments, as long as sleep latency remains in the normal range. Even severe insomniacs benefit from this treatment (Morin, Kowatch, & O'Shanick, 1990; Spielman, Saskin, & Thorpy, 1987).

Hypersomnia

Narcolepsy is the most widely studied disease of hypersomnia. It occurs in 1 out of 2000 individuals (Takahashi, 1999) and has two prominent symptoms (see Siegel, 2000). First, narcoleptics experience severe daytime sleepiness and repeated, brief (10- to 15-minute) daytime sleep episodes. Narcoleptics typically sleep only about an hour per day more than average; it is the inappropriateness of their sleep episodes that most clearly defines their condition. Most of us occasionally fall asleep on the beach, in front of the television, or in that most *soporific* (sleep-promoting) of all daytime sites: the large, dimly lit lecture hall. But narcoleptics fall asleep in the middle of a conversation, while eating, while making love, or even while scuba diving.

The second prominent symptom of narcolepsy is cataplexy. **Cataplexy** is characterized by recurring losses of muscle tone during wakefulness, often triggered by an emotional experience. In its mild form, it may simply force the patient to sit down for a few seconds until it passes. In its extreme form, the patient drops to the ground as if shot and remains there for a minute or two, fully conscious.

In addition to the two prominent symptoms of narcolepsy (daytime sleep attacks and cataplexy), narcoleptics often experience two other symptoms: sleep paralysis and hypnagogic hallucinations. **Sleep paralysis** is the inability to move (paralysis) when falling asleep or waking up. **Hypnagogic hallucinations** are dreamlike experiences during wakefulness. Sleep paralysis and hypnagogic hallucinations are occasionally experienced by many people. Have you experienced them?

Three lines of evidence suggested to early researchers that narcolepsy results from an abnormality in the mechanisms that trigger REM sleep. First, unlike normal people, narcoleptics often go directly into REM sleep when they fall asleep. Second and third, narcoleptics often experience dreamlike states and loss of muscle tone during wakefulness.

Advances have been made in research on narcolepsy, thanks to the existence of a strain of dogs that suffer from the disorder. In one study, Siegel and colleagues (1991) recorded the activity of the **nucleus magnocellularis**—a structure of the caudal reticular formation that controls muscle relaxation during REM sleep. In normal dogs, this structure was active only during REM sleep; in the narcoleptic dogs, it also became active during their narcoleptic attacks.

[4]From *Some Must Watch while Some Must Sleep* by William E. Dement, published by Portable Stanford Books, Stanford Alumni Association, Stanford University. Reprinted by permission.

For centuries, neuropathologists had screened the brains of deceased narcoleptics looking for brain damage but had found nothing; similarly, no brain damage was found in the first studies of the narcoleptic dogs. Siegel and colleagues (1999) wondered whether researchers had failed to find narcolepsy-related brain damage because they had been looking at the wrong time in the disease process. After diagnosis, narcoleptics get no worse, suggesting that the brain damage might be complete at this point. If this were the case, by the time a patient died, any debris from the damage would have been removed by glial cells, and the loss of cells would have been obscured by the normal neural degeneration associated with aging. By examining the brains of dogs that had recently developed narcolepsy, Siegel and colleagues found obvious damage in the basal forebrain region and the amygdala.

An exciting recent advance in the study of narcolepsy is also attributable to narcoleptic dogs (see Takahashi, 1999). Lin and colleagues (1999), after 10 years of studying the genetics of the narcoleptic dogs, finally isolated the gene that causes the disorder. The gene encodes a receptor protein that binds to a neuropeptide called **orexin** (Kilduff & Peyron, 2000). In response to this discovery, Chemielli and colleagues (1999) bred *knockout mice* with a dysfunctional gene for the orexin-binding protein. These mice display the symptoms of narcolepsy.

When narcolepsy occurs in an identical twin, the probability that the other twin will be narcoleptic is only 25%. This finding suggests that environmental factors normally play a major role in the brain damage associated with narcolepsy. Perhaps exposure to a neurotoxin damages the orexin system.

■ REM-Sleep–Related Disorders

Several sleep disorders are specific disorders of REM sleep; these are classified as *REM-sleep–related disorders.* Even narcolepsy, which is usually classified as a disorder of hypersomnia, can reasonably be considered to be a REM-sleep–related disorder—for reasons you have just encountered.

Occasionally, patients are discovered who have little or no REM sleep. Although this disorder is rare, it is important because of its theoretical implications. Lavie and others (1984) described a patient who had suffered a brain injury that presumably involved damage to the REM-sleep generator in the pontine reticular formation. The most important finding of this case study was that the patient did not appear to be adversely affected by his lack of REM sleep. After receiving his injury, he completed high school, college, and law school and now has a thriving law practice.

Some patients experience REM sleep without core muscle atonia. It has been suggested that the function of REM-sleep atonia is to prevent the acting out of dreams. This theory receives support from case studies of people who suffer from this disorder.

The Case of the Sleeper Who Ran Over a Tackle

I was a halfback playing football, and after the quarterback received the ball from the center he lateraled it sideways to me and I'm supposed to go around end and cut back over tackle and—this is very vivid—as I cut back over tackle there is this big 280-pound tackle waiting, so I, according to football rules, was to give him my shoulder and bounce him out of the way.... [W]hen I came to I was standing in front of our dresser and I had [gotten up out of bed and run and] knocked lamps, mirrors and everything off the dresser, hit my head against the wall and my knee against the dresser. (Schenck et al., 1986, p. 294)

Presumably, REM sleep without atonia is caused by damage to the nucleus magnocellularis or to an interruption of its output. Supporting this hypothesis is the fact that lesions of the caudal reticular formation often induce a similar disorder in cats:

The cat, which is standing . . . may attack unknown enemies, play with an absent mouse, or display flight behavior. There are orienting movements of the head or eyes toward imaginary stimuli, although the animal does not respond to visual or auditory stimuli. (Jouvet, 1972, pp. 236–237)

14.11 The Effects of Long-Term Sleep Reduction

You have already learned in this chapter that answering the question of how much sleep we need requires a particular kind of research. Most studies of sleep deprivation have been studies of short-term deprivation—that is, of a few days or less. This type of research serves an important function, but it provides little insight into how much sleep people really need because virtually all of the subjects in these studies have been inefficient sleepers. Clearly, the only way to discover minimal sleep requirements is to study healthy human subjects who have maximized the efficiency of their sleep by voluntarily following regular, long-term, programs of reduced sleep. Because they are so time-consuming, few of these critical studies have been conducted; but there have been enough of them for a clear pattern of results to have emerged. I think you will by amazed by the results.

There have been two kinds of long-term sleep-reduction studies: studies in which the subjects sleep nightly and studies in which subjects sleep by napping. Following a brief discussion of these two kinds of studies, the chapter concludes with my own personal experience of long-term sleep reduction.

■ | Long-Term Reduction of Nightly Sleep

There have been two studies in which healthy subjects have reduced their nightly sleep for several weeks or longer. In one (Webb & Agnew, 1974), a group of 16 subjects slept for only 5.5 hours per night for 60 days, with only one detectable deficit on an extensive battery of mood, medical, and performance tests: a slight deficit on a test of auditory vigilance.

In the other systematic study of long-term sleep reduction (Friedman et al., 1977; Mullaney et al., 1977), 8 subjects reduced their nightly sleep by 30 minutes every 2 weeks until they reached 6.5 hours per night, then by 30 minutes every 3 weeks until they reached 5 hours, and then by 30 minutes every 4 weeks thereafter. After a subject indicated a lack of desire to reduce sleep further, the person slept for 1 month at the shortest duration of nightly sleep that was achieved, then for 2 months at the shortest duration plus 30 minutes. Finally, each subject slept each night for 1 year for however long the person preferred. The minimum duration of nightly sleep achieved during this experiment was 5.5 hours for 2 subjects, 5.0 hours for 4 subjects, and an impressive 4.5 hours for 2 subjects. In each of the subjects, a reduction in sleep time was associated with an increase in sleep efficiency: a decrease in the amount of time it took the subjects to fall asleep after going to bed, a decrease in the number of nighttime awakenings, and an increase in the proportion of stage 4 sleep. After the subjects had reduced their sleep to 6 hours per night, they began to experience daytime sleepiness, and this became a problem as sleep time was further reduced. Nevertheless, there were no deficits on any of the mood, medical, or performance tests given to the subjects throughout the experiment. The most encouraging result was that during a follow-up 1 year later, all subjects were sleeping less than they had previously—between 7 and 18 hours less each week—with no excessive sleepiness.

■ | Long-Term Sleep Reduction by Napping

Most mammals and human infants display **polyphasic sleep cycles;** that is, they regularly sleep more than once per day. In contrast, most adult humans display **monophasic sleep cycles;** that is, they sleep once per day. Nevertheless, most adult humans do display polyphasic cycles of sleepiness, with periods of sleepiness occurring in late afternoon and late morning (Stampi, 1992a). Have you ever experienced them?

Do adult humans need to take sleep in one continuous period per day, or can they sleep effectively in several naps as human infants and other mammals do? Which of the two sleep patterns is more efficient? Research has shown that naps have recuperative powers out of proportion with their brevity (e.g., Gillberg et al., 1996; Horne & Reyner, 1996; Naitoh, 1992), suggesting that polyphasic sleep might be particularly efficient.

Interest in the value of polyphasic sleep was stimulated by the legend that Leonardo da Vinci managed to generate a steady stream of artistic and engineering accomplishments during his life by napping for 15 minutes every 4 hours, thereby limiting his sleep to 1.5 hours per day. As unbelievable as this may seem, it has been replicated in several experiments (see Stampi, 1992b). Here are the main findings of these truly mind-boggling experiments. First, the subjects required a long time, about 2 weeks, to adapt to a polyphasic sleep schedule. Second, once adapted to polyphasic sleep, the subjects were content and displayed no deficits on the performance tests that they received. Third, Leonardo's 4-hour schedule works quite well, but in unstructured working situations (e.g., as in around-the-world solo sailboat races), subjects often vary the duration of the cycle without feeling negative consequences. Fourth, most subjects display a strong preference for particular sleep durations (e.g., 25 minutes) and refrain from sleeping too little, which leaves them unrefreshed, or too much, which leaves them groggy for several minutes when they awake—an effect called *sleep inertia.* Fifth, at first most of the sleep is slow-wave sleep, but eventually the subjects return to their usual relative proportions of REM and slow-wave sleep; however, REM and slow-wave sleep seldom occur during the same nap.

The following are the words of artist Giancarlo Sbragia, who adopted Leonardo's sleep schedule:

> This schedule was difficult to follow at the beginning. . . . It took about 3 wk to get used to it. But I soon reached a point at which I felt a natural propensity for sleeping at this rate, and it turned out to be a thrilling and exciting experience.
>
> . . . How beautiful my life became: I discovered dawns, I discovered silence, and concentration. I had more time for studying and reading—far more than I did before. I had more time for myself, for painting, and for developing my career. (Sbragia, 1992, p. 181)

■ | Long-Term Sleep Reduction: A Personal Case Study

I began this chapter 4 weeks ago with both zeal and trepidation. I was fascinated by the idea that I could wring 2 or 3 extra hours of living out of each day by sleeping less, and I hoped that adhering to a sleep-reduction program while writing about sleep would create an enthusiasm for the subject that would color my writing and be passed on to you. On the other hand, I was more than a little concerned about the negative effect that losing 3 hours of sleep per night might have on me.

The Case of the Author Who Reduced His Sleep

Rather than using the gradual stepwise reduction method of Friedman and his colleagues, I jumped directly into my 5-hours-per-night sleep schedule. This proved to be less difficult than you might think. I took advantage of a trip to the East Coast from my home on the West Coast to reset my circadian clock. While I was in the East, I got up at 7:00 A.M., which is 4:00 A.M. on the West Coast, and I just kept on the same schedule when I got home. I decided to add my extra waking hours to the beginning of my day rather than to the end so there would be no temptation for me to waste them; there are not too many distractions around this university at 5:00 A.M.

Figure 14.15 is a record of my sleep times for the 4-week period that it took me to write a first draft of this chapter. I didn't quite meet my goal of sleeping less than 5 hours every night, but I didn't miss by much: My overall mean was 5.05 hours per night. Notice that in the last week, there was a tendency for my circadian clock to run a bit slow; I began sleeping in until 4:30 A.M. and staying up until 11:30 P.M.

What were the positives and negatives of my experience? The main positive was the added time to do things: Having an extra 21 hours per week was wonderful. Furthermore, because my daily routine was out of synchrony with everybody else's, I spent little time sitting in rush-hour traffic. The only negative of the experience was sleepiness. It was no problem during the day, when I was active. However, staying awake during the last hour before I went to bed—an hour during which I usually engaged in sedentary activities, such as reading—was at times a problem. This is when I became personally familiar with the phenomenon of microsleeps, and it was then that I required some assistance in order to stay awake. Going to bed and falling asleep each night became a fleeting but satisfying experience.

I began this chapter with the question: How much sleep do we need? Then, I gave you my best professorial it-could-be-this, it-could-be-that answer. However, that was a month ago. Now, after experiencing sleep reduction firsthand, I am less inclined toward wishy-washiness on the topic of sleep. The fact that most committed subjects who are active during the day can reduce their sleep to about 5.5 hours per night without great difficulty or major adverse consequences suggested to me that the answer is 5.5 hours of sleep. But that was before I reviewed the research on napping and polyphasic sleep schedules. Now, I must revise my estimate downward—substantially.

FIGURE 14.15 Sleep record of Pinel during a 4-week sleep-reduction program.

Themes Revisited

The evolutionary perspective theme played a prominent role in this chapter. You learned how thinking about the adaptive function of sleep and comparing sleep in different species have led to interesting insights. Also, you saw how research into the physiology and genetics of sleep has been conducted on nonhuman species.

The thinking-about-biopsychology theme pervaded this chapter. The major purpose of the chapter was to encourage you to reevaluate conventional ideas about sleep.

Has this chapter changed your thinking about sleep? Writing it changed mine.

Finally, the clinical implications theme received emphasis in the section on sleep disorders. Perhaps most exciting and interesting were the recent breakthroughs in the understanding of the genetics and physiology of narcolepsy.

ON THE CD

Looking for more information about the topics in this chapter? For recommended additional readings, see Hard Copy for Chapter 14.

Log On

- **http://faculty.washington.edu/chudler/sleep.html** A general review of sleeping, this link includes EEG traces for different sleep stages and an animation of REM (sleep, not the band!).

- **http://www.SleepQuest.com/** This site from SleepQuest, a group devoted to the study of sleeping disorders, and Dr. William Dement, a pioneer in sleep research, includes a demonstration of sleep apnea and a Q–A forum with Dr. Dement.

- **http://www.sfn.org/briefings/rem_sleep.html** The Society for Neuroscience's Brain Briefings presents a thorough overview of REM sleep.

- **http://www.uwm.edu/People/johnchay/sl.htm** A Shockwave-based animation shows a running record of EEG, EOG, and EMG recordings and a "patient" in a sleep lab. You can wake the "virtual patient" during various stages of the experiment to observe changes in his/her sleep and electrophysiological activity.

Think about It

1. Do you think your life could be improved by changing when or how long you sleep each day? In what ways? What negative effects do you think such changes might have on you?

2. Some people like to stay up late, some people like to get up early, others like to do both, and still others like to do neither. Design a sleep-reduction program that is tailored to your own preferences and lifestyle and that is consistent with the research literature on circadian cycles and sleep deprivation. The program should produce the greatest benefits for you with the least discomfort.

3. How has reading about sleep research changed your views about sleep? Give three specific examples.

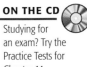

ON THE CD

Studying for an exam? Try the Practice Tests for Chapter 14.

4. Given the evidence that the long-term use of benzodiazepines actually contributes to the problems of insomnia, why are they so commonly prescribed for its treatment?

5. Your friend tells you that everybody needs 8 hours of sleep per night; she points out that every time she stays up late to study, she feels lousy the next day. Convince her that she is wrong.

Key Terms

Activation-synthesis theory
  (p. 355)
Alpha waves *(p. 352)*
Antihypnotic drugs *(p. 371)*
Basal forebrain region *(p. 367)*
Benzodiazepines *(p. 371)*
Carousel apparatus *(p. 362)*
Cataplexy *(p. 374)*
Cerveau isolé preparation
  (p. 365)
Circadian clock *(p. 369)*
Circadian rhythms *(p. 357)*
Circadian theories of sleep
  (p. 356)
Delta waves *(p. 352)*
Desynchronized EEG *(p. 365)*
Electroencephalogram (EEG)
  (p. 352)
Electromyogram (EMG)
  (p. 352)

Electrooculogram (EOG)
  (p. 352)
Emergent stage 1 EEG *(p. 352)*
Encéphale isolé preparation
  (p. 365)
5-Hydroxytryptophan (5-HTP)
  (p. 371)
Free-running period *(p. 358)*
Free-running rhythms *(p. 358)*
Hypersomnia *(p. 373)*
Hypnagogic hallucinations
  (p. 374)
Hypnotic drugs *(p. 371)*
Iatrogenic *(p. 373)*
Initial stage 1 EEG *(p. 352)*
Insomnia *(p. 373)*
Internal desynchronization
  (p. 358)
Jet lag *(p. 359)*
Lucid dreams *(p. 355)*

Melatonin *(p. 371)*
Microsleeps *(p. 361)*
Monophasic sleep cycles
  (p. 376)
Narcolepsy *(p. 374)*
Nocturnal myoclonus *(p. 374)*
Nucleus magnocellularis
  (p. 374)
Orexin *(p. 375)*
Parachlorophenylalanine
  (PCPA) *(p. 367)*
Pineal gland *(p. 372)*
Polyphasic sleep cycles *(p. 376)*
Raphé nuclei *(p. 367)*
Recuperation theories
  of sleep *(p. 356)*
REM sleep *(p. 354)*
Restless legs *(p. 374)*
Reticular activating system
  (p. 365)

Sleep apnea *(p. 374)*
Sleep paralysis *(p. 374)*
Slow-wave sleep (SWS) *(p. 354)*
Somnambulism *(p. 355)*
Suprachiasmatic nuclei (SCN)
  (p. 369)
Tricyclic antidepressant drugs
  (p. 363)
Zeitgebers *(p. 358)*

ON THE CD
Need some help studying the key terms for this chapter? Check out the electronic flash cards for Chapter 14.

chapter 15

Drug Addiction and the Brain's Reward Circuits

Chemicals That Harm with Pleasure

Drug addiction is a serious problem in most parts of the world. For example, in the United States alone, over 60 million people are addicted to nicotine, alcohol, or both; 5.5 million are addicted to illegal drugs; and many millions more are addicted to prescription drugs. Pause for a moment and think about the sheer magnitude of the grief represented by such figures—hundreds of millions of sick and suffering people worldwide. Think also about what these figures may mean for you personally. The incidence of drug addiction is so high that it is almost certain that you, or somebody dear to you, will be adversely affected by drugs. Perhaps it has happened already.

This chapter introduces you to some basic pharmacological principles and concepts, compares the effects of five common addictive drugs, and reviews the research on the neural mechanisms of addiction. You likely already have strong views about drug addiction; thus, as you progress through this chapter, it is particularly important that you do not let your thinking be clouded by preconceptions. In particular, it is important that you do not fall into the trap of assuming that a drug's legal status has much to say about its safety. You will be less likely to assume that legal drugs are safe and illegal drugs are dangerous if you re-member that most laws governing drug abuse in various parts of the world were enacted in the early 1900s or earlier, long before there was any scientific research on the topic.

People's tendency to equate drug legality with drug safety was recently conveyed to me in a particularly ironic fashion: I was invited to address a convention of high school teachers on the topic of drug abuse. When I arrived at the convention center to give my talk, I was escorted to a special suite, where I was encouraged to join the executive committee in a round of drug taking—the drug being a special high-proof single-malt whiskey. Later, the irony of the situation had its full impact. As I stepped to the podium under the influence of a psychoactive drug (the whiskey), I looked out through the haze of cigarette smoke at an audience of educators who had invited me to speak to them because they were concerned about the unhealthy impact of drugs on their students. The welcoming applause gradually gave way to the melodic tinkling of ice cubes in liquor glasses, and I began. They did not like what I had to say.

ON THE CD

In the *Thinking about Drugs* module, Pinel welcomes you to this chapter and discusses some common misconceptions about drug addiction—while he is under the influence of a mind-altering chemical.

15.1 Basic Principles of Drug Action

This section focuses on the basic principles of drug action, with an emphasis on **psychoactive drugs**—drugs that influence subjective experience and behavior by acting on the nervous system.

Drug Administration and Absorption

Drugs are usually administered in one of four ways: by oral ingestion, by injection, by inhalation, or by absorption through the mucous membranes of the nose, mouth, or rectum. The route of administration influences the rate at which and the degree to which the drug reaches its sites of action.

INGESTION ■ The oral route is the preferred route of administration for many drugs. Once they are swallowed, drugs dissolve in the fluids of the stomach and are carried to the intestine, where they are absorbed into the bloodstream. However, some drugs readily pass through the stomach wall (e.g., alcohol), and these take effect sooner because they do not have to reach the intestine to be absorbed. Drugs that are not readily absorbed from the digestive tract or that are broken down into inactive metabolites before they can be absorbed must be taken by some other route.

The two main advantages of the oral route of administration over other routes are its ease and relative safety. Its main disadvantage is its unpredictability: Absorption from the digestive tract into the bloodstream can be greatly influenced by such difficult-to-gauge factors as the amount and type of food in the stomach.

INJECTION ■ Drug injection is common in medical practice because the effects of injected drugs are strong, fast, and predictable. Drug injections are typically made *subcutaneously (SC)*, into the fatty tissue just beneath the skin; *intramuscularly (IM)*, into the large muscles; or *intravenously (IV)*, directly into veins at points where they run just beneath the skin. Many addicts prefer the intravenous route because the bloodstream delivers the drug directly to the brain. However, the speed and directness of the intravenous route are mixed blessings; after an intravenous injection, there is little or no opportunity to counteract the effects of an overdose, an impurity, or an allergic reaction. Furthermore, many addicts develop scar tissue, infections, and collapsed veins at the few sites on their bodies where there are large accessible veins.

INHALATION ■ Some drugs can be absorbed into the bloodstream through the rich network of capillaries in the lungs. Many anesthetics are typically administered by *inhalation,* as are tobacco and marijuana. The two main shortcomings of this route are that it is difficult to precisely regulate the dose of inhaled drugs, and many substances damage the lungs if chronically inhaled.

ABSORPTION THROUGH MUCOUS MEMBRANES ■ Some drugs can be administered through the mucous membranes of the nose, mouth, and rectum. Cocaine, for example, is commonly self-administered through the nasal membranes (snorted)—but not without damaging them.

■ Drug Penetration of the Central Nervous System

Once a drug enters the bloodstream, it is carried in the blood to the blood vessels of the central nervous system. Fortunately, a protective filter, the *blood–brain barrier,* makes it difficult for many potentially dangerous bloodborne chemicals to pass from the blood vessels of the CNS into its neurons.

■ Mechanisms of Drug Action

Psychoactive drugs influence the nervous system in many ways (see Koob & Bloom, 1988). Some drugs (e.g., alcohol and many of the general anesthetics) act diffusely on neural membranes throughout the CNS. Others act in a more specific way: by binding to particular synaptic receptors; by influencing the synthesis, transport, release, or deactivation of particular neurotransmitters; or by influencing the chain of chemical reactions elicited in postsynaptic neurons by the activation of their receptors (see Chapter 4).

■ Drug Metabolism and Elimination

The actions of most drugs are terminated by enzymes synthesized by the *liver.* These liver enzymes stimulate the conversion of active drugs to nonactive forms—a process referred to as **drug metabolism.** In many cases, drug metabolism eliminates a drug's ability to pass through lipid membranes of cells so that it can no longer penetrate the blood–brain barrier. In addition to the deactivating effects of drug metabolism, small amounts of some psychoactive drugs are passed from the body in urine, sweat, feces, breath, and mother's milk.

■ Drug Tolerance

Drug tolerance is a state of decreased sensitivity to a drug that develops as a result of exposure to it. Drug tolerance can be demonstrated in two ways: by showing that a given dose of the drug has less effect than it had before drug exposure or by showing that it takes more of the drug to produce the same effect. In essence, what this means is that drug tolerance is a shift in the *dose-response curve* (a graph of the magnitude of the effect of different doses of the drug) to the right (see Figure 15.1).

There are three important points to remember about the specificity of drug tolerance. The first is that exposure to one drug can produce tolerance to other drugs that act by the same mechanism; this is known as **cross tolerance.** The second is that drug tolerance often develops to some effects of a drug but not to others. Failure to understand this second point can have tragic consequences for people who think that because they have become tolerant to some effects of a drug (e.g., to the nauseating effects of alcohol or tobacco), they are tolerant to all of them. In fact, tolerance may develop to some effects of a drug while sensitivity to other effects increases—increases in sensitivity to drugs are called **sensitization** (Robinson, 1991). The third important point about the specificity of drug tolerance is that it

FIGURE 15.1 Drug tolerance: A shift in the dose-response curve to the right as a result of exposure to the drug.

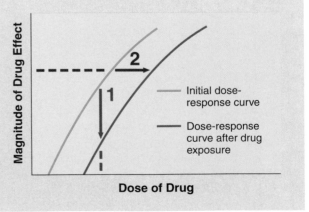

Drug tolerance is a shift in the dose-response curve to the right. Therefore,

1 In tolerant subjects, the same dose has less effect

2 In tolerant subjects, a greater dose is required to produce the same effect

Magnitude of Drug Effect

— Initial dose-response curve

— Dose-response curve after drug exposure

Dose of Drug

is not a unitary phenomenon; that is, there is no single mechanism that underlies all examples of it. When a drug is administered at active doses, many kinds of adaptive changes can occur to reduce its effects.

Two categories of changes underlie drug tolerance: metabolic and functional. Drug tolerance that results from changes that reduce the amount of drug getting to its sites of action is called **metabolic tolerance.** Drug tolerance that results from changes that reduce the reactivity of the sites of action to the drug is called **functional tolerance.**

Tolerance to psychoactive drugs is largely functional. Functional tolerance to psychoactive drugs can result from several different types of neural changes. For example, exposure to a psychoactive drug can reduce the number of receptors for it, decrease the efficiency with which it binds to existing receptors, or diminish the impact of receptor binding on the activity of the cell.

Drug Withdrawal Effects and Physical Dependence

After significant amounts of a drug have been in the body for a period of time (e.g., several days), its sudden elimination can trigger an illness called a **withdrawal syndrome.** The effects of drug withdrawal are virtually always opposite to the initial effects of the drug. For example, the withdrawal of anticonvulsant drugs often triggers convulsions, and the withdrawal of sleeping pills often produces insomnia. Individuals who suffer withdrawal reactions when they stop taking a drug are said to be **physically dependent** on that drug.

The fact that withdrawal effects are frequently opposite to the initial effects of the drug suggests that withdrawal effects may be produced by the same neural changes that produce drug tolerance (see Figure 15.2). According to this theory, exposure to a drug produces compensatory changes in the nervous system that offset the drug's effects and produce tolerance. Then, when the drug is eliminated from the body, these compensatory neural changes, without the drug to offset them, manifest themselves as withdrawal symptoms opposite to the initial effects of the drug.

The severity of withdrawal symptoms depends on the particular drug in question, on the duration and degree of the preceding drug exposure, and on the speed with which the drug is eliminated from the body. In general, longer exposure to greater doses followed by more rapid elimination produces greater withdrawal effects.

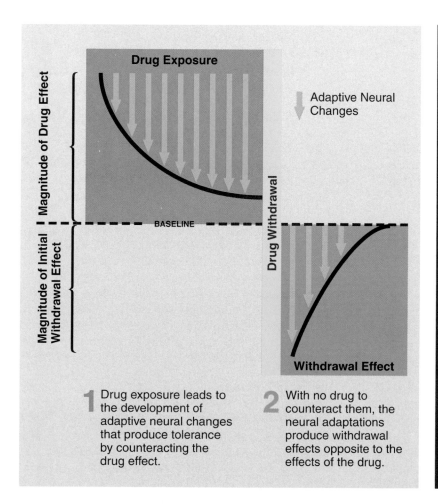

FIGURE 15.2 The relation between drug tolerance and withdrawal effects. The same adaptive neurophysiological changes that develop in response to drug exposure and produce drug tolerance manifest themselves as withdrawal effects once the drug is removed. As the neurophysiological changes develop, tolerance increases; as they subside, the severity of the withdrawal effects decreases.

1 Drug exposure leads to the development of adaptive neural changes that produce tolerance by counteracting the drug effect.

2 With no drug to counteract them, the neural adaptations produce withdrawal effects opposite to the effects of the drug.

Addiction: What Is It?

Addicts are habitual drug users, but not all habitual drug users are addicts. **Addicts** are those habitual drug users who continue to use a drug despite its adverse effects on their health and social life and despite their repeated efforts to stop using it.

The greatest confusion about the nature of addiction concerns its relation to physical dependence. Many people equate the two: They see addicts as people who are trapped on a merry-go-round of drug taking, withdrawal symptoms, and further drug taking to combat the withdrawal symptoms. Although appealing in its simplicity, this conception of drug addiction is wrong. Addicts sometimes take drugs to prevent or alleviate withdrawal symptoms, but this is

rarely the primary motivating factor in their addiction. If it were, addicts could be easily cured by hospitalizing them for a few days, until their withdrawal symptoms subsided. However, most addicts renew their drug taking even after months of enforced abstinence. This is an important issue, and it will be revisited later in the chapter.

When physical dependence was believed to be the major cause of addiction, the term *psychological dependence* was coined to refer to exceptions to this general rule. **Psychological dependence** was said to be the cause of any compulsive drug taking that occurred in the absence of physical dependence. However, now that it is clear that physical dependence is not the major motivating factor in addiction, there is little need for a special category of psychological dependence (see Leshner, 1997).

15.2 Role of Learning in Drug Tolerance and Drug Withdrawal

An important line of psychopharmacologic research has shown that learning plays a major role in both drug tolerance and drug withdrawal. This research has contributed substantially to an understanding of tolerance and withdrawal, but its impact has been more far-reaching: It has established that efforts to understand the effects of psychoactive drugs without considering the experience and behavior of the subjects will provide only partial answers.

Research on the role of learning in drug tolerance has focused on three phenomena: contingent drug tolerance, conditioned drug tolerance, and conditioned withdrawal effects. These phenomena are discussed in the following subsections.

Contingent Drug Tolerance

Contingent drug tolerance refers to demonstrations that tolerance develops only to drug effects that are actually experienced. Most studies of contingent drug tolerance employ the **before-and-after design.** In before-and-after experiments, two groups of subjects receive the same series of drug injections and the same series of repeated tests, but the subjects in one group receive the drug before each test of the series and those in the other group receive the drug after each test. At the end of the experiment, all subjects receive the same dose of the drug followed by the test so that the degree to which the drug disrupts test performance in the two groups can be compared.

My colleagues and I (e.g., Pinel, Mana, & Kim, 1989) have used the before-and-after design to study contin-

gent tolerance to the anticonvulsant effect of alcohol. In our study, two groups of rats received exactly the same regimen of alcohol injections: one injection every 2 days for the duration of the experiment. During the tolerance development phase, the rats in one group received each alcohol injection 1 hour before a mild convulsive amygdala stimulation so that the anticonvulsant effect of the alcohol could be experienced on each trial. The rats in the other group received their injections 1 hour after each convulsive stimulation so that the anticonvulsant effect could not be experienced. At the end of the experiment, all of the subjects received a test injection of alcohol, followed 1 hour later by a convulsive stimulation so that the amount of tolerance to the anticonvulsant effect of alcohol could be compared in the two groups. As Figure 15.3 illustrates, the rats that received alcohol on each trial before a convulsive stimulation became almost totally tolerant to alcohol's anticonvulsant effect, whereas those that received the same injections and stimulations in the reverse order developed no tolerance whatsoever to alcohol's anticonvulsant effect. Contingent drug tolerance has been demonstrated for many other drug effects in many species (see Poulos & Cappell, 1991).

Conditioned Drug Tolerance

Whereas studies of contingent drug tolerance focus on what subjects do while they are under the influence of drugs, studies of conditioned drug tolerance focus on the situations in which drugs are taken. **Conditioned drug**

FIGURE 15.3 Contingent tolerance to the anticonvulsant effect of alcohol. The rats that received alcohol on each trial *before* a convulsive stimulation became tolerant to its anticonvulsant effect; those that received the same injections *after* a convulsive stimulation on each trial did not become tolerant. (Adapted from Pinel, Mana, & Kim, 1989.)

tolerance refers to demonstrations that tolerance effects are maximally expressed only when a drug is administered in the same situation in which it has previously been administered (see Mitchell, Basbaum, & Fields, 2000; Weise-Kelley & Siegel, 2001).

In one demonstration of conditioned drug tolerance (Crowell, Hinson, & Siegel, 1981), two groups of rats received 20 alcohol and 20 saline injections in an alternating sequence, 1 injection every other day. The only difference between the two groups was that the rats in one group received all 20 alcohol injections in a distinctive test room and the 20 saline injections in their colony room, while the rats in the other group received the alcohol in the colony room and the saline in the distinctive test room. At the end of the injection period, the tolerance of all rats to the *hypothermic* (temperature-reducing) effects of alcohol was assessed in both environments. As Figure 15.4 on page 386 illustrates, tolerance was observed only when the rats were injected in the environment that had previously been paired with alcohol administration. There have been dozens of other demonstrations of the *situational specificity of drug tolerance:* The effect is large, reliable, and general.

The situational specificity of drug tolerance led Siegel and his colleagues to propose that addicts may be particularly susceptible to the lethal effects of a drug *overdose* when the drug is administered in a new context. Their hypothesis is that addicts become tolerant when they repeatedly self-administer their drug in the same environment and, as a result, begin taking larger and larger doses to counteract the diminution of drug effects. Then, if the addict administers the usual massive dose in an unusual situation, tolerance effects are not present to

counteract the effects of the drug, and there is a greater risk of death from overdose. In support of this hypothesis, Siegel and colleagues (1982) found that many more heroin-tolerant rats died following a high dose of heroin administered in a novel environment than in their usual injection environment. Heroin kills by suppressing respiration.

Of the several noteworthy theories that have been proposed to account for the situational specificity of drug tolerance (see Baker & Tiffany, 1985; Eikelboom & Stewart, 1982; Paletta & Wagner, 1986), Siegel's theory has been the most influential. Siegel views each incidence of drug administration as a Pavlovian conditioning trial in which various environmental stimuli that regularly predict the administration of the drug (e.g., pubs, washrooms, needles, other addicts) are conditional stimuli and the drug effects are unconditional stimuli. The central assumption of the theory is that conditional stimuli that predict drug administration come to elicit conditional responses opposite to the unconditional effects of the drug. Siegel has termed these hypothetical opposing conditional responses **conditioned compensatory responses.** The theory is that as the stimuli that repeatedly predict the effects of a drug come to elicit greater and greater conditioned compensatory responses, they increasingly counteract the unconditional effects of the drug and produce situationally specific tolerance.

Although tolerance develops to many drug effects, sometimes the opposite—sensitization—occurs. *Drug sensitization,* like drug tolerance, can be situationally specific (see Arvanitogiannis, Sullivan, & Amir, 2000). For example, Anagnostaras and Robinson (1996) demonstrated the situational specificity of sensitization to the

FIGURE 15.4 The situational specificity of tolerance to the hypothermic effects of alcohol. (Adapted from Crowell et al., 1981.)

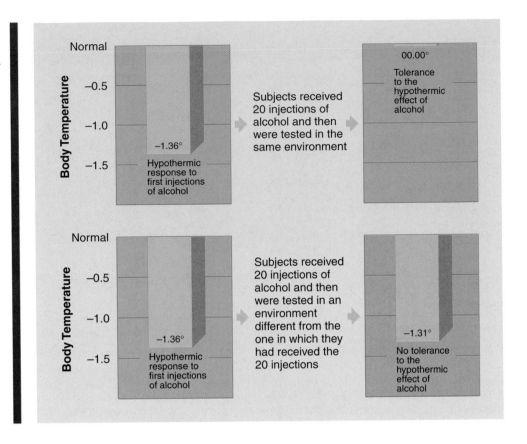

Conditioned Withdrawal Effects

As you have just learned, Siegel's conditioned compensatory response theory suggests that when a drug is repeatedly administered in the same environment, that environment begins to elicit responses that counteract the drug effects and lead to the development of tolerance. One prediction of this theory is that in the absence of the drug, the drug environment should elicit effects opposite to the original effects of the drug. Withdrawal effects that are elicited by the drug environment or by other drug-associated cues are **conditioned withdrawal effects.**

There have been many demonstrations of conditioned withdrawal effects. For example, Krank and Perkins (1993) administered two injections each day to three groups of rats. One group of rats received a morphine injection each day in a distinctive test environment and a saline injection in their home cages; another group received saline injections in the test environment and morphine injections in their home cages; and the third group received saline injections in both the test environment and their home cages. After 10 injection days (i.e., after 20 injections), all injections ceased, the rats were placed in the distinctive test environment, and the morphine withdrawal reactions were assessed. The results are presented in Figure 15.5. The rats that had received morphine injections in the distinctive test environment displayed substantially more morphine withdrawal symptoms than did the rats that had received morphine injections in their home cages and the rats that had received only saline injections.

Thinking about Drug Conditioning

In any situation in which drugs are repeatedly administered, conditioned effects are inevitable. That is why it is particularly important to understand them. However, most theories of drug conditioning have a serious problem: They have difficulty predicting the direction of the conditioned effects. For example, Siegel's conditioned compensatory response theory predicts that conditioned drug effects will always be opposite to the unconditioned effects of the drug, but there are many documented in-

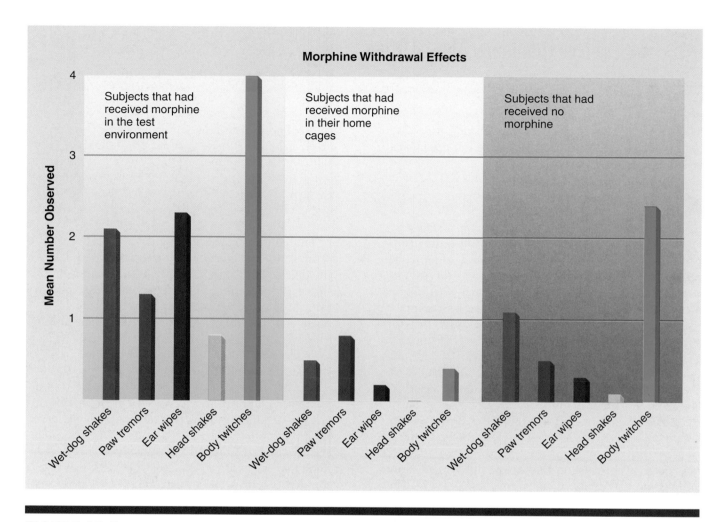

FIGURE 15.5 Conditioned morphine withdrawal effects in rats. Being placed in an environment in which they had previously experienced the effects of morphine elicited morphine withdrawal effects in rats. (Adapted from Krank & Perkins, 1993.)

stances in which conditional stimuli elicit responses similar to those of the drug.

Ramsay and Woods (1997) contend that much of the confusion about conditioned drug effects stems from a misunderstanding of Pavlovian conditioning. In particular, they criticize the common assumption that the unconditional stimulus in a drug-tolerance experiment is the drug and that the unconditional response is whatever change in physiology or behavior the experimenter happens to be recording. They argue instead that the unconditional stimulus (i.e., the stimulus to which the subject reflexively reacts) is the disruption of neural functioning that has been directly produced by the drug, and that the unconditional responses are the various neurally mediated compensatory reactions to the unconditional stimulus.

This change in perspective makes a big difference. For example, in the previously described alcohol tolerance experiment by Crowell and others (1981), alcohol was designated as the unconditional stimulus and the resulting hypothermia as the unconditional response. Instead, Ramsay and Woods would argue that the unconditional stimulus was the hypothermia directly produced by the exposure to alcohol, whereas the compensatory changes that tended to counteract the reductions in body temperature were the unconditional responses. The important point about all of this is that once one determines the unconditional stimulus and unconditional response, it is easy to predict the direction of the conditional response in any drug-conditioning experiment: The conditional response is always similar to the unconditional response. Moreover, Ramsay and Woods would argue that when the unconditional response counteracts the unconditional stimulus, as is usually the case, conditioning produces tolerance; whereas when the unconditional response augments the unconditional stimulus, conditioning produces sensitization.

15.3 Five Commonly Abused Drugs

This section focuses on the hazards of chronic use of five commonly abused drugs: tobacco, alcohol, marijuana, cocaine, and the opiates.

Tobacco

When a cigarette is smoked, **nicotine**—the major psychoactive ingredient of tobacco—and some 4,000 other chemicals, collectively referred to as *tar,* are absorbed through the lungs. Approximately 76 million Americans have consumed nicotine in the last month.

Because considerable tolerance develops to some of the immediate effects of tobacco, the effects of smoking a cigarette on nonsmokers and smokers can be quite different. Nonsmokers often respond to a few puffs of a cigarette with various combinations of nausea, vomiting, coughing, sweating, abdominal cramps, dizziness, flushing, and diarrhea. In contrast, smokers report that they are more relaxed, more alert, and less hungry after a cigarette.

There is no question that heavy smokers are drug addicts in every sense of the word (Jones, 1987). The compulsive drug craving, which is the major defining feature of addiction, is readily apparent in any habitual smoker who has run out of cigarettes or who is forced by circumstance to refrain from smoking for several hours. Furthermore, habitual smokers who stop smoking experience a variety of withdrawal effects, such as depression, anxiety, restlessness, irritability, constipation, and difficulties in sleeping and concentrating.

About 70% of all people who experiment with smoking become addicted—this figure compares unfavorably with 10% for alcohol and 30% for heroin. Twin studies (Lerman et al., 1999; True et al., 1999) indicate that nicotine addiction has a major genetic component. The heritability estimate is about 65%. Moreover, only about 20% of all attempts to stop smoking are successful for 2 years or more (Schelling, 1992). Can you think of any other psychoactive drug that is self-administered almost continually—even while the addicts are walking along the street?

The consequences of long-term tobacco use are alarming. **Smoker's syndrome** is characterized by chest pain, labored breathing, wheezing, coughing, and a heightened susceptibility to infections of the respiratory tract. Chronic smokers are highly susceptible to a variety of potentially lethal lung disorders, including pneumonia, *bronchitis* (chronic inflammation of the bronchioles of the lungs), *emphysema* (loss of elasticity of the lung from chronic irritation), and lung cancer. Although the increased risk of lung cancer receives the greatest publicity, smoking also increases the risk of cancer of the larynx (voice box), mouth, esophagus, kidneys, pancreas, bladder, and stomach. Smokers also run a greater risk of developing a variety of cardiovascular diseases, which may culminate in heart attack or stroke. About 450,000 Americans die each year from smoking-related disorders.

Many smokers claim that they smoke despite the adverse effects because smoking reduces tension. However, smokers are actually more tense than nonsmokers: Their levels of tension are reasonably normal while they are smoking, but they increase markedly between cigarettes. Thus, the apparent relaxant effect of smoking merely reflects the temporary reversal of the stress caused by the smoker's addiction (see Parrott, 1999).

Sufferers from Buerger's disease provide a shocking illustration of the addictive power of nicotine. **Buerger's disease** is a condition in which the blood vessels, especially those supplying the legs, are constricted whenever nicotine enters the bloodstream:

> If a patient with this condition continues to smoke, gangrene may eventually set in. First a few toes may have to be amputated, then the foot at the ankle, then the leg at the knee, and ultimately at the hip. Somewhere along this gruesome progression gangrene may also attack the other leg. Patients are strongly advised that if they will only stop smoking, it is virtually certain that the otherwise inexorable march of gangrene up the legs will be curbed. Yet surgeons report that it is not at all uncommon to find a patient with Buerger's disease vigorously puffing away in his hospital bed following a second or third amputation operation. (Brecher, 1972, pp. 215–216)

The adverse effects of tobacco smoke are unfortunately not restricted to those who smoke. There is now strong evidence that individuals who live or work with smokers are more likely to develop heart disease and cancer than those who don't. Even the unborn are vulnerable: Smoking during pregnancy increases the likelihood of miscarriage, stillbirth, and early death of the child. The levels of nicotine in the blood of breastfed infants are often as great as those in the blood of their smoking mothers.

Alcohol

Approximately 104 million Americans have consumed alcohol in the last month, 13 million of these are heavy users, and over 100,000 die each year from alcohol-related diseases and accidents. Alcohol is involved in roughly 3% of all deaths in the United States, including deaths from birth defects, ill health, accidents, and violence.

Because alcohol molecules are small and soluble in both fat and water, they invade all parts of the body. Alcohol is classified as a **depressant** because at moderate-to-high doses it depresses neural firing; however, at low doses it can stimulate neural firing and facilitate social interaction. Alcohol addiction has a major genetic component (McGue, 1999): Heritability estimates are about 55%.

With moderate doses, the alcohol drinker experiences various degrees of cognitive, perceptual, verbal, and motor impairment, as well as a loss of control that can lead to a variety of socially unacceptable actions. High doses result in unconsciousness; and if blood levels reach 0.5%, there is a risk of death from respiratory depression. The telltale red facial flush of alcohol intoxication is produced by the dilation of blood vessels in the skin; this dilation increases the amount of heat that is lost from the blood to the air and leads to a decrease in body temperature (*hypothermia*). Alcohol is also a *diuretic;* that is, it increases the production of urine by the kidneys.

Alcohol, like many addictive drugs, produces both tolerance and physical dependence. The livers of heavy

drinkers metabolize alcohol more quickly than do the livers of nondrinkers, but this increase in metabolic efficiency contributes only slightly to overall alcohol tolerance; most alcohol tolerance is functional. Alcohol withdrawal often produces a mild syndrome of headache, nausea, vomiting, and tremulousness, which is euphemistically referred to as a *hangover.*

A full-blown alcohol withdrawal syndrome comprises three phases. The first phase begins about 5 or 6 hours after the cessation of a long bout of heavy drinking and is characterized by severe tremors, agitation, headache, nausea, vomiting, abdominal cramps, profuse sweating, and sometimes hallucinations. The defining feature of the second phase, which typically occurs between 15 and 30 hours after cessation of drinking, is convulsive activity. The third phase, which usually begins a day or two after the cessation of drinking and lasts for 3 or 4 days, is called **delirium tremens (DTs).** The DTs are characterized by disturbing hallucinations, bizarre delusions, agitation, confusion, *hyperthermia* (high temperature), and *tachycardia* (rapid heartbeat). The convulsions and the DTs produced by alcohol withdrawal can be lethal.

Alcohol attacks almost every tissue in the body (see Anderson et al., 1993). Chronic alcohol consumption produces extensive brain damage (Hayakawa et al., 1992) and, as you learned in Chapter 1, **Korsakoff's syndrome**—a neuropsychological disorder that is characterized by severe memory loss, sensory and motor dysfunction, and severe *dementia* (intellectual deterioration). Chronic alcohol consumption also causes extensive scarring, or **cirrhosis,** of the liver, which is the major cause of death among heavy alcohol users. Alcohol erodes the muscles of the heart and thus increases the risk of heart attack. It irritates the lining of the digestive tract and, in so doing, increases the risk of oral and liver cancer, stomach ulcers, *pancreatitis* (inflammation of the pancreas), and *gastritis* (inflammation of the stomach). And not to be forgotten is the carnage that alcohol produces on our highways and in our homes. (The devastating effect of alcohol on the families of addicts was emphasized to me by a student who had grown up with an alcoholic parent and who asked me to stress this adverse effect.

Like nicotine, alcohol readily penetrates the placental membrane and affects the fetus. The result is that the offspring of mothers who consume substantial quantities of alcohol during pregnancy can develop **fetal alcohol syndrome (FAS).** The FAS child suffers from some or all of the following symptoms (Streissgarth et al., 1999): brain damage, mental retardation, poor coordination, poor muscle tone, low birth weight, retarded growth, and/or physical deformity. The period of vulnerability to FAS corresponds to the developmental stage of *synaptogenesis,* which begins about 6 months after conception.

Alcohol affects the brain in many ways. For example it reduces the flow of calcium ions into neurons by acting on ion channels, interferes with second messenger systems inside neurons, and disrupts GABAergic and glutaminergic transmission (see Ikonomidou et al., 2000).

■ | Marijuana

Marijuana is the name commonly given to the dried leaves and flowers of **Cannabis sativa**—the common hemp plant. Approximately, 2 million Americans have used marijuana in the last month. The usual mode of consumption is to smoke these leaves in a *joint* (a cigarette of marijuana) or a pipe; but marijuana is also effective when ingested orally, if first baked into an oil-rich substrate, such as a chocolate brownie, to promote absorption from the gastrointestinal tract.

The psychoactive effects of marijuana are largely attributable to a constituent called **THC** (delta-9-tetrahydrocannabinol). However, marijuana contains over 80 *cannabinoids* (chemicals of the same chemical class as THC), which may also be psychoactive (see Kephalas et al., 1976). Most of the cannabinoids are found in a sticky resin covering the leaves and flowers of the plant, which can be extracted and dried to form a dark corklike material called **hashish.** Hashish can be further processed into an extremely potent product called *hash oil.*

Written records of marijuana use go back 6,000 years in China, where its stems were used to make rope, its seeds were used as a grain, and its leaves and flowers were used for their psychoactive and medicinal effects.

In the Middle Ages, cannabis cultivation spread from the Middle East into Western Europe; however, in Europe, the plant was grown primarily for the manufacture of rope, and its psychoactive properties were largely forgotten. During the period of European imperialism, rope was in high demand for sailing vessels. In 1611, the American colonies responded to this demand by growing cannabis as a cash crop; George Washington was one of the more notable cannabis growers.

The practice of smoking the leaves of *Cannabis sativa* and the word *marijuana* itself seem to have been

introduced to the southern United States in the early part of the 20th century by Mexican immigrants; and the drug gradually became popular among certain subgroups, such as the poor in city ghettos and jazz musicians. In 1926, an article appeared in a New Orleans newspaper exposing the "menace of marijuana," and soon similar stories were appearing in newspapers all over the United States under titles such as "The Evil Weed," "The Killer Drug," and "Marijuana Madness." The population was told that marijuana turns normal people into violent, drug-crazed criminals who rapidly become addicted to heroin.

The result of the misrepresentation of the effects of marijuana by the U.S. news media was the enactment of many laws against the drug. In many states, marijuana was legally classified a **narcotic** (a legal term generally used to refer to opiates), and punishment for its use was dealt out accordingly. However, the structure of the active constituents of marijuana and their physiological and behavioral effects bear no resemblance to those of the other narcotics; thus, legally classifying marijuana as a narcotic was akin to passing a law that red is green.

The popularization of marijuana smoking among the middle and upper classes in the 1960s stimulated a massive program of research; yet there is still considerable confusion about marijuana among the general population. One of the difficulties in characterizing the effects of marijuana is that they are subtle, difficult to measure, and greatly influenced by the social situation:

> At low, usual "social" doses, the intoxicated individual may experience an increased sense of well-being: initial restlessness and hilarity followed by a dreamy, carefree state of relaxation; alteration of sensory perceptions including expansion of space and time; and a more vivid sense of touch, sight, smell, taste, and sound; a feeling of hunger, especially a craving for sweets; and subtle changes in thought formation and expression. To an unknowing observer, an individual in this state of consciousness would not appear noticeably different. (National Commission on Marijuana and Drug Abuse, 1972, p. 68)

Although the effects of typical social doses of marijuana are subtle, high doses do impair psychological functioning. Short-term memory is impaired, and the ability to carry out tasks involving multiple steps to reach a specific goal declines. Speech becomes slurred, and meaningful conversation becomes difficult. A sense of unreality, emotional intensification, sensory distortion, and motor impairment are also common. However, even after high doses, an unexpected knock at the door can often bring about the return of a reasonable semblance of normal behavior.

In the light of the documented effects of marijuana, the earlier claims that marijuana would trigger a wave of violent crimes in the youth of America seem absurd. It is difficult to imagine how anybody could believe that the red-eyed, gluttonous, sleepy, giggling products of common social doses of marijuana would be likely to commit violent criminal acts. In fact, marijuana actually curbs aggressive behavior (Tinklenberg, 1974).

What are the hazards of long-term marijuana use? The main problems appear to be respiratory (see Zimmer & Morgan, 1997). The minority of marijuana smokers who continually smoke the drug tend to have deficits in respiratory function (e.g., Tilles et al., 1986), and they are more likely to develop a chronic cough, bronchitis, and asthma (Abramson, 1974).

Some authors list four other adverse effects of regular marijuana use; however, in each case, the evidence is either indirect, inconsistent, or incomplete (see Mendelson, 1987). First, there have been reports that chronic marijuana smoking lowers the plasma *testosterone* levels of males (e.g., Kolodny et al., 1974); but the effects are slight, and several studies have failed to replicate them. Second, there has been some suggestion that marijuana can adversely influence the *immune system*, but it has yet to be demonstrated that marijuana smokers are more susceptible to infection than are comparable nonsmokers. Third, because *tachycardia* (rapid heart rate) is one effect of marijuana, there has been some concern that marijuana consumption might cause cardiovascular problems; but, again, there is no direct evidence for this hypothesis. There is evidence, however, that marijuana use can trigger attacks in individuals who already have heart pathology. Fourth, many people have hypothesized that the relaxation produced by marijuana could reach pathological proportions and produce what is generally referred to as the **amotivational syndrome.** The evidence that occasional marijuana use causes a significant amotivational syndrome is far from strong (see Mendelson et al., 1976): No significant difference was found between the grade point averages of marijuana smokers and those of nonsmokers in a study of 2,000 college students (Brill & Christie, 1974). Nevertheless, it seems likely that continual marijuana use would be associated with some decline in productivity, assuming that the user was a productive person in the first place.

The addiction potential of marijuana is low. Most people who use marijuana do so only occasionally, and most who use it as youths curtail their use in their 30s and 40s. Tolerance to marijuana develops during periods of sustained use (Babor et al., 1975); however, withdrawal symptoms (e.g., nausea, diarrhea, sweating, chills, tremor, restlessness, sleep disturbance) are extremely rare, except in contrived laboratory situations in which massive oral doses are administered.

Some effects of marijuana have been shown to be of clinical benefit. It has been used, often illegally, to block the nausea of cancer patients undergoing chemotherapy and to stimulate the appetites of patients who have lost their appetites. Marijuana has also been shown to block seizures (Corcoran, McCaughran, & Wada, 1978), to dilate the

bronchioles of asthmatics, and to decrease the severity of *glaucoma* (a disorder characterized by an increase in the pressure of the fluid inside the eye); but it is not normally prescribed for these purposes.

Because THC is fat-soluble, it was initially assumed that it influenced the brain by inserting itself directly into neural membranes. However, we now know that THC binds to receptors that are particularly dense in the basal ganglia, hippocampus, cerebellum, and neocortex (Howlett et al., 1990); presumably, it exerts most of its effects through this mechanism. The cloning of the gene for the THC receptor (Matsuda et al., 1990) triggered a search for an endogenous THC-like chemical that binds to the receptor. Such a chemical has been isolated, its structure has been characterized (Devane et al., 1992) and named *anandamide* (which means "internal bliss"), but its function is still unknown (Di Marzo et al., 1998).

I cannot end this discussion of marijuana (*Cannabis sativa*) without telling you the following story:

> You can imagine how surprised I was when my colleague went to his back door, opened it, and yelled, "Sativa, here Sativa, dinner time."
>
> "What was that you called your dog?" I asked as he returned to his beer.
>
> "Sativa," he said. "The kids picked it. I think they learned about it at school; a Greek goddess or something. Pretty, isn't it? And catchy too: Every kid on the street seems to remember her name."
>
> "Yes," I said. "Very pretty."

▪ Cocaine and Other Stimulants

Stimulants are drugs whose primary effect is to produce general increases in neural and behavioral activity. Although stimulants all have a similar profile of effects, they differ greatly in their potency. Coca-Cola is a mild commercial stimulant preparation consumed by many people around the world. Today, its stimulant action is attributable to *caffeine,* but when it was first introduced, "the pause that refreshes" packed a real wallop in the form of small amounts of cocaine. **Cocaine** and its derivatives are the most commonly abused stimulants, and thus they are the focus of this discussion.

Cocaine is prepared from the leaves of the coca bush, which is found primarily in Peru and Bolivia. For centuries, a crude extract called *coca paste* has been made directly from the leaves and eaten. Today, it is more common to treat the coca paste and extract *cocaine hydrochloride,* the nefarious white powder that is referred to simply as *cocaine* and typically consumed by snorting or by injection. Cocaine hydrochloride may be converted to its base form by boiling it in a solution of baking soda until the water has evaporated. The impure residue of this process is **crack,** which is a potent, cheap, smokable form of cocaine. Crack has rapidly become the preferred form of the drug for many cocaine users. However, because crack is impure, variable, and consumed by smoking, it is difficult to study and most research on cocaine derivatives has thus focused on pure cocaine hydrochloride. Approximately 1.5 million Americans used cocaine or crack in the last month.

Cocaine hydrochloride is an effective local anesthetic and was once widely prescribed as such until it was supplanted by synthetic analogues such as *procaine* and *lidocaine.* It is not, however, cocaine's anesthetic actions that are of interest to users. People eat, smoke, snort, or inject cocaine or its derivatives in order to experience its psychological effects. Users report being swept by a wave of well-being; they feel self-confident, alert, energetic, friendly, outgoing, fidgety, and talkative; and they have less than their usual desire for food and sleep.

Like alcohol, cocaine hydrochloride is frequently consumed in *binges* (see Gawin, 1991). Cocaine addicts tend to go on so-called **cocaine sprees,** binges in which extremely high levels of intake are maintained for periods of a day or two. During a cocaine spree, users become increasingly tolerant to the euphoria-producing effects of cocaine. Accordingly, larger and larger doses are often administered. The spree usually ends when the cocaine is gone or when it begins to have serious toxic effects.

Extremely high blood levels of cocaine are reached during cocaine sprees. The results commonly include sleeplessness, tremors, nausea, and psychotic behavior. The syndrome of psychotic behavior observed during cocaine sprees is called **cocaine psychosis.** It is similar to, and has often been mistakenly diagnosed as, *paranoid schizophrenia.*

During cocaine sprees, there is a risk of loss of consciousness and death from seizures (Earnest, 1993), respiratory arrest, or stroke (Kokkinos & Levine, 1993). Although tolerance develops to most effects of cocaine (e.g., to the euphoria), repeated cocaine exposure sensitizes subjects (i.e., makes them even more responsive) to its motor and convulsive effects (see Robinson & Berridge, 1993).

Cocaine snorting can damage the nasal membranes, and cocaine smoking can damage the lungs; but both routes are safer than IV injection. Fatalities from cocaine overdose are most likely to follow IV injection.

Although cocaine is extremely addictive, the withdrawal effects triggered by abrupt termination of a cocaine spree are mild (Miller, Summers, & Gold, 1993). Common cocaine withdrawal symptoms include a negative mood swing and insomnia.

Cocaine facilitates catecholaminergic transmission. It does this by blocking the reuptake of *catecholamines* (dopamine, norepinephrine, and epinephrine) into presynaptic neurons. Its effects on dopaminergic transmission seem to play the major role in mediating its euphoria-inducing effects.

There is considerable confusion about the effects of cocaine and its derivatives on human fetuses. Soon after crack use became popular, newspaper headlines began to proclaim that the use of this drug by pregnant women was a major problem: "Crack Baby Syndrome Destroys Brains of a Generation." According to the stories, the children of female crack users were being born with severe brain damage and behavioral problems. How should a thinking person with some knowledge of the complexities of biopsychological research (i.e., you) react to such a claim?

It should be readily apparent that these stories violate one of the major rules of scientific thinking: Correlational studies cannot provide unambiguous evidence for causal conclusions. In this instance, because pregnant crack users also tend to use alcohol, tobacco, and other drugs, to feed and care for their children less well than nonusers, to receive poor medical support, and to lie about their drug taking, the observation of problems in their children cannot with confidence be attributed to fetal cocaine exposure. Over 100 studies of the effects of fetal cocaine exposure on cognitive development have been done, many using sophisticated statistical procedures to sort out confounding factors and histochemical procedures to reliably identify the amount of cocaine use from an analysis of the babies' hair. And the conclusion based on all this work? Fetal cocaine exposure does cause significant deficits in cognitive development, but these are much more subtle than first claimed (Lester, LaGasse, & Seifer, 1998); for example, the 375,000 affected children born each year in the United States will experience an average decline of 3.26 IQ points.

Cocaine and its various derivatives are not the only commonly abused stimulants. **Amphetamine** (speed) and its relatives also present major health problems. Amphetamine has been in wide illicit use since the 1960s—it is usually consumed orally in the potent form called *d-amphetamine* (dextroamphetamine). The effects of *d*-amphetamine are comparable to those of cocaine; for example, it produces a syndrome of psychosis called *amphetamine psychosis.*

In the 1990s, *d*-amphetamine was supplanted as the favored amphetaminelike drug by several more potent relatives. One is *methamphetamine* (see Cho, 1990).

Methamphetamine (meth) is commonly used in its even more potent, smokable, crystalline form (ice or crystal). Another potent relative of amphetamine is *3,4-methylenedioxymethamphetamine* (MDMA, or ecstasy), which is taken orally. Relatively little is known about the particular dangers of these amphetaminelike drugs; however, both methamphetamine and ecstasy have been shown to destroy serotonergic neurons in animal models. Because it is widely used in the "rave" culture, ecstasy is commonly associated with the adverse consequences of overexercise on the dance floor: dehydration, exhaustion, muscle breakdown, overheating, and convulsions (Julien, 1996; Wills, 1997).

■ The Opiates: Heroin and Morphine

Opium—the sap that exudes from the seeds of the opium poppy—has several psychoactive ingredients. Most notable are **morphine** and **codeine,** its weaker relative. Morphine, codeine, and other drugs that have similar structures or effects are commonly referred to as the **opiates.** The opiates have a clear Jekyll-and-Hyde character. On their Dr. Jekyll side, the opiates are unmatched as **analgesics** (painkillers), and they are also extremely effective in the treatment of cough and diarrhea. But, unfortunately, the kindly Dr. Jekyll brings with him the evil Mr. Hyde—the risk of addiction.

Archeological evidence suggests that the practice of eating opium became popular in the Middle East sometime before 4000 B.C., and then it spread throughout Africa, Europe, and Asia (see Berridge & Edwards, 1981; Latimer & Goldberg, 1981). Three historic events fanned the flame of opiate addiction. First, in 1644, the Emperor of China banned tobacco smoking, and many Chinese tobacco smokers tried smoking opium and liked it. Because smoking opium has a greater effect on the brain than does eating it, many more people became addicted to opium as the practice of opium smoking slowly spread to other countries. Second, morphine, the most potent constituent of opium, was first isolated in 1803, and it became available commercially in the 1830s. Third, the hypodermic needle was invented in 1856, and soon injured soldiers (e.g., those of the American Civil War) were introduced to morphine through a needle; during this era, morphine addiction was known as *soldiers' disease.*

Most people are surprised to learn that until the early 1900s, opium was legally available and consumed in great quantity in many parts of the world, including Europe and North America. Opium was available in cakes, candies, and wines, as well as in a variety of over-the-counter medicinal offerings. Opium potions such as *laudanum* (a very popular mixture of opium and alcohol), *Godfrey's Cordial,* and *Dalby's Carminative* were very popular. (The word *carminative* should win first prize for making a sow's ear at least sound like a silk purse: A carminative is a drug that expels gas from the digestive tract, thereby reducing stomach cramps and flatulence. *Flatulence* is the obvious pick for second prize.) There were even over-the-counter opium potions just for baby. Potions such as *Mrs. Winslow's Soothing Syrup* and the aptly labeled *Street's Infant Quietness* were popular in many households. Although pure morphine could not be purchased without a prescription in the early 1900s, it was so frequently prescribed by physicians for so many different maladies that morphine addiction was common among those who could afford doctors.

The **Harrison Narcotics Act,** passed in 1914, made it illegal to sell or use opium, morphine, or cocaine in the United States. However, the act did not include the semisynthetic opiate **heroin.** Heroin had been synthesized in 1870 by the addition of two acetyl groups to the morphine molecule, which greatly increased its ability to penetrate the blood–brain barrier. In 1898, heroin was marketed by the Bayer Drug Company; it was freely available without prescription and was widely advertised as a super aspirin. Tests showed that it was a more potent analgesic than morphine and that it was less likely to induce nausea and vomiting. Moreover, the Bayer Drug Company, on the basis of flimsy evidence, claimed that heroin was not addictive; this is why it was not covered by the Harrison Narcotics Act.

The consequence of this omission was that opiate addicts in the United States, forbidden by law to use opium or morphine, turned to the readily available and much more potent heroin; and the flames of addiction were further fanned. In 1924, the U.S. Congress made it illegal for anybody to possess, sell, or use heroin. Unfortunately, the laws enacted to stamp out opiate addiction in the United States have been far from successful: An estimated 130,000 Americans currently use heroin, and organized crime flourishes on the proceeds.

The effect of opiates most valued by addicts is the *rush* that follows intravenous injection. The *heroin rush* is a wave of intense abdominal, orgasmic pleasure that evolves into a state of serene, drowsy euphoria. Many opiate users, drawn by these pleasurable effects, begin to use the drug more and more frequently. Then, once they reach a point where they keep themselves drugged much of the time, tolerance and physical dependence develop and contribute to the problem. Opiate tolerance encourages addicts to progress to higher doses, to more potent drugs (e.g., heroin), and to more direct routes of administration (e.g., IV injection); and physical dependence adds to the already high motivation to take the drug.

Although opiates are highly addictive, the direct health hazards of chronic exposure are surprisingly minor. The main risks are constipation, pupil constriction, menstrual irregularity, and reduced libido (sex drive). Many opiate addicts have taken pure heroin or morphine for years with no serious ill effects. In fact,

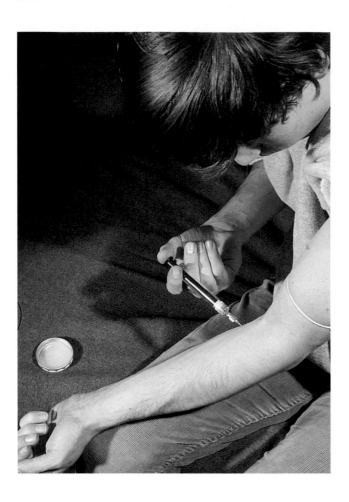

opiate addiction is more prevalent among doctors, nurses, and dentists than among other professionals (e.g., Brewster, 1986):

> An individual tolerant to and dependent upon an opiate who is socially or financially capable of obtaining an adequate supply of good quality drug, sterile syringes and needles, and other paraphernalia may maintain his or her proper social and occupational functions, remain in fairly good health, and suffer little serious incapacitation as a result of the dependence. (Julien, 1981, p. 117)

> One such individual was Dr. William Steward Halsted, one of the founders of Johns Hopkins Medical School and one of the most brilliant surgeons of his day . . . known as "the father of modern surgery." And yet, during his career he was addicted to morphine, a fact that he was able to keep secret from all but his closest friends. In fact, the only time his habit caused him any trouble was when he was attempting to reduce his dosage. (McKim, 1986, p. 197)

The classic opiate withdrawal syndrome usually begins 6 to 12 hours after the last dose. The first withdrawal sign is typically an increase in restlessness; the addict begins to pace and fidget. Watering eyes, running nose, yawning, and sweating are also common during the early stages of opiate withdrawal. Then, the addict often falls into a fitful sleep, which typically lasts for several hours. After the sleep is over, the original symptoms may be joined in extreme cases by chills, shivering, profuse sweating, gooseflesh, nausea, vomiting, diarrhea, cramps, pains, dilated pupils, tremor, and muscle spasms. The gooseflesh skin and leg spasms of the opiate withdrawal syndrome are the basis for the expressions "going cold turkey" and "kicking the habit." The symptoms of opiate withdrawal are typically most severe in the second or third day after the last injection, and by the seventh day they have all but disappeared.

The symptoms of opiate withdrawal are not trivial (see Koob, Maldonado, & Stinus, 1992), but their severity has been widely exaggerated. Opiate withdrawal is about as serious as a bad case of the flu—a far cry from the convulsions, delirium, and risk of death associated with alcohol withdrawal:

> Opiate withdrawal is probably one of the most misunderstood aspects of drug use. This is largely because of the image of withdrawal that has been portrayed in the movies and popular literature for many years. . . . Few addicts . . . take enough drug to cause the . . . severe withdrawal symptoms that are shown in the movies. Even in its most severe form, however, opiate withdrawal is not as dangerous or terrifying as withdrawal from barbiturates or alcohol. (McKim, 1986, p. 199)

Most risks of opiate addiction are indirect—that is, not attributable to the drug itself. Many are risks that arise out of the battle between the relentless addictive power of opiates and the attempts of governments to eradicate addiction by making drugs illegal. The opiate addicts who cannot give up their habit—treatment programs report success rates of only 10%—are caught in the middle. Because most opiate addicts must purchase their morphine and heroin from illicit dealers at greatly inflated prices, those who are not wealthy become trapped in a life of poverty and petty crime. They are poor, they are undernourished, they receive poor medical care, they are often driven to prostitution, and they run great risk of contracting AIDS and other infections from unsafe sex and unsterile needles. Moreover, they never know for sure what they are injecting: Some street drugs are poorly processed, and virtually all have been *cut* (stretched by the addition of some similar-appearing substance) to some unknown degree.

A case in point is death from heroin overdose. Overdose deaths are a risk any time addictive drugs are routinely administered via the intravenous route, but it is clear that the very laws designed to prevent heroin addiction are complicit in heroin-overdose deaths. The laws force addicts to buy their drugs from unreliable sources, and, as a result, waves of overdose deaths occur when shipments of contaminated drugs hit the street. Paradoxically, similar waves of deaths occur when shipments of particularly pure heroin hit the street—because addicts select doses on the basis of their previous experience with heroin that has been heavily cut.

The opiates, like marijuana, seem to exert their effects by binding to particular receptors whose normal function is to bind to endogenous chemicals. The endogenous chemicals that bind to opiate receptors are called *endorphins,* and about 20 different kinds have been identified.

Comparison of the Hazards of Tobacco, Alcohol, Marijuana, Cocaine, and Heroin

One way of comparing the adverse effects of tobacco, alcohol, marijuana, cocaine, and heroin is to compare the prevalence of their use in society as a whole. In terms of this criterion, it is clear that tobacco and alcohol have a far greater negative impact than do marijuana, cocaine, and heroin (see Figure 15.6). Another method of comparison is to base it on death rates: Tobacco has been implicated in the deaths of approximately 450,000 Americans per year; alcohol, in approximately 100,000 per year; and all other drugs combined, in about 40,000 per year.

But what about the individual drug user? Who is taking greater health risks: the cigarette smoker, the alcohol drinker, the marijuana smoker, the cocaine user, or the heroin user? You now have the information to answer this question. Complete the Demonstration on page 396, which will help you appreciate the positive impact that studying biopsychology is having on your understanding of important issues. Would you have ranked the health risks of these drugs in the same way before you began this chapter?

The Drug Dilemmas: Striking the Right Balance

Drug abuse is currently a serious problem. In the United States alone, recreational drugs contribute to

several hundred thousand deaths each year, and the public must bear the brunt of the crime and violence that is perpetrated by addicts who are forced to steal and prostitute themselves to fuel their expensive habits. Also, the public must bear the economic burdens of increased medical care, increased law enforcement, and decreased productivity—close to $100 billion annually.

Several eminent psychopharmacologists and political scientists evaluated the U.S. approach to drug control; they all recommended sweeping changes (see Goldstein & Kalant, 1990; Jarvik, 1990; Nadelman, 1989). Each of these experts concluded that the system of drug control in the United States is both poorly conceived and ineffective. The following quotes provide glimpses of their disenchantment with a system that treats addiction as a crime, rather than a disease, and that tries to combat it by reducing the supply and punishing the users:

> The investment of more than 70% of the federal [U.S.] drug control money into supply reduction seems misplaced. . . . Curtailing the supply of demanded drugs has been compared to squeezing a balloon: constrict it in one place and it expands somewhere else. . . . An example is the expansion of the California marijuana crop after the availability of Mexican marijuana was reduced. (Jarvik, p. 339)

> The greatest beneficiaries of the drug laws are . . . drug traffickers. More than half of all organized crime revenues are believed to derive from the illicit drug business. (Nadelman, p. 941)

> Drug treatment programs remain notoriously underfunded, turning away tens of thousands of addicts seeking help even as increasing billions of dollars are spent to arrest, prosecute, and imprison illegal drug . . . users. (Nadelman, p. 942)

The experts recommend solutions to the drug problem that are different from those preferred by the

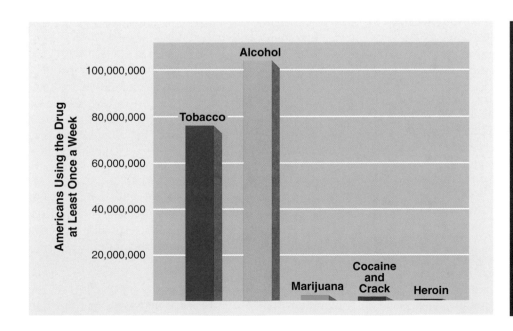

FIGURE 15.6 Prevalence of drug use in the United States. Figures are based on a 2000 survey of people 12 years of age and over who live in households and used the drug in question at least once in the last month.

Demonstration

List the major direct health hazards of the following five drugs. Omit the indirect hazards that result from the drugs' legal or social status.

Tobacco	Alcohol	Marijuana	Cocaine	Heroin
1. _____	1. _____	1. _____	1. _____	1. _____
2. _____	2. _____	2. _____	2. _____	2. _____
3. _____	3. _____	3. _____	3. _____	3. _____
4. _____	4. _____	4. _____	4. _____	4. _____
5. _____	5. _____	5. _____	5. _____	5. _____
6. _____	6. _____	6. _____	6. _____	6. _____

On the basis of comparisons among your lists, rank the five drugs in terms of their overall health risks.

Most Hazardous 1. _____

2. _____

3. _____

4. _____

Least Hazardous 5. _____

American public. The experts say (1) that there is no way of stopping the supply—every major drug bust merely increases the street prices of drugs and encourages more illicit suppliers to enter the market; (2) that it makes little sense to persecute and punish the sick and the weak; and (3) that it is hypocritical to take severe measures against some drugs while allowing others that are more dangerous to be openly advertised. In contrast to the views of the experts, surveys suggest that the U.S. public, frustrated with the drug problem and not understanding the issues, wants even more money to be spent on the approaches that have proven to be so ineffective (see MacCoun, 1998).

Here are some of the specific recommendations that have been made by the experts:

1. The only way of reducing recreational drug use is by reducing the demand. Some of the billions that are currently being spent on arresting and supporting drug users in crowded jails would be better spent on education, research, and social programs.
2. More emphasis should be placed on caring for addicts than on persecuting them.
3. Unlike the current laws, the laws that govern drug use should be enforceable and should be tailored to the hazards of each drug.
4. Judges should be given greater discretion in sentencing. For example, the current 5-year minimum sentence for anybody caught sharing a small amount of heroin or cocaine with a friend is unduly harsh.
5. All cigarette and alcohol advertising should be curtailed.
6. The possession of small amounts of marijuana for personal use has been legalized in some parts of the country; the effects of this legalization should be carefully monitored. If it does not lead to a significant increase in use, other states should follow suit to allow the legal system to focus on more serious problems.
7. Finally, lessons should be learned from countries that have taken alternative approaches to drug control. For example, in 1976, Holland removed criminal penalties for possession and small-scale sales of marijuana, with no resulting increases in the use of marijuana or more dangerous drugs (see MacCoun & Reuter, 1997).
8. Experimental clinics should be established. In them, addicts, as a first step in their treatment, should be provided with their drug. The potential advantages of such programs are many: They would encourage addicts to enter treatment; they would bring addicts in contact with health care professionals who are experienced in dealing with the health problems of addicts (e.g., AIDS and malnutrition); they would allow some addicts who have not been able to shake their habits to live reasonably normal, productive lives; and they would reduce the amount of drug-related crime.

The most important current research effort on the treatment of heroin addiction is the Swiss experiment. In

1995, the Swiss government established—despite substantial opposition from the public—a series of clinics in which, as part of a total treatment package, resident heroin addicts are supplied with heroin injections on request (once doses have been checked for safety by physicians). The Swiss government also funded a major research program to evaluate the clinics. The first wave of research reports have been published, and the results have been uniformly positive: Addicts are no longer a presence in the streets and parks; drug-related crime has substantially declined; the physical and social well-being of the addicts has improved; there has been no increase in heroin use by the addicts; and some addicts have voluntarily reduced or curtailed their heroin use (see Perneger et al., 1998, 2000). The Swiss public was convinced by these results; in a recent plebiscite (referendum), the clinics were endorsed by a clear majority of voters. What do you think?

One does not normally find a discussion of legal and social policy in a biopsychology textbook. Please excuse my digression, but I believe that the drug problem is a serious one and that biopsychologists have important things to say about it. They have a responsibility to bring the relevant research literature to the attention of policy makers and the educated public. Unfortunately, although scientists have been speaking out against the so-called war on drugs for over a decade, little has changed in the United States and many other countries.

15.4 Biopsychological Theories of Addiction

This section of the chapter introduces two diametrically different theories of addiction: Are addicts driven to take drugs by an internal need, or are they drawn to take drugs by their anticipated positive effects? I am sure you will recognize from preceding chapters that this is the same fundamental question that has been the focus of biopsychological research on the motivation to eat and sleep.

Physical-Dependence Theories of Addiction

Early attempts to explain the phenomenon of drug addiction attributed it to physical dependence. According to the **physical-dependence theory of addiction,** physical dependence traps addicts in a vicious circle of drug taking and withdrawal symptoms. The idea was that drug users whose intake has reached a level sufficient to induce physical dependence are driven by their withdrawal symptoms to self-administer the drug each time they attempt to curtail their intake.

Early drug addiction treatment programs were based on the physical-dependence theory of addiction. They attempted to break the vicious circle of drug taking by gradually withdrawing drugs from addicts in a hospital environment. Unfortunately, once discharged, almost all detoxified addicts return to their former drug-taking habits—**detoxified addicts** are addicts who have no drugs in their bodies and who are no longer experiencing withdrawal symptoms.

The failure of detoxification as a treatment for addiction is not surprising, for two reasons. First, some highly addictive drugs, such as cocaine and amphetamines, do not produce severe withdrawal distress (see Gawin, 1991). Second, the pattern of drug taking routinely displayed by many addicts involves an alternating cycle of binges and detoxification (Mello & Mendelson, 1972). There are a variety of reasons for this pattern of drug use. For example, some addicts adopt it because weekend binges are compatible with their work schedules, others adopt it because they do not have enough money to use drugs continuously, others have it forced on them because their binges often land them in jail, and others have it forced on them by their repeated unsuccessful efforts to shake their habit. However, whether detoxification is by choice or necessity, it does not stop addicts from renewing their drug-taking habits (see Leshner, 1997).

A more recent physical-dependence theory of drug addiction attempts to account for the fact that addicts frequently relapse after lengthy drug-free periods by pointing to the fact that withdrawal symptoms can be conditioned. According to this theory, when addicts who have remained drug-free for a considerable period of time return to a situation in which they have previously experienced the drug, conditioned withdrawal effects opposite to the effects of the drug (conditioned compensatory responses) are elicited. These effects are presumed to result in a powerful craving for the drug to counteract them.

The theory that *relapse* is motivated primarily by an attempt to counteract conditioned withdrawal effects encounters two major problems. One is that many of the effects elicited by environments that have previously been associated with drug administration are similar to those of the drug rather than being antagonistic to them. The second is that experimental animals and addicts often display a preference for drug-predictive cues, even when no drug is forthcoming (e.g., Bozarth & Wise, 1981; Mucha et al., 1982; White, Sklar, & Amit, 1977). For example, some detoxified heroin addicts called *needle freaks* derive pleasure from sticking an empty needle into themselves. It therefore seems unlikely that conditioned withdrawal effects are the major motivating factors in drug relapse.

Positive-Incentive Theories of Addiction

The failure of physical-dependence theories to account for the major aspects of addiction has lent support to the theory that the primary reason most addicts take drugs is not to escape or avoid the unpleasant consequences of withdrawal or conditioned withdrawal, but rather to obtain the drugs' positive effects. This **positive-incentive theory of addiction** acknowledges that addicts may sometimes self-administer drugs to suppress withdrawal symptoms or to escape from other unpleasant aspects of their existence, but it holds that the primary factor in most cases of addiction is the craving for the positive-incentive (pleasure-producing) properties of the drugs (McAuliffe et al., 1986; Stewart, de Wit, & Eikelboom, 1984). Anecdotal support for this view comes from the statements of some addicts—for example:

> I'm just trying to get high as much as possible. . . . If I could get more money, I would spend it all on drugs. All I want is to get loaded. I just really like shooting dope. I don't have any use for sex; I'd rather shoot dope. I like to shoot dope better than anything else in the world.

One positive-incentive theory of addiction is based on the idea that the positive-incentive value of addictive drugs increases (i.e., is sensitized) with drug use. Robinson and Berridge (1993, 2000) have suggested that in addiction-prone individuals, the use of drugs sensitizes their positive-incentive value, thus rendering the user highly motivated to consume drugs and to seek drug-associated stimuli. A key point of Robinson and Berridge's **incentive-sensitization theory** deserves emphasis: They argue that it isn't the pleasure (liking) of drug taking per se that is the basis of addiction; it is the anticipated pleasure (wanting) of drug taking (i.e., the drug's positive-incentive value). Initially, a drug's positive-incentive value is closely tied to its pleasurable effects; but tolerance often develops to the pleasurable effects, whereas the addict's wanting for the drug is sensitized. Thus, in chronic addicts, the positive-incentive value of the drug is often out of proportion with the pleasure actually derived from it: Many addicts are miserable, their lives are in ruins, and the drug effects are not that great anymore; but they crave the drug more than ever (see Berridge & Robinson, 1995; Nesse & Berridge, 1997).

15.5 Intracranial Self-Stimulation and the Pleasure Centers of the Brain

Rats, humans, and many other species will administer brief bursts of electrical stimulation to specific sites in their own brains (see Figure 15.7). This phenomenon is known as **intracranial self-stimulation (ICSS),** and the

FIGURE 15.7 A rat pressing a lever to obtain rewarding brain stimulation.

brain sites capable of mediating the phenomenon are often called *pleasure centers.*

Olds and Milner (1954), the discoverers of intracranial self-stimulation, argued that the specific brain sites that mediate self-stimulation are those that normally mediate the pleasurable effects of natural rewards (e.g., food, water, and sex). Accordingly, researchers have studied the self-stimulation of various brain sites in order to map the neural circuits that mediate the experience of pleasure. Because the pleasure-producing effects of drugs are now believed to play a major causal role in addiction, this section focuses on these cerebral pleasure circuits.

Fundamental Characteristics of Intracranial Self-Stimulation

It was initially assumed that intracranial self-stimulation was a unitary phenomenon—that is, that its fundamental properties were the same regardless of the site of stimulation. Most early studies of intracranial self-stimulation involved septal or lateral hypothalamic stimulation because the rates of self-stimulation from these sites are spectacularly high: Rats typically press a lever thousands of times per hour for stimulation of these sites, stopping only after they become exhausted. However, the self-stimulation of many other brain structures has been documented.

Early studies of intracranial self-stimulation suggested that lever pressing for brain stimulation was fundamentally different from lever pressing for natural reinforcers such as food or water. Two puzzling observations contributed to this view. First, despite their extremely high response rates, many rats stopped pressing the self-stimulation lever almost immediately when the current delivery mechanism was shut off. This finding was puzzling because high rates of operant responding are generally assumed to indicate that the reinforcer is particularly pleasurable, whereas rapid rates of extinction are usually assumed to indicate that it is not. Would you stop pressing a lever that had been delivering $100 bills the first few times that a press did not produce one? Second, experienced self-stimulators often did not recommence lever pressing when they were returned to the apparatus after being briefly removed from it. In such cases, the rats had to be **primed** to get them going again: The experimenter simply pressed the lever a couple of times, to deliver a few free stimulations, and the hesitant rat immediately began to self-stimulate at a high rate once again.

These differences between lever pressing for rewarding lateral hypothalamic or septal stimulation and lever pressing for food or water seemed to discredit Olds and Milner's original theory that intracranial self-stimulation involves the activation of natural reward circuits in the brain. However, several lines of research indicate that the circuits mediating intracranial self-stimulation are natural reward circuits. Let's consider three of these.

First, brain stimulation through electrodes that mediate self-stimulation often elicits a natural motivated behavior such as eating, drinking, maternal behavior, or copulation in the presence of the appropriate goal object.

Second, producing increases in natural motivation (for example, by food or water deprivation, by hormone injections, or by the presence of prey objects) often increases self-stimulation rates (e.g., Caggiula, 1970).

And third, it became clear that differences between the situations in which the rewarding effects of brain stimulation and those of natural rewards were usually studied contribute to the impression that these effects are qualitatively different. For example, comparisons between lever pressing for food and lever pressing for brain stimulation are usually confounded by the fact that subjects pressing for brain stimulation are nondeprived and by the fact that the lever press delivers the reward directly and immediately. In contrast, in studies of lever pressing for natural rewards, subjects are often deprived, and they press a lever for a food pellet or drop of water that they then must approach and consume to experience rewarding effects. This point was illustrated by a clever experi-

ment (Panksepp and Trowill, 1967) that compared lever pressing for brain stimulation and lever pressing for a natural reinforcer in a situation in which the usual confounds were absent. In the absence of the confounds, some of the major differences between lever pressing for food and lever pressing for brain stimulation disappeared. When nondeprived rats pressed a lever to inject a small quantity of chocolate milk directly into their mouths through an intraoral tube, they behaved remarkably like self-stimulating rats: They quickly learned to lever press, they pressed at high rates, they extinguished quickly, and some even had to be primed.

■ Mesotelencephalic Dopamine System and Intracranial Self-Stimulation

The mesotelencephalic dopamine system plays an important role in intracranial self-stimulation. The **mesotelencephalic dopamine system** is a system of dopaminergic neurons that projects from the mesencephalon (the midbrain) into various regions of the telencephalon. As Figure 15.8 on page 400 indicates, the neurons that compose the mesotelencephalic dopamine system have their cell bodies in two midbrain nuclei—the **substantia nigra** and the **ventral tegmental area.** Their axons project to a variety of telencephalic sites, including specific regions of the prefrontal neocortex, the limbic cortex, the olfactory tubercle, the amygdala, the septum, the dorsal striatum, and, in particular, the **nucleus accumbens,** nucleus of the ventral striatum.

Most of the axons of dopaminergic neurons having their cell bodies in the substantia nigra project to the dorsal striatum; this component of the mesotelencephalic dopamine system is called the *nigrostriatal pathway.* It is degeneration in this pathway that is associated with Parkinson's disease.

Most of the axons of dopaminergic neurons having their cell bodies in the ventral tegmental area project to various cortical and limbic sites. This component of the mesotelencephalic dopamine system is called the *mesocorticolimbic pathway.* Although there is some intermingling of the neurons between these two dopaminergic pathways (Gardner & Ashby, 2000; White, 1996), it is the particular neurons that project from the ventral tegmental area to the nucleus accumbens that have been most frequently implicated in the rewarding effects of brain stimulation, natural rewards, and addictive drugs.

The results of several kinds of studies have supported the view that the mesocorticolimbic pathway plays an important role in mediating intracranial self-stimulation:

1. Many brain sites at which self-stimulation occurs are part of the mesotelencephalic dopamine system (see Routtenberg, 1978). Some self-stimulation sites that do not contain dopaminergic neurons have been shown to project directly to the mesotelencephalic

FIGURE 15.8 The mesotelencephalic dopamine system in
the human brain, consisting of the
nigrostriatal pathway (red) and
the mesocorticolimbic pathway
(green). (Adapted from Klivington,
1992.)

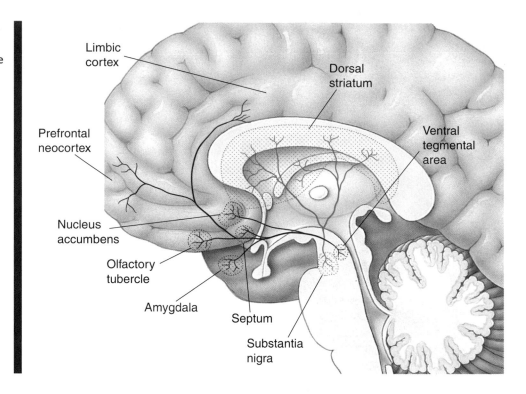

dopamine system (see Shizgal & Murray, 1989; Yeomans, Mathur, & Tampakeras, 1993).

2. In *cerebral dialysis studies,* microsamples of extracellular fluid are continuously drawn from a particular
area of the brain as the subject behaves, and the fluid
is later subjected to chemical analysis. Such studies
have shown that intracranial self-stimulation is often
associated with an increase in dopamine release in
the mesocorticolimbic pathway. For example, Phillips

and colleagues (1992) and Fiorino and colleagues
(1993) found increased dopamine release in the nucleus accumbens when rats engaged in self-stimulation of the ventral tegmental area (see Figure 15.9).

3. Dopamine agonists have been shown to increase intracranial self-stimulation (e.g., Colle & Wise, 1988);
dopamine antagonists, to decrease self-stimulation.

4. Lesions of the mesocorticolimbic pathway have been
shown to disrupt intracranial self-stimulation.

FIGURE 15.9 The increase in dopamine
release from the nucleus accumbens
during consecutive periods of intracranial
self-stimulation. (Adapted from Phillips et al.,
1992.)

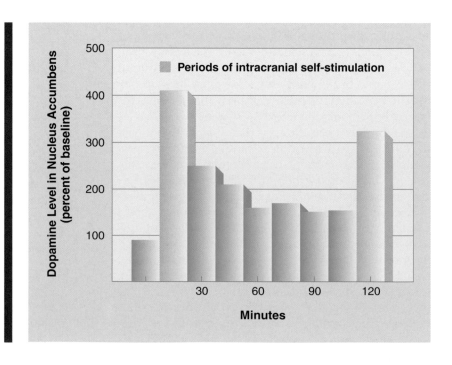

15.6 Neural Mechanisms of Motivation and Addiction

The search for the neural mechanisms of drug addiction has focused on the mesocorticolimbic pathway. This focus resulted from two influences: first, the increasing appreciation that the pleasurable effects of drugs, rather than the alleviation of withdrawal effects, are the major factors in addiction; and second, the discovery that the mesocorticolimbic pathway plays a principal role in intracranial self-stimulation.

The effort to understand the neural basis of addiction has been inextricably linked to the study of the neural mechanisms of natural forms of motivation (e.g., hunger and sexual motivation). It is clear that brain mechanisms did not evolve for the purpose of mediating addiction; therefore, the key to understanding the neural mechanisms of addiction lies in understanding natural motivational mechanisms and how they are co-opted and warped by addictive drugs (Nesse & Berridge, 1997).

◼ Two Key Methods for Measuring Drug-Produced Reinforcement

Most of the research on the neural mechanisms of addiction has been conducted in nonhumans. Because of the presumed role of the positive-incentive value of drugs in addiction, methods used to measure the rewarding effects of drugs in nonhumans have played a key role in this research. Two such methods have played particularly important roles: the drug self-administration paradigm and the conditioned place-preference paradigm. They are illustrated in Figure 15.10.

In the **drug self-administration paradigm,** laboratory rats or primates press a lever to inject drugs into themselves through implanted cannulas. They readily learn to self-administer intravenous injections of drugs to which humans become addicted. Furthermore, once they have learned to self-administer an addictive drug, their drug taking often mimics in major respects the drug taking of human addicts. Studies in which microinjections have been self-administered directly into particular brain structures have proved particularly enlightening.

In the **conditioned place-preference paradigm,** rats repeatedly receive a drug in one compartment (the *drug compartment*) of a two-compartment box. Then, during the test phase, the rat is placed in the box drug-free, and the proportion of time it spends in the drug compartment, as opposed to the equal-sized but distinctive *control compartment,* is measured. Rats usually prefer the

drug compartment over the control compartment when the drug compartment has been associated with the effects of drugs to which humans become addicted. The main advantage of the conditioned place-preference paradigm is that the subjects are tested drug-free, which means that the measure of the incentive value of a drug is not confounded by other effects the drug might have

Drug Self-Administration

From infusion pump

The rat presses the lever to self-inject a drug, either into an area of its brain or into general circulation.

Conditioned Place Preferences

A rat repeatedly receives a drug in one of two distinctive compartments. Then, on the test, the tendency of the rat, now drug-free, to prefer the drug compartment is assessed.

FIGURE 15.10 Two behavioral paradigms that are used extensively in the study of the neural mechanisms of addiction: the drug self-administration paradigm and the conditioned place-preference paradigm.

on behavior (see Carr, Fibiger, & Phillips, 1989; Van der Kooy, 1987).

Evidence of the Involvement of Dopamine in Drug Addiction

In the 1970s, following much research on the role of dopamine in intracranial self-stimulation, experiments began to implicate dopamine in the rewarding effects of natural reinforcers and addictive drugs. For example, in rats, dopamine antagonists blocked the self-administration of, or conditioned preference for, several different addictive drugs; and they reduced the reinforcing effects of food. These findings suggested that dopamine signaled something akin to reward value or pleasure.

Strong evidence that dopamine is involved in the drug-induced pleasure experienced by human addicts comes from a study by Volkow and colleagues (1997). They administered various doses of radioactively labeled cocaine to addicts and asked the addicts to rate the resulting "high." They also used positron emission tomography (PET) to measure the degree to which the labeled cocaine bound to dopamine transporters. **Dopamine transporters** are molecules in the presynaptic membrane of dopaminergic neurons that attract dopamine molecules in the synaptic cleft and deposit them back inside the neuron—cocaine has its agonistic effects on dopamine by binding to these transporters and blocking reuptake. The intensity of the "highs" experienced by the addicts was correlated with the degree to which cocaine bound to the dopamine transporters—no high at all was experienced unless the drug bound to 50% of the dopamine transporters.

Focus on the Nucleus Accumbens

Once evidence had accumulated linking dopamine to natural reinforcers and drug-induced reward, investigators began to explore particular sites in the mesocorticolimbic dopamine pathway. Their findings soon focused attention on the nucleus accumbens. Events occurring in the nucleus accumbens and dopaminergic input to it from the ventral tegmental area were most clearly related to the experience of reward and pleasure.

The following are four of the findings from research on laboratory animals that focused attention on the nucleus accumbens (see Ikemoto & Panksepp, 1999; Spanagel & Weiss, 1999):

1. Laboratory animals self-administered microinjections of addictive drugs (e.g., cocaine, amphetamine, and morphine) directly into the nucleus accumbens.

2. Microinjections of addictive drugs into the nucleus accumbens produced a conditioned place preference for the compartment in which they were administered (e.g., White & Hiroi, 1993).

3. Lesions to either the nucleus accumbens or the ventral tegmental area blocked the self-administration of drugs into general circulation or the development of drug-associated conditioned place preferences (e.g., Kelsey, Carlezon, & Falls, 1989: Roberts & Koob, 1982; Roberts et al., 1980).

4. Both the self-administration of addictive drugs and the experience of natural reinforcers are associated with elevated levels of extracellular dopamine in the nucleus accumbens (e.g., Bradberry et al., 2000; Fibiger, 1993; Tanda, Pontieri, & Chiara, 1997).

The involvement of the nucleus accumbens has also been demonstrated by research on human subjects. In one study, healthy human subjects were given an IV injection of amphetamine (Drevets et al., 2001). As dopamine levels in the nucleus accumbens increased in response to the amphetamine injection, the subjects reported a parallel increase in their experience of euphoria.

Changing View of the Nucleus Accumbens: A Role in Predicting Reward

As a result of the early research, it was believed that the nucleus accumbens was the reward center in the brain: that dopaminergic activity of the nucleus accumbens mediated the reinforcing effects of all addictive drugs and natural reinforcers. This view is now changing. There is still a consensus, and a great deal of evidence, that the nucleus accumbens is involved in reward, but evidence is rapidly accumulating that these effects are more complex and subtle than first assumed (see Kesner, 1999).

Most influential in the thinking of researchers about function of the nucleus accumbens have been reports that extracellular dopamine levels in this brain area increase in response to stimuli that indicate that a reward will soon be delivered. For example, Phillips and colleagues (e.g., Fiorino, Coury, & Phillips, 1997) found that the sound of a buzzer that signaled the imminent presentation of a food reward produced a surge in extracellular dopamine levels in the nucleus accumbens and that the presence of a receptive female increased such levels even before copulation commenced. Similarly, Weiss and colleagues (2000) taught rats that they could self-administer cocaine by pressing a lever only when a tone sounded; once the rats learned the predictive relationship, the tone itself produced increases in extracellular dopamine in the nucleus accumbens. The discovery that its extracellular dopamine levels surge in

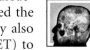

response to stimuli that predict reward suggests that the role of the nucleus accumbens is not to mediate the experience of pleasure but rather to predict pleasure.

Schultz (1997) recorded the activity of individual dopaminergic neurons in the ventral tegmental area of monkeys. He found that dopaminergic neurons responded to rewards only when the rewards were presented unpredictably—as in the early stages of a conditioning experiment. If a reward was expected—as in the late stages of a conditioning experiment—the reward itself did not increase the activity of dopaminergic neurons, but the conditional stimulus that predicted the reward did.

Role of the Nucleus Accumbens in Addiction

In view of the role of the nucleus accumbens in predicting reward, the nucleus accumbens and associated structures are presumed to play a role in addiction. The main input into the nucleus accumbens is the dopaminergic input from the ventral tegmental area, but significant input also comes from the *amygdala* and *prefrontal cortex*. The amygdala seems to be involved in the function of conditioned reinforcers, and prefrontal cortex provides the context for reward by supplying information about ongoing events and behaviors (e.g., Kalivas & Nakamura, 1999).

How does this circuit involving the nucleus accumbens produce addiction? Nobody knows. However, the incentive-sensitization theory of Robinson and Berridge (2000) is guiding the search for the answer—see Robbins and Everitt (1999). As you learned previously, Robinson and Berridge believe that addictive drugs have one thing in common: They all produce sensitization. More specifically, they all produce sensitization in the mechanisms mediating the positive-incentive value of drugs (i.e., the wanting of drugs). This can occur even when there are decreases in the rewarding effects of drugs (i.e., the liking for drugs). Under natural conditions, wanting things is closely related to how rewarding they are. However, addictive drugs act directly on the motivational circuits of the brain, and sensitization produces a wanting for drugs that is all out of normal proportion. So, the search is on. Investigators are looking for examples of drug-induced sensitization in the nucleus accumbens—examples that increase the positive-incentive value of the drugs that produced the sensitization.

15.7 A Noteworthy Case of Addiction

To illustrate in a more personal way some of the things you have learned about addiction, this chapter concludes with a case study of one addict. The addict was Sigmund Freud, a man of great significance to psychology.

Freud's case is particularly important for two reasons. First, it shows that nobody, no matter how powerful their intellect, is immune to the addictive effects of drugs. Second, it allows comparisons between the two drugs of addiction with which Freud had problems.

The Case of Sigmund Freud

In 1883, a German army physician prescribed cocaine, which had recently been isolated, to Bavarian soldiers to help them deal with the demands of military maneuvers. When Freud read about this, he decided to procure some of the drug.

In addition to taking cocaine himself, Freud pressed it on his friends and associates, both for themselves and for their patients. He even sent some to his fiancée. In short, by today's standards, Freud was a public menace.

Freud's famous essay "Song of Praise" was about cocaine and was published in July 1884. Freud wrote in such glowing terms about his own personal experiences with cocaine that he created a wave of interest in the drug. But within a year, there was a critical reaction to Freud's premature advocacy of the drug. As evidence accumulated that cocaine was highly addictive and produced a psychosis-like state at high doses, so too did published criticisms of Freud.

Freud continued to praise cocaine until the summer of 1887, but soon thereafter he suddenly stopped all use of cocaine—both personally and professionally. Despite the fact that he had used cocaine for 3 years, he seems to have had no difficulty stopping.

Some 7 years later, in 1894, when Freud was 38, his physician and close friend ordered him to stop smoking because it was causing a heart arrhythmia. Freud was a heavy smoker; he smoked approximately 20 cigars per day.

Freud did stop smoking, but 7 weeks later he started again. On another occasion, Freud stopped for

14 months, but at the age of 58, he was still smoking 20 cigars a day—and still struggling against his addiction. He wrote to friends that smoking was adversely affecting his heart and making it difficult for him to work . . . yet he kept smoking.

In 1923, at the age of 67, Freud developed sores in his mouth. They were cancerous. When he was recovering from oral surgery, he wrote to a friend that smoking was the cause of his cancer . . . yet he kept smoking.

In addition to the cancer, Freud began to experience severe heart pains (tobacco angina) whenever he smoked . . . still he kept smoking.

At 73, Freud was hospitalized for his heart condition and stopped smoking. He made an immediate recovery. But 23 days later, he started to smoke again.

In 1936, at the age of 79, Freud was experiencing more heart trouble, and he had had 33 operations to deal with his recurring oral cancer. His jaw had been entirely removed and replaced by an artificial one. He was in constant pain, and he could swallow, chew, and talk only with difficulty . . . yet he kept smoking.

Freud died of cancer in 1939. Imagine his many years of suffering and its effect on his family and friends. Do you smoke? Do people you love smoke?

Themes Revisited

Two of this book's themes received strong emphasis in this chapter because they are integral to its major objective: to sharpen your thinking about the effects of addiction on health. These two themes are the thinking-about-biopsychology and the clinical implications themes.

The evolutionary perspective theme was also highlighted frequently in this chapter, largely because of the nature of biopsychological research on drug addiction. Because of the risks associated with the administration of addictive drugs and with the direct manipulation of brain structures, the majority of biopsychological studies of drug addiction involve nonhumans—mostly rats and monkeys. Also, in studying the neural mechanisms of addiction, there is a need to maintain an evolutionary perspective. It is important not to lose sight of the fact that brain mechanisms did not evolve to support addiction; they evolved to serve natural adaptive functions and have somehow been co-opted by addictive drugs.

Some of the most exciting recent research on the mechanisms of addiction has employed the methods of cognitive neuroscience. The cognitive neuroscience theme arose in this chapter when functional brain-imaging techniques were used to measure cocaine binding and dopamine release in the living human brain. This research has confirmed the results of experiments on other species.

ON THE CD

Looking for more information about the topics in this chapter? For recommended additional readings, see Hard Copy for Chapter 15.

Log On

- **http://www.dancesafe.org/slideshow/** This slideshow and explanation of the effects of MDMA (ecstasy) includes a discussion of the drug's effects (e.g., euphoria, heightened sensory processing, increased empathy) and their relation to depression and neurotoxicity.

- **http://www.pet.bnl.gov/images.html** A collection of animations and PET images compellingly illustrates the effects of cocaine, nicotine, and other drugs of abuse on the brain.

- **http://www.niaaa.nih.gov/** This is a useful source of information on alcohol abuse; check out the "Graphics Gallery" link for images about fetal alcohol syndrome and effects of alcohol on the nervous system.

- **http://www.nida.nih.gov/NIDAHome.html** The home page for the U.S. National Institute on Drug Abuse includes information on most drugs of abuse, as well as links to illustrations of the effects of these drugs on the nervous system.

- **http://www.samhsa.gov/search/search.html** The home page of the Substance Abuse and Mental Health Services Administration includes the 2000 National Household Survey on Drug Abuse.

Think about It

1. There are many misconceptions about drug abuse. Describe three. What do you think are the reasons for these misconceptions?

2. A man who had been a heroin user for many years was found dead of an overdose at a holiday resort. He appeared to have been in good health, and no foul play was suspected. What factors might have led to his death?

3. If you had an opportunity to redraft the current legislation related to drug abuse in the light of what you have learned in this chapter, what changes would you make? Explain.

4. Speculate. How might recent advances in the study of the mesotelencephalic dopamine system eventually lead to effective treatments?

5. Does somebody you love use a hard drug such as nicotine or alcohol? Now that you know the truth about these drugs, do you feel ethically obligated to help? What should you do?

ON THE CD
Studying for an exam? Try the Practice Tests for Chapter 15.

6. Although my primary purpose in writing this chapter was to explain the biopsychology of addiction, it was not my only purpose. My other purpose was to provide you with a way of thinking about addiction that might be of benefit to you and those around you. Imagine my dismay, then, when I received an e-mail message suggesting that this chapter was making things worse for addicts. According to this message, explicit photographs and discussion of addiction induce craving in addicts who have stopped taking drugs (perhaps by inducing conditioned compensatory responses), thus encouraging them to recommence their drug taking. Discuss this argument, and consider its implications for the design of televised antidrug campaigns.

Key Terms

Addicts (p. 384)
Amotivational syndrome (p. 391)
Amphetamine (p. 392)
Analgesics (p. 393)
Before-and-after design (p. 384)
Buerger's disease (p. 388)
Cannabis sativa (p. 390)
Cirrhosis (p. 389)
Cocaine (p. 392)
Cocaine psychosis (p. 392)
Cocaine sprees (p. 392)
Codeine (p. 393)
Conditioned compensatory responses (p. 385)
Conditioned drug tolerance (p. 384)
Conditioned place-preference paradigm (p. 401)
Conditioned withdrawal effects (p. 386)

Contingent drug tolerance (p. 384)
Crack (p. 392)
Cross tolerance (p. 382)
Delirium tremens (DTs) (p. 389)
Depressant (p. 389)
Detoxified addicts (p. 397)
Dopamine transporters (p. 402)
Drug metabolism (p. 382)
Drug self-administration paradigm (p. 401)
Drug tolerance (p. 382)
Fetal alcohol syndrome (FAS) (p. 389)
Functional tolerance (p. 383)
Harrison Narcotics Act (p. 393)
Hashish (p. 390)
Heroin (p. 393)

Incentive-sensitization theory (p. 398)
Intracranial self-stimulation (ICSS) (p. 398)
Korsakoff's syndrome (p. 389)
Mesotelencephalic dopamine system (p. 399)
Metabolic tolerance (p. 383)
Morphine (p. 393)
Narcotic (p. 390)
Nicotine (p. 388)
Nucleus accumbens (p. 399)
Opiates (p. 393)
Opium (p. 393)
Physical-dependence theory of addiction (p. 397)
Physically dependent (p. 383)
Positive-incentive theory of addiction (p. 398)
Primed (p. 399)

Psychoactive drugs (p. 381)
Psychological dependence (p. 384)
Sensitization (p. 382)
Smoker's syndrome (p. 388)
Stimulants (p. 391)
Substantia nigra (p. 399)
THC (p. 390)
Ventral tegmental area (p. 399)
Withdrawal syndrome (p. 383)

ON THE CD
Need some help studying the key terms for this chapter? Check out the electronic flash cards for Chapter 15.

chapter 16

Lateralization, Language, and the Split Brain

The Left Brain and the Right Brain of Language

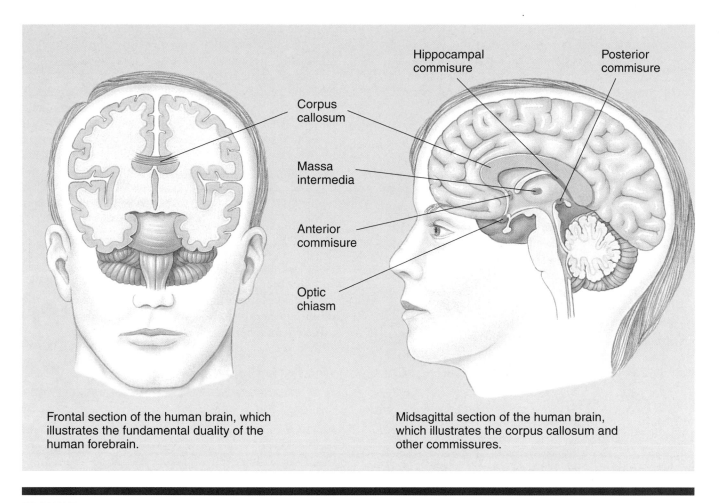

Frontal section of the human brain, which illustrates the fundamental duality of the human forebrain.

Midsagittal section of the human brain, which illustrates the corpus callosum and other commissures.

FIGURE 16.1   The cerebral hemispheres and cerebral commissures.

With the exception of a few midline orifices, we have two of almost everything—one on the left and one on the right. Even the brain, which most people view as the unitary and indivisible basis of self, reflects this general principle of bilateral duplication. In its upper reaches, the brain comprises two structures, the left and right cerebral hemispheres, which are entirely separate except for the **cerebral commissures** connecting them. The fundamental duality of the human forebrain and the location of the cerebral commissures are illustrated in Figure 16.1.

Although the left and right hemispheres are similar in appearance, there are major differences between them in function. This chapter is about these differences, a topic commonly referred to as **lateralization of function.** The study of **split-brain patients**—patients whose left and right hemispheres have been separated by **commissurotomy**—is a major focus of discussion. Another focus is the cortical localization of language abilities in the left hemisphere; language abilities are the most highly lateralized of all cognitive abilities.

You will learn in this chapter that your left and right hemispheres have different abilities and that they have the capacity to function independently—to have different thoughts, memories, and emotions. Accordingly, this chapter will challenge the concept you have of yourself as a unitary being. I hope you both enjoy it.

16.1 Cerebral Lateralization of Function: Introduction

In 1836, Marc Dax, an unknown country doctor, presented a short report at a medical society meeting in France. It was his first and only scientific presentation. Dax was struck by the fact that of the 40 or so brain-damaged patients with speech problems whom he had seen during his career, not a single one had damage restricted to the right hemisphere. His report aroused little interest, and Dax died the following year unaware that he had anticipated one of the most important areas of modern neuropsychological research.

Aphasia, Apraxia, and Left-Hemisphere Damage

One reason Dax's paper had little impact was that most of his contemporaries believed that the brain acted as a whole and that specific functions could not be attributed to particular parts of it. This view began to change 25 years later, when Paul Broca reported his postmortem examination of two aphasic patients. **Aphasia** is a brain-damage–produced deficit in the ability to produce or comprehend language.

Both of Broca's patients had a left-hemisphere lesion that involved an area in the frontal cortex just in front of the face area of the primary motor cortex. Broca at first did not realize that there was a relation between aphasia and the side of the brain damage; he had not heard of Dax's report. However, by 1864, Broca had performed postmortem examinations on seven more aphasic patients, and he was struck by the fact that, like his first two, they all had damage to the *inferior prefrontal cortex* of the left hemisphere—which by then had become known as **Broca's area** (see Figure 16.2).

FIGURE 16.2 The location of Broca's area: in the inferior left prefrontal cortex, just anterior to the face area of the left primary motor cortex.

In the early 1900s, another example of *cerebral lateralization of function* was discovered. Hugo-Karl Liepmann found that **apraxia,** like aphasia, is almost always associated with left-hemisphere damage, despite the fact that its symptoms are *bilateral* (involving both sides of the body). Apraxic patients have difficulty performing movements when asked to perform them out of context, even though they often have no difficulty performing the same movements when they are not thinking about doing so.

The combined impact of the evidence that the left hemisphere plays a special role in both language and voluntary movement led to the concept of *cerebral dominance.* According to this concept, one hemisphere—usually the left—assumes the dominant role in the control of all complex behavioral and cognitive processes, and the other plays only a minor role. This concept led to the practice of referring to the left hemisphere as the **dominant hemisphere** and the right hemisphere as the **minor hemisphere.**

Tests of Cerebral Lateralization

Early research on the cerebral lateralization of function compared the effects of left-hemisphere and right-hemisphere lesions. Now, however, other techniques are also used for this purpose. The sodium amytal test, the dichotic listening test, and functional brain imaging are three of them.

SODIUM AMYTAL TEST ■ The **sodium amytal test** of language lateralization (Wada, 1949) is often given to patients prior to neurosurgery. The neurosurgeon uses the results of the test to plan the surgery; every effort is made to avoid damaging areas of the cortex that are likely to be involved in language. The sodium amytal test involves the injection of a small amount of sodium amytal into the carotid artery on one side of the neck. The injection anesthetizes the hemisphere on that side for a few minutes, thus allowing the capacities of the other hemisphere to be assessed. During the test, the patient is asked to recite well-known series (e.g., letters of the alphabet, days of the week, months of the year) and to name pictures of common objects. Then, an injection is administered to the other side, and the test is repeated. When the hemisphere that is dominant for speech, usually the left hemisphere, is anesthetized, the patient is rendered completely mute for a minute or two; then once the ability to talk returns, there are errors of serial order and naming. In contrast, when the minor speech hemisphere, usually the right, is anesthetized, mutism often does not occur at all, and errors are few.

DICHOTIC LISTENING TEST ■ Unlike the sodium amytal test, the **dichotic listening test** is noninvasive;

thus it can be administered to healthy subjects. In the standard dichotic listening test (Kimura, 1961), three pairs of spoken digits are presented through earphones; the digits of each pair are presented simultaneously, one to each ear. For example, a subject might hear the sequence 3, 9, 2 through one ear and at the same time 1, 6, 4 through the other. The subject is then asked to report all of the digits. Kimura found that most people report slightly more of the digits presented to the right ear than the left, which is indicative of left-hemisphere dominance for language. In contrast, Kimura found that all the patients who had been identified by the sodium amytal test as right-hemisphere dominant for language performed better with the left ear than the right.

Why does the superior ear on the dichotic listening test indicate the dominance of the contralateral hemisphere? Kimura argued that although the sounds from each ear are projected to both hemispheres, the contralateral connections are stronger and take precedence when two different sounds are simultaneously competing for access to the same cortical auditory centers.

FUNCTIONAL BRAIN IMAGING ■ Lateralization of function has also been studied using functional brain-imaging techniques. While the subject engages in some activity, such as reading, the activity of the brain is monitored by positron emission tomography (PET) or functional magnetic resonance imaging (fMRI). On language tests, functional brain-imaging techniques typically reveal greater activity in the left hemisphere than in the right hemisphere (e.g., Belin et al., 1998).

Speech Laterality and Handedness

Two early large-scale lesion studies clarified the relation between the cerebral lateralization of speech and handedness. One study involved military personnel who suffered brain damage in World War II (Russell & Espir, 1961), and the other focused on neurological patients who underwent unilateral excisions for the treatment of neurological disorders (Penfield & Roberts, 1959). In both studies, approximately 60% of **dextrals** (right-handers) with left-hemisphere lesions and 2% of those with right-hemisphere lesions were diagnosed as aphasic; the comparable figures for **sinestrals** (left-handers) were about 30% and 24%, respectively. These results indicate that the left hemisphere is dominant for language-related abilities in almost all dextrals and in the majority of sinestrals; they also indicate that sinestrals are more variable than dextrals with respect to language lateralization.

Results of the sodium amytal test have confirmed the relation between handedness and language lateralization that was first observed in early lesion studies. For

example, Milner (1974) found that almost all right-handed patients without early left-hemisphere damage were left-hemisphere dominant for speech (92%), that most left-handed and ambidextrous patients without early left-hemisphere damage were left-hemisphere dominant for speech (69%), and that early left-hemisphere damage decreased left-hemisphere dominance for speech in left-handed and ambidextrous patients (30%).

In interpreting Milner's figures it is important to remember that sodium amytal tests are administered only to people who are experiencing brain dysfunction, that early brain damage can cause the lateralization of speech to shift to the other hemisphere (see Maratsos & Matheny, 1994; Stiles, 1998), and that many more people are left-hemisphere dominant to start with. Considered together, these points suggest that Milner's findings likely underestimate the proportion of left-hemisphere dominant individuals among healthy members of the general population.

Sex Differences in Brain Lateralization

Interest in the possibility that the brains of females and males differ in their degree of lateralization was stimulated by McGlone's (1977, 1980) studies of unilateral stroke victims. McGlone found that male victims of unilateral strokes were three times more likely to suffer from aphasia than female victims. She found that male victims of left-hemisphere strokes had deficits on the Wechsler Adult Intelligence Scale (WAIS) verbal subtests, whereas male victims of right-hemisphere strokes had deficits on the WAIS performance subtests. And she found that female victims of unilateral strokes had the same deficits on the WAIS regardless of the side of the stroke. On the basis of these three findings, McGlone concluded that the brains of males are more lateralized than the brains of females.

McGlone's hypothesis of sex difference in brain lateralization has been widely embraced, and it has been used to explain almost every imaginable behavioral difference between the sexes. But support for McGlone's hypothesis has been mixed. Some other researchers have failed to confirm her report of a sex difference in the effects of unilateral brain lesions (see Inglis & Lawson, 1982), whereas some functional brain-imaging studies have supported such a difference (e.g., Jaeger et al., 1998; Kansaku, Yamaura, & Kitazawa, 2000). Females, more than males, tend to use both hemispheres in the performance of language-related tasks.

So far, you have learned about four methods of studying cerebral lateralization of function. The next section describes a fifth.

16.2 The Split Brain

In the early 1950s, the **corpus callosum**—the largest cerebral commissure—constituted a paradox of major proportions. Its size, an estimated 200 million axons, and its central position, right between the two cerebral hemispheres, implied that it performed an extremely important function; yet research in the 1930s and 1940s seemed to suggest that it did nothing at all. The corpus callosum had been cut in monkeys and in several other laboratory species, but the animals seemed no different after the surgery than they had been before. Similarly, human patients who were born without a corpus callosum seemed perfectly normal. In the early 1950s, Roger Sperry and his colleagues were intrigued by this paradox.

Groundbreaking Experiment of Myers and Sperry

The solution to the puzzle of the corpus callosum was provided in 1953 by an experiment on cats by Myers and Sperry. The experiment made two astounding theoretical points. First, it showed that one function of the corpus callosum is to transfer learned information from one hemisphere to the other. Second, it showed that when the corpus

callosum is cut, each hemisphere can function independently; each split-brain cat appeared to have two brains. If you find the thought of a cat with two brains provocative, you will almost certainly be bowled over by similar observations about split-brain humans. But I am getting ahead of myself. Let's first consider the research on cats.

In their experiment, Myers and Sperry trained cats to perform a simple visual discrimination. On each trial, each cat was confronted by two panels, one with a circle on it and one with a square on it. The relative positions of the circle and square (right or left) were varied randomly from trial to trial, and the cats had to learn which symbol to press in order to get a food reward. Myers and Sperry correctly surmised that the key to split-brain research was to develop procedures for teaching and testing one hemisphere at a time. Figure 16.3 illustrates the method they used to isolate visual-discrimination learning in one hemisphere of the cats. There are two routes by which visual information can cross from one eye to the contralateral hemisphere: via the corpus callosum or via the optic chiasm. Accordingly, in their key experimental group, Myers and Sperry *transected* (cut completely through) both the optic chiasm and the corpus callosum of each cat and put a patch on one eye. This restricted all incoming visual information to the hemisphere ipsilateral to the uncovered eye.

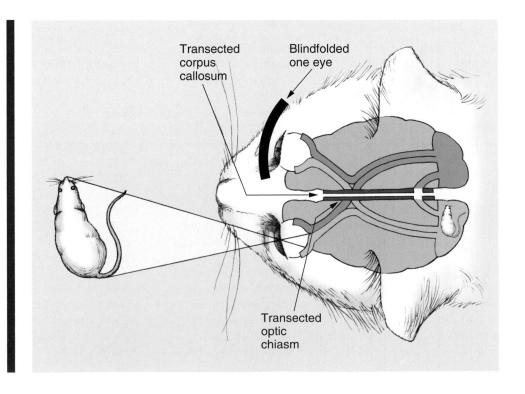

FIGURE 16.3 Restricting visual information in cats to one hemisphere. To restrict visual information to one hemisphere, Myers and Sperry (1) cut the corpus callosum, (2) cut the optic chiasm, and (3) blindfolded one eye. This restricted the visual information to the hemisphere ipsilateral to the uncovered eye.

Transected corpus callosum

Blindfolded one eye

Transected optic chiasm

The results of Myers and Sperry's experiment are illustrated in Figure 16.4. In the first phase of the study, all cats learned the task with a patch on one eye. The cats in the key experimental group (those with both the optic chiasm and the corpus callosum transected) learned the simple discrimination as rapidly as did unlesioned control cats or control cats with either the corpus callosum or the optic chiasm transected, despite the fact that cutting the optic chiasm produced a **scotoma**—an area of blindness—involving the entire medial half of each retina. This result suggested that one hemisphere working alone can learn simple tasks as rapidly as two hemispheres working together.

More surprising were the results of the second phase of Myers and Sperry's experiment, during which the

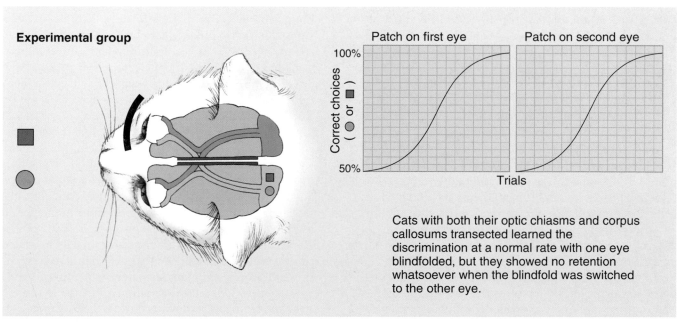

FIGURE 16.4 Schematic illustration of Myers and Sperry's (1953) groundbreaking split-brain experiment. There were four groups: (1) the key experimental group with both the optic chiasm and corpus callosum transected, (2) a control group with only the optic chiasm transected, (3) a control group with only the corpus callosum transected, and (4) an unlesioned control group. The performance of the three control groups did not differ, so they are illustrated here together.

patch was transferred to each cat's other eye. The transfer of the patch had no effect on the performance of the intact control cats or of the control cats with either the optic chiasm or the corpus callosum transected; these subjects continued to perform the task with close to 100% accuracy. In contrast, transferring the eye patch had a devastating effect on the performance of the experimental cats. In effect, it blindfolded the hemisphere that had originally learned the task and tested the knowledge of the other hemisphere, which had been blindfolded during initial training. When the patch was transferred, the performance of the experimental cats dropped immediately to baseline (i.e., to 50% correct); and then the cats relearned the task with no savings whatsoever, as if they had never seen it before. Myers and Sperry concluded that each cat brain has the capacity to act as two separate brains and that the function of the corpus callosum is to transmit information between them.

Myers and Sperry's startling conclusions about the fundamental duality of the brain and the information-transfer function of the corpus callosum have been confirmed in a variety of species with a variety of test procedures. For example, split-brain monkeys cannot perform tasks requiring fine tactual discriminations (e.g., rough versus smooth) or fine motor responses (e.g., unlocking a puzzle) with one hand if they have learned them with the other—provided that they are not allowed to watch their hands, which would allow the information to enter both hemispheres. There is no transfer of fine tactual and motor information in split-brain monkeys because the somatosensory and motor fibers involved in fine sensory and motor discriminations are all contralateral.

Commissurotomy in Human Epileptics

In the first half of the 20th century, when the normal function of the corpus callosum was still a mystery, it was known that epileptic discharges often spread from one hemisphere to the other through the corpus callosum. This fact and the fact that cutting the corpus callosum had proven in numerous studies to have no obvious effect on performance outside the contrived conditions of Sperry's laboratory led two neurosurgeons, Vogel and Bogen, to initiate a program of *commissurotomy* for the treatment of severe intractable cases of epilepsy.

The rationale underlying therapeutic commissurotomy—which typically involves transecting the corpus callosum and leaving the smaller commissures intact—was that the severity of the patient's convulsions might be reduced if the discharges could be limited to the hemisphere of their origin. The therapeutic benefits of commissurotomy turned out to be even greater than anticipated: Despite the fact that commissurotomy is performed in only the most severe cases, many commissurotomized patients do not experience another major convulsion.

The evaluation of the split-brain patient's neuropsychological status was placed in the capable hands of Sperry and his associate Gazzaniga. They began by developing a battery of tests based on the same methodological strategy that had proved so informative in their studies of laboratory animals: delivering information to one hemisphere while keeping it out of the other.

They could not use the same visual-discrimination procedure that had been used in studies of split-brain laboratory animals (i.e., cutting the optic chiasm and blindfolding one eye) because cutting the optic chiasm produces a scotoma. Instead, they employed the procedure illustrated in Figure 16.5. Each patient was asked to fixate on the center of a display screen; then, visual stimuli were flashed onto the left or right side of the screen for 0.1 second. The 0.1-second exposure time was long enough for the subjects to perceive the stimuli but short enough to preclude the confounding effects of eye movement. All stimuli thus presented in the left visual field were transmitted to the right visual cortex, and all stimuli thus presented in the right visual field were transmitted to the left visual cortex.

Fine tactual and motor tasks were performed by each hand under a ledge. This procedure was used so that the nonperforming hemisphere, that is, the ipsilateral hemisphere, could not monitor the performance via the visual system.

The results of the tests on split-brain patients have confirmed the research with split-brain laboratory animals in one major respect, but not in another. Like split-brain laboratory animals, human split-brain patients seem to have two independent brains, each with its own stream of consciousness, abilities, memories, and emotions (e.g., Gazzaniga, 1967; Gazzaniga & Sperry, 1967; Sperry, 1964). But unlike the brains of split-brain laboratory animals, the brains of split-brain patients are far from equal in their ability to perform certain tasks. Most notably, the left hemisphere of most split-brain patients is capable of speech, whereas the right hemisphere is not.

Before I recount some of the key results of the tests on split-brain humans, let me give you some advice. Some students become confused by the results of these tests because their tendency to think of the human brain as a single unitary organ is deeply engrained. If you become confused, think of each split-brain patient as two separate subjects: Ms. or Mr. Right Hemisphere, who understands a few simple instructions but cannot speak, who receives sensory information from the left visual field and left hand, and who controls the fine motor responses of the left hand; and Ms. or Mr. Left Hemisphere, who is verbally adept, who receives sensory information from the right visual field and right hand, and who controls the fine motor responses of the right hand. In everyday life, the behavior of split-brain subjects is reasonably normal because their two brains go through life together and acquire much of the same information; however, in the neuropsychological laboratory, major

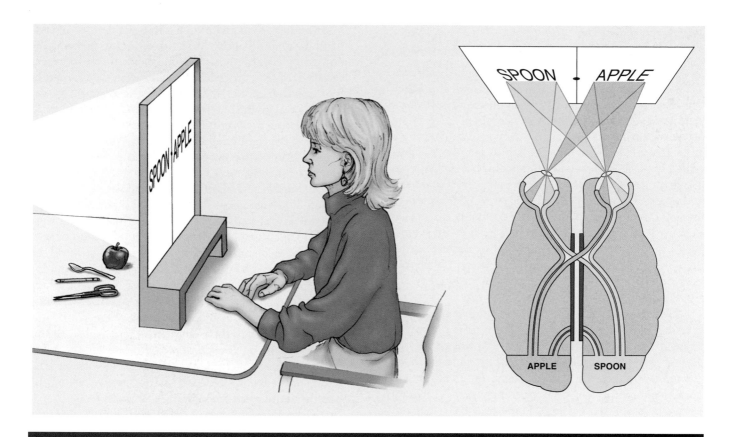

FIGURE 16.5 The testing procedure that was used to evaluate the neuropsychological status of split-brain patients. Visual input goes from each visual field to the contralateral hemisphere; fine tactual input goes from each hand to the contralateral hemisphere; and each hemisphere controls the fine motor movements of the contralateral hand.

discrepancies in what the two hemispheres learn can be created. As you are about to find out, this situation has some interesting consequences.

Evidence That the Hemispheres of Split-Brain Patients Function Independently

If a picture of an apple were flashed in the right visual field of a split-brain patient, the left hemisphere could do one of two things to indicate that it had received and stored the information. Because it is the hemisphere that speaks, the left hemisphere could simply tell the experimenter that it saw a picture of an apple. Or the patient could reach under the ledge with the right hand, feel the test objects that are there, and pick out the apple. Similarly, if the apple were presented to the left hemisphere by being placed in the patient's right hand, the left hemisphere could indicate to the experimenter that it was an apple either by saying so or by putting the apple down and picking out another apple with the right hand from the test objects under the ledge. If, however, the nonspeaking right hemisphere were asked to indicate the identity of an object that had previously been presented

to the left hemisphere, it could not do so. Although objects that have been presented to the left hemisphere can be accurately identified with the right hand, performance is no better than chance with the left hand.

When test objects are presented to the right hemisphere either visually (in the left visual field) or tactually (in the left hand), the pattern of responses is entirely different. A patient asked to name an object flashed in the left visual field is likely to claim that nothing appeared on the screen. (Remember that it is the left hemisphere who is talking and the right hemisphere who has seen the stimulus.) A patient asked to name an object placed in the left hand is usually aware that something is there, presumably because of the crude tactual information carried by ipsilateral somatosensory fibers, but is unable to say what it is. Amazingly, all the while the patient is claiming (i.e., all the while that the left hemisphere is claiming) the inability to identify a test object presented in the left visual field or left hand, the left hand (i.e., the right hemisphere) can identify the correct object. Imagine how confused the patient must become when, in trial after trial, the left hand can feel an object and then fetch another just like it from a collection of test items under the ledge, while the left hemisphere is vehemently claiming that it does not know the identity of the test object.

Cross-Cuing

Although the two hemispheres of a split-brain subject have no means of direct neural communication, they sometimes communicate with each other indirectly by a process called **cross-cuing.** An example of cross-cuing occurred during a series of tests designed to determine whether the left hemisphere could respond to colors presented in the left visual field. To test this possibility, a red or a green stimulus was presented in the left visual field, and the split-brain subject was asked to verbally report the color: red or green. At first, the patient performed at a chance level on this task (50% correct); but after a time, performance improved appreciably, thus suggesting that the color information was somehow being transferred over neural pathways from the right hemisphere to the left. However, this proved not to be the case:

We soon caught on to the strategy the patient used. If a red light was flashed and the patient by chance guessed red, he would stick with that answer. If the flashed light was red, and the patient by chance guessed green, he would frown, shake his head and then say, "Oh no, I meant red." What was happening was that the right hemisphere saw the red light and heard the left hemisphere make the guess "green." Knowing that the answer was wrong, the right hemisphere precipitated a frown and a shake of the head, which in turn cued in the left hemisphere to the fact that the answer was wrong and that it had better correct itself! . . . The realization that the neurological patient has various strategies at his command emphasizes how difficult it is to obtain a clear neurological description of a human being with brain damage. (Gazzaniga, 1967, p. 27)

Learning Two Things at Once

In most of the classes I teach, there is a student who fits the following stereotype. He sits—or rather sprawls—near the back of the class; and despite good grades, he tries to create the impression that he is above it all by making sarcastic comments. I am sure you recognize him—and it is almost always a him. Such a student inadvertently triggered an interesting discussion in one of my classes. His comment went something like this: "If getting my brain cut in two could create two separate brains, perhaps I should get it done so that I could study for two different exams at the same time."

The question raised by this comment is a good one. If the two hemispheres of a split-brain patient are capable of total independence, then they should be able to learn two different things at the same time. Can they? Indeed they can. For example, in one test, two different visual stimuli appeared simultaneously on the test screen—let's say a pencil in the left visual field and an orange in the right visual field. The subject was asked to simultaneously reach

into two bags—one with each hand—and grasp in each hand the object that was on the screen. After grasping the objects, but before withdrawing them, the subject was asked to tell the experimenter what was in the two hands; the subject (i.e., the left hemisphere) replied, "Two oranges." Much to the bewilderment of the verbal left hemisphere, when the hands were withdrawn, there was an orange in the right hand and a pencil in the left. The two hemispheres of the split-brain subject had learned two different things at exactly the same time.

In another test in which two visual stimuli were presented simultaneously—again, let's say a pencil to the left visual field and an orange to the right—the subjects were asked to pick up the presented object from an assortment of objects on a table, this time in full view. As the right hand reached out to pick up the orange under the direction of the left hemisphere, the right hemisphere saw what was happening and thought an error was being made (remember that the right hemisphere saw a pencil). On some trials, the right hemisphere dealt with this problem in the only way that it could: The left hand shot out, grabbed the right hand away from the orange, and redirected it to the pencil. This response is called the **helping-hand phenomenon.**

Yet another example of simultaneous learning in the two hemispheres involves the phenomenon of **visual completion.** As you may recall from Chapter 7, subjects with scotomas are often unaware of them because their brains have the capacity to fill them in (to complete them) by using information from the surrounding areas of the visual field. In a sense, each hemisphere of a split-brain patient is a subject with a scotoma covering the entire ipsilateral visual field.

The ability of each hemisphere of a split-brain subject to simultaneously and independently engage in completion has been demonstrated in studies using the **chimeric figures test**—named after *Chimera,* a mythical monster composed of the combined parts of different animals. Levy, Trevarthen, and Sperry (1972) flashed photographs composed of the fused half faces of two different people onto the center of a screen in front of their split-brain subjects. The subjects were then asked to describe what they saw or to indicate what they saw by pointing to it in a series of photographs of intact faces. Amazingly, each subject (i.e., each left hemisphere) reported seeing a complete, bilaterally symmetrical face, even when asked such leading questions as "Did you notice anything peculiar about what you just saw?" When the subjects were asked to describe what they saw, they usually described a completed version of the half that had been presented to the right visual field (i.e., the left hemisphere).

The Z Lens

Once it was firmly established that the two hemispheres of each split-brain patient can function independently, it became clear that the study of split-brain patients provided a unique opportunity to compare the abilities of left and right hemispheres. However, early studies of the lateralization of function in split-brain patients were limited by the fact that visual stimuli requiring more than 0.1 second to perceive could not be studied using the conventional method for restricting visual input to one hemisphere. This methodological barrier was eliminated by Zaidel in 1975. Zaidel developed a lens, called the **Z lens,** that limits visual input to one hemisphere of split-brain patients while they scan complex visual material such as the pages of a book. As Figure 16.6 illustrates, the Z lens is a contact lens that is opaque on one side (left or right). Because it moves with the eye, it permits visual input to enter only one hemisphere, irrespective of eye movement. Zaidel used the Z lens to compare the ability of the left and right hemispheres of split-brain patients to perform various tests.

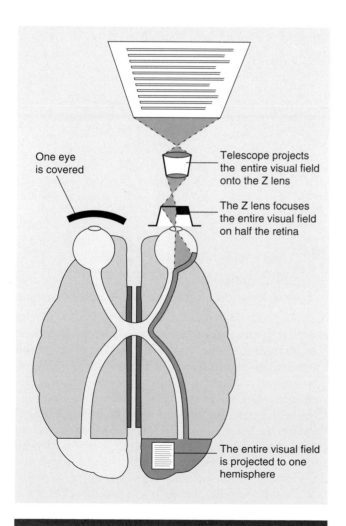

FIGURE 16.6 The Z lens, which was developed by Zaidel to study functional asymmetry in split-brain patients. It is a contact lens that is opaque on one side (left or right), so that visual input reaches only one hemisphere.

The usefulness of the Z lens is not restricted to purely visual tests. For example, here is how it has been used to compare the ability of the left and right hemispheres to comprehend speech. Because each ear projects to both hemispheres, it is not possible to present spoken words to only one hemisphere. Thus, to assess the ability of a hemisphere to comprehend spoken words or sentences, Zaidel presented them to both ears, and then he asked the subject to pick the correct answer or to perform the correct response under the direction of visual input to only that hemisphere. For example, to test the ability of the right hemisphere to understand oral commands, the subjects were given an oral instruction (such as "Put the green square under the red circle"), and then the right hemisphere's ability to comprehend the direction was tested by allowing only the right hemisphere to observe the colored tokens while the task was being completed.

Dual Mental Functioning and Conflict in Split-Brain Patients

In most split-brain patients, the right hemisphere does not seem to have a strong will of its own; the left hemisphere seems to control most everyday activities. However, in other patients, the right hemisphere takes a more active role in controlling behavior. In these latter cases, there can be serious conflicts between the left and right hemispheres. Patient 2C (let's call him Peter) was such a case (Joseph, 1988).

The Case of Peter, the Split-Brain Patient Tormented by Conflict

At the age of 8, Peter began to suffer from complex partial seizures. Antiepileptic medication was ineffective, and at 20, he received a commissurotomy, which greatly improved his condition but did not completely block his seizures. A sodium amytal test administered prior to surgery showed that he was left-hemisphere dominant for language.

Following surgery, Peter, unlike most other split-brain patients, was not able to respond with the left side of his body to verbal input. When asked to make whole-body movements (e.g., "Stand like a boxer") or movements of the left side of his body (e.g., "Touch your left ear with your left hand"), he could not respond correctly. Apparently, his left hemisphere could not, or would not, control the left side of his body via contralateral fibers. During such tests, Peter—or, more specifically, Peter's left hemisphere—often remarked that he hated the left side of his body.

The independent, obstinate, and sometimes mischievous behavior of Peter's right hemisphere often caused him (his left hemisphere) considerable frustration. He (his left hemisphere) complained that his left hand would turn off television shows that he was enjoying, that his left leg would not always walk in the intended direction, and that his left arm would sometimes perform embarrassing, socially unacceptable acts (e.g., striking a relative).

In the laboratory, he (his left hemisphere) sometimes became angry with his left hand, swearing at it,

striking it, and trying to force it with his right hand to do what he (his left hemisphere) wanted. In these cases, his left hand usually resisted his right hand and kept performing as directed by his right hemisphere. In these instances, it was always clear that the right hemisphere was behaving with intent and understanding and that the left hemisphere had no clue why the despised left hand was doing what it was doing.

16.3 Differences between the Left and Right Hemispheres

So far in this chapter, you have learned about five methods of studying cerebral lateralization of function: unilateral lesions, the sodium amytal test, the dichotic listening test, functional brain imaging, and studies of split-brain patients. This section takes a look at some of the major functional differences between the left and right cerebral hemispheres that have been discovered using these methods. Because the verbal and motor abilities of the left hemisphere are readily apparent (see Beeman & Chiarello, 1998; Reuter-Lorenz & Miller, 1998), most recent research on the lateralization of function has focused on uncovering the special abilities of the right hemisphere.

Slight Biases versus All-or-None Hemispheric Differences

Before I introduce you to some of the differences between the left and right hemispheres, I need to clear up a common misconception: For many functions, there are no differences between the hemispheres; and when functional differences do exist, these tend to be slight biases in favor of one hemisphere or the other—not absolute differences (see Brown & Kosslyn, 1993). Disregarding these facts, the popular media inevitably portray left–right cerebral differences as absolute. As a result, it is widely believed that various abilities reside exclusively in one hemisphere or the other. For example, it is widely believed that the left hemisphere has exclusive control over language and the right hemisphere has exclusive control over emotion and creativity. The most disturbing thing about this misrepresentation is that educational programs are sometimes inspired by it.

Language-related abilities provide a particularly good illustration of the fact that lateralization of function is statistical rather than absolute. Language is the most lateralized of all cognitive abilities. Yet, even in this

most extreme case, lateralization is far from total; there is substantial language-related activity in the right hemisphere. Following are three illustrations of this point: First, on the dichotic listening test, subjects who are left-hemisphere dominant for language tend to identify more digits with the right ear than the left ear, but this right-ear advantage is only slight, 55% to 45%. Second, in most split-brain patients, the left hemisphere is dominant for language, but the right hemisphere can understand many spoken or written words and simple sentences (see Baynes & Gazzaniga, 1997; Zaidel, 1987). And third, although there is considerable variability among split-brain patients in the performance of their right hemisphere on tests of language comprehension (Gazzaniga, 1998), the language abilities of their right hemispheres tend to be comparable to those of a preschool child.

Some Examples of Lateralization of Function

Table 16.1 lists some of the abilities that have been shown to be lateralized. They appear in two columns: those that are controlled more by the left hemisphere and those that are controlled more by the right hemisphere. The study of lateralization of function has put the archaic notion of left-hemisphere dominance to rest. The right hemisphere has been shown to be functionally superior to the left in several respects. The three best-documented domains of right-hemisphere superiority are spatial ability, emotion, and musical ability. Also, the right hemisphere is superior in performing some memory tasks. Before discussing these four superiorities of the right hemisphere, let's take a look at an unexpected superiority of the left hemisphere.

SUPERIORITY OF THE LEFT HEMISPHERE IN CONTROLLING IPSILATERAL MOVEMENT ■ One interesting and unexpected lateralized function was revealed

Table 16.1   Abilities that Display Cerebral Lateralization of Function

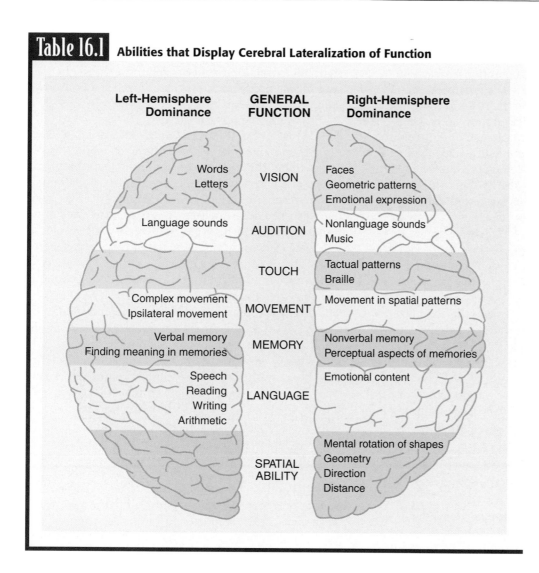

Left-Hemisphere Dominance	GENERAL FUNCTION	Right-Hemisphere Dominance
Words Letters	VISION	Faces Geometric patterns Emotional expression
Language sounds	AUDITION	Nonlanguage sounds Music
	TOUCH	Tactual patterns Braille
Complex movement Ipsilateral movement	MOVEMENT	Movement in spatial patterns
Verbal memory Finding meaning in memories	MEMORY	Nonverbal memory Perceptual aspects of memories
Speech Reading Writing Arithmetic	LANGUAGE	Emotional content
	SPATIAL ABILITY	Mental rotation of shapes Geometry Direction Distance

by functional brain-imaging studies (see Haaland & Harrington, 1996). When complex, cognitively driven movements are made by one hand, most of the activity is observed in the *contralateral* hemisphere, as expected. However, some activation is also observed in the *ipsilateral* hemisphere, and these ipsilateral effects are substantially greater in the left hemisphere than in the right (Kim et al., 1993). Consistent with this observation is the fact that left-hemisphere lesions are more likely than right-hemisphere lesions to be associated with ipsilateral motor problems.

SUPERIORITY OF THE RIGHT HEMISPHERE IN SPATIAL ABILITY
■ In a classic early study, Levy (1969) placed a three-dimensional block of a particular shape in either the right hand or the left hand of her split-brain subjects. Then, after they had thoroughly *palpated* (tactually investigated) it, she asked them to point to the two-dimensional test stimulus that best represented what the three-dimensional block would look like if it were made of cardboard and unfolded. She found a right-hemisphere superiority on this task, and she found

that the two hemispheres seemed to go about the task in different ways. The performance of the left hand and right hemisphere was rapid and silent, whereas the performance of the right hand and left hemisphere was hesitant and often accompanied by a running verbal commentary that was difficult for the subjects to inhibit. Levy concluded that the right hemisphere is superior to the left at spatial tasks. This conclusion has been frequently confirmed (e.g., Funnell, Corballis, & Gazzaniga, 1999; Kaiser at al., 2000), and it is consistent with the finding that disorders of spatial perception (e.g., contralateral neglect—see Chapters 7 and 8) tend to be associated with right-hemisphere damage.

SUPERIORITY OF THE RIGHT HEMISPHERE IN THE EXPERIENCE OF EMOTION
■ According to the old concept of left-hemisphere dominance, the right hemisphere is incapable of emotion. This presumption has been proven false. Indeed, analysis of the effects of unilateral brain lesions indicates that the right hemisphere is superior to the left at perceiving both facial expression (Bowers et al., 1985) and mood (Tompkins & Mateer, 1985).

Sperry, Zaidel, and Zaidel (1979) used the Z lens to assess the behavioral reactions of the right hemispheres of split-brain patients to various emotion-charged images: photographs of relatives; of pets; of themselves; and of political, historical, and religious figures and emblems. Their behavioral reactions were appropriate, thus indicating that right hemispheres are capable of emotional expression. In addition, there was an unexpected finding: The emotional content of images presented to the right hemisphere was reflected in the patients' speech as well as in their nonverbal behavior. This suggested that emotional information was somehow being passed from the right to the verbal left hemisphere of the split-brain subjects. The ability of emotional reactions, but not visual information, to be passed from the right hemisphere to the left hemisphere created a bizarre situation. A subject's left hemisphere often reacted with the appropriate emotional verbal response to an image that had been presented to the right hemisphere, even though it did not know what the image was.

Consider the following remarkable exchange (paraphrased from Sperry, Zaidel, & Zaidel, 1979, pp. 161–162). The patient's right hemisphere was presented with an array of photos, and the patient was asked if one was familiar. He pointed to the photo of his aunt.

Experimenter: "Is this a neutral, a thumbs-up, or a thumbs-down person?"
Patient: With a smile, he made a thumbs-up sign and said, "This is a happy person."
Experimenter: "Do you know him personally?"
Patient: "Oh, it's not a him, it's a her."
Experimenter: "Is she an entertainment personality or an historical figure?"
Patient: "No, just . . ."
Experimenter: "Someone you know personally?"
Patient: He traced something with his left index finger on the back of his right hand, and then he exclaimed, "My aunt, my Aunt Edie."
Experimenter: "How do you know?"
Patient: "By the E on the back of my hand."

Pause and think about the experiences and thoughts of these two hemispheres as each struggled to perform the task.

SUPERIORITY OF THE RIGHT HEMISPHERE IN MUSICAL ABILITY

Kimura (1964) compared the performance of 20 right-handers on the standard, digit version of the dichotic listening test with their performance on a version of the test involving the dichotic presentation of melodies. In the melody version of the test, Kimura simultaneously played two different melodies—one to each ear—and then asked the subjects to identify the two they had just heard from four that were subsequently played to them through both ears. The right ear (i.e., the left hemisphere) was superior in the perception of digits, whereas the left ear (i.e.,

the right hemisphere) was superior in the perception of melodies. This is consistent with the observation that right temporal lobe lesions are more likely to disrupt music discriminations than are left temporal lobe lesions.

HEMISPHERIC DIFFERENCE IN MEMORY

Both the left and right hemispheres have the ability to remember, but they seem to go about the task of remembering in different ways (see Gazzaniga, 1998). Although this hemispheric difference in memory style has been demonstrated in several ways, it is particularly well illustrated by the performance of split-brain patients on the following task. In this task, the left or right hemispheres of split-brain patients are tested separately. The task is to guess which of two lights—top or bottom—will come on next, based on the hemisphere's memory of recent trials. The top light comes on 80% of the time in random sequence, but the subjects are not given this information. The fact that the top light comes on more than the bottom is quickly discovered by intact control subjects; however, because they try to figure out the nonexistent rule that predicts the exact sequence, they are correct only 68% of the time—even though they could score 80% if they always selected the top light.

The left hemispheres of split-brain subjects perform like intact controls: They attempt to find deeper meaning in their memories and as a result perform poorly on this task. In contrast, right hemispheres, like rats, do not try to interpret their memories and readily learn to maximize their correct responses by always selecting the top light. The left hemisphere attempts to place its experiences in a larger context, while the right hemisphere attends strictly to the perceptual aspects of the stimulus (Metcalfe, Funnell, & Gazzaniga, 1995).

■ What Is Lateralized—Broad Clusters of Abilities or Individual Cognitive Processes?

Take another look at Table 16.1, which summarizes major examples of cerebral lateralization of function. Before you encountered this table for the first time, I alerted you to one way in which examples of cerebral lateralization are commonly misinterpreted: They reflect slight hemispheric biases, not all-or-none differences. Now that you have had the opportunity to digest the information in Table 16.1, I want to issue a second warning about it.

You have undoubtedly encountered some of this information before: Is there a single educated person in this society who does not know that the left hemisphere is the logical language hemisphere and the right hemisphere is the emotional spatial hemisphere? The information in tables like 16.1 summarizes the results of many studies and thus serves a useful function if it is not taken too literally. The problem is that it is almost always taken too literally. Let me explain.

Early theories of cerebral laterality tended to ascribe complex clusters of mental abilities to one hemisphere or the other. The left hemisphere tended to perform better on language tests, so it was presumed to be dominant for language-related abilities; the right hemisphere tended to perform better on some spatial tests, so it was presumed to be dominant for space-related abilities; and so on. Perhaps this was a reasonable first step, but now the general view among researchers is that this approach is simplistic, illogical, and inconsistent with the evidence.

The problem is that categories such as language, emotion, musical ability, and spatial ability are each composed of dozens of different individual cognitive activities, and there is no reason to assume that all those activities associated with a general English label (e.g., spatial ability) will necessarily be lateralized in the same hemisphere. The inappropriateness of broad categories of cerebral lateralization has been further confirmed by recent evidence. How is it possible to argue that all language-related abilities are lateralized in the left hemisphere, when the right hemisphere has proved superior in perceiving the intonation of speech and the identity of the speaker (Beeman & Chiarello, 1998)? Indeed, notable exceptions to all broad categories of cerebral lateralization have emerged.

As a result of mounting evidence of the inappropriateness of broad categories of cerebral lateralization, many researchers are taking a different approach. They are basing their studies of cerebral lateralization on the work of cognitive psychologists, who have broken down complex cognitive tasks—such as reading, judging space, and remembering—into their *constituent cognitive processes*. Once the laterality of the individual cognitive elements has been determined, it is possible to predict the laterality of cognitive tasks based on the specific cognitive elements that compose them. The research of Chabris and Kosslyn (1998) is an excellent example of this new approach:

> Consider the problems of (a) assessing whether one object is above or below another and (b) assessing whether two objects are greater or less than 1 foot apart. Both are spatial tasks, so early theories might have predicted that the right hemisphere would be superior at both. Yet both require a verbal response . . . , so perhaps the left hemisphere would be better . . . in each case. But if the left hemisphere is better, could this instead be because of the "analytical" processing required to compare two elements? It is clear that the coarse conceptualizations offered by early theories shed little light on even such apparently similar tasks as these.

Chabris and Kosslyn therefore took a different approach to predicting the laterality of these two simple spatial judgments. They based their research on the cognitive theory of Kosslyn (1994). Kosslyn found evidence that separate processes in the visual system judge differ-

ent types of spatial relations between objects: There is a process for making categorical judgments about the spatial relations (e.g., left/right, above/below) and one for making precise judgments of the spatial relations between objects in terms of their distance and angle from each other. Because the process for making *categorical spatial judgments* is dominant in the left hemisphere and the process for making *coordinate* (distance and angles) *spatial judgments* is dominant in the right hemisphere, Chabris and Kosslyn predicted that the left hemisphere would be superior in judging whether an object is above or below another and that the right hemisphere would be better in judging whether two objects are greater or less than a foot apart. They were right.

Anatomical Asymmetries of the Brain

Casual inspection suggests that the left and right hemispheres are mirror images of one another, but they are not; many anatomical differences between them have been documented. Most effort has been expended trying to document anatomical asymmetries in areas of cortex that are important for language (see Figure 16.7). Three of these areas are the planum temporale, Heschl's gyrus, and the frontal operculum. The **planum temporale** is the area of temporal lobe cortex that lies in the posterior region of the lateral fissure; it is thought to play a role in the comprehension of language and is often referred to as *Wernicke's area*. **Heschl's gyrus** is located in the lateral fissure just anterior to the planum temporale in the temporal lobe; it is the location of primary auditory cortex. The **frontal operculum** is the area of frontal lobe cortex that lies just in front of the face area of the primary

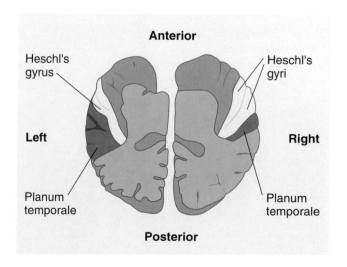

FIGURE 16.7 Two language areas of the cerebral cortex that display neuroanatomical asymmetry: the planum temporale (Wernicke's area) and Heschl's gyrus (primary auditory cortex).

motor cortex; in the left hemisphere, it is the location of Broca's area.

Because the planum temporale, Heschl's gyrus, and the frontal operculum are all involved in language-related activities, one might expect that they would all be larger in the left hemisphere than in the right in most subjects; but they aren't. The left planum temporale does tend to be larger on the left, but in only 65% of human brains (Geschwind & Levitsky, 1968). In contrast, the cortex of Heschl's gyrus tends to be larger on the right, primarily because there are often two Heschl's gyri in the right hemisphere and only one in the left. The laterality of the frontal operculum is less clear. The area of the frontal operculum that is visible on the surface of the brain tends to be larger on the right; but when the cortex buried within sulci of the frontal operculum is considered, there tends to be a greater volume of frontal operculum cortex on the left (Falzi, Perrone, & Vignolo, 1982).

A word of caution is in order. It is tempting to conclude that the tendency for the planum temporale to be larger in the left hemisphere predisposes the left hemisphere for language dominance. Indeed, the finding that the left planum temporale is larger than the right in fetal brains (Wada, Clarke, & Hamm, 1975) is consistent with this view. However, because most studies of neuroanatomical asymmetry are conducted at autopsy, there is no evidence that people with well-developed anatomical asymmetries tend to have more lateralized language functions. In fact, there is a substantial discrepancy between the proportion of the population that has been reported to have a larger left planum temporale (about 65%) and the proportion that is left-hemisphere dominant for language (over 90%).

Techniques for imaging the living human brain have made it easier to look for correlations between particular neuroanatomical asymmetries and particular performance measures. Such studies are important because they have the potential for revealing the functional advantages of cerebral lateralization. One such study is that of Schlaug and colleagues (1995). They used structural magnetic resonance imaging (MRI) to measure the asymmetry of the planum temporale and relate it to the presence of *perfect pitch* (the ability to identify the pitch of individual musical notes). The planum temporale was found to be more lateralized to the left hemisphere in musicians with perfect pitch than in nonmusicians or in musicians without perfect pitch (see Figure 16.8).

Most studies of anatomical asymmetries of the brain have measured differences in gross neuroanatomy, comparing the sizes of particular gross structures in the left and right hemispheres. Recently, however, anatomists have started to study differences in cellular structure between corresponding areas of the two hemispheres that have been found to differ in function (see Gazzaniga, 2000). One such study was conducted by Galuske and colleagues (2000). They compared the organization of the microcircuitry in part of Wernicke's area with its organization in the same part of the right hemisphere. They found that the areas in both hemispheres are organized into regularly spaced columns of interconnected neurons and that the columns are interconnected by medium-range axons. The columns are the same diameter in both hemispheres, but they are about 20% further apart in the left hemisphere and are interconnected by longer axons. Presumably, the particular way in

FIGURE 16.8 The anatomical asymmetry detected in the planum temporale of musicians by magnetic resonance imaging. In most people, the planum temporale is larger in the left hemisphere than in the right; this difference was found to be greater in musicians with perfect pitch than in either musicians without perfect pitch or control subjects. (Adapted from Schlaug et al., 1995.)

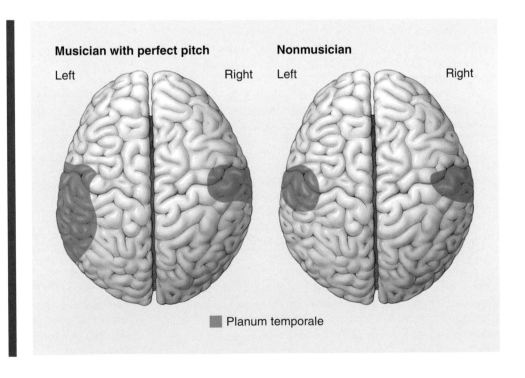

Musician with perfect pitch — Left / Right   Nonmusician — Left / Right

■ Planum temporale

which the columns are organized in Wernicke's area is adapted for the processing of language signals.

Theories of Cerebral Asymmetry

Several theories have been proposed to explain why cerebral asymmetry evolved. All of them are based on the same general premise: that it is advantageous for areas of the brain that perform similar functions to be located in the same hemisphere. However, each theory of cerebral asymmetry postulates a different distinction between left and right hemisphere function. The following are three prominent theories of cerebral asymmetry.

ANALYTIC–SYNTHETIC THEORY ■ One theory of cerebral asymmetry is the analytic–synthetic theory. The *analytic–synthetic theory of cerebral asymmetry* holds that there are two basic modes of thinking, an analytic mode and a synthetic mode, which have become segregated during the course of evolution in the left and right hemispheres, respectively. According to this theory,

> . . . the left hemisphere operates in a more logical, analytical, computerlike fashion, analyzing stimulus information input sequentially and abstracting the relevant details, to which it attaches verbal labels; the right hemisphere is primarily a synthesizer, more concerned with the overall stimulus configuration, and organizes and processes information in terms of gestalts, or wholes. (Harris, 1978, p. 463)

Although the analytic–synthetic theory has been the darling of pop psychology, its vagueness is a problem. Because it is not possible to specify the degree to which any task requires either analytic or synthetic processing, it has been difficult to subject the analytic–synthetic theory to empirical tests.

MOTOR THEORY ■ A second theory of cerebral asymmetry is the motor theory (see Kimura, 1979). According to the *motor theory of cerebral asymmetry,* the left hemisphere is specialized not for the control of speech per se but for the control of fine movements, of which speech is only one category. Support for this theory comes from reports that lesions that produce aphasia also produce other motor deficits. For example, Kimura (1987) found a correlation between the disruption of language abilities by lesions and the disruption of voluntary nonspeech oral movements by the same lesions; Kimura and Watson (1989) found that left frontal lesions produced deficits in the ability to make both individual speech sounds and individual facial movements, whereas left temporal and parietal lesions produced deficits in the ability to make sequences of speech sounds and sequences of facial movements; and Wolff and others (1990) found that subjects with reading disabilities also had difficulty performing a finger-tapping test.

LINGUISTIC THEORY ■ A third theory of cerebral asymmetry is the linguistic theory. The *linguistic theory of cerebral asymmetry* posits that the primary role of the left hemisphere is language—in contrast to the analytic–synthetic and motor theories, which view language as a secondary specialization residing in the left hemisphere because of its primary specialization for synthetic thought and skilled motor activity, respectively.

The linguistic theory of cerebral asymmetry is based to a large degree on the study of deaf people who use American Sign Language (a sign language with a structure similar to spoken language) and then suffer unilateral brain damage (see Hickok, Bellugi, & Klima, 2001). W.L. was such a case (Corina et al., 1992).

The Case of W.L., the Man Who Experienced Aphasia for Sign Language

W.L. is a congenitally deaf, right-handed male. He has two deaf, signing brothers and grew up using American Sign Language. Until his stroke, he had relied on sign language as his primary means of communication with his spouse, relatives, and friends.

W.L. has a history of cardiovascular disease; and 7 months prior to testing, he was admitted to hospital complaining of right-side weakness and motor problems. A CT scan revealed a large frontotemporoparietal lesion. At that time, W.L.'s wife noticed that he was making many uncharacteristic errors in signing and was having difficulty understanding the signs of others.

Fortunately, W.L.'s neuropsychologists managed to obtain a 2-hour videotape of an interview with him recorded 10 months before his stroke, which served as a valuable source of prestroke performance measures. Formal poststroke neuropsychological testing confirmed that W.L. had suffered a specific loss in his ability to use and understand sign language. The fact that he could produce and understand complex pantomime gestures suggested that his sign-language aphasia was not the result of motor or sensory deficits, and the results of cognitive tests suggested that it was not the result of general cognitive deficits.

The case of W.L. is particularly important because it illustrates a striking dissociation between two kinds of communicative gestures: linguistic (sign) gestures and nonlinguistic (pantomime) gestures. The fact that left-hemisphere damage can disrupt the use of sign language but not pantomime gestures argues strongly that the fundamental specialization of the left hemisphere is language.

Evolution of Cerebral Lateralization of Function

Cerebral lateralization is often assumed to be an exclusive feature of the hominid brain. One theory of the evolution of cerebral asymmetry is based on the motor theory of cerebral asymmetry: Left-hemisphere dominance for motor control is thought to have evolved in early hominids in response to their use of tools, and then the propensity for vocal language is thought to have subsequently evolved in the left hemisphere because of its greater motor dexterity. This theory of the evolution of cerebral lateralization of function is challenged by reports of handedness in non-human primates.

The first studies of hand preference in nonhuman primates found that some individual monkeys tended to use one hand more than the other but that there was no general tendency for the right to be preferred over the left (Colell, Segarra, & Sabater-Pi, 1995). However, more recently, there have been several reports that some nonhuman primates display a right-hand preference for certain tasks (see Hopkins, 1996). For example, Hopkins (1995) found that chimpanzees tended to use their right hands to extract peanut butter from a transparent tube; Westergaard and Suomi (1996), using the same task, found a right-hand preference in rhesus monkeys but not in tufted capuchins. Such demonstrations of handedness in nonhuman primates rule out the possibility that tool use by early hominids was the major factor in the evolution of cerebral lateralization of function.

Hand preference is not the only evidence of cerebral lateralization of function in nonhuman primates. In some nonhuman primate species, the left hemispheres have been found to be dominant for the production (see Owren, 1990) and discrimination (Heffner & Heffner, 1984) of communicative vocalizations, and the cortical area homologous to Wernicke's area has been found to be larger in the left hemisphere (Gannon et al., 1998). Moreover, in some nonhuman primate species, the right hemisphere has proven to be superior in the discrimination of facial identity and expression (Vermeire, Hamilton, & Erdmann, 1998). All these findings indicate that the evolution of cerebral laterality preceded the evolution of humans.

Interestingly, the motor circuit controlling singing in male canaries is more developed on the left side of their brains (see Mooney, 1999). Because birds are not part of the evolutionary lineage of humans—birds evolved from reptiles in a separate branch—this finding indicates either that cerebral laterality evolved prior to the branching or that the advantages of cerebral laterality led to its independent evolution in more than one species.

16.4 Cortical Localization of Language: The Wernicke-Geschwind Model

So far, this chapter has focused on the functional asymmetry of the brain, with an emphasis on the lateralization of language-related functions. At this point, it shifts its focus from language lateralization to language localization. In contrast to language lateralization, which refers to the relative control of language-related functions by the left and right hemispheres, *language localization* refers to the location within the hemispheres of the circuits that participate in language-related activities.

Like most introductions to language localization, the following discussion begins with the *Wernicke-Geschwind model*, the predominant theory of language localization. Because most of the research on the localization of language has been conducted and interpreted within the context of this model, reading about the localization of language without a basic understanding of the Wernicke-Geschwind model would be like watching a game of chess without knowing the rules—not a very fulfilling experience.

Historical Antecedents of the Wernicke-Geschwind Model

The history of the localization of language and the history of the lateralization of function began at the same point, with Broca's assertion that a small area in the inferior portion of the left prefrontal cortex (Broca's area) is the center for speech production. Broca hypothesized that programs of articulation are stored within this area and that speech is produced when these programs activate the adjacent area of the precentral gyrus, which controls the muscles of the face and oral cavity. According to Broca, damage restricted to Broca's area should disrupt speech production without producing deficits in language comprehension.

The next major event in the study of the cerebral localization of language occurred in 1874, when Carl Wernicke (pronounced "VER-ni-key") concluded on the basis of 10 clinical cases that there is a language area in the left temporal lobe just posterior to the primary auditory cortex (i.e., in the left planum temporale). This second language area, which Wernicke argued was the cortical area of language comprehension, subsequently became known as **Wernicke's area.**

Wernicke suggested that selective lesions of Broca's area produce a syndrome of aphasia whose symptoms are primarily **expressive**—characterized by normal comprehension of both written and spoken language and by speech that retains its meaningfulness despite being slow, labored, disjointed, and poorly articulated. This hypothetical form of aphasia became known as **Broca's aphasia.** In contrast, Wernicke suggested that selective lesions of Wernicke's area produce a syndrome of aphasia whose deficits are primarily **receptive**—characterized by poor comprehension of both written and spoken language and speech that is meaningless but still retains the superficial structure, rhythm, and intonation of normal speech. This hypothetical form of aphasia became known as **Wernicke's aphasia,** and the normal-sounding but nonsensical speech of Wernicke's aphasia became known as **word salad.**

The following are examples of the kinds of speech that are presumed to be associated with selective damage to Broca's and Wernicke's areas (Geschwind, 1979, p. 183):

> **Broca's aphasia:** A patient who was asked about a dental appointment replied haltingly and indistinctly: "Yes . . . Monday . . . Dad and Dick . . . Wednesday nine o'clock . . . 10 o'clock . . . doctors . . . and . . . teeth."

> **Wernicke's aphasia:** A patient who was asked to describe a picture that showed two boys stealing cookies reported smoothly: "Mother is away here working her work to get her better, but when she's looking the two boys looking in the other part. She's working another time."

Wernicke reasoned that damage to the pathway connecting Broca's and Wernicke's areas—the **arcuate fasciculus**—would produce a third type of aphasia, one he called **conduction aphasia.** He contended that comprehension and spontaneous speech would be largely intact in patients with damage to the arcuate fasciculus but that they would have difficulty repeating words that had just been heard.

The left **angular gyrus**—the area of left temporal and parietal cortex just posterior to Wernicke's area—is another cortical area that has been implicated in language. Its role in language was recognized in 1892 by Dejerine on the basis of the postmortem examination of one special patient. The patient suffered from **alexia** (the inability to read) and **agraphia** (the inability to write). What made this case special was that the alexia and agraphia were exceptionally pure: Although the patient could not read or write, he had no difficulty speaking or understanding speech. Dejerine's postmortem examination revealed damage in the pathways connecting the visual cortex with the left angular gyrus. He concluded that the left angular gyrus is responsible for comprehending language-related visual input, which is received directly from the adjacent left visual cortex and indirectly from the right visual cortex via the corpus callosum.

During the era of Broca, Wernicke, and Dejerine, there were many influential scholars (e.g., Freud, Head, and Marie) who opposed their attempts to localize various language-related abilities to specific neocortical areas. In fact, advocates of the holistic approach to brain function gradually gained the upper hand, and interest in the cerebral localization of language waned. However, in the mid 1960s, Norman Geschwind (1970) revived the old localizationist ideas of Broca, Wernicke, and Dejerine, added some new data and insightful interpretation, and melded the mix into a powerful theory: the Wernicke-Geschwind model.

The Wernicke-Geschwind Model

The following are the seven components of the **Wernicke-Geschwind model:** primary visual cortex, angular gyrus, primary auditory cortex, Wernicke's area, arcuate fasciculus, Broca's area, and primary motor cortex—all in the left hemisphere. They are shown in Figure 16.9 on page 424.

The following two examples illustrate how the Wernicke-Geschwind model is presumed to work (see Figure 16.10 on page 424). First, when you are having a conversation, the auditory signals triggered by the speech of the other person are received by your primary auditory cortex and conducted to Wernicke's area, where they are comprehended. If a response is in order, Wernicke's area generates the neural representation of the thought underlying the reply, and it is transmitted to Broca's area via the left arcuate fasciculus. In Broca's area, this signal activates the appropriate program of articulation that drives the appropriate neurons of your primary motor cortex and ultimately your muscles of articulation. Second, when you are reading aloud, the signal received by your primary visual cortex is transmitted to your left angular gyrus, which translates the visual form of the word into its auditory code and transmits it to Wernicke's area for comprehension. Wernicke's area then triggers the appropriate responses in your arcuate fasciculus, Broca's area, and motor cortex, respectively, to elicit the appropriate speech sounds.

FIGURE 16.9 The seven components of the Wernicke-Geschwind model.

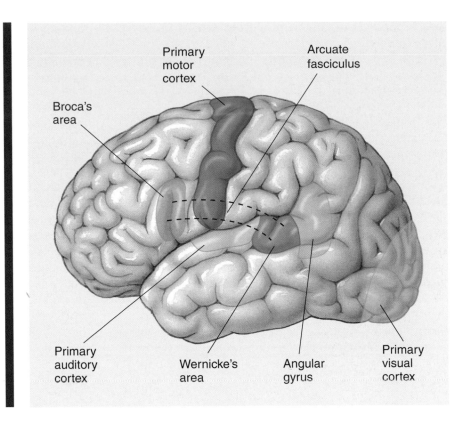

FIGURE 16.10 How the Wernicke-Geschwind model works in responding to a heard question and in reading aloud.

BrainScan

Before proceeding to the following evaluation of the Wernicke-Geschwind model, scan your brain to confirm that you understand its fundamentals. The correct answers are provided at the bottom of this page. Review material related to your errors and omissions before proceeding.

According to the Wernicke-Geschwind model, the following seven areas of the left cerebral cortex play a role in language-related activities:

1. The _____ gyrus translates the visual form of a read word into an auditory code.

2. The _____ cortex controls the muscles of articulation.

3. The _____ cortex perceives the written word.

4. _____ area is the center for language comprehension.

5. The _____ cortex perceives the spoken word.

6. _____ area contains the programs of articulation.

7. The left _____ carries signals from Wernicke's area to Broca's area.

16.5 Evaluation of the Wernicke-Geschwind Model

Unless you are reading this text from back to front, you should have read the preceding description of the Wernicke-Geschwind model with some degree of skepticism. By this point in the text, you will almost certainly recognize that any model of a complex cognitive process that involves a few localized neocortical centers joined in a serial fashion by a few arrows is sure to have major shortcomings, and you will appreciate that the neocortex is not divided into neat compartments whose cognitive functions conform to vague concepts such as language comprehension, speech motor programs, and conversion of written language to auditory language. Initial skepticism aside, the ultimate test of a theory's validity is the degree to which its predictions are consistent with the empirical evidence.

Before we examine this evidence, I want to emphasize one point. The Wernicke-Geschwind model was initially based on case studies of aphasic patients with strokes, tumors, and penetrating brain injuries. Damage in such cases is often diffuse, and it inevitably encroaches on subcortical fibers coursing through the lesion site to other areas of the brain (see Bogen & Bogen, 1976). For

example, illustrated in Figure 16.11 on page 426 is the extent of the cortical damage in one of Broca's two original cases (see Mohr, 1976).

Effects of Damage to Various Areas of Cortex on Language-Related Abilities

In view of the fact that the Wernicke-Geschwind model grew out of the study of patients with cortical damage, it is appropriate to begin evaluating it by assessing its ability to predict the language-related deficits produced by damage to various parts of the cortex.

SURGICAL REMOVAL OF CORTICAL TISSUE ■ The study of patients in whom discrete areas of cortex have been surgically removed has proved particularly informative with regard to understanding the cortical localization of language. This is because the location and extent of these patients' lesions can be derived with reasonable accuracy from the surgeon's report. The study of neurosurgical patients has not confirmed the predictions of the Wernicke-Geschwind model by any stretch of the imagination. See the six cases summarized in Figure 16.12 on page 426.

Surgery that destroys all of Broca's area but little surrounding tissue typically has no lasting effects on speech

FIGURE 16.11 The extent of brain damage in one of Broca's two original patients. Like this patient, most aphasic patients have diffuse brain damage. It is thus difficult to determine from studying them the precise location of particular cortical language areas. (Adapted from Mohr, 1976.)

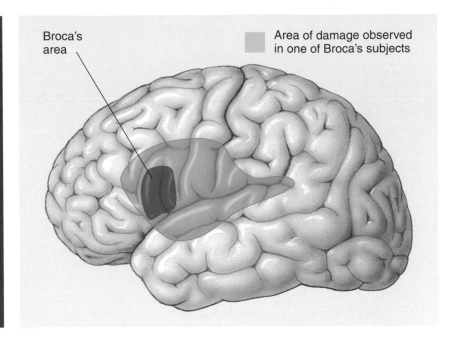

Broca's area

Area of damage observed in one of Broca's subjects

Case J.M. No speech difficulties for 2 days after his surgery, but by Day 3 he was almost totally aphasic; 18 days after his operation he had no difficulty in spontaneous speech, naming, or reading, but his spelling and writing were poor.

Case H.N. After his operation, he had a slight difficulty in spontaneous speech, but 4 days later he was unable to speak; 23 days after surgery, there were minor deficits in spontaneous speech, naming, and reading aloud, and a marked difficulty in oral calculation.

Case J.C. There were no immediate speech problems; 18 hours after his operation he became completely aphasic, but 21 days after surgery, only mild aphasia remained.

Case P.R. He had no immediate speech difficulties; 2 days after his operation, he had some language-related problems, but they cleared up.

Case D.H. This operation was done in two stages; following completion of the second stage, no speech-related problems were reported.

Case A.D. He had no language-related problems after his operation, except for a slight deficit in silent reading and writing.

FIGURE 16.12 The lack of permanent disruption of language-related abilities after surgical excision of the classic Wernicke-Geschwind language areas. (Adapted from Penfield & Roberts, 1959.)

(Penfield & Roberts, 1959; Rasmussen & Milner, 1975; Zangwill, 1975). Some speech problems were observed after Broca's excisions, but their temporal course suggested that they were products of postsurgical *edema* (swelling) in the surrounding neural tissue rather than of the *excision* (cutting out) of Broca's area per se. Prior to the use of effective anti-inflammatory drugs, patients with excisions of Broca's area often regained consciousness with their language abilities fully intact only to have serious language-related problems develop over the next few hours and then subside in the following weeks. Similarly, permanent speech difficulties were not produced by discrete surgical lesions to the arcuate fasciculus, and permanent alexia and agraphia were not produced by surgical lesions restricted to the cortex of the angular gyrus (Rasmussen & Milner, 1975).

The consequences of surgical removal of Wernicke's area are less well documented; surgeons have been hesitant to remove it in light of Wernicke's dire predictions. Nevertheless, in some cases, a good portion of Wernicke's area has been removed without lasting language-related deficits (e.g., Ojemann, 1979; Penfield & Roberts, 1959).

Supporters of the Wernicke-Geschwind model argue that, despite the precision of surgical excision, negative evidence obtained from the study of the effects of brain surgery should be discounted. They argue that the brain pathology that warranted the surgery may have reorganized the control of language by the brain.

ACCIDENTAL OR DISEASE-RELATED BRAIN DAMAGE

Hécaen and Angelergues (1964) rated the articulation, fluency, comprehension, naming ability, ability to repeat spoken sentences, reading, and writing of 214 right-handed patients with small, medium, or large accidental or disease-related lesions to the left hemisphere. The extent and location of the damage in each case were estimated by either postmortem histological examination or visual inspection during subsequent surgery. Figure 16.13 summarizes the deficits found by Hécaen and Angelergues in patients with relatively localized damage to one of five different regions of left cerebral cortex.

Hécaen and Angelergues found that small lesions to Broca's area seldom produced lasting language deficits and that those restricted to Wernicke's area sometimes did not produce such deficits. Medium-sized lesions did produce some deficits; but in contrast to the predictions of the Wernicke-Geschwind model, problems of articulation were just as likely to occur following medium-sized parietal or temporal lesions as they were following comparable lesions in the vicinity of Broca's area. All other symptoms that

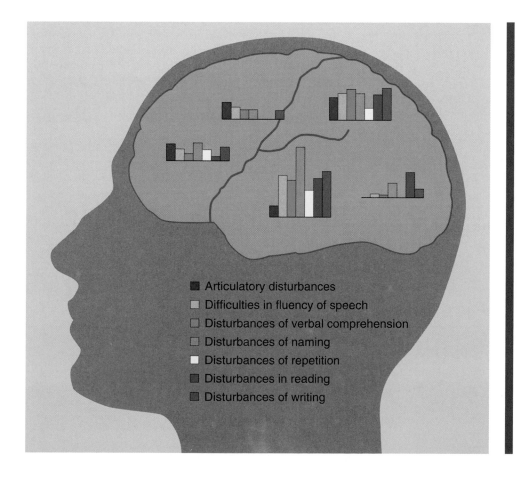

FIGURE 16.13 The relative effects on language-related abilities of damage to one of five general areas of left-hemisphere cortex. (Adapted from Hécaen & Angelergues, 1964.)

■ Articulatory disturbances
□ Difficulties in fluency of speech
□ Disturbances of verbal comprehension
□ Disturbances of naming
□ Disturbances of repetition
■ Disturbances in reading
■ Disturbances of writing

were produced by medium-sized lesions were more likely to appear following parietal or temporal lesions than following frontal damage.

Consistent with the Wernicke-Geschwind model, large lesions (those involving three lobes) in the anterior areas of the brain were more likely to be associated with articulation problems than were large lesions in the posterior areas of the brain. It is noteworthy that none of the 214 subjects displayed syndromes of aphasia that were either totally expressive (Broca's aphasia) or totally receptive (Wernicke's aphasia).

CT AND STRUCTURAL MRI SCANS OF APHASIC PATIENTS ■ Since the development of computed tomography (CT) and structural magnetic resonance imaging (MRI), it has been possible to visualize the brain damage of living aphasic patients (see Damasio, 1989). In early CT studies by Mazzocchi and Vignolo (1979) and Naeser and colleagues (1981), none of the aphasic patients had cortical damage restricted to Broca's and Wernicke's areas, and all had extensive damage to subcortical white matter. Consistent with the Wernicke-Geschwind model, large anterior lesions of the left hemisphere were more likely to produce deficits in language expression than were large posterior lesions, and large posterior lesions were more likely to produce deficits in language comprehension than were large anterior lesions. Also, in both studies, **global aphasia**—a severe disruption of all language-related abilities—was associated with very large left-hemisphere lesions that involved both anterior and posterior cortex as well as substantial portions of subcortical white matter.

The findings of Damasio's (1989) structural MRI study were similar to those of the aforementioned CT studies, with one important addition. Damasio found a few aphasic patients whose damage was restricted to the medial frontal lobes (to the supplementary motor area and the anterior cingulate cortex), an area not included in the Wernicke-Geschwind model. Similarly, several CT and MRI studies have found cases of aphasia resulting from damage to subcortical structures (see Alexander, 1989)—for example, to the left subcortical white matter, the left basal ganglia, or the left thalamus (e.g., Naeser et al., 1982).

■ Electrical Stimulation of the Cortex and Localization of Language

The first large-scale electrical brain-stimulation studies of humans were conducted by Penfield and his colleagues in the 1940s at the Montreal Neurological Institute (see Feindel, 1986). One purpose of the studies was to map the language areas of each patient's brain so that tissue involved in language could be avoided during the surgery. The mapping was done by assessing the responses of conscious patients who were under local anesthetic to stimulation applied to various points on the cortical surface. The description of the effects of each stimulation were dictated to a stenographer—this was before the days of tape recorders—and then a tiny numbered card was dropped on the stimulation site for subsequent photography.

Figure 16.14 illustrates the responses to stimulation of a 37-year-old right-handed epileptic patient. He had started to have seizures about 3 months after receiving a blow to the head; at the time of his operation, in 1948, he had been suffering from seizures for 6 years, despite efforts to control them with medication. In considering his responses, remember that the cortex just posterior to the central fissure is primary somatosensory cortex and that the cortex just anterior to the central fissure is primary motor cortex.

Because electrical stimulation of the cortex is much more localized than a brain lesion, it has been a useful method for testing predictions of the Wernicke-Geschwind model. Penfield and Roberts (1959) published the first large-scale study of the effects of cortical stimulation on speech. They found that sites at which stimulation blocked or disrupted speech in conscious neurosurgical patients were scattered throughout a large expanse of frontal, temporal, and parietal cortex, rather than being restricted to the Wernicke-Geschwind areas (see Figure 16.15 on page 430). They also found no tendency for particular kinds of speech disturbances to be elicited from particular areas of the cortex: Sites at which stimulation produced disturbances of pronunciation, confusion of counting, inability to name objects, or misnaming of objects were pretty much intermingled. Right-hemisphere stimulation almost never disrupted speech.

In a more recent series of cortical stimulation studies, Ojemann and his colleagues (see Ojemann, 1983) assessed naming, reading of simple sentences, short-term verbal memory, ability to mimic movements of the face and mouth, and ability to recognize **phonemes**—individual speech sounds—during cortical stimulation. They found (1) that the areas of cortex at which stimulation could disrupt language extended far beyond the boundaries of the Wernicke-Geschwind language areas, (2) that each of the language tests was disrupted by stimulation at widely scattered sites, and (3) that there were major differences among the subjects in the organization of language abilities.

Because the disruptive effects of stimulation at a particular site were frequently quite specific (i.e., disrupting only a single test), Ojemann suggested that the language cortex is organized like a mosaic, with the discrete columns of tissue performing a particular function being widely distributed throughout the language areas of cortex.

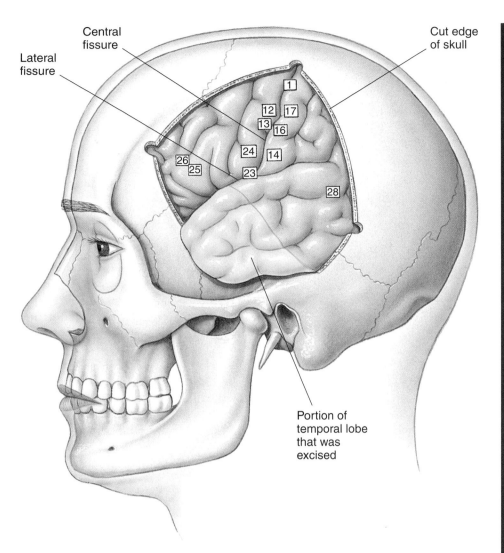

Central fissure

Lateral fissure

Cut edge of skull

Portion of temporal lobe that was excised

FIGURE 16.14 The responses of the left hemisphere of a 37-year-old epileptic to electrical stimulation. Numbered cards were placed on the brain during surgery to mark the sites where brain stimulation had been applied. (Adapted from Penfield & Roberts, 1959.)

1 Tingling in the right thumb and a slight movement

12 Quivering of the jaw in a sidewise manner

13 Pulling of jaw to right

14 Sensation in the jaw and lower lip

16 Tingling in the right side of tongue

17 Sensation in right upper lip

23 Stimulation, applied while the patient was talking, stopped his speech. After cessation of stimulation, he said that he had been unable to speak despite trying.

24 The patient tried to talk, his mouth moved, but he made no sound.

25 The patient had initial difficulty, but eventually he named a picture of a butterfly.

26 The patient said, "Oh, I know what it is" in response to a picture of a foot. "That is what you put in your shoes." After termination of the stimulation, he said, "foot."

28 The patient became unable to name the pictures as soon as the electrode was placed here. The EEG revealed seizure activity in the temporal lobe. When the seizure discharges stopped, the patient spoke at once. "Now I can talk," he said, and he correctly identified the picture of a butterfly.

Current Status of the Wernicke-Geschwind Model

Empirical evidence has supported the Wernicke-Geschwind model in two general respects. First, the evidence has confirmed that important roles are played in language by Broca's and Wernicke's areas; many aphasics

have diffuse cortical damage that involves one or both of these areas. Second, there is a tendency for aphasias associated with anterior damage to involve deficits that are more expressive and those associated with posterior damage to involve deficits that are more receptive.

However, the evidence has not been supportive of the specific predictions of the Wernicke-Geschwind model. First, damage restricted to the boundaries of the

FIGURE 16.15 The wide distribution of left hemisphere sites where cortical stimulation either blocked speech or disrupted it. (Adapted from Penfield & Roberts, 1959.)

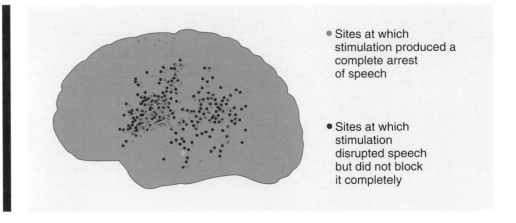

• Sites at which stimulation produced a complete arrest of speech

• Sites at which stimulation disrupted speech but did not block it completely

Wernicke-Geschwind cortical areas often has little lasting effect on the use of language. Second, brain damage that does not include any of the Wernicke-Geschwind areas can produce aphasia. Third, Broca's and Wernicke's aphasias rarely exist in the pure forms implied by the Wernicke-Geschwind model; aphasia virtually always involves both expressive and receptive symptoms (see Benson, 1985). Fourth, there seem to be major differences in the localization of cortical language areas in different individuals.

Despite these problems, the Wernicke-Geschwind model has been an extremely important theory. It guided the study and clinical diagnosis of aphasia for over a quarter of a century. Indeed, clinical neuropsychologists still use *Broca's aphasia* and *Wernicke's aphasia* as diagnostic categories, but with an understanding that the syndromes are much less selective and the precipitating damage much more diffuse and variable than implied by the model (Alexander, 1997).

Because of the lack of empirical support for its major predictions, the Wernicke-Geschwind model has been largely supplanted by a new approach to the study of the cerebral mechanisms of language and their dysfunctions. The last two sections of this chapter focus on this approach, called the *cognitive neuroscience approach.*

16.6 The Cognitive Neuroscience Approach to Language

The cognitive neuroscience approach is currently dominating research on language and its disorders. What is this approach, and how does it differ from the traditional (Wernicke-Geschwind) approach? The following are three related ideas that define the cognitive neuroscience approach to language. Although these ideas were originally premises, or assumptions, that directed cognitive neuroscience research on language, each one is now supported by a substantial amount of evidence (see Patterson & Ralph, 1999; Saffran, 1997).

Premise 1: Language-related behaviors are mediated by activity in those particular areas of the brain that are involved in the specific cognitive processes required for the behaviors. The Wernicke-Geschwind model theorized that particular areas of the brain involved in language were each dedicated to a specific, but complex, activity such as speech, comprehension, or reading. But cognitive neuroscience research has found that each of these activities can itself be broken down into

constituent cognitive processes, which may be organized in different parts of the brain (Neville & Bavelier, 1998). Accordingly, these constituent cognitive processes, not the general Wernicke-Geschwind activities, appear to be the appropriate level of analysis. Cognitive neuroscientists typically divide the cognitive processes involved in language into three categories of activity: **phonological analysis** (analysis of the sound of language), **grammatical analysis** (analysis of the structure of language), and **semantic analysis** (analysis of the meaning of language).

Premise 2: The areas of the brain involved in language are not dedicated solely to that purpose (Nobre & Plunkett, 1997). In the Wernicke-Geschwind model, large areas of left cerebral cortex were thought to be dedicated solely to language, whereas the cognitive neuroscience approach assumes that many of the constituent cognitive processes involved in language also play roles in other behaviors (see Bischoff-Grethe et al., 2000). For example, some of the areas of the brain that participate in short-term memory and visual pattern recognition are clearly involved in reading as well.

Premise 3: Because many of the areas of the brain that perform specific language functions are also parts of other functional systems, these areas are likely to be small, widely distributed, and specialized (Neville & Bavelier, 1998). In contrast, the language areas of the Wernicke-Geschwind model are assumed to be large, circumscribed, and homogeneous.

In addition to these three premises, the cognitive neuroscience approach to language is distinguished from the traditional approach by its methodology. The Wernicke-Geschwind model rested heavily on the analysis of brain-damaged patients, whereas researchers using the cognitive neuroscience approach also have at their disposal an increasing array of techniques—most notably, functional brain imaging—for studying the localization of language in healthy subjects.

Functional Brain Imaging and Language

Functional brain-imaging techniques have revolutionized the study of the localization of language. In the last decade, there have been numerous PET and fMRI studies of subjects engaging in various language-related activities. I have selected two to describe to you. As you are about to learn, I selected them because they are of high quality, have interesting findings, and feature two different approaches. The first is the fMRI study of silent reading by Bavelier and colleagues (1997); the second is the PET study of naming objects by Damasio and colleagues (1996).

BAVELIER'S fMRI STUDY OF READING ■ Bavelier and colleagues used fMRI to measure the brain activity of healthy subjects while they read silently. The researchers' general purpose was not to break down reading into its constituent cognitive processes or elements but to get a sense of the extent of cortical involvement in reading.

The methodology of Bavelier and colleagues was noteworthy in two respects. First, they used a particularly sensitive fMRI machine that allowed them to identify areas of activity with more accuracy than in most previous studies and without having to average the scores of several subjects (see Chapter 5). Second, they recorded activity during the reading of sentences—rather than during the simpler, controllable, and unnatural activities most often used in functional brain-imaging studies of language (e.g., listening to individual words).

The subjects in Bavelier and colleagues' study viewed sentences displayed on a screen. Interposed between pe-

riods of silent reading were control periods, during which the subjects were presented with strings of consonants. The differences in activity during the reading and control periods served as the basis for calculating the areas of cortical activity associated with reading. Because of the computing power required for the detailed analyses, only the lateral cortical surfaces were monitored.

Let's begin by considering the findings observed in individual subjects on individual trials, before any averaging took place. Three important points emerged from this analysis. First, the areas of activity were patchy; that is, they were tiny areas of activity separated by areas of inactivity. Second, the patches of activity were variable; that is, the areas of activity differed from subject to subject and even from trial to trial in the same subject. Third, although some activity was observed in the classic Wernicke-Geschwind areas, it was widespread over the lateral surfaces of the brain. The widespread, spotty activity over the left cortex is consistent with the basic premises of the cognitive neuroscience approach and with previous research—in particular, with brain stimulation studies of language.

Figure 16.16 on page 432 illustrates the reading-related increases of activity averaged over all the trials and subjects in the study by Bavelier and colleagues—as they are typically reported. The averaging creates the false impression that large, homogeneous expanses of tissue were active during reading, whereas the patches of activity induced on any given trial comprised only between 5% and 10% of the illustrated areas. Still, two points are clear: First, although there was significant activity in the right hemisphere, there was far more activity in the left hemisphere; second, the activity extended far beyond those areas predicted by the Wernicke-Geschwind model to be involved in silent reading (e.g., activity in Broca's area and motor cortex would not have been predicted).

DAMASIO'S PET STUDY OF NAMING ■ In contrast to the purpose of the study by Bavelier and colleagues, which was to assess the extent of activity associated with silent reading, the objective of Damasio and colleagues (1996) was to look selectively at the temporal-lobe activity involved in naming objects within particular categories.

Damasio and colleagues recorded the PET activity in the left temporal lobes of healthy subjects while they named images presented on a screen. The images were of three different types: famous faces, animals, and tools. To get a specific measure of the temporal-lobe activity involved in naming, they subtracted from the activity recorded during this task the activity recorded while the subjects judged the orientation of the images. The researchers focused on the left temporal lobes of the subjects to permit a more fine-grained PET analysis.

Naming objects activated the left temporal lobe outside the classic Wernicke's language area. Remarkably, the

Left Hemisphere

Right Hemisphere

Active

Very active

FIGURE 16.16 The areas in which reading-associated increases in activity were observed in the fMRI study of Bavelier and colleagues (1997). These maps were derived by averaging the scores of all subjects, each of whom displayed patchy increases of activity in 5–10% of the indicated areas on any particular trial.

precise area that was activated by the naming depended on the category: Famous faces, animals, and tools each activated a slightly different area. In general, the areas for naming famous faces, animals, and tools are arrayed from anterior to posterior along the middle portions of the left temporal lobe.

Damasio and colleagues have not been the only ones to report category-specific naming-related activity in the left temporal lobes (see Nobre & Plunkett, 1997); Martin and colleagues (1996) reported a similar finding. More-

over, the existence of category-specific lexical areas in the left temporal lobes has been supported by the analysis of aphasic patients with damage in that area. Some patients have naming difficulties that are specific to particular categories (see Kurbat & Farah, 1998), and specific deficits in naming famous faces, animals, and tools have been shown to correspond to the three areas of the left temporal lobe that were identified by the PET study (Damasio et al., 1996).

16.7 The Cognitive Neuroscience Approach and Dyslexia

This, the final section of the chapter, looks further at the cognitive neuroscience approach introduced in the preceding section. It focuses on dyslexia, one of the major subjects of cognitive neuroscience research.

Dyslexia is a pathological difficulty in reading, one that does not result from general visual, motor, or intellectual deficits. There are two fundamentally different types of dyslexias: *developmental dyslexias*, dyslexias that become apparent when a child is learning to read; and *acquired dyslexias*, dyslexias that are caused by brain damage in individ-

uals who were already capable of reading. Developmental dyslexia is a widespread problem; for example, approximately 15% of English-speaking males and 5% of English-speaking females fail to learn to read despite normal visual, motor, and intellectual abilities (Shaywitz, 1996).

Although the causes of acquired dyslexia are usually apparent, the causes of developmental dyslexia are not. The problem in discovering the causes of developmental dyslexia is not that no abnormalities have been discovered in the brains of individuals suffering from the disorder. Many differences between the brains of dyslex-ics and normal readers have been reported (see Farmer & Klein, 1995). For example, dyslexics often do not display the usual left-larger-than-right asymmetry in the size of the planum temporale.

Although many structural abnormalities have been identified in the brains of patients suffering from devel-opmental disorders, three problems have impeded the discovery of the neural basis of developmental dyslexia. First, although many abnormalities have been reported in the brains of developmental dyslexics, none seems to play a critical role in the disorder. Second, there are sev-eral types of developmental dyslexia, and these are likely to have different causes. Third, it is difficult to rule out the possibility that particular brain "abnormalities" ob-served in developmental dyslexics are the result, rather than the cause, of the disorder; perhaps the lack of read-ing experience causes the brains of dyslexics to develop differently than those of normal readers.

There is a genetic component to developmental dy-slexia; it has a heritability estimate of about 0.5. It has been suggested that the disorder may be caused by the early ex-posure of genetically susceptible individuals to a virus or a toxin, but there is no strong evidence for this notion.

Developmental Dyslexia: Cultural Diversity and Biological Unity

Although it is well established that developmental dyslexia is influenced by genetic factors and is associated with abnormalities of brain function, it has long been considered by many to be a psychological rather than a neural disorder. Why? Because developmental dyslexia is influenced by culture.

For many years, those whose thinking was warped by the physiology-or-psychology dichotomy (see Chapter 2) assumed that because developmental dyslexia is influenced by culture, it could not possibly be a brain disorder. Paulesu and colleagues (2001) recently used the cognitive neuroscience ap-proach to drive the final nail into the coffin of this mis-guided way of thinking about dyslexia.

The work of Paulesu and colleagues is based on the remarkable finding that about twice as many English speakers as Italian speakers are diagnosed as dyslexic. This fact has to do with the complexity of the respective languages. English consists of 40 phonemes (individual speech sounds), which can be spelled, by one count, in 1120 different ways. In contrast, Italian is composed of 25 phonemes, which can be spelled in 33 different ways. As a result, Italian-speaking children learn to read much more quickly than English-speaking children and are less likely to develop reading disorders.

Paulesu and colleagues (2000) began by comparing PET activity in the brains of normal English-speaking and Italian-speaking adults. These researchers hypothe-sized that since the cognitive demands of reading aloud are different for Italian- and English-speaking subjects, they should use different parts of their brains while reading. That is exactly what the researchers found. Although the same general areas were active during reading in both groups, Italian readers displayed more activity in the left superior tem-poral lobe, whereas English readers displayed more ac-tivity in the left inferior temporal and frontal lobes.

Next, Paulesu and colleagues (2001) turned their at-tention to developmental dyslexia. They recorded PET scans of the brains of normal and dyslexic British, French, and Italian university students while the subjects read individual words in their own language— university students were used to rule out lack of access to education as a possible confounding factor. Despite the fact that the Italian dyslexics had less severe reading problems, all three groups of dyslexics displayed the same pattern of abnormal PET activity when reading: less than normal reading-related activity in the posterior region of the temporal lobe, near its boundary with the occipital lobe. Thus, although dyslexia can manifest itself differently in people who speak different languages, the underlying neural pathol-ogy appears to be the same.

Cognitive Neuroscience Analysis of Reading Aloud: Deep and Surface Dyslexia

Cognitive psychologists have long recognized that reading aloud can be accomplished in two entirely different ways. One is by a **lexical procedure,** which is based on specific stored information that has been acquired about written words: The reader simply looks at the word, recognizes it, and says it. The other way reading can be accomplished is by a **phonetic procedure:** The reader looks at the word, recognizes the letters, sounds them out, and says the word. The lexical pro-cedure dominates in the reading of familiar words; the phonetic procedure dominates in the reading of un-familiar words.

This simple cognitive analysis of reading aloud has proven useful in understanding the symptoms of two different kinds of dyslexia resulting from brain damage. These two different classes of acquired dyslexia are *sur-face dyslexia* and *deep dyslexia.* Similar syndromes are ob-served for developmental dyslexia, but they tend to be less severe.

In cases of **surface dyslexia,** patients have lost their ability to pronounce words based on their specific memories of the words (i.e., they have lost the *lexical procedure*), but they can still apply rules of pronunciation in their reading (i.e., they can still use the *phonetic procedure*). Accordingly, they retain their ability to pronounce words whose pronunciation is consistent with common rules (e.g., *fish, river,* or *glass*) and their ability to pronounce non-words according to common rules of pronunciation (e.g., *spleemer* or *twipple*); but they have great difficulty pronouncing words that do not follow common rules of pronunciation (e.g., *have, lose,* or *steak*). The errors they make often involve the misapplication of common rules of pronunciation; for example, *have, lose,* and *steak* are typically pronounced as if they rhyme with *cave, hose,* and *beak.*

In cases of **deep dyslexia,** patients have lost their ability to apply rules of pronunciation in their reading (i.e., they have lost the *phonetic procedure*), but they can still pronounce familiar concrete words based on their specific memories of them (i.e., they can still use the *lexical procedure*). Accordingly, they are completely incapable of pronouncing nonwords and have difficulty pronouncing uncommon words and words whose meaning is abstract. In attempting to pronounce words, patients with deep dyslexia try to react to them by using various lexical strategies, such as responding to the overall look of the word, the meaning of the word, or the derivation of the word. This leads to a characteristic pattern of errors. A patient with deep dyslexia might say "quill" for *quail* (responding to the overall look of the word), "hen" for *chicken* (responding to the meaning of the word), or "wise" for *wisdom* (responding to the derivation of the word).

I used to have difficulty keeping these two syndromes straight. Now I remember which is which by reminding myself that surface dyslexics have difficulty reacting to the overall shape of the word, which is metaphorically more superficial (less deep) than a problem in applying rules of pronunciation, which is experienced by deep dyslexics.

Where are the lexical and phonetic procedures performed in the brain? Much of the research attempting to answer this question has focused on the study of deep dyslexia. Deep dyslexics most often have extensive damage to the left-hemisphere language areas, suggesting that the disrupted phonetic procedure is widely distributed in the frontal and temporal areas of the left hemisphere. But which part of the brain maintains the lexical procedure in deep dyslexics? There have been two theories, both of which have received some support.

One theory is that the surviving lexical abilities of deep dyslexics are mediated by activity in surviving parts of the left-hemisphere language areas. Evidence for this theory comes from the observation of such activity during reading (Laine et al., 2000; Price et al., 1998). The other theory is that the surviving lexical abilities of deep dyslexics are mediated by activity in the right hemisphere. Support for this view comes from the following remarkable case study of Patterson, Vargha-Khadem, & Polkey, 1989.

The Case of N.I., the Woman Who Read with Her Right Hemisphere

Prior to the onset of her illness, N.I. was a healthy girl. At the age of 13, she began to experience periods of aphasia, and several weeks later, she suffered a generalized convulsion. She subsequently had many convulsions, and her speech and motor abilities deteriorated badly. CT scans indicated ischemic brain damage to the left hemisphere.

Two years after the onset of her disorder, N.I. was experiencing continual seizures and blindness in her right visual field, and there was no meaningful movement or perception in her right limbs. In an attempt to relieve these symptoms, a total left **hemispherectomy** was performed; that is, her left hemisphere was totally removed. Her seizures were totally arrested by this surgery.

The reading performance of N.I. is poor, but she displays a pattern of retained abilities strikingly similar to those displayed by deep dyslexics or split-brain patients reading with their right hemispheres. For example, she recognizes letters but is totally incapable of translating them into sounds; she can read concrete familiar words; she cannot pronounce even simple nonsense words (e.g., *neg*); and her reading errors indicate that she is reading on the basis of the meaning and appearance of words rather than by translating letters into sounds (e.g., when presented with the word *fruit*, she responded, "Juice . . . it's apples and pears and . . . fruit"). In other words, she suffers from a severe case of deep dyslexia.

The case of N.I. completes the circle: The chapter began with a discussion of language and lateralization of function, and the case of N.I. concludes it on the same note.

Themes Revisited

In positioning the themes icons throughout this chapter, I learned something. I learned why this is one of my favorite chapters. This chapter has more themes icons than any other chapter—it contributes most to developing the themes of the book. Indeed, several passages in this chapter are directly relevant to more than one of the themes, which made placing the icons difficult.

The clinical implications theme is the most prevalent because much of what we know about the lateralization of function and the localization of language in the brain comes from the study of neuropsychological patients. Currently, however, the cognitive neuroscience approach is playing a particularly prominent role in the study of the localization of language, which is why the cognitive neuroscience theme was also prevalent, particularly in the second half of the chapter.

Because lateralization of function and language localization are often covered by the popular media,

they have become integrated into pop culture, and many widely held ideas about these subjects are overly simplistic. In this chapter, the thinking-about-biopsychology icons mark aspects of laterality and language about which it is particularly important that you think clearly.

Evolutionary analysis has not played a major role in the study of the localization of language, largely because humans are the only species with well-developed language. However, it has played a key role in trying to understand why cerebral lateralization of function evolved in the first place, and the major breakthrough in understanding the split-brain phenomenon came from comparative research.

ON THE CD
Looking for more information about the topics in this chapter? For recommended additional readings, see Hard Copy for Chapter 16.

Log On

■ **http://www.macalester.edu/~psych/whathap/UBNRP/ Split_Brain/Split_Brain_Consciousness.html** This detailed look at the split-brain procedure includes a review of the pioneering work of Sperry, Gazzaniga, and others.

■ **http://faculty.washington.edu/chudler/lang.html** A useful summary of the Wernicke-Geschwind model and re-

cent language-related brain-imaging work by Ojemann and others can be found here.

■ **http://www.sfn.org/briefings/dyslexia.html** The Society for Neuroscience presents a brief review of current research on the neural basis of dyslexia.

Think about It

1. Design an experiment to show that it is possible for a split-brain student to study for an English exam and a geometry exam at the same time by using a Z lens.

2. The decision to perform commissurotomies on epileptic patients turned out to be a good one; the decision to perform prefrontal lobotomies on mental patients (see Chapter 1) turned out to be a bad

one. Was this just the luck of the draw? Discuss.

3. Design a fMRI study to identify the areas of the brain involved in comprehending speech.

4. Why do you think cerebral lateralization of function evolved?

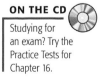

ON THE CD
Studying for an exam? Try the Practice Tests for Chapter 16.

Key Terms

Agraphia *(p. 423)*
Alexia *(p. 423)*
Angular gyrus *(p. 423)*
Aphasia *(p. 408)*
Apraxia *(p. 408)*
Arcuate fasciculus *(p. 423)*
Broca's aphasia *(p. 423)*
Broca's area *(p. 408)*
Cerebral commissures *(p. 407)*
Chimeric figures test *(p. 414)*
Commissurotomy *(p. 407)*
Conduction aphasia *(p. 423)*
Corpus callosum *(p. 410)*
Cross-cuing *(p. 414)*
Deep dyslexia *(p. 434)*

Dextrals *(p. 409)*
Dichotic listening test *(p. 408)*
Dominant hemisphere *(p. 408)*
Dyslexia *(p. 432)*
Expressive *(p. 423)*
Frontal operculum *(p. 419)*
Global aphasia *(p. 428)*
Grammatical analysis
    (p. 430)
Helping-hand phenomenon
    (p. 414)
Hemispherectomy *(p. 434)*
Heschl's gyrus *(p. 419)*
Lateralization of function
    (p. 407)

Lexical procedure *(p. 433)*
Minor hemisphere *(p. 408)*
Phonemes *(p. 428)*
Phonetic procedure *(p. 433)*
Phonological analysis *(p. 430)*
Planum temporale *(p. 419)*
Receptive *(p. 423)*
Scotoma *(p. 411)*
Semantic analysis *(p. 430)*
Sinestrals *(p. 409)*
Sodium amytal test *(p. 408)*
Split-brain patients *(p. 407)*
Surface dyslexia *(p. 433)*
Visual completion *(p. 414)*
Wernicke's aphasia *(p. 423)*

Wernicke's area *(p. 423)*
Wernicke-Geschwind model
    (p. 423)
Word salad *(p. 423)*
Z lens *(p. 415)*

ON THE CD

Need some help studying the key terms for this chapter? Check out the electronic flash cards for Chapter 16.

chapter 17

Biopsychology of Emotion, Stress, and Health

Fear, the Dark Side of Emotion

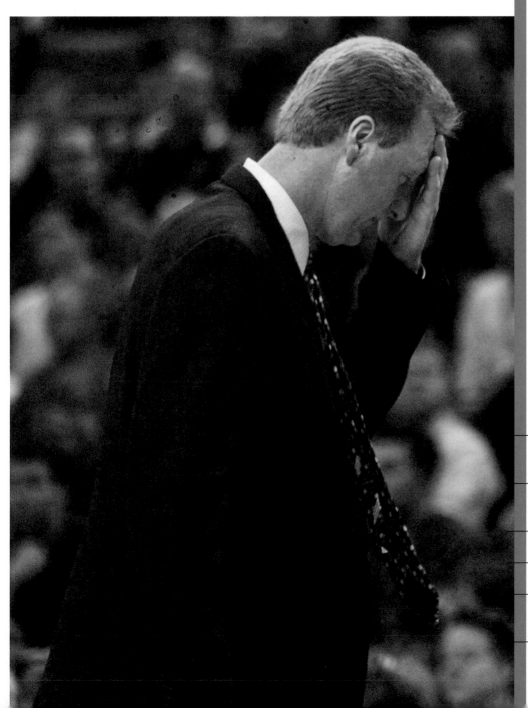

This chapter is about the biopsychology of emotion, stress, and health. It begins with a general introduction to the biopsychology of emotion and gradually focuses on the dark end of the emotional spectrum: fear. Biopsychological research on emotions has concentrated on fear not because biopsychologists are a scary bunch, but because fear has three important qualities: It is the easiest emotion to infer from behavior; it plays an important adaptive function in motivating the avoidance of threatening situations; and the stress associated with chronic fear increases our susceptibility to a wide range of disorders. These include physical disorders such as ulcers and infections, which you will learn about in this chapter, and numerous psychological disorders, which you will learn about in the next.

17.1 Biopsychology of Emotion: Introduction

This section provides a general introduction to the biopsychology of emotion by reviewing several of the classic early discoveries, the role of the autonomic nervous system in emotional experience, and the facial expression of emotion.

Early Landmarks in the Biopsychological Investigation

This subsection describes, in chronological sequence, six early landmarks in the biopsychological investigation of emotion. It begins with the 1848 case of Phineas Gage.

The Mind-Blowing Case of Phineas Gage

In 1848, Phineas Gage, a 25-year-old construction foreman for the Rutland and Burlington Railroad, was the victim of a tragic accident. In order to lay new tracks, the terrain had to be leveled, and Gage was in charge of the blasting. His task involved drilling holes in the rock, pouring some gun powder into each hole, covering it with sand, and tamping the material down with a large tamping iron before detonating it with a fuse. On the fateful day, the gunpowder exploded while Gage was tamping it, launching the 3-cm-thick, 90-cm-long tamping iron through his face, skull, and brain and out the other side.

Amazingly, Gage survived his accident, but he survived it a changed man. Before the accident, Gage had been a responsible, intelligent, socially well-adapted person, who was well liked by his friends and fellow workers. Once recovered, he appeared to be as able-bodied and intellectually capable as before, but his personality and emotional life had totally changed. Formerly a religious, respectful, reliable man, Gage became irreverent and impulsive. In particular, his abundant profanity offended many. He became so unreliable and undependable that he soon lost his job, and was never again able to hold a responsible position.

Gage became an itinerant, roaming the country for a dozen years until his death in San Francisco. His bizarre accident and apparently successful recovery made headlines around the world, but his death went largely unnoticed and unacknowledged.

Gage was buried next to the offending tamping iron. Five years later, neurologist John Harlow was granted permission from Gage's family to exhume the body and tamping iron to study them. Since then, Gage's skull and the tamping iron have been on display in the Warren Anatomical Medical Museum at Harvard University.

In 1994, Damasio and her colleagues brought the power of computerized reconstruction to bear on Gage's classic case. They began by taking an X-ray of the skull and measuring it precisely, paying particular attention to the position of the entry and exit holes. From these measurements, they reconstructed the accident and determined the likely region of Gage's brain damage (see Figure 17.1). It was apparent that the damage to Gage's brain affected both *medial prefrontal lobes*, which we now know are involved in planning and emotion.

DARWIN'S THEORY OF THE EVOLUTION OF EMOTION ■ The first major event in the study of the biopsychology of emotion was the publication in 1872 of Darwin's book *The Expression of Emotions in Man and Animals*. In it, Darwin argued, largely on the basis of anecdotal evidence, that particular emotional responses, such as human facial expressions, tend to accompany the same emotional states in all members of a species.

Darwin believed that expressions of emotion, like other behaviors, are products of evolution; he therefore tried to understand them by comparing them in different species. From such interspecies comparisons, Darwin developed a

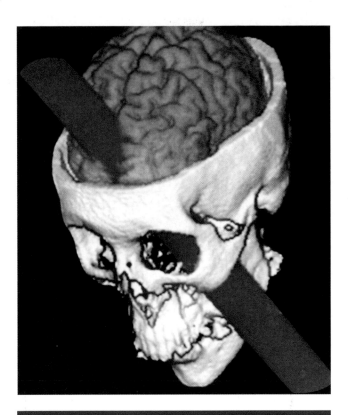

FIGURE 17.1 A reconstruction of the brain injury of Phineas Gage. The damage focused on the medial prefrontal lobes. (Adapted from Damasio et al., 1994.)

theory of the evolution of emotional expression that was composed of three main ideas: (1) Expressions of emotion evolve from behaviors that indicate what an animal is likely to do next; (2) if the signals provided by such behaviors benefit the animal that displays them, they will evolve in ways that enhance their communicative function, and their original function may be lost; and (3) opposite messages are often signaled by opposite movements and postures (the *principle of antithesis*).

Consider how Darwin's theory accounts for the evolution of *threat displays*. Originally, facing one's enemies, rising up, and exposing one's weapons were the components of the early stages of combat. But once enemies began to recognize these behaviors as signals of impending aggression, a survival advantage accrued to attackers that could communicate their aggression most effectively and intimidate their victims without actually fighting. As a result, elaborate threat displays evolved, and actual combat declined.

To be most effective, signals of aggression and submission must be clearly distinguishable; thus they tended to evolve in opposite directions. For example, gulls signal aggression by pointing their beaks at one another and submission by pointing their beaks away from one another; primates signal aggression by staring and submission by averting their gaze. Figure 17.2 is a reproduction of the actual woodcuts that Darwin used in his 1872 book to illustrate this principle of antithesis in dogs.

JAMES-LANGE AND CANNON-BARD THEORIES ■

The first physiological theory of emotion was proposed independently by James and Lange in 1884. According to the **James-Lange theory,** emotion-inducing sensory stimuli are received and interpreted by the cortex, which triggers changes in the visceral organs via the autonomic nervous system and in the skeletal muscles via the somatic nervous system. Then, the autonomic and somatic responses trigger the experience of emotion in the brain.

Aggression

Submission

FIGURE 17.2 Two woodcuts from Darwin's 1872 book, *The Expression of Emotions in Man and Animals,* that he used to illustrate the principle of antithesis. The aggressive posture of dogs features ears forward, back up, hair up, and tail up; the submissive posture features ears back, back down, hair down, and tail down.

In effect, what the James-Lange theory did was to reverse the usual commonsense way of thinking about the causal relation between the experience of emotion and its expression. James and Lange argued that the autonomic activity and behavior that are triggered by the emotional event (e.g., rapid heartbeat and running away) produce the feeling of emotion, not vice versa.

In the early 1900s, Cannon proposed an alternative to the James-Lange theory of emotion, and it was subsequently extended and promoted by Bard. According to the **Cannon-Bard theory,** emotional stimuli have two independent excitatory effects: They excite both the feeling of emotion in the brain and the expression of emotion in the autonomic and somatic nervous systems. Accordingly, the Cannon-Bard theory, in contrast to the James-Lange theory, views emotional experience and emotional expression as parallel processes that have no direct causal relation.

The James-Lange and Cannon-Bard theories make different predictions about the role of feedback from autonomic and somatic nervous system activity in emotional experience. According to the James-Lange theory, emotional experience depends entirely on feedback from autonomic and somatic nervous system activity; according to the Cannon-Bard theory, emotional experience is totally independent of such feedback. Both extreme positions have proved to be incorrect. On the one hand, it seems that the autonomic and somatic feedback is not necessary for the experience of emotion: Human patients whose autonomic and somatic feedback has been largely eliminated by a broken neck are capable of a full range of emotional experiences (e.g., Lowe & Carroll, 1985). On the other hand, there have been numerous reports—some of which you will soon encounter—that autonomic and somatic responses to emotional stimuli can influence emotional experience.

Failure to find unqualified support for either the James-Lange or the Cannon-Bard theory has led to a third theory. According to this theory, each of the three principal factors in an emotional response—the perception of the emotion-inducing stimulus, the autonomic and somatic responses to the stimulus, and the experience of the emotion—influences the other two (see Figure 17.3).

SHAM RAGE ■ In the late 1920s, Bard (1929) discovered that **decorticate** cats—cats whose cortex has been removed—respond aggressively to the slightest provocation: After a light touch, they arch their backs, erect their hair, growl, hiss, and expose their teeth.

The aggressive responses of decorticate animals are abnormal in two respects: They are inappropriately severe, and they are not directed at particular targets. Bard referred to the exaggerated, poorly directed aggressive responses of decorticate animals as **sham rage.**

Sham rage can be elicited in cats whose cerebral hemispheres have been removed down to, but not in-

cluding, the hypothalamus; but it cannot be elicited if the hypothalamus is also removed. On the basis of this observation, Bard concluded that the hypothalamus is critical for the expression of aggressive responses and that the function of the cortex is to inhibit and direct these responses.

LIMBIC SYSTEM AND EMOTION ■ In 1937, Papez (pronounced "Payps") proposed that emotional expression is controlled by several interconnected neural structures that he referred to as the limbic system. The **limbic system** is a collection of nuclei and tracts that borders the thalamus (*limbic* means "border"). Figure 17.4 on page 442 illustrates some of its key structures: the amygdala, mammillary body, hippocampus, fornix, cingulate cortex, septum, olfactory bulb, and hypothalamus (see Macchi, 1989). Papez proposed that emotional states are expressed through the action of the other limbic structures on the hypothalamus and that they are experienced through the action of the limbic structures on the cortex.

KLUVER-BUCY SYNDROME ■ In 1939, Kluver and Bucy observed a striking *syndrome* (pattern of behavior) in monkeys that had had their anterior temporal lobes removed. This syndrome, which is commonly referred to as the **Kluver-Bucy syndrome**, includes the following behaviors: the consumption of almost anything that is edible, increased sexual activity often directed at inappropriate objects, a tendency to repeatedly investigate familiar objects, a tendency to investigate objects with the mouth, and a lack of fear. Monkeys that could not be handled before surgery were transformed by bilateral anterior temporal lobectomy into tame subjects that showed no fear whatsoever—even in response to snakes, which terrify normal monkeys. In primates, most of the symptoms of the Kluver-Bucy syndrome appear to result from amygdala damage.

The Kluver-Bucy syndrome has been observed in several species. Following is a description of the syndrome in a human patient with a brain infection.

A Human Case of Kluver-Bucy Syndrome

He exhibited a flat affect, and although originally restless, ultimately became remarkably placid. He appeared indifferent to people or situations. He spent much time gazing at the television, but never learned to turn it on; when the set was off, he tended to watch reflections of others in the room on the glass screen. On occasion he became facetious, smiling inappropriately and mimicking the gestures and actions of others. Once initiating an imitative series, he would perseverate copying all movements made by another for extended periods of time. . . .

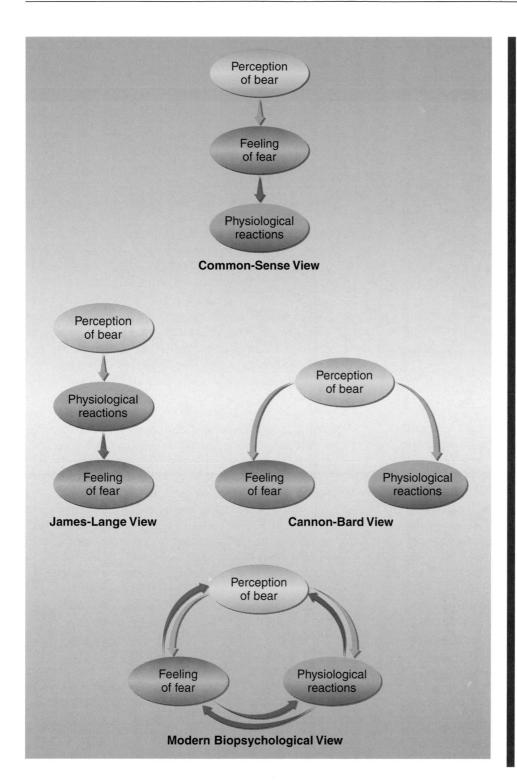

He engaged in oral exploration of all objects within his grasp, appearing unable to gain information via tactile or visual means alone. All objects that he could lift were placed in his mouth and sucked or chewed. . . .

Although vigorously heterosexual prior to his illness, he was observed in hospital to make advances toward other male patients. . . . [H]e never made advances toward women, and, in fact, his apparent reversal of sexual polarity prompted his fiancée to sever their relationship. (Marlowe, Mancall, & Thomas, 1985, pp. 55–56)

The six early landmarks in the study of brain mechanisms of emotion just reviewed are listed in Table 17.1 on page 442.

■ Emotions and the Autonomic Nervous System

Research on the role of the autonomic nervous system (ANS) in emotion has focused on two issues: the

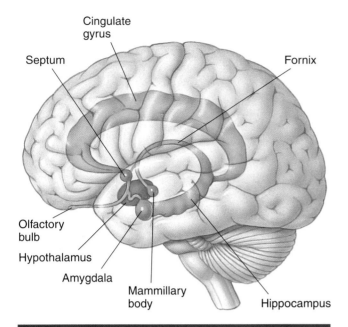

FIGURE 17.4 The location of the major limbic system structures. In general, they are arrayed near the midline in a ring around the thalamus. (See also Figure 3.30.)

Table 17.1	Biopsychological Investigation of Emotion: Six Early Landmarks
EVENT	**DATE**
Case of Phineas Gage	1848
Darwin's theory of the evolution of emotion	1872
James-Lange and Cannon-Bard theories	about 1900
Discovery of sham rage	1929
Limbic-system theory of emotion	1937
Discovery of Kluver-Bucy syndrome	1939

degree to which specific patterns of ANS activity are associated with specific emotions and the effectiveness of ANS measures in polygraphy (lie detection).

EMOTIONAL SPECIFICITY OF THE AUTONOMIC NERVOUS SYSTEM ■ The James-Lange and Cannon-Bard theories differ in their views of the emotional specificity of the autonomic nervous system. The James-Lange theory says that different emotional stimuli induce different patterns of ANS activity and that these different patterns produce different emotional experiences. In contrast, the Cannon-Bard theory claims that all emotional stimuli produce the same general pattern of sympathetic activation, which prepares the organism for action (i.e., increased heart rate, increased blood pressure, pupil dilation, increased flow of blood to the muscles, increased respiration, and increased release of epinephrine and norepinephrine from the adrenal medulla).

The experimental evidence suggests that the specificity of ANS reactions lies somewhere between the extremes of total specificity and total generality (Levenson, 1994). There is ample evidence that not all emotions are associated with the same pattern of ANS activity (see Ax, 1955); however, there is insufficient evidence to make a strong case for the view that each emotion is characterized by a different pattern of ANS activity.

POLYGRAPHY ■ **Polygraphy** is a method of interrogation that employs autonomic nervous system indexes of emotion to infer the truthfulness of the subject's responses. Polygraph tests administered by skilled examin-

ers can be useful additions to normal interrogation procedures, but they are not infallible (Iacono & Patrick, 1987).

The main problem in evaluating the effectiveness of polygraphy is that it is rarely possible in real-life situations to know for certain whether the suspect is guilty or innocent. Consequently, many studies of polygraphy have employed the *mock-crime procedure:* Volunteer subjects participate in a mock crime and are then subjected to a polygraph test by an examiner who is unaware of their "guilt" or "innocence." The usual interrogation method is the **control-question technique,** in which the physiological response to the target question (e.g., "Did you steal that purse?") is compared with the physiological responses to control questions whose answers are known (e.g., "Have you ever been in jail before?"). The assumption is that lying will be associated with greater sympathetic activation. The average success rate in various mock-crime studies using the control-question technique is about 80%.

Despite being commonly referred to as *lie detection,* polygraphy detects emotions, not lies. Consequently, it is likely more difficult to detect lies in real life than in experiments. In real-life situations, questions such as "Did you steal that purse?" are likely to elicit a reaction from all suspects, regardless of their guilt or innocence, making it difficult to detect deception. Lykken (1959) developed the **guilty-knowledge technique** to circumvent this problem. In order to use this technique, the polygrapher must have a piece of information concerning the crime that would be known only to the guilty person. Rather than attempting to catch the suspect in a lie, the polygrapher simply assesses the suspect's reaction to a list of actual and contrived details of the crime. Innocent parties, because they have no knowledge of the crime, react to all such details in the same way; the guilty react differentially.

In one study of the guilty-knowledge technique (Lykken, 1959), subjects waited until the occupant of an office went to the washroom. Then, they entered her office, stole her purse from her desk, removed the money, and left the purse in a locker. The critical part of the interrogation went something like this: "Where do you think we found the purse? In the washroom? . . . In a locker? . . . Hanging on a coat rack? . . . " Even though electrodermal activity was the only measure of ANS activity used in this study, 88% of the mock criminals were correctly identified; more importantly, none of the innocent parties was judged guilty.

■ Emotions and Facial Expression

Ekman and his colleagues have been preeminent in the study of facial expression (see Ekman, 1992, 1993). They began in the 1960s by analyzing hundreds of films and photographs of people experiencing various real emotions. From these, they compiled an atlas of the facial expressions that are normally associated with different emotions (Ekman & Friesen, 1975). The facial expressions in Ekman and Friesen's atlas are not photographs of people experiencing genuine emotions. They are photographs of models who were instructed to contract specific facial muscles on the basis of Ekman and Friesen's analysis. For example, to produce the facial expression for surprise, models were instructed to pull their brows upward so as to wrinkle their forehead, to open their eyes wide so as to reveal white above the iris, to slacken the muscles around their mouth, and to drop their jaw. Try it.

UNIVERSALITY OF FACIAL EXPRESSION ■ Despite Darwin's assertion that people in all parts of the world make similar facial expressions, it was widely believed that facial expressions are learned and culturally variable. Then, several empirical studies showed that people of different cultures do indeed make similar facial expressions in similar situations and that they can correctly identify the emotional significance of facial expressions displayed by people from cultures other than their own (e.g., Ekman, Sorenson, & Friesen, 1969; Hejmadi, Davidson, & Rozin, 2000; Izard, 1971). The most convincing of these studies was a study of the members of an isolated New Guinea tribe who had had little or no contact with the outside world (Ekman & Friesen, 1971). Although these findings support Darwin's view of the universality of facial expressions, they do not deny the possibility of minor cultural differences.

PRIMARY FACIAL EXPRESSIONS ■ Ekman and Friesen concluded that the facial expressions of the following six emotions are primary: surprise, anger, sadness, disgust, fear, and happiness. They further concluded that all other facial expressions of genuine emotion are composed of predictable mixtures of the six primaries. In Figure 17.5, Ekman himself illustrates the six primary facial expressions and the combination of two of them to form a nonprimary expression.

Surprise Anger Sadness

Disgust Fear Happiness

Combination of sadness and happiness

FIGURE 17.5 Examples of the six facial expressions that Ekman and Friesen (1975) considered to be primary: surprise, anger, sadness, disgust, fear, and happiness. All other emotional facial expressions were considered to be combinations of these six. For example, shown here on the right is an expression you might make while visiting a sick friend; it is a combination of sadness in the upper half of the face and happiness in the lower half.

FIGURE 17.6 The effects of facial expression on the feeling of emotion. Subjects reported feeling more happy and less angry when they viewed slides while making a happy face, and less happy and more angry when they viewed slides while making an angry face. (Adapted from Rutledge & Hupka, 1985.)

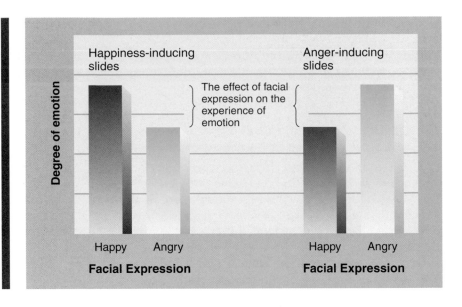

FACIAL FEEDBACK HYPOTHESIS

Is there any truth to the old idea that putting on a happy face can make you feel better? Research suggests that there is (see Adelmann & Zajonc, 1989). The hypothesis that our facial expressions influence our emotional experience is called the **facial feedback hypothesis.**

In a test of the facial feedback hypothesis, Rutledge and Hupka (1985) instructed subjects to assume one of two patterns of facial contractions while they viewed a series of slides; the patterns corresponded to happy or angry faces, although the subjects were unaware of it. The subjects reported that the slides made them feel more happy and less angry when they were making happy faces, and less happy and more angry when they were making angry faces (see Figure 17.6). Why don't you try it? Pull your eyebrows down and together; raise your upper eyelids and tighten your lower eyelids, and narrow your lips and press them together. Now, hold this expression for a few seconds. If it makes you feel slightly angry, you have just experienced the effect of facial feedback.

VOLUNTARY CONTROL OF FACIAL EXPRESSION

Because we can exert voluntary control over our facial muscles, it is possible to inhibit true facial expressions and to substitute false ones. There are many reasons for choosing to put on a false facial expression. Some of them are positive (e.g., putting on a false smile to reassure a worried friend), and some are negative (e.g., putting on a false smile to disguise a lie). In either case, it is difficult to fool an expert.

There are two ways of distinguishing true expressions from false ones (Ekman, 1985). First, *microexpressions* (brief facial expressions) of the real emotion often break through the false one. Such microexpressions last only about 0.05 second, but with practice they can be detected without the aid of slow-motion photography. Second, there are often subtle differences between genuine facial expressions and false ones that can be detected by skilled observers.

The most widely studied difference between a genuine and a false facial expression was first described by the French anatomist Duchenne in 1862. Duchenne said that the smile of enjoyment could be distinguished from deliberately produced smiles by consideration of the two facial muscles that are contracted during genuine smiles: *orbicularis oculi,* which encircles the eye and pulls the skin from the cheeks and forehead toward the eyeball, and *zygomaticus major,* which pulls the lip corners up (see Figure 17.7. According to Duchenne, the zygomati-

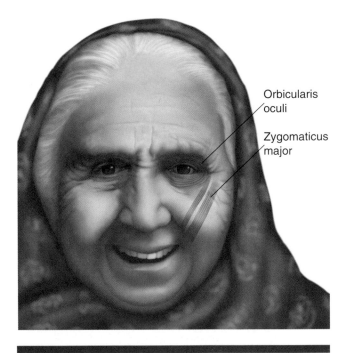

FIGURE 17.7 The orbicularis oculi and zygomaticus major, two muscles that contract during genuine (Duchenne) smiles. Because the lateral portion of the orbicularis oculi is difficult for most people to contract voluntarily, fake smiles usually lack this component.

cus major can be controlled voluntarily, whereas the or-bicularis oculi is normally contracted only by genuine pleasure. Thus inertia of the orbicularis oculi in smiling unmasks a false friend—a fact you would do well to remember. Ekman named the genuine smile the **Duchenne smile** (see Ekman & Davidson, 1993).

Not all emotions are accompanied by changes in facial expression—as any good poker player will tell you. However, *facial electromyography (EMG)* can detect changes in the motor input to facial muscles that are too slight to produce observable changes in muscle contraction (see Tassinary & Cacioppo, 1992). For example, Cacioppo and colleagues (1986) recorded the EMG activity of several facial muscles while the subjects viewed slides. Although facial expressions were seldom evoked, the EMG activity was related to how much the subjects reported they liked each slide. For example, the smile muscles—the orbicularis oculi and the zygomaticus

major—tended to be more active while the subjects were viewing slides that they judged to be pleasant.

A recent study by Dimberg, Thunberg, and Elmehed (2000) assessed the effect of the observation of facial expressions on the facial muscles of the observer. These researchers found that people tend to mimic the facial expressions they see in others, even if they are not consciously aware of what they are seeing. The researchers presented either a happy or an angry face for 30 milliseconds and then immediately replaced the target expression with a neutral expression. None of the subjects reported being aware of the briefly presented target expression; they were aware of only the neutral expression. Yet, facial EMG revealed that those who had been presented with a happy face as the target expression made subtle happy faces, whereas those who had been presented with an angry face made subtle angry faces.

17.2 Fear, Defense, and Aggression

Biopsychological research on emotion has focused to a large degree on fear and defensive behaviors. One reason for this focus—which will become more apparent as the chapter progresses—is the major role played by the stressful effects of chronic fear in the development of disease (see Adamec, 1997). **Fear** is the emotional reaction to threat; it is the motivating force for defensive behaviors. **Defensive behaviors** are behaviors whose primary function is to protect the organism from threat or harm. In contrast, **aggressive behaviors** are behaviors whose primary function is to threaten or harm.

Types of Aggressive and Defensive Behaviors

Considerable progress in the understanding of aggressive and defensive behaviors has come from the research of Blanchard and Blanchard (see 1989, 1990) on the *colony-intruder model of aggression and defense* in rats. Blanchard and Blanchard have derived rich descriptions of rat intraspecific aggressive and defensive behaviors by studying the interactions between the **alpha male**—the dominant male—of an established mixed-sex colony and a small male intruder:

The alpha approaches the stranger and sniffs at its perianal area. . . . If the intruder is an adult male, the alpha's sniff leads to piloerection [involuntary bristling of hairs]. . . .

Shortly after piloerecting, the alpha male usually bites the intruder, and the intruder runs away. The alpha chases after it, and after one or two additional bites, the intruder stops running and turns to face its attacker. It rears up on its hind legs, using

its forelimbs to push off the alpha. . . . However, rather than standing nose to nose with the "boxing" intruder, the attacking rat abruptly moves to a lateral orientation, with the long axis of its body perpendicular to the front of the defending rat. . . . It moves sideways toward the intruder, crowding and sometimes pushing it off balance. If the defending rat stands solid against this "lateral attack" movement, the alpha may make a quick lunge forward and around the defender's body to bite at its back. In response to such a lunge, the defender usually pivots on its hind feet, in the same direction as the attacker is moving, continuing its frontal orientation to the attacker. If the defending rat moves quickly enough, no bite will be made.

However, after a number of instances of the lateral attack, and especially if the attacker has succeeded in biting the intruder, the stranger rat may roll backward slowly from the boxing position, to lie on its back. The attacker then takes up a position on top of the supine animal, digging with its forepaws at the intruder's sides. If the attacker can turn the other animal over, or expose some portion of its back, . . . it bites. In response to these efforts, the defender usually moves in the direction of the attacker's head, rolling slightly on its back to continue to orient its ventrum [front] toward the alpha, and continuing to push off with both forelimbs and hindlimbs. Although all four legs and abdomen of the defending rat are exposed, the attacker does not bite them. This sequence of bites, flight, chasing, boxing, lateral attack, lying on the back, and standing on top is repeated . . . until the stranger rat is removed. (Blanchard & Blanchard, 1984, pp. 8–9)[1]

---

[1] From "Affect and Aggression: An Animal Model Applied to Human Behavior," by D. C. Blanchard and R. J. Blanchard, in *Advances in the Study of Aggression*, Vol. 1, 1984, edited by D. C. Blanchard and R. J. Blanchard. San Diego: Academic Press. Copyright 1984 by Academic Press. Reprinted by permission.

Another excellent example of gaining insight from careful measurement of defensive and aggressive behaviors is the study of Pellis and colleagues (1988). They began by videotaping interactions between cats and mice. They found that different cats reacted to mice in different ways: Some were efficient mouse killers, some reacted defensively, and some seemed to play with the mice. Careful analysis of the "play" sequences led to two important conclusions. The first conclusion was that, in contrast to the common belief, cats do not play with their prey; the cats that appeared to be playing with the mice were simply vacillating between attack and defense. The second conclusion was that one can best understand each cat's interactions with mice by locating the interactions on a linear scale, with total aggressiveness at one end, total defensiveness at the other, and various proportions of the two in between.

Pellis and colleagues tested their conclusions by reducing the defensiveness of the cats with an antianxiety drug. As predicted, the drug moved each cat along the scale toward more efficient killing. Cats that avoided mice before the injection played with them after the injection, those that played with them before the injection killed them after the injection, and those that killed them before the injection killed them more quickly after the injection. The next time you play with a cat, take the opportunity to analyze the cat's behavior in the light of Pellis's observations.

The defensive and aggressive behaviors of rats have been divided into categories on the basis of three differ-

ent criteria: (1) their *topography* (form), (2) the situations that elicit them, and (3) their apparent function. Several of these categories are described in Table 17.2.

The analysis of aggressive and defensive behaviors has led to the development of the **target-site concept**—the idea that the aggressive and defensive behaviors of an animal are often designed to attack specific sites on the body of another animal while protecting specific sites on its own. For example, the behavior of a socially aggressive rat (e.g., lateral attack) appears to be designed to deliver bites to the defending rat's back and to protect its own face, the likely target of a defensive attack. Conversely, most of the maneuvers of the defending rat (e.g., boxing) appear to be designed to protect the target site on its back.

The discovery that aggressive and defensive behaviors occur in a variety of stereotypical species-common forms was the necessary first step in the identification of their neural bases. Because the different categories of aggressive and defensive behaviors are mediated by different neural circuits, little progress was made in identifying these circuits before the categories were delineated (see Davis, Rainnie, & Cassell, 1994; Kalin, 1993). For example, the lateral septum was once believed to inhibit all aggression, because lateral septal lesions rendered laboratory rats notoriously difficult to handle—the behavior of the lesioned rats was commonly referred to as *septal aggression* or *septal rage*. However, we now know that lateral septal lesions do not

Table 17.2 Categories of Aggressive and Defensive Behaviors in Rats

AGGRESSIVE BEHAVIORS

Predatory aggression	The stalking and killing of members of other species for the purpose of eating them. Rats kill prey, such as mice and frogs, by delivering bites to the back of the neck.
Social aggression	Unprovoked aggressive behavior that is directed at a conspecific for the purpose of establishing, altering, or maintaining a social hierarchy. In mammals, social aggression occurs primarily among males. In rats, it is characterized by piloerection, lateral attack, and bites directed at the defender's back.

DEFENSIVE BEHAVIORS

Intraspecific defense	Defense against social aggression. In rats, it is characterized by freezing and flight and by various behaviors, such as boxing, that are specifically designed to protect the back from bites.
Defensive attacks	Attacks that are launched by animals when they are cornered by threatening conspecifics or members of other species. In rats, they include lunging, shrieking, and biting attacks that are usually directed at the face of the attacker.
Freezing and flight	Responses that many animals use to avoid attack. For example, if a human approaches a wild rat, it will often freeze until the human penetrates its safety zone, whereupon it will explode into flight.
Maternal defensive behaviors	The behaviors by which mothers protect their young. Despite their defensive function, they are similar to male social aggression in appearance.
Risk assessment	Behaviors that are performed by animals in order to obtain specific information that helps them defend themselves more effectively. For example, rats that have been chased by a cat into their burrow do not emerge until they have spent considerable time at the entrance scanning the surrounding environment.
Defensive burying	Rats and other rodents spray sand and dirt ahead with their forepaws to bury dangerous objects in their environment, to drive off predators, and to construct barriers in burrows.

increase experimenter-directed aggression: Rats with lateral septal lesions do not initiate more attacks at the experimenter if they are left undisturbed. They are more defensive, not more aggressive.

Aggression and Testosterone

The fact that social aggression in many species occurs more commonly among males than among females is usually explained with reference to the organizational and activational effects of testosterone. The brief period of testosterone release that occurs around birth in genetic males is thought to organize their nervous systems along masculine lines and hence to create the potential for male patterns of social aggression to be activated by the high testosterone levels that are present after puberty. These organizational and activational effects have been demonstrated in many nonprimate mammalian species. For example, neonatal castration of male mice eliminates the ability of testosterone injections to induce social aggression in adulthood, and adult castration eliminates social aggression in males that do not receive testosterone replacement injections.

In contrast to the research on nonprimates, attempts to demonstrate the organizational and activational effects of testosterone on the aggressive behavior of humans have been mixed. In human males, aggressive behavior does not increase at puberty as testosterone levels increase, it is not eliminated by castration, and it is not increased by testosterone injections that raise blood levels of testosterone to high, but normal, levels (see Albert, Walsh, & Jonik, 1993). However, a few studies have found that violent male criminals and aggressive male athletes tend to have slightly higher testosterone levels than normal (see Bernhardt, 1997). This weak correlation may indicate that aggressive encounters increase testosterone, rather than vice versa (see Archer, 1991).

The fact that human aggression is not strongly related to testosterone levels could mean that its hormonal and neural regulation differ from that in nonprimate mammalian species. However, Albert, Walsh, and Jonik (1993) believe that the evidence favors a different conclusion. They contend that the confusion has arisen because the researchers who study human aggression often fail to appreciate the difference between defensive aggression and social aggression. Most aggressive outbursts in humans are overreactions to real or perceived threat, and they are thus more appropriately viewed as defensive attack than social aggression. Consequently, the failure to find positive correlations between human aggressive behavior and testosterone levels is consistent with the failure to find positive correlations between defensive attack and testosterone levels in other species.

17.3 Stress and Health

When the body is exposed to harm or threat, the result is a cluster of physiological changes that is generally referred to as *the stress response*—or just **stress.** All *stressors,* whether psychological (e.g., dismay at the loss of one's job) or physical (e.g., long-term exposure to cold), produce a similar core pattern of physiological changes; however, it is *chronic psychological stress* (e.g., in the form of chronic fear) that has been most frequently implicated in ill health.

The Stress Response

Hans Selye (pronounced "SELL-yay") first described the stress response in the 1950s, and he quickly recognized its dual nature. In the short term, it produces adaptive changes that help the animal respond to the stressor (e.g., mobilization of energy resources, inhibition of inflammation, and resistance to infection); in the long term, however, it produces changes that are maladaptive (e.g., enlarged adrenal glands).

Selye attributed the stress response to the activation of the *anterior-pituitary adrenal-cortex system.* He concluded that stressors acting on neural circuits (see Herman & Cullinan, 1997) stimulate the release of **adrenocorticotropic hormone (ACTH)** from the anterior pituitary, that the ACTH in turn triggers the release of **glucocorticoids** from the **adrenal cortex,** and that the glucocorticoids produce many of the effects of the stress response. The level of circulating glucocorticoids is the most commonly employed physiological measure of stress.

With his emphasis on the role of the anterior-pituitary adrenal-cortex system in stress, Selye largely ignored the contributions of the sympathetic nervous system. Stressors also activate the sympathetic nervous system, thereby increasing the amounts of epinephrine and norepinephrine released from the **adrenal medulla.**

Most modern theories of stress (see Stanford & Salmon, 1993) acknowledge the major roles of both systems (see Figure 17.8).

The magnitude of the stress response depends not only on the stressor and the individual; it also depends on the strategies the individual adopts to cope with the stress (McEwen, 1994). For example, in a study of women awaiting surgery for possible breast cancer, the levels of stress were lower in those who had convinced themselves to think about their problem in certain ways. Those who had convinced themselves either that they could not possibly have cancer, that their prayers were certain to be answered, or that it was counterproductive to worry about it experienced less stress (Katz et al., 1970).

From the perspective of psychological science, the major contribution of Selye's stress response was that it provided a mechanism by which psychological factors can influence physical illness. All kinds of common psychological stressors (e.g., losing a job, preparing for an examination, ending a re-

lationship) are associated with high circulating levels of glucocorticoids, epinephrine, and norepinephrine; and these in turn have been implicated in many physical disorders (Salovey et al., 2000). For example, fear or stress prior to surgery has been associated with slower postsurgical recovery, including delays in wound healing (Kiecolt-Glaser et al., 1998).

The relation between chronic fear, stress, and ill health is readily apparent in animals undergoing subordination stress. Virtually all mammals—particularly males—experience threats from *conspecifics* (members of the same species) at certain points in their lives. When conspecific threat becomes an enduring feature of daily life, the result is **subordination stress.** Subordination stress is most readily studied in social species that form stable *dominance hierarchies* (pecking orders). What do you think happens to subordinate male rodents who are continually attacked by more dominant males? Several studies (see Blanchard et al., 1993; Delville, Melloni, & Ferris, 1998) have reported that animals exposed to subordination stress are more likely to attack juveniles, to have testes that are reduced in size, to have shorter life spans, and to have lower levels of testosterone and higher levels of corticosterone (a glucocorticoid).

■ Stress and Gastric Ulcers

Stress has long been implicated in the development of gastric ulcers. **Gastric ulcers** are painful lesions to the lining of the stomach and duodenum, which in extreme cases can be life-threatening. In the United States alone, about 500,000 new cases are reported each year (see Livingston & Guth, 1992). Gastric ulcers occur more commonly in people living in stressful situations, and stressors (e.g., confinement to a restraint tube for a few hours) can produce these ulcers in laboratory animals.

For decades, gastric ulcers were regarded as the prototypical *psychosomatic disease* (physical disease with incontrovertible evidence of a psychological cause). However, this view seemed to change with the report that gastric ulcers are caused by bacteria. Indeed, it has been claimed that the ulcer-causing bacteria (*Helicobacter pylori*) are responsible for all cases of gastric ulcers except those caused by nonsteroidal anti-inflammatory agents such as aspirin (Blaser, 1996). This seemed to rule out stress as a causal factor in such ulcers, but a careful consideration of the evidence suggests otherwise (Overmier & Murison, 1997).

The facts do not deny that *H. pylori* damages the stomach wall or that antibiotic treatment of gastric ulcers helps many sufferers. The facts do, however, suggest that *H. pylori* infection alone is insufficient to produce the disorder in most people. Although it is true that most patients with gastric ulcers display signs of *H. pylori* infec-

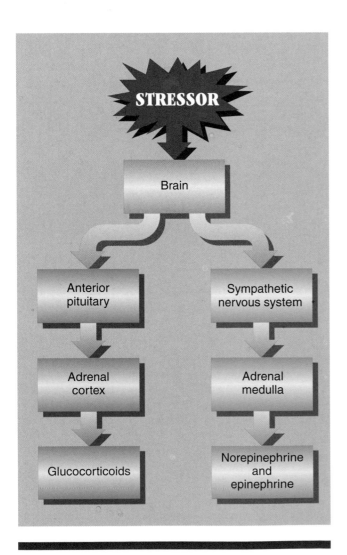

FIGURE 17.8 The two-system view of the stress response.

tion, so too do 75% of healthy control subjects. Also, although it is true that antibiotics improve the condition of many patients with gastric ulcers, so do psychological treatments—and they do it without reducing signs of *H. pylori* infection. Apparently, there is another factor that increases the susceptibility of the stomach wall to damage from *H. pylori,* and this factor is likely to be stress.

Psychoneuroimmunology: Stress, the Immune System, and the Brain

A major breakthrough in the study of stress and health came with the discovery that stress can reduce a person's resistance to infection. This finding had a great impact on the field of psychology, because it showed that stress could play a role in infectious diseases, which up to that point had been regarded as "strictly physical." In so doing, it opened up a vast area of medicine to psychological input (see Cohen, 1996; Cohen & Herbert, 1996). The theoretical and clinical implications of the finding that stress can increase susceptibility to infection were so great that the discovery contributed in the early 1980s to the emergence of a new field of biopsychological research. That field is **psychoneuroimmunology**—the study of interactions among psychological factors, the nervous system, and the immune system (see Maier, Watkins, & Fleshner, 1994). Psychoneuroimmunological research has focused on three important questions, which will be discussed later in this section. First is an introduction to the immune system.

IMMUNE SYSTEM ■ Microorganisms of every description revel in the warm, damp, nutritive climate of your body (see Ploegh, 1998). Your **immune system** keeps your body from being overwhelmed by these invaders. Before it can take any action against an invading micro-organism, the immune system must have some way of distinguishing foreign cells from body cells. That is why **antigens**—protein molecules on the surface of a cell that identify it as native or foreign—play a major role in specific immune reactions (see Beck & Habicht, 1996; Nossal, 1993).

Immune system barriers to infection are of two sorts. First, there are nonspecific barriers, those that act generally and quickly against most invaders. These barriers include mucous membranes, which destroy many foreign micro-organisms, and **phagocytosis**—the process by which foreign micro-organisms and debris are consumed and destroyed by *phagocytes* (specialized body cells that consume foreign micro-organisms and debris)—see Figure 17.9 on page 450. Second, there are specific barriers, those that act specifically against particular strains of invaders. The specific barriers are of two types—cell-mediated and antibody-mediated—each defended by a different class of lymphocytes. **Lymphocytes** are specialized white blood cells that are produced in bone marrow and are stored in the lymphatic system. **Cell-mediated immunity** is directed by **T cells** (T lymphocytes); **antibody-mediated immunity** is directed by **B cells** (B lymphocytes).

The cell-mediated immune reaction begins when a **macrophage**—a type of large phagocyte—ingests a foreign micro-organism. The macrophage then displays the micro-organism's antigens on the surface of its cell membrane (see Figure 17.10 on page 451), and this attracts T cells. Each T cell has two kinds of receptors on its surface, one for molecules that are normally found on the surface of macrophages and other body cells, and one for a specific foreign antigen. There are millions of different receptors for foreign antigens on T cells, but there is only one kind on each T cell, and there are only a few T cells with each kind of receptor. After the micro-organism has been ingested and its antigens have been displayed, a T cell with a receptor for the foreign antigen binds to the surface of the infected macrophage, which initiates a series of reactions (Grakoui et al., 1999; Malissen, 1999). Among these reactions is the multiplication of the bound T cell, which creates more T cells with the specific receptor necessary to destroy all invaders that contain the target antigens and all body cells that have been infected by the invaders.

The antibody-mediated immune reaction begins when a B cell binds to a foreign antigen for which it contains an appropriate receptor. This causes the B cell to multiply and to synthesize a lethal form of its receptor molecules. These lethal receptor molecules, called **antibodies,** are released into the intracellular fluid, where they bind to the foreign antigens and destroy or deactivate the micro-organisms that possess them. Memory B cells for the specific antigen are also produced during the process; these cells have a long life and accelerate antibody-mediated immunity if there is a subsequent infection by the same organism (see Ahmed & Gray, 1996).

Cell-mediated immunity and antibody-mediated immunity are illustrated in Figure 17.10. Both processes take several days the first time a particular foreign antigen is recognized, but responses to subsequent invasions of micro-organisms with the same antigen are much faster thanks to the memory T cells and B cells. This is why *inoculation* (the injection of small samples of an infective micro-organism into healthy individuals) is often an effective preventive measure against the effects of subsequent infection.

Now that you have been introduced to the immune system, it is time to turn to a consideration of psychoneuroimmunological research. It has focused on the following three questions.

HOW DOES STRESS INCREASE SUSCEPTIBILITY TO INFECTION? ■ Many studies have documented the adverse effects of stress on various aspects of immune

FIGURE 17.9 Phagocytosis: A macrophage hunts down and destroys a bacterium.

function, both in humans and in laboratory animals (see Kiecolt-Glaser & Glaser, 2001). In laboratory animals, stressors such as electric shocks, social defeat, overcrowding, the odor of stressed conspecifics, loud noise, and maternal separation have been shown to depress immune function. In humans, the list includes final examinations, sleep deprivation, divorce, bereavement, and caring for a relative who has Alzheimer's disease. However, it has been more difficult than you might think to prove that the effects of stress on immune function are large enough to increase the rate or severity of infectious diseases (see Ader, 2001).

Numerous studies have reported *positive correlations* between stress and ill health in human subjects; for example, students in one study reported more respiratory infections during their final examination period (Glaser et al., 1987). However, causal interpretation of such correlations is never straightforward: Subjects may report more illness during times of stress because they expect to be more ill, because their experience of illness during times of stress is more unpleasant, or because the stress caused changes in their behavior that increased susceptibility to infection (e.g., changes in diet, drug use, or sleep patterns). In contrast, the causal effect of stress on the susceptibility to infectious diseases has been demonstrated in many well-controlled experiments on laboratory animals. Together, the two lines of evidence—the human correlational studies and the controlled laboratory experiments—leave little doubt that stress does increase susceptibility to at least some infectious diseases.

The mechanisms by which stress increases susceptibility to infection have been difficult to specify. The reason is that there are so many possibilities. Stress produces widespread changes in the body through its effects on the anterior-pituitary adrenal-cortex system and the sympathetic adrenal medulla system, and there are innumerable mechanisms

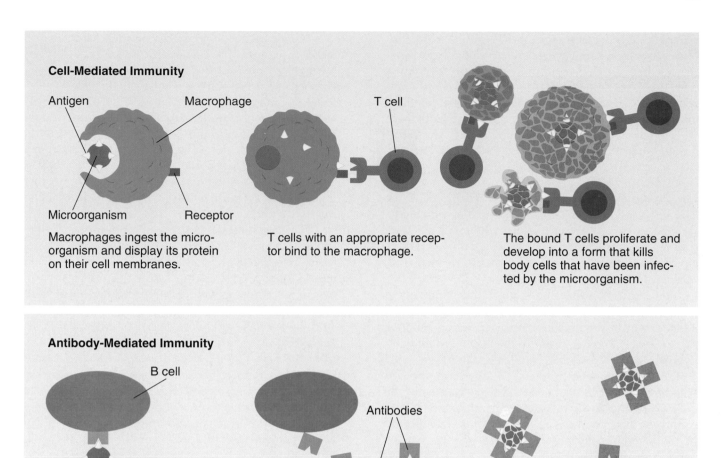

Cell-Mediated Immunity

Antigen   Macrophage   T cell

Microorganism   Receptor

Macrophages ingest the micro-organism and display its protein on their cell membranes.

T cells with an appropriate receptor bind to the macrophage.

The bound T cells proliferate and develop into a form that kills body cells that have been infected by the microorganism.

Antibody-Mediated Immunity

B cell

Antibodies

Antigen   Microorganism

Foreign antigens are bound by B cells with an appropriate receptor.

The B cells replicate and develop into a form that releases antibodies to the antigen.

The antibodies bind to the antigens and kill or deactivate the microorganism.

FIGURE 17.10   Specific barriers to infection: Cell-mediated immunity and antibody-mediated immunity. In cell-mediated immunity, microorganisms or body cells that they have invaded are killed by T cells; in antibody-mediated immunity, microorganisms are killed by antibodies produced by B cells.

by which these effects could influence immune function. For example, both T cells and B cells have receptors for glucocorticoids. In addition, many of the neuropeptides that are released by neurons are also released by cells of the immune system. Conversely, *cytokines,* a class of signaling chemicals originally thought to be produced only by cells of the immune system, have recently been found to be produced in the nervous system (Salzet, Vieau, & Day, 2000).

Although most psychoneuroimmunological research has focused on the role that psychological factors, such as stress, can play in susceptibility to infection, it is important to recognize that this is only half the story. The other half is the effect that infection can have on psychological processes. Maier and Watkins (2000) have suggested that much of the seemingly spontaneous day-

to-day variability in people's behavior, mood, and cognitive efficiency may have its roots in variations in the activity of the immune system—people are continually encountering foreign proteins and mounting immune responses to them without being aware of it. It is widely recognized that hormones are important regulators of brain and behavior; preliminary evidence suggests that cytokines and other signal chemicals of the immune system can play a similar role.

HOW DOES MATERNAL CARE INFLUENCE THE STRESS RESPONSE? ■ To understand the influence of stress on health, it is important to consider the severity of each individual's stress response: Those individuals who react most strongly to stressful events are most likely to experience adverse effects on their health. Accordingly, researchers have paid particular attention to early experiences that can change an individual's stress response (see Francis & Meaney, 1999). One productive line of research has focused on the effects of postnatal handling on the development of stress responses in rodents.

Handling rat pups for a few minutes per day during the first few weeks of their lives has a variety of salutary (health-promoting) effects (see Sapolsky, 1997). The majority of these effects seem to result from a decrease in the magnitude of the handled pups' responses to stressful events, which lasts through adulthood. For example, as adults, rats that were handled as pups display smaller increases in circulating glucocorticoids in response to stressors (see Francis & Meaney, 1999).

It is remarkable that a few hours of handling early in life could have such a significant and lasting effect on the development of the nervous system. However, handling itself does not directly produce the effect. Liu and colleagues (1997) found that handled rats were groomed (licked) more by their mothers, and they hypothesized that the salutary effects of handling are stimulated by the extra grooming rather than by the handling itself. They confirmed this hypothesis by showing that unhandled rat pups that received the most grooming from their mothers developed the profile of decreased glucocorticoid release observed in handled pups. These effects seem to have been produced by an increase in negative feedback from increased glucocorticoid receptors in the hippocampus.

In combination with the finding that rat mothers that are themselves most reactive to stress provide the poorest maternal care to their offspring, the discovery that normal variations in maternal care can have lasting effects on the stress responses of offspring has extremely important theoretical implications (Meaney, 2001). It provides a nongenetic mechanism by which behavioral tendencies can be passed from generation to generation.

WHAT ADVERSE EFFECTS DOES STRESS HAVE ON THE HIPPOCAMPUS? ■ Many of the effects of stress on behavior and health are mediated by the effects of glucocorticoids on the brain. The finding that the hippocampus has a particularly dense population of glucocorticoid receptors focused attention on the effects of stress on this brain structure (see McEwen, 2000b). Remarkably, stress has been found to have adverse effects on the hippocampal anatomy of laboratory animals (see Kim & Yoon, 1998; McEwen, 2000a). A period of stress lasting only a few hours can induce structural changes in the adult hippocampus that can last a month or more. The two changes that have been most thoroughly investigated are (1) the shrinking of hippocampal dendrites and (2) the blockage of hippocampal *neurogenesis* (formation of new neurons).

The shrinking of hippocampal dendrites has been demonstrated in several species following both physical (e.g., restraint) and psychosocial (e.g., exposure of a subordinate male to a dominant male) stress (see McEwen, 2000a). Specifically, the dendrites of *pyramidal neurons* in the *CA3 region* of the hippocampus (see Chapter 11) are both reduced in length and show less branching following a period of stress. This effect on the hippocampus seems to be mediated by the increase in glucocorticoids, because high doses of *corticosterone* (one of the glucocorticoids) can have a similar effect.

The adverse effects of stress on hippocampal neurogenesis have also been demonstrated in several species (see McEwen, 2000a). For example, Gould and colleagues (1998) found that stress blocks the normal creation of new hippocampal *granule cells* (see Chapter 11) in adult male monkeys. They exposed some male monkeys to stress by placing them for 1 hour in an unfamiliar monkey colony, where they became targets of social aggression from the high-ranking male residents; this experience substantially reduced the creation of new hippocampal granule cells in the stressed monkeys.

Four important points about research on stress and the adult hippocampus warrant emphasis here because of their important implications:

1. The adverse effects of stress on the hippocampus are great enough to have behavioral consequences. Exposure to stress disrupts the performance of tasks that are mediated by the hippocampus (e.g., performance on the radial-arm maze).

2. The finding that increased maternal grooming produces lasting reductions in reactivity to stress raises the possibility that maternal care could provide protection against hippocampal damage. Indeed, rats handled as pups and subsequently groomed intensively by their mothers suffered less hippocampal cell loss and fewer memory deficits in old age (Meaney et al., 1988).

3. Comparison of the adverse effects that various kinds of stressors have on the hippocampus indicates that natural stressors (e.g., threat from dominant conspecifics or predators) produce more hippocampal pathology than experimenter-applied stressors (e.g., restraint).

4. There seems to be a large gender difference in the negative impact of stress on the hippocampus. Most studies of the effects of stress on the hippocampus have been conducted with males; the few studies of females have not found such effects (e.g., Galea et al., 1997; Falconer & Galea, 2000). The reason may be the fact that *estradiol* has been shown to promote neurogenesis (Ormerod & Galea, 2001; Tanapat et al., 1999) and to promote recovery from brain damage (Garcia-Segura, Azcoitia, & DonCarlos, 2001).

BrainScan

This chapter is about to change direction: The remaining sections focus on those structures of the brain that mediate the experience of emotion. Accordingly, this is an appropriate point at which to pause and scan your brain to see whether it has retained the introductory material on emotion, fear, and stress. Fill in each of the following blanks with the most appropriate term. The correct answers are provided at the bottom of this page. Before continuing, review material related to your errors and omissions.

1. The theory that the subjective experience of emotion is triggered by ANS responses is called the _____ theory.

2. The pattern of aggressive responses observed in decorticate animals is called _____.

3. Between the amygdala and the fornix in the limbic ring is the _____ . _____.

4. A Duchenne smile, but not a false smile, involves contraction of the _____.

5. Aggression directed by the alpha male of a colony at a male intruder is called _____ aggression.

6. The usual target site of rat defensive attacks is the _____ of the attacking rat.

7. Testosterone increases _____ aggression.

8. Glucocorticoids are released from the _____ _____ as part of the stress response.

9. Stressors increase the release of epinephrine and norepinephrine from the _____ _____.

10. When threats from conspecifics become an enduring feature of daily life, the result is _____.

11. The study of the interactions among psychological factors, the nervous system, and the immune system is called _____.

12. T cells and B cells are involved in cell-mediated and _____ immune reactions, respectively.

13. As adults, rats groomed intensely by their mothers as pups display decreased _____ release in response to stressors.

14. Stress shrinks hippocampal _ _ _____ and blocks hippocampal _____.

Clearly, research on the adverse effects of stress on the brain is in its early stages, but rapid progress is being made and the implications are immense. Partially motivating such research is the finding that the human brain, particularly the hippocampus, displays signs of atrophy following severe, chronic stress (see Sapolsky, 1996; Yehuda, 1997).

17.4 Fear Conditioning

In the past decade, much of the research on the neural mechanisms of emotion has focused on fear conditioning, largely in rats. **Fear conditioning** is the establishment of fear in response to a previously neutral stimulus (the *conditional stimulus*) by presenting it, usually several times, before the delivery of an aversive stimulus (the *unconditional stimulus*). Fear conditioning has been the preferred method of studying fear because the source of fear is always unambiguous (the unconditional stimulus) in fear-conditioning

experiments, and because the development of the fear response can be investigated systematically (see Maren, 2001).

Brain Scan answers: (1) James-Lange, (2) sham rage, (3) hippocampus, (4) orbicularis oculi, (5) social, (6) face, (7) social, (8) adrenal cortex, (9) adrenal medulla, (10) subordination stress, (11) psychoneuroimmunology, (12) antibody-mediated, (13) glucocorticoid, (14) dendrites, neurogenesis.

In the usual fear-conditioning experiment, the subject, typically a rat, hears a tone (conditional stimulus) and then receives a mild electric shock to its feet (unconditional stimulus). After several pairings of the tone and the shock, the rat responds to the tone with a variety of defensive behaviors (e.g., freezing and increased susceptibility to startle) and sympathetic nervous system responses (e.g., increased heart rate and blood pressure). LeDoux and his colleagues have mapped the neural mechanism that mediates this form of auditory fear conditioning (see LeDoux, 2000a, 2000b).

Amygdala and Fear Conditioning

LeDoux and his colleagues began their search for the neural mechanisms of auditory fear conditioning by making lesions in the auditory pathways of rats. They found that bilateral lesions to the *medial geniculate nucleus* (the auditory relay nucleus of the thalamus) blocked fear conditioning to a tone, but bilateral lesions to the auditory cortex did not. This indicated that for auditory fear conditioning to occur, it is necessary for signals elicited by the tone to reach the medial geniculate nucleus but not the auditory cortex. It also indicated that a pathway from the medial geniculate nucleus to a structure other than the auditory cortex plays a key role in fear conditioning. This pathway proved to be the pathway from the medial geniculate nucleus to the amygdala. Lesions of the amygdala, like

lesions of the medial geniculate nucleus, blocked fear conditioning. The amygdala receives input from all sensory systems, and it is believed to be the structure in which the emotional significance of sensory signals is learned and retained.

Several pathways carry signals from the amygdala to brain stem structures that control the various emotional responses. For example, a pathway to the periaqueductal gray of the midbrain elicits appropriate defensive responses (see Bandler & Shipley, 1994), whereas another pathway to the lateral hypothalamus elicits appropriate sympathetic responses.

The fact that auditory cortex lesions do not disrupt fear conditioning to simple tones does not mean that the auditory cortex is not involved in auditory fear conditioning. There are two pathways from the medial geniculate nucleus to the amygdala: the direct one, which you have already learned about, and an indirect one that projects via the auditory cortex (Romanski & LeDoux, 1992). Both routes are capable of mediating fear conditioning to simple sounds; if only one is destroyed, conditioning progresses normally. However, only the cortical route is capable of mediating fear conditioning to complex sounds (Jarrell et al., 1987).

Figure 17.11 illustrates the circuit of the brain that is thought to mediate fear conditioning to auditory conditional stimuli (see LeDoux, 1994). Sound signals from the medial geniculate nucleus of the thalamus reach the amygdala either directly or via the auditory cortex. The amygdala assesses the emotional significance of the

FIGURE 17.11 The structures that are thought to mediate the sympathetic and behavioral responses conditioned to an auditory conditional stimulus.

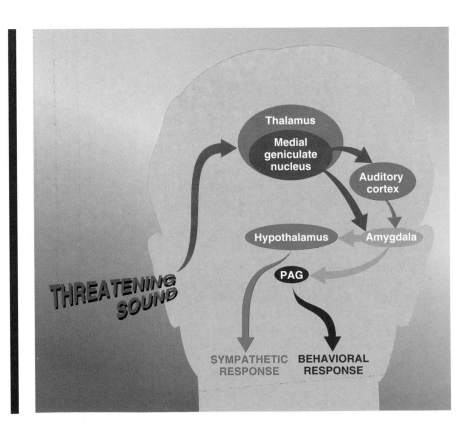

sound on the basis of previous encounters with it, and then the amygdala activates the appropriate response circuits—for example, behavioral circuits in the lateral hypothalamus and sympathetic circuits in the periaque-ductal gray.

■ Anatomy of the Amygdala: A General Comment

The preceding discussion has probably left you with the impression that the amygdala is a single brain structure; it isn't. It is actually a cluster of many nuclei, often referred to as the *amygdala complex*. The amygdala is composed of a dozen or so major regions, which are themselves divided into subregions. Each of these subregions is structurally distinct and has different connections. Making things potentially even more confusing is the fact that the anatomy of the amygdala is so complex that there is no general consensus about how to divide it into its components or what to call them (see LeDoux, 2000b).

Don't worry! I have not raised this issue here because I expect you to master the intricacies of amygdalar anatomy. I merely want you to be able to put what you have learned about the amygdala in context and to appreciate current research on fear conditioning. So far, all evidence suggests that the amygdala plays a critical role in fear conditioning; thus researchers are focusing on its internal circuitry. Researchers are currently tracing input into the amygdala from sensory pathways signaling the presence of a conditional stimulus and studying how, through conditioning, this input activates circuits within the amygdala that trigger pathways to structures outside the amygdala that ultimately produce the fear response (see LeDoux, 2000a, 2000b).

■ Contextual Fear Conditioning and the Hippocampus

Environments, or *contexts*, in which fear-inducing stimuli are encountered can themselves come to elicit fear. For example, if you repeatedly encountered a bear on a particular trail in the forest, the trail itself would elicit fear in you. The process by which benign contexts come to elicit fear through their association with fear-inducing stimuli is called **contextual fear conditioning.**

Contextual fear conditioning has been produced in the laboratory in two ways. First, it has been produced by the conventional fear-conditioning procedure, which we just discussed. For example, if a rat repeatedly receives a footshock following a conditional stimulus, such as a tone, the rat will become fearful of the conditional context (the test chamber) as well as the tone. Second, contextual fear conditioning have been produced by delivering aversive stimuli in a particular context in the absence of any other conditional stimulus. For example, if a rat receives footshocks in a distinctive test chamber, the rat will become fearful of that chamber.

In view of the fact that the hippocampus plays a key role in memory for spatial location, it is reasonable to expect that it would be involved in contextual fear conditioning. This seems to be the case (see LeDoux, 2000a). Two kinds of lesion studies have implicated the hippocampus in contextual fear conditioning. First, bilateral hippocampal lesions made *before* conditioning block the development of a fear response to the context without blocking the development of a fear response to the explicit conditional stimulus (e.g., a tone). Second, bilateral hippocampal lesions made shortly *after* conditioning block the retention of the fear response to the context without disrupting retention of the fear response to the explicit conditional stimulus.

17.5 Brain Mechanisms of Human Emotion

So far in this chapter, you have been introduced to various prominent lines of biopsychological research on emotion. These lines of research have provided you with glimpses of the neural mechanisms of emotion, often in nonhuman species. This, the final section of the chapter, focuses exclusively on the brain mechanisms of emotion in humans.

Most recent studies of the brain mechanisms of emotion in humans are of two types: neuropsychological studies of emotional changes in brain-damaged patients

(see Kolb & Taylor, 2000) and functional brain-imaging studies of healthy subjects (see Dolen & Morris, 2000; Whalen, 1998). The strength of this contemporary research is that it generally confirms and extends the research conducted on nonhuman species. Specifically, recent studies of the brain mechanisms of emotion have repeatedly confirmed the involvement of the amygdala and the prefrontal cortex—although they have not been so kind to the limbic theory (see LeDoux, 2000b; Calder, Lawrence, & Young, 2001).

The study of the brain mechanisms of human emotion is in its early stages. Consequently, most of the progress has been made in discovering the complexities of the problem, rather than providing simple answers. In the following subsections, three such advances are described. Notice that in each case, the amygdala and the prefrontal cortex have been implicated.

■ Specific Brain Structures Play Specific Roles in Emotion

Early theories of the neural mechanisms of emotion (e.g., the limbic system theory) were based on the premise that the activity of a single neural circuit mediates all emotional experience. The results of two lines of recent research have challenged this premise (see Calder, Lawrence, & Young, 2001). First, particular brain structures have been found to be involved in only some human emotions; for example, the amygdala appears to be particularly involved in fear. Second, a particular brain structure found to be involved in a single emotion is not necessarily involved in all aspects of that emotion. For example, effective social behavior depends on the ability to perceive (receive) emotional social signals and the ability to produce (send) them; the human amygdala seems to be more involved in the perception of social fear than in its production. Consider the following case (Anderson & Phelps, 2000).

The Case of S.P., the Woman Who Couldn't Perceive Fear

At the age of 48, S.P. had her right amygdala and adjacent tissues removed for the treatment of epilepsy. Because her left amygdala had been damaged, she in effect had a bilateral amygdalar lesion.

Following her surgery, S.P. had an above average I.Q., and her perceptual abilities were generally normal. Of particular relevance was the fact that she had no difficulty in identifying faces or extracting information from them (e.g., information about age or gender). However, S.P. did have a severe postsurgical deficit in recognizing facial expressions of fear and less striking deficits in recognizing facial expressions of disgust, sadness, and happiness.

In contrast, S.P. had no difficulty specifying which emotion would go with particular sentences. Also, she had no difficulty expressing various emotions using facial expressions upon request.

This case is consistent with previous reports that the human amygdala is specifically involved in perceiving facial expressions of emotion, particularly of

fear (e.g., Broks et al., 1998; Calder et al., 1996). Because S.P. had damage to structures other than her amygdala, it was not possible to determine the extent to which that other damage contributed to the disruption in her perception of facial expressions other than fear.

The case of S.P. is similar to reported cases of Urbach-Wiethe disease (see Aggleton & Young, 2000). **Urbach-Wiethe disease** is a genetic disorder that often results in *calcification* (hardening by conversion to calcium carbonate, the main component of bone) of the amygdala and surrounding anterior medial temporal-lobe structures in both hemispheres. One Urbach-Wiethe patient with bilateral amygdalar damage was found to have lost the ability to recognize facial expressions of fear (Adolphs et al., 1994). Indeed, she could not describe fear-inducing situations or draw fearful expressions although she had no difficulty on tests involving other emotions.

Evidence for the involvement of specific brain structures in particular emotions has also come from research on the prefrontal cortex. For example, Northoff and colleagues (2000) found that the medial and lateral portions of prefrontal cortex respond differently to pictures designed to elicit different emotions. Functional MRIs indicated that negative emotions produce strong medial prefrontal activation, whereas positive emotions produce strong lateral prefrontal activation.

■ The Right Hemisphere Is More Involved Than the Left in Human Emotion

The investigation of neuropsychological brain damage provides a means of studying the cerebral lateralization of human emotion, and so does whole-brain functional brain imaging. Both of these types of research often find a general tendency for structures in the right hemisphere to play a greater role in emotion than structures in the left hemisphere do. However, whether or not there is right-hemisphere dominance depends on the structures under consideration and the particular aspect of emotion under study. Consider the following lines of research.

There are many reports that the right hemisphere is dominant for the perception of emotion—from both facial expression and **prosody** (emotional tone of voice). However, this does not mean that the left hemisphere does not play a role or that all structures of the right hemisphere play a greater role than their corresponding structures in the left hemisphere. For example, Kolb and Taylor (1988) found that the perception of emotion from facial expression was disrupted by right temporal lesions but not at all by left temporal lesions, whereas right and left frontal lesions produced equivalent disruption (see Figure 17.12).

The results of a PET study of the perception of fear from prosody make a similar point (Morris, Scott, & Dolan, 1999). The right amygdala and right prefrontal cortex responded more to fearful speech than did their left-hemisphere counterparts, but the right temporal lobe responded less than the left temporal lobe.

The study of lateralization in the production of emotional expression tells a similarly complex story: Whether or not there is right-hemisphere dominance depends on the part of the hemisphere under consideration. For example, although there is a general right-hemisphere dominance for the production of emotional expression, right frontal and left frontal lesions have been found to have an equivalent disruptive effect on such expression (Kolb & Taylor, 2000).

The general right-hemisphere dominance for producing emotional facial expressions is suggested by a careful study of the emotional expressions themselves. Facial expressions appear to develop sooner and to be of greater magnitude on the left side of the face, which is controlled by the right hemisphere. Remarkably, the same asymmetry of emotional expressions has been documented in monkeys (Hauser, 1993)—see Figure 17.13 on page 458.

■ Individual Differences in the Neural Mechanisms of Emotion

Unlike those parts of the brain that play major sensory and motor roles, the parts that play a role in emotion seem to vary substantially from person to person. This, of course, greatly complicates the search for the neural mechanisms of emotion. Let's consider two lines of research and one case study that have illustrated individual differences in the organization of the neural mechanisms of emotion.

First, Adolphs and colleagues (1999) tested the ability of nine neuropsychological patients with bilateral amygdalar damage to correctly identify facial expressions of emotion. As others had reported, these researchers found that the group of patients as a whole had difficulty identifying facial expressions of fear. However, there were substantial differences among the subjects: Some also had difficulty identifying other negative emotions, but two had no deficits whatsoever in identifying facial expressions. Remarkably, structural MRIs revealed that both of these two subjects had total bilateral amygdalar lesions. Subsequent testing of these two subjects showed that, in addition to having no deficits in identifying facial expressions of emotion, they had no deficits in judging the similarity of pairs of emotional expressions (Hamann & Adolphs, 1999).

Second, Canli and colleagues (2001) used functional MRIs to compare the reactions of healthy women who scored high on personality scales of *extraversion* with those of women who scored high on *neuroticism*. These scales were selected because of their relation to emotion—people high on the extraversion scale have a tendency toward positive emotional reaction; people high on the neuroticism scale have a tendency toward negative emotional reaction. The reactivity of various parts of the brain to pleasant images was found to be correlated with the degree of extraversion; reactivity to negative images was correlated with

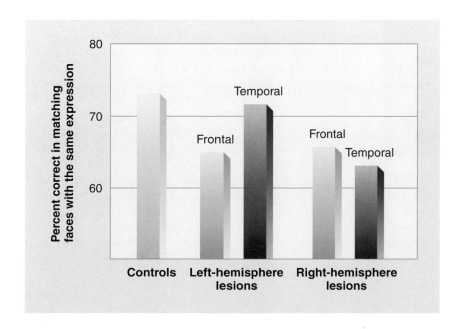

FIGURE 17.12 The ability of control subjects and patients with cortical damage to match photographs of faces on the basis of expression. (Adapted from Kolb & Taylor, 1988.)

FIGURE 17.13 A frame-by-frame illustration of a fear grimace in a rhesus monkey (redrawn with permission of Hauser, 1993). Notice that the expression begins on the left side and is of greater magnitude there, thus suggesting right-side dominance for facial expression.

the degree of neuroticism. The finding that the brains of people with different personalities react differently to emotional stimuli suggests that efforts to identify brain reactions to emotional stimuli must consider differences among the subjects.

The following case study ends the chapter by emphasizing the point that the brain mechanisms of emotion differ from person to person. Fortunately, the reactions of Charles Whitman to brain damage are atypical.

The Case of Charles Whitman, the Texas Tower Sniper

After having lunch with his wife and his mother, Charles Whitman went home and typed a letter of farewell—perhaps as an explanation for what would soon happen.

He stated in his letter that he was having many compelling and bizarre ideas. Psychiatric care had been no help. He asked that his brain be autopsied after he was through; he was sure that they would find the problem.

By all reports, Whitman had been a good person. An Eagle Scout at 12 and a high school graduate at 17, he then enlisted in the Marine Corps, where he established himself as expert marksman. After his discharge, he entered the University of Texas to study architectural engineering.

Nevertheless, in the evening of August 1, 1966, Whitman killed his wife and mother. He professed love for both of them, but he did not want them to face the aftermath of what was to follow.

The next morning, at about 11:30, Whitman went to the Tower of the University of Texas, carrying six guns, ammunition, several knives, food, and water. He clubbed the receptionist to death and shot four more people on his way to the observation deck. Once on the deck, he opened fire on people crossing the campus and on nearby streets. He was deadly, killing people as far as 300 meters away—people who assumed they were out of range.

At 1:24 that afternoon, the police fought their way to the platform and shot Whitman to death. All told, 17 people, including Whitman, had been killed, and another 31 had been wounded (Helmer, 1986).

An autopsy was conducted. Whitman was correct: They found a walnut-sized tumor in his right amygdala.

Themes Revisited

Two of the book's themes were especially prevalent in this chapter. The clinical implications theme appeared frequently because brain-damaged patients have taught us much about the neural mechanisms of emotion and because emotions have a major impact on health. The evolutionary thinking theme occurred almost as frequently because comparative research and the consideration of evolutionary pressures have also had a major impact on current thinking about the biopsychology of emotion.

Current understanding of the biopsychology of emotion is largely the result of the convergence of evolutionary, comparative, and clinical research; however, the cognitive neuroscience approach is starting to play a major role in the study of the neural mechanisms of emotion. Accordingly, the cognitive neuroscience theme came up several times late in the chapter.

The thinking-about-biopsychology theme appeared five times, when the text emphasized the importance of thinking clearly about the use of polygraphy in lie detection, about the critical interpretation of reports of correlations between stress and ill health, about the possibility of susceptibility to stress being communicated from generation to generation by maternal care, and about the complex structure of the amygdala.

Log On

- **http://www.epub.org.br/cm/n05/mente/limbic_i.htm** From the Brain and Mind site, this page is a review of the limbic system and its role in emotion.

- **http://helping.apa.org/daily/neurala.html** Psychology in Daily Life presents an interesting article on the effects of exercise on central noradrenergic activity and the ability to deal with stress.

- **http://www.dana.org/books/radiotv/eyb_0399.cfm** Here is a transcript from a radio show that sponsored by the Dana Alliance and focused on the effects of stress on health; many key researchers in the area participated.

- **http://www.dana.org/books/radiotv/gm_0300.cfm** This second radio-show transcript focuses on emotions and the brain.

- **http://www.cns.nyu.edu/home/ledoux/** This home page for the lab of Dr. Joseph LeDoux describes his work on the neural bases of emotion and includes links to related sites.

Think about It

1. With practice, you could become an expert in the production and recognition of facial expressions. How could you earn a living with these skills?

2. Does the target-site concept have any relevance to human aggression, defense, and play fighting?

3. Genes are not the only means by which behavioral tendencies can be passed from generation to generation. Discuss, with reference to maternal care and susceptibility to stress.

4. The amygdala is not a single structure. Discuss.

5. Evidence suggests that emotion is a right-hemisphere phenomenon. Discuss.

6. Research on emotion has focused on fear. Why?

Key Terms

Adrenal cortex *(p. 447)*
Adrenal medulla *(p. 447)*
Adrenocorticotropic hormone (ACTH) *(p. 447)*
Aggressive behaviors *(p. 445)*
Alpha male *(p. 445)*
Antibodies *(p. 449)*
Antibody-mediated immunity *(p. 449)*
Antigens *(p. 449)*
B cells *(p. 449)*
Cannon-Bard theory *(p. 440)*
Cell-mediated immunity *(p. 449)*

Contextual fear conditioning *(p. 455)*
Control-question technique *(p. 442)*
Decorticate *(p. 440)*
Defensive behaviors *(p. 445)*
Duchenne smile *(p. 445)*
Facial feedback hypothesis *(p. 444)*
Fear *(p. 445)*
Fear conditioning *(p. 453)*
Gastric ulcers *(p. 448)*
Glucocorticoids *(p. 447)*

Guilty-knowledge technique *(p. 442)*
Immune system *(p. 449)*
James-Lange theory *(p. 439)*
Kluver-Bucy syndrome *(p. 440)*
Limbic system *(p. 440)*
Lymphocytes *(p. 449)*
Macrophage *(p. 449)*
Phagocytosis *(p. 449)*
Polygraphy *(p. 442)*
Prosody *(p. 456)*
Psychoneuroimmunology *(p. 449)*
Sham rage *(p. 440)*

Stress *(p. 443)*
Subordination stress *(p. 448)*
Target-site concept *(p. 446)*
T cells *(p. 449)*
Urbach-Wiethe disease *(p. 456)*

ON THE CD

Need some help studying the key terms for this chapter? Check out the electronic flash cards for Chapter 17.

Biopsychology of Psychiatric Disorders

The Brain Unhinged

This chapter is about the biopsychology of *psychiatric disorders*. Before we begin, let's consider the answers to two fundamental questions: What are psychiatric disorders? How do they differ from neuropsychological disorders, which you learned about in Chapter 10?

Defining psychiatric disorders is fairly straightforward: A **psychiatric disorder** (or psychological disorder) is a disorder of psychological function sufficiently severe to require treatment by a psychiatrist or clinical psychologist. Explaining how psychiatric disorders differ from neuropsychological disorders is more difficult because there really are no clear-cut differences between the two types of disorders.

The convention of viewing psychological disorders as being of two fundamentally different types—psychiatric or neuropsychological—is the product of the archaic mind–brain (psychology–biology) dichotomy, discussed in Chapter 2. Neuropsychological disorders are those that were assumed to be products of dysfunctional brains; psychiatric disorders are those that were assumed to be products of dysfunctional minds in the absence of brain pathology. As you will learn in this chapter, there is now plenty of evidence that psychiatric disorders are disorders of dysfunctional brains, and thus the main reason for distinguishing between psychiatric and neuropsychological disorders no longer exists (see Hyman, 2000).

Still, the conventional categories of neuropsychological and psychiatric disorders persist, and there tend to be some differences between them. For example, psychiatric disorders tend to be influenced more by experiential factors (e.g., stress), tend to be the product of more subtle forms of brain pathology, and tend to be less well understood.

This chapter begins with discussion of the biopsychological research on four psychiatric disorders: schizophrenia, affective (emotional) disorders, anxiety disorders, and Tourette's syndrome. In each case, you will learn how advances in understanding the neural mechanisms of the disorder have gone hand in hand with the development of therapeutic drugs. In each of the four cases, the initial breakthrough was the fortuitous discovery of an effective drug; then, study of the drug's mechanisms led to theories of the disorder's neural mechanisms and the development of drugs that are even more effective. The chapter ends with a discussion of the steps involved in establishing the efficacy of new *psychotherapeutic* drugs.

18.1 Schizophrenia

The term *schizophrenia* means the splitting of psychic functions. The term was coined in the early 1900s to describe what was assumed at that time to be the primary symptom of the disorder: the breakdown of integration among emotion, thought, and action.

Schizophrenia is the disease that is most commonly associated with the concept of madness. It attacks about 1% of individuals of all races and cultural groups, typically beginning in adolescence or early adulthood. Schizophrenia occurs in many forms, but the case of Lena introduces you to some of its common features (Meyer & Salmon, 1988).

The Case of Lena, the Catatonic Schizophrenic

Lena's mother was hospitalized with schizophrenia when Lena was 2. She died in the hospital under peculiar circumstances, a suspected suicide. As a child, Lena displayed periods of hyperactivity; as an adolescent, she was viewed by others as odd. Although she enjoyed her classes and got good grades, she seldom established relationships with her fellow students. Lena rarely dated. However, she married her husband only a few months after meeting him. He was a quiet man who tried to avoid fuss or stress at all costs and who was attracted to Lena because she was quiet and withdrawn.

Shortly after their marriage, Lena's husband noticed that Lena was becoming even more withdrawn. She would sit for hours barely moving a muscle. He also found her having lengthy discussions with nonexistent persons.

About 2 years after he first noticed her odd behavior, Lena's husband found her sitting on the floor in an odd posture staring into space. She was totally unresponsive. When he tried to move her, Lena displayed *waxy flexibility*—that is, she reacted like a mannequin, not resisting movement but holding her new position until she was moved again. At that point, he took her to the hospital, where her disorder was immediately diagnosed as *stuporous catatonic schizophrenia* (schizophrenia characterized by long periods of immobility and waxy flexibility).

In the hospital, Lena displayed a speech pattern that is displayed by many schizophrenics; *echolalia* (a speech pattern characterized by repetition of some or all of what has just been heard).

Doctor: How are you feeling today?
Lena: I am feeling today, feeling the feelings today.
Doctor: Are you still hearing the voices?
Lena: Am I still hearing the voices, voices?

What Is Schizophrenia?

The major difficulty in studying and treating schizophrenia is accurately defining it (Peralta & Cuesta, 2000). Its symptoms are complex and diverse; they overlap greatly with those of other psychiatric disorders, and they frequently change during the progression of the disorder (see Andreasen, 1994; Heinrichs, 1993). As a result, there have been many attempts to break schizophrenia down into several disorders, but none of these attempts has proved successful.

The following are common symptoms of schizophrenia, but none of them appears in all cases. Indeed, the recurrence of only one of these symptoms for 8 months is grounds for the diagnosis of schizophrenia:

Bizarre delusions. Delusions of being controlled (e.g., "Martians are making me think evil thoughts"), delusions of persecution (e.g., "My mother is trying to poison me"), delusions of grandeur (e.g., "Michael Jordan admires my sneakers").

Inappropriate affect. Failure to react with an appropriate level of emotionality to positive or negative events (Keltner, Kring, & Bonanno, 1999; Kring, 1999).

Hallucinations. Imaginary voices telling the person what to do or commenting negatively on the person's behavior.

Incoherent thought. Illogical thinking, peculiar associations among ideas, or belief in supernatural forces.

Odd behavior. Long periods with no movement (*catatonia*), a lack of personal hygiene, talking in rhymes, avoiding social interaction, echolalia.

Causal Factors in Schizophrenia

In the first half of the 20th century, the cloak of mysticism began to be removed from mental illness by a series of studies that established schizophrenia's genetic basis. First, it was discovered that although only 1% of the population develops schizophrenia, the probability of schizophrenia's occurring in a close biological relative (i.e., in a parent, child, or sibling) of a schizophrenic is about 10%, even if the relative was adopted shortly after birth by a healthy family (e.g., Kendler & Gruenberg, 1984; Rosenthal et al., 1980). Then, it was discovered that the concordance rates for schizophrenia are higher in identical twins (45%) than in fraternal twins (10%)—see Holzman and Matthyse (1990) and Kallman (1946). Finally, adoption studies have shown that the risk of schizophrenia is increased by the presence of the disorder in biological parents but not by its presence in adoptive parents (Gottesman & Shields, 1982).

The fact that the concordance rate for schizophrenia in identical twins is substantially less than 100% suggests that differences in experience contribute significantly to differences among people in the development of schizophrenia. The current view is that some people inherit a potential for schizophrenia, which may or may not be activated by experience. Supporting this view is a recent comparison of the offspring of a large sample of identical twins who were themselves discordant for schizophrenia (i.e., one had the disorder and one did not); the incidence of schizophrenia was as great in the offspring of the nonschizophrenic twins as in the offspring of the schizophrenic twins (Gottesman & Bertelsen, 1989).

It is clear that schizophrenia has multiple causes. Regions on several different chromosomes have been implicated in the vulnerability to schizophrenia (Brzustowicz et al., 2000; Cowan et al., 2000; Pulver, 2000). Also, a variety of early experiential factors have been implicated in the development of schizophrenia—for example, infections, autoimmune reactions, toxins, traumatic injury, and stress. Such experiential factors are thought to exert their effects on the development of schizophrenia by affecting the course of neurodevelopment. Exposure to stressors is common just before a schizophrenic episode, and several

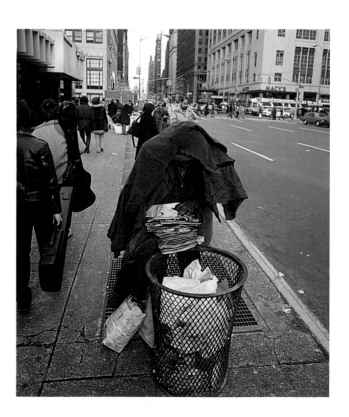

investigators have found correlations between the severity of the stressors and the severity of the subsequent schizophrenic symptoms (see Kring, 2001; Norman & Malla, 1993).

Discovery of the First Antischizophrenic Drugs

The first major breakthrough in the study of the biochemistry of schizophrenia was the accidental discovery in the early 1950s of the first antischizophrenic drug, **chlorpromazine.** Chlorpromazine was developed by a French drug company as an antihistamine. Then, in 1950, a French surgeon noticed that chlorpromazine given prior to surgery to counteract swelling had a calming effect on some of his patients, and he suggested that it might have a calming effect on difficult-to-handle psychotic patients. His suggestion proved to be incorrect, but the research it triggered led to the discovery that chlorpromazine alleviates schizophrenic symptoms: Agitated schizophrenics were calmed by chlorpromazine, and emotionally blunt schizophrenics were activated by it. Don't get the idea that chlorpromazine cures schizophrenia. It doesn't. But in many cases it reduces the severity of schizophrenic symptoms enough to allow institutionalized patients to be discharged.

Shortly after the antischizophrenic action of chlorpromazine was first documented, an American psychiatrist became interested in reports that the snakeroot plant had long been used in India for the treatment of mental illness. He gave **reserpine**—the active ingredient of the snakeroot plant—to his schizophrenic patients and confirmed its antischizophrenic action. Reserpine is no longer used in the treatment of schizophrenia because it produces a dangerous decline in blood pressure at the doses needed for the treatment.

Although the chemical structures of chlorpromazine and reserpine are dissimilar, their antischizophrenic effects are similar in two major respects. First, the antischizophrenic effect of both drugs is manifested only after a patient has been medicated for 2 or 3 weeks. Second, the onset of the antischizophrenic effect of the medication is usually associated with motor effects similar to the symptoms of Parkinson's disease: tremors at rest, muscular rigidity, and a general decrease in voluntary movement. These similarities suggested to researchers that chlorpromazine and reserpine were acting through the same mechanism, one that was related to Parkinson's disease.

Dopamine Theory of Schizophrenia

Paradoxically, the next major breakthrough in the study of schizophrenia came from research on Parkin-

son's disease. In 1960, it was reported that the *striatums* (caudates plus putamens) of persons dying of Parkinson's disease had been depleted of dopamine (Ehringer & Hornykiewicz, 1960). This finding suggested that a disruption of dopaminergic transmission might produce Parkinson's disease and, because of the relation between Parkinson's disease and the antischizophrenic effects of chlorpromazine and reserpine, also suggested that antischizophrenic drug effects might be produced in the same way. Thus was born the *dopamine theory of schizophrenia*—the theory that schizophrenia is caused by too much dopamine and, conversely, that antischizophrenic drugs exert their effects by decreasing dopamine levels.

Lending instant support to the dopamine theory of schizophrenia were two already well-established facts. First, the antischizophrenic drug reserpine was known to deplete the brain of dopamine and other monoamines by breaking down their synaptic vesicles. Second, drugs such as amphetamine and cocaine, which can trigger schizophrenic episodes in normal subjects, were known to increase the extracellular levels of dopamine and other monoamines in the brain.

An important step in the evolution of the dopamine theory of schizophrenia came in 1963, when Carlsson and Lindqvist assessed the effects of chlorpromazine on extracellular levels of dopamine and its *metabolites* (molecules that are created when another molecule is broken down). Although they expected to find that chlorpromazine, like reserpine, depletes the brain of dopamine, they didn't. The extracellular levels of dopamine were unchanged by chlorpromazine, and the extracellular levels of its metabolites were increased. The researchers concluded that both chlorpromazine and reserpine antagonize transmission at dopamine synapses but that they do it in different ways—reserpine by depleting the brain of dopamine and chlorpromazine by binding to dopamine receptors. Carlsson and Lindqvist argued that chlorpromazine is a **false transmitter** (receptor blocker) at dopamine synapses—that is, that it binds to dopamine receptors without activating them and that, in so doing, keeps dopamine from activating them (see Figure 18.1). The researchers further postulated that the lack of activity at postsynaptic dopamine receptors sent a feedback signal to the presynaptic cells that increased their release of dopamine, which was broken down in the synapses. This explained why dopaminergic activity was reduced while extracellular levels of dopamine stayed about the same and extracellular levels of its metabolites were increased. Carlsson and Lindqvist's findings led to an important revision of the dopamine theory of schizophrenia: Rather than high dopamine levels per se, the main factor in schizophrenia was presumed to be high levels of activity at dopamine receptors.

In the mid-1970s, Snyder and his colleagues (Creese, Burt, & Snyder, 1976) assessed the degree to which the various antischizophrenic drugs that had been developed

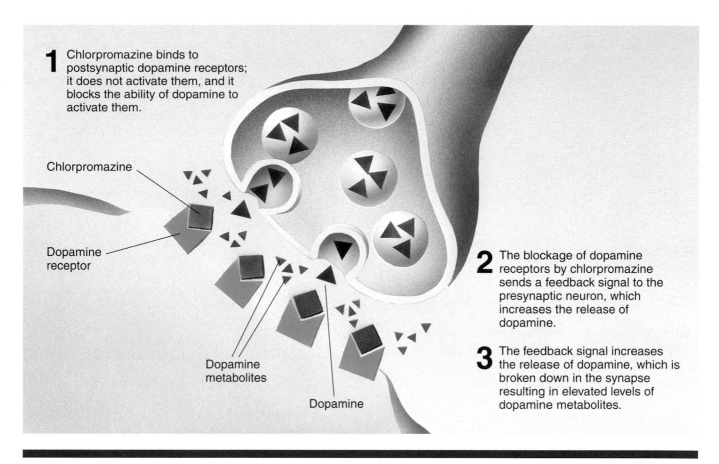

1 Chlorpromazine binds to postsynaptic dopamine receptors; it does not activate them, and it blocks the ability of dopamine to activate them.

Chlorpromazine

Dopamine receptor

Dopamine metabolites

Dopamine

2 The blockage of dopamine receptors by chlorpromazine sends a feedback signal to the presynaptic neuron, which increases the release of dopamine.

3 The feedback signal increases the release of dopamine, which is broken down in the synapse resulting in elevated levels of dopamine metabolites.

FIGURE 18.1   Chlorpromazine, a false transmitter at dopamine synapses.

by that time bind to dopamine receptors. First, they added radioactively labeled dopamine to samples of dopamine-receptor-rich neural membrane obtained from calf striatums. Then, they rinsed away the unbound dopamine molecules from the samples and measured the amount of radioactivity left in them to obtain a measure of the number of dopamine receptors. Next, in other samples, they measured each drug's ability to block the binding of radioactive dopamine to the sample, the assumption being that the drugs with a high affinity for dopamine receptors would leave fewer sites available for the dopamine. In general, they found that chlorpromazine and the other effective antischizophrenic drugs had a high affinity for dopamine receptors, whereas ineffective antischizophrenic drugs had a low affinity. There were, however, several major exceptions, one of them being haloperidol. Although **haloperidol** was one of the most potent antischizophrenic drugs of its day, it had a relatively low affinity for dopamine receptors.

A solution to the haloperidol puzzle came with the discovery that dopamine binds to more than one receptor subtype—five have been identified (Hartmann & Civelli, 1997). It turned out that chlorpromazine and the other antischizophrenic drugs in the same chemical class (the **phenothiazines**) all bind effectively to both D_1 and D_2 receptors, whereas haloperidol and the other antischizo-

phrenic drugs in its chemical class (the **butyrophenones**) all bind effectively to D_2 receptors but not to D_1 receptors.

This discovery of the selective binding of butyrophenones to D_2 receptors led to an important revision in the dopamine theory of schizophrenia. It suggested that schizophrenia is caused by hyperactivity specifically at D_2 receptors, rather than at dopamine receptors in general. Snyder and his colleagues (see Snyder, 1978) subsequently confirmed that the degree to which **neuroleptics**—antischizophrenic drugs—bind to D_2 receptors is highly correlated with their effectiveness in suppressing schizophrenic symptoms (see Figure 18.2 on page 466). For example, the butyrophenone *spiroperidol* had the greatest affinity for D_2 receptors and the most potent antischizophrenic effect.

The D_2 receptor version of the dopamine theory is currently the most widely recognized theory of the neural basis of schizophrenia. The major events in its development are summarized in Table 18.1 on page 466.

Current Research on the Neural Basis of Schizophrenia

Although the evidence implicating D_2 receptors in schizophrenia is strong, the dopamine theory as it

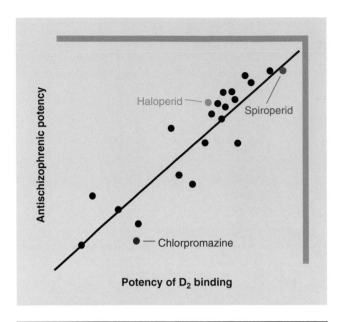

FIGURE 18.2 The positive correlation between the ability of various neuroleptics to bind to D_2 receptors and their clinical potency. (Adapted from Snyder, 1978.)

Table 18.1	The Key Events That Led to the Development and Refinement of the Dopamine Theory of Schizophrenia
Early 1950s	The antischizophrenic effects of both chlorpromazine and reserpine were documented and related to their Parkinsonian side effects.
Late 1950s	The brains of recently deceased Parkinson's patients were found to be depleted of dopamine.
Early 1960s	It was hypothesized that schizophrenia was associated with excessive activity at dopaminergic synapses.
1960s and early 1970s	Chlorpromazine and other clinically effective neuroleptics were found to act as false transmitters at dopamine synapses.
Mid-1970s	The affinity of neuroleptics for dopamine receptors was found to be only roughly correlated with their antischizophrenic potency.
Late 1970s	The binding of existing antischizophrenic drugs to D_2 receptors was found to be highly correlated with their antischizophrenic potency.

currently stands leaves some major questions unanswered. Let's consider four major questions about the theory that have been the focus of recent research.

ARE D_2 RECEPTORS THE ONLY RECEPTORS INVOLVED IN SCHIZOPHRENIA? ■

The development of *atypical neuroleptic drugs* (antischizophrenic drugs that are not primarily D_2 receptor blockers) has challenged the view that D_2 receptors are the only receptors involved in schizophrenia. For example, **clozapine** is effective in the treatment of schizophrenia; yet, unlike *typical neuroleptics*, it does not have a high affinity for D_2 receptors or produce parkinsonian side effects (see Meltzer et al., 1990). The effectiveness of clozapine and other atypical neuroleptics thus suggests that D_2 receptors are not the only receptors involved in schizophrenia. Clozapine, for example, has an affinity for D_1 receptors, D_4 receptors, and several serotonin receptors, as well as for D_2 receptors.

The effectiveness of atypical neuroleptics seemed to constitute a serious challenge to the dopamine theory of schizophrenia, but it has proven to be less problematic than anticipated. There are two major reasons for this. First, all atypical neuroleptics have been found to bind to D_2 receptors—although, by definition, this is not their primary binding site (see Lewis & Lieberman, 2000; Seeman & Kapur, 2000). Second, other lines of research, in addition to the receptor-binding studies, have provided independent support for the dopamine theory. For example, Abi-Dargham and colleagues (2000) used a brain-imaging procedure to establish that recently diagnosed

schizophrenics not previously exposed to neuroleptics have more D_2 receptors and more extracellular dopamine than nonschizophrenic subjects—see Seeman and Kapur (2000).

From a clinical perspective, the introduction of clozapine and other atypical neuroleptics has been beneficial (see Tollefson et al., 2001). These drugs are often useful in treating schizophrenics who have not responded to typical neuroleptics, and they produce fewer, or at least different, side effects. Accordingly, they are often invaluable alternatives to typical neuroleptics.

WHY DOES IT TAKE SEVERAL WEEKS OF NEUROLEPTIC THERAPY TO AFFECT SCHIZOPHRENIC SYMPTOMS? ■

The dopamine theory of schizophrenia has difficulty explaining why it takes several weeks of neuroleptic therapy to alleviate schizophrenic symptoms when dopaminergic transmission is effectively blocked within hours. This discrepancy indicates that the blockage of dopamine receptors is not the specific mechanism by which schizophrenic symptoms are alleviated. It appears that blocking dopamine receptors triggers some slow-developing compensatory change in the brain that is the key factor in the therapeutic effect. One theory is that this critical slow-acting change is the *dopamine-cell depolarization block* (Grace et al., 1997). Neuroleptics initially increase the firing of dopaminergic neurons, but eventually, at about the time that the therapeutic effects are manifested, there is a general decrease in their firing. This decrease is the dopamine-cell depolarization block.

WHAT PARTS OF THE BRAIN ARE INVOLVED IN SCHIZOPHRENIA? ■

Brain-imaging studies of schizophrenic patients typically reveal widespread abnormalities, including an abnormally small cerebral cortex and abnormally large cerebral ventricles (see Frith & Dolan, 1998). However, although the brain damage is widespread, it is not evenly distributed. For example, cortical damage is most prevalent in prefrontal, cingulate, and medial temporal cortex. Surprisingly, though, there is little evidence of structural damage to dopaminergic circuits (see Egan & Weinberger, 1997; Nopoulis et al., 2001).

One major question about the brain pathology of schizophrenics is whether or not it is developmental: Do the brains of schizophrenics develop abnormally, or do they develop normally and then suffer some type of damage? Two types of indirect evidence suggest that schizophrenia is a developmental disorder (see Harrison, 1997; Raedler, Knable, & Weinberger, 1998): First, there are no obvious signs of ongoing neural degeneration in the brains of schizophrenics; second, the brain pathology associated with schizophrenia seems to be largely devel-

oped when the disorder is first diagnosed (see Lewis & Lieberman, 2000).

WHY ARE NEUROLEPTICS EFFECTIVE AGAINST ONLY SOME SCHIZOPHRENIC SYMPTOMS? ■
Neuroleptics do not improve the condition of all schizophrenics, and when they do have therapeutic effects, they do not act equally on all symptoms. In general, neuroleptics are more effective in the treatment of *positive schizophrenic symptoms* (such as incoherence, hallucinations, and delusions), which are assumed to be caused by increased neural activity, than they are in the treatment of *negative schizophrenic symptoms* (such as blunt affect and poverty of speech), which are assumed to be caused by decreased neural activity. Accordingly, it has been suggested that positive schizophrenic symptoms are produced by D_2 hyperactivity and that negative schizophrenic symptoms are produced by structural pathology.

18.2 Affective Disorders: Depression and Mania

All of us have experienced depression. Depression is a normal reaction to grievous loss such as the loss of a loved one, the loss of self-esteem, the loss of personal possessions, or the loss of health. However, there are people

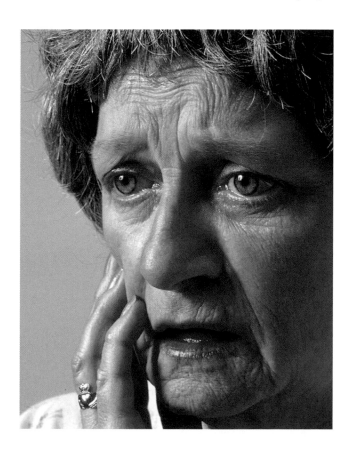

whose tendency toward depression is out of proportion. These people repeatedly fall into the depths of despair, often for no apparent reason; and their depression can be so extreme that it is almost impossible for them to meet the essential requirements of their daily lives—to keep a job, to maintain social contacts, or even to maintain an acceptable level of personal hygiene. It is these people who are said to be suffering from clinical **depression.** The case of P.S. introduces you to some of the main features of clinical depression (Spitzer et al., 1983).

The Case of P.S., the Weeping Widow

P.S. was a 57-year-old widow and mother of four. She was generally cheerful and friendly and known for her meticulous care of her home and children. She took great pride in having reared her children by herself following the death of her husband 14 years earlier.

For no apparent reason, her life began to change. She suddenly appeared more fatigued, less cheerful, and more lackadaisical about her housework. Over the ensuing weeks, she stopped going to church and cancelled all of her regular social engagements, including the weekly family dinner, which she routinely hosted. She started to spend all her time sleeping or rocking back and forth and sobbing in her favorite chair. She wasn't eating, bathing, or changing her clothes. And her house was rapidly becoming a garbage dump. She

CHAPTER 18 *Biopsychology of Psychiatric Disorders*

woke up every morning at about 3:00 A.M. and was unable to get back to sleep.

Things got so bad that her two children who were still living with her called her oldest son for advice. He drove from the nearby town where he lived. What he found reminded him of an episode about 10 years earlier, when his mother had attempted suicide by slitting her wrists.

At the hospital, P.S. answered few questions. She cried throughout the admission interview and sat rocking in her chair wringing her hands and rolling her head up towards the ceiling. When asked to explain what was bothering her, she just shook her head no.

She was placed on a regimen of antidepressant medication. Several weeks later, she was discharged, much improved.

Categories of Affective Disorders

Depression is not the only *affective disorder* (psychotic disorder of emotion). The other is **mania,** which is in many respects the opposite of depression. Mania is an affective disorder characterized by overconfidence, impulsivity, distractibility, and high energy.

During periods of mild mania, people are talkative, energetic, impulsive, positive, and very confident. In this state, they can be very effective at certain jobs and can be great fun to be with. But when mania becomes extreme, it is a serious clinical problem. The florid manic often awakens in a state of unbridled enthusiasm, with an outflow of incessant chatter that careens nonstop from topic to topic. No task is too difficult. No goal is unattainable. This confidence and grandiosity, coupled with high energy, distractibility, and a leap-before-you-look impulsiveness, result in a continual series of disasters. Mania often leaves behind it a trail of unfinished projects, unpaid bills, and broken relationships.

Many depressive patients experience periods of mania. Those who do are said to suffer from **bipolar affective disorder.** Those depressives who do not experience periods of mania are said to suffer from **unipolar affective disorder.**

Depression is often divided into two categories. Depression triggered by a negative experience (e.g., the death of a friend, the loss of a job) is called **reactive depression;** depression with no apparent cause is called **endogenous depression.**

The high incidence of affective disorders in industrialized Western societies has been well documented. About 6% of people suffer from unipolar affective disorder at some point in their lives, and about 1% suffer from

ON THE CD

The module called *Recognizing Mood Disorders (Affective Disorders)* includes a general overview of affective disorders and a 45-second audio clip of a patient describing one such disorder.

bipolar affective disorder. Unipolar affective disorder tends to be twice as prevalent in women as in men, but there is no sex difference in the incidence of bipolar affective disorder. About 10% of those suffering from affective disorders commit suicide (see Culbertson, 1997; Weissman & Olfson, 1995).

Although there is less information about the incidence of affective disorders in nonindustrialized societies, there are indications that culture may play a major role in the disorders—or at least in the tendency to seek treatment for them. For example, in Chile and China, many times more women than men seek treatment for depression (see Kleinman & Cohen, 1997).

Causal Factors in Affective Disorders

Genetic factors contribute to differences among people in the development of affective disorders (see MacKinnon, Jamison, & DePaulo, 1997). Twin studies of affective disorders suggest a concordance rate of about 60% for identical twins and 15% for fraternal twins, whether they are reared together or apart. Although there are many exceptions, there is a tendency for affected twins to suffer from the same type of disorder, unipolar or bipolar; and the concordance rates for bipolar disorders tend to be higher than those for unipolar disorders.

Most of the research on the causal role of experience in affective disorders has focused on the role of stress in the etiology of depression. Several studies have shown that stressful experiences can trigger attacks of depression in already depressed individuals. For example, Brown (1993) found that over 84% of a large sample of patients seeking treatment for depression had experienced severe stress in the preceding year, in comparison to 32% of a group of control subjects. However, it has been more difficult to confirm the hypothesis that early exposure to stress increases the likelihood of developing depression in adulthood (Kessler, 1997).

Discovery of Antidepressant Drugs

Four classes of drugs have been developed for the treatment of affective disorders: monoamine oxidase inhibitors, tricyclic antidepressants, lithium, and selective monoamine-reuptake inhibitors.

MONOAMINE OXIDASE INHIBITORS ■ **Iproniazid,** the first antidepressant drug, was originally developed for the treatment of tuberculosis; for which it proved to be a dismal flop. However, interest in the antidepressant potential of the drug was kindled by the observation that it left patients with tuberculosis less depressed about their disorder. As a result, iproniazid was tested on a mixed group of psychiatric patients and was found to be effective against depression. It was first marketed as an antidepressant drug in 1957.

Iproniazid is a monoamine agonist; it increases the levels of monoamines (e.g., norepinephrine and serotonin) by inhibiting the activity of *monoamine oxidase (MAO),* the enzyme that breaks down monoamine neurotransmitters in the cytoplasm of the neuron. **MAO inhibitors** have several side effects; the most dangerous is known as the **cheese effect.** Foods such as cheese, wine, and pickles contain an amine called *tyramine,* which is a potent elevator of blood pressure. Normally, these foods have little effect on blood pressure, because tyramine is rapidly metabolized in the liver by MAO. However, people who take MAO inhibitors and consume tyramine-rich foods run the risk of strokes caused by surges in blood pressure.

TRICYCLIC ANTIDEPRESSANTS ■ The **tricyclic antidepressants** are so named because of their antidepressant action and because their chemical structures include a three-ring chain. **Imipramine,** the first tricyclic antidepressant, was initially thought to be an antischizophrenic drug. However, when its effects on a mixed sample of psychiatric patients were assessed, its antidepressant effect was immediately obvious. Tricyclic antidepressants block the reuptake of both serotonin and norepinephrine, thus increasing their levels in the brain. They are a safer alternative to MAO inhibitors.

LITHIUM ■ The discovery of the ability of **lithium**—a simple metallic ion—to block mania is yet another important pharmacological breakthrough that was made by accident. John Cade, an Australian psychiatrist, mixed the urine of manic patients with lithium to form a soluble salt; then he injected the salt into a group of guinea pigs to see if it would induce mania. As a control, he injected lithium into another group. Instead of inducing mania, the urine solution seemed to calm the guinea pigs; and because the lithium control injections had the same effect, Cade concluded that lithium, not uric acid, was the calming agent. In retrospect, Cade's conclusion was incredibly foolish. We now know that at the doses he used, lithium salts produce extreme nausea. To Cade's untrained eye, his subjects' inactivity may have looked like calmness. But the subjects weren't calm; they were sick. In any case, flushed with what he thought was the success of his guinea pig experiments, in 1954 Cade tried lithium on a group of 10 manic patients, and it proved remarkably effective.

There was little immediate reaction to Cade's report. Few scientists were impressed by Cade's scientific credentials, and few drug companies were interested in spending millions of dollars to evaluate the therapeutic potential of a metallic ion that could not be protected by a patent. Accordingly, the therapeutic potential of lithium was not fully appreciated until the late 1960s, when it was it was discovered that the ion—in addition to acting against mania—reduced the depression of

some bipolar patients. Consequently, for a time, lithium was the treatment of choice for bipolar affective disorder.

Today, lithium is still widely used in the treatment of mania, but it has largely been supplanted in the treatment of bipolar affective disorder by new drugs that are more consistently effective against depression. Lithium's therapeutic effects are thought to be mediated by its agonistic effects on serotonin function.

SELECTIVE MONOAMINE-REUPTAKE INHIBITORS ■ In the late 1980s, a new class of drugs—the selective serotonin-reuptake inhibitors (SSRIs)—was introduced for treating depression. Selective serotonin-reuptake inhibitors exert agonistic effects on serotonergic transmission by blocking the reuptake of serotonin from synapses—see Figure 18.3 on page 470.

Fluoxetine, which is marketed under the name **Prozac,** was the first selective serotonin-reuptake inhibitor. Prozac's structure is a slight variation of that of imipramine and other tricyclic antidepressants, and in fact Prozac is no more effective than imipramine in treating depression. Nevertheless, it was immediately embraced by the psychiatric community and has been prescribed in many millions of cases.

The remarkable popularity of Prozac is attributable to two things. First, Prozac has few side effects; second, it is effective against a wide range of psychological disorders in addition to depression. Because Prozac is so effective against disorders that were once considered to be the exclusive province of psychotherapy (e.g., lack of self-esteem, fear of failure, excessive sensitivity to criticism, and inability to experience pleasure), it has had a major impact on the fields of psychiatry and clinical psychology.

The success of Prozac spawned the introduction of two kinds of imitators for the treatment of affective disorders: new selective serotonin-reuptake inhibitors (e.g., Paxil, Zoloft, Luvox, Remeron) and a similar class of drugs, the selective norepinephrine-reuptake inhibitors (SNRIs). These have proven to be as effective as selective serotonin-reuptake inhibitors in the treatment of depression.

■ Neural Mechanisms of Depression

The search for the neural mechanisms of affective disorders has focused on depression. However, the fact that depression and mania often occur in the same patients—that is, in those with bipolar affective disorder—and the fact that some drugs act against both of these disorders suggest that the mechanisms of the two are closely related.

MONOAMINE THEORY OF DEPRESSION ■ The most widely accepted theory of depression is the *monoamine theory.* The monoamine theory of depression holds that depression is associated with underactivity at serotonergic and noradrenergic synapses. It is based on

FIGURE 18.3 Blocking of serotonin reuptake by fluoxetine (Prozac).

the fact that monoamine oxidase inhibitors, tricyclic antidepressants, selective serotonin-reuptake inhibitors, and selective norepinephrine-reuptake inhibitors are all agonists of serotonin, norepinephrine, or both.

The monoamine theory of depression has been supported by the results of some autopsy studies (see Nemeroff, 1998). Certain subtypes of norepinephrine and serotonin receptors have been found to be elevated in depressed individuals who have not received pharmacological treatment. This implicates a deficit in monoamine release: When an insufficient amount of a neurotransmitter is released at a synapse, there are usually compensatory increases in the number of receptors for that neurotransmitter. This process of compensatory proliferation of receptors is called **up-regulation.**

The monoamine theory of depression has difficulty accounting for two important facts, though (Wong & Licinio, 2001): the fact that extracellular monoamine levels are elevated within hours of the onset of drug therapy, whereas the drugs usually have to be taken for 3 or more weeks before therapeutic effects are first observed, and the fact that serotonergic and adrenergic agonists have equivalent therapeutic effects. To explain these observations, the current working hypothesis is that following a period of chronic exposure, both serotonin and norepinephrine agonists influence the expression of the same set of genes (Wong & Licinio, 2001).

DIATHESIS–STRESS MODEL OF DEPRESSION ■ A second prominent theory of depression is the *diathesis–stress model.* According to this theory (see Nemeroff,

1998), some people inherit a **diathesis** (genetic susceptibility) which is incapable of initiating the disorder by itself. The central idea of the diathesis–stress model is that if susceptible individuals are exposed to stress early in life, their systems become permanently sensitized, and they over-react to mild stressors for the rest of their lives.

The main support for this theory comes from evidence that the endocrine systems of depressed people react abnormally to stress (see Brown, Rush, & McEwen, 1999; Holsboer, 2000; Young et al., 2000). Depressed individuals synthesize more hypothalamic *corticotropin-releasing hormone,* release more *adrenocorticotropic hormone* from the anterior pituitary, and release more *glucocorticoids* from the adrenal cortex. Moreover, injections of *dexamethasone,* a synthetic glucocorticoid, do not reduce the release of glucocorticoids by negative feedback in many depressed patients as they do in normal subjects.

One hypothesis has linked the hippocampus to the diathesis–stress model (see Jacobs, van Praag, & Gage, 2000). You may recall from earlier chapters that the hippocampus is one of the few areas of the mammalian brain where new neurons are created throughout adulthood. Exposure to stress blocks this *neurogenesis* in the hippocampus. Accordingly, it has been proposed that the blocking of hippocampal neurogenesis triggers depression.

■ Antidepressant Effect of Sleep Deprivation

I would be remiss if I did not point out one of the most puzzling findings about the treatment of depression: More than 50% of depressed patients display dramatic improvements after one night of sleep deprivation (Demet et al., 1999). The antidepressant action of sleep deprivation cannot be explained by current theories of depression. Also, the finding is of little therapeutic relevance because the depression returns once the patients return to their normal sleep pattern. However, studying how sleep deprivation reduces depression may lead to a better understanding of the neural mechanism of depression and to the development of new antidepressant drugs.

Functional Brain Imaging and Affective Disorders

Unlike schizophrenics, patients suffering from affective disorders display no obvious brain damage.

Accordingly, functional, rather than structural, brain-imaging methods are typically used to visualize differences in the brains of living patients suffering from affective disorders (Davidson et al., 1999).

Not surprisingly, studies using fMRI and PET changes have implicated in depression those brain structures involved in emotion—see Chapter 17. For example, during attacks of depression, reduced activity has been observed in the amygdala (Drevets et al., 1992) and in parts of the prefrontal lobes (e.g., Drevets et al., 1997). The functional brain-imaging studies of affective disorders have a weakness, however. There is no way of knowing whether the observed changes are a cause or an effect of the disorders.

18.3 Anxiety Disorders

Anxiety—chronic fear that persists in the absence of any direct threat—is a common psychological correlate of stress. Anxiety is adaptive if it motivates effective coping behaviors; however, when it becomes so severe that it disrupts normal functioning, it is referred to as an **anxiety disorder.** All anxiety disorders are associated with feelings of anxiety (e.g., fear, worry, despondency) and with a variety of physiological stress reactions—for example, *tachycardia* (rapid heartbeat), *hypertension* (high blood pressure), nausea, breathing difficulty, sleep disturbances, and high glucocorticoid levels.

Anxiety disorders are the most prevalent of all psychiatric disorders; in Great Britain, for example, 1 in 5 women and 1 in 10 men take antianxiety medication each year (Dunbar, Perera, & Jenner, 1989). An estimated 25% of people suffer from an anxiety disorder at some point in their lives.

The case of M.R., a woman who was afraid to leave her home, serves to introduce anxiety.

The Case of M.R., the Woman Who Was Afraid To Go Out

M.R. was a 35-year-old woman who developed a pathological fear of leaving home. The onset of her problem was sudden. Following an argument with her husband, she went out to mail a letter and cool off, but before she could accom-

plish her task, she was overwhelmed by dizziness and fear. She immediately struggled back to her house and rarely left it again, for about 2 years. Then, she gradually started to improve.

Her recovery was abruptly curtailed, however, by the death of her sister and another argument with her husband. Following the argument, she tried to go shopping, panicked, and had to be escorted home by a stranger. Following that episode, she was not able to leave her house by herself without experiencing an anxiety attack. Shortly after leaving home by herself, she would feel dizzy and sweaty, and her heart would start to pound; at that point, she would flee home to avoid a full-blown panic attack.

Although M.R. could manage to go out if she was escorted by her husband or one of her children, she felt anxious the entire time. Even with an escort, she was terrified of crowds—crowded stores, restaurants, or movie theaters were out of the question.

Four Classes of Anxiety Disorders

There are four major classes of anxiety disorders: generalized anxiety disorders, phobic anxiety disorders, panic disorders, and obsessive-compulsive disorders.

Generalized anxiety disorders are characterized by stress responses and extreme feelings of anxiety that occur in the absence of any obvious precipitating stimulus. **Phobic anxiety**

disorders are similar to generalized anxiety disorders except that they are triggered by exposure to particular objects (e.g., birds, spiders) or situations (e.g., crowds, darkness). **Panic disorders** are characterized by rapid-onset attacks of extreme fear and severe symptoms of stress (e.g., choking, heart palpitations, shortness of breath); they are often components of generalized anxiety and phobic disorders, but they also occur as separate disorders. **Obsessive-compulsive disorders** are characterized by frequently recurring, uncontrollable, anxiety-producing thoughts (obsessions) and impulses (compulsions). Responding to them—for example, by repeated compulsive hand washing—is a means of dissipating the anxiety associated with them.

M.R., the woman who was afraid to go out, suffered from a particularly common phobic anxiety disorder: agoraphobia. **Agoraphobia** is the pathological fear of public places and open spaces.

Etiology of Anxiety Disorders

Because anxiety disorders are often triggered by identifiable stressful events and because the anxiety is often focused on particular objects or situations, the role of experience in shaping the disorder is often readily apparent (see Anagnostaras, Craske, & Fanselow, 1999). For example, in addition to having agoraphobia, M.R. was obsessed by her health—particularly by high blood pressure, although hers was in the normal range. The fact that both her

grandfather and father suffered from high blood pressure and died of heart attacks clearly shaped this component of her disorder.

Like other psychiatric disorders, anxiety disorders have a significant genetic component. The concordance rates for various anxiety disorders are substantially higher for identical twins than for fraternal twins. Still, although identical twins have the same genetic susceptibility to anxiety disorders, the timing and focus of their attacks often reflect their individual experiences.

Pharmacological Treatment of Anxiety Disorders

Two classes of drugs are effective against anxiety disorders: benzodiazepines and serotonin agonists.

BENZODIAZEPINES ■ Benzodiazepines such as *chlordiazepoxide* (Librium) and *diazepam* (Valium) are widely prescribed for the treatment of anxiety disorders. They are also prescribed as hypnotics (sleep-inducing drugs), anticonvulsants, and muscle relaxants. Indeed, benzodiazepines are the most widely prescribed psychoactive drugs; approximately 10% of adult North Americans are currently taking them. The benzodiazepines have several adverse side effects: sedation, ataxia (disruption of motor activity), tremor, nausea, addiction, and a withdrawal reaction that includes rebound anxiety.

The behavioral effects of benzodiazepines are thought to be mediated by their agonistic action on $GABA_A$ receptors. Benzodiazepines bind to a $GABA_A$ receptor at a different site than the one at which GABA molecules bind and, in so doing, increase the binding of GABA molecules to the receptor (see Figure 4.18). $GABA_A$ receptors are distributed widely throughout the brain.

SEROTONIN AGONISTS ■ Serotonin agonists are also widely used in the treatment of anxiety disorders. For example, *buspirone*, which is often prescribed for the treatment of anxiety, has selective agonist effects at one subtype of serotonin receptor, the 5-HT_{1A} receptor. The main advantage of buspirone over the benzodiazepines is its specificity: It produces *anxiolytic* (antianxiety) effects without producing ataxia, muscle relaxation, and sedation, the common side effects of the benzodiazepines. Presumably, the selectivity of its behavioral effects is attributable to its selective pattern of binding.

The serotonin agonists that are used to treat depression (e.g., monoamine oxidase inhibitors, tricyclic antidepressants, and selective serotonin-reuptake inhibitors) also have anxiolytic effects. The selective serotonin-reuptake inhibitors are commonly used in the treatment of anxiety disorders.

Animal Models of Anxiety

Animal models have played an important role in the study of anxiety and in the assessment of the anxiolytic potential of new drugs (see Green, 1991; Treit, 1985). These models typically involve animal defensive behaviors, the implicit assumption being that defensive behaviors are motivated by fear and that fear and anxiety are similar states. Three animal behaviors that model anxiety are elevated-plus-maze performance, defensive burying, and risk assessment.

In the *elevated-plus-maze test,* rats are placed on a four-armed plus-sign-shaped maze that is 50 centimeters above the floor. Two arms have sides and two arms have no sides, and the measure of anxiety is the proportion of time the rats spend in the enclosed arms, rather than venturing onto the exposed arms (see Pellow et al., 1985).

In the *defensive-burying test* (see Figure 5.25), rats are shocked by a wire-wrapped wooden dowel mounted on the wall of a familiar test chamber. The measure of anxiety is the amount of time the rats spend spraying bedding material from the floor of the chamber at the source of the shock with forward thrusting movements of their head and forepaws (see Treit et al., 1993).

In the *risk-assessment test,* after a single brief exposure to a cat on the surface of a laboratory burrow system, rats flee to their burrows and freeze. Then, they engage in a variety of risk-assessment behaviors (e.g., scanning the surface from the mouth of the burrow or exploring the surface in a cautious stretched posture) before their behavior returns to normal (see Blanchard, Blanchard, & Rodgers, 1991; Blanchard et al., 1990). The measures of anxiety are the amounts of time that the rats spend in freezing and in risk assessment.

The elevated-plus-maze, defensive-burying, and risk-assessment tests of anxiety have all been validated by demonstrations that benzodiazepines reduce the various indexes of anxiety used in the tests, whereas nonanxiolytic drugs usually do not. There is a potential problem with this line of evidence, however. The potential problem stems from the fact that many cases of anxiety do not respond well to benzodiazepine therapy. Accordingly, existing animal models of anxiety may be models of benzodiazepine-sensitive anxiety rather than of anxiety in general, and thus the models may not be sensitive to anxiolytic drugs that act by a different (i.e., a nonGABA-ergic) mechanism. For example, the atypical anxiolytic *buspirone* does not have a reliable anxiolytic effect in the elevated-plus-maze test.

Neural Bases of Anxiety Disorders

Like current theories of the neural bases of schizophrenia and depression, current theories of the neural bases of anxiety disorders rest heavily on the analysis of therapeutic drug effects. The fact that many anxiolytic drugs are agonists at either GABA$_A$ receptors (e.g., the benzodiazepines) or serotonin receptors (e.g., buspirone and Prozac) has focused attention on the possible role in anxiety disorders of deficits in both GABAergic and serotonergic transmission.

Speculations about the brain structures involved in anxiety disorders have focused on the amygdala because of the central role it plays in fear and defensive behavior (see LeDoux, 1995). In support of the involvement of the amygdala in anxiety disorders are the following findings: The amygdala has a high concentration of GABA$_A$ receptors, local infusion of benzodiazepines into the amygdala produces anxiolytic effects in laboratory animals, and local injections of GABA antagonists into the amygdala can block the anxiolytic effects of *systemic* (into general circulation) injections of benzodiazepines (see Davis, Rainnie, & Cassell, 1994).

Brain-imaging studies of patients suffering from anxiety have not revealed obvious structural pathology in the amygdala or any other brain structure. In contrast, many functional changes have been reported, but so far none has been consistently replicated. One likely problem may be that crude diagnostic categories inevitably cloud brain images that are obtained by averaging observations from several subjects (Reiman et al., 2000).

18.4 Tourette's Syndrome

Tourette's syndrome is the last of the four psychiatric disorders discussed in this chapter. It differs from the first three (schizophrenia, affective disorders, and anxiety) in the specificity of its effects. And they are as interesting as they are specific. The case of R.G. introduces you to Tourette's syndrome (see Spitzer et al., 1983).

The Case of R.G.—Barking Mad

When R.G. was 15, he developed *tics* (involuntary twitchlike movements). For the first week, his tics took the form of involuntary blinking, but after that they started to involve other parts of the body, particularly his arms and legs.

R.G. and his family were religious, so it was particularly distressing when his tics became verbal. He began to curse repeatedly and involuntarily. Involuntary cursing is a common symptom of Tourette's syndrome and of several other psychiatric and neurological disorders (Van Lancker & Cummings, 1999). R.G. also started to bark like a dog. Finally, he developed echolalia: When his mother said, "Dinner is ready," he responded, "Is ready, is ready."

Prior to the onset of R.G.'s symptoms, he was an A student, apparently happy and with an outgoing, engaging personality. Once his symptoms developed, he was jeered at, imitated, and ridiculed by his schoolmates. He responded by becoming anxious, depressed, and withdrawn. His grades plummeted.

Once R.G. was taken to a psychiatrist by his parents, his condition was readily diagnosed—the symptoms of Tourette's syndrome are unmistakable. Medication eliminated 99% of his symptoms, and once his disorder was explained to him and he realized he was not mad, he resumed his former outgoing manner.

What Is Tourette's Syndrome?

Tourette's syndrome is a disorder of **tics** (involuntary, repetitive, stereotyped movements or vocalizations) (Jankovic, 2001; Leckman et al., 2001). It typically begins in childhood with simple motor tics, such as eye blinking or head movements, but the symptoms develop over time, becoming more complex and severe. Common complex motor tics include making lewd gestures, hitting, touching objects, squatting, hopping, and twirling. Common verbal tics include inarticulate sounds (e.g., barking, coughing, grunting), *coprolalia* (uttering obscenities), *echolalia* (repetition of another's words), and *palilalia* (repetition of one's own words).

Tourette's syndrome develops in approximately 0.7% of children and is three times more frequent in males than in females. There is a major genetic component: Concordance rates are 55% for identical twins and 8% for fraternal twins (see Pauls, 2001).

The majority of patients with Tourette's syndrome also display signs of *attention-deficit–hyperactivity disorder*, obsessive-compulsive disorder, or both (Sheppard et al., 1999). For example, R.G. was obsessed by odd numbers and refused to sit in even-numbered seats.

Although the tics of Tourette's syndrome are involuntary, they can be suppressed for brief periods of time with great concentration and effort from the patient. However, if they are suppressed, a discomfort or tension builds up in the body, which is eventually released in the

form of a bout of particularly frequent and intense tics. Imagine how difficult it would be to get on with your life if you frequently grabbed your genitals and started barking like a dog. No matter how intelligent, capable, and kind you were inside, not many people would be willing to socialize with or employ you (see Kushner, 1999).

Impediments to the Study of the Neuropathology of Tourette's Syndrome

Little is known about the neural mechanisms of Tourette's syndrome, in part because of several major impediments that make studying them difficult (see Swerdlow & Young, 2001). The following are three of these: First, there are no animal models of Tourette's syndrome; as a result, controlled experiments are difficult, and studies that involve direct manipulation of the brain are impossible. Second, no particular genes have been implicated in the development of the disorder, and thus a potentially important source of clues about its neurochemical basis is absent. Third, because of the involuntary movements that characterize the disorder, brain imaging is difficult and must be restricted to brief periods during which patients are capable of controlling their tics.

Brain Mechanisms of Tourette's Syndrome

Little information can be gleaned about Tourette's syndrome from published postmortem neuropathological investigations. Remarkably, this literature describes only seven cases, and all of these are complicated by ambiguities of diagnosis and the coexistence of other disorders, such as epilepsy (see Swerdlow & Young, 2001).

This shortage of postmortem studies of the brains of Tourette's patients is not a chance situation. Tourette's patients typically receive most of their medical care in childhood, when they first display signs of the disorder and the symptoms are most severe. Thus, when they die, they are usually no longer in contact with the specialists who treated them as children, and thus their brains are rarely examined for links to Tourette's syndrome. Consequently, the few brains that have been subjected to postmortem study have been brains of atypical Tourette's patients who were receiving neurological care just prior to their death.

Many abnormalities have been reported in functional brain images of Tourette's patients who are actively suppressing their tics. However, most of these abnormalities have not been replicated—with two exceptions (Peterson, 2001). First, abnormalities are almost always observed in the basal ganglia. Second, abnormalities are commonly observed in the cortex, particularly in areas of limbic and association cortex. You may recall that the basal ganglia are part of a major feedback circuit: They receive input from many areas of the cortex, and much of their output goes to the thalamus, which in turn projects back to many areas of the cortex. The results of functional brain-imaging studies suggest that the neuropathology of Tourette's syndrome lies in this circuit.

■ Treatment of Tourette's Syndrome

Although tics are the defining feature of Tourette's syndrome, treatment typically begins by focusing on other aspects of the disorder. First, the patient, family members, friends, and teachers, are educated about the nature of the syndrome. Second, the treatment focuses on the ancillary emotional problems (e.g., anxiety and depression). Once these first two steps have been taken, attention turns to treating the symptoms.

The tics of Tourette's syndrome are usually treated with *neuroleptics* (the D_2 receptor blockers that are used in the treatment of schizophrenia). Although there have been few controlled studies of the effectiveness of various neuroleptics, physicians report that typical neuroleptics are often effective; the efficacy of atypical neuroleptics in the treatment of Tourette's syndrome has yet to be established (see Lang, 2001).

The success of D_2 receptor blockers in the treatment of Tourette's syndrome is consistent with the hypothesis that the disorder is related to an abnormality of the basal ganglia–thalamus–cortex feedback circuit. In particular, the efficacy of these drugs implicates the *striatum*, which

is the target of many of the dopaminergic projections into the basal ganglia. The current hypothesis is that Tourette's syndrome is a neurodevelopmental disorder that results from excessive dopaminergic innervation of the striatum and the associated limbic cortex (see Jankovic, 2001).

The Case of P.H., the Neuroscientist with Tourette's Syndrome

Tourette's syndrome has been P.H.'s problem for more than three decades (Hollenbeck, 2001). Taking advantage of his position as a medical school faculty member, he regularly offers a series of lectures on the topic. Along with students, many other Tourette's patients and their families are attracted to his lectures.

Encounters with Tourette's patients of his own generation taught P.H. a real lesson. He was astounded to learn that most of them did not have his thick skin. About half of them were still receiving treatment for psychological wounds inflicted during childhood.

For the most part, these patients' deep-rooted pain and anxiety did not result from the tics themselves. They derived from being ridiculed and tormented by others and from the self-righteous advice repeatedly offered by well-meaning "clods." The malfunction may be in the basal ganglia, but in reality this is more a disorder of the onlooker than of the patient.

There is no character, howsoever good and fine, but it can be destroyed by ridicule, howsoever poor and witless.

MARK TWAIN

18.5 Clinical Trials: Development of New Psychotherapeutic Drugs

Almost daily, the news media report exciting discoveries that appear to be pointing to effective new therapeutic drugs or treatments. But most often, the promise does not materialize. For example, almost 50 years after the revolution in molecular biology began, not a single form of gene therapy is yet in use. The reason is that the journey of a drug or other medical treatment from promising basic research to useful reality is excruciatingly complex, time-consuming, and expensive.

You have no true appreciation of the difficulties of developing psychotherapeutic drugs after reading the preceding sections of this chapter because, so far, the chapter has focused on early drug discoveries and their

role in the development of theories of psychiatric dysfunction. As you have seen, in the early years, the development of psychotherapeutic drugs was largely a hit-or-miss process. New drugs were tested on patient populations with little justification and then quickly marketed to an unsuspecting public, often before it was discovered that they were ineffective for their original purpose.

Things have changed. The testing of experimental drugs on human subjects and their subsequent release for sale are now strictly regulated by government agencies.

The process of gaining permission from the government to market a new psychotherapeutic drug begins with the synthesis of the drug, the development of procedures for synthesizing it economically, and the collection of evidence from nonhuman subjects showing that the drug is likely safe for human consumption and has potential therapeutic benefits. These initial steps take a long time—at least 5 years—and only if the evidence is sufficiently promising is permission granted to proceed to clinical trials. **Clinical trials** are studies conducted on human subjects to assess the therapeutic efficacy of an untested drug or other treatment. This entire process is summarized in Table 18.2.

This final section of the chapter focuses on the process of conducting clinical trials. But before we begin, I want to emphasize the critical role played by research on nonhuman subjects in the development of effective therapeutic drugs for human patients. Without a solid foundation of comparative research, it is extremely difficult to gain governmental permission to begin clinical trials.

■ Clinical Trials: The Three Phases

Once approval has been obtained from the appropriate government agencies, clinical trials of a new drug with therapeutic potential can commence. Clinical trials are conducted in three separate phases: (1) screening for safety, (2) establishing the testing protocol, and (3) the final tests (see Zivin, 2000).

SCREENING FOR SAFETY ■ The purpose of the first phase of a clinical trial is to determine whether the drug is safe for human use and, if it is, to determine how much of the drug can be tolerated. Administering the drug to humans for the first time is always a risky process because there is no way of knowing for certain how they will respond. The subjects in phase 1 are typically healthy paid volunteers. Phase 1 clinical trials always begin with tiny injections, which are gradually increased as the tests proceed. The reactions of the subjects are meticulously monitored, and once strong adverse reactions are observed, phase 1 is curtailed. It usually requires about 1.5 years and $10 million to complete phase 1.

ESTABLISHING THE TESTING PROTOCOL ■ The purpose of the second phase of a clinical trial is to establish the *protocol* (the conditions) under which the final tests are likely to provide a clear result. For example, in phase 2, researchers hope to discover which doses are likely to be therapeutically effective, how frequently they should be administered, how long they need to be administered to have a therapeutic effect, what benefits are likely to occur, and which patients are likely to be helped.

Table 18.2 Phases of Drug Development

TIME	BASIC RESEARCH	
At least 5 years	Discovery of the drug, development of efficient methods of synthesis, and testing with animal models	
About 1 year	**Application to begin clinical trials and the review of basic research by government agency**	
	HUMAN CLINICAL TRIALS	**COST**
About 1.5 years	**Phase I** Screening for safety and finding the maximum safe dose	About $10 million
About 2 years	**Phase II** Establishing most effective doses and schedules of treatment	About $20 million
About 3.5 years	**Phase III** Clear demonstrations that the drug is therapeutic	About $45 million
About 1.5 years	**Application to begin marketing and reviews of results of clinical trials by government agency**	
	SELLING TO THE PUBLIC	
Ongoing	Recovering development costs and continuing to monitor the safety of the drug	

Source: Adapted from Zivin (2000).

Phase 2 tests are conducted on patients suffering from the target disorder; the tests usually include *placebo control groups* (groups of subjects who receive a control substance rather than the drug), and their designs are *double blind*—that is, they are conducted so that neither the patients nor the physicians interacting with them know which treatment (drug or placebo) each patient has received. It typically requires about 2 years and $20 million to complete phase 2.

THE FINAL TESTS ■ Phase 3 of a clinical trial is typically a double-blind, placebo-control study on large numbers—often, many thousands—of patients suffering from the target disorder. The design of the phase 3 tests is based on the results of phase 2 so that the final tests are likely to demonstrate positive therapeutic effects, if these exist. The first test of the final phase is often not conclusive, but if it is promising, a second test based on a redesigned protocol may be conducted. In most cases, two independent successful tests are required to convince government regulatory agencies. A successful test is one in which the beneficial effects are substantially greater than the adverse side effects. The typical length of the final test phase is about 3.5 years, and the typical cost is about $45 million.

■ Controversial Aspects of Clinical Trials

The clinical trial process is not without controversy, as is clear from the following major focuses of criticism and debate (Zivin, 2000).

REQUIREMENT FOR DOUBLE-BLIND, PLACEBO CONTROLS ■ In most clinical trials, patients are assigned to drug or placebo groups randomly and do not know for sure which treatment they are receiving (see Woods et al., 2001). Accordingly, some patients whose only hope for recovery may be the latest experimental treatment will, without knowing it, receive the placebo. Drug companies and government agencies concede that this is true, but they argue that there can be no convincing evidence that the experimental treatment is effective until a double-blind, placebo-control trial is complete. Because psychiatric disorders often improve after a placebo, a double-blind, placebo-control procedure is essential in the evaluation of any psychotherapeutic drug.

THE NEED FOR ACTIVE PLACEBOS ■ The double-blind, placebo-control trial seems perfect for clinical testing, but it isn't (see Salamone, 2000). At therapeutic doses, many drugs have side effects that are obvious to people taking them, and thus the subjects in double-blind, placebo-control studies who receive the drug can be certain that they are

not in the placebo group. This knowledge may greatly contribute to the positive effects of the drug, independent of any real therapeutic effect. Accordingly, it is now widely recognized that an active placebo is better than an inert placebo as the control drug. **Active placebos** are control drugs that have no therapeutic effect but produce side effects similar to those produced by the drug under evaluation.

LENGTH OF TIME REQUIRED ■ Patients desperately seeking new treatments are frustrated by the amount of time needed for clinical trials. Accordingly, researchers, drug companies, and government agencies are striving to speed up the evaluation process, but without sacrificing the quality of the procedures designed to protect patients from ineffective treatments.

FINANCIAL ISSUES ■ The drug companies pay the scientists, physicians, technicians, assistants, and patients involved in drug trials. Considering the millions they spend and the fact that only 20% of the candidate drugs entering phase 1 testing ever gain final approval (Zivin, 2000), it should come as no surprise that drug companies are anxious to recoup their costs. In view of this pressure, many have questioned the impartiality of those conducting the trials. The scientists themselves have often complained that drug companies make them sign agreements that prohibit them from publishing or discussing negative findings without the consent of the sponsoring company.

■ Effectiveness of Clinical Trials

Despite the controversy that surrounds the clinical trial process, there is no question that it works.

> A long, dismal history tells of charlatans who make unfounded promises and take advantage of people at the time when they are least able to care for themselves. The clinical trial process is the most objective method ever devised to assess the efficacy of a treatment. It is expensive and slow, and in need of constant refinements, and oversight, but the process is trustworthy. (Zivin, 2000, p. 75)

Certainly, the clinical trial process is far from perfect. For example, concerns about the ethics of randomized double-blind, placebo-control studies are often warranted. Still, the vast majority of those in the medical and research professions accept that these studies are the essential critical test of any new therapy. This is particularly true of psychotherapeutic drugs because psychiatric disorders often respond to placebo treatments and because assessment of their severity is subjective and can be greatly influenced by the expectations of the therapist.

Everybody agrees that clinical trials are too expensive and take too long. But one expert responds to this concern in the following way: Clinical trials can be trustworthy, fast, or cheap; but in any one trial, only two of the three are possible (Zivin, 2000). Think about it.

It is important to realize that every clinical trial is carefully monitored as it is being conducted. Any time the results warrant it, changes to the research protocol are made to reduce costs and the time required to deliver an effective treatment to patients in need—particularly to the placebo subjects who participated in the clinical trials.

CONCLUSION ■ The chapter, and indeed the book, ends with the case of S.B., who suffers from bipolar affective disorder. S.B.'s case is appropriate here because S.B. benefited greatly from the clinical trial process and because S.B.'s case demonstrates the value of a biopsychological education that stresses clear thinking and the importance of taking responsibility for one's own health. You see, S.B. took a course similar to the one that you are currently taking, and the things that he learned in the course enabled him to steer his own treatment to a positive outcome.

The Case of S.B., the Biopsychology Student Who Took Control

I met S.B. when he was a third-year undergraduate. That year, he was a student in my biopsychology course, and he also volunteered to work in my laboratory. S.B. is a quiet, pleasant, shy person; he has an unassuming manner, but he is kind, knowledgeable, and intelligent, with broad interests. For example, I was surprised to learn that he was a skilled artist, interested in medical illustration, so we chatted at length about the illustrations in this book.

I was delighted to discover that S.B.'s grades confirmed my positive impression of him. He had the highest grades in the program. In addition, it soon became apparent that he had a real "touch" for research, so I invited him to become my graduate student. He accepted and has been truly exceptional. As you can tell, I am very proud of him.

S.B. is now going to describe his case to you in his own words. I wanted to tell you about him myself so that you would have a clear picture of his situation. As you are about to discover, S.B.'s view of himself, obscured by a black cloud of depression, often bears little relation to reality.

As an undergraduate student, I suffered from depression. Although my medication improved things somewhat, I still felt stupid, disliked, and persecuted. There were some

positives in my undergraduate years. Dr. Pinel was very good to me, and I liked his course. He always emphasized that the most important part of his course was learning to be an independent thinker, and I was impressed by how he had been able to diagnose his own brain tumor. I did not appreciate at the time just how important these lessons would be.

A few months after beginning graduate school, my depression became so severe that I could not function. My psychiatrist advised me to take a leave of absence, which I did. I returned a few months later, filled with antipsychotics and antidepressants, barely capable of keeping things together.

You can appreciate how pleased I was 2 years later, when I started to snap out of it. It occurred to me that I was feeling better than I had ever felt. My productivity and creativity increased. I read, wrote, and drew, and new ideas for experiments flooded into my head. Things were going so well that I found that I was sleeping only 2 or 3 hours a night, and my brain was so energized that my friends sometimes begged me to talk more slowly so that they could follow what I was saying.

But my euphoria soon came to an abrupt end. I was still energetic and creative, but the content of my ideas changed. My consciousness was again dominated by feelings of inferiority, stupidity, and persecution. Thoughts of suicide were a constant companion.

As a last resort, I called my psychiatrist, and when she saw me, she immediately had me committed. My diagnosis was bipolar affective disorder with a *mixed episode*. As she explained, mixed episodes are transition states between mania and depression and are associated with particularly high suicide rates.

Heavily sedated, I slept for much of the first week. When I came out of my stupor, two resident psychiatrists informed me that I would be placed on a mood stabilizer and would likely have to take it for the rest of my life. Two things made me feel uncomfortable about this. First, many patients in the ward were taking this drug, and they seemed like bloated zombies; second, my physicians seemed to know less about this drug and its mechanisms than I did. So I requested that they give me access to the hospital library so I could learn about my disorder and drug. In effect, I was pulling a "Pinel."

I was amazed by what I found. The drug favored by the residents had been shown several months before to be no more effective in the treatment of bipolar affective disorder than an active placebo. Moreover, a new drug that had recently cleared clinical trials was proving very effective with few side effects.

When I confronted my psychiatrists with this evidence, they were astounded and agreed to prescribe the new drug. Today, I am feeling well and am enjoying graduate school. I still find it difficult to believe that I had enough nerve to question my physicians and prescribe for myself. I never imagined that the lessons learned from this book would have such a positive impact on my life. I am glad that I could tell you my story, and I hope that you benefit from it.

Themes Revisited

This entire chapter focused on psychiatric disorders, so it should come as no surprise that the clinical implications theme was predominant. Nevertheless, the other three major themes of this book also received substantial coverage.

The thinking-about-biopsychology theme arose during the discussions of the differences between psychiatric and neuropsychological disorders and the reasons why postmortem studies of typical Tourette's patients are rare. The thinking-about-biopsychology theme also arose several times during the description of clinical trials.

The cognitive neuroscience theme was apparent in the discussion of functional brain-imaging studies of af-fective disorders, anxiety disorders, and Tourette's syndrome. Functional brain-imaging studies have been important in the study of these particular disorders because structural correlates have not been identified.

The evolutionary perspective theme came up twice: in the section on animal models of anxiety disorders and in the discussion of the important role played by research on nonhuman subjects in gaining official clearance to commence human clinical trials.

ON THE CD

Looking for more information about the topics in this chapter? For recommended additional readings, see Hard Copy for Chapter 18.

Log On

- **http://lexington-on-line.com/naf.html** The home page of the National Anxiety Foundation provides an overview of anxiety-related disorders and includes links to related sites.

- **http://www.mhsource.com/narsad/** This is the home page of the National Alliance for Research on Schizo-phrenia and Depression, which includes easy-to-read and accurate descriptions of these major psychiatric disorders.

- **http://www.sciam.com/1998/0698issue/0698nemeroff. html** In this *Scientific American* article, Dr. Charles Nemeroff discusses the neurobiology of depression.

Think about It

1. Blunders often play an important role in scientific progress. Discuss this with respect to the development of drugs for the treatment of psychiatric disorders.

2. The mechanism by which a disorder is alleviated is not necessarily opposite to the mechanism by which it was caused. Discuss this with respect to the evidence supporting current theories of schizophrenia, depression, and anxiety.

3. Discuss the diathesis–stress model of psychological disorders. Design an experiment to test the model.

4. Judge people by what they do, not by what they say. Discuss this recommendation with respect to Tourette's syndrome.

5. Tourette's syndrome is a disorder of onlookers. Explain and discuss.

6. Clinical trials are no more than excessive government bureaucracy. The prescription of drugs should be left entirely to the discretion of physicians. Discuss.

ON THE CD

Studying for an exam? Try the Practice Tests for Chapter 18.

Key Terms

Active placebos *(p. 477)*
Agoraphobia *(p. 472)*
Anxiety *(p. 471)*
Anxiety disorder *(p. 471)*
Benzpdiazepines *(p. 472)*
Bipolar affective disorder
  (p. 468)
Butyrophenones *(p. 465)*
Cheese effect *(p. 469)*
Chlorpromazine *(p. 464)*
Clinical trials *(p. 476)*
Clozapine *(p. 466)*
Depression *(p. 467)*

Diathesis *(p. 470)*
Endogenuous depression
  (p. 468)
False transmitter *(p. 464)*
Generalized anxiety disorders
  (p. 471)
Haloperidol *(p. 465)*
Imipramine *(p. 469)*
Iproniazid *(p. 468)*
Lithium *(p. 469)*
Mania *(p. 468)*
MAO inhibitors *(p. 469)*
Neuroleptics *(p. 465)*

Obsessive-compulsive
  disorders *(p. 472)*
Panic disorders *(p. 472)*
Phenothiazines *(p. 465)*
Phobic anxiety disorders
  (p. 471)
Prozac *(p. 469)*
Psychiatric disorder *(p. 462)*
Reactive depression *(p. 468)*
Reserpine *(p. 464)*
Tics *(p. 474)*
Tricyclic antidepressants
  (p. 469)

Unipolar affective disorder
  (p. 468)
Up-regulation *(p. 470)*

ON THE CD

Need some help studying the key terms for this chapter? Check out the electronic flash cards for Chapter 18.

Epilogue

I feel relieved to be finishing the edition that I began almost 2 years ago, and I am excited by the prospect of being able to speak to so many students like you through this edition and its CD. You must also feel relieved to be finishing this book; still, I hope that you feel a tiny bit of regret that our time together is over.

Like good friends, we have shared good times and bad. We have shared the fun and wonder of Rhonda, the dexterous cashier; the Nads basketball team; people who rarely sleep; the mamawawa assumption; split brains; and brain transplantation. But we have also been touched by many personal tragedies: for example, the victims of Alzheimer's disease and MPTP poisoning; the lost mariner; H.M.; the man who mistook his wife for a hat; Professor P., the biopsychologist who experienced brain surgery from the other side of the knife; and his graduate student, S.B., who guided the treatment of his own treatment. Thank you for allowing me to share *Biopsychology* with you. I hope you have found it to be an enriching experience.

Our mutual experiences have transcended space and time. Right now, I am sitting at my desk looking out over my garden and the Pacific Ocean, as the neighborhood finches celebrate the completion of this edition and the first wave of spring flowers with a song. It is 10:00 A.M. on Saturday, April 13, 2002. Where and when are you?

Appendixes

Appendix I

The Autonomic Nervous System

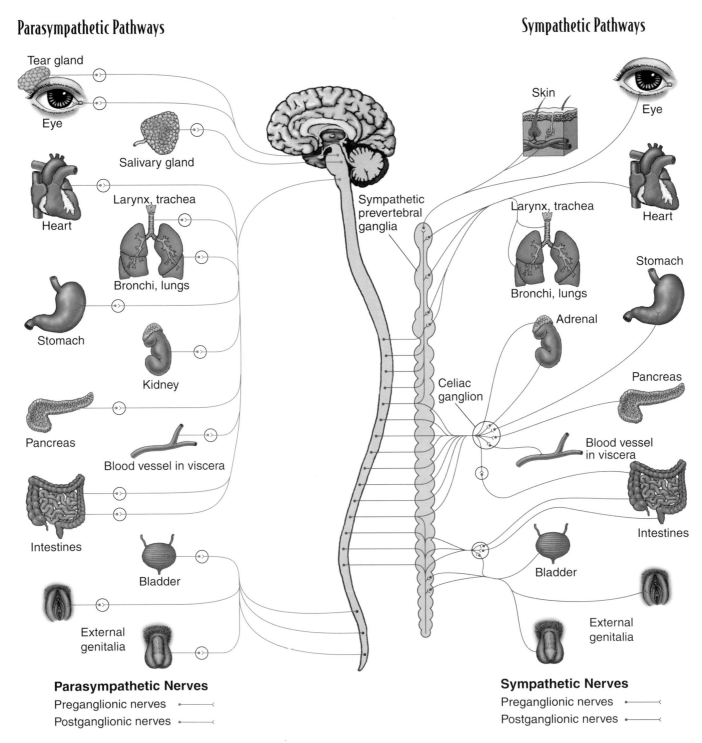

Parasympathetic Pathways

Tear gland

Eye

Salivary gland

Heart

Larynx, trachea

Bronchi, lungs

Stomach

Kidney

Pancreas

Blood vessel in viscera

Intestines

Bladder

External genitalia

Sympathetic Pathways

Skin

Eye

Heart

Sympathetic prevertebral ganglia

Larynx, trachea

Bronchi, lungs

Adrenal

Stomach

Celiac ganglion

Pancreas

Blood vessel in viscera

Intestines

Bladder

External genitalia

Parasympathetic Nerves

Preganglionic nerves

Postganglionic nerves

Sympathetic Nerves

Preganglionic nerves

Postganglionic nerves

Appendix II

Some Functions of Sympathetic and Parasympathetic Neurons

ORGAN	SYMPATHETIC EFFECT	PARASYMPATHETIC EFFECT
Salivary gland	Decreases secretion	Increases secretion
Heart	Increases heart rate	Decreases heart rate
Blood vessels	Constricts blood vessels in most organs	Dilates blood vessels in a few organs
Penis	Ejaculation	Erection
Iris radial muscles	Dilates pupils	No effect
Iris sphincter muscles	No effect	Constricts pupils
Tear gland	No effect	Stimulates secretion
Sweat gland	Stimulates secretion	No effect
Stomach and intestine	No effect	Stimulates secretion
Lungs	Dilates bronchioles; inhibits mucous secretion	Constricts bronchioles; stimulates mucous secretion
Arrector pili muscles	Erects hair and creates gooseflesh	No effect

Appendix III

The Cranial Nerves

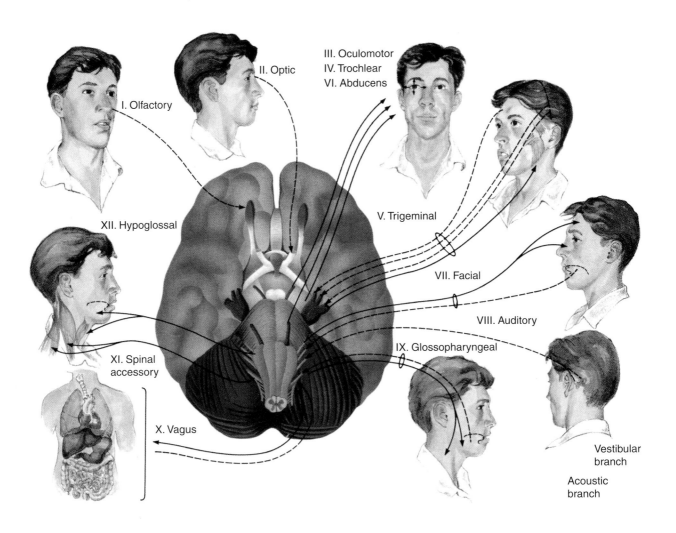

I. Olfactory

II. Optic

III. Oculomotor
IV. Trochlear
VI. Abducens

XII. Hypoglossal

V. Trigeminal

VII. Facial

VIII. Auditory

XI. Spinal
accessory

IX. Glossopharyngeal

X. Vagus

Vestibular
branch

Acoustic
branch

Functions of the Cranial Nerves

NUMBER	NAME	GENERAL FUNCTION	SPECIFIC FUNCTIONS
I	Olfactory	Sensory	Smell
II	Optic	Sensory	Vision
III	Oculomotor	Motor Sensory	Eye movement and pupillary constriction Sensory signals from certain eye muscles
IV	Trochlear	Motor Sensory	Eye movement Sensory signals from certain eye muscles
V	Trigeminal	Sensory Motor	Facial sensations Chewing
VI	Abducens	Motor Sensory	Eye movement Sensory signals from certain eye muscles
VII	Facial	Sensory Motor	Taste from anterior two-thirds of tongue Facial expression, secretion of tears, salivation, cranial blood vessel dilation
VIII	Auditory-Vestibular	Sensory	Audition; sensory signals from the organs of balance in the inner ear
IX	Glossopharyngeal	Sensory Motor	Taste from posterior third of tongue Salivation, swallowing
X	Vagus	Sensory Motor	Sensations from abdominal and thoracic organs Control over abdominal and thoracic organs and muscles of the throat
XI	Spinal Accessory	Motor Sensory	Movement of neck, shoulders, and head Sensory signals from muscles of the neck
XII	Hypoglossal	Motor Sensory	Tongue movements Sensory signals from tongue muscles

Appendix V

Nuclei of the Thalamus

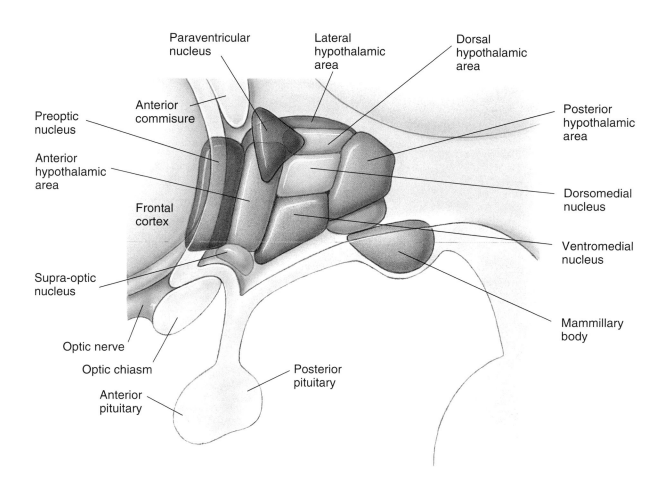

Paraventricular nucleus

Lateral hypothalamic area

Dorsal hypothalamic area

Anterior commisure

Preoptic nucleus

Posterior hypothalamic area

Anterior hypothalamic area

Frontal cortex

Dorsomedial nucleus

Ventromedial nucleus

Supra-optic nucleus

Mammillary body

Optic nerve

Optic chiasm

Posterior pituitary

Anterior pituitary

Appendix VII

Some of the Peptides That Have Been Found in Mammalian Neurons

Major Neuropeptides

Pituitary Peptides

Corticotropin

Growth hormone

Lipotropin

α-Melanocyte stimulating hormone

Oxytocin

Prolactin

Vasopressin

Gut Peptides

Cholecystokinin

Gastrin

Motilin

Pancreatic polypeptide

Secretin

Substance P

Vasoactive intestinal polypeptide

Miscellaneous Peptides

Angiotensin

Bombesin

Bradykinin

Carnosine

Glucagon

Insulin

Neuropeptide Y

Neurotensin

Proctolin

Hypothalamic Peptides

Luteinizing hormone-releasing hormone

Somatostatin

Thyrotropin-releasing hormone

Endorphins

Dynorphin

β-Endorphin

Met Enkephalin

Leu Enkephalin

Appendix VIII

Phases of the Human Menstrual Cycle

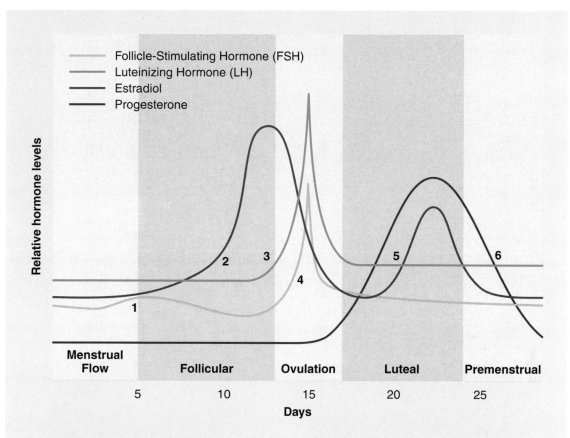

1 In response to an increase in FSH, small spheres of cells called ovarian follicles begin to grow around individual egg cells (ova).

2 The follicles begin to release estrogens such as estradiol.

3 The estrogens stimulate the hypothalamus to increase the release of LH and FSH from the anterior pituitary.

4 In response to the LH surge, one of the follicles ruptures and releases its ovum.

5 The ruptured follicle under the influence of LH develops into a corpus luteum (yellow body) and begins to release progesterone, which prepares the lining of the uterus for the implantation of a fertilized ovum.

6 Meanwhile, the ovum is moved into the fallopian tube by the rowing action of ciliated cells. If the ovum is not fertilized, progesterone and estradiol levels fall, the walls of the uterus are sloughed off as menstrual flow, and the cycle begins once again.

Glossary

Ablatio penis. Accidental destruction of the penis.

Absolute refractory period. A brief period (typically 1 to 2 milliseconds) after the initiation of an action potential during which it is impossible to elicit another action potential in the same neuron.

Absorption spectrum. A graph of the ability of a substance to absorb light of different wavelengths.

Absorptive phase. The metabolic phase during which the body is operating on the energy from a recently consumed meal and is storing the excess as body fat, glycogen, and proteins.

Accommodation. The process of adjusting the configuration of the lenses to bring images into focus on the retina.

Acetylcholinesterase. The enzyme that breaks down acetylcholine.

Achromatic colors. Black, white, and gray.

Action potential (AP). The firing of a neuron; a massive momentary change in the membrane potential from about –70 mV to about +50 mV.

Activation-synthesis theory. The theory that dream content reflects the cerebral cortex's inherent tendency to make sense of, and give form to, the random signals it receives from the brain stem during REM sleep.

Active placebos. Control drugs that have no therapeutic effect but produce side effects similar to those produced by the drug under evaluation.

Acuity. The ability to see the details of objects.

Addicts. Habitual drug users who continue to use a drug despite the adverse effects of the drug on their health and life and despite their repeated efforts to stop using it.

Adipsia. Complete cessation of drinking.

Adrenal cortex. The outer layer of the adrenal glands, which releases glucocorticoids in response to stressors as well as gonadal hormones in small amounts.

Adrenal medulla. The core of the adrenal glands, which releases epinephrine and norepinephrine in response to stressors.

Adrenocorticotropic hormone (ACTH). The anterior pituitary hormone that triggers the release of glucocorticoids from the adrenal cortex.

Adrenogenital syndrome. A sexual developmental disorder in which high levels of adrenal androgens, resulting from congenital adrenal hyperplasia, masculinize the bodies of genetic females.

Afferent nerves. Nerves that carry sensory signals to the central nervous system; sensory nerves.

Ageusia. The inability to taste.

Aggregation. The alignment of cells during neurodevelopment to form the various structures of the nervous system.

Aggressive behaviors. Behaviors whose primary function is to threaten or harm other organisms.

Agnosia. The inability to consciously recognize sensory stimuli of a particular class that is not attributable to a sensory deficit or to verbal or intellectual impairment.

Agonists. Drugs that facilitate the effects of a particular neurotransmitter.

Agoraphobia. Pathological fear of public places and open spaces.

Agraphia. A specific inability to write; one that does not result from general visual, motor, or intellectual deficits.

Alexia. A specific inability to read; one that does not result from general visual, motor, or intellectual deficits.

Alleles. The two genes that control the same trait.

All-or-none responses. Responses that are not graded, that occur full-blown or not at all.

Alpha fetoprotein. The protein present in the blood of perinatal rats that deactivates circulating estradiol by binding to it.

Alpha male. The dominant male of a colony.

Alpha waves. Regular, 8- to 12-per-second, high-amplitude EEG waves that typically occur during relaxed wakefulness and just before falling asleep.

Alzheimer's disease. The major cause of dementia in old age, characterized by neurofibrillary tangles, amyloid plaques, and neuron loss.

Amacrine cells. A layer of retinal neurons whose function is lateral communication.

Amino acid derivative hormones. Hormones that are simple modifications of individual amino acids.

Amino acids. The breakdown products of proteins.

Amotivational syndrome. Chronic lack of motivation produced by drug use.

Amphetamine. A stimulant drug whose effects are similar to those of cocaine.

Amphibians. Species that spend their larval phase in water and their adult phase on land.

Amygdala. A structure of the medial temporal lobe that plays a role in the memory for the emotional significance of experiences.

Anabolic steroids. Steroid drugs that are similar to testosterone and have powerful anabolic (growth-promoting) effects.

Analgesics. Drugs that reduce pain.

Analogous. Having a similar structure because of convergent evolution (e.g., a bird's wing and a bee's wing are analogous).

Androgenic insensitivity syndrome. The developmental disorder of genetic males in which a mutation to the androgen receptor gene renders their androgen receptors defective and causes them to develop female bodies.

Androgens. The class of steroid hormones that includes testosterone.

Androstenedione. The adrenal androgen that triggers the growth of pubic and axillary hair in human females.

Aneurysm. A pathological balloonlike dilation that forms in the wall of a blood vessel at a point where the elasticity of the vessel wall is defective.

Angular gyrus. The gyrus of the posterior cortex at the boundary between the temporal and parietal lobes, which in the left hemisphere is thought to play a role in reading.

Anorexia nervosa. An eating disorder that is characterized by a pathological fear of obesity and that results in health-threatening weight loss.

Anosmia. The inability to smell.

Anosognosia. The common failure of neurological patients to recognize their own symptoms.

Antagonistic muscles. Pairs of muscles that act in opposition.

Antagonists. Drugs that inhibit the effects of a particular neurotransmitter.

Anterior. Toward the nose end of a vertebrate.

Anterior cingulate cortex. The cortex of the anterior cingulate gyrus, which is involved in the emotional reaction to painful stimulation.

Anterior pituitary. The part of the pituitary gland that releases tropic hormones.

Anterograde amnesia. Loss of memory for events occurring after the amnesia-inducing brain injury.

Anterograde degeneration. The degeneration of the distal segment of a cut axon.

Anterolateral system. The division of the somatosensory system that ascends in the anterolateral portion of spinal white matter and carries signals related to pain and temperature.

Antibodies. Proteins that bind specifically to antigens on the surface of invading microorganisms and in so doing promote the destruction of the microorganisms.

Antibody-mediated immunity. The immune reaction by which B cells destroy invading microorganisms.

Antidromic conduction. Axonal conduction opposite to the normal direction; conduction from axon terminals back toward the cell body.

Antigens. Proteins on the surface of cells that identify them as native or foreign.

Antihypnotic drugs. Sleep-reducing drugs.

Anxiety. Fear that persists in the absence of direct threat.

Anxiety disorder. Anxiety that is so extreme and so pervasive that it disrupts normal functioning.

Aphagia. Complete cessation of eating.

Aphasia. A disturbance in the ability to use or comprehend language.

Apoptosis. Cell death that is actively induced by genetic programs; programmed cell death.

Appetizer effect. The increase in hunger that is produced by the consumption of small amounts of palatable food.

Applied research. Research that is intended to bring about some direct benefit to humankind.

Apraxia. A disorder in which patients have great difficulty performing movements when asked to do so out of context but can readily perform them spontanously in natural situations.

Arachnoid membrane. The meninx that is located between the dura mater and the pia mater and has the appearance of a gauzelike spiderweb.

Arcuate fasciculus. The major neural pathway between Broca's area and Wernicke's area.

Aromatization. The chemical process by which testosterone is converted to estradiol.

Arteriosclerosis. A condition in which blood vessels are blocked by the accumulation of fat deposits in their walls.

Asomatognosia. A deficiency in recognizing parts of one's own body that is produced by brain damage.

Aspiration. A lesion technique in which tissue is drawn off by suction through the tip of a glass pipette.

Association cortex. Areas of the cortex that receive input from more than one sensory system.

Astereognosia. A difficulty in recognizing objects by touch that is not attributable to a simple sensory deficit or to general intellectual impairment.

Astrocytes. Large, star-shaped glial cells that provide a supportive matrix for neurons in the central nervous system and are thought to play a role in the transfer of molecules from blood to CNS neurons.

Ataxia. Loss of motor coordination.

Atropine. A receptor blocker at muscarinic cholinergic synapses.

Auditory nerve. The branch of the eighth cranial nerve that carries auditory signals from the hair cells in the basilar membrane.

Autism. A neurodevelopmental disorder characterized by (1) a reduced ability to interpret the emotions and intentions of others, (2) a reduced capacity for social interaction and communication, and (3) a preoccupation with a single subject or activity.

Autonomic nervous system (ANS). The part of the peripheral nervous system that participates in the regulation of the body's internal environment.

Autoradiography. The technique of photographically developing brain slices that have been exposed to a radioactively labeled substance such as 2-DG so that regions of high uptake are visible on the brain slices.

Autoreceptors. Receptors, often on the presynaptic membrane, that are sensitive to a neuron's own neurotransmitter.

Axon hillock. The conical structure at the junction between the axon and cell body, where action potentials are normally generated.

B cells. B lymphocytes; lymphocytes that manufacture antibodies against antigens they encounter.

Basal forebrain region. The cholinergic area of the forebrain just in front of and above the hypothalamus.

Basal metabolic rate. The rate at which resting individuals utilize energy to maintain their bodily processes.

Basilar membrane. The membrane of the organ of Corti in which the hair cell receptors are embedded.

Before-and-after design. The experimental design used to demonstrate contingent drug tolerance; the experimental group receives the drug before each of a series of behavioral tests and the control group receives the drug after each test.

Behavioral paradigm. A single set of procedures developed for the investigation of a particular behavioral phenomenon.

Benign tumors. Tumors that are surgically removable with little risk of further growth in the body.

Benzodiazepines. A class of GABA agonists with anxiolytic, sedative, and anticonvulsant properties; drugs such as chlordiazepoxide (Librium) and diazepam (Valium).

Between-subjects design. An experimental design in which a different group of subjects is tested under each condition.

Betz cells. Large pyramidal neurons of the primary motor cortex that synapse directly on spinal motor neurons, mainly in the lower spinal cord.

Bilateral medial temporal lobectomy. The removal of the medial portions of both temporal lobes, including the hippocampus, the amygdala, and the adjacent cortex.

Binocular. Involving both eyes.

Binocular disparity. The difference in the position of the retinal image of the same object on the two retinas.

Biopsychology. The scientific study of the biology of behavior.

Bipolar affective disorder. A disorder of emotion in which the patient experiences periods of mania interspersed with periods of depression.

Bipolar cells. The cells in the middle layer of the retina.

Bipolar neuron. A neuron with two processes extending from its cell body.

Bisexual. Sexually attracted to members of both sexes.

Blind spot. The area on the retina where the axons of retinal ganglion cells gather together, penetrate the receptor layer, and leave the eye as the optic nerve.

Blindsight. The ability of some patients who are blind as a consequence of cortical damage to unconsciously see some aspects of their visual environments.

Blobs. Peglike, cytochrome oxidase–rich, dual-opponent color columns.

Blood–brain barrier. The mechanism that keeps certain toxic substances in the blood from penetrating cerebral neural tissue.

Blueprint hypothesis. The hypothesis that growing axons reach their correct targets by following chemical or mechanical trails through the developing nervous system.

Brain stem. The part of the brain on which the cerebral hemispheres rest; in general, it regulates reflex activities that are critical for survival (e.g., heart rate and respiration).

Bregma. A landmark on the surface of the skull that is commonly used as a reference point in stereotaxic surgery on rats.

Broca's aphasia. A hypothetical disorder of speech production with no associated deficits in language comprehension.

Broca's area. The area of the inferior prefrontal cortex of the left hemisphere hypothesized by Broca to be the center of speech production.

Buerger's disease. A nicotine-produced disease in which blood flow to the legs is restricted, the ultimate result being gangrene and amputation.

Bulimia nervosa. An eating disorder that is characterized by recurring cycles of fasting, bingeing, and purging without dangerous weight loss.

Butyrophenones. A class of antischizophrenic drugs that bind primarily to D_2 receptors.

CA1 subfield. The region of the hippocampus that is commonly damaged by cerebral ischemia.

Cafeteria diet. A diet offered to experimental animals that is composed of a wide variety of palatable foods.

Cannabis sativa. The common hemp plant and the source of marijuana.

Cannon-Bard theory. The theory that emotional experience and emotional expression are parallel processes that have no direct causal relation.

Cannula. A fine tube, such as a hypodermic needle, that is implanted in the body for the purpose of introducing or extracting substances.

Carousel apparatus. An apparatus used to study the effects of sleep deprivation in laboratory rats.

Cartesian dualism. The philosophical position of Descartes, who argued that the universe is composed of two elements: physical matter and the human mind.

Case studies. Studies that focus on a single case or subject.

Cataplexy. A disorder that is characterized by sudden losses of muscle tone during wakefulness and is often seen in cases of narcolepsy.

Cell-adhesion molecules (CAMs). Molecules on the surface of cells that have the ability to recognize specific molecules on the surface of other cells and bind to them.

Cell-mediated immunity. The immune reaction by which T cells destroy invading microorganisms.

Central canal. The small CSF-filled passage that runs the length of the spine.

Central nervous system (CNS). The portion of the nervous system within the skull and spine.

Central sensorimotor programs. Patterns of activity that are programmed into the sensorimotor system.

Cephalic phase. The metabolic phase during which the body prepares for food that is about to be absorbed.

Cerebellum. The metencephalic structure that has been shown to mediate the retention of Pavlovian eyeblink conditioning.

Cerebral angiography. A contrast X-ray technique for visualizing the cerebral circulatory system by infusing a radiopaque dye through a cerebral artery.

Cerebral aqueduct. The narrow channel that connects the third and fourth ventricles.

Cerebral commissures. Tracts that connect the left and right cerebral hemispheres.

Cerebral cortex. The layer of neural tissue covering the cerebral hemispheres of humans and other mammals.

Cerebral dialysis. A method for recording changes in brain chemistry in behaving animals; a tube with a short semipermeable section is implanted in the brain, and extracellular neurochemicals are continuously drawn off for analysis through the semipermeable section.

Cerebral hemorrhage. Bleeding in the brain.

Cerebral ischemia. An interruption of blood supply to the brain; a common cause of medial temporal lobe amnesia.

Cerebral ventricles. The four CSF-filled internal chambers of the brain: the two lateral ventricles, the third ventricle, and the fourth ventricle.

Cerebrospinal fluid (CSF). The colorless fluid that fills the subarachnoid space, the central canal, and the cerebral ventricles.

Cerebrum. The portion of the brain that sits on the brain stem; in general, it plays a role in complex adaptive processes (e.g., learning, perception, and motivation).

Cerveau isolé preparation. An experimental preparation in which the forebrain is disconnected from the rest of the brain by a midcollicular transection.

Change blindness. The difficulty perceiving major changes to unattended-to parts of a visual image when the changes are introduced during brief interruptions in the presentation of the image.

Cheese effect. The surges in blood pressure that occur when individuals taking MAO inhibitors consume tyramine-rich foods, such as cheese.

Chemoaffinity hypothesis. The hypothesis that growing axons are attracted to their appropriate targets by different chemicals released by the target sites.

Chimeric figures test. The test of visual completion in split-brain subjects that uses pictures composed of the left and right halves of two different faces.

Chlorpromazine. The first antischizophrenic drug.

Cholecystokinin (CCK). A peptide that is released by the gastrointestinal tract and is thought to function as a satiety signal.

Chordates. Animals with dorsal nerve cords.

Choroid plexuses. The networks of capillaries that protrude into the ventricles and continuously produce cerebrospinal fluid.

Chromatic colors. The hues—colors such as blue, green, and yellow.

Chromosomes. Threadlike genetic structures in the cell nucleus; each chromosome is a DNA molecule.

Ciliary muscles. The eye muscles that control the shape of the lenses.

Cingulate motor areas. Two areas of secondary motor cortex located in the cortex of the cingulate gyrus of each hemisphere.

Circadian clock. An internal timing mechanism that is capable of maintaining daily cycles of physiological change, even when there are no temporal cues from the environment.

Circadian rhythms. Diurnal (daily) cycles of body function.

Circadian theories of sleep. Theories based on the premise that sleep is controlled by an internal timing mechanism and is not a reaction to the adverse effects of wakefulness.

Cirrhosis. Scarring, typically of the liver.

Clinical. Pertaining to illness or treatment.

Clinical trials. Studies conducted on human subjects to assess the therapeutic efficacy of an untested drug or other treatment.

Clozapine. An antischizophrenic drug that does not produce many of the side effects of conventional neuroleptics and does not have a high affinity for D_2 receptors.

Cocaine psychosis. Psychotic behavior observed during a cocaine spree, similar in many respects to schizophrenic behavior.

Cocaine sprees. Binges of cocaine use.

Cocaine. A potent catecholamine agonist and stimulant that is highly addictive.

Cochlea. The long, coiled structure of the inner ear that houses the organ of Corti and its auditory receptors.

Cocktail-party phenomenon. The ability to unconsciously monitor the contents of one conversation while consciously focusing on another.

Cocontraction. The simultaneous contraction of antagonistic muscles.

Codeine. A weak psychoactive ingredient of opium.

Codon. A group of three consecutive nucleotide bases on a DNA or messenger RNA strand; each codon specifies the particular amino acid that is to be added to an amino acid chain during protein synthesis.

Coexistence The presence of more than one neurotransmitter in the same neuron.

Cognition. Higher intellectual processes such as thought, memory, attention, and complex perceptual processing.

Cognitive map theory. The theory that the main function of the hippocampus is to store memories of spatial location.

Cognitive neuroscience. A division of biopsychology that focuses on the use of functional brain imaging to study human cognition.

Collateral sprouting. The growth of axon branches from mature neurons, usually to postsynaptic sites abandoned by adjacent axons that have degenerated.

Colony–intruder paradigm. A paradigm for the study of aggressive and defensive behavior in male rats; a small male intruder rat is placed in an established colony in order to study the aggressive responses of the colony's alpha male and the defensive responses of the intruder.

Color constancy. The tendency of an object to appear the same color even when the wavelengths that it reflects change.

Columnar organization. The functional organization of the neocortex in vertical columns; the cells in each column form a mini circuit that performs a single function.

Commissurotomy. Severing of the cerebral commissures.

Comparative approach. The study of biological processes by comparing different species—usually from the evolutionary perspective.

Comparative psychology. The division of biopsychology that studies the evolution, genetics, and adaptiveness of behavior, often by using the comparative approach.

Complementary colors. Pairs of colors that produce white or gray when combined in equal measure; every color has a complementary color.

Completion. The visual system's automatic use of information obtained from receptors around a blind spot, or scotoma, to create a perception of the missing portion of the retinal image.

Complex cells. Neurons in the visual cortex that respond optimally to straight-edge stimuli in a certain orientation in any part of their receptive field.

Complex partial seizures. Seizures that are characterized by various complex psychological phenomena and are thought to result from temporal lobe discharges.

Component theory. The theory that the relative amount of activity produced in three different classes of cones by a light determines its perceived color (also called *trichromatic theory*).

Computed tomography (CT). A computer-assisted X-ray procedure that can be used to visualize the brain and other internal structures of the living body.

Concussion. Disturbance of consciousness following a blow to the head with no cerebral bleeding or obvious structural damage.

Conditioned compensatory responses. Physiological responses opposite to the effects of a drug that are elicited by stimuli that are regularly associated with experiencing the drug effects.

Conditioned defensive burying. The burial of a source of aversive stimulation by rodents.

Conditioned drug tolerance. Tolerance effects that are maximally expressed only when the drug is administered in situations in which it has previously been administered.

Conditioned place-preference paradigm. A test that assesses an animal's preference for environments in which it has previously experienced drug effects.

Conditioned taste aversion. The aversion developed by animals to the taste of food whose consumption has been followed by illness.

Conditioned withdrawal effects. Withdrawal effects that are elicited by the drug environment or by other drug-associated cues.

Conduction aphasia. Aphasia that is thought to result from damage to the neural pathway between Broca's area and Wernicke's area.

Cones. The visual receptors that mediate high-acuity color vision in good lighting.

Confounded variable. An unintended difference between the conditions of an experiment that could have affected the dependent variable.

Congenital. Present at birth.

Congenital adrenal hyperplasia. A congenital deficiency in the release of cortisol from the adrenal cortex, which leads to the excessive release of adrenal androgens.

Conspecifics. Members of the same species.

Constituent cognitive processes. Simple cognitive processes that combine to produce complex cognitive processes.

Contextual fear conditioning. The process by which benign contexts (situations) come to induce fear through their association with fear-inducing stimuli.

Contingent drug tolerance. Drug tolerance that develops as a reaction to the experience of the effects of drugs rather than to drug exposure alone.

Contralateral. Projecting from one side of the body to the other.

Contralateral neglect. A disturbance of the patient's ability to respond to visual, auditory, and somatosensory stimuli on the side of the body opposite to a site of brain damage, usually the left side of the body following damage to the right parietal lobe.

Contrast enhancement. The enhancement of the perception of edges.

Contrast X-ray techniques. X-ray techniques that involve the injection of a radiopaque substance into a structure to make it visible on an X-ray photograph.

Contrecoup injuries. Contusions that occur on the side of the brain opposite to the side of a blow.

"Control of behavior" versus "conscious perception" theory. The theory that the dorsal stream mediates the control of behavior by visual input and the ventral stream mediates conscious vision.

Control-question technique. A lie-detection technique in which the polygrapher compares the responses to target questions with the responses to control questions.

Contusions. Closed-head injuries that involve damage to the cerebral circulatory system and produce bleeding.

Convergent evolution. The evolution of similar solutions to the same environmental demands by unrelated species.

Converging operations. The use of several research approaches to solve a single problem.

Convolutions. Folds on the surface of the cerebral hemispheres.

Convulsions. Motor seizures.

Coolidge effect. The fact that a copulating male who becomes incapable of continuing to copulate with one sex partner can often recommence copulating with a new sex partner.

Copulation. Sexual intercourse.

Corpus callosum. The largest cerebral commissure.

Corticofugal pathways. Descending pathways in sensory systems that conduct signals from cortical to subcortical structures.

Crack. A potent, cheap, smokable base form of cocaine.

Cranial nerves. The 12 pairs of nerves extending from the brain (e.g., the optic nerves, the olfactory nerves, and the vagus nerves).

Cross section. Section cut at a right angle to any long, narrow structure.

Cross tolerance. Tolerance that develops to the effects of one drug as the result of exposure to another drug.

Cross-cuing. Nonneural communication between hemispheres that have been separated by commissurotomy.

Crossing over. The exchange of sections between pairs of chromosomes during the first stage of meiosis.

Cryogenic blockade. The temporary elimination of neural activity in an area of the brain by cooling the area with a cryoprobe.

Curare. A blocker of nicotinic cholinergic synapses that produces paralysis by blocking transmission at neuromuscular junctions.

Cytochrome oxidase. An enzyme present in particularly high concentrations in the mitochondria of dual-opponent color cells of the visual cortex.

Decorticate. Lacking a cortex.

Decussate. To cross over to the other side of the brain.

Deep dyslexia. A reading disorder in which the phonetic procedure is disrupted while the lexical procedure is not.

Defeminizes. Suppresses or disrupts female characteristics.

Defensive behaviors. Behaviors whose primary function is protection from threat or harm.

Delayed nonmatching-to-sample test. A test in which the subject is presented with an unfamiliar sample object and then, after a delay, is presented with a choice between the sample object and an unfamiliar object, where the correct choice is the unfamiliar object.

Delirium tremens (DTs). The phase of the alcohol withdrawal syndrome characterized by hallucinations, delusions, and extremely agitated behavior.

Delta waves. The largest, slowest EEG waves.

Demasculinizes. Suppresses or disrupts male characteristics.

Dementia. General intellectual deterioration.

Dendritic spines. Tiny buds on dendrites, which are the location of many dendritic synapses; their function seems to be to restrict certain synaptic effects in the postsynaptic neuron to the vicinity of the synapse.

2-Deoxyglucose (2-DG). A substance similar to glucose that is taken up by active neurons and accumulates in them because, unlike glucose, it cannot be used by neurons as a source of energy.

Deoxyribonucleic acid (DNA). The double-stranded, coiled molecule of genetic material; a chromosome.

Dependent variable. The variable measured by the experimenter to assess the effect of the independent variable.

Depolarize. To decrease the membrane potential.

Deprenyl. A monoamine oxidase inhibitor that has been shown to retard the development of Parkinson's disease.

Depressant. A drug that depresses neural activity and behavior.

Depression. A normal reaction to grievous loss; when depression is excessive, disruptive, and recurring, it is classified as a psychiatric disorder.

Dermatome. An area of the body that is innervated by the left and right dorsal roots of one segment of the spinal cord.

Desynchronized EEG. Low-amplitude, high-frequency EEG.

Detoxified addicts. Addicts who have none of the drug to which they are addicted in their body and who are no longer experiencing withdrawal symptoms.

Dextrals. Right-handers.

Diathesis. An inherited susceptibility, such as in the diathesis–stress model of depression.

Dichotic listening test. A test of language lateralization in which two sequences of three spoken digits are presented simultaneously to each ear and the subject is asked to report all of the digits heard.

Dichotomous traits. Traits that occur in one form or the other, never in combination.

Diet-induced thermogenesis. The homeostasis-defending increases in body temperature that are associated with increases in body fat.

Digestion. The process by which food is broken down and absorbed through the lining of the gastrointestinal tract.

Digit span. The longest sequence of random digits that can be repeated correctly 50% of the time—most people have a digit span of 7.

Dihydrotestosterone. An androgen that cannot be aromatized to estrogen.

Directed synapses. Synapses at which the site of neurotransmitter release and the receptor sites on the postsynaptic membrane are in close proximity.

Distal segment. The segment of a cut axon between the cut and the axon terminals.

Diuretic. A drug that increases the production of urine.

DNA-binding proteins. Proteins that bind to DNA molecules and in so doing either induce or block gene expression.

Dominant hemisphere. A term used in the past to refer to the left hemisphere, based on the incorrect assumption that the left hemisphere is dominant in all complex activities.

Dominant trait. The trait of a dichotomous pair that is expressed in the phenotypes of heterozygous individuals.

Dopamine transporters. Molecules in the presynaptic membrane of dopaminergic neurons that attract dopamine molecules in the synaptic cleft and deposit them back inside the neuron.

Dorsal. Toward the surface of the back of a vertebrate or toward the top of the head.

Dorsal-column medial-lemniscus system. The division of the somatosensory system that ascends in the dorsal portion of the spinal white matter and carries signals related to touch and proprioception.

Dorsal columns. The somatosensory tracts that ascend in the dorsal portion of the spinal cord white matter.

Dorsal horns. The two dorsal arms of the spinal gray matter.

Dorsal stream. The group of visual pathways that flows out of the primary visual cortex to the dorsal prestriate cortex to the posterior parietal cortex; according to one theory, its function is the control of visually guided behavior.

Dorsolateral corticorubrospinal tract. The descending motor tract that synapses in the red nucleus of the midbrain, decussates, and descends in the dorsolateral spinal white matter.

Dorsolateral corticospinal tract. The motor tract that leaves the primary motor cortex, descends to the medullary pyramids, decussates, and then descends in the contralateral dorsolateral spinal white matter.

Dorsolateral prefrontal association cortex. The area of the prefrontal association cortex that plays a role in the evaluation of external stimuli and the initiation of complex voluntary motor responses.

Down syndrome. A disorder associated with the presence of an extra chromosome 21, resulting in disfigurement and mental retardation.

Drug metabolism. The conversion of a drug from its active form to a nonactive form.

Drug self-administration paradigm. A test of the addictive potential of drugs in which animals can inject drugs into themselves by pressing a lever.

Drug tolerance. A state of decreased susceptibility to a drug that develops as a result of exposure to the drug.

Dual-opponent color cells. Neurons that respond to the differences in the wavelengths of light stimulating adjacent areas of their receptive field.

Duchenne smile. A genuine smile, one that includes contraction of the orbicularis oculi muscles.

Duodenum. The upper portion of the intestine through which most of the glucose and amino acids are absorbed into the bloodstream.

Duplexity theory. The theory that cones and rods mediate photopic and scotopic vision, respectively.

Dura mater. The tough outer meninx.

Dynamic contraction. Contraction of a muscle that causes the muscle to shorten.

Dynamic phase. The first phase of the VMH syndrome, characterized by grossly excessive eating and weight gain.

Dyslexia. A specific pathological difficulty in reading, one that does not result from general visual, motor, or intellectual deficits.

Efferent nerves. Nerves that carry motor signals from the central nervous system to the skeletal muscles or internal organs.

Ejaculation. Ejection of sperm.

Electrocardiogram (ECG or EKG). A recording of the electrical activity of the heart.

Electroconvulsive shock (ECS). An intense, brief, diffuse, seizure-inducing current administered to the brain via large electrodes attached to the scalp.

Electroencephalogram (EEG). A measure of the electrical activity of the brain, commonly recorded through scalp electrodes.

Electroencephalography. A procedure for recording the gross electrical activity of the brain through disk-shaped electrodes, which in humans are usually taped to the surface of the scalp.

Electromyogram (EMG). A measure of the electrical activity of muscles.

Electromyography. A procedure for recording the gross electrical discharges of muscles.

Electron microscopy. A technique used to study the fine details of cellular structure.

Electrooculogram (EOG). A measure of eye movement.

Electrooculography. A procedure for recording eye movements through electrodes placed around the eye.

Elevated plus maze. A test of defensiveness or anxiety in rats that assesses the tendency of rats to avoid the two open arms of a plus-sign-shaped maze mounted some distance above the floor of a lab.

Embolism. The blockage of blood flow in a smaller blood vessel by a plug that was formed in a larger blood vessel and carried by the bloodstream to the smaller one.

Emergent stage 1 EEG. All periods of stage 1 sleep EEG except initial stage 1; it is associated with REM.

Encapsulated tumors. Tumors that grow within their own membrane.

Encéphale isolé preparation. An experimental preparation in which the brain is separated from the rest of the nervous system by a transection of the caudal brain stem.

Encephalitis. The inflammation associated with brain infection.

Endocrine glands. Ductless glands that release hormones into the general circulation of the body.

Endogenous depression. Depression that appears not to have been triggered by a negative experience.

Endorphins. Endogenous (internally produced) opiate analgesics.

Engram. The physiological change in the brain that is induced by learning and stores the memory of the experience.

Enzymatic degradation. The breakdown of chemicals by enzymes—one of the two mechanisms for deactivating released neurotransmitters.

Enzymes. Chemicals that stimulate or inhibit chemical reactions without directly participating in them.

Epidemiology. The study of factors that influence the distribution of a disease in the general population.

Epilepsy. A neurological disorder characterized by spontaneously recurring seizures.

Epileptic auras. Psychological symptoms that precede the onset of a convulsion.

Epileptogenesis. Development of epilepsy.

Episodic memories. Explicit memories of the particular events and experiences of one's life.

Estradiol. The most common estrogen.

Estrogens. The class of steroid hormones that includes estradiol.

Estrous cycle. The cycle of sexual receptivity and non-receptivity displayed by many female mammals.

Estrus. The portion of the estrous cycle characterized by fertility and sexual receptivity (*estrus* is a noun and *estrous* an adjective).

Ethological research. The study of animal behavior in its natural environment.

Ethology. The study of the behavior of animals in their natural environments.

Event-related potentials (ERPs). The EEG waves that regularly accompany certain psychological events.

Evolutionary perspective. The approach that focuses on the environmental pressures that likely led to the evolution of the characteristics (e.g., of brain and behavior) of current species.

Evolve. To undergo gradual orderly change.

Exaptation. A characteristic that evolved because it performed one function but was then co-opted to perform another.

Excitatory postsynaptic potentials (EPSPs). Graded postsynaptic depolarizations, which increase the likelihood that an action potential will be generated.

Exocrine glands. Glands that secrete chemicals into ducts that carry them to the surface of the body.

Exocytosis. The process of releasing a neurotransmitter.

Experimental autoimmune encephalomyelitis. A model of multiple sclerosis that can be induced in laboratory animals by injecting them with myelin and a preparation that stimulates the body's immune system.

Explicit memories. Conscious memories.

Expressive. Pertaining to the generation of language; that is, pertaining to writing or talking.

Extensors. Muscles that act to straighten or extend a joint.

Exteroceptive sensory systems. The five sensory systems that interpret stimuli from outside the body: vision, hearing, touch, smell, and taste.

Facial feedback hypothesis. The hypothesis that our facial expressions can influence how we feel.

False transmitter. A receptor blocker; a chemical that binds to a synaptic receptor without activating it and, in so doing, blocks the action of the neurotransmitter.

Far-field potentials. EEG signals recorded in attenuated form at the scalp because they originate far away—for example, in the brain stem.

Fasciculation. The tendency of growing axons to follow the route of preceding axons.

Fasting phase. The metabolic phase that begins when energy from the preceding meal is no longer sufficient to meet the immediate needs of the body and during which energy is extracted from fat and glycogen stores.

Fear conditioning. Establishing fear of a previously neutral conditional stimulus by pairing it with an aversive unconditional stimulus.

Fear. The emotion that is normally elicited by the presence or expectation of threatening stimuli.

Feminizes. Enhances or produces female characteristics.

Fetal alcohol syndrome (FAS). A syndrome produced by prenatal exposure to alcohol and characterized by mental retardation, low birth weight, and a variety of other physical abnormalities.

Fitness. The ability of an organism to survive and contribute its genes to the next generation.

Flavor. The combined impression of taste and smell.

Flexors. Muscles that act to bend or flex a joint.

Follicle-stimulating hormone (FSH). The gonadotropic hormone that stimulates development of ovarian follicles.

Fourier analysis. A mathematical procedure for breaking down a complex wave form (e.g., an EEG signal) into component sine waves of varying frequency.

Fovea. The central indentation of the retina, which is specialized for high-acuity vision.

Fraternal twins. Twins that develop from different zygotes and thus are no more similar than any pair of siblings; dizygotic twins.

Free fatty acids. The main source of the body's energy during the fasting phase; released from body fat stores.

Free nerve endings. Cutaneous receptors that are composed of nerve endings without specialized structures on them; they detect cutaneous pain and changes in skin temperature.

Free-running period. The duration of one cycle of a free-running rhythm.

Free-running rhythms. Circadian rhythms that do not depend on environmental cues to keep them running on a regular schedule.

Frontal eye field. A small area of prefrontal cortex that plays a role in the control of eye movements.

Frontal operculum. The neuroanatomical designation for the area of prefrontal cortex that in the left hemisphere roughly corresponds to Broca's area.

Frontal sections. Any slices of brain tissue cut in a plane that is parallel to the face; also termed *coronal sections*.

Functional MRI (fMRI). A magnetic resonance imaging technique for measuring brain activity.

Functional segregation. Organization into different areas, each of which performs a different function; for example, in sensory systems, different areas of secondary and association cortex analyze different aspects of the same sensory stimulus.

Functional tolerance. Tolerance resulting from a reduction in the reactivity of the nervous system (or other sites of action) to a drug.

Gametes. Egg cells and sperm cells.

Ganglia. Clusters of neuronal cell bodies in the peripheral nervous system (singluar *ganglion).*

Gastric ulcers. Lesions to the lining of the stomach or duodenum, a common consequence of stress.

Gate-control theory. The theory that neural signals that descend from the brain can activate neural gating circuits in the spinal cord to block incoming pain signals.

Gene. A unit of inheritance; for example, the section of a chromosome that controls the synthesis of one protein.

Gene expression. The production of the protein specified by a particular gene.

Gene knockout techniques. Procedures for creating organisms that lack a particular gene.

Gene maps. Maps that indicate the relative positions of genes along a chromosome.

Gene replacement techniques. Procedures for creating organisms in which a particular gene has been deleted and replaced with another.

General paresis. The insanity and intellectual deterioration resulting from syphilitic infection.

Generalizability. The degree to which the results of a study can be applied to other individuals or situations.

Generalized anxiety disorders. Anxiety disorders that are not precipitated by any obvious event.

Generalized seizures. Seizures that involve the entire brain.

Genitals. The external reproductive organs.

Genotype. The traits that an organism can pass on to its offspring through its genetic material.

Glial cells. The supportive cells of the central nervous system.

Global amnesia. Amnesia for information in all sensory modalities.

Global aphasia. Almost total elimination of all language-related abilities.

Glucagon. A pancreatic hormone that promotes the release of free fatty acids from adipose tissue and their use as the body's primary fuel.

Glucocorticoids. Steroid hormones that are released from the adrenal cortex in response to stressors.

Gluconeogenesis. The process by which glucose is synthesized from the breakdown products of the body's protein.

Glucose. The simple sugar breakdown product of complex starches and sugars; it is the body's primary, directly utilizable source of energy.

Glucostatic theory. The theory that eating is controlled by deviations from a hypothetical blood glucose set point.

Glutamate. The brain's most prevalent exitatory neurotransmitter, whose excessive release causes much of the brain damage resulting from cerebral ischemia.

Golgi complex. Structures in the cell bodies and buttons of neurons that package neurotransmitters and other molecules in vesicles.

Golgi stain. A neural stain that completely darkens a few of the neurons in each slice of tissue, thereby revealing their silhouettes.

Golgi tendon organs. Receptors that are embedded in tendons and are sensitive to the amount of tension in the muscles to which their tendons are attached.

Gonadectomy. The surgical removal of the gonads (testes or ovaries); castration.

Gonadotropin. The anterior pituitary hormone that stimulates the release of hormones from the gonads.

Gonadotropin-releasing hormone. The hypothalamic releasing hormone that controls the release of the two gonadotropic hormones from the anterior pituitary.

Gonads. The testes and ovaries.

Graded responses. Responses whose magnitude is indicative of the magnitude of the stimuli that induce them.

Grammatical analysis. Analysis of a language in terms of its rules of sentence structure.

Grand mal seizure. A seizure whose symptoms are loss of consciousness, loss of equilibrium, and a violent tonic-clonic convulsion.

Growth cone. Amoebalike structure at the tip of each growing axon or dendrite that guides its growth to its appropriate target.

Growth hormone. The anterior pituitary hormone that acts directly on bone and muscle tissue to produce the pubertal growth spurt.

Guilty-knowledge technique. A lie-detection technique in which the polygrapher records autonomic nervous system responses to a list of control and crime-related information known only to the criminal and the examiners.

Hair cells. The receptors of the auditory system.

Haloperidol. A butyrophenone antischizophrenic drug.

Harrison Narcotics Act. The act, passed in 1914, that made it illegal to sell or use opium, morphine, or cocaine in the United States.

Helping-hand phenomenon. The redirection of one hand of a split-brain patient by the other hand.

Hematoma. A bruise.

Hemianopsic. Having a scotoma that covers half the field of vision.

Hemispherectomy. The removal of one cerebral hemisphere.

Heritability estimate. A numerical estimate of the proportion of variability that occurred in a particular trait in a particular study and that resulted from the genetic variation among the subjects in that study.

Heroin. A powerful semisynthetic opiate.

Heschl's gyrus. The temporal lobe gyrus that is the location of primary auditory cortex.

Heterosexual. Sexually attracted to members of the other sex.

Heterozygous. Possessing two different genes for a particular trait.

Hierarchical organization. Organization into a series of levels that can be ranked with respect to one another; for example, primary cortex, secondary cortex, and association cortex perform progressively more detailed analyses.

Hippocampus. A structure of the medial temporal lobes that plays a role in memory for spatial location.

Homeostasis. The stability of an organism's internal environment.

Hominids. The family of primates that includes *Homo sapiens* (humans), *Homo erectus,* and *Australopithecus.*

Homologous. Having a similar structure because of a common evolutionary ancestor (e.g., a human's arm and a bird's wing are homologous).

Homosexual. Sexually attracted to members of the same sex.

Homozygous. Possessing two identical genes for a particular trait.

Horizontal cells. A layer of retinal neurons whose function is lateral communication.

Horizontal sections. Any slices of brain tissue cut in a plane that is parallel to the top of the brain.

Hormones. Chemicals released by the endocrine system into general circulation.

Human genome project. The international effort to construct a detailed map of the human chromosomes.

Huntington's disease. A progressive terminal disorder of motor and intellectual function that is produced in adulthood by a dominant gene.

H-Y antigen. The protein hormone that stimulates the cells of the medullary portion of the primordial gonads to proliferate and develop into testes.

5-Hydroxytryptophan (5-HTP). The precursor of serotonin.

Hyperphagia. Excessive eating.

Hyperpolarize. To increase the membrane potential.

Hypersomnia. Disorders characterized by excessive sleep or sleepiness.

Hypertension. Chronically high blood pressure.

Hypnagogic hallucinations. Vivid dreamlike states that some people occasionally experience just as they are falling asleep.

Hypnotic drugs. Sleep-promoting drugs.

Hypothalamopituitary portal system. The vascular network that carries hormones from the hypothalamus to the anterior pituitary.

Hypoxia. Shortage of oxygen supply to tissue—for example, to the brain.

Iatrogenic. Physician-created.

Identical twins. Twins that develop from the same zygote and are thus genetically identical; monozygotic twins.

Imipramine. The first tricyclic antidepressant drug.

Immune system. The system that protects the body against infectious microorganisms.

Immunocytochemistry. A procedure for locating particular proteins in the brain by labeling their antibodies with a dye or radioactive element and then exposing slices of brain tissue to the labeled antibodies.

Implicit memories. Memories that are expressed by improved performance without conscious recall or recognition.

Impotent. Unable to achieve a penile erection.

In situ hybridization. A technique for locating particular proteins in the brain; molecules that bind to the mRNA that directs the synthesis of the target protein are synthesized; then these ligands are labeled, and brain slices are exposed to them.

Incentive-sensitization theory. Theory that addictions develop when drug use sensitizes the neural circuits mediating "wanting" of the drug—not necessarily "liking" for the drug.

Incomplete-pictures test. A test of memory involving the improved ability to identify fragmented figures that have been previously observed.

Independent variable. The difference between experimental conditions that is arranged by the experimenter.

Induction. The process of causing an enduring change in the nervous system.

Inferior. Toward the bottom of the primate head or brain.

Inferior colliculi. The structures of the tectum that receive auditory input from the superior olives.

Inferotemporal cortex. The cortex of the inferior temporal lobe, an area of secondary visual cortex that is involved in object recognition.

Infiltrating tumors. Tumors that grow diffusely through surrounding tissue.

Inhibitory factors. Hypothalamic hormones thought to regulate anterior pituitary hormones by inhibiting their release.

Inhibitory postsynaptic potentials (IPSPs). Graded postsynaptic hyperpolarizations, which decrease the likelihood that an action potential will be generated.

Initial stage 1 EEG. The period of the stage 1 EEG that occurs at the onset of sleep; it is not associated with REM.

Insomnia. Disorders of initiating and maintaining sleep.

Instinctive behaviors. Behaviors that occur in all like members of a species, even when there seems to have been no opportunity for them to have been learned.

Insulin. A pancreatic hormone that facilitates the entry of glucose into cells and the conversion of bloodborne fuels to forms that can be stored.

Integration. Adding or combining a number of individual signals into one overall signal.

Internal desynchronization. The cycling on different schedules of the free-running circadian cycles of two different processes.

Interneurons. Neurons whose processes are contained within a single brain structure; neurons with short axons or no axons at all.

Intracranial self-stimulation (ICSS). The repeated performance of a response that delivers electrical stimulation to certain sites in the brain.

Intrafusal motor neuron. A motor neuron that innervates an intrafusal muscle.

Intrafusal muscle. A threadlike muscle that adjusts the tension on a muscle spindle.

Intromission. Insertion of the penis into the vagina.

Ion channels. Pores in membranes through which specific ions pass.

Ionotropic receptors. Receptors that are associated with ligand-activated ion channels.

Ions. Positively or negatively charged particles.

Iproniazid. The first antidepressant drug; a monoamine oxidase inhibitor.

Ipsilateral. On the same side of the body.

Isometric contraction. Contraction of a muscle that increases the force of its pull but does not shorten the muscle.

James-Lange theory. The theory that emotional experience results from the brain's perception of the pattern of autonomic and somatic nervous system responses elicited by emotional stimuli.

Jet lag. The adverse effects on body function of zeitgebers being accelerated during eastern flights or decelerated during western flights.

Ketones. Breakdown products of fat that can be used as a source of energy for the brain when glucose is in short supply.

Kindling phenomenon. The progressive development and intensification of convulsions elicited by a series of periodic low-intensity stimulations—most commonly by daily electrical stimulations to the amygdala.

Kluver-Bucy syndrome. The syndrome of behavioral changes (e.g., lack of fear and hypersexuality) that is induced in primates by bilateral damage to the anterior temporal lobes.

Korsakoff's syndrome. A neuropsychological disorder that is common in alcoholics and whose primary symptom is severe memory loss.

Lateral. Away from the midline of the body and toward the body's lateral surfaces.

Lateral geniculate nuclei. The six-layered thalamic structures that receive input from the retinas and transmit their output to the primary visual cortex.

Lateral hypothalamus (LH). The area of the hypothalamus once thought to be the feeding center.

Lateral inhibition. Inhibition of adjacent neurons or receptors in a topographic array.

Lateralization of function. The unequal representation of a particular psychological function in the two hemispheres of the brain.

L-Dopa. The chemical precursor of dopamine, which is used in the treatment of Parkinson's disease.

Leaky-barrel model. A settling-point model of body-fat regulation.

Learning. The brain's ability to change in response to its experience.

Leptin. A protein normally synthesized in fat cells; it is thought to act as a negative feedback fat signal, reducing consumption.

Leucotome. Any one of the various surgical devices used for performing lobotomies—*leucotomy* is another word for lobotomy.

Lexical procedure. A procedure for reading aloud that is based on stored information acquired about the pronunciation of specific words.

Ligand. A molecule that binds to another molecule; neurotransmitters are ligands of their receptors.

Limbic system. A collection of interconnected nuclei and tracts that circles the thalamus and is widely assumed to play a role in emotion.

Linkage. The tendency for traits that are encoded on the same chromosome to be inherited together.

Lipids. Fats.

Lipogenesis. The production of body fat.

Lipolysis. The breakdown of body fat.

Lipostatic theory. The theory that eating is controlled by deviations from a hypothetical body-fat set point.

Lithium. A metallic ion that is used in the treatment of bipolar affective disorder.

Lobectomy. An operation in which a lobe, or a major part of one, is removed from the brain.

Lobotomy. An operation in which a lobe, or a major part of one, is separated from the rest of the brain by a large cut but is not removed.

Long-term potentiation (LTP). The enduring facilitation of synaptic transmission that occurs following activation of a synapse by high-intensity, high-frequency stimulation of the presynaptic neurons.

Lordosis. The intromission-facilitating, arched-back, tail-to-the-side posture of female rodent sexual receptivity.

Lordosis quotient. The proportion of mounts that elicit lordosis.

Lucid dreams. Dreams in which the dreamer is aware that she or he is dreaming and can influence the course of the dream.

Luteinizing hormone (LH). The gonadotropic hormone that causes the developing ovum to be released from its follicle.

Lymphocytes. Specialized white blood cells that play important roles in the body's immune reactions.

Macrophage. A large phagocyte that plays a role in cell-mediated immunity.

Magnetic resonance imaging (MRI). A procedure in which high-resolution images of the structures of the living brain are constructed from the measurement of waves that hydrogen atoms emit when they are activated by radio-frequency waves in a magnetic field.

Magnetoencephalography (MEG). A technique for recording changes produced in magnetic fields around the head by changes in underlying patterns of neural activity.

Magnocellular layers. The layers of the lateral geniculate nuclei that are composed of large neurons; the bottom two layers (also called *M layers*).

Malignant tumors. Tumors that may continue to grow in the body even after attempted surgical removal.

Mammals. Species whose young are fed from mammary glands.

Mania. An affective disorder in which the patient is impulsive, overconfident, highly energetic, and distractible.

MAO inhibitors. Drugs that increase the level of monoamine neurotransmitters by inhibiting the action of monoamine oxidase.

Masculinizes. Enhances or produces male characteristics.

Medial. Toward the midline of the body.

Medial diencephalic amnesia. Amnesia that is associated with damage to the medial diencephalon (e.g., Korsakoff's amnesia).

Medial dorsal nuclei. The thalamic relay nuclei of the olfactory system.

Medial geniculate nuclei. The auditory thalamic nuclei that receive input from the inferior colliculi and project to primary auditory cortex.

Medial lemniscus. The somatosensory pathway between the dorsal column nuclei and the ventral posterior nucleus of the thalamus.

Medial preoptic area. The area of the hypothalamus that includes the sexually dimorphic nuclei and that plays a key role in the control of male sexual behavior.

Medial temporal lobe amnesia. Amnesia associated with bilateral damage to the medial temporal lobes; its major feature is anterograde amnesia for explicit memories in combination with preserved intellectual functioning.

Mediodorsal nuclei. A pair of medial diencephalic nuclei in the thalamus, damage to which is thought to be responsible for many of the memory deficits associated with Korsakoff's syndrome.

Meiosis. The process of cell division that produces cells (e.g., egg cells and sperm cells) with half the chromosomes of the parent cell.

Melatonin. A hormone synthesized from serotonin in the pineal gland.

Membrane potential. The difference in electrical charge between the inside and the outside of a cell.

Memory. The brain's ability to store and access the learned effects of its experiences.

Memory consolidation. The transfer of short-term memories to long-term storage.

Meninges. The three protective membranes that cover the brain and spinal cord (singular *meninx).*

Meningiomas. Tumors that grow between the meninges.

Meningitis. Inflammation of the meninges, usually caused by bacterial infection.

Menstrual cycle. The hormone-regulated cycle in women of follicle growth, egg release, uterus lining buildup, and menstruation.

Mesoderm layer. The middle of the three cell layers in the developing embryo.

Mesotelencephalic dopamine system. The ascending projections of dopamine-releasing neurons from the substantia nigra and ventral tegmental area of the mesencephalon into various regions of the telencephalon.

Messenger RNA. The strands of RNA that are transcribed from DNA and direct the synthesis of proteins.

Metabolic tolerance. Tolerance that results from a reduction in the amount of a drug getting to its sites of action.

Metabotropic receptors. Receptors that are associated with signal proteins and G proteins.

Metastatic tumors. Tumors that originate in one organ and spread to another.

Microelectrodes. Extremely fine recording electrodes, which are used for intracellular recording.

Microsleeps. Brief periods of sleep that occur in sleep-deprived subjects while they remain sitting or standing.

Microspectrophotometry. A technique that has been used to measure the absorption spectrum of the photopigment contained in a single cone.

Migration. The movement of cells from their site of creation in the ventricular zone of the neural tube to their ultimate location in the mature nervous system.

Minor hemisphere. A term used in the past to refer to the right hemisphere, based on the incorrect assumption that the left hemisphere is dominant in all complex activities.

Mitochondria. The energy-generating, DNA-containing structures in each cell's cytoplasm.

Mitosis. The process of cell division that produces cells with the same number of chromosomes as the parent cell.

Monocular. Involving only one eye.

Monogamy. A pattern of mate bonding in which one male bonds with only one female.

Monophasic sleep cycles. Sleep cycles that regularly involve only one period of sleep per day, typically at night.

Morgan's Canon. The rule that the simplest possible interpretation for a behavioral result should be given precedence.

Morphine. The major psychoactive ingredient in opium.

Morris water maze. A pool of milky water with a goal platform invisible just beneath its surface; it is used to study the ability of rats to learn spatial locations.

Morris water maze test. A widely used test of spatial memory in which rats must learn to swim directly to a platform hidden just beneath the surface of a circular pool of murky water.

Motor end-plate. The receptive area on a muscle fiber at a neuromuscular junction.

Motor equivalence. The ability of the sensorimotor system to carry out the same basic movement in different ways that involve different muscles.

Motor homunculus. The somatotopic map of the human primary motor cortex.

Motor pool. All of the motor neurons that innervate the fibers of a given muscle.

Motor units. A single motor neuron and all of the muscle fibers that are innervated by it.

MPTP. A neurotoxin that produces a disorder in primates that is similar to Parkinson's disease.

Müllerian system. The embryonic precursors of the female reproductive ducts.

Müllerian-inhibiting substance. The testicular hormone that causes the precursors of the female reproductive ducts to degenerate and the testes to descend.

Multiple sclerosis (MS). A progressive disease of the CNS myelin.

Multipolar neuron. A neuron with more than two processes emanating from its cell body.

Mumby box. An apparatus that is used in a rat version of the delayed nonmatching-to-sample test.

Muscle spindles. Receptors that are embedded in muscle tissue and are sensitive to changes in muscle length.

Mutations. Accidental alterations in genes that arise during chromosome duplication.

Myelin stains. Stains that selectively dye the sheaths of myelinated axons.

Narcolepsy. A disorder of hypersomnia characterized by repeated, brief daytime sleep attacks.

Narcotic. A legal classification of certain drugs, mostly opiates.

Nasal hemiretina. The half of each retina next to the nose.

Natural selection. The idea that heritable traits that are associated with high rates of survival and reproduction are preferentially passed on to future generations.

Nature–nurture issue. The debate about the relative contributions of nature (genes) and nurture (experience) to the behavioral capacities of individuals.

NEAT. Nonexercise activity thermogenesis, which is generated by activities such as fidgeting and the maintenance of posture.

Necrosis. Passive cell death, which is characterized by inflammation.

Negative feedback systems. Systems in which feedback from changes in one direction elicit compensatory effects in the opposite direction.

Nerve growth factor (NGF). A neurotrophin that attracts the growing axons of the sympathetic nervous system and promotes their survival.

Nerves. Bundles of axons in the peripheral nervous system.

Neural crest. The structure formed by cells breaking off from the neural groove during the formation of the neural tube; it develops into the peripheral nervous system.

Neural plate. A small patch of ectodermal tissue on the dorsal surface of the vertebrate embryo, from which the neural groove, the neural tube, and, ultimately, the mature nervous system develop.

Neural proliferation. The rapid increase in the number of neurons that occurs following the formation of the neural tube.

Neural regeneration. The regrowth of damaged neurons.

Neural tube. The tube formed in the vertebrate embryo when the edges of the neural groove fuse; it develops into the central nervous system.

Neuroanatomy. The study of the structure of the nervous system.

Neurochemistry. The study of the chemical bases of neural activity.

Neuroendocrinology. The study of the interactions between the nervous system and the endocrine system.

Neuroleptics. Drugs that alleviate schizophrenic symptoms.

Neuromuscular junctions. The synapses of a motor neuron on a muscle.

Neurons. Cells of the nervous system that are specialized for receiving and transmitting electrochemical signals.

Neuropathology. The study of nervous system disorders.

Neuropharmacology. The study of the effects of drugs on neural activity.

Neurophysiology. The study of the functions and activities of the nervous system.

Neuropsychology. The division of biopsychology that studies the psychological effects of brain damage in human patients.

Neuroscience. The scientific study of the nervous system.

Neurotoxins. Neural poisons.

Neurotrophins. Chemicals that are supplied to developing neurons by their targets and that promote their survival.

Nicotine. The major psychoactive ingredient of tobacco.

Nigrostriatal pathway. The pathway along which axons from the substantia nigra project to the striatum.

Nissl stain. A neural stain that has an affinity for structures of neural cell bodies.

Nitric oxide. A soluable-gas neurotransmitter that is thought to serve as a retrograde messenger in the production of LTP-maintaining changes in presynaptic neurons.

NMDA (N-methyl-D-aspartate) receptors. Glutamate receptors that play key roles in the development of stroke-induced brain damage and long-term potentiation at glutaminergic synapses.

Nocturnal myoclonus. Periodic sleep-disrupting twitching of the legs during sleep.

Nodes of Ranvier. The gaps in axonal myelin.

Nondirected synapses. Synapses at which the site of neurotransmitter release and the target site are not close together.

Nuclei. The DNA-containing structures of cells; also, clusters of neuronal cell bodies in the central nervous system (singular *nucleus).*

Nucleotide bases. A class of chemical substances that includes adenine, thymine, guanine, and cytosine—the constituents of the genetic code.

Nucleus accumbens. A nucleus of the ventral striatum and a major terminal of the mesocorticolimbic dopamine pathway.

Nucleus magnocellularis. The nucleus of the caudal reticular formation that promotes relaxation of the core muscles during REM sleep and during cataplectic attacks.

Nutritive density. Calories per unit volume of food.

Ob/ob mice. Mice that are homozygous for the mutant ob gene; their body fat produces no leptin, and they become very obese.

Obsessive-compulsive disorders. Anxiety disorders characterized by recurring uncontrollable thoughts and impulses.

Off-center cells. Neurons that respond to lights shone in the center of their receptive fields with "off" firing and to lights shone in the periphery of their fields with "on" firing.

Olfactory bulbs. The first cranial nerves, whose output goes primarily to the amygdala and piriform cortex.

Olfactory mucosa. The mucous membrane that lines the upper nasal passages and contains the olfactory receptor cells.

Oligodendrocytes. Glial cells that myelinate axons of the central nervous system; also known as oligodendroglia.

Ommatidia. The visual receptors of the horseshoe crab.

On-center cells. Cells that respond to lights shone in the center of their receptive fields with "on" firing and to lights shone in the periphery of their fields with "off" firing.

Ontogeny. The development of individuals through their life span.

Open-field test. A method for recording and scoring the activity of an animal in a large, barren chamber.

Operant conditioning paradigm. A paradigm in which the rate of a particular voluntary response is increased by reinforcement or decreased by punishment.

Operator genes. Short segments of DNA that determine whether or not messenger RNA will be transcribed from associated structural genes.

Opiates. Morphine, codeine, heroin, and other chemicals with similar structures or effects.

Opium. The sap that exudes from the opium poppy.

Opponent-process theory. The theory that a receptor or neuron signals one color when it responds in one way (e.g., by increasing its firing rate) and signals its complementary color when it responds in the opposite way (e.g., by decreasing its firing rate).

Optic tectum. The main destination of visual neurons in lower vertebrates.

Orbitofrontal cortex. The cortex of the inferior frontal lobes, which receives olfactory input from the thalamus.

Orchidectomy. The removal of the testes.

Orexin. A neuropeptide that has been implicated in narcolepsy in dogs and in knockout mice.

Organ of Corti. The auditory receptor organ, comprising the basilar membrane, the hair cells, and the tectorial membrane.

Orthodromic conduction. Axonal conduction in the normal direction; conduction from the cell body toward the terminal buttons.

Ossicles. The three small bones of the middle ear: the malleus, the incus, and the stapes.

Oval window. The cochlear membrane that transfers vibrations from the ossicles to the fluid of the cochlea.

Ovariectomy. The removal of the ovaries.

Ovaries. The female gonads.

Oxytocin. One of the two major hormones of the posterior pituitary, which in females stimulates contractions of the uterus during labor and the ejection of milk during suckling.

P300 wave. The positive EEG wave that usually occurs about 300 msec after a momentary stimulus that has considerable meaning for the subject.

Pacinian corpuscles. The largest and most deeply positioned cutaneous receptors, which are sensitive to sudden displacements of the skin.

Paired-image subtraction technique. Using PET and fMRI to locate constituent cognitive processes in the brain by producing an image of the difference in brain activity associated with two cognitive tasks that differ in terms of a single constituent cognitive process.

Panic disorders. Anxiety disorders characterized by recurring rapid-onset attacks of extreme fear that are often associated with choking, heart palpitations, and shortness of breath.

Parachlorophenylalanine (PCPA). A chemical that blocks the synthesis of serotonin and produces insomnia in cats.

Parallel processing. The simultaneous analysis of a signal in different ways by the multiple parallel pathways of a neural network.

Parasympathetic nerves. Those motor nerves of the autonomic nervous system that project from the brain (as components of cranial nerves) or from the sacral region of the spinal cord.

Paraventricular nuclei. Hypothalamic nuclei that play a role in eating and synthesize hormones released by the posterior pituitary.

Parkinson's disease. A movement disorder that is associated with degeneration of dopaminergic neurons in the nigrostriatal pathway.

Partial seizures. Seizures that do not involve the entire brain.

Parvocellular layers. The layers of the lateral geniculate nuclei that are composed of small neurons; the top four layers (also called *P layers*).

Patellar tendon reflex. The stretch reflex that is elicited when the patellar tendon is struck.

Pavlovian conditioning paradigm. A paradigm in which the experimenter pairs an initially neutral stimulus (conditional stimulus) with a stimulus (unconditional stimulus) that elicits a reflexive response (unconditional response); after several pairings, the neutral stimulus elicits a response (conditional response).

Peptide hormones. Hormones that are short strings of amino acids.

Peptides. Short chains of amino acids, some of which function as neurotransmitters.

Perception. The higher-order process of integrating, recognizing, and interpreting complex patterns of sensations.

Periaqueductal gray (PAG). The gray matter around the cerebral aqueduct, which contains opiate receptors and activates a descending analgesia circuit.

Perimetry test. The procedure used to map scotomas.

Peripheral nervous system (PNS). The portion of the nervous system outside the skull and spine.

Perseveration. The tendency to continue making a formerly correct response that is currently incorrect.

Petit mal seizure. A generalized seizure that is characterized by a disturbance of consciousness and a 3-per-second spike-and-wave EEG discharge.

Phagocytosis. The consumption of dead tissue and invading microorganisms by specialized body cells (phagocytes).

Phantom limb. The vivid perception that an amputated limb still exists.

Phenothiazines. A class of antischizophrenic drugs that bind effectively to both D_1 and D_2 receptors.

Phenotype. An organism's observable traits.

Phenylketonuria (PKU). A neurological disorder whose symptoms are vomiting, seizures, hyperactivity, hyper-irritability, mental retardation, and high levels of phenyl-pyruvic acid in the urine.

Phenylpyruvic acid. A substance that is found in abnormally high concentrations in the urine of those suffering from phenylketonuria.

Pheromones. Odors that are released by an animal and elicit specific patterns of behavior in its conspecifics.

Phobic anxiety disorders. Anxiety disorders characterized by extreme, largely irrational fears of specific objects or situations.

Phonemes. Individual speech sounds.

Phonetic procedure. A procedure for reading aloud that involves the application of a language's rules of pronunciation.

Phonological analysis. Sound-related analysis of a language.

Photopic spectral sensitivity curve. The graph of the sensitivity of cone-mediated vision to different wavelengths of light.

Photopic vision. Cone-mediated vision, which predominates when lighting is good.

Phylogeny. The evolutionary development of species.

Physical-dependence theory of addiction. The theory that the main factor that motivates drug addicts to keep taking drugs is the prevention or termination of withdrawal symptoms.

Physically dependent. Being in a state in which the discontinuation of drug taking will induce withdrawal effects.

Physiological psychology. The division of biopsychology that studies the neural mechanisms of behavior through direct manipulation of the brains of nonhuman animal subjects in controlled experiments.

Pia mater. The delicate, innermost meninx.

Pineal gland. The endocrine gland that is the human body's sole source of melatonin.

Pioneer growth cones. The first growth cones to travel along a particular route in the developing nervous system.

Piriform cortex. The area of medial temporal cortex that receives direct olfactory input.

Pituitary stalk. The structure connecting the hypothalamus and the pituitary.

Place cells. Neurons that develop place fields—that is, that come to fire rapidly only when the subject is in a particular place in a familiar test environment.

Planum temporale. An area of the temporal lobe that in the left hemisphere roughly corresponds to Wernicke's area.

Plethysmography. Measuring changes in the volume of blood in a part of the body.

Polyandry. A pattern of mate bonding in which one female bonds with more than one male.

Polygraphy. A method of interrogation in which autonomic nervous system indexes of emotion are used to infer the truthfulness of the responses.

Polygyny. A pattern of mate bonding in which one male bonds with more than one female; the most prevalent form of mate bonding in mammals.

Polyphasic sleep cycles. Sleep cycles that regularly involve more than one period of sleep per day.

Positive-incentive theory. The theory that behaviors (e.g., eating and drinking) are motivated by their anticipated pleasurable effects.

Positive-incentive theory of addiction. The theory that the primary factor in most cases of addiction is a craving for the pleasure-producing effects of drugs.

Positive-incentive value. The anticipated pleasure involved in the performance of a particular behavior, such as eating a particular food or drinking a particular beverage.

Positron emission tomography (PET). A technique for visualizing the activity in the brain by measuring the accumulation of radioactive 2-deoxyglucose (2-DG) or radioactive water in the various regions of the brain.

Posterior. Toward the tail end of a vertebrate or toward the back of the head.

Posterior parietal cortex. An area of association cortex that receives input from the visual, auditory, and somatosensory systems and is involved in the perception of spatial location and guidance of voluntary behavior.

Posterior pituitary. The part of the pituitary gland that contains the terminals of hypothalamic neurons.

Postsynaptic inhibition. A form of inhibition that reduces a neuron's responsiveness to all excitatory synaptic inputs.

Posttraumatic amnesia (PTA). Amnesia produced by a nonpenetrating head injury (e.g., by a blow to the head that does not penetrate the skull).

Prefrontal lobes. The large areas, left and right, at the very front of the brain.

Prefrontal lobotomy. A surgical procedure in which the connections between the prefrontal lobes and the rest of the brain are cut as a treatment for mental illness.

Premotor cortex. The area of secondary motor cortex that lies between the supplementary motor area and the lateral fissure.

Prestriate cortex. The area of secondary visual cortex just anterior to the primary visual cortex.

Presynaptic inhibition. A form of inhibition that selectively reduces a neuron's responsiveness to specific synaptic input; it is mediated by excitatory axoaxonal synapses.

Primary motor cortex. The cortex of the precentral gyrus, which is the major point of departure for motor signals descending from the cerebral cortex into lower levels of the sensorimotor system.

Primary sensory cortex. An area of sensory cortex that receives most of its input directly from the thalamic relay nuclei of one sensory system.

Primary visual cortex. The area of the cortex that receives direct input from the lateral geniculate nuclei (also called *striate cortex*).

Primates. One of 14 different orders of mammals; there are five families of primates: prosimians, New-World monkeys, Old-World monkeys, apes, and hominids.

Primed. Induced to resume self-stimulation by a few "free" stimulations.

Proceptive behaviors. Behaviors that serve to attract the sexual advances of the other sex.

Progesterone. A progestin that prepares the uterus and breasts for pregnancy.

Progestins. The class of gonadal hormones that includes progesterone.

Prosody. Emotional tone of voice.

Prosopagnosia. Visual agnosia for faces.

Protein hormones. Hormones that are long strings of amino acids.

Proteins. Long chains of amino acids.

Proximal segment. The segment of a cut axon between the cut and the cell body.

Prozac. The trade name of fluoxetine, the widely prescribed selective serotonin-reuptake inhibitor that is effective against depression and various anxiety disorders.

Psychiatric disorder. A disorder of psychological function sufficiently severe to require treatment by a psychiatrist or a clinical psychologist.

Psychoactive drugs. Drugs that influence subjective experience and behavior by acting on the nervous system.

Psychological dependence. Compulsive drug taking that occurs in the absence of physical dependence.

Psychoneuroimmunology. The study of interactions among psychological factors, the nervous system, and the immune system.

Psychopharmacology. The division of biopsychology that studies the effects of drugs on the brain and behavior.

Psychophysiology. The division of biopsychology that studies the relation between physiological activity and psychological processes in human subjects by noninvasive methods.

Pulsatile hormone release. The typical pattern of hormone release, which occurs in large pulses or surges several times a day.

Punch-drunk syndrome. The psychological disturbances that result from repeated concussions.

Pure research. Research motivated primarily by the curiosity of the researcher and done solely for the purpose of acquiring knowledge.

Purkinje effect. In intense light, red and yellow wavelengths look brighter than blue or green wavelengths of equal intensity; in dim light, blue and green wavelengths look brighter than red and yellow wavelengths of equal intensity.

Pyramidal cell layer. The major layer of cell bodies in the hippocampus.

Pyramidal cells. Large cortical multipolar neurons with a pyramid-shaped cell body, an apical dendrite, and a long axon.

Quasiexperimental studies. Studies of subjects who have been exposed to the conditions of interest in the real world; such studies have the appearance of experiments but are not true experiments because potential confounded variables have not been controlled.

Radial arm maze. A maze in which several arms radiate out from a central starting chamber; it is commonly used to study spatial learning in rats.

Radial arm maze test. A widely used test of rats' spatial ability in which the same arms are baited on each trial, and the rats must learn to visit only the baited arms only one time on each trial.

Radial glial cells. Glial cells that exist in the neural tube only during the period of neural migration; they form a matrix along which developing neurons migrate.

Raphé nuclei. A cluster of serotonin-producing nuclei running in a thin strip down the midline of the caudal reticular formation.

Reactive depression. Depression that is precipitated by a negative experience.

Receptive. Pertaining to the comprehension of language.

Receptive field. The area (e.g., on the retina) within which it is possible for the appropriate stimulus to influence the firing of the neuron.

Receptor blockers. Antagonistic drugs that bind to postsynaptic receptors without activating them and block the access of the usual neurotransmitter.

Receptor subtypes. Different classes of receptors to which the same neurotransmitter can bind.

Receptors. Cells that are specialized to receive chemical, mechanical, or radiant signals from the environment; also proteins that include binding sites for particular neurotransmitters.

Recessive trait. The trait of a dichotomous pair that is not expressed in the phenotype of heterozygous individuals.

Reciprocal innervation. The principle of spinal cord circuitry that causes a muscle to automatically relax when a muscle that is antagonistic to it contracts.

Recuperation theories of sleep. Theories based on the premise that being awake disturbs the body's homeostasis and the function of sleep is to restore it.

Recurrent collateral inhibition. The inhibition of a neuron that is produced by its own activity via a collateral branch of its axon and an inhibitory interneuron.

Reference memory. Memory for the general principles and skills that are required to perform a task.

Relative refractory period. A period after the absolute refractory period during which a higher-than-normal amount of stimulation is necessary to make a neuron fire.

Releasing factors. Suspected (hypothesized) hypothalamic releasing hormones that have not yet been isolated.

Releasing hormones. Hypothalamic hormones that stimulate the release of hormones from the anterior pituitary.

REM sleep. The stage of sleep characterized by rapid eye movements, loss of core muscle tone, and emergent stage 1 EEG.

Repetition priming tests. Tests of implicit memory; in one example, a list of words is presented, then fragments of the original words are presented and the subject is asked to complete them.

Replacement injections. Injections of a hormone whose natural release has been curtailed by the removal of the gland that normally releases it.

Replication. The process by which the DNA molecule duplicates itself.

Reserpine. The first monoamine antagonist to be used in the treatment of schizophrenia; it is the active ingredient of the snakeroot plant.

Response-chunking hypothesis. The idea that practice combines the central sensorimotor programs that control individual responses into programs that control sequences of responses (chunks of behavior).

Resting potential. The steady membrane potential of a neuron at rest, usually about −70 mV.

Restless legs. Tension or uneasiness in the legs that keeps people from falling asleep.

Reticular activating system. The hypothetical arousal system in the reticular formation.

Reticular formation. A complex network of nuclei in the core of the brain stem that contains, among other things, motor programs for complex species-common movements such as walking and swimming.

Retina-geniculate-striate pathway. The major visual pathway from the retina to the striate cortex (primary visual cortex) via the lateral geniculate nuclei of the thalamus.

Retinal ganglion cells. The neurons in the retina whose axons leave the eyeball and form the optic nerve.

Retinex theory. Land's theory that the color of a surface is determined by its reflectance; with the visual system calculating the reflectance of the surfaces in a scene by comparing the ability of adjacent surfaces to reflect short, medium, and long wavelengths.

Retinotopic. Organized, like the primary visual cortex, according to a map of the retina.

Retrograde amnesia. Loss of memory for information learned before the amnesia-inducing brain injury.

Retrograde degeneration. Degeneration of the proximal segment of a cut axon.

Reuptake. The more common of the two mechanisms for deactivating a released neurotransmitter.

Rhinal cortex. An area of medial temporal cortex adjacent to the amygdala and hippocampus.

Rhodopsin. The photopigment of rods.

Ribonucleic acid (RNA). A molecule that is similar to DNA except that it has the nucleotide base uracil and a phosphate and ribose backbone.

Ribosome. A structure in the cell's cytoplasm that reads the genetic code from strands of messenger RNA.

Rods. The visual receptors that mediate achromatic, low-acuity vision under dim light.

Saccades. The rapid movements of the eyes between fixations.

Sagittal sections. Any slices of brain tissue cut in a plane that is parallel to the side of the brain.

Saltatory conduction. Conduction of an action potential from node to node down a myelinated axon.

Satellite cells. The supportive cells of the peripheral nervous system.

Satiety. The motivational state that terminates a meal.

Savants. Intellectually handicapped individuals who nevertheless display amazing and singular cognitive or artistic abilities; savant abilities are sometimes associated with autism.

Schwann cells. The satellite cells that compose the myelin sheaths of PNS axons and promote their regeneration.

Scientific inference. The logical process by which observable events are used to infer the properties of unobservable events.

Scotoma. An area of blindness produced by damage to, or disruption of, part of the visual system.

Scotopic spectral sensitivity curve. The graph of the sensitivity of rod-mediated vision to different wavelengths of light.

Scotopic vision. Rod-mediated vision, which predominates in dim light.

Scrotum. The sac that holds the male testes.

Second messenger. A chemical synthesized in a neuron in response to the binding of a neurotransmitter to a metabotropic receptor in its cell membrane.

Secondary motor cortex. Areas of the cerebral cortex that receive much of their input from association cortex and send much of their output to primary motor cortex.

Secondary sensory cortex. Areas of sensory cortex that receive most of their input from the primary sensory cortex of one system or from other areas of secondary cortex of the same system.

Secondary sex characteristics. Structural features, other than the reproductive organs, that distinguish men from women.

Selective attention. The ability to focus on a small subset of the multitude of stimuli that are being received at any one time.

Self-stimulation paradigm. A paradigm in which animals press a lever to administer reinforcing electrical stimulation to their own brains.

Semantic analysis. Meaning-related analysis of a language.

Semantic memories. Explicit memories of general facts and knowledge.

Semicircular canals. The receptive organs of the vestibular system.

Sensation. The simple process of detecting the presence of stimuli.

Sensitive period. The period during the development of a particular trait, usually early in life, when a particular experience is likely to change the course of its development.

Sensitivity. In vision, the ability to detect the presence of dimly lit objects.

Sensitization. An increase in the sensitivity to a drug effect that develops as the result of exposure to the drug.

Sensorimotor phase. The second of the two phases of birdsong development, during which juvenile birds progress from subsongs to adult songs.

Sensory evoked potential. A change in the electrical activity of the brain that is elicited by the momentary presentation of a sensory stimulus.

Sensory feedback. Sensory signals that are produced by a response and are often used to guide the continuation of the response.

Sensory phase. The first of the two phases of birdsong development, during which young birds do not sing but form memories of the adult songs they hear.

Sensory-specific satiety. The fact that the consumption of a particular food produces more satiety for foods of the same taste than for other foods.

Set point. The value of a physiological parameter that is maintained constantly by physiological or behavioral mechanisms; for example, the body's energy resources are often assumed to be maintained at a constant optimal level by compensatory changes in hunger.

Set-point assumption. The assumption that hunger is typically triggered by the decline of the body's energy reserves below their set point.

Settling point. The point at which various factors that influence the level of some regulated function achieve an equilibrium.

Sex chromosomes. The pair of chromosomes that determine an individual's sex: XX for a female and XY for a male.

Sex-linked traits. Traits that are influenced by genes on the sex chromosomes.

Sexually dimorphic nucleus. The nucleus in the medial preoptic area of rats that is larger in males than in females.

Sham eating. The experimental protocol in which an animal chews and swallows food, which immediately exits its body through a tube implanted in its esophagus.

Sham rage. The exaggerated, poorly directed aggressive responses of decorticate animals.

Signal averaging. A method of increasing the signal-to-noise ratio by reducing background noise.

Simple cells. Neurons in the visual cortex that respond maximally to straight-edge stimuli in a certain position and orientation.

Simple partial seizures. Partial seizures in which the symptoms are primarily sensory or motor or both.

Simultanagnosia. A disorder characterized by the inability to attend to more than one thing at a time.

Sinestrals. Left-handers.

Sine-wave grating. An array of equally spaced, parallel, alternating dark and light stripes that is created by varying the light across the grating in a sine-wave pattern.

Skeletal muscle (extrafusal muscle). Striated muscle that is attached to the skeleton and is usually under voluntary control.

Skin conductance level (SCL). The steady level of skin conductance associated with a particular situation.

Skin conductance response (SCR). The transient change in skin conductance associated with a brief experience.

Sleep apnea. A condition in which sleep is repeatedly disturbed by momentary interruptions in breathing.

Sleep paralysis. A sleep disorder characterized by an attack of paralysis just as a person is falling asleep.

Slow-wave sleep (SWS). Stages 3 and 4 of sleep, which are characterized by the largest and slowest EEG waves.

Smoker's syndrome. The chest pain, labored breathing, wheezing, coughing, and heightened susceptibility to infections of the respiratory tract commonly observed in tobacco smokers.

Sodium amytal test. A test involving the anesthetization of first one hemisphere and then the other to determine which hemisphere plays the dominant role in language.

Sodium–potassium pumps. Active transport mechanisms that pump Na^+ ions out of neurons and K^+ ions in.

Solitary nucleus. The medullary relay nucleus of the gustatory system.

Somatic nervous system (SNS). The part of the peripheral nervous system that interacts with the external environment.

Somatosensory homunculus. The somatotopic map that constitutes the primary somatosensory cortex.

Somatotopic. Organized, like the primary somatosensory cortex, according to a map of the surface of the body.

Somnambulism. Sleepwalking.

Spandrels. Nonadaptive characteristics that evolve because they are related to evolutionary changes that are adaptive.

Spatial-frequency theory. The theory that the visual cortex encodes visual patterns in terms of their component sine-wave gratings.

Spatial resolution. Ability of a recording technique to detect differences in spatial location (e.g., to pinpoint a location in the brain).

Spatial summation. The integration of signals that occur at different sites on the neuron.

Species. A group of organisms that is reproductively isolated from other organisms; the members of one species cannot produce fertile offspring by mating with members of other species.

Species-common behaviors. Behaviors that are displayed in the same manner by virtually all like members of a species.

Spindle afferent neurons. Neurons that carry signals from muscle spindles into the spinal cord via the dorsal root.

Split-brain patients. Commissurotomized patients.

Stabilized retinal image. A retinal image that does not shift across the retina when the eye moves.

Static phase. The second phase of the VMH syndrome, during which the grossly obese animal regulates its body weight.

Stellate cells. Small star-shaped cortical interneurons with short axons.

Stem cells. Developing cells that have the potential to develop into various kinds of mature cells; stem cells in the developing nervous system can become various kinds of neurons or glial cells.

Stereognosis. The process of identifying objects by touch.

Stereotaxic atlas. A three-dimensional map of the brain that is used to determine coordinates for stereotaxic surgery.

Stereotaxic instrument. A device for performing stereotaxic surgery, composed of two parts: a head holder and an electrode holder.

Steroid hormones. Hormones that are synthesized from cholesterol.

Stimulants. Drugs that produce general increases in neural and behavioral activity.

Stress. The physiological response to physical or psychological threat.

Stretch reflex. A reflexive counteracting reaction to an unanticipated external stretching force on a muscle.

Striatum. A structure of the basal ganglia that is the terminal of the dopaminergic nigrostriatal pathway and is damaged in Parkinson's patients; it seems to play a role in memory for consistent relationships between stimuli and responses in multiple-trial tasks.

Strokes. Sudden-onset cerebrovascular disorders that cause brain damage.

Structural genes. Genes that contain the information required for the synthesis of a particular protein.

Subarachnoid space. The space beneath the arachnoid membrane; it contains many large blood vessels and cerebrospinal fluid.

Subjective contours. Perceived visual contours that do not exist.

Subordination stress. Stress experienced by animals, typically males, that are continually attacked by higher-ranking conspecifics.

Substantia nigra. The midbrain nucleus of the meso-telencephalic dopamine system that is a major source of the nigrostriatal pathway; it degenerates in cases of Parkinson's disease.

Superior. Toward the top of the primate head or brain.

Superior olives. Medullary nuclei that play a role in sound localization.

Supplementary motor area. The area of secondary motor cortex that is within and adjacent to the longitudinal fissure.

Suprachiasmatic nuclei (SCN). Nuclei of the hypothalamus that control the circadian cycles of various body functions.

Supraoptic nuclei. One of the two pairs of hypothalamic nuclei in which the hormones of the posterior pituitary are synthesized.

Surface dyslexia. A reading disorder in which the lexical procedure is disrupted while the phonetic procedure is not.

Sympathetic nerves. Those motor nerves of the autonomic nervous system that project from the CNS in the lumbar and thoracic areas of the spinal cord.

Synaptic vesicles. Small spherical membranes that store neurotransmitter molecules and release them into the synaptic cleft.

Synaptogenesis. The formation of new synapses.

Synergistic muscles. Pairs of muscles that produce a movement in the same direction.

T cells. T lymphocytes; lymphocytes that bind to foreign microorganisms and cells that contain them and, in so doing, destroy them.

Tardive dyskinesia (TD). A motor disorder that results from chronic use of certain antipsychotic drugs.

Target-site concept. The idea that many of the species-specific sequences of attack and defense can be reduced to the fact that animals are trying to attack a specific site on the other animal's body, to protect a specific site on their own, or both.

Taste buds. Clusters of taste receptors.

Tectorial membrane. The cochlear membrane that rests on the hair cells.

Tectum. The division of the midbrain that comprises the superior and inferior colliculi and receives auditory and visual information about spatial location.

Temporal hemiretina. The half of each retina next to the temple.

Temporal resolution. Ability of a recording technique to detect differences in time (i.e., to pinpoint when an event occurred).

Temporal summation. The integration of neural signals that occur at different times on the same neuron.

Testes. The male gonads.

Testosterone. The most common androgen.

THC. Delta-9-tetrahydrocannabinol, the main psychoactive ingredient of marijuana.

Thigmotaxic. Tending to stay near the walls of an open field.

3-per-second spike-and-wave discharge. The characteristic EEG of the petit mal seizure.

Threshold of excitation. The level of depolarization at the axon hillock necessary to generate an action potential, usually about −65 mV.

Thrombosis. The blockage of blood flow by a plug (a thrombus) at the site of its formation.

Thyrotropin. The anterior pituitary hormone that stimulates the release of hormones from the thyroid gland.

Thyrotropin-releasing hormone. The hypothalamic hormone that stimulates the release of thyrotropin from the anterior pituitary.

Tics. Involuntary, repetitive, stereotyped movements or vocalizations; the defining feature of Tourette's syndrome.

Token test. A preliminary test of language deficits that involves following verbal instructions to touch or move tokens of different shapes, sizes, and colors.

Tonotopic. Organized, like the primary auditory cortex, according to the frequency of sound.

Topographic gradient hypothesis. The hypothesis that axonal growth is guided by the relative position of the cell bodies on intersecting gradients, rather than by point-to-point coding of neural connections.

Totipotent. Capable of developing into any type of mature body cell.

Toxic psychosis. Psychiatric disturbance that is caused by exposure to toxic chemicals.

Tracts. Bundles of axons in the central nervous system.

Transduction. The conversion of one form of energy to another.

Transfer RNA. Molecules of RNA that carry amino acids to ribosomes during protein synthesis; each kind of amino acid is carried by a different kind of transfer RNA molecule.

Transgenic. Containing the genes of another species, which have been implanted there for research purposes.

Transgenic mice. Mice into which the genetic material of another species has been introduced.

Transneuronal degeneration. Degeneration of a neuron caused by damage to another neuron to which it is linked by synapses.

Transorbital lobotomy. A prefrontal lobotomy performed with a cutting instrument inserted through the eye socket.

Tricyclic antidepressant drugs. A class of drugs that are commonly prescribed for the treatment of depression; they selectively suppress REM sleep.

Tricyclic antidepressants. Drugs with an antidepressant action and a three-ring structure.

True-breeding lines. Breeding lines in which interbred members always produce offspring with the same trait, generation after generation.

Tumor (neoplasm). A mass of cells that grows independently of the rest of the body.

Tympanic membrane. The eardrum.

Unipolar affective disorder. A depressive disorder in which the patient does not experience periods of mania.

Unipolar neuron. A neuron with one process emanating from its cell body.

Up-regulation. The increase in a neurotransmitter's receptors in response to decreased release of that neurotransmitter.

Urbach-Wiethe disease . A genetic disorder that often results in the calcification of the amygdala and surrounding brain structures.

Vasopressin. One of the two major hormones of the posterior pituitary, which facilitates reabsorption of water by kidneys; also called antidiuretic hormone.

Ventral. Toward the chest surface of a vertebrate, or toward the bottom of the head.

Ventral horns. The two ventral arms of the spinal gray matter.

Ventral posterior nucleus. A thalamic relay nucleus in both the somatosensory and gustatory systems.

Ventral stream. The group of visual pathways that flows out of the primary visual cortex to the ventral prestriate cortex to the inferotemporal cortex; according to one theory, its function is conscious visual perception.

Ventral tegmental area. The midbrain nucleus of the mesotelencephalic dopamine system that is a major source of the mesoscorticolimbic pathway.

Ventricular zone. The region adjacent to the ventricle in the developing neural tube; the zone where neural proliferation occurs.

Ventromedial cortico-brainstem-spinal tract. The indirect ventromedial motor pathway, which descends bilaterally from the primary motor cortex to several interconnected brain stem motor structures and then descends in the ventromedial portions of the spinal cord.

Ventromedial corticospinal tract. The direct ventromedial motor pathway, which descends ipsilaterally from the primary motor cortex directly into the ventromedial areas of the spinal white matter.

Ventromedial hypothalamus (VMH). The area of the hypothalamus that was once thought to be the satiety center.

Ventromedial nucleus. A hypothalamic nucleus that is involved in female sexual behavior.

Vertebrates. Chordates that possess spinal bones.

Vestibular nucleus. The brain stem nucleus that receives information about balance from the semicircular canals.

Vestibular system. The sensory system that detects changes in the direction and intensity of head movements and that contributes to the maintenance of balance through its output to the motor system.

Visual agnosia. A failure to recognize visual stimuli that is not attributable to sensory, verbal, or intellectual impairment.

Visual completion. The completion or filling in of a scotoma by the brain.

Voltage-activated ion channels. Ion channels that open and close in response to changes in the membrane potential.

Wechsler Adult Intelligence Scale (WAIS). A widely used test of general intelligence.

Wernicke-Geschwind model. An influential cortical model of language localization.

Wernicke's aphasia. A hypothetical disorder of language comprehension with no associated deficits in speech production.

Wernicke's area. The area of the left temporal cortex hypothesized by Wernicke to be the center of language comprehension.

"Where" versus "what" theory. The theory that the dorsal stream mediates the perception of where things are and the ventral stream mediates the perception of what things are.

Williams syndrome. A neurodevelopmental disorder characterized by severe mental retardation, accompanied by preserved language and social skills.

Wisconsin Card Sorting Test. A neuropsychological test that evaluates a patient's ability to remember that previously learned rules of behavior are no longer effective and to learn to respond to new rules.

Withdrawal reflex. The reflexive withdrawal of a limb when it comes in contact with a painful stimulus.

Withdrawal syndrome. The illness brought on by the elimination from the body of a drug on which the person is physically dependent.

Within-subjects design. An experimental design in which the same subjects are tested under each condition.

Wolffian system. The embryonic precursors of the male reproductive ducts.

Word salad. Speech that has the overall sound and flow of fluid speech but is totally incomprehensible.

Working memory. Temporary memory necessary for the successful completion of the task on which one is currently working.

Z lens. A contact lens that is opaque on one side (left or right) and thus allows visual input to enter only one hemisphere of a split-brain subject, irrespective of eye movement.

Zeitgebers. Environmental cues, such as the light-dark cycle, that entrain circadian rhythms.

Zeitgeist. The general intellectual climate of a culture.

Zygote. The cell formed from the fusion of a sperm cell and an ovum.

Abi-Dargham, A., Rodenhiser, J., Printz, D., Zea-Ponce, Y., Gil, R., Kegeles, L. S., Weiss, R., Cooper, T. B., Mann, J. J., Van Heertum, R. L., Gorman, J. M. (2000). Increased baseline occupancy of D$_2$ receptors by dopamine in schizophrenia. *Proceedings of the National Academy of Science, USA, 97,* 8104–8109.

Abramson, H. A. (1974). Editorial: Respiratory disorders and marijuana use. *Journal of Asthma Research, 11,* 97.

Acker, W., Ron, M. A., Lishman, W. A., & Shaw, G. K. (1984). A multivariate analysis of psychological, clinical and CT scanning measures in detoxified chronic alcoholics. *British Journal of Addiction, 79,* 293–301.

Adamec, R. (1990). Kindling, anxiety and limbic epilepsy: Human and animal perspectives. In J. A. Wada (Ed.), *Kindling 4* (pp. 329–341). New York: Plenum Press.

Adamec, R. (1997). Introduction to neurobiology of defense. *Neuroscience and Biobehavioral Reviews, 21,* 729–731.

Adams, J. M., & Cory, S. (1998). The Bcl-2 protein family: Arbiters of cell survival. *Science, 281,* 1322–1326.

Adelmann, P. K., & Zajonc, R. B. (1989). Facial efference and the experience of emotion. *Annual Review of Psychology, 40,* 249–280.

Ader, R. (2001). Psychoneuroimmunology. *Current Direction in Psychological Science, 10,* 94–98.

Adkins-Regan, E. (1988). Sex hormones and sexual orientation in animals. *Psychobiology, 16,* 335–347.

Adolphs, R., Tranel, D., Damasio, H., & Damasio, A. (1994). Impaired recognition of emotion in facial expressions following bilateral damage to the human amygdala. *Nature, 372,* 669–672.

Adolphs, R., Tranel, D., Hamann, S., Young, A. W., Calder, A. J., Phelps, E. A., Anderson, A., Lee, G. P., & Damasio, A. R. (1999). Recognition of facial emotion in nine individuals with bilateral amygdala damage. *Neuropsychologia, 37,* 1111–1117.

Aggleton, J. P., & Young, A. W. (2000). The enigma of the amygdala: On its contribution to human emotion. In R. D. Lane & L. Nadel (Eds.), *Cognitive neuroscience of emotion* (pp. 106–128). New York: Oxford University Press.

Aglioti, S., Smania, N., & Peru, A. (1999). Frames of reference for mapping tactile stimuli in brain-damaged patients. *Journal of Cognitive Neuroscience, 11,* 67–79.

Agnew, N., & Demas, M. (1998, September). Preserving the Laetoli footprints. *Scientific American, 279,* 46–55.

Ahmed, R., & Gray, D. (1996). Immunological memory and protective immunity: Understanding their relation. *Science, 272,* 54–60.

Åkerstedt, R., & Gillberg, M. (1981). The circadian variation of experimentally displaced sleep. *Sleep, 4,* 159–169.

Albert, D. J., Walsh, M. L., & Jonik, R. H. (1993). Aggression in humans: What is its biological foundation? *Neuroscience and Biobehavioral Reviews, 17,* 405–425.

Albin, R. L., & Tagle, D. A. (1995). Genetics and molecular biology of Huntington's disease. *Trends in Neurosciences, 18,* 11–14.

Albright, T. D. (1995). "My most true mind thus makes mine eye untrue." *Trends in Neurosciences, 18,* 331–333.

Aldridge, J. W., & Berridge, K. C. (1998). Coding of serial order by neostriatal neurons: A "natural action" approach to movement sequence. *Journal of Neuroscience, 18,* 2777–2787.

Alexander, M. P. (1989). Clinical-anatomical correlations of the aphsia following predominantly subcortical lesions. In H. Goodglas (Ed.), *Handbook of neuropscyhology, II, part 2.* New York: Elsevier.

Alexander, M. P. (1997). Aphasia: Clinical and anatomic aspects. In T. E. Feinberg & M. J. Farah (Eds.), *Behavioral neurology and neuropsychology* (pp. 133–149). New York: McGraw-Hill.

Allegretta, M., Nicklas, J. A., Sriram, S., & Albertini, R. J. (1990). T cells responsive to myelin basic protein in patients with multiple sclerosis. *Science, 247,* 718–720.

Allen, G., Buxton, R. B., Wong, E. C., & Courchesne, E. (1997). Attentional activation of the cerebellum independent of motor involvement. *Science, 275,* 1940–1943.

Allen, L. S., Hines, M., Shryne, J. E., & Gorski, R. A. (1989). Two sexually dimorphic cell groups in the human brain. *Journal of Neuroscience, 9,* 497–506.

Allsop, T. E., & Fazakerley, J. K. (2000). Altruistic cell suicide and the specialized case of the virus-infected nervous system. *Trends in Neurosciences, 23,* 284–290.

Anagnostaras, S. G., & Robinson, T. E. (1996). Sensitization to the psychomotor stimulant effects of amphetamine: Modulation by associative learning. *Behavioral Neuroscience, 110 (6),* 1397–1414.

Anagnostaras, S. G., Craske, M. G., & Fanselow, M. S. (1999). Anxiety: At the intersection of genes and experience. *Nature Reviews Neuroscience, 2,* 780–782.

Anch, A. M., Browman, C. P., Mitler, M. M., & Walsh, J. K. (1988). *Sleep: A scientific perspective.* Englewood Cliffs, NJ: Prentice Hall.

Andersen, R. A., Snyder, L. H., Bradley, D.C., & Xing, J. (1997). Multimodal representation of space in the posterior parietal cortex and its use in planning movements. *Annual Review of Neuroscience, 20,* 303–330.

Anderson, A. K., & Phelps, E. A. (2000). Expression without recognition: Contributions of the human amygdala to emotional communication. *Psychological Science, 11,* 106–111.

Anderson, P., Cremona, A., Paton, A., Turner, C., & Wallace, P. (1993). The risk of alcohol. *Addiction, 88,* 1493–1508.

Anderson, R. H., Fleming, D. E., Rhees, R. W., & Kinghorn, E. (1986). Relationships between sexual activity, plasma testosterone, and the volume of the sexually dimorphic nucleus of the preoptic area in prenatally stressed and non-stressed rats. *Brain Research, 370,* 1–10.

Andreasen, N. C. (1994). The mechanisms of schizophrenia. *Current Opinion in Neurobiology, 4,* 245–251.

Andreassi, J. L. (1989). *Psychophysiology: Human behavior and physiological response.* Hillsdale, NJ: Erlbaum.

Antonini, A., & Stryker, M. P. (1993). Rapid remodeling of axonal arbors in the visual cortex. *Science, 260,* 1819–1821.

Apkarian, A. V. (1995). Functional imaging of pain: New insights regarding the role of the cerebral cortex in human pain perception. *Seminars in the Neurosciences, 7,* 279–293.

Archer, J. (1991). The influence of testosterone on human aggression. *British Journal of Psychology, 82,* 1–28.

Arieli, A., Sterkin, A., Grinvald, A., & Aertsen, A. (1996). Dynamics of ongoing activity: Explanation of the large variability in evoked cortical responses. *Science, 273,* 1868–1870.

Arvanitogiannis, A., Sullivan, J., & Amir, S. (2000). Time acts as a conditioned stimulus to control behavioral sensitization to amphetamine in rats. *Neuroscience, 101,* 1–3.

Aserinsky, E., & Kleitman, N. (1953). Regularly occurring periods of eye motility and concomitant phenomena, during sleep. *Science, 118,* 273–274.

Ashkenazi, A., & Dixit, V. M. (1998). Death receptors: Signaling and modulation. *Science, 281,* 1305–1308.

Assanand, S., Pinel, J. P. J., & Lehman, D. R. (1998a). Personal theories of hunger and eating. *Journal of Applied Social Psychology, 28,* 998–1015.

Assanand, S., Pinel, J. P. J., & Lehman, D. R. (1998b). Teaching theories of hunger and eating: Overcoming students' misconceptions. *Teaching Psychology, 25,* 44–46.

Attenburrow, M. E. J., Cowen, P. J., & Sharpely, A. L. (1996). Low dose melatonin improves sleep in healthy middle-aged subjects. *Psychopharmacology, 126,* 179–181.

Ax, A. F. (1955). The physiological differentiation between fear and anger in humans. *Psychosomatic Medicine, 15,* 433–442.

Axel, R. (1995, October). The molecular logic of smell. *Scientific American, 273,* 154–159.

Babor, T. F., Mendelson, J. H., Greenberg, I., & Kuehnle, J. C. (1975). Marijuana consumption and tolerance to physiological and subjective effects. *Archives of General Psychiatry, 32,* 1548–1552.

Bailey, J. M., Pillard, R. C., Neale, M. C., & Agyei, Y. (1993). Heritable factors influence sexual orientation in women. *Archives of General Psychiatry, 50,* 217–223.

Bailey, M. J., & Pillard, R. C. (1991). A genetic study of male sexual orientation. *Archives of General Psychiatry, 48,* 1089–1096.

Baker, B. J., & Booth, D. A. (1989). Preference conditioning by concurrent diets with delayed proportional reinforcement. *Physiology & Behavior, 46,* 585–590.

Baker, T. B., & Tiffany, S. T. (1985). Morphine tolerance as habituation. *Psychological Review, 92,* 78–108.

Ball, G. F., & Hulse, S. H. (1998). Birdsong. *American Psychologist, 53,* 37–58.

Balthazart, J., & Ball, G. F. (1998). New insights into the regulation and function of brain estrogen synthase (aromatase). *Trends in Neurosciences, 21,* 243–249.

Bancroft, J., Sanders, D., Davidson, D., & Warner, P. (1983). Mood, sexuality, hormones and the menstrual cycle: III. Sexuality and the role of androgens. *Psychosomatic Medicine, 45,* 509–516.

Bandler, R., & Shipley, M. T. (1994). Columnar organization in the midbrain periaqueductal gray: Modules for emotional expression? *Trends in Neuroscience, 17,* 379–389.

Bankiewicz, K. S., Plunkett, R. J., Jaconowitz, D. M., Porrino, L., di Porzio, U., London, W. T., Kopin, I. J., & Oldfield, E. H. (1990). The effect of fetal mesencephalon implants on primate MPTP-induced Parkinsonianism: Histochemical and behavioral studies. *Journal of Neuroscience, 72,* 231–244.

Bard P. (1929). The central representation of the sympathetic system. *Archives of Neurology and Psychiatry, 22,* 230–246.

Baron, J. C. (1989). Depression of energy metabolism in distant brain structures: Studies with positron emission tomography in stroke patients. *Seminars in Neurology, 9,* 281–285.

Bartoshuk, L. M., & Beauchamp, G. K. (1994). Chemical senses. *Annual Review of Psychology, 45,* 419–449.

Basbaum, A. I., & Fields, H. L. (1978). Endogenous pain control mechanisms: Review and hypothesis. *Annals of Neurology, 4,* 451–462.

Bashir, Z. I., & Collingridge, G. L. (1992). Synaptic plasticity: Long-term potentiation in the hippocampus. *Current Opinion in Neurobiology, 2,* 328–335.

Bastiani, M. J., Doe, C. Q., Helfand, S. L., & Goodman, C. S. (1985). Neuronal specificity and growth cone guidance in grasshopper and Drosophila embryos. *Trends in Neurosciences, 8,* 257–266.

Baum, M. J., Erskine, M. S., Kornberg, E., & Weaver, C. E. (1990). Prenatal and neonatal testosterone exposure interact to affect differentiation of sexual behavior and partner preference in female ferrets. *Behavioral Neuroscience, 104,* 183–198.

Bauman, M. L., Filipek, P. A., & Kemper, T. L. (1997). Early infantile autism. *International Review of Neurobiology, 41,* 367–386.

Baura, G., Foster, D., Porte, D., Kahn, S. E., Bergman, R. N., Cobelli, C., & Schwartz, M. W. (1993). Saturable transport of insulin from plasma into the central nervous system of dogs in vivo: A mechanism for regulated insulin delivery to the brain. *Journal of Clinical Investigations, 92,* 1824–1830.

Bavelier, D., Corina, D., Jessard, P., Padmanabhan, S., Clark, V. P., Karni, A., Pinster, A., Braun, A., Lalwani, A., Rauschecker, J. P., Turner, R., & Neville, H. (1997). Sentence reading: A functional MRI study at 4 Telsa. *Journal of Cognitive Neuroscience, 9,* 664–686.

Baxter, M. G., & Chiba, A. A. (1999). Cognitive functions of the basal forebrain. *Current Opinion in Neurobiology, 9,* 178–183.

Baynes, K., & Gazzaniga, M. S. (1997). Callosal disconnection. In T. E. Feinberg & M. J. Farah (Eds.), *Behavioral neurology and neuropsychology* (pp. 419–425). New York: McGraw-Hill.

Bechara, A., Tranel, D., Damasio, H., Adolphs, R., Rockland, C., & Damasio, A. R. (1995). Double dissociation of conditioning and declarative knowledge relative to the amygdala and hippocampus in humans. *Science, 269,* 1115–1118.

Beck, G., & Habicht, G. S. (1996, November). Immunity and invertebrates. *Scientific American, 275,* 60–66.

Beeman, M. J., & Chiarello, C. (1998). Complementary right- and left-hemisphere language comprehension. *Current Directions in Psychological Science, 7,* 2–8.

Behrmann, M., & Haimson, C. (1999). The cognitive neuroscience of visual attention. *Current Opinion in Neurobiology, 9,* 158–163.

Belin, P., Silbovicius, M., Crozier, S., Thivard, L., Masure, M-C., & Samson, Y. (1998). Lateralization of speech and auditory temporal processing. *Journal of Cognitive Neuroscience, 10,* 536–540.

Bellugi, U., Lichtenberger, L., Mills, D., Galaburda, A., & Korenberg, J. R. (1999). Bridging cognition, the brain and molecular genetics: Evidence from Williams syndrome. *Trends in Neurosciences, 22,* 197–207.

Benington, J. H., & Heller, H. C. (1999). Implications of sleep deprivation experiments for our understanding of sleep homeostasis. *Sleep, 22,* 1033–1043.

Bennett, E. L., Diamond, M. C., Krech, D., & Rosenzweig, M. R. (1964). Chemical and anatomical plasticity of brain. *Science, 146,* 610–619.

Benson, D. F. (1985). Aphasia. In K. M. Heilman & E. Valenstein (Eds.), *Clinical neuropsychology* (pp. 17–47). New York: Oxford University Press.

Benton, A. L. (1994). Neuropsychological assessment. *Annual Review of Psychology, 45,* 1–23.

Bernhardt, P. C. (1997). Influences of serotonin and testosterone in aggression and dominance: Convergence with social psychology. *Current Directions in Psychological Science, 6,* 44–48.

Bernstein, I. L., & Webster, M. M. (1980). Learned taste aversion in humans. *Physiology & Behavior, 25,* 363–366.

Bernstein, L. J., & Robertson, L. C. (1998). Illusory conjunctions of color and motion with shape following bilateral parietal lesions. *Psychological Science, 9,* 167–175.

Berridge, K. C., & Robinson, T. E. (1995). The mind of an addicted brain: Neural sensitization of wanting versus liking. *Current Directions in Psychological Science, 4,* 71–76.

Berridge, V., & Edwards, G. (1981). *Opium and the people: Opiate use in nineteenth-century England.* New York: St. Martin's Press.

Bertranpetit, J. (2000). Genome, diversity, and origins: The Y chromosome as a storyteller. *Proceedings of the National Academy of Science, U.S.A., 97,* 6927–6929.

Billington, C. J., & Levine, A. S. (1992). Hypothalamic neuropeptide Y regulation of feeding and energy metabolism. *Current Opinion in Neurobiology, 2,* 847–851.

Binks, P. G., Waters, W. F., & Hurry, M. (1999). Short-term total sleep deprivations does not selectively impair higher cortical functioning. *Sleep, 22,* 328–334.

Bischoff-Grethe, A., Proper, S. M., Mao, H., Daniels, K. A., & Berns, G. S. (2000). Conscious and unconscious processing of nonverbal predictability in Wernicke's area. *Journal of Neuroscience, 20,* 1975–1981.

Bishop, D. V. M., (1999). An innate basis for language? *Science, 286,* 2283–2355.

Björklund, A., & Lindvall, O. (2000). Cell replacement therapies for central nervous system disorders. *Nature, 3,* 537–544.

Blackmore, S. (1991). Lucid dreaming: Awake in your sleep? *Skeptical Inquirer, 15,* 362–370.

Blanchard, D.C., & Blanchard, R. J. (1984). Affect and aggression: An animal model applied to human behavior. In D.C. Blanchard & R. J. Blanchard (Eds.), *Advances in the study of aggression* (pp. 1–62). Orlando, FL: Academic Press.

Blanchard, D.C., & Blanchard, R. J. (1988). Ethoexperimental approaches to the biology of emotion. *Annual Review of Psychology, 39,* 43–68.

Blanchard, D.C., & Blanchard, R. J. (1990). Behavioral correlates of chronic dominance-subordination relationships of male rats in a seminatural situation. *Neuroscience and Biobehavioral Reviews, 14,* 455–462.

Blanchard, D.C., Blanchard, R. J., & Rodgers, R. J. (1991). Risk assessment and animal models of anxiety. In *Animal models in psychopharmacology: Advances in pharmacological sciences.* Basel: Birkhauser Verlag.

Blanchard, D.C., Blanchard, R. J., Tom, P., & Rodgers, R. J. (1990). Diazepam changes risk assessment in an anxiety/defense test battery. *Psychopharmacology, 101,* 511–518.

Blanchard, D.C., Sakai, R. R., McEwen, B., Weiss, S. M., & Blanchard, R. J. (1993). Subordination stress: Behavioral, brain, and neuroendocrine correlates. *Behavioural Brain Research, 58,* 113–121.

Blanchard, R. J., & Blanchard, D.C. (1989). Anti-predator defensive behaviors in a visible burrow system. *Journal of Comparative Psychology, 103,* 70–82.

Blaser, M. J. (1996, February). The bacteria behind ulcers. *Scientific American, 275,* 104–107.

Blaustein, J. D., King, J. C., Toft, D. O., & Turcotte, J. (1988). Immunocytochemical localization of estrogen-induced progestin receptors in guinea pig brain. *Brain Research, 474,* 1–15.

Blessing, W. W. (1997). Inadequate frameworks for understanding bodily homeostasis. *Trends in Neurosciences, 20,* 235–239.

Bliss, T. V. P., & Lømø, T. (1973). Long-lasting potentiation of synaptic transmission in the dentate area of the anaesthetized rabbit following stimulation of the perforant path. *Journal of Physiology, 232,* 331–356.

Bloch, G. J., & Gorski, R. A. (1988). Cytoarchitectonic analysis of the SDN-POA of the intact and gonadectomized rat. *Journal of Comparative Neurology, 275,* 604–612.

Bloch, G. J., & Mills, R. (1995). Prepubertal testosterone treatment of neonatally gonadectomized male rats: Defeminization and masculinization of behavioral and endocrine function in adulthood. *Neuroscience and Behavioral Reviews, 19,* 187–200.

Bloch, G. J., Mills, R., & Gale, S. (1995). Prepubertal testosterone treatment of female rats: Defeminization of behavioral and endocrine function in adulthood. *Neuroscience and Biobehavioral Reviews, 19,* 177–186.

Blundell, J. E., & Halford, J. C. G. (1998). Serotonin and appetite regulation. *CNS Drugs, 9,* 473–495.

Bodis-Wollner, I., & Pfeiffer, R. F. (Eds.). (1998). Parkinson's disease. [Special issue]. *Clinical Neuroscience, 5*(2).

Bogen, J. G., & Bogen, G. M. (1976). Wernicke's region—Where is it? *Annals of the New York Academy of Science, 280,* 834–843.

Bolles, R. C. (1980). Some functionalist thought about regulation. In F. M. Toates & T. R. Halliday (Eds.), *Analysis of motivational processes* (pp. 63–75). London: Academic Press.

Bolz, J. (1994). Cortical circuitry in a dish. *Current Opinion in Neurobiology, 4,* 545–549.

Bonnet, M. H., & Arand, D. L. (1996). Insomnia—nocturnal sleep disruption—daytime fatigue: The consequences of a week of insomnia. *Sleep, 19,* 453–461.

Booth, D. A. (1981). The physiology of appetite. *British Medical Bulletin, 37,* 135–140.

Booth, D. A., Fuller, J., & Lewis, V. (1981). Human control of body weight: Cognitive or physiological? Some energy-related perceptions and misperceptions. In L. A. Cioffi (Ed.), *The body weight regulatory system: Normal and disturbed systems* (pp. 305–314). New York: Raven Press.

Borbély, A. A. (1981). The sleep process: Circadian and homeostatic aspects. *Advances in Physiological Sciences, 18,* 85–91.

Borbély, A. A. (1983). Pharmacological approaches to sleep regulation. In A. R. Mayes (Ed.), *Sleep mechanisms and functions in humans and animals* (pp. 232–261). Wokingham, England: Van Nostrand Reinhold.

Borbély, A. A., Baumann, F., Brandeis, D., Strauch, I., & Lehmann, D. (1981). Sleep deprivation: Effect on sleep stages and EEG power density in man. *Electroencephalography and Clinical Neurophysiology, 51,* 483–493.

Borszcz, G. S. (1999). Differential contributions of medullary, thalamic, and amygdaloid serotonin to the antinociceptive action of morphine administered into the periaqueductal gray: A model of morphine analgesia. *Behavioral Neuroscience, 113,* 612–631.

Bouchard, T. J., Jr. (1998). Genetic and environmental influences on adult intelligence and special mental abilities. In *Human biology,* v. 70, pp. 257–279. Michigan: Wayne State University Press.

Bouchard, T. J., Jr., & Pedersen, N. (1998). Twins reared apart: Nature's double experiment. In *On the Way to Individuality: Current Methodological Issues in Behavioral Genetics.* E. L. Grigorenko and S. Scarr, eds. New Jersey: Nova.

Boucsein, W. (1992). *Electrodermal activity.* New York: Plenum Press.

Boulos, Z., & Terman, M. (1980). Food availability and daily biological rhythms. *Neuroscience and Biobehavioral Reviews, 4,* 119–131.

Bowers, D., Bauer, R. M., Coslett, H. B., & Heilman, K. M. (1985). Processing of face by patients with unilateral hemisphere lesions. I. Dissociations between judgements of facial affect and facial identity. *Brain Cognition, 4,* 258–272.

Bozarth, M. A., & Wise R. A. (1981). Heroin reward is dependent on a dopaminergic substrate. *Life Sciences, 29,* 1881–1886.

Brackett, N. L., & Edwards, D. A. (1984). Medial preoptic connections with the midbrain tegmentum are essential for male sexual behavior. *Physiology & Behavior, 32,* 79–84.

Bradberry, C. W., Barrett-Larimore, R. L., Jatlow, P., & Rubino, S. R., (2000). Impact of self-administered cocaine and cocaine cues on extracellular dopamine in mesolimbic and sensorimotor striatum in rhesus monkeys. *Journal of Neuroscience, 20,* 3874–3883.

Brady, J. V. (1993). Behavior analysis applications and interdisciplinary research strategies. *American Psychologist, 48,* 435–440.

Braun, C., Schweizer, R., Elbert, T., Birbaumer, N., & Taub, E. (2000). Differential activation in somatosensory cortex for different discrimination tasks. *Journal of Neuroscience, 20,* 446–450.

Brecher, E. M. (1972). *Licit and illicit drugs.* Boston: Little, Brown.

Breedlove, S. M. (1994). Sexual differentiation of the human nervous system. *Annual Review of Psychology, 45,* 389–418.

Breitner, J. C. S. (1990). Life table methods and assessment of familial risk in Alzheimer's disease. *Archives of General Psychiatry, 47,* 395–396.

Bremer, F. (1936). Nouvelles recherches sur le mécanisme du sommeil. *Comptes Rendus de la Société de Biologie, 22,* 460–464.

Bremer, F. L. (1937). L'activité cérébrale au cours du sommeil et de la narcose. Contribution à l'étude du mécanisme du sommeil. *Bulletin de l'Académie Royale de Belgique, 4,* 68–86.

Bremer, J. (1959). *Asexualization.* New York: Macmillan.

Brenman, J. E., & Bredt, D. S. (1997). Synaptic signaling by nitric oxide. *Current Opinion in Neurobiology, 7,* 374–378.

Brewster, J. M. (1986). Prevalence of alcohol and other drug problems among physicians. *Journal of the American Medical Association, 255,* 1913–1920.

Bridgeman, B., Van der Heijden, A. H. C., & Velichkovsky, B. M. (1994). A theory of visual stability across saccadic eye movements. *Behavioral and Brain Sciences, 17,* 247–292.

Brill, N. Q., & Christie, R. L. (1974). Marihuana use and psychosocial adaptation. *Archives of General Psychiatry, 31,* 713–719.

Brittle, E. R., & Waters, M. G. (2000). ER-to-Golgi traffic—this bud's for you. *Science, 289,* 403–448.

Broberg, D. J., & Bernstein, I. L. (1989). Cephalic insulin release in anorexic women. *Physiology & Behavior, 45,* 871–875.

Broks, P., Young, A. W., Maratos, E. J., Coffey, P. J., Calder, A. J., Isaac, C. L., Mayes, A. R., Hodges, J. R., Montaldi, D., Cezayirli, E., Roberts, N., & Hadley, D. (1998). Face processing impairments after encephalitis: Amygdala damage and recognition of fear. *Neuropsychologia, 36,* 59–70.

Bronson, F. H., & Matherne, C. M. (1997). Exposure to anabolic-androgenic steroids shortens life span of male mice. *Medicine and Science in Sports and Exercise, 29,* 615–619.

Brooks, M. J., & Melnik, G. (1995). The refeeding syndrome: An approach to understanding its complications and preventing its occurrence. *Pharmacotherapy, 15,* 713–726.

Brooks, V. B. (1986). *The neural basis of motor control.* New York: Oxford University Press.

Brou, P., Sciascia, T. R., Linden, L., & Lettvin, J. Y. (1986, September). The colors of things. *Scientific American, 255,* 84–91

Brown, E. S., Rush, A. J., & McEwen, B. S. (1999). Hippocampal remodeling and damage by corticosteroids: Implications for mood disorders. *Neuropsychopharmacology, 21,* 474–484.

Brown, G. W. (1993). The role of life events in the aetiology of depressive and anxiety disorders. In S. C. Stanford & S. Salmon (Eds.), *Stress: From synapse to syndrome* (pp. 23–50). San Diego: Academic Press.

Brown, L. L., Schneider, J. S., & Lidsky, T. I. (1997). Sensory and cognitive functions of the basal ganglia. *Current Opinion in Neurobiology, 7,* 157–163.

Brown, M. W., & Aggleton, J. P. (2001). Recognition memory: What are the roles of perirhinal cortex and hippocampus? *Nature Reviews Neuroscience, 2,* 51–61.

Brown, R. E. (1994). *An introduction to neuroendocrinology.* Cambridge, England: Cambridge University Press.

Brown, T. H., Chapman, P. F., Kairiss, E. W., & Keenan, C. L. (1988). Long-term synaptic potentiation. *Science, 242,* 724–728.

Brownell, K. D., & Rodin, J. (1994). The dieting maelstrom: Is it possible and advisable to lose weight? *American Psychologist, 49,* 781–791.

Brüning, J. C., Gautam, D., Burks, D. J., Gillette, J., Schubert, M., Orban, P. C., Klein, R., Krone, W., Müller-Wieland, D., & Kahn, C. R. (2000). Role of brain insulin receptor in control of body weight and reproduction. *Science, 289,* 2122–2125.

Brunner, D. P., Dijk, D-J., Tobler, I., & Borbély, A. A. (1990). Effect of partial sleep deprivation on sleep stages and EEG power spectra: Evidence for non-REM and REM sleep homeostasis. *Electroencephalography and Clinical Neurophysiology, 75,* 492–499.

Brzustowicz, L. M., Hodgkinson, K. A., Chow, E. W. C., Honer, W. G., & Bassett, A. S. (2000). Location of a major susceptibility locus for familial schizophrenia on chromosome 1q21-q22. *Science, 288,* 678–682.

Bucci, T. J. (1992). Dietary restriction: Why all the interest? An overview. *Laboratory Animal, 21,* 29–34.

Buck, L. B. (1996). Information coding in the vertebrate olfactory system. *Annual Reviews in Neuroscience, 19,* 517–544.

Buckley, M. J., & Gaffan, D. (1998). Perirhinal cortex ablation impairs visual object identification. *Journal of Neuroscience, 18 (6),* 2268–2275.

Bunin, M. A., & Wightman, R. M. (1999). Paracrine neurotransmission in the CNS: involvement of 5-HT. *Trends in Neurosciences, 22,* 377–382.

Buonomano, D. V. (1999). Distinct functional types of associative long-term potentiation in neocortical and hippocampal pyramidal neurons. *Journal of Neuroscience, 19,* 6748–6754.

Buonomano, D. V., & Merzenich, M. M. (1998). Cortical plasticity: from synapses to maps. *Annual Reviews of Neuroscience, 21,* 149–186.

Burke, A. C., & Feduccia, A. (1997). Developmental patterns and the identification of homologies in the avian hand. *Science, 278,* 666–668.

Burns, R. S., Chiueh, C. C., Markey, S. P., Ebert, M. H., Jacobowitz, D. M., & Kopin, I. J. (1983). A primate model of Parkinsonism: Selective destruction of dopaminergic neurons in the pars compacta of the substantia nigra by N-methyl-4-phenyl-1,2,3,6-tetrahydropyridine. *Proceedings of the National Academy of Sciences, USA, 80,* 4546–4550.

Buss, D. M. (1992). Mate preference mechanisms: Consequences for partner choice and intrasexual competition. In J. M. Barkow, L. Cosmides, & J. Tooby (Eds.), *The adapted mind* (pp. 249–265). New York: Oxford University Press.

Buss, D. M., Haselton, M. G., Shackelford, T. K., Bleske, A. L., & Wakefield, J. C. (1998). Adaptations, exaptations, and spandrels. *American Psychologist, 53,* 533–548.

Bussey, T. J., Warburton, E. C., Aggleton, J. P., & Muir, J. L. (1998). Fornix lesions can facilitate acquisition of the transverse patterning task: A challenge for "configural" theories of hippocampal function. *Journal of Neuroscience, 18 (4),* 1622–1631.

Butters, N., & Delis, D.C. (1995). Clinical assessment of memory disorders in amnesia and dementia. *Annual Review of Psychology, 46,* 493–523.

Butterworth, R. F., Kril, J. J., & Harper, C. G. (1993). Thiamine-dependent enzyme changes in the brains of alcoholics: Relationship to the Wernicke-Korsakoff syndrome. *Alcoholism: Clinical and Experimental Research, 17,* 1084–1088.

Byne, W. (1994, May). The biological evidence challenged: Even if genetic and neuroanatomical traits turn out to be correlated with sexual orientation, causation is far from proved. *Scientific American, 270,* 50–55.

Cabanac, M. (1971). Physiological role of pleasure. *Science, 173,* 1103–1107.

Cabeza, R., & Nyberg, L. (1997). Imaging cognition: An empirical review of PET studies with normal subjects. *Journal of Cognitive Neuroscience, 9:1,* 1–26.

Cabeza, R., & Nyberg, L. (2000). Imaging cognition II: An empirical review of 275 PET and fMRI studies. *Journal of Cognitive Neuroscience 12:1,* 1–47.

Cacioppo, J. T., Petty, R. E., Losch, M., & Kim, H. S. (1986). Electromyographic activity over facial muscle regions can differentiate the valence and intensity of emotional reactions. *Journal of Personality and Social Psychology, 50,* 260–268.

Cade, J. F. J. (1949). Lithium salts in treatment of psychotic excitement. *Medical Journal of Australia, 2,* 349–352.

Caggiula, A. R. (1970). Analysis of the copulation-reward properties of posterior hypothalamic stimulation in male rats. *Journal of Comparative and Physiological Psychology, 70,* 399–412.

Cain, D. P. (1986). The transfer phenomenon in kindling. In J. A. Wada (Ed.), *Kindling 3* (pp. 231–245). New York: Raven Press.

Cain, D. P. (1997). LTP, NMDA, genes and learning. *Current Opinion in Neurobiology, 7,* 235–242.

Calder, A. J., Lawrence, A. D., & Young, A. W. (2001). Neuropsychology of fear and loathing. *Nature Reviews Neuroscience, 2,* 352–363.

Calder, A. J., Young, A. W., Rowland, D., Perrett, D. I., Hodges, J. R., & Etcoff, N. L. (1996). Facial emotion recognition after bilateral amygdala damage: Differentially severe impairment of fear. *Cognitive Neuropsychology, 13,* 699–745.

Calles-Escandon, J., & Horton, E. S. (1992). The thermogenic role of exercise in the treatment of morbid obesity: A critical evaluation. *American Journal of Clinical Nutrition, 55,* 533S-537S.

Callwood, J. (1990). *The sleepwalker.* Toronto: Lester & Orpen Dennys Ltd.

Calmon, G., Roberts, N., Eldridge, P., & Thirion, J-P. (1998). Automatic quantification of changes in the volume of brain structures. *Lectures Notes in Computer Science, 1496,* 761–769.

Calne, S., Schoenberg, B., Martin, W., Uitti, J., Spencer, P., & Calne, D. B. (1987). Familial Parkinson's disease: Possible role of environmental factors. *Canadian Journal of Neurological Sciences, 14,* 303–305.

Cameron, H. A., Woolley, C. S., McEwen, B. S., & Gould, E. (1993). Differentiation of newly born neurons and glia in the dentate gyrus of the adult rat. *Neuroscience, 56,* 337–344.

Caminiti, R., Ferraina, S., & Mayer, A. B. (1998). Visuomotor transformations: Early cortical mechanisms of reaching. *Current Opinion in Neurobiology, 8,* 753–761.

Campfield, L. A., & Smith, F. J. (1990). Transient declines in blood glucose signal meal initiation. *International Journal of Obesity, 14* (Supplement 3), 15–33.

Campfield, L. A., Smith, F. J., Gulsez, Y. Devos, R., & Burn, P. (1995). Mouse Ob protein: evidence for a peripheral signal linking adiposity and central neural networks. *Science, 269,* 546–550.

Canli, T., Zhao, Z., Desmond, J. E., Kang, E., Gross, J., & Gabrieli, J. D. E. (2001). An fMRI study of personality influences on brain reactivity to emotional stimuli. *Behavioral Neuroscience, 115,* 33–42.

Cannon, W. B., & Washburn, A. L. (1912). An explanation of hunger. *American Journal of Physiology, 29,* 441–454.

Carlson, N. R. (1994). *Physiology of behavior* (5th ed.). Boston, MA: Allyn and Bacon.

Carlsson, A., & Linqvist, M. (1963). Effect of chlorpromazine or haloperidol on formation of 3-methoxytyramine and normetanephrine in mouse brains. *Acta Pharmacologica et Toxicologica, 20,* 140–144.

Carr, G. D., Fibiger, H. C, & Phillips, A. G. (1989). Conditioned place preference as a measure of drug reward. In J. M. Liebman & S. J. Cooper (Eds.), *The neuropharmacological basis of reward* (pp. 264–319). Oxford: Clarendon Press.

Carroll, D. (1984). *Biofeedback in practice.* New York: Longman Group.

Carter, R. J., Lione, L. A., Humby, T., Mangiarini, L., Mahal, A., Bates, G. P., Dunnett, S. B., & Morton, A. J. (1999). Characterization of progressive motor deficits in mice transgenic for the human Huntington's disease mutation. *Journal of Neuroscience, 19,* 3248–3257.

Caselli, R. J. (1997). Tactile agnosia and disorders of tactile perception. In T. E. Feinberg & M. J. Farah (Eds.), *Behavioral neurology and neuropsychology* (pp. 277–288). New York: McGraw-Hill.

Cassone, V. M. (1990). Effects of melatonin on vertebrate circadian systems. *Trends in Neurosciences, 13 (11),* 457–467.

Castro, C. A., Silbert, L. H., McNaughton, B. L., & Barnes, C. A. (1989). Recovery of spatial learning deficits after decay of electrically induced synaptic enhancement in the hippocampus. *Nature, 342,* 545–548.

Cesare, P., & McNaughton, P. (1997). Peripheral pain mechanisms. *Current Opinion in Neurobiology, 7,* 493–499.

Chabris, C. F., & Kosslyn, S. M. (1998). How do the cerebral hemispheres contribute to encoding spatial relations? *Current Directions in Psychological Science, 7,* 8–14.

Changeux, J.-P. (1993, November). Chemical signaling in the brain. *Scientific American, 269,* 58–62.

Chan-Ling, T., & Stone, J. (1991). Factors determining the morphology and distribution of astrocytes in the cat retina: A "contact-spacing" model of astrocyte interaction. *Journal of Comparative Neurology, 303,* 387–399.

Chavez, M., Seeley, R. J., & Woods, S. C. (1995). A comparison between the effects of intraventricular insulin and intraperitoneal LiCl on three measures sensitive to emetic agents. *Behavioral Neuroscience, 109,* 547–550.

Chemielli, R. M., Willie, J. T., Sinton, C. M., Elmquist, J. K., Scammell, T., Lee, C., Richardson, J. A., Williams, S. C., Xiong, U., Kisanuki, Y., Fitch, T. E., Nakzato, M., Hammer, R. E., Saper, C. B., & Yanagisawa, M. (1999). Narcolepsy in orexin knockout mice: Molecular genetics of sleep regulation. *Cell, 98,* 437–451.

Chen, W. R., Midtgaard, J., & Shepherd, G. M. (1997). Forward and backward propagation of dendritic impulses and their synaptic control in mitral cells. *Science, 278,* 463–466.

Cheney, D. L., & Seyfarth, R. M. (1992). Précis of how monkeys see the world. *Behavioral and Brain Sciences, 15,* 135–182

Cheng, J., Cao, Y., & Olson, L. (1996). Spinal cord repair in adult paraplegic rats: Partial restoration of hind limb function. *Science, 273,* 510–451.

Cherkow, H., & Murtha, S. (1997). PET activation and language. *Clinical Neuroscience, 4,* 78–86.

Cho, A. K. (1990). Ice: A new dosage form of an old drug. *Science, 249,* 631–634.

Chorover, S. L., & Schiller, P. H. (1965). Short-term retrograde amnesia in rats. *Journal of Comparative and Physiological Psychology, 59,* 73–78.

Christoff, K., & Gabrieli, J. D. E. (2000). The frontopolar cortex and human cognition: Evidence for a rostrocaudal hierarchical organization within the human prefrontal cortex. *Psychobiology, 28,* 168–186.

Clapham, D. E. (1994). Direct G protein activation of ion channels. *Annual Review of Neuroscience, 17,* 441–464.

Clements, J. D., Lester, R. A. J., Tong, G., Jahr, C. E., & Westbrook, G. L. (1992). The time course of glutamate in the synaptic cleft. *Science, 258,* 1498–1501.

Clifton, P. G. (2000). Meal patterning in rodents: Psychopharmacological and neuroanatomical studies. *Neuroscience and Biobehavioral Reviews, 24,* 213–222.

Cohen, S. (1996). Psychological stress, immunity, and upper respiratory infections. *Current Directions in Psychological Science, 5,* 86–90.

Cohen, S., & Herbert, T. B. (1996). Health psychology: Psychological factors and physical disease from the perspective of human psychoneuroimmunology. *Annual Review of Psychology, 47,* 113–142.

Cohen, Y. E., & Knudsen, E. I. (1999). Maps versus clusters: Different representations of auditory space in the midbrain and forebrain. *Trends in Neuroscience, 22,* 128–135.

Colapinto, J. (2000). *As nature made him: The boy who was raised as a girl.* New York: Harper Collins.

Colarelli, S. M. (1998). Psychological interventions in organizations. *American Psychologist, 53,* 1044–1056.

Colell, M., Segarra, M. D., & Sabater-Pi, J. (1995). Manual laterality in chimpanzees (*Pan troglodytes*) in complex tasks. *Journal of Comparative Psychology, 109,* 298–307.

Coleman, D. L. (1979). Obesity genes: beneficial effects in heterozygous mice. *Science, 203,* 663–665.

Colle, L. M., & Wise, R. A. (1988). Effects of nucleus accumbens amphetamine on lateral hypothalamic brain stimulation reward. *Brain Research, 459,* 361–368.

Collier, G. (1986). The dialogue between the house economist and the resident physiologist. *Nutrition and Behavior, 3,* 9–26.

Collier, G. H. (1980). An ecological analysis of motivation. In F. M. Toates & T. R. Halliday (Eds.), *Analysis of motivational processes* (pp. 125–151). London: Academic Press.

Collins, F. S., Guyer, M. S., Chakravarti, A. (1997). Variations on a theme: Cataloging human DNA sequence variation. *Science, 278,* 1580–1581.

Collins, F. S., Patrinos, A., Jordan, E., Chakravarti, A., Gesteland, R., Walters, L., and the members of the DOE and NIH planning groups (1998). New goals for the U.S. human genome project: 1998–2003. *Science, 282,* 682–689.

Colombo, M., & Broadbent, N. (2000). Is the avian hippocampus a functional homologue of the mammalian hippocampus? *Neuroscience and Biobehavioral Reviews, 24,* 465–484.

Cook, G., Tannahill, D., & Keynes, R. (1998). Axon guidance to and from choice points. *Current Opinion in Neurobiology, 8,* 64–72.

Cooper, R. M., & Zubek, J. P. (1958). Effects of enriched and restricted early environments on the learning ability of bright and dull rats. *Canadian Journal of Psychology, 12,* 159–164.

Corbetta, M., Miezin, F. M., Dobmeyer, S., Shulman, G. L., & Petersen, S. E. (1990). Attentional modulation of neural processing of shape, color, and velocity in humans. *Science, 248,* 1556–1559.

Corcoran, M., McCaughran Jr., J. A., & Wada, J. A. (1978). Antiepileptic and prophylactic effects of tetrahydrocannabinols in amygdaloid kindled rats. *Epilepsia, 19,* 47–55.

Corina, D. P., Poizner, H., Bellugi, U., Feinberg, T., Dowd, D., & O'Grady-Batch, L. (1992). Dissociation between linguistic and nonlinguistic gestural systems: A case for compositionality. *Brain and Language, 43,* 414–447.

Corkin, S. (1968). Acquisition of motor skill after bilateral medial temporal-lobe excision. *Neuropsychologia, 6,* 255–265.

Corkin, S., Milner, B., & Rasmussen, R. (1970). Somatosensory thresholds. *Archives of Neurology, 23,* 41–59.

Corsi, P. I. (1991). *The enchanted loom: Chapters in the history of neuroscience.* New York: Oxford.

Corwin, J. T., & Warchol, M. E. (1991). Auditory hair cells. *Annual Review of Neuroscience, 14,* 301–333.

Coslett, H. B. (1997). Acquired dyslexia. In T. E. Feinberg & M. J. Farah (Eds.), *Behavioral neurology and neuropsychology* (pp. 209–218). New York: McGraw-Hill.

Courtney, S. M., & Ungerleider, L. G. (1997). What fMRI has taught us about human vision. *Current Opinion in Neurobiology, 7,* 554–561.

Cowan, W. M. (1979). The development of the brain. *Scientific American, 241,* 113–133.

Cowan, W. M., Harter, D. H., & Kandel, E. R. (2000). The emergence of modern neuroscience: Some implications for neurology and psychiatry. *Annual Review of Neuroscience, 23,* 343–391.

Crabbe, J. C., Wahlsten, D., & Dudek, B. C. (1999). Genetics of mouse behavior: Interactions with laboratory environment. *Science, 284,* 1670–1672.

Craig, A. D., Reiman, E. M., Evans, A., & Bushnell, M. C. (1996). Functional imaging of an illusion of pain. *Nature, 384,* 258–260.

Crair, M. C. (1999). Neuronal activity during development: Permissive or instructive? *Current Opinion in Neurobiology, 9,* 88–93.

Crair, M. C., Gillespie, D.C., & Stryker, M. P. (1998). The role of visual experience in the development of columns in cat visual cortex. *Science, 279,* 566–570.

Creese, I., Burt, D. R., & Snyder, S. H. (1976). Dopamine receptor binding predicts clinical and pharmacological potencies of antischizophrenic drugs. *Science, 192,* 481–483.

Crisp, A. H. (1983). Some aspects of the psychopathology of anorexia nervosa. In P. L. Darby, P. E. Garfinkel, D. M. Garner, & D. V. Coscina (Eds.), *Anorexia nervosa: Recent developments in research* (pp. 15–28). New York: Alan R. Liss.

Crowell, C. R., Hinson, R. E., & Siegel, S. (1981). The role of conditional drug responses in tolerance to the hypothermic effects of ethanol. *Psychopharmacology, 73,* 51–54.

Crusio, W. M. (1996). Gene-targeting studies: new methods, old problems. *Trends in Neurosciences, 19,* 186–187.

Culbertson, F. M. (1997). Depression and gender. *American Psychologist, 52,* 25–31.

Curran, T., & Schacter, D. L. (1997). Amnesia: Cognitive neuropsychological aspects. In T. E. Feinberg & M. J. Farah (Eds.), *Behavioral neurology and neuropsychology* (pp. 463–472). New York: McGraw-Hill.

Curtiss, S. (1977). *Genie: a psycholinguistic study of modern-day "wild child."* New York: Academic Press

Czeisler, C. A., Duffy, J. F., Shanahan, T. L., Brown, E. N., Mitchell, J. F., Rimmer, D. W., Ronda, J. M., Silva, E. J., Allan, J. S., Emens, J. S., Kijk, D-J., & Kronauer, R. E. (1999). Stability, precision, and near-24-hour period of the human circadian pacemaker. *Science, 284,* 2177–2181.

D'Almeida, V., Hipólide, D.C., Azzalis, L. A., Lobo, L. L., Junqueira, V. B. C., & Tufik, S. (1997). Absence of oxidative stress following paradoxical sleep deprivation in rats. *Neuroscience Letters, 235,* 25–28.

Daly, M., & Wilson, M. (1983). *Sex, evolution, and behavior.* Boston, MA: Allard Grant Press.

Damasio, A. R. (1999, December). How the brain creates the mind. *Scientific American, 281,* 112–117.

Damasio, A. R. (1999, December). The end of nature versus nurture. *Scientific American, 281,* 112–117.

Damasio, H. (1989). Neuroimaging contributions to the understanding of aphasia. In F. Boller & J. Grafman (Eds.), *Handbook of neuropsychology,* Vol. 2 (pp. 3–46). New York: Elsevier.

Damasio, H., Grabowski, T. J., Frank, R., Galaburda, A. M., & Damasio, A. R. (1994). The return of Phineas Gage: Clues about the brain from the skull of a famous patient. *Science, 264,* 1102–1105.

Damasio, H., Grabowski, T. J., Tranel, D., Hichwa, R. D., & Damasio, A. R. (1996). A neural basis for lexical retrieval. *Nature, 380,* 499–505.

Darian-Smith, I., Burman, K., & Darian-Smith, C. (1999). Parallel pathways mediating manual dexterity in the macaque. *Experimental Brain Research, 128,* 101–108.

Darlison, M. G., & Richter, D. (1999). Multiple genes for neuropeptides and their receptors: co-evolution and physiology. *Trends in Neurosciences, 22,* 81–88.

Darnell, J. E., Jr. (1997). STATS and gene regulation. *Science, 277,* 1630–1635.

Daum, I., & Schugens, M. M. (1996). On the cerebellum and classical conditioning. *Current Directions in Psychological Science, 5,* 58–61.

Davidson, J. M. (1980). Hormones and sexual behavior in the male. In D. T. Krieger & J. C. Hughes (Eds.), *Neuroendocrinology* (pp. 232–238). Sunderland, MA: Sinauer Associates.

Davidson, J. M., Kwan, M., & Greenleaf, W. J. (1982). Hormonal replacement and sexuality in men. *Clinics in Endocrinology and Metabolism, 11,* 599–623.

Davidson, R. J., Abercrombie, H., Nitschke, J. B., & Putnam, K. (1999). Regional brain function, emotion and disorders of emotion. *Current Opinion in Neurobiology, 9,* 228–234.

Davis, M., Rainie, D., & Cassell, M. (1994). Neurotransmission in the rat amygdala related to fear and anxiety. *Trends in Neuroscience, 17,* 208–214.

Dawson, D., & Encel, N. (1993). Melatonin and sleep in humans. *Journal of Pineal Research, 15,* 1–2.

Deadwyler, S. A., & Hampson, R. E. (1995). Ensemble activity and behavior: What's the code? *Science, 270,* 1316–1318.

DeCatanzaro, Muir, C., Spironello, E., Binger, T., & Thomas, J. (2000). Intense arousal of novel male mice in proximity to previously inseminated females: Inactivation of males via chlorpromazine does not diminish the capacity to disrupt pregnancy. *Psychobiology, 28,* 110–114.

De Gelder, B. (2000). More to seeing than meets the eye. *Science, 289,* 1148–1208.

De Gennaro, L., Ferrara, M., & Bertini, M. (2000). Muscle twitch activity during REM sleep: Effect of sleep deprivation and relation with rapid eye movement activity. *Psychobiology, 28,* 432–436.

De Jonge, F. H., Louwerse, A. L., Ooms, M. P., Evers, P., Endert, E., & van de Poll, N. E. (1989). Lesions of the SDN-POA inhibit sexual behavior of male Wistar rats. *Brain Research Bulletin, 23,* 483–492.

De Keyser, J., Sulter, G., Luiten, P. G. (1999). Clinical trials with neuroprotective drugs in acute ischaemic stroke: Are we doing the right thing? *Trends in Neurosciences, 22,* 535–540.

de Kruif, P. (1945). *The male hormone.* New York: Harcourt, Brace.

Delville, Y., Melloni, Jr., R. H., & Ferris, C. F. (1998). Behavioral and neurobiological consequences of social subjugation during puberty in golden hamsters. *Journal of Neuroscience, 18,* 2667–2672.

Dement, W. C. (1960). The effect of dream deprivation. *Science, 131,* 1705–1707.

Dement, W. C. (1978). *Some must watch while some must sleep.* New York: W. W. Norton.

Dement, W. C., & Kleitman, N. (1957). The relation of eye movement during sleep to dream activity: An objective method for the study of dreaming. *Journal of Experimental Psychology, 53,* 339–553.

Dement, W. C., & Wolpert, E. A. (1958). The relation of eye movements, body motility and external stimuli to dream content. *Journal of Experimental Psychology, 55,* 543–553.

Dement, W. C., Mitler, M., & Henriksen, S. (1972). Sleep changes during chronic administration of parachorophenylalanine. *Revue Canadianne de Biologie, 31,* 239–246.

Demet, E. M., Chicz-Demet, A., Fallon, J. H., & Sokolski, K. N. (1999). Sleep deprivation therapy in depressive illness and Parkinson's disease. *Progressive Neuro-Psychopharmacology & Biological Psychiatry, 23,* 753–784.

De Renzi, E. (1997). Visuospatial and constructional disorders. In T. E. Feinberg, and M. J. Farah (Eds.), *Behavioral Neurology and Neuropsychology* (pp. 297–308). New York: McGraw-Hill.

Dess, N. K., & Chapman, C. D. (1998). "Humans and animals"? On saying what we mean. *Psychological Science, 9: 2,* 156–157.

Deutch, A. Y., & Roth, R. H. (1999). Neurotransmitters. In M. J. Zigmond, F. E. Bloom, S. C. Landis, J. L. Roberts, & L. R. Squire (Eds.), *Fundamental neuroscience* (pp. 193–234). New York: Academic Press.

DeValois, R. L., & DeValois, K. K. (1988). *Spatial vision.* New York: Oxford University Press.

Devane, W. A., Hanusÿ, L., Breuer, A., Pertwee, R. G., Stevenson, L. A., Griffin, G., Gibson, D., Mandelbaum, A., Etinger, A., & Mechoulam, R. (1992). Isolation and structure of a brain constituent that binds to the cannabinoid receptor. *Science, 258,* 1946–1949.

de Waal, F. B. M. (1999, December). The end of nature versus nurture. *Scientific American, 281,* 94–99.

Dewsbury, D. A. (1988). The comparative psychology of monogamy. In D. W. Leger (Ed.), Comparative perspectives in modern psychology: *Nebraska Symposium on Motivation, Vol. 35* (pp. 1–50). Lincoln: University of Nebraska Press.

Dewsbury, D. A. (1990). *Contemporary issues in comparative psychology.* Sunderland, MA: Sinauer.

Dewsbury, D. A. (1991). Psychobiology. *American Psychologist, 46,* 198–205.

Diamond, A. (1985). Development of the ability to use recall to guide action, as indicated by infants' performance on AB. *Child Development, 56,* 868–863.

Diamond, A. (1991). Neuropsychological insights into the meaning of object concept development. In S. Carey & R. Gelman (Eds.), *The epigenesis of mind: Essays on biology and cognition* (pp. 67–110). Hillsdale, NJ: Lawrence Erlbaum.

Diamond, A., Prevor, A., Callender, G., & Druin, D. P. (1997). *Prefrontal cortex cognitive deficits in children treated early and continuously for PKU*. Chicago: University of Chicago Press.

Diamond, M. C. (1986). I want a girl just like the girl . . . *Discover, 7*, 65–68.

Diamond, M., & Sigmundson, H. K. (1997). Sex reassignment at birth: Long-term review and clinical implications. *Archives of Pediatric and Adolescent Medicine, 151*, 298–304.

DiCarlo, J. J., & Johnson, K. O. (2000). Spatial and temporal structure of receptive fields in primate somatosensory area 3b: Effects of stimulus scanning direction and orientation. *Journal of Neuroscience, 20*, 495–510.

DiCarlo, J. J., Johnson, K. O., & Hsaio, S. S. (1998). Structure of receptive fields in area 3b of primary somatosensory cortex in the alert monkey. *Journal of Neuroscience, 18*, 2626–2645.

DiFiglia, M., Sapp, E., Chase, K. O., Davies, S. W., Bates, G. P., Vonsattel, J. P., & Aronin, N. (1997). Aggregation of Huntington in neuronal intranuclear inclusions and dystrophic neurites in brain. *Science, 277*, 1990–1993.

Di Marzo, V., Melck, D., Bisogno, T., & De Petrocellis, L. (1998). Endocannabinoids: endogenous cannabinoid receptor ligands with neuromodulatory action. *Trends in Neurosciences, 21*, 521–528.

Dimberg, U., Thunberg, M., & Elmehed, K. (2000). Unconscious facial reactions to emotional facial expressions. *Psychological Science, 11*, 86–89.

Dinges, D. F., Pack, F., Williams, K., Gillen, K. A., Powell, J. W., Ott, G. E., Aptowicz, C., Pack, A. I. (1997). Cumulative sleepiness, mood disturbance, and psychomotor vigilance performance decrements during a week of sleep restricted to 4–5 hours per night. *Sleep, 20*, 267–277.

Di Pelligrino, G. D., & Wise, S. P. (1991). Neurophysiological comparison of three distinct regions in the primate frontal lobe. *Brain, 114*, 951–978.

Dirgnagl, U., Iadecola, C., & Moskowitz, M. A. (1999). Pathobiology of ischaemic stroke: An integrated view. *Trends in Neurosciences, 22*, 391–397.

Dixon, M. J., Bub, D. N., & Arguin, M. (1998). Semantic and visual determinants of face recognition in a prosopagnosic patient. *Journal of Cognitive Neuroscience, 10*, 362–376.

Dobelle, W. H., Mladejovsky, M. G., & Girvin, J. P. (1974). Artificial vision for the blind: Electrical stimulation of visual cortex offers hope for a functional prosthesis. *Science, 183*, 440–444.

Dodd, J., Jessel, T. M., & Placzek, M. (1998). The when and where of floor plate induction. *Science, 282*, 1654–1658

Dolen, R. J., & Morris, J. S. (2000). The functional anatomy of innate and acquired fear: Perspectives from neuroimaging. In R. D. Lane, & L. Nadel, (Eds.), *Cognitive neuroscience of emotion* (pp. 225–241). New York: Oxford University Press.

Donoghue, J. P. (1995). Plasticity of adult sensorimotor representations. *Current Opinion in Neurobiology, 5*, 749–754.

Doty, R. L. (1986). Gender and endocrine-related influences on human olfactory perception. In H. Meiselman & R. S. Rivlin (Eds.), *Clinical measurement of taste and smell* (pp. 377–413). New York: Macmillan.

Doupe, A. J. (1993). A neural circuit specialized for vocal learning. *Current Opinion in Neurobiology, 3*, 104–110.

Drachman, D. A., & Arbit, J. (1966). Memory and the hippocampal complex. *Archives of Neurology, 15*, 52–61.

Drevets, W. C., Gautier, C., Price, J. C., Kupfer, D. J., Kinahan, P. E., Grace, A. A., Price, J. L., & Mathis, C. A. (2001). Amphetamine-induced dopamine release in human ventral striatum correlates with euphoria. *Biological Psychiatry, 49*, 81–96.

Drevets, W. C., Price, J. L., Simpson, J. R., Jr., Todd, R. D., Reich, T., Vannier, M., & Raichle, M. (1997). Subgenual prefrontal cortex abnormalities in mood disorders. *Nature, 386*, 824–827.

Drevets, W. C., Videen, T. O., Price, J. L., Preskorn, S. H., Carmichael, T., & Raichle, M. E. (1992). A functional anatomical study of unipolar depression. *Journal of Neuroscience, 12*, 3628–3641.

Drewnowski, A., Halmi, K. A., Pierce, B., Giibbs, J., & Smith, G. P. (1987). Taste and eating disorders. *American Journal of Clinical Nutrition, 46*, 442–450.

Driver, J., & Mattingly, J. B. (1996). Selective attention in humans: normality and pathology. *Current Opinion in Neurobiology, 5*, 191–197.

Drummey, A. B., & Newcombe, N. (1995). Remembering versus knowing the past: Children's explicit and implicit memories for pictures. *Journal of Experimental Child Psychology, 59*, 540–565.

Duchamp-Viret, P., Chaput, M. A., & Duchamp, A. (1999). Odor response properties of rat olfactory receptor neurons. *Science, 284*, 2171–2174.

Dunbar, G. C., Perera, M. H., & Jenner, F. A. (1989). Patterns of benzodiazepine use in Great Britain as measured by a general population survey. *British Journal of Psychiatry, 155*, 836–841.

Duncan, J., & Owen, A. M. (2000). Common regions of the human frontal lobe recruited by diverse cognitive demands. *Trends in Neurosciences, 23*, 475–483

Duva, C. A., Kornecook, T. J., & Pinel, J. P. J. (2000). Animal models of medial temporal lobe amnesia: The myth of the hippocampus. In M. Haug & R. E. Whalen (Eds.), *Animal models of human emotion and cognition* (pp. 197–214). Washington: American Psychological Association.

Earnest, D. J., Liang, F-Q., Ratcliff, M., & Cassone, V. M. (1999). Immortal time: Circadian clock properties of rat suprachiasmatic cell lines. *Science, 283*, 693–695.

Earnest, M. P. (1993). Seizures. *Neurologic Complications of Drug and Alcohol Abuse, 11*, 563–575.

Easter, S. S., Jr., Purves, D., Rakic, P., & Spitzer, N. C. (1985). The changing view of neural specificity. *Science, 230*, 507–511.

Ebner, T. J. (1998). A role for the cerebellum in the control of limb movement velocity. *Current Opinion in Neurobiology, 8*, 762–769.

Edwards, F. A. (1995). LTP—a structural model to explain the inconsistencies. *Trends in Neurosciences, 18*, 250–255.

Egan, M. F., & Weinberger, D. R. (1997). Neurobiology of schizophrenia. *Current Opinion in Neurobiology, 7*, 701–707.

Ehrhardt, A. A., Epstein, R., & Money, M. (1968). Fetal androgens and female gender identity in the early-treated androgenital syndrome. *Johns Hopkins Medical Journal, 122*, 160–167.

Ehrhardt, A. A., Meyer-Bahlburg, H. F. L., Rosen, L. R., Feldman, J. F., Veridiano, N. P., Zimmerman, I., & McEwen, B. S. (1985). Sexual orientation after prenatal exposure to exogenous estrogen. *Archives of Sexual Behavior, 14*, 57–77.

Ehringer, H., & Hornykiewicz, O. (1960). Verteilung von Noradrenalin und Dopamin (3-Hydroxytyramin) im gehirn des Menschen und ihr Verhalten bei Erkrankungen des Extrapyramidalen Systems. *Klinische Wochenschrift, 38*, 1236–1239.

Eichenbaum, H. (1996). Learning from LTP: A comment on recent attempts to identify cellular and molecular mechanisms of memory. *Learning & Memory, 3*, 61–73.

Eichenbaum, H. (1997). How does the brain organize memories? *Science, 277*, 330–332.

Eichenbaum, H. (1999). Conscious awareness, memory and the hippocampus. *Nature, 2*, 775–776.

Eidelberg, E. (1987). Flexion reflexes. In G. Adelman (Ed.), *Encyclopedia of neuroscience, I* (pp. 431–432). Boston, MA: Birkhäuser.

Eikelboom, R., & Stewart, J. (1982). Conditioning of drug-induced physiological responses. *Psychological Review, 89,* 507–528.

Eilers, J., & Konnerth, A. (1997). Dendritic signal integration. *Current Opinion in Neurobiology, 7,* 385–390.

Eitan, S., Solomon, A., Lavie, V., Yoles, E., Hirschberg, D. L., Belkin, M., & Schwartz, M. (1994). Recovery of visual response of injured adult rat optic nerves treated with transglutaminase. *Science, 264,* 1764–1768.

Ekman, P. (1985). *Telling lies.* New York: Norton.

Ekman, P. (1992). Facial expressions of emotion: New findings, new questions. *Psychological Science, 3,* 34–38.

Ekman, P., & Davidson, R. J. (1993). Voluntary smiling changes regional brain activity. *Psychological Science, 4,* 342–345.

Ekman, P., & Friesen, W. V. (1971). Constants across cultures in the face and emotion. *Journal of Personality and Social Psychology, 17,* 124–129.

Ekman, P., & Friesen, W. V. (1975). *Unmasking the face: A guide to recognizing emotions from facial clues.* Englewood Cliffs, NJ: Prentice-Hall.

Ekman, P., Sorenson, E. R., & Friesen, W. V. (1969). Pan-cultural elements in facial displays of emotions. *Science, 164,* 86–88.

Elbert, T., Pantev, C., Wienbruch, C., Rockstroh, B., & Taub, E. (1995). Increased cortical representation of the fingers of the left hand in string players. *Science, 270,* 305–307.

Elena, S. F., Cooper, V. S., & Lenski, R. E. (1996). Punctuated evolution cased by selection of rare beneficial mutations. *Science, 272,* 1802–1807.

Ellis, L., & Ames, M. A. (1987). Neurohormonal functioning and sexual orientation: A theory of homosexuality-heterosexuality. *Psychological Bulletin, 101,* 233–258.

Emerich, D. F. (2000). Clinical trials with neuroprotective drugs in acute ischaemic stroke: Are we doing the right thing? (Letter to the editor). *Trends in Neurosciences, 23,* 245–246.

Engel, S. A. (1999). Using neuroimaging to measure mental representations: Finding color-opponent neurons in visual cortex. *Current Directions in Psychological Science, 8,* 23–27.

Enns, J. T., & DiLollo, V. (1997). Object substitution: A new form of masking in unattended visual locations. *Psychological Science, 8,* 135–139.

Erikkson, P. S., Perfilieva, E., Björk-Eriksson, T., Alborn, A., Nordberg, C., Peterson, D. A., & Gage, F. H. (1998). Neurogenesis in the adult human hippocampus. *Nature Medicine, 4,* 1313–1317.

Ervin, G. N., Mosher, J. T., Birkemo, L. S., & Johnson, M. F. (1995). Multiple, small doses of cholecystokinin octapeptide are more efficacious at inducing taste aversion conditioning than single, large doses. *Peptides, 16,* 539–545.

Evan, G., & Littlewood, T. (1998). A matter of life and cell death. *Science, 281,* 1317–1320.

Everitt, B. J., & Herbert, J. (1972). Hormonal correlates of sexual behavior in sub-human primates. *Danish Medical Bulletin, 19,* 246–258.

Everitt, B. J., & Robbins, T. W. (1997). Central cholinergic systems and cognition. *Annual Review of Psychology, 48,* 649–684.

Everitt, B. J., & Stacey, P. (1987). Studies of instrumental behavior with sexual reinforcement in male rats (*Rattus norvegicus*): II. Effects of preoptic area lesions, castration, and testosterone. *Journal of Comparative Psychology, 101,* 407–419.

Everitt, B. J., Herbert, J., & Hamer, J. D. (1971). Sexual receptivity of bilaterally adrenalectomized female rhesus monkeys. *Physiology & Behavior, 8,* 409–415.

Falconer, E. M., & Galea, L. A. M. (2000). Sex differences in the expression of defensive behaviors due to acute or chronic predator odor exposure is related to cell proliferation in the dentate gyrus of adult rats. *Society for Neuroscience Abstracts, 847.10.*

Falzi, G., Perrone, P., & Vignolo, L. A. (1982). Right-left asymmetry in anterior speech region. *Archives of Neurology, 39,* 239–240.

Farah, M. J. (1990). *Visual agnosia: Disorders of object recognition and what they tell us about normal vision.* Cambridge, MA: MIT Press.

Farmer, M. E., & Klein, R. M. (1995). The evidence for a temporal processing deficit linked to dyslexia: A review. *Psychonomic Bulletin and Review, 2,* 460–493.

Farooqi, I. S., Jebb, S. A.., Langmack, G., Lawrence, E., Cheetham, C. H., Prentice, A. M., Hughes, I. A., McCamish, M. A., & O'Rahilly, S. (1999). Effects of recombinant leptin therapy in a child with congenital leptin deficiency. *New England Journal of Medicine, 341,* 879–884.

Fazeli, S., & Walsh, F. S. (1996). The role of cell adhesion molecules during the development and regeneration of the neuromuscular system. *Seminars in the Neurosciences, 8,* 367–377.

Fazio, F., Perani, D., Gilardi, Colombo, F., Cappa, S. F., Vallar, G., Bettinardi, V., Paulesu, E., Alberoni, M., Bressi, S., Franceschi, M., & Lenzi, G. L. (1992). *Journal of Cerebral Blood Flow and Metabolism, 12,* 353–358.

Feinberg, T. E., & Farah, M. J. (Eds.) (1997). *Behavioral neurology and neuropsychology.* New York: McGraw-Hill.

Feindel, W. (1986). Electrical stimulation of the brain during surgery for epilepsy—historical highlights. In G. P. Varkey (Ed.), *Anesthetic considerations for craniotomy in awake patients* (pp. 75–87). Boston: Little, Brown.

Fentress, J. C. (1973). Development of grooming in mice with amputated forelimbs. *Science, 179,* 704–705.

Ferrara, M., De Gennaro, L., & Bertini, M. (1999). The effects of slow-wave sleep (SWS) deprivation and time of night on behavioral performance upon awakening. *Physiology & Behavior, 68,* 55–61.

Fibiger, H. C. (1993). Mesolimbic dopamine: An analysis of its role in motivated behavior. *Seminars in the Neurosciences, 5,* 321–327.

Fields, R. D., & Itoh, K. (1996). Neural cell adhesion molecules in activity-dependent development and synaptic plasticity. *Trends in Neurosciences, 19,* 473–480.

Fillion, T. J., & Blass, E. M. (1986). Infantile experience with suckling odors determines adult sexual behavior in male rats. *Science, 231,* 729–731.

Fink, G., Sumner, B., Rosie, R., Wilson, H., & McQueen, J. (1999). Androgen actions on central serotonin neurotransmission: relevance for mood, mental state and memory. *Behavioural Brain Research, 105,* 53–68.

Finlay, B. L., & Darlington, R. B. (1995). Linked regularities in the development and evolution of Mammalian brains. *Science, 268,* 1578–1584.

Fiorino, D. F., Coury, A., Fibiger, H. C., & Phillips, A. G. (1993). Electrical stimulation of reward sites in the ventral tegmental area increases dopamine transmission in the nucleus accumbens of the rat. *Behavioural Brain Research, 55,* 131–141.

Fiorino, D. F., Coury, A., & Phillips, A. G. (1997). Dynamic changes in nucleus accumbens dopamine efflux during the Coolidge effect in male rats. *Journal of Neuroscience, 17,* 4849–4855.

Flament, D., Ellermann, J. M., Kim, S-G., Ugurbil, K., & Ebner, T. J. (1996). Functional magnetic resonance imaging of cerebellar activation during the learning of a visuomotor dissociation task. *Human Brain Mapping, 4,* 210–226.

Floresco, S. B., Seamans, J. K., & Phillips, A. G. (1997). Selective roles for hippocampal, prefrontal cortical, and ventral striatal circuits in radial-arm maze tasks with or without a delay. *Journal of Neuroscience, (17) 5,* 1880–1890.

Foulkes, N. S., Borjigin, J. Snyder, S. H., & Sassone-Corsi, P. (1997). Rhythmic transcription: The molecular basis of circadian melatonin synthesis. *Trends in Neurosciences, 20,* 487–492.

Francis, D. D., & Meaney, M. J. (1999). Maternal care and the development of stress responses. *Current Opinion in Neurobiology, 9,* 128–134.

Fraser, S. P., Suh, Y-H., & Djamgoz, M. B. A. (1997). Ionic effects of the Alzheimer's disease ß-amyloid precursor protein and its metabolic fragments. *Trends in Neurosciences, 20,* 67–72.

Frederikse, M. E., Lu, A., Aylward, E., Barta, P., & Pearlson (1999). Sex differences in the inferior parietal lobule. *Cerebral Cortex, 9,* 896–901.

Freedman, M. S., Lucas, R. J., Soni, B., von Schantz, M., Muñoz, M., David-Gray, Z., & Foster, R. (1999). Regulation of mammalian circadian behavior by non-rod, non-cone, ocular photoreceptors. *Science, 284,* 502–504.

Friedman, J., Globus, G., Huntley, A., Mullaney, D., Naitoh, P., & Johnson, L. (1977). Performance and mood during and after gradual sleep reduction. *Psychophysiology, 14,* 245–250.

Friedman-Hill, S. R., Robertson, L. C., & Treisman, A. (1995). Parietal contributions to visual feature binding: Evidence from a patient with bilateral lesions. *Science, 269,* 853–855.

Frith, C., & Dolan, R. J. (1998). Images of psychopathology. *Current Opinion in Neurobiology, 8,* 259–262.

Funnell, M. G., Corballis, P. M., & Gazzaniga, M. S. (1999). *Neuropsychologia, 37,* 1143–1154.

Fuster, J. M. (2000). The prefrontal cortex of the primate: A synopsis. *Psychobiology, 28,* 125–131.

Gabrieli, J. D. E., Corkin, S., Mickel, S. F., & Growdon, J. H. (1993). Intact acquisition and long-term retention of mirror-tracing skill in Alzheimer's disease and in global amnesia. *Behavioral Neuroscience, 107,* 899–910.

Gackenbach, J., & LaBerge, S. (Eds.). (1988). *Conscious mind, sleeping brain.* New York: Plenum.

Gaffan, D. (1974). Recognition impaired and association in the memory of monkeys after transection of the fornix. *Journal of Comparative and Physiological Psychology, 86,* 1100–1109.

Gage, F. H. (2000). Mammalian neural stem cells. *Science, 287,* 1433–1438.

Galea, L. A. M., McEwen, B. S., Tanapat, P., Keak, T., Spencer, R. L., & Dhabhar, F. S. (1997). Sex differences in dendritic atrophy of CA3 pyramidal neurons in response to chronic restraint stress. *Neuroscience, 81,* 689–697.

Galef, B. G. (1989). Laboratory studies of naturally-occurring feeding behaviors: Pitfalls, progress and problems in ethnoexperimental analysis. In R. J. Blanchard, P. F. Brain, D.C. Blanchard, & S. Parmigiani (Eds.), *Ethnoexperimental approaches to the study of behavior* (pp. 51–77). Dordrecht, The Netherlands: Kluwer Academic Publishers.

Galef, B. G. (1995). Food selection: problems in understanding how we choose foods to eat. *Neuroscience and Biobehavioral Reviews, 20,* 67–73.

Galef, B. G. (1996). Social enhancement of food preferences in Norway rats: A brief review. In *Social learning in animals: The roots of culture* (pp. 49–64). New York: Academic Press.

Galef, B. G., & Sherry, D. F. (1973). Mother's milk: A medium for transmission of cues reflecting the flavor of mother's diet. *Journal of Comparative and Physiological Psychology, 83,* 374–378.

Galef, B. G., & Wright, T. J. (1995). Groups of naive rats learn to select nutritionally adequate foods faster than do isolated naive rats. *Animal Behavior, 49,* 403–409.

Galef, B. G., Whishkin, E. E., & Bielavska, E. (1997). Interaction with demonstrator rats changes observer rats' affective responses to flavors. *Journal of Comparative Psychology, 111,* 393–398.

Gallup, G. G. (Jr.) (1983). Toward a comparative psychology of mind. In R. L. Mellgren (Ed.), *Animal cognition and behavior* (pp. 473–505). New York: North-Holland Publishing.

Galuske, R. A. W., Schlote, W., Bratzke, H., & Singer, W. (2000). Interhemispheric asymmetries of the modular structure in human temporal cortex. *Science, 289,* 1946–1949.

Gannon, P. J., Holloway, R. L., Broadfield, D.C., & Braun, A. R. (1998). Asymmetry of chimpanzee planum temporale: Humanlike pattern of Wernicke's brain language area homolog. *Science, 279,* 220–222.

Gao, E., & Suga, N. (2000). Experience-dependent plasticity in the auditory cortex and the inferior colliculus of bats: Role of the corticofugal system. *Proceedings of the National Academy of Sciences U.S.A., 97,* 8081–8086.

Garcia, J., & Koelling, R. A. (1966). Relation of cue to consequence in avoidance learning. *Psychonomic Science, 4,* 123–124.

Garcia-Segura, L. M., Azcoitia, I., & DonCarlos, L. L. (2001). Neuroprotection by estradiol. *Progress in Neurobiology, 63,* 29–60.

Gardner, E. L., & Ashby, C. R. (2000). Heterogeneity of the mesotelencephalic dopamine fibers: Physiology and pharmacology. *Neuroscience and Biobehavioral Reviews, 24,* 115–118.

Gauthier, I., Behrmann, M., & Tarr, M. J. (1999). Can face recognition really be dissociated from object recognition? *Journal of Cognitive Neuroscience, 11,* 349–370.

Gauthier, I., Skudlarski, P., Gore, J. C., & Anderson, A. W. (2000). Expertise for cars and birds recruits brain areas involved in face recognition. *Nature, 3,* 191–197.

Gawin, F. H. (1991). Cocaine addiction: Psychology and neurophysiology. *Science, 251,* 1580–1586.

Gaze, R. M., & Sharma, S. C. (1970). Axial differences in the reinnervation of the goldfish optic tectum by regenerating optic nerve fibres. *Experimental Brain Research, 10,* 171–181.

Gaze, R. M., Keating, M. J., Ostberg, A., & Chung, S. H. (1979). The relationship between retinal and tectal growth in larval Xenopus: Implications for the development of the retino-tectal projection. *Journal of Embryology and Experimental Morphology, 53,* 103–143.

Gazzaniga, M. S. (1967, August). The split brain in man. *Scientific American, 217,* 24–29.

Gazzaniga, M. S. (1998, July). The split brain revisited. *Scientific American, 278,* 51–55.

Gazzaniga, M. S. (2000). Regional differences in cortical organization. *Science, 289,* 1887–1888.

Gazzaniga, M. S., & Sperry, R. W. (1967). Language after section of the cerebral commissure. *Brain, 90,* 131–148.

Gearhart, J. (1998). New potential for human embryonic stem cells. *Science, 282,* 1061–1062.

Georgopoulos, A. P. (1991). Higher order motor control. *Annual Review of Neuroscience, 14,* 361–377.

Georgopoulos, A. P. (1995). Current issues in directional motor control. *Trends in Neurosciences, 18,* 506–510.

Gerlai, R. (1996). Gene-targeting studies of mammalian behavior: is it the mutation or the background genotype? *Trends in Neurosciences, 19,* 177–181.

Gerlai, R., & Clayton, N. S. (1999). Analyzing hippocampal function in transgenic mice: An ethological perspective. *Trends in Neurosciences, 22:2,* 47–51.

Geschwind, N. (1970). The organization of language and the brain. *Science, 170,* 940–944.

Geschwind, N. (1979, September). Specializations of the human brain. *Scientific American, 241,* 180–199.

Geschwind, N., & Levitsky, W. (1968). Human brain: Left-right asymmetries in temporal speech region. *Science, 161,* 186–187.

Gevins, A., Leong, H., Smith, M. E., Le, J., & Du, R. (1995). Mapping cognitive brain function with modern high-resolution electroencephalography. *Trends in Neurosciences, 18,* 429–436.

Gibbs, J., Young, R. C., & Smith, G. P. (1973). Cholecystokinin decreases food intake in rats. *Journal of Comparative and Physiological Psychology, 84,* 488–495.

Gibson, A. D., & Garbers, D. L. (2000). Guanylyl cyclases as a family of putative odorant receptors. *Annual Review of Neuroscience, 23,* 417–439.

Gilbert, C. D., & Wiesel, T. N. (1992). Receptive field dynamics in adult primary visual cortex. *Nature, 356,* 150–152.

Gillberg, M., Kecklund, G., Axelsson, J., & Åkerstedt, T. (1996). The effects of a short daytime nap after restricted night sleep. *Sleep, 19,* 570–575.

Gillette, M. U., & McArthur, A. J. (1996). Circadian actions of melatonin at the suprachiasmatic nucleus. *Behavioural Brain Research, 73,* 135–139.

Gilliam, T. C., Gusella, J. F., & Lehrach, H. (1987). Molecular genetic strategies to investigate Huntington's disease. *Advances in Neurology, 48,* 17–29.

Gingrich, J. R., & Roder, J. (1998). Inducible gene expression in the nervous system of transgenic mice. *Annual Review of Neuroscience, 21,* 377–405.

Gladue, B. A. (1994). The biopsychology of sexual orientation. *Current Directions in Psychological Science, 3,* 150–154.

Glaser, R., Rice, J., Sheridan, J., Fertel, R., Stout, J., Speicher, C., Pinsky, D., Koture, M., Post, A., Beck, M., & Kiecolt-Glaser, J. K. (1987). Stress-related immune suppression: Health implications. *Brain, Behavior & Immunity, 1,* 7–20.

Gleeson, J. G., & Walsh, C. A. (2000). Neuronal migration disorders: From genetic diseases to developmental mechanisms. *Trends in Neurosciences, 23,* 352–359.

Glickstein, M. (2000). How are visual areas of the brain connected to motor areas for the sensory guidance of movement? *Trends in Neurosciences, 23,* 613–617.

Goddard, G. V., McIntyre, D.C., & Leech, C. K. (1969). A permanent change in brain function resulting from daily electrical stimulation. *Experimental Neurology, 25,* 295–330.

Goedert, M. (1993). Tau protein and the neurofibrillary pathology of Alzheimer's disease. *Trends in Neurosciences, 16,* 460–465.

Gold, R. M., Jones, A. P., Sawchenko, P. E., & Kapatos, G. (1977). Paraventricular area: Critical focus of a longitudinal neurocircuitry mediating food intake. *Physiology & Behavior, 18,* 1111–1119.

Goldberg, J. L., & Barres, B. A. (2000). The relationship between neuronal survival and regeneration. *Annual Reviews of Neuroscience, 23,* 576–612.

Goldman, S. A., & Nottebohm, F. (1983). Neuronal production, migration, and differentiation in a vocal control nucleus of the adult female canary brain. *Proceedings of the National Academy of Sciences, USA, 80,* 2390–2394.

Goldman-Rakic, P. S., & Selemon, L. D. (1990). New frontiers in basal ganglia research. *Trends in Neurosciences, 13,* 241–244.

Goldman-Rakic, P. S., Bates, J. F., & Chafee, M. V. (1992). The prefrontal cortex and internally generated motor acts. *Current Opinion in Neurobiology, 2,* 830–835.

Goldowitz, D., & Hamre, K. (1998). The cells and molecules that make a cerebellum. *Trends in Neurosciences, 21,* 375–382.

Goldstein, A., & Kalant, H. (1990). Drug policy: Striking the right balance. *Science, 249,* 1513–1521.

Goldstein, I. (2000, August). Male sexual circuitry. *Scientific American, 283,* 70–75.

Gollin, E. S. (1960). Developmental studies of visual recognition of incomplete objects. *Perceptual Motor Skills, 11,* 289–298.

Gollinick, P. D., & Hodgson, D. R. (1986). The identification of fiber types in skeletal muscle: A continual dilemma. *Exercise and Sport Sciences Reviews, 14,* 81–10

Golman, S. S., & Luskin, M. B. (1998). Strategies utilized by migrating neurons of the postnatal vertebrate forebrain. *Trends in Neurosciences, 21,* 107–114.

Goodale, M. A. (1993). Visual pathways supporting perception and action in the primate cerebral cortex. *Current Opinion in Neurobiology, 3,* 578–585.

Goodale, M. A., & Milner, A. D. (1992). Separate visual pathways for perception and action. *Trends in Neurosciences, 15,* 20–25.

Goodale, M. A., Milner, A. D., Jakobson, L. S., & Carey, D. P. (1991). A neurological dissociation between perceiving objects and grasping them. *Nature, 349,* 154–156.

Goodenough, D. R., Shapiro, A., Holden, M., & Steinschriber, L. (1959). A comparison of "dreamers" and "nondreamers": Eye movements, electroencephalograms, and the recall of dreams. *Journal of Abnormal and Social Psychology, 59,* 295–303.

Gorski, R. A. (1980). Sexual differentiation in the brain. In D. T. Krieger & J. C. Hughes (Eds.), *Neuroendocrinology* (pp. 215–222). Sunderland, MA: Sinauer.

Gorski, R. A., Gordom, J. H., Shryne, J. E., & Southam, A. M. (1978). Evidence for a morphological sex difference within the medial preoptic area of the rat brain. *Brain Research, 148,* 333–346.

Gottesmann, I. I., & Bertelsen, A. (1989). Confirming unexpressed genotypes for schizophrenia. *Archives of General Psychiatry, 46,* 867–872.

Gottesmann, I. I., & Shields, J. (1982). *Schizophrenia: The epigenetic puzzle.* Cambridge, UK: Cambridge University Press.

Gottlieb, G. (2000). Environmental and behavioral influences on gene activity. *Current Directions in Psychological Science, 9,* 93–97.

Gould, E., Reeves, A. J., Graziano, M. S. A., & Gross, C. G. (1999). Neurogenesis in the neocortex of adult primates. *Science, 286,* 548–552.

Gould, E., Tanapat, P., McEwen, B. S., Flügge, G., & Fuchs, E. (1998). Proliferation of granule cell precursors in the dentate gyrus of adult monkeys is diminished by stress. *Proceedings of the National Academy of Science (USA), 95,* 3168–3171.

Goy, R. W., & McEwen, B. S. (1980). *Sexual differentiation of the brain.* Cambridge, MA: MIT Press.

Grace, A., Bunney, B. S., Moore, H., & Todd, C. L. (1997). Dopamine-cell depolarization block as a model for the therapeutic actions of antipsychotic drugs. *Trends in Neuroscience, 20,* 31–37.

Grady, K. L., Phoenix, C. H., & Young, W. C. (1965). Role of the developing rat testis in differentiation of the neural tissues mediating mating behavior. *Journal of Comparative and Physiological Psychology, 59,* 176–182.

Graff-Radford, N., Damasio, H., Yamada, T., Eslinger, P. J., & Damasio, A. R. (1985). Nonhaemorrhagic thalamic infarction. *Brain, 108,* 485–516.

Grakoui, A., Bromley, S. K., Sumen, C., Davis, M. M., Shaw, A. S., Allen, P. M., & Dustin, M. L., (1999). The imunological synapse: A molecular machine controlling T cell activation. *Science, 285,* 221–227.

Grant, P. R. (1991, October). Natural selection and Darwin's finches. *Scientific American, 265,* 82–87.

Grant, S. G. N., & Silva, A. J. (1994). Targeting learning. *Trends in Neurosciences, 17,* 71–79.

Graybiel, A. M. (1995). Building action repertoires: memory and learning functions of the basal ganglia. *Current Opinion in Neurobiology, 5,* 733–741.

Graybiel, A. M., Aosaki, T., Flaherty, A. W., & Kimura, M. (1994). The basal ganglia and adaptive motor control. *Science, 265,* 1826–1831.

Graziano, M. S. A., Gross, C. G. (1998). Spatial maps for the control of movement. *Current Opinion in Neurobiology, 8,* 195–201.

Green, D. R., & Reed, J. C. (1998). Mitochondria and apoptosis. *Science, 281,* 1309–1316.

Green, S. (1991). Benzodiazepines, putative anxiolytics and animal models of anxiety. *Trends in Neuroscience, 14,* 101–103.

Greene, P. E., Fahn, S., Tsai, W. Y., Winfield, H., Dillon, S., Kao, R., Winfield, L., Eidelberg, D., Breeze, R. E., & Freed, C. R. (1999). Double-blind controlled trial of human embryonic dopaminergic tissue transplants in advanced Parkinson's disease: Long-term unblinded follow-up phase. *Neurology, 52* (suppl 2).

Grillner, S. (1985). Neurobiological bases of rhythmic motor acts in vertebrates. *Science, 228,* 143–149.

Grilly, D. M. (1998). *Drugs and human behavior* (3rd ed.). Boston: Allyn & Bacon.

Grimson, W. E. L., Kikinis, R., Jolesz, F. A., & Black, P. McL. (1999, June). Virtual-reality technology. *Scientific American, 280,* 63–69.

Groos, G. (1983). *Regulation of the circadian sleep-wake cycle.* Sleep 1982, 6th European Congress on Sleep Research (Zurich, 1982) (pp. 19–29). Basel: Karger.

Groos, G., & Hendricks, J. (1982). Circadian rhythms in electrical discharge of rat suprachiasmatic neurones recorded in vitro. *Neuroscience Letters, 34,* 283–288.

Gross, C. G., & Sergent, J. (1992). Face recognition. *Current Opinion in Neurobiology, 2,* 156–161.

Gross, C. G., Desimone, R., Albright, T. X., & Schwarz, E. L. (1985). Inferior temporal cortex and pattern recognition. In C. Chagas, R. Gattass, & C. Gross (Eds.), *Pattern recognition mechanisms* (pp. 179–201). Berlin: Springer-Verlag.

Grossman, E., Donnelly, Price, R., Pickens, D., Morgan, V. Neighbor, G., & Blake, R. (2000). Brain areas involved in perception of biological motion. *Journal of Cognitive Neuroscience, 12,* 711–720.

Grunt, J. A., & Young, W. C. (1952). Differential reactivity of individuals and the response of the male guinea pig to testosterone propionate. *Endocrinology, 51,* 237–248.

Guo, Y., & Udin, S. B. (2000). The development of abnormal axon trajectories after rotation of one eye in xenopus. *Journal of Neuroscience, 20,* 4189–4197.

Gur, R. C., Mozley, L. H., Mozley, P. D., Resnick, S. M., Karp, J. S., Alavi, A., Arnold, S. E., & Gur, R. E. (1995). Sex differences in regional cerebral glucose metabolism during a resting state. *Science, 267,* 528–531.

Gur, R. C., Turetsky, B. I., Matsui, M., Yan, M., Bilker, W., Hughett, P., & Gur, R. E. (1999). Sex differences in brain gray and white matter in healthy young adults: Correlations with cognitive performance. *Journal of Neuroscience, 19,* 4065–4072.

Gusella, J. F., & MacDonald, M. E. (1998). Huntingtin: a single bait hooks many species. *Current Opinion in Neurobiology, 8,* 425–430.

Gustafsson, J-Å. (1999). Seeking ligands for lonely orphan receptors. *Science, 284,* 1285–1286.

Haaland, K. Y., & Harrington, D. L. (1996). Hemispheric asymmetry of movement. *Current Opinion in Neurobiology, 6,* 796–800.

Haass, C., & De Strooper, B. (1999). The presenilins in Alzheimer's disease—proteolysis holds the key. *Science, 286,* 916–919.

Haffenden, A. M., & Goodale, M. A. (1998). The effect of pictorial illusion on prehension and perception. *Journal of Cognitive Neuroscience, 10,* 122–136.

Haimov, I., & Lavie, P. (1996). Melatonin—a soporific hormone. *Current Directions in Psychological Science, 5* (4), 106–111.

Haimov, I., Lavie, P., Laudon, M., Herer, P., & Zisapel, N. (1995). Melatonin replacement therapy of elderly insomniacs. *Sleep, 18,* 598–603.

Halford, J. C. G., & Blundell, J. E. (2000). Pharmacology of appetite suppression. In E. Jucker (Ed.), *Progress in Drug Research,* vol. 54 (pp. 25–58). Basel: Birkhäuser, Verlag.

Halford, J. C. G., & Blundell, J. E. (2000a). Serotonin drugs and the treatment of obesity. In T. G. Heffner & D. H. Lockwood (Eds.), *Obesity: Pathology and therapy* (pp. 155–176). Berlin: Springer-Verlag.

Halford, J. C. G., & Blundell, J. E. (2000b). Separate systems for serotonin and leptin in appetite control. *Annals of Medicine, 32,* 222–232.

Hall, G. L., Compston, A., & Scolding, N.J. (1997). Beta-interferon and multiple sclerosis. *Trends in Neurosciences, 20,* 63–67.

Hamann, S. B., & Adolphs, R. (1999). Normal recognition of emotional similarity between facial expressions following bilateral amygdala damage. *Neuropsychologia, 37,* 1135–1141.

Hamer, D. H., Hu, S., Magnuson, V. L., Hu, N., & Pattatucci, A. M. L. (1993). A linkage between DNA markers on the chromosome and male sexual orientation. *Science, 261,* 321–327.

Hammond, P. H., Merton, P. A., & Sutton, G. G. (1956). Nervous gradation of muscular contraction. *British Medical Bulletin, 12,* 214–218.

Happé, F., & Frith, U. (1996). The neuropsychology of autism. *Brain, 119,* 1377–1400.

Haqq, C. M., King, C.-Y., Ukiyama, E., Falsafi, S., Haqq, T. N., Donahoe, P. K., & Weiss, M. A. (1994). Molecular basis of mammalian sexual determination: Activation of Müllerian inhibiting substance gene expression by SRY. *Science, 266,* 1494–1500.

Harrington, M. E., Rusak, B., & Mistlberger, R. E. (1994). Anatomy and physiology of the mammalian circadian system. In M. H. Kryger, T. Roth, & W. C. Dement (Eds.), *Principles and practise of sleep medicine,* 2nd ed. (pp. 286–300). Philadelphia: W. B. Saunders.

Harris, G. W. (1955). *Neural control of the pituitary gland.* London: Edward Arnold Ltd.

Harris, G. W., & Levine, S. (1965). Sexual differentiation of the brain and its experimental control. *Journal of Physiology, 181,* 379–400.

Harris, K. M. (1995). How multiple-synapse boutons could preserve input specificity during an interneuronal spread of LTP. *Trends in Neurosciences, 18,* 365–369.

Harris, K. M., & Kater, S. B. (1994). Dendritic spines: Cellular specializations imparting both stability and flexibility to synaptic function. *Annual Review of Neuroscience, 17,* 341–371.

Harris, L. J. (1978). Sex differences in spatial ability: Possible environmental, genetic, and neurological factors. In M. Kinsbourne (Ed.), *Asymmetrical function of the brain* (p. 463). Cambridge, England: Cambridge University Press.

Harris, L. J., Clay, J., Hargreaves, F. J., & Ward, A. (1933). Appetite and choice of diet: The ability of the vitamin B deficient rat to discriminate between diets containing and lacking the vitamin. *Proceedings of the Royal Society of London (B), 113,* 161–190.

Harrison, P. J. (1997). Schizophrenia: A disorder of neurodevelopment? *Current Opinion in Neurobiology, 7,* 285–289.

Harrison, Y., & Horne, J. A. (1997). Sleep deprivation affects speech. *Sleep, 20,* 871–877.

Hartmann, D. S., & Civelli, O. (1997). Dopamine receptor diversity: Molecular and pharmacological perspectives. *Progressive Drug Research, 48,* 173–194.

Hartmann, E. L. (1973). *The functions of sleep.* Westford, MA: Murray Printing.

Harvey, P. H., & Krebs, J. R. (1990). Comparing brains. *Science, 249,* 140–145.

Hastings, M. H. (1997). Central clocking. *Trends in Neuroscience, 20,* 459–464.

Hata, Y., & Stryker, M. P. (1994). Control of thalamocortical afferent rearrangement by postsynaptic activity in developing visual cortex. *Science, 265,* 1732–1735.

Hauser, M. D. (1993). Right hemisphere dominance for the production of facial expression in monkeys. *Science, 261,* 475–478.

Hauser, M. D. (1999). Perseveration, inhibition and the prefrontal cortex: A new look. *Current Opinion in Neurobiology, 9,* 214–222.

Hauser, M. D. (2000). *Wild minds: What animals really think.* New York: Henry Holt.

Haüser, M., Spruston, N., & Stuart, G. J. (2000). Diversity and dynamics of dendritic signaling. *Science, 290,* 739–743.

Hayakawa, K., Kumagai, H., Suzuki, Y., Furusawa, N., Haga, T., Hoshi, T., Fujiwara, Y., & Yamaguchi, K. (1992). MRI imaging of chronic alcoholism. *Acta Radiologica, 33,* 201–206.

Haydon, P. G. (2001). Glia: Listening and talking to the synapse. *Neuroscience, 2,* 185–193.

Hazeltine, W. A. (1997, March). Discovering genes for new medicines. *Scientific American, 276,* 92–97.

Hebb, D. O. (1949). *The organization of behavior.* New York: John Wiley & Sons.

Hécaen, H., & Angelergues, R. (1964). Localization of symptoms in aphasia. In A. V. S. de Reuck & M. O'Connor (Eds.), *CIBA foundation symposium on the disorders of language* (pp. 222–256). London: Churchill Press.

Heffner, H. E., & Heffner, R. S. (1984). Temporal lobe lesions and perception of species-specific vocalizations by macaques. *Science, 226,* 75–76.

Heffner, H. E., & Masterton, R. B. (1990). Sound localization in mammals: Brainstem mechanisms. In M. Berkley & W. Stebbins (Eds.), *Comparative perception, Vol. I: Discrimination.* New York: Wiley & Sons.

Heilman, K. M., Watson, R. T., & Rothi, L. J. G. (1997). Disorders of skilled movements: Limb apraxia. In T. E. Feinberg & M. J. Farah (Eds.), *Behavioral neurology and neuropsychology* (pp. 227–236). New York: McGraw-Hill.

Heilman, K. M., Watson, R. T., & Valenstein, E. (1997). Neglect: Clinical and anatomic aspects. In T. E. Feinberg & M. J. Farah (Eds.), *Behavioral neurology and neuropsychology* (pp. 309–317). New York: McGraw-Hill.

Heinrichs, R. W. (1993). Schizophrenia and the brain. *American Psychologist, 48,* 221–233.

Hejmadi, A., Davidson, R. J, & Rozin, P. (2000). Exploring Hindu Indian emotion expressions: Evidence for accurate recognition by Americans and Indians. *Psychological Science, 11,* 183–187.

Helmer, W. J. (1986, February). The madman in the tower. *Texas Monthly.*

Henderson, J. M., & Hollingworth, A. (1999). The role of fixation position in detecting scene changes across saccades. *Psychological Science, 10,* 438–443.

Hendry, S. H. C., & Calkins, D. J. (1998). Neuronal chemistry and functional organization in the primate visual system. *Trends in Neurosciences, 21:8,* 344–349.

Henke, K., Kroll, N. E. A., Behniea, H., Amaral, D. G., Miller M. B., Rafal, R., & Gazzaniga, M. S. (1999). Memory lost and regained following bilateral hippocampal damage. *Journal of Cognitive Neuroscience, 11,* 682–697.

Hennessey, A. C., Camak, L., Gordon, F., & Edwards, D. A. (1990). Connections between the pontine central gray and the ventromedial hypothalamus are essential for lordosis in female rats. *Behavioral Neuroscience, 104,* 477–488.

Herrup, K., & Silver, J. (1994). Cortical development and topographic maps: Patterns of cell dispersion in developing cerebral cortex. *Current Opinion in Neurobiology, 4,* 108–111.

Hetherington, A. W., & Ranson, S. W. (1940). Hypothalamic lesions and adiposity in the rat. *Anatomical Record, 78,* 149–172.

Heuss, C., & Gerber, U. (2000). G-protein-independent signaling by G-protein-coupled receptors. *Trends in Neurosciences, 23,* 469–474.

Heymsfield, S. N., Greenberg, A. S., Fujioka, K., Dixon, R. M., Kushner, R., Hunt, T., Lubina, J. A., Patane, J., Self, B., Hunt, P., & McCamish, M. (1999). Recombinant leptin for weight loss in obese and lean adults. *Journal of the American Medical Association, 282,* 1568–1575.

Hickok, G., Bellugi, U., & Klima, E. S. (2001, June). Sign language in the brain: How does the human brain process language? New studies of deaf signers hint at an answer. *Scientific American, 284,* 58–65.

Hilgetag, C-C., O'Neill, M. A., & Young, M. P. (1996). Indeterminate organization of the visual system. *Science, 271,* 776–777.

Hobson, J. A. (1989). *Sleep.* New York: Scientific American Library.

Hobson, J. A., Pace-Schott, E. F., Stickgold, R., & Kahn, (1998). To dream or not to dream? Relevant data from new neuroimaging and electrophysiological studies. *Current Opinion in Neurobiology, 8 (2),* 239–244.

Hockfield, S., & Kalb, R. G. (1993). Activity-dependent structural changes during neuronal development. *Current Opinion in Neurobiology, 3,* 87–92.

Hollenbeck, P. J. (2001). Insight and hindsight into Tourette syndrome. In D. J. Cohen, C. G. Goetz, & J. Jankovic (Eds.), *Tourette syndrome* (pp. 363–367). Philadelphia: Lippincott Williams & Wilkins.

Hollyday, M., & Hamburger, V. (1976). Reduction of the naturally occurring motor neuron loss by enlargement of the periphery. *Journal of Comparative Neurology, 170,* 311–320.

Holsboer, F. (2000). The corticosteroid receptor hypothesis of depression. *Neuropsychopharmacology, 23,* 477–501.

Holscher, C. (1997). Nitric oxide, the enigmatic neuronal messenger: its role in synaptic plasticity. *Trends in Neurosciences, 20,* 298–303.

Holt, C. E., & Harris, W. A. (1998). Target selection: Invasion, mapping and cell choice. *Current Opinion in Neurobiology, 8,* 98–105.

Holzman, P. S., & Matthyse, S. (1990). The genetics of schizophrenia: A review. *Current Directions in Psychological Science, 1,* 279–286.

Hopkins, W. D. (1995). Chimpanzee handedness revisited: 55 years since Finch (1941). *Psychonomic Bulletin & Review, 3,* 449–457.

Hopkins, W. D. (1996). Hand preferences for a coordinated bimanual task in 110 chimpanzees (*Pan troglodytes*): Cross-sectional analysis. *Journal of Comparative Psychology, 109 (3),* 291–297.

Horne, J. A. (1983). Sleep loss and "divergent" thinking ability. *Sleep, 11,* 528–536.

Horne, J. A., & Reyner, L. A. (1996). Counteracting driver sleepiness: Effects of napping, caffeine, and placebo. *Psychophysiology, 33,* 306–309.

Howlett, A. C., Bidaut-Russell, M., Devane, W. A., Melvin, L. S., Johnson, M. R., & Herkenham, M. (1990). The cannabinoid receptor: Biochemical, anatomical and behavioral characterization. *Trends in Neurosciences, 13,* 420–423.

Hsiao, K., Chapman, P., Nilsen, S., Eckman, C., Harigaya, Y., Younkin, S., Yang, F., & Cole, G. (1996). Correlative memory deficits, Aß elevation, and amyloid plaques in transgenic mice. *Science, 274,* 99–102.

Hubel, D. H., & Wiesel, T. N. (1979, September). Brain mechanisms of vision. *Scientific American, 241,* 150–162.

Hubel, D. H., Wiesel, T. N., & LeVay, S. (1977). Plasticity of ocular dominance columns in the monkey striate cortex. *Philosophical Transactions of the Royal Society of London, 278,* 377–409.

Hubel, D. H., Wiesel, T. N., & Stryker, M. P. (1977). Orientation columns in macaque monkey visual cortex demonstrated by the 2-deoxyglucose autoradiographic technique. *Nature, 269,* 328–330.

Hugdahl, K. (1996). Cognitive influences on human autonomic nervous system function. *Current Opinion in Neurobiology, 6,* 252–258.

Hughes, J., Smith, T. W., Kosterlitz, H. W, Fothergill, L. A., Morgan, B. A., & Morris, H. R. (1975). Identification of two related pentapeptides from the brain with potent opiate agonist activity. *Nature, 258,* 577–581.

Hull, E. M., Lorrain, D. S., Du, J., Matuszewich, L., Lumley, L. A., Putnam, S. K., & Moses, J. (1999). Hormone-neurotransmitter interaction in the control of sexual behavior. *Behavioural Brain Research, 105,* 105–116.

Hume, K. I., & Mills, J. N. (1977). Rhythms of REM and slow wave sleep in subjects living on abnormal time schedules. *Waking and Sleeping, 1,* 291–296.

Humphrey, K. G., James, T. W., Gati, J. S., Menon, R. S., & Goodale, M. A. (1999). Perception of the McCollough effect correlates with activity in extrastriate cortex: A functional magnetic resonance imaging study. *Psychological Science, 10,* 444–448.

Hurlbert, A. (1991). Deciphering the color code. *Nature, 349,* 191–193.

Hustvedt, B. E., & Løvø, A. (1972). Correlation between hyperinsulinemia and hyperphagia in rats with ventromedial hypothalamic lesions. *Acta Physiologica Scandinavica, 84,* 29–33.

Huttenlocher, P. R. (1994). Synaptogenesis, synapse elimination, and neural plasticity in human cerebral cortex. In C. A. Nelson (Ed.), *Threats to optimal development: The Minnesota Symposium on child psychology,* vol. 27, 35–54. Hillsdale, NJ: Lawrence Erlbaum.

Hyman, S. (2000). Mental illness: Genetically complex disorders of neural circuitry and neural communication. *Neuron, 28,* 321–323.

Iacono, W. G. (1985). Psychophysiologic markers in psychopathology: A review. *Canadian Psychology, 26,* 96–111.

Iacono, W. G., & Koenig, W. G. R. (1983). Features that distinguish the smooth-pursuit eye-tracking performance of schizophrenic, affective-disorder, and normal individuals. *Journal of Abnormal Psychology, 92,* 29–41.

Iacono, W. G., & Patrick, C. J. (1987). What psychologists should know about lie detection. In I. B. Weiner & A. K. Hess (Eds.), *Handbook of forensic psychology* (pp. 460–489). New York: John Wiley & Sons.

Iadecola, C. (1993). Regulation of the cerebral microcirculation during neural activity: Is nitric oxide the missing link? *Trends in Neurosciences, 16,* 206–214.

Ibáñez, C. F. (1998). Emerging themes in structural biology of neurotrophic factors. *Trends in Neurosciences, 21,* 438–444.

Ikemoto, S., & Panksepp, J. (1999). The role of nucleus accumbens dopamine in motivated behavior: A unifying interpretation with special reference to reward-seeking. *Brain Research Reviews, 31,* 6–41.

Ikonomidou, C., Bittigau, P., Ishimaru, M. J., Wozniak, D. F., Koch, C., Geenz, K., Price, M. T., Stefovska, V., Hörster, F., Tenkova, T., Dikranian, K., & Olney, J. W. (2000). Ethanol-induced apoptotic neurodegeneration and fetal alcohol syndrome. *Science, 287,* 1056–1060.

Illert, M., & Kummel, H. (1999). Reflex pathways from large muscle spindle afferents and recurrent axon collaterals to motorneurones of wrist and digit muscles: A comparison in cats, monkeys and humans. *Experimental Brain Research, 128,* 13–19.

Inglis, J., & Lawson, J. S. (1982). A meta-analysis of sex- differences in the effects of unilateral brain damage on intelligence test results. *Canadian Journal of Psychology, 36,* 670–683.

Inouye, S. I., & Kawamura, H. (1982). Characteristics of a circadian pacemaker in the suprachiasmatic nucleus. *Journal of Comparative Psychology, 146,* 153–160.

Institute of Laboratory Animal Resources: Commission on Life Sciences (1996). *Guide for the care and use of laboratory animals.* Washington: National Academy Press.

Iriki, A., Pavlides, C., Keller, A., & Asanuma, H. (1989). Long-term potentiation in the motor cortex. *Science, 24 5,* 1385–1387.

Irwin, D. E. (1996). Integrating information across saccadic eye movements. *Current Directions in Psychological Science, 5,* 94–100.

Ishai, A., Ungerleider, L. G., Martin, A., & Haxby, J. V. (2000). The representation of objects in the human occipital and temporal cortex. *Journal of Cognitive Neuroscience, 12,* Supplement 2, 35–51,

Itoh, K., Stevens, B., Schachner, M., & Fields, R. D. (1995). Regulated expression of the neural cell adhesion molecule L1 by specific patterns of neural impulses. *Science, 270,* 1369–1372.

Iwamura, Y. (1998). Hierarchical somatosensory processing. *Current Opinion in Neurobiology, 8,* 522–528.

Iwaniuk, A. N., & Whishaw, I.Q. (2000). On the origin of skilled forelimb movements. *Trends in Neurosciences, 23,* 372–376.

Izard, C. E. (1971). *The face of emotion.* New York: Appleton-Century-Crofts.

Jacobs, B. L., van Praag, H., & Gage, F. H. (2000, July). Depression and the birth and death of brain cells. *American Scientist, 88,* 340–345.

Jaeger, J. J., Lockwood, A. H., Van Valin, R. D., Kemmerer, D. L., Murphy, B. W., & Wack, D. S. (1998). Sex differences in brain regions activated by grammatical and reading tasks. *NeuroReport, 9,* 2803–2807.

Jakel, R. J., & Maragos, W. F. (2000). Neuronal cell death in Huntington's disease: A potential role for dopamine. *Trends in Neurosciences, 23,* 239–245.

Jankovic, J. (2001). Tourette's syndrome. *New England Journal of Medicine, 345,* 1184–1192.

Jarrell, T. W., Gentile, C. G., Romanski, L. M., McCabe, P. M., & Schneiderman, N. (1987). Involvement of cortical and thalamic auditory regions in retention of differential bradycardia conditioning to acoustic conditioned stimuli in rabbits. *Brain Research, 412,* 285–294.

Jarvik, M. E. (1990). The drug dilemma: Manipulating the demand. *Science, 250,* 387–392.

Jeannerod, M., & Decety, J. (1995). Mental motor imagery: a window into the representational stages of action. *Current Opinion in Neurobiology, 5,* 727–732.

Jeannerod, M., Arbib, M. A., Rizzolatti, G., & Sakarta, H. (1995). Grasping objects: The cortical mechanisms of visuomotor transformation. *Trends in Neurosciences, 18:7,* 314–327.

Jenkins, I. H., Brooks, D. J., Bixon, P. D., Frackowiak, R. S. J., & Passingham, R. E. (1994). Motor sequence learning: a study with positron emission tomography. *Journal of Neuroscience, 14 (6),* 3775–3790.

Jenkins, W. M., & Merzenich, M. M. (1987). Reorganization of neocortical representations after brain injury: A neurophysiological model of the bases of recovery from stroke. *Progressive Brain Research, 71,* 249–266.

Jog, M. S., Kubota, Y., Connolly, C. I., Hillegaart, V., & Graybiel, A. M. (1999). Building neural representations of habits. *Science, 286,* 1745–1749.

Johnson, M. H. (1997). *Developmental cognitive neuroscience: An introduction.* Cambridge, MA: Blackwell Publishers.

Johnston, D. (1997). A missing link? LTP and learning. *Science, 278,* 401–402.

Johnston, T. D. (1987). The persistence of dichotomies in the study of behavioral development. *Developmental Review, 7,* 149–182.

Jones, E. G. (2000). Cortical and subcortical contributions to activity-dependent plasticity in primate somatosensory cortex. *Annual Review of Neuroscience* (pp. 1–37). Palo Alto, CA: Annual Reviews.

Jones, H. S., & Oswald, I. (1966). Two cases of healthy insomnia. *Electroencephalography and Clinical Neurophysiology, 24,* 378–380.

Jones, H. W., & Park, I. J. (1971). A classification of special problems in sex differentiation. In D. Bergsma (Ed.), *The clinical delineation of birth defects. Part X: The endocrine system* (pp. 113–121). Baltimore: Williams and Wilkins.

Jones, R. T. (1987). Tobacco dependence. In H. Y. Meltzer (Ed.), *Psychopharmacology: The third generation of progress* (pp. 1589–1596). New York: Raven Press.

Joseph, R. (1988). Dual mental functioning in a split-brain patient. *Journal of Clinical Psychology, 44,* 771–779.

Jost, A. (1972). A new look at the mechanisms controlling sex differentiation in mammals. *Johns Hopkins Medical Journal, 130,* 38–53.

Jouvet, M. (1972). The role of monoamines and acetylcholine-containing neurons in the regulation of the sleep-waking cycle. *Ergebnisse der Physiologie, 64,* 166–307.

Jouvet, M., & Renault, J. (1966). Insomnie persistante après lésions des noyaux du raphé chez le chat. *Comptes Rendus de la Société de Biologie (Paris), 160,* 1461–1465.

Julien, R. M. (1981). *A primer of drug action* (p. 117). San Francisco: W. H. Freeman.

Julien, R. M. (1996). *A primer of drug action: A concise, nontechnical guide to the actions, uses, and side effects of psychoactive drugs.* New York: W. H. Freeman.

Juusola, M., French, A. S., Uusitalo, R. O., & Weckström, M. (1996). Information processing by graded-potential transmission through tonically active synapses. *Trends in Neurosciences, 19,* 292–297.

Kaas, J. H., Hackett, T. A., & Tramo, M. J. (1999). Auditory processing in primate cerebral cortex. *Current Opinion in Neurobiology, 9,* 164–170.

Kaas, J. H., Krubtzer, L. A., Chino, Y. M., Langston, A. L., Polley, E. H., & Blair, N. (1990). Reorganization of retinotopic cortical maps in adult mammals after lesions of the retina. *Science, 248,* 229–231.

Kaas, J. H., Nelson, R. J., Sur, M., & Merzenich, M. M. (1981). Organization of somatosensory cortex in primates. In F. O. Schmitt, F. G. Worden, G. Adelman, & S. G. Dennis (Eds.), *The organization of the cerebral cortex* (pp. 237–261). Cambridge, MA: MIT Press.

Kagawa, Y. (1978). Impact of westernization on the nutrition of Japanese: Changes in physique, cancer, longevity, and centenarians. *Preventive Medicine, 7,* 205–217.

Kaiser, J., Lutzenberger, W., Preissl, H., Ackermann, H., & Birbaumer, N. (2000). Right-hemisphere dominance for the processing of sound-source lateralization. *Journal of Neuroscience, 20,* 6631–6639.

Kalaska, J. F., Scott, S. H., Cisek, P., & Sergio, L. E. (1997). Cortical control of reaching movements. *Current Opinion in Neurobiology, 7,* 849–859.

Kalil, R. E. (1989, December). Synapse formation in the developing brain. *Scientific American, 261,* 76–85.

Kalin, N. H. (1993, May). The neurobiology of fear. *Scientific American, 268,* 94–101.

Kalivas, P. W., & Nakamura, M. (1999). Neural systems for behavioral activation and reward. *Current Opinion in Neurobiology, 9,* 223–227.

Kallman, F. J. (1946). The genetic theory of schizophrenia: An analysis of 691 schizophrenic twin index families. *American Journal of Psychiatry, 103,* 309–322.

Kalynchuk, L. E. (2000). Long-term amygdala kindling in rats as a model for the study of interictal emotionality in temporal lobe epilepsy. *Neuroscience and Biobehavioral Reviews, 24,* 691–704.

Kalynchuk, L. E., Pinel, J. P. J., Treit, D., & Kippin, T. E. (1997). Changes in emotional behavior produced by long-term amygdala kindling in rats. *Biological Psychiatry, 41,* 438–451.

Kandel, E. R., & Squire, L. R. (2000). Neuroscience: Breaking down barriers to the study of brain and mind. *Science, 290,* 1113–1120.

Kansaku, K., Yamaura, A., & Kitazawa, S. (2000). Sex differences in lateralization revealed in the posterior language areas. *Cerebral Cortex, 10,* 866–872.

Kanwisher, N., & Downing, P. (1998). Separating the wheat from the chaff. *Science, 282,* 57–58.

Kapur, N. (1997). *Injured brains of medical minds.* Oxford: Oxford University Press.

Karacan, I., Williams, R. L., Finley, W. W., & Hursch, C. J. (1970). The effects of naps on nocturnal sleep: Influence on the need for stage-1 REM and stage-4 sleep. *Biological Psychiatry, 2,* 391–399.

Karni, A., Tanne, D., Rubenstein, B. S., Askensy, J. J. M., & Sagi, D. (1994). Dependence on REM sleep of overnight improvement of a perceptual skill. *Science, 265,* 679–682

Karsch, F. J. (1987). Central actions of ovarian steroids in the feedback regulation of pulsatile secretion of luteinizing hormone. *Annual Review of Physiology, 49,* 365–382.

Kasai, H. (1999). Comparative biology of Ca^{2+}-dependent exocytosis: implications of kinetic diversity for secretory function. *Trends in Neurosciences, 22:2,* 88–93.

Kastner, S., De Weerd, P., Desimone, R., & Ungerleider, L. G. (1998). Mechanisms of directed attention in the human extrastriate cortex as revealed by functional MRI. *Science, 282,* 108–112

Katz, J. L., Ackamn, P., Rothwax, Y., Sachar, E. J., Weiner, H., Hellman, L., & Gallagher, T. F. (1970). Psychoendocrine aspects of cancer of the breast. *Psychosomatic Medicine, 32,* 1–18.

Katz, L. C., & Shatz, C. J. (1996). Synaptic activity and the construction of cortical circuits. *Science, 274,* 1133–1138.

Kavanagh, G. L., & Kelly, J. B. (1988). Hearing in the ferret (*Mustela putorius*): Effects of primary auditory cortical lesions on thresholds for pure tone detection. *Journal of Neurophysiology, 60,* 879–888.

Kelsey, J. E., Carlezon, W. A., Jr., & Falls, W. A. (1989). Lesions of the nucleus accumbens in rats reduce opiate reward but do not alter context-specific opiate tolerance. *Behavioral Neuroscience, 103,* 1327–1334.

Kelso, S. R., Ganong, A. H., & Brown, T. H. (1986). Hebbian synapses in hippocampus. *Proceedings of the National Academy of Sciences, USA, 83,* 5326–5330.

Keltner, D., Kring, A. M., & Bonanno, G. A. (1999). Fleeting signs of the course of life: facial expression and personal adjustment. *Current Directions in Psychological Science, 8,* 18–22.

Kempermann, G., & Gage, F. H. (May, 1999). New nerve cells for the adult brain. *Scientific American, 282:* 48–53.

Kendler, K. S., & Gruenberg, A. M. (1984). An independent analysis of the Danish adoption study of schizophrenia: VI. The relationship between psychiatric disorders as defined by DSM-III in the relatives and adoptees. *Archives of General Psychiatry, 41,* 555–564.

Kentridge, R. W., Heywood, C. A., & Weiskrantz, L. (1997). Residual vision in multiple retinal locations within a scotoma: implications for blindsight. *Journal of Cognitive Neuroscience, 9,* 191–202.

Kephalas, T. A., Kiburis, J., Michael, C. M., Miras, C. J., & Papadakis, D. P. (1976). Some aspects of cannabis smoke chemistry. In G. G. Nahas (Ed.), *Marihuana: Chemistry, biochemistry, and cellular effects* (pp. 39–49). New York: Springer-Verlag.

Kerr, R. A. (1996). New mammal data challenge evolutionary pulse theory. *Science, 273,* 431–432.

Kesner, R. (Ed.). (1999). Nucleus accumbens: Behavioral and cognitive function [Special issue]. *Psychobiology, 27,* (2).

Kessler, D. S., & Melton, D. A. (1994). Vertebrate embryonic induction: Mesodermal and neural patterning. *Science, 266,* 596–604.

Kessler, R. C. (1997). The effects of stressful life events on depression. *Annual Review of Psychology, 48,* 191–214.

Keys, A., Broz, J., Henschel, A. Mickelsen, O., Taylor H. L. (1950). *The biology of human starvation.* Minneapolis: The University of Minnesota Press.

Kiecolt-Glaser, J. K., & Glaser, R. (2001). Stress and immunity: Age enhances the risks. *Current Directions in Psychological Science, 10,* 18–221.

Kiecolt-Glaser, J. K., Page, G. G., Marucha, P. T., MacCallum, R. C., & Glaser, R. (1998). Psychological influences on surgical recovery. *American Psychologist, 53,* 1209–1218.

Kiehl, K. A., Liddle, P. F., Smith, A. M., Mendrek, A., Forster, B. B., & Hare, R. D. (1999). Neural pathways involved in the processing of concrete and abstract words. *Human Brain Mapping, 7,* 225–233.

Kilduff, T. S., & Peyron, C. (2000). The hypocretin/orexin ligand-receptor system: Implications for sleep and sleep disorders. *Trends in Neurosciences, 23,* 359–365.

Killacky, H. P. (1995). Evolution of the human brain: A neuroanatomical perspective. In M. S. Gazzaniga (Ed.), *The cognitive neurosciences.* Cambridge: MIT Press.

Kim, D-S., Duong, T. Q., & Kim, S-G. (2000). High-resolution mapping of iso-orientation columns by fMRI. *Nature, 3:2,* 164–169.

Kim, J. J., & Thompson, R. F. (1997). Cerebellar circuits and synaptic mechanisms involved in classical eyeblink conditioning. *Trends in Neurosciences, 20,* 177–181.

Kim, J. J., & Yoon, K. S. (1998). Stress: Metaplastic effects in the hippocampus. *Trends in Neuroscience, 21,* 505–509.

Kim, S-G., Ashe, J., Hendrich, K., Ellermann, J. M., Merkle, H., Ugurbil, K., & Georgopoulos, A. P. (1993). Functional magnetic resonance imaging of motor cortex: Hemispheric asymmetry and handedness. *Science, 261,* 615–617.

Kimberg, D. Y., D'Esposito, M., & Farah, M. J. (1997). Frontal lobes: Cognitive neuropsychological aspects. In T. E. Feinberg & M. J. Farah (Eds.), *Behavioral neurology and neuropsychology* (pp. 409–418). New York: McGraw-Hill.

Kimberg, D. Y., D'Esposito, M., & Farah, M. J. (1998). Cognitive functions in the prefrontal cortex—working memory and executive control. *Current Directions in Psychological Science, 6,* 185–192.

Kimble, G. A. (1989). Psychology from the standpoint of a generalist. *American Psychologist, 44,* 491–499.

Kimura, D. (1961). Some effects of temporal-lobe damage on auditory perception. *Canadian Journal of Psychology, 15,* 156–165.

Kimura, D. (1964). Left-right differences in the perception of melodies. *Quarterly Journal of Experimental Psychology, 16,* 355–358.

Kimura, D. (1973, March). The asymmetry of the human brain. *Scientific American, 228,* 70–78.

Kimura, D. (1979). Neuromotor mechanisms in the evolution of human communication. In H. E. Steklis & M. J. Raleigh (Eds.), *Neurobiology of social communication in primates* (pp. 197–219). New York: Academic Press.

Kimura, D. (1987). Sex differences, human brain organization. In G. Adelman (Ed.), *Encyclopedia of neuroscience,* Vol. II. Boston: Birkhäuser.

Kimura, D., & Watson, N. (1989). The relation between oral movement control and speech. *Brain and Language, 37,* 565–690.

King, A. J., Schnupp, J. W. H., & Thompson, I. D. (1998). Signals from the superficial layers of the superior colliculus enable the development of the auditory space map in the deeper layers. *Journal of Neuroscience, 18,* 9394–9408.

King, D. P., & Takahashi, J. S. (2000). Molecular genetics of circadian rhythms in mammals. *Annual Review of Neuroscience, 23,* 723–742.

Kinnamon, S. C., & Margolskee, R. F. (1996). Mechanisms of taste transduction. *Current Opinion in Neurobiology, 6,* 506–513.

Klawans, H. L. (1990). *Newton's madness: Further tales of clinical neurology.* New York: Harper & Row.

Kleinman, A., & Cohen, A. (1997, March). Psychiatry's global challenge: An evolving crisis in the developing world signals the need for a better understanding of the links between culture and mental disorders. *Scientific American, 276,* 86–89.

Kleitman, N. (1963). *Sleep and wakefulness.* Chicago: University of Chicago Press.

Klivington, K. A. (Ed.) (1992). *Gehirn und Geist.* Heidelberg: Spektrum Akademischer Verlag.

Kluver, H., & Bucy, P. C. (1939). Preliminary analysis of the temporal lobes in monkeys. *Archives of Neurology and Psychiatry, 42,* 979–1000.

Knoth, R. L., & Mair, R. G. (1991). Response latency and accuracy on a pretrained nonmatching-to-sample task in rats recovered from pyrithiamine-induced thiamine deficiency. *Behavioral Neuroscience, 105,* 375–385.

Knowlton, B. J., Mangels, J. A., & Squire, L. R. (1996). A neostriatal habit learning system in humans. *Science, 273,* 1399–1402.

Knudsen, E. I. (1998). Capacity for plasticity in the adult owl auditory system expanded by juvenile experience. *Science, 279,* 1531–1533.

Knudsen, E. I., & Brainard, M S. (1991). Visual instruction of the neural map of auditory space in the developing optic tectum. *Science, 253,* 85–87.

Koch, C., & Braun, J. (1996). Towards the neuronal correlate of visual awareness. *Current Opinion in Neurobiology, 6,* 158–164.

Kogure, T., & Kogure, K. (1997). Molecular and biochemical events within the brain subjected to cerebral ischemia (targets for therapeutic intervention). *Clinical Neuroscience, 4,* 179–183.

Kokkinos, J., & Levine, S. R. (1993). Stroke. *Neurologic Complications of Drug and Alcohol Abuse, 11,* 577–590.

Kolb, B. (1989). Brain development, plasticity, and behavior. *American Psychologist, 44,* 202–212.

Kolb, B., & Taylor, L. (1988). Facial expression and the neocortex. *Society for Neuroscience Abstracts, 14,* 219.

Kolb, B., & Taylor, L. (2000). Facial expression, emotion, and hemispheric organization. In R. D. Lane & L. Nadel (Eds.), *Cognitive neuroscience of emotion* (pp. 62–83). New York: Oxford University Press.

Kolb, B., & Whishaw, I. Q. (1990). *Fundamentals of human neuropsychology* (3rd ed.). New York: Freeman.

Kollar, E. J., & Fisher, C. (1980). Tooth induction in chick epithelium: Expression of quiescent genes for enamel synthesis. *Science, 207,* 993–995.

Kolodny, R. C., Masters, W. H., Kolodner, R. M., & Toro, G. (1974). Depression of plasma testosterone levels after chronic intensive marihuana use. *New England Journal of Medicine, 290,* 872–874.

Koob, G. F., & Bloom, F. E. (1988). Cellular and molecular mechanisms of drug dependence. *Science, 242,* 715–723.

Koob, G. F., Maldonado, R., & Stinus, L. (1992). Neural substrates of opiate withdrawal. *Trends in Neurosciences, 15,* 186–191.

Koolhaas, J. M., Schuurman, T., & Wierpkema, P. R. (1980). The organization of intraspecific agonistic behaviour in the rat. *Progress in Neurobiology, 15,* 247–268.

Koopmans, H. S. (1981). The role of the gastrointestinal tract in the satiation of hunger. In L. A. Cioffi, W. B. T. James, & T. B. Van Italie (Eds.), *The body weight regulatory system: Normal and disturbed mechanisms* (pp. 45–55). New York: Raven Press.

Kornack, D. R., & Rakic, P. (1999). Continuation of neurogenesis in the hippocampus of the adult macaque monkey. *Proceedings of the National Academy of Sciences, USA, 96,* 5768–5773.

Kosslyn, S. M. (1994). *Image and brain: The resolution of the imagery debate.* Cambridge, MA: MIT Press.

Kosslyn, S. M., & Andersen, R. A. (1992). *Frontiers in cognitive neuroscience.* Cambridge, MA: MIT Press.

Kourtzi, Z., & Kanwisher, N. (2000). Activation in Human MT/MST by static images with implied motion. *Journal of Cognitive Neuroscience 12,* 48–55.

Koutalos, Y., & Yau, K-W. (1993). A rich complexity emerges in phototransduction. *Current Opinion in Neurobiology, 3,* 513–519.

Krank, M. D., & Perkins, W. L. (1993). Conditioned withdrawal signs elicited by contextual cues for morphine administration. *Psychobiology, 21,* 113–119.

Krieglstein, J. (1997). Mechanisms of neuroprotective drug actions. *Clinical Neuroscience, 4,* 184–193.

Kring, A. M. (1999). Emotion in schizophrenia: Old mystery, new understanding. *Current Directions in Psychological Science, 8,* 160–163.

Kring, A. M. (2001). Emotion and psychopathology. In T. J. Mayne & G. A. Bonanno (Eds.), *Emotions: Current issues and future direction* (pp. 337–360). New York: Guilford Press.

Kuan, C-Y., Roth, K. A., Flavel, R. A., & Rakic, P. (2000). Mechanisms of programmed cell death in the developing brain. *Trends in Neurosciences, 23,* 291–297.

Kuczmarski, R. J. (1992). Prevalence of overweight and weight gain in the United States. *American Journal of Clinical Nutrition, 55,* 495S-502S.

Kuhar, M. J., & Dall Vechia, S. E. (1999). CART peptides: Novel addiction-and feeding-related neuropeptides. *Trends in Neurosciences, 22,* 316–320.

Kurbat, M. A., & Farah, M. J. (1998). Is the category-specific deficit for living things spurious? *Journal of Cognitive Neuroscience, 10,* 355–361.

Kushner, H. I. (1999). A cursing brain? The histories of Tourette syndrome. Cambridge, MA: Harvard University Press.

Kuwada, J. Y. (1986). Cell recognition by neuronal growth cones in a simple vertebrate embryo. *Science, 233,* 740–746.

LaBerge, S., Greenleaf, W., & Kedzierski, B. (1983). Physiological responses to dreamed sexual activity during lucid REM sleep. *Psychophysiology, 20,* 454–455.

Laine, M., Salmelin, R., Helenius, P., & Marttila, R. (2000). Brain activation during reading in deep dyslexia: An MEG study. *Journal of Cognitive Neuroscience, 12,* 622–634.

Lance-Jones, C., & Landmesser, L. (1980). Motor neuron projection patterns in the chick hind limb following early partial spinal cord reversals. *Journal of Physiology, 302,* 559–580.

Land, E. H. (1977, April). The retinex theory of color vision. *Scientific American, 237,* 108–128.

Lang, A. E. (2001). Update on the treatment of tics. In D. J. Cohen, C. G. Goetz, & J. Jankovic (Eds.), *Tourette syndrome* (pp. 355–362). Philadelphia: Lippincott Williams & Wilkins.

Langston, J. W. (1985). MPTP and Parkinson's disease. *Trends in Neurosciences, 8,* 79–83.

Langston, J. W., & Palfreman, J. (1996). *The case of the frozen addicts.* New York: Vintage Books.

Langston, J. W., Forno, L. S., Robert, C. S., & Irwin, I. (1984). Selective nigral toxicity after systemic administration of 1-methyl-4-phenyl-1,2,3,6-tetrahydropyridine (MPTP) in the squirrel monkey. *Brain Research, 292,* 390–394.

Lapierre, O., & Dumont, M. (1995). Melatonin treatment of a non-24-hour sleep-wake cycle in a blind retarded child. *Biological Psychiatry, 38,* 119–122.

Larkman, A. U., & Jack, J. J. B. (1995). Synaptic plasticity: Hippocampal LTP. *Current Opinion in Neurobiology, 5,* 324–334.

Lashley, K. S. (1941). Patterns of cerebral integration indicated by the scotomas of migraine. *Archives of Neurology and Psychiatry, 46,* 331–339.

Lathe, R. (1996). Mice, gene-targeting and behaviour: More than just genetic background. *Trends in Neurosciences, 19,* 183–186

Latimer, D., & Goldberg, J. (1981). *Flowers in the blood.* New York: Franklin Watts.

Laurent, G. (1997). Olfactory processing: maps, time and codes. *Current Opinion in Neurobiology, 7,* 7547–553.

Lavie, P., Pratt, H., Scharf, B., Peled, R., & Brown, J. (1984). Localized pontine lesion: Nearly total absence of REM sleep. *Neurology, 34,* 1118–1120.

Lawrence, D. G., & Kuypers, H. G. J. M. (1968a). The functional organization of the motor system in the monkey: I. The effects of bilateral pyramidal lesions. *Brain, 91,* 1–14.

Lawrence, D. G., & Kuypers, H. G. J. M. (1968b). The functional organization of the motor system in the monkey: II. The effects of lesions of the descending brain-stem pathways. *Brain, 91,* 15–36.

Leakey, M., & Walker, A. (1997, June). Early hominid fossils from Africa: a new species of Australopithccus, the ancestor of Homo, pushes back the origins of bipedalism to some four million years ago. *Scientific American, 276,* 74–79.

Leckman, J. F., Peterson, B. S., King, R. A., Scahill, L., & Cohen, D. J. (2001). Phenomenology of tics and natural history of tic disorders. In D. J. Cohen, C. G. Goetz, & J. Jankovic (Eds.), *Tourette syndrome* (pp. 1–14). Philadelphia: Lippincott Williams & Wilkins.

Lederhendler, I., & Schulkin, J. (2000). Behavioral neuroscience challenges for the era of molecular biology. *Trends in Neurosciences, 23,* 451–454.

LeDoux, J. E. (1992). Brain mechanisms of emotion and emotional learning. *Current Opinion in Neurobiology, 2,* 191–197.

LeDoux, J. E. (1994, June). Emotion, memory and the brain. *Scientific American, 270,* 50–57.

LeDoux, J. E. (1995). Emotion: Clues from the brain. *Annual Review of Psychology, 46,* 209–235.

LeDoux, J. E. (2000a). Cognitive-emotional interactions: Listen to the brain. In R. D. Lane & L. Nadel (Eds.), *Cognitive neuroscience of emotion* (pp.129–155). New York: Oxford University Press.

LeDoux, J. E. (2000b). Emotion circuits in the brain. *Annual Review of Neuroscience, 23,* 155–184.

Leech, C. K., & McIntyre, D.C. (1976). Kindling rates in inbred mice: An analog to learning? *Behavioral Biology, 16,* 439–452.

Leibowitz, S. F. (1992). Neurochemical-neuroendocrine systems in the brain controlling macronutrient intake and metabolism. *Trends in Neurosciences, 15,* 491–497.

Leibowitz, S. F., Akabayashi, A., & Wang, J. (1998). Obesity on a high-fat diet: role of hypothalamic galanin in neurons of the anterior paraventricular nucleus projecting to the median eminence. *Journal of Neuroscience, 18 (7),* 2709–2719.

Leibowitz, S. F., Hammer, N.J., & Chang, K. (1981). Hypothalamic paraventricular nucleus lesions produce overeating and obesity in the rat. *Physiology & Behavior, 27,* 1031–1040.

Leiner, H. C., Leiner, A. L., & Dow, R. S. (1995). The underestimated cerebellum. *Human Brain Mapping, 2,* 244–254.

Lemon, R. N. (1999). Neural control of dexterity: what has been achieved? *Experimental Brain Research, 128,* 6–12.

Lenhoff, H. M., Wang, P. P., Greenberg, F., & Bellugi, U. (December, 1997). Williams syndrome and the brain. *Scientific American, 279,* 68–73.

Lennox, W. G. (1960). *Epilepsy and related disorders.* Boston: Little, Brown.

Lerman, C., Caporaso, N. E., Audrain, J., Main, D., Bowman, E. D., Lockshin, B., Boyd, N. R., & Shields, P. G. (1999). Evidence suggesting the role of specific genetic factors in cigarette smoking. *Health Psychology, 18,* 14–20.

Leshner, A. I. (1997). Addiction is a brain disease, and it matters. *Science, 278,* 45–46.

Lester, B. M., LaGasse, L. L., & Seiffer, R. (1998). Cocaine exposure and children: The meaning of subtle effects. *Science, 282,* 633–634.

Lester, G. L. L., & Gorzalka, B. B. (1988). Effect of novel and familiar mating partners on the duration of sexual receptivity in the female hamster. *Behavioral and Neural Biology, 49,* 398–405.

Leung, L. S., Ma, J., & McLachlan, R. S. (2000). Behaviors induced or disrupted by complex partial seizures. *Neuroscience and Biobehavioral Reviews, 24,* 763–775.

LeVay, S. (1991). A difference in hypothalamic structure between heterosexual and homosexual men. *Science, 253,* 1034–1037.

LeVay, S., & Hamer, D. H. (1994, May). Evidence for a biological influence in male homosexuality. *Scientific American, 270,* 44–49.

LeVay, S., Hubel, D. H., & Wiesel, T. N. (1975). The pattern of ocular dominance columns in Macaque visual cortex revealed by a reduced silver stain. *Journal of Comparative Neurology, 159,* 559–576.

Levenson, R. W. (1994). The search for autonomic specificity. In P. Ekman & R. J. Davidson (Eds.), *The nature of emotion: Fundamental questions* (pp. 252–257). New York: Oxford University Press.

Levi-Montalcini, R. (1952). Effects of mouse motor transplantation on the nervous system. *Annals of the New York Academy of Sciences, USA, 55,* 330–344.

Levi-Montalcini, R. (1975). NGF: An uncharted route. In F. G. Worden, J. P. Swazey, & G. Adelman (Eds.), *The neurosciences: Paths of discovery* (pp. 245–265). Cambridge, MA: MIT Press.

Levin, H. S. (1989). Memory deficit after closed-head injury. *Journal of Clinical and Experimental Neuropsychology, 12,* 129–153.

Levin, H. S., Papanicolaou, A., & Eisenberg, H. M. (1984). Observations on amnesia after non-missile head injury. In L. R. Squire & N. Butters (Eds.), *Neuropsychology of memory* (pp. 247–257). New York: Guilford Press.

Levine, J. A., Eberhardt, N. L., & Jensen, M. D. (1999). Role of nonexercise activity thermogenesis in resistance to fat gain in humans. *Science, 283,* 212–214.

Levitt, P., Harvey, J. A., Friedman, E., Simansky, K., & Murphy, E. H. (1997). New evidence for neurotransmitter influences on barren development. *Trends in Neurosciences, 20,* 269–274.

Levy, J. (1969). Possible basis for the evolution of lateral specialization of the human brain. *Nature, 224,* 614–615.

Levy, J., Trevarthen, C., & Sperry, R. W. (1972). Perception of bilateral chimeric figures following hemispheric deconnection. *Brain, 95,* 61–78.

Lewis, D. A., & Lieberman, J. A. (2000). Catching up on schizophrenia: Natural history and neurobiology. *Neuron, 25,* 325–334.

Lewy, A. J., Ahmed, S., & Sack, R. L. (1996). Phase shifting the human circadian clock using melatonin. *Behavioural Brain Research, 73,* 131–134.

Lezak, M. D. (1997). Principles of neuropsychological assessment. In T. E. Feinberg & M. J. Farah (Eds.), *Behavioral neurology and neuropsychology* (pp. 43–54). New York: McGraw-Hill.

Li, Y., Field, P., & Raisman, G. (1997). Repair of adult rat corticospinal tract by transplants of olfactory ensheathing cells. *Science, 277,* 2000–2002.

Lin, L., Faraco, J., Li, R., Kadotani, H., Rogers, W., Lin, X., Qiu, X., de Jong, P. J., Nishino, S., & Mignot, E. (1999). The sleep disorder canine narcolepsy is caused by a mutation in the hypocretin (orexin) receptor 2 gene. *Cell, 98,* 365–376.

Lin, X. Y., & Glanzman, D. L. (1994). Hebbian induction of long-term potentiation of *Aplysia* sensorimotor synapses: partial requirement for activation of an NMDA-related receptor. *Proceedings of Royal Society of London (B). 255,* 215–221.

Linden, D. J., & Routtenberg, A. (1989). The role of protein kinase C in long-term potentiation: A testable model. *Brain Research Reviews, 14,* 279–296.

Linder, M. E., & Gilman, A. G. (1992, July). G proteins. *Scientific American, 267,* 56–65.

Lindsay, P. H., & Norman, D. A. (1977). *Human information processing* (2nd ed.). New York: Academic Press.

Lindsey, D. B., Bowden, J., & Magoun, H. W. (1949). Effect upon the EEG of acute injury to the brain stem activating system. *Electroencephalography and Clinical Neurophysiology, 1,* 475–486.

Lipert, J., Bauder, H., Miltner, W. H. R., Taub, E., & Weiller, C. (2000). Treatment-induced cortical reorganization after stroke in humans. *Stroke, 31,* 1210–1216.

Lishman, W. A. (1990). Alcohol and the brain. *British Journal of Psychiatry, 156,* 635–644.

Liu, D., Dorio, J., Tannenbaum, B., Caldji, C., Francis, D., Freedman, A., Sharma, S., Pearson, D., Plotsky, P. M., & Meaney, M. J. (1997). Maternal care, hippocampal glucocorticoid receptors, and hypothalamic-pituitary-adrenal responses to stress. *Science, 277,* 1659–1662.

Livingston, E. H., & Guth, P. H. (1992). Peptic ulcer disease: Wounds in the walls of the stomach develop only after elaborate cellular and molecular defensive mechanisms are breached. *American Scientist, 80,* 592–598.

Livingstone, M. S., & Hubel, D. H. (1984). Anatomy of physiology of a color system in the primate visual cortex. *Journal of Neuroscience, 4,* 309–356.

Livingstone, M. S., & Hubel, D. S. (1988). Segregation of form, color, movement, and depth: Anatomy, physiology, and perception. *Science, 240,* 740–749.

Livingstone, M. S., & Tsao, D. Y. (1999). Receptive fields of disparity-selective neurons in macaque striate cortex. *Nature Reviews Neuroscience, 2,* 825–832.

Lo, Y-J., & Poo, M-M. (1991). Activity-dependent synaptic competition in vitro: Heterosynaptic suppression of developing synapses. *Science, 254,* 1019–1022.

Logothetis, N. (1998). Object vision and visual awareness. *Current Opinion in Neurobiology, 8,* 536–544.

Logothetis, N. K., & Sheinberg, D. L. (1996). Visual object recognition. *Annual Review of Neuroscience, 19,* 577–621.

Lombardino, A. J., & Nottebohm, F. (2000). Age at deafening affects the stability of learned song in adult male zebra finches. *Journal of Neuroscience, 20,* 5054–5064.

Loomis, A. L., Harvey, E. N., & Hobart, G. (1936). Electrical potentials of the human brain. *Journal of Experimental Psychology, 19,* 249–279.

Losick, R., & Shapiro, L. (1998). Bringing the mountain to Mohammed. *Science, 282,* 1430–1431.

LoTurco, J. L. (2000). Neural circuits in the 21st century: Synaptic networks of neurons and glia. *Proceedings of the National Academy of Science, U.S.A., 97,* 8196–8197.

Lotze, M., Montoya, P., Erb, M., Hülsmann, E., Flor, H., Klose, U., Birbaumer, N., & Grodd, W. (1999). Activation of cortical and cerebellar motor areas during executed and imagined hand movements: An fMRI study. *Journal of Cognitive Neuroscience, 11,* 491–501.

Lowe, M. R. (1993). The effects of dieting on eating behavior: A three-factor model. *Psychological Bulletin, 114,* 100–121.

Lowrey, P. L., Shimomura, K., Antoch, M. P., Yamazaki, S., Zemenides, P. D., Ralph, M. R., Menaker, M., & Takahashi, J. S. (2000). Positional syntenic cloning and functional characterization of the mammalian circadian mutation *tau. Science, 288,* 483–491.

Lozano, A. M., Lang, A. E., Hutchison, W. D., & Dostrovsky, J. O. (1998). New developments in understanding the etiology of Parkinson's disease and in its treatment. *Current Opinion in Neurobiology, 8,* 783–790.

Lu, J., Greco, M. A., Shiromani, P., & Saper, C. B. (2000). Effect of lesions of the ventrolateral preoptic nucleus on NREM and REM sleep. *Journal of Neuroscience, 20,* 3830–3842.

Lucas F., & Sclafani, A. (1989). Flavor preferences conditioned by intragastric fat infusions in rats. *Physiology & Behavior, 46,* 403–412.

Lucas, R. J., Freedman, M. S., Muñoz, M., Garcia-Fernández, & Foster, R. G. (1999). Regulation of the mammalian pineal by non-rod, non-cone, ocular photoreceptors. *Science, 284,* 505–507.

Lucidi, F., Devoto, A., Violani, C., Mastracci, P., & Bertini, M. (1997). Effects of different sleep duration on delta sleep in recovery nights. *Psychophysiology, 34,* 227–233.

Lykken, D. T. (1959). The GSR in the detection of guilt. *Journal of Applied Psychology, 43,* 385–388.

Macchi, G. (1989). Anatomical substrate of emotional reactions. In F. Boller & J. Grafman (Eds.), *Handbook of neuropsychology,* Vol. 3 (pp. 283–304). New York: Elsevier.

MacCoun, R. J. (1998). Toward a psychology of harm reduction. *American Psychologist, 53,* 1199–1208.

MacCoun, R., & Reuter, P. (1997). Interpreting Dutch cannabis policy: Reasoning by analogy in the legalization debate. *Science, 278,* 47–52.

MacDonald, M. E., & Gusella, J. F. (1996). Huntington's disease: Translating a CAG repeat into a pathogenic mechanism. *Current Opinion in Neurobiology, 6,* 638–643.

Macdonald, R. L., & Olsen, R. (1994). $GABA_A$ receptor channels. *Annual Review of Neuroscience, 17,* 569–602.

MacDougall-Shackleton, S. A. & Ball, G. F. (1999), Comaparative studies of sex differences in the song-control system of songbirds. *Trends in Neurosciences, 22:10,* 432–436.

MacKinnon, D. F., Jamison, K. R., & DePaulo, J. R. (1997). Genetics of manic depressive illness. *Annual Review of Neuroscience, 20,* 355–373.

MacLusky, N.J., & Naftolin, F. (1981). Sexual differentiation of the central nervous system. *Science, 211,* 1294–1302.

Maguire, A. A., Burgess, N., Donnett, J. G., Frackowiak, R. S. J., Frith, C. D., & O'Keefe, J. (2000). Knowing where and getting there: A human navigation network. *Science, 280,* 921–924.

Maguire, E. A., Frith, C. D., Burgess, N., Donnett, J. G., & O'Keefe, J. (1998). Knowing where things are: Parahippocampal involvement in encoding object locations in virtual large-scale space. *Journal of Cognitive Neuroscience, 19,* 61–76.

Maier, S. F., & Watkins, L. R. (2000). The immune system as a sensory system: Implications for psychology. *Current Directions in Psychological Science, 9,* 98–102.

Maier, S. R., Watkins, L. R., & Fleshner, M. (1994). Psychoneuroimmunology: The interface between behavior, brain, and immunity. *American Psychologist, 49,* 1004–1017.

Mair, R. G., Knoth, R. L., Rabenchuk, S. A., & Langlais, P. J. (1991). Impairment of olfactory, auditory, and spatial serial reversal learning in rats recovered from pyrithiamine-induced thiamine deficiency. *Behavioral Neuroscience, 105,* 360–374.

Mair, R. G., Otto, T. A., Knoth, R. L., & Langlais, P. J. (1991). Analysis of aversively conditioned learning and memory in rats recovered from pyrithiamine-induced thiamine deficiency. *Behavioral Neuroscience, 105,* 351–359.

Malgaroli, A., Ting, A. E., Wendland, B., Bergamaschi, A., Villa, A., Tsien, R. W., & Scheller, R. H. (1995). Presynaptic component of long-term potentiation visualized at individual hippocampal synapses. *Science, 268,* 1624–1628.

Malinow, R. (1994). LTP: Desperately seeking resolution. *Science, 266,* 1195–1196.

Malissen, B. (1999). Dancing the immunological two-step. *Science, 285,* 207–208.

Malsbury, C. W. (1971). Facilitation of male rat copulatory behavior by electrical stimulation of the medial preoptic area. *Physiology & Behavior, 7,* 797–805.

Malsbury, C. W., & Pfaff, D. W. (1974). Neural and hormonal determinants of mating behavior in adult male rats. A review. In L. V. DiCara (Ed.), *Limbic and autonomic nervous system research* (pp. 85–136). New York: Plenum Press.

Manson, J. E., Willett, W. C., Stampfer, M. J., Colditz, G. A., Hunter, D. J., Hankinson, S. E., Hennekens, C. H., & Speizer, F. E. (1995). Body weight and mortality among women. *New England Journal of Medicine, 333,* 677–685.

Maratsos, M., & Matheny, L. (1994). Language specificity and elasticity: Brain and clinical syndrome studies. *Annual Review of Psychology, 45,* 487–516.

Maren, S. (2001). Neurobiology of Pavlovian fear conditioning. In *Annual Reviews of Neuroscience* (pp. 893–897). Palo Alto, CA: Annual Reviews.

Mark, V. H., Ervin, F. R., & Yakolev, P. I. (1962). The treatment of pain by stereotaxic methods. 1st International Symposium on Stereoencephalotomy (Philadelphia, 1961). *Confina Neurologica, 22*, 238–245.

Marlowe, W. B., Mancall, E. L., & Thomas, J. J. (1985). Complete Kluver-Bucy syndrome in man. *Cortex, 11*, 53–59.

Martin, A., Wiggs, C. L., Ungerleider, L. G., & Haxby, J. V. (1996). Neural correlates of category-specific knowledge. *Nature, 379*, 649–652.

Martin, J. B. (1987). Molecular genetics: Applications to the clinical neurosciences. *Science, 238*, 765–772.

Martin, R. J., White, B. D., & Hulsey, M. G. (1991). The regulation of body weight. *American Scientist, 79*, 528–541.

Martin, R. L., Roberts, W. V., & Clayton, P. J. (1980). Psychiatric status after a one-year prospective follow-up. *Journal of the American Medical Association, 244*, 350–353.

Martin, S. J., Grimwood, P. D., & Morris, R. G. M. (2000). Synaptic plasticity and memory: An evaluation of the hypothesis. *Annual Reviews of Neuroscience, 23*, 649–711.

Masoro, E. J. (1988). Minireview: Food restriction in rodents: An evaluation of its role in the study of aging. *Journal of Gerontology, 43*, 59–64.

Masterton, R. B. (1992). Role of the central auditory system in hearing: The new direction. *Trends in Neurosciences, 15*, 280–285.

Matsuda, L. A., Lolait, S. J., Brownstein, M. J., Young, A. C., & Bonner, T. I. (1990). Structure of a cannabinoid receptor and functional expression of the cloned DNA. *Nature, 346*, 561–564.

Matthews, P. B. C. (1991). The human stretch reflex and the motor cortex. *Trends in Neurosciences, 3*, 87–91.

Mazzocchi, F., & Vignolo, L. A. (1979). Localisation of lesions in aphasia: Clinical-CT scan correlations in stroke patients. *Cortex, 15*, 627–654.

McAuliffe, W. E., Feldman, B., Friedman, R., Launer, E., Magnuson, E., Mahoney, C., Santangelo, S., Ward, W., & Weiss, R. (1986). Explaining relapse to opiate addiction following successful completion of treatment. In F. M. Tims & C. G. Leukefield (Eds.), *Relapse and recovery in drug abuse: National Institute on Drug Abuse Research Monograph Series* (Vol. 72, pp. 136–156). Rockville, MA: National Institute on Drug Abuse Research Monograph Series 72.

McCann, T. S. (1981). Aggression and sexual activity of male southern elephant seals, *Mirounga leonina. Journal of Zoology, 195*, 295–310.

McClearn, G. E., Johansson, B., Berg, S., Pedersen, N. L., Ahern, F., Petrill, S. A., & Plomin, R. (1997). *Science, 276*, 1560–1563.

McClintock, M. K., & Herdt, G. (1996). Rethinking puberty: The development of sexual attraction. *Current Directions in Psychological Science, 5*, 178–183.

McCormick, D. A. (1999). Membrane potential and action potential. In M. J. Zigmond, F. E. Bloom, S. C. Landis, J. L. Roberts, & L. R. Squire (Eds.) *Fundamental Neuroscience* (pp. 129–154). Academic Press: New York.

McDonald, J. W., Liu, X-Z., Qu, Y., Liu, S., Mickey, S. K., Turetsky, D., Gottlieb, D. I., & Choi, D. W. (1999). Transplanted embryonic stem cells survive, differentiate and promote recovery in injured rat spinal cord. *Nature Medicine, 5*, 1410–1412.

McDonald, R. J., & White, N. M. (1993). Triple dissociation of memory systems: Hippocampus, amygdala, and dorsal striatum. *Behavioral and Neural Biology, 59*, 107–119.

McDonald, R. J., & White, N. M. (1993). Triple dissociation of memory systems: Hippocampus, amygdala, and dorsal striatum. *Behavioral and Neural Biology, 59*, 107–119.

McEwen, B. (1994). Introduction: Stress and the nervous system. *Seminars in the Neurosciences, 6*, 195–196.

McEwen, B. S. (1983). Gonadal steroid influences on brain development and sexual differentiation. In R. O. Greep (Ed.), *Reproductive physiology IV*. Baltimore: University Park Press.

McEwen, B. S. (1987). Sexual differentiation. In G. Adelman (Ed.), *Encyclopedia of neuroscience, Vol. II* (pp. 1086–1088). Boston, MA: Birkhäuser.

McEwen, B. S. (2000a). Effects of adverse experiences for brain structure and function. *Biological Psychiatry, 48*, 721–731.

McEwen, B. S. (2000b). The neurobiology of stress: From serendipity to clinical relevance. *Brain Research, 886*, 172–189.

McFarland, H. F. (1996). Complexities in the treatment of autoimmune disease. *Science, 274*, 2037–2038.

McGinty, D. J., & Sterman, M. B. (1968). Sleep suppression after basal forebrain lesions in the cat. *Science, 160*, 1253–1255.

McGlone, J. (1977). Sex differences in the cerebral organization of verbal functions in patients with unilateral brain lesions. *Brain, 100*, 775–793.

McGlone, J. (1980). Sex differences in human brain asymmetry: A critical survey. *Behavioral and Brain Sciences, 3*, 215–263.

McGue, M. (1999). The behavioral genetics of alcoholism. *Current Directions in Psychological Science, 8*, 109–115.

McKim, W. A. (1986). *Drugs and behavior: An introduction to behavioral pharmacology.* Englewood Cliffs, NJ: Prentice-Hall.

McNally, G. P. (1999). Pain facilitatory circuits in the mammalian central nervous system: Their behavioral significance and role in morphine analgesic tolerance. *Neuroscience and Biobehavioral Reviews, 23*, 1059–1078.

Meaney, M. J. (2001). Maternal care, gene expression, and the transmission of individual differences in stress reactivity across generations. *Annual Review of Neuroscience, 24*, 1161–1192.

Meaney, M. J., Aitken, D. H., van Berkel, C., Bhatnagar, S., & Sapolsky, R. M. (1988). Effect of neonatal handling on age-related impairments associated with the hippocampus. *Science, 239*, 766–768.

Meddis, R. (1977). *The sleep instinct.* London: Routledge & Kegan Paul.

Mello, N. K., & Mendelson, J. H. (1972). Drinking patterns during work-contingent and noncontingent alcohol acquisition. *Psychosomatic Medicine, 34*, 139–165.

Meltzer, L. D., et al. (1990). Clinical efficacy of clozapine in the treatment of schizophrenia. *Clinical Neuropharmacology, 13 (supplement 2)*, 259–260.

Melzack, R. (1992, April). Phantom limbs. *Scientific American, 266*, 120–126.

Melzack, R., & Wall, P. D. (1965). Pain mechanisms: A new theory. *Science, 150*, 971–979.

Melzack, R., & Wall, P. D. (1982). *The challenge of pain* (pp. 16–17). London: Penguin Books Ltd.

Mendelson, J. H. (1987). Marijuana. In H. Y. Meltzer (Ed.), *Psychopharmacology: The third generation of progress* (pp. 1565–1571). New York: Raven Press.

Mendelson, J. H., Kuehnle, J. C., Greenberg, I., & Mello, N. K. (1976). The effects of marihuana use on human operant behavior: Individual data. In M. C. Braude and S. Szara (Eds.), *The pharmacology of marihuana* (pp. 643–653). New York: Raven Press.

Mervis, C. B., Robinson, B. F., Bertrand, J., Morris, C. A., Klein-Tasman, B. P., & Armstrong, S. C. (2000). The Williams syndrome cognitive profile. *Brain and Cognition, 44*, 604–628.

Metcalfe, J., Funnell, M., & Gazzaniga, M. S. (1995). Right hemisphere memory veridicality: Studies of a split-brain patient. *Psychological Science, 6*, 157–165.

Meurnier, M., Murray, E. A., Bachevalier, J., & Mishkin, M. (1990). Effects of perirhinal cortical lesions on visual recognition memory in rhesus monkeys. *Society for Neuroscience Abstracts, 17,* 337.

Meyer, R. G., & Salmon, P. (1988). *Abnormal psychology,* 2nd ed. Boston: Allyn & Bacon.

Middleton, F. A., & Strick, P. L. (1994). Anatomical evidence for cerebellar and basal ganglia involvement in higher cognitive function. *Science, 266,* 458–461.

Miller, G. L., & Knudsen, E. I. (1999). Early visual experience shapes the representation of auditory space in the forebrain gaze fields of the barn owl. *Journal of Neuroscience, 19,* 2326–2336.

Miller, N. E., Bailey, C. J., & Stevenson, J. A. F. (1950). Decreased "hunger" but increased food intake resulting from hypothalamic lesions. *Science, 112,* 256–259.

Miller, N. S., Summers, G. L., & Gold, M. S. (1993). Cocaine dependence: Alcohol and other drug dependence and withdrawal characteristics. *Journal of Addictive Diseases, 12,* 25–35.

Milner, B. (1965). Memory disturbances after bilateral hippocampal lesions. In P. Milner & S. Glickman (Eds.), *Cognitive processes and the brain* (pp. 104–105). Princeton, NJ: D. Van Nostrand Co.

Milner, B. (1971). Interhemispheric differences in the localization of psychological processes in man. *British Medical Bulletin, 27,* 272–277.

Milner, B. (1974). Hemispheric specialization: Scope and limits. In F. O. Schmitt and F. G. Worden (Eds.), *The neurosciences: Third study program* (pp. 75–89). Cambridge, MA: MIT Press.

Milner, B., Corkin, S., & Teuber, H. L. (1968). Further analysis of the hippocampal amnesic syndrome: 14-year follow-up study of H. M. *Neuropsychologia, 6,* 317–338.

Milner, D., & Goodale, M. A. (1993). Visual pathways to perception and action. *Progress in Brain Research, 95,* 317–337.

Milner, P. M. (1993, January). The mind and Donald O. Hebb. *Scientific American, 268,* 124–129.

Milner, P. M., & White, N. M. (1987). What is physiological psychology? *Psychobiology, 15,* 2–6.

Mishkin, M., & Appenzeller, T. (1987). The anatomy of memory. *Scientific American, 256,* 80–89.

Mishkin, M., & Delacour, J. (1975). An analysis of short-term visual memory in the monkey. *Journal of Experimental Psychology: Animal Behavior Processes, 1,* 326–334.

Mistlberger, R. E. (1993). Circadian properties of anticipatory activity to restricted water access in suprachiasmatic-ablated hamsters. *American Journal of Physiology, 263,* 22–29.

Mistlberger, R. E. (1994). Circadian food-anticipatory activity: Formal models and physiological mechanisms. *Neuroscience and Biobehavioral Reviews, 18,* 171–195.

Mistlberger, R. E., de Groot, M. H. M., Bossert, J. M., & Marchant, E. G. (1996). Discrimination of circadian phase in intact and suprachiasmatic nuclei-ablated rats. *Brain Research, 739,* 12–18.

Mitchell, J. M., Basbaum, A. I., & Fields, H. L. (2000). A locus and mechanism of action for associative morphine tolerance. *Nature Reviews Neuroscience, 3,* 47–53.

Mogil, J. S., Yu, L., & Basbaum, A. I. (2000). Pain genes? Natural variation and transgenic mutants. *Annual Review of Neuroscience, 23,* 777–811.

Mohr, J. P. (1976). Broca's area and Broca's aphasia. In H. Whitaker & H. A. Whitaker (Eds.), *Studies in neurolinguistics,* Vol. 1 (pp. 201–235). New York: Academic Press.

Molday, R. S., & Hsu, Y-T. (1995). The cGMP-gated channel of photoreceptor cells: its structural properties and role in phototransduction. *Behavioral and Brain Sciences, 18,* 441–451.

Mombaerts, P. (1996). Targeting olfaction. *Current Opinion in Neurobiology, 6,* 481–486.

Money, J. (1975). Ablatio penis: Normal male infant sex-reassigned as a girl. *Archives of Sexual Behavior, 4* (1), 65–71.

Money, J., & Ehrhardt, A. A. (1972). *Man & woman, boy & girl.* Baltimore: Johns Hopkins University Press.

Mooney, R. (1999). Sensitive periods and circuits for learned birdsong. *Current Opinion in Neurobiology, 9,* 121–127.

Moore, R. Y. (1982). The suprachiasmatic nucleus and the organization of a circadian system. *Trends in Neurosciences, 5,* 404–407.

Moore, R. Y. (1996). Neural control of the pineal gland. *Behavioural Brain Research, 73,* 125–130.

Moore, R. Y. (1999). A clock for the ages. *Science, 284,* 2101–2177.

Moran, J., & Desimone, R. (1985). Selective attention gates visual processing in the extrastriate cortex. *Science, 229,* 782–784.

Morgan, T. H., Sturtevant, A. H., Muller, H. J., & Bridges, C. B. (1915). *The mechanism of Mendelian heredity.* New York: Henry Holt.

Mori, K. (1995). Relation of chemical structure to specificity of response in olfactory glomeruli. *Current Opinion in Neurobiology, 5,* 467–474.

Mori, N., & Wada, J. A. (1990). Does electrical and excitatory amino acid kindling share a common neurobiological mechanism? In J. A. Wada (Ed.), *Kindling 4* (pp. 209–222). New York: Plenum Press.

Morin, C. M., Kowatch, R. A, & O'Shanick, G. (1990). Sleep restriction for the inpatient treatment of insomnia. *Sleep, 13,* 183–186.

Morris, J. S., Scott, S. K., & Dolan, R. J. (1999). Saying it with feeling: Neural responses to emotional vocalizations. *Neuropsychologia, 37,* 1155–1163.

Morris, M. K., Bowers, D., Chatterjee, A., & Heilman, K. M. (1992). Amnesia following a discrete basal forebrain lesion. *Brain, 115,* 1827–1847.

Morris, N. M., Udry, J. R., Khan-Dawood, F., & Dawood, M. Y. (1987). Marital sex frequency and midcycle female testosterone. *Archives of Sexual Behavior, 16,* 27–37.

Morris, R. G. M. (1981). Spatial localization does not require the presence of local cues. *Learning and Motivation, 12,* 239–260.

Moruzzi, G., & Magoun, H. W. (1949). Brain stem reticular formation and activation of the EEG. *Electroencephalography and Clinical Neurophysiology, 1,* 455–473.

Moscovitch, M., Winocur, G., & Behrmann, M. (1997). What is special about face recognition? Nineteen experiments on a person with visual object agnosia and dyslexia but normal face recognition. *Journal of Cognitive Neuroscience, 9* (5), 555–604.

Moser, M-B., & Moser, E. I. (1998). Distributed encoding and retrieval of spatial memory in the hippocampus. *Journal of Neuroscience, 18,* 7535–7542.

Mosher, J. T., Birkemo, L., S., Johnson, M. F., & Ervin, G. N. (1998). Sulfated chlecystokinin (26–33) induces mild taste aversion conditioning in rats when administered by three different routes. *Peptides, 19,* 849–857.

Mountcastle, V. B., & Powell, T. P. S. (1959). Neural mechanisms subserving cutaneous sensibility with special references to the role of afferent inhibition in sensory perception and discrimination. *Bulletin of Johns Hopkins Hospital, 105,* 201–232.

Mouret, J., Bobillier, P., & Jouvet, M. (1968). Insomnia following parachlorophenylalanin in the rat. *European Journal of Pharmacology, 5,* 17–22.

Mrosovsky, N., & Salmon, P. A. (1987). A behavioral method for accelerating re-entrainment of rhythms to new light-dark cycles. *Nature, 330,* 372–373.

Mucha, R. F., Van der Kooy, D., O'Shaughnessy, M., & Bucenieks, P. (1982). Drug reinforcement studied by the use of place conditioning in rat. *Brain Research, 243,* 91–105.

Mühlnickel, W., Elbert, T., Taub, E., & Flor, H. (1998). Reorganization of auditory cortex in tinnitus. *Proceedings of the National Academy of Sciences, USA, 95,* 10340–10343.

Muir, G. D., & Steeves, J. D. (1997). Sensorimotor stimulation to improve locomotor recovery after spinal cord injury. *Trends in Neurosciences, 20,* 72–77.

Mullaney, D. J., Johnson, L. C., Naitoh, P., Friedman, J. K., & Globus, G. G. (1977). Sleep during and after gradual sleep reduction. *Psychophysiology, 14,* 237–244.

Mumby, D. G., & Pinel, J. P. J. (1994). Rhinal cortex lesions impair object recognition in rats. *Behavioral Neuroscience, 108,* 11–18.

Mumby, D. G., Pinel, J. P. J., & Wood, E. R. (1989). Nonrecurring items delayed nonmatching-to-sample in rats: A new paradigm for testing nonspatial working memory. *Psychobiology, 18,* 321–326.

Mumby, D. G., Wood, E. R., & Pinel, J. P. J. (1992). Object-recognition memory is only mildly impaired in rats with lesions of the hippocampus and amygdala. *Psychobiology, 20,* 18–27.

Mumby, D. G., Wood, E. R., Duva, C. A., Kornecook, T. J., Pinel, J. P. J., & Phillips, A. G. (1996). Ischemia-induced object-recognition deficits in rats are attenuated by hippocampal ablation before or soon after ischemia. *Behavioral Neuroscience, 110* (2), 266–281.

Murphy, G. G., & Glanzman, D. L. (1997). Mediation of classical conditioning in *Aplysia californica* by long-term potentiation of sensorimotor synapses. *Science, 278,* 467–471.

Murphy, M. R., & Schneider, G. E. (1970). Olfactory bulb removal eliminates mating behavior in the male golden hamster. *Science, 157,* 302–304.

Murphy, P. C., Duckett, S. G., & Sillito, A. M. (1999). Feedback connections to the lateral geniculate nucleus and cortical response properties. *Science, 286,* 1552–1554.

Murray, E. A. (1996). What have ablation studies told us about the neural substrates of stimulus memory? *Seminars in the Neurosciences, 8,* 13–22.

Myers, R. E., & Sperry, R. W. (1953). Interocular transfer of a visual form discrimination habit in cats after section of the optic chiasma and corpus callosum. *American Association of Anatomists: Abstracts of Papers from Platform,* p. 351.

Nadel, L., & Moscovitch, M. (1997). Memory consolidation, retrograde amnesia and the hippocampal complex. *Current Opinion in Neurobiology, 7,* 217–227.

Nadelmann, E. A. (1989). Drug prohibition in the United States: Costs, consequences, and alternatives. *Science, 245,* 939–947.

Naeser, M. A., Alexander M. P., Helm-Estabrooks, N., Levine, H. L., Laughlin, S. A., & Geschwind, N. (1982). Aphasia with predominantly subcortical lesion sites. *Archives of Neurolinguistics, 39,* 2–14.

Naeser, M. A., Hayward, R. W., Laughlin, S. A., & Zatz, L. M. (1981). Quantitative CT scan studies in aphasia. *Brain and Language, 12,* 140–164.

Naitoh, P. (1992). Minimal sleep to maintain performance: The search for sleep quantum in sustained operations. In C. Stampi (Ed.), *Why we nap: Evolution, chronobiology, and functions of polyphasic and ultrashort sleep.* Boston: Birkhäuser.

Nathans, J. (1989, February). The genes for color vision. *Scientific American, 260,* 42–49.

National Commission on Marijuana and Drug Abuse (1972). R. P. Schafer, Chairman. *Marijuana: A signal of misunderstanding.* New York: New American Library.

Nauta, W. J. H., & Feirtag, M. (1986). *Fundamental neuroanatomy.* New York: W. H. Freeman.

Naya, Y., Yoshida, M., & Miyashita, Y. (2001). Backward spreading of memory-retrieval signal in the primate temporal cortex. *Science, 291,* 661–664.

Neher, E., & Sakmann, B. (1992, March). The patch clamp technique. *Scientific American, 266,* 44–51.

Nelson, C. A. (1999). Neural plasticity and human development. *Current Directions in Psychological Science, 8,* 42–45.

Nemeroff, C. B. (1998, June). The neurobiology of depression. *Scientific American, 278,* 42–49.

Nesse, R. M., & Berridge, K. C. (1997). Psychoactive drug use in evolutionary perspective. *Science, 278,* 63–66.

Nesse, R. M., & Williams, G. C. (1998, November). Evolution and the origins of disease. *Scientific American, 278,* 86–93.

Netter, F. H. (1962). *The CIBA collection of medical illustrations: Vol. 1. The nervous system.* New York: CIBA.

Neve, R. L., & Robakis, N. K. (1998). Alzheimer's disease: A re-examination of the amyloid hypothesis. *Trends in Neurosciences, 21,* 15–19.

Neville, H., & Bavelier, D. (1998). Neural organization and plasticity of language. *Current Opinion in Neurobiology, 8,* 254–258.

Newcombe, N., & Fox, N. (1994). Infantile amnesia: Through a glass darkly. *Child Development, 65,* 31–40.

Newcombe, N. S., Drummey, A. B., Fox, N. A., Lie, E., & Ottinger-Alberts, W. (2000). Remembering early childhood: How much, how, and why (or why not). *Current Directions in Psychological Science, 9,* 55–58.

Newsom-Davis, J., & Vincent, A. (1991). Antibody-medicated neurological disease. *Current Opinion in Neurobiology, 1,* 430–435.

Nguyen, P. V., Abel, T., & Kandel, E. R. (1994). Requirement of a critical period of transcription for induction of a late phase of LTP. *Science, 265,* 1104–1106.

Nicoll, R. A., & Malenka, R. C. (1998). A tale of two transmitters. *Science, 281,* 360–424.

Nijhawan, D., Honarpour, N., & Wang, X. (2000). Apoptosis in neural development and disease. *Annual Review of Neuroscience, 23,* 73–89.

Nobre, A. C., & Plunkett, K. (1997). The neural system of language: Structure and development. *Current Opinion in Neurobiology, 7,* 262–268.

Nopoulis, P. C., Ceilley, J. W., Gailis, E. A., & Andreasen, N. C. (2001). An MRI study of midbrain morphology in patients with schizophrenia: Relationship to psychosis, neuroleptics, and cerebellar neural circuitry. *Biological Psychiatry, 49,* 13–19.

Norman, R. M. G., & Malla, A. K. (1993). Stressful life events and schizophrenia I: A review of the research. *British Journal of Psychiatry, 162,* 161–166.

Northcutt, R. G., & Kaas, J. H. (1995). The emergence and evolution of mammalian neocortex. *Trends in Neurosciences, 18:9,* 373–418.

Northoff, G., Richter, A., Gessner, M., Schlagenhauf, F., Fell, J., Baumgart, F., Kaulisch, T., Kötter, R., Stephan, K. E., Leschinger, A., Hagner, T., Bargel, B., Witzel, T., Hinrichs, H., Bogerts, B., Scheich, H., & Heinze, H-J. (2000). Functional dissociation between medial and lateral prefrontal cortical spatiotemporal activation in negative and positive emotions: A combined FMRI/MEG study. *Cerebral Cortex, 10,* 93–107.

Noselli, S., & Perrimon, N. (2000). Are there close encounters between signaling pathways? *Science, 290,* 68–69.

Nossal, G. J. V. (1993, September). Life, death and the immune system: By defining and defending the self, the immune system makes life possible; malfunction causes illness and death. Study of the system provides a unifying view of biology. *Scientific American, 269,* 53–62.

Nudo, R. J., Jenkins, W. M., & Merzenich, M. M. (1996). Repetitive microstimulation alters the cortical representation of movements in adult rats. *Somatosensory Motor Research, 7,* 463–483.

Nyberg, L., Habib, R., McIntosh, A. R., & Tulving, E. (2000). Reactivation of encoding-related brain activity during memory retrieval. *Proceedings of the National Academy of Sciences, USA, 97,* 11120–11124.

Nykamp, K., Rosenthal, L., Folkerts, M., Roehrs, T., Guido, P., & Roth, T. (1998). The effects of REM sleep deprivation on the level of sleepiness/alertness. *Sleep, 21,* 609–614

O'Banion, M. K., Coleman, P. D., & Callahan, L. M. (1994). Regional neuronal loss in aging and Alzheimer's disease: A brief review. *Seminars in the Neurosciences, 6,* 307–314.

O'Callaghan, M. A. J., & Carroll, D. (1982). *Psychosurgery: A scientific analysis.* Ridgewood, NJ: George A. Bogdaen & Son, Inc.

Ohzawa, I. (1998). Mechanisms of stereoscopic vision: The disparity energy model. *Current Opinion in Neurobiology, 8,* 509–515.

Ojemann, G. A. (1979). Individual variability in cortical localization of language. *Journal of Neurosurgery, 50,* 164–169.

Ojemann, G. A. (1983). Brain organization for language from the perspective of electrical stimulation mapping. *Behavioral and Brain Sciences, 2,* 189–230.

O'Keefe, J. (1993). Hippocampus, theta, and spatial memory. *Current Opinion in Neurobiology, 3,* 917–924.

O'Keefe, J., & Dostrovsky, J. (1971). The hippocampus as a spatial map: Preliminary evidence from unit activity in the freely-moving rat. *Brain Research, 34,* 171–175.

O'Keefe, J., & Nadel, L. (1978). *The hippocampus as a cognitive map.* Oxford: The Clarendon Press.

O'Keefe, J., & Speakman, A. (1987). Single unit activity in the rat hippocampus during a spatial memory task. *Experimental Brain Research, 68,* 1–27.

Olds, J., & Milner, P. (1954). Positive reinforcement produced by electrical stimulation of septal area and other regions of rat brain. *Journal of Comparative and Physiological Psychology, 47,* 419–427.

O'Leary, D. D. M.., Ruff, N. L., & Dyck, R. H. (1994). Development, critical period plasticity, and adult reorganization of mammalian somatosensory systems. *Current Opinion in Neurobiology, 4,* 535–544.

Olton, D. S., & Samuelson, R. J. (1976). Remembrance of places: Spatial memory in rats. *Journal of Experimental Psychology: Animal Behavior Processes, 2,* 97–116.

O'Neill, L., Murphy, M., & Gallager, R. B. (1994). What are we? Where did we come from? Where are we going? *Science, 263,* 181–184.

Ormerod, B. K., & Galea, L. A. M. (2001a). Mechanism and function of adult neurogenesis. In C. A. Shaw & J. C. McEachern (Eds.), *Towards a theory of neuroplasticity* (pp. 85–100). Philadelphia: Taylor & Francis.

Ormerod, B. K., & Galea, L. A. M. (2001b). Reproductive status influences cell proliferation and cell survival in the dentate gyrus of adult female meadow voles: A possible regulatory role for estradiol. *Neuroscience, 102,* 369–379.

Ormerod, B. K., Falconer, E. M., & Galea, L. A. M. (in press 2001). *Neurogenesis. Encyclopedia of cognitive science.* London: Macmillan Reference Ltd.

Overmier, J. B., & Murison, R. (1997). Animal models reveal the "psych" in the psychosomatics of peptic ulcers. *Current Directions in Psychological Science, 6,* 180–184.

Owen, A. M., Lee, A. C. H., & Williams, E. J. (2000). Dissociating aspects of verbal working memory within the human

frontal lobe: Further evidence for a "process-specific" model of lateral frontal organization. *Psychobiology, 28,* 146–155.

Owren, M. J. (1990). Acoustic classification of alarm calls by vervet monkeys (*Cercopithecus aethiops*) and humans (*Homo sapiens*): II. Synthetic calls. *Journal of Comparative Psychology, 104,* 29–40.

Pääbo, S. (1995). The Y chromosome and the origin of all of us (men). *Science, 268,* 1141–1142.

Paletta, M. S., & Wagner, A. R. (1986). Development of context specific tolerance to morphine: Support for a dual-process interpretation. *Behavioral Neuroscience, 100,* 611–623.

Paller, K. A., Acharya, A., Richardson, B. C., Plaisant, O., Shimamura, A. P., Reed, B. R., & Jagust, W. J. (1997). Functional neuroimaging of cortical dysfunction in alcoholic Korsakoff's syndrome. *Journal of Cognitive Neuroscience, 9,* 277–293.

Panksepp, J., & Trowill, J. A. (1967). Intraoral self-injection: II. The simulation of self-stimulation phenomena with a conventional reward. *Psychonomic Science, 9,* 407–408.

Papez, J. W. (1937). A proposed mechanism of emotion. *Archives of Neurology and Psychiatry, 38,* 725–743.

Parker, S. T., Mitchell, R. W., & Boccia, M. L. (1994). *Self-awareness in animals and humans: Developmental perspectives.* New York: Cambridge University Press.

Parnas, H., Segel, L., Dudel, J., & Parnas, I. (2000). Autoreceptors, membrane potential and the regulation of transmitter release. *Trends in Neurosciences, 23,* 60–68.

Parnavelas, J. G. (2000). The origin and migration of cortical neurons: New vistas. *Trends in Neurosciences, 23,* 123–131.

Parrott, A. C. (1999). Does cigarette smoking *cause* stress? *American Psychologist, 54,* 817–820.

Parsons, L. M., Fox, P. T., Downs, J. H., Glass, T., Hirsch, T. B., Martin, C. C., Jerabek, P. A., & Lancaster, J. L. (1995). Use of implicit motor imagery for visual shape discrimination as revealed by PET. *Nature, 375,* 54–58.

Paterson, S. J., Brown, J. H., Gsödl, M. K., Johnson, M. H., & Karmiloff-Smith, A. (1999). *Science, 286,* 2355–2358.

Patterson, K., & Ralph, M. A. L. (1999). Selective disorders of reading? *Current Opinion in Neurobiology, 9,* 235–239.

Patterson, K., Vargha-Khadem, F., & Polkey, C. E. (1989). Reading with one hemisphere. *Brain, 112,* 39–63.

Patton, G. C. (1988). The spectrum of eating disorders in adolescence. *Journal of Psychosomatic Research, 32,* 579–584.

Paulesu, E., Démonet, J.-F., Fazio, F., McCrory, E., Chanoine, V., Brunswick, N., Cappa, S. F., Cossu, G., Habib, M., Frith, C. D., & Frith, U. (2001). Dyslexia: Cultural diversity and biological unity. *Science, 291,* 2165–2167.

Paulesu, E., McCrory, E., Fazio, F., Menoncello, L., Brunswick, N., Cappa, S. F., Cotelli, M., Cossu, G., Corte, F., Lorusso, M., Pesenti, S., Gallagher, A., Perani, D., Price, C., & Frith, C. D. (2000). A cultural effect on brain function. *Nature Reviews Neuroscience, 3,* 91–96.

Pauls, D. L. (2001). Update on the genetics of Tourette syndrome. In D. J. Cohen, C. G. Goetz, & J. Jankovic (Eds.), *Tourette syndrome* (pp. 281–293). Philadelphia: Lippincott Williams & Wilkins.

Paulson, H. L., & Fischbeck, K. H. (1996). Trinucleotide repeats in neurogenetic disorders. *Annual Review of Neuroscience, 19,* 79–107.

Paxinos, G. (Ed.). (1990). *The human nervous system.* New York: Harcourt Brace Jovanovich.

Pearlman, A. L., Faust, P. L., Hatten, M. E., & Brunstrom, J. E. (1998). New directions for neuronal migration. *Current Opinion in Neurobiology, 8,* 45–54.

Pellis, S. M., & Pellis, V. C. (1993). Influence of dominance on the development of play fighting in pairs of male Syrian golden hamsters (*Mesocricetus auratus*). *Aggressive Behavior, 19,* 293–302.

Pellis, S. M., O'Brien, D. P., Pellis, V. C., Teitelbaum, P., Wolgin, D. L., & Kennedy, S. (1988). Escalation of feline predation along a gradient from avoidance through "play" to killing. *Behavioral Neuroscience, 102,* 760–777.

Pellow, S., Chopin, P., File, S. E., & Briley, M. (1985). Validation of open:closed arm entries in an elevated plus-maze as a measure of anxiety in the rat. *Journal of Neuroscience Methods, 14,* 149–167.

Penfield, W., & Boldrey, E. (1937). Somatic motor and sensory representations in cerebral cortex of man as studied by electrical stimulation. *Brain, 60,* 389–443.

Penfield, W., & Evans, J. (1935). The frontal lobe in man: A clinical study of maximum removals. *Brain, 58,* 115–133.

Penfield, W., & Roberts, L. (1959). *Speech and brain mechanisms* (pp. 133–191). Princeton, NJ: Princeton University Press.

Peralta, V., & Cuesta, M. J. (2000). Clinical models of schizophrenia: A critical approach to competing conceptions. *Psychopathology, 33,* 252–258.

Percival, J. E., Horne, J. A, & Tilley, A. J. (1983). Effects of sleep deprivation on tests of higher cerebral functioning. *Sleep 1982. 6th European Congress on Sleep Research* (Zurich, 1982). (pp. 390–391). Basel: Karger.

Perneger, T. V., Giner, F., Del Rio, M., & Mino, A. (1998). Randomised trial of heroin maintenance programme for addicts who fail in conventional drug treatments. *British Medical Journal, 317,* 350–351.

Perneger, T. V., Mino, A., Giner, F., & Broers, B. (2000). Patterns of opiate use in a heroin maintenance programme. *Psychopharmacology, 152,* 7–13.

Pert, C. B., Snowman, A. M., & Snyder, S. H. (1974). Localization of opiate receptor binding in presynaptic membranes of rat brain. *Brain Research, 70,* 184–188.

Peterhans, E., & von der Heydt, R. (1991). Subjective contours—bridging the gap between psychophysics and physiology. *Trends in Neurosciences, 14,* 112–119.

Peters, M., & Brooke, J. (1998). Conduction velocity in muscle and cutaneous afferents in humans. *Journal of Motor Behavior, 30,* 285–287.

Petersen, S. E., Fox, P. T., Posner, M. I., Mintun, M., & Raichle, M. E. (1988). Positron emission tomographic studies of the cortical anatomy of single-word processing. *Nature, 331,* 585–589.

Peterson, A. T., Soberon, J., & Sanchez-Cordero, V. (1999). Conservatism of ecological niches in evolutionary time. *Science, 285,* 1265–1267.

Peterson, B. S. (2001). Neuroimaging studies of Tourette syndrome: A decade of progress. In D. J. Cohen, C. G. Goetz, & J. Jankovic (Eds.) *Tourette syndrome* (pp. 179–196). Philadelphia: Lippincott Williams & Wilkins.

Petrides, M. (1996). Lateral frontal cortical contribution to memory. *Seminars in the Neurosciences, 8,* 57–63.

Petrides, M. (2000). Dissociable roles of mid-dorsolateral prefrontal and anterior inferotemporal cortex in visual working memory. *Journal of Neuroscience, 20,* 7496–7503.

Pfaff, D., & Modianos, D. (1985). Neural mechanisms of female reproductive behavior. In N. Adler, D. Pfaff, & R. W. Goy (Eds.), *Handbook of behavioral neurobiology, Vol. 7, reproduction* (pp. 423–493). New York: Plenum Press.

Pfeiffer, C. A. (1936). Sexual differences of the hypophyses and their determination by the gonads. *American Journal of Anatomy, 58,* 195–225.

Phillips, A. G., Coury, A., Fiorino, D., LePiane, F. G., Brown, E., & Fibiger, H. C. (1992). Self-stimulation of the ventral tegmental area enhances dopamine release in the nucleus accumbens:

A microdialysis study. *Annals of the New York Academy of Sciences, 654,* 199–206.

Phoenix, C. H., Goy, R. W., Gerall, A. A., & Young, W. C. (1959). Organizing action of prenatally administered testosterone propionate on the tissues mediating mating behavior in the female guinea pig. *Endocrinology, 65,* 369–382.

Pigott, S., & Milner, B. (1993). Memory for different aspects of complex visual scenes after unilateral temporal- or frontal-lobe resection. *Neuropsychologia, 31,* 1–15.

Pilar, G., Landmesser, L., & Burstein, L. (1980). Competition for survival among developing ciliary ganglion cells. *Journal of Neurophysiology, 43,* 233–254.

Pinel, J. P. J. (1969). A short gradient of ECS-produced amnesia in a one-trial appetitive learning situation. *Journal of Comparative and Physiological Psychology, 68,* 650–655.

Pinel, J. P. J. (1981). Spontaneous kindled motor seizures in rats. In J. A. Wada (Ed.), *Kindling, 2* (pp. 179–192). New York: Raven Press.

Pinel, J. P. J., & Edwards, M. E. (1998). *A colorful introduction to the anatomy of the human brain.* Boston: Allyn & Bacon.

Pinel, J. P. J., & Mana, M. J. (1989). Adaptive interactions of rats with dangerous inanimate objects: Support for a cognitive theory of defensive behavior. In R. J. Blanchard, P. F. Brain, D.C. Blanchard, & S. Parmigiani (Eds.), *Ethoexperimental approaches to the study of behavior* (pp. 137–150). Dordrecht, The Netherlands: Kluwer Academic Publishers.

Pinel, J. P. J., & Treit, D. (1978). Burying as a defensive response in rats. *Journal of Comparative and Physiological Psychology, 92,* 708–712.

Pinel, J. P. J., Assanand, S., & Lehman, D. R. (2000). Hunger, eating, and ill health. *American Psychologist, 55,* 1105–1116.

Pinel, J. P. J., Mana, M. J., & Kim, C. K., (1989). Effect-dependent tolerance to ethanol's anticonvulsant effect on kindled seizures. In R. J. Porter, R. H. Mattson, J. A. Cramer, & I. Diamond (Eds.), *Alcohol and seizures: Basic mechanisms and clinical implications* (pp. 115–125). Philadelphia: F. A. Davis.

Pi-Sunyer, R. X., Kissileff, H. R., Thornton, J., & Smith, G. P. (1982). C-terminal octapeptide of cholecystokinin decreases food intake in obese men. *Physiological Behavior, 29,* 27–630.

Pleim, E. T., & Barfield, R. J. (1988). Progesterone versus estrogen facilitation of female sexual behavior by intracranial administration to female rats. *Hormones and Behavior, 22,* 150–159.

Ploegh, H. L. (1998). Viral strategies of immune evasion. *Science, 280,* 248–252.

Plomin, R. (1995). Molecular genetics and psychology. *Current Direction in Psychological Science, 4,* 114–117.

Plomin, R. (2000, September). Psychology in a post-genomics world: It will be more important than ever. *Observer: American Psychological Society, 13,* 3 & 27.

Plomin, R., & DeFries, J. C. (1998, May). The genetics of cognitive abilities and disabilities. *Scientific American, 278,* 62–69.

Plomin, R., & Neiderhiser, J. M. (1992). Genetics and experience. *Current Directions in Psychological Science, 1,* 160–163.

Plomin, R., Fulker, D. W., Corley, R., & DeFries, J. C. (1997). Nature, nurture, and cognitive development from 1 to 16 years: A parent-offspring adoption study. *Psychological Science, 8:6,* 442–447.

Pons, T. P., Garraghty, P. E., Ommaya, A. K., Kaas, J. H., Taub, E., & Mishkin, M. (1991). Massive cortical reorganization after sensory deafferentation in adult macaques. *Science, 252,* 1857–1860.

Pope, H. G., & Katz, D. L. (1987). Bodybuilder's psychosis. *Lancet, 1* (8537), 863.

Pope, H. G., Jr, Kouri, E. M., & Hudson, J. I. (2000). Effects of supraphysiologic doses of testosterone on mood and aggression in normal men. *Archives of General Psychiatry, 57,* 133–140.

Porter, R., & Lemon, R. N. (1993). *Corticospinal function and voluntary movement.* Monographs of the Physiological Society, no. 45. New York: Oxford University Press.

Posner, M. I., & Raichle, M. E. (1994). *Images of the mind.* New York: Scientific American Library.

Post, R. M., Weiss, S. R. B., Clark, M., Nakajima, T., & Pert, A. (1990). Amygdala versus local anesthetic kindling: Differential anatomy, pharmacology, and clinical implications. In J. A. Wada (Ed.), *Kindling 4* (pp. 357–369). New York: Plenum Press.

Postle, B. R., & D'Esposito, M. (2000). Evaluating models of the topographical organization of working memory function in frontal cortex with even-related fMRI. *Psychobiology, 28,* 132–145.

Postle, B. R., Corkin, S., & Growdon, J. H. (1996). Intact implicit memory for novel patterns in Alzheimer's disease. *Learning & Memory, 3,* 305–312.

Potts, R. (1996). Evolution and climate variability. *Science, 273,* 922.

Poulos, C. X., & Cappell, H. (1991). Homeostatic theory of drug tolerance: A general model of physiological adaptation. *Psychological Review, 98,* 390–408.

Powers, J. B., Newman, S. W., & Bergondy, M. L. (1987). MPOA and BNST lesions in male Syrian hamsters: Differential effects on copulatory and chemoinvestigatory behaviors. *Behavioral Brain Research, 23,* 181–195.

Powley, T. L., Opsahl, C. A., Cox, J. E., & Weingarten, H. P. (1980). The role of the hypothalamus in energy homeostasis. In P. J. Morgane & J. Panksepp (Eds.), *Handbook of the hypothalamus—3A: Behavioral studies of the hypothalamus* (pp. 211–298). New York: Marcel Dekker.

Price, C. J., Howard, D., Patterson, K., Warburton, E. A., Friston, K. J., & Frackowiak, R. S. J. (1998). A functional neuroimaging description of two deep dyslexic patients. *Journal of Cognitive Neuroscience, 10,* 303–315.

Price, D. D. (2000). Psychological and neural mechanisms of the affective dimension of pain. *Science, 288,* 1769–1772.

Price, R. A., & Gottesman, I. I. (1991). Body fat in identical twins reared apart: Roles for genes and environment. *Behavioral Genetics, 21,* 1–7.

Pritchard, R. M. (1961, June). Stabilized images on the retina. *Scientific American, 204,* 72–78.

Pritchard, T. C., Macaluso, D. A., & Eslinger, P. J. (1999). Taste perception in patients with insular cortex lesions. *Behavioral Neuroscience, 113,* 663–671.

Psychobiology, 27, June (1999).

Pulver, A. E. (2000). Search for schizophrenia vulnerability genes. *Biological Psychiatry, 47,* 221–230.

Pusey, A., Williams, J., & Goodall, J. (1997). The influence of dominance rank on the reproductive success of female chimpanzees. *Science, 277,* 828–830.

Racine, R. J., & Burnham, W. M. (1984). The kindling model. In P. A. Schwartzkroin & H. Wheal (Eds.), *Electrophysiology of epilepsy* (pp. 153–171). London: Academic Press.

Racine, R. J., Burnham, W. M., Gartner, J. G., & Levitan, D. (1973). Rates of motor seizure development in rats subjected to electrical brain stimulation: Strain and interstimulation interval effects. *Electroencephalography and Clinical Neurophysiology, 35,* 553–556.

Raedler, T. J., Knable, M. B., & Weinberger, D. R. (1998). Schizophrenia as a developmental disorder of the cerebral cortex. *Current Opinion in Neurobiology, 8,* 157–161.

Raichle, M. E. (1994, April). Visualizing the mind. *Scientific American, 2,* 58–64.

Raisman, G. (1997). An urge to explain the incomprehensible: Geoffrey Harris and the discovery of the neural control of the pituitary gland. *Annual Review of Neuroscience, 20,* 533–566.

Raisman, G., & Field, P. M. (1971). Sexual dimorphism in the neuropil of the preoptic area of the rat and its dependence on neonatal androgens. *Brain Research, 54,* 1–29.

Rakic, P. (1979). Genetic and epigenetic determinants of local neuronal circuits in the mammalian central nervous system. In F. O. Schmitt & F. G. Worden (Eds.), *The neurosciences: Fourth study program.* Cambridge, MA: MIT Press.

Ralph, M. R., & Menaker, M. (1988). A mutation of the circadian system in golden hamsters. *Science, 241,* 1255–1227.

Ralph, M. R., Foster, T. G., Davis, F. C., & Menaker, M. (1990). Transplanted suprachiasmatic nucleus determines circadian period. *Science, 247,* 975–978.

Ramachandran, V. S. (1992, May). Blind spots. *Scientific American, 260,* 86–91.

Ramachandran, V. S., & Blakeslee, S. (1998). *Phantoms in the brain.* New York: William Morrow.

Ramachandran, V. S., & Rogers-Ramachandran, D. (2000). Phantom limbs and neuronal plasticity. *Archives of Neurology, 57,* 317–320.

Ramsay, D. S., & Woods, S. C. (1997). Biological consequences of drug administration: Implications for acute and chronic tolerance. *Psychological Review, 104 (1),* 170–193.

Rao, S. C., Rainer, G., & Miller, E. K. (1997). Integration of what and where in the primate prefrontal cortex. *Science, 276,* 821–824.

Rasmussen, T., & Milner, B. (1975). Clinical and surgical studies of the crerbral speech areas in man. In K. J. Zulch, O. Creutzfeldt, & G. C. Galbraith (Eds.), *Cerebral localization* (pp. 258–263). New York: Springer-Verlag.

Ratliff, F. (1972, June). Contour and contrast. *Scientific American, 226,* 90–101.

Ratnasuriya, R. H., Eisler, I., Szmukler, G. I., & Russell, G. F. M. (1991). Anorexia nervosa: Outcome and prognostic factors after 20 years. *British Journal of Psychiatry, 158,* 495–502.

Rauschecker, J. P. (1999). Auditory cortical plasticity: A comparison with other sensory systems. *Trends in Neurosciences, 22,* 74–80.

Rauschecker, J. P., Tian, B., & Hauser, M. (1995). Processing of complex sounds in the macaque nonprimary auditory cortex. *Science, 268,* 111–114.

Ravussin, E., & Danforth, E. Jr. (1999). Beyond sloth—physical activity and weight gain. *Science, 283,* 184–185.

Raymond, J. L., Lisberger, S. G., & Mauk, M. D. (1996). The cerebellum: A neuronal learning machine? *Science, 272,* 1126–1131.

Raynor, H. A., & Epstein, L. H. (2001). Dietary variety, energy regulation, and obesity. *Psychological Bulletin, 127,* 325–341.

Reame, N., Sauder, S. E., Kelch, R. P., & Marshall, J. C. (1984). Pulsatile gonadotropin secretion during the human menstrual cycle: Evidence for altered frequency of gonadotropin releasing hormone secretion. *Journal of Clinical Endocrinology and Metabolism, 59,* 328.

Reber, P. J., Knowlton, B. J., & Squire, L. R. (1996). Dissociable properties of memory system: differences in the flexibility of declarative and nondeclarative knowledge. *Behavioral Neuroscience, 110 (5),* 861–871.

Rechtschaffen, A. (1998). Current perspectives on the function of sleep. *Perspectives in Biology and Medicine, 41 (3),* 359–390.

Rechtschaffen, A., & Bergmann, B. M. (1995). Sleep deprivation in the rat by the disk-over-water method. *Behavioural Brain Research, 69,* 55–63.

Rechtschaffen, A., & Kales, A. (1968). *A manual of standardized terminology, techniques and scoring systems for sleep stages of human subjects.* Washington, DC: U.S. Government Printing Office.

Rechtschaffen, A., Gilliland, M. A., Bergmann, B. M., & Winter, J. B. (1993). Physiological correlates of prolonged sleep deprivation in rats. *Science, 221,* 182–184.

Redd, M., & de Castro, J. M. (1992). Social facilitation of eating: Effects of social instruction on food intake. *Physiology & Behavior, 52,* 749–754.

Reddy, P. H., Williams, M., & Tagle, D. A. (1999). Recent advances in understanding the pathogenesis of Huntington's disease. *Trends in Neurosciences, 22,* 248–255.

Reh, T. A., & Constantine-Paton, M. (1984). Retinal ganglion cell terminals change their projection sites during larval development of *Rana pipiens. Journal of Neuroscience, 4,* 442–457.

Reid, R. C., & Alonso, J-M. (1996). The processing and encoding of information in the visual cortex. *Current Opinion in Neurobiology, 6,* 475–480.

Reiman, E. M., Lane, R. D., Ahern, G. L., Schwartz, G. E., & Davidson, R. J. (2000). Positron emission tomography in the study of emotion, anxiety, and anxiety disorders. In R. D. Lane & L. Nadel (Eds.), *Cognitive neuroscience of emotion* (pp. 389–406). New York: Oxford University Press.

Reiner, W. (1997). To be male or female—that is the question. *Archives of Pediatry and Adolescent Medicine, 151,* 224–225.

Rensberger, B. (2000). The nature of evidence. *Science, 289,* 61.

Rensink, R. A., O'Regan, J. K., & Clark, J. J. (1997). To see or not to see: the need for attention to perceive changes in scenes. *Psychological Science, 8:5,* 368–373.

Reuter-Lorenz, P. A., & Miller, A. C. (1998). The cognitive neuroscience of human laterality: Lessons from the bisected brain. *Current Directions in Psychological Science, 7,* 15–20.

Revusky, S. H., & Garcia, J. (1970). Learned associations over long delays. In G. H. Bower & J. T. Spence (Eds.), *The psychology of learning and motivation, vol. 4* (pp. 1–85). New York: Academic Press.

Reynolds, D. V. (1969). Surgery in the rat during electrical analgesia induced by focal brain stimulation. *Science, 164,* 444–445.

Rice, G., Anderson, C., Risch, N., & Ebers, G. (1999). Male homosexuality: Absence of linkage to microsatellite markers at Xq28. *Science, 284,* 665–667.

Rice, W. R. (1994). Degeneration of a nonrecombining chromosome. *Science, 263,* 230–232.

Richards, W. (1971, May). The fortification illusions of migraines. *Scientific American, 224,* 89–97.

Richter, C. P. (1967). Sleep and activity: Their relation to the 24-hour clock. *Proceedings of the Association for Research on Nervous and Mental Disorders, 45,* 8–27.

Richter, C. P. (1971). Inborn nature of the rat's 24-hour clock. *Journal of Comparative and Physiological Psychology, 75,* 1–14.

Rijntjes, M., Dettmers, C., Büchel, C., Kiebel, S., Frackowiak, R. S. J., & Weiller, C. (1999). A blueprint for movement: Functional and anatomical representations in the human motor system. *Journal of Neuroscience, 19,* 8043–8048.

Rindi, G. (1989). Alcohol and thiamine of the brain. *Alcohol & Alcoholism, 24,* 493–495.

Rizzolatti, G., Fogassi, L., & Gallese, V. (1997). Parietal cortex: From sight to action. *Current Opinion in Neurobiology, 7,* 562–567.

Robbins, T. W., & Everitt, B. J. (1999). Interaction of the dopaminergic system with mechanisms of associative learning and cognition: Implications for drug abuse. *Psychological Science, 10,* 199–202.

Roberts, D.C. S., & Koob, G. F. (1982). Disruption of cocaine self-administration following 6-hydroxydopamine lesions of the ventral tegmental area in rats. *Pharmacology Biochemistry & Behavior, 17,* 901–904.

Roberts, D.C. S., Koob, G. F., Klonoff, P., & Fibiger, H. C. (1980). Extinction and recovery of cocaine self-administration following 6-hydroxydopamine lesions of the nucleus accumbens. *Pharmacology Biochemistry & Behavior, 12,* 781–787.

Robinson, T. E. (1991). Persistent sensitizing effects of drugs on brain dopamine systems and behavior: Implications for addiction and relapse. In J. Barchas and S. Korenman (Eds.), *The biological basis of substance abuse and its therapy.* New York: Oxford University Press.

Robinson, T. E., & Berridge, K. C. (1993). The neural basis of drug craving: An incentive-sensitization theory of addiction. *Brain Research Reviews, 18,* 247–291.

Robinson, T. E., & Berridge, K. C. (2000). The psychology and neurobiology of addiction: An incentive-sensitization view. *Addiction, 95 (supplement 2),* 91–117.

Robinson, T. E., & Justice, J. B. (Eds.). (1991). *Microdialysis in the neurosciences. Vol. 7, Techniques in the neural and behavioral sciences.* Elsevier: Amsterdam.

Rodier, P. M. (February, 2000). The early origins of autism. *Scientific American, 284,* 56–63.

Rodin, J. (1985). Insulin levels, hunger, and food intake: an example of feedback loops in body weight regulation. *Health Psychology, 4,* 1–24.

Rodríguez-Monzo, G., Pellicer, F. Larsson, K., & Fernández-Guasti, A. (2000). Stimulation of the medial preoptic area facilitates sexual behavior but does not reverse sexual satiation. *Behavioral Neuroscience, 114,* 553–560.

Roe, A. W., Pallas, S. L., Hahm, J-O., & Sur, M. (1990). A map of visual space induced in primary auditory cortex. *Science, 250,* 818–820.

Rogers, P. J., & Blundell, J. E. (1980). Investigation of food selection and meal parameters during the development of dietary induced obesity. *Appetite, 1,* 85–88.

Roland, P. E., & Zilles, K. (1996). Functions and structures of the motor cortices in humans. *Current Opinion in Neurobiology, 6,* 773–781.

Rolls, B. J. (1986). Sensory-specific satiety. *Nutrition Reviews, 44,* 93–101.

Rolls, B. J. (1990). The role of sensory-specific satiety in food intake and food selection. In E. D. Capaldi & T. L. Powley (Eds.), *Taste, experience, & feeding* (pp. 28–42). Washington, DC: American Psychological Association.

Rolls, B. J., Rolls, E. T., Rowe, E. A., & Sweeney, K. (1981). Sensory specific satiety in man. *Physiology & Behavior, 27,* 137–142.

Rolls, E. T. (1981). Central nervous mechanisms related to feeding and appetite. *British Medical Bulletin, 37,* 131–134.

Rolls, E. T., Robertson, R. G., & Georges-François, P. (1995). The representation of space in the primate hippocampus. *Society for Neuroscience Abstracts, 21,* 1492.

Romanski, L. M., & LeDoux, J. E. (1992). Equipotentiality of thalamo-cortico-amygdala projections as auditory conditioned stimulus pathways. *Journal of Neuroscience, 12,* 4501–4509.

Rosa, M. G. P., Tweedale, R., & Elston, G. N. (2000). Visual responses of neurons in the middle temporal area of new world monkeys after lesions of striate cortex. *Journal of Neuroscience, 20,* 5552–5563.

Rosen, A. C., Rao, S. M., Caffarra, P., & Scaglioni, A. (1999). Neural basis of endogenous and exogenous spatial orienting: A functional MRI study. *Journal of Cognitive Neuroscience, 11,* 135–152.

Rosenthal, D., Wender, P. H., Kety, S. S., Welner, J., & Schulsinger, F. (1980). The adopted-away offspring of schizophrenics. *American Journal of Psychiatry, 128,* 87–91.

Ross, J., Morrone, M. C., & Burr, D.C. (1989). The conditions for the appearance of Mach bands. *Vision Research, 29,* 669–715.

Rothman, J. E., & Orci, L. (1996, March). Budding vesicles in living cells. *Scientific American, 274,* 70–75.

Rothwell, J. C., Traub, M. M., Day, B. L., Obeso, J. A., Thomas, P. K., & Marsden, C. D. (1982). Manual motor performance in a deafferented man. *Brain, 105,* 515–542.

Rothwell, N.J., & Stock, M. J. (1982). Energy expenditure derived from measurements of oxygen consumption and energy balance in hyperphagic, "cafeteria"-fed rats. *Journal of Physiology, 324,* 59–60.

Routtenberg, A. (1978, November). The reward system of the brain. *Scientific American, 239,* 154–164.

Routtenberg, A. (1997). Measuring memory in a mouse model of Alzheimer's disease. *Science, 277,* 839–841.

Rowland, N. E. (1990). Sodium appetite. In E. D. Capaldi & T. L. Powley (Eds.), *Taste, experience, and feeding* (pp. 94–104). Washington, DC: American Psychological Association.

Roy, M., & Sapolsky, R. (1999). Neuronal apoptosis in acute necrotic insults: Why is this subject such a mess? *Trends in Neurosciences, 22,* 419–422.

Rozin, P. N., & Schulkin, J. (1990). Food selection. In E. M. Stricker (Ed.), *Handbook of behavioral neurobiology* (pp. 297–328). New York: Plenum Press.

Rozin, P., Dow, S., Moscovitch, M., & Rajaram, S. (1998). What causes humans to begin and end a meal? A role for memory for what has been eaten, as evidenced by a study of multiple meal eating in amnesic patients. *Psychological Science, 9,* 392–396.

Rudy, J. W., & Sutherland, R. J. (1992). Configural and elemental associations and the memory coherence problem. *Journal of Cognitive Neuroscience, 4,* 208–216.

Rusak, B., & Groos, G. (1982). Suprachiasmatic stimulation phase shifts rodent circadian rhythms. *Science, 215,* 1407–1409.

Rushworth, M. F. S. (2000). Anatomical and functional subdivision within the primate lateral prefrontal cortex. *Psychobiology, 28,* 187–196.

Russell, W. R., & Espir, M. I. E. (1961). *Traumatic aphasia—a study of aphasia in war wounds of the brain.* London: Oxford University Press.

Rutledge, L. L., & Hupka, R. B. (1985). The facial feedback hypothesis: Methodological concerns and new supporting evidence. *Motivation and Emotion, 9,* 219–240.

Rutter, M. L. (1997). Nature-nurture integration: The example of antisocial behavior. *American Psychologist, 52,* 390–398.

Rymer, R. (1993). *Genie.* New York: Harper Collins

Sacks, O. (1985). *The man who mistook his wife for a hat and other clinical tales.* New York: Summit Books.

Saffran, E. M. (1997). Aphasia: Cognitive neuropsychological aspects. In T. E. Feinberg, & M. J. Farah, (Eds.), *Behavioral neurology and neuropsychology* (pp. 133–149). New York: McGraw-Hill.

St. George-Hyslop, P. H. (December, 2000). Piecing together Alzheimer's. *Scientific American, 283,* 76–83.

Sakata, H., Taira, M., Kusunoki, M., Murata, A., & Tanaka, Y. (1997). The TINS lecture. The parietal association cortex in depth perception and visual control of hand action. *Trends in Neurosciences, 20,* 350–357.

Sakuma, Y., & Pfaff, D. W. (1979). Mesencephalic mechanisms for the integration of female reproductive behavior in the rat. *American Journal of Physiology, 237,* 285–290.

Sakurai, T., Amemiya, A., Ishil, M., Matsuzaki, I., Chemelli, R. M., Tanaka, H., Williams, S. C., Richardson, J. A., Koslowski, G.

P., Wilson, S., Arch, J. R. S., Buckingham, R. E., Haynes, A. C., Carr, S. A., Annan, R. S., McNulty, D. E., Liu, W-S., Terrett, J. A., Elshourbagy, N. A., Bergsma, D. J., & Yanagisawa, M. (1998). Orexins and orexin receptors: A family of hypothalamic neuropeptides and G protein-coupled receptors that regulate feeding behavior. *Cell, 92,* 573–585.

Salamone, J. D. (2000). A critique of recent studies on placebo effects of antidepressants: Importance of research on active placebos. *Psychopharmacology, 152,* 1–6.

Salmon, D. P., & Butters, N. (1995). Neurobiology of skill and habit learning. *Current Opinion in Neurobiology, 5,* 184–190.

Salovey, P., Rothman, A. J., Detweiler, J. B., & Steward, W. T. (2000). Emotional states and physical health. *American Psychologist, 55,* 110–121.

Salzet, M., Vieau, D., & Day, R. (2000). Crosstalk between nervous and immune systems through the animal kingdom: Focus on opioids. *Trends in Neuroscience, 23,* 550–555.

Sanders, D., & Bancroft, J. (1982). Hormones and the sexuality of women—the menstrual cycle. *Clinics in Endocrinology and Metabolism, 11,* 639–659.

Sanes, J. N., & Donoghue, J. P. (2000). Plasticity and primary motor cortex. In *Annual Review of Neuroscience,* (pp. 393–415). Palo Alto, CA: Annual Reviews.

Sanes, J. N., Donoghue, J. P., Thangaraj, V., Edelman, R. R., & Warach, S. (1995). Shared neural substrates controlling hand movements in human motor cortex. *Science, 268,* 1775–1777.

Sanes, J. N., Suner, S., & Donoghue, J. P. (1990). Dynamic organization of primary motor cortex output to target muscles in adult rats. I. Long-term patterns of reorganization following motor or mixed peripheral nerve lesions. *Experimental Brain Research, 79,* 479–491.

Sapolsky, R. M. (1996). Why stress is bad for your brain. *Science, 273,* 749–750.

Sapolsky, R. M. (1997). The importance of a well-groomed child. *Science, 277,* 1620–1622.

Sarter, M., Berntson, G. G., & Cacioppo, J. T. (1996). Brain imaging and cognitive neuroscience toward strong inference in attributing function to structure. *American Psychologist, 51,* 13–21.

Sastry, B. R., Goh, J. W., & Auyeung, A. (1986). Associative induction of posttetanic and long-term potentiation in CA1 neurons of rat hippocampus. *Science, 232,* 988–990.

Sawada, H., & Shimohama, S. (2000). Neuroprotective effects of estradiol in mesencephalic dopaminergic neurons. *Neuroscience and Biobehavioral Reviews, 24,* 143–147.

Sawle, G. V., & Myers, R. (1993) The role of positron emission tomography in the assessment of human neurotransplantation. *Trends in Neurosciences, 16,* 172–176.

Sbragia, G. (1992). Leonardo da Vinci and ultrashort sleep: Personal experience of an eclectic artist. In C. Stampi (Ed.), *Why we nap: Evolution, chronobiology, and functions of polyphasic and ultrashort sleep.* Boston: Birkhaüser.

Schally, A. V., Kastin, A. J., & Arimura, A. (1971). Hypothalamic follicle-stimulating hormone (FSH) and luteinizing hormone (LH)-regulating hormone: Structure, physiology, and clinical studies. *Fertility and Sterility, 22,* 703–721.

Schärli, H. Harman, A. M., & Hogben, J. H. (1999b). Residual vision in a subject with damaged visual cortex. *Journal of Cognitive Neuroscience, 11,* 502–510.

Schärli, H., Harman, A. M., & Hogben, J. H. (1999a). Blindsight in subjects with homonymous visual field defects. *Journal of Cognitive Neuroscience, 11,* 52–66.

Schatzman, M., Worsley, A., & Fenwich, P. (1988). Correspondence during lucid dreams between dreamed and actual events. In J.

Gackenbach and S. LaBerge (Eds.), *Conscious mind, sleeping brain* (pp. 67–103). New York: Plenum.

Scheiber, M. H. (1999). Somatotopic gradients in the distributed organization of the human primary motor cortex hand area: Evidence from small infarcts. *Experimental Brain Research, 128,* 139–148.

Scheiber, M. H., & Poliakov, A. V. (1998). Partial inactivation of the primary motor cortex hand area: Effects on individuated finger movements. *Journal of Neuroscience, 18,* 9038–9054.

Schelling, T. C. (1992). Addictive drugs: The cigarette experience. *Science, 255,* 430–433.

Schenck, C. H., Bundlie, S. R., Ettinger, M. G., & Mahowald, M. W. (1986). Chronic behavioral disorders of human REM sleep: A new category of parasomnia. *Sleep, 9,* 293–308.

Schieber, M. H., & Hibbard, L. S. (1993). How somatotopic is the motor cortex hand area? *Science, 261,* 489–492.

Schiffman, S. S., & Erickson, R. P. (1980). The issue of primary tastes versus a taste continuum. *Neuroscience and Biobehavioral Reviews, 4,* 109–117.

Schinder, A. F., & Poo, M-M. (2000). The neurotrophin hypothesis for synaptic plasticity. *Trends in Neurosciences, 23,* 639–645.

Schlaug, G., Jäncke, L., Huang, Y., & Steinmetz, H. (1995). In vivo evidence of structural brain asymmetry in musicians. *Science, 267,* 699–701.

Schnapf, J. L., & Baylor, D. A. (1987, April). How photoreceptor cells respond to light. *Scientific American, 256,* 40–47.

Schreiner, C. E. (1992). Functional organization of the auditory cortex: Maps and mechanisms. *Current Opinion in Neurobiology, 2,* 516–521.

Schreiner, C. E., Read, H. L., & Sutter, M. L. (2000). Modular organization of frequency integration in primary auditory cortex. *Annual Review of Neuroscience, 23,* 501–529.

Schulman, H., & Hyman, S. E. (1999). Intracellular signaling. In M. J. Zigmond, F. E. Bloom, S. C. Landis, J. L. Roberts, & L. R. Squire (Eds.), *Fundamental neuroscience* (pp. 269–316). New York: Academic Press.

Schultz, W. (1997). Dopamine neurons and their role in reward mechanisms. *Current Opinion in Neurobiology, 7,* 191–197.

Schwartz, A. B. (1994). Distributed motor processing in cerebral cortex. *Current Opinion in Neurobiology, 4,* 840–846.

Schwartz, M. W. (2000). Staying slim with insulin in mind. *Science, 289,* 2066–2067.

Schwartz, M. W., Peskind, E., Raskind, M., Nicolson, M., Moore, J., Morawiecki, A., Boyko, E. J., & Porte, D. J. (1996a). Cerebrospinal fluid leptin levels: Relationship to plasma levels and to adiposity in humans. *Nature Medicine, 2,* 589–593.

Schwartz, M. W., Seeley, R. J., Campfield, L. A., Burn, P., & Baskin, D. G. (1996b). Identification of hypothalamic targets of leptin action. *Journal of Clinical Investigation, 98,* 1101–1106.

Sclafani, A. (1990). Nutritionally based learned flavor preferences in rats. In E. D. Capaldi & T. L. Powley (Eds.), *Taste, experience, and feeding* (pp. 139–156). Washington, DC: American Psychological Association.

Scoville, W. B., & Milner, B. (1957). Loss of recent memory after bilateral hippocampal lesions. *Journal of Neurology, Neurosurgery and Psychiatry, 20,* 11–21.

Searle, J. R. (2000). Consciousness. *Annual Review of Neuroscience, 23,* 557–578.

Searle, L. V. (1949). The organization of hereditary maze-brightness and maze-dullness. *Genetic Psychology Monographs, 39,* 279–325.

Seeley, R. J., & Schwartz, M. W. (1997). The regulation of energy balance: Peripheral hormonal signals and hypothalamic neuropeptides. *Current Directions in Psychological Science, 6,* 39–44.

Seeley, R. J., van Dijk, G., Campfield, L. A., Smith, F. J., Nelligan, J. A., Bell, S. M., Baskin, D. G., Woods, S. C., & Schwartz, M. W. (1996). The effect of intraventricular administration of leptin (Ob protein) in food intake and body weight in the rat. *Hormone and Metabolic Research, 28,* 664–668.

Seeman, P., & Kapur, S. (2000). Schizophrenia: More dopamine, more D$_2$ receptors. *Proceedings of the National Academy of Science, USA, 97,* 7673–7675.

Segev, I., & London, M. (2000). Untangling dendrites with quantitative models. *Science, 290,* 744–749.

Segev, I., & Rall, W. (1998). Excitable dendrites and spines: earlier theoretical insights elucidate recent direct observations. *Trends in Neurosciences, 21:11,* 453–460.

Seitz, R. J., Roland, P. E., Bohm, C., Greitz, T., & Stone-Elanders, S. (1990). Motor learning in man: A positron emission tomographic study. *NeuroReport, 1,* 17–20.

Sejnowski, T. J. (1997). The year of the dendrite. *Science, 275,* 178–213.

Selkoe, D. J. (1991, November). Amyloid protein and Alzheimer's. *Scientific American, 265,* 68–78.

Seminars in Neuroscience, 9 (Issue 3/4, 1997).

Seminars in the Neurosciences, 5 (October 1993).

Serrien, D. J., & Weisendanger, M. (1999). Role of the cerebellum in tuning anticipatory and reactive grip force responses. *Journal of Cognitive Neuroscience, 11,* 672–681.

Shadmehr, R., & Holcomb, H. H. (1997). Neural correlates of motor memory consolidation. *Science, 277,* 821–825.

Shapiro, B. H., Levine, D.C., & Adler, N. T. (1980). The testicular feminized rat: A naturally occurring model of androgen independent brain masculinization. *Science, 209,* 418–420.

Sharpe, L. T., & Stockman, A. (1999). Rod pathways: the importance of seeing nothing. *Trends in Neurosciences, 22,* 497–504.

Shaw, P. J., Cirelli, C., Greenspan, R. J., Tononi, G. (2000). Correlates of sleep and waking in *Drosophila melanogaster. Science, 287,* 1834–1837.

Shaywitz, S. E. (1996, November). Dyslexia. *Scientific American, 275,* 98–104.

Shepherd, G. M., & Erulkar, S. D. (1997). Centenary of the synapse: From Sherrington to the molecular biology of the synapse and beyond. *Trends in Neurosciences, 20,* 385–392.

Sheppard, D. M., Bradshaw, J. L., Purcell, R., & Pantelis, C. (1999). Tourette's and comorbid syndromes: Obsessive compulsive and attention deficit hyperactivity disorder: A common etiology? *Clinical Psychology Review, 19,* 531–552.

Sherin, J. E., Shiromani, P. J., McCarley, R. W., & Saper, C. B. (1996). Activation of ventrolateral preoptic neurons during sleep. *Science, 271,* 216–219.

Sherry, D. F., Vaccarino, A. L., Buckenham, K., & Herz, R. S. (1989). The hippocampal complex of food-storing birds. *Brain, Behavior, and Evolution, 34,* 308–317.

Sherwin, B. B. (1985). Changes in sexual behavior as a function of plasma sex steroid levels in post-menopausal women. *Maturitas, 7,* 225–233.

Sherwin, B. B. (1988). A comparative analysis of the role of androgen in human male and female sexual behavior: Behavioral specificity, critical thresholds, and sensitivity. *Psychobiology, 16,* 416–425.

Sherwin, B. B., Gelfand, M. M., & Brender, W. (1985). Androgen enhances sexual motivation in females: A prospective crossover study of sex steroid administration in the surgical menopause. *Psychosomatic Medicine, 47,* 339–351.

Sheth, B. R., Sharma, J., Chenchal Rao, S., & Sur, M. (1996). Orientation maps of subjective contours in visual cortex. *Science, 274,* 2110–2115.

Shimura, T., & Shimokochi, M. (1990). Involvement of the lateral mesencephalic tegmentum in copulatory behavior of male rats: Neuron activity in freely moving animals. *Neuroscience Research, 9,* 173–183.

Shizgal, P., & Murray, B. (1989). Neuronal basis of intracranial self-stimulation. In J. M. Liebman & S. J. Cooper (Eds.), *The neuropharmacological basis of reward* (pp. 106–163). Oxford: Clarendon Press.

Shors, T. J., & Matzel, L. D. (1997). Long-term potentiation: What's learning got to do with it? *Behavioral and Brain Sciences, 20,* 597–655.

Shoulson, I. (1998). Experimental therapeutics of neurodegenerative disorders: Unmet needs. *Science, 282,* 1072–1074.

Shouse, M. N., King, A., Langer, J., Vreeken, T., King, K., & Richkind, M. (1990). The ontogeny of feline temporal lobe epilepsy: Kindling a spontaneous seizure disorder in kittens. *Brain Research, 525,* 215–224.

Siegel, J. M. (1983). A behavioral approach to the analysis of reticular formation unit activity. In T. E. Robinson (Ed.), *Behavioral approaches to brain research* (pp. 94–116). New York: Oxford University Press.

Siegel, J. M. (2000, January). Narcolepsy. *Scientific American, 282,* 77–81

Siegel, J. M., Nienhuis, R., Fahringer, H. M., Paul, R., Shiromani, P., Dement, W. C., Mignot, E., & Chui, C. (1991). Neuronal activity in narcolepsy: Identification of cataplexy-related cells in the medial medulla. *Science, 252,* 1315–1318.

Siegel, J. M., Nienhuis, R., Gulyani, S., Ouyang, S., Wu, M. F., Mignot, E., Switzer, R. C., McMurry, G., Cornford, M. (1999). Neuronal degeneration in canine narcolepsy. *Journal of Neuroscience, 19,* 248–257.

Siegel, S., Hinson, R. E., Krank, M. D., & McCully, J. (1982). Heroin 'overdose' death: Contribution of drug-associated environmental cues. *Science, 216,* 436–437.

Sigmund, M. J., Bloom, F. E., Landis, S. C., Roberts, J. L., & Squire, L. R. (1999). *Fundamental neuroscience.* New York: Academic Press.

Silva, A. J., Paylor, R., Wehner, J. M., & Tonegawa, S. (1992). Impaired spatial learning in a-calcium-calmodulin kinase II mutant mice. *Science, 257,* 206–211.

Sinclair, S. V., & Mistlberger, R. E. (1997). Scheduled activity reorganizes circadian phase of Syrian hamsters under full and skeleton photoperiods. *Behavioural Brain Research, 87,* 127–137.

Singer, J. (1968). Hypothalamic control of male and female sexual behavior. *Journal of Comparative and Physiological Psychology, 66,* 738–742.

Skelton, R. W., Scarth, A. S., Wilkie, D. M., Miller, J. J., & Phillips, A. G. (1987). Long-term increases in dentate granule cell responsivity accompany operant conditioning. *Journal of Neuroscience, 7,* 3081–3087.

Skovronksy, D. M., Zhang, B., Kung, M-P., Hung, H. F., Trojanowski, J. Q., & Lee, V. M.-Y. (2000). *In vivo* detection of amyloid plaques in a mouse model of Alzheimer's disease. *Proceedings of the National Academy of Sciences, USA, 97,* 7609–7614.

Sladek, J. R., Jr., Redmond, D. E., Jr., Collier, T. J., Haber, S. N., Elsworth, J. D., Deutch, A. Y., & Roth, R. H. (1987). Transplantation of fetal dopamine neurons in primate brain reverses MPTP induced parkinsonism. In F. J. Seil, E. Herbert, & B. M. Carlson (Eds.), *Progress in brain research* (Vol. 71, pp. 309–323). New York: Elsevier.

Sluder, G., & McCollum, D. (2000). The mad ways of meiosis. *Science, 289,* 254–255.

Small, M. F. (1992). Female choice in mating. *American Scientist, 80,* 142–151.

Smith, D. V., & Margolskee, R. F. (March, 2001). Making sense of taste. *Scientific American, 284,* 32–39.

Smith, E. E. (2000). Neural bases of human working memory. *Current Directions in Psychological Science, 9,* 45–49.

Smith, E. E., & Jonides, J. (1999). Storage and executive processes in the frontal lobes. *Science, 283,* 1657–1661.

Snyder, S. H. (1978). Neuroleptic drugs and neurotransmitter receptors. *Journal of Clinical and Experimental Psychiatry, 133,* 21–31.

Snyder, S. H., & Bredt, D. S. (1992, May). Biological roles of nitric oxide. *Scientific American, 266,* 68–77.

Sohal, R. S., & Weindruch, R. (1996). Oxidative stress, caloric restriction, and aging. *Science, 273,* 59–68.

Soloman, S. M., & Kirby, D. F. (1990). The refeeding syndrome: A review. *Journal of Parenteral and Enteral Nutrition, 14,* 90–97.

Spanagel, R., & Weiss, F. (1999). The dopamine hypothesis of reward: Past and current status. *Trends in Neurosciences, 22,* 521–527.

Spear, L. P. (2000). Neurobehavioral changes in adolescence. *Current Directions in Psychological Science, 9,* 111–114.

Sperry, R. W. (1943). Effect of 180° rotation of the retinal field on visuomotor coordination. *Journal of Experimental Zoology, 92,* 263–279.

Sperry, R. W. (1963). Chemoaffinity in the orderly growth of nerve fiber patterns and connections. Proceedings of the National Academy of Sciences, USA, 50, 703–710.

Sperry, R. W. (1964, January). The great cerebral commissure. *Scientific American, 210,* 42–52.

Sperry, R. W. (1993). The impact and promise of the cognitive revolution. *American Psychologist, 48,* 878–885.

Sperry, R. W., Zaidel, E., & Zaidel, D. (1979). Self recognition and social awareness in the deconnected minor hemisphere. *Neuropsychologia, 17,* 153–166.

Spielman, A. J., Saskin, P., & Thorpy, M. J. (1987). Treatment of chronic insomnia by restriction of time in bed. *Sleep, 10,* 45–56.

Spillman, L., & Werner, J. S. (1996). Long-range interactions in visual perception. *Trends in Neurosciences, 19,* 428–434.

Spitzer, H., Desimone, R., & Moran, J. (1988). Increased attention enhances both behavioral and neuronal performance. *Science, 240,* 338–340.

Spitzer, R. L., Skodol, A. E., Gibbon, M., & Williams, J. B. W. (1983). *Psychopathology: A case book.* New York: McGraw-Hill.

Squire, L. R. (1987). *Memory and brain* (p. 139). New York: Oxford University Press.

Squire, L. R., & Alvarez, P. (1995). Retrograde amnesia and memory consolidation: A neurobiological perspective. *Current Opinion in Neurobiology, 5,* 169–177.

Squire, L. R., & Spanis, C. W. (1984). Long gradient of retrograde amnesia in mice: Continuity with the findings in humans. *Behavioral Neuroscience, 98,* 345–348.

Squire, L. R., & Zola-Morgan, S. (1985). The neuropsychology of memory: New links between humans and experimental animals. *Annals of the New York Academy of Sciences, 444,* 137–149.

Squire, L. R., & Zola-Morgan, S. (1991). The medial temporal lobe memory system. *Science, 253,* 1380–1386.

Squire, L. R., Amaral, D. G., Zola-Morgan, S., Kritchevsky, M., & Press, G. (1989). Description of brain injury in the amnesic patient N. A. based on magnetic resonance imaging. *Experimental Neurology, 105,* 23–35.

Squire, L. R., Slater, P. C., & Chace, P. M. (1975). Retrograde amnesia: Temporal gradient in very long term memory following electroconvulsive therapy. *Science, 187,* 77–79.

Stampi, C. (1992a). Evolution, chronobiology, and functions of polyphasic and ultrashort sleep: Main issues. In C. Stampi (Ed.), *Why we nap: Evolution, chronobiology, and functions of polyphasic and ultrashort sleep*. Boston: Birkhäuser.

Stampi, C. (1992b). *Why we nap: Evolution, chronobiology, and functions of polyphasic and ultrashort sleep*. Boston: Birkhäuser.

Stanford, S. C., & Salmon, P. (1993). *Stress: From synapse to syndrome*. London: Academic Press.

Stanley, E. F. (1997). The calcium channel and the organization of the presynaptic transmitter release face. *Trends in Neurosciences, 20,* 404–409.

Stefano, G. B., Goumon, Y., Casares, F., Cadet, P., Fricchione, G. L., Rialas, C., Peter, D., Sonetti, D., Guarna, M., Welters, I. D., & Bianchi, E. (2000). Endogenous morphine. *Trends in Neurosciences, 23,* 436–442.

Steinmetz, J. E. (1998). The localization of a simple type of learning and memory: The cerebellum and classical eyeblink conditioning. *Current Directions in Psychological Science, 7,* 72–77.

Steinmetz, M. A. (1998). Contributions of posterior parietal cortex to cognitive functions in primates. *Psychobiology, 26,* 109–118.

Stepanski, E., Lamphere, J., Badia, P., Zorick, F., & Roth, T. (1984). Sleep fragmentation and daytime sleepiness. *Sleep 7,* 18–26.

Stepanski, E., Lamphere, J., Roehrs, T., Zorick, F., & Roth, T. (1987). Experimental sleep fragmentation in normal subjects. *International Journal of Neuroscience, 33,* 207–214.

Steriade, M., & Hobson, J. A. (1976). Neuronal activity during the sleep-waking cycle. *Progress in Neurobiology, 6,* 155–376.

Stewart, J., de Wit, H., & Eikelboom, R. (1984). Role of unconditioned and conditioned drug effects in the self-administration of opiates and stimulants. *Psychological Review, 91,* 251–268.

Stewart, M. G., Harrison, E., Rusakov, D. A., Richter-Levin, G., & Maroun, M. (2000). Re-structuring of synapses 24 hours after induction of long-term potentiation in the dentate gyrus of the rat hippocampus *in vivo. Neuroscience, 100,* 221–227.

Stiles, J. (1998). The effects of early focal brain injury on lateralization of cognitive function. *Current Directions in Psychological Science, 7,* 21–26.

Stirling, R. V., & Dunlop, S. A. (1995). The dance of the growth cones—where to next? *Trends in Neurosciences, 18,* 111–115.

Stoekli, E. T., & Landmesser, L. T. (1998). Axon guidance at choice points. *Current Opinion in Neurobiology, 8,* 73–79.

Streissgarth, A. P, Barr, H. M., Bookstein, F. L., Sampson, P. D., & Carmichael Olson, H. (1999). The long-term neurocognitive consequences of prenatal alcohol exposure: A 14-year study. *Psychological Science, 10,* 186–190.

Strömland, K., Nordin, V., Miller, M., Åkerström, & Gillberg, C. (1994). Autism in thalicomide embryopathy: A population study. *Developmental Medicine and Child Neurology, 36,* 351–356.

Strub, R. L., & Black, F. W. (1997). The mental status exam. In T. E. Feinberg & M. J. Farah (Eds.), *Behavioral neurology and neuropsychology* (pp. 25–42). New York: McGraw-Hill.

Sunday, S. R., & Halmi, K. A. (1990). Taste perceptions and hedonicas in eating disorders. *Physiology and Behavior, 48,* 587–594.

Susman, R. L. (1994). Fossil evidence for early hominid tool use. *Science, 265,* 1570–1573.

Svendsen, C. N., & Smith, A. G. (1999). New prospects for human stem-cell therapy in the nervous system. *Trends in Neurosciences, 22,* 357–364.

Swaab, D. F., & Fliers, E. (1985). A sexually dimorphic nucleus in the human brain. *Science, 188,* 1112–1115.

Swaab, D. F., & Hofman, M. A. (1995). Sexual differentiation of the human hypothalamus in relation to gender and sexual orientation. *Trends in Neuroscience, 18,* 264–270.

Swaab, D. F., Zhou, J. N., Ehlhart, T., & Hofman, M. A. (1994). Development of vasoactive intestinal polypeptide neurons in the human suprachiasmatic nucleus in relation to birth and sex. *Developmental Brain Research, 79,* 249–259.

Swanson, L. W. (2000). What is the brain? *Trends in Neurosciences, 23,* 519–527.

Swanson, L. W., & Petrovich, G. D. (1998). What is the amygdala? *Trends in Neurosciences, 21,* 323–331.

Sweeney, M. E., Hill, P. A., Baney, R., & DiGirolamo, M. (1993). Severe vs. moderate energy restriction with and without exercise in the treatment of obesity: Efficiency of weight loss. *American Journal of Clinical Nutrition, 57,* 127–134.

Swerdlow, N. R., & Young, A. B. (2001). Neuropathology in Tourette syndrome: An update. In D. J. Cohen, C. G. Goetz, & J. Jankovic (Eds.), *Tourette syndrome* (pp. 151–161). Philadelphia: Lippincott Williams & Wilkins.

Takahashi, J. S. (1999). Narcolepsy genes wake up the sleep field. *Science, 285,* 2076–2077.

Tanaka, A. (1972). A progressive change of behavioral and electroencephalographic response to daily amygdaloid stimulations in rabbits. *Fukuoka Acta Medica, 63,* 152–163.

Tanaka, K. (1996). Inferotemporal cortex and object vision. *Annual Review of Neuroscience, 19,* 109–139.

Tanapat, P., Hastings, N. B., Reeves, A. J., & Gould, E. (1999). Estrogen stimulates a transient increase in the number of new neurons in the dentate gyrus of the adult female rat. *Journal of Neuroscience, 19,* 5792–5801.

Tanda, G., Pontieri, F. E., & Chiara, G. D. (1997). Cannabinoid and heroin activation of mesolimbic dopamine transmission by a common opioid receptor mechanism. *Science, 276,* 2048–2049.

Tanji, J. (1996). New concepts of the supplementary motor area. *Current Opinion in Neurobiology, 6,* 782–787.

Tank, D. W., Sugimori, M., Connoer, J. A., & Llinás, R. R. (1998). Spatially resolved calcium dynamics of mammalian Purkinje cells in cerebellar slice. *Science, 242,* 7733–777.

Tassinary, L. G., & Cacioppo, J. T. (1992). Unobservable facial actions and emotion. *Psychological Science, 3,* 28–33.

Tattersall, I. (1997, April). Out of Africa again . . . and again? *Scientific American, 276,* 60–67.

Taub, J. M., & Berger, R. J. (1973). Performance and mood following variations in the length and timing of sleep. *Psychophysiology, 10,* 559–570.

Taylor, J. R., Elsworth, J. D., Roth, J. R., Sladek, J. R., Jr., & Redmond, D. E., Jr. (1990). Cognitive and motor deficits in the acquisition of an object retrieval/detour task in MPTP-treated monkeys. *Brain, 113,* 617–637.

Teitelbaum, P. (1957). Random and food-directed activity in hyperphagic and normal rats. *Journal of Comparative and Physiological Psychology, 50,* 486–490.

Teitelbaum, P. (1961). Disturbances in feeding and drinking behavior after hypothalamic lesions. In M. R. Jones (Ed.), *Nebraska Symposium on motivation* (pp. 39–69). Lincoln: University of Nebraska Press.

Teitelbaum, P., & Epstein, A. N. (1962). The lateral hypothalamic syndrome: Recovery of feeding and drinking after lateral hypothalamic lesions. *Psychological Review, 69,* 74–90.

Temple, S., & Alvarez-Buylla, A. (1999). Stem cells in the adult mammalian central nervous system. *Current Opinion in Neurobiology, 9,* 135–141.

Teskey, G. C., & Valentine, P. A. (1998). Post-activation potentiation in the neocortex of awake freely moving rats. *Neuroscience & Biobehavioral Reviews, 22,* 195–207.

Tessier-LaVigne, M., & Goodman, C. S. (1996). The molecular biology of axon guidance. *Science, 274,* 1123–1132.

Tessier-Lavigne, M., & Placzek, M. (1991). Target attraction: Are developing axons guided by chemotropism? *Trends in Neurosciences, 14,* 303–310.

Tetrud, J. W., & Langston, J. W. (1989). The effect of deprenyl (Selegiline) on the natural history of Parkinson's disease. *Science, 245,* 519–522.

Teuber, H.-L. (1975). Recovery of function after brain injury in man. In *Outcomes of severe damage to the nervous system. Ciba Foundation Symposium 34.* Amsterdam: Elsevier North-Holland.

Teuber, H.-L., Battersby, W. S., & Bender, M. B. (1960). Recovery of function after brain injury in man. In *Outcome of severe damage to the nervous system. Ciba Foundation Symposium 34.* Amsterdam: Elsevier North-Holland.

Teuber, H-L., Milner, B., & Vaughan, H. G., Jr. (1968). Persistent anterograde amnesia after stab wound of the basal brain. *Neuropsychologia, 6,* 267–282.

Thach, W. T. (1996). On the specific role of the cerebellum in motor learning and cognition: Clues from PET activation and lesion studies in man. *Behavioral and Brain Sciences, 19,* 411–431.

Thoenen, H. (1995). Neurotrophins and neuronal plasticity. *Science, 270,* 593–598.

Thompson, R. F., & Krupa, J. J. (1994). Organization of memory traces in the mammalian brain. *Annual Review of Neuroscience, 17,* 519–549.

Thureson-Klein, A. K., & Klein, R. L. (1990). Exocytosis from neuronal large dense-cored vesicles. *International Review of Cytology, 121,* 67–126.

Tilles, D., Goldenheim, P., Johnson, D.C., Mendelson, J. H., Mello, N. K., & Hales, C. A. (1986). Marijuana smoking as cause of reduction in single-breath carbon monoxide diffusing capacity. *American Journal of Medicine, 80,* 601–606.

Timberlake, W. (1993). Animal behavior: A continuing synthesis. *Annual Review of Psychology, 44,* 675–708.

Tinklenberg, J. R. (1974). Marijuana and human aggression. In L. L. Miller (Ed.), *Marijuana, effects on human behavior* (pp. 339–358). New York: Academic Press.

Toates, F. M. (1981). The control of ingestive behaviour by internal and external stimuli—A theoretical review. *Appetite, 2,* 35–50.

Tollefson, G. D., Birkett, M. A., Kiesler, G. M., Wood, A. J., & The Lilly Resistant Schizophrenia Study Group (2001). Double-blind comparison of Olanzapine versus Clozapine in schizophrenic patients clinically eligible for treatment with Clozapine. *Biological Psychiatry, 49,* 52–63.

Tompkins, C. A., & Mateer, C. A. (1985). Right hemisphere appreciation of intonational and linguistic indications of affect. *Brain and Language, 24,* 185–203.

Tonge, D. A., & Golding, J. P. (1993). Regeneration and repair of the peripheral nervous system. *Seminars in the Neurosciences, 5,* 385–390.

Toni, N. Buchs, P.-A., Nikonenko, I., Bron, C. R., & Muller, D. (1999). LTP promotes formation of multiple spine synapses between a single axon terminal and a dendrite. *Nature, 402,* 421–425

Tootell, R. B. H., Dale, A. M., Sereno, M. I., & Malach, R. (1996). New images from human visual cortex. *Trends in Neurosciences, 19,* 481–489.

Tosini, G., & Menacker, M. (1996). Circadian rhythms in cultured mammalian retina. *Science, 272,* 419–421.

Townsend, J., Courchesne, E., Covington, J., Westerfield, M., Singer Harris, N., Lyden, P., Lowry, T. P., & Press, G. A. (1999). Spatial attention deficits in patients with acquired or developmental cerebellar abnormality. *Journal of Neuroscience, 19,* 5632–5643.

Tramontin, A. D., & Brenowitz, E. A. (2000). Seasonal plasticity in the adult brain. *Trends in Neurosciences, 23:6,* 251–258.

Tramontin, A. D., Hartman, V. N.,& Brenowitz, E. A. (2000). Breeding conditions induce rapid and sequential growth in adult avian song control circuits: a model of seasonal plasticity in the brain. *The Journal of Neuroscience, 20:2,* 854–861.

Tranel, D., & Damasio, A. R. (1985). Knowledge without awareness: An autonomic index of facial recognition by prosopagnosics. *Science, 228,* 1453–1454.

Treit, D. (1985). Animal models for the study of anti-anxiety agents: A review. *Neuroscience and Biobehavioral Reviews, 9,* 203–222.

Treit, D. (1987). RO 15–1788, CGS 8216, picrotoxin, pentylenetetrazol: Do they antagonize anxiolytic drug effects through an anxiogenic action? *Brain Research Bulletin, 19,* 401–405.

Treit, D., Robinson, A., Rotzinger, S., & Pesold, C. (1993). Anxiolytic effects of serotonergic interventions in the shock-probe burying test and the elevated plus-maze test. *Behavioural Brain Research, 54,* 23–34.

Trends in Pharmacological Science, 13 (May 1992).

Trivers, R. L. (1972). Parental investment and sexual selection. In B. Campbell (Ed.), *Sexual selection and the descent of man.* Chicago: Aldine.

True, W. R., Xian, H., Scherrer, J. F., Madden, P. A. F., Bucholz, K. K., Heath, A. C., Eisen, S. A., Lyons, M. J., Goldberg, J., & Tsuang (1999). Common genetic vulnerability for nicotine and alcohol dependence in men. *Archives of General Psychiatry, 56,* 655–661.

Tryon, R. C. (1934). Individual differences. In Moss, F. A. (Ed.), *Comparative psychology* (pp. 409–448). New York: Prentice-Hall.

Tsien, J. Z. (2000, April). Building a brainier mouse. *Scientific American, 282,* 62–68.

Tsodyks, M., Kenet, T., Grinval, A., & Arieli, A. (1999). Linking spontaneous activity of single cortical neurons and the underlying functional architecture. *Science, 286,* 1943–1946.

Tucker, J., Nixon, P. D., Rushworth, M., Harding, A. E., Jahanshahi, M., Quinn, N. P., Thompson, P. D., & Passingham, R. E. (1996). Associative learning in patients with cerebellar ataxia. *Behavioral Neuroscience, 110 (6),* 1229–1234.

Turkenburg, J. L., Swaab, D. F., Endert, E., Louwerse, A. L., & van de Poll, N. E. (1988). Effects of lesions of the sexually dimorphic nucleus on sexual behavior of testosterone-treated female Wistar rats. *Brain Research Bulletin, 329,* 195–203.

Turkheimer, E. (2000). Three laws of behavior genetics and what they mean. *Current Directions in Psychological Science, 9:5,* 160–164.

Turner, R. (1995). Functional mapping of the human brain with magnetic resonance imaging. *Seminars in the Neurosciences, 7,* 179–195.

Ullian, E. M., Sapperstein, S. K., Christopherson, K. S., & Barres, B. A. (2001). Control of synapse number by glia. *Science, 291,* 657–661.

Ulrich, R. E. (1991). Commentary: Animal rights, animal wrongs and the question of balance. *Psychological Science, 2,* 197–201.

Ungerleider, L. G., & Haxby, J. V. (1994). "What" and "where" in the human brain. *Current Opinion in Neurobiology, 4,* 157–165.

Ungerleider, L. G., & Mishkin, M. (1982). Two cortical visual systems. In D. J. Ingle, M. A. Goodale, & R. J. W. Mansfield

(Eds.), *Analysis of visual behavior* (pp. 549–586). Cambridge, MA: MIT Press.

Valenstein, E. S. (1973). *Brain control.* New York: John Wiley and Sons.

Valenstein, E. S. (1980). *The psychosurgery debate: Scientific, legal, and ethical perspectives.* San Francisco: W. H. Freeman and Co.

Valenstein, E. S. (1986). *Great and desperate cures: The rise and decline of psychosurgery and other radical treatments for mental illness.* New York: Basic Books.

Vallee, R. B., & Bloom, G. S. (1991). Mechanisms of fast and slow axonal transport. *Annual Review of Neuroscience, 14,* 59–92.

Van der Kooy, D. (1987). Place conditioning: A simple and effective method for assessing the motivational properties of drugs. In M. A. Bozarth (Ed.), *Methods of assessing the reinforcing properties of abused drugs* (pp. 229–240). New York: Springer-Verlag.

Vanderwolf, C. H. (1988). Cerebral activity and behavior: Control by central cholinergic and serotonergic systems. *International Review of Neurobiology, 30,* 225–340.

Van Essen, D.C., Anderson, C. H., & Felleman, D. J. (1992). Information processing in the primate visual system: An integrated systems perspective. *Science, 255,* 419–423.

VanHelder, T., & Radomski, M. W. (1989). Sleep deprivation and the effect on exercise performance. *Sports Medicine, 7,* 235–247.

Van Lancker, D., & Cummings, J. L. (1999). Expletives: Neurolinguistic and neurobehavioral perspectives on swearing. *Brain Research Reviews, 31,* 83–104.

Van Praag, H., Christie, B. R., Sejnowski, T. J., & Gage, F. H. (1999). Running enhances neurogenesis, learning, and long-term potentiation in mice. *Proceedings of the National Academy of Sciences, USA, 19,* 13427–13431.

van Vactor, D. (1998). Adhesion and signaling in axonal fasciculation. *Current Opinion in Neurobiology, 8,* 80–86.

Vargha-Khadem, F., Gadian, D. G., Watkins, K. E., Connelly, A., van Paesschen, W., & Mishkin, M. (1997). Differential effects of early hippocampal pathology on episodic and semantic memory. *Science, 277,* 376–380.

Vermeij, G. J. (1996). Animal origins. *Science, 274,* 525–526.

Vermeire, B. A., Hamilton, C. R., & Erdmann, A. L. (1998). Right-hemisphere superiority in split-brain monkeys for learning and remembering facial discriminations. *Behavioral Neuroscience, 112,* 1048–1061.

Vertes, R. P. (1983). Brainstem control of the events of REM sleep. *Progress in Neurobiology, 22,* 241–288.

Vicario, D. S. (1991). Neural mechanisms of vocal production in songbirds. *Current Opinion in Neurobiology, 1,* 595–600.

Volkow, N. D., Wang, G. J., Fischman, M. W., Foltin, R. W., Fowler, J. S., Abumrad, N. N., Vitkun, S., Logan, J., Gatley, S. J., Pappas, N. Hitzemann, R., & Shea, C. E. (1997). Relationship between subjective effects of cocaine and dopamine transporter occupancy. *Nature, 386,* 827–830.

Voogd, J., & Glickstein, M. (1998). The anatomy of the cerebellum. *Trends in Neurosciences, 21,* 370–374.

Wada, J. A. (1949). A new method for the determination of the side of cerebral speech dominance. *Igaku to Seibutsugaku, 14,* 221–222.

Wada, J. A. (1990a). Erosion of kindled epileptogenesis and kindling-induced long-term seizure suppressive effect in primates. In J. A. Wada (Ed.), *Kindling 4* (pp. 382–394) New York: Plenum Press.

Wada, J. A. (Ed.). (1990b). *Kindling 4.* Plenum Press: New York.

Wada, J. A., & Sato, M. (1974). Generalized convulsive seizures induced by daily electrical stimulation of the amygdala in cats: Correlative electrographic and behavioral features. *Neurology, 24,* 565–574.

Wada, J. A., Clarke, R., & Hamm, A. (1975). Cerebral hemispheric asymmetry in humans. *Archives of Neurology, 32,* 239–246.

Wada, J. A., Sato, M., & Corcoran, M. E. (1974). Persistent seizure susceptibility and recurrent spontaneous seizures in kindled cats. *Epilepsia, 15,* 465–478.

Wakayama, T., Tabar, V., Rodriguez, I., Perry, A. C. F., Studer, L., & Mombaerts, P. (2001). Differentiation of embryonic stem cell lines generated from adult somatic cells by nuclear transfer. *Science, 292,* 740–743.

Wald, G. (1964). The receptors of human color vision. *Science, 145,* 1007–1016.

Walford, R. L., & Walford, L. (1994) *The anti-aging plan.* New York: Four Walls Eight Windows.

Wallace, D. C. (1997, August). Mitochondrial DNA in aging and disease. *Scientific American, 277,* 40–47.

Walmsley, B., Alvarez, f. J., & Fyffe, E. W. (1998). Diversity of structure and function at mammalian central synapses. *Trends in Neurosciences, 21:2,* 81–88.

Wan, H., Aggleton, J. P., Brown, M. W. (1999). Different contributions of the hippocampus and perirhinal cortex to recognition memory. *Journal of Neuroscience, 19,* 1142–1148.

Wang, W., Meadows, L. R. den Haan, J. M. M., Sherman, N. E., Chen, Y., Blokland, E., Shabanowitz, J. Agulnik, A. I., Hendrickson, R. C., Bishop, C. E., Hunt, D. F., Goulmy, E., & Engelhard, V. H. (1995). Human H-Y: A male-specific histocompatibility antigen derived from the SMCY protein. *Science, 269,* 1588–1590.

Watson, J. B. (1930). *Behaviorism.* New York: W. W. Norton.

Wauquier, A., Ashton, D., & Melis, W. (1979). Behavioral analysis of amygdaloid kindling in beagle dogs and the effects of clonazepam, diazepam, phenobarbital, diphenylhydantoin, and flunarizine on seizure manifestation. *Experimental Neurology, 64,* 579–586.

Waxham, M. N. (1999). Neurotransmitter receptors. In M. J. Zigmond, F. E. Bloom, S. C. Landis, J. L. Roberts, & L. R. Squire (Eds.) *Fundamental neuroscience* (pp. 235–268). New York: Academic Press.

Webb, W. B. (1973). Selective and partial deprivation of sleep. In W. P. Koella & P. Levin (Eds.), *Sleep: Physiology, biochemistry, psychology, pharmacology, clinical implications* (pp. 176–204). Basel: Karger.

Webb, W. B., & Agnew, H. W. (1967). Sleep cycling within the twenty-four hour period. *Journal of Experimental Psychology, 74,* 167–169.

Webb, W. B., & Agnew, H. W. (1970). Sleep stage characteristics of long and short sleepers. *Science, 163,* 146–147.

Webb, W. B., & Agnew, H. W. (1974). The effects of a chronic limitation of sleep length. *Psychophysiology, 11,* 265–274.

Webb, W. B., & Agnew, H. W. (1975). The effects on subsequent sleep of an acute restriction of sleep length. *Psychophysiology, 12,* 367–370.

Weeks, R. A., Gerloff, C., Dalakas, M., & Hallett, M. (1999). PET study of visually and non-visually guided finger movements in patients with severe pan-sensory neuropathies and healthy controls. *Experimental Brain Research, 128,* 291–302.

Weiller, C., & Rijntjes, M. (1999). Learning, plasticity, and recovery in the central nervous system. *Experimental Brain Research, 128,* 134–138.

Weindruch, R. (1996, January). Caloric restriction and aging. *Scientific American, 274,* 46–52.

Weindruch, R., & Walford, R. L. (1988). *The retardation of aging and disease by dietary restriction.* Springfield, IL: Charles C. Thomas.

Weindruch, R., Walford, R. L., Fligiel, S., & Guthrie, D. (1986). The retardation of aging in mice by dietary restriction:

Longevity, cancer, immunity, and lifetime energy intake. *Journal of Nutrition, 116,* 641–654.

Weingarten, H. P. (1983). Conditioned cues elicit feeding in sated rats: A role for learning in meal initiation. *Science, 220,* 431–433.

Weingarten, H. P. (1984). Meal initiation controlled by learned cues: Basic behavioral properties. *Appetite, 5,* 147–158.

Weingarten, H. P. (1985). Stimulus control of eating: Implications for a two-factor theory of hunger. *Appetite, 6,* 387–401.

Weingarten, H. P. (1990). Learning, homeostasis, and the control of feeding behavior. In E. D. Capaldi & T. L. Powley (Eds.), *Taste, experience, and feeding* (pp. 14–27). Washington, DC: American Psychological Association.

Weingarten, H. P., & Kulikovsky, O. T. (1989). Taste-to-post-ingestive consequence conditioning: Is the rise in sham feeding with repeated experience a learning phenomenon? *Physiology & Behavior, 45,* 471–476.

Weingarten, H. P., Chang, P. K., & Jarvie, K. R. (1983). Reactivity of normal and VMH-lesion rats to quinine-adulterated foods: Negative evidence for negative finickiness. *Behavioral Neuroscience, 97,* 221–233.

Weintraub, S., & Mesulam, M.-M. (1989). Neglect: Hemispheric specialization, behavioral components and anatomical correlates. In F. Boller & J. Grafman (Eds.), *Handbook of neuropsychology, 2.* New York: Elsevier Science Publishers.

Weise-Kelley, L., & Siegel, S. (2001). Self-administration cues as signals: Drug self-administration and tolerance. *Journal of Experimental Psychology, 27,* 125–136.

Weiskrantz, L. (1996). Blindsight revisited. *Current Opinion in Neurobiology, 6:* 215–220.

Weiskrantz, L., Warrington, E. K., Sanders, M. D., & Marshall, J. (1974). Visual capacity in the hemianopic field following a restricted occipital ablation. *Brain, 97,* 709–728.

Weiss, F., Maldonado-Vlaar, Parsons, L. H., Kerr, T. M., Smith, D. L., & Ben-Shahar, O. (2000). Control of cocaine-seeking behavior by drug-associated stimuli in rats: Effects on recovery of extinguished operant-responding and extracellular dopamine levels in amygdala and nucleus accumbens. *Proceedings of the National Academy of Sciences, 97,* 4321–4326.

Weissman, M. M., & Olfson, M. (1995). Depression women: Implications for health care research. *Science, 269,* 799–801.

Wekerle, H. (1993). Experimental autoimmune encephalomyelitis as a model of immune-mediated CNS disease. *Current Opinion in Neurobiology, 3,* 779–784.

Weliky, M., & Katz, C. (1997). Disruption of orientation tuning in visual cortex by artificially correlated neuronal activity. *Nature, 386,* 680–685.

Wenning, A. (1999). Sensing effectors make sense. *Trends in Neurosciences, 22,* 550–555.

Wessinger, C. M., Fendrich, R., & Gazzaniga, M. S. (1997). Islands of residual vision in hemianopic patients. *Journal of Cognitive Neuroscience, 9 (2),* 203–221.

West, M. J., Slomianka, L., & Gunderson, H. J. G. (1991). Unbiased stereological estimation of the total number of neurons in the subdivisions of the rat hippocampus using the optical fractionator. *Anatomical Record, 231,* 482–497.

Westergaard, G. C., & Suomi, S. J. (1996). Hand preference for a bimanual task in tufted capuchins (*Cebus apella*) and rhesus macaques (*Macaca mullata*). *Journal of Comparative Psychology, 110,* 406–411.

Wever, R. A. (1979). *The circadian system of man.* Andechs: Max-Planck-Institut fur Verhaltensphysiologie.

Whalen, P. J. (1998). Fear, vigilance, and ambiguity: Initial neuroimaging studies of the human amygdala. *Current Directions in Psychological Science, 7,* 177–188.

Wheeler, M. E., Petersen, S. E., & Buckner, R. L. (2000). Memory's echo: Vivid remembering reactivates sensory-specific cortex. *Proceedings of the National Academy of Sciences, USA, 97,* 11125–11129.

White, F. J. (1996). Synaptic regulation of mesocorticolimbic dopamine neurons. *Annual Review of Neuroscience, 19,* 405–536.

White, N. M. (1997). Mnemonic functions of the basal ganglia. *Current Opinion in Neurobiology, 7,* 164–169.

White, N. M., & Hiroi, N. (1993). Amphetamine conditioned cue preference and the neurobiology of drug seeking. *Seminars in the Neurosciences, 5,* 329–336.

White, N., Sklar, L., & Amit, Z. (1977). The reinforcing action of morphine and its paradoxical side effect. *Psychopharmacology, 52,* 63–66.

Whitelaw, V., & Hollyday, M. (1983). Position-dependent motor innervation of the chick hindlimb following serial and parallel duplications of limb segments. *Journal of Neuroscience, 3,* 1216–1225.

Wichmann, T., & DeLong, M. R. (1996). Functional and pathophysiological models of the basal ganglia. *Current Opinion in Neurobiology, 6,* 751–758.

Willett, W. C. (1994). Diet and health: What should we eat? *Science, 264,* 532–537.

Williams, J., Merritt, J., Rittenhouse, C., & Hobson, J. A. (1992). Bizarreness in dreams and fantasies: Implications for the activation-synthesis hypothesis. *Consciousness and Cognition, 1,* 172–185.

Williams, M. (1970). *Brain damage and the mind.* Baltimore: Penguin Books.

Willingham, D. B. (1999). The neural basis of motor-skill learning. *Current Directions in Psychological Science, 8,* 178–182.

Wills, S. (1997). *Drugs of abuse.* Cambridge: Pharmaceutical Press.

Wilson, B. A. (1998). Recovery of cognitive functions following nonprogressive brain injury. *Current Opinion in Neurobiology, 8,* 281–287.

Wilson, G. T, Heffernan, K., & Black, C. M. D. (1996). Eating disorders. In E. J. Mash & R. A. Barkley (Eds.), *Child psychopathology* (pp. 541–571). New York: Guilford Press.

Wilson, M. A., & McNaughton, B. L. (1993). Dynamics of the hippocampal ensemble code for space. *Science, 261,* 1055–1058.

Wiltstein, S. (1995). Quarry KO'd by dementia. *The Vancouver Sun,* October 26, 135.

Winocur, G., Oxbury, S., Roberts, R., Agnetti, V., & Davis, C. (1984). Amnesia in a patient with bilateral lesions to the thalamus. *Neurophysiologia, 22,* 123–143.

Winson, J. (1993). The biology and function of rapid eye movement sleep. *Current Opinion in Neurobiology, 3,* 243–248.

Wirtshafter, D., & Davis, J. D. (1977). Set points, settling points, and the control of body weight. *Physiology & Behavior, 19,* 75–78.

Witelson, S. F. (1991). Neural sexual mosaicism: Sexual differentiation of the human temporo-parietal region for functional asymmetry. *Psychoneuroendocrinology, 16,* 133–153.

Wodak, A., Richmond, R., & Wilson, A. (1990). Thiamin fortification and alcohol. *Medical Journal of Australia, 152,* 97–99.

Wolff, P. H., Michel, G. F., Ovrut, M., & Drake, C. (1990). Rate and timing precision of motor coordination in developmental dyslexia. *Developmental Psychology, 26,* 349–359.

Wong, M-L., & Licinio, J. (2001). Research and treatment approaches to depression. *Nature Reviews Neuroscience, 2,* 343–351.

Wood, B., & Collard, M. (1999). The human genus. *Science, 284,* 65–71.

Wood, E. R., Mumby, D. G., Pinel, J. P. J., & Phillips, A. G. (1993). Impaired object recognition memory in rats following ischemia-induced damage to the hippocampus. *Behavioral Neuroscience, 107,* 51–62.

Woods, S. C. (1991). The eating paradox: How we tolerate food. *Psychological Review, 98,* 488–505.

Woods, S. C., & Ramsay, D. S. (2000). Pavlovian influences over food and drug intake. *Behavioural Brain Research, 110,* 175–182.

Woods, S. C., & Strubbe, J. H. (1994). The psychology of meals. *Psychonomic Bulletin & Review, 1,* 141–155.

Woods, S. C., Lotter, E. C., McKay, L. D., & Porte, D., Jr. (1979). Chronic intracerebroventricular infusion of insulin reduces food intake and body weight of baboons. *Nature, 282,* 503–505.

Woods, S. W., Stolar, M., Sernyak, M. J., & Charney, D. S. (2001). Consistency of atypical antipsychotic superiority to placebo in recent clinical trials. *Biological Psychiatry, 49,* 64–70.

Wu, L-G., & Saggau, P. (1997). Presynaptic inhibition of elicited neurotransmitter release. *Trends in Neurosciences, 20,* 204–212.

Xu, D., Bureau, Y., McIntyre, D.C., Nicholson, D. W., Liston, P., Zhu, Y., Gong, W. G., Crocker, S. J., Korneluk, R. G., & Robertson, G. S. (1999). Attenuation of ischemia-induced cellular and behavioral deficits by X chromosome-linked inhibitor of apoptosis protein overexpression in the rat hippocampus. *Journal of Neuroscience, 19,* 5026–5033.

Yabuta, N. H., & Callaway, E. M. (1998). Functional streams and local connections of layer 4C neurons in primary visual cortex of the Macaque monkey. *Journal of Neuroscience, 18:22,* 9489–9499.

Yang, L-Y., & Clemens, L. G. (2000). MPOA lesions affect female pacing of copulation in rats. *Behavioral Neuroscience, 114,* 1191–1202.

Yehuda, R. (1997). Stress and glucocorticoid. *Science, 275,* 1662–1664.

Yeomans, J. S., Mathur, A., & Tampakeras, M. (1993). Rewarding brain stimulation: Role of tegmental cholinergic neurons that activate dopamine neurons. *Behavioral Neuroscience, 107,* 1077–1087.

Yesalis, C. E., & Bahrke, M. S. (1995). Anabolic-androgenic steroids: Current issues. *Sports Medicine, 19,* 326–340.

Yoon, M. (1971). Reorganization of retinotectal projection following surgical operations on the optic tectum in goldfish. *Experimental Neurology, 33,* 395–411.

Yoshihara, Y., Nagao, H., & Mori, K. (2001). Sniffing out odors with multiple dendrites. *Science, 291,* 835–836.

Youdim, M. B. H., & Riederer, P. (1997, January). Understanding Parkinson's disease. *Scientific American, 276,* 52–59.

Young, E. A., Lopez, J. F., Murphy-Weinberg, V., Watson, S. J., & Akil, H. (2000). Hormonal evidence for altered responsiveness to social stress in major depression. *Neuropsychopharmacology, 23,* 411–418.

Young, M. W. (2000a). Marking time for a kingdom. *Science, 288,* 451–453.

Young, M. W. (2000b, March). The tick-tock of the biological clock. *Scientific American, 282,* 64–71.

Yuan, L-L., & Ganetsky, B. (1999). A glial-neuronal signaling pathway revealed by mutations in a neurexin-related protein. *Science, 283,* 1343–1344.

Yuste, R., Majewska, A., & Holthoff, K. (2000). From form to function: Calcium compartmentalization in dendritic spines. *Nature, 3:7,* 653–659.

Zaidel, E. (1975). A technique for presenting lateralized visual input with prolonged exposure. *Vision Research, 15,* 283–289.

Zaidel, E. (1987). Language in the disconnected right hemisphere. In G. Adelman (Ed.), *Encyclopedia of neuroscience* (pp. 563–564). Cambridge, MA: Birkhäuser.

Zangwill, O. L. (1975). Excision of Broca's area without persistent aphasia. In K. J. Zulch, O. Creutzfeldt, & G. C. Galbraith (Eds.), *Cerebral localization* (pp. 258–263). New York: Springer-Verlag.

Zeki, S. (1993a). *A vision of the brain.* Oxford: Blackwell Scientific Publication.

Zeki, S. (1993b). The visual association cortex. *Current Opinion in Neurobiology, 3,* 155–159.

Zhang, Y., Proenca, R., Maffie, M., Barone, M., Leopold, L., & Friedman, J. M. (1994). Positional cloning of the mouse obese gene and its human homologue. *Nature, 372,* 425–432.

Zimitat, C., Kril, J., Harper, C. G., & Nixon, P. F. (1990). Progression of neurological disease in thiamin-deficient rats is enhanced by ethanol. *Alcohol, 7,* 493–501.

Zimmer, L., & Morgan, J. P. (1997). *Marijuana myths marijuana facts: A review of the scientific evidence.* Lindesmith Center: New York.

Zivin, J. A. (2000, April). Understanding clinical trials, *Scientific American, 282,* 69–75.

Zivin, J. A., & Choi, D. W. (1991, July). Stroke therapy. *Scientific American, 265,* 56–63.

Zola-Morgan, S. M., Squire, L. R., Amaral, D. G., & Suzuki, W. A. (1989). Lesions of perirhinal and parahippocampal cortex that spare the amygdala and hippocampal formation produce severe memory impairment. *Journal of Neuroscience, 9,* 4355–4370.

Zola-Morgan, S., Squire, L. R., & Amaral, D. G. (1986). Human amnesia and the medial temporal region: Enduring memory impairment following a bilateral lesion limited to field CA1 of the hippocampus. *Journal of Neuroscience, 6,* 2950–2967.

Zola-Morgan, S., Squire, L. R., & Mishkin, M. (1982). The neuroanatomy of amnesia: Amygdala-hippocampus versus temporal stem. *Science, 218,* 1337–1339.

Zola-Morgan, S., Squire, L. R., Rempel, N. L., Clower, R. P., & Amaral, D. G. (1992). Enduring memory impairment in monkeys after ischemic damage to the hippocampus. *Journal of Neuroscience, 12,* 2582–2596.

Zucker, K. J., Bradley, S. J., Oliver, G., Blake, J., Fleming, S., & Hood, J. (1996). Psychosexual development of women with congenital adrenal hyperplasia. *Hormones and Behavior, 30,* 300–318.

Zucker, R. S. Kullman, D. M., & Bennett, M. (1999). Release of neurotransmitters. In M. J. Zigmond, F. E. Bloom, S. C. Landis, J. L. Roberts, & L. R. Squire (Eds.), *Fundamental neuroscience* (pp. 155–192). Academic Press: New York.

Zusho, H. (1983). Posttraumatic anosmia. *Archives of Ontolaryngology, 4,* 252–256.

Credits

courtesy of the Department of Neurology and Image Analysis Facility, University of Iowa. **Fig. 17.5,** Reprinted by permission of the Human Interaction Laboratory/Dr. Eckman and Dr. Friesen (1975). **Fig. 17.9,** Lennart Nilsson/Bonnierforlagen AB. **p. 461,** © Jonathan Knowles/Getty Images/FPG International. **p. 463,** © Jan Halaska/Photo Researchers, Inc. **p. 467,** © SIU School of Medicine/Bruce Coleman, Inc. **p. 472,** © Will Hart.

ILLUSTRATION CREDITS

Fig. 1.3, Schneck-DePippo Graphics. **Figs. 1.4, 1.6, 1.8,** Frank Forney. **Figs. 1.7, 1.9,** William C. Ober and Claire W. Garrison. **Fig. 2.1,** William C. Ober and Claire W. Garrison. **Figs. 2.3, 2.4, 2.10, 2.11, 2.13, 2.15, 2.16, 2.21, 2.22, 2.24,** Schneck-DePippo Graphics. **Fig. 2.7,** Leo Harrington. **Figs. 2.17, 2.18, 2.19,** Illustrious Interactive. **Fig. 2.20,** Frank Forney. **Fig. 2.25, p. 48,** Omegatype Typography Inc. **Fig. 3.1,** Adrienne Lehmann. **Figs. 3.2, 3.4, 3.5, 3.7, 3.16, 3.17, 3.19, 3.22, 3.31, 3.32,** Schneck-DePippo Graphics. **Figs. 3.3, 3.18, 3.20, 3.23, 3.24, 3.25, 3.26, 3.27, 3.28, 3.30,** William C. Ober and Claire Garrison. **Figs. 3.6, 3.8, 3.9, 3.10,** Mark Lefkowitz. **Fig. 4.1,** Illustrious Interactive. **Figs. 4.2, 4.3, 4.4, 4.5, 4.6, 4.7, 4.14, 4.15,** Schneck-DePippo Graphics. **Figs. 4.8, 4.9, 4.11, 4.12, 4.16, 4.17,** Frank Forney. **Figs. 4.10, 4.18,** Mark Lefkowitz. **Figs. 5.2, 5.8, 5.9, 5.10, 5.13, 5.14, 5.15, 5.17, 5.24,** Schneck-DePippo Graphics. **Figs. 5.16, 5.22,** Frank Forney. **Fig. 6.1,** Omegatype Typography Inc. **Figs. 6.2, 6.9, 6.12, 6.13, 6.14, 6.15, 6.16, 6.17, 6.18, 6.19, 6.23, 6.24, 6.25,** Schneck-DePippo Graphics. **Figs. 6.5, 6.8, 6.10, 6.11, 6.22, 6.26, 6.27, 6.28, 6.29,** Celadon Digital Studios. **Figs. 7.1, 7.2, 7.4,** Leo Harrington. **Figs. 7.3, 7.16, 7.21, 7.23, 7.27,** William C. Ober and Claire W. Garrison. **Fig. 7.5,** Academy Artworks. **Figs. 7.6, 7.13, 7.15, 7.18, 7.26,** Illustrious Interactive. **Figs. 7.7, 7.9, 7.11, 7.12, 7.20, 7.22, 7.24, 7.25,** Schneck-DePippo Graphics. **Fig. 7.8,** Frank Forney.

Figs. 7.14, 7.17, Adrienne Lehmann. **Fig. 8.1,** Leo Harrington. **Figs. 8.2, 8.7, 8.8, 8.15,** Schneck-DePippo Graphics. **Figs. 8.3, 8.4, 8.5, 8.10, 8.11, 8.12, 8.13, 8.14, 8.16, 8.17,** Frank Forney. **Fig. 8.6,** William C. Ober and Claire W. Garrison. **Figs. 9.1, 9.2, 9.3, 9.5, 9.8, 9.9,** Illustrious Interactive. **Figs. 9.6, 9.11,** Frank Forney. **Fig. 9.7,** Schneck-DePippo Graphics. **Fig. 10.5,** Mark Lefkowitz. **Figs. 10.13, 10.14, 10.19, 10.20,** Schneck-DePippo Graphics. **Figs. 10.15, 10.16, 10.17,** Illustrious Interactive. **Fig. 10.18,** Academy Artworks. **Fig. 10.21,** Frank Forney. **Figs. 11.1, 11.5,** Illustrious Interactive. **Figs. 11.2, 11.3, 11.12,** Frank Forney. **Figs. 11.4, 11.6, 11.7, 11.8, 11.9, 11.10, 11.13, 11.14, 11.15, 11.16, 11.17, 11.18,** Schneck-DePippo Graphics. **Fig. 12.1,** Gale Mueller. **Figs. 12.2, 12.3, 12.4, 12.5, 12.6, 12.7, 12.9, 12.12, 12.13, 12.15,** Schneck-DePippo Graphics. **Figs. 12.8, 12.10, 12.11,** Academy Artworks. **Fig. 12.14,** Frank Forney. **Figs. 13.1, 13.5, 13.7, 13.10, 13.13, 13.15,** Schneck-DePippo Graphics. **Fig. 13.2,** William C. Ober and Claire W. Garrison. **Figs. 13.3, 13.4,** Adrienne Lehmann. **Figs. 13.6, 13.12,** Illustrious Interactive. **Fig. 13.8,** Frank Forney. **Fig. 13.9,** Gale Mueller. **Figs. 14.2, 14.6, 14.7, 14.8, 14.9, 14.10, 14.11, 14.12, 14.13, 14.15,** Schneck-DePippo Graphics. **Figs. 14.3, 14.5, 14.14,** Illustrious Interactive. **Figs. 15.1, 15.2, 15.3, 15.4, 15.5, 15.6, 15.7, 15.9,** Schneck-DePippo Graphics. **Figs. 15.8, 15.10,** Frank Forney. **Figs. 16.1, 16.2, 16.9, 16.10, 16.11,** William C. Ober and Claire W. Garrison. **Figs. 16.3, 16.4, 16.5, 16.6, 16.16, Table 16.1,** Frank Forney. **Figs. 16.7, 16.13,** Illustrious Interactive. **Figs. 16.8, 16.12, 16.14, 16.15,** Schneck-DePippo Graphics. **Figs. 17.2, 17.3, 17.6, 17.8, 17.10, 17.12,** Schneck-DePippo Graphics. **Fig. 17.4,** William C. Ober and Claire W. Garrison. **Figs. 17.7, 17.13,** Frank Forney. **Fig. 17.11,** Illustrious Interactive. **Figs. 18.1, 18.3,** Mark Lefkowitz. **Fig. 18.2,** Schneck-DePippo Graphics. **Appendix I,** Frank Forney. **Appendix VIII,** Schneck-DePippo Graphics.

Name Index

Martin, B. J ., 362
Martin, J. B., 251
Martin, R. J., 313
Martin, R. L., 342
Martin, S. J., 294
Masoro, E. J., 313
Masterton, R. B., 172, 175, 176
Mateer, C. A., 417
Matheny, L., 409
Matherne, C. M., 343
Mathur, A., 400
Matsubara, J., 63, 120
Matsuda, L. A., 391
Matthews, P. B. C., 212
Matthyse, S., 463
Mattingley, J. B., 190
Matzel, L. D., 291
Mauk, M. D., 204
Mayer, A. B., 197
Mazziotta, J. C., 108
Mazzocchi, F., 428
McArthur, A. J., 372
McAuliffe, W. E., 398
McCann, T. S., 26
McCaughran, J. A., Jr., 391
McClearn, G. E., 49
McClintock, M. K., 347
McCollum, D., 36
McCormick, D. A., 86
McDonald, J. W., 264
McDonald, R. J., 204, 286
McEwen, B., 448
McEwen, B. S., 335, 344, 452, 470
McFarland, H. F., 251
McGinty, D. J., 368
McGlone, J., 409
McGue, M., 389
McIntyre, D. C., 255
McKim, W. A., 394
McLachlin, R. S., 255
McNally, G. P., 185
McNaughton, B. L., 286
McNaughton, P., 183
Meaney, M. J., 452
Meddis, R., 351
Melis, W., 255
Mello, N. K., 397
Melloni, R. H., Jr., 448
Melnik, G., 321
Melton, D. A., 224
Meltzer, L. D., 466
Melzack, R., 183, 184, 264
Menacker, M., 370
Menaker, M., 371
Mendel, G., 34, 35
Mendelson, J. H., 391, 397
Merton, P. A., 14
Merzenich, M. M., 260
Mesulam, M-M., 198
Metcalfe, J., 418
Meunier, M., 284
Meyer, R. G., 462
Middleton, F. A., 204
Midtgaard, J., 89
Miller, A. C., 416
Miller, E. K., 200
Miller, G. L., 233
Miller, N. E., 308
Miller, N. S., 392
Mills, J. N., 364
Mills, R., 335, 336, 345
Milner, A. D., 170

Milner, B., 181, 270, 271, 275, 279, 286, 409, 427
Milner, D., 170
Milner, P., 78, 398
Milner, P. M., 4
Mishkin, M., 168, 280, 281, 284
Mistlberger, R. E., 358, 359, 370
Mitchell, J. M., 385
Mitchell, R. W., 21
Mitler, M., 367
Miyashita, Y., 287
Mladejovsky, M. G., 145
Modianos, D., 346
Mogul, J. S., 121
Mohr, J. P., 425, 426
Molday, R. S., 143
Mombaerts, P., 186
Money, J., 338, 339, 340
Money, M., 338
Moniz, E., 8, 15
Mooney, R., 45, 422
Moore, R. Y., 358, 369, 372
Moran, J., 190
Morgan, J. P., 391
Morgan, T. H., 36
Mori, K., 186
Mori, N., 255
Morin, C. M., 374
Morris, J. S., 455, 457
Morris, M. K., 276
Morris, N. M., 342
Morris, R. G. M., 130, 294
Morrone, M. C., 146
Moruzzi, G., 365
Moscovitch, M., 171, 279
Moser, E. I., 279
Moser, M-B., 279
Mosher, J. T., 312
Moskowitz, M. A., 243
Mountcastle, V. B., 180
Mouret, J., 367
Mrosovsky, N., 359, 360
Mucha, R. F., 397
Mühlnickel, W., 234
Muir, G. D., 264
Mullaney, D. J., 364, 376
Mumby, D. G., 283, 284, 285
Murison, R., 448
Murphy, G. G., 291
Murphy, M., 27
Murphy, M. R., 186
Murphy, P. C., 165
Murray, B., 400
Murray, E. A., 284
Myers, R., 263
Myers, R. E., 411

Nadel, L., 279, 287
Nadelman, E. A., 395
Naeser, M. A., 428
Naftolin, F., 341
Nagao, H., 186
Naitoh, P., 376
Nakamura, M., 403
National Commission on Mari-
   juana and Drug Abuse, 390
Nauta, W. J. H., 62
Naya, Y., 287
Neher, E., 8
Neiderhiser, J. M., 49
Nemeroff, C. B., 470, 479
Nesse, R. M., 31, 398, 401

Netter, F. H ., 144
Neve, R. L., 255
Neville, H., 430, 431
Newcombe, N., 294
Newcombe, N. S., 294
Newman, S. W., 345
Newsom-Davis, J., 246
Nguyen, P. V., 293
Nicoll, R. A., 90
Nijhawan, D., 247
Nissl, F., 61
Nobre, A. C., 430, 432
Nopoulos, P. C., 467
Norman, D. A., 140
Norman, R. M. G., 464
Northcutt, R. G., 70
Northoff, G., 456
Noselli, S., 93
Nossal, G. J. V., 449
Nottebohm, F., 45, 234
Nudo, R. J., 264
Nyberg, L., 109, 168, 287
Nykamp, K., 364

O'Banion, M. K., 253
O'Callaghan, M. A. J., 16
Ohzawa, I., 150
Ojemann, G. A., 427, 428
O'Keefe, J., 286, 287
Olds, J., 78, 398
O'Leary, D. D. M., 260
Olfson, M., 468
Olsen, R., 101
Olson, L., 263
Olton, D. S., 129
O'Neill, L., 27
O'Neill, M. A., 162
Orci, L., 90
O'Regan, J. K., 189
Ormerod, B. K., 234, 452
O'Shanick, G., 374
Oswald, I., 352, 364
Otto, T. A., 12
Overmier, J. B., 448
Owen, A. M., 288, 289
Owren, M. J., 422

Pääbo, S., 30
Paletta, M. S., 385
Paller, K. A., 275
Panksepp, J., 399, 402
Papanicolaou, A., 276
Papez, J. W., 440
Park, I. J., 337
Parker, S. T., 21
Parnas, H., 93
Parnavelas, J. G., 224
Parrott, A. C., 388
Parsons, L. M., 202
Paterson, S. J., 237
Patrick, C. J., 442
Patterson, K., 430, 434
Patton, G. C., 320
Paulesu, E., 433
Pauls, D. L., 474
Paulson, H. L., 250
Pavlov, I., 8
Pearlman, A. L., 224
Pedersen, N., 47
Pellis, S. M., 446
Pellis, V. C., 446
Pellow, S., 128, 473

Penfield, W., 179, 202, 203, 288, 409, 426, 427, 428, 429, 430
Peralta, V., 463
Percival, J. E., 362
Perera, M. H., 471
Perkins, W. L., 386, 387
Perneger, T. V., 397
Perriman, N., 93
Perrone, P., 420
Pert, C. B., 98
Peru, A., 200
Peterhans, E., 167, 168
Peters, M., 88
Petersen, S. E., 126, 287
Peterson, A. T., 27
Peterson, B. S., 474
Petrides, M., 288, 289
Petrovich, G. D., 73
Peyron, C., 375
Pfaff, D., 346
Pfaff, D. W., 345, 346
Pfeiffer, C. A., 333
Pfeiffer, R. F., 250
Phelps, E. A., 456
Phelps, M. E., 108
Phillips, A. G., 115, 400, 402
Phoenix, C. H., 335
Pigott, S., 286
Pilar, G., 229
Pillard, R. C., 346
Pinel, J. P. J., 130, 255, 278, 284, 285, 301, 303, 312, 317, 384, 385
Pi-Sunyer, R. X., 312
Placzek, M., 224, 226
Pleim, E. T., 346
Ploegh, H. L., 449
Plomin, R., 40, 44, 48, 49
Plunkett, K., 430, 432
Poliakov, A. V., 202
Polkey, C. E., 434
Pons, T. P., 260, 265
Pontieri, F. E., 402
Poo, M-M., 232, 233
Pope, H. G., 342, 343
Porter, R., 206
Posner, M. I., 126
Post, R. M., 255
Postle, B. R., 276, 289
Potts, R., 31
Poulos, C. X., 384
Powell, T. P. S., 180
Powers, J. B., 345
Powley, T. L., 309
Price, C. J., 434
Price, D. D., 184
Price, R. A., 317
Pritchard, R. M., 141
Pritchard, T. C., 188
Pulver, A. E., 463
Pusey, A., 26

Quarry, J., 244, 245

Racine, R. J., 255
Radomski, M. W., 362
Raedler, T. J., 467
Raichle, M. E., 108, 126, 127
Rainer, G., 200
Rainnie, D., 446, 473
Raisman, G., 263, 328, 344
Rakic, P., 73, 234

Subject Index

Putative neurotransmitter, 97–98
Pyramidal cells, 71, 273–274
Pyramidal neurons, 452

Quasiexperimental studies, 7

Rabies, 246
Radial arm maze test, 129, 286
Radial glial cells, 224
Radio-frequency lesions, 115
Random motion, 81
Raphé nuclei, 367–368
Rapid eye movement (REM), 352. *See also* REM sleep
Reactive depression, 468
Receptive aphasia, 423
Receptive fields
    of somatosensory neurons, 180, 182
    of visual neurons, 147–154
Receptors, 92–94
    auditory, 174
    cutaneous, 177
    and depression, 470
    locating, 119–120
    metabotropic, 92, 93, 94
    muscarinic, 101
    in muscles, 210
    NMDA, 243–244, 291–292
    olfactory, 186
    and opiates, 394–395
    progesterone, 346
    in retina, 136–143
    and schizophrenia, 464–466
    taste, 187–188
    and THC, 391
Receptor blockers, 100, 464, 465
Receptor subtypes, 92
Recessive trait, 35
Reciprocal innervation, 212–214
Recording methods, 110–114
Recuperation theories of sleep, 356
Recurrent collateral inhibition, 214
Red nucleus, 68, 206
Reference memory, 286
Reflectance, 158
Refractory periods, 87
Regeneration, neural, 257–259, 262–263
Rehabilitative training, 264–265
Reinforcement, 128
Relapse, 397
Relative refractory period, 87
Releasing factors, 329–330
Releasing hormones, 330–331, 333, 336
REM sleep, 352, 354–355
    disorders of, 375
    loss of, 362–364
Renshaw cells, 214
Reorganization, neural, 259–261
Repetition priming tests, 125, 272
Replacement injections, 340–341
Replication, 39
Repolarization of action potential, 87
Reproductive barrier, 27
Reproductive organs. *See* Genitals; Gonads
Reptiles, evolution of, 27

Reptilian stare, 80
Research methods, 13. *See also* Cognitive neuroscience
    behavioral, 122–130
    biopsychological, 5–8
    ethological, 11
    invasive, 114–118
    neuroanatomical techniques as, 61–64
    pharmacological, 118–121
    psychophysiological, 110–114
Reserpine, 464
Response-chunking hypothesis, 217
Resting potential, 81–83. *See also* Membrane potential
Restless legs, 374
Reticular activating system, 67, 206, 365–367
Reticular formation, 67, 206, 368–369
Reticulum, endoplasmic, 58
Retina, 134–143, 226
Retina-geniculate-striate pathway, 144–145, 148, 158
Retinal ganglion cells, 136, 226
Retinex theory, 158
Retinohypothalamic tracts, 370, 371
Retinotopic organization, 144–145
Retrograde amnesia, 270, 275, 276–279
Retrograde degeneration, 257, 258
Retrograde tracing methods, 63
Reuptake, 94–95
Reversible lesions, 115, 116
Rhinal cortex, 280–285
Rhodopsin, 142–143
Ribonucleic acid (RNA), 40
Ribosomes, 40, 58, 90
Right parietal lobe, 21
Rising phase of action potential, 87
Risk-assessment test, 473
RNA, 40
Rods, 137–143
Rostral, 63
Rotary-pursuit test, 270, 272
Round window, 174
Ruffini endings, 177
Rush, 393

Saccades, 141
Sacral region, 52
Sagittal sections of brain, 64
Saltatory conduction, 88
Satellite cells, 56
Satiety, 305–312
Savants, 235
SC injections, 381
Scalp electroencephalography, 110–112, 248
Scanning electron microscope, 62
Schizophrenia, 392, 462–467
Schwann cells, 56, 60, 258–259
Scientific inference, 12–14
SCL, 113
SCN, 369–370
Scotomas, 165–167, 411
Scotopic spectral sensitivity curve, 140, 141, 142

Scotopic vision, 138
SCR, 113
Scrotum, 332
Second messenger, 93
Secondary auditory cortex, 176–177
Secondary gustatory cortex, 188
Secondary motor cortex, 197–198, 201–202
Secondary sensory cortex, 162
Secondary sex characteristics, 336
Secondary somatosensory cortex (SII), 178, 179, 182
Secondary visual cortex, 165, 167, 168
Sectioning, 115, 116
Selective attention, 189–192
Selective bonding, 33
Selective breeding, 43
Selective norepinephrine-reuptake inhibitors (SNRIs), 469
Selective serotonin-reuptake inhibitors (SSRIs), 469, 470, 472
Self-awareness, 21–22
Self-stimulation paradigm, 128
Semantic analysis, 430
Semantic memory, 125, 272
Semantics, 125
Semicircular canals, 174, 175
Seminal vesicles, 332
Sensation, 163
Sensitive period of development, 45
Sensitivity, 135, 138, 140
Sensitization, 382, 385–386, 398
Sensorimotor association cortex, 197–200
Sensorimotor phase of birdsong development, 45
Sensorimotor spinal circuits, 209–215
Sensorimotor system, 195–197, 215–219
Sensory evoked potential, 111
Sensory feedback, 196
Sensory phase of birdsong development, 45
Sensory relay nuclei, 68
Sensory-specific satiety, 306–307
Sensory system, exteroceptive, 162–165. *See also* Audition; Smell; Taste; Touch; Vision
Sensory theory of sleep, 365–367
Septal aggression, 446
Septal rage, 446
Septum, 73
Serial system, 164
Serotonergic neurons, 184
Serotonin, 96, 312, 319–320, 371–372, 469, 470, 472
Set point, 298, 301–303, 312–316
Settling point, 314–316
Sex chromosomes, 36–38, 326
Sex hormones, 325–337, 340–343
Sex-linked traits, 36–38, 336
Sexual behavior, 340–343
    and the hypothalamus, 343–346
    tests of, 128
Sexual development, 327, 331–337
Sexual identity, 339

Sexual orientation, 346–348
Sexually dimorphic nucleus, 344–345
Sham eating, 305–306
Sham rage, 440
Shift work, 359
Signal averaging, 111, 126–127
Signal proteins, 56
Signal-to-noise ratio, 126
Simple cells, 148, 150
Simple partial seizures, 249
Simultanagnosia, 192
Sinestrals, 409
Sine-wave grating, 152–154
Single-test approach, 12–123
Situational specificity, 385–386
Skeletal muscle, 210, 211, 213, 214
Skin conductance level (SCL), 113
Skin conductance response (SCR), 113
Sleep
    disorders of, 373–375
    and drugs, 371–373
    loss of, 359–365, 375–377, 470–471
    measures of, 352–353
    NREM, 354
    physiology of, 365–369
    REM. *See* REM sleep
    theories of, 356, 365–367
Sleep apnea, 374
Sleep inertia, 376
Sleep paralysis, 374
Sleep restriction therapy, 374
Sleep spindle, 352
Sleepwalking, 355
Slow-wave sleep (SWS), 354
Smell, 185–187, 188–189
Smoker's syndrome, 388
Snakeroot plant, 464
SNRIs, 469
Social dominance, 26
Social-learning theory of sexual identity, 339
Sodium amytal test, 124, 408
Sodium–potassium pumps, 83
Soldiers' disease, 393
Solitary nucleus, 187
Soluble gases, 95, 96–97
Soma, 57, 89
Somatic nervous system (SNS), 52–53
Somatosensory agnosia, 18, 182
Somatosensory homunculus, 179–180, 182
Somatosensory system, 177–185
Somatotopic organization, 179, 202
Somnambulism, 355
Sound localization, 176–177
Sound waves, 172–177
Spandrels, 31
Spatial-frequency theory, 152–154
Spatial memory, 286–287
Spatial resolution, 107, 111
Spatial summation, 84, 85
Species, 27
Species-common behaviors, 127–128
Spectral sensitivity curve, 140
Speed, 392–393
Sperm, 222, 326